UNIVERSITY CASEBOOK SERIES®

LAW OF TORTS
CASES AND MATERIALS

SIXTH EDITION

by

HARRY SHULMAN
Late Dean of the Law School and Sterling Professor of Law
Yale University

FLEMING JAMES, JR.
Late Sterling Professor Emeritus of Law
Yale University

OSCAR S. GRAY
Jacob A. France Professor Emeritus of Torts
University of Maryland

DONALD G. GIFFORD
Edward M. Robertson Research Professor of Law
University of Maryland

FOUNDATION
PRESS

© 1942, 1952, 1976, 2003 FOUNDATION PRESS
© 2010 By THOMSON REUTERS/FOUNDATION PRESS
© 2015 LEG, Inc. d/b/a West Academic
    444 Cedar Street, Suite 700
    St. Paul, MN 55101
    1-877-888-1330

Printed in the United States of America

ISBN: 978-1-60930-267-2

Mat #41378480

PREFACE

This is the sixth edition of a casebook that has changed both the teaching of torts and the law of torts itself. In 1942, Dean Harry Shulman and Professor Fleming James, Jr. of the Yale Law School presented the first edition, derived in part from materials previously used at Yale by Shulman and Walton Hamilton, an economist, and among the first to systematically apply economic principles to the study of law. In the preface to the first edition, Shulman and James wrote:

> While the focus of tort law is the adjustment of relationships between individuals, the quality of the adjustment here, as in all law, is referred to its effects upon the social good. Otherwise it would seem wasteful to spend social wealth and energy merely to shift money from the pocket of the defendant to that of the plaintiff. * * *

> In this casebook, * * * we have tried to present the material in such a fashion as to emphasize social consequences and to invite inquiry and criticism as to underlying assumptions. The student should be constantly aware that the law is concerned not so much with rule or doctrine as with problems in human relations, that the problem must be understood before rule or doctrine can be properly fashioned or applied. * * *

During the 1960s and 1970s, tort law changed dramatically in the direction implicitly suggested by the earlier editions of the casebook with, for example, the widespread adoption of strict products liability and the substitution of comparative fault for contributory negligence. The second edition, published in 1952, had been among the first casebooks to contain a chapter on a new category of tort liability, "Suppliers of Goods and Remote Contracts,"[1] in other words, products liability. Further, in articles published during the 1940s and 1950s, James championed numerous changes in tort law, many of which would materialize during the decades to come. James justified his proposals by applying and analyzing the principles of loss distribution and loss minimization that still feature prominently in the chapters that follow.[2]

The casebook's greatest impact, however, was on the students who studied it. James's students included many future judges and professors (as well as outstanding lawyers), among them, Senior United States Court of Appeals Judge and Yale Professor (formerly Dean) Guido Calabresi. Judge Calabresi recounts how he "first fell in love with the subject fifty-five years ago in Fleming James's torts class."[3] He praises James as "a great torts teacher," but also credits the casebook, which he would later use (and continues to use) teaching Torts at the Yale Law School for more than a half-century.[4]

---

[1] Harry Shulman & Fleming James, Jr., Cases and Materials on the Law of Torts 718–823 (2d ed. 1952).

[2] See Donald G. Gifford, The Death of Causation: Mass Products Torts' Incomplete Incorporation of Social Welfare Principles, 41 Wake Forest L. Rev. 943, 967–69 (2006).

[3] Guido Calabresi, Comments by the Honorable Guido Calabresi, 8 Ind. Health L. Rev. 333, 333 (2010/2011).

[4] Guido Calabresi, Calabresi's The Costs of Accidents: A Generation of Impact on Law and Scholarship: Neologisms Revisited, 64 Md. L. Rev. 736, 739–40 (2005).

The preface to the first edition is strikingly contemporary despite the transformation of tort law during the intervening decades. This latest edition builds upon its predecessors in examining the basic issue of whether there should be liability for accidental injuries even in the absence of fault. At the same time, the cases and other teaching materials have been selected to expose students to a wide variety of ideological perspectives on this issue and on other aspects of tort law instead of viewing them through a single ideological lens. We explicitly consider competing theories of tort liability, including both the instrumental perspective presented in the earlier editions and corrective justice or civil recourse models.

Unlike most torts casebooks, this one does not begin with a study of intentional torts. We begin with *Ives v. South Buffalo Railway Co.*, *infra* pages 3–15, which students initially find challenging but later frequently acknowledge was the most beneficial place to start their study. We then turn our attention to strict liability torts. Professors frequently express frustration that their students do not recognize the importance of the interplay between rules and policy in the everyday practice of law. By beginning the study of tort law with intentional torts, however, many torts professors exacerbate their students' tendencies to view the law as merely the syllogistic application of rules. A recent study of more than 450 students at eight law schools found "that students who begin their study of torts with strict liability experience a greater shift toward understanding the judge's role as being influenced by social, economic, and ideological factors and a sense of fairness and less as a process of rule application than do students who begin their study with either intentional torts or negligence."[5]

The new edition reflects the changes in the law brought about by the recent adoptions of the various parts of the *Restatement (Third) of Torts*. It also considers the United States Supreme Court's increasing involvement—unprecedented in recent memory—in various aspects of tort law including products liability, global climate change, the Alien Tort Statute, and, in the context of an opinion considering the First Amendment rights of protestors at military funerals, even intentional infliction of emotional distress. This edition also includes more notes, questions, and textual discussion to make the casebook more accessible to students.

It is our privilege to present this classic yet remarkably contemporary casebook to students as they enter the wonderfully engaging world of torts and to their professors, who are fortunate to guide them on the journey.

OSCAR S. GRAY

DONALD G. GIFFORD

Baltimore, Maryland
January 2015

---

[5] Donald G. Gifford, Joseph L. Kroart III, Brian Jones & Cheryl Cortemeglia, What's on First? Organizing the Casebook and Molding the Mind, 45 Ariz. St. L.J. 97, 130 (2013).

EXPLANATORY NOTES AND ACKNOWLEDGMENTS

This casebook consists largely of excerpts from judicial opinions and additional materials written by others. We have tried to represent these writings faithfully and accurately. Obviously they have been edited to include only relevant portions and to reduce the length of these materials. Deletions of text from a case opinion or from other materials are marked by triple asterisks ("* * *").

Legal opinions proceed from an analysis of legal authorities— generally previous cases thought to be binding or persuasive or both, statutes, regulations, law review articles and books—that are identified or "cited" in the opinions. To include every citation mentioned in these materials, however, would make them far too voluminous and might distract the student from the flow of the author's reasoning. On the other hand, to delete all citations without any reference to them would create the appearance that the precedents have nothing to do with the conclusions reached by these authorities. For these reasons, citations to authorities are included when we think they may be important to a student's understanding of the law. Where citations have been deleted, the deletions are marked by a single asterisk ("*"). In some instances we have taken the liberty of changing the form of citations to make them more consistent with others in the book or to add the date of the opinion or citations to parallel reporters. In the notes throughout the book, the classic torts treatise, Fowler V. Harper, Fleming James, Jr. and Oscar S. Gray, *Harper, James and Gray on Torts* (3d ed. 2006–2008), is abbreviated as *Harper, James and Gray on Torts*. Finally, we have re-paragraphed a number of opinions in order to make them easier for the modern reader to follow.

We are grateful to our faculty colleagues who used previous editions of this casebook in teaching their Torts classes and have generously shared their suggestions and corrections, especially Peter Cartensen of Wisconsin, Andy Levy and Bill Reynolds of Maryland, Rob Rhee of Florida, and David Super of Georgetown. We have been assisted by a dedicated and competent group of Maryland student research assistants including Monica Basche, Kelsey Harrer, James Houghton, Jane Kalinina, Laura Koman, Stephen Rigg, and Kellsi Wallace. We also express our appreciation to Maxine Grosshans of the Thurgood Marshall Law Library for her superb reference services. Finally, we thank Dean Donald Tobin, former Dean Phoebe A. Haddon, and Director of Information Technologies Gregory Smith for making available the facilities and support of the University of Maryland Carey School of Law.

We also thank the authors and copyright holders of the following books, articles, and other materials for allowing their writings to be included in this text:

American Law Institute, selected provisions of Restatement (Second) of Torts (1965); Restatement (Second) of Torts (1979); Restatement (Third) of Torts: Products Liability (1998); Restatement (Third) of Torts: Apportionment of Liability (2000); Restatement (Third) of Torts: Liability for Physical and Emotional Harm (2010 & 2012); Restatement (Third) of Torts: Intentional Torts to Persons (Discussion

Draft, April 4, 2014); and Restatement (Third) of Torts: Liability for Economic Harm (Tentative Draft No. 2, 2014).

Anderson, James M., Paul Heaton & Stephen J. Carroll, The U.S. Experience with No-Fault Automobile Insurance: A Retrospective 1–2, 8, 14–15, 35, 63, 68, 69, 74, 79, 82, 83, 86, 92, 97, 105, 110–11, 115, 117–19, 120–21, 124–25, 127–28, 133 (Santa Monica, CA: RAND. © RAND 2010. Reprinted by permission).

Calabresi, Guido, Concerning Cause and the Law of Torts: An Essay for Harry Kalven, Jr., 43 U. Chi. L. Rev. 69, 71–72 (1975). © 1975 by the University of Chicago Law Review.

Calabresi, Guido, Some Thoughts on Risk Distribution and the Law of Torts, 70 Yale L.J. 499, 499–500 517–18, 543–45 (1961). Reprinted by permission of The Yale Law Journal Company and William S. Hein Company from The Yale Law Journal, Vol. 110, pages 527–541.

Calabresi, Guido, The Costs of Accidents: A Legal and Economic Analysis 135–38 (1970). © 1970 by the Yale University Press. Reprinted by permission.

Carroll, Stephen J., and James S. Kakalik, No-Fault Automobile Insurance: A Policy Perspective, 4–7, 9 (RAND Institute for Civil Justice, 1991). Santa Monica, CA: RAND. © RAND 1991. Reprinted by permission.

Epstein, Richard A., A Theory of Strict Liability, 2 J. Legal Stud. 151,198–99 (1973). © 1972 by The University of Chicago. All rights reserved.

Feinberg, Kenneth R., The BP Gulf Oil Spill and the Quest for Complete Justice: Unconventional Responses to Unique Catastrophes, 45 Akron L. Rev. 575, 577–79, 582 (2012). Reprinted by permission.

Fischer, David A. & Robert H. Jerry II, Teaching Torts Without Insurance: A Second-Best Solution, 45 St. Louis Univ. L.J. 857, 859–870 (2001). Reprinted by permission.

Gifford, Donald G. & Christopher J. Robinette, Apportioning Liability: Time to End Contributory Negligence and Joint and Several Liability, 73 Md. L. Rev. 701, 759–60 (2014). Reprinted by permission.

Gifford, Donald G., William L. Reynolds & Andrew M. Murad, A Case Study in the Superiority of the Purposive Approach to Statutory Interpretation 64 S.C. L. Rev. 221, 222, 224, 246–62 (2012). Reprinted by permission.

Gifford, Donald G. The Peculiar Challenges Posed by Latent Diseases Resulting from Mass Products, 64 Md. L. Rev. 613, 648–49 (2003). Reprinted by permission.

Harper, Fowler, Fleming James, Jr. & Oscar S. Gray, Harper, James and Gray on Torts §§ 1.28, 3.16, 5.9A, 5.26, 7.8, 11.2, 12.2, 16.13 & 16.13 n.4, 20.5 n.45, 20.6(5), and 27.6 (3d ed. 2006–2008). © 2006–2008 by Oscar S. Gray. Reprinted by permission.

Holmes, Oliver Wendell, THE COMMON LAW, 76–78, 86, 88, 96, 97–99 (1881; Howe ed. 1963). Reprinted by permission of the publisher from THE COMMON LAW by Oliver Wendell Holmes, edited by Mark DeWolfe Howe, Cambridge, Mass. Harvard University Press, © 1963 by the President and Fellows of Harvard College.

James, Fleming, Jr., Memorandum, The Element of Fault in Private Nuisance (Tentative Draft No. 16, 1970), copyright © 1970 by the American Law Institute. Reprinted with permission of the American Law Institute.

Jerry, Robert H. II, and Douglas R. Richmond, Understanding Insurance Law §§ 60B & 65 (5th ed. 2012). Reprinted by permission of LexisNexis.

Noah, Lars, Advertising Prescription Drugs to Consumers: Assessing the Regulatory and Liability Issues, 32 Ga. L. Rev. 141, 157–59, 173, 179 (1997). Reprinted with permission of the Georgia Law Review.

Noonan, John T. Jr., Persons and Masks of the Law: Cardozo, Holmes, Jefferson, and Wythe as Makers of the Masks, 111–51 (2002). Reprinted by permission.

O'Connell, Jeffrey, A "Neo No-Fault" Contract In Lieu of Tort: Preaccident Guarantees of Postaccident Settlement Offers, 73 Cal. L. Rev. 898, 906,913 (1985). © 1985 by The University of California. Reprinted from California Law Review.

Polinsky, A. Mitchell & Steven Shavell, The Uneasy Case for Product Liability, 123 Harv. L. Rev. 1437, 1469–70 (2010). Reprinted by permission.

Posner, Richard A., A Theory of Negligence, 1 J. Legal Stud. 29, 32–34 (1972). © 1972 by The University of Chicago. All rights reserved.

Rhee, Robert J., Loss of Chance, Probabilistic Cause, and Damage Calculations: The Error in *Matsuyama v. Birnbaum* and the Majority Rule of Damages in Many Jurisdictions More Generally, 1 Suffolk U. L. Rev. Online 39, 4-9–9-9, (2013), *available at* http://suffolklawreview.org/wp-content/uploads/2013/03/Rhee_Web_PDF.pdf.   Reprinted   by permission.

Samuelson, Paul A. & William D. Nordhaus, Economics 286–87 (19th ed. 2009). Reprinted by permission.

Sugarman, Stephen D., Doing Away With Tort Law, 73 Cal. L. Rev. 555 (1985). © 1985 by the University of California, Berkeley. Reprinted by permission of the California Law Review. This article originally appeared at 73 Cal. L. Rev. 558 (1985).

Todd, Stephen, Privatization of Accident Compensation: Policy and Politics in New Zealand, 39 Washburn L.J. 404 (2000). Reprinted by permission.

Wilkinson, Bryce, New Zealand's Failed Experiment with State Monopoly Accident Insurance, 2 Green Bag 2d 45 (1998). Reprinted by permission.

Witt, John Fabian, Toward A New History of American Accident Law: Classical Tort Law and the Cooperative First-Party Insurance Movement, 114 Harv. L. Rev. 690, 693–95, 719–22, 759, 766–67 (2001). © 2001 by the Harvard Law Review Association.

SUMMARY OF CONTENTS

TABLE OF CONTENTS

TABLE OF CASES

The principal cases are in bold type.

TABLE OF RESTATEMENT SECTIONS

Restatement (Second) of Torts (1977)

Restatement (Second) of Torts (1979)

Restatement (Third) of Torts: Products Liability (1998)

Restatement (Third) of Torts: Intentional Torts to Persons (Discussion Draft, April 4, 2014)

Restatement (Third) of Unfair Competition (1995)

LAW OF TORTS

CASES AND MATERIALS

SIXTH EDITION

CHAPTER 1

BASES OF LIABILITY FOR ACCIDENTAL HARM

A. INTRODUCTION

Chapters 1 through 13 of this casebook address primarily losses resulting from accidental injuries of a physical nature to person or property. By accidental, we mean that the injury is the more or less incidental (and usually undesired) by-product of carrying on legitimate activities of one sort or another.

Modern industrialized societies provide the setting for staggering numbers of accidental injuries to people and property. Millions of Americans are injured accidentally each year, nearly 100,000 fatally.[a] The cost of personal injury accidents exceeds $175 billion annually in medical, employment, and other economic losses, not to mention the intangible costs, such as emotional distress and suffering resulting from physical pain.

A central focus of tort law is whether the costs of accidents should be shifted from the party that originally sustained them to another party that caused the accident. In this connection a subsidiary issue has assumed considerable importance: the relevance of "fault" (in the sense of culpability) to the allocation of accident costs.

Excerpt, John Fabian Witt, Toward a New History of American Accident Law: Classical Tort Law and the Cooperative First Party Insurance Movement
114 Harv. L. Rev. 690, 693–95, 719–22, 759, 766–67 (2001).

* * * [T]he great waves of industrialization in the American economy have always been, and will surely always remain, a central interpretive tool in explaining changes in the nineteenth- and twentieth-century law of torts. * * * In the second half of the nineteenth century, the United States experienced an accident crisis like none the world had ever seen and like none any Western nation has witnessed since. By the turn of the century, one worker in fifty was killed or disabled for at least four weeks each year because of a work-related accident. In the population as a whole, roughly one in every thousand Americans died by accident each year. In dangerous industries, accident rates were considerably higher. * * * The most extraordinary rates of death and injury appear to have been reached in the anthracite coal mines of Pennsylvania, where each year during the 1860s and 1870s six percent of the workforce was killed, six percent permanently crippled, and six percent seriously but temporarily disabled. By comparison to other Western economies, accident rates in the late nineteenth- and

---

early twentieth-century United States were remarkably high. Railroad fatalities, for example, were four times more frequent per train-mile in the United States than in England. And by comparison to today, rates of accidental death at the turn of the century were astronomical. The annual accidental death rate of one in one thousand for the population as a whole in the United States in 1900 is as great as that of the single most dangerous occupation (lumber and timber work) at the opening of the twenty-first century. * * * The common law of torts emerged in these years—for the first time—as an accident law regime. * * *

It is clear that nineteenth-century observers believed that the number of accidental injuries was increasing rapidly. Moreover, they were certain that the cause of the perceived increase in injury rates was the increased mechanization of industrial life. Muckraking journalists of the early twentieth century, of course, voiced this complaint quite vigorously. "The radical revolution in industrial methods," contended a typical article in the New York magazine *The Independent*, "has involved a vast increase of danger to the laborers." Accidental death and injury, wrote another journalist, were "the inevitable concomitants of high-speed machine production." * * *

* * * [T]he industrial revolution devised myriad new and unfamiliar mechanisms for inflicting harm on the human body. If age-old sources of injury, illness, and premature death had been more or less integrated into the fabric of everyday life, new industrial causes of accident and death stood out in bold relief against the background of traditional and familiar sources of human suffering. * * * [W]hile ancient and familiar sources of tragedy appeared to be caused by some combination of natural forces, acts of God, and fate, railroad accidents seemed to have human causes that were direct and immediate. As Carroll Wright of the Massachusetts Bureau of Labor Statistics observed in 1883, disability and death arising out of age-old sources could be chalked up to mere chance. In railroad accidents, by contrast, Wright claimed that most Americans believed that "[n]o man dies without a cause, though the cause and the causer may remain alike unknown." * * *

Even as late as the mid-nineteenth century, remarkably few Americans sued for personal injuries. Randolph Bergstrom found that in New York City in 1870 * * * a total of thirteen personal injury suits [were filed] for the entire year, some thirteen years after the abolition of the party disqualification rule in New York. By 1890, however, the number of accident suits being litigated in New York courts had grown almost eight-fold, and by 1910 that number had grown again by more than a factor of four. * * *

As late as the early 1880s, students of American industrial accidents believed that accidents were almost always the result of someone's fault. "Every death upon a railroad," explained Carroll Wright in 1883, "like every death by violence, is the result of somebody's negligence or willfulness." By the turn of the century, however, it seemed increasingly unlikely in many instances that accidents could be traced to any human fault. The New York Bureau of Labor Statistics claimed that "in modern industry," with its "extremely complicated machinery," it was "impossible to locate the responsibility" in work accident cases. In Maryland in 1902, the legislature announced that in "perilous occupations . . . unavoidable or trade risk is responsible for at least ninety-five per cent" of fatal accidents. * * *

Ives v. South Buffalo Railway Co.
Court of Appeals of New York, 1911.
201 N.Y. 271, 94 N.E. 431.

This is an action brought by an employee against his employer to recover compensation under article 14–a of the Labor Law, being chapter 674 of the Laws of 1910, entitled "An act to amend the labor law, in relation to workmen's compensation in certain dangerous employments."

The complaint alleges, in substance, that on the second day of September 1910, while the plaintiff was engaged in his work as a switchman on defendant's steam railroad, he was injured solely by reason of a necessary risk or danger of his employment; that at the time of the commencement of the action he had been totally incapacitated for labor for a period of three weeks, and that such incapacity would continue for four weeks longer, and demands judgment for compensation in accordance with the provisions of said act for a period of five weeks. The answer, after admitting all the allegations of the complaint, pleads as a defense the unconstitutionality of article 14–a of the Labor Law, upon the ground that it contravenes certain provisions of the Federal and State Constitutions. The plaintiff demurred to this defense on the ground that it was insufficient in law upon the face thereof. The issue of law thus presented was tried at Special Term, where the demurrer was sustained. Final judgment was entered upon this decision, and the defendant appealed to the Appellate Division, where the judgment was affirmed by a divided court. * * *

■ WERNER, J. In 1909 the legislature passed a law (Chapter 518) providing for a commission of fourteen persons, six of whom were to be appointed by the governor, three by the president of the senate from the senate, and five by the speaker of the assembly from the assembly, "to make inquiry, examination and investigation into the working of the law in the State of New York relative to the liability of employers to employees for industrial accidents, and into the comparative efficiency, cost, justice, merits and defects of the laws of other industrial states and countries, relative to the same subject, and as to the causes of the accidents to employees." The act contained other provisions germane to the subject and provided for a full and final report to the legislature of 1910, if practicable, and if not practicable then to the legislature of 1911, with such recommendations for legislation by bill or otherwise as the commission might deem wise or expedient. Such a commission was appointed and promptly organized by the election of officers and the appointment of sub-committees, the chairman being Senator Wainwright, from whom it has taken the name of the "Wainwright Commission," by which it is popularly known.

No word of praise could overstate the industry and intelligence of this commission in dealing with a subject of such manifold ramifications and of such far-reaching importance to the state, to employers, and to employees. We cannot dwell in detail upon the many excellent features of its comprehensive report, because the limitations of time and space must necessarily confine us to such of its aspects as have a necessary relation to the legal questions which we are called upon to decide. As the result of its labors the commission recommended for adoption the bill which, with slight changes, was enacted into law by the Legislature of 1910, under the designation of article 14–a of the Labor Law. This act is modeled upon the English Workmen's Compensation Act of 1897, which has since been extended so as to cover every kind of occupational injury. Our commission has frankly stated in its report that the classification of the industries which will be immediately affected by the present statute is only tentative, and that other more extended classifications will probably be recommended to the legislature for its action.

The statute, judged by our common-law standards, is plainly revolutionary. Its central and controlling feature is that every employer who is engaged in any of the classified industries shall be liable for any injury to a workman arising out of and in the course of the employment by "a necessary risk or danger of the employment or one inherent in the nature thereof; . . . provided that the employer shall not be liable in respect of any injury to the workman which is caused in whole or in part by the serious and willful misconduct of the workman."[a] This rule of liability, stated in another form, is that the employer is responsible to the employee for every accident in the course of the employment, whether the employer is at fault or not, and whether the employee is at fault or not, except when the fault of the employee is so grave as to constitute serious and willful misconduct on his part.

The radical character of this legislation is at once revealed by contrasting it with the rule of the common law, under which the employer is liable for injuries to his employee only when the employer is guilty of some act or acts of negligence which caused the occurrence out of which the injuries arise, and then only when the employee is shown to be free from any negligence which contributes to the occurrence. The several judicial and statutory modifications of this broad rule of the common law we shall further on have occasion to mention. Just now our purpose is to present in sharp juxtaposition the fundamentals of these two opposing rules, namely, that under the common law an employer is liable to his injured employee only when the employer is at fault and the employee is free from fault; while under the new statute the employer is liable, although not at fault, even when the employee is at fault, unless this latter fault amounts to serious and willful misconduct. The reasons for this departure from our long-established law and usage are summarized in the language of the commission as follows:

> *First,* that the present system in New York rests on a basis that is economically unwise and unfair, and that in operation

---

[a]   [Eds.' note] The amount of compensation that might be recovered under the act was limited: it was computed on the basis of average weekly wages. Law of June 25, 1910, ch. 674, § 219, 1910 New York Laws 1945 (repealed 1913). Another section (§ 218) preserved all existing rights of action at common law or under statute but provided that any action brought under the act would bar any other recovery. Section 219–d provided that claims under the act might be settled, arbitrated, or might be the basis for an action at law in any court of appropriate jurisdiction. For a brief description of how workers compensation systems operate today, see Fowler V. Harper, Fleming James, Jr. & Oscar S. Gray, Harper, James and Gray on Torts, § 11.2, *infra* pages 15–16.

it is wasteful, uncertain, and productive of antagonism between workmen and employers.

Second, that it is satisfactory to none and tolerable only to those employers and workmen who practically disregard their legal rights and obligations, and fairly share the burden of accidents in industries.

Third, that the evils of the system are most marked in hazardous employments, where the trade risk is high and serious accidents frequent.

Fourth, that, as matter of fact, workmen in the dangerous trades do not, and practically cannot, provide for themselves adequate accident insurance, and, therefore, the burden of serious accidents falls on the workmen least able to bear it, and brings many of them and their families to want.

This indictment of the old system is followed by a statement of the anticipated benefits under the new statute as follows:

These results can, we think, be best avoided by compelling the employer to share the accident burden in intrinsically dangerous trades, since by fixing the price of his product the shock of the accident may be borne by the community. In those employments which have not so great an element of danger, in which, speaking generally, there is no such imperative demand for the exercise of the police power of the state for the safeguarding of its workers from destitution and its consequences, we recommend, as the first step in this change of system, such amendment of the present law as will do away with some of its unfairness in theory and practice, and increase the workman's chance of recovery under the law. With such changes in the law we couple an elective plan of compensation which, if generally adopted, will do away with many the evils of the present system. Its adoption will, we believe, be profitable to both employers and employees, and prove to be the simplest way for the State to change its system of liability without disturbance of industrial conditions. Not the least of the motives moving us is the hope that by these means a source of antagonism between employer and employed, pregnant with danger for the State, may be eliminated.

This quoted summary of the report of the commission to the Legislature, which clearly and fairly epitomizes what is more fully set forth in the body of the report, is based upon a most voluminous array of statistical tables, extracts from the works of philosophical writers and the industrial laws of many countries, all of which are designed to show that our own system of dealing with industrial accidents is economically, morally, and legally unsound. Under our form of government, however, courts must regard all economic, philosophical, and moral theories, attractive and desirable though they may be, as subordinate to the primary question whether they can be molded into statutes without infringing upon the letter or spirit of our written constitutions. In that respect we are unlike any of the countries whose industrial laws are referred to as models for our guidance. Practically all of these countries are so called constitutional monarchies in which, as in England, there is no written constitution, and the Parliament or law-making body is supreme. In our country the federal and state constitutions are the charters which demark the extent and the limitations of legislative power; and while it is true that the rigidity of a written constitution may at times prove to be a hindrance to the march of progress, yet more often its stability protects the people against the frequent and violent fluctuations of that which, for want of a better name, we call public opinion.

* * * The new statute, as we have observed, is totally at variance with the common-law theory of the employer's liability. Fault on his part is no longer an element of the employee's right of action. This change necessarily and logically carries with it the abrogation of the "fellow-servant" doctrine, the "contributory negligence" rule, and the law relating to the employee's assumption of risks. * * *

The "fellow-servant" rule is one of judicial origin engrafted upon the common law for the protection of the master against the consequences of negligence in which he has no part. In its early application to simple industrial conditions it had the support of both reason and justice. By degrees it was extended until it became evident that under the enormous expansion and infinite complexity of our modern industrial conditions the rule gave opportunity, in many instances, for harsh and technical defenses. * * *

The law of contributory negligence has the support of reason in any system of jurisprudence in which the fault of one is the basis of liability for injury to another. Under such a system it is at least logical to hold that one who is himself to blame for his injuries should not be permitted to entail the consequences upon another who has not been negligent at all, or whose negligence would not have caused the injury if the one injured had been free from fault. * * *

Under the common law the employee was also held to have assumed the ordinary and obvious risks incident to the employment, as well as the special risks arising out of dangerous conditions which were known and appreciated by him. This doctrine, too, has been modified by statute so that * * * the employee is presumed to have assented to the necessary risks of the occupation or employment and no others; and these necessary risks are defined as those only which are inherent in the nature of the business and exist after the employer has exercised due care in providing for the safety of his employees, and has complied with the laws affecting or regulating the business or occupation for the greater safety of employees. * * *

This legislation is challenged as void under the fourteenth amendment to the federal Constitution and under section 6, art. 1 of our state Constitution, which guarantee all persons against deprivation of life, liberty, or property without due process of law. We shall not stop to dwell at length upon definitions of "life," "liberty," "property," and "due process of law." They are simple and comprehensive in themselves, and have been so often judicially defined that there can be no misunderstanding as to their meaning. "Process of law" in its broad sense means law in its regular course of administration through courts of justice, and that is but another way of saying that every man's right to life, liberty, and property is to be disposed of in accordance with those ancient and fundamental principles which were in existence when our constitutions were adopted. "Due process of law implies the right of the person affected thereby to be present before the tribunal which pronounces judgment upon the question of life, liberty or property in its most comprehensive sense, to be heard by testimony or otherwise, and to have the right of controverting by proof every material fact which bears upon the question of right in the matter involved. If any question of fact or liability be conclusively presumed against him this is not due process of law." Zeigler v. S. & N. Ala. R.R. Co., 58 Ala. 594 (1877). Liberty has been authoritatively defined as "the right of one to use his faculties in all lawful ways, to live and work where he will, to earn his livelihood in any lawful calling, and to pursue any lawful trade or avocation," Matter of Jacobs, 98 N.Y. 98, 106, 50 Am. Rep. 636 (1885); and the right of property as "the right to acquire, possess and enjoy it in any way consistent with the equal rights of others and the just exactions and demands of the state." Bertholf v. O'Reilly, 74 N.Y. 509, 515, 30 Am.Rep. 323 (1878). The several industries and occupations enumerated in the statute before us are concededly lawful within any of the numerous definitions which might be referred to, and have always been so. They are, therefore, under the constitutional protection.

One of the inalienable rights of every citizen is to hold and enjoy his property until it is taken from him by due process of law. When our Constitutions were adopted, it was the law of the land that no man who was without fault or negligence could be held liable in damages for injuries sustained by another. That is still the law, except as to the employers enumerated in the new statute, and as to them it provides that they shall be liable to their employees for personal injury by accident to any workman arising out of and in the course of the employment which is caused in whole or in part, or is contributed to, by a necessary risk or danger of the employment or one inherent in the nature thereof, except that there shall be no liability in any case where the injury is caused in whole or in part by the serious and willful misconduct of the injured workman. It is conceded that this is a liability unknown to the common law and we think it plainly constitutes a deprivation of liberty and property under the federal and state Constitutions, unless its imposition can be justified under the police power which will be discussed under a separate head.

In arriving at this conclusion we do not overlook the cogent economic and sociological arguments which are urged in support of the statute. There can be no doubt as to the theory of this law. It is based upon the proposition that the inherent risks of an employment should in justice be placed upon the shoulders of the employer, who can protect himself against loss by insurance and by such an addition to the price of his wares as to cast the burden ultimately upon the consumer; that indemnity to an injured employee should be as much a charge upon the business as the cost of replacing or repairing disabled or defective machinery, appliances, or tools; that, under our present system, the loss falls immediately upon the employee who is almost invariably unable to bear it, and ultimately upon the community which is taxed for the support of the indigent; and that our present system is uncertain, unscientific, and wasteful, and fosters a spirit of antagonism between employer and employee which it is to the interests of the state to remove. We have already admitted the strength of this appeal to a recognized and widely prevalent sentiment, but we think it is an appeal which must be made to the people and not to the courts.

The right of property rests not upon philosophical or scientific speculations nor upon the commendable impulses of benevolence or charity, nor yet upon the dictates of natural justice. The right has its foundation in the fundamental law. That can be changed by the people, but not by legislatures. In a government like ours theories of public goods or necessity are often so plausible or sound as to command popular approval, but courts are not permitted to forget that the law is the only chart by which the ship of state is to be guided. Law as used in this sense means the basic law, and not the very act of legislation which deprives the citizen of his rights, privileges or property. Any other view would lead to the absurdity that the Constitutions protect only those rights which the legislatures do not take away. If such economic and sociologic arguments as are here advanced in support of this statute can be allowed to subvert the fundamental idea of property, then there is no private right entirely safe, because there is no limitation upon the absolute discretion of legislatures, and the guarantees of the Constitution are a mere waste of words. Wynehamer v. People, 13 N.Y. 378 (1856); Taylor v. Porter, 4 Hill 140, 145, 40 Am.Dec. 274 (1843); Norman v. Heist, 5 Watts. & Serg. (Pa.) 171, 40 Am.Dec. 493 (1843); Hoke v. Henderson, 4 Dev. 15, 15 N.C. 1 (1833). As stated by Judge Comstock in the case of Wynehamer v. People, "these constitutional safeguards, in all cases, require a judicial investigation, not to be governed by a law specially enacted to take away and destroy existing rights, but confined to the question whether, under the pre-existing rule of conduct, the right in controversy has been lawfully acquired and is lawfully possessed."

If the argument in support of this statute is sound we do not see why it cannot logically be carried much further. Poverty and misfortune from every cause are detrimental to the state. It would probably conduce to the welfare of all concerned if there could be a more equal distribution of wealth. Many persons have much more property than they can use to advantage and many more find it impossible to get the means for a comfortable existence. If the legislature can say to an employer, "you must compensate your employee for an injury not caused by you or by your fault," why can it not go further and say to the man of wealth, "you have more property than you need and your neighbor is so poor that he can barely subsist; in the interest of natural justice you must divide with your neighbor so that he and his dependents shall not become a charge upon the State?"

The argument that the risk to an employee should be borne by the employer because it is inherent in the employment, may be economically sound, but it is at war with the legal principle that no employer can be compelled to assume a risk which is inseparable from the work of the employee, and which may exist in spite of a degree of care by the employer far greater than may be exacted by the most drastic law. If it is competent to impose upon an employer, who has omitted no legal duty and has committed no wrong, a liability based solely upon a legislative fiat that his business is inherently dangerous, it is equally competent to visit upon him a special tax for the support of hospitals and other charitable institutions, upon the theory that they are devoted largely to the alleviation of ills primarily due to his business. In its final and simple analysis that is taking the property of A and giving it to B, and that cannot be done under our Constitutions. Practical and simple illustrations of the extent to which this theory of liability might be carried could be multiplied *ad infinitum*, and many will readily occur to the thoughtful reader.

There is, of course, in this country no direct legal authority upon the subject of the liability sought to be imposed by this statute, for the theory is not merely new in our system of jurisprudence, but plainly antagonistic to its basic idea. The English authorities are of no assistance to us, because in the king's courts the decrees of the Parliament are the supreme law of the land, although they are interesting in their disclosures of the paternalism which logically results from a universal employers' liability based solely upon the relation of employer and employee, and not upon fault in the employer.

There are a few American cases, however, which clearly state the legal principle which, we think, is applicable to the case at bar, and with a brief reference to them we shall close this branch of the discussion. In the nitroglycerine case, Parrot v. Wells, Fargo & Co., 15 Wall. 524, 21 L.Ed. 206 (1872), the plaintiff, who was the common landlord of the defendants and other tenants, sought to hold the defendants liable for damages occasioned to the premises occupied by the other tenants, by an explosion of nitroglycerine which had been delivered to the defendants as common carriers for shipment. It appeared that the defendants were innocently ignorant of the contents of the packages containing the dangerous explosives, and that they were guilty of no negligence in receiving or handling them. Upon these facts the Federal Supreme Court held that it was a case of unavoidable accident for which no one was legally responsible.

In Ohio & Mississippi Ry. Co. v. Lackey, 78 Ill. 55 (1875), the question was whether the railroad company was liable under a statute which provided that "every railroad company running cars within this State shall be liable for all the expense of the coroner and his inquest, and the burial of all persons who may die on the cars, or who may be killed by collision, or other accident occurring to such cars, or otherwise." In speaking of the effect of that section of the law Mr. Justice Breese observed: "An examination of the section will show that no default, or negligence of any kind, need be established against the railroad company, but they are mulcted in heavy charges if, notwithstanding all their care and caution, a death should occur on one of their cars, no matter how caused, even if by the party's own hand. Running of trains by these corporations is lawful and of great public benefit. It is not claimed that the liability attaches for the violation of any law, the omission of any duty or the want of proper care or skill in running their trains. The penalty is not aimed at anything of this kind. We say penalty, for it is in the nature of a penalty, and there is a constitutional inhibition against imposing penalties where no law has been violated or duty neglected. Neither is pretended in this case, nor are they in the contemplation of the statute. A passenger on a train dies from sickness. He is a man of wealth. Why should his burial expenses be charged to the railroad company? There is neither reason nor justice in it; and if he be poor, having not the means for a decent burial, the general law makes ample provision for such cases." To the same effect are the numerous cases arising under statutes passed by different states imposing upon railroad corporations absolute liability for killing or injuring upon their rights of way horses, cattle, etc., by running over them, in which this liability was held to constitute a deprivation of property without due process of law. Jensen v. Union Pacific Ry. Co., 6 Utah 253, 21 P. 994 (1889); Zeigler v. South & North Alabama Ry. Co., 58 Ala. 594 (1877). *

A different interpretation has been given to statutes imposing upon railroad corporations the duty to fence their rights of way, under which the liability is imposed for failure to obey the command of the statutes. Quackenbush v. Wis. & M. R.R. Co., 62 Wis. 411, 22 N.W. 519 (1885). * "But even such statutes," says Black in his work on Constitutional Law (2d ed. p. 351), "cannot go beyond the imposition of such a penalty in cases where the fault lies at the door of the company. If the law attempts to make such companies liable for accidents which were not caused by their negligence or disobedience of the law, but by the negligence of others or by uncontrollable causes, or does not give the company an opportunity to show these facts in its own defense, it is void."

We conclude, therefore, that in its basic and vital features the right given to the employee by this statute, does not preserve to the employer the "due process" of law guaranteed by the Constitutions, for it authorizes the taking of the employer's property without his consent and without his fault. * * *

If we are warranted in concluding that the new statute violates private right by taking the property of one and giving it to another without due process of law, that is really the end of this case. But the auspices under which this legislation was enacted, no less than its intrinsic importance, entitle its advocates to the fullest consideration of every argument in its support, and we, therefore, take up the discussion of the police power under which this law is sought to be justified. The police power is, of course, one of the necessary attributes of civilized government. In its most comprehensive sense it embraces the whole system by which the state seeks to preserve the public order, to prevent offenses against the law, to insure to citizens in their intercourse with each other the enjoyment of their own so far as is reasonably consistent with a like enjoyment of rights by others. Under it persons and property are subjected to all kinds of restraints and burdens in order to secure the general comfort, health and prosperity of the state. But it is a power which is always subject to the Constitution, for in a constitutional government limitation is the abiding principle, exhibited in its highest form in the Constitution as the deliberative judgment of the people, which moderates every claim of right and controls every use of power. In the language of Chief Justice Shaw, in Commonwealth v. Alger, 7 Cush. 53, 85, 61 Mass. 53, 85 (1851): "It is much easier to perceive and realize the existence and sources of this power than to mark its boundaries or prescribe limits to its exercise." It covers a multitude of things that are designed to protect life, limb, health, comfort, peace, and property according to the maxim *sic utere tuo ut alienum non laedas*, but its exercise is justified only when it appears that the interests of the public generally, as distinguished from those of a particular class, require it, and when the means used are reasonably necessary for the accomplishment of the desired end, and are not unduly oppressive. *

In order to sustain legislation under the police power the courts must be able to see that its operation tends in some degree to prevent some offense or evil, or to preserve public health, morals, safety, and welfare. If it discloses no such purpose, but is clearly calculated to invade the liberty and property of private citizens, it is plainly the duty of the courts to declare it invalid; for legislative assumption of the right to direct the channel into which the private energies of the citizen may flow, or legislative attempt to abridge or hamper the right of the citizen to pursue, unmolested and without unreasonable regulation, any lawful calling or avocation which he may choose, has always been condemned under our form of government.

Concrete illustrations of what may and what may not be done under the police power are to be found in this very Labor Law of which the new statute is a part. As this statute stood before article 14–a was added, it regulated electric work, the operation of elevators, work on scaffolds, work with explosives and compressed air, the construction of tunnels and railroad work. It regulated the hours of work in certain employments; it directed the payment of wages in cash at specified periods; it provided for the protection of employees engaged in the erection of buildings; it compelled the employer to guard dangerous and exposed machinery and to construct fire escapes and ventilating appliances; it required him to provide toilet facilities, pure drinking water, and sanitary arrangements and prohibited the employment of women, and of children under certain ages, in specified occupations; it regulated the hours of labor of minors; it modified the fellow-servant rule, the law of contributory negligence and the assumption of risks; and, in short, it imposed upon the employer many restrictions and duties which were unknown to the common law. Broadly classified, all these and similar statutory provisions which are designed, in one way or another, to conserve the health, safety or morals of the employees and to increase the duties and responsibilities of the employer, are rules of conduct which properly fall within the sphere of the police power. * But the new addition to the Labor Law is of quite a different character. It does nothing to conserve the health, safety or morals of the employees, and it imposes upon the employer no new or affirmative duties or responsibilities in the conduct of his business. Its sole purpose is to make him liable for injuries which may be sustained wholly without his fault, and solely through the fault of the employee, except where the latter fault is such as to constitute serious and willful misconduct. Under this law, the most thoughtful and careful employer, who has neglected no duty, and whose workshop is equipped with every possible appliance that may make for the safety, health and morals of his employees, is liable in damages to any employee who happens to sustain injury through an accident which no human being can foresee or prevent, or which, if preventable at all, can only be prevented by the reasonable care of the employee himself.

That this is the unmistakable theory and purpose of the act is made perfectly plain by the recital in section 215, which sets forth that from the nature, conditions, or mean of prosecution of the work in the employments which are classified a dangerous, "extraordinary risks to the life and limb of workmen engaged therein are inherent, necessary or substantially unavoidable, and as to each of which employments it is deemed necessary to establish a new system of compensation for accidents to workmen." And to make the matter still more plain, the learned counsel for the commission argues in his brief that "if it is competent for the legislature to say to the employer in a dangerous trade, 'use the utmost care in giving your workmen safe work, so that no act of yours, or implement of yours, or work that you set them to do shall hurt them, and if you fail you shall be liable in damages,' if it is competent to make such a law, then it is equally competent to say as in this new act directly, 'you shall be responsible for all damages caused by unsafe condition of work,' and that is just what the liability for trade risks under the new act means."

In this argument the learned counsel ignores, or at least misses, as we think, the vital distinction between legislation which imposes upon an employer a legal duty, for the failure to perform which he may be penalized or rendered liable in damages, and legislation which makes him liable notwithstanding he has faithfully observed every duty imposed upon him by law. * * *

* * * Conceding, as we do, that it is within the range of proper legislative action to give a workman two remedies for a wrong when he had but one before, we ask, by what stretch of the police power is the legislature, authorized to give a remedy for no wrong? If, before the passage of this law, the employer had a right to a jury trial upon the question of liability, where and how did he lose it? Can it be taken from him by the mere assertion that this statute only reverses the common-law doctrine that the employee assumes the risk of his employment? It would be quite as logical and effective to argue that this legislation only reverses the laws of nature, for in everything within the sphere of human activity the risks which are inherent and unavoidable must fall upon those who are exposed to them. * * *

In support of this new statute we are also asked to consider the supposed analogies of the laws of deodands; the common-law liability of the husband for the torts of his wife; the liability of the master for the acts of his servant; and the liability of a ship for the care and maintenance of sick or disabled seamen. From the historical point of view, these subjects might be very entertainingly elaborated, but for the practical purposes of this discussion they may be very briefly disposed of. If the law of deodands was ever imported into this country it has never, to our knowledge, found expression in a single statute or judicial decision.[b] It was one of those primitive conceptions of justice under

---

    [b]   [Eds.' note] But see Act of March 31, 1868, sec. 5, 15, Stat. 58, 59, which provides for forfeiture of any distillery and distilling apparatus "used by" a distiller who shall "attempt to defraud the United States of the tax on * * * spirits;" and Dobbins' Distillery v. United States, 96 U.S. 395, 24 L.Ed. 637 (1877), where the distillery had been fraudulently operated by a lessee, but the statute was applied against the assertedly innocent lessor as well: "Nothing can be plainer * * * than * * * that the offense therein defined is attached primarily to the distillery, * * * without any regard whatsoever to the personal misconduct or responsibility of the owner * * * ." As recently as 1996, the United States Supreme Court upheld the constitutionality of the forfeiture of property used to engage in a public nuisance against the due process claims of an innocent owner. In Bennis v. Michigan, 516 U.S. 442, 116 S.Ct. 994, 134 L.Ed.2d 68 (1996), the petitioner was the joint owner, along with her husband, of an automobile seized by the state after her husband was arrested and convicted for engaging in sexual activity with a prostitute in the vehicle. The Supreme Court found that although the

which a chattel which caused the death of a human being was forfeited to the king. We are unable to see what bearing it can have upon the question whether, under our Constitutions, it is due process of law to render a man liable for damages when he has been guilty of no fault.

Quite as far-fetched seems the argument based upon the common-law liability of the husband for the torts of his wife. Under the common-law unity of husband and wife, the latter was presumed to act under the compulsion of the former; and the wife could never be sued alone. As the marriage vested the husband with the personal property of the wife, it was simply logical that he should pay her obligations. So with the liability of the master for the acts of his servant, the whole theory is expressed in the maxim *qui facit per alium facit per se.* He who acts through another acts himself. How do these illustrations support the principle of liability without fault? Could a husband or master be held liable under the common law when the wife or servant had been guilty of no wrong? Would the common law have denied to the husband or master the right to prove that no tort had been committed by the wife or servant?

The admiralty cases of The Osceola, 189 U.S. 158, 23 S.Ct. 483, 47 L.Ed. 760 (1903), The City of Alexandria, 17 F. 390 (S.D.N.Y. 1883), and the case of Scarff v. Metcalf, 107 N.Y. 211, 13 N.E. 796 (1887), seem to us equally inapplicable as authorities for the proposition that the law recognizes liability without fault. It is common knowledge that the contracts and services of seamen are exceptional in character. A seaman engages for the voyage. He is subject to physical discipline, and exposed to hardships and dangers peculiar to the sea. He is, in effect, a co-adventurer with the master, and shares in the risks of shipwreck and capture, often losing his wages by casualties which do not affect workmen on land. For these and many other obvious reasons the maritime law has wisely and benevolently built up peculiar rights and privileges for the protection of the seaman which are not cognizable in the common law. When he is sick or injured he is entitled to be cared for at the expense of the ship, and, for the failure of the master to perform his duty in this regard, the ship or the owner is liable. That is a right given to the seaman, and a duty enjoined upon the master, by the plainest dictates of justice, which arises out of the necessities of the case; and, because of the reason of the rule, the right and duty cease when the contract has terminated and the seaman has been returned to the port of shipment or discharge, or has been furnished with means to do so. But, beyond this duty on the part of the master or owner, there seems to be no liability whatever for injuries sustained by the seaman in the course of his work. We think it may confidently be asserted that within the whole range of the maritime law there will be found no rule which renders master, owner, or ship liable in damages for an injury sustained by the seaman without fault on the part of any one, or without any fault except his own. The case of Scarff v. Metcalf, *supra,* was not disposed of upon any such theory, but was based upon the

---

petitioner was an innocent owner of the property, and was not aware of the use of the automobile by her husband for illegal purposes, the seizure of the auto under state forfeiture laws did not violate the due process clause of the Fourteenth Amendment. Accordingly, the petitioner was not entitled to recover the auto or any portion of its value.

neglect of the master to perform the duty of caring for the injured seaman imposed by the maritime law. * * *

Great reliance is placed upon the case of St. Louis & San Francisco Ry. Co. v. Mathews, 165 U.S. 1, 17 S.Ct. 243, 41 L.Ed. 611 (1897), in support of the contention that there may be liability where there is no delinquency. That was an action brought by an owner of land adjoining the defendant's railroad to recover damages for the destruction of his dwelling house and other buildings, caused by fire which spread from sparks emitted by the defendant's locomotives. The action was brought under a statute of the state of Missouri which provided that "each railroad corporation, owning or operating a railroad in this state, shall be responsible in damages to every person and corporation whose property may be injured or destroyed by fire communicated, directly or indirectly, by locomotive engines in use upon the railroad owned or operated by such railroad corporation; and each such railroad corporation shall have an insurable interest in the property upon the route of the railroad owned or operated by it, and may procure insurance thereon in its own behalf, for its protection against such damages." The statute was upheld as being within the legislative power of the state. That decision is amply supported by a number of reasons which have no application to the controversy at bar. To begin with, the Constitution of Missouri contained a clause, which was in force when the railroad company obtained its charter, providing that "the exercise of the police power of the state shall never be abridged, or so construed as to permit corporations to conduct their business in such manner as to infringe the equal rights of individuals, or the general well-being of the state." Missouri Const. art. 12, § 5. Another ample reason is found in the fact that railroads alone "have the privilege of taking a narrow strip of land from each owner, without his consent, along the route selected for the track, and of traversing the same at all hours of the day and night, and at all seasons whether wet or dry, with locomotive engines that scatter fire along the margin of the land not taken, thereby subjecting all combustible property to extraordinary hazard of loss." Grissell v. Housatonic R.R. Co., 54 Conn. 447, 9 A. 137 (1886). * * * A legislature may, if it chooses, make it a condition of the right to run carriages propelled the agency of fire, that the corporation employing them shall be responsible for all injuries which fire may cause. Ingersoll and Quigley v. Stockbridge & Pittsfield R.R. Co., 8 Allen 438, 90 Mass. 438 (1864); Grand Trunk Ry. Co. v. Richardson, 91 U.S. 454, 23 L.Ed. 356 (1875).

And, finally, these statutes are designed to protect the rights of those who have no contractual relations to the corporations which inflict the injury. In such a case, when both parties are equally faultless, the legislature may properly consider it to be just that the duty of insuring private property against loss or injury caused by the use of the dangerous instruments should rest up the railroad company, which employs the instruments and creates the peril for its own profit, rather than upon the owner of the proper who has no control over or interest in these instruments. Quite aside from the considerations which support such a statutory liability against railroad corporations, it may be added that it is in no sense an extension of the rule of the common law to modern conditions, but in reality a return to the original common-law doctrine under which every person who permitted fire started by him to escape beyond his house or close was liable to every one who suffered loss or injury thereby. The severity of that early English rule was moderated by numerous statutes, among which are 6 Anne and 14 Geo. III. As to these two last-mentioned statutes it has been held that they became by adoption a part of the common law of this state, * under which neither individuals nor corporations are liable for escaping fire unless there is negligence. * * *

The judgment of the Appellate Division should be reversed and judgment directed for the defendant, with costs in all courts. * * *

Excerpt, Fowler V. Harper, Fleming James, Jr. & Oscar S. Gray, Harper, James and Gray on Torts, § 11.2
(3d ed. 2007).

In the field of industrial accidents, society has for the most part specifically provided by statute for compensating accident victims without regard to fault. Workers' (or, as they were traditionally called, workmen's) compensation acts, enacted by the legislatures of all the states and by the District of Columbia and the federal government, afford compensation to industrial workers for wage loss and medical expenses incurred as a result of accidental injuries, sometimes including diseases, arising out of and in the course of employment. * * *

The compensation features of the acts disregard the presence or absence of negligence on the part of the employer or the employee. Instead, compensation is based on a principle of liability without fault, recovery being broadly provided for injuries arising out of and in the course of employment. * The amount of compensation is governed by the workers' pay and the period of incapacity or by schedules in the case of certain named specific injuries. * In case of permanent total incapacity, for instance, disability payments typically amount to two-thirds of the worker's pre-injury pay, subject, however, to a specified maximum. Medical expenses are also to be defrayed by the employer. Compensation is payable to the injured employee (or his dependents in case of death) in installments. This method of payment is thought to serve best, in most cases, the economic interests of wage earners and their families by ensuring a steady income to the beneficiaries and protecting them against the hazards of managing a capital sum. * Discretion is commonly vested in the Commissioner, however, to award a lump sum in exceptional cases. * The compensation under these acts is usually the exclusive remedy of the employee and dependents against the employer, in lieu of any amounts that might otherwise have been recovered in a lawsuit for injuries covered by the acts. *

Workers' compensation systems are intended to provide not only the certainty of an award, but also substantial assurance that it will be paid. This they do by requiring employers either to procure insurance covering liability under the acts or to furnish proof of financial ability to compensate their workers for accidental injury. * As a rule insurance is placed with private stock or mutual companies although, in some states, state insurance funds have been established that compete with the private insurance companies, and in a few states the business of insuring against industrial accidents is a state monopoly. *

In the majority of states the workers' compensation acts are administered by special agencies. Most states have special single-administrator agencies or multimember commissions operating on a statewide basis. * * *

If the injured employee's claim is not contested, the worker and the employer or its insurer may in most states agree on the compensation to be paid, but the agreement must usually be approved by the workers' compensation agency; in other "direct-payment" states, uncontested payments begin and continue without an agreement, but the agency may still supervise the process. * If the parties are in dispute, the compensation authority (in states other than those with court administration), after sending notice to all interested parties, will hold a hearing and decide all the issues on the facts presented, determining the amount of compensation to be paid and the method of payment. * In the conduct of the hearings, the hearing officer is not bound by common law rules of evidence. Relatively informal rules prevail. * * *

NOTES

1. *More Facts about the Accident and the Litigation.* The *Ives* opinion provides only the sparsest facts regarding the accident leading to Earl Ives's injury and the extent of the harm he experienced. At the moment he was injured, Ives, an experienced switchman, was standing on the thirty-second car of a thirty-five-car train that was loaded with coke, a distilled residue of coal used in the production of iron and steel. Ives himself had given a signal to the engineer to proceed forward in order to "take up the slack" in the train, but the resulting jarring motion caused Ives to fall off the car and sustain a sprained ankle, as well as bruises and other injuries. See John Fabian Witt, The Accidental Republic: Crippled Workingmen, Destitute Widows, and the Remaking of American Law 164 (2004). The injuries were comparatively slight when compared with the disabling injuries described by Professor Witt in the excerpt from his article presented at the beginning of this chapter.

Why do you suppose that Ives and his attorney filed for benefits under the workers' compensation system instead of under the common law, as they had the right to do under the New York law? What defenses would the South Buffalo Railway have had to a common law tort claim?

2. *The Tort Litigation Process.* In *Ives*, how did the plaintiff begin his legal action, and how did the defendant respond? Did the defendant contest the accuracy of the facts alleged by the plaintiff? What does it mean when the opinion tells us that the plaintiff "demurred" to the defense presented by the defendant? For a succinct overview of the tort litigation process, see Appendix, "The Litigation Process," *infra* pages 975–979. You will want to repeatedly refer back to this Appendix during your first weeks of study to help you understand the various procedural contexts in which the substantive tort issues considered in the opinions excerpted in this casebook arise.

3. *Federal and State Constitutions.* The opinion states that the defendant challenged the constitutionality of the New York Workers' Compensation statute under the due process clauses of both the federal and the state constitutions. The members of the New York General Assembly and the lawyers who provided legal advice to them evidently thought that the newly enacted article 14–a of the Labor Law was constitutional. Why does the view of the New York Court of Appeals prevail over that of the democratically elected legislature? See Marbury v. Madison, 5 U.S. 137, 2 L.Ed. 60 (1803).

4. *Sources of Compensation for Accidental Injury.* The tort system as a whole (which does not include workers' compensation) reportedly compensates accident victims for less than five percent of their total economic losses. See Neal Feigenson, Legal Blame: How Jurors Think and Talk about Accidents 9 (2000). In addition to recovery under tort law and workers' compensation benefits, what other sources of compensation for accidental losses exist in modern society? Despite a variety of sources of compensation for accidental losses, "victims themselves and their families absorb nearly 40% of medical costs and two thirds of lost wages." *Id.*

5. *Comparing the Goals of Workers' Compensation and the Tort System.* The opinion includes excerpts from the report of the Wainwright Commission that outline the reasons for replacing the common law of torts governing workplace injuries with a workers' compensation system. What were the goals of the proposed workers' compensation system?

You intuitively might think that holding employers liable for workplace injuries, even in the absence of fault, reduces their incentives to be careful: "If I am forced to pay for my employees' injuries even when I am without fault, why should I be careful?" The evidence suggests that these concerns are not well-founded. In a leading study, economist Don Dewees and his co-authors report:

> We conclude that the operation of the workers' compensation system does reduce worker injury rates and that for high-risk industries and risk-rated firms this reduction is substantial, although the absolute magnitude of the effect is subject to enormous uncertainty. We accept the evidence that this effect is greater than that created by the tort system or that created by U.S. federal occupational safety and health regulation.

Don Dewees *et al.*, Exploring the Domain of Accident Law: Taking the Facts Seriously 382 (1996). What might explain this finding?

Obviously, there is no commission report that recounts the goals of the common law tort system that emerged over many centuries. Today's legal scholars offer two different perspectives on the goals of the tort system.

Instrumental conceptions of tort law, notably law and economics, focus on tort law's impact on society and the economy, that is, in achieving policy objectives. The two most important of these objectives are "loss minimization"—deterring future conduct that causes harm—and "loss distribution"—distributing the costs of accidents in a manner that inflicts "less pain" than if the accident costs were borne solely by the original victim. See Guido Calabresi, The Costs of Accidents 27–28, 68 (1970); see also Richard A. Posner, Economic Analysis of the Law 213–17 (8th ed. 2011). For more on loss minimization and loss distribution, see Note 2 following Taber v. Maine, *infra* pages 114–117, and Excerpt, Guido Calabresi, Some Thoughts on Risk Distribution and the Law of Torts, 70 Yale L.J. 499, 499–500, 517–18, 543–45 (1961) *reprinted infra* pages 120–122.

Note the similarity between the loss distribution function of workers' compensation and the prominent role played by the same objective in the instrumental conception of tort law. In the decades following the adoption of workers' compensation, scholars led by Fleming James, Jr., one of the original co-editors of this casebook, promoted the transposition of the goal of loss distribution from the workers' compensation system to the common law of torts. See, e.g., Fleming James, Jr., Accident Liability Reconsidered: The Impact of Liability Insurance, 57 Yale L.J. 549, 550 (1948). Many of the pro-plaintiff changes in tort law during the last third of the twentieth century suggest the influence of the instrumental theory.

In contrast, the corrective justice and civil recourse perspectives on tort law are both derived from moral philosophy. The two approaches are separate and distinct from each other, but these distinctions are subtle and should not overly concern you at this point. Corrective justice theory holds that when a wrongdoer injures a victim, this creates a duty on the part of the injurer to make the victim whole. See Ernest J. Weinrib, The Idea of Private Law 56–81 (1995). Civil recourse theory attempts to explain the more nuanced and sophisticated tort law that operates in today's world. It argues that the duty to repair the wrong or compensate the victim does not arise automatically, but rather exists only as prescribed by tort law. In other words, there is a distinction between a moral duty of repair and a state-imposed affirmative duty to compensate. As we will see throughout the course, in some instances, tort law declines to impose upon the defendant a duty to repair the loss, either wholly or in part; conversely, in other instances, tort law may impose remedies that are not aimed at making the victim whole. See Benjamin C. Zipursky, Civil Recourse, Not Corrective Justice, 91 Geo. L.J. 695, 699, 710 (2003).

Many of the opinions in this casebook evince the continuing tension between the civil recourse/corrective justice and the instrumental conceptions of tort law. Are the two approaches to tort law necessarily mutually exclusive? See Izhak Englard, The Costs of Accidents: A Retrospect View from the Cathedral, 64 Md. L. Rev. 355, 361 (2005) (arguing that judges, in a single mental process, simultaneously consider instrumental and civil recourse goals).

For a critique of the tort system arguing that it achieves neither its instrumental nor its corrective justice goals, see Excerpt, Stephen D. Sugarman, Doing Away with Tort Law, 73 Cal. L. Rev. 558 (1985), *infra* pages 668–671.

6. *The Law and the Legal Process.* Our primary interest in *Ives* is not the constitutionality of the New York workers' compensation statute. While the constitutionality of workers' compensation statutes is no longer in doubt, the opinion states a proposition that, to the extent that it may be true, would be fundamental to tort law. The extent to which liability may be imposed without "fault" is still subject to disagreement. The view has been tenaciously held that "fault" is requisite to tort liability and may be dispensed with only in exceptional cases. This debate will be illuminated in the materials that follow.

For our purposes, the *Ives* opinion is here largely for an additional purpose—to serve as an introduction to law and legal analysis. What is law and how does one find it? We read the legislation and know what to do if the legislation is law. But in some cases that is not enough because a higher law—for example, a constitution—may make what seems to be law not law at all. We read the constitution and find that the liability must not be such as to deprive the defendant of property "without due process of law." What is due process and where do we find that out? The court directs us to judicial decisions made at the time of and prior to the adoption of the relevant constitution. How was the law found or made in those decisions? Is the law frozen as of that time or is change permissible? The court states that some change is surely permissible, but other change is not. How can we tell into which category a particular change falls?

The *Ives* court makes its respectful bow to "the cogent economic and sociological arguments," "philosophical or scientific speculations," "the commendable impulses of benevolence or charity," and "the dictates of natural justice." But such appeals "must be made to the people and not to the courts." Are the courts asses? Are they not at all concerned with economic or sociological consequences or the impulses of morality and philosophy? What is the relation between these social factors and so-called "legal" factors? Upon what considerations does a court decide a new case?

Ives was concededly a case of first impression. There was no precedent precisely on point. In its search for light from prior judicial decisions, the court necessarily had to look to prior cases that were in many respects different from the one before it. Almost never are two cases precisely alike. At least the parties are different—they may be of different height, age, race, or economic status. Precedents therefore provide differences and similarities by which to compare the case in hand. Is it enough to find just one similarity or difference? Or must we look for *significant* differences or *significant* similarities? And, we may have to determine whether the differences outweigh the similarities or vice versa. But how do we determine significance and the weight to which it is entitled?

Again, is it enough if we discover one prior decision with overpowering similarity or must we look for a "course" or "line" of decisions, to determine a consistent generalization of many cases? We study the decisions through the opinions of the courts that made them. How much are we to be influenced by what is said in the opinions? Some opinions are well written and cogent. Others are confused, illogical, or otherwise unpersuasive. Can we disregard decisions resulting from such poor reasoning? How far can we accept or rely upon the statements in one opinion if what it states was decided in a prior case?

Reconsider the opinion in *Ives*. The court makes a number of statements of historical fact, for example, that when "our constitutions were adopted it was the law of the land that no man who was without fault or negligence could be held liable in damages for injuries sustained by another." Is the court's history accurate? What if it is wrong? Is there evidence in the opinion itself that casts doubt on the proposition? The court also interprets quotations from other opinions. Do the interpretations seem indubitable?

The court relies on prior decisions that are in many respects different from the case in hand. Are the similarities significant enough to justify the reliance or are the differences significant enough to distinguish the cases? The court also distinguishes cases urged by the plaintiff. Are the differences stated enough to distinguish them or are there significant enough similarities to justify reliance? Is significance a matter of ineluctable logic or choice? If the latter, what influences choice? Are "economic" or "sociological" differences or similarities relevant? Is the time factor—difference in general outlook and public opinion between two periods of time—relevant?

Questions of this character are raised by *Ives* and will recur throughout our study.

7. *The Context of the Times and the Eventual Acceptance of the Constitutionality of Workers' Compensation Legislation.* The *Ives* opinion was announced on March 24, 1911. One of the greatest tragedies—and turning points—in American labor history occurred the following day.

On March 25, 1911, 146 workers, most of them Jewish and Italian immigrant women and girls between the ages of thirteen and twenty-three, died in less than fifteen minutes in a fire at the Triangle Shirtwaist factory near Washington Square in New York City. See generally Robert A. Slayton, Empire Statesman: The Rise and Redemption of Al Smith 89–100 (2001); Leon Stein, The Triangle Fire (1962); *The Triangle Factory Fire,* Kheel Center for Labor-Management Documentation and Archives, http://www.ilr.cornell.edu/trianglefire (last visited September 26, 2014). The fire began shortly before 4:30 p.m. on the eighth floor and it spread quickly, fed by thousands of pounds of rags and other fabric. Most of the deaths occurred on the ninth floor, where the doors to the fire escape were locked shut. The majority of the victims were suffocated or burned to death inside the building, but many others died when they leaped to the pavement below:

> The girls rushed to the windows and looked down at Greene Street, 100 feet below them. Then one poor little creature jumped. There was a plate glass protection over part of the sidewalk, but she crashed through it, wrecking it and breaking her body into a thousand pieces.

New York Times, March 26, 1911, p.1.

The two owners of the company were charged with manslaughter, but were acquitted. The families of the victims brought twenty-three individual civil suits. They culminated in judicial awards that averaged $75 per death.

Nine days after the fire, Local 25 of the International Ladies Garment Workers' Union organized a rally in memory of the workers. The number of those who marched was variously estimated at between 120,000 and 400,000. Within a month, the governor of New York appointed the Factory Investigating Commission which conducted statewide hearings into the condition of working people. It was co-chaired by Robert F. Wagner, later a United States Senator and a principal author of the Fair Labor Standards Act of 1938 and the National Labor Relations Act (the "Wagner Act"), and Alfred E. Smith, later governor of New York and Democratic nominee for the presidency, and included Samuel Gompers, the president of the American Federation of Labor. The Commission's work ultimately resulted in the passage of important factory safety legislation, the constitutionality of which the courts upheld. The Triangle Shirtwaist Fire is now regarded as a turning point in the struggle for social justice and workers' rights. See Stein, *supra,* at 48. The public reaction to the fire, moreover, combined with the public reaction to the nearly simultaneous release of the *Ives* opinion, led to an amendment to the New York Constitution designed to permit workers' compensation legislation.

A slightly revised statute pursuant to that amendment was upheld by the New York Court of Appeals in 1915 without discussion. Between the 1911 decision of that court in *Ives* and its decision in White v. New York C. & H. R.R. Co., 216 N.Y. 653, 110 N.E. 1051 (1915), there intervened not only the public turmoil that followed the Triangle Shirtwaist fire, the amendment of the state constitution, and the enactment of new compensation legislation, but also changes in the membership of the Court of Appeals. Only two of the seven judges who sat on the *Ives* case (not including Judge Werner) participated in the *White* decision. Among the new judges sitting in 1915 were Benjamin N. Cardozo and Samuel Seabury. (Seabury later attained national prominence as a social reformer for investigating and exposing judicial and political corruption in New York.).

In New York Central Railroad Co. v. White, 243 U.S. 188, 37 S.Ct. 247, 61 L.Ed. 667 (1917), the United States Supreme Court upheld the constitutionality of the New York workers' compensation statute under the federal Constitution. ("No person has a vested interest in any rule of law, entitling him to insist it shall remain unchanged for his benefit.").

The *Ives* decision thus stood at the end of one era of American political, economic, and legal culture, and before the vast changes that began with the post-*Ives* acceptance of workers' compensation legislation and later characterized the New Deal and the decades to follow. See Witt, *supra*, at 154, 186.

8. *Judge William E. Werner.* It might be guessed that Judge William E. Werner's decision in *Ives* reflects the personal viewpoint of someone from a privileged background. The reality is more complicated. When Judge Werner's parents died when he was fourteen years old, he worked as an iron molder's apprentice and, during his twenties, in a tin-stamping plant. Politically, his early heroes included President Abraham Lincoln and other, more radical, abolitionists. In remarks delivered in 1901, he characterized " 'workmen,' not the 'money kings,' " as the " 'real producers.' " He denounced " 'the pharisees of commerce' who 'wax fat at the expense of * * * the poor and helpless consumers.' " John Fabian Witt, The Accidental Republic: Crippled Workingmen, Destitute Widows, and the Remaking of American Law 155–57 (2004). He very much hoped that President Theodore Roosevelt, a progressive, who as governor had appointed him to the Court of Appeals, would appoint him to the United States Supreme Court. *Id.* at 158. Roosevelt, however, emerged as one of the harshest critics of the *Ives* decision. *Id.* at 175.

Despite his humble origins, Judge Werner believed that the salvation of American society lay in individual effort, not organized labor, large enterprises run by professional managers or what he regarded as class-based and paternalistic reform legislation. As Professor Witt writes, "[I]n his tort decisions, Werner adopted an approach typical to late-nineteenth-century classical tort law, one that was concerned first and foremost with the articulation and defense of the boundaries of freedom of action." *Id.* at 161.

9. *Facts, Presumptions, and Law.* To state that a defendant is liable under certain circumstances—as for example, if he is negligent and his negligence proximately causes the harm, or that he is not liable under converse circumstances—is to state that the trier of the facts must be satisfied as to the existence or nonexistence of those circumstances. But in accident litigation the relevant circumstances are generally not facts that can be established beyond peradventure, and the trier of facts does not make a private, independent investigation. The parties to the litigation must undertake to persuade the trier. Therefore, the determination of who bears the risk of non-persuasion, that is, who loses if the trier is not satisfied as to what the circumstances were, is a matter of prime importance. Lawyers know that it is not enough to be convinced as to what the facts are; they must worry about whether and how to prove the facts at the trial. So in studying the cases in this text, you must consider not merely the facts upon which liability or immunity are based, but also how those facts are established. You must develop an acute awareness of procedure and method at every point; for judgments are rendered not automatically or by omniscient powers, but by human beings informed only through certain processes.

In Western & Atlantic Railroad v. Henderson, 279 U.S. 639, 49 S.Ct. 445, 73 L.Ed. 884 (1929), the plaintiff sued for the death of her husband who had died when the truck he was driving was struck by a train. An applicable Georgia statute provided:

> A railroad company shall be liable for any damages done to persons, stock, or other property by the running of the locomotives, or cars, or other machinery of such company, or for damage done by any person in the employment and service of such company, unless the company shall make it appear that their agents have exercised all ordinary and reasonable care and diligence, the presumption in all cases being against the company.

Ga. Civ. Code § 2780 (1910).

Why do you think that the Georgia legislature passed such a law? To what social problems was it addressed?

The Supreme Court held that this statutory presumption in favor of liability was unconstitutional under the due process clause of the Fourteenth Amendment. The Court ruled the statute was arbitrary and unreasonable because there was no rational connection between the fact proved, that is, the collision between the train and the motor vehicle, and the inference to be drawn as to the ultimate fact in issue, which the Court assumed to be whether the accident was caused by the negligence of the railroad company. Is this what the statute requires?

Thus, the case holds that the plaintiff, as a constitutional requirement, bears the risk of not persuading the trier that the harm was caused by negligence on the part of the defendant. It does so notwithstanding an explicit statutory provision establishing the railroad's liability upon proof of damage done "by the running of" the locomotives, etc., without reference to a requirement that plaintiff prove negligence on the railroad's part. The plaintiff is to lose not only when the trier is persuaded that the harm was not so caused, but also when the trier is not persuaded either way, when the evidence is "in equipoise." As an original proposition, why should this be so? Why must the plaintiff establish the conditions of liability rather than the defendant establish the conditions of non-liability?

The court in *Henderson* requires a "rational connection between what is proved and what is to be inferred." Does the decision in this case in effect create a presumption that a railroad crossing accident is not caused by the negligence of the railroad company? Does the decision mean that the Georgia legislature could not constitutionally make a railroad company liable for harm resulting from a crossing accident without reference to fault on the part of the company?

It is now established that a state may render an employer liable to his employee for an accident in the course of employment whether or not the employee's negligence caused it. Would a statute be unconstitutional if it provided that in case of such a "work accident" the employer shall be presumed to have been negligent? Would the connection be rational? Logical? What is the difference in result between saying (a) the defendant is liable though he has not been at fault and (b) the defendant is presumed to have been at fault? Is the Georgia statute harsher or more lenient on the railroad than a statute imposing liability without fault?

We shall consider from time to time in this course the extent to which the proposition advanced by the *Henderson* court accords with common law doctrines of an earlier day, or with more recent developments in American law.

10. *Federal Employers' Liability Act.* Today, state workers' compensation statutes similar to the one declared to be unconstitutional in *Ives* govern liability for most workplace injuries. However, injuries sustained by at least two groups of workers are handled differently. See generally Harper, James and Gray on Torts § 11.2 n.23. Under the Federal Employers' Liability Act (FELA), 35 Stat. 65, 45 U.S.C. §§ 51–60 (2012), enacted in 1908, an injured railroad worker must prove negligence on the part of the employer in order to recover, but certain defenses that previously aided the employer are either eliminated or modified. The traditional rule of contributory negligence, where the employee was precluded from recovery if he had been at fault, even in cases in which the employer was also at fault, was replaced by a rule of comparative negligence, under which the employee was allowed to recover but his damages were reduced in proportion to his own fault. The fellow servant rule, under which the employer was not responsible for harm caused to an employee by the negligence of another employee, was abolished for FELA cases. The defense of assumption of risk was eliminated in actions under the FELA by an amendment enacted in 1939. Coverage of the FELA was extended to merchant seamen by the Jones Act in 1920. See 41 Stat. 1007, 46 U.S.C. § 30104 (2012). Railroad workers and merchant seamen apparently would resist any attempt to replace their remedies under these acts with the no-fault provisions of workers' compensation. See Grant Gilmore & Charles Black, Jr., The Law of Admiralty 427 (2d ed. 1975); Lloyd Larson, Changing Concepts in Workmen's Compensation Coverage, in Report of the National Workshop on Rehabilitation and Workmen's Compensation 35–37 (1971); Jerry J. Phillips, FELA Revisited, 52 Md. L. Rev. 1063 (1993).

B. EARLIER DEVELOPMENTS

Excerpt, Edmund M. Morgan & Francis X. Dwyer, Introduction to the Study of Law
79–81 (2d ed. 1948).

FORMS OF ACTION

After the Norman Conquest * * * the king's courts gradually absorbed all the judicial business of the kingdom. The method by which litigation was drawn into the royal tribunals was the issuance of a royal mandate, commonly called an original writ, that is, a writ originating an action or lawsuit. The development of the system of original writs may be briefly summarized as follows: At the beginning of the Norman period the jurisdiction actually exercised by the royal courts was very narrow. But the king had the power to draw to his courts, by the issuance of special writs, each manufactured for a particular case, such causes as he desired; and he exercised this power with increasing frequency. Under Henry II [who reigned 1154–1189] the royal judicial power was greatly extended. A royal writ was necessary to compel a man to answer for his freehold. Actions for the recovery of possession of realty in the king's court were invented. In a steadily growing number of other classes of cases, the king through his chancery was issuing writs as of course. Indeed it began to look as if the royal courts, either through writs of course or special writs created for the purpose, might provide a remedy for every wrong. Under John a slight check occurred; but under Henry III the stream of writs issuing from chancery rapidly widened. As early as 1244 the barons and prelates protested. Gradually it was being perceived that the king by his invention of new writs was legislating and was frequently creating new rights. Finally in 1258 the barons extracted from the king, in the Provisions of Oxford, the pledge that his chancellor should be under oath to "seal no writs, excepting writs of course, without the commandment of the king and of his council, who shall be present." Thereafter no new writs could be granted by the chancery; and this meant that, so far as the royal courts were concerned, a litigant whose case could not be brought within the confines of a formed writ was remediless. * * *

Importance of the Forms of Action. When the medieval litigant or his lawyer applied to chancery for a formed writ, he was in effect asking for a mandate to the royal judges to take jurisdiction of and to try a cause of action properly falling within the limits of that writ. The writ was no general order or authorization to try the validity of any claim which the plaintiff might choose to assert against the defendant. If plaintiff had selected and secured a writ in debt, he could not expect the judges to try a case in trespass. As Pollock and Maitland put it:[3]

> The metaphor which likens the chancery to a shop is trite; we will liken it to an armoury. It contains every weapon of medieval warfare from the two-handed sword to the poniard. The man who has a quarrel with his neighbor comes thither to choose his weapon. The choice is large; but he must remember that he will not be able to change weapons in the middle of the combat and also that every weapon has its proper use and may be put to none other. If he selects a sword, he must observe the rules of sword-play; he must not try to use his cross-bow as a mace. To drop metaphor, our plaintiff is not merely choosing a writ, he is choosing an action, and every action has its own rules.

And this remained true as long as the formulary system endured. Professor Maitland, in pointing out the practical importance of distinguishing between the several forms of action, said:[a]

---

[3]   2 Frederick Pollock & Frederic William Maitland, History of English Law 561 (2d ed. 1905); see also F.W. Maitland, Equity and the Forms of Action 298 (1910).

[a]   [Eds.' note] *Id.* For a brief history of writ procedure in the twelfth and thirteenth centuries see John Hamilton Baker, An Introduction to English Legal History 53 *et seq.* (4th ed. 2002), and R.C. van Caenegem, The Birth of the English Common Law ch. 2 (2nd ed. 1989).

"A form of action" has implied a particular original process, a particular *mesne* process, a particular final process, a particular mode of pleading, of trial, of judgment. But further to a very considerable degree the substantive law administered in a given form of action has grown up independently of the law administered in other forms. Each procedural pigeon-hole contains its own rules of substantive law, and it is with great caution that we may argue from what is found in one to what will probably be found in another; each has its own precedents. It is quite possible that a litigant will find that his case will fit some two or three of these pigeon-holes. If that be so he will have a choice, which will often be a choice between the old, cumbrous, costly, on the one hand, the modern, rapid, cheap, on the other. Or again he may make a bad choice, fail in his action, and take such comfort as he can from the hints of the judges that another form of action might have been more successful. The plaintiff's choice is irrevocable; he must play the rules of the game that he has chosen. Lastly he may find that, plausible as his case may seem, it just will not fit any one of the receptacles provided by the courts and he may take to himself the lesson that where there is no remedy there is no wrong.

NOTE

Common Law Pleading. Under the formulary system, the technical challenge to counsel was not limited to the applicability of the writs to the claims. It extended as well to the rules of pleading, and in particular to the rules governing defendants' denials of liability. An understanding of the substantive liability rules of the day can often be deduced from the ancient cases only after decoding the procedural aspects of the litigation. The defensive pleading technicalities were, to the modern eye, incredibly complex. For an overview, simplified but still more detailed than can be conveniently summarized here, see Joseph H. Koffler & Alison Reppy, Handbook of Common Law Pleading ch. 22 (1969).

For present purposes it may suffice to note a distinction between two general categories of denial (or "traverse"), although the number of specific types of denial was greater. One, sometimes called a "general" denial, conveyed the sense that is captured in modern criminal practice by ideas like mistaken identity or alibi, i.e., "I didn't do it" or "I wasn't there" or "It was somebody else." The other, sometimes identified with terms like "special" or "confession and avoidance" or "justification," was a "Yes, but . . ." plea. It conceded defendant's involvement in the incident but sought to excuse it, such as through a modern claim of self-defense. The facts involved in real accidents, however, do not always arrange themselves so as to make clear which of these categories of defensive pleading should apply. Just as a plaintiff with a meritorious claim on the facts could lose for picking the wrong writ, defendant with a meritorious defense could lose for pleading it according to a form deemed inappropriate to the theory of defense.

The form of denial chosen was often signaled by the use of certain formal Latin tag-labels. One used for the general denial was "*actio non,*" i.e., "Not my act" or "It didn't happen." Another, used for special (or other non-general) traverse, such as confession and avoidance, was *"absque hoc,"* or "without this," in the sense of "Apart from this . . . "—for instance, "I did shoot X; apart from this, I was an officer of the law defending Y from X's armed attack. . . ." This tag conceded the facts recited in the complaint, but set out additional facts as the grounds on which the defense was based.

Weaver v. Ward
King's Bench, 1616.
80 Eng.Rep. 284, Hobart 134.

Weaver brought an action of trespass of assault and battery against Ward. The defendant pleaded, that he was amongst others by the commandment of the Lords of the Council a trained soldier in London, of the band of one Andrews captain; and so was the plaintiff, and that they were skirmishing with their musquets charged with powder for their exercise *in re militari*, against another captain and his band; and as they were so skirmishing, the defendant *casualiter* & *per infortunium* & *contra voluntatem suam*, in discharging of his piece did hurt and wound the plaintiff, which is the same, & c. *absque hoc*, that he was guilty *aliter sive alio modo*. And upon demurrer by the plaintiff, judgment was given for him; for though it were agreed, that if men tilt or turney in the presence of the King, or if two masters of defence playing their prizes kill one another, that this shall be no felony; or if a lunatick kill a man, or the like, because felony must be done *animo felonico*: yet in trespass, which tends only to give damages according to hurt or loss, it is not so; and therefore if a lunatick hurt a man, he shall be answerable in trespass: and therefore no man shall be excused of a trespass (for this is the nature of an excuse, and not of a justification, *prout ei bene licuit*) except it may be judged utterly without his fault.

As if a man by force take my hand and strike you, or if here the defendant had said, that the plaintiff ran across his piece when he was discharging, or had set forth the case with the circumstances, so as it had appeared to the Court that it had been inevitable, and that the defendant had committed no negligence to give occasion to the hurt.

NOTE

The Case of Thorns. In The Case of Thorns, Y.B. 6 Edw. 4, fol. 7, pl. 18 (1466), Brian, J., stated:

> * * * And so if a man makes an assault upon me and I cannot avoid him, and he wants to beat me, and I in defence of myself raise my stick and strike him, and in raising it I hurt some man who is behind my back, this man will have an action against me. And yet it was lawful for me to raise my stick to defend myself, and it was against my will that I hurt him. * * *

(dicta), reprinted in Courtney Stanhope Kenny, A Selection of Cases Illustrative of the English Law of Tort 379, 380–81 (1904).

Note the discussion of *Weaver v. Ward* in Francis Bohlen, Liability in Tort of Infants and Insane Persons, 23 Mich. L. Rev. 9, 16 (1924), in which the author views the case as the court's beginning "to feel its way to a recognition of the excuse of 'inevitable accident.'"

Dickenson v. Watson

King's Bench, 1682.
84 Eng.Rep. 1218, T. Jones 205.

The plaintiff brought error on a judgment in the Court of the sheriffs of the City of York, in trespass for an assault, battery, and wounding of the plaintiff's eye, by discharging of a gun charged with powder and hail-shot, by which he lost the sight of his eye. The defendant pleaded *actio non*, because he is, and at the time of the trespass was an officer appointed for collecting the duty of hearth-money, and for the better discharge of his office, and more sure custody, and keeping of the money by him collected and to be collected, he provided himself with fire-arms, and having one of his pistols in his hands, and intending to discharge it *ne aliquod damnum eveniret,* he discharged it *(nemine in opposito vis. existente)* and while he discharged it, the plaintiff *casualiter viam illam proeterivit, & si aliquod malum ei inde accideret hoc fuit contra voluntat.* of the defendant. *Quoe est eadem transgressio.* Upon this the plaintiff demurred, and judgment was given for him; whereupon error was brought and judgment was affirmed, nothing being urged besides the sufficiency of the plea. But the Court held it to be insufficient; for in trespass the defendant shall not be excused without unavoidable necessity, which is not shown here. Besides, the defendant did not traverse *absq; [absque] hoc quod aliter seu alio modo,* as was done in the case of Weaver and Ward, Hob. 134. And yet judgment there given for the plaintiff.

NOTE

From where might a cynical observer surmise that defendant's counsel in *Dickenson v. Watson* got the idea for the defense he pleaded? Why did it not succeed?

Gibbons v. Pepper

King's Bench, 1695.
91 Eng.Rep. 922, 1 Ld. Ray. 38.

Trespass, assault and battery. The defendant pleads, that he rode upon a horse in the King's highway, and that his horse being affrighted ran away with him, persons standing in the way, among whom the plaintiff stood; so that he could not stop the horse; that there were several persons standing in the way, among whom the plaintiff stood; and that he called to them to take care, but that notwithstanding, the plaintiff did not go out of the way, but continued there; so that the defendant's horse ran over the plaintiff against the will of the defendant; *quae est eadem transgressio,* & c. The plaintiff demurred. And Serjeant Darnall for the defendant argued, that if the defendant in his justification shews that the accident was inevitable, and that the negligence of the defendant did not cause it, judgment shall be given for him. To prove which he cited Hob. 344, Weaver vers. Ward. Mo. 864, p1. 1192. 2 Roll. Abr. 548. 1 Brownl. Prec. 188.

Northey for the plaintiff said, that in all these cases the defendant confessed a battery, which he afterwards justified; but in this case he justified a battery, which is no battery. Of which opinion was the whole

Court; for if I ride upon a horse, and J. S. whips the horse, so that he runs away with me and runs over any other person, he who whipped the horse is guilty of the battery, and not me. But if I by spurring was the cause of such accident, then I am guilty. In the same manner, if A. takes the hand of B. and with it strikes C., A. is the trespasser, and not B. And, *Per Curiam*, the defendant might have given this justification in evidence, upon the general issue pleaded. And therefore judgment was given for the plaintiff.

NOTES

1. *An Act.* The Restatement (Second) of Torts § 2 (1965) defines "act" as "an external manifestation of the actor's will." Section 8 further defines "unavoidable accident * * * to denote the fact that the harm * * * is not caused by any tortious act * * *." See Steudle v. Rentchler, 64 Ill. 161 (1872) (boys frightened defendant's horse, which ran away and injured plaintiff); Cunningham v. Pitzer, 2 W.Va. 264 (1867) (trespass committed by soldier under military compulsion).

2. *Voluntary.* Liability in trespass, as well as in case, had to be based on some *voluntary* conduct of the defendant. Of course, voluntary conduct can nearly always be shown if we look far enough back in the sequence of events. Pepper, we may assume, voluntarily went out to ride on the day that proved so eventful and by free choice rode to the place where his horse was frightened. Would these acts support liability in trespass? In an action on the case? What of the voluntary act of continuing to drive a car when sleepy? When drunk? For more on the distinction between trespass and trespass on the case, see *Scott v. Shepherd, infra* pages 30–34, and pages 34–35, Note 2.

Hall v. Fearnley

Queen's Bench, 1842.
114 Eng.Rep. 761, 3 Q.B. 919.

Trespass for driving defendant's cart and horse with great violence against plaintiff, and thereby knocking him down, bruising and wounding him, &c.

Plea, not guilty.

On the trial, before Wightman, J., at the Middlesex sittings in Hilary term 1842, it was proved that the plaintiff was walking on a narrow part of the pavement in a public street, where there was a considerable curvature in it. The defendant was driving a cart in the road near the pavement at the edge of which the plaintiff was walking. The case for the plaintiff was that there was want of due care on the part of the defendant who had driven so close to the pavement as to knock the plaintiff down, and run over and break his leg. The defendant endeavoured to shew that the plaintiff had slipped from the curb stone at the moment when the cart was passing, and had so got his leg under the wheel. The defendant called no witnesses.

Wightman, J. told the jury that the question for them was, whether the injury was occasioned by unavoidable accident or by the defendant's default; and that, if they thought the plaintiff had accidentally slipped off the pavement as the defendant's cart was passing, and had been run over in consequence of such accident, they ought to find for the defendant. Verdict for defendant.

In the same term Crowder obtained a rule *nisi* for a new trial on the ground that the Judge had misdirected the jury, by telling them that, on the issue, if the injury was accidental, the defendant was entitled to a verdict.

Knowles now shewed cause. The jury have in effect negatived all fault on the part of the defendant. This was an inevitable accident, as in Gibbon v. Pepper (2 Salk. 637), where the defendant's horse ran away with the rider, and struck the plaintiff, and the Court held it to be no trespass, and therefore properly evidence under not guilty. The new rules of pleading make no alteration in pleadings for trespass to the person; and the case therefore stands on the old forms of pleading. This was in fact no assault or battery at all; for to constitute one some degree of negligence is always necessary; 3 Starkie on Evidence, 1119, 3d ed. Gough v. Bryan (2 M. & W. 770), is to the same effect. There a special plea, alleging collision by the improper driving of the plaintiff himself, and concluding to the country, was held to be bad as amounting to the general issue. Griffin v. Parsons (1 Selw. N. P. 25, 26, note (1), 10th ed.), reported in Selwyn's Nisi Prius, tit. Assault and Battery, sect. 1, shews that a seizure of the person is not necessarily an assault, but that the animus with which the act was done is material; therefore, on a replication denying a prior assault, evidence was admitted to shew that the alleged assault was only to part the defendant and another who were fighting. It is at all events evidence in mitigation.

■ [LORD DENMAN, C.J. If the plaintiff has suffered damage by a trespass not justified, the defendant should pay the whole amount without inquiry into the question of animus. The case would be different, if the defendant was not a voluntary agent. So it may be different where an action on the case for negligence is brought, and the negligence is denied; there negligence is the fact in issue.]

Crowder (with whom was H. S. Cooper) contra. The case of *Gibbon v. Pepper*, as reported in Lord Raymond's Reports (Gibbons v. Pepper, 1 Ld. Raym. 38), appears to have been one of mere involuntary accident occasioned by the act of a third person in frightening the defendant's horse. A flash of lightning may have the same effect, and would certainly exculpate the rider from all blame. But here there was nothing inevitable. Weaver v. Ward (Hob. 134, 5th ed.), is in point. There an accidental injury done by a soldier who was exercising was held to be actionable, for there was nothing to shew that it was unavoidable. Griffin v. Parsons, (1 Selw. N. P. 25, 26, note (1), 10th ed.), is only a *Nisi Prius* case, and the doctrine contained is against the current of authorities. Milman v. Dolwell (2 Camp. 378), and Knapp v. Salsbury (2 Camp. 500), also shew that, if the trespass is in fact committed, the fact of its being excusable by some accident or by negligence of the plaintiff is matter for a special plea. [He was then stopped by the Court.]

■ LORD DENMAN, C.J. The authorities shew that if the accident had resulted entirely from a superior agency, that would have been a defence, and might have been proved under the general issue; but a defence admitting that the accident resulted from an act of the defendant would not have been so provable.

■ COLERIDGE, J. Any defence, which admits the trespass complained of to be the act of the defendant, must be pleaded specially.

■ WIGHTMAN, J. The act of the defendant was prima facie unjustifiable, and required an excuse to be shewn. When the motion in this case was first made, I had in my recollection the case of Wakeman v. Robinson (1 Bing. 213). It was there agreed that an involuntary act might be a defence on the general issue. The decision indeed turned on a different point; but the general proposition is laid down. I think the omission to plead the defence here deprived the defendant of the benefit of it, and entitled the plaintiff to recover.

Rule absolute for a new trial.

NOTE

Trespass for Assault and Battery and Fault. Apparently in no reported common law action of trespass for assault and battery did the defendant actually prevail upon a showing that the injury, though caused directly by his voluntary act, did not result from any fault on his part. Can it therefore be said that want of fault was unavailable as a defense to an action for trespass? See, e.g., John Hamilton Baker, An Introduction to English Legal History 402–05 (4th ed. 2002). If freedom from fault was at all a defense to such an action, then who had the burden of pleading or proving it? Compare this situation with the one that Georgia tried to bring about by statute, invalidated in *Western & Atlantic Railway Co. v. Henderson*, discussed *supra* page 22–23.

Scott v. Shepherd

Common Pleas, 1773.

95 Eng.Rep. 1124, 3 Wils. 403.

This is an action of trespass and assault, wherein the plaintiff declares, that the defendant on the 28th day of October, 1770, with force and arms, (to wit) with sticks, staves, clubs and fists, made an assault upon the plaintiff at Taunton, in the county of Somerset, and greatly bruised, wounded, and ill treated him, so that his life was greatly despaired of, and then and there threw, casted and tossed a lighted squib, consisting of gunpowder and other combustible materials, at and against the said plaintiff, and struck the said plaintiff on the face therewith, and so greatly burnt one of the eyes of the said plaintiff, that the plaintiff underwent and suffered great and excruciating pain and torment for a long time, (to wit) for the space of six months then next following, and afterwards wholly lost his said eye. * * *

The defendant by his guardian pleaded not guilty, whereupon issue being joined, this cause came on to be tried at the last Summer Assizes for the county of Somerset, before Mr. Justice Nares; when it appeared by the plaintiff's evidence, that in the evening of the 28th day of October, 1770, at Milborne Port in the said county, it being the day the fair was held there, the defendant threw a lighted serpent, being a large squib, consisting of gunpowder and other combustible materials, from the street into the market-house, which is a covered building, supported by arches, and inclosed at one end, but open at the other end and on both sides, when a large concourse of people were then assembled; and that the said lighted serpent or squib, so thrown by the defendant, fell upon the standing there of one William Yates, who was then exposing to sale gingerbread, cakes, pies, and other pastry wares upon his said standing; that one James Willis instantly, and to prevent injury to himself and to the said wares of the said William Yates, took the said lighted serpent or squib from off the said standing and then threw it across the said market-house, when it fell upon another standing there, of one James Ryall, on which he was also exposing the same sort of wares to sale; that the said James Ryall instantly, and to save himself and his said goods from being injured, took up the said lighted serpent or squib from off the said standing, and then threw it to another part of the said market-house, and in so throwing it struck the plaintiff then in said market-house in the face therewith, and the said lighted serpent or squib so striking against the plaintiff's face, and the combustible matter therein then bursting put out one of the plaintiff's eyes.

Upon this evidence the jury found a verdict for the plaintiff with £100. damages, subject to the opinion of this Court; whether upon these facts this action is maintainable against the defendant.

Serjeant Glynn [for the plaintiff].—It was objected at the trial that the plaintiff had mistaken his action, that trespass *vi et armis* will not lie, because the damage the plaintiff received was not done immediately by the defendant, but was consequential. * * * In answer to this, I insist, that whoever does a *tortious* act is answerable in trespass * * * for all the consequences. * * *

Serjeant Burland for the defendant. * * *

■ NARES, JUSTICE, for the Plaintiff.—The question is, whether, upon the facts proved at the trial, which have been reported, and before stated, this action of trespass of assault and battery *vi et armis* doth not well lie against the defendant? Or whether it should not have been an action upon the case against him, upon a supposal that the injury done to the plaintiff was consequential and not immediate?

I am of opinion that this action of trespass *vi et armis* doth well lie against the defendant.—The nature of the act, the time and place when and where it was done, make it highly probable that some personal damage would immediately happen thereby to somebody then present in a crowded market house on the fair-day; and I think the act in itself was illegal at common law; but the stat. 9 & 10 W. 3, ch. 7, which makes the throwing of squibs in any publick street, & c. a common nuisance, and gives a forfeiture for so doing, puts it out of doubt that the act was unlawful.

It is objected that the plaintiff's eye was not put out by the immediate act of the defendant but by the immediate act of James Ryall, and therefore this action will not lie against the defendant, but would well have laid against Ryall.

I answer, that the act of throwing the squib into the market-house was of a mischievous nature, and bespeaks a bad intention, and whether the plaintiff's eye was put out mediately or immediately thereby, the defendant, who first threw the squib, is answerable in this action: but supposing the defendant had no bad or mischievous intention when he threw the squib, yet as the injury done was not inevitable, this action well lies against him; for the *malus animus* of a defendant is not necessary to be alleged, proved or taken into consideration in this action; "but in felony it shall be considered, as where a man shoots (with a bow) arrows at butts and kills a man it is not felony, and it should be construed that he had no intent to kill him; and so of a tyler upon a house who with a tyle kills a man unknowingly, it is not felony: but where a man shoots at butts, and wounds a man, although that it be against his will, he shall be said to be a trespasser. 21 Hen. 7, 28a."—If the injury done be not inevitable, the person who doth it, or is the immediate cause thereof, even by accident, misfortune, and against his will, is answerable in this action of trespass *vi et armis*; so is 1 Stran. 596, Underwood versus Hewson. Hob. 134, Weaver versus Ward. Sir Thomas Jones, 205, Dickenson versus Watson. 6 Ed. 4, 7, 8. Sir Thomas Raym. 422. 4 Mod. 404, 5.—If the act in the first instance be unlawful, trespass will lie; but if the act is prima facie lawful, and the prejudice to another is not immediate, but consequential, it must be an action upon the case, and this is the distinction laid down by the Lord Chief Justice Raymond in Reynolds versus Clarke, 1 Stran. 635. 2 Lord Raym. 1399, S.C. In the case at Bar, the act in the first instance done by the defendant was unlawful, therefore trespass *vi et armis* well lies against him; every subsequent act in throwing the squib by Yates, and Ryall, did partake of the nature of the first act, and was *quasi causa causata* immediately and *instanter*. In the case of *The Prior of Spalding* in trespass against defendants for putting earth and mud into his sewer, whereby the water therein was stopped in its course and surrounded 40 acres of his land adjoining; it was objected that trespass *vi et armis* did not lie, and prayed judgment of the writ; but by Thirning Chief Justice, although the surrounding the land with water was not against the peace, yet the putting the earth and mud into the sewer may be against the peace; and the defendants have done what they ought not to have done, wherefore they must answer. 12 Hen. 4, 3a. There are some cases where one may have either trespass *vi et armis*, or an action upon the case, as Hob. 180, Wheatley versus Stone. Cro. Jac. 122, 43, Dent versus Oliver.—"If a man be riding on the way, and another man striketh his horse by which the rider falleth and is hurt, he which is cast off his horse shall have trespass against the other" (whereby I suppose is meaned trespass *vi et armis*), F.N.B. 89 E. and 90 K., 91 A. 8vo. Edit.—The stroke is given to the horse, and not to the rider, but he is instantly hurt by the fall, in consequence of the act of striking the horse.

It is objected that the squib, after it was thrown by the defendant, had a new direction given to it, whereby the plaintiff was injured, but was not hurt by the defendant's throwing it.—I answer, that the defendant was the first actor, and the cause of the cause of the putting out the eye of the plaintiff, the act was not compleat until the explosion; if a man turns out a mad bull, ox, or any other wild or mischievous beast towards A. who turns the brute towards B. who turns it again towards C. whom it hurts, he who was the first actor and turned out the beast is answerable in trespass *vi et armis* for the injury done to C.— But suppose the death of a man ensues from turning out such a wild beast by the owner, who knows it to be mischievous, the owner of the beast is guilty of murder, Rex versus Huggins, 2 Ld. Raym. 1583.—If a man doth an unlawful act, he shall be answerable for the consequences of it. 1 Ld. Raym. 480, per Holt Chief Justice. 5 Mod. 427, S.C. and S.P.

I shall conclude with what the Lord Chief Justice Wilmot, and the Court said in the case of Slater versus Baker and Stapleton, 1 Wilson, 362, where it was objected that the defendants ought to have been charged as trespassers *vi et armis*, and not as trespassers upon the case; the Court said, "that the plaintiff in that case ought to receive a satisfaction, [d]eemed to be admitted, so we will not look with eagle's eyes to see whether the evidence applies exactly or not to the case, when we can see the plaintiff has obtained a verdict for such damages as he deserves, but we will establish such verdict if possible:" so I am of opinion the plaintiff ought to have judgment.

■ BLACKSTONE, JUSTICE.—I am of a different opinion. I take it here is no verdict; the declaration and special case are stated for the opinion of the Court, whether the facts in the case amount to an assault and battery *vi et armis* by the defendant upon the plaintiff?

The declaration alleges that the defendant threw, cast and tost a lighted squib against the plaintiff, and struck him on the face therewith, whereby he lost his eye; this is laid as an immediate injury done by defendant to the plaintiff, which is the gist of this action of assault and battery; for if the injury received from the act of the defendant was not immediate, but a consequence, trespass *vi et armis* will not lie, but it must be an action on the case. * * *

The lawfulness or unlawfulness of an act is not the criterion between these two actions, for a man may become an immediate trespasser *vi et armis*, by doing a lawful act; as if a man doing an act lawful in itself, hurts another by accident, misfortune, and against the will of the actor, yet he shall be answerable in trespass *vi et armis* for immediate injury done; unless the injury was inevitable, 27 Hen. 7, 28a. 1 Stran. 596, and many other cases in the books to this purpose. Trespass on the case will lie for doing an unlawful act, if the damage sustained thereby be not immediate but consequential, 11 Mod. 108. The first act in the present case (I allow) was unlawful; but the squib by the first act did not strike the plaintiff, the first act was compleat when it lay on Yates' stall, afterwards Willis a byestander threw it across the market-house, it fell on the stall of another man who threw it to another part of the market-house and struck the plaintiff therewith and put out his eye. Willis who took up the squib and threw it across the market-house is not answerable in trespass *vi et armis*, for he did that act to prevent injury to himself, and did no harm to any body. Willis and Yates gave the squib two new directions, acting as free agents, not by the instigation, command, request, or as servants of the defendant, but in defence of their persons, so the injury which happened to the plaintiff was the consequence of, and not done immediately by the first act of the defendant.

■ GOULD, JUSTICE.—I differ with my Brother Blackstone, but with the utmost respect to his sentiments. I think that neither Willis nor Ryall are liable to an action in this case; if that be so, and this action will not lie against the defendant Shepherd who did the first act, which was unlawful, the plaintiff who has been greatly injured will be without remedy. The damage done did instantly arise by and from the act of the defendant: Willis and Ryall in defence of themselves and their goods, being in a state of fear, without power of recollection, instantly tossed and threw the squib away from themselves, what they did was inevitable, as it seemeth to me. Suppose a burning squib thrown into a coach passing along the street, and one of the persons therein throws it out, and the like misfortune as this happens; surely the person throwing the squib out of the coach might justify or excuse himself by pleading; though this is not so strong a case I think as the present. The defendant is the only wrong doer; his act put Willis and Ryall under an inevitable necessity of acting as they did, so neither of them is liable to an action: upon the whole I am of opinion judgment must be for the plaintiff.

■ LORD CHIEF JUSTICE DE GREY. The distinction between actions of trespass on the case, and trespass *vi et armis* should be most carefully and precisely observed, otherwise we shall introduce much confusion and uncertainty; this is that kind of injury where the distinction is very nice. It strikes me thus; trespass *vi et armis* lies against the person from whom an injury is received by force. So the question is, whether this personal injury was received by the plaintiff by force from the defendant? Or whether the injury was received from, or resulting from a new force of another?

The real or true question (I think) is not whether the first act of throwing the squib by the defendant was lawful or not; for I see, that in doing a lawful act, trespass *vi et armis* will, in some cases, lie against the actor; and yet there are cases where trespass *vi et armis* will not lie against a person for doing an unlawful act. * * *

The throwing the squib by the defendant was an unlawful act at common law, the squib had a natural power and tendency to do mischief indiscriminately; but what mischief, or where it would fall, none could know; the fault *egrediture e persona* of him who threw the squib, it would naturally produce a defence to be made by every person in danger of being hurt thereby, and no line can be drawn as to the mischief likely to happen to any person in such danger; the two persons Willis and Ryall, did not act with or in combination with the defendant, and their removal of the squib for fear of danger to themselves seems to me to be a continuation of the first act of the defendant until the explosion of the squib; no man contracts guilt in defending himself; the second and third men were not guilty of any trespass, but all the injury was done by the first act of the defendant; here I lay the stress, and here I differ with my brother Blackstone; for I conceived all the facts of throwing the squib must be considered as one single act, namely the act of the defendant; the same as if it had been a cracker made with gunpowder which had bounded and rebounded again and again before it struck out the plaintiff's eye. I am of opinion that judgement must be for the plaintiff, and the postea was accordingly delivered to him, by the opinion of three judges against one.

NOTES

1. *The Role of Directness in Trespass.* Suppose a philanthropist grabs a bystander to shield himself from a terrorist dynamiter? See Laidlaw v. Sage, 2 A. D. 374, 37 N.Y.S. 770 (1896), rev'd for insufficient evidence of causation, 158 N.Y. 73, 52 N.E. 679 (1899).

2. *Trespass and "Case."* The relevance of the concepts of immediacy, force, and negligence to trespass and case was further considered, *inter*

alia, in Leame v. Bray, (1803) 102 Eng.Rep. (K.B.) 724, 3 East 593. Defendant had negligently driven his horse-drawn carriage into plaintiff's carriage, causing plaintiff's driver to be thrown to the ground, the horses to run away with the plaintiff's carriage, and plaintiff to jump for his life, fracturing his collarbone. No "blame" was "imputable" to the defendant except that on a dark night when the parties could not see each other, he had driven on the wrong side of the road. Defendant contended that the injury here was "consequential and not immediately flowing from the forcible act of the defendant" and that, therefore, the only proper remedy was by an action on the case, not trespass *vi et armis*, no willfulness having been shown. The court held that trespass did lie, notwithstanding defendant's negligence, and seemed to satisfy itself as to the requirement for immediacy in trespass on the basis of the continuity of activities resulting from defendant's application of force. For instance, Le Banc, J.:

> * * * [W]here the injury is immediate on the act done, there trespass lies; but where it is not immediate on the act done, but consequential, there the remedy is in case. And the distinction is well instanced by the example put of a man's throwing a log into the highway: if at the time of its being thrown, it hit any person, it is trespass; but if after it be thrown, any person going along the road receive an injury by falling over it as it lies there, it is case. Neither does the degree of violence with which the act is done make any difference: for if the log were put down in the most quiet way upon a man's foot, it would be trespass; but if thrown into the road with whatever violence, and one afterwards fall over it, it is case and not trespass. So here, if the defendant had simply placed his chaise in the road, and the plaintiff had run against it in the dark, the injury would not have been direct but in consequence only of the defendant's previous improper act. Here however the defendant was driving the carriage at the time with the force necessary to move it along, and the injury to the plaintiff happened from that immediate act: therefore the remedy must be trespass, and all the cases will support that principle.

> It is chiefly in actions for running down vessels at sea that difficulties may occur; because certainly the force which occasions the injury is not so immediate from the act of the person steering. The immediate agents of the force are the wind and waves, and the personal act of the party rather consists in putting the vessel in the way to be so acted upon: and whether that may make any difference in that case I will not now take upon me to determine. But here, where the personal force is immediately applied to the horse and carriage, the things acted upon and causing the damage, like a finger to the trigger of a gun, the injury is immediate from the act of driving, and trespass is the proper remedy for an immediate injury done by one to another: but where the injury is only consequential from the act done, there it is case.

The converse proposition, that case could lie where injury was immediate but occasioned by negligence, was established in Williams v. Holland, (1833) 10 Bing. 112 (Common Pleas), despite earlier indications to the contrary, Day v. Edwards, (1794) 101 Eng.Rep. (K.B.) 361, 5 Term Rep. 648.

3. *Damages as a Requirement of Recovery.* At common law, if a plaintiff established the elements of trespass, she was entitled to at least nominal damages. In trespass on the case, damages were usually an essential element of liability. Joseph H. Koffler & Alison Reppy, Handbook of Common Law Pleading 170, 185 (1969); compare Restatement (Second) of Torts § 328A(d) (1965) (damages required for recovery in negligence), and § 519 and cmts. d, e (1977) (damages required for recovery in strict liability for abnormally dangerous activities), with First Nat'l Bank of Des Plaines v. Amco Eng'g Co., 32 Ill.App.3d 451, 454, 335 N.E.2d 591, 594 (1975) (no damages required for liability in trespass to real property).

4. *Liability without Fault at Common Law.* What do these early English cases suggest about the statements in *Ives* that the idea of liability without fault was unheard of at common law and at the time the American Constitution was adopted? Consider the following analysis of these cases from Harper, James and Gray on Torts § 12.2:

> In trespass * * *, the gist of the action was certainly not fault. The notion was, rather, that one whose affirmative act directly caused the harm should ordinarily pay for it. Now it is perfectly true that this form of action was often used to redress the clearest type of wrongs, such as deliberate beatings and woundings, and the allegations in all cases savored of this kind of situation. But trespass was also the appropriate remedy for direct accidental harms. And a prima facie case in trespass was made out by showing that defendant's voluntary act directly produced the injury. This did not mean that liability for injuries so caused was absolute. The defendant might justify even an intentional hurting of the plaintiff by showing that it was done in self-defense, or to repel a trespass, or to effect a lawful arrest, for example. And there have been suggestions from early times that the defendant could excuse himself by showing that the injury was caused through "inevitable accident." But it was never clear just what constituted an "inevitable accident." The phrase was sometimes used to describe a situation where there was really no voluntary act on the part of defendant at all "as if a man by force take my hand and strike you"; and such a state of facts was inconsistent with even a prima facie trespass and could be shown under the general issue. But the phrase seems also to have been used to refer to cases where defendant was utterly without fault, though the harm was caused by a voluntary act. This must be gathered from dicta; there is not a single recorded case before the nineteenth century in which a defendant successfully pleaded and proved such an excuse in an action of trespass. On the other hand, the pleas that were unsuccessful fell short of ruling out all possibilities of negligence as we know it today. Thus in *Dickinson v. Watson*, where the defendant accidentally shot the plaintiff, the defendant pleaded that he lawfully had the gun; that he discharged it intending no harm to happen, and when no one was in sight; that as he did so the plaintiff came into the way. But it was not alleged that the presence of people in the vicinity was unlikely.

From the decisions, these conclusions seem warranted:

(1) The gist of liability in trespass was that the defendant's act directly produced the injury;

(2) If the defendant affirmatively pleaded and proved the complete absence of any fault, such as intention or carelessness on his part, it is possible this may have defeated the action at the trial court, but even here, there is no written opinion clearly disallowing the plaintiff's recovery because of an absence of fault; and

(3) The concept of negligence was not sufficiently developed before the nineteenth century that the plaintiff was required to plead and prove negligence in a trespass action or the defendant was allowed to defeat recovery by pleading and proving the absence of negligence.

For further reading on these issues, see John Hamilton Baker, An Introduction to English Legal History 60–64, 402–05 (4th ed. 2002); S.F.C. Milsom, Historical Foundations of the Common Law 295–313 (2d ed. 1981); Charles O. Gregory, Trespass to Negligence to Absolute Liability, 37 Va. L. Rev. 359 (1951). Be mindful, however, of Professor Gregory's admonition, "It is stuff like this that drives a torts professor mad and which convinces his students at the threshold of their professional training that the law is a crazy mess." *Id.* at 379.

Brown v. Kendall

Supreme Judicial Court of Massachusetts, 1850.
60 Mass. 292, 6 Cush. 292.

This was an action of trespass for assault and battery, originally commenced against George K. Kendall, the defendant, who died pending the suit, and his executrix was summoned in.

It appeared in evidence, on the trial, which was before Wells, C.J., in the court of common pleas, that two dogs, belonging to the plaintiff and the defendant, respectively, were fighting in the presence of their masters; that the defendant took a stick about four feet long, and commenced beating the dogs in order to separate them; that the plaintiff was looking on, at the distance of about a rod, and that he advanced a step or two towards the dogs. In their struggle, the dogs approached the place where the plaintiff was standing. The defendant retreated backwards from before the dogs, striking them as he retreated; and as he approached the plaintiff, with his back towards him, in raising his stick over his shoulder, in order to strike the dogs, he accidentally hit the plaintiff in the eye, inflicting upon him a severe injury.

Whether it was necessary or proper for the defendant to interfere in the fight between the dogs; whether the interference, if called for, was in proper manner, and what degree of care was exercised by each party on the occasion; were the subject of controversy between the parties, upon all the evidence in the case, of which the foregoing is an outline.

The defendant requested the judge to instruct the jury, that "if both the plaintiff and defendant at the time of the blow were using ordinary care, or if at that time the defendant was using ordinary care and the plaintiff was not, or if at that time both plaintiff and defendant were not using ordinary care, then the plaintiff could not recover." * * *

The judge [declined to give the instructions, as above requested but] left the case to the jury under the following instructions:

> If the defendant, in beating the dogs, was doing a necessary act, or one which it was his duty under the circumstances of the case to do, and was doing it in a proper way; then he was not responsible in this action, provided he was using ordinary care at the time of the blow. If it was not a necessary act; if he was not in duty bound to attempt to part the dogs, but might with propriety interfere or not as he chose; the defendant was responsible for the consequences of the blow, unless it appeared that he was in the exercise of extraordinary care, so that the accident was inevitable, using the word inevitable not in a strict but a popular sense.

> If, however, the plaintiff, when he met with the injury, was not in the exercise of ordinary care, he cannot recover, and this rule applies, whether the interference of the defendant in the fight of the dogs was necessary or not. If the jury believe, that it was the duty of the defendant to interfere, then the burden of proving negligence on the part of the defendant, and ordinary care on the part of the plaintiff, is on the plaintiff. If the jury believe, that the act of interference in the fight was unnecessary, then the burden of proving extraordinary care on the part of the defendant or want of ordinary care on the part of the plaintiff, is on defendant.

The jury under these instructions returned a verdict for the plaintiff; whereupon the defendant alleged exceptions. * * *

■ SHAW, C.J. This is an action of trespass, *vi et armis,* brought by George Brown against George K. Kendall, for an assault and battery. * * * The facts set forth in the bill of exceptions preclude the supposition, that the blow, inflicted by the hand of the defendant upon the person of the plaintiff, was intentional. The whole case proceeds on the assumption, that the damage sustained by the plaintiff, from the stick held by the defendant, was inadvertent and unintentional; and the case involves the question how far, and under what qualifications, the party by whose unconscious act the damage was done is responsible for it. We use the term "unintentional" rather than involuntary, because in some of the cases, it is stated, that the act of holding and using a weapon or instrument, the movement of which is the immediate cause of hurt to another, is a voluntary act, although its particular effect in hitting and hurting another is not within the purpose or intention of the party doing the act.

It appears to us, that some of the confusion in the cases on this subject has grown out of the long-vexed question, under the rule of the common law, whether a party's remedy, where he has one, should be sought in an action of the case, or of trespass. This is very distinguishable from the question, whether in a given case, any action will lie. The result of these cases is, that if the damage complained of is the immediate effect of the act of the defendant, trespass *vi et armis* lies; if consequential only, and not immediate, case is the proper remedy. *

In these discussions, it is frequently stated by judges, that when one receives injury from the direct act of another, trespass will lie. But we think this is said in reference to the question, whether trespass and not case will lie, assuming that the facts are such, that some action will lie. These dicta are no authority, we think, for holding, that damage received by a direct act of force from another will be sufficient to maintain an action of trespass, whether the act was lawful or unlawful, and neither wilful, intentional, or careless. In the principal case cited, Leame v. Bray, 3 East, 593, the damage arose from the act of the defendant, in driving on the wrong side of the road, in a dark night, which was clearly negligent if not unlawful. In the course of the argument of that case, (p. 595,) Lawrence, J., said: "There certainly are cases in the books, where, the injury being direct and immediate, trespass has been holden to lie, though the injury was not intentional." The term "injury" implies something more than damage; but, independently of that consideration, the proposition may be true, because though the injury was unintentional, the act may have been unlawful or negligent, and the cases cited by him are perfectly consistent with that supposition. So the same learned judge in the same case says, (p. 597,) "No doubt trespass lies against one who drives a carriage against another, whether done wilfully or not." But he immediately adds, "Suppose one who is driving a carriage is negligently and heedlessly looking about him, without attending to the road when persons are passing, and thereby runs over a child and kills him, is it not manslaughter? and if so, it must be trespass; for every manslaughter includes trespass;" showing what he understood by a case not wilful. * * *

In using this term, ordinary care, it may be proper to state, that what constitutes ordinary care will vary with the circumstances of cases. In general, it means that kind and degree of care, which prudent and cautious men would use, such as is required by the exigency of the case, and such as is necessary to guard against probable danger. A man, who should have occasion to discharge a gun, on an open and extensive marsh, or in a forest, would be required to use less circumspection and care, than if he were to do the same thing in an inhabited town, village, or city. To make an accident, or casualty, or as the law sometimes states it, inevitable accident, it must be such an accident as the defendant could not have avoided by the use of the kind and degree of care necessary to the exigency, and in the circumstances in which he was placed.

We are not aware of any circumstances in this case, requiring a distinction between acts which it was lawful and proper to do, and acts of legal duty. There are cases, undoubtedly, in which officers are bound to act under process, for the legality of which they are not responsible, and perhaps some others in which this distinction would be important. We can have no doubt that the act of the defendant in attempting to part the fighting dogs, one of which was his own, and for the injurious acts of which he might be responsible, was a lawful and proper act, which he might do by proper and safe means. If, then, in doing this act, using due care and all proper precautions necessary to the exigency of the case, to avoid hurt to others, in raising his stick for that purpose, he accidentally hit the plaintiff in his eye, and wounded him, this was the result of pure accident, or was involuntary and unavoidable, and therefore the action would not lie. Or if the defendant was chargeable with some negligence, and if the plaintiff was also chargeable with negligence, we think the plaintiff cannot recover without showing that the damage was caused wholly by the act of the defendant and that the plaintiff's own negligence did not contribute as an efficient cause to produce it. * * *

The court is of opinion that [the instructions to the jury] were not conformable to law. If the act of hitting the plaintiff was unintentional, on the part of the defendant and done in the doing of a lawful act, then the defendant was not liable, unless it was done in the want of exercise of due care adapted to the exigency of the case, and therefore such want of due care became part of the plaintiff's case, and the burden of proof was on the plaintiff to establish it. *

Perhaps the learned judge, by the use of the term extraordinary care, in the above charge, explained as it is by the context, may have intended nothing more than that increased degree of care and diligence, which the exigency of particular circumstances might require, and which men of ordinary care and prudence would use under like circumstances, to guard against danger. If such was the meaning of this part of the charge, then it does not differ from our views, as above explained. But we are of opinion, that the other part of the charge, that the burden of proof was on the defendant, was incorrect. Those facts which are essential to enable the plaintiff to recover, he takes the burden of proving. The evidence may be offered by the plaintiff or by the defendant; the question of due care, or want of care, may be essentially connected with the main facts, and arise from the same proof; but the effect of the rule, as to the burden of proof, is this, that when the proof is all in, and before the jury, from whatever side it comes, and whether directly proved, or inferred from circumstances, if it appears that the defendant was doing a lawful act, and unintentionally hit and hurt the plaintiff, then unless it also appears to the satisfaction of the jury, that the defendant is chargeable with some fault, negligence, carelessness, or want of prudence, the plaintiff fails to sustain the burden of proof, and is not entitled to recover.

New trial ordered.

NOTES

1. *The Importance of Brown v. Kendall in American Law.* Cases such as *Scott v. Shepherd* illustrate the preoccupation of eighteenth century judges in accident cases with the technical requirements of the forms of action, rather than with substantive issues of fault. Counsel's difficulties were compounded by the inability at that time to plead in the alternative. If plaintiff's counsel chose the wrong writ, the action was dismissed with prejudice. See S.F.C. Milsom, Historical Foundations of the Common Law 396–400 (2d ed. 1981).

Brown v. Kendall effectively eliminated the difference between trespass and case in Massachusetts, and it stated a requirement that, to prevail in trespass, a plaintiff must prove "want of due care." It does not necessarily follow that "want of due care" had previously been a traditional requirement in an action on the case. Instead, it has been contended by Professor Morton Horwitz that, at least in American courts before the early years of the nineteenth century, the opinions in accident cases did not require proof of negligence in actions either on the case or in trespass. Thereafter, he argues, both actions for trespass and on case were transformed within a few short decades, about the time of *Brown v. Kendall,* to require proof of want of care, in a "flowering of the negligence action having nothing to do with any earlier recognition of a substantive distinction between writs." Morton Horwitz, The Transformation of American Law, 1780–1860, 90–94 (1977). This transformation occurred within the century before *Ives*, well after the American Revolution and the adoption of our federal Constitution.

2. *The Possible Relationship between the Emergence of the Negligence Regime and Economic Growth in the Nineteenth Century.* The onset of industrialization in nineteenth century America resulted in a huge increase in the number of accidental injuries. For the past quarter-century, leading American legal historians and tort scholars have debated the extent to which the substance of fundamental tort principles changed during this same period of time and whether any such transformation was motivated by a desire to promote emerging industry by relieving it from more strict liability rules previously applied by the courts.

According to Professor Horwitz, those seeking economic expansion in America in the late decades of the eighteenth century and the early decades of the nineteenth century viewed the prospect of tort liability as a major concern. Morton Horwitz, The Transformation of American Law, 1780–1860, 67–69 (1977). Horwitz finds that the prevailing liability standard at the turn of the nineteenth century was a strict liability standard favoring compensation. By mid-nineteenth century, he concludes, a negligence standard prevailed:

> * * * [T]he law of negligence became a leading means by which the dynamic and growing forces in American society were able to challenge and eventually overwhelm the weak and relatively powerless segments of the American economy. After 1840 the principle that one could not be held liable for socially useful activity exercised with due care became a commonplace of American law. In the process, the conception of property gradually changed from the eighteenth century view that dominion over land above all conferred the power to prevent others from interfering with one's quiet enjoyment of property to the nineteenth century assumption that the essential attribute of property ownership was the power to develop one's property regardless of the injurious consequences to others.

Further, according to Horwitz, this "subsidization" occurred through the legal system, rather than through the legislative process, because antebellum statesmen believed that subsidy through the judicial system more easily disguised the political choices being made than a more transparent and overt process of subsidization through legislative action.

In two subsequent writings, Professor Gary Schwartz disagreed with three major assertions of the Horwitz thesis and concluded that "[t]he nineteenth century's negligence standard developed naturally, without major rejection of pre-existing or proposed rules of strict liability; moreover, with the important exception of worker injury cases, nineteenth-century tort law tended to be generous in affirming the tort liabilities of emerging industry." Gary Schwartz, The Character of Early American Tort Law, 36 UCLA L. Rev. 641, 641 (1989); see also Gary Schwartz, Tort Law and the Economy in Nineteenth-Century America: A Reinterpretation, 90 Yale L.J. 1717 (1981). Schwartz rejected Horwitz's analysis that American courts at the beginning of the nineteenth century encountered "a strong set of preexisting pro-liability common law rules." 36 UCLA L. Rev. at 678. Further, while he agreed that negligence law was the "dominant standard" by the mid-nineteenth century, he argued that it was "by no means the exclusive liability standard."

3. *Classical Liberal Thought and the Origins of Negligence.* An alternative, but not necessarily mutually exclusive explanation for the emergence of the negligence standard during the mid-nineteenth century finds its origins in classical liberal thought. See John Fabian Witt, Toward a New History of American Accident Law: Classical Tort Law and the Cooperative First Party Insurance Movement, 114 Harv. L. Rev. 690, 734–43 (2001). According to Witt:

> The central proposition of nineteenth-century political liberalism was the idea that individuals may act as they choose, consistent with the like rights of others. * * * A negligence standard would allow individuals to act freely with their rights, without compromising those rights by charging them with the costs of harms that they could not reasonably avoid.

Id. at 736, 738.

Similarly, James Barr Ames, a Harvard Law School professor who published the first torts casebook in 1871, saw the emergence of fault in nineteenth century tort law as "bringing our system of law more and more into harmony with moral principles . . ." James B. Ames, Law and Morals, 22 Harv. L. Rev. 97, 113 (1908). At the same time the law of negligence was developing, American society experienced an increasing focus on religious and moral matters in other areas. For example, Witt suggests that Thomas Cooley, the author of an influential nineteenth-century torts treatise, may have been influenced by " 'the most extravagant religious revivalism, antimasonry, abolition, millennialism, prohibition, spiritualism, woman's rights, the Mormon church, [and] the Millerites . . .' " that swept through the " 'Burned-Over District' " of western New York where he grew up. Witt, *supra*, at 742 (quoting Peter F. Walker, Moral Choices: Memory, Desire, and Imagination in Nineteenth-Century American Abolition 337 (1978)). According to Witt:

> Cooley's torts treatise * * * drew inspiration from the Burned-Over District's reform ideal of moral autonomy. So long as an actor remained within the bounds of his legal rights and duties he was, in Cooley's conception, unchargeable by the state for harms falling on others. Thus the "lawful and proper exercise by one man of his rights" was never grounds for liability.

Id. at 743.

4. *The Legacy of the Forms of Action in English Law.* The elimination of all distinctions between trespass and case in English law was much more gradual than in the United States. In Williams v. Holland [1833] 10 Bing 112, Tindal, C.J., held that a plaintiff could choose to bring claims for most injuries, even direct ones (excepting willful harms) in case. The plaintiff was no longer forced to make the choice, often fatal to his action in the past, between trespass and case by deciding whether the injury had been "direct" or "consequential." See M. J. Prichard, Trespass, Case and the Rule in *Williams v. Holland,* 22 Cambridge L.J. 234 (1964). As a result of this decision, trespass became more and more associated with willful injuries. John Hamilton Baker, An Introduction to English Legal History 413 (4th ed. 2002).

Nevertheless, actions in trespass for accidental injuries continued to be brought in England without a requirement of fault. In Holmes v. Mather, (1875) L.R. 10 Ex. 261, the defendant's horses, having been frightened by a dog, had run away with their carriage and knocked the plaintiff down. The plaintiff sued in two counts, negligence and trespass, and the defendant pleaded not guilty. The jury found "no negligence in any one." Bramwell B. ruled that the trespass action was accordingly not maintainable, stating, "For the convenience of mankind in carrying on the affairs of life, people as they go along roads must expect, or put up with, such mischief as reasonable care on the part of others cannot avoid. * * * [I]f the act that does an injury is an act of direct force *vi et armis,* trespass is the proper remedy (if there is any remedy) where the act is wrongful, either being willful or as being the result of negligence. Were the act not wrongful for either of these reasons, no action is maintainable, though trespass would be the proper form of action if it were wrongful." He also concluded that the driver was not "immediately doing the act which did the mischief." * * *

It has been argued that Baron Bramwell was assuming that wrongfulness was a necessary element in prima facie trespass, and that this reflected a general understanding of nineteenth century common law lawyers, prevalent before 1875, that trespass would not lie except for a wrongful act. Justice Diplock, as he then was, so contended in Fowler v. Lanning, [1959] 1 Q.B. 426. Most scholarly opinion had tended otherwise, assuming instead that, before *Holmes v. Mather*, negligence was relevant to trespass only as an affirmative defense, and not as a necessary element of the cause of action. It is clear in any event that a substantial body of English opinion considered *Holmes v. Mather* to have established a special exception for highway cases, perhaps based on the suggestion, reflected in Bramwell's opinion, that highway travelers voluntarily assume the risks of non-wrongful accident. Until 1959, it was widely thought in England that while plaintiff must plead and prove negligence in actions of trespass arising from highway accidents, defendants must prove freedom from negligence in trespass arising otherwise. See, e.g., Stanley v. Powell, [1891] 1 Q.B. 86. Not until 1959 did a British high court judge rule that an allegation "the defendant shot the plaintiff" (without alleging wilfulness, negligence, or any other circumstances, "indeed with what weapon, from bow and arrow to atomic warhead") fails to state a cause of action, Fowler v. Lanning, [1959] 1 Q.B. 426.

Indeed, in England loose ends as to a residual distinction between "trespass" and "negligence" lingered for purposes of statutes of limitation until Letang v. Cooper, [1965] 1 Q.B. 232 (C.A.). Thereafter, there remained some Commonwealth opinion to the effect that a tort of "negligent trespass" survives as a different cause of action from "negligence". See, e.g., F.A.

Trindade, Some Curiosities of Negligent Trespass to the Person: A Comparative Study, 20 Int'l & Comp. L.Q. 706 (1971).

Excerpt, Oliver Wendell Holmes, Jr., The Common Law
76–78 (Mark DeWolfe Howe ed., 1963) (1881).

To return to the example of the accidental blow with a stick lifted in self-defence, there is no difference between hitting a person standing in one's rear and hitting one who was pushed by a horse within range of the stick just as it was lifted, provided that it was not possible, under the circumstances, in the one case to have known, in the other to have anticipated, the proximity. In either case there is wanting the only element which distinguishes voluntary acts from spasmodic muscular contractions as a ground of liability. In neither of them, that is to say, has there been an opportunity of choice with reference to the consequence complained of,—a chance to guard against the result which has come to pass. A choice which entails a concealed consequence is as to that consequence no choice.

The general principle of our law is that loss from accident must lie where it falls, and this principle is not affected by the fact that a human being is the instrument of misfortune. But relatively to a given human being anything is accident which he could not fairly have been expected to contemplate as possible, and therefore to avoid. In the language of the late Chief Justice Nelson of New York: "No case or principle can be found, or if found can be maintained, subjecting an individual to liability for an act done without fault on his part. . . . All the cases concede that an injury arising from inevitable accident, or, which in law or reason is the same thing, from an act that ordinary human care and foresight are unable to guard against is but the misfortune of the sufferer, and lays no foundation for legal responsibility." If this were not so, any act would be sufficient, however remote, which set in motion or opened the door for a series of physical sequences ending in damage; such as riding the horse, in the case of the runaway, or even coming to a place where one is seized with a fit and strikes the plaintiff in an unconscious spasm. Nay, why need the defendant have acted at all, and why is it not enough that his existence has been at the expense of the plaintiff? The requirement of an act is the requirement that the defendant should have made a choice. But the only possible purpose of introducing this moral element is to make the power of avoiding the evil complained of a condition of liability. There is no such power where the evil cannot be foreseen. Here we reach the argument from policy, and I shall accordingly postpone for a moment the discussion of trespasses upon land, and of conversions, and will take up the liability for cattle separately at a later stage.

A man need not, it is true, do this or that act,—the term *act* implies a choice,—but he must act somehow. Furthermore, the public generally profits by individual activity. As action cannot be avoided, and tends to the public good, there is obviously no policy in throwing the hazard of what is at once desirable and inevitable upon the actor.

The state might conceivably make itself a mutual insurance company against accidents, and distribute the burden of its citizens' mishaps among all its members. There might be a pension for paralytics, and state aid for those who suffered in person or estate from tempest or wild beasts. As between individuals it might adopt the mutual insurance principle *pro tanto,* and divide damages when both were in fault, as in the *rusticum judicium* of the admiralty, or it might throw all loss upon the actor irrespective of fault. The state does none of these things, however, and the prevailing view is that its cumbrous and expensive machinery ought not to be set in motion unless some clear benefit is to be derived from disturbing the status quo. State interference is an evil, where it cannot be shown to be a good. Universal insurance, if desired, can be better and more cheaply accomplished by private enterprise. The undertaking to redistribute losses simply on the ground that they resulted from the defendant's act would not only be open to these objections, but, as it is hoped the preceding discussion has shown, to the still graver one of offending the sense of justice. Unless my act is of a nature to threaten others, unless under the circumstances a prudent man would have foreseen the possibility of harm, it is no more justifiable to make me indemnify my neighbor against the consequences, than to make me do the same thing if I had fallen upon him in a fit, or to compel me to insure him against lightning. * * *

NOTE

Compare Holmes' views with those expressed by Guido Calabresi & A. Douglas Melamed in Property Rules, Liability Rules, and Inalienability: One View of the Cathedral, 85 Harv. L. Rev. 1089, 1091 (1972):

> When a loss is left where it falls in an auto accident, it is not because God so ordained it. Rather it is because the state has granted the injurer an entitlement to be free of liability and will intervene to prevent the victim's friends, if they are stronger, from taking compensation from the injurer. The loss is shifted in other cases because the state has granted an entitlement to compensation and will intervene to prevent the stronger injurer from rebuffing the victim's request for compensation.

Consider also the views expressed in Guido Calabresi, The Costs of Accidents, 261–63 (1970) and in George Fletcher, Fairness and Utility in Tort Theory, 85 Harv. L. Rev. 537, 564 *et seq.* (1972).

C. THE CHALLENGE TO THE COMMON LAW POSED BY ACCIDENTAL INJURY

Excerpt, Jeremiah Smith, Sequel to Workmen's Compensation Acts

27 Harv. L. Rev. 344, 363–67 (1914).

Of what has heretofore been said this is the sum: The result reached in many cases under the Workmen's Compensation Acts is absolutely incongruous with the results reached under the modern common law as to various persons whose cases are not affected by these statutes. For this difference there is no satisfactory reason.

It is believed that the incongruities heretofore pointed out, resulting from the difference between the statute and the modern common law, will not be permitted to continue permanently without protest. The public are not likely to be "content for long under the contradictory systems." In the end, one or the other of the two conflicting theories is likely to prevail. There is no probability, during the present generation, of a repeal of the Workmen's Compensation Acts. Indeed, the tendency is now in the direction of extension, rather than repeal, of this species of legislation. The only present available method to remove the inconsistency is by bringing about a change in the existing common law, either by legislation or by judicial decisions.

As to legislation (aided perhaps by constitutional amendments); there may be an attempt to bring about State Insurance, not confined to harm suffered by hired laborers. It may extend to an "outsider," who suffers harm from the non-culpable conduct of persons carrying on a business in which he is not a participant. It may not be confined to the case where there is, in the chain of antecedents, the non-culpable conduct of some human being other than the damaged person himself. It may include the case of an independent workman, who is hurt by pure accident, without any human agency other than his own, while conducting his own business on his own account; e.g., a small farmer, or a blacksmith who runs his forge without an assistant.

A State Insurance Law may not merely insure against accident, but also against disease, either contracted in the service of another or while the claimant was working on his own account.

It may include damage wholly due to a natural cause, such as a stroke of lightning.

Whether legislation of the above descriptions *ought* to be enacted is a question upon which no opinion is here intimated. Our immediate point is, that the present Workmen's Compensation legislation will inevitably give rise to a plausible agitation for such further legislation.

As to a change in the common law, to be brought about by judicial decisions:

There may be an attempt to induce judges to repudiate the fundamental doctrine of the modern common law of torts that fault is generally requisite to liability, and to go back to the ancient common-law doctrine that an innocent actor must answer for harm caused by his non-culpable conduct.

Or the judges may be urged to adopt a middle or compromise view; that, as between two non-culpable actors, the loss shall be equally divided.

Several questions arise:

1.   Can the judges change the law?
2.   Ought they to change the law?
3.   Will they change the law?

The objection may be raised that judges cannot make, or change, law; not merely that they cannot alter statute law, a result which is admittedly beyond their power; but that they cannot make or alter law on subjects not dealt with by the legislature.

There are at least three different theories as to judicial lawmaking.

1. That judges cannot "make" law; that they merely discover and apply law which has always existed.

2. (A middle view.) That judges can and do make new law on subjects not covered by previous decisions; but that judges cannot unmake old law, cannot even change an existing rule of "judge-made" law.

3. That judges can and do make new law; and also can and do unmake old law; i.e., law previously laid down by themselves or by their judicial predecessors.

We prefer the third view. But if the second view is adopted, the result here would not be to sustain and preserve unaltered (unless by legislation) the common law as declared by the courts in A.D. 1900 but, instead, to sustain the law as formerly declared in A.D. 1400 by the judges of that day. If judges have no power to change (i.e., if they cannot change) law "made" by their judicial predecessors, then of course, they have not legally done that which they had no legal power to do (that which they could not do). Hence it would follow that the common law of 1400 is still in force; and that the decisions in more recent times, purporting to establish a contrary rule (i.e., the rule now known as the modern common-law doctrine), are simply instances of judicial usurpation.

But, as already intimated, we prefer the third view, that judges can and do make new law and unmake old law. Under this view the judges have heretofore changed the law of A.D. 1400 to the law of A.D. 1900, and still have now the power to change it back again. Assuming, then, that the judges can turn the hands of the legal clock back five centuries, the questions remain:

Ought they to make the change?

Will they make the change?

As to whether the change will be made: it is safe to say that, while it may take place, yet it is not likely to be done directly and avowedly. When courts change the substantive law, they generally do so very gradually, and often attempt to conceal (or perhaps unconsciously conceal) the fact of change by using various "fiction phrases."

Judges, however, are not insensible to public opinion; and legislation, evidencing public opinion, has a reflex action on courts.

Even if courts should shrink from directly and avowedly changing the law, the result could be, to a considerable extent, accomplished by indirect methods. By a very liberal construction of the *res ipsa loquitur* doctrine; by a broad view as to what constitutes prima facie evidence of negligence; and by inverting the burden of proof (putting on defendant the burden of proving that he was not negligent),—the court could go far towards practically reversing the common law of A.D. 1900 in a large proportion of cases.

Whether this change *ought* to be made (whether it is expedient for either courts or legislatures to make it) is a problem of immense importance, which we here make no attempt to solve. At the very beginning it was said: "The object of this paper is to give notice of an impending question of great importance; not to give an answer to the question, but to show how and why it arises at the present time."

NOTE

Varying Perspectives on the Role of the Common Law Judge. How do you think that the members of the *Ives* court viewed their roles as judges? Did they believe, in Smith's words, that they were "making" the law or "discovering" the law? Did Chief Judge Shaw in *Brown v. Kendall* view his role in the same manner? To what extent do you suppose judges are capable of accurately answering this question about themselves? For one notable judge's attempts to address such issues, see Benjamin Cardozo, The Nature of the Judicial Process (1921).

CHAPTER 2

TRADITIONAL FORMS OF LIABILITY WITHOUT FAULT

This chapter explores various traditional bases of liability other than fault that have found expression from time to time in our statutory and judge-made law. *Ives v. South Buffalo Railway Co.* suggested that tort liability must ordinarily rest on fault, and claimed historical sanction for this proposition. The succeeding materials showed that in the common law action of trespass, fault was not the dominant theme, though it grew in importance along with the development of the action on the case until the attitude disclosed in *Ives* became prevalent.

We do not suggest that a common set of considerations or policies runs through all these cases in this chapter; indeed quite the reverse. Our purpose is to point out the variety of objectives and aims which have been sought through the device of making one person pay for another's damage, or refusing to do so, regardless of fault. It is hoped that this will stimulate examination of the suitability and efficacy of the strict liability device in promoting social objectives in a variety of social and economic contexts.

A. RECOVERY FOR DAMAGES CAUSED BY A PARTY ACTING UNDER NECESSITY

Vincent v. Lake Erie Transportation Co.

Supreme Court of Minnesota, 1910.
109 Minn. 456, 124 N.W. 221.

■ O'BRIEN, J. The steamship Reynolds, owned by the defendant, was for the purpose of discharging her cargo on November 27, 1905, moored to plaintiffs' dock in Duluth. While the unloading of the boat was taking place a storm from the northeast developed, which at about ten o'clock p.m., when the unloading was completed, had so grown in violence that the wind was then moving at fifty miles per hour and continued to increase during the night. There is some evidence that one, and perhaps two, boats were able to enter the harbor that night, but it is plain that navigation was practically suspended from the hour mentioned until the morning of the 29th, when the storm abated, and during that time no master would have been justified in attempting to navigate his vessel, if he could avoid doing so. After the discharge of the cargo the Reynolds signaled for a tug to tow her from the dock, but none could be obtained because of the severity of the storm. If the lines holding the ship to the dock had been cast off, she would doubtless have drifted away; but, instead, the lines were kept fast, and as soon as one parted or chafed it was replaced, sometimes with a larger one. The vessel lay upon the outside of the dock, her bow to the east, the wind and waves striking her starboard quarter with such force that she was constantly being lifted and thrown against the dock, resulting in its damage, as found by the jury, to the amount of $500.

We are satisfied that the character of the storm was such that it would have been highly imprudent for the master of the Reynolds to have attempted to leave the dock or to have permitted his vessel to drift away from it. One witness testified upon the trial that the vessel could have been warped into a slip, and that, if the attempt to bring the ship into the slip had failed, the worst that could have happened would be that the vessel would have been blown ashore upon a soft and muddy bank. The witness was not present in Duluth at the time of the storm, and, while he may have been right in his conclusions, those in charge of the dock and the vessel at the time of the storm were not required to use the highest human intelligence, nor were they required to resort to every possible experiment which could be suggested for the preservation of their property. Nothing more was demanded of them than ordinary prudence and care, and the record in this case fully sustains the contention of the appellant that, in holding the vessel fast to the dock, those in charge of her exercised good judgment and prudent seamanship.

It is claimed by the respondent that it was negligence to moor the boat at an exposed part of the wharf, and to continue in that position after it became apparent that the storm was to be more than usually severe. We do not agree with this position. The part of the wharf where the vessel was moored appears to have been commonly used for that purpose. It was situated within the harbor at Duluth, and must, we think, be considered a proper and safe place, and would undoubtedly have been such during what would be considered a very severe storm. The storm which made it unsafe was one which surpassed in violence any which might have reasonably been anticipated.

The appellant contends by ample assignments of error that, because its conduct during the storm was rendered necessary by prudence and good seamanship under conditions over which it had no control, it cannot be held liable for any injury resulting to the property of others, and claims that the jury should have been so instructed. An analysis of the charge given by the trial court is not necessary, as in our opinion the only question for the jury was the amount of damages which the plaintiffs were entitled to recover, and no complaint is made upon that score.

The situation was one in which the ordinary rules regulating property rights were suspended by forces beyond human control, and if, without the direct intervention of some act by the one sought to be held liable, the property of another was injured, such injury must be attributed to the act of God, and not to the wrongful act of the person sought to be charged. If during the storm the Reynolds had entered the harbor, and while there had become disabled and been thrown against the plaintiffs' dock, the plaintiffs could not have recovered. Again, if while attempting to hold fast to the dock the lines had parted, without any negligence, and the vessel carried against some other boat or dock in the harbor, there would be no liability upon her owner. But here those in charge of the vessel deliberately and by their direct efforts held her in such a position that the damage to the dock resulted, and, having thus preserved the ship at the expense of the dock, it seems to us that her owners are responsible to the dock owners to the extent of the injury inflicted.

In Depue v. Flatau, 100 Minn. 299, 111 N.W. 1 (1907), this court held that where the plaintiff, while lawfully in the defendants' house, became so ill that he was incapable of traveling with safety, the defendants were responsible to him in damages for compelling him to leave the premises. If, however, the owner of the premises had furnished the traveler with proper accommodations and medical attendance, would he have been able to defeat an action brought against him for their reasonable worth?

In Ploof v. Putnam, 81 Vt. 471, 71 A. 188 (1908), the supreme court of Vermont held that where, under stress of weather, a vessel was without permission moored to a private dock at an island in Lake Champlain owned by the defendant, the plaintiff was not guilty of trespass, and that the defendant was responsible in damages because his representative upon the island unmoored the vessel, permitting it to drift upon the shore, with resultant injuries to it. If, in that case, the vessel had been permitted to remain, and the dock had suffered an injury, we believe the shipowner would have been held liable for the injury done.

Theologians hold that a starving man may, without moral guilt, take what is necessary to sustain life; but it could hardly be said that the obligation would not be upon such person to pay the value of the property so taken when he became able to do so. And so public necessity, in times of war or peace, may require the taking of private property for public purposes; but under our system of jurisprudence compensation must be made.

Let us imagine in this case that for the better mooring of the vessel those in charge of her had appropriated a valuable cable lying upon the dock. No matter how justifiable such appropriation might have been, it would not be claimed that, because of the overwhelming necessity of the situation, the owner of the cable could not recover its value.

This is not a case where life or property was menaced by any object or thing belonging to the plaintiffs, the destruction of which became necessary to prevent the threatened disaster. Nor is it a case where, because of the act of God, or unavoidable accident, the infliction of the injury was beyond the control of the defendant, but is one where the defendant prudently and advisedly availed itself of the plaintiffs' property for the purpose of preserving its own more valuable property, and the plaintiffs are entitled to compensation for the injury done.

Order affirmed.

■ LEWIS, J. I dissent. It was assumed on the trial before the lower court, that appellant's liability depended on whether the master of the ship might in the exercise of reasonable care, have sought a place of safety before the storm made it impossible to leave the dock. The majority opinion assumes that the evidence is conclusive that appellant moored its boat at respondents' dock pursuant to contract, and that the vessel was lawfully in position at the time the additional cables were fastened to the dock, and the reasoning of opinion is that, because appellant made use of the stronger cables to hold the boat in position, it became liable under the rule that it had voluntarily made use of the property of another for the purpose of saving its own.

In my judgment, if the boat was lawfully in position at the time the storm broke, and the master could not, in the exercise of due care, have left that position without subjecting his vessel to the hazards of the storm, then the damage to the dock, caused by the pounding of the boat, was the result of an inevitable accident. If the master was in the exercise of due care, he was not at fault. The reasoning of the opinion admits that if the ropes, or cables, first attached to the dock had not parted, or if, in the first instance, the master had used the stronger cables, there would be no liability. If the master could not, in the exercise of reasonable care, have anticipated the severity of the storm and sought a place of safety before it became impossible, why should he be required to anticipate the severity of the storm, and, in the first instance, use the stronger cables?

I am of the opinion that one who constructs a dock to the navigable line of waters, and enters into contractual relations with the owner of a vessel to moor at the same, takes the risk of damage to his dock by a boat caught there by a storm, which event could not have been avoided in the exercise of due care, and further, that the legal status of the parties in such a case is not changed by renewal of cables to keep the boat from being cast adrift at the mercy of the tempest.

NOTES

1. *Trespass to Land.* Was the defendant in *Vincent* entitled to dock his boat and keep it attached to the pier as he did? Was he a trespasser?

Trespass to land has been defined as "an actionable invasion of a possessor's interest in the exclusive possession of land." See Martin v. Reynolds Metals Co., *infra* pages 101–07. Trespass to land is ordinarily said to require that the actor "intentionally" enters the land, e.g., Restatement (Second) of Torts § 158 (1965); "enters" is deemed to include "the presence upon the land of a third person or thing which the actor has caused to be or to remain there." *Id.* at cmt. b. Restatement (Third) of Torts: Liability for Physical and Emotional Harm § 1 indicates that "[a] person acts with the intent to produce a consequence if: (a) the person acts with the purpose of producing that consequence; or (b) the person acts knowing that the consequence is substantially certain to result." Restatement (Third) of Torts: Liability for Physical and Emotional Harm § 1 (2010). See also Restatement (Second) of Torts §§ 164–66, e.g., *id.* at § 164, cmt. a: "In order to be liable for a trespass on land * * * it is necessary only that the actor intentionally be upon any part of the land in question. It is not necessary that he intend to invade the possessor's interest in the exclusive possession of his land and, therefore, that he know his entry to be an intrusion. If the actor is and intends to be upon the particular piece of land in question, it is immaterial that he honestly and reasonably believes that he has the consent of the lawful possessor to enter, or, indeed, that he himself is its possessor."

2. *Incomplete Privilege.* In Ploof v. Putnam, 81 Vt. 471, 71 A. 188 (1908), the Vermont Supreme Court only two years before *Vincent* held that when agents of the defendant unmoored the plaintiff's boat from defendant's dock and returned it to the stormy waters of Lake Champlain, the defendant was liable for the subsequent loss of the boat, notwithstanding defendant's claim of privilege to use force to repel a trespass. The court reasoned that "necessity, and an inability to control movements inaugurated in the proper exercise of a strict right, will justify entries upon land and interferences with personal property that would otherwise have been trespasses." In its opinion, the Vermont Supreme Court cited an early English case holding that "[i]f one have a way over the land of another for his beasts to pass, and the beasts, being properly driven, feed the grass by morsels in passing, or run out of the way and are promptly pursued and brought back, trespass will not lie. See Vin. Ab. Trespass, K. a, pl. 1." 81 Vt. at 474, 71 A. at 189. Is this consistent with *Vincent*?

The privilege in *Vincent v. Lake Erie Transportation* is often described as an "incomplete privilege." See Restatement (Second) of Torts § 197 (1965); Francis H. Bohlen, Incomplete Privilege to Inflict Intentional Invasions of Interests of Property and Personality, 39 Harv. L. Rev. 307 (1926).

3. *Restitution.* A slightly different but closely related interpretation of *Vincent v. Lake Erie Transportation* is that it represents an application of the principle of restitution: a body of rules that includes the doctrine of "unjust enrichment," that is, that the ship owner should not be able to save his ship at the expense of the dock owner without paying for damage to her dock.

4. *Economic Realities.* Who are probably the real parties in interest in the *Vincent* situation? Who bears the loss if plaintiff wins? If plaintiff loses? Does it matter who wins or loses here?

The Mayor of New York v. Lord
New York Court for the Correction of Errors, 1837.
18 Wend. 126.

■ By the CHANCELLOR. The only real question in this case is, whether the lessee of the store, which was destroyed by direction of the public authorities of the city of New York, during the great fire, is entitled, upon a fair construction of the statute on this subject, to compensation for the actual loss or damages which he sustained by the destruction of his goods, which, as such lessee, he had in the store at the time it was blown up; which loss, according to the finding of the jury, under the decision and charge of Judge Irving, must be considered as the direct and necessary consequence of the destruction of the store at the time and under the particular circumstances in which such destruction thereof took place or was effected. * * *

The principle appears to be well settled, that in a case of actual necessity, to prevent the spreading of a fire, the ravages of a pestilence, the advance of a hostile army, or any other great public calamity, the private property of an individual may be lawfully taken and used or destroyed, for the relief, protection or safety of the many, without subjecting those, whose duty it is to protect the public interests, by whom or under whose direction such private property was taken or destroyed, to personal liability for the damage which the owner has thereby sustained. Where the same extent of loss or injury would have been sustained by the individual, as the necessary consequence of the fire or other public calamity, if his property had not been thus taken and destroyed for the protection of others, it may be considered as at the least doubtful whether he has any equitable claim to compensation, either from the public in general or from that portion of the community for whose particular benefit or protection his private property was taken or sacrificed; for in such a case, although others have been benefitted, he has in fact sustained no damage thereby. It is very clear that the individual could not claim compensation *for such a loss*, under the statute we are now considering, which limits the amount of the assessment to *damages* actually sustained by the pulling down and destruction of the building.

On the other hand, it is very evident that if the private property of an individual, the whole or a part of which might otherwise have been saved to the owner, is taken or destroyed for the benefit of the public, or of the inhabitants of a particular county, city, town, or other smaller section of the community, those for whose supposed benefit the sacrifice was made, ought in equity and justice to make good the loss which the individual has sustained for the common benefit of all. It is upon this great principle of natural equity that maritime contributions are founded; as in the case of a *jettison*, where the property of an individual is cast into the sea, or otherwise sacrificed, with a view to the safety of the vessel and the residue of the cargo, during an impending peril. In that case the vessel and freight and the residue of the cargo, which are thus saved by the sacrifice of a part, all contribute ratably to make good the loss to the individual whose property has been sacrificed for the common benefit. But where the jettison does not divert the impending evil, so that the same loss would have occurred to the individual by the same peril, if his property had not been thus sacrificed, he has no claim for contribution from the owners of the vessel and the residue of the cargo, who have all shared with him in a common calamity. * * *

NOTE

Public Necessity. How does the situation in *The Mayor of New York v. Lord* differ from that in *Vincent*? Can the decisions of public authorities to destroy property to protect the public be given more deference than the decision of a private individual to protect herself or her property? Should it matter from the perspective of the property owner when he seeks compensation for his loss?

Most courts hold that in cases of "public necessity," the plaintiff is not entitled to compensation for the loss of his property. E.g., United States v. Caltex, Inc., 344 U.S. 149, 73 S.Ct. 200, 97 L.Ed. 157 (1952); Restatement (Second) of Torts § 196 (1965). In *United States v. Caltex*, the United States Army destroyed an oil refinery in the Philippines to keep it from falling into the hands of the advancing Japanese army. The United States Supreme Court held that the destruction was privileged and not a compensable taking for public use. Under English law there is no such privilege. Burmah Oil Co., Ltd. v. Lord Advocate, [1964] 2 All E.R. 348.

B. ABNORMALLY DANGEROUS ACTIVITIES

Fletcher v. Rylands

Court of Exchequer, 1865.
34 L.J. Rep., N.S. 177, 159 All E.R. 737.

[Plaintiff was a tenant of certain beds of coal lying under certain land belonging to the Earl of Wilton. By arrangement with Lord Wilton, plaintiff in 1850 sank a pit for the mining of coal under other lands lying to the north of those first mentioned. This was called the "Red House Pit," and the colliery worked thereby the "Red House Colliery."

In 1860 the defendants, proprietors of a mill near the Red House Colliery, made a reservoir, to supply their mill with water, in certain other lands of Lord Wilton, lying northwest of the colliery.

The coal under the site of the reservoir and between it and the colliery had been partially worked at some time or other beyond living memory, but this was not known to defendants, or to anyone employed by them in selecting their site or constructing their reservoir. These old coal workings communicated with the plaintiff's coal workings.]

In the course of constructing and excavating for the bed of the reservoir, five old shafts running vertically downwards were met with in the portion of land selected for the site of the reservoir. At the time they were so met with, the sides or walls of at least three of them were constructed of timber, and were still in existence, but the shafts themselves were filled up with marl or soil of the same kind as the marl or soil which immediately surrounded them; and it was not known to or suspected by the defendants, or any of the persons employed by them in or about the planning or constructing of the reservoir that they were (as they afterwards proved to be) shafts which had been made for the purpose of getting the coal under the land in which the reservoir was made, or that they led down to coal workings under the site of the reservoir.

For the selection of the site of the reservoir, and for the planning and constructing thereof, it was necessary that the defendants should employ an engineer and contractors, and *they did employ for those purposes a competent engineer and competent contractors* by and under whom the site was selected, and the reservoir was planned and constructed; and, *on the part of the defendants themselves, there was no personal negligence or default whatever* in or about or in relation to the selection of the site, or in or about the planning or construction of the reservoir; *but, in point of fact, reasonable and proper care and skill were not exercised by or on the part of the persons so employed by them* with reference to the shafts so met with as aforesaid, to provide for the sufficiency of the reservoir, to bear the pressure of water which, when filled to the height proposed, it would have to bear.

The reservoir was completed about the beginning of December 1860, when the defendants caused the same to be partially filled with water; and on the morning of the 11th of December in the same year, whilst the reservoir was so partially filled, one of the shafts which had been so met with as aforesaid gave way and burst downwards; in consequence of which the water of the reservoir flowed into the old coal workings underneath, and by means of the underground communications * * * large quantities of the water so flowing from the reservoir as aforesaid found their way into the coal workings in the Red House Colliery, and by reason thereof the said colliery became and was flooded, and the working thereof was obliged to be and was for a time necessarily suspended. * * * [Later the colliery was abandoned.]

The question for the opinion of the Court was, whether the plaintiff was entitled to recover damages from the defendants by reason of the matters stated in the case. * * *

■ BRAMWELL, B.—* * * [This] case is singularly wanting in authority, and, therefore, while it is always desirable to ascertain the principle on which a case depends, it is especially so here.

Now, what is the plaintiff's right? He had the right to work his mines to their extent, leaving no boundary between himself and the next owner. By so doing, he subjected himself to all consequences resulting from natural causes; among others, to the influx of all water naturally flowing in; but he had a right to be free from what has been called foreign water—that is, water artificially brought or sent to him directly, or indirectly by its being sent to where it would flow to him. * * *

I proceed to deal with the arguments the other way. It is said, there must be a trespass or nuisance with negligence. I do not agree with that, and I think Bonomi v. Backhouse, 9 H.L. Cas. 903; s. c. 27 Law J. Rep. (N.S.) Q.B. 378, and *ante*, Q.B. 181, shews the contrary. But why is not this a trespass?—see Gregory v. Piper, 9 B. & C. 591. Wilfulness is not material—see Leame v. Bray, 3 East, 593. Why is it not a nuisance? The nuisance is not in the reservoir, but in the water escaping. As in *Bonomi v. Backhouse*, the act was lawful, the mischievous consequence was a wrong. Where two carriages come in collision, if there is no negligence in either, it is as much the act of the one driver as of the other that they meet. * * * The old common law liability for fire created a liability beyond what I contend for here. * * *

I think, therefore, on the plain ground that the defendants have caused water to flow into the plaintiff's mines, which, but for the defendants' act, would not have gone there, this action is maintainable. I think that the defendants' innocence, whatever may be its moral bearing on the case, is immaterial in point of law. But I may as well add, that if the defendants did not know what would happen, their agents knew that there were old shafts on their land; knew, therefore, that they must lead to old workings; knew that those old workings might extend in any direction, and, consequently, knew damage might happen. The defendants surely are as liable as their agents would be. Why should not both be held to act at their peril? But I own, this seems to me, rather to enforce the rule, that knowledge and wilfulness are not necessary to make the defendant liable, than to give the plaintiff a separate ground of action. My judgment is for the plaintiff.

■ MARTIN, B.—* * * First, I think there was no trespass. In the judgment of my Brother Bramwell, to which I shall hereafter refer, he seems to think the act of the defendants was a trespass; but I cannot concur, as * * * it seems to me that the cases cited by him, namely, Leame v. Bray, 3 East 593, and Gregory v. Piper, 9 B. & C. 591, prove the contrary. I think the true criterion of trespass is laid down in the judgment in the former case, namely, that to constitute trespass, the act doing the damage must be immediate, and that if the damage be not immediate but consequential, which I think the present was, it is not trespass.

Secondly, I think there was no nuisance in the ordinary and generally understood meaning of that word, that is to say, something hurtful or injurious to the senses. The making a pond for holding water is a nuisance to no one. The digging a reservoir in [sic] a man's own land is a lawful act. It does not appear that there was any embankment, or that the water in the reservoir was ever above the level of the natural surface of the land; but the water escaped from the bottom of the reservoir, and, in ordinary course, would descend by gravitation into the defendants' own land, and they did not know of the existence of the old workings.

To hold the defendants liable, would therefore make them insurers against the consequence of a lawful act upon their own land, when they had no reason to believe or suspect that any damage was likely to ensue. No case was cited in which the question has arisen as to real property; but as to personal property the question arises every day, and there is no better established rule of law than that, when damage is done to personal property, or even to the person, by collision either upon land or at sea, there must be negligence in the party doing the damage to render him legally responsible; and, if there be no negligence, the party sustaining the damage must bear with it. The existence of this rule is proved by the exceptions to it, namely, the cases of the innkeeper and the common carrier of goods for hire, who are *quasi* insurers. These cases are said to be by the custom of the realm, treating them as exceptions from the ordinary rule of law. In the absence of authority to the contrary, I can see no reason why damage to real property should be governed by a different rule or principle than damage to personal property. There is an instance, also, of damage to real property, where the party causing it was at common law liable upon the custom of the realm as a *quasi* insurer; namely, in the case of the master of a house, if a fire had kindled there, and consumed the house of another. In such case the master of the house was liable at common law without proof of negligence on his part. * This seems to be an exception from the ordinary rule at law; and, in my opinion, affords an argument that in other cases such as the present there must be negligence to create a liability. * * *

There then arises the second question, namely, does it make any difference that reasonable and proper care and skill were not exercised by the engineer and contractors employed by the defendant (they being competent persons) with reference to the shafts, which were five old shafts running vertically downwards in that portion of the land selected for the reservoir, but which were not known or suspected by any one to be (as they afterwards proved to be) shafts which had been made for the purpose of getting coal under the land beneath the reservoir, or to lead to coal under it? Now, assuming that the want of reasonable and proper care and skill by the engineer and contractors constituted in point of law want of reasonable and proper skill by the defendants themselves (which is by no means a clear proposition), I nevertheless think that the defendants are not responsible. The assumed facts are these: The defendants dig a reservoir in their own land; they do not know or suspect that their doing it in the manner they did would do any damage to their neighbour: is there any authority to shew that the law casts upon them a liability for damage, should it occur? In my opinion there is authority to the contrary. Prima facie a man may excavate a reservoir for water in his own land. Whether he does so carefully and skilfully would seem to be his own concern; and, if he be ignorant that any fact exists which makes it dangerous to his neighbour, it is difficult to see what duty is imposed upon him to take any peculiar care, or use any particular skill in the matter. When a man does an act upon his close, which of itself is lawful, but is alleged to be wrongful towards an adjoining neighbour by reason of the existence of some underground openings between their two closes, reason and good sense would seem to require that he should know or have the means of knowledge of the existence of the openings. How can a man be said to be negligent when he is ignorant of the existence of the circumstances which require the exercise of care? * * *

[The opinion of POLLOCK, C. B. is omitted.]

Judgment for the defendants.

Rylands v. Fletcher

Exchequer Chamber, 1866.
L.R. 1 Excheq. 265.

■ BLACKBURN, J. * * * We have come to the conclusion that the opinion of Bramwell, B., was right, and that the answer to the question should be that the plaintiff was entitled to recover damages from the defendants, by reason of the matters stated in the case, and consequently, that the judgment below should be reversed. * * *

The plaintiff, though free from all blame on his part, must bear the loss, unless he can establish that it was the consequence of some default for which the defendants are responsible. The question of law therefore arises, what is the obligation which the law casts on a person who, like the defendants, lawfully brings on his land something which, though harmless whilst it remains there, will naturally do mischief if it escape out of his land. It is agreed on all hands that he must take care to keep in that which he has brought on the land and keeps there, in order that it may not escape and damage his neighbours, but the question arises whether the duty which the law casts upon him, under such circumstances, is an absolute duty to keep it in at his peril, or is, as the majority of the Court of Exchequer have thought, merely a duty to take all reasonable and prudent precautions, in order to keep it in, but no more. If the first be the law, the person who has brought on his land and kept there something dangerous, and failed to keep it in, is responsible for all the natural consequences of its escape. If the second be the limit of his duty, he would not be answerable except on proof of negligence, and consequently would not be answerable for escape arising from any latent defect which ordinary prudence and skill could not detect.

Supposing the second to be the correct view of the law, a further question arises subsidiary to the first, viz., whether the defendants are not so far identified with the contractors whom they employed, as to be responsible for the consequences of their want of care and skill in making the reservoir in fact insufficient with reference to the old shafts, of the existence of which they were aware, though they had not ascertained where the shafts went to.

We think that the true rule of law is, that the person who for his own purposes brings on his lands and collects and keeps there anything likely to do mischief if it escapes, must keep it in at his peril, and, if he does not do so, is prima facie answerable for all the damage which is the natural consequence of its escape. He can excuse himself by showing that the escape was owing to the plaintiffs' default; or perhaps that the escape was the consequence of vis major, or the act of God; but as nothing of this sort exists here, it is unnecessary to inquire what excuse would be sufficient. The general rule, as above stated, seems on principle just. The person whose grass or corn is eaten down by the escaping cattle of his neighbour, or whose mine is flooded by the water from his neighbour's reservoir, or whose cellar is invaded by the filth of his neighbour's privy, or whose habitation is made unhealthy by the fumes and noisome vapours of his neighbour's alkali works, is damnified without any fault of his own; and it seems but reasonable and just that the neighbour, who has brought something on his own property which was not naturally there, harmless to others so long as it is confined to his own property, but which he knows to be mischievous if it gets on his neighbour's, should be obliged to make good the damage which ensues if he does not succeed in confining it to his own property. But for his act in bringing it there no mischief could have accrued, and it seems but just that he should at his peril keep it there so that no mischief may accrue, or answer for the natural and anticipated consequences. And upon authority, this we think is established to be the law whether the things so brought be beasts, or water, or filth, or stenches.

The case that has most commonly occurred, and which is most frequently to be found in the books, is as to the obligation of the owner of cattle which he has brought on his land, to prevent their escaping and doing mischief. The law as to them seems to be perfectly settled from early times; the owner must keep them in at his peril, or he will be answerable for the natural consequences of their escape; that is with regard to tame beasts, for the grass they eat and trample upon, though not for any injury to the person of others, for our ancestors have settled that it is not the general nature of horses to kick, or bulls to gore; but if the owner knows that the beast has a vicious propensity to attack man, he will be answerable for that too.

* * * In the recent case of Cox v. Burbidge, 13 C.B. N.S. at 438, 32 L.J. (C.P.) 89, Williams, J., says, "I apprehend the general rule of law to be perfectly plain. If I am the owner of an animal in which by law the right of property can exist, I am bound to take care that it does not stray into the land of my neighbour, and I am liable for any trespass it may commit, and for the ordinary consequences of that trespass. Whether or not the escape of the animal is due to my negligence is altogether immaterial." * * *

As has been already said, there does not appear to be any difference in principle, between the extent of the duty cast on him who brings cattle on his land to keep them in, and the extent of the duty imposed on him who brings on his land, water, filth, or stenches, or any other thing which will, if it escape, naturally do damage, to prevent their escaping and injuring his neighbor. * * *

No case has been found in which the question as to the liability for noxious vapours escaping from a man's works by inevitable accident has been discussed, but the following case will illustrate it. Some years ago several actions were brought against the occupiers of some alkali works at Liverpool for the damage alleged to be caused by the chlorine fumes of their works. The defendants proved that they at great expense erected contrivances by which the fumes of chlorine were condensed, and sold as muriatic acid, and they called a great body of scientific evidence to prove that this apparatus was so perfect that no fumes possibly could escape from the defendants' chimneys. The jury * * * being satisfied that the mischief was occasioned by chlorine, drew the conclusion that it had escaped from the defendants' works somehow, and in each case found for the plaintiff. No attempt was made to disturb these verdicts on the ground that the defendants had taken every precaution which prudence or skill could suggest to keep those fumes in, and that they could not be responsible unless negligence were shewn; yet, if the law be as laid down by the majority of the Court of Exchequer, it would have been a very obvious defence. If it had been raised, the answer would probably have been that the uniform course of pleading in actions on such nuisances is to say that the defendant caused the noisome vapours to arise on his premises, and suffered them to come on the plaintiff's, without stating there was any want of care or skill in the defendant, and that the case of Tenant v. Goldwin, 1 Salk. 21, 360, 2 Ld. Raym. 1089, 6 Mod. 311, shewed that this was founded on the general rule of law, that he whose stuff it is must keep it that it may not trespass. There is no difference in this respect between chlorine and water; both will, if they escape, do damage, the one by scorching, and the other by drowning, and he who brings them there must at his peril see that they do not escape and do that mischief. What is said by Gibbs, C.J., in Sutton v. Clarke, 6 Taunt. at 44, though not necessary for the decision of the case, shews that that very learned judge took the same view of the law that was taken by Lord Holt.

But it was further said by Martin, B., that when damage is done to personal property, or even to the person, by collision, either upon land or at sea, there must be negligence in the party doing the damage to render him legally responsible; and this is no doubt true, and as was pointed out by Mr. Mellish during his argument before us, this is not confined to cases of collision, for there are many cases in which proof of negligence is essential, as for instance, where an unruly horse gets on the footpath of a public street and kills a passenger: Hammack v. White, 11 C.B. N.S. 588, 31 L.J. (C.P.) 129; or where a person in a dock is struck by the falling of a bale of cotton which the defendant's servants are lowering, Scott v. London Dock Company, 3 H. & C. 596, 34 L.J. (Ex.) 17, 220; and many other similar cases may be found. But we think these cases distinguishable from the present. Traffic on the highways, whether by land or sea, cannot be conducted without exposing those whose persons or property are near it to some inevitable risk; and that being so, those who go on the highway, or have their property adjacent to it, may well be held to do so subject to their taking upon themselves the risk of injury from that inevitable danger; and persons who by the license of the owner pass near to warehouses where goods are being raised or lowered, certainly do so subject to the inevitable risk of accident. In neither case, therefore, can they recover without proof of want of care or skill occasioning the accident; and it is believed that all the cases in which inevitable accident has been held an excuse for what prima facie was a trespass, can be explained on the same principle, viz., that the circumstances were such as to shew that the plaintiff had taken that risk upon himself. But there is no ground for saying that the plaintiff here took upon himself any risk arising from the uses to which the defendants should choose to apply their land. He neither knew what these might be, nor could he in any way control the defendants, or hinder their building what reservoirs they liked, and storing up in them what water they pleased, so long as the defendants succeeded in preventing the water which they there brought from interfering with the plaintiff's property.

The view which we take of the first point renders it unnecessary to consider whether the defendants would or would not be responsible for the want of care and skill in the persons employed by them, under the circumstances stated in the case. * * *

Judgment for the plaintiff.

Rylands v. Fletcher

House of Lords, 1868.
[1868] L.R. 3 H.L. 330.

■ THE LORD CHANCELLOR (LORD CAIRNS):— * * * My Lords, the principles on which this case must be determined appear to me to be extremely simple. The Defendants, treating them as the owners or occupiers of the close on which the reservoir was constructed, might lawfully have used that close for any purpose for which it might in the ordinary course of the enjoyment of land be used; and if, in what I may term the natural user of that land, there had been any accumulation of water, either on the surface or underground, and if, by the operation of the laws of nature, that accumulation of water had passed off into the close occupied by the Plaintiff, the Plaintiff could not have complained that that result had taken place. If he had desired to guard himself against it, it would have lain upon him to have done so, by leaving, or by interposing, some barrier between his close and the close of the Defendants in order to have prevented that operation of the laws of nature. * * *

On the other hand if the Defendants, not stopping at the natural use of their close, had desired to use it for any purpose which I may term a nonnatural use, for the purpose of introducing into the close that which in its natural condition was not in or upon it, for the purpose of introducing water either above or below ground in quantities and in a manner not the result of any work or operation on or under the land,— and if in consequence of their doing so, or in consequence of any imperfection in the mode of their doing so, the water came to escape and to pass off into the close of the Plaintiff, then it appears to me that that which the Defendants were doing they were doing at their own peril; and, if in the course of their doing it, the evil arose to which I have referred, the evil, namely, of the escape of the water and its passing away to the close of the Plaintiff and injuring the Plaintiff, then for the consequence of that, in my opinion, the Defendants would be liable. * * *

My Lords, these simple principles, if they are well founded, as it appears to me they are, really dispose of this case.

The same result is arrived at on the principles referred to by Mr. Justice Blackburn in his judgment, in the Court of Exchequer Chamber. * * *

My Lords, in that opinion, I must say I entirely concur. Therefore, I have to move your Lordships that the judgment of the Court of Exchequer Chamber be affirmed, and that the present appeal be dismissed with costs.

■ LORD CRANWORTH:—My Lords, I concur with my noble and learned friend in thinking that the rule of law was correctly stated by Mr. Justice Blackburn in delivering the opinion of the Exchequer Chamber. If a person brings, or accumulates, on his land anything which, if it should escape, may cause damage to his neighbour, he does so at his peril. If it does escape, and cause damage, he is responsible, however careful he may have been, and whatever precautions he may have taken to prevent the damage. * * *

Judgment of the Court of Exchequer Chamber affirmed.

NOTES

1. *Basis of Holding.* What is the basis of the holding in the Court of Exchequer according to Baron Bramwell? In the Exchequer Chamber, according to Justice Blackburn? In the House of Lords, according to Lord Cairns? Why is it not a simple trespass case? Why is the defendant not liable for the negligence of the contractor who built the reservoir?

It is sometimes emphasized that the harmful agent must have been brought onto the land by the defendant. E.g., Pennsylvania Coal Co. v. Sanderson, 113 Pa. 126, 6 A. 453 (1886). Whether Lord Cairns intended to require more, i.e., that the use of the land be "unnatural," or only that the harmful agent be artificially on the land, rather than naturally so, is not clear from his opinion. Presumably agriculture would be considered a "natural" use, yet, as Blackburn points out, there has traditionally been strict liability for crop damage by escaping cattle. Nevertheless, decisions often purport to turn on a characterization of the use, e.g., Rickards v. Lothian, [1913] A.C. 263, [1911–1913] All E.R. 71 (P.C.) (supplying water to houses "ordinary and proper" use, so no liability for overflowing residential wash basin in absence of negligence); Duncans v. Regina [1966] Ex. C.R. 1080 (Can. Exch.) (strict liability for sewage); Attorney-General v. Corke, [1933] Ch. 89, 94–95 (leasing land for gypsy encampment "abnormal use," so landowner enjoined under *Rylands* from permitting the gypsies to commit unsanitary nuisances on neighbor's land); Mihalchuk v. Ratke, [1966] 57 D.L.R. (2d) 269 (Sask. Q.B.) (spraying of crops from air unnatural use, as contrasted with customary boom spraying behind tractor); Mason v. Levy Auto Parts of Eng. Ltd., [1967] 2 Q.B. 530 (bringing combustible materials onto land is nonnatural use, based on quantities of such materials, the method of storage, and the character of the neighborhood, so strict liability for escape of mysteriously caused fire).

In England, the applicability of *Rylands* to personal injuries has been questioned, and the doctrine has been generally confined to escapes from defendant's land, Read v. J. Lyons & Co., [1947] A.C. 156, [1946] 2 All E.R. 471. American courts, however, sometimes have imposed strict liability predicated on *Rylands* for personal injury. See, e.g., Siegler v. Kuhlman, 81 Wash.2d 448, 502 P.2d 1181 (1972) (motorist killed by explosion from gasoline spilled on highway from defendant's trailer tank).

2. *American Reception.* "A significant majority of the states actually accepted *Rylands* in the late nineteenth and early twentieth centuries, at the height of the 'era of fault.'" See Jed Handelsman Shugerman, Note, The Floodgates of Strict Liability: Bursting Reservoirs and the Adoption of *Fletcher v. Rylands* in the Gilded Age, 110 Yale L.J. 333 (2000); see also, e.g., Ball v. Nye, 99 Mass. 582 (1868), Cahill v. Eastman, 18 Minn. 324 (1872).

Some American courts—particularly in the northeastern industrialized states—were more guarded in their response to the strict liability principles of *Rylands*. For example, in Losee v. Buchanan, 51 N.Y. 476 (1873), the New York Court of Appeals rejected the strict liability principle of *Rylands* in a case in which the defendant manufacturer's steam boiler exploded into the air, landing on several of the plaintiff's buildings. The court justified the limitation of liability to accidents caused by defendant's fault in the following terms:

> By becoming a member of civilized society, I am compelled to give up many of my natural rights, but I receive more than a compensation from the surrender by every other man of the same rights. * * * We must have factories, machinery, dams, canals and railroads. They are demanded by the manifold wants of mankind, and lay at the basis of all our civilization. If I have any of these upon my lands, and they are not a nuisance and are not so managed as to become such, I am not responsible for any damage they accidentally and unavoidably do my neighbor. He receives his compensation for such damage by the general good, in which he shares, and the right which he has to place the same things upon his lands.

Id. at 484–85. Compare Spano v. Perini Corp., *infra* pages 65–67.

Similarly, Brown v. Collins, 53 N.H. 442 (1873), rejected *Rylands* because it would "impose a penalty upon efforts, made in a reasonable, skillful, and careful manner, to rise above a condition of barbarism." *Rylands* was even rejected by some American courts as a precedent for fact situations very similar to those of *Rylands* itself. For example, in Turner v. Big Lake Oil Co., 128 Tex. 155, 96 S.W.2d 221 (1936), the Supreme Court of Texas rejected *Rylands* where damage was caused by the escape of impounded water:

> In Texas we have conditions very different from those which obtain in England. A large portion of Texas is an arid or semi-arid region. * * * The country is almost without streams; and without the storage of water from rainfall in basins constructed for the purpose, or to hold waters pumped from the earth, the great livestock industry of West Texas must perish. No such condition obtains in England. With us the storage of water is a natural or necessary and common use of the land, necessarily within the

contemplation of the State and its grantees when grants were made, and obviously the rule announced in *Rylands v. Fletcher*, predicated upon different conditions, can have no application here.

Id. at 165, 96 S.W.2d at 226.

More recently, as environmental concerns have grown in the United States, American courts increasingly follow *Rylands*. E.g., N.J. Dep't of Envtl. Prot. v. Ventron Corp., 94 N.J. 473, 468 A.2d 150 (1983); Cities Serv. Co. v. State, 312 So.2d 799 (Fla.Dist.Ct.App.1975).

3. *Public Compensation for Victims of Crimes, Riots, and Wars.* The various opinions in *Rylands* cite as precedents ancient English cases such as those involving damages to real property caused by straying animals. Other examples of strict liability in English law date from as early as the thirteenth century. Legislation passed at that time was directed at the unwillingness of the inhabitants of a number of disorderly counties to capture and convict local brigands who robbed travelers. 13 Edw. I, St. 2, c. 2 (1285). Sections 22–24 of the Code of Hammurabi (circa 2250 B.C.) contained a similar provision, requiring compensation of loss by the city and the governor in whose jurisdiction a crime was committed, if the brigand was not captured.

The English statute made inhabitants collectively liable for the amount robbed unless the thieves were caught within forty days—without regard to the fault of any inhabitant who would have to pay, either in respect of the robbery or the failure to arrest the thief. This was changed in the sixteenth century, both to reduce the liability of the inhabitants to one-half of the amount stolen, and to alter somewhat the basis of liability to that of a communal negligence in failing to catch the villains—rather than strict liability—standard. 27 Eliz., c. 13 (1584). The liability applied only where "negligence, fault, or defect of pursuit . . . should happen to be," but it continued to apply to all the inhabitants of the "city or such Hundred" (a political subdivision) in question, without regard to the personal fault of any individual inhabitant. Although the primary objective of these statutes appears to have been to encourage the prompt arrest and prosecution of thieves, compare how the principle of loss distribution operates in these statutes in a way similar to that in the workers' compensation system described in Chapter 1.

Today many states have enacted statutes providing compensation to victims of crimes. E.g., Wis. Stat. § 949.001 *et seq.* (2014). A number of jurisdictions specifically provide compensation for victims of riots and mob violence. See, e.g., Md. Code Ann. Pub. Safety §§ 14–1001 to 14–1004 (2014); Mass. Gen. Laws Ann., ch. 269, § 8 (2014). Other legislatures have repealed statutes providing state compensation for victims of riots, believing such statutes to be "an anachronism in modern law" as the risk of mob violence is covered by private insurance policies, not local citizens. See, e.g., Gates v. Superior Ct., 32 Cal.App.4th 481, 496–500, 38 Cal.Rptr.2d 489, 496–99 (1995).

Spano v. Perini Corp.

Court of Appeals of New York, 1969.
25 N.Y.2d 11, 302 N.Y.S.2d 527, 250 N.E.2d 31.

■ FULD, CHIEF JUDGE. The principal question posed on this appeal is whether a person who has sustained property damage caused by blasting on nearby property can maintain an action for damages without a showing that the blaster was negligent. Since 1893, when this court decided the case of Booth v. Rome, W. & O. T. R. R. Co., 140 N.Y. 267, 35 N.E. 592 (1893), it has been the law of this State that proof of negligence was required unless the blast was accompanied by an actual physical invasion of the damaged property—for example, by rocks or other material being cast upon the premises. We are now asked to reconsider that rule.

The plaintiff Spano is the owner of a garage in Brooklyn which was wrecked by a blast occurring on November 27, 1962. There was then in that garage, for repairs, an automobile owned by the plaintiff Davis which he also claims was damaged by the blasting. * * * It is undisputed that, on the day in question * * * the defendants had set off a total of 194 sticks of dynamite at a construction site which was only 125 feet away from the damaged premises. Although both plaintiffs alleged negligence in their complaints, no attempt was made to show that the defendants had failed to exercise reasonable care or to take necessary precautions when they were blasting. Instead, they chose to rely, upon the trial, solely on the principle of absolute liability. * * * At the close of the plaintiff Spano's case, when defendants' attorney moved to dismiss the action on the ground, among others, that no negligence had been proved, the trial judge expressed the view that the defendants could be held liable even though they were not shown to have been careless. The case then proceeded, with evidence being introduced solely on the question of damages and proximate cause. Following the trial, the court awarded damages of some $4,400 to Spano and of $329 to Davis. * * *

The Appellate Division affirmed; it called attention to a decision in the Third Department, * in which the court observed that "[i]f Booth is to be overruled, 'the announcement thereof should come from the authoritative source and not in the form of interpretation or prediction by an intermediate appellate court.'"

In our view, the time has come for this court to make that "announcement" and declare that one who engages in blasting must assume responsibility, and be liable without fault, for any injury he causes to neighboring property.

The concept of absolute liability in blasting cases is hardly a novel one. The overwhelming majority of American jurisdictions have adopted such a rule. * * * We need not rely solely however upon out-of-state decisions in order to attain our result. Not only has the rationale of the *Booth* case, 140 N.Y. 267, 35 N.E. 592, *supra*, been overwhelmingly rejected elsewhere but it appears to be fundamentally inconsistent with earlier cases in our own court which had held, long before *Booth* was decided, that a party was absolutely liable for damages to neighboring property caused by explosions. See, e.g., Hay v. Cohoes Co., 2 N.Y. 159 (1849); Heeg v. Licht, 80 N.Y. 579 (1880). In the *Hay* case, for example, the defendant was engaged in blasting an excavation for a canal and the force of the blasts caused large quantities of earth and stones to be thrown against the plaintiff's house, knocking down his stoop and part of his chimney. The court held the defendant *absolutely* liable for the damage caused, stating, 2 N.Y. at 160–61:

> It is an elementary principle in reference to private rights, that every individual is entitled to the undisturbed possession and lawful enjoyment of his own property. The mode of enjoyment is necessarily limited by the rights of others—otherwise it might be made destructive of their rights altogether. Hence the maxim *sic utere tuo, &c.* The defendants had the right to dig the canal. The plaintiff the right to the undisturbed possession of his property. If these rights conflict, the former must yield to the latter, as the more important of the two, since, upon grounds of public policy, it is better that one man should surrender a particular use of his land, than that another should be deprived of the beneficial use of his property altogether, which might be the consequence if the privilege of the former should be wholly unrestricted. The case before us illustrates this principle. For if the defendants in excavating their canal, in itself a lawful use of their land, could, in the manner mentioned by the witnesses, demolish the stoop of the plaintiff with impunity, they might, for the same purpose, on the exercise of reasonable care, demolish his house, and thus deprive him of all use of his property.

Although the court in *Booth* drew a distinction between a situation—such as was presented in the *Hay* case—where there was "a physical invasion" of, or trespass on, the plaintiff's property and one in which the damage was caused by "setting the air in motion, or in some other unexplained way," * it is clear that the court, in the earlier cases, was not concerned with the particular manner by which the damage was caused but by the simple fact that any explosion in a built-up area was likely to cause damage. Thus, in Heeg v. Licht, 80 N.Y. 579, *supra*, the court held that there should be absolute liability where the damage was caused by the accidental explosion of stored gunpowder, even in the absence of a physical trespass:

> The defendant had erected a building and stored materials therein, which from their character were liable to and actually did explode, causing injury to the plaintiff. The fact that the explosion took place tends to establish that the magazine was dangerous and liable to cause damage to the property of persons residing in the vicinity. . . . The fact that the magazine was liable to such a contingency, which could not be guarded against or averted by the greatest degree of care and vigilance, evinces its dangerous character, . . . In such a case, the rule which exonerates a party engaged in a lawful business, when free from negligence, has no application.

Such reasoning should, we venture, have led to the conclusion that the *intentional* setting off of explosives—that is, blasting—in an area in which it was likely to cause harm to neighboring property similarly results in absolute liability. However, the court in the *Booth* case rejected such an extension of the rule for the reason that "[t]o exclude the defendant from blasting to adapt its lot to the contemplated uses, at the instance of the plaintiff, would not be a compromise between conflicting rights, but an extinguishment of the right of the one for the benefit of the other." * The court expanded on this by stating, "This sacrifice, we think, the law does not exact. Public policy is promoted by the building up of towns and cities and the improvement of property. Any unnecessary restraint on freedom of action of a property owner hinders this."

This rationale cannot withstand analysis. The plaintiff in *Booth* was not seeking, as the court implied, to "exclude the defendant from blasting" and thus prevent desirable improvements to the latter's property. Rather, he was merely seeking compensation for the damage which was inflicted upon his own property as a result of that blasting. The question, in other words, was not *whether* it was lawful or proper to engage in blasting but *who* should bear the cost of any resulting damage—the person who engaged in the dangerous activity or the innocent neighbor injured thereby. Viewed in such a light, it clearly appears that *Booth* was wrongly decided and should be forthrightly overruled.

In more recent cases, our court has already gone far toward mitigating the harsh effect of the rule laid down in the *Booth* case. Thus, we have held that negligence can properly be inferred from the mere fact that a blast has caused extensive damage, even where the plaintiff is unable to show "the method of blasting or the strength of the charges or the character of the soil or rock." Schlansky v. Augustus V. Riegel, Inc., 9 N.Y.2d 493, 497, 215 N.Y.S.2d 52, 54, 174 N.E.2d 730, 732. * But, even under this liberal interpretation of *Booth*, it would still remain possible for a defendant who engages in blasting operations— which he realizes are likely to cause injury—to avoid liability by showing that he exercised reasonable care. Since blasting involves a substantial risk of harm no matter the degree of care exercised, we perceive no reason for ever permitting a person who engages in such an activity to impose this risk upon nearby persons or property without assuming responsibility therefor. * * *

Yommer v. McKenzie

Court of Appeals of Maryland, 1969.
255 Md. 220, 257 A.2d 138.

■ SINGLEY, JUDGE. Mr. and Mrs. McKenzie, the plaintiffs below, live at Little Crossing in Garrett County. Their immediate neighbors are the defendants, Mr. and Mrs. Yommer, who operate a grocery store and gasoline filling station. On 17 December 1967, Mr. McKenzie noticed a "smell" in his well water which, on analysis, proved to be caused by the presence of gasoline in the well. McKenzie complained to Yommer, who arranged to have one of his storage tanks removed and replaced in January 1968. However, it was not until the McKenzies had a filter and water softener installed in April of 1968 that it was possible for them to use the water for cooking and bathing. At the time of the trial of the case in December of 1968 there was testimony that the McKenzies were still bringing drinking water from Grantsville, about a mile distant.

The McKenzies, alleging a nuisance, sued the Yommers for damages and recovered a verdict of $3,500. The Yommers had moved for a directed verdict at the end of the plaintiffs' case and renewed their motion at the end of the entire case. The Yommers have appealed from the judgment entered on the verdict, assigning as error the trial court's refusal to direct a verdict in their favor. We shall affirm.

The thrust of the Yommers' argument is threefold: (i) that the establishment of a gasoline filling station does not constitute a nuisance; (ii) that the McKenzies failed to show that the damage they sustained was occasioned by the Yommers' negligence in the operation of the filling station. * * *

The argument that the McKenzies must prove negligence in order to recover fails to take into account the doctrine of strict liability imposed by the rule of *Rylands v. Fletcher* which has been adopted by our prior decisions. * Dean Prosser states the rule of the English cases "[T]hat the defendant will be liable when he damages another by a thing or activity unduly dangerous and inappropriate to the place where it is maintained, in the light of the character of that place and its surroundings." W[illiam L.] Prosser, Torts § 77 (3d ed. 1964). * * * Or, as Mr. Justice Sutherland put it in describing a nuisance in Euclid, Ohio v. Ambler Co., 272 U.S. 365, 388, 47 S.Ct. 114, 118, 71 L.Ed. 303 (1926), "[It is] merely a right thing in the wrong place, like a pig in the parlor instead of the barnyard."

Restatement of Torts § 519 (1938) relied on by the Yommers, limits the applicability of the rule of *Rylands v. Fletcher* to what it terms an "ultrahazardous activity" and incorporates a caveat, "The Institute expresses no opinion as to whether the construction and use of a large tank or artificial reservoir in which a large body of water or other fluid is collected is or is not an ultrahazardous activity." W[illiam L.] Prosser, Torts § 77, is critical of the ultrahazardous activity concept which

> . . . goes beyond the English rule in ignoring the relation of the activity to its surroundings, and falls short of it in the insistence on extreme danger and the impossibility of eliminating it with all possible care. The shift of emphasis is not at all reflected in the American cases, which have laid quite as much stress as the English ones upon the place where the thing is done.

Restatement (Second) of Torts, * for which Dean Prosser is the Reporter, §§ 519–20, provides more guidance for us than its predecessor. For the "ultrahazardous activity" test an "abnormally dangerous activity" test has been substituted. The effect of this change is to enlarge the circumstances under which the rule of strict liability will apply. As the Reporter pointed out to the American Law Institute:

> "Ultrahazardous," as it is defined in the old Section, is misleading. There is probably no activity whatever, unless it be the use of atomic energy, which is not perfectly safe if the *utmost* care is used—which would of course include the choice of an absolutely safe place to carry it on.

Restatement (Second) of Torts, Note to Institute at 57.

The black letter of new § 520 sets out the definition:

520. Abnormally Dangerous Activities

In determining whether an activity is abnormally dangerous, the following factors are to be considered:

(a) Whether the activity involves a high degree of risk of some harm to the person, land or chattels of others;

(b) Whether the gravity of the harm which may result from it is likely to be great;

(c) Whether the risk cannot be eliminated by the exercise of reasonable care;

(d) Whether the activity is not a matter of common usage;

(e) Whether the activity is inappropriate to the place where it is carried on; and

(f) The value of the activity to the community. * * *

The fifth and perhaps most crucial factor under the Institute's guidelines as applied to this case is the appropriateness of the activity in the particular place where it is being carried on. No one would deny that gasoline stations as a rule do not present any particular danger to the community. However, when the operation of such activity involves the placing of a large tank adjacent to a well from which a family must draw its water for drinking, bathing and laundry, at least that aspect of the activity is inappropriate to the locale, even when equated to the value of the activity.

In the Reporter's notes concerning the new rule of the Restatement, he is careful to make a distinction which is applicable to this case. While in the first Restatement no position was taken on the issue of the storage of water and other liquids, Restatement (Second) of Torts takes a different view:

The thing which stands out from the cases is that the important thing about the activity is not that it is extremely dangerous in itself, but that it is abnormally so in relation to its surroundings.

The same is true of the storage of gasoline, or other inflammable liquids, in large quantities. In a populated area this is a matter of strict liability. * But in an isolated area it is not. *

The same distinction is found in the cases of water stored in quantity, as in a reservoir. *Rylands v. Fletcher* was a case of a reservoir in Lancashire, which was primarily coal mining country; and the basis of the decision in the House of Lords was clearly that this was a "non-natural" use of the particular land. . . . Where water is stored in large quantity in [a] dangerous location in a city, there [h]as been strict liability. *

Restatement (Second) of Torts, Note to Institute at 57–58.

We accept the test of appropriateness as the proper one: that the unusual, the excessive, the extravagant, the bizarre * are likely to be non-natural uses which lead to strict liability. * * * It is apparent to us that the storage of large quantities of gasoline immediately adjacent to a private residence comes within this rule and relieved the McKenzies of the necessity of proving negligence. * * *

NOTES

1. *The American Law Institute and Restatements.* In reaching its decision, the Maryland Court of Appeals relied on Section 520 of the Restatement (Second) of Torts (1977). Because most tort law is judge-made common law that develops incrementally as issues arise in specific cases, there is no comprehensive codification of tort law enacted by any legal authority. Further, tort law varies from one state to another.

The American Law Institute (ALI) was founded in 1923 with the goal of reducing the uncertainty and complexity in American law stemming from the lack of agreement on fundamental principles of the common law and the variations in the law among the states. The membership of the ALI consists of distinguished judges, lawyers, and law professors chosen by the existing membership.

"Restatements" of law are probably the most influential of the ALI's undertakings. Periodically, the ALI "restates" or summarizes and clarifies the law in a particular field. Subsequent revisions of the restatements in a field are referred to as "second restatements" or "third restatements." The ALI adopts restatements only after extensive study, review, and debate. Each restatement project is led by a "Reporter" who prepares the initial drafts, in consultation with a small group of heavily involved "Advisers" and a larger group of members who constitute a "Consultative Group." Once a draft restatement is completed, it is submitted to the general membership for approval. Restatements are intended to describe the common law as it exists, but when the law of various jurisdictions conflicts—which often is the case—the ALI is not obligated to count jurisdictions and follow the majority approach. Instead, the ALI can adopt the approach it regards as better reasoned. Although restatements are not binding authority in any jurisdiction, they are highly persuasive and frequently cited authorities in tort cases.

2. *Typical Fact Patterns of Abnormally Dangerous Activities.* Perhaps as a reaction to the amorphous, open-ended rule of the Restatement (Second) of Torts, in practice cases finding liability for abnormally dangerous activities often fall within certain fairly well-defined groupings. Liability under this theory, for example is common when injuries result from the following activities:

   a.   Hazardous waste disposal, see, e.g., Shockley v. Hoechst Celanese Corp., 793 F.Supp. 670 (D.S.C.1992);

   b.   Gasoline storage in residential areas, see, e.g., City of Northglenn, Colo. v. Chevron U.S.A., Inc., 519 F.Supp. 515 (D.Colo.1981);

   c.   Toxic chemicals and gases, see, e.g., Langlois v. Allied Chem. Corp., 258 La. 1067, 249 So.2d 133 (1971);

   d.   Blasting and storage of explosives, see, e.g., Exner v. Sherman Power Const. Co., 54 F.2d 510 (2d Cir.1931); Yukon Equip., Inc. v. Fireman's Fund Ins. Co., 585 P.2d 1206 (Alaska 1978); and

   e.   Escape of water and other liquids, see, e.g., Clark-Aiken Co. v. Cromwell-Wright Co., 367 Mass. 70, 323 N.E.2d 876 (1975). Many jurisdictions, however, deny liability in these cases. E.g., Dye v. Burdick, 262 Ark. 124, 553 S.W.2d 833 (1977).

3. *Aviation.* In its early years, aviation was regarded as an activity justifying the imposition of strict liability. In 1934, the Restatement of Torts took the position that aerial navigation was an "ultrahazardous activity" giving rise to strict liability for personal injury or property damage caused thereby on the ground, § 520, cmt. d. Most cases in recent decades have rejected this conclusion and require a showing of negligence before a plaintiff on the ground can recover for damage caused by a crash. See, e.g., Crosby v. Cox Aircraft Co., 109 Wash.2d 581, 746 P.2d 1198 (1987); see generally Harper, James, and Gray on Torts § 14.13.

Indiana Harbor Belt Railroad Co. v. American Cyanamid Co.

United States Court of Appeals for the Seventh Circuit, 1990.
916 F.2d 1174.

■ POSNER, CIRCUIT JUDGE, American Cyanamid Company, the defendant in this diversity tort suit governed by Illinois law, is a major manufacturer of chemicals, including acrylonitrile, a chemical used in large quantities in making acrylic fibers, plastics, dyes, pharmaceutical chemicals, and other intermediate and final goods. On January 2, 1979, at its manufacturing plant in Louisiana, Cyanamid loaded 20,000 gallons of liquid acrylonitrile into a railroad tank car that it had leased from the North American Car Corporation. The next day, a train of the Missouri Pacific Railroad picked up the car at Cyanamid's siding. * * * The Missouri Pacific train carried the car north to the Blue Island railroad yard of Indiana Harbor Belt Railroad, the plaintiff in this case, a small switching line that has a contract with Conrail to switch cars from other lines to Conrail, in this case for travel east. The Blue Island yard is in the Village of Riverdale, which is just south of Chicago and part of the Chicago metropolitan area.

The car arrived in the Blue Island yard on the morning of January 9, 1979. Several hours after it arrived, employees of the switching line noticed fluid gushing from the bottom outlet of the car. The lid on the outlet was broken. After two hours, the line's supervisor of equipment was able to stop the leak by closing a shut-off valve controlled from the top of the car. No one was sure at the time just how much of the contents of the car had leaked, but it was feared that all 20,000 gallons had, and since acrylonitrile is flammable at a temperature of 30 degrees Fahrenheit or above, highly toxic, and possibly carcinogenic, * the local authorities ordered the homes near the yard evacuated. The evacuation lasted only a few hours, until the car was moved to a remote part of the yard and it was discovered that only about a quarter of the acrylonitrile had leaked. Concerned nevertheless that there had been some contamination of soil and water, the Illinois Department of Environmental Protection ordered the switching line to take decontamination measures that cost the line $981,022.75, which it sought to recover by this suit.

One count of the two-count complaint charges Cyanamid with having maintained the leased tank car negligently. The other count asserts that the transportation of acrylonitrile in bulk through the

Chicago metropolitan area is an abnormally dangerous activity, for the consequences of which the shipper (Cyanamid) is strictly liable to the switching line, which bore the financial brunt of those consequences because of the decontamination measures that it was forced to take. After the district judge denied Cyanamid's motion to dismiss the strict liability count, * the switching line moved for summary judgment on that count—and won. * * *

The question whether the shipper of a hazardous chemical by rail should be strictly liable for the consequences of a spill or other accident to the shipment en route is a novel one in Illinois. * * * The parties agree that * * * the Supreme Court of Illinois would treat as authoritative the provisions of the Restatement governing abnormally dangerous activities. The key provision is section 520, which sets forth six factors to be considered in deciding whether an activity is abnormally dangerous and the actor therefore strictly liable.

The roots of section 520 are in nineteenth-century cases. The most famous one is *Rylands v. Fletcher,* * but a more illuminating one in the present context is Guille v. Swan, 19 Johns. (N.Y.) 381 (1822). A man took off in a hot-air balloon and landed, without intending to, in a vegetable garden in New York City. A crowd that had been anxiously watching his involuntary descent trampled the vegetables in their endeavor to rescue him when he landed. The owner of the garden sued the balloonist for the resulting damage, and won. Yet the balloonist had not been careless. In the then state of ballooning it was impossible to make a pinpoint landing.

Guille is a paradigmatic case for strict liability. (a) The risk (probability) of harm was great, and (b) the harm that would ensue if the risk materialized could be, although luckily was not, great (the balloonist could have crashed into the crowd rather than into the vegetables). The confluence of these two factors established the urgency of seeking to prevent such accidents. (c) Yet such accidents could not be prevented by the exercise of due care; the technology of care in ballooning was insufficiently developed. (d) The activity was not a matter of common usage, so there was no presumption that it was a highly valuable activity despite its unavoidable riskiness. (e) The activity was inappropriate to the place in which it took place—densely populated New York City. The risk of serious harm to others (other than the balloonist himself, that is) could have been reduced by shifting the activity to the sparsely inhabited areas that surrounded the city in those days. (f) Reinforcing (d), the value to the community of the activity of recreational ballooning did not appear to be great enough to offset its unavoidable risks.

These are, of course, the six factors in section 520. They are related to each other in that each is a different facet of a common quest for a proper legal regime to govern accidents that negligence liability cannot adequately control. The interrelations might be more perspicuous if the six factors were reordered. One might for example start with (c), inability to eliminate the risk of accident by the exercise of due care. * The baseline common law regime of tort liability is negligence. When it is a workable regime, because the hazards of an activity can be avoided by being careful (which is to say, non-negligent), there is no need to switch to strict liability. Sometimes, however, a particular type of accident cannot be prevented by taking care but can be avoided, or its consequences minimized, by shifting the activity in which the accident occurs to another locale, where the risk or harm of an accident will be less ((e)), or by reducing the scale of the activity in order to minimize the number of accidents caused by it ((f)). * * * The greater the risk of an accident ((a)) and the costs of an accident if one occurs ((b)), the more we want the actor to consider the possibility of making accident-reducing activity changes; the stronger, therefore, is the case for strict liability. Finally, if an activity is extremely common ((d)), like driving an automobile, it is unlikely either that its hazards are perceived as great or that there is no technology of care available to minimize them; so the case for strict liability is weakened.

The largest class of cases in which strict liability has been imposed under the standard codified in the Restatement (Second) of Torts involves the use of dynamite and other explosives for demolition in residential or urban areas. Restatement, § 519, cmt. d. * * * Explosives are dangerous even when handled carefully, and we therefore want blasters to choose the location of the activity with care and also to explore the feasibility of using safer substitutes (such as a wrecking ball), as well as to be careful in the blasting itself. Blasting is not a commonplace activity like driving a car, or so superior to substitute methods of demolition that the imposition of liability is unlikely to have any effect except to raise the activity's costs.

Against this background we turn to the particulars of acrylonitrile. Acrylonitrile is one of a large number of chemicals that are hazardous in the sense of being flammable, toxic, or both; acrylonitrile is both, as are many others. * * * Every shipper of any of these materials would therefore [under the logic of the opinion below] be strictly liable for the consequences of a spill or other accident that occurred while the material was being shipped through a metropolitan area. The plaintiff's lawyer further acknowledged the irrelevance, on her view of the case, of the fact that Cyanamid had leased and filled the car that spilled the acrylonitrile; all she thought important is that Cyanamid introduced the product into the stream of commerce that happened to pass through the Chicago metropolitan area. Her concession may have been incautious. One might want to distinguish between the shipper who merely places his goods on his loading dock to be picked up by the carrier and the shipper who, as in this case, participates actively in the transportation. But the concession is illustrative of the potential scope of the district court's decision.

No cases recognize so sweeping a liability. Several reject it, though none has facts much like those of the present case. * * *

Siegler v. Kuhlman, 81 Wash.2d 448, 502 P.2d 1181 (1972), also imposed strict liability on a transporter of hazardous materials, but the circumstances were again rather special. A gasoline truck blew up, obliterating the plaintiff's decedent and her car. The court emphasized that the explosion had destroyed the evidence necessary to establish whether the accident had been due to negligence; so, unless liability was strict, there would be no liability—and this as the very consequence of the defendant's hazardous activity. * * * We shall see that a further distinction of great importance between the present case and *Siegler* is

that the defendant there was the transporter, and here it is the shipper.
* * *

So we can get little help from precedent, and might as well apply section 520 to the acrylonitrile problem from the ground up. To begin with, we have been given no reason, whether the reason in *Siegler* or any other, for believing that a negligence regime is not perfectly adequate to remedy and deter, at reasonable cost, the accidental spillage of acrylonitrile from rail cars. * Acrylonitrile could explode and destroy evidence, but of course did not here, making imposition of strict liability on the theory of the *Siegler* decision premature. More important, although acrylonitrile is flammable even at relatively low temperatures, and toxic, it is not so corrosive or otherwise destructive that it will eat through or otherwise damage or weaken a tank car's valves although they are maintained with due (which essentially means, with average) care. No one suggests, therefore, that the leak in this case was caused by the *inherent* properties of acrylonitrile. It was caused by carelessness—whether that of the North American Car Corporation in failing to maintain or inspect the car properly, or that of Cyanamid in failing to maintain or inspect it, or that of the Missouri Pacific when it had custody of the car, or that of the switching line itself in failing to notice the ruptured lid, or some combination of these possible failures of care. Accidents that are due to a lack of care can be prevented by taking care; and when a lack of care can (unlike *Siegler*) be shown in court, such accidents are adequately deterred by the threat of liability for negligence.

It is true that the district court purported to find as a fact that there is an inevitable risk of derailment or other calamity in transporting "large quantities of anything." This is not a finding of fact, but a truism: anything can happen. The question is, how likely is this type of accident if the actor uses due care? For all that appears from the record of the case or any other sources of information that we have found, if a tank car is carefully maintained the danger of a spill of acrylonitrile is negligible. If this is right, there is no compelling reason to move to a regime of strict liability, especially one that might embrace all other hazardous materials shipped by rail as well. This also means, however, that the *amici curiae* who have filed briefs in support of Cyanamid cry wolf in predicting "devastating" effects on the chemical industry if the district court's decision is affirmed. If the vast majority of chemical spills by railroads are preventable by due care, the imposition of strict liability should cause only a slight, not as they argue a substantial, rise in liability insurance rates, because the incremental liability should be slight. The *amici* have momentarily lost sight of the fact that the feasibility of avoiding accidents simply by being careful is an argument *against* strict liability.

This discussion helps to show why *Siegler* is indeed distinguishable. * * * There are so many highway hazards that the transportation of gasoline by truck is, or at least might plausibly be thought, inherently dangerous in the sense that a serious danger of accident would remain even if the truckdriver used all due care. * * * Which in turn means, contrary to our earlier suggestion, that the plaintiff really might have difficulty invoking *res ipsa loquitur*, because a gasoline truck might well blow up without negligence on the part of the driver. The plaintiff in this case has not shown that the danger of a comparable disaster to a tank car filled with acrylonitrile is as great and might have similar consequences for proof of negligence. And to repeat a previous point, if the reason for strict liability is fear that an accident might destroy the critical evidence of negligence we should wait to impose such liability until such a case appears.

The district judge and the plaintiff's lawyer make much of the fact that the spill occurred in a densely inhabited metropolitan area. Only 4,000 gallons spilled; what if all 20,000 had done so? Isn't the risk that this might happen even if everybody were careful sufficient to warrant giving the shipper an incentive to explore alternative routes? Strict liability would supply that incentive. But this argument overlooks the fact that, like other transportation networks, the railroad network is a hub-and-spoke system. And the hubs are in metropolitan areas. Chicago is one of the nation's largest railroad hubs. In 1983, the latest date for which we have figures, Chicago's railroad yards handled the third highest volume of hazardous-material shipments in the nation. * * * With most hazardous chemicals (by volume of shipments) being at least as hazardous as acrylonitrile, it is unlikely—and certainly not demonstrated by the plaintiff—that they can be rerouted around all the metropolitan areas in the country, except at prohibitive cost. Even if it were feasible to reroute them one would hardly expect shippers, as distinct from carriers, to be the firms best situated to do the rerouting. * * *

The difference between shipper and carrier points to a deep flaw in the plaintiff's case. Unlike *Guille*, and unlike *Siegler*, and unlike the storage cases, beginning with *Rylands* itself, here it is not the actors— that is, the transporters of acrylonitrile and other chemicals—but the manufacturers, who are sought to be held strictly liable. * A shipper can in the bill of lading designate the route of his shipment if he likes, * but is it realistic to suppose that shippers will become students of railroading in order to lay out the safest route by which to ship their goods? Anyway, rerouting is no panacea. Often it will increase the length of the journey, or compel the use of poorer track, or both. When this happens, the probability of an accident is increased, even if the consequences of an accident if one occurs are reduced; so the expected accident cost, being the product of the probability of an accident and the harm if the accident occurs, may rise. * It is easy to see how the accident in this case might have been prevented at reasonable cost by greater care on the part of those who handled the tank car of acrylonitrile. It is difficult to see how it might have been prevented at reasonable cost by a change in the activity of transporting the chemical. This is therefore not an apt case for strict liability. * * *

In emphasizing the flammability and toxicity of acrylonitrile rather than the hazards of transporting it, as in failing to distinguish between the active and the passive shipper, the plaintiff overlooks the fact that ultrahazardousness or abnormal dangerousness is, in the contemplation of the law at least, a property not of substances, but of activities: not of acrylonitrile, but of the transportation of acrylonitrile by rail through populated areas. * Natural gas is both flammable and poisonous, but the operation of a natural gas well is not an ultrahazardous activity. * Whatever the situation under products liability law (section 402A of the

Restatement), the manufacturer of a product is not considered to be engaged in an abnormally dangerous activity merely because the product becomes dangerous when it is handled or used in some way after it leaves his premises, even if the danger is foreseeable. * The plaintiff does not suggest that Cyanamid should switch to making some less hazardous chemical that would substitute for acrylonitrile in the textiles and other goods in which acrylonitrile is used. Were this a feasible method of accident avoidance, there would be an argument for making manufacturers strictly liable for accidents that occur during the shipment of their products (how strong an argument we need not decide). Apparently it is not a feasible method.

The relevant activity is transportation, not manufacturing and shipping. This essential distinction the plaintiff ignores. But even if the defendant is treated as a transporter and not merely a shipper, the plaintiff has not shown that the transportation of acrylonitrile in bulk by rail through populated areas is so hazardous an activity, even when due care is exercised, that the law should seek to create—perhaps quixotically—incentives to relocate the activity to nonpopulated areas, or to reduce the scale of the activity, or to switch to transporting acrylonitrile by road rather than by rail, perhaps to set the stage for a replay of *Siegler v. Kuhlman.* It is no more realistic to propose to reroute the shipment of all hazardous materials around Chicago than it is to propose the relocation of homes adjacent to the Blue Island switching yard to more distant suburbs. It may be less realistic. Brutal though it may seem to say it, the inappropriate use to which land is being put in the Blue Island yard and neighborhood may be, not the transportation of hazardous chemicals, but residential living. The analogy is to building your home between the runways at O'Hare.

The briefs hew closely to the Restatement, whose approach to the issue of strict liability is mainly *allocative* rather than *distributive.* By this we mean that the emphasis is on picking a liability regime (negligence or strict liability) that will control the particular class of accidents in question most effectively, rather than on finding the deepest pocket and placing liability there. At argument, however, the plaintiff's lawyer invoked distributive considerations by pointing out that Cyanamid is a huge firm and the Indiana Harbor Belt Railroad a fifty-mile-long switching line that almost went broke in the winter of 1979, when the accident occurred. Well, so what? A corporation is not a living person but a set of contracts the terms of which determine who will bear the brunt of liability. Tracing the incidence of a cost is a complex undertaking which the plaintiff sensibly has made no effort to assume, since its legal relevance would be dubious. We add only that however small the plaintiff may be, it has mighty parents: it is a jointly owned subsidiary of Conrail and the Soo line.

The case for strict liability has not been made. Not in this suit in any event. We need not speculate on the possibility of imposing strict liability on shippers of more hazardous materials, such as * * * bombs, * * * any more than we need differentiate (given how the plaintiff has shaped its case) between active and passive shippers. We noted earlier that acrylonitrile is far from being the most hazardous among hazardous materials shipped by rail in highest volume. Or among materials shipped, period. * * *

Ordinarily when summary judgment is denied, the movant's rights are not extinguished; the case is simply set down for trial. If this approach were followed here, it would require remanding the case for a trial on whether Cyanamid should be held strictly liable. Yet that would be a mistake. The parties have agreed that the question whether the transportation of acrylonitrile through densely populated areas is abnormally dangerous is one of law rather than of fact; and trials are to determine facts, not law. More precisely—for there is no sharp line between "law" and "fact"—trials are to determine adjudicative facts rather than legislative facts. The distinction is between facts germane to the specific dispute, which often are best developed through testimony and cross-examination, and facts relevant to shaping a general rule, which, as the discussion in this opinion illustrates, more often are facts reported in books and other documents not prepared specially for litigation or refined in its fires. Again the line should not be viewed as hard and fast. If facts critical to a decision on whether a particular activity should be subjected to a regime of strict liability cannot be determined with reasonable accuracy without an evidentiary hearing, such a hearing can and should be held, though we can find no reported case where this was done. Some courts treat the question whether an activity is abnormally dangerous as one of fact, and then there must be an evidentiary hearing to decide it. * * * Here we are concerned with cases in which the question is treated as one of law but in which factual disputes of the sort ordinarily resolved by an evidentiary hearing may be germane to answering the question. An evidentiary hearing would be of no use in the present case, however, because the plaintiff has not indicated any facts that it wants to develop through such a hearing. * * *

Reversed and remanded, with directions.

NOTE

Rejection of the Multiple Factor Analysis for Determining the Abnormally Dangerous Nature of an Activity. The multiple factor analysis provided by Restatement (Second) of Torts § 520 (1977) has been heavily criticized since its adoption. Even Professor William Prosser, Reporter for the Second Restatement, criticized the section because, as he stated, he "always intensely disliked sections which put factors to be taken into account." 41 A.L.I. Proc. 455 (1964). Prosser asked, "which of these factors are to be given priority[, and] * * * [w]hat is the importance of each of them?" His conclusion was "the only answer that can be given is it all depends."

The Restatement (Third) of Torts: Liability for Physical and Emotional Harm (2010) responded to such criticisms by dropping the multiple factor approach—returning to a more rule-like format—and eliminating consideration of both the appropriateness of the location of the activity and its social value:

§ 20. Abnormally Dangerous Activities. * * *

  (b) An activity is abnormally dangerous if:

    (1) the activity creates a foreseeable and highly significant risk of physical harm even when reasonable care is exercised by all actors; and

(2)   the activity is not one of common usage.

Restatement (Third) of Torts: Liability for Physical and Emotional Harm § 20 (2010).

C. NUISANCE

Bohan v. Port Jervis Gas-Light Co.

Court of Appeals of New York, 1890.
122 N.Y. 18, 25 N.E. 246.

[Action to recover damages for the maintenance by the defendant of an alleged nuisance on its premises, and to restrain its continuance. At the trial of this case before a jury plaintiff gave no evidence of negligence on the part of defendant either in the construction or maintenance of its works or the conduct of its business. For failure to give such proof, defendant moved to dismiss the complaint and excepted to the denial of this motion.]

■ BROWN, J. * * * The court charged the jury that, to constitute a nuisance, it was essential that the smells and odors from the defendant's works should be sufficient "to contaminate and pollute the air, and substantially interfere with the plaintiff's enjoyment of her property," and that the question for them to determine was, "Did the odor pollute the air so as to substantially render plaintiff's property unfit for comfortable enjoyment?" An exception was taken by the defendant to this part of the charge.

The rule stated by the learned trial judge was in accordance with all the authorities. If one carry [sic] on a lawful trade or business in such a manner as to prove a nuisance to his neighbor, he must answer in damages, and it is not necessary to a right of action that the owner should be driven from his dwelling; it is enough that the enjoyment of life and property be rendered uncomfortable. *

It was claimed by the defendant, and the court refused a request to charge, "that unless the jury should find that the works of the defendant were defective, or that they were out of repair, or that the persons in charge of manufacturing gas at these works were unskillful and incapable, their verdict should be for the defendant;" and "that if the odors which affect the plaintiff are those that are inseparable from the manufacture of gas with the most approved apparatus, and with the utmost skill and care, and do not result from any defects in the works, or from want of care in their management, the defendant is not liable." An exception to this ruling raises the principal question discussed in the case. While every person has exclusive dominion over his own property and may subject it to such uses as will subserve his wishes and private interests, he is bound to have respect and regard for his neighbor's rights. The maxim *"Sic utere tuo ut alienum non laedas"* limits his power. He must make a reasonable use of his property, and a reasonable use can never be construed to include those uses which produce destructive vapors and noxious smells, and that result in material injury to the property and to the comfort of the existence of those who dwell in the neighborhood.

The reports are filled with cases where this doctrine has been applied, and it may be confidently asserted that no authority can be produced, holding that negligence is essential to establish a cause of action for injuries of such a character. * * * The principle, that one cannot recover for injuries sustained from lawful acts done on one's own property without negligence and without malice, is well founded in the law. Everyone has the right to the reasonable enjoyment of his own property, and so long as the use to which he devotes it violates no rights of others, there is no legal cause of action against him. The wants of mankind demand that property be put to many and various uses and employments, and one may have upon his property any kind of lawful business, and so long as it is not a nuisance, and is not managed so as to become such, he is not responsible for any damage that his neighbor accidently and unavoidably sustains. Such losses the law regards as *damnum absque injuria*. And under this principle, if the steam boiler on the defendant's property, or the gas retort, or the naphtha tanks had exploded and injured the plaintiff's property, it would have been necessary for her to prove negligence, on the defendant's part, to entitle her to recover. Losee v. Buchanan, 51 N.Y. 476 (1873). But where the damage is the necessary consequence of just what the defendant is doing, or is incident to the business itself, or the manner in which it is conducted, the law of negligence has no application and the law of nuisance applies. * The exception to the refusal to charge the first proposition above quoted was not, therefore, well taken.

It is contended, however, by the defendant that the acts of the legislature relating to gas companies are a protection from liability for consequential injuries flowing from the manufacture of gas, or the prosecution of the business, when want of care forms no element of the cause of injury; and it is sought to apply to this case the broad principle that that which the law authorizes cannot be a nuisance, although it may occasion damages to individual rights and property. The cases cited to sustain this proposition are ones where municipal corporations were engaged in grading and improving public streets and highways. Or where the act causing the injury was done by corporations in the construction of works upon property acquired under the power of eminent domain. * In these cases, in doing the acts complained of, the defendants acted in the performance of a public duty, imposed upon them by the legislature, or in the exercise of a right conferred by law; and it is well settled that persons appointed or authorized by law to perform a public duty, or to do acts of a public character, are not answerable for consequential damages, if they act within their jurisdiction, and with care and skill. * This principle cannot, however, be applied to cases like the one under consideration. * * *

It may be conceded that the business of manufacturing and distributing gas through the public streets for public and private use is a business of a public character, and the individual possessing such right has a franchise granted by the state for a public object, and that it meets a public necessity, for which the state may make provision. But the state has not seen fit to confer upon the corporations formed under the act cited, the power of eminent domain, and they cannot, therefore, locate their works where they will. In their ability to acquire real estate upon which to establish their manufactory, they have no greater power than any citizen of the state; and, having acquired property, they rest under the same obligation as other citizens to make a reasonable use of it, and to respect and regard the rights of their neighbors. The proposition contended for by the learned counsel for the defendant has in recent years received full consideration in the courts of England and of this country, and the rule is now established that the statutory authority which will justify an injury to private property and afford immunity for acts which would otherwise be a nuisance, must be express, or must be a clear and unquestionable implication from powers expressly conferred; and it must appear that the legislature contemplated the doing of the very act which occasioned the injury. * * * The legislature may authorize acts which would otherwise be a nuisance when they affect or relate to matters in which the public have an interest, or over which the public have control, such as highways or public streams. In such cases the legislative authorization exempts from liability to suits civil or criminal at the instance of the state, but it does not affect the claims of private citizens for damages for any special inconvenience and special discomfort not experienced by the public at large. * These views lead to the conclusion that the defendant obtained no immunity from liability for consequential injuries sustained by property surrounding its works by reason of its incorporation, or the privileges conferred upon the business by the acts of the legislature, and that the facts of the case do not take it out of the operation of the rules of law applicable to ordinary common-law nuisances.

The legislature has given to the corporations created to manufacture gas the right to lay down their conductors in the public streets, subject to the control and regulation of the municipal authorities; and, for acts done in the execution of that privilege, they are exempt from prosecution at the suit of the people.

The choice, however, of the place to locate their works, and the selection of materials from which to manufacture gas, has been left to the corporations, and those things must be performed with reference to the rights of others. * * * We think the proof permitted the conclusion that the defendant had created a nuisance, and that there was no error in the charge of the court or the refusal to charge.

The judgment must be affirmed. * * *

NOTES

1. *Relationship between Trespass and Nuisance.* The Restatement (Second) of Torts defines private nuisance as "a non-trespassory invasion of another's interest in the private use and enjoyment of land," as distinguished from trespass, an invasion by "unprivileged entry or intrusion" of an interest in the exclusive possession of land. See Restatement § 821D (1979). Comment *e* to § 821D makes it clear that the same conduct can constitute both trespass and nuisance:

> There may, however, be some overlapping of the causes of action for trespass and private nuisance. An invasion of the possession of land normally involves some degree of interference with its use and enjoyment and this is true particularly when some harm is inflicted upon the land itself. The cause of action for trespass has traditionally included liability for incidental harms of this nature. If the interference with the use and enjoyment of the land is a

significant one, sufficient in itself to amount to a private nuisance, the fact that it arises out of or is accompanied by a trespass will not prevent recovery for the nuisance, and the action may be maintained upon either basis as the plaintiff elects or both. Thus the flooding of the plaintiff's land, which is a trespass, is also a nuisance if it is repeated or of long duration. * * *

See also Martin v. Reynolds Metals Co., *infra* pages 101–107.

2. *Relationship between Fault and Liability.* The amorphous and sometimes inconsistent treatment of nuisance cases by the courts poses real difficulty for those attempting to articulate principles governing this field of liability. Consider the history of the treatment in nuisance by the drafters of the Restatement provisions. Section 822 of the first Restatement of Torts suggested a distinction between intentional and unintentional invasions. For the latter there would be liability only if the invasion were "otherwise actionable under the rules governing liability for negligent, reckless or ultrahazardous conduct." If the invasion was "intentional" (either "for the purpose" of causing the harm, or known to be "resulting or * * * substantially certain to result" from the actor's conduct, e.g., typical industrial pollution), there would be liability only if it were also "unreasonable," i.e., "unless the utility of the actor's conduct outweighs the gravity of the harm." Restatement of Torts §§ 825–26. When a similar formulation was proposed for Restatement Second, a dissenting memorandum was submitted by one of the Advisers, Professor Fleming James, Jr., one of the original editors of this casebook:[a]

> * * * The Restatement has built * * * an elaborate edifice for weighing in all cases the utility of defendant's enterprise * * * against the gravity of the harm inflicted on plaintiff's interest. * * *
>
> This line of reasoning is, of course, quite in keeping with the late nineteenth and earlier twentieth century urge to reduce all tort liability to terms of fault. * * * But this reasoning unduly simplifies the matter by leaving out of account a basis of liability without fault the recognition of which gives greater flexibility to the law of nuisance and better explains some lines of cases than the Restatement's procrustean insistence on fault (except where conduct is abnormally dangerous).
>
> * * * [W]here an actor's conduct will inevitably cause damage to another he may nevertheless be privileged to pursue it if its social utility is great enough. But where the actor is also the beneficiary of the conduct, the law may render his privilege incomplete; it may make him pay for the actual harm caused by its exercise. This, it is submitted, is the proper explanation of liability in some cases of nuisance * * * where the invasion of plaintiff's interest is so substantial that he should not be compelled to suffer it without compensation even though defendant's conduct entails no fault and is not abnormally dangerous. * * * The reasoning has been accepted in a number of American decisions. A rather dramatic example is *Madison v. Ducktown Sulphur, Copper & Iron Co.*,[33]

---

[a] [Eds.' note] Fleming James, Jr., Memorandum, The element of fault in private nuisance, Restatement (Second) of Torts (Tent. Draft No. 16, 1970), at 131.

[33] 113 Tenn. 331, 83 S.W. 658 (1904).

where the court specifically found that defendant's activity (open-air roasting of ores) was lawful and the only known method of conducting the operation; that defendants had used every method to eliminate the emissions, spending large sums for the purpose; and that "There is no place more remote to which the operations referred to could be transferred." * The lands of the farmer-plaintiffs were "all thin mountain lands, of little agricultural value," located from 2–8 miles from the plants in the mountains around Ducktown. * Fumes and smoke from defendant's operations badly damaged the plaintiff's timber and crops. Defendants showed the utility of their operations and their economic value to the community. The court denied the injunction sought but ordered the award of damages, explaining: ". . . in the case of conflicting rights, where neither party can enjoy his own without in some measure restricting the liberty of the other in the use of property, the law must make the best arrangement it can between the contending parties, with a view to preserving to each one the largest measure of liberty possible under the circumstance * * *." This reasoning is surely inconsistent with a finding of fault on Ducktown's part; yet it was held in damages. In a number of other American cases defendants have been held liable in damages for substantial harm inflicted on plaintiff's property interest, although their operations have been lawful and carefully conducted in a suitable place. * * * Several of them use the reasoning of incomplete privilege or inverse condemnation. And recently there have been similar rulings made on this basis awarding damages against airports for serious invasions of nearby land caused by low non-trespassory flights necessary for landing and taking off. * * *

The Restatement accepts abnormal danger as an appropriate basis for strict liability. The justification for it is the high degree of *risk* of injury caused by legitimate but dangerous activity. * But if high risk of harm is a sufficient basis for strict liability, then the certainty (or substantial certainty) of harm in the cases under discussion is an even stronger basis for it. * * * The foregoing reasoning would lead to the following rules:

> * * * "Where the harm is inadvertently or unintentionally caused, liability will be imposed only if the invasion is negligent or reckless or actionable as an abnormally dangerous activity. This is the same as the Restatement rule.

> Where the invasion is intentional, liability will be imposed if the defendant's conduct has been unreasonable. * * *

> Where the invasion is intentional, liability will be imposed even where the condition or conduct causing it is socially useful, is maintained and conducted with all due care and in a suitable and convenient location, if the harm caused is unreasonably great. This departs from Restatement rule but accords with what is believed to be the weight of judicial authority. This again involves weighing of utility against harm but within limits. * * * Persons who live in business or manufacturing districts must not, in Mellor's often quoted words 'Stand upon extreme rights and bring actions in

respect of every matter of annoyance.' But where material physical injury is inflicted upon persons or property or where annoyance is serious and long continued so as 'visibly to diminish the value of the property and the enjoyment of it,' then 'a thing of value has been taken from the plaintiff for the benefit of the defendant as the representative of the public, and for that thing compensation must be made.' "

In partial response to this memorandum, as well as to suggestions from Professor (later Judge) Robert Keeton, another adviser, Section 826 was added to the Restatement (Second) in 1979 to supplement Section 822:

§ 822.   General Rule.

One is subject to liability for a private nuisance if, but only if, his conduct is a legal cause of an invasion of another's interest in the private use and enjoyment of land, and the invasion is either

(a)   intentional and unreasonable, or

(b)   unintentional and otherwise actionable under the rules controlling liability for negligent or reckless conduct, or for abnormally dangerous conditions or activities.

§ 826.   Unreasonableness of Intentional Invasion.

An intentional invasion of another's interest in the use and enjoyment of land is unreasonable if

(a)   the gravity of the harm outweighs the utility of the actor's conduct, or

(b)   the harm caused by the conduct is serious and the financial burden of compensating for this and similar harm to others would not make the continuation of the conduct not feasible.

Public Service Co. of Colorado v. Van Wyk

Supreme Court of Colorado, 2001.
27 P.3d 377.

■ MARTINEZ, JUSTICE. This case presents the issue of whether the Colorado Public Utilities Commission's (PUC) approval of electrical line upgrades by the Public Service Company of Colorado (PSCo) precluded claims by adjacent property owners for * * * nuisance against PSCo based on those upgrades. This case also presents the issue of whether the class-action complaint, filed by Mark and Erica Van Wyk and all others similarly situated (collectively the Van Wyks), stated claims sufficient for relief against PSCo. * * *

In 1989, PUC granted PSCo's application to increase the voltage from 115 to 230 kilovolts (kV) on one of its above-ground electric lines in Douglas County (the Daniels Park Line). * * * Upon completion of the upgrade, the Van Wyks, owners and residents of property adjacent to the upgraded Daniels Park Line, sued PSCo in the district court on behalf of themselves and all owners of property adjacent to or within three hundred feet of the line. * The Van Wyks' complaint asserted [a] claim[ ] of * * * nuisance * * * stemming from the upgrade of the line.

The Van Wyks' complaint alleged that the Daniels Park Line is noisy, particularly during times of high humidity, rain, and snow. * * * [T]he Van Wyks allege that PSCo acted intentionally to create a nuisance by transmitting 230kV of electricity through the line, thereby creating noise, an electromagnetic field, and radiation particles. Based on these claims, the Van Wyks sought money damages from PSCo. In response to the Van Wyks' complaint, PSCo filed a * * * motion to dismiss for failure to state a claim, and the district court dismissed the Van Wyks' complaint. * * * The court of appeals reversed the district court decision. * The court of appeals held that PUC's approval of the upgrade of the Daniels Park Line is not dispositive of the Van Wyks' common law tort claim[ ]. * * * Additionally, the court of appeals concluded that the Van Wyks adequately alleged * * * [nuisance] in their complaint. * * * We granted certiorari to review these court of appeals' determinations which reversed the district court's decisions. * * *

We begin our analysis of this case with the question of preclusion. PSCo argues that permitting the Van Wyks to pursue claims for damages for trespass and nuisance in the district court is inconsistent with PUC's authority to regulate utilities. PSCo claims that, under Article XXV of the Colorado Constitution and section 40–4–102, 11 C.R.S. (2000), PUC has the exclusive jurisdiction to balance various public and private interests affected by the actions of public utilities. PSCo suggests that if individuals are permitted recovery in private tort actions against utility companies for acting in a manner consistent with PUC approval, PUC's authority can essentially be overruled by a district court. * * *

We have upheld the rule * * * that PUC regulations and adjudications generally preempt local government in decisions concerning utilities. * The need for such preemption stems from the fact that "the regulation of public utilities in the interest of public safety and convenience is a matter of state-wide concern." City of Craig v. Pub. Util. Comm'n, 656 P.2d 1313, 1316 (Colo.1983). * * * Furthermore, it has been established that judicial action that undermines agency authority is generally disfavored. * PUC, acting as an administrative agency, has been endowed with legislative authority in public utility matters. * * *

The district court's holding that the Van Wyks' claims were precluded by PUC's approval of the Daniels Park Line upgrade effectively determined that PUC's decision was an adjudication of the Van Wyks' property rights. Such a determination is contrary to our conclusion in *City of Craig* that PUC's valid exercise of its statutory authority leaves the issue of the property interest to the affected parties. * While the pertinent PUC ruling concerns the authorization granted to PSCo to upgrade the Daniels Park Line, * the questions presented by the Van Wyks in this case demand an adjudication of property rights which were not addressed by PUC's decision. * * *

Here, the Van Wyks seek an adjudication based on their claim[ ] of * * * nuisance. * * * [N]uisance * * * [is a] tort claim[ ] related to property rights and damages to property and property owners. Since we have held that PUC does not have the authority to adjudicate property rights, it logically follows that PUC also does not have authority to adjudicate questions related to damages stemming from property ownership and torts committed against either the property or the owner. Thus, because the Van Wyks seek a determination of * * * damages related to their property and property holdings, through their * * * nuisance tort claim[ ], they are not seeking to re-litigate PUC's decision in another forum. * Therefore, we conclude that the Van Wyks are not precluded from seeking an adjudication of their property rights and torts related to those rights with regard to the upgrade of the Daniels Park Line. * * *

C.   Nuisance

* * * The nuisance alleged by the Van Wyks is the continuous and constant transmission of 230kV of electric power through the Daniels Park Line. * In the complaint, the Van Wyks allege that the Daniels Park Line emits continual, unreasonably loud noises that increase during times of high humidity, rain, or snow. They further allege that the electrical line emits high amounts of radiation and an electromagnetic field, both of which encroach upon their land. As a result of these intrusions, the Van Wyks allege that the value of their property has depreciated, they have suffered mental distress, and they have lost the quiet use and enjoyment of their land. * * *

A claim for nuisance is predicated upon a substantial invasion of a plaintiff's interest in the use and enjoyment of his property when such invasion is: (1) intentional and unreasonable; (2) unintentional and otherwise actionable under the rules for negligent or reckless conduct; or (3) so abnormal or out of place in its surroundings as to fall within the principle of strict liability. Restatement (Second) Torts § 822. * Stated differently, the elements of a claim of nuisance are an intentional, negligent, or unreasonably dangerous activity resulting in the unreasonable and substantial interference with a plaintiff's use and enjoyment of her property. * To maintain a successful nuisance claim, a plaintiff must establish that the defendant has unreasonably interfered with the use and enjoyment of her property. * The question of unreasonableness is an issue of fact and should, therefore, be left to the determination of the trier of fact. Restatement (Second) of Torts, § 826 cmt. b. In making any determination of unreasonableness, the trier of fact must weigh the gravity of the harm and the utility of the conduct causing that harm. *Id.* at cmt. d. Generally, to be unreasonable, an interference must be significant enough that a normal person in the community would find it offensive, annoying, or inconvenient. *Id.* at § 821F *.

We agree with PSCo's assertion that the Van Wyks' complaint alleges an intentional, and not negligent or strict liability, nuisance. As such, we examine whether the Van Wyks have adequately alleged that PSCo has intentionally and unreasonably interfered, in a significant way, with the use and enjoyment of their property. * * * PSCo relies on the Restatement (Second) of Torts section 825, which provides that conduct resulting in an invasion of the plaintiff's interest in the use and enjoyment of her property is intentional if a defendant acts for the purpose of causing such invasion, or knows that such invasion is the result of, or is substantially certain to result from, his conduct. * * *

[T]he Van Wyks argue that PSCo committed the tort of intentional nuisance by continuing to transmit electricity through the line after gaining knowledge that the transmission of that power resulted in a possible nuisance. While it is not entirely clear from the Van Wyks' complaint whether PSCo was ever actually made aware of the alleged invasion interfering with the use and enjoyment of the Van Wyks' property, we must view the complaint in the light most favorable to the plaintiff. * The allegation in the complaint that "Public Service Company has refused to discuss compensation or make any offers of payment to the property owners" suggests that the property owners made PSCo aware of the alleged invasion interfering with the use and enjoyment of the property, and that despite that notice, PSCo continued to transmit electricity through the line at 230 kV.

Accordingly, the Van Wyks' complaint alleges that PSCo has intentionally and unreasonably continued to transmit electricity through the Daniels Park Line with awareness of the invasion interfering in the Van Wyks' use and enjoyment of their property. Whether that allegation sufficiently alleges the tort of intentional nuisance is also dependent upon the Van Wyks' allegations concerning the unreasonableness of the invasion of their substantial interest in the use and enjoyment of their land resulting from that act. Because PUC considered the noise and electromagnetic fields that would probably be emitted by the line and determined that the upgrade of the line was reasonable, we next compare the unreasonableness alleged by the Van Wyks to that PUC determination.

As we noted above, the interference complained of by the Van Wyks must be a substantial invasion interfering with the use and enjoyment of the land, and reducing the value of the land. * A determination that the social utility of the act causing the invasion that interferes with the use and enjoyment of the land does not outweigh the harm of that invasion is necessary for a finding of unreasonableness. Restatement (Second) of Torts § 826. Although the determination of unreasonableness is ultimately an issue of fact, Restatement (Second) of Torts § 826 cmt. b, we are concerned here with whether the allegation is sufficient to state a claim. * * *

In its determination that the increase in noise levels likely to be occasioned by the transmission line upgrade was reasonable, * * * PUC * * * depended upon testimony that the audible noise from the proposed upgraded line would be reasonable because noise complaints generally arise only at noise levels exceeding those found on lines similar to the proposed upgrade here. No fact finding was made as to actual noise levels, or as to whether the line here, once transmitting electricity, would actually produce noise levels at or below the levels of similar lines. Thus, PUC did not quantify the noise level it deemed to be reasonable, but simply determined that the noise that it anticipated was not unreasonable. * * *

While the complaint in this case does not quantify how the electromagnetic fields and noise interfere with their use and enjoyment of the property, we infer that the Van Wyks are alleging that the fields and noise exceed what PUC considered to be reasonable. Because PUC's determination as to reasonableness here lacked any specificity with respect to electromagnetic fields and noise, the Van Wyks' claim goes beyond that PUC determination by alleging that the invasion that interferes with the use and enjoyment of their land is unreasonable, without making more specific allegations. As such, the Van Wyks' allegations that the unreasonableness of conducting electricity through the Daniels Park Line at 230kV is beyond the scope of the previous PUC determination. * * *

[W]e next consider the intent requirement of the nuisance claim. * * * As stated above, the Restatement (Second) of Torts section 825 defines "intentional invasion" as one where the actor acted for the purpose of causing the invasion interfering with the use and enjoyment of the plaintiff's land, or knew that the invasion interfering with the use and enjoyment of the land is the result of, or is substantially certain to result from, his conduct. * * * [W]e adopt the rule of intentional nuisance as defined in section 825 of the Restatement (Second) of Torts. Contrary to PSCo's argument, the mere fact that we adopt the rule here that a defendant must act with intent to create the nuisance, or knowing that the nuisance will result, or is substantially likely to result from his conduct, does not automatically render the Van Wyks' complaint insufficient. On the contrary, we note that the defendant's intent to act in such a way that an invasion interfering with the use and enjoyment of the plaintiff's property occurs is not limited to the initial act or motivation behind that act. Indeed, if a defendant, with notice that an invasion interfering with the use and enjoyment of the plaintiff's property has occurred, or is substantially certain to occur, continues his conduct without regard to the invasion interfering with the use and enjoyment of the plaintiff's property, that defendant's conduct will be the proper basis for an intentional nuisance cause of action. *

Thus, if PSCo knew of the allegedly unreasonable invasions interfering with the use and enjoyment of the Van Wyks' property, and if, as we are required to assume, all of the averments of fact made by the Van Wyks are true, then the Van Wyks' complaint properly states a claim for intentional nuisance against PSCo. As we note above, the Van Wyks' complaint satisfies both of the requirements necessary to allege a nuisance. First, the Van Wyks made the allegation of unreasonableness beyond the scope of the PUC reasonableness determination. Second, the Van Wyks alleged that PSCo was made aware of the invasions interfering with the use and enjoyment of the Van Wyks' property, which were beyond the scope of what PUC had determined to be reasonable, and yet continued to conduct electricity through the line, thereby continuing to cause the invasions interfering with the use and enjoyment of the Van Wyks' property. * * * Thus, the nuisance section of the Van Wyks' complaint sufficiently states a claim. * Accordingly, we hold that the district court improperly dismissed the Van Wyks' nuisance claim. * * *

In light of our holdings here, we conclude that the district court erred in determining that PUC's decision precluded the Van Wyks from pursuing an adjudication of their * * * tort claim[ ]. We further conclude that the district court * * * improperly dismissed the Van Wyks' claim of intentional nuisance. * * *

■ MULLARKEY, CHIEF JUSTICE, concurring in part and dissenting in part. * * * [T]o be liable for an intentional nuisance, a party's activities must be both intentional and unreasonable. Restatement (Second) of Torts § 822 cmt. a ("[An] invasion may be intentional but reasonable. . . . [In such case] there is no liability.") This rule is necessary given the pressures inherent in contemporary society:

> Not every intentional and significant invasion of a person's interest in the use and enjoyment of land is actionable. . . . Practically all human activities unless carried on in a wilderness interfere to some extent with others . . . and these interferences range from mere trifling annoyances to serious harms. It is an obvious truth that each individual in a community must put up with a certain amount of annoyance, inconvenience and interference. . . . The very existence of organized society depends upon the principle of "give and take, live and let live," and therefore the law of torts does not attempt to impose liability or shift the loss in every case in which one person's conduct has some detrimental effect on another

Id. at § 822. * * *

The Restatement (Second) of Torts explains that an intentional invasion of another's interest in the use and enjoyment of land is unreasonable if "the gravity of the harm outweighs the utility of the actor's conduct." *Id.* at § 826. Thus, a determination of the unreasonableness of an invasion "is a problem of relative values," and requires a comparative evaluation of the interests of the person harmed, the actor, and the community as a whole. *Id.* at cmts. b, c. These conflicting interests must be evaluated from an objective legal standpoint, rather than from the point of view of the individual parties involved. *Id.* at cmt. c.

In determining the degree of harm suffered, a court must consider the extent and character of the harm, the social value given to the type of use or enjoyment invaded, and the character of the neighborhood affected. *Id.* at § 827. Factors to be considered in determining the utility of the conduct include the social value of the conduct, the suitability of the conduct to the character of the locality, and the impracticality of preventing or avoiding the invasion. *Id.* at § 828. * * *

NOTE

Displacement. One set of issues considered by the court involves the impact of the previous decisions by the Public Utility Commission (PUC), an administrative agency established by the legislature to regulate utilities. The court notes that "PUC regulations and adjudications generally preempt local government in decisions concerning utilities," but then concludes that "because the Van Wyks seek a determination of * * * damages related to their property and property holdings, through their * * * nuisance tort claim[], they are not seeking to re-litigate PUC's decision in another forum." Would a decision in favor of the plaintiffs in this case possibly have a regulatory effect on the defendant's conduct in a way that could be inconsistent with the regulations established by the PUC? Is not the PUC the body charged with the responsibility for regulating such matters and presumably with the requisite expertise?

Similar issues arose more recently in American Electric Power Co. v. Connecticut, 564 U.S. ___, 131 S.Ct. 2527, 180 L.Ed.2d 435 (2011). Eight states joined several other plaintiffs in suing five major electric power companies, alleging that their greenhouse gas emissions contributed to global warming and violated the federal common law of interstate nuisance. The plaintiffs sought injunctive relief requiring the gradual reduction in the amount of greenhouse gas emissions from the defendants' utility plants. Despite the fact that the Environmental Protection Agency had not begun to regulate greenhouse gas emissions at the time the plaintiffs' complaint was filed, the Court held that the Congressionally-enacted "Clean Air Act and the EPA actions it authorizes displace any federal common law right to seek abatement of carbon-dioxide emissions from fossil-fuel fired power plants." *Id.* at ___, 131 S.Ct. at 2537, 180 L.Ed.2d at 447. The Court explained:

> The Clean Air Act is no less an exercise of the legislature's "considered judgment" concerning the regulation of air pollution because it permits emissions until EPA acts. * The critical point is that Congress delegated to EPA the decision whether and how to regulate carbon-dioxide emissions from power plants; the delegation is what displaces federal common law. Indeed, were EPA to decline to regulate carbon-dioxide emissions altogether at the conclusion of its ongoing rulemaking, the federal courts would have no warrant to employ the federal common law of nuisance to upset the agency's expert determination. * * *
>
> It is altogether fitting that Congress designated an expert agency, here, EPA, as best suited to serve as primary regulator of greenhouse gas emissions. The expert agency is surely better equipped to do the job than individual district judges issuing ad hoc, case-by-case injunctions. Federal judges lack the scientific, economic, and technological resources an agency can utilize in coping with issues of this order. * Judges may not commission scientific studies or convene groups of experts for advice, or issue rules under notice-and-comment procedures inviting input by any interested person, or seek the counsel of regulators in the States where the defendants are located. Rather, judges are confined by a record comprising the evidence the parties present. Moreover, federal district judges, sitting as sole adjudicators, lack authority to render precedential decisions binding other judges, even members of the same court.
>
> Notwithstanding these disabilities, the plaintiffs propose that individual federal judges determine, in the first instance, what amount of carbon-dioxide emissions is "unreasonable," * and then decide what level of reduction is "practical, feasible and economically viable." * These determinations would be made for the defendants named in the two lawsuits launched by the plaintiffs. Similar suits could be mounted, counsel for the States and New York City estimated, against "thousands or hundreds or tens" of other defendants fitting the description "large contributors" to carbon-dioxide emissions. *

Id. at ___, 131 S.Ct. at 2537, 180 L.Ed.2d at 449. As of this writing, the Court has yet to decide whether federal legislation and regulations bar *state* tort actions against emitters of greenhouse gases.

Can the two decisions be distinguished on the basis that the plaintiffs in *American Electric Power Co.* sought injunctive relief while the *Van Wyck* plaintiff sought only damages?

Similar issues will arise when we consider whether federal regulation in various contexts "preempts" state tort law claims. See *infra* pages 629–644.

Boomer v. Atlantic Cement Co.

Court of Appeals of New York, 1970.
26 N.Y.2d 219, 309 N.Y.S.2d 312, 257 N.E.2d 870.

■ BERGAN, J. Defendant operates a large cement plant near Albany. These are actions for injunction and damages by neighboring land owners alleging injury to property from dirt, smoke and vibration emanating from the plant. A nuisance has been found after trial, temporary damages have been allowed; but an injunction has been denied.

The public concern with air pollution arising from many sources in industry and in transportation is currently accorded ever wider recognition accompanied by a growing sense of responsibility in State and Federal Governments to control it. Cement plants are obvious sources of air pollution in the neighborhoods where they operate.

But there is now before the court private litigation in which individual property owners have sought specific relief from a single plant operation. The threshold question raised by the division of view on this appeal is whether the court should resolve the litigation between the parties now before it as equitably as seems possible; or whether, seeking promotion of the general public welfare, it should channel private litigation into broad public objectives.

A court performs its essential function when it decides the rights of parties before it. Its decision of private controversies may sometimes greatly affect public issues. Large questions of law are often resolved by the manner in which private litigation is decided. But this is normally an incident to the court's main function to settle controversy. It is a rare exercise of judicial power to use a decision in private litigation as a purposeful mechanism to achieve direct public objectives greatly beyond the rights and interests before the court.

Effective control of air pollution is a problem presently far from solution even with the full public and financial powers of government. In large measure adequate technical procedures are yet to be developed and some that appear possible may be economically impracticable.

It seems apparent that the amelioration of air pollution will depend on technical research in great depth; on a carefully balanced consideration of the economic impact of close regulation; and of the actual effect on public health. It is likely to require massive public expenditure and to demand more than any local community can accomplish and to depend on regional and interstate controls.

A court should not try to do this on its own as a by-product of private litigation and it seems manifest that the judicial establishment is neither equipped in the limited nature of any judgment it can pronounce nor prepared to lay down and implement an effective policy for the elimination of air pollution. This is an area beyond the circumference of one private lawsuit. It is a direct responsibility for government and should not thus be undertaken as an incident to solving a dispute between property owners and a single cement plant—one of many—in the Hudson River valley. * * *

The total damage to plaintiffs' properties is, however, relatively small in comparison with the value of defendant's operation and with the consequences of the injunction which plaintiffs seek. [Permanent damages for all plaintiffs were found to total $185,000. Defendant had invested over $45,000,000 in plant and employed over 300 people.]

The ground for the denial of injunction, notwithstanding the finding both that there is a nuisance and that plaintiffs have been damaged substantially, is the large disparity in economic consequences of the nuisance and of the injunction. This theory cannot, however, be sustained without overruling a doctrine which has been consistently reaffirmed in several leading cases in this court and which has never been disavowed here, namely that where a nuisance has been found and where there has been any substantial damage shown by the party complaining an injunction will be granted. [See opinion of Judge Werner in Whalen v. Union Bag & Paper Co., 208 N.Y. 1, 101 N.E. 805 (1913).] * * *

[T]o follow the rule literally in these cases would be to close down the plant at once. This court is fully agreed to avoid that immediately drastic remedy; the difference in view is how best to avoid it. * One alternative is to grant the injunction but postpone its effect to a specified future date to give opportunity for technical advances to permit defendant to eliminate the nuisance; another is to grant the injunction conditioned on the payment of permanent damages to plaintiffs which would compensate them for the total economic loss to their property present and future caused by defendant's operations. For reasons which will be developed the court chooses the latter alternative.

If the injunction were to be granted unless within a short period—e.g., 18 months—the nuisance be abated by improved methods, there would be no assurance that any significant technical improvement would occur.

The parties could settle this private litigation at any time if defendant paid enough money and the imminent threat of closing the plant would build up the pressure on defendant. If there were no improved techniques found, there would inevitably be applications to the court at Special Term for extensions of time to perform on showing of good faith efforts to find such techniques.

Moreover, techniques to eliminate dust and other annoying by-products of cement making are unlikely to be developed by any research the defendant can undertake within any short period, but will depend on the total resources of the cement industry nationwide and throughout the world. The problem is universal wherever cement is made.

For obvious reasons the rate of the research is beyond control of defendant. If at the end of 18 months the whole industry has not found a technical solution a court would be hard put to close down this one cement plant if due regard be given to equitable principles.

On the other hand, to grant the injunction unless defendant pays plaintiffs such permanent damages as may be fixed by the court seems to do justice between the contending parties. All of the attributions of economic loss to the properties on which plaintiffs' complaints are based will have been redressed.

The nuisance complained of by these plaintiffs may have other public or private consequences, but these particular parties are the only ones who have sought remedies and the judgment proposed will fully redress them. * * *

Thus it seems fair to both sides to grant permanent damages to plaintiffs which will terminate this private litigation. The theory of damage is the "servitude on land" of plaintiffs imposed by defendant's nuisance. See United States v. Causby, 328 U.S. 256, 261, 262, 267, 66 S.Ct. 1062, 1065, 1066, 1068, 90 L.Ed. 1206, 1210, 1211, 1213 (1946), where the term "servitude" addressed to the land was used by Justice Douglas relating to the effect of airplane noise on property near an airport.

The judgment, by allowance of permanent damages imposing a servitude on land, which is the basis of the actions, would preclude future recovery by plaintiffs or their grantees. * * *

■ JASEN, J. (dissenting). * * * I see grave dangers in overruling our long-established rule of granting an injunction where a nuisance results in substantial continuing damage. In permitting the injunction to become inoperative upon the payment of permanent damages, the majority is, in effect, licensing a continuing wrong. It is the same as saying to the cement company, you may continue to do harm to your neighbors so long as you pay a fee for it. Furthermore, once such permanent damages are assessed and paid, the incentive to alleviate the wrong would be eliminated, thereby continuing air pollution of an area without abatement. * * *

This kind of inverse condemnation * may not be invoked by a private person or corporation for private gain or advantage. Inverse condemnation should only be permitted when the public is primarily served in the taking or impairment of property. * The promotion of the interests of the polluting cement company has, in my opinion, no public use or benefit. * * *

Spur Industries, Inc. v. Del E. Webb Development Co.

Supreme Court of Arizona, 1972.
108 Ariz. 178, 494 P.2d 700.

[Spur's feedlot was established in 1956, about two miles south of a retirement community. In 1959 there were 25 cattle feeding operations within a seven-mile radius of Spur. About then Webb started acquiring land for urban development in the vicinity of the retirement community, and Spur also expanded.]

■ CAMERON, VICE CHIEF JUSTICE. * * * Accompanied by an extensive advertising campaign, homes were first offered by Del Webb in January 1960 and the first unit to be completed was south of Grand Avenue and approximately 2½ miles north of Spur. By 2 May 1960, there were 450 to 500 houses completed or under construction. At this time, Del Webb did not consider odors from the Spur feed pens a problem and Del Webb continued to develop in a southerly direction, until sales resistance became so great that the parcels were difficult if not impossible to sell. * * *

By December 1967, Del Webb's property had extended south to Olive Avenue and Spur was within 500 feet of Olive Avenue to the north. * Del Webb filed its original complaint alleging that in excess of 1,300 lots in the southwest portion were unfit for development for sale as residential lots because of the operation of the Spur feedlot.

Del Webb's suit complained that the Spur feeding operation was a public nuisance because of the flies and the odor which were drifting or being blown by the prevailing south to north wind over the southern portion of Sun City. At the time of the suit, Spur was feeding between 20,000 and 30,000 head of cattle, and the facts amply support the finding of the trial court that the feed pens had become a nuisance to the people who resided in the southern part of Del Webb's development. The testimony indicated that cattle in a commercial feedlot will produce 35 to 40 pounds of wet manure per day, per head, or over a million pounds of wet manure per day for 30,000 head of cattle, and that despite the admittedly good feedlot management and good housekeeping practices by Spur, the resulting odor and flies produced an annoying if not unhealthy situation as far as the senior citizens of southern Sun City were concerned. There is no doubt that some of the citizens of Sun City were unable to enjoy the outdoor living which Del Webb had advertised and that Del Webb was faced with sales resistance from prospective purchasers as well as strong and persistent complaints from the people who had purchased homes in that area. * * *

We have no difficulty * * * in agreeing with the conclusion of the trial court that Spur's operation was an enjoinable public nuisance as far as the people in the southern portion of Del Webb's Sun City were concerned.

§ 36–601, subsec. A reads as follows: * * *

> The following conditions are specifically declared public nuisances dangerous to the public health:
>
> 1. Any condition or place in populous areas which constitutes a breeding place for flies, rodents, mosquitoes and other insects which are capable of carrying and transmitting disease-causing organisms to any person or persons. * * *

It is clear that as to the citizens of Sun City, the operation of Spur's feedlot was both a public and a private nuisance. They could have successfully maintained an action to abate the nuisance. Del Webb, having shown a special injury in the loss of sales, had a standing to bring suit to enjoin the nuisance. * * *

A suit to enjoin a nuisance sounds in equity and the courts have long recognized a special responsibility to the public when acting as a court of equity * * *. In addition to protecting the public interest * * * courts of equity are concerned with protecting the operator of a lawfully, albeit noxious, business from the result of a knowing and willful encroachment by others near his business. In the so-called "coming to the nuisance" cases, the courts have held that the residential landowner may not have relief if he knowingly came into a neighborhood reserved for industrial or agricultural endeavors and has been damaged thereby * * *.

Were Webb the only party injured, we would feel justified in holding that the doctrine of "coming to the nuisance" would have been a bar to the relief asked by Webb, and, on the other hand, had Spur located the feedlot near the outskirts of a city and had the city grown toward the feedlot, Spur would have to suffer the cost of abating the nuisance as to those people locating within the growth pattern of the expanding city * * *. We agree, however, with the Massachusetts court that:

> The law of nuisance affords no rigid rule to be applied in all instances. It is elastic. It undertakes to require only that which is fair and reasonable under all the circumstances. In a commonwealth like this, which depends for its material prosperity so largely on the continued growth and enlargement of manufacturing of diverse varieties, "extreme rights" cannot be enforced. . . .

Stevens v. Rockport Granite Co., 216 Mass. 486, 488, 104 N.E. 371, 373 (1914).

There was no indication in the instant case at the time Spur and its predecessors located in western Maricopa County that a new city would spring up, full-blown, alongside the feeding operation and that the developer of that city would ask the court to order Spur to move because of the new city. Spur is required to move not because of any wrongdoing on the part of Spur, but because of a proper and legitimate regard of the courts for the rights and interests of the public.

Del Webb, on the other hand, is entitled to the relief prayed for (a permanent injunction), not because Webb is blameless, but because of the damage to the people who have been encouraged to purchase homes in Sun City. It does not equitably or legally follow, however, that Webb, being entitled to the injunction, is then free of any liability to Spur if Webb has in fact been the cause of the damage Spur has sustained. It does not seem harsh to require a developer, who has taken advantage of the lesser land values in a rural area as well as the availability of large tracts of land on which to build and develop a new town or city in the area, to indemnify those who are forced to leave as a result.

Having brought people to the nuisance to the foreseeable detriment of Spur, Webb must indemnify Spur for a reasonable amount of the cost of moving or shutting down. It should be noted that this relief to Spur is limited to a case wherein a developer has, with foreseeability, brought into a previously agricultural or industrial area the population which makes necessary the granting of an injunction against a lawful business and for which the business has no adequate relief. * * *

NOTE

"Coming to the Nuisance." "[I]t is generally not a defense to an action for a nuisance that plaintiff 'came to the nuisance' by acquiring property in the vicinity of defendant's premises with knowledge of the nuisance. [See Restatement (Second) of Torts § 840D (1979).] If such conduct on plaintiff's part deprived him of his remedy, that fact would virtually allow defendant, by his wrongful conduct, to condemn part of the value of neighboring land

without compensation. The fact that plaintiff moved to a nuisance is not, however, altogether irrelevant in determining whether there was a nuisance." Harper, James and Gray on Torts § 1.28. Traditionally, for instance, one who moved to an industrial area would be expected to put up with more in the way of pollution and noise than one living in a rural area. Because the value of land near nuisances often is discounted to reflect the nuisance, nuisances disproportionately affect those with limited resources. In recent years, the environmental justice movement has emerged to advocate on behalf of low-income groups who disproportionately bear the burden of environmental nuisances.

State v. Lead Industries Ass'n

Supreme Court of Rhode Island, 2008.
951 A.2d 428.

■ WILLIAMS, CHIEF JUSTICE. * * * It is undisputed that lead poisoning constitutes a public health crisis that has plagued and continues to plague this country, particularly its children. * * * There seems to be little public debate that exposure to lead can have a wide range of effects on a child's development and behavior. Contact with low levels of lead may lead to "permanent learning disabilities, reduced concentration and attentiveness and behavior problems, problems which may persist and adversely affect the child's chances for success in school and life." * * * Children exposed to elevated levels of lead can suffer from comas, convulsions, and even death.

Lead was widely used in residential paints in the United States until the mid-1970s. There is no doubt that lead-based paint is the primary source of childhood lead exposure. In the United States, children most often are lead-poisoned by ingesting lead paint chips from deteriorating walls or inhaling lead-contaminated surface dust. * * *

On October 12, 1999, the Attorney General, on behalf of the state filed a ten-count complaint against eight former lead pigment manufacturers * * *. The state alleged that the manufacturers or their predecessors-in-interest had manufactured, promoted, distributed, and sold lead pigment for use in residential paint, despite that they knew or should have known, since the early 1900s, that lead is hazardous to human health. * * * As such, the state asserted, defendants were liable for public nuisance * * *. The state also requested equitable relief to protect children in Rhode Island. * The state sought compensatory and punitive damages, in addition to an order requiring defendants to (1) abate lead pigment in all Rhode Island buildings accessible to children and (2) fund educational and lead-poisoning prevention programs.

In January 2000, defendants moved to dismiss all counts of the state's complaint * * *. The trial justice dismissed several other counts * * *. Eventually, only the state's public nuisance claim proceeded to trial. After a seven-week trial, however, the jury was deadlocked and the trial justice declared a mistrial. * * *[T]he second trial proceeded * * *. The jury* * * found that the "cumulative presence of lead pigment in paints and coatings on buildings throughout the State of Rhode Island" constituted a public nuisance. * * * On March 16, 2007, the court entered a judgment of abatement in favor of the state against defendants, Millennium, NL, and Sherwin-Williams, from which they appeal. * * *

Today, public nuisance and private nuisance are separate and distinct causes of action, but both torts are inextricably linked by their joint origin as a common writ, dating to twelfth-century English common law. See * Donald G. Gifford, Public Nuisance as a Mass Products Liability Tort, 71 U. Cin. L. Rev. 741, 790–91, 794 (2003). In its earliest form, nuisance was a criminal writ used to prosecute individuals or require abatement of activities considered to "be '*nocumentum iniuriousum propter communem et publicam utiliatem*'—a nuisance by reason of the common and public welfare." *Id.* at 793–94. * Public nuisance, or common nuisance as it originally was called, was "an infringement of the rights of the Crown." Restatement (Second) of Torts § 821B, cmt. a (1979). Although the earliest cases involved encroachments on the royal domain, public nuisance law evolved to include "the invasion of the rights of the public." By the fourteenth century, courts began to apply public nuisance principles to protect rights common to the public, including "roadway safety, air and water pollution, disorderly conduct, and public health * * *." See Richard O. Faulk & John S. Gray, Alchemy in the Courtroom? The Transmutation of Public Nuisance Litigation, 2007 Mich. St. L. Rev. 941, 951 (2007). Nuisance became a "flexible judicial remedy" that allowed courts to address conflicts between land use and social welfare at a time when government regulations had not yet made their debut.

It was not until the sixteenth century that the crime of public nuisance largely was transformed into the tort that is familiar in our courts today. * However, additional parameters were necessary to limit the reach of the new tort. A private party seeking to bring a public nuisance claim was required to demonstrate that he or she had "suffered a 'particular' or 'special' injury that was not common to the public." *Id.*; see also Restatement (Second) Torts § 821B, cmt. a (1979). Ultimately, "[a]t common law public nuisance came to cover a large, miscellaneous and diversified group of minor offenses * * *." Restatement (Second) of Torts § 821B, cmt. b. Notably, all these offenses involved an "interference with the interests of the community at large—interests that were recognized as rights of the general public entitled to protection." *Id.*

Public nuisance as it existed in English common law made its way to Colonial America without change. * In time, public nuisance became better known as a tort, and its criminal counterpart began to fade away in American jurisprudence. As state legislatures started enacting statutes prohibiting particular conduct and setting forth criminal penalties there was little need for the broad, vague, and anachronistic crime of nuisance. * * *

This Court has defined public nuisance as "an unreasonable interference with a right common to the general public." Citizens for Preservation of Waterman Lake v. Davis, 420 A.2d 53, 59 (R.I.1980). * "[I]t is behavior that unreasonably interferes with the health, safety, peace, comfort or convenience of the general community." Put another way, "public nuisance is an act or omission which obstructs or causes inconvenience or damage to the public in the exercise of rights common to all." Iafrate v. Ramsden, 96 R.I. 216, 222, 190 A.2d 473, 476 (1963).*

Although this Court previously has not had the opportunity to address all the elements of public nuisance, to the extent that we have addressed this common law cause of action, our definition largely is consistent with that of many other jurisdictions, the Restatement (Second) of Torts, and several scholarly commentators. The Restatement (Second) defines public nuisance, in relevant part, as follows:

> (1) A public nuisance is an unreasonable interference with a right common to the general public. (2) Circumstances that may sustain a holding that an interference with a public right is unreasonable include the following: (a) Whether the conduct involves a significant interference with the public health, the public safety, the public peace, the public comfort or the public convenience * * *.

Restatement (Second) Torts § 821B. * * *

This Court recognizes three principal elements that are essential to establish public nuisance: (1) an unreasonable interference; (2) with a right common to the general public; (3) by a person or people with control over the instrumentality alleged to have created the nuisance when the damage occurred. * * *

Unreasonable Interference

Whether an interference with a public right is unreasonable will depend upon the activity in question and the magnitude of the interference it creates. Activities carried out in violation of state laws or local ordinances generally have been considered unreasonable if they interfere with a public right. * Activities that do not violate the law but that nonetheless create a substantial and continuing interference with a public right also generally have been considered unreasonable. See, e.g., Wood v. Picillo, 443 A.2d 1244, 1245–48 (R.I.1982) (chemical dump that emitted noxious odors and eventually caught fire, causing multiple explosions and groundwater contamination); Lapre v. Kane, 69 R.I. 504, 507–09, 36 A.2d 92, 94–95 (1944) (swine operation that emitted noxious odors and required that large quantities of "swill" be transported and dumped onto property); Braun v. Iannotti, 54 R.I. 469, 469–70, 175 A. 656, 657 (1934) (greenhouse that continually emitted smoke); Blomen v. N. Barstow Co., 35 R.I. 198, 199–200, 211, 85 A. 924, 924–25 (1913) ("drop or hammer" that caused noise and vibration that could be felt at some distance). * * *

Public Right

* * * This Court also has emphasized the requirement that "the nuisance must affect an interest common to the general public, rather than peculiar to one individual, or several." Iafrate, 96 R.I. at 222, 190 A.2d at 476 (quoting [William L.] Prosser, Torts, ch. 14, § 72 at 402). * * * The Restatement (Second) provides further assistance in defining a public right.

> A public right is *one common to all members of the general public.* It is collective in nature and not like the individual right that everyone has not to be assaulted or defamed or defrauded or negligently injured. Thus the pollution of a stream that merely deprives fifty or a hundred lower riparian

owners of the use of the water for purposes connected with their land does not for that reason alone become a public nuisance. If, however, the pollution prevents the use of a public bathing beach or kills the fish in a navigable stream and so deprives all members of the community of the right to fish, it becomes a public nuisance.

Restatement (Second) of Torts § 821B cmt. g.

* * * As the Restatement (Second) makes clear, a public right is more than an aggregate of private rights by a large number of injured people. See *id.*; see also City of Chicago v. American Cyanamid Co., 355 Ill. App. 3d 209, 215, 291 Ill. Dec. 116, 121, 823 N.E.2d 126, 131 (2005) (a public right is not "an assortment of claimed private individual rights"). Rather, a public right is the right to a public good, such as "an indivisible resource shared by the public at large, like air, water, or public rights of way." Am. Cyanamid Co., 291 Ill. Dec. at 121, 823 N.E.2d at 131. Unlike an interference with a public resource,

> [t]he manufacture and distribution of products rarely, if ever, causes a violation of a public right as that term has been understood in the law of public nuisance. Products generally are purchased and used by individual consumers, and any harm they cause—even if the use of the product is widespread and the manufacturer's or distributor's conduct is unreasonable—is not an actionable violation of a public right. * * * The sheer number of violations does not transform the harm from individual injury to communal injury.

Gifford, 71 U. Cin. L. Rev. at 817. * * *

Control

As an additional prerequisite to the imposition of liability for public nuisance, a defendant must have *control* over the instrumentality causing the alleged nuisance *at the time the damage occurs.* * * *

Indeed, control at the time the damage occurs is critical in public nuisance cases, especially because the principal remedy for the harm caused by the nuisance is abatement. See * City of Manchester v. Nat'l Gypsum Co., 637 F.Supp. 646, 656 (D.R.I. 1986). ("The defendants, after the time of manufacture and sale, no longer had the power to abate the nuisance. Therefore, a basic element of the tort of nuisance is absent, and the plaintiff cannot succeed on this theory of relief."). * * *

Recently, the New Jersey Supreme Court similarly held that control at the time the damage occurs is a time-honored element of public nuisance. In re Lead Paint Litigation, 191 N.J. 405, 429, 924 A.2d 484, 499 (2007). In ruling that the manufacturers of lead pigment could not be held liable for nuisance under New Jersey law, the high court of that state emphasized that "a public nuisance, by definition, is related to conduct, performed in a location within the actor's control * * *." See also * Gifford, 71 U.Cin.L.Rev. at 820 ("The essence of public nuisance law * * * is ending the harmful conduct. This is impossible for the manufacturer or distributor who has relinquished possession by selling or otherwise distributing the product."). *

Causation

* * * Causation is a basic requirement in any public nuisance action; such a requirement is consistent with the law of torts generally. * A defendant will be held liable in public nuisance only if the conduct complained of actually *caused* an interference with a public right. * * * In addition to proving that a defendant is the cause-in-fact of an injury, a plaintiff must demonstrate proximate causation. * * *

Another Attribute of Public Nuisance

* * * A common feature of public nuisance is the occurrence of a dangerous condition at a specific location. This Court has recognized that the existence of a nuisance depends in large part on its location, and, to date, the actions for nuisance in this jurisdiction have been related to *land*. See, e.g., Wood, 443 A.2d at 1245–46 (dump site on the defendant's property). * * * See also In re Lead Paint Litigation, 924 A.2d at 495 ("[P]ublic nuisance has historically been tied to conduct on one's own land or property as it affects the rights of the general public.").

* * * Professor William L. Prosser, the highly respected authority on the law of torts, remarked that "[i]f 'nuisance' is to have any meaning at all, it is necessary to dismiss a considerable number of cases which have applied the term to matters not connected either with land or with any public right, as mere aberration * * *." Prosser and Keeton on the Law of Torts, § 86 at 618. * Unlike private nuisance, public nuisance does not necessarily involve an interference with a particular *individual's* use and enjoyment of his or her land. In re Lead Paint Litigation, 924 A.2d at 495–96 (citing Restatement (Second) of Torts § 821B, cmt. h). Rather, public nuisance typically arises on a defendant's land and interferes with a public right. For example, a nuisance may originate on a defendant's land as in the case of a mosquito pond, or an activity conducted on a defendant's land may interfere with a right of the general public, as in a stream-polluting business. *

Whether the Presence of Lead Paint Constitutes a Public Nuisance

After thoroughly reviewing the complaint filed by the state in this case, we are of the opinion that the trial justice erred in denying defendants' motion to dismiss. * * * Even considering the allegations of fact as set forth in the complaint, we cannot ascertain allegations in the complaint that support each of these elements. The state's complaint alleges simply that "[d]efendants created an environmental hazard that continues and will continue to unreasonably interfere with the health, safety, peace, comfort or convenience of the residents of the [s]tate, thereby constituting a public nuisance." Absent from the state's complaint is any allegation that defendants have interfered with a public right as that term long has been understood in the law of public nuisance. Equally problematic is the absence of any allegation that defendants had control over the lead pigment at the time it caused harm to children.

* * * A necessary element of public nuisance is an interference with a public right—those indivisible resources shared by the public at large, such as air, water, or public rights of way. The interference must deprive all members of the community of a right to some resource to

which they otherwise are entitled. See Restatement (Second) of Torts § 821B, cmt. g. The Restatement (Second) provides much guidance in ascertaining the fine distinction between a public right and an aggregation of private rights. "Conduct does not become a public nuisance merely because it interferes with the use and enjoyment of land by a large number of persons." *Id.* *

Although the state asserts that the public's right to be free from the hazards of unabated lead had been infringed, this contention falls far short of alleging an interference with a public right as that term traditionally has been understood in the law of public nuisance. The state's allegation that defendants have interfered with the "health, safety, peace, comfort or convenience of the residents of the [s]tate" standing alone does not constitute an allegation of interference with a public right. * The term public right is reserved more appropriately for those indivisible resources shared by the public at large, such as air, water, or public rights of way. * Expanding the definition of public right based on the allegations in the complaint would be antithetical to the common law and would lead to a widespread expansion of public nuisance law that never was intended. * * *

In the words of one commentator:

> Despite the tragic nature of the child's illness, the exposure to lead-based paint usually occurs within the most private and intimate of surroundings, his or her own home. Injuries occurring in this context do not resemble the rights traditionally understood as public rights for public nuisance purposes—obstruction of highways and waterways, or pollution of air or navigable streams.

Gifford, 71 U. Cin. L. Rev. at 818.

The enormous leap that the state urges us to take is wholly inconsistent with the widely recognized principle that the evolution of the common law should occur gradually, predictably, and incrementally. Were we to hold otherwise, we would change the meaning of public right to encompass all behavior that causes a widespread interference with the private rights of numerous individuals. * * *

Even had the state adequately alleged an interference with a right common to the general public, which we conclude it did not, the state's complaint also fails to allege any facts that would support a conclusion that defendants were in control of the lead pigment at the time it harmed Rhode Island's children.

The state filed suit against defendants in their capacity "either as the manufacturer of * * * lead pigment * * * or as the successors in interest to such manufacturers" for "the cumulative presence of lead pigment in paints and coatings in or on buildings throughout the [s]tate of Rhode Island." For the alleged public nuisance to be actionable, the state would have had to assert that defendants not only manufactured the lead pigment but also controlled that pigment at the time it caused injury to children in Rhode Island—and there is no allegation of such control. * * *

The New Jersey Supreme Court, in rejecting the public nuisance claims against lead pigment manufacturers wrote that "[w]e cannot help but agree with the observation that, were we to find a cause of action here, 'nuisance law would become a monster that would devour in one gulp the entire law of tort.' " In re Lead Paint Litigation, 924 A.2d at 505. * * *

For the foregoing reasons, we conclude that the trial justice erred in denying defendants' motion to dismiss.

NOTES

1. *Traditional Public Nuisance.* Traditional examples of public nuisance encompass everything from the obstruction of highways to houses of prostitution or gambling establishments that disturb public morals and decency. During recent decades, public nuisance actions increasingly have been successful against those who pollute. E.g., Philadelphia Elec. Co. v. Hercules, Inc., 762 F.2d 303 (3d Cir.1985); Tadjer v. Montgomery Cnty., 300 Md. 539, 552–53, 479 A.2d 1321, 1327–28 (1984). A more recent trend is the filing of public nuisance actions, usually unsuccessful, against persons whose conduct is alleged to be more broadly detrimental to the public welfare. In addition to the principal case, see People ex rel. Gallo v. Acuna, 14 Cal.4th 1090, 60 Cal.Rptr.2d 277, 929 P.2d 596 (1997) (gang members) and Texas v. American Tobacco Co., 14 F.Supp.2d 956 (E.D.Tex.1997) (tobacco products).

2. *Hazardous Waste (CERCLA).* The Comprehensive Environmental Response, Compensation, and Liability Act (CERCLA), 42 U.S.C. § 9607 (2012) can best be seen as a federal statutory response to the problems traditionally addressed by private and public nuisance law and, indeed, as an extension of nuisance law. CERCLA allows the federal or state government to sue to collect the costs of cleaning up hazardous wastes and damages to natural resources. Unlike most federal environmental statutes, it does not regulate to prevent environmental degradation prospectively. Instead, like tort law, it allows the party that has borne the costs of the environmental harm to collect damages.

The statute imposes a strict liability standard and, indeed, holds liable, among others, "the owner and operator of a vessel or a facility" and "any person who at the time of disposal of any hazardous substance owned or operated any facility at which such hazardous substances were disposed of," even if it cannot be proven that such parties deposited the hazardous substances. Defenses are limited to damages caused *solely* by an act of God, an act of war, or the actions of a third party. How does this standard compare with traditional strict liability? With the requirement often articulated in public nuisance cases that the instrumentality causing the harm must be in the possession or control of the defendant?

D. TRESPASS

Martin v. Reynolds Metals Co.

Supreme Court of Oregon, En Banc, 1959.
221 Or. 86, 342 P.2d 790.

■ O'CONNELL, JUSTICE. This is an action of trespass. The plaintiffs allege that during the period from August 22, 1951 to January 1, 1956 the defendant, in the operation of its aluminum reduction plant near Troutdale, Oregon, caused certain fluoride compounds in the form of gases and particulates to become airborne and settle upon the plaintiff's land rendering it unfit for raising livestock during that period. Plaintiffs allege that their cattle were poisoned by ingesting the fluorides which contaminate the forage and water on their land. They sought damages in the amount of $450,000 for the loss of use of their land for grazing purposes and for the deterioration of the land through the growth of brush, trees and weeds resulting from the lack of use of the premises for grazing purposes. * * * The plaintiffs and the defendant each moved for a directed verdict, whereupon the trial court found that the plaintiffs had suffered damage in the amount of $71,500 in the loss of use of their land and $20,000 for the deterioration of their land and entered judgment accordingly. * * *

In the course of the pleadings the defendant raised the issue as to whether the complaint alleged a cause of action in trespass. The defendant contended that at most a cause of action in nuisance was stated. The trial court accepted the plaintiff's theory of the case. The principal assignments of error rest upon the defendant's contention that the trial court was mistaken in identifying the defendant's invasion of the plaintiffs' land as a trespass; that there was not sufficient evidence to establish a cause of action under any theory, but that if the court should find the evidence sufficient to give rise to liability the defendant's conduct constituted a nuisance and not a trespass.

Through appropriate pleadings the defendant set up the two-year statute of limitations applicable to nontrespassory injuries to land. * If the defendant's conduct created a nuisance and not a trespass the defendant would be liable only for such damage as resulted from its conduct during a period of two years immediately preceding the date upon which plaintiffs' action was instituted. On the other hand, if the defendant's conduct resulted in a trespass upon plaintiff's land the six-year statute of limitations provided for in Or. Rev. Stat. § 12.808 would be applicable and plaintiffs would be entitled to recover damages resulting from the trespasses by defendant during the period from August 22, 1951 to January 1, 1956.

The gist of the defendant's argument is as follows: a trespass arises only when there has been a "breaking and entering upon real property," constituting a direct, as distinguished from a consequential, invasion of the possessor's interest in land; and the settling upon the land of fluoride compounds consisting of gases, fumes and particulates is not sufficient to satisfy these requirements. * * *

There is evidence to prove that during the period from August, 1951, to January, 1956 the emanation of fluorides from defendant's plant averaged approximately 800 pounds daily. Some of this discharge was deposited upon the plaintiff's land. * * * We must determine, however, whether all or only a part of this damage may be shown; all, if the invasion constitutes a trespass, a part only (i.e., the damage which resulted within the two-year period of the statute of limitations) if the invasion was a nuisance and not a trespass.

Trespass and private nuisance are separate fields of tort liability relating to actionable interference with the possession of land. They may be distinguished by comparing the interest invaded; an actionable invasion of a possessor's interest in the exclusive possession of land is a trespass; an actionable invasion of a possessor's interest in the use and enjoyment of his land is a nuisance. *

The same conduct on the part of a defendant may and often does result in the actionable invasion of both of these interests, in which case the choice between the two remedies is, in most cases, a matter of little consequence. Where the action is brought on the theory of nuisance alone the court ordinarily is not called upon to determine whether the conduct would also result in a trespassory invasion. In such cases the courts' treatment of the invasion solely in terms of the law of nuisance does not mean that the same conduct could not also be regarded as a trespass. Some of the cases relied upon by the defendant are of this type; cases in which the court holds that the interference with the plaintiff's possession through soot, dirt, smoke, cinders, ashes and similar substances constitute a nuisance, but where the court does not discuss the applicability of the law of trespass to the same set of facts. *

However, there are cases which have held that the defendant's interference with plaintiff's possession resulting from the settling upon his land of effluents emanating from defendant's operations is exclusively nontrespassory. * Although in such cases the separate particles which collectively cause the invasion are minute, the deposit of each of the particles constitutes a physical intrusion and, but for the size of the particle, would clearly give rise to an action of trespass. The defendant asks us to take account of the difference in size of the physical agency through which the intrusion occurs and relegate entirely to the field of nuisance law certain invasions which do not meet the dimensional test, whatever that is. * * *

Thus it has been held that causing shot from a gun to fall upon the possessor's land is a trespass. * The dropping of particles of molten lead upon the plaintiff's land has been held to be a trespass. * And the defendant was held liable in trespass where spray from a cooling tower on the roof of its theater fell upon the plaintiff's land. * The deposit of soot and carbon from defendant's mill upon plaintiff's land was held to be a trespass in Young v. Fort Frances Pulp and Paper Co., Canada 1919, 17 Ont.Wkly. Notes 6. And liability on the theory of trespass has been recognized where the harm was produced by the vibration of the soil or by the concussion of the air which, of course, is nothing more than the movement of molecules one against the other. * * *

The view recognizing a trespassory invasion where there is no "thing" which can be seen with the naked eye undoubtedly runs counter to the definition of trespass expressed in some quarters. * It is quite possible that in an earlier day when science had not yet peered into the molecular and atomic world of small particles, the courts could not fit an invasion through unseen physical instrumentalities into the requirement that a trespass can result only from a *direct* invasion. But in this atomic age even the uneducated know the great and awful force contained in the atom and what it can do to a man's property if it is released. In fact, the now famous equation $E=mc^2$ has taught us that mass and energy are equivalents and that our concept of "things" must be reframed. If these observations on science in relation to the law of trespass should appear theoretical and unreal in the abstract, they become very practical and real to the possessor of land when the unseen force cracks the foundation of his house. The force is just as real if it is chemical in nature and must be awakened by the intervention of another agency before it does harm.

If, then, we must look to the character of the instrumentality which is used in making an intrusion upon another's land we prefer to emphasize the object's energy or force rather than its size. Viewed in this way we may define trespass as any intrusion which invades the possessor's protected interest in exclusive possession, whether that intrusion is by visible or invisible pieces of matter or by energy which can be measured only by the mathematical language of the physicist.

We are of the opinion, therefore, that the intrusion of the fluoride particulates in the present case constituted a trespass.

The defendant argues that our decision in Amphitheaters, Inc. v. Portland Meadows, 184 Or. 336, 345, 198 P.2d 847, 851 (1948), requires a contrary conclusion. In discussing the distinction between trespass and nuisance the court referred to a difference between "a cannon ball and a ray of light" indicating that the former but not the latter could produce a trespassory invasion. The court also said "The mere suggestion that the casting of light upon the premises of a plaintiff would render a defendant liable without proof of any actual damage, carries its own refutation." * We do not regard this statement as a pronouncement that a trespass can *never* be caused by the intrusion of light rays or other intangible forces; more properly the case may be interpreted as stating that the conduct of the defendant in a particular case may not be actionable if it does not violate a legally protected interest of the plaintiff. The court states that the defendant is not liable *without proof of actual damage*. In that case the plaintiff contended that he had suffered damage in the form of a less efficient cinema screen due to the defendant's lights. In denying recovery the court found that there was no damage, apparently because whatever harm the plaintiff suffered was *damnum absque injuria*.

In every case in which trespass is alleged the court is presented with a problem of deciding whether the defendant's intrusion has violated a legally protected interest of the plaintiff. * * * In some cases the solution can be based upon the ground that the defendant's conduct is not substantial enough to be regarded as a trespassory intrusion. Thus, the casting of a candle beam upon the screen of a drive-in theater would not constitute an actionable invasion, simply because the intrusion is so trifling that the law will not consider it and the principle *de minimis non curat lex* is applicable. In some cases the solution may be arrived at by admitting that the intrusion is substantial but refusing to recognize that plaintiff has a legally protected interest in the particular possessory use as against the particular conduct of the defendant. And so the glare of flood lights upon an adjoining owner's cinema screen, as in the *Amphitheaters* case, may not be a trespass, not because the intrusion is trifling, but because the law does not wish to protect such a use from an invasion, whether the cause of the interference be viewed as a physical intrusion or as a nontrespassory act and covered by the law of nuisance.

The *Amphitheaters* case can be explained in terms of this latter point of view, i.e., that the glare of the defendant's lights could be regarded as an intrusion within the law of trespass, but that the plaintiff had no right to treat the intrusion as actionable in view of the nature of plaintiff's use and the manner in which the defendant interfered with it. Had the defendant purposely, and not as an incidence of his own legitimate use, directed the rays of light against the plaintiff's screen the court might well have taken the position that the plaintiff could have recovered in a trespass action. These illustrations demonstrate that the tort of trespass involves a weighing process, similar to that involved in the law of nuisance, although to a more limited extent than in nuisance and for a different purpose, i.e., in the one case to define the possessor's interest in exclusive possession, and in the other to define the possessor's interest in use and enjoyment.

As stated earlier, normally no inquiry is made in the trespass cases as to whether the plaintiff's interest in making a particular use of his property is within the protection provided for under the law of trespass, because traditionally the interest has been regarded as one clearly entitled to protection in the trespass field. There are adjudicated cases which have refused to find a trespass where the intrusion is clearly established but where the court has felt that the possessor's interest should not be protected. Thus it has been held that the flight of aircraft over the surface of plaintiff's land does not constitute a trespass unless the intrusion interferes with the present enjoyment of property. Hinman v. Pacific Air Transport, 84 F.2d 755 (9th Cir.1936). The same result would seem to follow if the intrusion interfered with the present use of the land but where such use was not entitled to legal protection as against the socially desirable conduct of the defendant. Here it is apparent that the law of trespass and the law of nuisance come very close to merging. This is so because when inquiry is made as to whether the plaintiff's interest falls within the ambit of trespass law the courts look at the interference with the plaintiff's *use and enjoyment* of his land to determine whether his interest in *exclusive possession* should be protected and thus the two torts coalesce.

The *Amphitheaters* case may also be viewed as a pronouncement that a possessor's interest is not invaded by an intrusion which is so trifling that it cannot be recognized by the law. Inasmuch as it is not necessary to prove actual damage in trespass the magnitude of the intrusion ordinarily would not be of any consequence. But there is a point where the entry is so lacking in substance that the law will refuse to recognize it, applying the maxim *de minimis non curat lex*. Thus it would seem clear that ordinarily the casting of a grain of sand upon another's land would not be a trespass. And so too the casting of diffused light rays upon another's land would not ordinarily constitute a trespass. Conceivably such rays could be so concentrated that their entry upon the possessor's land would result in a trespassory invasion. An appropriate illustration is found in Watson v. Mississippi River Power Co., 174 Iowa 23, 32, 156 N.W. 188, 191 (1916) where the court said:

> . . . If, for example, a person interests himself in solar phenomena, and, while experimenting with a powerful sunglass, he accidentally focuses the instrument upon some inflammable material on the lot of his nextdoor [sic] neighbor, starting a blaze which results in injury and loss to the latter, can it be said there was no trespass, no actual invasion of the neighbor's premises?

But where the light is cast upon the plaintiff's premises in a manner which does no actual damage or causes no interference in any way with a legitimate use of the premises then there is no reason for recognizing an invasion of the plaintiff's possessory interest. Here again it is important to point out that the tort of trespass is composed of components which include the character (including the magnitude) of the defendant's conduct in causing an intrusion and the character (including the magnitude) of the harm visited on the plaintiff in interfering with his interest in the exclusive possession of the premises. Consequently the question as to whether a ray of light or any other intrusion is so unsubstantial that it is to be disregarded under the *de minimis* principle cannot be looked at solely from the standpoint of the defendant's conduct, but it must be evaluated with reference to the nature of the plaintiff's interest. * * * Once recognizing that actual damage need not be shown in making out an actionable invasion, the plaintiff's right to insist upon freedom from interference with his possession seems almost limitless.

But there are limits and they can be found, if only vaguely, in the reasons for protecting the possessory interest of the landholder where no actual damage is suffered. * * * The modern law of trespass can be understood only as it is seen against its historical background. Originally all types of trespass, including trespass to land, was [sic] punishable under the criminal law because the trespasser's conduct was regarded as a breach of the peace. When the criminal and civil aspect of trespass were separated, the civil action for trespass was colored by its past, and the idea that the peace of the community was put in danger by the trespasser's conduct influenced the courts' ideas of the character of the tort. Therefore, relief was granted to the plaintiff where he was not actually damaged, partly at least as a means of discouraging disruptive influences in the community * * *. If then, we find that an act on the part of the defendant in interfering with the plaintiff's possession, does, or is likely to result in arousing conflict between them, that act will characterize the tort as a trespass, assuming of course that the other elements of the tort are made out. * * *

Probably the most important factor which describes the nature of the interest protected under the law of trespass is nothing more than a feeling which a possessor has with respect to land which he holds. It is a sense of ownership; a feeling that what one owns or possesses should not be interfered with, and that it is entitled to protection through law. This being the nature of the plaintiff's interest, it is understandable why actual damage is not an essential ingredient in the law of trespass. As pointed out in Fowler V. Harper & Fleming James, Jr., Torts § 1.8 (1956), the rule permitting recovery in spite of the absence of actual damages "is probably justified as a vindicatory right to protect the possessor's proprietary or dignitary interest in his land."

We think that a possessor's interest in land as defined by the considerations recited above may, under the appropriate circumstances, be violated by a ray of light, by an atomic particle, or by a particulate of fluoride and contrariwise, if such interest circumscribed by these considerations is not violated or endangered, the defendant's conduct, even though it may result in a physical intrusion, will not render him liable in an action of trespass. Amphitheaters, Inc. v. Portland Meadows, *supra.*

We hold that the defendant's conduct in causing chemical substances to be deposited upon the plaintiff's land fulfilled all of the requirements under the law of trespass. * * *

It is also urged that the trial court erred in failing to enter a special finding requested by the defendant. The requested finding in effect stated that it was impossible in the operation of an aluminum reduction plant to capture all fluorides which are created in the manufacturing process; that the fume collection system was in operation during the period in question; and that it was the most efficient of the systems known in aluminum reduction plants in the United States.

* * * The complaint alleged that the defendant "carelessly, wantonly and willfully continuously caused to be emitted," from its plant the poisonous compounds. This allegation was denied in the defendant's answer. The issue thus raised, as to the character of defendant's conduct in making the intrusion upon plaintiff's land, would be material only with respect to the claim for punitive damages which * * * was rejected by the trial court. Since we hold that the intrusion in this case constituted a trespass it is immaterial whether the defendant's conduct was careless, wanton and willful or entirely free from fault. Therefore, the refusal to enter the requested finding is not error.

The judgment of the lower court is affirmed.

NOTES

1. *Trespass to Land.* We encourage you to review the basic requirements of liability for trespass to land presented earlier at page 52, Note 1.

2. *Contrasting Decisions.* With *Martin*, compare Johnson v. Paynesville Farmers Union Coop. Oil Co., 817 N.W.2d 693 (Minn.2013), holding that when defendant applied pesticides to his fields, which subsequently drifted onto the plaintiff's organic crops, the defendant was potentially liable only for nuisance and not for trespass:

> ... [T]respass claims address tangible invasions of the right to exclusive possession of land, and nuisance claims address invasions of the right to use and enjoyment of land. The Johnsons do not allege that a tangible object invaded their land. The Johnsons' claim is that the Cooperative's actions have prevented them from *using* their land as an organic farm, not that any action of the Cooperative has prevented the Johnsons from possessing any part of their land. The Johnsons' claim is one for nuisance, not trespass.

Id. at 705. Compare also Babb v. Lee Cnty. Landfill SC, LLC, 405 S.C. 129, 146, 747 S.E.2d 468, 477 (2013) ("The traditional common law rule, the dimensional test, provides that a trespass only exists where the invasion of land occurs through a physical tangible object.... Under that rule, intangible matter or energy, such as smoke, noise, light, and vibration are insufficient to constitute a trespass."). See also *supra* pages 80–81, Note 1.

E. ANIMALS

Behrens v. Bertram Mills Circus Ltd.

Queen's Bench Division, 1957.
2 Q.B. 1.

[Plaintiffs operated a funfair concession between defendant's circus ring and the elephant house. Plaintiffs' manager and ticket seller brought his daughter to the funfair; she brought her small dog Simba. As the elephant procession passed the ticket booth, Simba got loose and ran out barking and snapping, frightening the elephants. One, Bullu, trumpeted in panic. Simba ran into plaintiff's booth. Bullu followed, knocking down the front of the booth, which caused physical injury and shock to plaintiffs. Simba was killed.]

■ DEVLIN, J. read the following judgment: * * * [P]laintiffs rely upon * * * breach of the absolute duty laid upon the keeper of a dangerous animal to confine and control it * * *. A person who keeps an animal with knowledge (*scienter retinuit*) of its tendency to do harm is strictly liable for damage it does if it escapes; he is under an absolute duty to confine or control it so that it shall not do injury to others. All animals *ferae naturae*, that is, all animals which are not by nature harmless, such as a rabbit, or have not been tamed by man and domesticated, such as a horse, are conclusively presumed to have such a tendency, so that the scienter need not in their case be proved. All animals in the second class *mansuetae naturae* are conclusively presumed to be harmless until they have manifested a savage or vicious propensity; proof of such a manifestation is proof of scienter and serves to transfer the animal, so to speak, out of its natural class into the class of *ferae naturae*. * * * No doubt in its time [this "primitive rule"] was a great improvement on the still more primitive notion that only the animal was "liable" for the harm it did. But now this sort of doctrine with all its rigidity—its conclusive presumptions and categorisations—is outmoded * * *.

The particular rigidity in the scienter action which is involved in this case—there are many others which are not—is the rule that requires the harmfulness of the offending animal to be judged not by reference to its particular training and habits, but by reference to the general habits of the species to which it belongs. The law ignores the world of difference between the wild elephant in the jungle and the trained elephant in the circus. The elephant Bullu is in fact no more dangerous than a cow; she reacted in the same way as a cow would do to the irritation of a small dog; if perhaps her bulk made her capable of doing more damage, her higher training enabled her to be more swiftly checked. But I am compelled to assess the defendants' liability in this case in just the same way as I would assess it if they had loosed a wild elephant into the funfair. This is a branch of the law, which * * * has been settled by authority rather than by reason. * * *

NOTES

1. *Scope of Risk.* Suppose that the defendant keeps a rattlesnake in a secure cage in his backyard. The rattlesnake escapes when the cage is

destroyed by a tornado of unprecedented ferocity, the likes of which no one could have predicted. An hour or two later, a three-year-old toddler, playing in the cul-de-sac adjoining defendant's property, trips over the rattlesnake and breaks his arm. Will the parents of the toddler be able to recover from the defendant on a strict liability basis? See Restatement (Third) of Torts: Liability for Physical and Emotional Harm § 22 cmt. f (2010).

2. *Domestic Animals.* Personal injuries caused by the bites of dogs or other animals often are covered by statutes that frequently impose strict liability, even for domestic animals. Why would legislatures be inclined to impose strict liability in this area?

3. *Known Vicious Tendencies.* Restatement (Third) of Torts: Liability for Physical and Emotional Harm § 23 (2010) states that the owner or possessor of an animal will be held strictly liable if she "knows or has reason to know" that her animal has "dangerous tendencies abnormal" for a domestic animal. However, this provision is not a codification of the old adage that "every dog is entitled to one free bite." For example, the owner of a large dog that routinely greets guests by jumping on them may be held strictly liable when the dog bites someone. How does liability under this standard differ from liability for negligence?

What about subspecies and varieties of animals known to be particularly dangerous, including, arguably, pit bulls? According to the Restatement, "[p]it bulls * * * may be somewhat more likely to attack persons than are other breeds; when a pit bull does attack a person, the attack is likely to be ferocious." *Id.* at cmt. e. A majority of courts have not (at least at the time of this writing) applied strict liability to owners of pit bulls. *Id.*; but see Tracey v. Soleksy, 427 Md. 627, 636, 50 A.3d 1075, 1079 (2012) (imposing a strict liability standard on both tenants owning, harboring, or controlling pit bulls and their landlords if the landlords "have knowledge of the presence of a pit bull * * * or should have had such knowledge"), *superseded by statute*, Md. Code Ann. Cts. & Jud. Proc. § 3–1901 (2014) ("the common law liability relating to attacks by dogs against humans that existed on April 1, 2012, is retained * * * without regard to the breed or heritage of the dog"). What policies might lie behind the court's imposition of liability on landlords?

Remember that even if the requirements for imposing strict liability are not present, the owner or possessor of the domesticated animal may still be held liable for negligence.

4. *Damage to Property.* The traditional common law held that owners of domestic animals, including cattle, were strictly liable for their trespasses on the land of others. In what ways are the justifications for this rule evident in the reasoning of *Rylands v. Fletcher?*

This rule of strict liability no longer applies in some western states of the United States. Why? What would the implications of a strict liability rule have been for large-scale cattle ranching? See Harper, James and Gray on Torts § 14.9.

F. VICARIOUS LIABILITY

Sword v. NKC Hospitals, Inc.

Supreme Court of Indiana, 1999.
714 N.E.2d 142.

■ SELBY, J. * * * Diana Sword lives in southern Indiana. On April 24, 1991, Diana Sword and her husband entered Norton [Norton Children's Hospital, the defendant] in Louisville, Kentucky for the delivery of their first child. * * * Sword * * * made arrangements to go to Norton through her obstetrician's office. Norton aggressively marketed its services to the public. It stated in brochures that its Women's Pavilion is "the most technically sophisticated birthplace in the region." * Norton also advertised that it offers:

> [I]nstant access to the specialized equipment and facilities, as well as to physician specialists in every area of pediatric medicine and surgery. Every maternity patient has a private room *and the full availability of a special anesthesiology team, experienced and dedicated exclusively to OB patients.*

One brochure stated that:

> The Women's Pavilion medical staff includes the only physicians in the region who specialize exclusively in obstetrical anesthesiology. They are immediately available within the unit 24 hours a day *and are experts in administering continuous epidural anesthesia.*

At some point during her labor, an anesthesiologist came into Sword's room. He explained the epidural procedure and how it would make her feel. * * * As the anesthesiologist was preparing to begin the procedure, he was called out of the room. Five to ten minutes later, a second anesthesiologist, Dr. Luna, came into Sword's room to administer the epidural. The parties do not dispute that Dr. Luna practiced medicine at Norton as an independent contractor. After verifying that the previous anesthesiologist had explained the procedure to Sword, Dr. Luna began the epidural procedure. As Sword sat on the bed and leaned forward, Dr. Luna began inserting the epidural tubing. Dr. Luna first inserted the tubing near the top of Sword's neck. Shortly thereafter, Dr. Luna removed the epidural tubing "because it did not take" and then reinserted it in Sword's lower back. *

Soon after the delivery of her healthy baby, Sword began to have headaches which recur every four to six weeks. When the headaches occur, Sword is very sensitive to light and sound. In addition to the headaches, she also feels a numbness in her back where the second epidural was administered. Sword alleges that these symptoms are a result of Dr. Luna's negligent placement of the epidural tubing and that Norton is liable. * * *

The principal issue in this case is whether, under Indiana law, Norton can be held liable for the alleged negligence of an independent contractor anesthesiologist. Sword is seeking to hold Norton liable for the alleged negligence which caused her injuries. There are no allegations of direct corporate negligence, that is, that the hospital itself was negligent. Because the alleged negligence was not committed by

Norton, but instead by a physician working at Norton, Sword must present a theory by which a court can find the hospital vicariously liable for the actions of a physician who practices there. * * *

Vicarious liability is "indirect legal responsibility." * It is a legal fiction by which a court can hold a party legally responsible for the negligence of another, not because the party did anything wrong but rather because of the party's relationship to the wrongdoer. * * *

Respondeat superior is the applicable tort theory of vicarious liability. Under *respondeat superior*, an employer, who is not liable because of his own acts, can be held liable "for the wrongful acts of his employee which are committed within the scope of employment." * In this context, "employer" and "employee" are often stated in broader terms as "master" and "servant." *

One important aspect in applying *respondeat superior* is differentiating between those who are servants and those who are independent contractors. A servant is defined in the following general manner: one who is employed by a master to perform personal services and whose physical conduct is subject to the right to control by the master. * It is the employer's right to control that generally separates a servant from an independent contractor. * An independent contractor can, therefore, be defined as "a person who contracts with another to do something for him but who is not controlled by the other nor subject to the other's right to control with respect to his physical conduct in the performance of the undertaking." *

It is important to distinguish between servants and independent contractors in the tort context * because, while a master can be held liable for a servant's negligent conduct under *respondeat superior*, a master generally cannot be held liable for the negligence of an independent contractor. * The theory behind non-liability for independent contractors is that it would be unfair to hold a master liable for the conduct of another when the master has no control over that conduct. See Restatement (Second) of Torts § 409 cmt. b. *

Apparent agency is a doctrine based in agency law. It is most often associated with contracts and the ability of an agent with "apparent authority" to bind the principal to a contract with a third party. * Apparent authority "is the authority that a third person reasonably believes an agent to possess because of some manifestation from his principal." * The manifestation must be made by the principal to a third party and reasonably cause the third party to believe that an individual is an agent of the principal and to act upon that belief. * The manifestations can originate from direct or indirect communication. * They can also originate from advertisements to the community. *

In certain instances, apparent or ostensible agency also can be a means by which to establish vicarious liability. * * * One enunciation of this doctrine is set forth in the Restatement (Second) of Agency § 267, which provides that:

> *One who represents that another is his servant or other agent and thereby causes a third person justifiably to rely upon the care or skill of such apparent agent* is subject to liability to the third person for harm caused by the lack of care or skill of the one appearing to be a servant or other agent as if he were such.

[hereinafter "Section 267"]. Under a Section 267 analysis, if, because of the principal's manifestations, a third party reasonably believes that in dealing with the apparent agent he is dealing with the principal's servant or agent and exposes himself to the negligent conduct because of the principal's manifestations, then the principal may be held liable for that negligent conduct. * * *

In the area of hospital liability, there has been an ongoing movement by courts to use apparent or ostensible agency as a means by which to hold hospitals vicariously liable for the negligence of some independent contractor physicians. * Many of these cases employ the doctrine of apparent agency when the plaintiff was negligently injured by a physician's actions while visiting the hospital's emergency room. * Courts, however, also have employed the doctrine of apparent agency to hold a hospital liable for assertedly negligent acts committed in non-emergency room settings, including negligent acts committed by anesthesiologists. * * * While the language employed by these courts sometimes varies, generally they have employed tests which focus primarily on two basic factors. The first factor focuses on the hospital's manifestations and is sometimes described as an inquiry whether the hospital "acted in a manner which would lead a reasonable person to conclude that the individual who was alleged to be negligent was an employee or agent of the hospital." Kashishian v. Port, 167 Wis.2d 24, 39, 481 N.W.2d 277, 284–85 (1992). * Courts considering this factor often ask whether the hospital "held itself out" to the public as a provider of hospital care, for example, by mounting extensive advertising campaigns. * In this regard, the hospital need not make express representations to the patient that the treating physician is an employee of the hospital; rather a representation also may be general and implied. See, e.g., * Pamperin v. Trinity Mem'l Hosp., 144 Wis.2d 188, 423 N.W.2d 848, 856 (1988) (presuming that the hospital held itself out as a medical care provider unless the hospital expressly provided notice to the patient that independent contractors provide the care).

The second factor focuses on the patient's reliance. It is sometimes characterized as an inquiry as to whether "the plaintiff acted in reliance upon the conduct of the hospital or its agent, consistent with ordinary care and prudence." Kashishian, 167 Wis.2d 24, 39–40, 481 N.W.2d at 285. * Courts considering this factor sometimes ask whether, because of the hospital's manifestations, the plaintiff believed that the hospital was providing the pertinent medical care as opposed to simply acting as a situs for the physician to provide health care as an independent contractor. * Other courts, however, seem to employ a less subjective form of reliance or even to presume reliance absent any evidence that the patient knew or should have known that the physician was not an employee of the hospital and that it is the physician and not the hospital who is responsible for his medical care. * An example of a situation where a patient might be in a position to know that the physician was an independent contractor may exist if the patient establishes an independent relationship with the physician or selects a particular physician in advance of going to the hospital. * Even in such circumstances, however, the courts have reasoned that the patient may not have had reason to know of the contractual arrangements between the physician and the hospital. *

Central to both of these factors—that is, the hospital's manifestations and the patient's reliance—is the question of whether the hospital provided notice to the patient that the treating physician was an independent contractor and not an employee of the hospital. *

In the present case, Sword argues that, under the doctrine of apparent or ostensible agency, Norton is vicariously liable for the actions of its apparent agent Dr. Luna, whom the parties agree was an independent contractor. The Court of Appeals held that Dr. Luna could be an apparent agent of Norton, and that there were genuine issues of material fact in dispute on this question. * * * We agree with the conclusion of the Court of Appeals and now, in the specific context of a hospital setting, expressly adopt the formulation of apparent or ostensible agency set forth in the Restatement (Second) of Tort [sic] section 429.

Under Section 429, as we read and construe it, a trier of fact must focus on the reasonableness of the patient's belief that the hospital or its employees were rendering health care. This ultimate determination is made by considering the totality of the circumstances, including the actions or inactions of the hospital, as well as any special knowledge the patient may have about the hospital's arrangements with its physicians. We conclude that a hospital will be deemed to have held itself out as the provider of care unless it gives notice to the patient that it is not the provider of care and that the care is provided by a physician who is an independent contractor and not subject to the control and supervision of the hospital. A hospital generally will be able to avoid liability by providing meaningful written notice to the patient, acknowledged at the time of admission. See Cantrell v. Northeast Georgia Med. Ctr., 235 Ga.App. 365, 508 S.E.2d 716, 719–20 (1998) (concluding that hospital did not hold physician out as its employee as evidenced by conspicuous signs posted in hospital's registration area and express language in the patient consent to treatment form); Valdez v. Pasadena Healthcare Management, Inc., 975 S.W.2d 43, 48 (Tex.App.1998) (finding written notice, signed by the patient, that physician served as an independent contractor was sufficient to release hospital from liability for physician's medical malpractice). Under some circumstances, such as in the case of a medical emergency, however, written notice may not suffice if the patient had an inadequate opportunity to make an informed choice.

As to the meaning and importance of reliance in this specific context, we agree with the cases that hold that if the hospital has failed to give meaningful notice, if the patient has no special knowledge regarding the arrangement the hospital has made with its physicians, and if there is no reason that the patient should have known of these employment relationships, then reliance is presumed. *

Applying this test here, we conclude that there are genuine material issues of fact in dispute as to whether Dr. Luna was an apparent or ostensible agent of Norton and whether Norton may be held liable for any of Dr. Luna's asserted negligent acts. First, there is nothing in this record which indicates that the hospital did anything to put plaintiff on notice that it was her physician, an independent contractor, who was responsible for her medical care and not the hospital. * Second, this is clearly not a case where plaintiff selected her own anesthesiologist prior to admission, for she specifically testified that she did not know who would administer the epidural until just before the procedure, and if she had any special knowledge of the hospital's employment arrangement with Dr. Luna or with the hospital's general employment practices with respect to physicians, it is not apparent on this record. Finally, Norton held itself out, through an extensive advertising campaign, as a full-service hospital which specializes in obstetric care. * * *

Based on this record and under Section 429 as we construe it today, there are clearly genuine issues of material fact as to whether Dr. Luna is an apparent agent of Norton. The trial court erred when it entered summary judgment for defendant on this issue. * * *

Taber v. Maine

United States Court of Appeals for the Second Circuit, 1995.
67 F.3d 1029.

■ CALABRESI, CIRCUIT JUDGE * * * The facts are simple enough and not disputed. On the morning of April 13, 1985, Robert S. Maine, ("Maine") a Navy serviceman on active duty at the U.S. Naval Ship Repair Facility on the island of Guam, went on liberty after having completed a grueling 24 hour duty shift. While on liberty he was free to leave the base as he pleased and travel up to 50 miles away. He could also be recalled for duty at any time.

Maine decided to have a good time. By noon, he was relaxing at an on-base beach party and drinking beer with Navy friends. Later that afternoon, he purchased two six-packs of beer at the base PX with his Navy comrade, Karin Conville ("Conville"), and returned with her to his barracks to drink several more cans. At dinnertime, Maine accompanied friends to the enlisted men's club, where he consumed two cocktails with his meal. After dinner, he attended a barracks party in the room of a superior officer, with several other superior officers present. There, Maine drank three or four more beers and—when he left to return to his own barracks at about 11:00 p.m.—Conville and another Navy comrade named Jean Buquet noticed that he seemed to be drunk. At around 11:30 p.m., Maine had difficulty sleeping and decided to drive off base to get something to eat. Feeling tired, he aborted his snack mission and tried to return to base. On the way back, he caused the accident that injured Scott A. Taber ("Taber").

Taber was an enlisted Seabee—a construction worker in the United States Navy—and was stationed at Camp Covington, Guam. At 6:00 p.m. on Friday, April 12th, he too went on liberty. * * * Shortly before midnight, [Taber's civilian friend, Estelita] Stills and Taber left for Stills's house and their weekend of rest and recreation. As fate would have it, they never got there. While they were driving on the public roadway toward Stills's house, Maine crashed into them, injuring Taber severely.

Two years later, Taber started this action for damages under the Federal Tort Claims Act ("FTCA"), 28 U.S.C. §§ 1346(b), 2671, in the United States District Court for the Western District of New York. * * * Naming both Maine and the United States Government as defendants, Taber complained that he was injured as a result of Maine's negligent driving and that, because Maine was acting within the scope of his Naval employment when he caused the accident, the government was liable on a theory of *respondeat superior*. The government moved for summary judgment on the grounds that, as a matter of law, Maine's conduct fell outside the scope of his military service and that, therefore, the government was not liable for Taber's injuries. * * * Judge Larimer granted summary judgment to the government because "Maine's drunk driving incident on April 13, 1985, was not in the line of duty and therefore the United States is not liable under the doctrine of *respondeat superior*." * * * The action proceeded against Maine, however. After a bench trial in which Maine appeared pro se, the district court found Maine liable for negligence and assessed Taber's damages at $300,000. A final judgment was entered and Taber appealed. * * *

The FTCA allows civil actions against the government based on the negligent acts or omissions of its employees, * including those of members of the Armed Services who are acting "in the line of duty." * The courts have uniformly equated the FTCA's "line of duty" language with the phrase "scope of employment," as that concept is defined by the *respondeat superior* law of the jurisdiction in which the accident occurred. * Because the accident in this case happened in Guam, we must follow Guam's law of *respondeat superior*. Since the law of Guam is anything but certain, however, that is easier said than done.

Where the law of Guam is unclear, the Ninth Circuit, serving as Guam's highest appellate court, * has instructed courts to look to California law for guidance. * * * It seems clear to us that California law (and by implication the law of Guam) would hold the government vicariously liable for Maine's actions. California was one of the first states in the nation to adopt an expansive reading of the *respondeat superior* doctrine. As early as 1961, commentators noted that California had taken the lead in equating the scope of *respondeat superior* liability to the traditionally broader coverage mandated by workers' compensation statutes. Thus, California employers were subject to liability for injuries to third parties caused by the behavior of their employees whenever the employees' acts "arose out of or in the course of" their employment relationship. See Guido Calabresi, Some Thoughts on Risk Distribution and the Law of Torts, 70 Yale L.J. 499, 545 (1961).

This approach to *respondeat superior* is * * * evident in numerous California cases * * *. For example, in Rodgers v. Kemper Construction Co., 50 Cal. App. 3d 608, 124 Cal. Rptr. 143 (1975), a subcontractor was held vicariously liable for an assault committed by two of its employees who had lounged around drinking for several hours in what was, ironically, called the "dry house" (a rest area/locker room located on the job site). On a Friday night after their work shift had ended, the employees, though free to go home, stayed in the dry house and got drunk. Later they went outside and got in a fight with the plaintiffs. * In finding *respondeat superior* liability, the court stated that "the inquiry should be whether the risk was one 'that may be fairly regarded as typical of or broadly incidental' to the enterprise undertaken by the employer." * * * The court further noted that under California law,

> where social or recreational pursuits on the employer's
> premises after hours are endorsed by the express or implied

permission of the employer and are "conceivably" of some benefit to the employer or, even in the absence of proof of benefit, if such activities have become "a customary incident of the employment relationship," an employee engaged in such pursuits after hours is still acting within the scope of his employment.

* * * In *Rodgers*, the subcontractor "customarily permitted employees to remain on the premises in or about the dry house long after their work shift had ended" and it was also "customary, particularly on Friday evenings, for employees to sit around the dry house after their work shift and talk and drink beer, often . . . joined by their supervisors." * Because it "was neither unusual nor unreasonable" for the assailants to be on the job site drinking before the assault, and because such drinking in the dry house "was a customary incident of the employment relationship," the court ruled that their related tortious actions fell within the scope of their employment. * * * Similarly, in Childers v. Shasta Livestock Auction Yard, Inc., 190 Cal.App. 3d 792, 235 Cal.Rptr. 641 (1987), * * * [t]he court * * * explicitly linked the scope of liability under *respondeat superior* to that which would make an employer liable to an employee under the workers' compensation laws. *Id.* at 801, 235 Cal.Rptr. at 644. Consistently with these cases, the Ninth Circuit has, itself, read California's law of *respondeat superior* broadly. * * *

The district court below tried to distinguish these authorities on the ground that the drinking in *Rodgers* and *Childers* took place at the work site while Maine's supposedly did not. We disagree. The drinking in both *Rodgers* and *Childers* occurred at work-site rest areas (the "dry house" and the business office, respectively)—not on the assembly line. Similarly, although Maine did not drink while working at the Naval Ship Repair Facility, he drank at an on-base beach party, at the enlisted men's club, and in the barracks—all of which were located on his base. These places were as much on-site rest areas as the ones involved in both *Rodgers* and *Childers*.

The government understandably seeks to rely on an older conception of *respondeat superior*. This view of the doctrine required a close link between the acts of the "agent" and "profit" accruing to the master before vicarious liability attaches to the latter. See Restatement (Second) of Agency § 228 (1984). But today this position is in hasty retreat, if not rout. Thus *Rodgers* and *Childers* held that the employer-benefit requirement is met whenever broad potential effects on morale and customer relations exist, or where the employer has implicitly permitted or endorsed the recreational practices that led to the harm. * * *

Of course drinking by servicemembers can be viewed as important to military morale, just as drinking was apparently instrumental to good employee morale and customer relations in *Rodgers* and *Childers*. Hence, "employer-benefit" can be adduced in all these cases. But in the end, "employer-benefit" is significant only because it is one way of showing that the harm that drinking causes can properly be considered a cost of the employer's enterprise.

California courts have said that the doctrine of *respondeat superior* is "*concerned with the allocation of the cost of industrial injury.*" Childers, 190 Cal. App. 3d at 801, 235 Cal. Rptr. at 644 (emphasis added). The issue is simply whether the employee's "conduct is not so unusual or startling that it would seem unfair to include the loss resulting from it *among other costs* of the employer's business." Rodgers, 50 Cal. App. 3d at 619, 124 Cal. Rptr. at 149 (emphasis added). * * * Here, it is undisputed that drinking on base during off-duty hours was a commonplace, if not an officially condoned activity. It certainly was a customary incident of Maine's employment relationship with the Navy, as that element is described in *Rodgers*. * And in the context of the military mission, an occasional drunken service member who leaves government premises and causes damage is a completely foreseeable event, in the sense that it is a reasonably obvious risk of the general enterprise. As such, we do not think that it would be either "unfair" or the slightest bit unreasonable to impose that cost on the government. * To the contrary, given the pervasive control that the military exercises over its personnel while they are on a base, it is totally in keeping with the doctrine of *respondeat superior* to allocate the costs of base operations to the government. * * *4

As the leading Torts treatise has put it, "the integrating principle" of *respondeat superior* is "that the employer should be liable for those faults that may be fairly regarded as risks of his business, whether they are committed in furthering it or not." F. Harper, F. James & O. Gray, The Law of Torts § 26.8 (2d ed. 1986) * * *. Judge Friendly made the same point most elegantly in [Ira S.] *Bushey* & Sons, Inc. v. United States], "The proclivity of seamen to find solicitude by copious resort to the bottle," he wrote, "has been noted in opinions too numerous to warrant citation. Once all this is granted, it is immaterial that [the coastguardsman's] precise action was not to be foreseen." 398 F.2d at 172. After all, the government "cannot justly disclaim responsibility for accidents which may fairly be said to be characteristic of its activities." *

We believe the law of Guam reaches the same conclusion. Accordingly, we hold that the government is vicariously liable for Maine's conduct. * * *

NOTES

1. *Federal Tort Claims Act.* The Federal Tort Claims Act grants federal district courts exclusive jurisdiction to hear claims against the United States under the Act. 28 U.S.C. § 1346(b) (2012). Before filing suit, a claimant must file an administrative claim with the agency concerned within two years after the claim accrues. § 2401(b). Trial is without a jury. §§ 1346(b), 2402. Punitive damages are prohibited, § 2674, and attorneys' fees are limited. § 2678. See Soldano v. United States, *infra* pages 524–29.

---

4   We make no pronouncement on drunkenness in general. Our point here is simply that drinking on base during off-duty hours was a customary incident of Maine's employment relationship with the Navy. This "on-base" drinking included an on-base beach party, cocktails at the enlisted personnel club, and drinking at a barracks party in the room of a superior officer, all on the day of the off-base accident. It is these on-base activities that bring this case within the ambit of *Rodgers* and *Childers*, and therefore impose *respondeat superior* liability on the government. We find instructive the example offered by Judge Friendly, albeit in an admiralty context in *Bushey*, indicating that employer liability would not be imposed for an off-base tort resulting from drinking at an off-base bar. Like Judge Friendly, we would not deem such an activity incident to the employment relationship. See Ira S. Bushey & Sons, Inc. v. United States, 398 F.2d 167, 172 (2d Cir.1968).

2.   *Justifications for Strict Vicarious Liability.* Why should the employer be strictly liable under the doctrine of vicarious liability? Justice Holmes, no fan of the doctrine, explained it as a

> * * * survival from ancient times of doctrines which in their earlier form embodied certain rights and liabilities of heads of families based on substantive grounds which have disappeared long since, and that in modern days these doctrines have been generalized into a fiction, which, although nothing in the world but a form of words, has reacted upon the law and has tended to carry its anomalies still farther. That fiction is, of course, that, within the scope of the agency, principal and agent are one.

Oliver W. Holmes, Agency, 4 Harv. L. Rev. 345, 345 (1891).

In writing about vicarious liability in 1916, Thomas Baty opined: "In hard fact, the real reason for employers' liability is * * * [that] the damages are taken from a deep pocket." Thomas Baty, Vicarious Liability 154 (1916). Seven years later, Young B. Smith, subsequently Dean of the Columbia Law School, explained vicarious liability as follows:

> Why, then, should the master be responsible?

> A reason which occurs to the writer is that which has been offered in justification of workmen's compensation statutes. In substance it is the belief that it is socially more expedient to spread or distribute among a large group of the community the losses which experience has taught are inevitable in the carrying on of industry, than to cast the loss upon a few.[34]

Young B. Smith, Frolic and Detour, 23 Colum. L. Rev. 444, 456 (1923). See also Excerpt, Guido Calabresi, Some Thoughts on Risk Distribution and the Law of Torts, 70 Yale L.J. 499, 499–500, 517–18, 543–45 (1961), reprinted *infra* at 120–22.

While these scholars explained strict vicarious liability largely on *loss distribution* grounds, Warren Seavey, an authority on the law of agency, justified it on grounds of *loss minimization*:

> Perhaps the strongest reason which can be given for the imposition of "absolute" liability applies even more strongly in the case of vicarious liability, that is, the fact that one who is responsible for all consequences is more apt to take precautions to prevent injurious consequences from arising. If the law requires a

---

[34]   The justification of this policy is that the loss to wage-earners resulting from the accidents of industry should be regarded as an expense of production which the employer should bear as he bears the other expenses of production and which, since the burden falls on all employers alike, he will be able normally to recover in the somewhat high prices he will obtain for his goods.

H[enry] Seager, Principles of Economics 601 (1918).

> To the economist, the necessity of such legislation is abundantly evident. It is simply that the needs of the modern state require that the burden of loss of life, or personal injury in industry, shall be charged to the expenses of production, shall be borne, that is to say, by the employer. He knows well enough that eventually the cost will be paid by the community in the form of increased prices, but that is something it is not unwilling to pay.

[Harold] Laski, The Basis of Vicarious Liability, 26 Yale L.J. 105, 126 (1916).

[Next, the note sets forth the justifications for strict employer liability included in the excerpts of the Report of the Wainwright Commission quoted in the *Ives* opinion, *supra*, pages 4–5.]

perfect score in result, the actor is more likely to strive for that than if the law requires only the ordinary precautions to be taken; the cases where, either *de jure* or *de facto*, an actor is made absolutely liable for consequences indicate that this reason plays a very large part. * * *

[R]espondent superior results in greater care in the selection and instruction of servants than would be used otherwise. * * * Because of this financial liability, it appears safe to assume that an employer can and does bring a pressure to bear upon his employees which has a greater effect upon them than would the chance of their being made defendants in suits, which, if action were permitted only against them, ordinarily would not be brought. The pressure upon the employee is thus twofold. * * * The history of the * * * Workmen's Compensation Acts, showing a decreasing mortality in an increasingly dangerous environment, indicates that the proper place to apply pressure is on the employer.

Warren Seavey, Speculations as to "Respondeat Superior," Harvard Legal Essays, 447–49 (1934). See also Richard A. Posner, A Theory of Negligence, 1 J. Legal Stud. 29, 42–43 (1972).

3. *"Frolic and Detour."* "The master is only liable where the servant is acting in the course of his employment. If he was going out of his way, against his master's implied commands, when driving on his master's business, he will make his master liable; but if he was going on a frolic of his own, without being at all on his master's business, the master will not be liable." Joel v. Morison, 6 Car. & P. 501, 503, 172 E. R. 1338, 1339 (1834). The distinction is not always easy. For example, in Bejma v. Dental Dev. & Mfg Co., 356 F.2d 227 (6th Cir.1966), a traveling salesman used his own automobile and was reimbursed for mileage, including authorized weekend trips home. He caused a traffic accident while driving home, but in the wrong direction and drunk, for the Labor Day weekend. The employer was held vicariously liable. Compare Keppel Bus Co. v. Sa'ad bin Ahmad [1974] 2 All E.R. 700 (Privy Council) where the employer was held not liable for a Singapore bus driver's physical attack, while collecting fares, on a seated passenger who had previously remonstrated with him concerning the conductor's rudeness to elderly lady. The court held that the conductor was not within the scope of his employment, reasoning that he was not carrying out his duty of maintaining order because there was at the time of his attack no disorder on the bus.

Consider also the question of whether the employee's conduct must have furthered the interests of the employer or whether, as Judge Calabresi concludes, vicarious liability is warranted whenever the injury results from risks that may fairly be regarded as being characteristic of the employer's business. See West v. Waymire, 114 F.3d 646, 649 (7th Cir.1997) (per Posner, C.J.: "[W]hen the employee is a male police officer whose employer has invested him with intimidating authority to deal in private with troubled teen-aged girls, his taking advantage of the opportunity that authority and proximity and privacy give him to extract sexual favors from these girls should be sufficiently within the orbit of his employer-conferred powers to bring the doctrine of *respondeat superior* into play, * * * even though he is not acting to further the employer's goals but instead is on a frolic of his own. We want the police department to supervise its officers in this domain with especial care, and so we do not impose on the plaintiffs the burden of establishing negligent supervision"). Compare Andrews v. United States, 732 F.2d 366 (4th Cir.1984) (where government physician's assistant who persuaded patient that sexual relations were part of the treatment did not believe so himself, the assistant's acts were deemed not done to further his master's business, and therefore not within scope of employment; government nevertheless subject to liability for physician's negligent failure to supervise the treatment properly); Lisa M. v. Henry Mayo Newhall Mem. Hosp., 12 Cal.4th 291, 48 Cal.Rptr.2d 510, 907 P.2d 358 (1995) (hospital not liable for employee's sexual battery on patient after conducting ultrasound examination, on ground that culprit's motivation did not result from the employment). See generally Patrick Atiyah, Vicarious Liability in the Law of Torts (1967).

Excerpt, Guido Calabresi, Some Thoughts on Risk Distribution and the Law of Torts
70 Yale L.J. 499, 499–500, 517–18, 543–45 (1961).

* * * [W]hile many people have talked about "risk distribution," and some have even used it as a basis for proposed modifications in the law of torts, * few have in recent years attempted to examine in any depth just what it is they are striving for when they say "distribute losses." * They could mean one of three things. Do they wish as broad a spreading of all losses, both interpersonally and intertemporally, as is possible? Or do they want the burden of losses to be borne by those classes of people "most able" to pay? Or do they seek something entirely different—that those "enterprises" which give rise to a loss "should" bear the burden, whether or not this accomplishes the prior two aims? The answer, I suppose, is that sometimes they mean each of these things, and at other times all of them. Unfortunately, these goals are not always consistent with each other. They are, moreover, supported by quite different ethical and economic postulates. * * *

The justification for allocation of losses on a non-fault basis which is found most often among legal writers is that if losses are broadly spread—among people and over time—they are least harmful. * * *

The advantages of interpersonal loss spreading would probably be stated in terms of two propositions; (a) that taking a large sum of money from one person is more likely to result in economic dislocation, and therefore in secondary or avoidable losses, than taking a series of small sums from many people, * and (b) that even if the total economic dislocation is the same, many small losses are preferable to one large one, simply because people feel they suffer less if 10,000 of them lost $1 than if one loses $10,000.

While the first of these propositions is an empirical generalization not too difficult to accept, the second is in its precise terms a variant of the economist's theory of the diminishing marginal utility of money. This theory has been in substantial disfavor among modern economists. The reason for this disfavor is illustrated by recent studies which have indicated, for example, that a loss of a relatively small amount of money, if it results in a change in social status, may be nearly as significant to an individual as a much larger loss which causes an approximately equal change in his social position. On the other hand, a relatively small loss, if it can be borne without giving up certain symbols of social status—be they the house on the right street or the television set—feels infinitely smaller to people than an only slightly larger loss which does involve a change in status. * While this indicates the weaknesses of such a strict utilitarian pain-pleasure analysis as the marginal utility of money theory, with its implication that a loss of $5 divided among five people necessarily hurts less than $5 on one person, it does not detract much from the basic justification for loss spreading. We need merely take an additional step and recognize that social dislocations, like economic dislocations, will occur more frequently if one person bears a heavy loss than if many people bear light ones. One can, of course, conceive of situations where the extra $1 charged to one thousand people would be one thousand straws which would break one thousand backs and ruin one thousand homes or businesses, while $1,000 charged to one person would only ruin him, albeit thoroughly. But such situations seem mildly unlikely. *

The economic bases of inter-*temporal* loss spreading are not dissimilar. There is less danger of economic dislocation, and hence of secondary losses, if losses are spread over time. Social dislocations are also less likely if individuals can buy their risk-of-loss burden on a long term credit plan.

Thus, there are substantial reasons for allocating losses in ways which spread the burden over as many people and over as long a time as is possible. If these were the only aims in allocating losses, however, the most desirable plan would be some sort of governmental accident relief program spread over the population through taxes * * *. But in view of the conflict between this system and the best system from the standpoint of resource allocations—enterprise liability—a government-responsibility plan should not be embraced without some consideration of what loss spreading is in fact accomplished by enterprise liability.

Insofar as enterprise liability places the burden of accidents on the most likely insurer, it accomplishes directly a fair amount of both interpersonal and intertemporal loss spreading. * * *

Respondeat superior—like workmen's compensation, to which it has often been analogized—was the forerunner of modern enterprise liability. * * * Respondeat superior applies it to injuries to third parties, while workmen's compensation applies it to the worker himself. The effect * * * in terms of the justifications for enterprise liability is clear. The master is the best insurer, both in the sense of being able to obtain insurance at the lower rates and in the sense of being most aware of the risk. * Consequently, he is the best primary risk spreader. * * * Equally strong allocation-of-resources arguments can be made. Unless wages reflect the risk of injuries the true cost of labor in an industry is not shown. Similarly, the failure to show injury costs means that the prices of the goods the industry sells understate their true costs, and that too much is produced in that industry compared to those which are less accident prone. * * *

The similarities between workmen's compensation and *respondeat superior* have led some writers to urge that the "scope of employment" rule of *respondeat superior* be read as broadly as the "arising out of and in the course of employment" test of workmen's compensation. * On the basis of the theories analyzed here this is, of course, justified. These theories would suggest that *all* injuries caused by workmen which arise out of and in the course of their employment should result in the master's liability—whether or not the injury resulted from some activity which benefited the employer or was authorized by him, and whether it occurred through the servant's willfulness or through his negligence. * Since insurance is probably available in each case, and since secondary risk spreading is certainly the same in each, there seems no reason for the distinctions on risk-spreading or "deep pocket" grounds. Similarly, allocation of resources would tend to support liability. For a cost of an activity is not any the less real because the employee was not authorized to undertake it, or because he acted willfully. * If it arose out of an enterprise it should be just as chargeable to that enterprise as negligent torts; both should be reflected in prices. Of course, allocation of resources is not so exact or powerful a justification that it really matters too much where the line is drawn between activities arising, and those not arising, out of an enterprise; so long as it is in the general area. But since the other justifications are in accord with what formally seems the most "correct" line from the standpoint of resources it seems fair to say that allocation of resources also supports equating "scope of employment" and "arising out of or in the course of employment." To this extent courts like those in California, which have taken the lead in moving in this direction, have properly applied risk-distribution theories. *

This discussion, however, does not tell us why *respondeat superior* is in fact limited to injuries caused through the servant's *fault*. There is, of course, no answer to this question in terms of the theories analyzed in this article, any more than there is an answer to why extra-hazardous activities are limited as they are, or to why tort liability generally retains a semi-fault basis. The answer must be found in the broad justifications for the fault requirement. * * *

Maloney v. Rath

Supreme Court of California, In Bank, 1968.
69 Cal.2d 442, 71 Cal.Rptr. 897, 445 P.2d 513.

■ TRAYNOR, CHIEF JUSTICE. Plaintiff brought this action to recover damages for injuries to her person and property incurred in an automobile accident. She appeals from an adverse judgment and from an order denying her motion for judgment notwithstanding the verdict on the issue of liability.

Plaintiff stopped her car in a left-turn lane to wait for a traffic signal to change. Defendant turned into the left-turn lane behind plaintiff and stepped on her brake pedal. Defendant's brakes failed, and a collision ensued. Defendant neither knew nor had reason to know that her brakes were defective until they failed. The failure was caused by a rupture in a hydraulic hose that gave no warning to defendant of its impending occurrence. Defendant had the brakes completely overhauled by Peter Evanchik of Pete's Chevron Station about three months before the accident. Later, about two weeks before the accident, the car was involved in another collision, and defendant's husband had Evanchik inspect and repair it. Nothing was done to the brakes at that time. Defendant's expert witness testified that the brakes failed because of a hole in the hydraulic hose that was caused by rubbing of the hose against the right front wheel. The rubbing resulted from faulty installation of the hose at the time the brakes were overhauled. A qualified person inspecting the brakes before they failed would have detected the faulty installation and the evidence of the rubbing.

At the time of the accident section 26300 of the Vehicle Code provided that every motor vehicle "shall be equipped with brakes adequate to control the movement of the vehicle and to stop and hold the vehicle," and section 26453 provided that all "brakes and component parts thereof shall be maintained ... in good working order." * A defendant's failure to comply with these provisions gives rise to a presumption of negligence that he may rebut by proof "that he did what might reasonably be expected of a person of ordinary prudence, acting under similar circumstances, who desired to comply with the law." Alarid v. Vanier, 50 Cal.2d 617, 624, 327 P.2d 897, 900 (1958). *

Defendant offered sufficient evidence to rebut the presumption that she was negligent. The brakes had been overhauled three months before the accident; the car was inspected for damage and repaired after another accident in the interim; and the brakes gave no warning to defendant of their impending failure. Moreover, she was not negligent in failing to discover the faulty installation of or the growing damage to the hose, for those defects would be apparent only to a mechanic.

Plaintiff contends, however, that proof that defendant was not herself negligent should not absolve her from liability for the damage caused by the failure of her brakes. She contends that the court should reconsider the *Alarid* decision and hold that a motorist is strictly liable for damage caused by a brake failure or hold that the duty to exercise reasonable care to maintain adequate brakes is non-delegable.

We adhere to the holding of the *Alarid* case that a violation of a safety provision of the Vehicle Code does not make the violator strictly liable for damage caused by the violation. * * * It does not follow, however, that the duty to exercise reasonable care to maintain brakes so that they comply with the provisions of the Vehicle Code can be delegated. This issue was not raised or considered in the *Alarid* case. * * * We believe * * * that the law governing non-delegable duties dictates imposing such a duty here.

Unlike strict liability, a non-delegable duty operates, not as a substitute for liability based on negligence, but to assure that when a negligently caused harm occurs, the injured party will be compensated by the person whose activity caused the harm and who may therefore properly be held liable for the negligence of his agent, whether his agent was an employee or an independent contractor. To the extent that recognition of non-delegable duties tends to insure that there will be a financially responsible defendant available to compensate for the negligent harms caused by that defendant's activity, it ameliorates the need for strict liability to secure compensation. * * *

[W]e have found non-delegable duties in a wide variety of situations and have recognized that the rules set forth in the Restatement of Torts with respect to such duties are generally in accord with California law. Such duties include those imposed by a public authority as a condition of granting a franchise; * the duty of a condemning agent to protect a severed parcel from damage; * the duty of a general contractor to construct a building safely; * the duty to exercise due care when an "... independent contractor is employed to do work which the employer should recognize as necessarily creating a condition involving an unreasonable risk of bodily harm to others unless special precautions are taken"; * the duty of landowners to maintain their property in a reasonably safe condition * and to comply with applicable safety ordinances * and the duty of employers and suppliers to comply with the safety provisions of the Labor Code. *

Section 423 of the Restatement Second of Torts provides that "One who carries on an activity which threatens a grave risk of serious bodily harm or death unless the instrumentalities used are carefully ... maintained, and who employs an independent contractor to ... maintain such instrumentalities, is subject to the same liability for physical harm caused by the negligence of the contractor in ... maintaining such instrumentalities as though the employer had himself done the work of ... maintenance." Section 424 provides that "One who by statute or by administrative regulation is under a duty to provide specified safeguards or precautions for the safety of others is subject to liability to the others for whose protection the duty is imposed for harm caused by the failure of a contractor employed by him to provide such safeguards or precautions." Both of these sections point to a non-delegable duty in this case. The statutory provisions regulating the maintenance and equipment of automobiles constitute express legislative recognition of the fact that improperly maintained motor vehicles threaten "a grave risk of serious bodily harm or death." The responsibility for minimizing that risk or compensating for the failure to do so properly rests with the person who owns and operates the vehicle. He is the party primarily to be benefited by its use; he selects the contractor and is free to insist upon one who is financially responsible and to demand indemnity from him; the cost of his liability insurance that distributes the risk is properly attributable to his activities; and the discharge of the duty to exercise reasonable care in the maintenance of his vehicle is of the utmost importance to the public. *

In the present case it is undisputed that the accident was caused by a failure of defendant's brakes that resulted from her independent contractor's negligence in overhauling or in thereafter inspecting the brakes. Since her duty to maintain her brakes in compliance with the provisions of the Vehicle Code is non-delegable, the fact that the brake failure was the result of her independent contractor's negligence is no defense.

The judgment and the order denying the motion for judgment notwithstanding the verdict on the issue of liability are reversed and the case is remanded to the trial court for a new trial on the issue of damages only.

NOTES

1. *Nondelegable Duties.* According to a comment to the *Restatement (Third) of Torts*:

No single definition or set of standards exists for determining when a nondelegable duty arises. The concept of nondelegable duty reflects the notion that, in certain situations, the actor has a responsibility that should not be considered discharged when the actor, albeit with reasonable care, hires a contractor to perform the work. This responsibility could stem from several sources, including a statutory obligation, the actor's status, or the nature of the risk that the actor has set in motion.

Restatement (Third) of Torts: Liability for Physical and Emotional Harm §57 cmt. b (2012).

As illustrated by the principal case, duties imposed by state safety statutes sometimes are regarded as nondelegable, but often they are not. The duties owed by possessors of land to invitees (for example, customers, among others; see *infra* pages 221–22), e.g., Thomas v. E-Z Mart Stores, Inc., 102 P.3d 133, 136–137 (Okla.2004), and to adjacent landowners, e.g., Restatement (Second) of Torts § 422 cmt. a (1965), often are regarded as nondelegable. Finally, defendants owe a nondelegable duty whenever the activity is an "inherently dangerous" one, e.g., Miller v. Westcor Ltd. Pship., 171 Ariz. 387, 831 P.2d 386 (Ct.App. 1991) (liability of landowner for negligence of independent contractor in conducting fireworks display), but once again, the exact line delineating an inherently dangerous activity often is far from clear.

Is holding the defendant in *Maloney* liable on the basis of a nondelegable duty the same as imposing strict liability?

2. *Family Purpose Doctrine.* A married person is no longer vicariously liable for torts committed by a spouse. Similarly, except for liability imposed by statute, see e.g., Md. Code Crim. Proc. § 11–604 (2014) (parental liability for restitution for minor's criminal acts), parents typically are not liable for torts committed by their minor children.

The "family purpose" or "family car" doctrine provides that a family member who owns or otherwise controls the automobile may be held liable, without any fault on her or his part, whenever a child or other family member tortiously causes harm. See Harper, James and Gray on Torts §26.15. How do the justifications for the family purpose doctrine compare with those underlying vicarious liability of the employer?

CHAPTER 3

THE ANATOMY OF FAULT

This chapter focuses attention on "fault" as a basis of liability, particularly that type of fault known as "negligence." All the cases reprinted proceed on the assumption that negligence on the part of the defendant is a prerequisite of the liability sought to be imposed. Our concern is with what this thing, "negligence," is. The word is an ordinary one common in everyday language, but that is not to say that its legal connotations and meaning are clear or indisputable. Our search is not for dictionary definition but for function and operation. We wish to see who makes the determination, for example, judge or jury, how the decision maker is informed for or limited in the performance of that function, what factors enter into the determination, and how the determination may be checked or reviewed. We may then appraise this method of allocating the costs of accidents.

A. THE NATURE OF NEGLIGENCE

Frederick v. City of Detroit, Department of Street Railways

Supreme Court of Michigan, 1963.
370 Mich. 425, 121 N.W.2d 918.

■ SOURIS, JUSTICE. Plaintiff seeks reversal of an adverse jury verdict and denial of her subsequent motion for new trial on the ground that the trial judge instructed the jury improperly on the degree of care owed by a common carrier to its passengers. The case went to the jury on plaintiff's theory that defendant negligently permitted the rubber flooring of its bus to become worn and dirt to accumulate thereon and that it negligently omitted to provide a railing for the support of passengers alighting from its bus to the street. It was her claim that while leaving the bus she slipped on the worn, dirty flooring and, absent a railing which she could grasp for support, fell to the ground and suffered injuries.

The language of the instruction challenged by plaintiff is as follows:

Now, I will say this to you at this point; that the D.S.R. [Department of Street Railways] is not liable unless they were negligent. They are not an insurer. They are a common carrier. A common carrier has, in the vernacular, a higher degree,— owes a higher degree of care to its passengers than a person ordinarily owes to another person. Now, that definition is open to question; because the actual definition reads that they have the duty,—anyone has the duty to exercise due care. That is the general test of negligence. Do you exercise due care? And, what do you mean by "due care?" Due care means that amount of care that a reasonably prudent person would exercise under the circumstances then and there existing. But where the common carriers come into a different category, as it were, is the fact that it is more difficult for a common carrier to measure up to the standard of due care than it is for an ordinary person. The reason for that greater difficulty is precisely because he is a common carrier; he is carrying people for hire; and that makes him something less than an insurer, but someone who should exercise more care, in order to come up to the standard of due care, than an ordinary person. So, the Supreme Court in this state has sometimes referred—and I personally believe erroneously—to the fact that the common carrier owes a higher degree of care. I think that that is ultimately what it amounts to, but I think that is a very inaccurate way of stating it. They owe due care just like everybody else, but they have a harder time reaching that standard than the ordinary person does * * *. However, they do have that high standard to meet, that all public carriers have. They have to measure up to the test of due care owed by a bus company. * * *

What is negligence? I will define it. Negligence is the failure to use that amount of care that a reasonably prudent person would use under the circumstances. * * * You must ask yourselves, did the D.S.R. use the usual amount of care in this case that a common carrier, a reasonable common carrier, would and should use. That is the standard you go by when you are determining liability * * *.

   * [P]laintiff contends the trial judge erred in not clearly and concisely instructing the jury that she was owed a high degree of care, not just ordinary care, from the D.S.R. She claims that the instruction given, for all practical purposes, advised the jury that common carriers owe their passengers the same degree of care and diligence that others owe one another in the pursuit of their daily affairs. Without denying that the instruction can be read to impose upon carriers only a duty of due care as plaintiff contends, defendant maintains that it can, and should, be read as requiring no less than "a high degree of care," claimed by defendant to be a correct statement of its duty, by its reference to the greater difficulty a common carrier has in measuring up to a standard of due care than does an ordinary person and by its statement that a common carrier, because it carries people for hire, should exercise more care than an ordinary person. I agree with plaintiff that the instruction imposes upon defendant only the duty of due care, but that, in my view, is a correct statement of the law of this state, some of our prior opinions to the contrary notwithstanding and further notwithstanding the defendant's apparent reluctance to urge upon us such interpretation of the law more favorable to it than that which it uncritically assumes to be the law.

   We have recently expressed disapproval of contributory negligence instructions which expressly, or by fair inference, bar recovery by plaintiffs because of their own "slight negligence." * In those cases it was correctly conceded that the law imposed upon the plaintiffs no duty burden greater than ordinary or due care to avoid negligent injury to themselves and, hence, instructions which seemingly inferred the plaintiffs were barred from recovery for slight negligence or, put another way, for failure to exercise great care, were held erroneous. In this case of *Frederick*, however, while the parties assume that the law imposes upon the defendant a duty more stringent than due care,—a duty to exercise a high degree of care, or the highest degree of care for the safety of its fare paying passengers,—the law correctly stated requires no more than due care and, therefore, had the challenged instruction imposed a duty burden greater than due care, we would be obliged to strike it down * * *.

What an appellate court says in determining on review whether a trial record discloses factual compliance with the duty of reasonable care appropriately may be cast in terms of positive, comparative, or even superlative degrees, for then its task, as fact reviewer or determiner of fact sufficiency, is to apply the standard of reasonable care to the factual circumstances disclosed by the record,— circumstances which, because of the relation between the parties, because the instrument of harm is in the exclusive control of one party, or because the risk of physical harm is patently present, may reasonably require acts of great, greater or greatest diligence to meet the standard of care reasonable under such circumstances whereas other factual circumstances might reasonably require lesser acts of diligence. But its language thus used should not be, as it has been and is sought here to be, taken as a pronouncement of a different, more exacting, standard of care required of carriers nor should such appellate judicial language be considered appropriate for use in instructing juries. * The common law standard of reasonable care is constant although it "may require an infinite variety of precautions, or acts of care, depending upon the circumstances, and * * * it is primarily for the jury to say just what precautions were appropriate to the danger apparent in the case at hand." F. Harper & F. James, The Law of Torts, § 16.13. * * *

That the standard of care imposed in this state upon common carriers of passengers is the common law standard of due care was authoritatively announced for a unanimous Court almost 90 years ago by Mr. Justice Campbell, speaking for himself and Chief Justice Graves and Justices Cooley and Christiancy, in Michigan Central Railroad Company v. Coleman, 28 Mich. 440 (1874). * * * Justice Campbell * * * said that the care required in any business must be proportioned to its nature and risks, noting that railroading involves great risks and, therefore, requires great caution. But the railroader's required caution which may be extraordinary when "compared with the care needed in a business involving no possible human risk," is no greater than that of a railroad company of ordinary care. As I read Justice Campbell's opinion it means to me that, absent statutory standards to the contrary, a carrier of passengers is obliged to use due care, but that the actions which conform with or violate that standard of due care will vary according to the circumstances in which care is required to be exercised and will depend *upon jury determination* of what the reasonably prudent person in similar circumstances would consider reasonably necessary for the safety of passengers. When trial judges describe the *standard of duty* in terms of "high care," "higher care," "highest care" or the like, they impinge upon the jury's function as finders of fact. * * *

I would reaffirm the precepts of Michigan Central Railroad Company v. Coleman, *supra*, which endure in many of our sister states whose courts have carefully examined the carrier's liability at the common law and have resisted the now discredited theory that degrees of care or of negligence are recognized by the common law in such cases. * * *

* * * [T]he common law duty of due care * * * may be defined simply as the duty to exercise such diligence as would be exercised in the circumstances by a reasonably prudent carrier. It then becomes the function of the jury to determine from the evidence what action, if any, should have been taken or omitted in order to measure up to the standard of a reasonably prudent carrier in the same circumstances. By instructing the jury that high care or the highest care is required of carriers, a court impinges upon the jury's obligation to determine the carrier's compliance with its duty of due care by consideration of the proofs of what a reasonably prudent carrier would have done in the circumstances disclosed by the evidence. It is for the jury to decide as a matter of fact, and not for the court to decide as a matter of law, whether a reasonably prudent carrier in similar circumstance would exercise greater or lesser diligence in performance of its duty of due care owed to passengers than would a reasonably prudent person engaged in other pursuits not involving the risks inherent in a common carrier's business. * * *

Affirmed.

NOTES

1.   *The Standard of Care and the Jury.* As a practical matter, is one way of wording the jury instructions more likely than another to induce the jury to deliver a plaintiff's verdict? Five years before deciding the principal case, the Michigan Supreme Court stated:

> Care does not increase or diminish by calling it names. We think the abstract concept of reasonable care is in itself quite difficult enough to grapple with and apply in our law without our courts gratuitously conferring honorary degrees upon it. There is only *one* degree of care in the law, and that is the standard of care which may reasonably be required or expected under all the circumstances of a given situation * * *.

Spence v. Three Rivers Builders & Masonry Supply, Inc., 353 Mich. 120, 130, 90 N.W.2d 873, 878 (1958).

Why, then, do insurance carriers and physicians lobby legislatures to change the standards of care required to avoid liability in particular contexts? Many states, for example, enacted legislation, particularly in the 1920s and 1930s, known as "guest statutes," that reduced the standard of care required of an automobile owner or driver towards a social guest who is a passenger in an automobile. Harper, James and Gray on Torts § 16.15. Fifty years later, emergency room physicians in Florida sought and obtained legislative relief in the form of a lesser standard of care owed to their patients in order to reduce physicians' liability, believing this measure would make medical malpractice insurance more affordable and available. Fla. Stat. § 768.13 (2013).

What practical consequences result from the specificity of the language the court uses to instruct the jury?

2. *Degrees of Negligence.* With rare exceptions, orthodox doctrine today repudiates the notion of degrees of care. The most important exception is that a majority of courts require a common carrier to exercise "the highest degree of care and forethought consistent with the practical operation of the business." Harper, James and Gray on Torts § 16.14. Why? Compare this articulation with the principal case that would require different degrees of vigilance under the single standard of due care, depending on the hazards in the circumstances.

Similarly, in the case of a bailment, the requisite standard of care at common law varied according to the nature of the bailment. A bailment occurs when a person temporarily takes possession of the bailor's personal property, such as when a driver leaves his car with a valet. Traditionally,

> [W]here the bailment is for the exclusive benefit of the bailee, he is bound to use great care and is liable for slight negligence [for example, when another student allows you to borrow a spare laptop computer]; where the bailment is for the mutual benefit of the bailor and bailee [bailor leaves his car with a valet working in a paid parking garage], the latter must use ordinary care and is liable for ordinary negligence; where the bailment benefits the bailor only [your roommate brings your laptop computer, which you have forgotten, to school for your use], the bailee need use only slight care and is liable only for gross negligence. * * *

> But even here the tendency has been to get away from them and to regard the relationship between the parties as simply one of the circumstances in the light of which conduct is to be measured by the standard of reasonable care.

Harper, James and Gray on Torts § 16.13 & 16.13 n.4.

3. *Conduct in Emergencies.* Another circumstance affecting whether the defendant has acted reasonably in all the circumstances is whether his actions were taken in the midst of an emergency. As Judge Cardozo said, " 'Errors of judgment' * * * would not count against [the defendant] if they resulted 'from the excitement and confusion of the moment.' * The reason that was exacted of him was not the reason of the morrow. It was reason fitted and proportioned to the time and the event." Wagner v. Int'l Ry. Co., 232 N.Y. 176, 182, 133 N.E. 437, 438 (1921).

Should the trial court explicitly instruct the jury that an emergency situation might justify defendant's conduct when such conduct would constitute negligence in the absence of an emergency? Such instructions frequently are given. Compare Simonson v. White, 220 Mont. 14, 16, 713 P.2d 983, 984 (1986), where two passengers in an automobile driven by White sued both White and Phillips, the driver of the other automobile involved in the collision. Phillips, who allegedly had been drinking and driving at a high rate of speed, lost control of his car which then "somersaulted" and landed upside down in a pit adjacent to the highway. Shortly thereafter, White's car crested a hill, and he saw what he thought were headlights coming at him in his lane. White, in an effort to avoid what appeared to him to be an imminent collision, drove into the ditch, crashing into Phillips' vehicle. At trial, the court gave the jury the following "sudden emergency instruction" to assist them in evaluating White's conduct:

> You are instructed that when a person is faced with a sudden emergency which is not created by his own negligence, his conduct

is to be tested by what an ordinarily prudent person would have done under the same circumstances and he is not chargeable with negligence for failing to adopt the most judicious course as disclosed by subsequent events.

The Montana Supreme Court held that the trial court's instruction constituted error:

> There is no reason for this instruction to ever be given in an automobile accident case. It adds nothing to the established law applicable in any negligence case, that due care under the circumstances must be exercised. "The circumstances" includes the pressure and split-second decision-making which accompanies the crisis prior to some automobile accidents. Further, a driver is never held responsible for non-negligent actions which prove, with hindsight, to have been incorrect. The instruction adds nothing to the law of negligence and serves only to leave an impression in the minds of the jurors that a driver is somehow excused from the ordinary standard of care because an emergency existed. This is not the law. See W. P. Keeton, Prosser and Keeton on The Law of Torts § 33 (5th ed. 1984).

Consistent with *Simonson*, Restatement (Third) of Torts: Liability for Physical and Emotional Harm § 9 (2010) provides that "[i]f an actor is confronted with an unexpected emergency requiring rapid response, this is a circumstance to be taken into account in determining whether the actor's resulting conduct is that of the reasonably careful person." See also discussion of Eckert v. Long Island R.R., *infra* page 343, Note 6.

Blyth v. Birmingham Waterworks Co.

Court of Exchequer, 1856.
11 Ex 781, 25 L.J. Ex. 212, 156 Eng.Rep. 1047.

[T]he defendants were incorporated by * * * statute * for the purpose of supplying Birmingham with water. * * * The main-pipe opposite the house of the plaintiff was more than eighteen inches below the surface. The fire-plug was constructed according to the best known system, and the materials of it were at the time of the accident sound and in good order. * * *

On Feb. 24, a large quantity of water, escaping from the neck of the main, forced its way through the ground into the plaintiff's house. The apparatus had been laid down 25 years, and had worked well during that time. The defendants' engineer stated that the water might have forced its way through the brickwork round the neck of the main, and that the accident might have been caused by the frost, inasmuch as the expansion of the water would force up the plug out of the neck, and the stopper being encrusted with ice would not suffer the plug to ascend. One of the severest frosts on record set in on Jan. 15, 1855, and continued until after the accident in question. An encrustation of ice and snow had gathered about the stopper, and in the street all round, and also for some inches between the stopper and the plug. The ice had been observed on the surface of the ground for a considerable time before the accident. A short time after the accident, the company's turncock removed the ice from the stopper, took out the plug, and replaced it. The judge left it to the jury to consider whether the company had used proper care to prevent the accident. He thought, that, if the defendants had taken out the ice adhering to the plug, the accident would not have happened, and left it to the jury to say whether they ought to have removed the ice. The jury found a verdict for the plaintiff * * *.

■ ALDERSON, B. I am of opinion that there was no evidence to be left to the jury. The case turns upon the question whether the facts proved show that the defendants were guilty of negligence. Negligence is the omission to do something which a reasonable man, guided upon those considerations which ordinarily regulate the conduct of human affairs, would do, or doing something which a prudent and reasonable man would not do. The defendants might have been liable for negligence, if, unintentionally, they omitted to do that which a reasonable person would have done, or did that which a person taking reasonable precautions would not have done. A reasonable man would act with reference to the average circumstances of the temperature in ordinary years. The defendants had provided against such frosts as experience would have led men, acting prudently, to provide against; and they are not guilty of negligence, because their precautions proved insufficient against the effects of the extreme severity of the frost of 1855, which penetrated to a greater depth than any which ordinarily occurs south of the polar regions. Such a state of circumstances constitutes a contingency against which no reasonable man can provide. The result was an accident, for which the defendants cannot be held liable.

■ MARTIN, B. I think that the direction was not correct, and that there was no evidence for the jury. The defendants are not responsible, unless there was negligence on their part. To hold otherwise would be to make the company responsible as insurers.

■ BRAMWELL, B. The Act of Parliament directed the defendants to lay down pipes, with plugs in them, as safety-valves, to prevent the bursting of the pipes. The plugs were properly made, and of proper material; but there was an accumulation of ice about this plug, which prevented it from acting properly. The defendants were not bound to keep the plugs clear. It appears to me that the plaintiff was under quite as much obligation to remove the ice and snow which had accumulated, as the defendants. However that may be, it appears to me that it would be monstrous to hold the defendants responsible because they did not foresee and prevent an accident, the cause of which was so obscure, that it was not discovered until many months after the accident had happened.

National Food Stores, Inc. v. Union Electric Co.

Missouri Court of Appeals, 1973.
494 S.W.2d 379.

■ McMILLAN, JUDGE. * * * National sued Union Electric for damages that resulted from the spoilage of certain perishable food items kept in its stores, because of an interruption by Union Electric of its electrical service to National. A jury verdict for $5800.00 was found for National. Upon Union Electric's motion * * *, the court * * * set aside the verdict because there was no basis for legal liability * * *.

In June and July 1966 the City of St. Louis experienced a record breaking heat wave. The high temperatures put a great stress upon the capacity of Union Electric to meet the power needs of both its city and county consumers. * * * In recognition of the gravity of the situation, Union Electric put into effect its five phase "Emergency Load Reduction of Power Curtailment" plan.

At 7:55 A.M., 11 July 1966, Union Electric (Phase One) disconnected service to its "interruptable customers." For these contract customers neither reasons nor notices were necessary. Phase Two, which was a 5% voltage reduction, was not used. At 10:00 A.M., the same morning, the power drain continued; therefore, Union Electric (Phase Three) began to contact its 200 largest industrial consumers, and on a voluntary basis requested that each of them reduce their power consumption. By 12:30 P.M., all had been contacted.

At 1:47 P.M., the same afternoon, Union Electric (skipping Phase Four, which provided for a general notice to the general public by the media) put into operation Phase Five, which called for the involuntary curtailment of service periodically to certain specified geographical areas throughout the entire St. Louis Metropolitan area. It was the Phase Five interruption, without notice to National, which National claims resulted in spoilage to its food stuff in various stores throughout the area.

Union Electric contends * * * that it owed no duty to National to advise it of an interruption of electrical service to each of its stores before an interruption occurred * * *.

Generally speaking, an electric power company which undertakes to supply current, although not an insurer of service, has an obligation to provide a patron with adequate and continuous service, arising either from express contract, a regulatory enactment, or implied contract and the supplier is, ordinarily at least, subject to a duty to exercise reasonable care to fulfill such obligation. * * * There are cases that hold when the action is based upon negligence, power suppliers are relieved from liability for unintended interruptions, either as a matter of general principle or because of an express contractual or regulatory provision, where the interruption resulted from an "Act of God" or from circumstances beyond the control of the supplier. * * *

While the instant case is not a breakdown by an "Act of God" or from circumstances beyond the control of the supplier as outlined in the above cases, this case does involve the cessation of power by the supplier due to an emergency situation over which the supplier had no control. We concede that under the conditions existing on the morning of 11 July 1966 Union Electric was justified in its decision to cut off service in various portions of the area throughout the afternoon and evening of that day and into July 12. However, the fact of an emergency does not relieve Union Electric of its general duty to exercise reasonable care to avoid undue harm to its consumers where the harm is reasonably foreseeable. Union Electric says there was no duty to advise National of the interruption of power.

In Heaven v. Pender, 11 Q.B.D. 503 (1883), Brett, M.R., afterwards Lord Esher, made the first attempt to state a formula of duty as follows:

. . . that whenever one person is by circumstances placed in such a position with regard to another, that every one of ordinary sense who did think would at once recognize that if he did not use ordinary care and skill in his own conduct with regard to those circumstances he would cause danger of injury to the person or property of the other, a duty arises to use ordinary care and skill to avoid such danger.

* * * So, in our opinion, Union Electric was by virtue of its own charter placed in a position to its customers so that if it did not use ordinary care in the exercise of its franchise numerous injuries to both person and property could reasonably occur. * * * In Langley v. Pacific Gas & Electric Co., 41 Cal.2d 655, 660–62, 262 P.2d 849, 849–50 (1953), an owner of a trout hatchery sued to recover damages as a result of the death of 78,000 trout. Plaintiff claimed that the electric power necessary to pump water into the hatchery had gone off for about five hours due to a failure of defendant's voltage regulator. As a result of the power interruption the fish did not get sufficient water and died. The evidence showed that plaintiff had advised the defendant of the necessity of a continuous flow of power, and that defendant had agreed to notify them of the outage. Granted, the *Langley* case was founded upon contract, however, Justice Traynor clearly sets forth the general standard of conduct required of a public utility when he states:

. . . defendant agreed to furnish electricity in accordance with the applicable rules and regulations of the Public Utilities Commission . . . defendant contends that under these provisions its duty is limited to exercising reasonable diligence to furnish a continuous and sufficient supply of electricity, and that it is under no duty to exercise reasonable care or diligence to prevent loss from power failure when it is not legally responsible for the power failure itself. These provisions deal with the duty to supply power, and they make clear that defendant is not an insurer or guarantor of service. *In no way, however do they * abrogate defendant's general duty to exercise reasonable care in operating its system to avoid unreasonable risks of harm to . . . property of its customers.*

In the present case it is undisputed that defendant was not responsible for the power failure and that it exercised reasonable diligence to restore service. Accordingly, the question presented is whether . . . it could reasonably be concluded that its duty to exercise due care toward plaintiff in the operation of its system required it to give notice of the power failure when it knew that the failure to give notice would result in serious loss. In an analogous situation, a common carrier does not have a duty to transport goods immediately, but merely to use due diligence to deliver goods offered for shipment within a reasonable time . . . Nevertheless, . . . if the carrier is aware that causes of unusual delay exist of which the shipper is unaware, and does not inform the shipper of the facts, the carrier is liable for injuries caused by delay . . .

. . . By undertaking to supply electricity to plaintiff, defendant obligated itself to exercise reasonable care toward him, and failure to exercise such care has the characteristics of both a *breach of contract and a tort . . .*

* * * Public utilities occupy a unique position in our society. They furnish indispensable services while enjoying a privileged legal status. As consumers, our dependency upon their services is almost total. As such it is essential that such companies conduct themselves in a manner that does not take advantage of our dependency on them nor of the privileged status granted to them by the state legislature. While we do not propose that public utilities, in this instance an electrical company, are insurers or guarantors of the safety of persons or of their property, * we hold there is as a matter of law a duty on Union Electric to protect its customers from foreseeable damage from failure of electrical service.

* * * [T]he right to interrupt service in the face of an emergency is a far different thing from relieving a utility of liability where it fails to give a reasonable notice to its consumers of its intentions to interrupt services when the utility knows or could reasonably anticipate a situation that would make it necessary to interrupt service and the utility knows or should know that by so failing to give notice the interruptions might result in loss or harm to its consumers.

Under the evidence in this case, a jury could have reasonably found that Union Electric could have reasonably anticipated that the steadily deteriorating environmental situation on July 11, 1966, would necessitate the interruption of service to its customers. * * * [W]e find that Union Electric knew of the gravity of the situation and that it was well aware that it might have to have an area-wide cessation of power; therefore, we hold that it became a jury question as to whether Union Electric's failure to give a reasonable notice or warning of outages and interruptions of service was reasonably likely to cause harm or property loss to its consumers. It is a jury question as to whether or not the failure to give notice was a breach of that duty. * * *

NOTE

When is a Duty of Care Owed? The principal case quotes the language of the classic English case, *Heaven v. Pender,* on the issue of when a duty of reasonable care is owed. Brett's formulation was not accepted in his time. It was, however, later adapted by Lord Atkin in a classic House of Lords speech which became a landmark of twentieth-century English negligence law. This statement, in Donoghue v. Stevenson, [1932] A.C. 562, 579–82, [1932] All E.R. 1, 11–12, was delivered in a product liability case (a snail in a bottle of ginger beer), and represents the culmination in British law of a process of doctrinal evolution from preoccupation with remedies for particular offenses derived from common law writs toward a general theory of liability for negligence:

> * * * We are solely concerned with the question whether, as a matter of law in the circumstances alleged, the defender owed any duty to the pursuer to take care.
>
> It is remarkable how difficult it is to find in the English authorities statements of general application defining the relations between parties that give rise to the duty. The Courts are concerned with the particular relations which come before

them in actual litigation, and it is sufficient to say whether the
duty exists in those circumstances. The result is that the Courts
have been engaged upon an elaborate classification of duties as
they exist in respect of property, whether real or personal, with
further divisions as to ownership, occupation or control, and
distinctions based on the particular relations of the one side or the
other, whether manufacturer, salesman or landlord, customer,
tenant, stranger, and so on. In this way it can be ascertained at
any time whether the law recognizes a duty, but only where the
case can be referred to some particular species which has been
examined and classified. And yet the duty which is common to all
the cases where liability is established must logically be based
upon some element common to the cases where it is found to exist.
* * *

At present I content myself with pointing out that in English law
there must be, and is, some general conception of relations giving
rise to a duty of care, of which the particular cases found in the
books are but instances. The liability for negligence * * * is no
doubt based upon a general public sentiment of moral wrongdoing
for which the offender must pay. * * * The rule that you are to
love your neighbour becomes in law, you must not injure your
neighbour; and the lawyer's question, Who is my neighbour?
receives a restricted reply. You must take reasonable care to avoid
acts or omissions which you can reasonably foresee would be
likely to injure your neighbour. Who, then, in law is my
neighbour? The answer seems to be—persons who are so closely
and directly affected by my act that I ought reasonably to have
them in contemplation as being so affected when I am directing
my mind to the acts or omissions which are called in question.
This appears to me to be the doctrine of *Heaven v. Pender*, as laid
down by Lord Esher (then Brett M.R.) when it is limited by the
notion of proximity introduced by Lord Esher himself and A.L.
Smith, L.J. in Le Lievre v. Gould, [1893] 1 Q.B. 491, 497, 504.
Lord Esher says: "That case established that, under certain
circumstances, one man may owe a duty to another, even though
there is no contract between them. If one man is near to another,
a duty lies upon him not to do that which may cause a personal
injury to that other, or may injure his property." So A.L. Smith,
L.J.: "The decision of *Heaven v. Pender* was founded upon the
principle, that a duty to take due care did arise when the person
or property of one was in such proximity to the person or property
of another that, if due care was not taken, damage might be done
by the one to the other." I think that this sufficiently states the
truth if proximity be not confined to mere physical proximity; but
be used, as I think it was intended, to extend to such close and
direct relations that the act complained of directly affects a person
whom the person alleged to be bound to take care would know
would be directly affected by his careless act. * * *

While Lord Atkin's speech is not often quoted in the United States, it
reflects positions which are frequently at issue in American litigation. The
notion, for instance, that there is a general requirement to take care, rather
than a multiplicity of "duties" whose breach constitutes negligence, became
the dominant view among American courts during the twentieth century.

For example, the court in Wintersteen v. National Cooperage & Woodenware Co., 361 Ill. 95, 103, 197 N.E. 578, 582 (1935), stated:

> It is axiomatic that every person owes a duty to all persons to exercise ordinary care to guard against any injury which may naturally flow as a reasonably probable and foreseeable consequence of his act, and the law is presumed to furnish a remedy for the redress of every wrong. This duty to exercise ordinary care to avoid injury to another does not depend upon contract, privity of interest, or the proximity of relationship between the parties. It extends to remote and unknown persons. *

Today, Restatement (Third) of Torts: Liability for Physical and Emotional Harm § 7 (2010) provides that "[a]n actor ordinarily has a duty to exercise reasonable care when the actor's conduct creates a risk of physical harm." However, the provision goes on to state that "[i]n exceptional cases, when an articulated countervailing principle or policy warrants denying or limiting liability in a particular class of cases, a court may decide that the defendant has no duty or that the ordinary duty of reasonable care requires modification."

The question of liability to whom remains a critical issue, and will be encountered repeatedly in the following materials. E.g., Palsgraf v. Long Island Ry. Co., *infra* pages 293–300; MacPherson v. Buick Motor Co., *infra* pages 576–79; and Ultramares Corp. v. Touche, *infra* pages 828–33 (three important Cardozo opinions).

Stockberger v. United States

United States Court of Appeals for the Seventh Circuit, 2003.
332 F.3d 479.

[See *infra* pages 441–444.]

Hover v. Barkhoof

Court of Appeals of New York, 1870.
44 N.Y. 113.

* * * This action is for the recovery of damages sustained by the plaintiff, by the falling of a bridge over a stream in the town of Florida * * * which was alleged to be in an unsafe condition through the neglect of the defendants, who were commissioners of highways of that town, whereby the horses, wagon and harness of the plaintiff were injured. * * *

The jury found for the plaintiff $200 damages. On appeal to the General Term the judgment entered on this verdict was affirmed, and the defendants have appealed therefrom to the Court of Appeals. * * *

■ LEONARD, C. * * * During the trial one of the defendants who had examined the bridge and contracted for repairs, being a witness for the defense, was asked, on their behalf, if he believed the defendants had made use of all of the means necessary to the safety of the bridge? The question was excluded, and the defendants excepted.

Their belief in the sufficiency of the means used, or of the structure, was of no consequence or materiality. The alleged neglect was a fact to be proven. The belief of the defendants as to the non-existence of the fact, did not tend to show how, in truth, the fact was or might be. The belief of the defendants, while it proved nothing as to the fact, might tend to mislead the mind of the jury. If the inquiry was for the purpose of proving that the defendants were not acting in bad faith or with malice, it was equally immaterial; the question was negligence or no negligence, as a fact. Mistaken belief in the soundness of the timbers, or the sufficiency of the repairs, did not tend to any conclusion as to the fact. * * *

There appears to be no error, and the judgment should be affirmed with costs.

B. THE REASONABLE PERSON

Vaughan v. Menlove
Common Pleas, 1837.
3 Bing. (N.C.) 468, 132 Eng.Rep. 490.

[Case. The declaration charged defendant with negligently maintaining a rick or stack of hay in such a way as to make spontaneous combustion unreasonably likely; that such combustion did take place and the fire consumed plaintiff's nearby cottages.]

At the trial it appeared that the rick in question had been made by the Defendant near the boundary of his own premises; that the hay was in such a state when put together, as to give rise to discussions on the probability of fire: that though there were conflicting opinions on the subject, yet during a period of five weeks, the Defendant was repeatedly warned of his peril; that his stock was insured; and that upon one occasion, being advised to take the rick down to avoid all danger, he said "he would chance it." He made an aperture or chimney through the rick; but in spite, or perhaps in consequence of this precaution, the rick at length burst into flames from the spontaneous heating of its materials; the flames communicated to the Defendant's barn and stables, and thence to the Plaintiff's cottages, which were entirely destroyed.

Patteson, J., before whom the cause was tried, told the jury that the question for them to consider, was, whether the fire had been occasioned by gross negligence on the part of the Defendant; adding, that he was bound to proceed with such reasonable caution as a prudent man would have exercised under such circumstances.

A verdict having been found for the Plaintiff, a rule *nisi* for a new trial was obtained, on the ground that the jury should have been directed to consider, not, whether the Defendant had been guilty of gross negligence with reference to the standard of ordinary prudence, a standard too uncertain to afford any criterion; but whether he had acted bonâ fide to the best of his judgment; if he had, he ought not to be responsible for the misfortune of not possessing the highest order of intelligence. The action under such circumstances, was of the first impression. * * *

R. V. Richards [on behalf of the defendant]: * * * Defendant had a right to place his stack as near to the extremity of his own land as he

pleased: * * * under that right, * * * he can only be called on to act bonâ
fide to the best of his judgment * * *. At all events what would have
been gross negligence ought to be estimated by the faculties of the
individual, and not by those of other men. The measure of prudence
varies so with the varying faculties of men, that it is impossible to say
what is gross negligence with reference to the standard of what is called
ordinary prudence. * * *

■ TINDAL, C. J. * * * [T]here is a rule of law which says you must so
enjoy your own property as not to injure that of another; and according
to that rule the Defendant is liable for the consequence of his own
neglect; and though the Defendant did not himself light the fire, yet
mediately, he is as much the cause of it as if he had himself put a
candle to the rick; for it is well known that hay will ferment and take
fire if it be not carefully stacked. * * *

It is contended, however, that the learned Judge was wrong in
leaving this to the jury as a case of gross negligence, and that the
question of negligence was so mixed up with reference to what would be
the conduct of a man of ordinary prudence that the jury might have
thought the latter the rule by which they were to decide; that such a
rule would be too uncertain to act upon; and that the question ought to
have been whether the Defendant had acted honestly and bonâ fide to
the best of his own judgment. That, however, would leave so vague a
line as to afford no rule at all, the degree of judgment belonging to each
individual being infinitely various: and though it has been urged that
the care which a prudent man would take, is not an intelligible
proposition as a rule of law, yet * * * [t]he care taken by a prudent man
has always been the rule laid down; as to the supposed difficulty of
applying it, a jury has always been able to say, whether, taking that
rule as their guide, there has been negligence on the occasion in
question.

Instead, therefore, of saying that the liability for negligence should
be co-extensive with the judgment of each individual, which would be as
variable as the length of the foot of each individual, we ought rather to
adhere to the rule which requires in all cases a regard to caution such
as a man of ordinary prudence would observe. That was in substance
the criterion presented to the jury in this case, and therefore the
present rule must be discharged. * * *

Excerpt, Oliver Wendell Holmes, Jr., The Common Law
86–88 (Mark DeWolfe Howe ed., 1963) (1881).

The standards of the law are standards of general application. The
law takes no account of the infinite varieties of temperament, intellect,
and education which make the internal character of a given act so
different in different men. It does not attempt to see men as God sees
them, for more than one sufficient reason. In the first place, the
impossibility of nicely measuring a man's powers and limitations is far
clearer than that of ascertaining his knowledge of law, which has been
thought to account for what is called the presumption that every man
knows the law. But a more satisfactory explanation is, that, when men
live in society, a certain average of conduct, a sacrifice of individual
peculiarities going beyond a certain point, is necessary to the general

welfare. If, for instance, a man is born hasty and awkward, is always having accidents and hurting himself or his neighbors, no doubt his congenital defects will be allowed for in the courts of Heaven, but his slips are no less troublesome to his neighbors than if they sprang from guilty neglect. His neighbors accordingly require him, at his proper peril, to come up to their standard, and the courts which they establish decline to take his personal equation into account.

The rule that the law does, in general, determine liability by blameworthiness, is subject to the limitation that minute differences of character are not allowed for. The law considers, in other words, what would be blameworthy in the average man, the man of ordinary intelligence and prudence, and determines liability by that. If we fall below the level in those gifts, it is our misfortune; so much as that we must have at our peril, for the reasons just given. But he who is intelligent and prudent does not act at his peril, in theory of law. On the contrary, it is only when he fails to exercise the foresight of which he is capable, or exercises it with evil intent, that he is answerable for the consequences.

There are exceptions to the principle that every man is presumed to possess ordinary capacity to avoid harm to his neighbors, which illustrate the rule, and also the moral basis of liability in general. When a man has a distinct defect of such a nature that all can recognize it as making certain precautions impossible, he will not be held answerable for not taking them. A blind man is not required to see at his peril; and although he is, no doubt, bound to consider his infirmity in regulating his actions, yet if he properly finds himself in a certain situation, the neglect of precautions requiring eyesight would not prevent his recovering for an injury to himself, and, it may be presumed, would not make him liable for injuring another. So it is held that, in cases where he is the plaintiff, an infant of very tender years is only bound to take the precautions of which an infant is capable; the same principle may be cautiously applied where he is defendant. * Insanity is a more difficult matter to deal with, and no general rule can be laid down about it. There is no doubt that in many cases a man may be insane, and yet perfectly capable of taking the precautions, and of being influenced by the motives, which the circumstances demand. But if insanity of a pronounced type exists, manifestly incapacitating the sufferer from complying with the rule which he has broken, good sense would require it to be admitted as an excuse.

NOTES

1. *Knowledge of the Reasonable Person.* Restatement (Third) of Torts: Liability for Physical and Emotional Harm § 11(c) (2010) states, "An actor's mental or emotional disability is not considered in determining whether conduct is negligent, unless the actor is a child." See *infra* pages 153–154. What knowledge is attributed by the law to the reasonable person? Consider comment *e* to Restatement (Second) of Torts § 290 (1965):

> * * * He is treated as though he were a reasonable man and, therefore, he is treated as though he knew those things which the reasonable man at that time and place would know even though the actor is himself excusably ignorant of them. As a reasonable man, the actor is required to possess such scientific knowledge as

is common among laymen at the time and in the community. Thus, he is required to know the ordinary operation of well-known natural laws. He is required, among other things, to know the poisonous qualities of many drugs, chemicals, and gases and the explosive or inflammable qualities of many chemical compounds and the intoxicating quality of certain liquids. So too, the actor as a reasonable man is required to know the ordinary operation of natural forces in the locality in which he lives which are likely to be affected by his conduct. Thus, a man living in the northern part of Minnesota is required to expect extremely cold temperature in early winter. A man living in the tropics is required to expect hot weather, even in winter. Every man should realize that heavy rainstorms are likely to produce floods in mountain streams. A Californian during the summer is not required to expect the fall of rain even though the morning is cloudy. On the other hand, a man living on the Atlantic coast may well be required to recognize that such conditions would make it imprudent to expose perishable goods to the risk of rain.

In general, the actor is required to know everything with respect to the risk of harm which is a matter of common knowledge in the community in which his conduct occurs. There is a close relation between the minimum standard of knowledge required in negligence cases and those matters of which a court will take judicial notice because they are generally known.

2. *Experts and Novices.* What if a defendant possesses special skills or knowledge? Is the professional race car driver or the veteran professional truck driver to be held to a different standard than the ordinary reasonably prudent driver? According to Restatement (Third) of Torts: Liability for Physical and Emotional Harm § 12 (2010), "If an actor has skills or knowledge that exceed those possessed by most others, these skills or knowledge are circumstances to be taken into account in determining whether the actor has behaved as a reasonably careful person." Some courts suggest a different conclusion. For example, in Capital Raceway Promotions, Inc. v. Smith, 22 Md.App. 224, 239, 322 A.2d 238, 246 (1974), the court stated: "Although the question has never been precisely asked or answered by our appellate courts, dicta strongly indicate that neither the inexperience of a novice nor the professional experience of a truck driver affects the standard of care required of a driver."

Memorial Hospital of South Bend, Inc. v. Scott

Supreme Court of Indiana, 1973.
261 Ind. 27, 300 N.E.2d 50.

■ HUNTER, JUSTICE. The instant case involves a negligence action brought against a hospital for injuries sustained by a patient. Plaintiff Scott was severely burned by hot water (140°F.) while he was using a hospital toilet. Plaintiff activated a bed pan flusher hot water knob (shoulder level) which was located in proximity to the toilet flusher (small of back level) and was inundated by the scalding water. The facts set out below are those found by the trial court in support of his granting plaintiff's motion to correct error. * * *

[T]he patient was suffering from multiple sclerosis, that his known and recorded symptoms were lack of muscular co-ordination, difficiulty [sic] with vision, weakness in right arm and leg and in grip of right hand, occasional difficulty in walking and in distinguishing shapes. The plaintiff had hand trembles or intention tremors, vertical nystagumus or involuntary oscillatory eyeball movements, that sometimes his eyes would not focus and he would have some difficulty maintaining his balance. That on the morning of the accident he was subject to a spinal puncture and he was given an injection of thorazine. That the internist was of the opinion that he himself would not drive an automobile for four hours after being injected with thorazine. That a normal consequence of spinal puncture and thorazine injection was a headache. That the plaintiff, appellee, at sometime more than hour [sic] after the thorazine injection expressed the desire to use the bathroom. He was never instructed or warned about the bed pan flusher appliance mounted above and behind the toilet stool. That he remembers attempting to flush the toilet while he remained seated because he wasn't sure he was completed with his toilet function. He remembered touching a knob, and then he remembers the hot water. * * *

In weighing the conflicting evidence, the trial court has concluded that the plaintiff, Scott, was not contributorily negligent. The reasons for this conclusion were based upon Scott's physical disabilities and the fact he had no knowledge of the bed pan flushing device and that he had no appreciation or awareness of a danger existing behind the toilet. The Court of Appeals decided as a matter of law that the reasons for granting a new trial were incorrect. The Court of Appeals held that the trial court did not apply the ordinary reasonable man test and, therefore, an inaccurate rule of law was applied in the court below. As enunciated by the Court of Appeals:

> Therefore, assuming that Scott did not have actual knowledge of the danger, *if it were shown by Memorial Hospital that a reasonable and prudent person in like or similar circumstances would have known and appreciated the danger, then Scott still could have been guilty of contributory negligence.* . . . 290 N.E.2d at 84–85. (Emphasis added.)

However, an examination of the record discloses that the trial court was cognizant of the proper test to be applied on the issue of contributory negligence. The trial court tendered the following instructions to the jury on this issue:

> Contributory negligence is the failure of a plaintiff to use reasonable care to avoid injury to himself which failure is a proximate cause of the injuries for which he seeks to recover.

> You are instructed that in determining ordinary care of Defendants as to Plaintiff in this case, you may consider the physical and mental ailments of Plaintiff which may have affected his ability to look after his own safety.

> Similarly, you may consider such physical and mental ailments of Plaintiff in determining his ordinary care on the issue of contributory negligence. * * *

In our opinion the trial court did apply the correct standard when granting the new trial. Further, the Court of Appeals has made an incomplete statement of the law of contributory negligence.

The general rule on the issue of the plaintiff's contributory negligence is that the plaintiff must exercise that degree of care that an ordinary reasonable man would exercise in like or similar circumstances. * Contributory negligence is conduct on the part of the plaintiff, contributing as a legal cause to the harm he has suffered, *which falls below the standard to which he is required to conform for his own protection.* Restatement (Second) of Torts § 463 (1965). Thus, the critical scope of inquiry here is an examination of the standard of care which Scott was required to exhibit. Lack of reasonable care is the factor upon which the presence or absence of negligence depends. * We hold that a departure from the general rule is required where the plaintiff is suffering from physical infirmities which impair his ability to function as an "ordinary reasonable man." The proper test to be applied in such cases is the test of a reasonable man *under the same disabilities and infirmities* in like circumstances. * * * Dean Prosser has treated negligence with authoritative analysis and lends this discussion:

> As to his physical characteristics, the reasonable man may be said to be identical with the actor. The man who is blind or deaf, or lame, or is otherwise physically disabled, is entitled to live in the world and to have allowance made by others for his disability, and he cannot be required to do the impossible by conforming to physical standards which he cannot met [sic]. * * * At the same time, the conduct of the [physically disabled] individual must be reasonable in the light of his knowledge of his infirmity, which is treated merely as one of the circumstances under which he acts. A blind man may be negligent in going into a place of known danger, just as one who knows that he is subject to epileptic fits, or is about to fall asleep, may be negligent in driving a car. It is sometimes said that a blind man must use a greater degree of care than one who can see; but it is now generally agreed that as a fixed rule this is inaccurate, and that the correct statement is merely that he must take the precautions, be they more or less, which the ordinary reasonable man would take if he were blind. In theory the standard remains the same, but it is sufficiently flexible to take his physical defects into account.

W[illiam L.] Prosser, Law of Torts, pp. 151–52 (4th ed. 1971). * * *

* * * As the rule is stated in C.J.S.:

> A person laboring under any physical disability increasing his liability to injury must nevertheless exercise ordinary care to avoid injury, and if he fails to exercise that degree of care, and such failure contributes proximately to cause his injury, he is guilty of contributory negligence. Such a person is not required to exercise a higher degree of care to that end than is required of a person under no disability; ordinary care is all that is required.

However, in determining whether such a person exercised ordinary care for his own safety, his disability is a circumstance to be considered. Thus, while it has been said that ordinary care is such care as an ordinarily prudent person with the same disability would exercise under the same or similar circumstances, it has also been held that it may be incumbent on one with a physical disability to put forth a greater degree of effort than would otherwise be necessary in order to attain that standard of care which is required of everyone.

65A C.J.S. Negligence § 142.

The Court of Appeals has extracted the general rule as to contributory negligence, but has not taken into account the facts and circumstances of the instant case. The correct test to be applied in determining Scott's standard of care is the test of a reasonably prudent man suffering from the same maladies and disabilities under like circumstances as those here. * * *

NOTE

Clumsiness. Suppose the driver of an automobile, accused of negligence resulting in an accident, argues that he is not liable because he possesses a physical disability, i.e., he is inherently clumsy? Is such an argument likely to prevail? See Restatement (Third) of Torts: Liability for Physical and Emotional Harm § 11 cmt. a (2010).

Hammontree v. Jenner

Court of Appeal of California, 1971.
20 Cal.App.3d 528, 97 Cal.Rptr. 739.

■ LILLIE, J. * * * The evidence shows that on the afternoon of April 25, 1967, defendant was driving his 1959 Chevrolet home from work; at the same time plaintiff Maxine Hammontree was working in a bicycle shop owned and operated by her and her husband; without warning defendant's car crashed through the wall of the shop, struck Maxine and caused personal injuries and damage to the shop.

Defendant claimed he became unconscious during an epileptic seizure losing control of his car. He did not recall the accident but his last recollection before it, was leaving a stop light after his last stop, and his first recollection after the accident was being taken out of his car in plaintiffs' shop. Defendant testified he has a medical history of epilepsy and knows of no other reason for his loss of consciousness except an epileptic seizure; prior to 1952 he had been examined by several neurologists whose conclusion was that the condition could be controlled and who placed him on medication; * * * thereafter he saw Dr. Hyatt every six months and then on a yearly basis several years prior to 1967; * * * defendant has continued to take medication as prescribed by his physician and has done everything his doctors told him to do to avoid a seizure; he had no inkling or warning that he was about to have a seizure prior to the occurrence of the accident. In 1955 or 1956 the Department of Motor Vehicles was advised that defendant was an epileptic and placed him on probation under which every six months he had to report to the doctor who was required to advise it in writing of defendant's condition. In 1960 his probation was changed to a once-a-year report. Dr. Hyatt testified that * * * he believed it was safe for defendant to drive.

Appellants [contend] that the trial court erred in refusing to grant their motion for summary judgment on the issue of liability and * * * that the trial court committed prejudicial error in refusing to give their jury instruction on absolute liability.[1]

Under the present state of the law found in appellate authorities beginning with Waters v. Pacific Coast Dairy, Inc., 55 Cal.App.2d 789, 791–93, 131 P.2d 588 (1942) (driver rendered unconscious from sharp pain in left arm and shoulder) through Ford v. Carew & English, 89 Cal.App.2d 199, 203–04, 200 P.2d 828, 830 (1948) (fainting spells from strained heart muscles), Zabunoff v. Walker, 192 Cal.App.2d 8, 11, 13 Cal.Rptr. 463, 465 (1961), (sudden sneeze), and Tannyhill v. Pacific Motor Trans. Co., 227 Cal.App.2d 512, 520, 38 Cal.Rptr. 774, 779 (1964) (heart attack), the trial judge properly refused the instruction. The foregoing cases generally hold that liability of a driver, suddenly stricken by an illness rendering him unconscious, for injury resulting from an accident occurring during that time rests on principles of negligence. However, herein during the trial plaintiffs withdrew their claim of negligence and, after both parties rested and before jury argument, objected to the giving of any instructions on negligence electing to stand solely on the theory of absolute liability. The objection was overruled and the court refused plaintiffs' requested instruction * * *.

Appellants seek to have this court override the established law of this state which is dispositive of the issue before us as outmoded in today's social and economic structure, particularly in the light of the now recognized principles imposing liability upon the manufacturer, retailer and all distributive and vending elements and activities which bring a product to the consumer to his injury, on the basis of strict liability in tort * * *. Drawing a parallel with these products liability cases, appellants argue, with some degree of logic, that only the driver affected by a physical condition which could suddenly render him unconscious and who is aware of that condition can anticipate the hazards and foresee the dangers involved in his operation of a motor vehicle, and that the liability of those who by reason of seizure or heart failure or some other physical condition lose the ability to safely operate and control a motor vehicle resulting in injury to an innocent person should be predicated on strict liability.

We decline to superimpose the absolute liability of products liability cases upon drivers under the circumstances here. The theory on which those cases are predicated is that manufacturers, retailers

---

[1] "When the evidence shows that a driver of a motor vehicle on a public street or highway loses his ability to safely operate and control such vehicle because of some seizure or health failure, that driver is nevertheless legally liable for all injuries and property damage which an innocent person may suffer as a proximate result of the defendant's inability to so control or operate his motor vehicle."

"This is true even if you find the defendant driver had no warning of any such impending seizure or health failure."

and distributors of products are engaged in the business of distributing goods to the public and are an integral part of the over-all producing and marketing enterprise that should bear the cost of injuries from defective parts. * This policy hardly applies here and it is not enough to simply say, as do appellants, that the insurance carriers should be the ones to bear the cost of injuries to innocent victims on a strict liability basis. In Maloney v. Rath, 69 Cal.2d 442, 71 Cal.Rptr. 897, 445 P.2d 513 (1968), * * * appellant urged that defendant's violation of a safety provision (defective brakes) of the Vehicle Code makes the violator strictly liable for damages caused by the violation. While reversing the judgment for defendant upon another ground, the California Supreme Court refused to apply the doctrine of strict liability to automobile drivers. The situation involved two users of the highway but the problems of fixing responsibility under a system of strict liability are as complicated in the instant case as those in *Maloney v. Rath* and could only create uncertainty in the area of its concern. * * *

The instruction tendered by appellants was properly refused for still another reason. Even assuming the merit of appellants' position under the facts of this case in which defendant knew he had a history of epilepsy, previously had suffered seizures and at the time of the accident was attempting to control the condition by medication, the instruction does not except from its ambit the driver who suddenly is stricken by an illness or physical condition which he had no reason whatever to anticipate and of which he had no prior knowledge.

The judgment is affirmed. * * *

Keller v. DeLong

Supreme Court of New Hampshire, 1967.
108 N.H. 212, 231 A.2d 633.

■ DUNCAN, JUSTICE. The plaintiff's intestate, a registered nurse who was twenty-eight years of age, died in consequence of injuries suffered at Tyngsboro, Massachusetts at approximately 11:40 P.M. on April 14, 1963, when her automobile, operated by the defendant, collided with a utility pole at the side of the highway. She and the defendant had left Laconia late in the afternoon of the same day. Until shortly before the accident, the decedent had done the driving. A stop had been made at Bow, at which time both parties had some beer to drink. Thereafter they had sandwiches at a restaurant in Concord, and then proceeded toward Lowell, Massachusetts with the decedent at the wheel. At some place near the Massachusetts line, the defendant took the wheel at the decedent's request, and the decedent went to sleep. The accident occurred a few miles from where the defendant commenced to drive.

The Trial Court found "that the sole cause of the accident was the fact that the defendant dozed off to sleep and did not awaken in time to avoid collision with the pole." It further found: "While the defendant had been drinking, the evidence does not convince me that he was unable properly to control the vehicle while awake or that he had difficulty in doing so before dozing off. Neither is it found that after he took the wheel he had any warning that he was going to fall asleep." The Court granted the defendant's request as follows: "After taking over the wheel, Carl DeLong had no advance warning that he was about to doze, but suddenly and unexpectedly dozed at the time of the occurrence of the accident." After reasoning that dozing as a passenger "does not mean that a person cannot keep awake when charged with the responsibility of driving," the Trial Court was "not convinced . . . that in taking over the wheel . . . under all the circumstances was anything different than the ordinary man of average prudence would have done and I therefore do not find the defendant was negligent in doing so."

Under principles which receive general recognition an operator of a motor vehicle who permits himself to fall asleep while driving is guilty of ordinary negligence if he has continued to drive without taking reasonable precautions against sleeping after premonitory symptoms of drowsiness or fatigue. * * *

We are of the opinion that in the case before us, the Trial Court erred in the application of the law to the evidence. The error is best illustrated by the finding made at the defendant's request: "After taking over the wheel, Carl DeLong had no advance warning that he was about to doze, but suddenly and unexpectedly dozed at the time of occurrence of the accident." The effect of this finding, and of the like finding made by the Court of its own motion, was to isolate selected portions of the evidence in disregard of the evidence upon which the Court found that the defendant had dozed on a "couple of occasions" before he undertook to drive, and was "drowsy just before taking the wheel."

This evidence disclosed ample warning to the defendant that he might fall asleep. It was not disputed that when he took the wheel, the windows of the automobile were closed, and the heater turned on. There was no evidence that he took any precaution to arouse himself before proceeding, whether by walking around the vehicle, opening windows, or reducing the heat. * * *

Under these circumstances, a finding that "after taking over the wheel" the defendant had "suddenly and unexpectedly dozed at the time of . . . the accident" cannot be sustained. Such an occurrence could not be unexpected in the absence of precaution to prevent it. * * * The plaintiff was entitled to have the defendant's care determined upon a basis of all of the evidence, rather than just what occurred after he took the wheel. * The verdict for the defendant must therefore be set aside. * * *

Gould v. American Family Mutual Insurance Co.

Supreme Court of Wisconsin, 1996.
198 Wis.2d 450, 543 N.W.2d 282.

■ BRADLEY, JUSTICE. Both the plaintiffs, Sheri and Scott Gould, and the defendant, American Family Mutual Insurance Company, seek review of a court of appeals' decision which reversed and remanded a judgment of the Circuit Court of St. Croix County, Eric J. Lundell, Judge. The judgment imposed liability against American Family for personal injuries caused by its insured, Roland Monicken, who was institutionalized suffering from Alzheimer's disease. * * * Monicken was diagnosed with Alzheimer's disease after displaying bizarre and irrational behavior. As a result of his deteriorating condition, his family was later forced to admit him to the St. Croix Health Care Center.

Sheri Gould was the head nurse of the center's dementia unit and took care of him on several occasions. Monicken's records from St. Croix indicate that he was often disoriented, resistant to care, and occasionally combative. When not physically restrained, he often went into other patients' rooms and sometimes resisted being removed by staff. On one such occasion, Gould attempted to redirect Monicken to his own room by touching him on the elbow. She sustained personal injuries when Monicken responded by knocking her to the floor. *

Gould and her husband brought suit against Monicken and his insurer, American Family. American Family admitted coverage and filed a motion for summary judgment, arguing that Monicken was incapable of negligence as a matter of law due to his lack of mental capacity. An affidavit of Monicken's treating psychiatrist filed in support of the motion stated that Monicken was unable to appreciate the consequences of his acts or to control his behavior. * * * [T]he court instructed the jury to disregard any evidence related to Monicken's mental condition and to determine his negligence under the objective reasonable person standard. * The jury found Monicken totally negligent and a judgment of liability was entered against American Family. *

The court of appeals * * * reversed the judgment, holding that "a person may not be held civilly liable where a mental condition deprives that person of the ability to control his or her conduct." * * * Both the Goulds and American Family petitioned this court for review. * * *

It is a widely accepted rule in most American jurisdictions that mentally disabled adults are held responsible for the torts they commit regardless of their capacity to comprehend their actions; they are held to an objective reasonable person standard. See generally, Restatement (Second) of Torts § 283B (1965); W. Page Keeton *et al.*, Prosser and Keeton on the Law of Torts, § 135 (1984). Legal scholars trace the origins of this rule to an English trespass case decided in 1616, at a time when strict liability controlled. *Id.* at 1072, citing Weaver v. Ward, 80 Eng.Rep. 284 (K.B. 1616).

When fault-based liability replaced strict liability, American courts in common law jurisdictions identified the matter as a question of public policy and maintained the rule imposing liability on the mentally disabled. Although early case law suggested that Wisconsin followed this trend, * this court specifically adopted the common law rule and the public policy justifications behind it in German Mut. Fire Ins. Soc'y v. Meyer, 218 Wis. 381, 385, 261 N.W. 211, 212 (1935).

In *Meyer*, the defendant was criminally charged with arson to a barn but was committed to a mental hospital after he was found to be insane. In the civil claim filed by the insurer who covered the loss, the defendant pled his insanity as a defense. * The court primarily relied on cases from other jurisdictions to conclude that insanity was not a defense for tort liability. *

In doing so the court quoted with approval the following statement of the general rule and public policy rationale behind it:

It is the well settled rule that a person *non compos mentis* is liable in damages to one injured by reason of a tort committed by him unless evil intent or express malice constitutes an essential element in the plaintiff's recovery. This rule is usually considered to be based on the principle that where a loss must be borne by one of two innocent persons, it shall be borne by him who occasioned it, and it has also been held that public policy requires the enforcement of the liability in order that those interested in the estate of the insane person, as relatives or otherwise, may be under inducement to restrain him and that tortfeasors may not simulate or pretend insanity to defend their wrongful acts causing damage to others. * * *

This court did not have occasion to address the issue again until Breunig v. American Family Ins. Co., 45 Wis.2d 536, 173 N.W.2d 619 (1970). In *Breunig*, Erma Veith was overcome with a mental delusion while driving and crossed the center line of a roadway, striking the plaintiff's vehicle. The plaintiff sued Veith's automobile liability insurer, and a jury returned a verdict finding her causally negligent on the theory that she had knowledge or forewarning of her mental delusions. On appeal, the insurer argued that Veith could not be negligent as a matter of law because she was unable to drive with a conscious mind based on the sudden mental delusion. This court created a limited exception to the common law rule, holding that insanity could be a defense in the rare case "where the [person] is suddenly overcome without forewarning by a mental disability or disorder which incapacitates him from conforming his conduct to the standards of a reasonable man under like circumstances." However, because this court concluded that there was sufficient evidence for the jury to find that Veith had forewarning of the mental delusions, she was not entitled to use her condition as a defense.

* * * In contrast to the broad dicta found in *Breunig*, the actual holding was very limited:

> All we hold is that a sudden mental incapacity equivalent in its effect to such physical causes as a sudden heart attack, epileptic seizure, stroke, or fainting should be treated alike and not under the general rule of insanity.

* * * Mental impairments and emotional disorders come in infinite types and degrees. As the American Law Institute recognized in its Restatement of Torts, a legitimate concern in formulating a test for mentally disabled persons in negligence cases is "[t]he difficulty of drawing any satisfactory line between mental deficiency and those variations of temperament, intellect and emotional balance which cannot, as a practical matter, be taken into account in imposing liability for damage done." Restatement (Second) of Torts, § 283B, cmt. b, illus. 1.

The difficulties encountered by the trier of fact in determining the existence, nature, degree, and effect of a mental disability may introduce into the civil law some of the issues that currently exist in the insanity defense in criminal law. We are wary of establishing a defense to negligence based on indeterminate standards of mental disability given the complexities of the various mental illnesses and the increasing rate at which new illnesses are discovered to explain behavior. * Further, while the traditional public policy rationale relied on by this court in *Meyer* in support of the common law rule are subject to criticism, * we remain hesitant to abandon the long-standing rule in favor of a broad rule adopting the subjective standard for all mentally disabled persons. * * *

Even though the jury determined that Monicken was negligent and that his negligence was a cause of the plaintiff's injuries, liability does not necessarily follow. Public policy considerations may preclude liability. * * * One recognized public policy reason for not imposing liability despite a finding of negligence is that allowance of recovery would place an unreasonable burden on the negligent tortfeasor. * As explained in detail below, this court concludes that the circumstances of this case totally negate the rationale behind the *Meyer* rule imposing liability on the mentally disabled, and therefore application of the rule would place an unreasonable burden on the institutionalized mentally disabled tortfeasor.

The first rationale set forth in *Meyer* is that "where a loss must be borne by one of two innocent persons, it shall be borne by him who occasioned it." Meyer, 218 Wis. at 385, 261 N.W. at 213. The record reveals that Gould was not an innocent member of the public unable to anticipate or safeguard against the harm when encountered. Rather, she was employed as a caretaker specifically for dementia patients and knowingly encountered the dangers associated with such employment. It is undisputed that Gould, as head nurse of the dementia unit, knew Monicken was diagnosed with Alzheimer's disease and was aware of his disorientation and his potential for violent outbursts. Her own notes indicate that Monicken was angry and resisted being removed from another patient's room on the day of her injury. * * *

Holding Monicken negligent under these circumstances places too great a burden on him because his disorientation and potential for violence is the very reason he was institutionalized and needed the aid of employed caretakers. Accordingly, we conclude that the first *Meyer* rationale does not apply in this case.

The second rationale used to justify the rule is that "those interested in the estate of the insane person, as relatives or otherwise, may be under inducement to restrain him. . . ." *Id.* at 385, 261 N.W. at 213. This rationale also has little application to the present case. Monicken's relatives did everything they could to restrain him when they placed him in a secured dementia unit of a restricted health care center. When a mentally disabled person is placed in a nursing home, long-term care facility, health care center, or similar restrictive institution for the mentally disabled, those "interested in the estate" of that person are not likely in need of such further inducement.

The third reason for the common law rule set forth in *Meyer* is to prevent tortfeasors from "simulat[ing] or pretend[ing] insanity to defend their wrongful acts. . . ." *Id.* This rationale is likewise inapplicable under the facts of this case. To suggest that Mr. Monicken would "simulate or pretend" the symptoms of Alzheimer's disease over a period of years in order to avoid a future tort liability is incredible. It is likewise difficult to imagine circumstances under which persons would feign the symptoms of a mental disability and subject themselves to commitment in an institution in order to avoid some future civil liability.

In sum, we agree with the Goulds that ordinarily a mentally disabled person is responsible for his or her torts. However, we conclude that this rule does not apply in this case because the circumstances totally negate the rationale behind the rule and would place an unreasonable burden on the negligent institutionalized mentally disabled. When a mentally disabled person injures an employed caretaker, the injured party can reasonably foresee the danger and is not "innocent" of the risk involved. By placing a mentally disabled person in an institution or similar restrictive setting, "those interested in the estate" of that person are not likely to be in need of an inducement for greater restraint. It is incredible to assert that a tortfeasor would "simulate or pretend insanity" over a prolonged period of time and even be institutionalized in order to avoid being held liable for damages for some future civil act. Therefore, we hold that a person institutionalized, as here, with a mental disability, and who does not have the capacity to control or appreciate his or her conduct cannot be liable for injuries caused to caretakers who are employed for financial compensation. * * *

NOTES

1. *Distinction between Physical and Mental Disabilities.* Why should the law's treatment of physical and mental disabilities differ? See generally Harper, James and Gray on Torts §§ 16.2, 16.7 & 16.8 (at notes 15 *et seq.*); compare Restatement (Third) of Torts: Liability for Physical and Emotional Harm §§ 11(a) & 11(c) (2010) . How should the law react to the increasing body of scientific evidence showing that emotional disabilities most often have an organic basis? See, e.g., Harry J.F. Korrell, The Liability of Mentally Disabled Tort Defendants, 19 Law. & Psychol. Rev. 1 (1995).

2. *Sudden Mental Incapacity.* What if a defendant experiences a sudden mental incapacity, such as a hallucination or psychotic episode? In *Gould,* the Wisconsin Supreme Court discusses an earlier Wisconsin case, Breunig v. American Family Ins. Co., 45 Wis.2d 536, 539, 173 N.W.2d 619, 622 (1970), in which the defendant's car veered across the center lane when "she believed that God was taking a hold of the steering wheel and was directing her car. She saw the truck coming and stepped on the gas in order to become airborne because she knew she could fly because Batman does it." As noted in *Gould,* the Wisconsin Supreme Court stated that insanity could be a defense " 'where the [person] is suddenly overcome without forewarning by a mental disability or disorder which incapacitates him from conforming his conduct to the standards of a reasonable man under like circumstances.' " This indication that a defendant might not be negligent if suffering from a sudden, delusional state has been frequently criticized, and most courts hold defendants liable, whether or not their mental illnesses or hallucinations were "sudden." See generally Restatement (Third) of Torts: Liability for Physical and Emotional Harm § 11 cmt. d (2010).

3. *Economic Realities.* On whom would the economic impact of a judgment against the defendant in *Breunig* fall? Or a judgment against the defendant in *Gould?*

Dellwo v. Pearson

Supreme Court of Minnesota, 1961.
259 Minn. 452, 107 N.W.2d 859.

■ LOEVINGER, JUSTICE. This case arises out of a personal injury to Jeanette E. Dellwo, one of the plaintiffs. She and her husband, the other plaintiff, were fishing on one of Minnesota's numerous and beautiful lakes by trolling at a low speed with about 40 to 50 feet of line trailing behind the boat. Defendant, a 12-year-old boy, operating a boat with an outboard motor, crossed behind plaintiffs' boat. Just at this time Mrs. Dellwo felt a jerk on her line which suddenly was pulled out very rapidly. The line was knotted to the spool of the reel so that when it had run out the fishing rod was pulled downward, the reel hit the side of the boat, the reel came apart, and part of it flew through the lens of Mrs. Dellwo's glasses and injured her eye. Both parties then proceeded to a dock where inspection of defendant's motor disclosed 2 to 3 feet of fishing line wound about the propeller.

The case was fully tried to the court and jury and submitted to the jury upon instructions which, in so far as relevant here, instructed the jury that: (1) In considering the matter of negligence the duty to which defendant is held is modified because he is a child, a child not being held to the same standard of conduct as an adult and being required to exercise only that degree of care which ordinarily is exercised by children of like age, mental capacity, and experience under the same or similar circumstances * * *.

A more important point involves the instruction that defendant was to be judged by the standard of care of a child of similar age rather than of a reasonable man. There is no doubt that the instruction given substantially reflects the language of numerous decisions in this and other courts. * However, the great majority of these cases involve the issue of contributory negligence and the standard of care that may properly be required of a child in protecting himself against some hazard. * The standard of care stated is proper and appropriate for such situations.

However, this court has previously recognized that there may be a difference between the standard of care that is required of a child in protecting himself against hazards and the standard that may be applicable when his activities expose others to hazards. * Certainly in the circumstances of modern life, where vehicles moved by powerful motors are readily available and frequently operated by immature individuals, we should be skeptical of a rule that would allow motor vehicles to be operated to the hazard of the public with less than the normal minimum degree of care and competence. *

To give legal sanction to the operation of automobiles by teen-agers with less than ordinary care for the safety of others is impractical today, to say the least. We may take judicial notice of the hazards of automobile traffic, the frequency of accidents, the often catastrophic results of accidents, and the fact that immature individuals are no less prone to accidents than adults. While minors are entitled to be judged by standards commensurate with age, experience, and wisdom when engaged in activities appropriate to their age, experience, and wisdom, it would be unfair to the public to permit a minor in the operation of a motor vehicle to observe any other standards of care and conduct than those expected of all others. A person observing children at play with toys, throwing balls, operating tricycles or velocipedes, or engaged in other childhood activities may anticipate conduct that does not reach an adult standard of care or prudence. * However, one cannot know whether the operator of an approaching automobile, airplane, or powerboat is a minor or an adult, and usually cannot protect himself against youthful imprudence even if warned. Accordingly, we hold that in the operation of an automobile, airplane, or powerboat, a minor is to be held to the same standard of care as an adult.

Undoubtedly there are problems attendant upon such a view. However, there are problems in any rule that may be adopted applicable to this matter. They will have to be solved as they may present themselves in the setting of future cases. The latest tentative revision of the Restatement of Torts proposes an even broader rule that would hold a child to adult standards whenever he engages "in an activity which is normally undertaken only by adults, and for which adult qualifications are required."[15] However, it is unnecessary to this case to adopt a rule in such broad form, and, therefore, we expressly leave open the question whether or not that rule should be adopted in this state. For the present it is sufficient to say that no reasonable grounds for differentiating between automobiles, airplanes, and powerboats appears, and that a rule requiring a single standard of care in the operation of such vehicles, regardless of the age of the operator, appears to us to be required by the circumstances of contemporary life.

Reversed and remanded for a new trial.

NOTE

Standard of Care for Children Engaged in "Adult" Activities. Should the concept of adult activities be extended beyond the operation of motor vehicles? Is a game of golf played by an 11-year-old an adult activity? See Neumann v. Shlansky, 58 Misc.2d 128, 294 N.Y.S.2d 628 (Cnty. Ct.1968). Deer hunting by a 17-year-old? See Purtle v. Shelton, 251 Ark. 519, 474 S.W.2d 123 (1971).

Courts commonly hold that children of very tender years are incapable of negligence. E.g., DeLuca v. Bowden, 42 Ohio St.2d 392, 329 N.E.2d 109 (1975) (children under 7); Clark v. Circus-Circus, Inc., 525 F.2d 1328 (9th Cir.1975); cf. Miller v. Graff, 196 Md. 609, 78 A.2d 220 (1951) (children under the age of five are incapable of contributory negligence as a matter of law). See also Alabama Power Co. v. Taylor, 293 Ala. 484, 306 So.2d 236 (1975) (evidentiary requirements as to capacity of children between ages of 7 and 14).

C. THE RESPECTIVE ROLES OF JUDGE AND JURY

Once negligence has been defined by reference to the activities of the reasonable person, one possible approach would be to allow the jury to decide whether the particular activities of the defendant in an individual case are within the realm of reasonable care. Who, after all,

---

[15] Restatement [Second], Torts, Tentative Draft No. 4, § 238A cmt. c. * * *

could better evaluate the characteristics of reasonable care than the jury? What disadvantages would result from this approach?

Courts, however, frequently define negligence more specifically by reference to custom and judicially adopted standards of care, as well as statutes, ordinances, and regulations. This section begins with the question of when it is appropriate for judges themselves to establish judicially created rules governing what may or may not constitute negligence in specific factual contexts. In addition, some courts misleadingly label their determinations of no liability (for breach of a duty of reasonable care) as instances in which the defendants owed "no duty" to plaintiffs in the first instance.

Lorenzo v. Wirth

Supreme Judicial Court of Massachusetts, 1898.
170 Mass. 596, 49 N.E. 1010.

■ HOLMES, J. This is an action for personal injuries suffered by the plaintiff in consequence of her stepping into an open coal hole. The coal hole was situated about 18 inches in front of a house held by the defendant under a lease, and upon land embraced in the lease. The house was set back from the street, and the coal hole was 2 feet or more outside the street line. But the paving over the space between the street line and the house was continuous with that of the street, and there was nothing in the usual conditions to give notice that it was not part of the street except the way in which it generally was used by tenants for the deposit of barrels, etc., and the fact that the steps of the house next to it on the side from which the plaintiff was coming came out to the line of the street.

At the time of the accident a coal wagon was backed up to the side wall in front of the premises, and coal which had been ordered by the defendant was being delivered from it by the servants of a coal dealer. One of these had uncovered the coal hole, and was shoveling the last of the coal out of the wagon upon the sidewalk. The other stood by the hole, doing such work as was necessary to help the coal pour down the hole. The coal covered the whole sidewalk from the wagon to near the house. The plaintiff, a Spanish woman, who, according to her own testimony never had seen coal put through a coal hole before, stepped upon the steps of the next building above mentioned, thence stepped upon the coal, and then with her other leg went into the coal hole, which was 30 inches from the corner of the steps. The judge was asked to direct a verdict for the defendant, which he refused to do, and the defendant excepted.

The question, in its common form is whether these facts show any evidence of negligence proper to be left to the jury. But it will be seen that it is not a question of evidence, in the ordinary sense. It is not whether there is anything tending to prove a disputed fact. The acts and omissions of the defendant as to the plaintiff are fully known and undisputed. The question is whether those acts and omissions made the defendant liable for the plaintiff's hurt,—in the common language of the law, whether they constituted a breach of duty to the plaintiff. It will be observed, further, that the facts on which the question arises are quite simple, and are likely to be repeated with slight variations as long as coal holes exist; that they are all matters of eyesight, capable of being photographed; and that theory must recognize that at some point the visible situation would be such as to warrant the defendant in assuming that the public were sufficiently warned, or, in other words, that the defendant would have done her whole duty. * It is true that blind men, and foreigners unused to our ways have a right to walk in the streets, and this fact must be taken into consideration in drawing the line of the defendant's duty; but the line, when drawn, is a physical line, so to speak,—it is a visible situation, in which all the arrangements or precautions which the law requires of a defendant are there, upon the ground.

In simple cases of this sort, courts have felt able to determine what, in every case, however complex, defendants are bound at their peril to know, and are presumed to know, namely, whether the given situation is on one or the other side of the line. The examples are numerous * * *. We think that the case at bar is not beyond our competence to decide. The greatest danger in attempting to do so is that of being misled by ready-made generalizations, and of thinking only in phrases to which, as lawyers, the judges have become accustomed, instead of looking straight at things and regarding the facts in all their concreteness as a jury would do. Too broadly generalized conceptions are a constant source of fallacy. Thus, it is easy to say that the continuity of the sidewalk was an invitation, and then to discuss in universals the duty of one who invites the public upon his land. But, invitation or no, the invitation is not the same, and the responsibility is not the same, when the place is seemingly in the middle of a clear highway, and looks safe and ready for travel to one who is walking straight along the open road, as it is where the place is in a snug corner, and is capable of being reached only by going over steps which manifestly are not part of the highway, and then by stepping into a pile of coal which surrounds the spot in question. Without considering whether, under such circumstances, the defendant would be freed from all duty in respect of the temporary dangers created by the coal dealer while he was doing his work *, it is the opinion of a majority of the court that she was not called on to stand guard, and to tell the public that they must not understand the continuity of the pavement under the coal, if they happened to know of it, as a present assurance that they might step blindly into the coal, and as a warranty that there was no coal hole in the place where the coal was pouring down. A heap of coal on a sidewalk in Boston is an indication, according to common experience, that there very possibly may be a coal hole to receive it. But, without saying that it always is a sufficient warning to look out for one, we are of opinion that as against a person coming from where the plaintiff came from, with a coal hole situated as this was, the coal in the condition shown, and the business of delivering then going on, in the absence of men with baskets or other indication of a different means of making the delivery, the defendant cannot be said to have been wanting in due care.

Exceptions sustained.

■ KNOWLTON, J. (dissenting). I am unable to agree to the opinion of the majority in this case. The building occupied by the defendant, and the adjoining buildings for a considerable distance towards the west, stood back from the line of the street about three feet and eight inches. The buildings in the other direction, with their projections, came out to the line of the street. The space in front of the defendant's building, and of the adjoining buildings towards the west, was paved with the same kind of material, and on the same level, all the way from the buildings to the curbstone, and was used as a sidewalk. The walk was not very wide, and there was nothing to mark the line of the street. In Holmes v. Drew, 151 Mass. 578, 580, 25 N.E. 22, 23 (1890), is this language:

> The jury might have inferred from the facts stated that the defendant laid out and paved the sidewalk on her own land in order that it should be used by the public as the sidewalk of the street, and allowed it to remain apparently the part of the street that was intended to be used by foot passengers. This would amount to an invitation to the public to enter upon, and use as a public sidewalk, the land so prepared; and the plaintiff, so using it, would have gone upon the defendant's land by her implied invitation, and she would owe to him the duty not to expose him to a dangerous condition of the walk, which reasonable care on her part would have prevented.

* * * I think that the jury might have found the circumstances under which the plaintiff was walking upon the sidewalk at the time of the accident to be such as entitled her to protection or warning against openings in it.

At the time of the accident the coal hole was being used for the defendant's benefit, by her authority. If this would ordinarily be attended with danger to the public, the defendant was bound to see that proper precautions were taken for their safety, even if the work was being done by an independent contractor. * * * There was testimony from several witnesses that the coal covered the sidewalk from the curbstone to the coal hole, and two others testified that it extended from the curbstone to the line of the defendant's house. The accident occurred at a little before 6 o'clock on the evening of November 15, and there was testimony that it was dark, and that there was no daylight. There was evidence from the plaintiff, and from another witness who was present, that they saw nobody about the coal hole before the accident. One of the two men who were delivering the coal was in the wagon, from which he had just shoveled the last of the coal, and was busy with his team, and he did not see the plaintiff until she was being lifted out of the hole. The other testified that he was about three feet from the coal hole; that he could not say what he was doing, that he thought his head was turned around, looking up Eliot Street towards Tremont Street, which was in the direction opposite to that from which the plaintiff was coming. He also said in his testimony: "I was not shoveling coal at that time. I was trying to keep myself on my feet. There was a throng of people going up there, each way."

Apparently the plaintiff was going as others were, except that they did not happen to step into the hole. According to her testimony, she had just come from Spain, and had never seen coal put into a cellar through a coal hole. Eliot Street is traveled by many persons. Besides the plaintiff, others might have been expected there who had never seen coal put through holes in sidewalks. The wagon was backed up to the curbstone, and there were electric cars and teams passing through the street. I think that the jury well might have found that a coal hole on a public sidewalk where a throng of persons was passing in each direction was left open on a dark evening, with coal scattered about it from the curbstone to the side of the defendant's building with a large two-horse wagon backed up against the curbstone, with nothing to indicate to pedestrians that there was an opening there, and with nobody to guard the hole or to warn them of danger. It seems to me that there was evidence of negligence on the part of those who left the hole open and unguarded.

What kind of conduct is required, under complex conditions, to reach the usual standard of due care, namely, the ordinary care of persons of common prudence, is a question of fact, to be determined according to the observation and experience of common men. Even when there is no conflict of testimony, if there are acts and omissions, of which some tend to show negligence, and others do not, the question whether there was negligence or not is, in my judgment, a question for a jury. This proposition I deem to be established by such unanimity of decision as to need no citation of authorities in support of it. I think the case was rightly submitted to the jury. * * *

Excerpt, Oliver Wendell Holmes, Jr., The Common Law
89, 96–99 (Mark DeWolfe Howe ed., 1963) (1881).

* * * The ideal average prudent man, whose equivalent the jury is taken to be in many cases, and whose culpability or innocence is the supposed test, is a constant, and his conduct under given circumstances is theoretically always the same. * * *

If, now, the ordinary liabilities in tort arise from failure to comply with fixed and uniform standards of external conduct, which every man is presumed and required to know, it is obvious that it ought to be possible, sooner or later, to formulate these standards at least to some extent, and that to do so must at last be the business of the court. It is equally clear that the featureless generality, that the defendant was bound to use such care as a prudent man would do under the circumstances, ought to be continually giving place to the specific one, that he was bound to use this or that precaution under these or those circumstances. The standard which the defendant was bound to come up to was a standard of specific acts or omissions, with reference to the specific circumstances in which he found himself. If in the whole department of unintentional wrongs the courts arrived at no further utterance than the question of negligence, and left every case, without rudder or compass, to the jury, they would simply confess their inability to state a very large part of the law which they required the defendant to know, and would assert, by implication, that nothing could be learned by experience. But neither courts nor legislatures have ever stopped at that point. * * *

The principles of substantive law which have been established by the courts are believed to have been somewhat obscured by having presented themselves oftenest in the form of rulings upon the sufficiency of evidence. When a judge rules that there is no evidence of negligence, he does something more than is embraced in an ordinary ruling that there is no evidence of a fact. He rules that the acts or omissions proved or in question do not constitute a ground of legal liability, and in this way the law is gradually enriching itself from daily life, as it should. * * *

No doubt, as has been said above, the averment that the defendant has been guilty of negligence is a complex one: first, that he has done or omitted certain things; second, that his alleged conduct does not come up to the legal standard. And so long as the controversy is simply on the first half, the whole complex averment is plain matter for the jury without special instructions, just as a question of ownership would be where the only dispute was as to the fact upon which the legal conclusion was founded. But when a controversy arises on the second half, the question whether the court or the jury ought to judge of the defendant's conduct is wholly unaffected by the accident, whether there is or is not also a dispute as to what that conduct was. If there is such a dispute, it is entirely possible to give a series of hypothetical instructions adapted to every state of facts which it is open to the jury to find. If there is no such dispute, the court may still take their opinion as to the standard. The problem is to explain the relative functions of court and jury with regard to the latter.

When a case arises in which the standard of conduct, pure and simple, is submitted to the jury, the explanation is plain. It is that the court, not entertaining any clear views of public policy applicable to the matter, derives the rule to be applied from daily experience, as it has been agreed that the great body of the law of tort has been derived. But the court further feels that it is not itself possessed of sufficient practical experience to lay down the rule intelligently. It conceives that twelve men taken from the practical part of the community can aid its judgment. * Therefore it aids its conscience by taking the opinion of the jury.

But supposing a state of facts often repeated in practice, is it to be imagined that the court is to go on leaving the standard to the jury forever? Is it not manifest, on the contrary, that if the jury is, on the whole, as fair a tribunal as it is represented to be, the lesson which can be got from that source will be learned? Either the court will find that the fair teaching of experience is that the conduct complained of usually is or is not blameworthy, and therefore, unless explained, is or is not a ground of liability; or it will find the jury oscillating to and fro, and will see the necessity of making up its mind for itself. There is no reason why any other such question should not be settled, as well as that of liability for stairs with smooth strips of brass upon their edges. The exceptions would mainly be found where the standard was rapidly changing, as, for instance, in some questions of medical treatment. *

If this be the proper conclusion in plain cases, further consequences ensue. Facts do not often exactly repeat themselves in practice; but cases with comparatively small variations from each other do. A judge who has long sat at *nisi prius* ought gradually to acquire a fund of experience which enables him to represent the common sense of the community in ordinary instances far better than an average jury. He should be able to lead and to instruct them in detail, even where he thinks it desirable, on the whole, to take their opinion. Furthermore, the sphere in which he is able to rule without taking their opinion at all should be continually growing.

Baltimore & Ohio Railroad Co. v. Goodman

Supreme Court of the United States, 1927.
275 U.S. 66, 48 S.Ct. 24, 72 L.Ed. 167.

■ HOLMES, JUSTICE. This is a suit brought by the widow and administratrix of Nathan Goodman against the petitioner for causing his death by running him down at a grade crossing. The defense is that Goodman's own negligence caused the death. At the trial, the defendant asked the Court to direct a verdict for it, but the request, and others looking to the same direction, were refused, and the plaintiff got a verdict and a judgment which was affirmed by the Circuit Court of Appeals. *

Goodman was driving an automobile truck in an easterly direction and was killed by a train running southwesterly across the road at a rate of not less than sixty miles an hour. The line was straight, but it is said by the respondent that Goodman "had no practical view" beyond a section house two hundred and forty-three feet north of the crossing until he was about twenty feet from the first rail, or, as the respondent argues, twelve feet from danger, and that then the engine was still obscured by the section house. He had been driving at the rate of ten or twelve miles an hour, but had cut down his rate to five or six miles at about forty feet from the crossing. It is thought that there was an emergency in which, so far as appears, Goodman did all that he could.

We do not go into further details as to Goodman's precise situation, beyond mentioning that it was daylight and that he was familiar with the crossing, for it appears to us plain that nothing is suggested by the evidence to relieve Goodman from responsibility for his own death. When a man goes upon a railroad track he knows that he goes to a place where he will be killed if a train comes upon him before he is clear of the track. He knows that he must stop for the train, not the train stop for him. In such circumstances it seems to us that if a driver cannot be sure otherwise whether a train is dangerously near he must stop and get out of his vehicle, although obviously he will not often be required to do more than to stop and look. It seems to us that if he relies upon not hearing the train or any signal and takes no further precaution he does so at his own risk. If at the last moment Goodman found himself in an emergency it was his own fault that he did not reduce his speed earlier or come to a stop. It is true * * * that the question of due care very generally is left to the jury. But we are dealing with a standard of conduct, and when the standard is clear it should be laid down once for all by the Courts. *

Judgment reversed. * * *

NOTES

1.   *A Biographical Note on Justice Holmes.* Concerning *Goodman,* a biographer of Holmes wrote, "Holmes' fondness for taking cases away from juries combined with the fact that he had never learned to drive an automobile to produce one of his most notorious opinions." G. Edward White, Justice Oliver Wendell Holmes: Law and the Inner Self 384 (1993). "Holmes was in his late sixties when automobiles first became available as a mode of transportation, and the Holmeses did not acquire an automobile

[driven by a chauffeur] until 1925, when Holmes was eighty-four." *Id.* at 568.

2. *Subsequent History.* In Pokora v. Wabash Ry. Co., 292 U.S. 98, 54 S.Ct. 580, 78 L.Ed. 1149 (1934), the United States Supreme Court again considered a case involving a railroad crossing collision with facts similar to those in *Goodman*. The court, speaking through Justice Cardozo, limited the holding in *Goodman* to its facts, stating:

> Standards of prudent conduct are declared at times by courts, but they are taken over from the facts of life. To get out of a vehicle and reconnoiter is an uncommon precaution, as everyday experience informs us. Besides being uncommon, it is very likely to be futile, and sometimes dangerous.

Justice Cardozo advised of the "need for caution in framing standards of behavior that amount to rules of law. The need is the more urgent when there is no background of experience out of which the standards have emerged. They are then, not the natural flowerings of behavior in its customary forms, but rules artificially developed, and imposed from without."

In more modern times, federal courts apply the substantive rules of state law to cases under diversity jurisdiction in the federal courts. See Erie R.R. Co. v. Tompkins, 304 U.S. 64, 58 S.Ct. 817, 82 L.Ed. 1188 (1938) (federal courts exercising diversity jurisdiction must follow state statutory law and the general common law of the state as interpreted by the state's highest court).

Excerpt, Richard M. Nixon, Changing Rules of Liability in Automobile Accident Litigation
3 Law and Contemp. Probs. 476, 477–78 (1936).

* * * In the days of poor roads and low speeds, the facts of an accident could be reconstructed in the courtroom with some degree of accuracy, and the problem of determining fault did not present unusual difficulties. But with high-powered cars and concrete highways, the probability that an accident—often the consequence of a fractional mistake in management—can and will be described accurately in court has become increasingly remote, especially where court congestion has delayed the time of trial. The consequent uncertainties as to the facts have given to the jury in those cases where it determines the question of fault an almost unrestricted power to choose between the litigants at bar. And the notorious tendency of that body to prefer the plaintiff, * especially as against the defendant suspected of carrying insurance, has made "taking the case away from the jury" one of the primary objectives of the defense counsel.

To this end they have invoked the power of the trial judge to direct a verdict for the defendant if the evidence clearly demonstrates either the plaintiff's fault or the defendant's freedom from fault. But so long as the standard of care is that which a reasonable man would have exercised under the circumstances, the opportunity for such a demonstration is obviously limited. Where, however, the standard of care governing a specific situation has become crystallized in a rule of law, e.g., that a driver approaching a railroad crossing must "stop, look, and listen," the power of the trial judge is materially increased for the evidence may clearly show whether that standard was observed by the party to whom it is applicable.

It is not surprising then that it has been around the standard of care that some of the most important battles of automobile tort law have been waged. And the conflict has been most acute with respect to the standard of care applicable to the plaintiff. A specific standard of care is, as a rule, a more rigorous requirement than the general standard of the "reasonable man." For plaintiff's counsel, already enjoying the favor of the jury, the need to obtain a directed verdict based upon a proved deviation from a specific standard is less important than for a defendant's counsel who will strive to wrest the case from the jury by seeking a directed verdict based on the plaintiff's failure to observe such a standard. It is in the rise and decline of those specific standards of care most frequently invoked against plaintiffs that the change in the rules of liability in automobile cases can best be marked. *

The specific standard of care in civil cases is usually either of judicial creation or adoption. When a judge has discovered through hearing a number of cases involving similar situations that certain conduct is generally blameworthy he may rule that a person guilty of such conduct is negligent as a matter of law. * If the appellate court approves his ruling, or if that court itself so rules, the standard becomes a rule of law to be followed in all future cases involving similar facts.

NOTE

The Possibility of Pervasive Juror Bias. Nixon argues that the jury has a "notorious tendency * * * to prefer the plaintiff." Such a bias is widely assumed by attorneys regularly trying torts cases. The limited empirical evidence that exists, however, suggests more even-handedness than might be thought. According to a comprehensive study of nationwide civil cases in 2005 conducted by the U.S. Department of Justice, plaintiffs won in 51.3 percent of all tort cases. Lynn Langton and Thomas H. Cohen, Bureau of Justice Statistics, Civil Bench and Jury Trials in State Courts, 2005, 3–4 (October 2008, rev. April 2009), *available at* http://www.bjs.gov/content/pub/pdf/cbjtsc05.pdf.

Broussard v. State

Supreme Court of Louisiana, 2013.
113 So.3d 175.

■ KNOLL, JUSTICE. * * * The Wooddale Tower ("the Tower") is a twelve-story, State-owned office building located in Baton Rouge. There are two elevators in the Tower's lobby. Sometime in 1998, the State contracted to have the Tower's roof repaired. This roofing project generated a large amount of dust and debris, which eventually settled and accumulated on the elevators' relay contacts, causing the elevators to operate erratically for several years. Most significantly, the Tower's elevators would often stop in a position uneven with floors of the building. These misalignments would create an offset between the elevator floor and the building floor ranging anywhere from a few inches to several feet.

Between 1999 and 2000, the State received multiple complaints from the Tower's tenants expressing their concern the malfunctioning elevators would eventually cause a serious accident. For instance, several employees from the Department of Social Services, an agency housed on the Tower's first floor, sent a memorandum to their supervisor on July 10, 2000, in which they * * * noted the elevators' frequent failure to stop in a position flush with the building's floors, stating this problem would often cause employees to trip when entering or exiting the elevators. * * *

On January 23, 2001, Broussard, a United Parcel Service ("UPS") delivery driver, sustained a serious back injury while maneuvering a loaded dolly into one of the Tower's misaligned elevators. Before this incident, Broussard worked for UPS eleven years, seven of which were as a delivery driver. During his tenure as a UPS driver, Broussard delivered parcels to the Tower on a daily basis. He was, therefore, familiar with the building and knew its elevators intermittently stopped at a level uneven with the building's floors.

On the morning of the accident, Broussard * * * loaded a standard-issue UPS dolly with six boxes of computer paper weighing approximately three hundred pounds. Broussard's objective was to deliver this paper to the Tower's eighth floor. He then entered the lobby with his delivery, where one of the elevators stood open with its floor elevated one and one-half to three inches above the lobby floor. Two individuals had entered the elevator before Broussard. One of them, Tammy Loupe, testified Broussard initially held the dolly in front of his body and attempted to *push* it onto the elevator. The offset between the elevator and lobby floors, however, impeded Broussard's momentum and prevented him from pushing the dolly forward. After his initial maneuver failed, Broussard turned around, stepped backwards into the elevator, and attempted to *pull* the dolly over the elevation. Broussard successfully pulled the dolly over the offset, but the inertia created by the pull caused him to lose control of the load and forcefully pushed him into the back wall of the elevator. The resulting impact caused Broussard to suffer a serious back injury * * *.

After the accident Broussard was unable to return to work for UPS. Because his doctors prohibited him from lifting over 70 pounds, Broussard was forced to obtain less strenuous, but lower-paying, employment. At the beginning of trial in August 2010, he was employed as a delivery driver for a dry cleaner.

* * * In his petition, Broussard alleged the State was negligent in failing to properly maintain and adequately repair * * * [the elevator], thereby creating an unreasonable risk of harm. * * * At the conclusion of trial, the jury returned a verdict in favor of Broussard, specifically finding (1) the offset between the elevator and lobby floors created an unreasonable risk of harm, (2) the State had a reasonable opportunity to remedy the defect but failed to do so, and (3) the defect was the proximate cause of Broussard's injuries. The jury then found Broussard 38% at fault in causing the accident and apportioned the remaining

62% to the State.[a] Ultimately, the jury awarded Broussard $1,589,890.23 in damages. After reducing these damages in proportion to Broussard's assigned percentage of fault, the District Court rendered a judgment consistent with the jury verdict in the amount of $985,732.56. The Court of Appeal reversed, holding the jury's determination the offset created an unreasonable risk of harm was manifestly erroneous. * * *

* * * The sole issue we must address here is whether the defect in the Tower's elevators created an unreasonable risk of harm * * *. The owner of a building is not responsible for all injuries resulting from any risk posed by the building. * Rather, the owner is only responsible for those injuries caused by a * * * condition * * * that presents an unreasonable risk of harm to others. * We have described the question of whether a defect presents an unreasonable risk of harm as "a disputed issue of mixed fact and law or policy that is peculiarly a question for the jury or trier of the facts." Reed v. Wal-Mart Stores, Inc., 708 So.2d 362, 364 (La.1998). * As a mixed question of law and fact, it is the fact-finder's role—either the jury or the court in a bench trial—to determine whether a defect is unreasonably dangerous. Thus, whether a defect presents an unreasonable risk of harm is "a matter wed to the facts" and must be determined in light of facts and circumstances of each particular case. * * *

* * * Under Louisiana law, a defendant generally does not have a duty to protect against an open and obvious hazard. * In order for a hazard to be considered open and obvious, this Court has consistently stated the hazard should be one that is open and obvious to all, i.e., everyone who may potentially encounter it. * Murray v. Ramada Inns, Inc., 521 So.2d 1123, 1136 (La.1988) ("[A] potentially dangerous condition that should be obvious to all comers is not, in all instances, unreasonably dangerous."). * * *

In order to avoid * * * overlap between the jury's role as fact-finder and the judge's role as lawgiver, we find the analytic framework for evaluating an unreasonable risk of harm is properly classified as a determination of whether a defendant breached a duty owed, rather than a determination of whether a duty is owed *ab initio*. It is axiomatic that the issue of whether a duty is owed is a question of law, and the issue of whether a defendant has breached a duty owed is a question of fact. * The judge decides the former, and the fact-finder—judge or jury—decides the latter. "In the usual case where the duty owed depends upon the circumstances of the particular case, analysis of the defendant's conduct should be done in terms of 'no liability' or 'no breach of duty.'" Pitre [v. Louisiana Tech. Univ.], 673 So.2d [585,] 596 (La.1996) (Lemmon, J., concurring). Because the determination of whether a defect is unreasonably dangerous necessarily involves a myriad of factual considerations, varying from case to case, Reed, 708 So.2d at 364, the cost-benefit analysis employed by the fact-finder in

---

[a]   [Eds.' note] Louisiana and 45 other states have adopted comparative fault. As you know, traditionally the plaintiff's contributory negligence was a total bar to plaintiff's recovery. Under comparative fault, however, the plaintiff's failure to use reasonable care to protect himself reduces, but does not eliminate his recovery. See *infra* pages 344–352.

making this determination[b] is more properly associated with the breach, rather than the duty, element of our duty-risk analysis. * Thus, while a defendant only has a duty to protect against unreasonable risks that are not obvious or apparent, the fact-finder * * * determines which risks are unreasonable and whether those risks pose an open and obvious hazard. In other words, the fact-finder determines whether a defendant has breached a duty to keep its property in a reasonably safe condition by failing to discover, obviate, or warn of a defect that presents an unreasonable risk of harm.

Applying these precepts to the case *sub judice*, we conclude the record contains a reasonable factual basis to support the jury's determination the offset presented an unreasonable risk of harm to Broussard. Moreover, the record supports a finding that the elevator's defective condition was not an open and obvious hazard, as the defect was not readily apparent to all who encountered it. * * *

* * * [W]e find the record clearly supports a finding the offset was not, under our jurisprudence, an open and obvious defect. To be sure, we have consistently echoed one central theme throughout our open and obvious jurisprudence: If the complained-of condition **should be obvious to all**, then it may not be unreasonably dangerous. * E.g., *Pitre*, 673 So.2d at 591. * Thus, in order to be open and obvious, the risk of harm should be apparent to all who encounter the dangerous condition. See, e.g., *id.* at 591–92 (light poles in the area where college students were sledding were visible to everyone and thus open and obvious); Oster v. Dep't of Transp. & Dev., State of La., 582 So.2d 1285, 1288 (La.1991) (ditch on shoulder of road readily discernable from a considerable distance and thus not unreasonably dangerous). * * *

The open and obvious inquiry thus focuses on the global knowledge of everyone who encounters the * * * dangerous condition, not the victim's actual or potentially ascertainable knowledge. Simply put, we would undermine our comparative fault principles if we allowed the fact-finder to characterize a risk as open and obvious based solely on the plaintiff's awareness of that risk. The plaintiff's knowledge or awareness of the risk created by the defendant's conduct should not operate as a total bar to recovery in a case where the defendant would otherwise be liable to the plaintiff. * Instead, comparative fault principles should apply, and the plaintiff's "awareness of the danger" is but one factor to consider when assigning fault to all responsible parties * * *.

In this case, there was a reasonable basis upon which the jury could conclude the defect in the Tower's elevators, while apparent to Broussard, was not "open and obvious to all." There is no dispute that Broussard was aware of the offset after it impeded his initial attempt to push the dolly onto the elevator. Moreover, Tammy Loupe, the woman who entered the elevator before Broussard, testified she too was aware of the offset. The record, however, contains numerous exhibits highlighting instances of State employees either tripping or falling on the elevators after failing to notice they were misaligned. * * * As numerous individuals—including those most familiar with the

---

[b] [Eds.' note] See *infra* pages 167–170 for consideration of the use of cost-benefit analysis in the negligence determination.

elevators, *i.e.*, State employees working at the Tower—failed to notice and tripped over the misaligned elevators, a fact-finder could reasonably infer the defect, while apparent to Broussard, was not open and obvious to all who encountered it. * * *

After considering the record in its entirety * * *, we hold a reasonable basis exists to support the jury's factual determination that a one and one-half to three inch offset between the floor of the elevator and the floor of the Tower's lobby presented an unreasonable risk of harm. We further find a reasonable factual basis exists to support a finding the elevator's defective condition was not an open and obvious hazard, as the defect was not readily apparent to all who encountered it. * * *

NOTES

1.   *"Duty."* In *Broussard*, the court concludes that the issue of whether the unevenness of the elevator floor and the lobby floor is an "open and obvious hazard * * * is more properly associated with the breach, rather than the duty, element" of negligence. Some courts today misleadingly characterize similar issues as ones of "duty." E.g., Georgia Pac., LLC v. Farrar, 432 Md. 523, 540–41, 69 A.3d 1028, 1039 (2013) (holding that there is "no duty" to warn members of household exposed to asbestos dust brought into home on clothes of family member who works in close proximity to asbestos products supplied by defendant; "Determining the existence of a duty requires the weighing of policy considerations, [including] * * * whether * * * there is a feasible way of carrying out that duty * * *. To impose a duty that either cannot feasibly be implemented or, even if implemented, would have no practical effect would be poor public policy indeed."; "[I]t is not at all clear how * * * manufacturers and suppliers of products containing asbestos could have directly warned household members who had no connection with the product * * * not to have contact with dusty work clothes of household members who were occupationally exposed to asbestos."). Are these issues better considered under the rubric of whether a "duty" exists or whether a defendant has breached its duty of reasonable care to foreseeable victims?

According to the Restatement (Third) of Torts: Liability for Physical and Emotional Harm (2010):

> Sometimes reasonable minds cannot differ about whether an actor exercised reasonable care[, and] * * * [i]n such cases, courts take the question of negligence away from the jury and determine that the party was or was not negligent as a matter of law. Courts sometimes inaptly express this result in terms of duty. Here, the rubric of duty inaccurately conveys the impression that the court's decision is separate from and antecedent to the issue of negligence. In fact, these cases merely reflect the one-sidedness of the facts bearing on negligence, and they should not be misunderstood as cases involving exemption from or modification of the ordinary duty of reasonable care.

Id. at §7 cmt. i. See also Marshall v. Burger King Corp., 222 Ill.2d 422, 443, 856 N.E.2d 1048, 1061 (2006) ("It is inadvisable for courts to conflate the concepts of duty and breach in this manner.").

2. *"Open and Obvious" Dangers.* Traditionally, many courts held that defendant landowners had "no duty" to warn of open and obvious dangers. E.g., GMC v. Hill, 752 So.2d 1186, 1188 (Ala.1999); City of Winder v. Girone, 265 Ga. 723, 724, 462 S.W.2d 704, 705 (1995). Compare Restatement (Third) of Torts: Liability for Physical and Emotional Harm § 51 cmt. k (2012) ("[T]he fact that a dangerous condition is open and obvious bears on the assessment of whether reasonable care was employed, but it does not pretermit the land possessor's liability").

3. *Liriano v. Hobart.* For more on both sets of issues raised by the opinions in *Lorenzo* and in *Broussard*—that is, (1) the defendant's obligation to warn of "obvious" hazards and (2) the respective roles of the judge and jury in such cases, see *Liriano v. Hobart, infra* pages 603–606.

D. NEGLIGENCE AND COST-BENEFIT COMPARISONS

Adams v. Bullock

Court of Appeals of New York, 1919.
227 N.Y. 208, 125 N.E. 93.

■ CARDOZO, J. The defendant runs a trolley line in the city of Dunkirk, employing the overhead wire system. At one point, the road is crossed by a bridge or culvert which carries the tracks of the Nickle [sic] Plate and Pennsylvania Railroads. Pedestrians often use the bridge as a short cut between streets, and children play on it. On April 21, 1916, the plaintiff, a boy of twelve years, came across the bridge, swinging a wire about eight feet long. In swinging it, he brought it in contact with the defendant's trolley wire, which ran beneath the structure. The side of the bridge was protected by a parapet eighteen inches wide. Four feet 7¾ inches below the top of the parapet, the trolley wire was strung. The plaintiff was shocked and burned when the wires came together. He had a verdict at Trial Term, which has been affirmed at the Appellate Division by a divided court.

We think the verdict cannot stand. The defendant in using an overhead trolley was in the lawful exercise of its franchise. Negligence, therefore, cannot be imputed to it because it used that system and not another. * There was, of course, a duty to adopt all reasonable precautions to minimize the resulting perils. We think there is no evidence that this duty was ignored. The trolley wire was so placed that no one standing on the bridge or even bending over the parapet could reach it. Only some extraordinary casualty, not fairly within the area of ordinary prevision, could make it a thing of danger. Reasonable care in the use of a destructive agency imports a high degree of vigilance. * But no vigilance, however alert, unless fortified by the gift of prophecy, could have predicted the point upon the route where such an accident would occur. It might with equal reason have been expected anywhere else. At any point upon the route a mischievous or thoughtless boy might touch the wire with a metal pole, or fling another wire across it. * If unable to reach it from the walk, he might stand upon a wagon or climb upon a tree. No special danger at this bridge warned the defendant that there was need of special measures of precaution. No like accident had occurred before. No custom had been disregarded. We think that ordinary caution did not involve forethought of this extraordinary peril. * * * There is, we may add, a distinction not to be ignored between electric light and trolley wires. The distinction is that the former may be insulated. Chance of harm, though remote, may betoken negligence, if needless. Facility of protection may impose a duty to protect. With trolley wires, the case is different. Insulation is impossible. Guards here and there are of little value. To avert the possibility of this accident and others like it at one point or another on the route, the defendant must have abandoned the overhead system, and put the wires underground. Neither its power nor its duty to make the change is shown. To hold it liable upon the facts exhibited in this record would be to charge it as an insurer. The judgment should be reversed, and a new trial granted, with costs to abide the event. * * *

NOTES

1.　*Balancing Risks and Benefits.* The Restatement (Third) of Torts provides:

> A person acts negligently if the person does not exercise reasonable care under all the circumstances. Primary factors to consider in ascertaining whether the person's conduct lacks reasonable care are the foreseeable likelihood that the person's conduct will result in harm, the foreseeable severity of any harm that may ensue, and the burden of precautions to eliminate or reduce the risk of harm.

Restatement (Third) of Torts: Liability for Physical and Emotional Harm § 3 (2010). Comment *a* to the Restatement further states:

> Because a "reasonably careful person" (or a "reasonably prudent person") is one who acts with reasonable care, the "reasonable care" standard for negligence is basically the same as a standard expressed in terms of the "reasonably careful person" (or the "reasonably prudent person").

The Reporters' Notes acknowledge that jury instructions "frequently explain the negligence standard in terms of the reasonably prudent person." *Id.*, Reporters' Note, cmt. d. Are the two tests identical?

2.　*A Negligence Formula?* To what extent can the issue of negligence be reduced to a cost-benefit analysis weighing the costs of preventing an accident against the benefits achieved in reducing the costs resulting from accidents?

In Conway v. O'Brien, 111 F.2d 611, 612 (2d Cir.1940), Judge Learned Hand said:

> The degree of care demanded of a person by an occasion is the resultant of three factors: the likelihood that his conduct will injure others, taken with the seriousness of the injury if it happens, and balanced against the interest which he must sacrifice to avoid the risk. All these are practically not susceptible of any quantitative estimate, and the second two are generally not so, even theoretically. For this reason a solution always involves some preference, or choice between incommensurables, and it is consigned to a jury because their decision is thought most likely to accord with commonly accepted standards, real or fancied.

In Judge Hand's much-cited opinion in United States v. Carroll Towing Co., 159 F.2d 169, 173 (2d Cir.1947), he applied the *Conway* analysis in an admiralty context, and added: "Possibly it serves to bring this notion into relief to state it in algebraic terms: if the probability be called P; the injury, L; and the burden, B; liability depends upon whether B is less than L multiplied by P: i.e., whether B [is] less than PL." See also Richard A. Epstein, A Theory of Strict Liability, 2 J. Legal Stud. 151, 154 *et seq.* (1973).

Despite Hand's disclaimer of quantifiability, his formulation has been explained in terms of concepts of cost-benefit analysis. See Richard A. Posner, A Theory of Negligence, 1 J. Legal Stud. 29, 32–34 (1972):

It is time to take a fresh look at the social function of liability for negligent acts. The essential clue, I believe, is provided by Judge Learned Hand's famous formulation of the negligence standard— one of the few attempts to give content to the deceptively simple concept of ordinary care. * * * Hand was adumbrating, perhaps unwittingly, * an economic meaning of negligence. Discounting (multiplying) the cost of an accident if it occurs by the probability of occurrence yields a measure of the economic benefit to be anticipated from incurring the costs necessary to prevent the accident. The cost of prevention is what Hand meant by the burden of taking precautions against the accident. It may be the cost of installing safety equipment or otherwise making the activity safer, or the benefit forgone by curtailing or eliminating the activity. If the cost of safety measures or of curtailment— whichever cost is lower—exceeds the benefit in accident avoidance to be gained by incurring that cost, society would be better off, in economic terms, to forgo accident prevention. A rule making the enterprise liable for the accidents that occur in such cases cannot be justified on the ground that it will induce the enterprise to increase the safety of its operations. When the cost of accidents is less than the cost of prevention, a rational profit-maximizing enterprise will pay tort judgments to the accident victims rather than incur the larger cost of avoiding liability. Furthermore, overall economic value or welfare would be diminished rather than increased by incurring a higher accident-prevention cost in order to avoid a lower accident cost. If, on the other hand, the benefits in accident avoidance exceed the costs of prevention, society is better off if those costs are incurred and the accident averted, and so in this case the enterprise is made liable, in the expectation that self-interest will lead it to adopt the precautions in order to avoid a greater cost in tort judgments.

One misses any reference to accident avoidance by the victim. If the accident could be prevented by the installation of safety equipment or the curtailment or discontinuance of the underlying activity by the victim at lower cost than any measure taken by the injurer would involve, it would be uneconomical to adopt a rule of liability that placed the burden of accident prevention on the injurer. Although not an explicit part of the Hand formula this qualification, as we shall see, is implicit in the administration of the negligence standard.

Compare Harper, James and Gray on Torts § 16.9 ("It should not * * * be thought that, in the evaluation of precautions, the common law's standard of reasonableness turns on rigorous cost-benefit analysis. * The tone of the common law's approach has been more moral than economic.").

3. *Comparative Efficiency of Strict Liability and Negligence.* One of the fundamental issues of tort law is whether a fault-based system or a strict liability standard will produce the lowest sum of accident costs, costs of preventing accidents, and transaction or administrative costs. In short, which standard is the most economically efficient, negligence or strict liability? The question is not a simple one, and many commentators have written extensively on the topic. E.g., Guido Calabresi, The Cost of Accidents (1970); Richard A. Epstein, Torts, 91–107 (1999); Richard A. Posner, Economic Analysis of Law 178–82, 606–07 (7th ed. 2007); Steven Shavell, Economic Analysis of Accident Law 24–25, 29, 31–32, 57–58, 210, 264–65 (1987); Izhak Englard, The System Builders: A Critical Appraisal of Modern American Tort Theory, 9 J. Legal Stud. 27, 51–56 (1980); Steven Shavell, Strict Liability Versus Negligence, 9 J. Legal Stud. 1 (1980).

A beginning point for analysis of this issue is the "Coase Theorem," named for its late author who subsequently was awarded the Nobel Memorial Prize in Economic Science. According to Professor Coase, in a world without significant transaction costs, the liability rule would not ultimately affect the level of safety precaution. R[onald] H. Coase, The Problem of Social Cost, 3 J.L. & Econ. 1 (1960). Instead, market negotiations between any potential actor and those who might be affected by his conduct would achieve the same equilibrium among the interests of all the parties—and hence the same outcome in terms of conduct—regardless of which party initially was assigned the costs of the accident by the legal system.

The necessary assumption behind the Coase Theorem is that transaction costs do not make negotiations between parties unfeasible. These costs include, *inter alia*, the lack of perfect information, the cost of obtaining information, and the administrative and similar costs of influencing the conduct of others, beyond the consideration which may be paid for changes of conduct (e.g., through theoretically legitimate market transactions sometimes called, non-pejoratively, "bribes"). A market without transaction costs is like a physical universe without friction: it does not exist, but thinking about it may advance understanding of that which does exist. Coase himself certainly understood the important effects of transaction costs. See Ronald Coase, The Firm, the Market, and the Law 6–7 (1988).

Professor (now Senior Circuit Judge for the United States Court of Appeals) Guido Calabresi has discussed in detail the effects of actual transaction costs as influencing whether any general rule for the allocation of accident costs, either predicated on negligence or not, will lead to optimality in resource allocation. The following example of such a discussion, from Guido Calabresi, The Costs of Accidents: A Legal and Economic Analysis 135–38 (1970), is intended, as is the Posner excerpt, to illustrate how economic analysis may assist in understanding the effect of legal rules, such as the negligence principle, but not to suggest that economic theory provides the sole benchmark for the evaluation of those rules:

* * * Since in reality transactions are often terribly expensive, it is often not worthwhile spending both the cost of the transaction and the amount needed to bribe someone else to diminish the accident-causing behavior. As a result, the accident cost is not avoided by society, while another allocation that could eliminate or lessen the transaction cost is available and would result in the avoidance of the accident cost. The aim of the pure market determination of which activity to hold liable is to find this other allocation.

An overly simple example may be in order. Suppose car-pedestrian accidents currently cost $100. Suppose also that if cars had spongy bumpers the total accident costs would only be $10. Suppose finally that spongy bumpers cost $50 more than the present bumpers. Assuming no transaction costs, spongy bumpers would become established regardless of who was held responsible for car-pedestrian accidents. If car manufacturers were liable they would prefer to spend $50 for the new bumpers plus $10 in accident damages, instead of $100 for accident damages. If pedestrians were held responsible and could foresee the costs, they would prefer to bribe the car manufacturers $50 to put in spongy bumpers and bear $10 in damages, rather than bear $100 in damages. Exactly the same result would occur if an arbitrary third party, e.g. television manufacturers, were held liable initially; they too could lessen costs to themselves by bribing car manufacturers to put in spongy bumpers. The result is the same simply because the cost of avoiding the accident is in all instances smaller than the cost of compensating for it. Wherever this is so, and wherever it costs nothing to bribe (and people have the necessary knowledge), the market will seek the cheapest way and avoid the accident.

Now let us alter the example to add transaction costs. Assume that any allocation other than leaving the cost where it falls (i.e., on the pedestrian) entails $5 in administrative costs. Assume also that for pedestrians to bribe anyone is very expensive, e.g. $65. (This is because it is costly to gather pedestrians together to bargain and to handle the problem of would-be free-loaders.[4]) Assume finally that it would cost television manufacturers $30 to bribe. What would happen in our example?

If car manufacturers were held liable, they would bear $100 in accident costs plus perhaps the $5 allocation cost. They could avoid this in the future by putting in spongy bumpers at $50, paying $10 in damages, and perhaps the same $5 in administrative costs (assuming for the sake of simplicity that

---

[4] The free-loader is the person who refuses to be inoculated against smallpox because given the fact that almost everyone else is inoculated, the risk of smallpox to him is less than the risk of harm from the inoculation. If enough people are free-loaders it becomes necessary to compel inoculation to avoid smallpox epidemics. The free-loader is also the person who refuses to join a union because the fact that most other workers are union members assures him of the benefits of unionization without the cost. The use of compulsion in these areas suggests that the problem of free-loaders is crucial whenever many people must agree to bear a cost in order to bring about a change favorable to all of them. It would not be crucial if nonpayers could be excluded from the benefits of the change, but such exclusion is often extremely expensive. It is precisely that expense which justifies compulsion. *

these remained constant). Clearly they would install spongy bumpers.

If pedestrians were held liable, they would bear $100 in accident costs. But to get spongy bumpers installed would cost them $50 (bribe) plus $65 (transaction costs), and they would still bear $10 in accident costs. Since $125 is more than $100, a change to spongy bumpers would not seem worth the expense. But the absence of spongy bumpers would in fact entail an unnecessary cost to society of the difference between $100 (accident costs when borne by pedestrians) and $65 (the cost to society when car manufacturers are held liable).

If television manufacturers were held liable, the figures would be $100 plus $5 with no spongy bumpers, compared with $50 (bribe) plus $30 (transaction costs) plus $10 (remaining accident costs) plus perhaps $5 (administrative costs). Since $95 is less than $105, spongy bumpers would probably be installed. But this result would have been achieved in a more expensive, less efficient way than if car manufacturers had been liable, for $30 in unnecessary transaction costs would have been imposed on society.

Clearly then, on the basis of our initial assumptions, it would be best to make automobile manufacturers liable.

4. *Transaction Costs and the Legal System.* Another series of transaction costs are those which relate to the "costs of administration" of either the negligence or the strict liability standard.

Consider, for example, the impact of litigation costs. The litigation system—with attorneys' fees for both parties, experts' fees, court costs and usually with insurance company administrative expenses and profits—is an inefficient way to transfer compensation from the party causing the injury to the party suffering the injury. A study of asbestos litigation shows that claimants receive 42 percent of the total amount spent on asbestos litigation, with defense legal fees and expenses accounting for 31 percent and the fees and expenses of plaintiffs' attorneys totally 27 percent. Stephen J. Carroll, et al., Asbestos Litigation (RAND Corp. 2005), *available at* http://www.rand.org/content/dam/rand/pubs/monographs/2005/ RAND_MG162.pdf. In other words, it takes approximately $2.32 to deliver one dollar in compensation to claimants. What does this mean for any attempt to use the tort system to internalize the results of these harms and encourage the optimal amount of loss minimization? See also *infra* pages 671–672.

On the other hand, under either a negligence or a strict liability standard, not all actionable injuries will result in a claim or litigation "in the real world." In a study of medical negligence in the state of New York, Professor Paul Weiler and his colleagues found that the ratio of the total number of negligence claims to the total number of actual incidents of medical negligence was only one to seven. Paul C. Weiler et al., A Measure of Malpractice 70, 73 (1993). Further, in the subset of cases in which independent medical experts identified medical negligence, only one out of every fifty victims pursued a negligence claim. We should expect that this failure to pursue all possible claims would be greater in a negligence system than in a strict liability system. Why? What does this suggest about the economic efficiency of a negligence standard?

Nor do courts and juries inevitably make accurate determinations of liability issues and perfect valuations of the damages suffered by victims. Tort lawyers on both sides of cases, for example, often admit that the chances for a plaintiff's verdict and the amount of damages awarded vary considerably from one locality to the next, depending largely on demographics. See *infra* pages 407–408, Note 5. The question, however, is whether there is, on balance, a natural bias in the adjudicative process one way or the other.

Finally, during the remainder of this course, you will consider many doctrines that substantively change the negligence standard from cost-benefit analysis to something else. What happens to "negligence as cost-benefit analysis" when the standard of care demanded is determined, or at least influenced, by other factors, such as custom and statutes? What happens to this hypothetical finely calibrated world of cost-benefit analysis, designed to yield the lowest possible sum of costs of accidents and accident prevention, when issues such as proximate cause and immunities limit defendants' liabilities? With all the factors involved, many pointing in opposite directions, is it possible to hypothesize at all as to whether the negligence system as it currently operates offers too little or too much incentive for accident avoidance? Whether a strict liability standard does so?

These issues suggest that a cost-benefit analysis does not operate in any finely calibrated way within the "real world" negligence system. Occasionally, the testimony of an expert witness on whether a particular safety precaution would have been justified follows the format of a cost-benefit analysis. More generally, however, the idea of achieving the optimally efficient level of safety precaution exists only as a transcendent goal lurking behind the negligence standard and indeed hovering over the entire torts process.

E. THE ROLE OF CUSTOM

Lehigh & Wilkes-Barre Coal Co. v. Hayes

Supreme Court of Pennsylvania, 1889.
128 Pa. 294, 18 A. 387.

* * * Trespass on the case by James Hayes and Ann Hayes, his wife, against the Lehigh & Wilkes-Barre Coal Company, a corporation, for the death of plaintiffs' son, a boy 14 years old, who worked in defendant's mine. It was alleged that defendant's negligence caused the accident, which occurred by drawing a car of coal from the chute where deceased was at work, thus causing a large quantity of coal to be precipitated on him, causing his death. Plaintiffs contended that defendant's servants at the mouth of the shaft should have notified deceased that they intended to draw the car, but it appeared that the latter had sent word by another employee that the car should be drawn out. There was a verdict for plaintiffs, damages assessed at $1,500, judgment accordingly, and defendant brings error. * * *

■ GREEN, J. Upon the trial of this cause no evidence was given by the plaintiff to show that the defendant's breaker, and the machinery used in crushing and screening coal, was in any manner defectively built, or that it was not built in the same manner and with the same appliances as are used in all similar structures. The single act of negligence in this regard alleged against the defendant was that it had no appliance and used no means or method by which warning could be given to persons working in the pocket that a draw was about to be made. No evidence was given to show that it was customary among coal operators to give any such warning in the conduct of their collieries. It follows that there was no proof that the defendant neglected any of the precautions which were usually observed in carrying on the business of crushing, screening, and shipping coal. But the defendant did give testimony of importance upon this subject. G. M. Williamson, the mine inspector for the district in which this colliery was situated, testified that there were 62 collieries, or openings, altogether, in the district, and that this breaker, with its chutes and pockets, was constructed in the usual, ordinary way in which such breakers are constructed in that region. He also said he did not know that there was in use in any of the collieries of the district any signaling apparatus to indicate when coal is about to be drawn out of a chute to be lowered into a car. Joseph Tyrell, another witness, whose business was building breakers, and who built this one, testified that the breaker was built in the usual way in which breakers are built in that region, and that he knew of no breaker in the region in which, prior to this accident, any apparatus or device was used to signal before coal was drawn from the chutes into cars. There was affirmative testimony, therefore, that this breaker was built in the usual way in which all breakers were built in that district; and that there was no custom or use, known to the witnesses, of having appliances of any kind to signal the drawing of coal from the chutes. Against this there was no opposing testimony whatever.

The rule in regard to the obligation of the employer, respecting the character of the tools and appliances furnished by him, has been repeatedly stated in the recent decisions of this court. Thus, in Railroad Co. v. Sentmeyer, 92 Pa. 276 (1880), we said that, when the employer furnished his employees "with tools and appliances which, though not the best possible, may, by ordinary care, be used without danger, he has discharged his duty, and is not responsible for accidents." In Payne v. Reese, 100 Pa. 301 (1882), we said: "An employer is not bound to furnish for his workmen the 'safest' machinery, nor to provide the 'best methods' for its operation, in order to save himself from responsibility for accidents resulting from its use. If the machinery be of an ordinary character, and such as can, with reasonable care, be used without danger to the employee, it is all that can be required from the employer. This is the limit of his responsibility, and the sum total of his duty." In Manufacturing Co. v. McCormick, 118 Pa. 519, 12 A. 273 (1888), we said: "The general rule requires of the master that he provide materials and implements for the use of his servant such as are ordinarily used by persons in the same business; but he is not required to secure the best known materials, or to subject such as he does provide to a chemical analysis in order to settle, by experiment, what remote and possible hazard may be incurred by their use." In Ship Building Works v. Nuttall, 119 Pa. 149 (1888), we held that the employer was under no obligation to give warning to his employees of the dangerous character of a circular saw, or to provide it with a spreader to prevent accidents. As to the spreader we said: "The testimony shows that such an attachment is not in general use, and that there is no general agreement among mill-owners or practical sawyers that it is a desirable or a useful attachment. It is not enough that some persons regard it as a valuable safeguard. The test is general use. Tried by this test the saw of the defendant is such a one as the company had a right to use, because it is such as is commonly used by mill-owners; and it was error to leave to the jury any question of negligence based on the failure to provide a spreader." Applying these principles to the facts of the present case we fail to discover any evidence of negligence on the part of the defendant, so far as the character of the breaker and its appliances is concerned, and hence we can find nothing upon which to support a verdict for the plaintiff.

It was argued that the defendant should have given a warning to the deceased that the coal was about to be drawn; but, in view of the fact that the plaintiff gave evidence tending to show that the boy sent out word that they should draw the coal, he being at that time in the chute, the necessity for any such warning does not appear. It was a matter of no consequence, so far as he was concerned, whether his message was communicated to the parties outside or not. He, at least, was bound to avoid a danger which he must have had knowledge was likely to occur immediately. We think a verdict for the defendant should have been directed upon all the testimony. We sustain the first, second, third, seventh, and eighth assignments. Judgment reversed.

La Sell v. Tri-States Theatre Corp.

Supreme Court of Iowa, 1943.
233 Iowa 929, 11 N.W.2d 36.

■ BLISS, JUSTICE. * * * The appellant, aged 64 years, weighing at the time about 223 pounds, accompanied by her daughter, and the latter's daughter, having paid the required admission, entered the Des Moines Theater, operated by the appellee, about 5 o'clock in the afternoon of June 8, 1941, to attend a moving picture show. Patrons, after passing through the entrance, traverse the lobby, foyer, and promenade, in succession, before taking their seats in the auditorium. * * * The entire floor of the auditorium extends from the stage toward the rear, south, on a gradually rising gradient or incline, until it reaches the third row of seats from the rear wall of the auditorium. From the elevation of this line, the level of the aisles gradually slopes downward toward the aisle entrances and coincides with the floor level of the promenade. But the level of the floor under the last three rows of seats in the auditorium, and between those parts of the aisles which slope southward and down, continues on a rising incline to the rear wall. As a result of this method of construction the passageway to the seats in the third row from the rear is on the same level as the aisle, and there is no step-up from the aisle into this passageway. But to enter the passageway to the seats in the second row from the back there is a step-up of approximately five inches, which continues as a ramp or upward-sloping way for a short distance into the passageway. Entrance from the aisle into the last row at the rear of the auditorium is in like manner except that the step-up is somewhat higher.

Appellant and her daughter and granddaughter entered the auditorium at aisle two, the second from the west wall. An usher, with a flashlight, seated them in the second row from the rear * * *. None of them had any difficulty in taking her seat, and the appellant testified that she did not notice the step-up. The usher did not call their attention to the step-up. * * * The picture was shown, as is customary, in partial darkness. After they had been in the theater for about three hours, the daughter went to the rest room. She almost fell in stepping to the aisle, but retained her balance. About five or ten minutes later, the appellant took hold of the granddaughter's hand with her left hand, and stepped toward the aisle. Not seeing the step-down because of darkness, and not knowing of its presence, and thinking there was no change in level of the floor on which she was walking, she lost her balance when her foot went to the aisle floor, and she fell forward, striking her head on the metal seat across the aisle. She had never been in this theater before.

[The opinion then describes at length the testimony of plaintiff's witnesses.]

[Witnesses for defendant testified that the end of the step was painted with white enamel; that there was a hooded light with a 15 watt bulb immediately under the end seat of the second row which would illuminate the white portion of the step; that there were other lights which would more or less illuminate the place in question.] No usher or anyone else testified for the appellee, respecting the above matters, excepting a theater architect, who stated that, "where it is necessary to have the level of the floor on which seats are placed above that which the aisle runs on, a step between the aisle and the floor on which the seats are placed is an approved method of construction." * * *

One ground of appellee's peremptory motion for a directed verdict is: "4. The theatre is constructed and lighted in an approved manner, and in accordance with the customary method of lighting and constructing theatres of similar character and nature." * * * Of these authorities, the appellee states: "Appellee respectfully submits that the above cases hold as a matter of law that it was not *per se* faulty construction for appellee to place the seats of the auditorium or theatre at a higher level than the aisle between them as such arrangement has advantages which are obvious; that there is nothing uncommon in this form of construction." * * * One witness testified that the lighting in appellee's theater was like that which he had seen in other moving picture theaters. There was also testimony that the use of a step to reach a row of seats was approved construction. All of this testimony was admitted without objection.

We do not agree with the contention of appellee that because its lighting and construction was in accord with the customary or standard practice of theaters generally, in these respects, that these issues of alleged negligence were issues of law for the court, rather than issues of fact for the jury. The standard of custom cannot be substituted for the legal standard of reasonable or ordinary care under the circumstances. Following an approved method is merely evidentiary and is not conclusive on the question of ordinary care. The standard of care is ordinary care under the circumstances, and not what others have done under like circumstances. Habitual practice of any number, for any period of time, cannot make a negligent act an act of due care and caution. * * * As said in Walgreen Texas Co. v. Shivers, 131 S.W.2d 650, 657 (Tex.App.1939): "The fact that appellee and other companies had habitually and customarily used the same does not, of itself, show that they had exercised ordinary care. * * * Evidence of such use by other persons engaged in the same kind of business is admissible upon the issues of ordinary care, but the question * * * is whether, under the facts of the particular case, there has been an absence of ordinary care." The rule was tersely stated by Justice Holmes in Texas & P. R. Co. v. Behymer, 189 U.S. 468, 470, 23 S.Ct. 622, 623, 47 L.Ed. 905, 906 (1903), thus: "What usually is done may be evidence of what ought to be done, but what ought to be done is fixed by a standard of reasonable prudence, whether it usually is complied with or not." * * * The rule is aptly stated by the able court of the Second Circuit speaking through Learned Hand, J., in The T. J. Hooper, 60 F.2d 737, 739, 740 (1932). The owners of cargoes in towed barges sued the barge owners and tug owners for the loss of the cargoes through the negligence of the defendants, in not having radio receiving sets through which they would have been warned of the approaching storm. The defendants contended that it was not the general practice to carry such sets. In affirming judgments for plaintiffs, the court said:

> Is it then a final answer that the business had not yet generally adopted receiving sets? There are, no doubt, cases where courts seem to make the general practice of the calling the standard of proper diligence; we have indeed given some currency to the notion ourselves. * Indeed in most cases reasonable prudence is in fact common prudence; but strictly it is never its measure; a whole calling may have unduly lagged in the adoption of new and available devices. It never may set its own tests, however persuasive may be its usages. Courts must in the end say what is required; there are precautions so imperative that even their universal disregard will not excuse their omission. *

Speaking of evidence of customary conduct and standard methods, J. Wigmore, in Evidence § 461 (1940), says: "The proper method is to receive it with an express caution that it is merely evidential and is not to serve as a legal standard." * * *

The impracticability and the probative weakness of the standard practice test of negligence is made manifest when you consider the great variety of theater construction, the diversity of lighting in capacity and shading, the variety, presence, and absence of balconies, pillars, etc., which cast shadows, the reflecting powers of the carpeting, tapestries, wall coloring, and numerous other factors. There is ordinarily no absolute test, where human conduct is a controlling factor, of either negligence or due care, in a particular instance, unless it is by statute or statutory construction. * * *

It would have been no unreasonable burden for the appellee to have discontinued the use of the two rows of seats containing the dangerous steps. They constituted approximately one twentieth of the main floor seating capacity. Their discontinuance might have reduced the net income slightly, but it would have entirely eliminated the danger. As it was, after the appellant was injured, on the advice and under the direction of its expert witness, who would not say whether the danger was thereby lessened, the appellee replaced the steps with ramps. When one goes into a hazardous business—and it must be conceded that a darkened theater has its hazards—he must take that into consideration, and assume the burdens, and take the precautions which a reasonably and ordinarily prudent person would use under all of the circumstances. The fact that partial darkness is essential to the conduct of the business does not exempt him from this duty of reasonable care, nor does it lighten his burden thereunder. In fact it requires him to increase his care and watchfulness if necessary to make it commensurate with, and in proportion to, the patent, and to the reasonably expectable and foreseeable dangers which may injure his invitees and patrons. Such increased care, nevertheless, is nothing more than the legal standard of ordinary, or reasonable, care. * * *

It appeared in the examination of appellee's theater architect that under his supervision the appellee's theater was remodeled somewhat, after the appellant's injury, by removing the step which caused the appellant's fall and other similar steps in the theater, and putting in their place ramps or gradually sloped inclines the lower ends of which were level and flush with the aisle floors. This expert witness had testified that the use of the steps was *necessary* and approved theater construction. The witness was cross-examined at length respecting this substitution and the reasons therefore, and the results effected. He admitted that both methods of construction were used. * * *

The matter of the discontinuance of the steps and the substitution of ramps had a very important relation to, and bearing upon, the claim of appellee, and the testimony of the expert that the step construction was necessary, and was approved construction. The jury was entitled to have the full benefit of the testimony relative to the remodeling, and all reasonable inferences deducible therefrom, with respect to this claim of the appellee and this testimony of the expert. Yet the court instructed the jury as follows: " * * * *and the fact that the building has been remodeled and changes made in the floor should not be considered by you in arriving at your verdict in this case.*" (Italics ours.) * * *

The italicized portion of Instruction 9 is clearly erroneous and prejudicial. The testimony respecting the remodeling, both direct, and cross-examination, was all in the record and went to the jury. It was competent, relevant, and material. The weight and probative value of this testimony and of all reasonable inferences therefrom were for the jury to consider, and the court invaded the province of the jury in instructing them to give no consideration to the testimony. We are not questioning the rule that generally subsequent repairs or changes in the place causing the injury cannot be shown to prove the alleged negligence. * * *

Reversed and remanded. * * *

NOTES

1. *Effect of Conformity with Custom.* These two cases, *Lehigh & Wilkes-Barre Coal Co. v. Hayes* and *La Sell v. Tri-States Theatre Corp.*, address the issue of whether correspondence with custom necessarily precludes a finding of negligence.

Does the answer to this question turn on our degree of confidence in the free market system to identify the optimal level of safety precaution? What argument would a believer in free market economics make about the role of custom in establishing the absence of negligence? Is it an accident that cases such as *La Sell,* which refuse to recognize correspondence with custom as a determinative defense to negligence, became increasingly common during and after the Progressive Era, the New Deal, and the rise of the regulatory state?

2. *Custom as Evidence of Standard.* As the *La Sell* opinion points out, courts today almost universally admit evidence of custom as tending to show inconclusively what conduct or what precautions are reasonable under the circumstances, provided that the custom meets the test of relevancy. See Harper, James and Gray on Torts § 17.3; see also George v. Morgan Constr. Co., 389 F.Supp. 253 (E.D.Pa.1975) and Kaiser v. Cook, 67 Wis.2d 460, 227 N.W.2d 50 (1975).

3. *Subsequent Repairs or Remodeling as Evidence of Negligence.* The general rule is that the plaintiff cannot admit evidence that the defendant repaired the mechanism or remodeled the premises that caused plaintiff's injury. E.g., Federal Rules of Evidence, Rule 407. Often, however, plaintiff's counsel argues for the admissibility of such evidence for other purposes, such as proving ownership or control over the place where the injury occurred or establishing the feasibility of precautions. How effective are instructions to the jury that caution them to limit consideration of such evidence to these specific purposes and not to consider it on the issue of whether the defendant was negligent?

The exclusion of evidence about post-accident precautions is often justified on the ground that its admissibility might deter defendants from taking precautions that would prevent future accidents. If the rule were otherwise, and you were counsel to a company that had notice of a hazardous condition on its premises, or in its products, would you advise your client to refrain from correcting the hazard if a pending lawsuit focused on this very condition?

Stevens v. Boston Elevated Ry. Co.

Supreme Judicial Court of Massachusetts, 1904.
184 Mass. 476, 69 N.E. 338.

[Actions in tort for injuries and death of a carriage driver in a funeral procession whose carriage was struck by one of defendant's street cars. Plaintiff had judgment and defendant alleges exceptions.]

The exception relied upon was as follows:

The plaintiff offered in evidence one of the rules in a certain book admitted by the defendant to be a book of rules issued by the defendant company to its motormen and conductors, and admitted to have been the book of rules that was in force on the day of the accident. The rule which the plaintiff offered was Rule 83, and was as follows:

Gong Ringing. The gong must always be sounded before starting, when starting, and before reaching, and at all street crossings, when passing other cars or vehicles, and at all points where vehicles or foot passengers are crossing or are liable to cross the tracks. * * * Upon approaching streets or crossings the power must be shut off and the car kept under perfect control. * * *

To the admission of this rule the defendant objected. The counsel for the plaintiff said: "I put it in as a rule of conduct for your motorman by which he is to be judged to some degree." The judge then said: "I suppose it is put upon the same ground that an ordinance is put upon as bearing upon the carelessness or negligence of the person by whom the rules are to be followed. I will admit the evidence and save Mr. Thompson his exception." The rule was then admitted in evidence. * * *

■ KNOWLTON, C.J. * * * It is contended by the defendant that there is no sound principle under which such evidence can be admitted. The evidence is somewhat analogous to proof of the violation of an ordinance or statute by the defendant or his servant which is always received as evidence, although not conclusive, of the defendant's negligence. * Such an ordinance or statute, enacted by a body representing the interests of the public, imposes prima facie upon everybody a duty of obedience. Disobedience is therefore a breach of duty, unless some excuse for it can be shown which creates a different duty, that, as between man and man, overrides the duty imposed by the statute or ordinance. Such disobedience in a matter affecting the plaintiff is always competent upon the question whether the defendant was negligent.

So, a rule made by a corporation for the guidance of its servants in matters affecting the safety of others is made in the performance of a duty, by a party that is called upon to consider methods, and determine how its business shall be conducted. Such a rule, made known to its servants, creates a duty of obedience as between the master and the servant, and disobedience of it by the servant is negligence as between the two. If such disobedience injuriously affects a third person, it is not to be assumed in favor of the master that the negligence was immaterial to the injured person, and that his rights were not affected by it. Rather ought it to be held an implication that there was a breach of duty towards him, as well as towards the master who prescribed the conduct that he thought necessary or desirable for protection in such cases. Against the proprietor of a business, the methods which he adopts for the protection of others are some evidence of what he thinks necessary or proper to insure their safety.

A distinction may well be made between precautions taken voluntarily before an accident, and precautions which are suggested and adopted after an accident. This distinction is pointed out in Columbia Railroad Company v. Hawthorne, 144 U.S. 202, 207, 208, 12 S.Ct. 591, 593, 36 L.Ed. 405, 406 (1892). Mr. Justice Gray, referring to changes made by a defendant after an accident, says in the opinion,

> It is now settled, upon much consideration, by the decisions of the highest courts of most of the states in which the question has arisen, that the evidence is incompetent, because the taking of such precautions against the future is not to be construed as an admission of responsibility for the past, has no legitimate tendency to prove that the defendant has been negligent before the accident happened, and is calculated to distract the minds of the jury from the real issue, and to create a prejudice against the defendant.

In Morse v. Minneapolis & St. Louis Railway, 30 Minn. 465, 468, 16 N.W. 358, 359 (1883), it is said, referring to the same subject, that "a person may have exercised all the care which the law required, and yet, in the light of his new experience, after an unexpected accident has occurred, and as a measure of extreme caution, he may adopt additional safeguards." * * *

Exceptions overruled.

NOTE

Private Rules as Evidence of Negligence. What argument is there that the violation of the defendant's own rules should not be admitted as evidence of negligence? Consider Fonda v. St. Paul City Ry. Co., 71 Minn. 438, 449–50, 74 N.W. 166, 169–70 (1898), in which the court held such rules inadmissible:

> Private rules of a master regulating the conduct of his servants in the management of his own business, although designed for the protection of others, stand on an entirely different footing from statutes and municipal ordinances designed for the protection of the public. The latter, as far as they go, fix the standard of duty towards those whom they were intended to protect, and a violation of them is negligence in law or per se. But a person cannot, by the adoption of private rules, fix the standard of his duty to others. That is fixed by law, either statutory or common. Such rules may require more, or they may require less, than the law requires; and whether a certain course of conduct is negligent, or the exercise of reasonable care, must be determined by the standard fixed by law, without regard to any private rules of the party. * * *

> The fallaciousness and unfairness of any such doctrine ought to be apparent on a moment's reflection. The effect of it is that, the more cautious and careful a man is in the adoption of rules in the management of his business in order to protect others, the worse he is off, and the higher the degree of care he is bound to exercise. A person may, out of abundant caution, adopt rules requiring of his employees a much higher degree of care than the law imposes. This is a practice that ought to be encouraged, and not discouraged. But, if the adoption of such a course is to be used against him as an admission, he would naturally find it to his interest not to adopt any rules at all.

Brune v. Belinkoff

Supreme Judicial Court of Massachusetts, 1968.
354 Mass. 102, 235 N.E.2d 793.

■ SPALDING, JUSTICE. In this action of tort for malpractice Theresa Brune (plaintiff) seeks to recover from the defendant because of alleged negligence in administering a spinal anesthetic. * * *

The plaintiff was delivered of a baby on October 4, 1958, at St. Luke's Hospital in New Bedford. During the delivery, the defendant, a specialist in anesthesiology practising in New Bedford, administered a spinal anesthetic to the plaintiff containing eight milligrams of pontocaine in one cubic centimeter of ten per cent solution of glucose. When the plaintiff attempted to get out of bed eleven hours later, she slipped and fell on the floor. The plaintiff subsequently complained of numbness and weakness in her left leg, an affliction which appears to have persisted to the time of trial. * * * There was ample evidence that her condition resulted from an excessive dosage of pontocaine.

There was medical evidence that the dosage of eight milligrams of pontocaine was excessive and that good medical practice required a dosage of five milligrams or less. There was also medical evidence, including testimony of the defendant, to the effect that a dosage of eight milligrams in one cubic centimeter of ten per cent dextrose was proper. There was evidence that this dosage was customary in New Bedford in a case, as here, of a vaginal delivery.[1]

The plaintiffs' exception to the refusal to give their first request for instruction and their exception to a portion of the charge present substantially the same question and will be considered together. The request reads: "As a specialist, the defendant owed the plaintiff the duty to have and use the care and skill commonly possessed and used by similar specialist[s] in like circumstances." The relevant portion of the charge excepted to was as follows:

[The defendant] must measure up to the standard of professional care and skill ordinarily possessed by others in his profession in the community, which is New Bedford, and its environs, of course, where he practices, having regard to the current state of advance of the profession. If, in a given case, it were determined by a jury that the ability and skill of the physician in New Bedford were fifty percent inferior to that which existed in Boston, a defendant in New Bedford would be required to measure up to the standard of skill and competence and ability that is ordinarily found by physicians in New Bedford.

The basic issue raised by the exceptions to the charge and to the refused request is whether the defendant was to be judged by the standard of doctors practising in New Bedford.

The instruction given to the jury was based on the rule, often called the "community" or "locality" rule first enunciated in Small v. Howard, 128 Mass. 131, a case decided in 1880. There the defendant, a general practitioner in a country town with a population of 2,500 was consulted by the plaintiff to treat a severe wound which required a considerable degree of surgical skill. In an action against the defendant for malpractice this court defined his duty as follows:

It is a matter of common knowledge that a physician in a small country village does not usually make a specialty of surgery, and, however well informed he may be in the theory of all parts of his profession, he would, generally speaking, be but seldom called upon as a surgeon to perform difficult operations. He would have but few opportunities of observation

---

[1]   The defendant testified that such variations as there were in the dosages administered in Boston and New York, as distinct from New Bedford, were due to differences in obstetrical technique. The New Bedford obstetricians use suprafundi pressure (pressure applied to the uterus during delivery) which "requires a higher level of anesthesia."

and practice in that line such as public hospitals or large cities would afford. The defendant was applied to, being the practitioner in a small village, and we think it was correct to rule that "he was bound to possess that skill only which physicians and surgeons of ordinary ability and skill, practising in similar localities, with opportunities for no larger experience, ordinarily possess; and he was not bound to possess that high degree of art and skill possessed by eminent surgeons practising in large cities, and making a specialty of the practice of surgery."

The rule in *Small v. Howard* has been followed and applied in a long line of cases, some of which are quite recent. * Although in some of the later decisions the court has said that the doctor must exercise the care prevailing in "the locality where he practiced" it is doubtful if the court intended to narrow the rule in *Small v. Howard* where the expression "similar localities" was used. *

The rationale of the rule of *Small v. Howard* is that a physician in a small or rural community will lack opportunities to keep abreast with the advances in the profession and that he will not have the most modern facilities for treating his patients. Thus, it is unfair to hold the country doctor to the standard of doctors practising in large cities. The plaintiffs earnestly contend that distinctions based on geography are no longer valid in view of modern developments in transportation, communication and medical education, all of which tend to promote a certain degree of standardization within the profession. Hence, the plaintiffs urge that the rule laid down in *Small v. Howard* almost ninety years ago now be reexamined in the light of contemporary conditions.

The "community" or "locality" rule has been modified in several jurisdictions and has been subject to critical comment in legal periodicals. *

One approach, in jurisdictions where the "same community rule" obtains, has been to extend the geographical area which constitutes the community. The question arises not only in situations involving the standard of care and skill to be exercised by the doctor who is being sued for malpractice, but also in the somewhat analogous situations concerning the qualifications of a medical expert to testify. See Sampson v. Veenboer, 252 Mich. 660, 666–67, 234 N.W. 170, 171–72 (1931) (expert from another State permitted to testify as to standards in Grand Rapids, in view of evidence that he was familiar with standards in similar localities). In Connecticut which has the "same locality rule," it was said by the Supreme Court of Errors, " * * * There is now no lack of opportunity for the physician or surgeon in smaller communities to keep abreast of the advances made in his profession, and to be familiar with the latest methods and practices adopted. It is not unreasonable to require that he have and exercise the skill of physicians and surgeons in similar localities in the same general neighborhood. It may not be sufficient if he exercise only that degree of skill possessed by other practitioners in the community in which he lives." Geraty v. Kaufman, 115 Conn. 563, 573–74, 162 A. 33, 36 (1932).

Other courts have emphasized such factors as accessibility to medical facilities and experience. See Tvedt v. Haugen, 70 N.D. 338,

294 N.W. 183 (1940), where the defendant doctor recognized that the plaintiff's injury required the care of a specialist but failed to call this to the attention of the plaintiff. The court said *:

> * * * Today, with the rapid methods of transportation and easy means of communication, the horizons have been widened, and the duty of a doctor is not fulfilled merely by utilizing the means at hand in the particular village where he is practicing. So far as medical treatment is concerned, the borders of the locality and community have, in effect, been extended so as to include those centers readily accessible where appropriate treatment may be had which the local physician, because of limited facilities or training, is unable to give. * * *

Other decisions have adopted a standard of reasonable care and allow the locality to be taken into account as one of the circumstances, but not as an absolute limit upon the skill required. See * Viita v. Fleming, 132 Minn. 128, 135–37, 155 N.W. 1077 (1916). In the case last cited the court said at page 137, 155 N.W. at page 1081, "Frequent meetings of medical societies, articles in the medical journals, books by acknowledged authorities, and extensive experience in hospital work put the country doctor on more equal terms with his city brother. * * * [W]e are unwilling to hold that he is to be judged only by the qualifications that others in the same village or similar villages possess."

Recently the Supreme Court of Washington (sitting en banc) virtually abandoned the "locality" rule in Pederson v. Dumouchel, Wash., 72 Wash.2d 73, 79, 431 P.2d 973, 978 (1967). * * * In the course of its well reasoned opinion the court said, "the 'locality rule' has no present-day vitality except that it may be considered as *one* of the elements to determine the degree of care and skill which is to be expected of the average practitioner of the class to which he belongs. The degree of care which must be observed is, of course, that of an average, competent practitioner acting in the same or similar circumstances. In other words, local practice within geographic proximity is one, but not the only factor to be considered. No longer is it proper to limit the definition of the standard of care which a medical doctor or dentist must meet solely to the practice or custom of a particular locality, a similar locality, or a geographic area." * * *

In cases involving specialists the Supreme Court of New Jersey has abandoned the "locality" rule. See Carbone v. Warburton, 11 N.J. 418, 426, 94 A.2d 680, 683 (1953), "[O]ne who holds himself out as a specialist must employ not merely the skill of a general practitioner, but also the special degree of skill normally possessed by the average physician who devotes special study and attention to the particular organ or disease or injury involved, having regard to the present state of scientific knowledge." *

* * * We are of opinion [sic] that the "locality" rule of *Small v. Howard* which measures a physician's conduct by the standards of other doctors in similar communities is unsuited to present day conditions. The time has come when the medical profession should no longer be Balkanized by the application of varying geographic standards in malpractice cases. Accordingly, *Small v. Howard* is hereby overruled. The present case affords a good illustration of the

inappropriateness of the "locality" rule to existing conditions. The defendant was a specialist practising in New Bedford, a city of 100,000, which is slightly more than fifty miles from Boston, one of the medical centers of the nation, if not the world. This is a far cry from the country doctor in *Small v. Howard*, who ninety years ago was called upon to perform difficult surgery. Yet the trial judge told the jury that if the skill and ability of New Bedford physicians were "fifty percent inferior" to those obtaining in Boston the defendant should be judged by New Bedford standards, "having regard to the current state of advance of the profession." This may well be carrying the rule of *Small v. Howard* to its logical conclusion, but it is, we submit, a *reductio ad absurdum* of the rule.

The proper standard is whether the physician, if a general practitioner, has exercised the degree of care and skill of the average qualified practitioner, taking into account the advances in the profession. In applying this standard it is permissible to consider the medical resources available to the physician as *one* circumstance in determining the skill and care required. Under this standard some allowance is thus made for the type of community in which the physician carries on his practice. *

One holding himself out as a specialist should be held to the standard of care and skill of the average member of the profession practising the specialty, taking into account the advances in the profession. And, as in the case of the general practitioner, it is permissible to consider the medical resources available to him. * * *

NOTES

1. *Correspondence with Custom as a Defense in Professional Malpractice.* Why is correspondence with custom a defense for physicians and other professionals when it is not available for most other defendants? See Clarence Morris, Custom and Negligence, 42 Colum. L. Rev. 1147, 1164–65 (1942).

Who is the "average" qualified practitioner? Are nearly half substandard? See Restatement (Second) of Torts § 299A cmt. e (1965).

Proof that the medical care that was given accorded with any among the practices accepted as proper by any responsible physicians qualified in the particular field ordinarily shields a doctor from malpractice liability.

An important consequence of the rule that customary practice is the standard of care is the requirement for expert testimony to establish the standard of care, including the related question of who is qualified to provide such testimony in connection with specialized medical treatment. For example, in Boyce v. Brown, 51 Ariz. 416, 421 77 P.2d 455, 457 (1938), the Arizona Supreme Court stated:

> * * * In order to sustain a verdict for the plaintiffs in an action for malpractice, the standard of medical practice * * * must be shown by affirmative evidence, and, unless there is evidence of such a standard, a jury may not be permitted to speculate as to what the required standard is, or whether the defendant has departed therefrom. * * * [N]egligence on the part of a physician or surgeon, by reason of his departure from the proper standard of practice, must be established by expert medical testimony, unless the

negligence is so grossly apparent that a layman would have no difficulty in recognizing it.

2. *The Necessity of Expert Testimony in Cases Other than Medical Negligence.* If expert testimony regarding the standard of care is required in most medical negligence cases, what about other negligence cases? The generally articulated rule is that "if the subject in question is so distinctly related to some science, profession, or occupation as to be beyond the ken of the average layperson, expert testimony is usually required to prove the standard of care." District of Columbia v. Hampton, 666 A.2d 30, 35 (D.C.App.1995). The court went on to say, however, that:

> Where negligent conduct is alleged in a context which is within the realm of common knowledge and everyday experience, the plaintiff is not required to adduce expert testimony either to establish the applicable standard of care or to prove that the defendant failed to adhere to it.

In *Hampton*, the natural parent of a foster child under the care of a foster parent, selected and supervised by the defendant, sued for the wrongful death of the child. Even though an autopsy revealed that the child died of blunt force injuries to the head, abdomen, and back, and a member of the foster parent's household admitted to striking the child, the court ruled that expert testimony was required on the issue of the standard of care for the foster parents. Is this holding sound?

Courts generally require expert testimony in malpractice cases against so-called "professionals" other than doctors. E.g., McConwell v. FMG of Kansas City, Inc., 18 Kan.App.2d 839, 861 P.2d 830 (1993) (lawyers); Atwater Creamery Co. v. Western Nat'l Mut. Ins. Co., 366 N.W.2d 271 (Minn. 1985) (insurance agents).

3. *Locality Rule or National Standard.* In the late 1960s and the 1970s, many courts followed the path of *Brune v. Belinkoff* and adopted a "national standard" for measuring custom instead of a local standard. Some states adopted a national standard for medical specialists while retaining a locality standard for general practitioners. See, e.g., Bruni v. Tatsumi, 46 Ohio St.2d 127, 346 N.E.2d 673 (1976).

During the late 1980s, many state legislatures, facing what they perceived to be a medical malpractice crisis, intervened in this arena. A few altered the standard of care required of health care professionals. One of the more unusual re-articulations of the standard for medical malpractice is that of Md. Code Ann., Cts. & Jud. Proc. § 3–2A–02(c)(1) (2014) which provides:

> * * * [T]he health care provider is not liable * * * unless it is established that the care given by the health care provider is not in accordance with the standards of practice among members of the same health care profession with similar training and experience situated in the same or similar communities * * *.

How would the statute function if it were interpreted literally?

4. *Liability Despite Correspondence with Custom.* Should there ever be liability for malpractice even when the doctor's actions conform with customary practice? In Helling v. Carey, 83 Wash.2d 514, 519 P.2d 981 (1974), the Supreme Court of Washington upheld a judgment against an ophthalmologist for failure to administer a glaucoma pressure test. The trial court had found that the test would have been cheap, easy, and harmless and would have prevented loss of the patient's sight. The undisputed medical evidence, however, showed that the custom among ophthalmologists was not to administer the test to patients less than 40 years of age. A concurring opinion on behalf of three justices suggested that the proper justification for holding the defendant liable was strict liability so as not to stigmatize defendants with moral blame when they had followed all the normal precautions of their profession. The Washington legislature quickly adopted legislation that functionally reversed the impact of *Helling v. Carey,* see Wash. Rev. Code § 4.24.290 (2013), and virtually all other courts have declined to follow *Helling.*

Courts sometimes avoid the impact of custom as a defense by finding that a decision or an action leading to injury was not a medical decision. For example, in Homere v. State, 48 A.D.2d 422, 370 N.Y.S.2d 246 (1975), the court found a state mental hospital liable for negligence in the release of a patient who subsequently attacked several people. The decision to discharge the patient had been made by three psychiatrists. Following their evaluation of the patient, but before his release, the patient became violent and disruptive. The court found that defendants were liable for not ordering another medical evaluation. The court stressed, however, "We impose liability upon the State not for an erroneous medical judgment, but rather for its failure to make anything other than a purely administrative decision to release Samules following the incidents of violence * * *."

Homere also states that the defendant "is not responsible for an honest error of professional judgment made by qualified and competent doctors in its employ." * Is this a correct statement of the standard of care for physicians? For anyone under a negligence standard? What does *Vaughan v. Menlove* suggest about this?

Canterbury v. Spence
Court of Appeals for the District of Columbia, 1972.
464 F.2d 772.

■ ROBINSON III, SPOTTSWOOD W., CIRCUIT JUDGE. * * * At the time of the events which gave rise to this litigation, appellant was nineteen years of age, a clerk-typist employed by the Federal Bureau of Investigation. In December, 1958, he began to experience severe pain between his shoulder blades. * He consulted two general practitioners, but the medications they prescribed failed to eliminate the pain. Thereafter, appellant secured an appointment with Dr. Spence, who is a neurosurgeon. Dr. Spence examined appellant in his office at some length but found nothing amiss. On Dr. Spence's advice appellant was x-rayed, but the films did not identify any [abnormality]. Dr. Spence then recommended that appellant undergo a myelogram—a procedure in which dye is injected into the spinal column and traced to find evidence of disease or other disorder—at the Washington Hospital Center.

Appellant entered the hospital on February 4, 1959. * The myelogram revealed a "filling defect" in the region of the fourth thoracic vertebra. * * * Dr. Spence told appellant that he would have to undergo a laminectomy—the excision of the posterior arch of the vertebra—to correct what he suspected was a ruptured disc. Appellant did not raise any objection to the proposed operation nor did he probe into its exact nature. * * * Appellant called his mother the day after the myelogram was performed and * * * [w]hen Mrs. Canterbury returned the call, Dr. Spence told her that the surgery was occasioned by a suspected ruptured disc. Mrs. Canterbury then asked if the recommended operation was serious and Dr. Spence replied "not anymore than any other operation." * * * Dr. Spence performed the laminectomy on February 11 * * *.

For approximately the first day after the operation appellant recuperated normally, but then suffered a fall and an almost immediate setback. Since there is some conflict as to precisely when or why appellant fell, * we reconstruct the events from the evidence most favorable to him. * Dr. Spence left orders that appellant was to remain in bed during the process of voiding. These orders were changed to direct that voiding be done out of bed, and the jury could find that the change was made by hospital personnel. Just prior to the fall, appellant summoned a nurse and was given a receptacle for use in voiding, but was then left unattended. Appellant testified that during the course of the endeavor he slipped off the side of the bed, and that there was no one to assist him, or side rail to prevent the fall. Several hours later, appellant began to complain that he could not move his legs and that he was having trouble breathing; paralysis seems to have been virtually total from the waist down. * * * At the time of the trial in April, 1968, appellant required crutches to walk [and] still suffered from urinal incontinence and paralysis of the bowels * * *.

II

Appellant filed suit in the District Court on March 7, 1963, four years after the laminectomy and approximately two years after he attained his majority. The complaint stated several causes of action against each defendant. Against Dr. Spence it alleged, among other things, negligence in the performance of the laminectomy and failure to inform him beforehand of the risk involved. Against the hospital the complaint charged negligent post-operative care in permitting appellant to remain unattended after the laminectomy, in failing to provide a nurse or orderly to assist him at the time of his fall, and in failing to maintain a side rail on his bed. The answers denied the allegations of negligence and defended on the ground that the suit was barred by the statute of limitations.

Pretrial discovery—including depositions by appellant, his mother and Dr. Spence—continuances and other delays consumed five years. At trial, disposition of the threshold question whether the statute of limitations had run was held in abeyance until the relevant facts developed. Appellant introduced no evidence to show medical and hospital practices, if any, customarily pursued in regard to the critical aspects of the case, and only Dr. Spence, called as an adverse witness, testified on the issue of causality. Dr. Spence described the surgical procedures he utilized in the two operations and expressed his opinion that appellant's disabilities stemmed from his pre-operative condition as symptomized by the swollen, non-pulsating spinal cord. He stated, however, that neither he nor any of the other physicians with whom he consulted was certain as to what that condition was, and he admitted that trauma can be a cause of paralysis. Dr. Spence further testified that even without trauma paralysis can be anticipated "somewhere in the nature of one percent" of the laminectomies performed, a risk he termed "a very slight possibility." He felt that communication of that risk to the patient is not good medical practice because it might deter patients from undergoing needed surgery and might produce adverse psychological reactions which could preclude the success of the operation.

At the close of appellant's case in chief, each defendant moved for a directed verdict and the trial judge granted both motions. * * *

We reverse. The testimony of appellant and his mother that Dr. Spence did not reveal the risk of paralysis from the laminectomy made out a prima facie case of violation of the physician's duty to disclose which Dr. Spence's explanation did not negate as a matter of law. There was also testimony from which the jury could have found that the laminectomy was negligently performed by Dr. Spence, and that appellant's fall was the consequence of negligence on the part of the hospital. The record, moreover, contains evidence of sufficient quantity and quality to tender jury issues as to whether and to what extent any such negligence was causally related to appellant's post-laminectomy condition. These considerations entitled appellant to a new trial. * * *

III

Suits charging failure by a physician * adequately to disclose the risks and alternatives of proposed treatment are not innovations in American law. They date back a good half-century, * and in the last decade they have multiplied rapidly. * * *

The root premise is the concept, fundamental in American jurisprudence, that "[e]very human being of adult years and sound mind has a right to determine what shall be done with his own body." * * * W[illiam L.] Prosser, Torts § 18 at 102 (3d ed. 1964); Restatement of Torts § 49 (1934). True consent to what happens to one's self is the informed exercise of a choice, and that entails an opportunity to evaluate knowledgeably the options available and the risks attendant upon each. * The average patient has little or no understanding of the medical arts, and ordinarily has only his physician to whom he can look for enlightenment with which to reach an intelligent decision. * From these almost axiomatic considerations springs the need, and in turn the requirement, of a reasonable divulgence by physician to patient to make such a decision possible.[15] * * *

The context in which the duty of risk-disclosure arises is invariably the occasion for decision as to whether a particular treatment procedure is to be undertaken. * * * To enable the patient to chart his course understandably, some familiarity with the therapeutic alternatives and their hazards becomes essential. * A reasonable revelation in these

---

[15] * * * In duty-to-disclose cases, the focus of attention is more properly upon the nature and content of the physician's divulgence than the patient's understanding or consent. Adequate disclosure and informed consent are, of course, two sides of the same coin—the former a *sine qua non* of the latter. But the vital inquiry on duty to disclose relates to the physician's performance of an obligation, while one of the difficulties with analysis in terms of "informed consent" is its tendency to imply that what is decisive is the degree of the patient's comprehension. As we later emphasize, the physician discharges the duty when he makes a reasonable effort to convey sufficient information although the patient, without fault of the physician, may not fully grasp it. * * *

respects is not only a necessity but, as we see it, is as much a matter of the physician's duty. It is a duty to warn of the dangers lurking in the proposed treatment, and that is surely a facet of due care. * It is, too, a duty to impart information which the patient has every right to expect.[27] * * *

It is well established that the physician must seek and secure his patient's consent before commencing an operation or other course of treatment. It is also clear that the consent, to be efficacious, must be free from imposition upon the patient. It is the settled rule that therapy not authorized by the patient may amount to a tort—a common law battery—by the physician. * And it is evident that it is normally impossible to obtain a consent worthy of the name unless the physician first elucidates the options and the perils for the patient's edification. * Thus the physician has long borne a duty, on pain of liability for unauthorized treatment, to make adequate disclosure to the patient. * * *

IV

Duty to disclose has gained recognition in a large number of American jurisdictions, * but more largely on a different rationale. The majority of courts dealing with the problem have made the duty depend on whether it was the custom of physicians practicing in the community to make the particular disclosure to the patient. * If so, the physician may be held liable for an unreasonable and injurious failure to divulge, but there can be no recovery unless the omission forsakes a practice prevalent in the profession. * We agree that the physician's noncompliance with a professional custom to reveal, like any other departure from prevailing medical practice, * may give rise to liability to the patient. We do not agree that the patient's cause of action is dependent upon the existence and nonperformance of a relevant professional tradition.

There are, in our view, formidable obstacles to acceptance of the notion that the physician's obligation to disclose is either germinated or limited by medical practice. To begin with, the reality of any discernible custom reflecting a professional consensus on communication of option and risk information to patients is open to serious doubt. * We sense the danger that what in fact is no custom at all may be taken as an affirmative custom to maintain silence * * *. We cannot gloss over the inconsistency between reliance on a general practice respecting divulgence and, on the other hand, realization that the myriad of variables among patients * makes each case so different that its omission can rationally be justified only by the effect of its individual circumstances. * Nor can we ignore the fact that to bind the disclosure obligation to medical usage is to arrogate the decision on revelation to the physician alone. * Respect for the patient's right of self-determination on particular therapy * demands a standard set by law

---

[27] * * * [T]he physician is not compelled to give his patient a short medical education; the disclosure rule summons the physician only to a reasonable explanation. * That means generally informing the patient in nontechnical terms as to what is at stake: the therapy alternatives open to him, the goals expectably to be achieved, and the risks that may ensue from particular treatment and no treatment. * So informing the patient hardly taxes the physician, and it must be the exceptional patient who cannot comprehend such an explanation at least in a rough way.

for physicians rather than one which physicians may or may not impose upon themselves. * * *

* * * We hold that the standard measuring performance of that duty by physicians, as by others, is conduct which is reasonable under the circumstances. *

V

Once the circumstances give rise to a duty on the physician's part to inform his patient, the next inquiry is the scope of the disclosure the physician is legally obliged to make. * * *

The larger number of courts, as might be expected, have applied tests framed with reference to prevailing fashion within the medical profession. * * * We have explored this rather considerable body of law but are unprepared to follow it. The duty to disclose, we have reasoned, arises from phenomena apart from medical custom and practice. * The latter, we think, should no more establish the scope of the duty than its existence. Any definition of scope in terms purely of a professional standard is at odds with the patient's prerogative to decide on projected therapy himself. * * *

In our view, the patient's right of self-decision shapes the boundaries of the duty to reveal. That right can be effectively exercised only if the patient possesses enough information to enable an intelligent choice. The scope of the physician's communications to the patient, then, must be measured by the patient's need, * and that need is the information material to the decision. Thus the test for determining whether a particular peril must be divulged is its materiality to the patient's decision: all risks potentially affecting the decision must be unmasked. * * *

Optimally for the patient, exposure of a risk would be mandatory whenever the patient would deem it significant to his decision, either singly or in combination with other risks. Such a requirement, however, would summon the physician to second-guess the patient, whose ideas on materiality could hardly be known to the physician. That would make an undue demand upon medical practitioners, whose conduct, like that of others, is to be measured in terms of reasonableness. * * *

From these considerations we derive the breadth of the disclosure of risks legally to be required. * * * In broad outline, we agree that "[a] risk is thus material when a reasonable person, in what the physician knows or should know to be the patient's position, would be likely to attach significance to the risk or cluster of risks in deciding whether or not to forego the proposed therapy." *

The topics importantly demanding a communication of information are the inherent and potential hazards of the proposed treatment, the alternatives to that treatment, if any, and the results likely if the patient remains untreated. The factors contributing significance to the dangerousness of a medical technique are, of course, the incidence of injury and the degree of the harm threatened. * A very small chance of death or serious disablement may well be significant; a potential disability which dramatically outweighs the potential benefit of the therapy or the detriments of the existing malady may summons [sic] discussion with the patient. *

There is no bright line separating the significant from the insignificant; the answer in any case must abide a rule of reason. Some dangers—infection, for example—are inherent in any operation; there is no obligation to communicate those of which persons of average sophistication are aware. * * * Whenever nondisclosure of particular risk information is open to debate by reasonable-minded men, the issue is for the finder of the facts. *

VI

Two exceptions to the general rule of disclosure have been noted by the courts. * * * The first comes into play when the patient is unconscious or otherwise incapable of consenting, and harm from a failure to treat is imminent and outweighs any harm threatened by the proposed treatment. When a genuine emergency of that sort arises, it is settled that the impracticality of conferring with the patient dispenses with need for it. * Even in situations of that character the physician should, as current law requires, attempt to secure a relative's consent if possible. * But if time is too short to accommodate discussion, obviously the physician should proceed with the treatment. *

The second exception obtains when risk-disclosure poses such a threat of detriment to the patient as to become unfeasible or contraindicated from a medical point of view. It is recognized that patients occasionally become so ill or emotionally distraught on disclosure as to foreclose a rational decision, or complicate or hinder the treatment, or perhaps even pose psychological damage to the patient. * * *

The physician's privilege to withhold information for therapeutic reasons must be carefully circumscribed, however, for otherwise it might devour the disclosure rule itself. The privilege does not accept the paternalistic notion that the physician may remain silent simply because divulgence might prompt the patient to forego therapy the physician feels the patient really needs. * * *

VII

No more than breach of any other legal duty does non-fulfillment of the physician's obligation to disclose alone establish liability to the patient. * * * [A]s in malpractice actions generally, * there must be a causal relationship between the physician's failure to adequately divulge and damage to the patient. *

A causal connection exists when, but only when, disclosure of significant risks incidental to treatment would have resulted in a decision against it. * The patient obviously has no complaint if he would have submitted to the therapy notwithstanding awareness that the risk was one of its perils. On the other hand, the very purpose of the disclosure rule is to protect the patient against consequences which, if known, he would have avoided by foregoing the treatment. * The more difficult question is whether the factual issue on causality calls for an objective or a subjective determination.

It has been assumed that the issue is to be resolved according to whether the fact-finder believes the patient's testimony that he would not have agreed to the treatment if he had known of the danger which later ripened into injury. * We think a technique which ties the factual conclusion on causation simply to the assessment of the patient's credibility is unsatisfactory. * * * In our view, this method of dealing with the issue on causation comes in second-best. It places the physician in jeopardy of the patient's hindsight and bitterness. It places the fact-finder in the position of deciding whether a speculative answer to a hypothetical question is to be credited. It calls for a subjective determination solely on testimony of a patient-witness shadowed by the occurrence of the undisclosed risk. *

Better it is, we believe, to resolve the causality issue on an objective basis: in terms of what a prudent person in the patient's position would have decided if suitably informed of all perils bearing significance. * If adequate disclosure could reasonably be expected to have caused that person to decline the treatment because of the revelation of the kind of risk or danger that resulted in harm, causation is shown, but otherwise not. * * *

VIII

* * * We now delineate our view on the need for expert testimony in non-disclosure cases. * * * Experts are ordinarily indispensable to identify and elucidate for the fact-finder the risks of therapy and the consequences of leaving existing maladies untreated. They are normally needed on issues as to the cause of any injury or disability suffered by the patient and, where privileges are asserted, as to the existence of any emergency claimed and the nature and seriousness of any impact upon the patient from risk-disclosure. * * *

It is evident that many of the issues typically involved in nondisclosure cases do not reside peculiarly within the medical domain. * * * Experts are unnecessary to a showing of the materiality of a risk to a patient's decision on treatment, or to the reasonably, expectable effect of risk disclosure on the decision. * * *

IX

We now confront the question whether appellant's suit was barred, wholly or partly, by the statute of limitations. The statutory periods relevant to this inquiry are one year for battery actions * and three years for those charging negligence. * For one a minor when his cause of action accrues, they do not begin to run until he has attained his majority. * Appellant was nineteen years old when the laminectomy and related events occurred, and he filed his complaint roughly two years after he reached twenty-one. Consequently, any claim in suit subject to the one-year limitation came too late.

Appellant's causes of action for the allegedly faulty laminectomy by Dr. Spence and allegedly careless post-operative care by the hospital present no problem. Quite obviously, each was grounded in negligence and so was governed by the three-year provision. * The duty-to-disclose claim appellant asserted against Dr. Spence, however, draws another consideration into the picture. * * *

* * * [Appellant's] interest in bodily integrity commanded protection, not only against an intentional invasion by an unauthorized operation * but also against a negligent invasion by his physician's dereliction of duty to adequately disclose. * Appellant has asserted and litigated a violation of that duty throughout the case. * That claim, like the others, was governed by the three-year period of limitation applicable to negligence actions * * *.

X

This brings us to the remaining question, common to all three causes of action: whether appellant's evidence was of such caliber as to require a submission to the jury. On the first, the evidence was clearly sufficient to raise an issue as to whether Dr. Spence's obligation to disclose information on risks was reasonably met or was excused by the surrounding circumstances. Appellant testified that Dr. Spence revealed to him nothing suggesting a hazard associated with the laminectomy. His mother testified that, in response to her specific inquiry, Dr. Spence informed her that the laminectomy was no more serious than any other operation. When, at trial, it developed from Dr. Spence's testimony that paralysis can be expected in one percent of laminectomies, it became the jury's responsibility to decide whether that peril was of sufficient magnitude to bring the disclosure duty into play. * There was no emergency to frustrate an opportunity to disclose, * and Dr. Spence's expressed opinion that disclosure would have been unwise did not foreclose a contrary conclusion by the jury. There was no evidence that appellant's emotional makeup was such that concealment of the risk of paralysis was medically sound.[138] Even if disclosure to appellant himself might have bred ill consequences, no reason appears for the omission to communicate the information to his mother, particularly in view of his minority. * The jury, not Dr. Spence, was the final arbiter of whether nondisclosure was reasonable under the circumstances. * * *

We are advertent to Dr. Spence's attribution of appellant's disabilities to his condition preexisting the laminectomy, but that was a matter for the jury. * * *

In sum, judged by legal standards, the proof militated against a directed verdict in Dr. Spence's favor. True it is that the evidence did not furnish ready answers on the dispositive factual issues, but the important consideration is that appellant showed enough to call for resolution of those issues by the jury. * * *

We conclude, lastly, that the case against the hospital should also have gone to the jury. The circumstances surrounding appellant's fall—the change in Dr. Spence's order that appellant be kept in bed, * the failure to maintain a side rail on appellant's bed, and the absence of any attendant while appellant was attempting to relieve himself—could certainly suggest to jurors a dereliction of the hospital's duty to exercise reasonable care for the safety and well-being of the patient. * * * To this may be added Dr. Spence's testimony that paralysis can be brought on by trauma or shock. All told, the jury had available a store of information enabling an intelligent resolution of the issues respecting the hospital. * * *

Reversed and remanded for a new trial.

---

[138] * With appellant's prima facie case of violation of duty to disclose, the burden of introducing evidence showing a privilege was on Dr. Spence. * Dr. Spence's opinion—that disclosure is medically unwise—was expressed as to patients generally, and not with reference to traits possessed by appellant. His explanation was:

I think that I always explain to patients the operations are serious, and I feel that any operation is serious. I think that I would not tell patients that they might be paralyzed because of the small percentage, one per cent, that exists. There would be a tremendous percentage of people that would not have surgery and would not therefore be benefited by it, the tremendous percentage that get along very well, 99 per cent.

NOTES

1. *Subsequent History of Case.* On remand to the trial court, the jury found for the defendant. On appeal, the Court of Appeals affirmed the decision, without opinion. 509 F.2d 537 (D.C.Cir.1975); see also Earl H. Davis, *Canterbury v. Spence et al.* and Informed Consent, Revisited. Three Years Later, 11 Forum 708, 711 (1976).

Substantial disagreement remains among courts as to whether the standard of care in informed consent cases is determined by medical custom, thus requiring expert testimony, see, e.g., Riedisser v. Nelson, 111 Ariz. 542, 544, 534 P.2d 1052, 1054 (1975); Roberts v. Young, 369 Mich. 133, 138–39, 119 N.W.2d 627, 629–30 (1963); Aiken v. Clary, 396 S.W.2d 668, 673–75 (Mo.1965), or whether juries may find negligence for failure to inform without expert testimony showing a divergence from medical custom. See, e.g., Pauscher v. Iowa Methodist Med. Ctr., 408 N.W.2d 355, 359–60 (Iowa 1987); Sard v. Hardy, 281 Md. 432, 447, 379 A.2d 1014, 1024 (1977).

In a number of jurisdictions, *Canterbury v. Spence* evoked legislative responses, often at the behest of doctors and insurance companies. E.g., New York Pub. Health Law § 2805–d (2014).

2. *Causation.* What two-step causation sequence must the plaintiff prove in order to recover under *Canterbury?*

What does causation mean when it is measured not by what an individual plaintiff would have done had he been warned but, instead, by what the reasonable person would have done? Is this causation as we usually think of it? Under either this so-called "objective test" of causation or under the "subjective test" of what a specific plaintiff would have done, how realistic is it to project how someone might have acted if he or she had been given different information?

Many courts reject the so-called "objective test" of causation articulated in *Canterbury v. Spence.* For example, in Arena v. Gingrich, 305 Or. 1, 4, 748 P.2d 547, 549 (1988), the Oregon Supreme Court, speaking through Justice Linde, held that "What the patient in fact would have done after a full explanation is a question about that patient's behavior, not about some other 'reasonable' patient's, a question of cause and effect that one might ask in contexts unrelated to any legal consequences." In response to concerns about the credibility of the plaintiff on this issue, Justice Linde responded, "Factfinders are not bound to take the patient's word on that question but may decide it themselves on the available evidence."

F. THE ROLE OF STATUTES

Professors Daniel A. Farber and Philip P. Frickey observe:

> It is commonplace that we live in a statutory era. A century ago, statutes were considered intrusions into the pristine order of the common law. * Today, legislatures are the primary source of law, and the statue books grow exponentially.

Daniel A. Farber & Philip P. Frickey, In the Shadow of the Legislature: The Common Law in the Age of the New Public Law, 89 Mich. L. Rev. 875, 875 (1991). As the late Judge Robert E. Keeton, himself a torts scholar, observed:

A fundamental characteristic of judging in late-20th century America is that very few court cases depend solely on common-law grounds. Legislatures have enacted so many statutes on so many subjects that in most cases at least one party invokes at least one statute.

Robert E. Keeton, Judging in the American Legal System 205 (1999).

Throughout your study, you already have seen numerous examples of statutes that explicitly modified, or even precluded, common law tort liability. In *Ives v. South Buffalo Railway Co.*, *supra*, you considered the initially unsuccessful attempt by the New York legislature to replace an entire category of tort claims with a no-fault compensation system. We learned that any such legislative modifications of tort liability must be constitutional. Indeed, the U.S. Supreme Court upheld the constitutionality of replacing common law liability with a workers' compensation system a few years after the decision in *Ives*. See *supra* pages 20–21, Note 7. The statute enacted by the Maryland General Assembly that altered the standard of care in negligence actions against physicians and other healthcare providers, quoted earlier in this chapter, is an example of a more narrowly drawn legislative modification of the common law. See *supra* page 186, Note 3.

In other instances, courts hold that even if statutes do not expressly prohibit or alter common law tort actions, they may impliedly preclude common law liability. For example, in Chapter 2, we noted a recent U.S. Supreme Court opinion which held that the Clean Air Act, and EPA actions pursuant to it, *displaced* a federal common law interstate nuisance action seeking to force defendants emitting greenhouse gases to reduce their emissions. See *supra* pages 88–90, Note. In Chapter 11, we will consider opinions in which the Supreme Court holds that federal statutes or regulations *preempt* state common law tort actions against manufacturers, either expressly, see Cipollone v. Liggett Group, Inc., *infra* pages 629–32, or impliedly, see Mut. Pharm. Co. v. Bartlett, *infra* pages 633–42.

Each of these examples of legislative enactments is one that benefits the defendant in a tort action. In this section, however, we turn to instances in which the plaintiff uses a statute, ordinance, or regulation to define the care owed by the defendant under the doctrine of negligence per se.

Martin v. Herzog

Court of Appeals of New York, 1920.
228 N.Y. 164, 126 N.E. 814.

■ CARDOZO, J. The action is one to recover damages for injuries resulting in death. Plaintiff and her husband, while driving toward Tarrytown in a buggy on the night of August 21, 1915, were struck by the defendant's automobile coming in the opposite direction. They were thrown to the ground, and the man was killed. At the point of the collision the highway makes a curve. The car was rounding the curve, when suddenly it came upon the buggy, emerging, the defendant tells us from the gloom. Negligence is charged against the defendant, the driver of the car, in that he did not keep to the right of the center of the highway. Highway Law, § 286, subd. 3, and section 332 (Consol. Laws, ch. 25). Negligence is charged against the plaintiff's intestate, the driver of the wagon, in that he was traveling without lights. Highway Law, § 329a, as amended by Laws 1915, ch. 367. There is no evidence that the defendant was moving at an excessive speed. There is none of any defect in the equipment of his car. The beam of light from his lamps pointed to the right as the wheels of his car turned along the curve toward the left; and, looking in the direction of the plaintiff's approach, he was peering into the shadow. The case against him must stand, therefore, if at all, upon the divergence of his course from the center of the highway. The jury found him delinquent and his victim blameless. The Appellate Division reversed, and ordered a new trial.

We agree with the Appellate Division that the charge to the jury was erroneous and misleading. The case was tried on the assumption that the hour had arrived when lights were due. It was argued on the same assumption in this court. In such circumstances, it is not important whether the hour might have made a question for the jury. * A controversy put out of the case by the parties is not to be put into it by us. We say this by way of preface to our review of the contested rulings. In the body of the charge the trial judge said that the jury could consider the absence of light "in determining whether the plaintiff's intestate was guilty of contributory negligence in failing to have a light upon the buggy as provided by law. I do not mean to say that the absence of light necessarily makes him negligent, but it is a fact for your consideration." The defendant requested a ruling that the absence of a light on the plaintiff's vehicle was "prima facie evidence of contributory negligence." This request was refused, and the jury were again instructed that they might consider the absence of lights as some evidence of negligence, but that it was not conclusive evidence. The plaintiff then requested a charge that "the fact that the plaintiff's intestate was driving without a light is not negligence in itself," and to this the court acceded. The defendant saved his rights by appropriate exceptions.

We think the unexcused omission of the statutory signals is more than some evidence of negligence. It *is* negligence in itself. Lights are intended for the guidance and protection of other travelers on the highway. Highway Law, § 329a. By the very terms of the hypothesis, to omit, willfully or heedlessly, the safeguards prescribed by law for the benefit of another that he may be preserved in life or limb, is to fall short of the standard of diligence to which those who live in organized society are under a duty to conform. That, we think, is now the established rule in this state. * Whether the omission of an absolute duty, not willfully or heedlessly, but through unavoidable accident, is also to be characterized as negligence, is a question of nomenclature into which we need not enter, for it does not touch the case before us. There may be times, when, if jural niceties are to be preserved, the two wrongs, negligence and breach of statutory duty, must be kept distinct in speech and thought. *

In the conditions here present they come together and coalesce. A rule less rigid has been applied where the one who complains of the omission is not a member of the class for whose protection the safeguard is designed. * Some relaxation there has also been where the safeguard is prescribed by local ordinance, and not by statute. * Courts have been reluctant to hold that the police regulations of boards and councils and other subordinate officials create rights of action beyond the specific penalties imposed. This has led them to say that the violation of a statute is negligence, and the violation of a like ordinance is only evidence of negligence. An ordinance, however, like a statute, is a law within its sphere of operation, and so the distinction has not escaped criticism. * Whether it has become too deeply rooted to be abandoned, even if it be thought illogical, is a question not now before us. What concerns us at this time is that, even in the ordinance cases, the omission of a safeguard prescribed by statute is put upon a different plane, and is held not merely some evidence of negligence, but negligence in itself. *

In the case at hand, we have an instance of the admitted violation of a statute intended for the protection of travelers on the highway, of whom the defendant at the time was one. Yet the jurors were instructed in effect that they were at liberty in their discretion to treat the omission of lights either as innocent or as culpable. They were allowed to "consider the default as lightly or gravely" as they would (Thomas, J., in the court below). They might as well have been told that they could use a like discretion in holding a master at fault for the omission of a safety appliance prescribed by positive law for the protection of a workman. * Jurors have no dispensing power, by which they may relax the duty that one traveler on the highway owes under the statute to another. It is error to tell them that they have. The omission of these lights was a wrong, and, being wholly unexcused, was also a negligent wrong. No license should have been conceded to the triers of the facts to find it anything else.

We must be on our guard, however, against confusing the question of negligence with that of the causal connection between the negligence and the injury. A defendant who travels without lights is not to pay damages for his fault, unless the absence of lights is the cause of the disaster. A plaintiff who travels without them is not to forfeit the right to damages, unless the absence of lights is at least a contributing cause of the disaster. To say that conduct is negligence is not to say that it is always contributory negligence. "Proof of negligence in the air, so to speak, will not do." F. Pollock, Torts 472 (10th ed. 1916).

We think, however, that evidence of a collision occurring more than an hour after sundown between a car and an unseen buggy, proceeding without lights, is evidence from which a causal connection may be inferred between the collision and the lack of signals. * If nothing else is shown to break the connection, we have a case, *prima facie* sufficient, of negligence contributing to the result.

There may, indeed, be times when the lights on a highway are so many and so bright that lights on a wagon are superfluous. If that is so, it is for the offender to go forward with the evidence, and prove the illumination as a kind of substituted performance. The plaintiff asserts that she did so here. She says that the scene of the accident was illumined by moonlight, by an electric lamp, and by the lights of the approaching car. Her position is that, if the defendant did not see the buggy thus illumined, a jury might reasonably infer that he would not have seen it anyhow. We may doubt whether there is any evidence of illumination sufficient to sustain the jury in drawing such an inference;

but the decision of the case does not make it necessary to resolve the doubt, and so we leave it open. It is certain that they were not required to find that lights on the wagon were superfluous. They might reasonably have found the contrary. They ought, therefore, to have been informed what effect they were free to give, in that event, to the violation of the statute. They should have been told, not only that the omission of the light was negligence, but that it was "*prima facie* evidence of contributory negligence," i.e., that it was sufficient in itself unless its probative force was overcome (Thomas, J., in court below) to sustain a verdict that the decedent was at fault. *

Here, on the undisputed facts, lack of vision, whether excusable or not, was the cause of the disaster. The defendant may have been negligent in swerving from the center of the road; but he did not run into the buggy purposely, nor was he driving while intoxicated, nor was he going at such a reckless speed that warning would of necessity have been futile. Nothing of the kind is shown. The collision was due to his failure to see at a time when sight should have been aroused and guided by the statutory warnings. Some explanation of the effect to be given to the absence of those warnings if the plaintiff failed to prove that other lights on the car or the highway took their place as equivalents, should have been put before the jury. The explanation was asked for and refused.

We are persuaded that the tendency of the charge, and of all the rulings, following it, was to minimize unduly, in the minds of the triers of the facts, the gravity of the decedent's fault. Errors may not be ignored as unsubstantial, when they tend to such an outcome. A statute designed for the protection of human life is not to be brushed aside as a form of words, its commands reduced to the level of cautions, and the duty to obey attenuated into an option to conform.

The order of the Appellate Division should be affirmed, and judgment absolute directed on the stipulation in favor of the defendant, with costs in all courts. * * *

NOTES

1. *Rationales of Negligence Per Se.* According to Judge Cardozo's opinion in *Martin,* why do courts accept the idea that the violation of a criminal or regulatory statute establishes the standard of care in a negligence action despite the fact that the statute does not explicitly provide for such liability? Consider the following rationales for negligence per se suggested in the Restatement (Third) of Torts:

> First, even when the legislature has not chosen to attach a liability provision to the prohibition it has imposed, as a matter of institutional comity it would be awkward for a court in a tort case to commend as reasonable that behavior that the legislature has already condemned as unlawful.

> Second, in ordinary tort cases, so long as reasonable minds can differ, the responsibility for determining whether a person's conduct is negligent is vested in the jury. One major reason for this is to take advantage of community assessments in making the negligence determination. Yet when the legislature has addressed the issue of what conduct is appropriate, the judgment

of the legislature, as the authoritative representative of the community, takes precedence over the views of any one jury.

Third, it must be recognized that the negligence standard encounters difficulty in dealing with problems of recurring conduct. When each jury makes up its own mind as to the negligence of that conduct, there are serious disadvantages in terms of inequality, high litigation costs, and failing to provide clear guidance to persons engaged in primary activity. * * * In general, statutes address conduct that conspicuously recurs in a way that brings it to the attention of the legislature. Negligence per se hence replaces decisionmaking by juries in categories of cases where the operation of the latter may be least satisfactory.

Furthermore, negligence per se has been settled doctrine in American tort law for many decades. Once settled, the doctrine functions as a default rule in terms of how the judiciary will assess the significance of a statute. The legislature, in enacting a safety statute, can be aware that a party's violation of the statute will result in negligence per se. Aware of this, the legislature can be deemed to accept this result * * *.

Restatement (Third) of Torts: Liability for Physical and Emotional Harm § 14 cmt. c (2010).

2. *Effect of Defective, Outdated, or Subsequently Enacted Statutes.* What if the applicable statute was enacted a century ago and seldom, if ever, enforced? Or what if it is not clear whether the applicable statute is still in effect? Should it matter? What if the statute in question has no legal effect? In Clinkscales v. Carver, 22 Cal.2d 72, 136 P.2d 777 (1943), a California court found the defendant negligent for going through a stop sign even though it was posted under an ordinance invalid for faulty publication. The court reasoned that "the legislative standard may nevertheless apply if it is an appropriate measure for the defendant's conduct." Statutes that are invalid because they contravene the federal or state constitutions, though, cannot provide the basis for the standard of care on a negligence per se theory. Harper, James and Gray on Torts § 17.6. Rejection of the statutory standard also may be appropriate when the law is so obscure, unknown, or outmoded as to make its adoption as a standard of care inequitable. See, e.g., Sweet v. Sisters of Providence in Washington, 895 P.2d 484, 493–94 (Alaska 1995).

3. *Statutory Purpose.* The general rule for negligence per se limits its applications to cases in which the plaintiff is among the class of individuals that the statute was intended to protect and the injuries are of the character of injuries which the statute was designed to prevent. See Gorris v. Scott, [1873–74] L.R. 9 Ex. 125, *infra* pages 287–289.

In Osborne v. McMasters, 40 Minn. 103, 41 N.W. 543 (1889), the court articulated a classic formulation of the negligence per se doctrine:

[W]here a statute or municipal ordinance imposes upon any person a specific duty for the protection or benefit of others, if he neglects to perform that duty he is liable to those for whose protection or benefit it was imposed for any injuries of the character which the statute or ordinance was designed to prevent, and which were proximately produced by such neglect.

Tedla v. Ellman

Court of Appeals of New York, 1939.
280 N.Y. 124, 19 N.E.2d 987.

■ LEHMAN, JUDGE. While walking along a highway, Anna Tedla and her brother, John Bachek, were struck by a passing automobile, operated by the defendant [Ellman]. She was injured and Bachek was killed. Bachek was a deaf-mute. His occupation was collecting and selling junk. His sister, Mrs. Tedla, was engaged in the same occupation. They often picked up junk at the incinerator of the village of Islip. At the time of the accident they were walking along "Sunrise Highway" and wheeling baby carriages containing junk and wood which they had picked up at the incinerator. It was about six o'clock, or a little earlier, on a Sunday evening in December. Darkness had already set in. Bachek was carrying a lighted lantern, or, at least, there is testimony to that effect. The jury found that the accident was due solely to the negligence of the operator of the automobile. The defendants do not, upon this appeal, challenge the finding of negligence on the part of the operator. They maintain, however, that Mrs. Tedla and her brother were guilty of contributory negligence as matter of law.

Sunrise Highway, at the place of the accident, consists of two roadways, separated by a grass plot. There are no footpaths along the highway and the center grass plot was soft. It is not unlawful for a pedestrian, wheeling a baby carriage, to use the roadway under such circumstances, but a pedestrian using the roadway is bound to exercise such care for his safety as a reasonably prudent person would use. The Vehicle and Traffic Law (Consol. Laws, ch. 71) provides that

> Pedestrians walking or remaining on the paved portion, or traveled part of a roadway shall be subject to, and comply with, the rules governing vehicles, with respect to meeting and turning out, except that such pedestrians shall keep to the left of the center line thereof, and turn to their left instead of right side thereof, so as to permit all vehicles passing them in either direction to pass on their right. Such pedestrians shall not be subject to the rules governing vehicles as to giving signals.

§ 85, subd. 6.

Mrs. Tedla and her brother did not observe the statutory rule, and at the time of the accident, were proceeding in easterly direction on the east bound or right-hand roadway. The defendants moved to dismiss the complaint on the ground, among others, that violation of the statutory rule constitutes contributory negligence as matter of law. * * * The trial judge left to the jury the question whether failure to observe the statutory rule was a proximate cause of the accident * * *. Upon this appeal, the only question presented is whether, as matter of law, disregard of the statutory rule that pedestrians shall keep to the left of the center line of a highway constitutes contributory negligence which bars any recovery by the plaintiff.

Vehicular traffic can proceed safely and without recurrent traffic tangles only if vehicles observe accepted rules of the road. Such rules, and especially the rule that all vehicles proceeding in one direction must keep to a designated part or side of the road—in this country the right-hand side—have been dictated by necessity and formulated by

observance would subject a person to danger which might be avoided by disregard of the general rule. * * *

The generally accepted rule and the reasons for it are set forth in the comment to section 286 of the Restatement of the Law of Torts:

> Many statutes and ordinances are so worded as apparently to express a universally obligatory rule of conduct. Such enactments, however, may in view of their purpose and spirit be properly construed as intended to apply only to ordinary situations and to be subject to the qualification that the conduct prohibited thereby is not wrongful if, because of an emergency or the like, the circumstances justify an apparent disobedience to the letter of the enactment. . . . The provisions of statutes, intended to codify and supplement the rules of conduct which are established by a course of judicial decision or by custom, are often construed as subject to the same limitations and exceptions as the rules which they supersede. Thus, a statute or ordinance requiring all persons to drive on the right side of the road may be construed as subject to an exception permitting travelers to drive on the other side, if so doing is likely to prevent rather than cause the accidents which it is the purpose of the statute or ordinance to prevent.

Even under that construction of the statute, a pedestrian is, of course, at fault if he fails without good reason to observe the statutory rule of conduct. The general duty is established by the statute, and deviation from it without good cause is a wrong and the wrongdoer is responsible for the damages resulting from his wrong. * * *

■ O'BRIEN and FINCH, JJ., dissent on the authority of Martin v. Herzog, 228 N.Y. 164, 126 N.E. 814 (1920).

NOTE

Violation of Statute? In *Tedla*, did the conduct of the pedestrians constitute an excusable violation of the statute or no violation at all? See Clarence Morris, The Role of Criminal Statutes in Negligence Actions, 49 Colum. L. Rev. 21 (1949), and Fleming James, Jr., Statutory Standards and Negligence in Accident Cases, 11 La. L. Rev. 95 (1950); see also Sparkman v. Maxwell, 519 S.W.2d 852 (Tex.1975).

As counsel for either party in *Tedla v. Ellman*, could you have anticipated this result less than twenty years after *Martin v. Herzog*?

Combs v. Los Angeles Railway Corp.

Supreme Court of California, in Bank, 1947.
29 Cal.2d 606, 177 P.2d 293.

■ EDMONDS, JUSTICE. * * * The accident occurred when a street car operated by the railway company collided with an automobile operated by Joseph Commodore. Combs was standing on the step of the car and the impact threw him to the street. He named both the corporation and Commodore as defendants. Each of them denied the charge of negligence and, as a separate defense, pleaded contributory negligence. As Combs explained the circumstances of his case, late in the afternoon, he and several other persons were standing at a loading zone waiting for a street car. When it arrived, he made no observation as to the number of persons which it carried, nor did he notice that the rear platform was crowded. However, he saw several persons riding on the rear step. He was the last person to board the car. He reached the second step and, after the car started, paid his fare to the conductor, received a transfer, and then endeavored to make his way to the platform. However, it was so crowded with passengers that he could not do so. As the street car approached the next stop, and while Combs was still on the second step, the car and the automobile of Commodore collided. The impact ripped the steps from the body of the car and Combs received injuries for which he now claims damages.

At the conclusion of the plaintiff's case, both defendants challenged the sufficiency of the evidence by motion for a nonsuit based upon the claim that the evidence conclusively established that, as a matter of law, Combs was guilty of contributory negligence. This motion was denied. Upon the same grounds, at the close of the trial, each defendant unsuccessfully moved for a directed verdict. The jury returned its verdict in favor of Combs and Commodore and against the railway company. The appeal of the corporation is from the judgment and from the order denying its motion for judgment notwithstanding the verdict.

The appellant contends that the evidence conclusively established that Combs was guilty of contributory negligence as a matter of law because of his violation of a section of the Municipal Code of the City of Los Angeles which makes it unlawful for one to "ride upon the fenders, steps, or running board of any street car or vehicle." (§ 80.47) * * *

* * * Combs contends that the issue of contributory negligence was properly left to the jury. * * * The instruction given by the court on its own motion is defended by Combs as being a correct statement of law. Considering the circumstances, he says, the violation of the ordinance created merely a presumption of negligence, and it was a question of fact as to whether the evidence was such as to excuse such violation.

The railway company's proposed charge to the jury reads as follows: "If you find from the evidence ... that at the time of the collision between the automobile and street car and immediately prior thereto, ... Combs was riding upon one or more of the steps of said street car, then ... Combs was ... [violating] the Municipal Code ... and as such was guilty of negligence as a matter of law. If you further find from the evidence that such negligence, if any, contributed proximately in any degree whatever, even the slightest, to the injuries sustained by ... Combs, then [he] is not entitled to recover ... against defendant ... corporation. ... "

The instruction given by the court as a modification of one submitted by the appellant is No. 149 of California Jury Instructions, Third Revised Edition. It reads:

Conduct which is in violation of the [Municipal] code sections just read to you constitutes negligence *per se*. This means that if * * * you do find, that any party to this action did so conduct himself, it requires a presumption that he was negligent. However, such presumption is not conclusive. It may be overcome by other evidence showing that under all the circumstances surrounding the event, the conduct in question was excusable, justifiable and such as might reasonably have been expected from a person of ordinary prudence. * * *

The court also advised the jury that "a presumption is a deduction which the law expressly directs to be made from particular facts. It may be controverted by other evidence, direct or indirect; but unless so controverted, the jury is bound to find in accordance with the presumption."

* * * The evidence concerning the injury to Combs required, first, a determination as to whether he had violated the ordinance and, if he had done so, the effect of such violation. The instruction refused by the court directed the jury to find that, if he did not comply with the mandate of the ordinance, he could not recover. Because of the omission of the important qualification that such conduct might be excused under certain circumstances, the court's ruling upon it was correct. *

The instruction given by the court was a complete and correct statement of the law. By it, the jury was first asked to determine whether Combs was "riding" upon the steps of the car. In view of the testimony of Combs that he was endeavoring to reach the rear platform and that the streetcar had traveled only a short distance before the collision, the fact of violation was correctly left to the jury. *

If he was violating the ordinance in that particular at the time of the accident, the jury was told, the question then to be answered was whether the circumstances showed an excuse for his conduct. Bearing upon that issue was the testimony of Combs that when he boarded the street car he did not make any observation as to how many people it was carrying, that he did not notice the crowded condition of the rear platform until the car was proceeding on its way, that he endeavored to make his way into the car but found it was impossible to do so, and that the car had not stopped when the step upon which he was riding was struck by the automobile of Commodore. From this evidence, the jury could find that Combs reasonably thought that the people in front of him would soon move up into the car, but subsequent events beyond his control prevented him from doing so. * * *

In many other situations a jury is directed that, if it finds certain facts to be true, a certain conclusion follows; however, if additional facts are found then a different determination must be made. The challenged instruction does nothing more than this. In other words, to tell jurors that violation of an ordinance gives rise to a rebuttable presumption of negligence is to say that they are authorized by the law to look behind, beyond, around and outside the violation to see if there are circumstances that justify or excuse the conduct. The statements merely complement each other. * * *

The verdict is an implied finding that, under the circumstances, the alleged violation of the ordinance was excusable and it is amply supported by the evidence.

The judgment is affirmed. * * *

■ CARTER, JUSTICE. I concur in the judgment of affirmance, but * * * I cannot agree with the legal theory upon which said opinion is based.

Once it is conceded, as it is in the majority opinion, that the violation of a penal statute or ordinance by one seeking to recover civil damages, does not necessarily bar a recovery, there is no common sense or logic in talking about presumptions or presumptive negligence arising from evidence of such violation. * * * Even when we consider a statute or ordinance relating to conduct directly involved in the accident, it is first a question of fact as to whether there has been a violation, second, whether such violation was a proximate cause of the accident, and third, if both of the foregoing are answered in the affirmative, whether such violation was excused or justified. There must necessarily be involved in the latter the question of whether or not the person charged with such violation acted as a reasonably prudent person under the circumstances. If so, he could not be guilty of negligence. So the test must be in every case, what would a reasonably prudent person have done under the circumstances? * * *

From the foregoing discussion it is obvious that any error which existed in the instruction complained of was more favorable to defendant than to the plaintiff, and defendant could not have suffered prejudice thereby.

■ TRAYNOR, JUSTICE. I dissent. In my opinion plaintiff was guilty of contributory negligence as a matter of law. * * * Before a verdict may be directed there must be not only a violation of the ordinance, but a causal relation between the conduct in violation of the ordinance and the injuries sustained by the plaintiff. The unconflicting evidence disclosed by the record shows that the automobile struck the side of the street car and ripped off the steps, including the step on which plaintiff was standing. If plaintiff had been standing on the platform or in the interior part of the car, he would not have been injured. No reasonable jury, therefore, could doubt that plaintiff's conduct in violation of the ordinance was in fact a contributing cause of his injuries. * * *

Since the uncontradicted evidence showed that plaintiff was contributively negligent as a matter of law and that this negligence was a contributing cause of plaintiff's injuries, defendant's motion for a directed verdict should have been granted. * * *

NOTES

1.   *Effect of Violations of Criminal Statutes.* What should be the effect of a violation of a criminal statute by a defendant (or a plaintiff on the issue of contributory negligence) in a negligence action? How does the majority of the California Supreme Court in *Combs v. Los Angeles Ry. Corp.* respond? What effect does Justice Carter prefer in his concurring opinion? Justice Traynor in his dissenting opinion?

The courts are as divided on this issue as the justices of the California Supreme Court. Probably a majority of American courts have adopted the rule that the unexcused violation of a criminal statutory standard is negligence per se, that is, negligence as a matter of law to be determined by the court. Harper, James and Gray on Torts § 17.6. In a substantial number of other jurisdictions, violation of a criminal statute is regarded only as evidence of negligence to be weighed by the jury. Finally, yet another group of jurisdictions follows the approach of the majority in *Combs* and holds that violation of a statute creates a rebuttable presumption of negligence. Most states that regard violation of a statute as establishing negligence as a matter of law recognize certain specific exceptions, including the impossibility of the defendant (or, in the case of contributory negligence, the plaintiff) complying with the statute or emergency circumstances justifying the statutory violation. Many of these same jurisdictions today recognize a larger group of excuses or justifications for failure to comply. See, e.g., Restatement (Third) of Torts: Liability for Physical and Emotional Harm §15 (2010). In these jurisdictions, the impact of the "negligence as a matter of law" standard more closely resembles that of the "rebuttable presumption" alternative than it once did.

To what extent does the articulation of the rule regarding the importance of a criminal statutory violation really make a difference? Do you suppose that excused violations in negligence per se jurisdictions frequently differ in practice from holding that a violation of a criminal statute constitutes a rebuttable presumption of negligence? From a rule that a violation of a criminal or regulatory statute is only evidence of negligence?

2. *Effect of Violations of Municipal Ordinances and Regulations.* Can a municipal ordinance be the basis for negligence per se? Most jurisdictions hold that it can. See, e.g., Breeding v. Dodson Trailer Repair, Inc., 679 S.W.2d 281 (Mo.1984); Nixon v. Mr. Property Mgmt. Co., 690 S.W.2d 546 (Tex.1985). Other courts, however, hold that violation of municipal ordinances constitutes only evidence of negligence. These courts reason that only the state has the authority to establish legal standards governing when one person can be liable to another. See cf., Bauer v. Female Acad. of the Sacred Heart, 97 N.Y.2d 445, 741 N.Y.S.2d 491, 767 N.E.2d 1136 (2002) (dicta).

Courts frequently hold that negligence per se also applies to violations of federal or state administrative regulations. See, e.g., Sammons v. Ridgeway, 293 A.2d 547 (Del.1972); Britton v. Wooten, 817 S.W.2d 443 (Ky.1991). Again, however, a few states view violations of regulations as only evidence of negligence. E.g., Glielmi v. Toys "R" Us, Inc., 62 N.Y.2d 664, 476 N.Y.S.2d 283, 464 N.E.2d 981 (1984).

3. *Distinction between Negligence Per Se and Private Cause of Action Under Statute.* In addition to providing the standard of care in a negligence per se claim, a federal or state statute sometimes also may create a private right of action, either expressly or impliedly. As the court stated in Loewy v. Stuart Drug & Surgical Supply, Inc., CCH Prod. Liab. Rep. ¶ 15,592 (S.D.N.Y.1999):

> At the heart of this dispute are two analytically related but legally distinct concepts: (1) implication of a private right of action from a statute that does not expressly create such a cause of action, and (2) importation of a standard of conduct from a statute, violation of which may be proof of negligence. Compare Restatement (Second) of Torts § 874A (1979) (implied rights of action), with *id.* at § 286 (negligence *per se*). Several courts have explicitly discussed the distinction, see, e.g., Pratico v. Portland Terminal Co., 783 F.2d 255, 265–67 (1st Cir.1985) (holding that although Occupational Health and Safety Act does not provide for a private right of action, its standards may be relevant for purposes of negligence *per se* actions) * * *.

In what circumstances does a federal statute provide an implied private right to recover damages? The United States Supreme Court has taken a somewhat guarded approach in considering when a private cause of action can be implied under a federal statute. In the leading case of Cort v. Ash, 422 U.S. 66, 95 S.Ct. 2080, 45 L.Ed.2d 26 (1975), the Court held that a stockholder did not have a private right of action for damages against a corporate director when the corporation made a contribution, illegal under federal law, to a presidential campaign. The Court identified four relevant factors in determining whether a private remedy is implicit in a federal statute where the statute does not expressly provide one:

> First, is the plaintiff "one of the class for whose *especial* benefit the statute was enacted," * * *? Second, is there any indication of legislative intent, explicit or implicit, either to create such a remedy or to deny one? * Third, is it consistent with the underlying purposes of the legislative scheme to imply such a remedy for the plaintiff? * And finally, is the cause of action one traditionally relegated to state law * * * so that it would be inappropriate to infer a cause of action based solely on federal law? *

For further reading on this distinction, see H. Miles Foy, III, Some Reflections on Legislation, Adjudication, and Implied Private Actions in the State and Federal Courts, 71 Cornell L. Rev. 501 (1986).

G. CONDUCT MORE EGREGIOUS THAN NEGLIGENCE

Sandler v. Commonwealth

Supreme Judicial Court of Massachusetts, 1995.
419 Mass. 334, 644 N.E.2d 641.

■ WILKINS, JUSTICE. In Molinaro v. Northbridge, 419 Mass. 278, 643 N.E.2d 1043 (1995), we reiterated our view that a governmental unit could be liable under G.L. c. 21, § 17C (1992 ed.), for its wanton or reckless conduct that caused harm to a member of the public who used government land that was available for recreational purposes without charge. In this case we deal with the question whether the evidence, viewed most favorably to the plaintiff, justified the submission of the plaintiff's case to the jury. * * *

The plaintiff was injured, not long after 5 P.M. on October 29, 1987, when he fell off his bicycle while attempting to pass through a tunnel under the Eliot Bridge in Cambridge. The tunnel is part of the Dr. Paul Dudley White Bikeway, along the Charles River, which is controlled by the Commonwealth through the Metropolitan District Commission ("MDC"). * The jury were warranted in concluding that the plaintiff's fall was caused by an uncovered, eight-inch wide, twelve-inch long drain in the unlit tunnel. The drain, which was about eight inches deep, had had a cover, and the tunnel was designed to be lit, but vandals had removed the drain cover and had made the lights inoperative. Before we discuss the evidence in detail, it is important that we define wanton or reckless conduct.

The judge used the words "willful, wanton, or reckless" in instructing the jury but defined them by the standard this court has used for wanton or reckless conduct. This was appropriate because willfulness in the sense of an intention to cause harm was not presented by the facts. * * * Wanton conduct may suggest arrogance, insolence, or heartlessness that reckless conduct lacks,* but the difference is likely not to be significant in most cases. Our recent practice has been simply to refer to reckless conduct as constituting the conduct that produces liability for what the court has traditionally called willful, wanton, or reckless conduct. *

Our long-standing custom has been to measure reckless conduct by the same test whether reckless conduct is alleged as the basis for liability in tort or as the basis for guilt of involuntary manslaughter. * Reckless conduct may consist of a failure to act, if there is a duty to act, as well as affirmative conduct. * We are concerned here with an alleged breach of a duty to remedy or guard against a known or reasonably knowable dangerous condition.[2]

Reckless failure to act involves an intentional or unreasonable disregard of a risk that presents a high degree of probability that substantial harm will result to another. * The risk of death or grave bodily injury must be known or reasonably apparent, and the harm must be a probable consequence of the defendant's election to run that risk or of his failure reasonably to recognize it. *

* * * [R]eckless conduct involves a degree of risk and a voluntary taking of that risk so marked that, compared to negligence, there is not just a difference in degree but also a difference in kind. * * * [R]eckless conduct must be based on a high degree of risk that death or serious bodily injury will result from a defendant's action or inaction when under a duty to act.

There is no doubt that the MDC through its employees was aware that a risk of harm was created by a chronically unlit tunnel with missing drain covers. An MDC employee testified that he did not know when the lights last worked. Another witness testified that he had not seen them illuminated in at least thirteen years. There was evidence that the lights were frequently broken, that they once had had protective devices which were now broken, and that they were broken and not working on the day of the accident. The MDC used only unattached drain covers, held in place only by gravity. The covers loosened over the years, did not fit the drains, and were frequently stolen by vandals. The MDC knew that at least one drain in the tunnel

---

[2] It is not essential that reckless conduct be defined in the same terms for both tort and criminal law purposes, as we have done in this Commonwealth. Under the Model Penal Code, for example, manslaughter includes a criminal homicide committed recklessly (Model Penal Code § 210.3 [1][a] [1980]), which is defined subjectively as a conscious disregard of a substantial and unjustifiable risk that conduct will cause the death of another. (*id.* at § 2.02[2][c]). Liability in tort for reckless disregard of safety is defined, on the other hand, in Restatement (Second) of Torts § 500 (1965), as including either an objective or a subjective element of knowledge of the risk:

> The actor's conduct is in reckless disregard of the safety of another if he does an act or intentionally fails to do an act which it is his duty to the other to do, knowing or having reason to know of facts which would lead a reasonable man to realize, not only that his conduct creates an unreasonable risk of physical harm to another, but also that such risk is substantially greater than that which is necessary to make his conduct negligent.

Our cases have followed this latter definition of recklessness. * * *

was often without a cover from January 1 to October 30, 1987. The cover of the particular drain that caused the plaintiff's injury was frequently stolen and was not in place following the accident. The MDC knew that the lack of a drain cover posed a danger to individuals. The MDC also knew that the regularly used tunnel was often flooded with water because of inadequate drainage.

There was evidence that the MDC, knowing of the danger posed by absent drain covers in the dark tunnel, did not respond reasonably. It had no policy for bikeway inspection, had no record of the existence or replacement of drain covers from January 1 to October 30, 1987, and did not have drain cover replacements on hand, although they were frequently stolen and there was room to store replacement covers in the tunnel closet. There was expert testimony that the design of the lighting and drainage in the tunnel was deficient and that feasible alternatives were available at reasonable costs, including vandal-resistant lighting and drains capable of being fastened. *

Nevertheless, the degree of the risk of injury in this case does not meet the standard that we have established for recklessness. While it is true that each case depends on its facts and that some cases are close to the line, this case, which involves a persistent failure to remedy defects in a tunnel on a traveled bikeway, simply does not present a level of dangerousness that warrants liability under G.L. c. 21, § 17C, for the MDC's inaction. In the margin, we summarize several of our civil cases in which the degree of risk of injury was so great that a finding of recklessness justifying tort liability was warranted.[4] * * *

The level of fault in this case, measured by the degree of risk of serious injury, is more consistent with our cases in which we have held that the evidence did not warrant a finding of wanton or reckless conduct. See, e.g., * Hawco v. Massachusetts Bay Transp. Auth., 398 Mass. 1006, 1007, 499 N.E.2d 295, 296–97 (1986) (defendant not reckless in leaving bus passenger at station where it appeared to bus driver that burglary was in progress). *

Judgment reversed.

NOTES

1. *Gross Negligence.* According to the Restatement (Third) of Torts: Liability for Physical and Emotional Harm § 2 comment *a*:

---

[4] Many of our cases involving reckless conduct justifying tort liability have involved the use of motor vehicles and the like. See, e.g., Sheehan v. Goriansky, 317 Mass. 10, 15, 56 N.E.2d 883, 885 (1944) (finding warranted that driver's conduct was reckless where driver knew that trespasser was on running board, increased speed, ran into pole, killing him); * Isaacson v. Boston, Worcester & N.Y. St. Ry., 278 Mass. 378, 390, 180 N.E. 118, 123 (1932) (finding that bus driver was reckless warranted where brakes were not functioning and driver was speeding in a forbidden lane, in violation of three separate laws); Leonard v. Conquest, 274 Mass. 347, 352, 174 N.E. 677, 678 (1931) (evidence warranted finding of recklessness where driver drove thirty miles an hour in lane designated for oncoming traffic on crowded narrow road, forcing oncoming car off road and into pole and thereby injuring other driver). * * *

Other cases, not involving vehicles but warranting a finding of recklessness include Freeman v. United Fruit Co., 223 Mass. 300, 302, 111 N.E. 789, 791 (1916) (deliberately throwing large, heavy roll of canvas stiffened with ice off deck from great height, thereby breaking plaintiff's leg). *

Terms conveying the idea of wrongdoing that is aggravated—even though following short of the wrongdoing involved in intentional torts—are common in the discourse of torts. Sometimes, the term used is "gross negligence." Taken at face value, this term simply means negligence that is especially bad. Given this literal interpretation, gross negligence carries a meaning that is less than recklessness.

Compare Yancey v. Lea, 354 N.C. 48, 52, 550 S.E.2d 155, 157 (2001) ("us[ing] the terms 'willfull and wanton conduct' and 'gross negligence' interchangeably to describe conduct that falls somewhere between ordinary negligence and intentional conduct").

2. *Implied Knowledge of Danger.* Courts disagree as to whether an implied knowledge of danger can provide the basis for a finding of willful misconduct. In Jones v. McDonald's Corp., 958 F.Supp. 234 (E.D.Pa.1997), the plaintiff was injured when she slipped on oil and grease while walking across the "drive-thru" lane at McDonald's. She alleged that the defendants' indifference to the risk constituted the level of willful and wanton misconduct required for an award of punitive damages even though the defendants had no actual knowledge of the greasy condition which created the high degree of risk. See *infra* pages 428–40 for discussion of punitive damages. The court found that the defendants were entitled to a summary judgment on the issue of punitive damages:

> * * * This inference tends to prove at most, however, that Defendants *should have known*—or that a reasonable person in their shoes would know—that patrons had a greater risk of slipping on oil or grease in this part of the lot than in others. In Pennsylvania, punitive damages may not be imposed on a defendant for a risk of which he should have been aware, but failed to appreciate. * * * Plaintiffs point to no evidence, * * * suggesting that Defendants were aware of any such risk, much less a high degree of risk, and acted in spite of it. *

Many courts take the position that subjective knowledge of the risk is not required. See, e.g., Begley v. Kohl & Madden Printing Ink Co., 157 Conn. 445, 254 A.2d 907 (1969); Miller v. General Motors Corp., 207 Ill.App.3d 148, 152 Ill.Dec. 154, 565 N.E.2d 687 (1990); see also Restatement (Second) of Torts § 500 (1965).

The Restatement (Third) of Torts: Liability for Physical and Harm § 2 (2010) suggests an intermediate position, as explained in comment *c*:

> Section 2 acknowledges appropriate differences between criminal recklessness and tort recklessness and also sets forth a standard for recklessness that is somewhat more restrictive than that included in the previous [Restatement (Second)] § 500. Under the latter, an actor can be found reckless whose only fault consists of the failure to draw an inference that a reasonable person would have drawn. Yet that fault is too limited and too ordinary to justify a finding of recklessness. This Section accordingly requires that the person either have knowledge of the danger or have knowledge of facts that would make the danger obvious to anyone in the actor's situation. If the danger is obvious, then any of three assessments is possible. The first is that the person in fact knew of the risk, even though direct proof of such knowledge may be

lacking; the obviousness of the danger can support an inference of the person's knowledge. The second possible assessment is that the actor—for fear of what might be learned—has, in a studied way, refused to consider the implications of the facts the actor knew. The language of "reckless indifference to risk" appropriately applies to such a person. A third assessment is that the actor's denial of actual knowledge of the danger, while sincere, is nevertheless disturbing. For example, consider the motorist who, late for a social occasion, drives 80 miles per hour on a crowded city street, giving no thought to the risk imposed on others on the street. In such a case, the person's failure to appreciate so obvious a risk is indicative of an attitude of indifference to risk. Whichever of these three assessments is most pertinent in the individual case, the obviousness of the danger serves to support a finding of recklessness.

3. *The Significance of Finding Willful and Wanton Conduct.* In addition to the rules involved in the above material, the notions of intentional or willful or wanton or reckless misconduct, or of some combination of such or similar epithets, may be useful to plaintiffs in personal injury litigation in a number of ways:

a. Damages may be enhanced, apart from the explicit award of exemplary damages, as discussed in the *Jones* case, Note 2 *supra*. The jury may be angered against a defendant and exercise unfavorably their discretion in awarding compensatory damages. It must be remembered that in any personal injury case many items of damage (e.g. pain, suffering, etc.) are incapable of exact measurement and rest pretty much in the jury's discretion. The court, of course, sets limits to this power but there is some evidence that courts themselves are more lenient toward plaintiffs in setting these limits where defendant's misconduct has been wanton, or worse. Ralph S. Bauer, The Degree of Defendant's Fault as Affecting the Administration of the Law of Excessive Compensatory Damages, 82 U. Pa. L. Rev. 583 (1934).

b. The effect of contributory or comparative negligence may be avoided or reduced. See *infra* page 342–43; Harper, James and Gray on Torts § 22.6.

c. In some jurisdictions, recovery may be possible for an undiscovered trespasser or licensee who could not recover under ordinary negligence. Cf. Cain v. Johnson, 755 A.2d 156, 160 (R.I. 2000), *infra* pages 537–42 ("[A] landowner owes a trespasser no duty except to refrain from willful or wanton conduct").

d. An employee may sometimes bring a tort action against an employer, notwithstanding the exclusivity of remedy provision of the state's worker's compensation statute. Cf. Iddings v. Mee-Lee, 82 Haw. 1, 919 P.2d 263 (1996) (recognizing similar principle in action against co-employee). See generally *supra* pages 15–16, on workers' compensation as the exclusive remedy against the employer for injuries arising from the course of employment.

e. Immunity of a parent from most suits by a minor child alleging tortious conduct by the parent may more readily be avoided in some jurisdictions where the parent's misconduct transcends negligence. See, e.g., Cowgill v. Boock, 189 Or. 282, 218 P.2d 445 (1950). See also generally *infra* pages 514–21.

f.   Judgments from claims involving willful and malicious conduct may not be dischargeable in bankruptcy under 11 U.S.C. § 523(a)(6) (2012).

g.   Occasionally the notion of reasonableness in the circumstances merges into the formulation of an atypical standard of care. In such cases, conduct that would be unreasonable for most people in most contexts appears to be not unreasonable for certain actors in unusual circumstances. While such a distinction can be sustained under the standard rubric of reasonable care in the circumstances, it is often addressed by a requirement that such actors be subject to liability only for "recklessness," "gross negligence," or something worse. See, e.g., District of Columbia v. Hawkins, 782 A.2d 293 (D.C.2001) (high-speed police chase; applicable statute provides for liability of drivers of emergency vehicles in emergency service only for "gross negligence"); Leonard ex rel. Meyer v. Behrens, 601 N.W.2d 76, 79 (Iowa 1999) ("[P]ersonal injury cases arising out of an athletic event [involving 'contact sports'] must be predicated on reckless disregard of safety"). Compare Lestina v. West Bend Mut. Ins. Co., 176 Wis.2d 901, 913, 501 N.W.2d 28, 33 (1993) ("Because it requires only that a person exercise ordinary care under the circumstances, the negligence standard is adaptable to a wide range of situations. An act or omission that is negligent in some circumstances might not be negligent in others. Thus the negligence standard, properly understood and applied, is suitable for cases involving recreational team contact sports."). See also Frederick v. City of Detroit, Dep't of Street Railways, *supra* pages 127–30.

H. PROOF OF THE BREACH: *RES IPSA LOQUITUR*

Most of this chapter addresses how courts define the duty of care that the defendant owes the plaintiff. Now we turn our attention briefly to what the plaintiff needs to prove in order to establish that the defendant violated a duty of care so as to justify liability to the plaintiff. In most instances, this is a matter of proving certain facts: What did the defendant actually do or fail to do? However, in this section, we consider how the use of circumstantial evidence to prove the defendant's lack of reasonable care evolved into the separate and distinct doctrine of *res ipsa loquitur*. The first three cases excerpted below trace the development of this doctrine. We then consider its modern scope and application in the cases that follow.

Winterowd v. Christensen

Supreme Court of Utah, 1926.
68 Utah 546, 251 P. 360.

■ CHERRY, J. * * * The defendant * * * operated a summer resort * * * called the Lagoon Resort, devoted to pleasure and amusements, to which the public was invited and for admission to which a fee was charged. In connection with the resort the defendant maintained and conducted a baseball grounds, including an elevated grand stand with seats for the use of persons attending the ball games played there. The ball grounds adjoined the resort proper, and was inclosed with a fence. Gates permitted entrance to the ball park from the resort. On July 20, 1922, there was a meeting of the members of the Railway Mail Associations of Salt Lake City and Ogden, at the Lagoon Resort, and as a part of the entertainment a baseball game was played on the ball grounds above described. There was proof that permission to use the ball grounds for the purpose had been granted by the defendant.

The plaintiff attended the meeting with her husband, and paid for admission to the resort. In the afternoon a baseball game, between rival teams of the Railway Mail Associations of Salt Lake City and Ogden, was being played. The gate between the resort proper and the ball grounds was open and persons in considerable numbers were passing into the ball grounds and taking seats in the grand stand to witness the game. The plaintiff's husband was one of the baseball players. The plaintiff entered the grounds through the gate, and, while walking in the grand stand to obtain a seat, upon a floor or platform elevated two or three feet from the ground, a board in the floor broke and gave way under her, causing her to fall and her foot and leg to drop through the floor, in which manner she sustained the injuries complained of.

It was shown that the defendant had had control and possession of the premises for several years, during which time baseball games were frequently played at the ball grounds in connection with outings and excursions to the resort. The board in the floor which broke under the plaintiff's weight was described as a "2 x 10 plank," which was "decomposed and dark, soggy, pithy." "It broke without any splinters at all." It was further described as "rotten" and breaking easily. That it appeared like it might have been rotten and defective when first put in the floor. The board was wet from rain at the time of the accident. A witness said "when dry it would be rather porous" and observable to a man making an ordinary inspection of it. * * * The trial court * * * sustained the motion [for nonsuit on the ground that there was no proof of negligence]. * * *

That the platform or floor was in an unsafe and dangerous condition was clearly made evident by the fact that the board which gave way was decomposed, and that it broke under the weight of one person. The particular fact of controlling importance is whether from the circumstances it can be fairly inferred that a reasonable inspection by defendant would have discovered the defect. As before seen, there was evidence that the board was decomposed and dark—porous when dry—and that the defective condition would be observable to a person making an ordinary inspection of it. The defect was not of recent origin. There was evidence tending to show it was old. This evidence, standing uncontradicted, and viewed in the light most favorable to the plaintiff, is, we think, sufficient, if believed and acted upon by the jury, to warrant the conclusion that there was a neglect of duty on the part of the defendant in not discovering and repairing the defect, and that therefore the question of the defendant's negligence should have been submitted to the jury.

It follows that the court erred in granting the nonsuit, for which reason the judgment is reversed and a new trial granted; costs to appellant. * * *

Welsh v. Cornell

Court of Appeals of New York, 1901.
168 N.Y. 508, 61 N.E. 891.

■ PER CURIAM. This was an action to recover for personal injuries sustained by the plaintiff, and alleged to have been caused by the negligence of the defendant. The plaintiff, his servant, was injured while in the defendant's employ by the breaking and falling of a portion of a clamp to which was attached the guy rope of a derrick owned by the defendant and in use upon his premises when the accident occurred. The plaintiff was at work under this guy rope, and immediately in front of a post to which it was attached by the clamp which gave way.

As negligence is not to be presumed, but must be proved to entitle the plaintiff to recover, it was necessary for him to show that the accident was the result of the defendant's negligence. It was the duty of the defendant to exercise reasonable and ordinary care to provide for the safety of his servants, and to furnish appliances that were reasonably safe and suitable for the purpose for which they were employed. Unless there is proof in this case showing the absence of ordinary care upon the part of the master in furnishing or maintaining the appliance which was broken, the plaintiff cannot recover.

Practically, the only facts established by any tangible or substantial proof were the plaintiff's injury, and that it was caused by the falling of a piece of the broken clamp. What occasioned the break was not shown, although there was some speculation or conjecture as to the cause. There was no proper proof, direct or inferential, that the clamp was made of defective iron, or that it was defectively made, or that it was not properly maintained, except such as might be inferred from the fact that it gave way. The only proof which even tended to show any defect in the clamp was that one witness testified that he glanced at the broken piece, that it looked like freshly-broken iron, and that on the corner there was a little bit of rust; but he finally refused to swear it was rust and testified that it might have been paint instead. The main portion of the plaintiff's evidence was that of experts, by whom he, at most, proved that the clamp would not have broken unless in some way defective, and that the defect which occasioned the break might have arisen from one of several causes, no one of which was proved to have existed. Nor was it proved that the defendant knew, or with reasonable diligence might have ascertained, the supposed defect. Upon that state of the evidence, the court dismissed the plaintiff's complaint upon the ground that he had failed to show any negligence on the part of the defendant. The judgment entered upon such dismissal was reversed by the Appellate Division by a divided court.

We think the trial judge was right, and that the reversal by the Appellate Division was not justified. A perusal of the evidence shows that the only proof relied upon by the plaintiff to establish the defendant's negligence was the mere speculations or conjecture of experts, with no sufficient proof upon which to base them. It is well established by the decisions of this court that parties may not enter the "realm of conjecture," and ask that a jury, in the absence of proof, may be allowed to guess that there was negligence on the part of a defendant. To entitle the plaintiff to recover in this case, it was necessary for him to establish by a fair preponderance of competent evidence that the accident which caused his injury was occasioned by the omission of the defendant to discharge some duty which rested upon him. This we think he failed to do, and that the disposition of the case by the trial court was proper, and should have been sustained.

We have patiently wandered through the maze of objections and exceptions contained in the record, but have found none which justified the learned Appellate Division in reversing the action of the trial court.

The order of the Appellate Division should be reversed, and the judgment entered upon the decision of the Trial Term affirmed, with costs in all the courts. * * *

Ristau v. E. Frank Coe Co.

Supreme Court of New York, Appellate Division, Second Department, 1907.
120 A. D. 478, 104 N.Y.S. 1059.

* * * The action was by servant against master for damages for negligence. The plaintiff was engaged in pushing by hand loaded trucks or cars along a track or tram on a trestle about 18 feet high. The product of the defendant's factory was thus taken from the factory to a storage place. The trestle collapsed and fell to the ground, and the plaintiff was thereby greatly injured. A nonsuit was granted on the plaintiff's case. [The plaintiff appealed.]

■ GAYNOR, J. The plaintiff proved the collapse of the trestle and rested, relying on the maxim the thing speaks for itself. No particular defect to cause the collapse of the trestle was apparent, and the plaintiff did not try to prove any. There was nothing but the bare fact that the trestle collapsed while in the ordinary use for which it was constructed, and that it had been built only three years. The nonsuit was error. The maxim applied to the case. The learned counsel for respondent argues, following the broad language of some opinions, that the maxim is made applicable in a given case, if at all, only by facts and circumstances indicating negligence in the defendant proved in connection with the happening of the accident itself, and that as this case is bare of such facts and circumstances, there is not sufficient evidence for the application of the maxim. The fault of this is that if there were other facts showing negligence, the maxim would not be needed as evidence to carry the case to the jury at all; it is only where there is nothing but the bare happening of the accident that the plaintiff needs and the law gives him the help of the maxim to escape a nonsuit.

This case is not distinguishable from the fall of scaffolds, floors, or other places to work. * There are cases in which it is apparent that the accident may have happened by some omission or commission by someone other than the defendant. In such a case the mere happening of the accident does not prove the cause of it, but leaves it open to conjecture. In such cases the maxim cannot apply. It applies only where the accident apparently could not have happened unless through some negligence of the defendant. * The judgment should be reversed. * * *

NOTES

1. *Bases for Inference of Negligence.* Is *Welsh* distinguishable from *Winterowd* and *Ristau*? Try to formulate the major premise in the proof or attempted proof of negligence in each of the cases. Which, if any, is clearly demanded by common experience?

Does proof of a defect's existence necessarily require a finding that the defendant was careless in failing to discover it? See, e.g., Levine v. Union & New Haven Trust Co., 127 Conn. 435, 17 A.2d 500 (1941); Miller v. Hickey, 368 Pa. 317, 81 A.2d 910 (1951).

2. *The Relationship between* Res Ipsa Loquitur *and Circumstantial Evidence.* The "maxim" referred to in *Ristau* is often expressed in its Latin form, *res ipsa loquitur*. Is *res ipsa loquitur* merely one kind of circumstantial evidence or is it a unique and distinctive doctrine?

In Ruerat v. Stevens, 113 Conn. 333, 155 A. 219 (1931), Ruerat showed that Stevens had called upon her and had been the only one to sit upon a davenport in the course of the evening, during which time he had smoked many cigarettes. After Stevens left, a fire broke out on the davenport and destroyed some of Ruerat's other furniture. She obtained a judgment for the damage and Stevens appealed, claiming there was no proof of his negligence and asserting that the *res ipsa loquitur* doctrine did not apply. In affirming the judgment, the court said:

> The doctrine is ordinarily relied upon in cases of accidents resulting from defective machines, vehicles, or apparatus, where the evidence as to the true cause of the accident is accessible to the defendant but not to the plaintiff. It does not change the burden of proof, but its application satisfies the plaintiff's duty of producing evidence sufficient to go to the jury. The distinctive function of the rule is to permit an inference of negligence from proof of the injury and the physical agency inflicting it, without proof of facts pointing to the responsible human cause. If the proof includes facts tending to show negligence, the doctrine becomes simply a specific application of the general principle that negligence can be proved by circumstantial evidence. Here the injury was the destruction of the furnishings in the plaintiff's living room, and the physical agency which caused the destruction was the fire. But the plaintiff's evidence goes beyond the mere proof that her property was destroyed by the fire. It includes evidence of the conduct of the defendant in placing the ash tray upon the inflammable arm of the davenport, and depositing his cigarette butts in it, and the evidence that when the plaintiff's daughter came into the room after defendant had left there were several butts in the tray, but not all that he had put down while he sat there. The defendant testified that he snuffed out all the cigarettes that he smoked on that occasion. The situation then was not one calling for the application of the *res ipsa loquitur* rule as a distinctive doctrine, but for the determination of whether the circumstantial evidence was sufficient to justify an inference that the fire was caused by the defendant's negligence.

Compare William L. Prosser, The Procedural Effect of *Res Ipsa Loquitur*, 20 Minn. L. Rev. 241, 257–58 (1936):

> [I]t should be clear that what we are dealing with [referring to the *res ipsa loquitur* doctrine] is nothing more than a matter of circumstantial evidence. * Negligence may be proved by circumstances, and in a *res ipsa* case * * * the circumstances are the evidence. * * * The ill-starred attempt to distinguish between the two, * and to say that one means more than the other, is * * * [the source of] the confusion.

Occasionally courts have held that a plaintiff must choose between pleading and proving *res ipsa loquitur*, or pleading and proving specific acts of negligence, on the theory that a plaintiff who has access to the facts necessary to prove breach of duty does not need *res ipsa loquitur*. This position has been largely repudiated, however, because the failure to prove one possible explanation of an accident does not eliminate other explanations, or even, in some cases, the explanation itself.

Colmenares Vivas v. Sun Alliance Insurance Co.

United States Court of Appeals for the First Circuit, 1986.
807 F.2d 1102.

■ BOWNES, CIRCUIT JUDGE. * * * On February 12, 1984, Jose Domingo Colmenares Vivas and his wife, Dilia Arreaza de Colmenares, arrived at the Luis Munoz Marin International Airport in Puerto Rico. They took an escalator on their way to the Immigration and Customs checkpoint on the second level. Mrs. Colmenares was riding the escalator on the right-hand side, holding the moving handrail, one step ahead of her husband. When the couple was about halfway up the escalator, the handrail stopped moving, but the steps continued the ascent, causing Mrs. Colmenares to lose her balance. Her husband grabbed her from behind with both hands and prevented her from falling, but in doing so, he lost his balance and tumbled down the stairs. Mr. and Mrs. Colmenares filed a direct action against the Sun Alliance Insurance Company (Sun Alliance), who is the liability insurance carrier for the airport's owner and operator, the Puerto Rico Ports Authority (Ports Authority). Sun Alliance brought a third-party contractual action against Westinghouse Electric Corporation (Westinghouse) based on a maintenance contract that required Westinghouse to inspect, maintain, adjust, repair, and replace parts as needed for the escalator and handrails, and to keep the escalator in a safe operating condition.

Six days before the trial was scheduled to begin, appellants filed a motion to amend their complaint to allege that Westinghouse was directly liable for their injuries. * * *

Appellants called four witnesses. The Ports Authority's contract and maintenance supervisor testified about his daily weekday inspections of the escalator, about the maintenance contract with Westinghouse, about inspection and maintenance procedures, and about the accident report and subsequent repair and maintenance of the escalator. * The Ports Authority's assistant chief of operations testified about the accident report. Appellants' testimony concerned the accident and their injuries.

Sun Alliance moved for a directed verdict. Appellants argued in opposition that the evidence presented was sufficient to show negligence and, in the alternative, that *res ipsa loquitur* should be applied to raise an inference that the Ports Authority had been negligent. * * * After hearing the parties' arguments, the court ruled that there was no evidence that the Ports Authority had been negligent, and that the case could not go to the jury based on *res ipsa loquitur* because at least one of the requirements for its application—that the injury-causing instrumentality was within the exclusive control of the defendant—was not met. * * *

Under Puerto Rico law, three requirements must be met for *res ipsa loquitur* ("the thing speaks for itself") to apply: "(1) the accident must be of a kind which ordinarily does not occur in the absence of someone's negligence; (2) it must be caused by an agency or instrumentality within the exclusive control of defendant; [and] (3) it must not be due to any voluntary action on the part of plaintiff." Community Partnership v. Presbyterian Hosp., 88 P.R.R. 379, 386 (1963). If all three requirements are met, the jury may infer that the defendant was negligent even though there is no direct evidence to that effect. *

A.   The First Requirement: Inference of Negligence

The first requirement that must be met for *res ipsa loquitur* to apply is that "the accident must be such that in the light of ordinary experience it gives rise to an inference that someone has been negligent." Community Partnership v. Presbyterian Hosp., 88 P.R.R. at 388–89. It is not clear to us whether the district court decided that this requirement was met, although the court did suggest that it was giving the benefit of the doubt on this question to the appellants. We hold that this requirement was met because an escalator handrail probably would not stop suddenly while the escalator continues moving unless someone had been negligent. *

This requirement would not be met if appellants had shown nothing more than that they had been injured on the escalator, because based on this fact alone it would not be likely that someone other than the appellants had been negligent. * Here, it was not disputed that the handrail malfunctioned and stopped suddenly, an event that foreseeably could cause riders to lose their balance and get injured. Thus, the evidence gave rise to an inference that someone probably had been negligent in operating or maintaining the escalator, and the first requirement for the application of *res ipsa loquitur* was met.

B.   The Second Requirement: Exclusive Control

The second requirement for *res ipsa loquitur* to apply is that the injury-causing instrumentality—in this case, the escalator—must have been within the exclusive control of the defendant. The district court found that this requisite was not met, despite the parties' stipulation that "[t]he escalator in question is property of and is under the control of the Puerto Rico Ports Authority." We agree that this stipulation was not by itself enough to satisfy the *res ipsa loquitur* requirement. It did not exclude the possibility that someone else also had control over the escalator; indeed, the stipulation said that Westinghouse maintained the escalator. We hold, however, that the Ports Authority effectively had exclusive control over the escalator because the authority in control of a public area has a nondelegable duty to maintain its facilities in a safe condition.

Few courts have required that control literally be "exclusive." See F[owler] Harper, F[leming] James & O[scar] Gray, The Law of Torts § 19.7 (2d ed. 1986). * * * The exclusive control requirement * * * should not be so narrowly construed as to take from the jury the ability to infer that a defendant was negligent when the defendant was responsible for the injury-causing instrumentality, even if someone else might also have been responsible. The purpose of the requirement is not to restrict the application of the *res ipsa loquitur* inference to cases in which there is only one actor who dealt with the instrumentality, but rather "to eliminate the possibility that the accident was caused by a *third party*." * It is not necessary, therefore, for the defendant to have had actual physical control; it is enough that the defendant, and not a third party, was ultimately responsible for the instrumentality. Thus, *res ipsa loquitur* applies even if the defendant shares responsibility with another, or if the defendant is responsible for the instrumentality even though someone else had physical control over it. * It follows that a defendant charged with a nondelegable duty of care to maintain an instrumentality in a safe condition effectively has exclusive control over it for the purposes of applying *res ipsa loquitur*. See Harper, James & Gray, *supra*, § 19.7 (exclusive control requirement met if defendant had nondelegable duty); * Restatement (Second) of Torts § 328D cmt. g (1965) (same). Unless the duty is delegable, the *res ipsa loquitur* inference is not defeated if the defendant had shifted physical control to an agent or contracted with another to carry out its responsibilities.

We hold that the Ports Authority could not delegate its duty to maintain safe escalators. There are no set criteria for determining whether a duty is nondelegable; the critical question is whether the responsibility is so important to the community that it should not be transferred to another. * The Ports Authority was charged with such a responsibility. It was created for a public purpose, which included the operation and management of the airport. * A concomitant of this authority is the duty to keep the facilities it operates in a reasonably safe condition. The public is entitled to rely on the Ports Authority—not its agents or contractors—to see that this is done. The Ports Authority apparently recognized this responsibility, for its maintenance and contract supervisor conducted daily weekday inspections of the escalators despite the maintenance contract with Westinghouse.

* * * Finally, an owner has a nondelegable duty to keep business premises safe for invitees. * Restatement (Second) of Torts § 344 (1965) (restating general principle that there is a nondelegable duty to keep business premises safe). These examples demonstrate a general tort law policy not to allow an entity to shift by contract its responsibility for keeping an area used by the public in a safe condition. It would be contrary to this policy to allow the owner and operator of an airport terminal to delegate its duty to keep its facility safe. We hold, therefore, that the district court erred in ruling that the exclusive control requirement was not met. *

C.   The Third Requirement: The Plaintiffs' Actions

The third requirement that must be met for *res ipsa loquitur* to apply is that the accident must not have been due to the plaintiff's voluntary actions. The district court found, and we agree, that there was no evidence that Mr. and Mrs. Colmenares caused the accident.

Indeed, there is no indication that they did anything other than attempt to ride the escalator in the ordinary manner. Therefore, we hold that all three requirements were met and that the jury should have been allowed to consider whether the Ports Authority was liable based on the permissible inference of negligence raised by the application of *res ipsa loquitur.* * * *

NOTES

1. Res Ipsa Loquitur *and the Restatement (Third) of Torts.* The Restatement (Third) of Torts: Liability for Physical and Emotional Harm § 17 (2010) addresses some of the same issues present in *Colmenares Vivas:*

> The factfinder may infer that the defendant has been negligent when the accident causing the plaintiff's physical harm is a type of accident that ordinarily happens as a result of the negligence of a class of actors of which the defendant is the relevant member.

2. *Exclusive Control.* Even before the adoption of the Third Restatement, the modern trend, exemplified by *Colmenares,* was to interpret the "exclusive control of the instrumentality" requirement for *res ipsa loquitur* in a common-sense manner that effectively eliminated other possible causes of the accident, even if literal exclusive control did not exist. When a soft-drink bottle explodes or contains a dead mouse, it is generally impossible to establish that the bottler had exclusive control of the instrumentality in the face of obvious handling by distributors, retailers, and the victim. The common sense inference still points to negligence by the bottler, however.

3. *Accident Ordinarily not Occurring without Negligence. Res ipsa loquitur* often applies where machinery or an appliance breaks or operates in an unusual way. The doctrine does not require expert testimony as to the likelihood that the accident resulted from defendant's negligence. In Kleinman v. Banner Laundry Co., 150 Minn. 515, 517–18, 186 N.W. 123, 124 (1921), for example, the court said:

> Boilers sometimes explode. Comparing the number of explosions with the extent of the use of boilers, explosions are not frequent. If they are kept in proper condition and repair, and if they are operated properly, explosions are unusual. Whether the *res ipsa* doctrine, which permits an inference of negligence from the fact of an explosion, should apply is largely a question of how justice in such cases is most practically and fairly administered. There is nothing legally illogical in permitting the inference to be drawn. Usually the party injured is without information upon which he may with certainty allege the exact cause, and is without direct proof. Perhaps the exact cause is incapable of ascertainment. The actual proof, if any, is with the party having the management of the instrumentality. These are practical considerations. We think the jury should have been permitted to draw an inference of negligence of the laundry company from the occurrence of the explosion. Though the holding may put us with the minority, we are content with it.

For application to airplane accidents, see Newing v. Cheatham, 15 Cal.3d 351, 124 Cal.Rptr. 193, 540 P.2d 33 (1975).

It is important to distinguish between the rarity of a phenomenon and its probable cause. Suppose the following facts:

- a bad outcome occurs only three times in every one million operations;
- negligence occurs only once per million operations; and
- further, a bad outcome occurs whenever negligence occurs.

Under these assumptions, an expert could swear that the likelihood of injury in the absence of negligence is small—as the chances are 2:1 that the cause is *not* negligence.

In Shepard v. United States, 811 F.Supp. 98 (E.D.N.Y.1993), the plaintiff's lingual nerve was severed during an extraction of a wisdom tooth, resulting in a permanent condition characterized by chronic numbness and difficulty in speaking. A dental resident in the second month of his surgical rotation performed the extraction without a supervisor present. The plaintiff was not able to establish exactly what went wrong during the surgery. Expert testimony, however, established that extraction by an experienced dental surgeon posed only "an infinitesimal risk," a risk in less than one case out of every 1,756 patients, but that an extraction by an unsupervised second month resident was riskier. The court held that in these circumstances the burden of explanation shifted to the defendant.

Sullivan v. Crabtree

Court of Appeals of Tennessee, 1953.
36 Tenn.App. 469, 258 S.W.2d 782.

■ FELTS, JUDGE. Plaintiffs sued for damages for the death of their adult son, Robert Sullivan, who was killed while a guest in a motor truck which swerved off the highway and overturned down a steep embankment. Suit was brought against both the owner and the driver of the truck, but a nonsuit was taken as to the owner, and the case went to trial against the driver alone. There was a verdict and judgment in his favor, and plaintiffs appealed in error.

The truck was a large trailer-tractor truck * * *. Its driver, Crabtree * * * permitted Sullivan to ride with him as a guest in the cab of the truck. * * *

The road on which he was driving was a paved first-class Federal-state highway (U.S. 41, Tenn. 2), but coming down the mountain from Monteagle to Pelham it had a number of moderate grades and pretty sharp curves. It was mid-afternoon, and the weather was dry and clear. As Crabtree was approaching a curve another truck overtook and passed him, and just after it did so, Crabtree's truck suddenly swerved from his right side over to his left, ran off the left shoulder, overturned down a steep embankment, and crushed Sullivan to death.

Defendant testified that there was some loose gravel on the road, which had perhaps been spilled there by trucks hauling gravel, and the pavement was broken a little on the right-hand side; and that when he "hit the edge of the curve on the right-hand side" he "lost control of the truck," and it turned from his right side across to the left, and ran off the left shoulder of the highway. On cross-examination he further said:

Q. Can you tell the Jury now what caused you to lose control of the truck and permit it to run off the road down the embankment?

A. No. The brakes could have gave way, or the brakes could have grabbed or it could have been a particular wheel grabbed, because on a tractor, if the brakes happen to grab on it, the load is so much heavier than the tractor, it whips either way and takes control of the tractor and you have nothing to do with it.

Q. Did that happen in this case?

A. It is possible. . . .

Q. You can't tell us just what did cause the accident or cause you to lose control of the truck?

A. Probably hitting the edge of the pavement or it could have been several different things. Like one going off the mountain, if it is pulled out with the wrecker, you don't know whether a hose got connected up in there and when you turned the curve break a hose, cut it, or break it loose. The brakes are cut on and off with a catch there like that, and it is easy for a hose to get loose.

Such being the undisputed facts, plaintiffs contend that defendant was guilty, as a matter of law, or [sic] negligence causing the death sued for, and that there was no evidence to support a verdict for defendant. They show a duty of care owing by defendant to the deceased under our rule that a driver must use ordinary care for the safety of his guest, * and to make out a breach of that duty, or proximate negligence, they invoke the rule of *res ipsa loquitur*.

They insist that the facts of this case brought it within the rule of *res ipsa loquitur* requiring a finding of negligence, in the absence of an explanation disproving negligence; that since there was no such explanation, since defendant did not know why he lost control of the truck or what caused the accident, the jury were bound to find that it was caused by his negligence and could not reasonably render a verdict in his favor. * * *

The maxim *res ipsa loquitur* means that the facts of the occurrence evidence negligence; the circumstances unexplained justify an inference of negligence. In the principle of proof employed, a case of *res ipsa loquitur* does not differ from an ordinary case of circumstantial evidence. *Res ipsa loquitur* is not an arbitrary rule but rather "a common sense appraisal of the probative value of circumstantial evidence." *

This maxim does not generally apply to motor vehicle accidents, but it may apply to such an accident where the circumstances causing it were within the driver's control and the accident was such as does not usually occur without negligence. So where a motor vehicle, without apparent cause, runs off the road and causes harm, the normal inference is that the driver was negligent, and *res ipsa loquitur* is usually held to apply. * * *

"A *res ipsa loquitur* case is a circumstantial evidence case which permits a jury to infer negligence from the mere occurrence of the accident itself." [William L.] Prosser, Res Ipsa Loquitur in California,

37 Cal. L. Rev. 183, 191 (1949). So after proof of the *rem* the adding of another fact or facts may supply the explanation and take the case out of the rule. For example, see Granert v. Bauer, 17 Tenn.App. 370, 373, 67 S.W.2d 748 (1933) (where driver ran out of road trying to miss a hole); Oliver v. Union Transfer Co., 17 Tenn.App. 694, 698, 71 S.W.2d 478 (1933) (where side of road caved in taking the bus with it).

So we agree with learned counsel for plaintiffs that the facts of this case brought it within the maxim *res ipsa loquitur*. The accident was such as does not usually occur without negligence, and the cause of it was in control of the driver, or rather it resulted from his loss of control of the truck, which he could not explain.

While we agree that these facts made a case of *res ipsa loquitur*, we do not agree that they, though unexplained, required an inference or finding of negligence, or that the jury could not reasonably refuse to find negligence and return a verdict for defendant, or that there was no evidence to support their verdict for him.

It is true there has been confusion in the cases as to the procedural effect of *res ipsa loquitur*, some cases giving it one and some another of these three different effects:

(1) It warrants an *inference* of negligence which the jury may draw or not, as their judgment dictates. *

(2) It raises a *presumption* of negligence which requires the jury to find negligence if defendant does not produce evidence sufficient to rebut the presumption. *

(3) It not only raises such a presumption but also *shifts the ultimate burden of proof* to defendant and requires him to prove by a preponderance of all the evidence that the injury was not caused by his negligence. * * *

The effect of a case of *res ipsa loquitur*, like that of any other case of circumstantial evidence, varies from case to case, depending on the particular facts of each case; and therefore such effect can no more be fitted into a fixed formula or reduced to a rigid rule than can the effect of other cases of circumstantial evidence. The only generalization that can be safely made is that, in the words of the definition of *res ipsa loquitur*, it affords "reasonable evidence," in the absence of an explanation by defendant, that the accident arose from this negligence.

The weight or strength of such "reasonable evidence" will necessarily depend on the particular facts of each case, and the cogency of the inference of negligence from such facts may of course vary in degree all the way from practical certainty in one case to reasonable probability in another.

In exceptional cases the inference may be so strong as to require a directed verdict for plaintiff, as in cases of objects falling from defendant's premises on persons in the highway, such as Byrne v. Boadle (1863), 2 H. & C. 722, 159 Eng. Reprint [Sic] 299 (a barrel of flour fell from a window of defendant's warehouse). *

In the ordinary case, however, *res ipsa loquitur* merely makes a case for the jury—merely permits the jury to choose the inference of defendant's negligence in preference to other permissible or reasonable inferences. *

We think this is true in the case before us. The cause of the death sued for was defendant's loss of control of the truck. This may have been due to his own negligence, or it may have been due to no fault of his—an unavoidable accident resulting from the brakes giving way or the breaking of some part of the control mechanism of the truck. Since such conflicting inferences might be reasonably drawn from the evidence, it was for the jury to choose the inference they thought most probable; and we cannot say that there was no evidence to support their verdict for defendant. * * *

NOTES

1.   *Procedural Effect of* Res Ipsa Loquitur. The majority of legal opinions regarding the procedural impact of *res ipsa loquitur* is in accord with *Sullivan v. Crabtree,* but many courts take different approaches. For example, in Kanter v. St. Louis, Springfield & Peoria R.R., 218 Ill.App. 565 (1920), the plaintiff sued on behalf of the decedent, a passenger riding an interurban railroad car owned, operated, and maintained by the defendant. The decedent was killed when the railroad car derailed. The court held that application of *res ipsa loquitur* created a presumption of negligence that entitled the plaintiff to a directed verdict in its favor unless the defendant presented evidence to overcome the presumption. The defendant presented evidence tending to prove that the derailment resulted from acts of vandalism, and the court found that this evidence overcame the prima facie case established by application of *res ipsa loquitur.* Nevertheless, the court upheld a jury verdict for the plaintiff because the plaintiff produced other evidence of negligence on the part of the defendant's employees in failing to detect the vandalized tracks and to stop the train in sufficient time to avoid the accident. The court found such evidence sufficient to constitute a breach of the common carrier's duty of "exercising the highest degree of care consistent with the practical operation of the road and the mode of conveyance adopted."

Yet another group of cases imposes an even greater burden on a defendant to overcome the effect of *res ipsa loquitur.* The next principal case, *Ybarra v. Spangard,* addresses this issue, among others. See *infra* page 230, Note 2.

For an explanation of the procedural effects of *res ipsa loquitur,* see Harper, James and Gray on Torts §§ 19.11–19.12.

2.   Res Ipsa Loquitur *and Automobile Accidents.* Most courts permit the application of *res ipsa loquitur* to the sudden departure of motor vehicles from their normal paths, in the absence of evidence of a cause other than the driver's negligence. See, e.g., Eaton v. Eaton, 119 N.J. 628, 640, 575 A.2d 858, 864–865 (1990) (doctrine applied). Compare Cuellar v. Garcia, 621 S.W.2d 646, 647–48 (Tex.App.1981) (application of doctrine denied; evidence of mechanical defect not attributable to driver).

Ybarra v. Spangard

Supreme Court of California, 1944.
25 Cal.2d 486, 154 P.2d 687.

■ GIBSON, CHIEF JUSTICE. * * * On October 28, 1939, plaintiff consulted defendant Dr. Tilley, who diagnosed his ailment as appendicitis, and made arrangements for an appendectomy to be performed by defendant Dr. Spangard at a hospital owned and managed by defendant Dr. Swift. Plaintiff entered the hospital, was given a hypodermic injection, slept, and later was awakened by Drs. Tilley and Spangard and wheeled into the operating room by a nurse whom he believed to be defendant Gisler, an employee of Dr. Swift. Defendant Dr. Reser, the anesthetist, also an employee of Dr. Swift, adjusted plaintiff for the operation, pulling his body to the head of the operating table and, according to plaintiff's testimony, laying him back against two hard objects at the top of his shoulders, about an inch below his neck. Dr. Reser then administered the anesthetic and plaintiff lost consciousness. When he awoke early the following morning he was in his hospital room attended by defendant Thompson, the special nurse, and another nurse who was not made a defendant.

Plaintiff testified that prior to the operation he had never had any pain in, or injury to, his right arm or shoulder, but that when he awakened he felt a sharp pain about half way between the neck and the point of the right shoulder. * * * The pain did not cease but spread down to the lower part of his arm, and after his release from the hospital the condition grew worse. He was unable to rotate or lift his arm, and developed paralysis and atrophy of the muscles around the shoulder. He received further treatments from Dr. Tilley until March, 1940, and then returned to work, wearing his arm in a splint on the advice of Dr. Spangard. * * * [Plaintiff's two medical experts testified that in their opinions, plaintiff's paralysis was the result of trauma.]

Plaintiff's theory is that the foregoing evidence presents a proper case for the application of the doctrine of *res ipsa loquitur,* and that the inference of negligence arising therefrom makes the granting of a nonsuit improper. Defendants take the position that, assuming that plaintiff's condition was in fact the result of an injury, there is no showing that the act of any particular defendant, nor any particular instrumentality, was the cause thereof. They attack plaintiff's action as an attempt to fix liability "en masse" on various defendants, some of whom were not responsible for the acts of others; and they further point to the failure to show which defendants had control of the instrumentalities that may have been involved. Their main defense may be briefly stated in two propositions: (1) that where there are several defendants, and there is a division of responsibility in the use of an instrumentality causing the injury, and the injury might have resulted from the separate act of either one of two or more persons, the rule of *res ipsa loquitur* cannot be invoked against any one of them; and (2) that where there are several instrumentalities, and no showing is made as to which caused the injury or as to the particular defendant in control of it, the doctrine cannot apply. We are satisfied, however, that these objections are not well taken in the circumstances of this case.

The doctrine of *res ipsa loquitur* has three conditions: "(1) the accident must be of a kind which ordinarily does not occur in the absence of someone's negligence; (2) it must be caused by an agency or instrumentality within the exclusive control of the defendant; (3) it must not have been due to any voluntary action or contribution on the part of the plaintiff." W. Prosser, Torts, p. 295 (1st ed. 1941). It is applied in a wide variety of situations, including cases of medical or dental treatment and hospital care. * * *

The present case is of a type which comes within the reason and spirit of the doctrine more fully perhaps than any other. The passenger sitting awake in a railroad car at the time of a collision, the pedestrian walking along the street and struck by a falling object or the debris of an explosion, are surely not more entitled to an explanation than the unconscious patient on the operating table. Viewed from this aspect, it is difficult to see how the doctrine can, with any justification, be so restricted in its statement as to become inapplicable to a patient who submits himself to the care and custody of doctors and nurses, is rendered unconscious, and receives some injury from instrumentalities used in his treatment. Without the aid of the doctrine a patient who received permanent injuries of a serious character, obviously the result of some one's negligence, would be entirely unable to recover unless the doctors and nurses in attendance voluntarily chose to disclose the identity of the negligent person and the facts establishing liability. * * *

The condition that the injury must not have been due to the plaintiff's voluntary action is of course fully satisfied under the evidence produced herein; and the same is true of the condition that the accident must be one which ordinarily does not occur unless some one was negligent. We have here no problem of negligence in treatment, but of distinct injury to a healthy part of the body not the subject of treatment, nor within the area covered by the operation. The decisions in this state make it clear that such circumstances raise the inference of negligence and call upon the defendant to explain the unusual result. *

The argument of defendants is simply that plaintiff has not shown an injury caused by an instrumentality under a defendant's control, because he has not shown which of the several instrumentalities that he came in contact with while in the hospital caused the injury; and he has not shown that any one defendant or his servants had exclusive control over any particular instrumentality. Defendants assert that some of them were not the employees of other defendants, that some did not stand in any permanent relationship from which liability in tort would follow, and that in view of the nature of the injury, the number of defendants and the different functions performed by each, they could not all be liable for the wrong, if any.

We have no doubt that in a modern hospital a patient is quite likely to come under the care of a number of persons in different types of contractual and other relationships with each other. For example, in the present case it appears that Drs. Smith, Spangard and Tilley were physicians or surgeons [sic] commonly placed in the legal category of independent contractors; and Dr. Reser, the anesthetist, and defendant Thompson, the special nurse, were employees of Dr. Swift and not of the other doctors. But we do not believe that either the number or relationship of the defendants alone determines whether the doctrine of *res ipsa loquitur* applies. Every defendant in whose custody the plaintiff was placed for any period was bound to exercise ordinary care to see that no unnecessary harm came to him and each would be liable for failure in this regard. Any defendant who negligently injured him, and any defendant charged with his care who so neglected him as to allow injury to occur, would be liable. The defendant employers would be liable for the neglect of their employees; and the doctor in charge of the operation would be liable for the negligence of those who became his temporary servants for the purpose of assisting in the operation.

In this connection, it should be noted that while the assisting physicians and nurses may be employed by the hospital, or engaged by the patient, they normally become the temporary servants or agents of the surgeon in charge while the operation is in progress, and liability may be imposed upon him for their negligent acts under the doctrine of *respondeat superior*. Thus a surgeon has been held liable for the negligence of an assisting nurse who leaves a sponge or other object inside a patient, and the fact that the duty of seeing that such mistakes do not occur is delegated to others does not absolve the doctor from responsibility for their negligence. *

It may appear at the trial that, consistent with the principles outlined above, one or more defendants will be found liable and others absolved, but this should not preclude the application of the rule of *res ipsa loquitur*. The control at one time or another, of one or more of the various agencies or instrumentalities which might have harmed the plaintiff was in the hands of every defendant or of his employees or temporary servants. This, we think, places upon them the burden of initial explanation. Plaintiff was rendered unconscious for the purpose of undergoing surgical treatment by the defendants; it is manifestly unreasonable for them to insist that he identify any one of them as the person who did the alleged negligent act.

The other aspect of the case which defendants so strongly emphasize is that plaintiff has not identified the instrumentality any more than he has the particular guilty defendant. Here, again, there is a misconception which, if carried to the extreme for which defendants contend, would unreasonably limit the application of the *res ipsa loquitur* rule. It should be enough that the plaintiff can show an injury resulting from an external force applied while he lay unconscious in the hospital; this is as clear a case of identification of the instrumentality as the plaintiff may ever be able to make.

An examination of the recent cases, particularly in this state, discloses that the test of actual exclusive control of an instrumentality has not been strictly followed, but exceptions have been recognized where the purpose of the doctrine of *res ipsa loquitur* would otherwise be defeated. Thus, the test has become one of right of control rather than actual control. In the bursting bottle cases where the bottler has delivered the instrumentality to a retailer and thus has given up actual control, he will nevertheless be subject to the doctrine where it is shown that no change in the condition of the bottle occurred after it left the bottler's possession, and it can accordingly be said that he was in constructive control. Escola v. Coca Cola Bottling Co., 24 Cal.2d 453, 150 P.2d 436 (1944). * * *

In the face of these examples of liberalization of the tests for *res ipsa loquitur*, there can be no justification for the rejection of the doctrine in the instant case. As pointed out above, if we accept the contention of defendants herein, there will rarely be any compensation for patients injured while unconscious. A hospital today conducts a highly integrated system of activities, with many persons contributing their efforts. There may be, e.g., preparation for surgery by nurses and interns who are employees of the hospital; administering of an anesthetic by a doctor who may be an employee of the hospital, an employee of the operating surgeon, or an independent contractor; performance of an operation by a surgeon and assistants who may be his employees, employees of the hospital, or independent contractors; and post surgical care by the surgeon, a hospital physician, and nurses. The number of those in whose care the patient is placed is not a good reason for denying him all reasonable opportunity to recover for negligent harm. It is rather a good reason for re-examination of the statement of legal theories which supposedly compel such a shocking result.

We do not at this time undertake to state the extent to which the reasoning of this case may be applied to other situations in which the doctrine of *res ipsa loquitur* is invoked. We merely hold that where a plaintiff receives unusual injuries while unconscious and in the course of medical treatment, all those defendants who had any control over his body or the instrumentalities which might have caused the injuries may properly be called upon to meet the inference of negligence by giving an explanation of their conduct.

The judgment is reversed.

NOTES

1. *Subsequent History of the Case.* At the subsequent retrial, all of the defendants testified that nothing untoward had happened during the operation. Nevertheless, the jury rendered a verdict against all defendants. 93 Cal.App.2d 43, 208 P.2d 445 (1949).

2. *Procedural Impact of* Ybarra v. Spangard. In Clark v. Gibbons, 66 Cal.2d 399, 58 Cal.Rptr. 125, 426 P.2d 525 (1967), the California Supreme Court clarified the procedural impact of *res ipsa loquitur* in *Ybarra* and in cases arising in similar factual contexts. As was the case in *Ybarra*, the justices in *Clark v. Gibbons* used *res ipsa loquitur* to hold multiple medical professionals—in this case, an anesthesiologist and an orthopedic surgeon—liable for the consequences of a surgery gone bad. The court held that the consequence of the application of *res ipsa loquitur* is substantially greater than merely allowing the jury to find a permissible inference of negligence, as it was in *Sullivan v. Crabtree, supra* pages 223–27. Instead, to avoid a finding of liability against him as a matter of law, "an individual doctor must go beyond showing that it was unlikely or not probable he was negligent and must establish that he is free from negligence by evidence which cannot be rationally disbelieved. Falling short of such a showing, it remains for the jury to determine whether the inference arising from the doctrine has been rebutted as to any particular doctor."

3. Res Ipsa Loquitur *in Medical Malpractice Cases.* The issue of whether or not *res ipsa loquitur* is available in medical malpractice cases sometimes appears to pose a dilemma. On one hand, most medical malpractice cases require the testimony of a medical expert on the issue of whether the defendant was negligent. If the jury is allowed to find negligence through the use of *res ipsa loquitur*, this requirement is bypassed and there is a risk that the defendant would be found negligent without a rational basis. On the other hand, *Ybarra* illustrates a variety of factors that would make the inability to use *res ipsa loquitur* in the surgical context particularly harsh.

Some courts reject the use of *res ipsa loquitur* in surgical cases, e.g., Barrett v. Emanuel Hosp., 64 Or.App. 635, 669 P.2d 835 (1983), but most courts allow its use in limited contexts. E.g., Fehrman v. Smirl, 20 Wis.2d 1, 22, 121 N.W.2d 255, 266 (1963) ("The general rule is that the doctrine of *res ipsa loquitur* may be invoked in medical malpractice actions only where a layman is able to say as a matter of common knowledge that the consequences of the professional treatment are not those which ordinarily result if due care is exercised.").

Is *Ybarra* better understood as a negligence case or as an opinion in which the Supreme Court of California uses *res ipsa loquitur* to impose liability without fault on the physicians and other medical personnel? Justice Tobriner, in his concurring opinion in *Clark v. Gibbons*, asserts that what the majority is actually doing in *Clark* (and implicitly in *Ybarra*) is using the doctrine of *res ipsa loquitur* to apply strict liability to at least some categories of medical malpractice. He finds that imposing such liability in the absence of proof of negligence, but purporting to do so under the negligence label, has the negative effect of stigmatizing physicians found liable. Instead, he argues for the explicit adoption of "[a] system openly imposing liability without any pretense of negligence" in similar cases:

> * * * In pursuing the laudable goal of shifting the losses occasioned by such accidents to the parties best able to protect against them through insurance, we have imposed the onus of negligence and malpractice upon capable and dedicated members of the medical profession, burdening the law of *res ipsa loquitur* with a sweep that is inaccurate, inefficient, and inequitable. * * * If public policy demands that defendants be held responsible for unexplained accidents without a reasoned finding of fault, such responsibility should be fixed openly and uniformly, not under the guise of negligence and at the discretion of a jury. *

> * * * Upon reexamining what seem to me the grave shortcomings of these varying formulations of *res ipsa loquitur* in surgical accident cases, I have concluded that the basic error lies in primary reliance upon the concept of negligence and that the courts should undertake a fundamental reassessment of the largely fictitious and often futile search for fault which presently characterizes medical injury litigation of the kind here involved.

> At the outset we must recognize that, in the present state of medical knowledge, risks which even the most cautious physician could not have prevented may lead to accidents which even the most expert cannot explain. Although the vast majority of medical practitioners are protected financially by liability insurance covering such accidents, * and although doctors and hospitals can readily transfer the cost of this insurance protection to their patients through higher medical fees, no technique yet devised can protect a doctor from the devastating impact which an adjudication of malpractice can have upon his professional standing. * Fearing that his competence may thus be impugned whenever he adopts a procedure difficult to justify to a lay jury, a surgeon may feel compelled to forego an unorthodox technique in order to protect his reputation from ruin. * Any system which

thus diverts the doctor's attention from the operating room to the courtroom leaves much to be desired. *

In light of the expansion of *res ipsa loquitur* * * * there can be little doubt that the net effect of the doctrine is to shift from plaintiffs to defendants the cost of a certain number of unexplainable accidents in which no meaningful basis exists for finding the defendants at fault. * Thus the concept of negligence as a prerequisite to medical liability now provides only sporadic and illusory protection for the physician. At the same time, insistence under all circumstances upon a nominal finding of fault frustrates the risk-shifting purpose of the *res ipsa* doctrine as currently applied since it stands as an occasionally insuperable obstacle to the financial protection of inexplicably injured patients.

A system openly imposing liability without any pretense of negligence in this narrow range of cases can avoid unwarranted imputations of fault while permitting the rational development of badly needed doctrine. Simultaneously, such a system can insure that the burdens of unexplained accidents will not fall primarily upon the helpless but will be borne instead by those best able to spread their cost among all who benefit from the surgical operations in which these misfortunes occur. * * *

Once the elusive and destructive search for an act or omission of "malpractice" has been restricted to those cases in which a negligent cause may actually be demonstrated, * a far higher percentage of all medical controversies will be settled out of court, without the "economic and emotional strain of protracted litigation requiring difficult or impossible proof." * In the relatively few cases which reach trial, the imposition of financial liability will not be aggravated by the ruinous consequences of a determination of malpractice unless the evidence points logically to such a finding.

We should not impose the stigma of negligence upon a doctor merely because an operation yields an uncommon and inexplicable result; in the present state of the medical art, the rarity of an event may well bear no relationship to negligence. Courts which ignore that fact in formulating the law of *res ipsa loquitur* unjustly penalize physicians and plunge the legal process into an abyss of uncertainty and obfuscation. Our proper concern for the financial protection of the patient gives us no warrant for faulting the doctor.

I must conclude that, in this limited category of cases, the attempt to fix liability exclusively in terms of traditional notions of fault has outlived its utility. Once it appears that an unexplained surgical accident has caused an unexpected injury, no useful end is advanced by rehearsing the ancient ritual of assessing blame.

Chief Justice Traynor, concurring and dissenting, echoed some of Justice Tobriner's analysis and warned that the application of *res ipsa loquitur* in medical cases will increase the prevalence of unwarranted "defensive medicine":

A physician's duty is to exercise that degree of care and skill ordinarily possessed and exercised by members of his profession under similar circumstances. * He does not guarantee a cure. The doctrine of *res ipsa loquitur* cannot properly be invoked to make him an insurer of the recovery of persons he treats. The Latin words cannot obliterate the fact that much of the functioning of the human body remains a mystery to medical science and that risks inherent in a given treatment may occur unexplainably though the treatment is administered skillfully. The occurrence of an injury that is a calculated risk of an approved course of conduct, standing alone, does not permit an inference of negligence. * * *

An anesthesiologist and a surgeon, confronted with one of the inherent risks of an operation not susceptible to advance calculation, may be found liable for any unfortunate consequence. In planning a course of action they may therefore feel compelled to consider not simply the best interests of the patient but the procedure that will be most readily justified to a lay jury.

4. *Application in Other Contexts.* In Samson v. Riesing, 62 Wis.2d 698, 215 N.W.2d 662 (1974), plaintiffs became ill with salmonella poisoning after eating turkey salad prepared by high school band parents. The evidence showed that nine separate parents cooked turkeys at their homes, and that salmonella poisoning cannot occur without negligent cooking of the turkey. Should *res ipsa loquitur* apply? How does the situation differ from that in *Ybarra*? Compare Dement v. Olin-Mathieson Chem. Corp., 282 F.2d 76 (5th Cir.1960) (action against separate suppliers of different components of dynamite charge that exploded prematurely); Jackson v. H.H. Robertson Co., Inc., 118 Ariz. 29, 574 P.2d 822 (1978) (action against two subcontractors following a construction site accident); additional cases cited in Anderson v. Service Merch. Co., 240 Neb. 873, 882–83, 485 N.W.2d 170, 177 (1992).

CHAPTER 4

CAUSATION AND ITS COUSINS

This section deals with the necessity of proving a link between the defendant's wrongful act, the injuries suffered by the plaintiff, and the *extent* of a defendant's liability for such injuries. For the most part, the problem concerns the limits within which the trier of fact *may* impose liability, though some attention has been given in the cases to the language in which instructions to the jury should be cast.

Issues of causation are bedeviled by confusing terminology. Sometimes the general subject is called "proximate cause" or "legal cause." Sometimes the term "proximate cause" is used in a more restrictive sense, under which causation issues are divided into sub-categories. Two of the more familiar of those sub-categories are called "cause in fact" and "proximate causation," the latter of which the Restatement (Third) of Torts, more descriptively, refers to as "scope of liability." Restatement (Third) of Torts: Liability for Physical and Emotional Harm § 29 cmt. b (2010). The first deals generally with the requirement that there be some link between defendant's tortious conduct and plaintiff's injury; ordinarily, the required link is that the conduct was a necessary antecedent of the injury. The second deals with the extent of defendant's liability, as the linkage becomes more and more attenuated.

A. CAUSE IN FACT

1. THE BASIC CONCEPT OF "BUT/FOR" CAUSATION

Wolf v. Kaufmann

Supreme Court of New York, Appellate Division, 1929.
227 A.D. 281, 237 N.Y.S. 550.

■ FINCH, J. * * * The action is in negligence to recover damages for the death of plaintiff's intestate. The plaintiff's cause of action is based upon the fact that the deceased was found injured and unconscious at the foot of a flight of stairs in premises owned by the defendants, coupled with the fact that the hallway was unlighted, in violation of section 76 of the Tenement House Law (as amended by Laws 1923, c. 796) which provides:

> Every light required by this section . . . shall be kept burning
> by the owner every night from sunset to sunrise throughout
> the year.

There was a sharp issue of fact as to whether the accident happened before or after sunset * * *.

A fatal defect exists, however, in the case of the plaintiff, in that, assuming the accident to have occurred after sunset and the hallway to have been unlighted, there is a total absence of proof of any causal connection between the accident and the absence of light. The deceased was shown to have entered the premises and was heard by tenants upon the stairs and in the hallway. Following a thud, also heard by tenants, he was found at the foot of the stairs. No one saw him fall. Without further proof, it would be solely a conjecture for a jury to draw the conclusion that the deceased fell down the stairs because of the absence of light.

A case closely analogous to the one at bar upon the facts, but containing an element not present in the case before us, serves to differentiate the case at bar from one where a failure to furnish light might be found to be a proximate cause of the accident. In Bornstein v. Faden, 149 A.D. 37, 133 N.Y.S. 608 (1912), aff'd 208 N.Y. 605, 102 N.E. 1099 (1913), the action was brought against the owner of a tenement house to recover for the death of a tenant due to the alleged negligence of the defendant in failing to light the public hallways as required by section 76 of the Tenement House Law.

In that case there was an eyewitness to the accident, who came out of an apartment with the decedent, and was within a few feet of her when she fell. This witness testified that the deceased was walking slowly with her hand on the railing, and that, as she turned to go down the stairs, she slipped and fell. The court held that the Legislature, in enacting section 76 of the Tenement House Law, contemplated that the light to be maintained should be sufficient to light the lower stairway and to enable people lawfully using the stairs, by exercising proper care, to see the steps and avoid slipping or missing their foothold. The court further held that the evidence tended to show that the decedent slipped, and that there was sufficient evidence of negligence on the part of the defendants to take the case to the jury, since the evidence there placed the decedent in the act of descending the stairs in the usual way, and that the absence of light sufficient to light the entire lower stairway created the inference that she slipped because of the darkness.

In the case at bar there is nothing to show that the accident occurred in the use of the stairs in the ordinary manner. In the absence of such proof, there are many possible conjectures for the accident. It follows that the order appealed from should be reversed in so far as it grants a new trial, with costs, and the complaint dismissed, with costs.[a]

Reynolds v. Texas & Pacific Railway Co.

Supreme Court of Louisiana, 1885.
37 La. Ann. 694.

■ FENNER, J. The plaintiff and his wife claim damages of the defendant company for injuries suffered by the wife and caused by the alleged negligence of the company.

---

[a]   [Eds.' note] Compare Ingersoll v. Liberty Bank of Buffalo, 278 N.Y. 1, 14 N.E.2d 828 (1938); Mutterperl v. Lake Spofford Hotel, Inc., 106 N.H. 538, 216 A.2d 35 (1965). In *Ingersoll*, Judge Finch ruled for the plaintiff in a case involving a fall down stairs, holding that causation "does not mean that plaintiff must eliminate every other possible cause." Instead, "it [was] enough that he shows facts and conditions from which * * * the causation of the accident * * * may be reasonably inferred" and the "question [is] one for the jury." * * * The plaintiff in *Mutterperl* recovered when she fell in a hotel room darkened by a power failure resulting from the negligence of the defendant. The court held that "it was not unreasonable for the jury to find from all the evidence and on the basis of their common experience that the cause of [the] fall was the darkened room * * *."

Mr. Reynolds, with his wife, sister-in-law, three small children and two * * * attendants, had purchased tickets as passengers on the defendant road, and were at the depot at Morrogh Station for the purpose of boarding the east-bound train, which was due at that station at about midnight, but, being behind time, did not reach there till about two o'clock in the morning. * * *

[The court decided that the evidence justified a finding of negligence in failing to sufficiently light the stairway down which plaintiff fell, in view of the lack of railing and the narrowness of the platform at the bottom of it.]

The train was behind time. Several witnesses testify that passengers were warned to "hurry up." Mrs. Reynolds, a corpulent woman, weighing two hundred and fifty pounds, emerging from the bright light of the sitting-room which naturally exaggerated the outside darkness, and hastening down these unlighted steps, made a misstep in some way and was precipitated beyond the narrow platform in front and down the slope beyond, incurring the serious injuries complained of.

Upon what grounds does the company claim exemption from liability? * * * It contends that, even conceding the negligence of the company [for failing to light the stairway], it does not follow that the accident to plaintiff was necessarily caused thereby, but that she might well have made the misstep and fallen even had it been broad daylight. We concede that this is possible, and recognize the distinction between *post hoc* and *propter hoc*. But where the negligence of the defendant greatly multiplies the chances of accident to the plaintiff, and is of a character naturally leading to its occurrence, the mere possibility that it might have happened without the negligence is not sufficient to break the chain of cause and effect between the negligence and the injury. Courts, in such matters, consider the natural and ordinary course of events, and do not indulge in fanciful suppositions. The whole tendency of the evidence connects the accident with the negligence.

[The judgment for plaintiff was affirmed.]

NOTES

1. *Another Slip and Fall Case.* In Fedorczyk v. Caribbean Cruise Lines, 82 F.3d 69 (3d Cir.1996), the plaintiff slipped and injured herself while taking a shower aboard a cruise ship. Non-skid surfaces on the floor of the shower/tub were not close enough together to prevent a slippery hazard, according to plaintiff's expert, and they violated the Consumer Products Safety Commission's standard for slip-resistant bathing facilities. The plaintiff, however, was unable to testify where her feet were at the time of the accident. The district court found, and the court of appeals affirmed, that the plaintiff failed to show that any negligence on the part of the defendant had caused her injury. The Court of Appeals concluded:

A portion of the bathtub had nonskid stripping and a portion of it did not have the stripping. No evidence presented tends to prove Fedorczyk was standing either on or off the stripping at the time she fell. Without such evidence, the jury is left to speculate whether Royal Cruise's negligence was the cause in fact of her injury. "A mere possibility of causation is not enough; and when the matter remains one of pure speculation or conjecture, or the probabilities are at best evenly balanced, it becomes the duty of the court to direct a verdict for the defendant." Restatement (Second) of Torts § 433B (1965).

Can *Fedorczyk* be distinguished from *Reynolds*? From *Wolf?*

2.   *Modern Trend.* Ultimately, of course, the issue is when the court will allow the jury to consider the issue of cause in fact. Notwithstanding *Fedorczyk*, the modern trend is for most courts to agree with *Reynolds*, and not with the more restrictive causation test of *Wolf*. A comment to the Restatement (Third) of Torts simply provides, "Of course, plaintiff need not prove defendant's tortious conduct was a cause of the harm with a high degree of certainty. The civil burden of proof merely requires a preponderance of the evidence, and the existence of other, plausible causal sets that cannot be ruled out does not by itself preclude plaintiff from satisfying the burden of proof on causation." Restatement (Third) of Torts: Liability for Physical and Emotional Harm § 28, cmt. b (2010).

Dillon v. Twin State Gas & Electric Co.

Supreme Court of New Hampshire, 1932.
85 N.H. 449, 163 A. 111.

[Plaintiff's decedent, a trespassing boy, fell off bridge and grabbed power company's charged high voltage line.]

■   ALLEN, J. * * * The defendant * * * makes the contention that it owed no duty of care to those not using the bridge in a rightful manner to make their wrongful use safe. If a duty might arise towards such a person as a workman painting the girders, yet it says there was none towards a boy in the decedent's position of climbing and mounting the girders without right. *

The present state of the law here in force does not support the claim. * * * A rule that no care is due one engaged in wrongful conduct is unreasonable without substantial qualifications. * * * [C]onceding * * * no right to mount the framework of a bridge in play, the defendant here may not be relieved from duty towards those of whose probable presence it had notice, however their conduct is to be regarded. * * *

If A's conduct towards B is wrongful, it should also be wrongful towards C if the only difference between B and C is that B is not, while C is, engaged in a wrong unrelated to A. C's wrong is not legally causal of his injury merely if it places him in the same position as B is in, and he should recover as well as B. Reasonable care is due both. The only qualification is that C's wrong might be a circumstance affecting A's care in his case. It may be that in reasonable conduct one will use less care towards wrongdoers than others. But the duty to use such care as the circumstances demand is not modified, and the difference is an issue of fact and not of law. * * *

If on a private road two stolen cars meet, one driven by its thief and with a passenger ignorant of the theft, and the other driven by an innocent purchaser from its thief and with a passenger aware of its theft, the varying wrongs of the drivers and passengers towards the owners of the cars would not be enough in any instance to affect their respective rights and duties to receive and use care. If the differences are circumstances affecting care, the standard of duty to use the care reasonably required is not lowered. Their wrongs towards the owners are not the causes of injury from negligence among themselves or from others, and recovery for the injury gives no profit from their own wrongdoing. * * *

The circumstances of the decedent's death give rise to an unusual issue of its cause. In leaning over from the girder and losing his balance he was entitled to no protection from the defendant to keep from falling. Its only liability was in exposing him to the danger of charged wires. If but for the current in the wires he would have fallen down on the floor of the bridge or into the river, he would without doubt have been either killed or seriously injured. Although he died from electrocution, yet, if by reason of his preceding loss of balance he was bound to fall except for the intervention of the current, he either did not have long to live or was to be maimed. In such an outcome of his loss of balance, the defendant deprived him, not of a life of normal expectancy, but of one too short to be given pecuniary allowance, in one alternative, and not of normal, but of limited, earning capacity, in the other.

If it were found that he would have thus fallen with death probably resulting, the defendant would not be liable, unless for conscious suffering found to have been sustained from the shock. In that situation his life or earning capacity had no value. To constitute actionable negligence there must be damage, and damage is limited to those elements the statute prescribes.

If it should be found that but for the current he would have fallen with serious injury, then the loss of life or earning capacity resulting from the electrocution would be measured by its value in such injured condition. Evidence that he would be crippled would be taken into account in the same manner as though he had already been crippled.

His probable future but for the current thus bears on liability as well as damages. Whether the shock from the current threw him back on the girder or whether he would have recovered his balance, with or without the aid of the wire he took hold of, if it had not been charged, are issues of fact, as to which the evidence as it stands may lead to different conclusions.

Exception overruled. * * *

NOTES

1. *Successive Independent Hazards.* Suppose plaintiff, a young professional athlete, is permanently disabled by defendant's negligence in a motoring accident at 2 p.m. on a highway near an airport to which the plaintiff was driving in order to catch a plane that crashes at 4:15 p.m. with no survivors. See generally Baker v. Willoughby, [1970] A.C. 467. Is this problem the same as that in Mayor of New York v. Lord, *supra* pages 53–54? See E.J. Cohn, Note, *Cutler v. Vauxhall Motors Ltd.*, [1970] 2 W.L.R. 961, 86 L.Q. Rev. 449. See also Buchalski v. Universal Marine Corp., 393 F.Supp. 246 (W.D.Wash.1975) (disabling heart attack after and unrelated to injury caused by fault of defendant); compare Victorson v. Milwaukee & Suburban Transp. Co., 70 Wis.2d 336, 234 N.W.2d 332 (1975) (disabling stroke after and unrelated to injuries for which defendant was liable).

What if thousands of fish were killed when the shutdown of a nuclear power plant that had been warming a stream caused a drop in water temperature fatal to the fish? The court found that the naturally cold water of the stream would have killed the fish anyway. New Jersey Dep't of Envtl. Prot. v. Jersey Cent. Power & Light Co., 69 N.J. 102, 351 A.2d 337 (1976). Should it have mattered that the fish were originally "lured" to the stream by the warmer waters created by the power plant?

2. *Continuing Exposure to Injurious Environmental Conditions.* If plaintiff's life expectancy is shortened by silicosis caused by wrongful exposure to industrial dust, liability for which is barred by a statute of limitations, and his remaining life expectancy is further reduced by additional exposures, as to which action is not barred, defendant is liable only for the further shortening caused by the exposure within the limitation period. Pieczonka v. Pullman Co., 89 F.2d 353 (2d Cir.1937); cf. Golden v. Lerch Bros., 203 Minn. 211, 218, 281 N.W. 249, 253 (1938).

3. *Medical Malpractice.* If it is clear that a patient would have died even if the doctor had not been negligent, is the doctor's malpractice a cause of the patient's death? Compare Barnett v. Chelsea and Kensington Hospital Management Committee [1969] 1 Q.B. 428 (arsenic poisoning; victim came to hospital too late, the court thought, to have been saved by proper treatment) with Rewis v. United States, 503 F.2d 1202 (5th Cir.1974) (doctor had misdiagnosed aspirin poisoning as virus and prescribed aspirin, but court resisted suggestions of experts that the victim would have died anyway).

Conversely, if a physician's malpractice aggravates a preexisting illness, she is theoretically liable only to the extent of the aggravation. As a practical matter, however, the burden may be placed on her to bear all the damages of the plaintiff's illness or injury following the negligent treatment unless she can establish a reasonable apportionment. Fosgate v. Corona, 66 N.J. 268, 330 A.2d 355 (1974). See also Matsuyama v. Birnbaum, 452 Mass. 1, 890 N.E.2d 819 (2008), *infra* pages 270–276.

2. CAUSE IN FACT IN TOXIC TORTS

Excerpt, Restatement (Third) of Torts: Liability for Physical and Emotional Harm § 28, Comment c (2010).

Cases involving toxic substances often pose difficult problems of proof of factual causation[,] * * * [including] proving the connection between a substance and development of a specific disease. In all of these cases, the requirement to prove factual causation remains the same; the plaintiff must prove it by a preponderance of the evidence * * *. In most traumatic-injury cases, the plaintiff can prove the causal role of the defendant's tortious conduct by observation, based upon reasonable inferences drawn from everyday experience and a close temporal and spatial connection between that conduct and the harm. Often, no other potential causes of injury exist. When a passenger in an automobile collision suffers a broken limb, potential causal explanations other than the collision are easily ruled out; common experience reveals that the forces generated in a serious automobile collision are capable of causing a fracture. By contrast, the causes of some diseases, especially those with significant latency periods, are generally much less well understood. * * *

Over the past several decades, courts have devoted a great deal of energy to the issue of causation in toxic-tort cases. Causation is a question of fact normally left to the jury, unless reasonable minds cannot differ. Appellate or trial-court review of jury findings affect the allocation of power between judges and juries. Until the early 1980s, a qualified expert witness's opinion that a toxic agent was a factual cause of the plaintiff's disease was treated as sufficient evidence. A few celebrated cases and case congregations, such as the Agent Orange and Bendectin litigations, led some courts to distrust juries' ability to resolve cases based on conflicting expert-opinion evidence. Courts began to scrutinize the scientific evidence employed and to examine carefully the bases for an expert's opinion on factual causation. * * *

These courts may be relying on a view that "science" presents "an objective" method of establishing that, in all cases, reasonable minds cannot differ on the issue of factual causation. Such a view is incorrect. First, scientific standards for the sufficiency of evidence to establish a proposition may be inappropriate for the law, which itself must decide the minimum amount of evidence permitting a reasonable (and, therefore, permissible) inference, as opposed to speculation that is not permitted. * Second, scientists report that an evaluation of data and scientific evidence to determine whether an inference of causation is appropriate requires judgment and interpretation. * * * There are instances in which although one scientist or group of scientists comes to one conclusion about factual causation, they recognize that another group that comes to a contrary conclusion might still be "reasonable." * * *

* * * The plaintiff must prove by a preponderance of the evidence that, but for the defendant's tortious conduct with respect to the toxic substance, the plaintiff would not have suffered harm. When group-based statistical evidence is proffered in a case, this means that the substance must be capable of causing the disease ("general causation") and that the substance must have caused the plaintiff's disease ("specific causation"). * * *

General causation. "General causation" exists when a substance is capable of causing a given disease. The concept developed because a prominent form of scientific methodology investigates causation on a group basis and therefore addresses whether an agent causes an increased incidence of disease in the group being studied. These studies proceed by comparing the incidence of disease in a group that has been exposed to the agent with the incidence of disease in a group of unexposed persons. The latter group's disease, thus, is attributable to causes other than the agent being studied. Traumatic-injury cases, by contrast, do not require this form of evidence because other causes that might explain the injury are absent, and we have a reasonably good understanding of the causal mechanisms involved from trauma to injury. * * *

Occasionally, courts have suggested or implied that a plaintiff cannot meet the burden of production on causation without epidemiologic evidence. Those cases often confronted a substantial body of epidemiologic evidence introduced by the defendant that tended to exonerate the agent as causal. Circumstances in individual cases, however, are sufficiently varied that almost all courts employ a more flexible approach to proof of causation—except in those cases with a substantial body of exonerative epidemiologic evidence. Epidemiologic studies are expensive and can take considerable time to design, conduct, and publish. For disease processes with long latency periods, valid studies cannot be performed until the disease has manifested itself. As a consequence, some plaintiffs may be forced to litigate long before epidemiologic research is available. * * *

Specific causation. "Specific causation" exists when exposure to an agent caused a particular plaintiff's disease. Sometimes proof of specific causation is easy and collapses into proof of general causation, as when there are no alternative causal agents for a disease, and the disease is said to be a "signature" of the substance. In other cases, however, specific causation remains an issue even though general causation is established.

Scientists who conduct group studies do not examine specific causation in their research. No scientific methodology exists for assessing specific causation for an individual based on group studies. Nevertheless, courts have reasoned from the preponderance-of-the-evidence standard to determine the sufficiency of scientific evidence on specific causation when group-based studies are involved. * * * Courts have reasoned that, when a group study finds that exposure to the agent causes an incidence in the exposed group that is more than twice the incidence in the unexposed group (i.e., a relative risk greater than two), the probability that exposure to an agent caused a similarly situated individual's disease is greater than 50 percent. Accordingly, when there is group-based evidence finding that exposure to an agent causes an incidence of disease in the exposed group that is more than twice the incidence in the unexposed group, the evidence is sufficient to satisfy the burden of production and permit submission of specific causation to a jury. In such a case, the factfinder may find that it is more likely than not that the substance caused the particular plaintiff's disease. The propriety of this "doubling" reasoning depends on group studies identifying a genuine causal relationship and a reasonably reliable measure of the increased risk. * * * [However,] any judicial requirement that plaintiffs must show a threshold increase in risk or a doubling in incidence in a group study in order to satisfy the burden of proof of specific causation is usually inappropriate. So long as there is adequate evidence of general causation, courts should permit the parties to attempt to show, based on the sorts of evidence described above, whether the plaintiff's disease was more likely than not caused by the agent. * * * When the sufficiency of the evidence to meet the burden of production is at issue, courts should consider all of the evidence that bears on the matters discussed above and determine whether, in light of the general standard for sufficiency * * *, the evidence would permit a reasonable jury to find that plaintiff's disease more probably than not was caused by exposure to the agent. * * *

Zuchowicz v. United States

United States Court of Appeals for the Second Circuit, 1998.
140 F.3d 381.

■ CALABRESI, CIRCUIT JUDGE. * * * This suit under the Federal Tort Claims Act, 28 U.S.C. §§ 1346(b), 2671–2680, was originally filed by Patricia Zuchowicz, who claimed to have developed primary pulmonary hypertension, a fatal lung condition, as a result of the defendant's negligence in prescribing an overdose of the drug Danocrine. Following Mrs. Zuchowicz's death in 1991, her husband, Steven, continued the case on behalf of his wife's estate, claiming that the defendant was responsible for her death. After a bench trial, the district court awarded the plaintiff $1,034,236.02 in damages.

The case statement recited above goes to the heart of the law of torts. A plaintiff claims to have developed a fatal condition as a result of a defendant's negligence in prescribing an excessive amount of a drug— a tragic injury allegedly caused by defendant's wrong. There is no doubt in the case before us either as to the injury or as to the defendant's wrong; both are conceded. The only issue is causation. * * *

The facts, as determined by the district court, are as follows. On February 18, 1989, Mrs. Zuchowicz filled a prescription for the drug Danocrine at the Naval Hospital pharmacy in Groton, Connecticut. The prescription erroneously instructed her to take 1600 milligrams of Danocrine per day, or twice the maximum recommended dosage. The defendant has stipulated that its doctors and/or pharmacists were negligent and violated the prevailing standard of medical care by prescribing this wrong dosage.

Mrs. Zuchowicz took the 1600 milligrams of Danocrine each day for the next month. Thereafter, from March 24 until May 30, she took 800 milligrams per day. While taking Danocrine she experienced abnormal weight gain, bloating, edema, hot flashes, night sweats, a racing heart, chest pains, dizziness, headaches, acne, and fatigue. On May 30, she was examined by an obstetrician/gynecologist in private practice who told her to stop taking the Danocrine. During the summer, she continued to experience severe fatigue and chest tightness and pain, and began having shortness of breath. In October 1989, she was diagnosed with primary pulmonary hypertension ("PPH"), a rare and fatal disease in which increased pressure in an individual's pulmonary artery causes severe strain on the right side of the heart. At the time she was diagnosed with the disease, the median life expectancy for PPH sufferers was 2.5 years. * * * Mrs. Zuchowicz was on the waiting list for a lung transplant when she became pregnant. Pregnant women are not eligible for transplants, and pregnancy exacerbates PPH. Mrs. Zuchowicz gave birth to a son on November 21, 1991. She died one month later, on December 31, 1991. * * *

Danocrine was approved by the Food and Drug Administration ("FDA") for use in dosages not to exceed 800 mg/day. Mrs. Zuchowicz was accidentally given a prescription instructing her to take twice this amount—1600 mg/day. According to Dr. D'Mowski no formal studies of the effects of Danocrine at such high doses have been performed, and very, very few women have received doses this high in any setting. * * *

The rarity of PPH, combined with the fact that so few human beings have ever received such a high dose of Danocrine, obviously impacted on the manner in which the plaintiff could prove causation. The number of persons who received this type of overdose was simply too small for the plaintiff to be able to provide epidemiological, or even anecdotal, evidence linking PPH to Danocrine overdoses. The plaintiff (Mrs. Zuchowicz's husband and executor), therefore, based his case primarily on the testimony of two expert witnesses, Dr. Richard Matthay, a physician and expert in pulmonary diseases, and Dr. Randall Tackett, a professor of pharmacology who has published widely in the field of the effects of drugs on vascular tissues. In rendering a judgment for the plaintiff, the district court relied heavily on the evidence submitted by these two experts. The defendant challenges both the admissibility and the sufficiency of their testimony.

* * * Dr. Matthay examined and treated Mrs. Zuchowicz. His examination included taking a detailed history of the progression of her disease, her medical history, and the timing of her Danocrine overdose and the onset of her symptoms. Dr. Matthay testified that he was confident to a reasonable medical certainty that the Danocrine caused Mrs. Zuchowicz's PPH. When pressed, he added that he believed the *overdose* of Danocrine to have been responsible for the disease. His conclusion was based on the temporal relationship between the overdose and the start of the disease and the differential etiology method of excluding other possible causes. * * * Dr. Matthay further testified that the progression and timing of Mrs. Zuchowicz's disease in relation to her overdose supported a finding of drug-induced PPH. Dr. Matthay emphasized that, prior to the overdose, Mrs. Zuchowicz was a healthy, active young woman with no history of cardiovascular problems, and that, shortly after the overdose, she began experiencing symptoms of PPH such as weight gain, swelling of hands and feet, fatigue, and shortness of breath. He described the similarities between the course of Mrs. Zuchowicz's illness and that of accepted cases of drug-induced PPH, and he went on to discuss cases involving classes of drugs that are known to cause other pulmonary diseases (mainly anti-cancer drugs). He noted that the onset of these diseases, which are recognized to be caused by the particular drugs, was very similar in timing and course to the development of Mrs. Zuchowicz's illness.

* * * Dr. Tackett testified that, to a reasonable degree of scientific certainty, he believed that the overdose of Danocrine, more likely than not, caused PPH in the plaintiff. * * *

A. Was the Admission of the Plaintiff's Experts' Testimony Manifestly Erroneous?

The defendant's first argument is that the district court erred in admitting the testimony of Dr. Tackett and Dr. Matthay. We review the district court's decision to admit or exclude expert testimony under a highly deferential abuse of discretion standard. * The Federal Rules of Evidence permit opinion testimony by experts when the witness is "qualified as an expert by knowledge, skill, experience, training, or education," and "[i]f scientific, technical, or other specialized knowledge will assist the trier of fact to understand the evidence or to determine a fact in issue." Fed. R. Evid. 702. * * *

Under Daubert v. Merrell Dow Pharmaceuticals, Inc., 509 U.S. 579, 597, 113 S.Ct. 2786, 2799, 125 L.Ed.2d 469 (1993), trial judges are charged with ensuring that expert testimony "both rests on a reliable foundation and is relevant to the task at hand." Thus, * * * *Daubert* and the Federal Rules of Evidence " * * * leave in place * * * [a] 'gatekeeper' role of the trial judge in screening such evidence." * Indeed *Daubert* strengthens this role, for it requires that judges make a "preliminary assessment of whether the reasoning or methodology underlying the testimony is scientifically valid and of whether that reasoning or methodology properly can be applied to the facts in issue." * The factors identified by the Supreme Court as relevant to this inquiry are: (1) whether the theory can be (and has been) tested according to the scientific method; (2) whether the theory or technique has been subjected to peer review and publication; (3) in the case of a particular scientific technique, the known or potential rate of error; and (4) whether the theory is generally accepted. * The Court emphasized, however, that these factors were not an exclusive or dispositive list of what should be considered, and that the trial court's inquiry should be a "flexible one." *

The question in this case is whether, in light of these factors, the district court's decision to admit the testimony of Dr. Matthay and Dr. Tackett was an abuse of discretion. * * * [T]he district court carefully undertook and fulfilled its role in making the evaluation required by *Daubert*—a "preliminary assessment of whether the reasoning or methodology underlying the testimony is scientifically valid and of whether that reasoning or methodology properly can be applied to the facts in issue." * Where, as in this case, the district court decides to admit the testimony of well-credentialed experts relying on scientific methodology, we should and will be reluctant to upset that decision as an abuse of discretion.

In the district court, the defendant made substantially the same arguments, regarding the validity of the methods used by Dr. Matthay and Dr. Tackett in reaching their conclusions, that it now raises on appeal. The district court rejected these arguments, stating that the plaintiff's experts "based their opinions on methods reasonably relied on by experts in their particular fields." We do not believe that the district court's decision in this regard was erroneous, let alone manifestly so.

B.   Were the District Court's Factual Findings with Respect to Causation Clearly Erroneous?

* * * The liability of the federal government under the Federal Tort Claims Act is determined according to the law of the state in which the injury occurred. * Connecticut law, therefore, provides the applicable standards in this case. A plaintiff alleging medical malpractice in Connecticut must first prove that the defendant negligently deviated from the customary standard of care. * * * In addition, "the plaintiff must establish a causal relationship between the physician's negligent actions or failure to act and the resulting injury by showing that the action or omission constituted a substantial factor in producing the injury." * This "substantial factor" causation requirement is the crux of the case before us. * * *

To meet the requirement that defendant's behavior was a substantial factor in bringing about the plaintiff's injury, the plaintiff must generally show: (a) that the defendant's negligent act or omission was a *but for* cause of the injury, (b) that the negligence was causally linked to the harm, and (c) that the defendant's negligent act or omission was proximate to the resulting injury. * * * In the case before us, as we shall see, neither the requirement of proximity nor that of causal link gives rise to any problems (though the presence of a strong causal link will prove to be highly significant). The case turns only on the difficulty of showing a *but for* cause. On whether, in other words, the plaintiff has sufficiently demonstrated: (a) that defendant's act in giving Mrs. Zuchowicz Danocrine was the source of her illness and death, and (b) that it was not just the Danocrine, but its negligent overdose that led to Mrs. Zuchowicz's demise. * * *

In seeking to show both components of *but for* causation, plaintiff's reliance on experts must meet the substantive requirements of Connecticut law. Under that law, "[t]he expert opinion that seeks to establish the causal connection between the injury and the alleged negligence 'must rest upon more than surmise or conjecture.' " * The expert must deal not in mere possibilities, but in "reasonable medical probabilit[ies]." * At the same time, it is well-established that causation "may be proved by circumstantial evidence," * and that "[t]he causal relation between an injury and its later physical effects may be established by the direct opinion of a physician, by his deduction by the process of eliminating causes other than the traumatic agency, or by his opinion based upon a hypothetical question."

4. Was Danocrine a *But For* Cause of Mrs. Zuchowicz's Illness and Death?

We hold that, on the basis of Dr. Matthay's testimony alone, the finder of fact could have concluded—under Connecticut law—that Mrs. Zuchowicz's PPH was, more likely than not, caused by Danocrine. While it was not possible to eliminate all other possible causes of pulmonary hypertension, the evidence presented showed that the experts had not only excluded all causes of secondary pulmonary hypertension, but had also ruled out all the previously known drug-related causes of PPH. In addition, Dr. Matthay testified, based on his expertise in pulmonary diseases, that the progression and timing of Mrs. Zuchowicz's illness in relationship to the timing of her overdose supported a finding of *drug-induced* PPH to a reasonable medical certainty. In this respect, we note that in the case before us, unlike many toxic torts situations, there was not a long latency period between the onset of symptoms and the patient's exposure to the drug that was alleged to have caused the illness. Rather, as Dr. Matthay testified, the plaintiff began exhibiting symptoms typical of drug-induced PPH shortly after she started taking the Danocrine. Under the circumstances, we cannot say that the fact finder was clearly erroneous in determining that, more probably than not, the Danocrine caused Mrs. Zuchowicz's illness.

5. Was the Overdose a *But For* Cause of Mrs. Zuchowicz's Illness and Death?

To say that Danocrine caused Mrs. Zuchowicz's injuries is only half the story, however. In order for the causation requirement to be met, a trier of fact must be able to determine, by a preponderance of the evidence, that the defendant's *negligence* was responsible for the injury. In this case, defendant's negligence consisted in prescribing an overdose of Danocrine to Mrs. Zuchowicz. For liability to exist, therefore, it is necessary that the fact finder be able to conclude, more probably than not, that the *overdose* was the cause of Mrs. Zuchowicz's illness and ultimate death. The mere fact that the exposure to Danocrine was likely responsible for the disease does not suffice.

The problem of linking defendant's negligence to the harm that occurred is one that many courts have addressed in the past. A car is speeding and an accident occurs. That the car was involved and was a cause of the crash is readily shown. The accident, moreover, is of the sort that rules prohibiting speeding are designed to prevent. But is this enough to support a finding of fact, in the individual case, that *speeding* was, in fact, more probably than not, the cause of the accident? The same question can be asked when a car that was driving in violation of a minimum speed requirement on a super-highway is rear-ended. Again, it is clear that the car and its driver were causes of the accident. And the accident is of the sort that minimum speeding rules are designed to prevent. But can a fact finder conclude, without more, that the driver's negligence in driving *too slowly* led to the crash? To put it more precisely—the defendant's negligence was strongly causally linked to the accident, and the defendant was undoubtedly a *but for* cause of the harm, but does this suffice to allow a fact finder to say that the defendant's *negligence* was a *but for* cause?

At one time, courts were reluctant to say in such circumstances that the wrong could be deemed to be the cause. They emphasized the logical fallacy of *post hoc, ergo propter hoc,* and demanded some direct evidence connecting the defendant's wrongdoing to the harm. See, e.g., Wolf v. Kaufmann, 227 A.D. 281, 282, 237 N.Y.S. 550, 551(1929) (denying recovery for death of plaintiff's decedent, who was found unconscious at foot of stairway which, in violation of a statute, was unlighted, because the plaintiff had offered no proof of "any causal connection between the accident and the absence of light").

All that has changed, however. And, as is so frequently the case in tort law, Chief Judge Cardozo in New York and Chief Justice Traynor in California led the way. In various opinions, they stated that: if (a) a negligent act was deemed wrongful *because* that act increased the chances that a particular type of accident would occur, and (b) a mishap of that very sort did happen, this was enough to support a finding by the trier of fact that the negligent behavior caused the harm. Where such a strong causal link exists, it is up to the negligent party to bring in evidence denying *but for* cause and suggesting that in the actual case the wrongful conduct had not been a substantial factor.

Thus, in a case involving a nighttime collision between vehicles, one of which did not have the required lights, Judge Cardozo stated that lights were mandated precisely to reduce the risk of such accidents occurring and that this fact sufficed to show causation unless the negligent party demonstrated, for example, that in the particular instance the presence of very bright street lights or of a full moon rendered the lack of lights on the vehicle an unlikely cause. See Martin v. Herzog, 228 N.Y. 164, 126 N.E. 814, 816 (1920). *

The general acceptance of this view is both signaled and explained by Prosser, which states categorically:

And whether the defendant's negligence consists of the violation of some statutory safety regulation, or the breach of a plain common law duty of care, the court can scarcely overlook the fact that the injury which has in fact occurred is precisely the sort of thing that proper care on the part of the defendant would be intended to prevent, and accordingly allow a certain liberality to the jury in drawing its conclusion.

W. Page Keeton, *et al.*, Prosser and Keeton on the Law of Torts § 41 at 270 (5th ed. 1984); see also Calabresi, *supra* note 6, at 71–73. * * *

The case before us is a good example of the above-mentioned principles in their classic form. The reason the FDA does not approve the prescription of new drugs at above the dosages as to which extensive tests have been performed is because all drugs involve risks of untoward side effects in those who take them. Moreover, it is often true that the higher the dosage the greater is the likelihood of such negative effects. At the approved dosages, the benefits of the particular drug have presumably been deemed worth the risks it entails. At greater than approved dosages, not only do the risks of tragic side effects (known and unknown) increase, but there is no basis on the testing that has been performed for supposing that the drug's benefits outweigh these increased risks. * It follows that when a negative side effect is demonstrated to be the result of a drug, and the drug was wrongly prescribed in an unapproved and excessive dosage (i.e. a strong causal link has been shown), the plaintiff who is injured has generally shown enough to permit the finder of fact to conclude that the excessive dosage was a substantial factor in producing the harm.

In fact, plaintiff's showing in the case before us, while relying on the above stated principles, is stronger. For plaintiff introduced some direct evidence of causation as well. On the basis of his long experience with drug-induced pulmonary diseases, one of plaintiff's experts, Dr. Matthay, testified that the timing of Mrs. Zuchowicz's illness led him to conclude that the overdose (and not merely Danocrine) was responsible for her catastrophic reaction.

Under the circumstances, we hold that defendant's attack on the district court's finding of causation is meritless. * * * Accordingly, the judgment of the district court is affirmed.

NOTE

Substantial Factor Test. Courts differ in their use of the "substantial factor" concept. Sometimes it is used as a test for determining cause in fact alone, sometimes as a composite requirement incorporating all of "but for" cause, causal link, and proximity, sometimes as a surrogate for proximity, and sometimes as a substitute for intermediate combinations. Regrettably, furthermore, "many courts indulge in random, standard definitions of proximate cause merely as a 'warm-up' exercise; formulas are collected indiscriminately and then often accorded no further consideration." Harper, James and Gray on Torts § 20.6 n.49. "What is needed is a separation between the issue of cause and all the other issues, which are often meritorious in themselves but too frequently parade meretriciously in the guise of cause. Perhaps this would affect substantive results only a little, but it would contribute much to clarity of thought." *Id*. at § 20.6. See also *infra* pages 333–334, Note 3.

3. MULTIPLE OR INDETERMINATE TORTFEASORS

Corey v. Havener

Supreme Judicial Court of Massachusetts, 1902.
182 Mass. 250, 65 N.E. 69.

Two actions of tort by the same plaintiff against different defendants for injuries to the plaintiff and to his wagon caused by the alleged negligence of both defendants each operating a separate gasoline motor tricycle at an illegal and dangerous rate of speed and frightening the plaintiff's horse. *

In the Superior Court the two cases were tried together before Pierce, J. It appeared, that the plaintiff, who was very deaf and could only hear by the use of an ear trumpet, was driving slowly in a wagon along Shrewsbury Street, a public street and main thoroughfare in Worcester; that the defendants came up from behind and passed the plaintiff at a high rate of speed one on each side; that each defendant was mounted on a motor tricycle with a gasoline engine making a loud noise and emitting steam, some of the plaintiff's witnesses saying that the machines emitted steam and smoke making a cloud about the defendants as they rode.

The plaintiff testified that his horse took fright when the defendants first passed but was under control and guidance until he overtook the defendants, and that running between them the horse shied and he then lost control. His wagon wheel struck another wagon going in the same direction, and the injuries to himself and his wagon occurred.

The plaintiff and each of his witnesses was asked on cross-examination if he could tell which defendant or which vehicle caused the horse to take fright, and each witness was unable to tell.

The defendants requested the judge to instruct the jury, that the evidence showing that they were on two separate vehicles entirely independent of each other, and there being two different suits for the same injury, the burden was on the plaintiff to show which one of the defendants, if either, was to blame; and that, if it was not clearly shown which one of the defendants caused the accident, the plaintiff could not recover.

The defendants also requested the judge to instruct the jury, that there being two defendants and two separate suits, and the cause of action against each being for the same injury, if the jury found for the plaintiff they must assess the full damages and determine against which defendant, and that they could not assess full damages against both, as that would be giving double damages.

The judge refused to give either of these instructions. The jury found for the plaintiff in each case and in each case assessed the damages in the sum of $700. The defendants alleged exceptions. * * *

■ LATHROP, J. The only question which arises in these cases is whether the judge erred in refusing to give the instructions requested. The bill of exceptions does not set forth what instructions were given, and we must assume that they were appropriate to the case as presented by the evidence, and were correct.

The verdict of the jury has established the fact that both of the defendants were wrongdoers. It makes no difference that there was no concert between them, or that it is impossible to determine what portion of the injury was caused by each. If each contributed to the injury, that is enough to bind both. Whether each contributed was a question for the jury. *

It makes no difference that the defendants were sued severally and not jointly. If two or more wrongdoers contribute to the injury, they may be sued either jointly or severally. * The first request for instructions was, therefore, rightly refused.

Nor was there any error in refusing to give the second request. If both defendants contributed to the accident, the jury could not single out one as the person to blame. There being two actions, the plaintiff was entitled to judgment against each for the full amount. There is no injustice in this, for a satisfaction of one judgment is all that the plaintiff is entitled to. *

NOTES

1.   *Joint and Several Liability.* In *Corey v. Havener*, the court holds that the two defendants are "jointly and severally" liable for plaintiff's injuries. Under this traditional doctrine of Anglo-American law, each of two or more defendants who is found liable for a single and indivisible harm to the plaintiff is subject to liability to the plaintiff for the entire harm. The plaintiff has the choice of collecting the entire judgment from one defendant, the entire judgment from another defendant, or recovering portions of the judgment from various defendants, as long as the plaintiff's entire recovery does not exceed the amount of the judgment.

In recent decades, either the courts or the state legislatures in most jurisdictions have modified or eliminated the concept of joint and several liability, generally at the behest of businesses (which frequently are sued) and insurance companies. The liability of joint tortfeasors, both to the plaintiff and among each other, is treated comprehensively at *infra* pages 387–97.

2.   *Concert of Action.* Justice Lathrop states that "[i]t makes no difference that there was no concert between [the two defendants]." However, suppose that the defendants had agreed before the accident that each of them would drive his motorized tricycle up alongside the plaintiff's carriage with the intent to scare the plaintiff's horses? In that case, joint and several liability might have been imposed under the doctrine of "concert of action." In Sindell v. Abbott Laboratories, 26 Cal.3d 588, 604, 163 Cal.Rptr. 132, 140, 607 P.2d 924, 932 (1980), the California Supreme Court explained concert of action as follows:

> The elements of this doctrine are prescribed in section 876 of the Restatement (Second) of Torts. The section provides, "For harm resulting to a third person from the tortious conduct of another, one is subject to liability if he (a) does a tortious act in concert

with the other or pursuant to a common design with him, or (b) knows that the other's conduct constitutes a breach of duty and gives substantial assistance or encouragement to the other so to conduct himself, or (c) gives substantial assistance to the other in accomplishing a tortious result and his own conduct, separately considered, constitutes a breach of duty to the third person." With respect to this doctrine, Prosser states that "those who, in pursuance of a common plan or design to commit a tortious act, actively take part in it, or further it by cooperation or request, or who lend aid or encouragement to the wrongdoer, or ratify and adopt his acts done for their benefit, are equally liable with him. Express agreement is not necessary, and all that is required is that there be a tacit understanding. . . ." W[illiam L.] Prosser, Law of Torts § 46 (4th ed. 1971).

In Clausen v. Carroll, 291 Ill. App. 3d 530, 684 N.E.2d 167 (1997), the court held that the driver of one of three cars engaged in a drag race could be held liable for the death of passengers in one of the other racing cars on a concert of action basis.

3. *Multi-Car Collisions.* In Haddigan v. Harkins, 441 F.2d 844 (3d Cir.1970), the decedent was killed when the automobile driven by her husband, in which she was a passenger, crashed through the median barrier of a four-lane highway. The automobile became wedged in the barrier, protruding into the oncoming lane, with its lights on. The court found the drivers of two oncoming cars, traveling in tandem for a distance of more than 100 yards with unobstructed visibility, were negligent for not avoiding—or even attempting to avoid—a collision. Decedent's automobile was struck in quick succession by both automobiles, and it was impossible to tell which collision killed her. The court held the defendants jointly and severally liable and commented that the defendant "would have us rule, apparently, that granting his car gave the decedent a whack and that in the same accident another car almost simultaneously gave her another whack, plaintiff must prove which whack killed her. Such is not the law." Suppose that each driver testified that it was the collision with the other driver that killed decedent?

Michie v. Great Lakes Steel Div., National Steel Corp.

United States Court of Appeals for the Sixth Circuit, 1974.
495 F.2d 213.

■ EDWARDS, CIRCUIT JUDGE. * * * Thirty-seven persons, members of thirteen families residing near LaSalle, Ontario, Canada, have filed a complaint against three corporations which operate seven plants in the United States immediately across the Detroit River from Canada. Plaintiffs claim that pollutants emitted by plants of defendants are noxious in character and that their discharge in the ambient air violates various municipal and state ordinances and laws. They assert that the discharges represent a nuisance and that the pollutants are carried by air currents onto their premises in Canada, thereby damaging their persons and property. Each plaintiff individually claims damages ranging from $11,000 to $35,000 from all three corporate defendants jointly and severally. There is, however, no assertion of joint action or conspiracy on the part of defendants. * * *

We believe the principal question presented by this appeal may be phrased thus: Under the law of the State of Michigan, may multiple defendants, whose independent actions of allegedly discharging pollutants into the ambient air thereby allegedly create a nuisance, be jointly and severally liable to multiple plaintiffs for numerous individual injuries which plaintiffs claim to have sustained as a result of said actions, where said pollutants mix in the air so that their separate effects in creating the individual injuries are impossible to analyze.

Appellants * * * quote and rely upon Restatement (First) of Torts § 881:

> Where two or more persons, each acting independently, create or maintain a situation which is a tortious invasion of a landowner's interest in the use and enjoyment of land by interfering with his quiet, light, air or flowing water, each is liable only for such proportion of the harm caused to the land or of the loss of enjoyment of it by the owner as his contribution to the harm bears to the total harm.

They also rely upon the comment under § 881:

> The rule stated in this Section is applicable whether or not there has been a physical or chemical union of materials and whether or not fumes or polluted matter sent out by the defendant have united with those sent out by others before entry upon the plaintiff's land, since the unity of the means by which the harm is caused does not prevent recovery. * * *

In Watts v. Smith, 375 Mich. 120, 134 N.W.2d 194 (1965), quoting Meier v. Holt, 347 Mich. 430, 80 N.W.2d 207 (1956), the Michigan Supreme Court said:

> Although it is not always definitely so stated the rule seems to have become generally established that, although there is no concert of action between tortfeasors, if the cumulative effects of their acts is a single indivisible injury which it cannot certainly be said would have resulted but for the concurrence of such acts, the actors are to be held liable as joint tortfeasors.

In Maddux v. Donaldson, 362 Mich. 425, 108 N.W.2d 33 (1961) the Michigan Supreme Court cites Landers v. East Texas Salt Water Disposal Co., 151 Tex. 251, 248 S.W.2d 731 (1952), a pollution case, in support of the above stated proposition. The court indicated that

> . . . [i]t is clear that there is a manifest unfairness in "putting on the injured party the impossible burden of proving the specific shares of harm done by each. . . . Such results are simply the law's callous dullness to innocent sufferers. One would think that the obvious meanness [sic] of letting wrongdoers go * * * free in such cases would cause the courts to think twice and to suspect some fallacy in their rule of law."

Plaintiffs contend that the *Maddux* and *Watts* language applies here since there is no possibility of dividing the injuries herein alleged to have occurred and that it is impossible to judge which of the alleged tortfeasors caused what harm.

* * * We believe that the issue was decided in the lengthy consideration given by the Michigan court in the *Maddux* case. There Justice Talbot Smith * * * in an opinion for the court majority * * * held:

> It is our conclusion that if there is competent testimony, adduced either by plaintiff or defendant, that the injuries are factually and medically separable, and that the liability for all such injuries and damages, or parts thereof, may be allocated with reasonable certainty to the impacts in turn, the jury will be instructed accordingly and mere difficulty in so doing will not relieve the triers of the facts of this responsibility. This merely follows the general rule that "where the independent concurring acts have caused distinct and separate injuries to the plaintiff, or where some reasonable means of apportioning the damages is evident, the courts generally will not hold the tortfeasors jointly and severally liable."
>
> But if, on the other hand, the triers of the facts conclude that they cannot reasonably make the division of liability between the tortfeasors, this is the point where the road of authority divides. Much ancient authority, not in truth precedent, would say that the case is now over, and that plaintiff shall take nothing. * * * The conclusion is erroneous. Such precedents are not apt. When the triers of the facts decide that they cannot make a division of injuries we have, by their own finding, nothing more or less than an indivisible injury, and the precedents as to indivisible injuries will control. They were well summarized in Cooley on Torts in these words: "Where the negligence of two or more persons concur in producing a single, indivisible injury, then such persons are jointly and severally liable, although there was no common duty, common design, or concert action."

Maddux, 362 Mich. at 432–33, 108 N.W.2d at 36. * * *

* * * Where the injury itself is indivisible, the judge or jury must determine whether or not it is practicable to apportion the harm among the tortfeasors. If not, the entire liability may be imposed upon one (or several) tortfeasors subject, of course, to subsequent right of contribution among the joint offenders. Perhaps the best summary of the rationale for such a rule is found in Harper and James:

> In the earlier discussion of the substantive liability of joint tort-feasors and independent concurring wrongdoers who have produced indivisible harm it was indicated that there were four categories into which these parties may be placed: situations in which (1) the actors knowingly join in the performance of the tortious act or acts; (2) the actors fail to perform a common duty owed to the plaintiff; (3) there is a special relationship between the parties (e.g., master and servant or joint entrepreneurs); (4) although there is no concerted action nevertheless the independent acts of several actors concur to produce indivisible harmful consequences.

While the Restatement of Torts contains a short and apparently simple statement of the rule in category four, this type of situation has caused a great deal of disagreement in the courts. Here joint and several liability is sometimes imposed for the harm caused by the independent concurring acts of a number of persons. In all the situations in which such recovery is permitted the court must find first that the harm for which the plaintiff seeks damages is "indivisible." This can mean that the harm is not even theoretically divisible (as death or total destruction of a building) or that the harm, while theoretically divisible, is single in a practical sense so far as the plaintiff's ability to apportion it among the wrongdoers is concerned (as where a stream is polluted as a result of refuse from several factories). In the first type of case almost uniformly courts will permit entire recovery from any or all defendants. There is conflict, however, in the second situation, with some well-reasoned recent cases recognizing that the plaintiff's right to recover for his harm should not depend on his ability to apportion the damage but that this is a problem which is properly left with the defendants themselves.

F. Harper & F. James, The Law of Torts § 10.1 at 697–98, 701–02 (1956). * * *

NOTE

Joinder and Joint and Several Liability: The Link between Procedure and Substance. At common law, the two concepts of procedural joinder and joint and several liability were coterminous: only tortfeasors who were jointly and severally liable under substantive law could be joined in the same lawsuit. See Harper, James and Gray on Torts § 10.1. Beginning in the mid-nineteenth century, however, reforms in procedural codes began to allow the joinder of all defendants where plaintiff's claims are "asserted against them jointly, severally, or in the alternative with respect to or arising out of the same transaction, occurrence, or series of transactions or occurrences; and any question of law or fact common to all defendants will arise in the action." Fed. R. Civ. Proc. 20(a)(2). These procedural changes facilitated changes in the substantive law as well.

Summers v. Tice

Supreme Court of California, in Bank, 1948.
33 Cal.2d 80, 199 P.2d 1.

■ CARTER, JUSTICE. * * * Plaintiff's action was against both defendants for an injury to his right eye and face as the result of being struck by bird shot discharged from a shotgun. * * * [P]laintiff and the two defendants were hunting quail on the open range. Each of the defendants was armed with a 12 gauge shotgun loaded with shells containing 7 ½ size shot. Prior to going hunting plaintiff discussed the hunting procedure with defendants, indicating that they were to exercise care when shooting and to "keep in line." In the course of hunting plaintiff proceeded up a hill, thus placing the hunters at the points of a triangle. The view of defendants with reference to plaintiff was unobstructed and they knew his location. Defendant Tice flushed a quail which rose in flight to a ten foot elevation and flew between plaintiff and defendants. Both defendants shot at the quail, shooting in plaintiff's direction. At that time defendants were 75 yards from plaintiff. One shot struck plaintiff in his eye and another in his upper lip. Finally it was found by the court that as the direct result of the shooting by defendants the shots struck plaintiff as above mentioned and that defendants were negligent in so shooting and plaintiff was not contributorily negligent. * * *

The problem presented in this case is whether the judgment against both defendants may stand. It is argued by defendants that they are not joint tortfeasors, and thus jointly and severally liable, as they were not acting in concert, and that there is not sufficient evidence to show which defendant was guilty of the negligence which caused the injuries—the shooting by Tice or that by Simonson. * * *

[The trial court] determined that the negligence of both defendants was the legal cause of the injury—or that both were responsible. Implicit in such finding is the assumption that the court was unable to ascertain whether the shots were from the gun of one defendant or the other or one shot from each of them. The one shot that entered plaintiff's eye was the major factor in assessing damages and that shot could not have come from the gun of both defendants. It was from one or the other only.

It has been held that where a group of persons are on a hunting party, or otherwise engaged in the use of firearms, and two of them are negligent in firing in the direction of a third person who is injured thereby, both of those so firing are liable for the injury suffered by the third person, although the negligence of only one of them could have caused the injury. * The same rule has been applied in criminal cases * and both drivers have been held liable for the negligence of one where they engaged in a racing contest causing an injury to a third person. * These cases speak of the action of defendants as being in concert as the ground of decision, yet it would seem they are straining that concept and the more reasonable basis appears in Oliver v. Miles, [110 So. 666 (Miss.1926)]. There two persons were hunting together. Both shot at some partridges and in so doing shot across the highway injuring plaintiff who was travelling on it. The court stated they were acting in concert and thus both were liable. The court then stated: "We think that . . . each is liable for the resulting injury to the boy, although no one can say definitely who actually shot him. *To hold otherwise would be to exonerate both from liability, although each was negligent, and the injury resulted from such negligence.*" Id. at 668. * * *

When we consider the relative position of the parties and the results that would flow if plaintiff was required to pin the injury on one of the defendants only, a requirement that the burden of proof on that subject be shifted to defendants becomes manifest. They are both wrongdoers—both negligent toward plaintiff. They brought about a situation where the negligence of one of them injured the plaintiff, hence it should rest with them each to absolve himself if he can. The injured party has been placed by defendants in the unfair position of pointing to which defendant caused the harm. If one can escape the other may also and plaintiff is remediless. Ordinarily defendants are in a far better position to offer evidence to determine which one caused the injury. This reasoning has recently found favor in this Court. In a quite analogous situation this Court held that a patient injured while unconscious on an operating table in a hospital could hold all or any of the persons who had any connection with the operation even though he could not select the particular acts by the particular person which led to his disability. Ybarra v. Spangard, 25 Cal.2d 486, 154 P.2d 687 (1944). There the Court was considering whether the patient could avail himself of *res ipsa loquitur,* rather than where the burden of proof lay, yet the effect of the decision is that plaintiff has made out a case when he has produced evidence which gives rise to an inference of negligence which was the proximate cause of the injury. It is up to the defendants to explain the cause of the injury. It was there said: "If the doctrine is to continue to serve a useful purpose, we should not forget that 'the particular force and justice of the rule, regarded as a presumption throwing upon the party charged the duty of producing evidence, consists in the circumstance that the chief evidence of the true cause, whether culpable or innocent, is practically accessible to him but inaccessible to the injured person.' " * Similarly in the instant case plaintiff is not able to establish which of defendants caused his injury. * * *

Cases are cited for the proposition that where two or more tortfeasors acting independently of each other cause an injury to plaintiff, they are not joint tortfeasors and plaintiff must establish the portion of the damage caused by each, even though it is impossible to prove the portion of the injury caused by each. * In view of the foregoing discussion it is apparent that defendants in cases like the present one may be treated as liable on the same basis as joint tortfeasors, and hence the last cited cases are distinguishable inasmuch as they involve independent tortfeasors.

In addition to that, however, it should be pointed out that the same reasons of policy and justice shift the burden to each of defendants to absolve himself if he can—relieving the wronged person of the duty of apportioning the injury to a particular defendant, apply here where we are concerned with whether plaintiff is required to supply evidence for the apportionment of damages. If defendants are independent tortfeasors and thus each liable for the damage caused by him alone, and, at least, where the matter of apportionment is incapable of proof, the innocent wronged party should not be deprived of his right to redress. The wrongdoers should be left to work out between themselves any apportionment. Some * * * cases refer to the difficulty of apportioning the burden of damages between the independent tortfeasors, and say that where factually a correct division cannot be made, the trier of fact may make it the best it can, which would be more or less a guess, stressing the factor that the wrongdoers are not in a position to complain of uncertainty. * * *

NOTES

1. *Restatement (Third).* See Restatement (Third) of Torts: Liability for Physical and Harm § 28(b) (2010):

> When the plaintiff sues all of multiple actors and proves that each engaged in tortious conduct that exposed the plaintiff to a risk of harm and that the tortious conduct of one or more of them caused

the plaintiff's harm but the plaintiff cannot reasonably be expected to prove which actor or actors caused the harm, the burden of proof, including both production and persuasion, on factual causation is shifted to the defendants.

2. *Shifting the Burden of Proof to a Single Defendant.* In Haft v. Lone Palm Hotel, 3 Cal.3d 756, 91 Cal.Rptr. 745, 478 P.2d 465 (1970), the California Supreme Court shifted the burden of proof on the issue of causation to the defendant. In that case, Mr. Haft and his five-year-old son drowned in a swimming pool owned and operated by the defendant Hotel for the benefit of its guests. The defendant violated specific California statutory provisions by failing to provide either a lifeguard or a sign advising guests of the absence of a lifeguard. Haft and his son drowned in an incident without witnesses, leaving their estate without any means of proving causation. The court shifted the burden to the defendant to prove that the absence of the lifeguard was not the proximate causation of the deaths, reasoning as follows:

> The main purpose of the lifeguard requirement is undoubtedly to aid those in danger, but an attentive guard does serve the subsidiary function of witnessing those accidents that do occur. The absence of such a lifeguard in the instant case thus not only stripped decedents of a significant degree of protection to which they were entitled, but also deprived the present plaintiffs of a means of definitively establishing the facts leading to the drownings.

Sindell v. Abbott Laboratories

Supreme Court of California, 1980.
26 Cal.3d 588, 163 Cal.Rptr. 132, 607 P.2d 924.

■ MOSK, J. * * * Plaintiff Judith Sindell brought an action against eleven drug companies and Does 1 through 100, on behalf of herself and other women similarly situated. The complaint alleges as follows:

Between 1941 and 1971, defendants were engaged in the business of manufacturing, promoting, and marketing diethylstilbesterol (DES), a drug which is a synthetic compound of the female hormone estrogen. The drug was administered to plaintiff's mother and the mothers of the class she represents,[1] for the purpose of preventing miscarriage. In 1947, the Food and Drug Administration authorized the marketing of DES as a miscarriage preventative, but only on an experimental basis, with a requirement that the drug contain a warning label to that effect.

DES may cause cancerous vaginal and cervical growths in the daughters exposed to it before birth, because their mothers took the drug during pregnancy. The form of cancer from which these daughters suffer is known as adenocarcinoma, and it manifests itself after a minimum latent period of 10 or 12 years. It is a fast-spreading and deadly disease, and radical surgery is required to prevent it from

---

[1]   The plaintiff class alleged consists of "girls and women who are residents of California and who have been exposed to DES before birth and who may or may not know that fact or the dangers" to which they were exposed. Defendants are also sued as representatives of a class of drug manufacturers which sold DES after 1941.

spreading. * * * Thousands of women whose mothers received DES during pregnancy are unaware of the effects of the drug. * * *

During the period defendants marketed DES, they knew or should have known that it was a carcinogenic substance, that there was a grave danger after varying periods of latency it would cause cancerous and precancerous growths in the daughters of the mothers who took it, and that it was ineffective to prevent miscarriage. Nevertheless, defendants continued to advertise and market the drug as a miscarriage preventative. They failed to test DES for efficacy and safety; the tests performed by others, upon which they relied, indicated that it was not safe or effective. In violation of the authorization of the Food and Drug Administration, defendants marketed DES on an unlimited basis rather than as an experimental drug, and they failed to warn of its potential danger. *

* * * As a result of the DES ingested by her mother, plaintiff developed a malignant bladder tumor which was removed by surgery. She suffers from adenosis and must constantly be monitored by biopsy or colposcopy to insure early warning of further malignancy.

The first cause of action alleges that defendants were jointly and individually negligent in that they manufactured, marketed and promoted DES as a safe and efficacious drug to prevent miscarriage, without adequate testing or warning, and without monitoring or reporting its effects.

A separate cause of action alleges that defendants are jointly liable regardless of which particular brand of DES was ingested by plaintiff's mother because defendants collaborated in marketing, promoting and testing the drug, relied upon each other's tests, and adhered to an industry-wide safety standard. DES was produced from a common and mutually agreed upon formula as a fungible drug interchangeable with other brands of the same product; defendants knew or should have known that it was customary for doctors to prescribe the drug by its generic rather than its brand name and that pharmacists filled prescriptions from whatever brand of the drug happened to be in stock. * * *

Plaintiff seeks compensatory damages of $1 million and punitive damages of $10 million for herself. For the members of her class, she prays for equitable relief in the form of an order that defendants warn physicians and others of the danger of DES and the necessity of performing certain tests to determine the presence of disease caused by the drug, and that they establish free clinics in California to perform such tests.

Defendants demurred to the complaint. * * * [T]he trial court sustained the demurrers of these defendants without leave to amend on the ground that plaintiff did not and stated she could not identify which defendant had manufactured the drug responsible for her injuries. Thereupon, the court dismissed the action. * * *

This case is but one of a number filed throughout the country seeking to hold drug manufacturers liable for injuries allegedly resulting from DES prescribed to the plaintiffs' mothers since 1947. * According to a note in the Fordham Law Review, estimates of the number of women who took the drug during pregnancy range from 1½ million to 3 million. Hundreds, perhaps thousands, of the daughters of these women suffer from adenocarcinoma, and the incidence of vaginal adenosis among them is 30 to 90 percent. Comment, DES and a Proposed Theory of Enterprise Liability, 46 Fordham L. Rev. 963, 964–67 (1978) [hereafter Fordham Comment]. Most of the cases are still pending. With two exceptions, * those that have been decided resulted in judgments in favor of the drug company defendants because of the failure of the plaintiffs to identify the manufacturer of the DES prescribed to their mothers. * * * The present action is another attempt to overcome this obstacle to recovery.

We begin with the proposition that, as a general rule, the imposition of liability depends upon a showing by the plaintiff that his or her injuries were caused by the act of the defendant or by an instrumentality under the defendant's control. * * *

There are, however, exceptions to this rule. Plaintiff's complaint suggests several bases upon which defendants may be held liable for her injuries even though she cannot demonstrate the name of the manufacturer which produced the DES actually taken by her mother. The first of these theories, classically illustrated by Summers v. Tice, 33 Cal.2d 80, 199 P.2d 1 (1948), places the burden of proof of causation upon tortious defendants in certain circumstances. The second basis of liability emerging from the complaint is that defendants acted in concert to cause injury to plaintiff. There is a third and novel approach to the problem, sometimes called the theory of "enterprise liability," but which we prefer to designate by the more accurate term of "industry-wide" liability,[9] which might obviate the necessity for identifying the manufacturer of the injury-causing drug. We shall conclude that these doctrines, as previously interpreted, may not be applied to hold defendants liable under the allegations of this complaint. However, we shall propose and adopt a fourth basis for permitting the action to be tried, grounded upon an extension of the *Summers* doctrine.

I

Plaintiff places primary reliance upon cases which hold that if a party cannot identify which of two or more defendants caused an injury, the burden of proof may shift to the defendants to show that they were not responsible for the harm. This principle is sometimes referred to as the "alternative liability" theory.

The celebrated case of Summers v. Tice, *supra*, a unanimous opinion of this court, best exemplifies the rule. In *Summers*, the plaintiff was injured when two hunters negligently shot in his direction. It could not be determined which of them had fired the shot which actually caused the injury to the plaintiff's eye, but both defendants were nevertheless held jointly and severally liable for the whole of the damages. * * *

Defendants assert that these principles are inapplicable here. First, they insist that a predicate to shifting the burden of proof under *Summers-Ybarra* is that the defendants must have greater access to information regarding the cause of the injuries than the plaintiff,

---

[9] The term "enterprise liability" is sometimes used broadly to mean that losses caused by an enterprise should be borne by it. [Howard C.] Klemme, Enterprise Liability Theory of Torts, 47 U. Colo. L. Rev. 153, 158 (1976).

whereas in the present case the reverse appears. Plaintiff does not claim that defendants are in a better position than she to identify the manufacturer of the drug taken by her mother or, indeed, that they have the ability to do so at all, but argues, rather, that *Summers* does not impose such a requirement as a condition to the shifting of the burden of proof. In this respect we believe plaintiff is correct. In *Summers*, the circumstances of the accident themselves precluded an explanation of its cause. To be sure, *Summers* states that defendants are "[o]rdinarily. . . in a far better position to offer evidence to determine which one caused the injury" than a plaintiff, * but the decision does not determine that this "ordinary" situation was present. Neither the facts nor the language of the opinion indicate that the two defendants, simultaneously shooting in the same direction, were in a better position than the plaintiff to ascertain whose shot caused the injury. As the opinion acknowledges, it was impossible for the trial court to determine whether the shot which entered the plaintiff's eye came from the gun of one defendant or the other. Nevertheless, burden of proof was shifted to the defendants.

Here, as in *Summers*, the circumstances of the injury appear to render identification of the manufacturer of the drug ingested by plaintiff's mother impossible by either plaintiff or defendants, and it cannot reasonably be said that one is in a better position than the other to make the identification. Because many years elapsed between the time the drug was taken and the manifestation of plaintiff's injuries she, and many other daughters of mothers who took DES, are unable to make such identification. * Certainly there can be no implication that plaintiff is at fault in failing to do so—the event occurred while plaintiff was *in utero*, a generation ago. *

On the other hand, it cannot be said with assurance that defendants have the means to make the identification. In this connection, they point out that drug manufacturers ordinarily have no direct contact with the patients who take a drug prescribed by their doctors. Defendants sell to wholesalers, who in turn supply the product to physicians and pharmacies. Manufacturers do not maintain records of the persons who take the drugs they produce, and the selection of the medication is made by the physician rather than the manufacturer. Nor do we conclude that the absence of evidence on this subject is due to the fault of defendants. While it is alleged that they produced a defective product with delayed effects and without adequate warnings, the difficulty or impossibility of identification results primarily from the passage of time rather than from their allegedly negligent acts of failing to provide adequate warnings. * * *

It is important to observe, however, that while defendants do not have means superior to plaintiff to identify the maker of the precise drug taken by her mother, they may in some instances be able to prove that they did not manufacture the injury-causing substance. In the present case, for example, one of the original defendants was dismissed from the action upon proof that it did not manufacture DES until after plaintiff was born.

Thus we conclude the fact defendants do not have greater access to information that might establish the identity of the manufacturer of the

DES which injured plaintiff does not per se prevent application of the *Summers* rule.

Nevertheless, plaintiff may not prevail in her claim that the *Summers* rationale should be employed to fix the whole liability for her injuries upon defendants, at least as those principles have previously been applied. * There is an important difference between the situation involved in *Summers* and the present case. There, all the parties who were or could have been responsible for the harm to the plaintiff were joined as defendants. Here, by contrast, there are approximately 200 drug companies which made DES, any of which might have manufactured the injury-producing drug. * * *

These arguments are persuasive if we measure the chance that any one of the defendants supplied the injury-causing drug by the number of possible tortfeasors. In such a context, the possibility that any of the five defendants supplied the DES to plaintiff's mother is so remote that it would be unfair to require each defendant to exonerate itself. There may be a substantial likelihood that none of the five defendants joined in the action made the DES which caused the injury, and that the offending producer not named would escape liability altogether. While we propose, *infra*, an adaptation of the rule in *Summers* which will substantially overcome these difficulties, defendants appear to be correct that the rule, as previously applied, cannot relieve plaintiff of the burden of proving the identity of the manufacturer which made the drug causing her injuries. *

II

The second principle upon which plaintiff relies is the so-called "concert of action" theory. * * * Plaintiff contends that her complaint states a cause of action under these principles. She alleges that defendants' wrongful conduct "is the result of planned and concerted action, express and implied agreements, collaboration in, reliance upon, acquiescence in and ratification, exploitation and adoption of each other's testing, marketing methods, lack of warnings . . . and other acts or omissions . . . " and that "acting individually and in concert, [defendants] promoted, approved, authorized, acquiesced in, and reaped profits from sales" of DES. These allegations, plaintiff claims, state a "tacit understanding" among defendants to commit a tortious act against her.

In our view, this litany of charges is insufficient to allege a cause of action under the rules stated above. The gravamen of the charge of concert is that defendants failed to adequately test the drug or to give sufficient warning of its dangers and that they relied upon the tests performed by one another and took advantage of each others' promotional and marketing techniques. These allegations do not amount to a charge that there was a tacit understanding or a common plan among defendants to fail to conduct adequate tests or give sufficient warnings, and that they substantially aided and encouraged one another in these omissions.

The complaint charges also that defendants produced DES from a "common and mutually agreed upon formula," allowing pharmacists to treat the drug as a "fungible commodity" and to fill prescriptions from whatever brand of DES they had on hand at the time. It is difficult to understand how these allegations can form the basis of a cause of action for wrongful conduct by defendants, acting in concert. The formula for DES is a scientific constant. It is set forth in the United States Pharmacopoeia, and any manufacturer producing that drug must, with exceptions not relevant here, utilize the formula set forth in that compendium. *

What the complaint appears to charge is defendants' parallel or imitative conduct in that they relied upon each others' testing and promotion methods. But such conduct describes a common practice in industry: a producer avails himself of the experience and methods of others making the same or similar products. Application of the concept of concert of action to this situation would expand the doctrine far beyond its intended scope and would render virtually any manufacturer liable for the defective products of an entire industry, even if it could be demonstrated that the product which caused the injury was not made by the defendant.

None of the cases cited by plaintiff supports a conclusion that defendants may be held liable for concerted tortious acts. They involve conduct by a small number of individuals whose actions resulted in a tort against a single plaintiff, usually over a short span of time, and the defendant held liable was either a direct participant in the acts which caused damage, * or encouraged and assisted the person who directly caused the injuries by participating in a joint activity. * * *

III

A third theory upon which plaintiff relies is the concept of industry-wide liability, or according to the terminology of the parties, "enterprise liability." This theory was suggested in Hall v. E. I. Du Pont de Nemours & Co., Inc., 345 F.Supp. 353 (E.D.N.Y.1972). In that case, plaintiffs were 13 children injured by the explosion of blasting caps in 12 separate incidents which occurred in 10 different states between 1955 and 1959. The defendants were six blasting cap manufacturers, comprising virtually the entire blasting cap industry in the United States, and their trade association. There were, however, a number of Canadian blasting cap manufacturers which could have supplied the caps. The gravamen of the complaint was that the practice of the industry of omitting a warning on individual blasting caps and of failing to take other safety measures created an unreasonable risk of harm, resulting in the plaintiffs' injuries. The complaint did not identify a particular manufacturer of a cap which caused a particular injury. *

The court reasoned as follows: there was evidence that defendants, acting independently, had adhered to an industry-wide standard with regard to the safety features of blasting caps, that they had in effect delegated some functions of safety investigation and design, such as labeling, to their trade association, and that there was industry-wide cooperation in the manufacture and design of blasting caps. In these circumstances, the evidence supported a conclusion that all the defendants jointly controlled the risk. Thus, if plaintiffs could establish by a preponderance of the evidence that the caps were manufactured by one of the defendants, the burden of proof as to causation would shift to all the defendants. The court noted that this theory of liability applied to industries composed of a small number of units, and that what would be fair and reasonable with regard to an industry of five or ten producers might be manifestly unreasonable if applied to a decentralized industry composed of countless small producers. *

Plaintiff attempts to state a cause of action under the rationale of *Hall*. She alleges joint enterprise and collaboration among defendants in the production, marketing, promotion and testing of DES, and "concerted promulgation and adherence to industry-wide testing, safety, warning and efficacy standards" for the drug. We have concluded above that allegations that defendants relied upon one another's testing and promotion methods do not state a cause of action for concerted conduct to commit a tortious act. Under the theory of industry-wide liability, however, each manufacturer could be liable for all injuries caused by DES by virtue of adherence to an industry-wide standard of safety. * * *

We decline to apply this theory in the present case. At least 200 manufacturers produced DES; *Hall*, which involved 6 manufacturers representing the entire blasting cap industry in the United States, cautioned against application of the doctrine espoused therein to a large number of producers. * Moreover, in *Hall*, the conclusion that the defendants jointly controlled the risk was based upon allegations that they had delegated some functions relating to safety to a trade association. There are no such allegations here, and we have concluded above that plaintiff has failed to allege liability on a concert of action theory.

* * * [Because] the government plays such a pervasive role in formulating the criteria for the testing and marketing of drugs, it would be unfair to impose upon a manufacturer liability for injuries resulting from the use of a drug which it did not supply simply because it followed the standards of the industry. *

IV

If we were confined to the theories of *Summers* and *Hall*, we would be constrained to hold that the judgment must be sustained. Should we require that plaintiff identify the manufacturer which supplied the DES used by her mother or that all DES manufacturers be joined in the action, she would effectively be precluded from any recovery. As defendants candidly admit, there is little likelihood that all the manufacturers who made DES at the time in question are still in business or that they are subject to the jurisdiction of the California courts. There are, however, forceful arguments in favor of holding that plaintiff has a cause of action.

In our contemporary complex industrialized society, advances in science and technology create fungible goods which may harm consumers and which cannot be traced to any specific producer. The response of the courts can be either to adhere rigidly to prior doctrine, denying recovery to those injured by such products, or to fashion remedies to meet these changing needs. Just as Justice Traynor in his landmark concurring opinion in Escola v. Coca Cola Bottling Co., 24 Cal.2d 453, 467–68, 150 P.2d 436 (1944), recognized that in an era of mass production and complex marketing methods the traditional standard of negligence was insufficient to govern the obligations of manufacturer to consumer, so should we acknowledge that some adaptation of the rules of causation and liability may be appropriate in these recurring circumstances. * * *

The most persuasive reason for finding plaintiff states a cause of action is that advanced in *Summers*: as between an innocent plaintiff and negligent defendants, the latter should bear the cost of the injury. Here, as in *Summers*, plaintiff is not at fault in failing to provide evidence of causation, and although the absence of such evidence is not attributable to the defendants either, their conduct in marketing a drug the effects of which are delayed for many years played a significant role in creating the unavailability of proof.

From a broader policy standpoint, defendants are better able to bear the cost of injury resulting from the manufacture of a defective product. As was said by Justice Traynor in *Escola*, "[t]he cost of an injury and the loss of time or health may be an overwhelming misfortune to the person injured, and a needless one, for the risk of injury can be insured by the manufacturer and distributed among the public as a cost of doing business." * The manufacturer is in the best position to discover and guard against defects in its products and to warn of harmful effects; thus, holding it liable for defects and failure to warn of harmful effects will provide an incentive to product safety. * * *

Where, as here, all defendants produced a drug from an identical formula and the manufacturer of the DES which caused plaintiff's injuries cannot be identified through no fault of plaintiff, a modification of the rule of *Summers* is warranted. * * * [W]e hold it to be reasonable in the present context to measure the likelihood that any of the defendants supplied the product which allegedly injured plaintiff by the percentage which the DES sold by each of them for the purpose of preventing miscarriage bears to the entire production of the drug sold by all for that purpose. * * *

If plaintiff joins in the action the manufacturers of a substantial share of the DES which her mother might have taken, the injustice of shifting the burden of proof to defendants to demonstrate that they could not have made the substance which injured plaintiff is significantly diminished. While 75 to 80 percent of the market is suggested as the requirement by the Fordham Comment, *supra* at 996, we hold only that a substantial percentage is required.

The presence in the action of a substantial share of the appropriate market also provides a ready means to apportion damages among the defendants. Each defendant will be held liable for the proportion of the judgment represented by its share of that market unless it demonstrates that it could not have made the product which caused plaintiff's injuries. * * *

Under this approach, each manufacturer's liability would approximate its responsibility for the injuries caused by its own products. Some minor discrepancy in the correlation between market share and liability is inevitable; therefore, a defendant may be held liable for a somewhat different percentage of the damage than its share of the appropriate market would justify. * * * [T]he difficulty of apportioning damages among the defendant producers in exact relation to their market share does not seriously militate against the rule we adopt. * * *

We are not unmindful of the practical problems involved in defining the market and determining market share, * but these are largely matters of proof which properly cannot be determined at the pleading stage of these proceedings. Defendants urge that it would be both unfair and contrary to public policy to hold them liable for plaintiff's injuries in the absence of proof that one of them supplied the drug responsible for the damage. Most of their arguments, however, are based upon the assumption that one manufacturer would be held responsible for the products of another or for those of all other manufacturers if plaintiff ultimately prevails. But under the rule we adopt, each manufacturer's liability for an injury would be approximately equivalent to the damage caused by the DES it manufactured. *

The judgments are reversed.

■ RICHARDSON, J. I respectfully dissent. In these consolidated cases the majority adopts a wholly new theory which contains these ingredients: The plaintiffs were not alive at the time of the commission of the tortious acts. They sue a generation later. They are permitted to receive substantial damages from multiple defendants without any proof that any defendant caused or even probably caused plaintiffs' injuries.

Although the majority purports to change only the required burden of proof by shifting it from plaintiffs to defendants, the effect of its holding is to guarantee that plaintiffs will prevail on the causation issue because defendants are no more capable of disproving factual causation than plaintiffs are of proving it. * * *

The applicable principles of causation are very well established. A leading torts scholar, Dean Prosser, has authoritatively put it this way: "An *essential* element of the plaintiff's cause of action for negligence, *or for that matter for any other tort*, is that there be some reasonable connection between the act or omission of the defendant and the damage which the plaintiff has suffered." W[illiam L.] Prosser, Torts § 41 (4th ed. 1971). * * *

The majority now expressly abandons the foregoing traditional requirement of some causal connection between defendants' act and plaintiffs' injury in the creation of its new modified industry-wide tort. Conceptually, the doctrine of absolute liability which heretofore in negligence law has substituted only for the requirement of a breach of defendant's duty of care, under the majority's hand now subsumes the additional necessity of a causal relationship.

According to the majority, in the present case plaintiffs have openly conceded that they are unable to identify the particular entity which manufactured the drug consumed by their mothers. In fact, plaintiffs have joined only *five* of the approximately *two hundred* drug companies which manufactured DES. * * * In the present case * * * it remains wholly speculative and conjectural whether *any* of the five named defendants actually caused plaintiffs' injuries. * * *

I believe that the scales of justice tip against imposition of this new liability because of the foregoing elements of unfairness to some defendants who may have had nothing whatever to do with causing any injury, the unwarranted preference created for this particular class of plaintiffs, the violence done to traditional tort principles by the drastic expansion of liability proposed, the injury threatened to the public interest in continued unrestricted basic medical research as stressed by the Restatement, and the other reasons heretofore expressed. * * *

Given the grave and sweeping economic, social, and medical effects of "market share" liability, the policy decision to introduce and define it should rest not with us, but with the Legislature which is currently considering not only major statutory reform of California product liability law in general, but the DES problem in particular. See Sen. Bill No. 1392 (1979–1980 Reg. Sess.), which would establish and appropriate funds for the education, identification, and screening of persons exposed to DES, and would prohibit health care and hospital service plans from excluding or limiting coverage to persons exposed to DES. An alternative proposal for administrative compensation, described as "a limited version of no-fault products liability" has been suggested by one commentator. Dale A. Coggins, Industry-Wide Liability, 13 Suffolk U. L. Rev. 980, 1019–21 (1979). Compensation under such a plan would be awarded by an administrative tribunal from funds collected "via a tax paid by all manufacturers." * In any event, the problem invites a legislative rather than an attempted judicial solution. * * *

NOTES

1. *Hymowitz v. Eli Lilly & Co.* Because the defendant could be excused from liability if it proved that it was not responsible for a particular victim's harm, it is possible to interpret *Sindell* as an opinion that merely shifts the burden of proof on the issue of causation to the defendant. In Hymowitz v. Eli Lilly & Co., 73 N.Y.2d 487, 541 N.Y.S.2d 941, 539 N.E.2d 1069 (1989), however, the New York Court of Appeals imposed true collective liability for the creation of risk when it held that a particular manufacturer of DES that could prove that its product could not have been the one that caused the harm to the particular victim nevertheless would be liable on a market share liability theory:

> [B]ecause liability here is based on the over-all [sic] risk produced, and not causation in a single case, there should be no exculpation of a defendant who, although a member of the market producing DES for pregnancy use, appears not to have caused a particular plaintiff's injury. It is merely a windfall for a producer to escape liability solely because it manufactured a more identifiable pill, or sold only to certain drugstores. These fortuities in no way diminish the culpability of a defendant for marketing the product, which is the basis of liability here. *

73 N.Y.2d at 512, 539 N.E.2d at 1078. The court conceded "the lack of a logical link between liability and causation in a single case." *Id.* at 513 n.3, 539 N.E.2d at 1078 n.3.

2. *Industry-wide Liability.* The court in *Sindell* rejected the idea of imposing liability on grounds of "industry-wide" liability or, as Judge Weinstein originally called it, "enterprise liability." In recent decades, courts have almost universally rejected this concept of collective liability. For example, in Ryan v. Eli Lilly & Co., 514 F.Supp. 1004 (D.S.C.1981), the court refused to apply enterprise liability and described it as "repugnant to the most basic tenets of tort law."

3. *"Third-Generation" DES Cases.* Tragically, the genetic damage caused by DES does not end with the harm to the daughter *in utero* when her mother took the drug but instead can be passed down to the original consumer's granddaughters. At least so far, the courts have refused to hold the DES manufacturer liable to the granddaughter. E.g., Enright v. Eli Lilly & Co., 77 N.Y.2d 377, 389, 570 N.E.2d 198, 204 (1991) (stating that "[f]or all we know, the rippling effects of DES exposure may extend for generations" and "it is our duty to confine liability within manageable limits."). Why? Compare, e.g., Ryan v. New York Central R.R. Co, *infra* at 281–283, and Palsgraf v. Long Island R.R. Co., *infra* at 293–303 (both majority and dissenting opinions).

Skipworth v. Lead Industries Association, Inc.

Supreme Court of Pennsylvania, 1997.
547 Pa. 224, 690 A.2d 169.

■ CAPPY, JUSTICE. * * * Dominique Skipworth ("Skipworth") was born on September 18, 1988. Between September 10, 1990 and May 8, 1991, she was hospitalized for lead poisoning on three separate occasions. She also received outpatient therapy for lead poisoning in August 1991, and again in June 1992. During this time, she resided at only one home, located at 2840 West Stiles Street in Philadelphia. This residence, which had been rented by Skipworth's guardian, Pandora Williams ("Williams"), was estimated to have been built circa 1870. Testing of Skipworth's residence revealed the presence of lead-based paint at various locations throughout the home.

On March 17, 1992, Skipworth filed an action through her legal guardian[s] * * * (collectively referred to as "Appellants") against several manufacturers of lead pigment ("the pigment manufacturers") and their alleged successors as well as a trade association, Lead Industries Association, Inc. ("LIA"). * Appellants alleged that Skipworth suffered physical and neuropsychological injuries as a result of lead poisoning from the lead paint in her home. Appellants stipulated that they could not identify the manufacturer of the lead pigment which Skipworth ingested, and admitted that they could not identify when such pigment was made, sold, or applied to her home. Appellants, however, alleged that they had identified and joined in this action substantially all of the manufacturers of lead pigment used in residential house paint from 1870 until production of lead pigment ceased in 1977. Appellants thus proceeded against the pigment manufacturers and LIA (collectively referred to as "Appellees") by invoking theories of collective liability, namely market share liability, alternate liability, conspiracy, and concert of action. Appellees filed a motion for summary judgment. The trial court granted Appellees' motion for summary judgment as to all counts of Appellants' complaint. * * *

The first question presented in this appeal is whether this court should adopt the market share liability theory in the context of lead poisoning cases. * The market share liability theory[3] provides an

---

[3] It would appear that this theory emanated from an article written by a law student. See Naomi Sheiner, Comment, DES and a Proposed Theory of Enterprise Liability, 46 Fordham L. Rev. 963 (1978).

exception to the general rule that a plaintiff must establish that the defendant proximately caused his or her injury. A sharply divided California Supreme Court was the first court to adopt this theory of liability. See Sindell v. Abbott Laboratories, 26 Cal.3d 588, 163 Cal.Rptr. 132, 607 P.2d 924 (1980). * * * The *Sindell* court stated that market share liability is appropriate where the following factors are present: all the named defendants are potential tortfeasors; the allegedly harmful products are identical and share the same defective qualities (or were "fungible"); the plaintiff is unable to identify which defendant caused her injury through no fault of her own; and, substantially all of the manufacturers which created the defective products during the relevant time are named as defendants. * The rationale for adopting this theory was that "each manufacturer's liability would approximate its responsibility for the injuries caused by its own products." *

Pennsylvania, on the other hand, follows the general rule that a plaintiff, in order to recover, must establish that a particular defendant's negligence was the proximate cause of her injuries. * Adoption of the market share liability theory would result in a significant departure from this rule. * Although we realize that there may arise a situation which would compel us to depart from our time-tested general rule, such a situation is not presented by the matter *sub judice.* Application of market share liability to lead paint cases such as this one would lead to a distortion of liability which would be so gross as to make determinations of culpability arbitrary and unfair.

The extent to which liability would be contorted in a lead pigment case were market share liability to be applied is brought into sharp focus when the facts presented by this case are compared with the situation presented by a typical DES case, which is the type of case for which this theory was created. Such a comparison has revealed to us two major factors which compel us to conclude that adoption of market share liability in the context of a lead pigment case would unacceptably distort liability. First, the relevant time period in question is far more extensive than the relevant time period in a DES case. In this case, Appellants cannot identify any particular application, or applications, of lead paint which have caused Skipworth's health problems. Thus, they "pinpoint" a more than one hundred year period from the date the house was built until the lead paint ceased being sold for residential purposes as the relevant time period. In contrast, the relevant time period in a DES case is necessarily limited to the nine months that the patient ingesting the product was pregnant.

The difficulty in applying market share liability where such an expansive relevant time period as one hundred years is at issue is that entities who could not have been the producers of the lead paint which injured Skipworth would almost assuredly be held liable. Over the one hundred year period at issue, several of the pigment manufacturers entered and left the lead paint market. * Thus, application of the market share theory to this situation would virtually ensure that certain pigment manufacturers would be held liable where they could not possibly have been a potential tortfeasor; therefore, the first prong of the *Sindell* test would not be met.

The second factor which persuades us that adoption of market share liability here would be inappropriate is that lead paint, as opposed to DES, is not a fungible product. All DES used for treatment of pregnant women was manufactured according to an identical formula and presented an identical risk of harm. In contrast, it is undisputed that lead pigments had different chemical formulations, contained different amounts of lead, and differed in potential toxicity. *

Appellants contend that "whether all of the lead pigment [the pigment manufacturers] manufactured was exactly the same, in every respect, [is] irrelevant. . . ." We do not see this problem being so easily dismissed. Uncontested evidence shows that differing formulae of lead paint result in differing levels of bioavailability[5] of the lead. * Because of differences in bioavailability, a child who ingests dust or chips of lead paint containing equal amounts of lead "derived from two lead paints will *not* generally develop equal elevation in internal lead level from the two paints. Rather, more highly bioavailable lead has a greater impact than lead in less bioavailable form." * Thus, differing formulae of lead paint has a direct bearing on how much damage a lead paint manufacturer's product would cause.

Contrary to Appellants' bald assertion that this is an irrelevant consideration, it is actually fatal to their claim that application of market share liability to these defendants would be appropriate. Market share liability is grounded on the premise that it ensures that "each manufacturer's liability would approximate its responsibility for the injuries caused by its own products." Sindell, 26 Cal.3d at 612, 163 Cal.Rptr. at 145, 607 P.2d at 937. Yet, in this case, apportioning liability based upon a manufacturer defendant's share of the market (even if it were possible to obtain an accurate statistic considering the lengthy relevant time period at question) would not serve to approximate that defendant's responsibility for injuries caused by its lead paint. For example, a manufacturer whose lead product had a lower bioavailability than average would have caused less damage than its market share would indicate. Thus, application of market share liability to such a manufacturer would impose on it disproportionately high share of the damages awarded.

As we find that application of market share liability to lead paint cases would grotesquely distort liability, we decline to apply it in this case. * * *

NOTES

1. *Extension of Market Share Liability beyond DES Cases.* For the reasons outlined in *Skipworth*, most courts have been reluctant to extend market share liability beyond the specific context of DES. See Donald G. Gifford & Paolo Pasicolan, Market Share Liability Beyond DES Cases: The Solution to the Causation Dilemma in Lead Paint Litigation?, 58 S.C. L. Rev. 115, 118 (2006).

---

[5] The term "bioavailability" refers to "the extent to which the lead is in a form which is easily internalized by the body, i.e., the extent to which it is in a form which can be physiologically transported through the lungs, gastrointestinal tract, skin, etc. and absorbed into the bloodstream. . . ." *

The most prominent exception to this general statement is Thomas v. Mallett, 285 Wis.2d 236, 701 N.W.2d 523 (2005), in which the Wisconsin Supreme Court allowed a lead poisoned child, through his guardian *ad litem*, to pursue litigation against lead pigment manufacturers on a "risk-contribution" basis that enabled the court to consider not only manufacturer's respective market shares, but also their degrees of respective culpability, in allocating liability among the defendants. The court held that "fungibility" does not require "chemical identity." In response to the defendants' argument that it was impossible for the trial court to determine each manufacturer's appropriate extent of liability, the court responded that they were "essentially arguing that their negligent conduct should be excused because they got away with it for too long." In dissent, Justice Wilcox wrote, "The end result of the majority opinion is that the defendants, lead pigment manufacturers, can be held liable for a product they may or may not have produced, which may or may not have caused the plaintiff's injuries, based on conduct that may have occurred 100 years ago when some of the defendants were not even a part of the relevant market." See Donald G. Gifford, The Death of Causation: Mass Products Torts' Incomplete Incorporation of Social Welfare Principles, 41 Wake Forest L. Rev. 943, 985–88 (2006) (evaluating the decision in *Thomas* critically).

2. *Determining Market Share.* One of the most difficult aspects of market share liability cases is the determination of market shares for various defendants. Should market share be determined on a national basis, see Hymowitz v. Eli Lilly & Co., 73 N.Y.2d 487, 541 N.Y.S.2d 941, 539 N.E.2d 1069 (1989), or on as specific a market basis as possible, see Conley v. Boyle Drug Co., 570 So.2d 275 (Fla.1990)? How easy is it to reconstruct market shares decades after the sales of the products causing the injury? Who pays for the market shares of those who have gone out of business? How should liability be apportioned when, as a practical matter, it proves impossible to determine relevant market shares? For alternative approaches, compare Collins v. Eli Lilly Co., 116 Wis.2d 166, 342 N.W.2d 37 (1984), with Abel v. Eli Lilly & Co., 418 Mich. 311, 343 N.W.2d 164 (1984). See Gifford & Pasicolan, *supra* Note 1.

4. RECOVERY FOR LOSS OF CHANCE

Matsuyama v. Birnbaum

Supreme Judicial Court of Massachusetts, 2008.
452 Mass. 1, 890 N.E.2d 819.

■ MARSHALL, C.J. We are asked to determine whether Massachusetts law permits recovery for a "loss of chance" in a medical malpractice wrongful death action, where a jury found that the defendant physician's negligence deprived the plaintiff's decedent of a less than even chance of surviving cancer. We answer in the affirmative.[3] As we later explain more fully, the loss of chance doctrine views a person's

---

[3] The loss of chance doctrine is also known as the "lost opportunity" doctrine. See Restatement (Third) of Torts: Liability for Physical Harm § 26 cmt. n (Proposed Final Draft No. 1, [April 6, 2005]). See generally [Joseph H.] King, Jr., Causation, Valuation, and Chance in Personal Injury Torts Involving Preexisting Conditions and Future Consequences, Yale L.J. 1353, 1365–366 (1981).

prospects for surviving a serious medical condition as something of value, even if the possibility of recovery was less than even prior to the physician's tortious conduct. Where a physician's negligence reduces or eliminates the patient's prospects for achieving a more favorable medical outcome, the physician has harmed the patient and is liable for damages. Permitting recovery for loss of chance is particularly appropriate in the area of medical negligence. Our decision today is limited to such claims.

* * * In response to special questions, the jury found the defendant physician negligent in misdiagnosing the condition of the decedent over a period of approximately three years. They found as well that the physician's negligence was a "substantial contributing factor" to the decedent's death. They awarded $160,000 to the decedent's estate for the pain and suffering caused by the physician's negligence, and $328,125 to the decedent's widow and son for the decedent's loss of chance. * The defendants appealed, asserting, among other things, that loss of chance was not cognizable under the Massachusetts wrongful death statute *, or otherwise. We granted their application for direct appellate review. * * *

[T]he defendant, Dr. Neil S. Birnbaum, a board-certified internist, * * * became the primary care physician of the decedent, Kimiyoshi Matsuyama, in July, 1995, when the forty-two year old Matsuyama presented himself for a routine physical examination. * * * Matsuyama's medical records at the time of his initial visit to Birnbaum disclosed complaints of gastric distress dating back to 1988. * * * During the physical Matsuyama complained, as Birnbaum testified at trial, of "heartburn and difficulty breathing associated with eating and lifting." Birnbaum testified that he was aware at the time that, as a person of Asian ancestry who * * * had a history of smoking, Matsuyama was at a significantly higher risk for developing gastric cancer than was the general population of the United States. * Nevertheless, Birnbaum did not order any tests to determine the cause of Matsuyama's complaints. Based on his physical examination alone, Birnbaum diagnosed Matsuyama with gastrointestinal reflux disease and recommended over-the-counter medications to relieve Matsuyama's symptoms. Birnbaum followed a similar course of action in October, 1996, when Matsuyama returned for a sick visit, complaining that his heartburn was worse and that he had gastric pain after eating.

In September, 1997, Matsuyama consulted Birnbaum about moles that had recently developed on his body. On visual inspection, Birnbaum made a diagnosis of "one benign seborrhea keratosis." * Birnbaum testified at trial that such moles are "common" and "not something that I would [have] overly been that fearful of."

Matsuyama next appeared for an office visit with Birnbaum on September 1, 1998, for a follow up to a recent urgent care visit and for concerns about a mole over his left eye. Birnbaum was aware at the time that on August, 24, 1998, Matsuyama had presented himself at Medical Associates's urgent care facility complaining of severe stomach pain during the previous forty-eight hours, which the urgent care physician had diagnosed as gastritis. Birnbaum made a clinical diagnosis of nonulcer dyspepsia, again without the benefit of any evaluative gastrointestinal tests.[11] However, he did order a test on Matsuyama to determine the presence of Helicobacter pylori (H. pylori), a bacteria associated with gastric cancer, among other gastric maladies. When the test came back positive for H. pylori, Birnbaum directed his nurse to inform Matsuyama of the test results and to call in medications to treat Matsuyama's H. pylori. Neither the nurse nor Birnbaum told Matsuyama about the association of H. pylori with gastrointestinal diseases, of which Birnbaum was aware. By this time, Birnbaum testified, gastritis "probably was my leading diagnosis," but he did not order an endoscopy with biopsy or an upper gastrointestinal series, which he knew would definitively confirm or rule out his diagnosis.

* * * [O]n May 3, 1999, when Matsuyama went to Birnbaum complaining of epigastric pain, vomiting, sudden weight loss, and premature feelings of fullness after eating[,] Birnbaum ordered a gastrointestinal series and an abdominal ultrasound, which revealed a two-centimeter mass in Matsuyama's stomach. Subsequent medical procedures confirmed the presence of infiltrative gastric adenoid carcinoma. * * * He succumbed to gastric cancer the following October, leaving his wife and his minor son.

In June, 2000, the plaintiff filed suit against Birnbaum and Medical Associates. Her complaint * * * alleged wrongful death * * * and negligence against both defendants. * Trial began in the Superior Court in July, 2004. The jury heard testimony from, among others, * the plaintiff's expert witness, Dr. Stuart Ira Finkel, a gastroenterologist. Finkel testified that, in his opinion, Birnbaum breached the applicable standard of care in evaluating and treating Matsuyama, resulting in Matsuyama's death. Specifically, Finkel opined that, in light of Matsuyama's complaints, symptoms, and risk factors, including the presence of H. pylori, his Japanese ancestry, his having lived in Japan or Korea for extended periods, his smoking history, and other well-known risk factors, an internist exercising the expected standard of care would have ordered an upper gastrointestinal series X-ray or an endoscopy, or referred Matsuyama to a specialist for endoscopy, beginning in 1995. The expert also testified that the appearance of Matsuyama's seborrheic keratosis in September, 1997, "could have and should have" triggered a suspicion of stomach cancer "right then and there." Finkel told the jury that if Birnbaum had ordered the appropriate testing on Matsuyama in 1995, the cancer "would have been diagnosed" and "treated in a timely fashion when it might still have been curable." As a result of Birnbaum's failure to make a timely diagnosis, Finkel opined, the cancer metastasized to an advanced, inoperable phase, resulting in Matsuyama's premature death.

In the course of his testimony, Finkel offered an extensive discussion of the tumor-lymph nodes-metastasis (TNM) method for classifying gastric cancer into separate "stages," from stage 0 to stage 4, with each higher stage signaling a more advanced cancer and carrying a statistically diminished chance for survival, as measured by the standard gastric cancer metric of five years cancer free after treatment. * * * Patients with stage 0, in which the cancer is confined to the

---

[11] Throughout the trial the jury heard evidence that gastritis and nonulcerative dyspepsia may be linked to gastric cancer.

stomach lining, have a better than 90% survival rate, * Finkel averred; at stage 1, the survival rate drops to between 60% and 80%; at stage 2, between 30% and 50%; at stage 3, between 10% and 20%; and at stage 4, less than 4%. * Finkel opined that, as a result of Birnbaum's breach of the standard of care, Matsuyama lost the opportunity of having gastric cancer "diagnosed and treated in a timely fashion when it might still have been curable."

* * * After a six-day trial, the case went to the jury. * * * [T]he jury found Birnbaum negligent in Matsuyama's treatment * * *. They also found that Birnbaum's negligence was a "substantial contributing factor" to Matsuyama's death[20] * * * Then, in response to a special jury question, * the jury awarded damages for loss of chance, which they calculated as follows: they awarded $875,000 as "full" wrongful death damages, * and found that Matsuyama was suffering from stage 2 adenocarcinoma at the time of Birnbaum's initial negligence and had a 37.5% chance of survival at that time. They awarded the plaintiff "final" loss of chance damages of $328,125 ($875,000 multiplied by .375). Judgment entered against the defendants, jointly and severally, on the negligence-wrongful death count in the amount of $328,125, later amended to $281,310. * * *

2. *Loss of chance.* Although we address the issue for the first time today, a substantial and growing majority of the States that have considered the question have indorsed the loss of chance doctrine, in one form or another, in medical malpractice actions. * We join that majority to ensure that the fundamental aims and principles of our tort law remain fully applicable to the modern world of sophisticated medical diagnosis and treatment.

The development of the loss of chance doctrine offers a window into why it is needed. The doctrine originated in dissatisfaction with the prevailing "all or nothing" rule of tort recovery. * Under the all or nothing rule, a plaintiff may recover damages only by showing that the defendant's negligence more likely than not caused the ultimate outcome, in this case the patient's death; if the plaintiff meets this burden, the plaintiff then recovers 100% of her damages. * Thus, if a patient had a 51% chance of survival, and the negligent misdiagnosis or treatment caused that chance to drop to zero, the estate is awarded *full* wrongful death damages. * On the other hand, if a patient had a 49% chance of survival, and the negligent misdiagnosis or treatment caused that chance to drop to zero, the plaintiff receives nothing. So long as the patient's chance of survival before the physician's negligence was less than even, it is logically impossible for her to show that the physician's negligence was the but-for cause of her death, so she can recover nothing. * Thus, the all or nothing rule provides a "blanket release from liability for doctors and hospitals any time there was less than a 50 percent chance of survival, regardless of how flagrant the negligence." * * *

Addressing the specific arguments advanced by the defendants is useful for delineating the proper shape of the doctrine. The defendants

---

[20] The judge instructed the jury that "substantial" "doesn't mean that Mr. Matsuyama's chance of survival was [50%] or greater, only that there was a fair chance of survival or cure had Dr. Birnbaum not been negligent and had he conformed to the applicable standard of care."

argue that the loss of chance doctrine "lowers the threshold of proof of causation" by diluting the preponderance of the evidence standard that "has been the bedrock of the Massachusetts civil justice system." Some courts have indeed approached the issue of how to recognize loss of chance by carving out an exception to the rule that the plaintiff must prove by a preponderance of the evidence that the defendant "caused" his injuries. See, e.g., Thompson v. Sun City Community Hosp., Inc., 141 Ariz. 597, 607–608, 688 P.2d 605 (1984) (adopting rule that "permits the case to go to the jury on the issue of causation with less definite evidence of probability than the ordinary tort case," and requiring jury to "find for the defendant unless they find a *probability* that defendant's negligence was a cause of plaintiff's injury."). We reject this approach. "It is fundamental that the plaintiff bears the burden of establishing causation by a preponderance of the evidence." Johnson v. Summers, 411 Mass. 82, 91, 577 N.E.2d 301 (1991). Therefore, in a case involving loss of chance, as in any other negligence context, a plaintiff must establish by a preponderance of the evidence that the defendant caused his injury.

However, "injury" need not mean a patient's death. Although there are few certainties in medicine or in life, progress in medical science now makes it possible, at least with regard to certain medical conditions, to estimate a patient's probability of survival to a reasonable degree of medical certainty. * That probability of survival is part of the patient's condition. When a physician's negligence diminishes or destroys a patient's chance of survival, the patient has suffered real injury. The patient has lost something of great value: a chance to survive, to be cured, or otherwise to achieve a more favorable medical outcome. * Thus we recognize loss of chance not as a theory of causation, but as a theory of injury. *

* * * In order to prove loss of chance, a plaintiff must prove by a preponderance of the evidence that the physician's negligence caused the plaintiff's likelihood of achieving a more favorable outcome to be diminished. That is, the plaintiff must prove by a preponderance of the evidence that the physician's negligence caused the plaintiff's injury, where the injury consists of the diminished likelihood of achieving a more favorable medical outcome. * The loss of chance doctrine, so delineated, makes no amendment or exception to the burdens of proof applicable in all negligence claims. * * *

In earlier periods, Massachusetts courts grappling with what we would now call loss of chance claims often lacked reliable expert evidence of what the patient's chances of survival or recovery would have been absent the alleged negligence. * More recently, as we noted above, at least for certain conditions, medical science has progressed to the point that physicians can gauge a patient's chances of survival to a reasonable degree of medical certainty, and indeed routinely use such statistics as a tool of medicine. * Reliable modern techniques of gathering and analyzing medical data have made it possible for fact finders to determine based on expert testimony—rather than speculate based on insufficient evidence—whether a negligent failure to diagnose a disease injured a patient by preventing the disease from being treated at an earlier stage, when prospects were more favorable. * The availability of such expert evidence on probabilities of survival makes it appropriate to recognize loss of chance as a form of injury. * Through appropriate expert evidence, a plaintiff in a medical malpractice case may be able to sustain her burden of showing that, as a result of defendant's negligence, a decedent suffered a diminished likelihood of achieving a more favorable medical outcome. * * *[33]

In sum, whatever difficulties may attend recognizing loss of chance as an item of damages in a medical malpractice action, these difficulties are far outweighed by the strong reasons to adopt the doctrine. * * *

4. *Damages.* Our conclusion that loss of chance is a separate, compensable item of damages in an action for medical malpractice does not fully resolve the issues on appeal. We must consider, among other things, how the loss of the likelihood of a more favorable outcome is to be valued. * * *

Courts adopting the loss of chance doctrine have arrived at different methods for calculating such damages. * The most widely adopted of these methods of valuation is the "proportional damages" approach. * Under the proportional damages approach, loss of chance damages are measured as "the percentage probability by which the defendant's tortious conduct diminished the likelihood of achieving some more favorable outcome." * The formula aims to ensure that a defendant is liable in damages only for the monetary value of the *portion* of the decedent's prospects that the defendant's negligence destroyed. In applying the proportional damages method, the court must first measure the monetary value of the patient's full life expectancy and, if relevant, work life expectancy as it would in any wrongful death case. But the defendant must then be held liable only for the portion of that value that the defendant's negligence destroyed. *

Deriving the damages for which the physician is liable will require the fact finder to undertake the following calculations: *

(1) The fact finder must first calculate the total amount of damages allowable for the death under the wrongful death statute, * or, in the case of medical malpractice not resulting in death, the full amount of damages allowable for the injury. This is the amount to which the decedent would be entitled if the case were *not* a loss of chance case: the full amount of compensation for the decedent's death or injury. *

(2) The fact finder must next calculate the patient's chance of survival or cure immediately preceding ("but for") the medical malpractice.

(3) The fact finder must then calculate the chance of survival or cure that the patient had as a result of the medical malpractice.

(4) The fact finder must then subtract the amount derived in step 3 from the amount derived in step 2.

(5) The fact finder must then multiply the amount determined in step 1 by the percentage calculated in step

---

[33] We do not decide today whether a plaintiff may recover on a loss of chance theory when the ultimate harm (such as death) has not yet come to pass. * * *

4 to derive the proportional damages award for loss of chance.

To illustrate, suppose in a wrongful death case that a jury found, based on expert testimony and the facts of the case, that full wrongful death damages would be $600,000 (step 1), that the patient had a 45% chance of survival prior to the medical malpractice (step 2), and that the physician's tortious acts reduced the chances of survival to 15% (step 3). The patient's chances of survival were reduced 30% (i.e., 45% minus 15%) due to the physician's malpractice (step 4), and the patient's loss of chance damages would be $600,000 multiplied by 30%, for a total of $180,000 (step 5). * * *

From our analysis thus far, it should be evident that the value of "the loss of opportunity to allow events to play out in order to see if the plaintiff's condition was in fact amenable to restoration," * is a matter beyond the average juror's ken; the evidence will necessarily come from experts. Expert testimony is required to ascertain what measure of a more favorable outcome is medically appropriate (for example, five-year survival as in this case), to determine what statistical rates of survival apply in what circumstances, for example, a 37.5% chance of survival, and to apply these rates to the particular clinical circumstances of the patient. * * *

Judgment affirmed.

NOTES

1. *Arguments against Recovery for Loss of Chance of Survival.* In Fennell v. Southern Maryland Hosp. Center, Inc., 320 Md. 776, 580 A.2d 206 (1990), the Maryland Court of Appeals denied recovery when the hospital's negligence deprived the plaintiff of a 40 percent chance of recovery. The court identified several arguments for rejecting "chance of survival" recovery. First, the court suggested that, under the logic of the loss of chance damages theory, the plaintiff should be entitled to some recovery if defendant's negligence reduced the chance of recovery from 40 percent to 10 percent, even if the plaintiff subsequently survived. Does this necessarily follow? Second, the Maryland Court of Appeals expressed concern that the numerical quantifications necessary for experts to prove the case for loss of survival would be "unreliable, misleading, easily manipulated, and confusing to a jury." Third, the court questioned the fairness of a result that a plaintiff suing on behalf of a decedent who had a 49 percent chance of survival would be entitled to recover 49 percent of the value of the decedent's life, but a plaintiff with a decedent with a 51 percent chance of recovery would be able to recover the entire value of the life. The court apparently considered it an absurd suggestion that, in the latter case, the plaintiff should recover only 51 percent of the damages. Compare Scafidi v. Seiler, 119 N.J. 93, 574 A.2d 398 (1990). Is it less unfair to allow the decedent with a 51 percent chance of recovery to recover all damages, but deny any recovery to the decedent who lost a 49 percent chance of recovery due to defendant's actions?

2. *Calculation of Damages.* Professor Robert Rhee argues that the calculation of damages by the *Matsuyama* court is incorrect:

The *Matsuyama* court and other courts have incorrectly calculated probabilistic causation, and the damage calculations derived therefrom are also wrong. The method of calculation endorsed in these cases is correct only in the special case when the malpractice reduced the chance of survival to zero. * * *

When malpractice reduces a less-than-probable chance of survival but there still remains a residual chance of survival after the negligence, the proper damage amount *cannot* be the product of the reduction in the chance of survival and the full value of the loss. For example, assume the exact hypothetical provided in *Matsuyama*: (1) full value of loss is $600,000; (2) the chance of survival before the negligence is 45%; and (3) the chance of survival after the negligence is 15%, which is the residual chance of survival after the negligence. The damage cannot be $180,000 (= 30% x $600,000) as *Matsuyama* suggests.

To see why, again imagine 100 people in the plaintiff's exact situation. How many of these people would have died naturally from the ailment? Fifty-five people, because the plaintiff had a 45% chance of survival before the malpractice. How many would have died from the malpractice? Thirty people, because the doctor reduced the chance of survival from 45% to 15%. How many people would have survived despite the negligence? Fifteen people, because there is still a 15% residual chance of survival after the negligence. Because these 15 people would have survived the natural ailment *and* the malpractice, they would have no injury and thus no legal claim. How many people would have died in total? Eighty-five people.

The reference class from which probability is calculated must be all injured people, which is 85 people and *not* 100 people. Of these unfortunate 85 people, 55 died from the natural ailment, and 30 died from the malpractice.

What, then, is the probabilistic causation attributable to the negligent doctor? The answer clearly cannot be 30%. The probabilistic causation attributable to the doctor's negligence must be: 30/85 = 35.3%. Thus, the damage calculation must be: 35.3% (reduction in chance) x $600,000 (full loss) = $211,765 (damages). The error in the hypothetical resulted in an undervaluation of damages of $31,765. * * *

The error in Matsuyama produces only a small difference between the erroneous damages and correct damages because the residual chance was so small. In other cases where the residual chance is large, the difference in damage amounts can be large. * * *

* * * [W]hen a person dies, which is a precondition to bringing a medical malpractice claim for loss of chance, we are no longer concerned with various states of future outcomes including the possibility of survival, but instead we are looking back in time to the *past*. The reference class is the group of dead plaintiffs, and should not include the class of people who survived (this last bit of uncertainty has been resolved). We have a past occurrence of death, and we must assign only two probabilities: $P(d_1)$ the probability that death resulted from the ailment, and $P(d_2)$ the probability that death resulted from negligence where $P(d_1) + P(d_2) = 1$. The residual chance of survival must be taken out of the

equation. The causation analysis must answer the question: Given that death occurred, what was the probability that it resulted from the negligence?

Damages should follow therefrom.

Robert J. Rhee, Loss of Chance, Probabilistic Cause, and Damage Calculations: The Error in *Matsuyama v. Birnbaum* and the Majority Rule of Damages in Many Jurisdictions More Generally, 1 Suffolk U. L. Rev. Online 39, 4-9–9-9, (2013), *available at* http://suffolklawreview.org/wp-content/uploads/2013/03/Rhee_Web_PDF.pdf.

5. CAUSAL LINKAGE

Green-Wheeler Shoe Co. v. Chicago, Rhode Island & Pacific Railway Co.

Supreme Court of Iowa, 1906.
130 Iowa 123, 106 N.W. 498.

■ MCCLAIN, C.J. In the agreed statement on which the case was tried without other evidence being introduced it is stipulated that the defendant was guilty of negligent delay in the forwarding of the goods of plaintiff from Ft. Dodge to Kansas City, where they were lost or injured on May 30, 1903, by a flood which was so unusual and extraordinary as to constitute an act of God, and that if there had been no such negligent delay the goods would not have been caught in the flood referred to or damaged thereby.

We have presented for our consideration, therefore, the simple question whether a carrier who by a negligent delay in transporting goods has subjected them, in the course of transportation, to a peril which has caused their damage or destruction, and for the consequence of which the carrier would not have been liable had there been no negligent delay intervening, is liable for the loss. On this question there is a well-recognized conflict in the authorities. In several well-considered cases decided by courts of high authority it was decided, while the question was still new, that the negligent delay of the carrier in transportation could not be regarded as the proximate cause of an ultimate loss by a casualty which in itself constituted an act of God, as that term is used in defining the carrier's exemption from liability, although had the goods been transported with reasonable diligence they would not have been subjected to such casualty, and these cases are very similar to the one before us inasmuch as the loss in each instance was due to the goods being overtaken by an unprecedented flood for the consequence of which the carrier would not be responsible. * These cases are predicated upon the view that if the carrier could not reasonably have foreseen or anticipated that the goods would be overtaken by such a casualty as a natural and probable result of the delay, then the negligent delay was not the proximate cause of the loss, and should be disregarded in determining the liability for such loss. A similar course of reasoning has been applied in other cases, where the loss has been due immediately to some cause such as accidental fire involving no negligence on the part of the carrier and within a valid exception in the bill of lading, but the goods have been brought within the peril stipulated against by negligent delay in transportation. * For similar reasons it has been held that loss of or injury to the goods by reason of their inherent nature, as by freezing or the like, will not render the carrier liable, even after negligent delay in transportation, if such casualty could not have been foreseen or anticipated as the natural and probable consequence of such delay. * * *

Now, while it is true that defendant could not have anticipated this particular flood and could not have foreseen that its negligent delay in transportation would subject the goods to such a danger, yet it is now apparent that such delay did subject the goods to the danger, and that but for the delay they would not have been destroyed; and defendant should have foreseen, as any reasonable person could foresee, that the negligent delay would extend the time during which the goods would be liable in the hands of the carrier to be overtaken by some such casualty, and would therefore increase the peril that the goods should be thus lost to the shipper. This consideration that the peril of accidental destruction is enhanced by the negligent extension of time during which the goods must remain in the carrier's control and out of the control of the owner, and during which some casualty may overtake them, has not, we think, been given sufficient consideration in the cases in which the carrier has been held not responsible for a loss for which he is not primarily liable, but which has overtaken the goods as a consequence of the preceding delay in their transportation. * * *

We are satisfied that the sounder reasons, supported by good authority, require us to hold that in this case the carrier is liable for the loss of and damage to plaintiff's goods, and justify the judgment of the trial court is therefore reversed.

Berry v. Sugar Notch Borough

Supreme Court of Pennsylvania, 1899.
191 Pa. 345, 43 A. 240.

■ FELL, J. The plaintiff was a motorman in the employ of the Wilkes-Barre & Wyoming Valley Traction Company on its line running from Wilkes Barre to the borough of Sugar Notch. The ordinance by virtue of which the company was permitted to lay its track and operate its cars in the borough of Sugar Notch contained a provision that the speed of the cars while on the streets of the borough should not exceed eight miles an hour. On the line of the road, and within the borough limits, there was a large chestnut tree, as to the condition of which there was some dispute at the trial. The question of the negligence of the borough in permitting it to remain must, however, be considered as set at rest by the verdict. On the day of the accident the plaintiff was running his car on the borough street in a violent windstorm, and as he passed under the tree it was blown down, crushing the roof of the car, and causing the plaintiff's injury.

There is some conflict of testimony as to the speed at which the car was running, but it seems to be fairly well established that it was considerably in excess of the rate permitted by the borough ordinance. We do not think that the fact that the plaintiff was running his car at a higher rate of speed than eight miles an hour affects his right to recover. It may be that in doing so he violated the ordinance by virtue of which the company was permitted to operate its cars in the streets of the borough, but he certainly was not, for that reason, without rights upon the streets. Nor can it be said that the speed was the cause of the accident, or contributed to it. It might have been otherwise if the tree had fallen before the car reached it, for in that case a high rate of speed might have rendered it impossible for the plaintiff to avoid a collision which he either foresaw or should have foreseen. Even in that case the ground for denying him the right to recover would be that he had been guilty of contributory negligence, and not that he had violated a borough ordinance. The testimony, however, shows that the tree fell upon the car as it passed beneath.

With this phase of the case in view, it was urged on behalf of the appellant that the speed was the immediate cause of the plaintiff's injury, inasmuch as it was the particular speed at which he was running which brought the car to the place of the accident at the moment when the tree blew down. This argument, while we cannot deny its ingenuity, strikes us, to say the least, as being somewhat sophistical. That his speed brought him to the place of the accident at the moment of the accident was the merest chance, and a thing which no foresight could have predicted. The same thing might as readily have happened to a car running slowly, or it might have been that a high speed alone would have carried him beyond the tree to a place of safety. It was also argued by the appellant's counsel that, even if the speed was not the sole efficient cause of the accident, it at least contributed to its severity, and materially increased the damage. It may be that it did. But what basis could a jury have for finding such to be the case? And, should they so find, what guide could be given them for differentiating between the injury done this man and the injury which would have been done a man in a similar accident on a car running at a speed of eight miles an hour or less?

The judgment is affirmed.

Excerpt, Guido Calabresi, Concerning Cause and the Law of Torts: An Essay for Harry Kalven, Jr.

43 U.Chi. L. Rev. 69, 71–72 (1975).

[W]hat role does causal language play in the achievement of certain goals [deterrence, cost-spreading, and distributional] that have come to be accepted as crucial to the law of torts?

To accomplish this function-oriented task it is useful to distinguish three concepts of "cause": "causal link," "*but for* cause," and "proximate cause."

The first concept, as I shall use it, is entirely predictive and empirical. There is a causal link between an act or activity and an injury when we conclude on the basis of the available evidence that the recurrence of that act or activity will increase the chances that the injury will also occur. There is a causal link between the failure to keep a light on at the top of a flight of stairs and a person falling down those stairs, whether or not a particular fall was in some other sense caused by the failure of lighting. * * *

The second concept of cause is the familiar one of *but for* or *sine qua non* cause. A *but for* cause * * * is any one of many acts or activities without which a particular injury would not have occurred. * * * [W]hile there is frequently an overlap between causal linkage and *but for* cause, the two concepts often diverge. The death of a person found with a broken neck at the foot of an unlighted staircase is causally linked to the absence of light even though it may be conclusively proved that the particular victim fell on the particular occasion because of a sudden dizzy spell that would have occurred with or without adequate lighting * * *.

* * * The final concept * * * of proximate cause * * * will embrace those presumably causally linked, usually (but by no means always) *but for* causes to which, in the absence of certain specified defenses, a particular legal system wishes to assign at least partial responsibility for an accident. Such a conclusory "definition" will obviously necessitate a discussion of what additional requirements, if any, must be met, under our current legal system and under each of the tort goals mentioned above, in order to conclude that an action is a proximate cause.

B. SCOPE OF LIABILITY (DUTY AND PROXIMATE CAUSATION)

1. LIMITING LIABILITY

Ryan v. New York Central Railroad Co.
Court of Appeals of New York, 1866.
35 N.Y. 210.

■ HUNT, J. * * * [T]he defendant, by the careless management, or through the insufficient condition, of one of its engines, set fire to its woodshed, and a large quantity of wood therein. The plaintiff's house, situated at a distance of one hundred and thirty feet from the shed, soon took fire from the heat and sparks, and was entirely consumed, notwithstanding diligent efforts were made to save it. A number of other houses were also burned by the spreading of the fire. The plaintiff brings this action to recover from the railroad company the value of his building thus destroyed. * * *

The question may be thus stated: A house in a populous city takes fire, through the negligence of the owner or his servant; the flames extend to and destroy an adjacent building: Is the owner of the first building liable to the second owner for the damage sustained by such burning?

It is a general principle that every person is liable for the consequences of his own acts. He is thus liable in damages for the proximate results of his own acts, but not for remote damages. It is not easy at all times to determine what are proximate and what are remote damages. In Thomas v. Winchester (2 Seld., 408), Judge Ruggles defines the damages for which a party is liable, as those which are the natural or necessary consequences of his acts. Thus, the owner of a loaded gun, who puts it in the hands of a child, by whose indiscretion it is discharged, is liable for the injury sustained by a third person from such discharge. * The injury is a natural and ordinary result of the folly of placing a loaded gun in the hands of one ignorant of the manner of using it, and incapable of appreciating its effects. The owner of a horse and cart, who leaves them unattended in the street, is liable for an injury done to a person or his property, by the running away of the horse. * The injury is the natural result of the negligence. * * * So if an engineer upon a steamboat or locomotive, in passing the house of A., so carelessly manages its machinery that the coals and sparks from its fires fall upon and consume the house of A., the railroad company or the steamboat proprietors are liable to pay the value of the property thus destroyed. * Thus far the law is settled and the principle is apparent. If, however, the fire communicates from the house of A. to that of B., and that is destroyed, is the negligent party liable for his loss? And if it spreads thence to the house of C., and thence to the house of D., and thence consecutively through the other houses, until it reaches and consumes the house of Z., is the party liable to pay the damages sustained by these twenty-four sufferers? The counsel for the plaintiff does not distinctly claim this, and I think it would not be seriously insisted that the sufferers could recover in such case. Where, then, is the principle upon which A. recovers and Z. fails?

* * * I prefer to place my opinion upon the ground that, in the one case, to wit, the destruction of the building upon which the sparks were thrown by the negligent act of the party sought to be charged, the result was to have been anticipated the moment the fire was communicated to the building; that its destruction was the ordinary and natural result of its being fired. In the second, third or twenty-fourth case, as supposed, the destruction of the building was not a natural and expected result of the first firing. That a building upon which sparks and cinders fall should be destroyed or seriously injured must be expected, but that the fire should spread and other buildings be consumed, is not a necessary or an usual result. That it is possible, and that it is not unfrequent, cannot be denied. The result, however, depends, not upon any necessity of a further communication of the fire, but upon a concurrence of accidental circumstances, such as the degree of the heat, the state of the atmosphere, the condition and materials of the adjoining structures and the direction of the wind. These are accidental and varying circumstances. The party has no control over them, and is not responsible for their effects.

My opinion, therefore, is, that this action cannot be sustained, for the reason that the damages incurred are not the immediate but the remote result of the negligence of the defendants. The immediate result was the destruction of their own wood and sheds; beyond that, it was remote. * * *

To sustain such a claim as the present, and to follow the same to its legitimate consequences, would subject to a liability against which no prudence could guard, and to meet which no private fortune would be adequate. Nearly all fires are caused by negligence, in its extended sense. In a country where wood, coal, gas and oils are universally used, where men are crowded into cities and villages, where servants are employed, and where children find their home in all houses, it is impossible that the most vigilant prudence should guard against the occurrence of accidental or negligent fires. A man may insure his own house or his own furniture, but he cannot insure his neighbor's building or furniture, for the reason that he has no interest in them. To hold that the owner must not only meet his own loss by fire, but that he must guarantee the security of his neighbors on both sides, and to an unlimited extent, would be to create a liability which would be the destruction of all civilized society. No community could long exist, under the operation of such a principle. In a commercial country, each man, to some extent, runs the hazard of his neighbor's conduct, and each, by insurance against such hazards, is enabled to obtain a reasonable security against loss. To neglect such precaution, and to call upon his neighbor, on whose premises a fire originated, to indemnify him instead, would be to award a punishment quite beyond the offense committed. It is to be considered, also, that if the negligent party is liable to the owner of a remote building thus consumed, he would also be liable to the insurance companies who should pay losses to such remote owners. * * *

The remoteness of the damage, in my judgment, forms the true rule on which the question should be decided, and which prohibits a recovery by the plaintiff in this case.

Judgment should be affirmed.

NOTES

1. *Proximate Cause in Fire Cases: A Question of Law or Fact?* Compare *Ryan* with Milwaukee & St. Paul Ry. Co. v. Kellogg, 94 U.S. 469, 24 L.Ed. 256 (1876). The defendant negligently allowed a fire to spread from its steamboat on the Mississippi River to its own grain elevator. The fire subsequently spread to the plaintiff's sawmill and lumber stacks, more than 500 feet away. The United States Supreme Court held that proximate cause is ordinarily a question for the jury and described the proper test of proximate cause as follows:

> In the nature of things, there is in every transaction a succession of events, more or less dependent upon those preceding, and it is the province of a jury to look at this succession of events or facts, and ascertain whether they are naturally and probably connected with each other by a continuous sequence, or are dissevered by new and independent agencies, and this must be determined in view of the circumstances existing at the time.

Id. at 476, 24 L.Ed. at 259.

2. *The Third Restatement and Scope of Liability.* The Restatement (Third) of Torts avoids the use of the term "proximate cause" and instead uses the more accurate and descriptive term "scope of liability": "Although the term 'proximate cause' has been in widespread use in judicial opinions, treatises, casebooks, and scholarship, the term is not * * * employed * * * because it is an especially poor one to describe the idea to which it is connected." Restatement (Third) of Torts: Liability for Physical and Emotional Harm, Chapter 6, Special Note on Proximate Cause (2010). The Third Restatement also dispenses with the Second Restatement's use of the umbrella term "legal cause" to include both cause in fact and proximate cause.

3. *The Relevance of Insurability.* To what extent is the *Ryan* outcome explainable on the grounds that accident law favors the broad distribution of losses and that fire losses to real property are prevalently covered by the owner's property insurance, whether or not the owner has a claim against a negligent tortfeasor for causing the fire? The court appears to endorse the first point with its observation that the tortfeasor cannot obtain property insurance on the victim's property, but obviously ignores the eventual availability of liability insurance, which was not available in 1866. In any event, it can be argued that the owner's property insurance is a more efficient vehicle for distributing the loss to any unit of property than would be the liability insurance of strangers, who are less able to value in advance the property that they might potentially damage or destroy than are the owners of that property. It should be noted that this case is one of several in which the outcomes of a tort claim of a type potentially applicable to conflagration is different from what might ordinarily be expected under general principles of tort law. See, e.g., H.R. Moch Co. v. Rensselaer Water Co., 247 N.Y. 160, 159 N.E. 896 (1928), *infra* 448–451. Compare Weinberg v. Dinger, 106 N.J. 469, 524 A.2d 366 (1987) (holding water company liable for losses caused by the negligent failure to maintain adequate water pressure for firefighting to the extent that insurance is available to pay such claims).

In re Polemis and Furness Withy & Co. Ltd.

Court of Appeal, 1921.
[1921] 3 K.B. 560.

■ Appeal by charters from an order of Sankey, J., on an award in the form of a Special Case.

[The owners of the Greek Steamship Thrasyvoulos sued the party that had chartered the ship to recover damages for the total loss of the steamship by fire. In the charter contract, the parties agreed that the chartering party would redeliver the ship to the owner in the "same good order and condition as when delivered to them," excepting for "fair wear and tear" and other specifically named perils. Among the other excepted perils were "loss or damage from fire on board in hulk or craft" and "any act, neglect, or default whatsoever of pilot, master, or crew in the management of navigation of the ship," all of whom were provided by the owner]. * * *

The vessel by the directions of the charterers * * * proceeded to Lisbon and was loaded with further cargo, consisting of cases of benzine and/or petrol and iron for Casablanca and other ports on the Morocco coast. She arrived at Casablanca on July 17, and there discharged a portion of her cargo. The cargo was discharged by Arab workmen and winchmen from the shore supplied and sent on board by the charterers' agents. The cargo in No. 1 hold included a considerable quantity of cases of benzine or petrol which had suffered somewhat by handling and/or by rough weather on the voyage, so that there had been some leakage from the tins in the cases into the hold.

On July 21 it had become necessary to shift from No. 1 lower hold a number of the cases of benzine which were required to be taken on by the ship to Safi, and for this purpose the native stevedores had placed heavy planks across the forward end of the hatchway in the 'tween decks using it as a platform in the process of transferring the cases from the lower hold to the 'tween decks. There were four or five of the Arab shore labourers in the lower hold filling the slings which, when filled, were hove up by means of the winch situated on the upper deck to the 'tween decks level of the platform on which some of the Arabs in the 'tween decks were working. In consequence of the breakage of the cases there was a considerable amount of petrol vapour in the hold.

In the course of heaving a sling of the cases from the hold the rope by which the sling was being raised or the sling itself came into contact with the boards placed across the forward end of the hatch, causing one of the boards to fall into the lower hold, and the fall was instantaneously followed by a rush of flames from the lower hold, and this resulted eventually in the total destruction of the ship.

The owners contended (so far as material) that the charterers were liable for the loss of the ship; that fire caused by negligence was not an excepted peril; and that the ship was in fact lost by the negligence of the stevedores, who were the charterers' servants, in letting the sling strike the board, knocking it into the hold, and thereby causing a spark which set fire to the petrol vapour and destroyed the ship.

The charterers contended that * * * there was no negligence for which the charterers were responsible, inasmuch as to let a board fall into the hold of the ship could do no harm to the ship and therefore was not negligence towards the owners; and that the danger and/or damage were too remote—i.e., no reasonable man would have foreseen danger and/or damage of this kind resulting from the fall of the board.

The three arbitrators made the following findings of fact:—

(a) That the ship was lost by fire.

(b) That the fire arose from a spark igniting petrol vapour in the hold.

(c) That the spark was caused by the falling board coming into contact with some substance in the hold.

(d) That the fall of the board was caused by the negligence of the Arabs (other than the winchmen) engaged in the work of discharging.

(e) That the said Arabs were employed by the charterers * * *, and that the said Arabs were the servants of the charterers.

(f) That the causing of the spark could not reasonably have been anticipated from the falling of the board, though some damage to the ship might reasonably have been anticipated.

(g) There was no evidence before us that the Arabs chosen were known or likely to be negligent.

(h) That the damages sustained by the owners through the said accident amount to the sum of 196,165£. 1s.11d. as shown in the second column of the schedule hereto[.]

Subject to the opinion of the Court on any questions of law arising the arbitrators awarded that the owners were entitled to recover from the charterers the before-mentioned sum. If the Court should be of opinion that the above award was wrong, then the arbitrators awarded that the owners should recover nothing from the charterers. Sankey, J. affirmed the award. The charterers appealed. * * *

■ BANKES, L.J. * * * These findings, are, no doubt, intended to raise the question [which of two views expressed in different precedents] is the correct one. * * * [T]he difference between the two views is this: According to the one view, the consequences which may reasonably be expected to result from a particular act are material only in reference to the question whether the act is or is not a negligent act; according to the other view, those consequences are the test whether the damages resulting from the act, assuming it to be negligent, are or are not too remote to be recoverable. * * * In Weld-Blundell v. Stephens, [1920] A.C. 983, Lord Sumner said:

> What are "natural, probable and necessary" consequences? Everything that happens, happens in the order of nature and is therefore "natural." Nothing that happens by the free choice of a thinking man is "necessary," except in the sense of predestination. To speak of "probable" consequence is to throw everything upon the jury. It is tautologous to speak of "effective" cause or to say that damages too remote from the cause are irrecoverable, for an effective cause is simply that which causes, and in law what is ineffective or too remote is not a cause at all. I still venture to think that direct cause is the best expression. * * * Direct cause excludes what is indirect, conveys the essential distinction, which *causa causans* and *causa sine qua non* rather cumbrously indicate and is consistent with the possibility of the concurrence of more direct causes than one, operating at the same time and leading to a common result. * As, however, these different epithets and formulae are used almost indiscriminately, something more must be done than to choose an epithet which has been used in a decided case. It is necessary to consider whether the facts of the case cited raise a question of causation belonging to the same category as that under discussion. * * *

In the present case the arbitrators have found as a fact that the falling of the plank was due to the negligence of the defendants' servants. The fire appears to me to have been directly caused by the falling of the plank. In these circumstances I consider that it is immaterial that the causing of the spark by the falling of the plank could not have been reasonably anticipated. The charterers' junior counsel sought to draw a distinction between the anticipation of the extent of damage resulting from a negligent act, and the anticipation of the type of damage resulting from such an act. He admitted that it could not lie in the mouth of a person whose negligent act had caused damage to say that he could not reasonably have foreseen the extent of the damage, but he contended that the negligent person was entitled to rely upon the fact that he could not reasonably have anticipated the type of damage which resulted from his negligent act. I do not think that the distinction can be admitted. Given the breach of duty which constitutes the negligence, and given the damage as a direct result of that negligence, the anticipations of the person whose negligent act has produced the damage appear to me to be irrelevant. I consider that the damages claimed are not too remote.

* * * For these reasons I think that the appeal fails, and must be dismissed with costs.

■ WARRINGTON, L.J. * * * The presence or absence of reasonable anticipation of damage determines the legal quality of the act as negligent or innocent. If it be thus determined to be negligent, then the question whether particular damages are recoverable depends only on the answer to the question whether they are the direct consequence of the act. * * * In the present case it is clear that the act causing the plank to fall was in law a negligent act, because some damage to the ship might reasonably be anticipated. If this is so then the charterers are liable for the actual loss, that being on the findings of the arbitrators the direct result of the falling board. * On the whole in my opinion the appeal must be dismissed with costs.

■ SCRUTTON, L.J. * * * The second defence is that the damage is too remote from the negligence, as it could not be reasonably foreseen as a consequence. On this head we were referred to a number of well-known cases in which vague language, which I cannot think to be really helpful, has been used in an attempt to define the point at which damage becomes too remote from, or not sufficiently directly caused by, the breach of duty, which is the original cause of action, to be recoverable. For instance, I cannot think it useful to say the damage must be the natural and probable result. This suggests that there are results which are natural but not probable, and other results which are probable but not natural. I am not sure what either adjective means in this connection; if they mean the same thing, two need not be used; if they mean different things, the difference between them should be defined. * * *

To determine whether an act is negligent, it is relevant to determine whether any reasonable person would foresee that the act would cause damage; if he would not, the act is not negligent. But if the act would or might probably cause damage, the fact that the damage it in fact causes is not the exact kind of damage one would expect is immaterial, so long as the damage is in fact caused sufficiently by the negligent act, and not by the operation of independent causes having no connection with the negligent act, except that they could not avoid its results. Once the act is negligent, the fact that its exact operation was not foreseen is immaterial. * * * In the present case it was negligent in discharging cargo to knock down the planks of the temporary staging, for they might easily cause some damage either to workmen, or cargo, or the ship. The fact that they did directly produce an unexpected result, a spark in an atmosphere of petrol vapour which caused a fire, does not relieve the person who was negligent from the damage which his negligent act directly caused. For these reasons the experienced arbitrators and the judge appealed from came, in my opinion, to a correct decision, and the appeal must be dismissed with costs.

Gorris v. Scott

Court of Exchequer, 1874.
L.R. 9 Exch. 125.

■ KELLY, C.B. This is an action to recover damages for the loss of a number of sheep which the defendant, a shipowner, had contracted to carry, and which were washed overboard and lost by reason (as we must take it to be truly alleged) of the neglect to comply with a certain order made by the Privy Council, in pursuance of the Contagious Diseases (Animals) Act, 1869. The Act was passed merely for sanitary purposes, in order to prevent animals in a state of infectious disease from communicating it to other animals with which they might come in contact. Under the authority of that Act, certain orders were made; amongst others, an order by which any ship bringing sheep or cattle from any foreign port to ports in Great Britain is to have the place occupied by such animals divided into pens of certain dimensions, and the floor of such pens furnished with battens or foot-holds. The object of this order is to prevent animals from being overcrowded, and so brought into a condition in which the disease guarded against would be likely to be developed. This regulation has been neglected, and the question is, whether the loss, which we must assume to have been caused by that neglect, entitles the plaintiffs to maintain an action.

The argument of the defendant is, that the Act has imposed penalties to secure the observance of its provisions, and that, according to the general rule, the remedy prescribed by the statute must be pursued; that although, when penalties are imposed for the violation of a statutory duty, a person aggrieved by its violation may sometimes maintain an action for the damage so caused, that must be in cases where the object of the statute is to confer a benefit on individuals, and to protect them against the evil consequences which the statute was designed to prevent, and which have in fact ensued; but that if the object is not to protect individuals against the consequences which have in fact ensued, it is otherwise; that if, therefore, by reason of the precautions in question not having been taken, the plaintiffs had sustained that damage against which it was intended to secure them, an action would lie, but that when the damage is of such a nature as was not contemplated at all by the statute, and as to which it was not intended to confer any benefit on the plaintiffs, they cannot maintain an action founded on the neglect. * * * [I]f we could see that it was the object, or among the objects of this Act, that the owners of sheep and cattle coming from a foreign port should be protected by the means described against the danger of their property being washed overboard, or lost by the perils of the sea, the present action would be within the principle.

But, looking at the Act, it is perfectly clear that its provisions were all enacted with a totally different view; there was no purpose, direct or indirect, to protect against such damage; but, as is recited in the preamble, the Act is directed against the possibility of sheep or cattle being exposed to disease on their way to this country. The preamble recites that "it is expedient to confer on Her Majesty's most honourable Privy Council power to take such measures as may appear from time to time necessary to prevent the introduction into Great Britain of contagious or infectious diseases among cattle, sheep, or other animals, by prohibiting or regulating the importation of foreign animals," and also to provide against the "spreading" of such diseases in Great Britain. Then follow numerous sections directed entirely to this object. Then comes section 75, which enacts that "the Privy Council may from time to time make such orders as they think expedient for all or any of the following purposes." What, then, are these purposes? They are "for securing for animals brought by sea to ports in Great Britain a proper supply of food and water during the passage and on landing," "for protecting such animals from unnecessary suffering during the passage and on landing," and so forth; all the purposes enumerated being calculated and directed to the prevention of disease, and none of them having any relation whatever to the danger of loss by the perils of the sea. That being so, if by reason of the default in question the plaintiffs' sheep had been overcrowded, or had been caused unnecessary suffering, and so had arrived in this country in a state of disease, I do not say that they might not have maintained this action. But the damage complained of here is something totally apart from the object of the Act of Parliament, and it is in accordance with all the authorities to say that the action is not maintainable.

■ PIGOTT, B. * * * The legislature never contemplated altering the relations between the owners and carriers of cattle, except for the purposes pointed out in the Act; and if the Privy Council had gone out of their way and made provisions to prevent cattle from being washed overboard, their act would have been *ultrà vires*. If, indeed, by reason of the neglect complained of, the cattle had contracted a contagious disease, the case would have been different. * * *

Judgment for the defendant.

NOTE

Federal Employers' Liability Act and Type of Risk. There is one major exception in American law to the rule of *Gorris v. Scott*. It relates to actions under the FELA (Federal Employers' Liability Act—cf. pages[ ]). In FELA cases, there is strict liability for harm caused in fact by violation of the Safety Appliance Acts or the Boiler Inspection Act. A line of cases has held that this liability requires cause-in-fact only, "without regard to whether the injury flowing from the breach was the injury the statute sought to prevent"—i.e., without regard to the rule of *Gorris v. Scott*.

In Kernan v. American Dredging Co., 355 U.S. 426, 78 S.Ct. 394, 2 L.Ed.2d 382 (1958), a seaman was killed when a kerosene lamp three feet from the deck of a scow ignited petroleum vapors on a river. A Coast Guard regulation had required the lamp to be at least eight feet high. Its purpose was to aid navigation, not to avoid the ignition of petroleum vapors, so the rule of *Gorris v. Scott* would appear to bar use of the regulation's violation as a basis for liability. But a statute, the Jones Act, had applied the FELA to seamen. In *Kernan*, the Supreme Court found that the seaman's claim was analogous to the claims under the FELA for the violation of the Safety Appliance Act and the Boiler Inspection Act. Therefore it applied that line of cases, which recognized liability under the FELA for violations of certain safety statutes, to the violation of the Coast Guard regulation, even though the accident was not of the type the regulation was enacted to prevent.

Brown v. Shyne

Court of Appeals of New York, 1926.
242 N.Y. 176, 151 N.E. 197.

■ LEHMAN, J. The plaintiff employed the defendant to give chiropractic treatment to her for a disease or physical condition. The defendant had no license to practice medicine, yet he held himself out as being able to diagnose and treat disease, and, under the provisions of the Public Health Law, * he was guilty of a misdemeanor. The plaintiff became paralyzed after she had received nine treatments by the defendant. She claims, and upon this appeal we must assume, that the paralysis was caused by the treatment she received. She has recovered judgment in the sum of $10,000 for the damages caused by said injury.

The plaintiff in her complaint alleges that the injuries were caused by the defendant's negligence. If negligence on the part of the defendant caused the injury, the plaintiff may recover the consequent damages. Though the defendant held himself out, and the plaintiff consulted him, as a chiropractor and not as a regular physician, he claimed to possess the skill requisite for diagnosis and treatment of disease, and in the performance of what he undertook to do he may be held to the degree of skill and care which he claimed to possess. At the trial the plaintiff gave testimony in regard to the manner in which she was treated. She supplemented this testimony by evidence that the treatment was not in accordance with recognized theory or practice; that it produced the injury which followed; and that a person qualified to treat disease should have foreseen that the treatment might have such result. Though her testimony was contradicted, the jury might well have resolved the conflict in her favor, and if the only question submitted to the jury had been whether or not this evidence showed that plaintiff's injury was caused by the defendant's negligence, the defendant could not complain of any substantial error at the trial. * * *

At the close of the plaintiff's case the plaintiff was permitted to amend the complaint to allege "that in so treating the plaintiff the defendant was engaged in the practice of medicine contrary to and in violation of the provisions of the Public Health Law of the State of New York in such case made and provided, he at the time of so treating plaintiff not being a duly licensed physician or surgeon of the State of New York." Thereafter the trial judge charged the jury that they might bring in a verdict in favor of the plaintiff if they found that the evidence established that the treatment given to the plaintiff was not in accordance with the standards of skill and care which prevail among those treating disease. He then continued:

> * * * I am going to allow you, if you think proper under the evidence in the case, to predicate negligence upon another theory. The public health laws of this State prescribe that no person shall practice medicine unless he is licensed so to do by the Board of Regents of this State and registered pursuant to statute. . . . This statute to which I have referred is a general police regulation. Its violation, and it has been violated by the defendant, is some evidence, more or less cogent, of negligence which you may consider for what it is worth, along with all the other evidence in the case. If the defendant attempted to treat the plaintiff and to adjust the vertebræ in her spine when he did not possess the requisite knowledge and skill as prescribed by the statute to know what was proper and necessary to do under the circumstances, or how to do it, even if he did know what to do, you can find him negligent.

In so charging the jury that from the violation of the statute the jury might infer negligence which produced injury to the plaintiff, the trial justice in my opinion erred.

The provisions of the Public Health Law prohibiting the practice of medicine without a license granted upon proof of preliminary training, and after examination intended to show adequate knowledge, are of course intended for the protection of the general public against injury which unskilled and unlearned practitioners might cause. If violation of the statute by the defendant was the proximate cause of the plaintiff's injury, then the plaintiff may recover upon proof of violation; if violation of the statute has no direct bearing on the injury, proof of the violation becomes irrelevant. For injury caused by neglect of duty imposed by the penal law there is civil remedy; but, of course, the injury must follow from the neglect.

Proper formulation of general standards of preliminary education and proper examination of the particular applicant should serve to raise the standards of skill and care generally possessed by members of the profession in this State; but the license to practice medicine confers no additional skill upon the practitioner, nor does it confer immunity from physical injury upon a patient if the practitioner fails to exercise care. Here, injury may have been caused by lack of skill or care; it would not have been obviated if the defendant had possessed a license yet failed to exercise the skill and care required of one practicing medicine. True, if the defendant had not practiced medicine in this State, he could not have injured the plaintiff, but the protection which the statute was intended to provide was against risk of injury by the unskilled or careless practitioner, and, unless the plaintiff's injury was caused by carelessness or lack of skill, the defendant's failure to obtain a license was not connected with the injury. * * *

The defendant in offering to treat the plaintiff held himself out as qualified to give treatment. He must meet the professional standards of skill and care prevailing among those who do offer treatment lawfully. If injury follows through failure to meet those standards, the plaintiff may recover. The provisions of the Public Health Law may result in the exclusion from practice of some who are unqualified. Even a skilled and learned practitioner who is not licensed commits an offense against the State; but against such practitioners the statute was not intended to protect, for no protection was needed, and neglect to obtain a license results in no injury to the patient and, therefore, no private wrong. The purpose of the statute is to protect the public against unfounded assumption of skill by one who undertakes to prescribe or treat for disease. In order to show that the plaintiff has been injured by defendant's breach of the statutory duty, proof must be given that defendant in such treatment did not exercise the care and skill which would have been exercised by qualified practitioners within the State, and that such lack of skill and care caused the injury. Failure to obtain a license as required by law gives rise to no remedy if it has caused no injury. No case has been cited where neglect of a statutory duty has given rise to private cause of action where it has not appeared that private injury has been caused by danger against which the statute was intended to afford protection, and which obedience to the statute would have obviated. * * *

Argument is made that, even if neglect of the statutory duty does not itself create liability, it tends to prove that injury was caused by lack of skill or care. That can be true only if logical inference may be drawn from defendant's failure to obtain or perhaps seek a license that he not only lacks the skill and learning which would enable him to diagnose and treat disease generally, but also that he lacks even the skill and learning necessary for the physical manipulation he gave to this plaintiff. Evidence of defendant's training, learning, and skill and the method he used in giving the treatment was produced at the trial, and upon such evidence the jury could base finding either of care or negligence, but the absence of a license does not seem to strengthen inference that might be drawn from such evidence, and *a fortiori* would not alone be a basis for such inference. Breach or neglect of duty imposed by statute or ordinance may be evidence of negligence only if there is logical connection between the proven neglect of statutory duty and the alleged negligence. * * *

For these reasons the judgments should be reversed and a new trial granted, with costs to abide the event.

■ CRANE, J. (dissenting). * * * The prohibition against practicing medicine without a license was for the very purpose of protecting the public from just what happened in this case. * * * The Public Health Law was intended to guard individual members of the public from the injuries which might result from resorting to unexamined practitioners. The violation of the law in this case has brought about the very thing which the Legislature has tried to prevent. * * *

I am convinced that the plaintiff in this case was a part of that public for whose benefit the Public Health Law * * * was passed. It was to prevent injury to such as she that the Legislature forbade the unlicensed practice of medicine. The plaintiff was injured through the defendant's disobedience of the law. He was treating her for laryngitis by pushing her vertebra. In pushing her vertebra and twisting her head, that is, by doing the very thing the law said he must not do, he caused paralysis. Thus by these authorities, the plaintiff could prove in connection with his acts that he was practicing medicine without a license, and such violation was, to say the least, some evidence of negligence. This is as far as the trial judge went in charging the jury. Personally, I am of the opinion that, where an injury is the direct and proximate result of practicing medicine without a license, a recovery can be had, as for an act negligent *per se;* but we do not need to go so far in this case. * * *

NOTE

Subsequent Legislative Enactment. Section 4504 of the New York Civil Practice Law and Rules (McKinney 2012) now provides:

(d) **Proof of negligence; unauthorized practice of medicine.** In any action for damages for personal injuries or death against a person not authorized to practice medicine under article 131 of the education law for any act or acts constituting the practice of medicine, when such act or acts were a competent producing proximate or contributing cause of such injuries or death, the fact that such person practiced medicine without being so authorized shall be deemed prima facie evidence of negligence.

Palsgraf v. Long Island Railroad Co.

Court of Appeals of New York, 1928.
248 N.Y. 339, 162 N.E. 99.

Appeal from a judgment of the Appellate Division of the Supreme Court in the second judicial department, entered December 16, 1927, affirming a judgment in favor of plaintiff entered upon a verdict. * * *

■ CARDOZO, CH. J. Plaintiff was standing on a platform of defendant's railroad after buying a ticket to go to Rockaway Beach. A train stopped at the station, bound for another place. Two men ran forward to catch it. One of the men reached the platform of the car without mishap, though the train was already moving. The other man, carrying a package, jumped aboard the car, but seemed unsteady as if about to fall. A guard on the car, who had held the door open, reached forward to help him in, and another guard on the platform pushed him from behind. In this act, the package was dislodged, and fell upon the rails. It was a package of small size, about fifteen inches long, and was covered by a newspaper. In fact it contained fireworks, but there was nothing in its appearance to give notice of its contents. The fireworks when they fell exploded. The shock of the explosion threw down some scales at the other end of the platform, many feet away. The scales struck the plaintiff, causing injuries for which she sues.

The conduct of the defendant's guard, if a wrong in its relation to the holder of the package, was not a wrong in its relation to the plaintiff, standing far away. Relatively to her it was not negligence at all. Nothing in the situation gave notice that the falling package had in it the potency of peril to persons thus removed. Negligence is not actionable unless it involves the invasion of a legally protected interest, the violation of a right. "Proof of negligence in the air, so to speak, will not do." Frederick Pollock, The Law of Torts 455 (11th ed. 1920); Martin v. Herzog, 228 N.Y. 164, 170, 126 N.E. 814 (1920). * "Negligence is the absence of care, according to the circumstances." Vaughan v. Taff Vale Ry. Co., 5 H. & N. 679, 688 (Willes, J.). *

The plaintiff as she stood upon the platform of the station might claim to be protected against intentional invasion of her bodily security. Such invasion is not charged. She might claim to be protected against unintentional invasion by conduct involving in the thought of reasonable men an unreasonable hazard that such invasion would ensue. These, from the point of view of the law, were the bounds of her immunity, with perhaps some rare exceptions, survivals for the most part of ancient forms of liability, where conduct is held to be at the peril of the actor. * If no hazard was apparent to the eye of ordinary vigilance, an act innocent and harmless, at least to outward seeming, with reference to her, did not take to itself the quality of a tort because it happened to be a wrong, though apparently not one involving the risk of bodily insecurity, with reference to someone else. "In every instance, before negligence can be predicated of a given act, back of the act must be sought and found a duty to the individual complaining, the observance of which would have averted or avoided the injury." W. Va.

Central R. Co. v. State, 96 Md. 652, 666, 54 A. 669, 671–72 (1903) (McSherry, C.J.). * The plaintiff sues in her own right for a wrong personal to her, and not as the vicarious beneficiary of a breach of duty to another.

A different conclusion will involve us, and swiftly too, in a maze of contradictions. A guard stumbles over a package which has been left upon a platform. It seems to be a bundle of newspapers. It turns out to be a can of dynamite. To the eye of ordinary vigilance, the bundle is abandoned waste, which may be kicked or trod on with impunity. Is a passenger at the other end of the platform protected by the law against the unsuspected hazard concealed beneath the waste? If not, is the result to be any different, so far as the distant passenger is concerned, when the guard stumbles over a valise which a truckman or a porter has left upon the walk? The passenger far away, if the victim of a wrong at all, has a cause of action, not derivative, but original and primary. His claim to be protected against invasion of his bodily security is neither greater nor less because the act resulting in the invasion is a wrong to another far removed.

In this case, the rights that are said to have been violated, the interests said to have been invaded, are not even of the same order. The man was not injured in his person nor even put in danger. The purpose of the act, as well as its effect, was to make his person safe. If there was a wrong to him at all, which may very well be doubted it was a wrong to a property interest only, the safety of his package. Out of this wrong to property, which threatened injury to nothing else, there has passed, we are told, to the plaintiff by derivation or succession a right of action for the invasion of an interest of another order, the right to bodily security. The diversity of interests emphasizes the futility of the effort to build the plaintiff's right upon the basis of a wrong to someone else. The gain is one of emphasis, for a like result would follow if the interests were the same. Even then, the orbit of the danger as disclosed to the eye of reasonable vigilance would be the orbit of the duty. One who jostles one's neighbor in a crowd does not invade the rights of others standing at the outer fringe when the unintended contact casts a bomb upon the ground. The wrongdoer as to them is the man who carries the bomb, not the one who explodes it without suspicion of the danger. Life will have to be made over, and human nature transformed, before prevision so extravagant can be accepted as the norm of conduct, the customary standard to which behavior must conform.

The argument for the plaintiff is built upon the shifting meanings of such words as "wrong" and "wrongful," and shares their instability. What the plaintiff must show is "a wrong" to herself; i.e., a violation of her own right, and not merely a wrong to someone else, nor conduct "wrongful" because unsocial, but not "a wrong" to anyone. We are told that one who drives at reckless speed through a crowded city street is guilty of a negligent act and therefore of a wrongful one irrespective of the consequences. Negligent the act is and wrongful in the sense that it is unsocial, but wrongful and unsocial in relation to other travelers, only because the eye of vigilance perceives the risk of damage. If the same act were to be committed on a speedway or a race course, it would lose its wrongful quality. The risk reasonably to be perceived defines the duty to be obeyed, and risk imports relation; it is risk to another or to others within the range of apprehension. *

This does not mean, of course, that one who launches a destructive force is always relieved of liability, if the force, though known to be destructive, pursues an unexpected path. "It was not necessary that the defendant should have had notice of the particular method in which an accident would occur, if the possibility of an accident was clear to the ordinarily prudent eye." Munsey v. Webb, 231 U.S. 150, 156, 34 S.Ct. 44, 45, 58 L.Ed. 162 (1913). * Some acts, such as shooting, are so imminently dangerous to anyone who may come within reach of the missile however unexpectedly, as to impose a duty of prevision not far from that of an insurer. Even today, and much oftener in earlier stages of the law, one acts sometimes at one's peril. * Under this head, it may be, fall certain cases of what is known as transferred intent, an act willfully dangerous to A resulting by misadventure in injury to B. * These cases aside, wrong is defined in terms of the natural or probable, at least when unintentional. *

The range of reasonable apprehension is at times a question for the court, and at times, if varying inferences are possible, a question for the jury. Here, by concession, there was nothing in the situation to suggest to the most cautious mind that the parcel wrapped in newspaper would spread wreckage through the station. If the guard had thrown it down knowingly and willfully, he would not have threatened the plaintiff's safety, so far as appearances could warn him. His conduct would not have involved, even then, an unreasonable probability of invasion of her bodily security. Liability can be no greater where the act is inadvertent.

Negligence, like risk, is thus a term of relation. Negligence in the abstract, apart from things related, is surely not a tort, if indeed it is understandable at all. * Negligence is not a tort unless it results in the commission of a wrong, and the commission of a wrong imports the violation of a right, in this case, we are told, the right to be protected against interference with one's bodily security. But bodily security is protected, not against all forms of interference or aggression, but only against some.

One who seeks redress at law does not make out a cause of action by showing without more that there has been damage to his person. If the harm was not willful, he must show that the act as to him had possibilities of danger so many and apparent as to entitle him to be protected against the doing of it though the harm was unintended. Affront to personality is still the keynote of the wrong. Confirmation of this view will be found in the history and development of the action on the case. Negligence as a basis of civil liability was unknown to medieval law. * For damage to the person, the sole remedy was trespass, and trespass did not lie in the absence of aggression, and that direct and personal. * Liability for other damage, as where a servant without orders from the master does or omits something to the damage of another, is a plant of later growth. * When it emerged out of the legal soil, it was thought of as a variant of trespass, an offshoot of the parent stock. This appears in the form of action, which was known as trespass on the case. * The victim does not sue derivatively, or by right of subrogation, to vindicate an interest invaded in the person of another.

Thus to view his cause of action is to ignore the fundamental difference between tort and crime. * He sues for breach of a duty owing to himself.

The law of causation, remote or proximate, is thus foreign to the case before us. The question of liability is always anterior to the question of the measure of the consequences that go with liability. If there is no tort to be redressed, there is no occasion to consider what damage might be recovered if there were a finding of a tort. We may assume, without deciding, that negligence, not at large or in the abstract, but in relation to the plaintiff, would entail liability for any and all consequences, however novel or extraordinary. * There is room for argument that a distinction is to be drawn according to the diversity of interests invaded by the act, as where conduct negligent in that it threatens an insignificant invasion of an interest in property results in an unforeseeable invasion of an interest of another order, as, e.g., one of bodily security. Perhaps other distinctions may be necessary. We do not go into the question now. The consequences to be followed must first be rooted in a wrong.

The judgment of the Appellate Division and that of the Trial Term should be reversed, and the complaint dismissed, with costs in all courts.

■ ANDREWS, J. (dissenting). * * * The result we shall reach depends upon our theory as to the nature of negligence. Is it a relative concept— the breach of some duty owing to a particular person or to particular persons? Or, where there is an act which unreasonably threatens the safety of others, is the doer liable for all its proximate consequences, even where they result in injury to one who would generally be thought to be outside the radius of danger? This is not a mere dispute as to words. We might not believe that to the average mind the dropping of the bundle would seem to involve the probability of harm to the plaintiff standing many feet away whatever might be the case as to the owner or to one so near as to be likely to be struck by its fall. If, however, we adopt the second hypothesis, we have to inquire only as to the relation between cause and effect. We deal in terms of proximate cause, not of negligence.

Negligence may be defined roughly as an act or omission which unreasonably does or may affect the rights of others, or which unreasonably fails to protect oneself from the dangers resulting from such acts. Here I confine myself to the first branch of the definition. Nor do I comment on the word "unreasonable." For present purposes it sufficiently describes that average of conduct that society requires of its members. * * *

But we are told that "there is no negligence unless there is in the particular case a legal duty to take care, and this duty must be one which is owed to the plaintiff himself and not merely to others." John A. Salmond, Law of Torts 24 (6th ed. 1924). This, I think too narrow a conception. Where there is the unreasonable act, and some right that may be affected there is negligence whether damage does or does not result. That is immaterial. Should we drive down Broadway at a reckless speed, we are negligent whether we strike an approaching car or miss it by an inch. The act itself is wrongful. It is a wrong not only to those who happen to be within the radius of danger but to all who might have been there—a wrong to the public at large. Such is the language of the street. * * * As was said by Mr. Justice Holmes many years ago: "The measure of the defendant's duty in determining whether a wrong has been committed is one thing, the measure of liability when a wrong has been committed is another." Spade v. Lynn & Boston R.R., 172 Mass. 488, 491, 52 N.E. 747, 748 (1899). Due care is a duty imposed on each one of us to protect society from unnecessary danger, not to protect A, B or C alone.

It may well be that there is no such thing as negligence in the abstract. "Proof of negligence in the air, so to speak, will not do." In an empty world negligence would not exist. It does involve a relationship between man and his fellows, but not merely a relationship between man and those whom he might reasonably expect his act would injure, rather, a relationship between him and those whom he does in fact injure. If his act has a tendency to harm someone, it harms him a mile away as surely as it does those on the scene. We now permit children to recover for the negligent killing of the father. It was never prevented on the theory that no duty was owing to them. A husband may be compensated for the loss of his wife's services. To say that the wrongdoer was negligent as to the husband as well as to the wife is merely an attempt to fit facts to theory. An insurance company paying a fire loss recovers its payment of the negligent incendiary. We speak of subrogation—of suing in the right of the insured. Behind the cloud of words is the fact they hide, that the act, wrongful as to the insured, has also injured the company. Even if it be true that the fault of father, wife, or insured will prevent recovery, it is because we consider the original negligence not the proximate cause of the injury. * * *

The proposition is this. Every one owes to the world at large the duty of refraining from those acts that may unreasonably threaten the safety of others. Such an act occurs. Not only is he wronged to whom harm might reasonably be expected to result, but he also who is in fact injured, even if he be outside what would generally be thought the danger zone. There needs be duty due the one complaining but this is not a duty to a particular individual because as to him harm might be expected. Harm to someone being the natural result of the act, not only that one alone, but all those in fact injured may complain. We have never, I think, held otherwise. Indeed in the *Di Caprio* case [Di Caprio v. New York Cent. R.R. Co., 231 N.Y. 94, 131 N.E. 746 (1921)], we said that a breach of a general ordinance defining the degree of care to be exercised in one's calling is evidence of negligence as to everyone. We did not limit this statement to those who might be expected to be exposed to danger. Unreasonable risk being taken, its consequences are not confined to those who might probably be hurt. * * *

The right to recover damages rests on additional considerations. The plaintiff's rights must be injured, and this injury must be caused by the negligence. We build a dam, but are negligent as to its foundations. Breaking, it injures property downstream. We are not liable if all this happened because of some reason other than the insecure foundation. But when injuries do result from our unlawful act, we are liable for the consequences. It does not matter that they are unusual, unexpected, unforeseen, and unforeseeable. But there is one limitation. The damages must be so connected with the negligence that the latter may be said to be the proximate cause of the former.

These two words have never been given an inclusive definition. What is a cause in a legal sense, still more what is a proximate cause, depend in each case upon many considerations, as does the existence of negligence itself. Any philosophical doctrine of causation does not help us. A boy throws a stone into a pond. The ripples spread. The water level rises. The history of that pond is altered to all eternity. It will be altered by other causes also. Yet it will be forever the resultant of all causes combined. Each one will have an influence. How great only omniscience can say. You may speak of a chain, or, if you please, a net. An analogy is of little aid. Each cause brings about future events. Without each the future would not be the same. Each is proximate in the sense it is essential. But that is not what we mean by the word. Nor on the other hand do we mean sole cause. There is no such thing.

Should analogy be thought helpful, however, I prefer that of a stream. The spring, starting on its journey, is joined by tributary after tributary. The river, reaching the ocean, comes from a hundred sources. No man may say whence any drop of water is derived. Yet for a time distinction may be possible. Into the clear creek, brown swamp water flows from the left. Later, from the right comes water stained by its clay bed. The three may remain for a space, sharply divided. But at last inevitably no trace of separation remains. They are so commingled that all distinction is lost.

As we have said, we cannot trace the effect of an act to the end, if end there is. Again, however, we may trace it part of the way. A murder at Serajevo may be the necessary antecedent to an assassination in London twenty years hence. An overturned lantern may burn all Chicago. We may follow the fire from the shed to the last building. We rightly say the fire started by the lantern caused its destruction.

A cause, but not the proximate cause. What we do mean by the word "proximate" is, that because of convenience, of public policy, of a rough sense of justice, the law arbitrarily declines to trace a series of events beyond a certain point. This is not logic. It is practical politics. Take our rule as to fires. Sparks from my burning haystack set on fire my house and my neighbor's. I may recover from a negligent railroad. He may not. Yet the wrongful act as directly harmed the one as the other. We may regret that the line was drawn just where it was, but drawn somewhere it had to be. We said the act of the railroad was not the proximate cause of our neighbor's fire. Cause it surely was. The words we used were simply indicative of our notions of public policy. Other courts think differently. But somewhere they reach the point where they cannot say the stream comes from any one source.

Take the illustration given in an unpublished manuscript by a distinguished and helpful writer on the law of torts. A chauffeur negligently collides with another car which is filled with dynamite, although he could not know it. An explosion follows. A, walking on the sidewalk nearby, is killed. B, sitting in a window of a building opposite, is cut by flying glass. C, likewise sitting in a window a block away, is similarly injured. And a further illustration. A nursemaid, ten blocks away, startled by the noise, involuntarily drops a baby from her arms to the walk. We are told that C may not recover while A may. As to B it is a question for court or jury. We will all agree that the baby might not. Because, we are again told, the chauffeur had no reason to believe his conduct involved any risk of injuring either C or the baby. As to them he was not negligent.

But the chauffeur, being negligent in risking the collision, his belief that the scope of the harm he might do would be limited is immaterial. His act unreasonably jeopardized the safety of any one who might be affected by it. C's injury and that of the baby were directly traceable to the collision. Without that, the injury would not have happened. C had the right to sit in his office, secure from such dangers. The baby was entitled to use the sidewalk with reasonable safety.

The true theory is, it seems to me, that the injury to C, if in truth he is to be denied recovery, and the injury to the baby is that their several injuries were not the proximate result of the negligence. And here not what the chauffeur had reason to believe would be the result of his conduct, but what the prudent would foresee, may have a bearing— may have some bearing, for the problem of proximate cause is not to be solved by any one consideration.

It is all a question of expediency. There are no fixed rules to govern our judgment. There are simply matters of which we may take account. We have in a somewhat different connection spoken of "the stream of events." We have asked whether that stream was deflected—whether it was forced into new and unexpected channels. * This is rather rhetoric than law. There is in truth little to guide us other than common sense.

There are some hints that may help us. The proximate cause, involved as it may be with many other causes, must be, at the least, something without which the event would not happen. The court must ask itself whether there was a natural and continuous sequence between cause and effect. Was the one a substantial factor in producing the other? Was there a direct connection between them, without too many intervening causes? Is the effect of cause on result not too attenuated? Is the cause likely, in the usual judgment of mankind, to produce the result? Or, by the exercise of prudent foresight, could the result be foreseen? Is the result too remote from the cause, and here we consider remoteness in time and space. * Clearly we must so consider, for the greater the distance either in time or space, the more surely do other causes intervene to affect the result. When a lantern is overturned, the firing of a shed is a fairly direct consequence. Many things contribute to the spread of the conflagration—the force of the wind, the direction and width of streets, the character of intervening structures, other factors. We draw an uncertain and wavering line, but draw it we must as best we can.

Once again, it is all a question of fair judgment, always keeping in mind the fact that we endeavor to make a rule in each case that will be practical and in keeping with the general understanding of mankind.

Here another question must be answered. In the case supposed, it is said, and said correctly, that the chauffeur is liable for the direct effect of the explosion, although he had no reason to suppose it would follow a collision. "The fact that the injury occurred in a different manner than that which might have been expected does not prevent the chauffeur's negligence from being in law the cause of the injury." But the natural results of a negligent act—the results which a prudent man would or should foresee—do have a bearing upon the decision as to proximate cause. We have said so repeatedly. What should be foreseen? No human foresight would suggest that a collision itself might injure one a block away. On the contrary, given an explosion, such a possibility might be reasonably expected. I think the direct connection, the foresight of which the courts speak, assumes prevision of the explosion, for the immediate results of which, at least, the chauffeur is responsible.

It may be said this is unjust. Why? In fairness he should make good every injury flowing from his negligence. Not because of tenderness toward him we say he need not answer for all that follows his wrong. We look back to the catastrophe, the fire kindled by the spark, or the explosion. We trace the consequences, not indefinitely, but to a certain point. And to aid us in fixing that point we ask what might ordinarily be expected to follow the fire or the explosion.

This last suggestion is the factor which must determine the case before us. The act upon which defendant's liability rests is knocking an apparently harmless package onto the platform. The act was negligent. For its proximate consequences the defendant is liable. If its contents were broken, to the owner; if it fell upon and crushed a passenger's foot, then to him; if it exploded and injured one in the immediate vicinity, to him also as to A in the illustration. Mrs. Palsgraf was standing some distance away. How far cannot be told from the record—apparently twenty-five or thirty feet, perhaps less. Except for the explosion, she would not have been injured. We are told by the appellant in his brief, "It cannot be denied that the explosion was the direct cause of the plaintiff's injuries." So it was a substantial factor in producing the result—there was here a natural and continuous sequence—direct connection. The only intervening cause was that instead of blowing her to the ground the concussion smashed the weighing machine which in turn fell upon her. There was no remoteness in time, little in space. And surely, given such an explosion as here, it needed no great foresight to predict that the natural result would be to injure one on the platform at no greater distance from its scene than was the plaintiff. Just how no one might be able to predict. Whether by flying fragments, by broken glass, by wreckage of machines or structures no one could say. But injury in some form was most probable.

Under these circumstances I cannot say as a matter of law that the plaintiff's injuries were not the proximate result of the negligence. That is all we have before us. The court refused to so charge. No request was made to submit the matter to the jury as a question of fact, even would that have been proper upon the record before us.

The judgment appealed from should be affirmed, with costs.

■ POUND, LEHMAN, and KELLOGG, JJ., concur with CARDOZO, C.J.

■ ANDREWS, J., dissents in opinion in which CRANE and O'BRIEN, JJ., concur.

NOTES

1. *Underlying Facts.* A considerable body of literature has been produced discussing the *Palsgraf* case and its underlying facts. Among the prominent examples are John T. Noonan, Jr., Persons and Masks of the Law: Cardozo, Holmes, Jefferson, and Wythe as Makers of the Masks, 111–51 (2002);

Richard A. Posner, Cardozo, A Study in Reputation, 33–48 (1993); William
L. Prosser, *Palsgraf* Revisited, 52 Mich. L. Rev. 1, 4–5 (1953). See also the
trial record reprinted at Austin Wakeman Scott & Robert Brydon Kent,
Cases and Other Materials on Civil Procedure 1061 (2d ed. 1967); and
"Bomb Blast Injures 13 in Station Crowd," N.Y. Times, Aug. 25, 1924, at p.
1, col. 5.

Some of commentators find "disturbing" the manner in which
"Cardozo's famous opinion reduced the complex facts of the case to a bare
minimum." Walter O. Weyrauch, Law as Mask: Legal Ritual and Relevance
66 Cal. L. Rev. 699, 704 (1978). Professor Noonan's account of the
underlying facts provides both greater details and a focus on the socio-
economic circumstances of the parties:

> "Plaintiff" * * * was forty-three and the mother of three children,
> of whom the younger two, then fifteen and twelve, were with her
> at the time of the accident. * * * She testified that * * * she was
> "all alone."
>
> At the time of the accident Helen Palsgraf lived in a basement flat
> * * * performing janitorial work in the apartment building, for
> which she was allowed ten dollars a month on her rent. She did
> day work outside the apartment, earning two dollars a day or
> about eight dollars a week. She spoke English intelligibly but not
> with complete grammatical correctness.
>
> The day of the accident was a hot Sunday in August. She was
> taking Elizabeth and Lilian to the beach. * * * As a train started
> to pull out, there was the noise of an explosion. Then, "Flying
> glass—a ball of fire came, and we were choked in smoke, and I
> says 'Elizabeth turn your back,' and with that the scale blew and
> hit me on the side."
>
> Fire engines and ambulances arrived. She was trembling. A
> policeman led her into the waiting room. A doctor from an
> ambulance gave her something to drink. She took a taxi home.
> * * *
>
> Helen Palsgraf had been hit by the scales on the arm, hip, and
> thigh. The chief perceptible effect of the accident, according to the
> doctors, was a stammer. Dr. Parshall said that she began to
> stutter and stammer about a week after the event. Dr. Hammond
> declared that "it was with difficulty that she could talk at all."
> * * * The neurologist took the position that the stammer was
> symptomatic of a deeper trauma, associated with the litigation
> itself. * * *
>
> The two most important facts of the case from Helen Palsgraf's
> perspective must have been the time it took to be heard and the
> size of the verdict she won. The accident took place August 24,
> 1924. * * * The trial took place on May 25 and 26, 1927. For
> anyone who has been injured and is awaiting compensation, two
> years and nine months is a very long time to wait. * * * When the
> trial was finally held, she won a verdict fourteen times her annual
> income. Even if she could keep only half for herself, she had a
> fortune in prospect. * * *

> The defendant * * * carried annually over 80 million passengers. Since 1900 it had been a subsidiary of the Pennsylvania Railroad, which owned 99.2 percent of its stock. * * *
>
> In 1924 the Long Island's total assets were valued at $114 million * * * The parent Pennsylvania had a net income of $48 million and assets of $1.7 billion * * *.

Noonan, *supra*, 126–28.

The critiques of Noonan and others on the whole do not do justice to Cardozo's serious and recurring concern for a fundamental problem in negligence law: how to provide limits to liability for harm caused in the course of more or less legitimate activity carried out more or less in good faith, and the shortcomings of conventional "proximate cause" doctrine to achieve this end fairly. See also Posner, *supra,* at 42–45 (defending Cardozo's treatment of the facts as the deliberate avoidance of details that could lead to spurious distinctions in later cases).

2.   *Was the Defendant Negligent at All?* In Petition of Kinsman Transit Co., 338 F.2d 708 (2d Cir. 1964), Judge Friendly suggests that perhaps the defendant Long Island Railroad was not negligent at all:

> There was exceedingly little evidence of negligence of any sort. The only lack of care suggested by the majority in the Appellate Division was that instead of endeavoring to assist the passenger, the guards "might better have discouraged and warned him not to board the moving train." * * * How much ink would have been saved over the years if the Court of Appeals had reversed Mrs. Palsgraf's judgment on the basis that there was no evidence of negligence at all.

Id. at 721 n.5.

Judge Friendly also considers why Judge Cardozo found that no duty was owed to Mrs. Palsgraf:

> The important question is what was the basis for Chief Judge Cardozo's conclusion that the Long Island Railroad owed no "duty" to Mrs. Palsgraf under the circumstances. Certainly there is no general principle that a railroad owes no duty to persons on station platforms not in immediate proximity to the tracks, as would have been quickly demonstrated if Mrs. Palsgraf had been injured by the fall of improperly loaded objects from a passing train. * Neither is there any principle that railroad guards who jostle a package-carrying passenger owe a duty only to him; if the package had contained bottles, the Long Island would surely have been liable for injury caused to close bystanders by flying glass or spurting liquid. The reason why the Long Island was thought to owe no duty to Mrs. Palsgraf was the lack of any notice that the package contained a substance demanding the exercise of any care toward anyone so far away; Mrs. Palsgraf was not considered to be within the area of apparent hazard created by whatever lack of care the guard had displayed to the anonymous carrier of the unknown fireworks.

Id. at 721.

3.   *Duty.* Earlier, we considered "duty" in the case of National Food Stores, Inc. v. Union Electric Co., *supra* pages 133–136, and pages 136–138,

Note, which discusses *Heaven v. Pender*. What is the relationship between these opinions considered earlier and Judge Cardozo's opinion in *Palsgraf*?

4. *Judge and Jury.* What is the practical consequence of whether the issue in *Palsgraf* is viewed from Judge Cardozo's perspective or Judge Andrews's? If you represent the plaintiff in a personal injury action, in most cases, which perspective would you prefer that your jurisdiction follow? Is it the judge or the jury that decides whether a duty is owed to the plaintiff? According to Restatement (Third) of Torts: Liability for Physical and Emotional Harm § 7 cmt. b (2010):

> Courts determine legislative facts necessary to decide whether a no-duty rule is appropriate in a particular category of cases. In most cases, the adjudicative facts that bear on whether a duty exists are not in dispute. When resolution of disputed adjudicative facts bears on the existence or scope of a duty, the case should be submitted to the jury with alternative instructions.

In comparison, who decides whether the defendant's tortious conduct was a proximate cause (within the scope of liability) of the plaintiff's injury? Restatement (Third) of Torts: Liability for Physical and Emotional Harm § 29 comment *q* (2010) provides:

> * * * [T]he court's role is to instruct the jury on the standard for scope of liability when reasonable minds can differ as to whether the type of harm suffered by the plaintiff is among the harms whose risks made the defendant's conduct tortious, and it is the function of the jury to determine whether the harm is within the defendant's scope of liability.

5. *Palsgraf under Competing Perceptions of Tort Law.* Is Judge Cardozo's conception of tort law more in line with an instrumental theory of tort law or a corrective justice/civil recourse theory? See *supra* pages 17–18, Note 5. How about Judge Andrews's conception of tort law?

Overseas Tankship (U.K.) Ltd. v. Morts Dock & Engineering Co. Ltd. (The Wagon Mound No. 1)

Privy Council, 1961.
[1961] A.C. 388.

The respondents at the relevant time carried on the business of ship-building, ship-repairing and general engineering at Morts Bay, Balmain, in the Port of Sydney. They owned and used for their business the Sheerlegs Wharf, a timber wharf * * *. In October and November, 1951, a vessel known as the *Corrimel* was moored alongside the wharf and was being refitted by the respondents. Her mast was lying on the wharf and a number of the respondents' employees were working both upon it and upon the vessel itself, using for that purpose electric and oxy-acetylene welding equipment. At the same time the appellants were charterers by demise of the s.s. *Wagon Mound*, an oil-burning vessel, which was moored * * * about 600 feet from the Sheerlegs Wharf. She was there * * * for the purpose of discharging gasoline products and taking in bunkering oil.

During the early hours of October 30, 1951, a large quantity of bunkering oil was, through the carelessness of the appellants' servants, allowed to spill into the bay, and by 10.30 on the morning of that day it had spread over a considerable part of the bay, being thickly concentrated in some places and particularly along the foreshore near the respondents' property. The appellants made no attempt to disperse the oil. * * *

When the respondents' works manager became aware of the condition of things in the vicinity of the wharf he instructed their workmen that no welding or burning was to be carried on until further orders. He enquired of the manager of the Caltex Oil Company, at whose wharf the *Wagon Mound* was then still berthed, whether they could safely continue their operations on the wharf or upon the *Corrimel*. The results of the enquiry coupled with his own belief as to the inflammability of furnace oil in the open led him to think that the respondents could safely carry on their operations. He gave instructions accordingly, but directed that all safety precautions should be taken to prevent inflammable material falling off the wharf into the oil.

For the remainder of October 30 and until about 2 p.m. on November 1 work was carried on as usual, the condition and congestion of the oil remaining substantially unaltered. But at about that time the oil under or near the wharf was ignited and a fire, fed initially by the oil, spread rapidly and burned with great intensity. The wharf and the *Corrimel* caught fire and considerable damage was done to the wharf and the equipment upon it.

The outbreak of fire was due, as the judge found, to the fact that there was floating in the oil underneath the wharf a piece of debris on which lay some smouldering cotton waste or rag which had been set on fire by molten metal falling from the wharf: that the cotton waste or rag burst into flames, that the flames from the cotton waste set the floating oil afire either directly or by first setting fire to a wooden pile coated with oil, and that after the floating oil became ignited the flames spread rapidly over the surface of the oil and quickly developed into a conflagration which severely damaged the wharf.

* * * The trial judge also made the all-important finding, which must be set out in his own words: "The raison d'être of furnace oil is, of course, that it shall burn, but I find the defendant did not know and could not reasonably be expected to have known that it was capable of being set afire when spread on water." This finding was reached after a wealth of evidence * * *. One other finding must be mentioned. The judge held that apart from damage by fire the respondents had suffered some damage from the spillage of oil in that it had got upon their slipways and congealed upon them and interfered with their use of the slips. He said: "The evidence of this damage is slight and no claim for compensation is made in respect of it. Nevertheless it does establish some damage, which may be insignificant in comparison with the magnitude of the damage by fire, but which nevertheless is damage which, beyond question, was a direct result of the escape of the oil."

It is upon this footing that their Lordships will consider the question whether the appellants are liable for the fire damage. * * * It is inevitable that first consideration should be given to the case of *In re Polemis and Furness Withy & Co. Ltd.*,[1] which will henceforward be referred to as *Polemis*. For it was avowedly in deference to that decision

---

[1]   1921] 3 K.B. 560; 37 T.L.R. 940, C.A. [See *supra* pages 284–287].

and to decisions of the Court of Appeal that followed it that the Full Court was constrained to decide the present case in favour of the respondents. * * *

If the line of relevant authority had stopped with *Polemis*, their Lordships might, whatever their own views as to its unreason, have felt some hesitation about overruling it. But it is far otherwise. It is true that both in England and in many parts of the Commonwealth that decision has from time to time been followed; but in Scotland it has been rejected with determination. It has never been subject to the express scrutiny of either the House of Lords or the Privy Council, though there have been comments upon it in those Supreme Tribunals. Even in the inferior courts judges have, sometimes perhaps unwittingly, declared themselves in a sense adverse to its principle. * * *

Enough has been said to show that the authority of *Polemis* has been severely shaken though lip-service has from time to time been paid to it. In their Lordships' opinion it should no longer be regarded as good law. It is not probable that many cases will for that reason have a different result, though it is hoped that the law will be thereby simplified, and that in some cases, at least, palpable injustice will be avoided. For it does not seem consonant with current ideas of justice or morality that for an act of negligence, however slight or venial, which results in some trivial foreseeable damage the actor should be liable for all consequences however unforeseeable and however grave, so long as they can be said to be "direct." It is a principle of civil liability, subject only to qualifications which have no present relevance, that a man must be considered to be responsible for the probable consequences of his act. To demand more of him is too harsh a rule, to demand less is to ignore that civilised order requires the observance of a minimum standard of behaviour.

This concept applied to the slowly developing law of negligence has led to a great variety of expressions which can, as it appears to their Lordships, be harmonised with little difficulty with the single exception of the so-called rule in *Polemis*. For, if it is asked why a man should be responsible for the natural or necessary or probable consequences of his act (or any other similar description of them) the answer is that it is not because they are natural or necessary or probable, but because, since they have this quality, it is judged by the standard of the reasonable man that he ought to have foreseen them. Thus it is that over and over again it has happened that in different judgments in the same case, and sometimes in a single judgment, liability for a consequence has been imposed on the ground that it was reasonably foreseeable or, alternatively, on the ground that it was natural or necessary or probable. The two grounds have been treated as coterminous, and so they largely are. But, where they are not, the question arises to which the wrong answer was given in *Polemis*. For, if some limitation must be imposed upon the consequences for which the negligent actor is to be held responsible—and all are agreed that some limitation there must be—why should that test (reasonable foreseeability) be rejected which, since he is judged by what the reasonable man ought to foresee, corresponds with the common conscience of mankind, and a test (the "direct" consequence) be substituted which leads to nowhere but the never-ending and insoluble problems of causation. "The lawyer," said

Sir Frederick Pollock, "cannot afford to adventure himself with philosophers in the logical and metaphysical controversies that beset the idea of cause." Yet this is just what he has most unfortunately done and must continue to do if the rule in *Polemis* is to prevail. * * *

In the same connection may be mentioned the conclusion to which the Full Court finally came in the present case. Applying the rule in *Polemis* and holding therefore that the unforeseeability of the damage by fire afforded no defence, they went on to consider the remaining question. Was it a "direct" consequence? Upon this J. Manning said: "Notwithstanding that, if regard is had separately to each individual occurrence in the chain of events that led to this fire, each occurrence was improbable and, in one sense, improbability was heaped upon improbability, I cannot escape from the conclusion that if the ordinary man in the street had been asked, as a matter of common sense, without any detailed analysis of the circumstances, to state the cause of the fire at Mort's Dock, he would unhesitatingly have assigned such cause to spillage of oil by the appellant's employees." Perhaps he would, and probably he would have added: "I never should have thought it possible." * * * After the event even a fool is wise. But it is not the hindsight of a fool; it is the foresight of the reasonable man which alone can determine responsibility. The *Polemis* rule by substituting "direct" for "reasonably foreseeable" consequence leads to a conclusion equally illogical and unjust.

At an early stage in this judgment their Lordships intimated that they would deal with the proposition which can best be stated by reference to the well-known dictum of Lord Sumner: "This however goes to culpability not to compensation." It is with the greatest respect to that very learned judge and to those who have echoed his words, that their Lordships find themselves bound to state their view that this proposition is fundamentally false.

It is, no doubt, proper when considering tortious liability for negligence to analyse its elements and to say that the plaintiff must prove a duty owed to him by the defendant, a breach of that duty by the defendant, and consequent damage. But there can be no liability until the damage has been done. It is not the act but the consequences on which tortious liability is founded. Just as (as it has been said) there is no such thing as negligence in the air, so there is no such thing as liability in the air. Suppose an action brought by A for damage caused by the carelessness (a neutral word) of B, for example, a fire caused by the careless spillage of oil. It may, of course, become relevant to know what duty B owed to A, but the only liability that is in question is the liability for damage by fire. It is vain to isolate the liability from its context and to say that B is or is not liable, and then to ask for what damage he is liable. For his liability is in respect of that damage and no other. If, as admittedly it is, B's liability (culpability) depends on the reasonable foreseeability of the consequent damage, how is that to be determined except by the foreseeability of the damage which in fact happened—the damage in suit? And, if that damage is unforeseeable so as to displace liability at large, how can the liability be restored so as to make compensation payable?

But, it is said, a different position arises if B's careless act has been shown to be negligent and has caused some foreseeable damage to A.

Their Lordships have already observed that to hold B liable for consequences however unforeseeable of a careless act, if, but only if, he is at the same time liable for some other damage however trivial, appears to be neither logical nor just. This becomes more clear if it is supposed that similar unforeseeable damage is suffered by A and C but other foreseeable damage, for which B is liable, by A only. A system of law which would hold B liable to A but not to C for the similar damage suffered by each of them could not easily be defended. Fortunately, the attempt is not necessary. For the same fallacy is at the root of the proposition. It is irrelevant to the question whether B is liable for unforeseeable damage that he is liable for foreseeable damage, as irrelevant as would the fact that he had trespassed on Whiteacre be to the question whether he has trespassed on Blackacre. Again, suppose a claim by A for damage by fire by the careless act of B. Of what relevance is it to that claim that he has another claim arising out of the same careless act? It would surely not prejudice his claim if that other claim failed: it cannot assist it if it succeeds. Each of them rests on its own bottom, and will fail if it can be established that the damage could not reasonably be foreseen. * * *

Their Lordships will humbly advise Her Majesty that this appeal should be allowed, and the respondents' action so far as it related to damage caused by the negligence of the appellants be dismissed with costs. * * *

NOTES

1. *The "Thin Skull Rule."* What if, as a result of the plaintiff's pre-existing physical condition, the defendant's negligence or other tortious conduct causes far greater injury to the plaintiff than it would to a person of ordinary physical vulnerability or sensitivity? The universal rule of tort law is that "the defendant takes his victim as he finds him." For example, in Smith v. Leech Brain & Co., [1962] 2 Q.B. 405, plaintiff's decedent was burned on the lip by a piece of molten metal as a result of defendant's negligence. As a result of similar incidents in the past, decedent had developed a susceptibility toward cancer. The burn, in fact, developed into cancer. The court acknowledged that death by cancer was not a foreseeable result of the burn, but nevertheless found that the defendant took his victim as he found him:

> The test is not whether these employers could reasonably have foreseen that a burn would cause cancer and that he would die. The question is whether these employers could reasonably foresee the type of injury he suffered, namely, the burn. What, in the particular case, is the amount of damage which he suffers as a result of that burn, depends upon the characteristics and constitution of the victim.

Suppose a driver strikes and kills a pedestrian in a shabby, skid row area of a city typically frequented by homeless winos, drunks, and drug-abusers. However, the deceased pedestrian is in fact the world's leading neurosurgeon, the mother of two adoring (and adorable) children, and the wife of a stay-at-home dad. Is the driver liable for the full amount of the family's losses under the wrongful death statute even though the defendant could never have foreseen such losses? See Schafer v. Hoffman, 831 P.2d

897 (Colo.1992) (discussing "shabby millionaire" doctrine as a corollary of thin-skull rule).

Can the thin skull rule and the shabby millionaire doctrine be reconciled with *Wagon Mound I*?

2. *Contemporaneous American Cases.* What implication, if any, should the *Palsgraf* decision hold for the issues considered in *Polemis*? During the 1960s, the questions reflected in *Polemis* were intensely considered not only in *Wagon Mound I*, but in the United States as well when defendants prevailed in litigation arising from the Texas City disaster, Republic of France v. United States, 290 F.2d 395 (5th Cir.1961). A cargo of Fertilizer Grade Ammonium Nitrate (FGAN) exploded, causing over 500 deaths, 3000 personal injuries, and "tremendous destruction" of property. The ship's master was found negligent in permitting the fire to start, and in failing to extinguish it early. The district court further found that he "should have foreseen and anticipated the danger of a disastrous fire, with the *possibility* of explosion," but that, "[f]rom the literature and information generally available * * * in the exercise of ordinary care, the Master could [not] have foreseen the probability of an explosion *of this sort*, even in the presence of fire." (emphasis by appellate court).

On appeal, defendants were held "not liable for any claim arising out of or consequent upon the explosion of the steamship." The court emphasized, in a split decision, that there had been no previous known instance of explosion of FGAN in storage or transit; that "it is only the operation of natural forces theretofore recognized as normal which one is charged with foreseeing;" and that "the explosion as distinguished from the fire, could not reasonably have been foreseen." The court also quoted a Supreme Court reference, in an earlier case involving somewhat different issues, to a Cardozo statement, in a products liability case not involving causation, that " '[t]here must be knowledge of a danger, not merely possible, but probable,' MacPherson v. Buick Motor Co., 217 N.Y. 382, 389, 111 N.E. 1050, 1053." (*infra* pages 576–579).

Then the wind shifted.

Hughes v. Lord Advocate
House of Lords, 1963.
[1963] A.C. 837, [1963] 2 W.L.R. 779, 107 S.J. 232, [1963] 1 All E.R. 705, 1963 S.C. (H.L.) 31, 1963 S.L.T. 150.

[Workers had left unguarded an open manhole covered by a tent, with paraffin-fueled burning warning lights. Two children entered, took and dropped a lamp. Paraffin (kerosene) spilled, vaporized, was ignited and exploded. The explosion knocked a child into the hole and spread hot paraffin, which burned him as he tried to get out. The court below, ruling for defendants, found that there was a low probability that this sequence of events should occur, and that it was so unforeseeable that a reasonable man would be excused if he disregarded it.]

■ LORD REID. * * * It was argued that the appellant cannot recover because the damage which he suffered was of a kind which was not foreseeable. * * * [T]he facts proved do not, in my judgment, support that argument. The appellant's injuries were mainly caused by burns, and it cannot be said that injuries from burns were unforeseeable. As a warning to traffic the workmen had set lighted red lamps round the tent which covered the manhole, and if boys did enter the dark tent it was very likely that they would take one of these lamps with them. If the lamp fell and broke it was not at all unlikely that the boy would be burned and the burns might well be serious. No doubt it was not to be expected that the injuries would be as serious as those which the appellant in fact sustained. But a defender is liable, although the damage may be a good deal greater in extent than was foreseeable. He can only escape liability if the damage can be regarded as differing in kind from what was foreseeable. * * * The cause of this accident was a known source of danger, the lamp, but it behaved in an unpredictable way. * * * [I]n my judgment, that affords no defence. I would therefore allow the appeal.

■ LORD JENKINS. * * * It is true that the duty of care expected in cases of this sort is confined to reasonably foreseeable dangers, but it does not necessarily follow that liability is escaped because the danger actually materialising is not identical with the danger reasonably foreseen and guarded against. * * * To my mind, the distinction drawn between burning and explosion is too fine to warrant acceptance. Supposing the pursuer had on the day in question gone to the site and taken one of the lamps, and upset it over himself, thus setting his clothes alight, the person to be considered responsible for protecting children from the dangers to be found there would presumably have been liable * * *. If there is a risk of such a fire as that, I do not think the duty of care * * * is prevented from coming into operation by the presence of the remote possibility of the more serious event of an explosion. * * *

■ LORD GUEST. * * * In order to establish a coherent chain of causation it is not necessary that the precise details leading up to the accident should have been reasonably foreseeable: it is sufficient if the accident which occurred is of a type which should have been foreseeable by a reasonably careful person * * *. An explosion is only one way in which burning can be caused. * * * [T]he explosion was an immaterial event in the chain of causation. It was simply one way in which burning might be caused by the potentially dangerous paraffin lamp. * * *

■ LORD PEARCE. * * * The obvious risks were burning and conflagration and a fall. All these in fact occurred, but unexpectedly the mishandled lamp instead of causing an ordinary conflagration produced a violent explosion. Did the explosion create an accident and damage of a different type from the misadventure and damage that could be foreseen? In my judgment it did not. The accident was but a variant of the foreseeable. It was, to quote the words of Denning L.J. in Roe v. Minister of Health,[59] "within the risk created by the negligence." No unforeseeable, extraneous initial occurrence fired the train. * * * [I]t would be, I think, too narrow a view to hold that those who created the risk of fire are excused from the liability for the damage by fire because it came by way of explosive combustion. The resulting damage, though severe, was not greater than or different in kind from that which might have been produced had the lamp spilled and produced a more normal conflagration in the hole. * * *

---

[59] [1954] 2 Q.B. 6] Q.B. 66, 85, [1954] 2 W.L.R. 915, [1954] 2 All E.R. 131, C.A..

Overseas Tankship (U.K.) Ltd. v. The Miller Steamship Co. Pty. (The Wagon Mound No. 2)

Privy Council, 1967.
[1967] 1 A.C. 617, [1966] 3 W.L.R. 498, [1966] 2 All E.R. 709.

[Action arising from the same accident as *Wagon Mound I*, at pages 303–07 above. In this case, the plaintiffs are the owners of ships that were damaged by the fire. Unlike Morts Dry Dock and Engineering Co., which was constrained by considerations of contributory negligence, these plaintiffs contended that the inflammability of the oil was foreseeable.]

■ LORD REID. * * * The findings of the learned trial judge are as follows:

(1) Reasonable people in the position of the officers of the *Wagon Mound* would regard the furnace oil as very difficult to ignite upon water. (2) Their personal experience would probably have been that this had very rarely happened. (3) If they had given attention to the risk of fire from the spillage, they would have regarded it as a possibility, but one which could become an actuality only in very exceptional circumstances. (4) They would have considered the chances of the required exceptional circumstances happening whilst the oil remained spread on the harbour waters, as being remote. (5) I find that the occurrence of damage to the plaintiff's property as a result of the spillage was not reasonably foreseeable by those for whose acts the defendant would be responsible. (6) I find that the spillage of oil was brought about by the careless conduct of persons for whose acts the defendant would be responsible. (7) I find that the spillage of oil was a cause of damage to the property of each of the plaintiffs. (8) Having regard to those findings, and because of finding (5), I hold that the claim of each of the plaintiffs, framed in negligence, fails. * * *

The crucial finding of Walsh J. in this case is in finding (5): that the damage was "not reasonably foreseeable by those for whose acts the defendant would be responsible." That is not a primary finding of fact but an inference from the other findings, and it is clear from the learned Judge's judgment that in drawing this inference he was to a large extent influenced by his view of the law. The vital parts of the findings of fact which have already been set out in full are (1) that the officers of the *Wagon Mound* * "would regard furnace oil as very difficult to ignite upon water"—not that they would regard this as impossible; (2) that their experience would probably have been "that this had very rarely happened"—not that they would never have heard of a case where it had happened, and (3) that they would have regarded it as a "possibility, but one which could become an actuality only in very exceptional circumstances"—not, as in *The Wagon Mound (No. 1)*, * that they could not reasonably be expected to have known that this oil was capable of being set afire when spread on water. The question which must now be determined is whether these differences between the findings in the two cases do or do not lead to different results in law.

In *The Wagon Mound (No. 1)* * the Board were not concerned with degrees of foreseeability because the finding was that the fire was not foreseeable at all. So Lord Simonds had no cause to amplify the statement that the "essential factor in determining liability is whether the damage is of such a kind as the reasonable man should have foreseen." * But here the findings show that some risk of fire would have been present to the mind of a reasonable man in the shoes of the ship's chief engineer. So the first question must be what is the precise meaning to be attached in this context to the words "foreseeable" and "reasonably foreseeable."

Before *Bolton v. Stone*[181] the cases had fallen into two classes: (1) those where, before the event, the risk of its happening would have been regarded as unreal either because the event would have been thought to be physically impossible or because the possibility of its happening would have been regarded as so fantastic or farfetched that no reasonable man would have paid any attention to it—"a mere possibility which would never occur to the mind of a reasonable man" (per Lord Dunedin in *Fardon v. Harcourt-Rivington*[182])—or (2) those where there was a real and substantial risk or chance that something like the event which happens might occur, and then the reasonable man would have taken the steps necessary to eliminate the risk.

Bolton v. Stone * posed a new problem. There a member of a visiting team drove a cricket ball out of the ground onto an unfrequented adjacent public road and it struck and severely injured a lady who happened to be standing in the road. That it might happen that a ball would be driven onto this road could not have been said to be a fantastic or far-fetched possibility: according to the evidence it had happened about six times in 28 years. And it could not have been said to be a far-fetched or fantastic possibility that such a ball would strike someone in the road: people did pass along the road from time to time. So it could not have been said that, on any ordinary meaning of the words, the fact that a ball might strike a person in the road was not foreseeable or reasonably foreseeable—it was plainly foreseeable. But the chance of its happening in the foreseeable future was infinitesimal. A mathematician given the data could have worked out that it was only likely to happen once in so many thousand years. The House of Lords held that the risk was so small that in the circumstances a reasonable man would have been justified in disregarding it and taking no steps to eliminate it.

But it does not follow that, no matter what the circumstances may be, it is justifiable to neglect a risk of such a small magnitude. A reasonable man would only neglect such a risk if he had some valid reason for doing so, e.g., that it would involve considerable expense to eliminate the risk. He would weigh the risk against the difficulty of eliminating it. If the activity which caused the injury to Miss Stone had been an unlawful activity, there can be little doubt but that *Bolton v. Stone* * would have been decided differently. In their Lordships' judgment *Bolton v. Stone* * did not alter the general principle that a person must be regarded as negligent if he does not take steps to eliminate a risk which he knows or ought to know is a real risk and not

---

[181] [1951] A.C. 850, [1951] 1 T.L.R. 977, [1951] 1 All E.R. 1078, H.L.
[182] [1932] 146 L.T. 391.

* * * [T]his does not dispose of the alternative argument that the manner in which several of the claimants were harmed, particularly by flood damage, was unforeseeable and that recovery for this may not be had—whether the argument is put in the forthright form that unforeseeable damages are not recoverable or is concealed under a formula of lack of "proximate cause." * * * Foreseeability of danger is necessary to render conduct negligent; whereas here the damage was caused by just those forces whose existence required the exercise of greater care than was taken—the current, the ice, and the physical mass of the *Shiras*, the incurring of consequences other and greater than foreseen does not make the conduct less culpable or provide a reasoned basis for insulation.[9] * The oft encountered argument that failure to limit liability to foreseeable consequences may subject the defendant to a loss wholly out of proportion to his fault seems scarcely consistent with the universally accepted rule that the defendant takes the plaintiff as he finds him and will be responsible for the full extent of the injury even though a latent susceptibility of the plaintiff renders this far more serious than could reasonably have been anticipated. *

The weight of authority in this country rejects the limitation of damages to consequences foreseeable at the time of the negligent conduct when the consequences are "direct," and the damage, although other and greater than expectable, is of the same general sort that was risked. * * * Other American courts, purporting to apply a test of foreseeability to damages, extend that concept to such unforeseen lengths as to raise serious doubt whether the concept is meaningful * * *.[10]

We see no reason why an actor engaging in conduct which entails a large risk of small damage and a small risk of other and greater damage, of the same general sort, from the same forces, and to the same class of persons, should be relieved of responsibility for the latter simply because the chance of its occurrence, if viewed alone, may not have been large enough to require the exercise of care. By hypothesis, the risk of the lesser harm was sufficient to render his disregard of it actionable; the existence of a less likely additional risk that the very forces against whose action he was required to guard would produce other and greater damage than could have been reasonably anticipated should inculpate him further rather than limit his liability. This does not mean that the

---

[9]   The contrasting situation is illustrated by the familiar instance[ ] * * * of the explosion of unlabeled rat poison, inflammable but not known to be, placed near a coffee burner. * Larrimore v. American Nat. Ins. Co., 184 Okl. 614, 89 P.2d 340 (1939). Exoneration of the defendant in such cases rests on the basis that a negligent actor is responsible only for harm the risk of which was increased by the *negligent aspect* of his conduct. * * * (emphasis added by editors).

[10]   An instance is In re Guardian Casualty Co., 253 App. Div. 360, 2 N.Y.S.2d 232, aff'd, 278 N.Y. 674, 16 N.E.2d 397 (1938), where the majority gravely asserted that a foreseeable consequence of driving a taxicab too fast was that a collision with another car would project the cab against a building with such force as to cause a portion of the building to collapse twenty minutes later, when the cab was being removed, and injure a spectator twenty feet away. Surely this is "straining the idea of foreseeability past the breaking point," [Francis H.] Bohlen, Book Review, 47 Harv. L. Rev. 556, 557 (1934), at least if the matter be viewed as of the time of the negligent act, as the supposedly symmetrical test of *The Wagon Mound* demands, [1961] 1 All E.R. at 415. On the other hand, if the issue of foreseeability is viewed as of the moment of impact, see [Warren A.] Seavey, Mr. Justice Cardozo and the Law of Torts, 52 Harv. L. Rev. 372, 385 (1939), the test loses functional significance since at that time the defendant is no longer able to amend his conduct so as to avert the consequences.

careless actor will always be held for all damages for which the forces that he risked were a cause in fact. Somewhere a point will be reached when courts will agree that the link has become too tenuous—that what is claimed to be consequence is only fortuity. Thus, if the destruction of the Michigan Avenue Bridge had delayed the arrival of a doctor, with consequent loss of a patient's life, few judges would impose liability on any of the parties here, although the agreement in result might not be paralleled by similar unanimity in reasoning; perhaps in the long run one returns to Judge Andrews' statement in Palsgraf, 248 N.Y. at 354–55, 162 N.E. at 104 (dissenting opinion). "It is all a question of expediency, . . . of fair judgment, always keeping in mind the fact that we endeavor to make a rule in each case that will be practical and in keeping with the general understanding of mankind."

It would be pleasant if greater certainty were possible, * but the many efforts that have been made at defining the *locus* of the "uncertain and wavering line," * are not very promising; what courts do in such cases makes better sense than what they, or others, say. Where the line will be drawn will vary from age to age; as society has come to rely increasingly on insurance and other methods of loss-sharing, the point may lie further off than a century ago. Here it is surely more equitable that the losses from the operators' negligent failure to raise the Michigan Avenue Bridge should be ratably borne by Buffalo's taxpayers than left with the innocent victims of the flooding; yet the mind is also repelled by a solution that would impose liability solely on the City and exonerate the persons whose negligent acts of commission and omission were the precipitating force of the collision with the bridge and its *sequelae*. We go only so far as to hold that where, as here, the damages resulted from the same physical forces whose existence required the exercise of greater care than was displayed and were of the same general sort that was expectable, unforeseeability of the exact developments and of the extent of the loss will not limit liability. Other fact situations can be dealt with when they arise. * * *

■ MOORE, CIRCUIT JUDGE. (concurring and dissenting): * * * I cannot agree, however, merely because "society has come to rely increasingly on insurance and other methods of loss-sharing" that the courts should, or have the power to, create a vast judicial insurance company which will adequately compensate all who have suffered damages. Equally disturbing is the suggestion that "[h]ere it is surely more equitable that the losses from the operators' negligent failure to raise the Michigan Avenue Bridge should be ratably borne by Buffalo's taxpayers than left with the innocent victims of the flooding." Under any such principle, negligence suits would become further simplified by requiring a claimant to establish only his own innocence and then offer, in addition to his financial statement, proof of the financial condition of the respective defendants. Judgment would be entered against the defendant which court or jury decided was best able to pay. Nor am I convinced that it should be the responsibility of the Buffalo taxpayers to reimburse the "innocent victims" in their community for damages sustained. In my opinion, before financial liability is imposed, there should be some showing of legal liability. * * *

My dissent is limited to that portion of the opinion which approves the awarding of damages suffered as a result of the flooding of various properties upstream. I am not satisfied with reliance on hindsight or on the assumption that since flooding occurred, therefore, it must have been foreseeable. * * *

If "foreseeability" be the test, I can foresee the likelihood that a vessel negligently allowed to break its moorings and to drift uncontrolled in a rapidly flowing river may well strike other ships, piers and bridges. Liability would also result on the "direct consequence" theory. However, to me the fortuitous circumstance of the vessels so arranging themselves as to create a dam is much "too tenuous." * * *

2.   INTERVENING AND SUPERSEDING CAUSES

This section analyzes how the conduct of another party, contributing as a cause in fact to the plaintiff's injury and occurring after the defendant's negligence, affects the liability of the original defendant. An "intervening cause" is one that takes effect after the conduct of the actor and operates in producing harm to the plaintiff. See Restatement (Third) of Torts: Liability for Physical and Emotional Harm § 34 cmt. b (2010). A "superseding cause" is an intervening cause that prevents the original tortfeasor from being held liable to the plaintiff. In short, "[t]hese terms are only conclusory labels."

The trick, of course, is figuring out when an intervening cause is also a superseding cause. As we shall see, most courts today talk about the foreseeability of the intervention as the factor that makes it non-superseding. It is important to remember that if the second actor's conduct is negligent and is a factual and proximate cause of the accident, then the original tortfeasor and the second actor will be jointly and severally liable. In many cases, however, the second actor may be judgment proof or beyond the jurisdiction of the court, so the potential liability of the original tortfeasor remains crucial to plaintiff's recovery.

NOTE

Last Wrongdoer Rule. In Vicars v. Wilcocks, (1806) 103 Eng.Rep. 244 (K.B), 8 East's Reports 1, the plaintiff was the victim of a slander spoken by the defendant to plaintiff's employer, who had fired the plaintiff because of the slander; the plaintiff then applied to a fourth person for another job, but was denied employment because he had been fired by his previous employer. The court found the discharge by the employer as having been wrongful (for reasons not made clear). It regarded both the defendant and the employer to have been wrongdoers, the defendant for the slander and the employer for the subsequent wrongful discharge. A modern court might well treat them as joint tortfeasors, each subject to liability for plaintiff's ultimate loss. But the King's Bench in 1806 treated defendant as not subject to liability for harm caused by the "illegal consequence" of the slander, the wrongful discharge—without inquiry as to whether that consequence should have been foreseeable to defendant.

Vicars reflects a concept that became known as the "last wrongdoer rule," an archaic notion that there can be only one "proximate" cause of an event and that it should be the one nearest in time to that event. It dates from a time when courts were reluctant to consider multiple causes for harms, and instead sought to identify a single responsible cause—in some sense the most significant cause, the one closest to the harm, hence the most "proximate." Where there was more than one wrongdoer, successive in time, there was a tendency for the wrongful conduct of the latest wrongdoer in the chain of events to be regarded as the sole proximate cause of the harm, thereby in effect erasing the potential liability of the earlier wrongdoer[s] whose wrongful acts had also contributed to plaintiff's loss.

The shortcomings of this view were appreciated long ago, as in Illidge v. Goodwin, (1831) 172 Eng.Rep. 934 (Assizes), 5 Carrington & Payne's Reports 100. There the defendant had carelessly parked a horse and cart outside a china shop, unattended, backed against the shop's window. This could be considered negligent because of the risk that something could cause the horse to move and break the window. The defendant claimed that a passerby had slapped the horse. This, the court held, would be no defense, even if true. The risk of "any mischief" was what made defendant's conduct negligent. The notion that could have been derived from *Vicars*, that a third-party slapper could be considered a "last wrongdoer," thereby erasing the defendant's earlier wrongdoing as a cause of plaintiff's loss, was not applied.

The last wrongdoer rule never commanded wide support as a test for limiting defendant's liability in ordinary negligence cases. Perhaps it is significant that the case where the rule first found expression was not a personal injury action at all, but one of the disfavored type of slander. Yet vestiges of this largely discredited doctrine linger in certain applications, e.g., a suit against a governmental unit for a highway defect when the accident was also contributed to by another wrongdoer, generally another driver. A leading torts treatise concludes:

> The last wrongdoer rule is subject to criticism where it is invoked. It reflects no vital modern policy, but only earlier mechanistic notions. And it is irreconcilable with large bodies of existing case law. The last wrongdoer is not always held liable for damage that ensures, on the other hand a wrongdoer who is not closest in point of time to the plaintiff's injury is often held liable. At best the last wrongdoer test yields a "correct" result only by chance.

Harper, James and Gray on Torts § 20.6(5). Several of the cases that follow in this section consider the question of whether the defendant can be held liable even though he is not the last wrongdoer.

Vesely v. Sager

Supreme Court of California, In Bank, 1971.
5 Cal.3d 153, 95 Cal.Rptr. 623, 486 P.2d 151.

■ WRIGHT, CHIEF JUSTICE. In this case we are called upon to decide whether civil liability may be imposed upon a vendor of alcoholic beverages for providing alcoholic drinks to a customer who, as a result of intoxication, injures a third person. * * *

Defendant Sager owned and operated the Buckhorn Lodge * * * and was engaged in the business of selling alcoholic beverages to the general public. Beginning about 10 p.m. on April 8, 1968, Sager served or permitted defendant O'Connell to be served large quantities of alcoholic beverages. At the time the beverages were served, Sager knew that O'Connell was becoming excessively intoxicated and that O'Connell was "incapable of exercising the same degree of volitional control over his consumption of intoxicants as the average reasonable person." Sager also knew that the only route leaving the Buckhorn Lodge was a very steep, winding, and narrow mountain road and that O'Connell was going to drive down that road. Nevertheless, Sager continued to serve O'Connell alcoholic drinks past the normal closing time of 2 a.m. until 5:15 a.m. on April 9. After leaving the lodge, O'Connell drove down the road, veered into the opposite lane, and struck plaintiff's vehicle. * * *

Defendant Sager demurred to the complaint on the ground that a "seller of intoxicating liquors is not liable for injuries resulting from intoxication" of a buyer thereof * * *. The trial court sustained the demurrer * * *. Plaintiff appeals. * * *

Until fairly recently, it was uniformly held that an action could not be maintained at common law against the vendor of alcoholic beverages for furnishing such beverages to a customer who, as a result of being intoxicated, injured himself or a third person. * The rationale for the common law rule was that the consumption and not the sale of liquor was the proximate cause of injuries sustained as a result of intoxication. * "The rule was based on the obvious fact that one cannot be intoxicated by reason of liquor furnished him if he does not drink it." * The common law rule has been substantially abrogated in many states by statutes which specifically impose civil liability upon a furnisher of intoxicating liquor under specified circumstances. * California, however, has not enacted similar legislation. * * *

[V]arious courts in other jurisdictions have reevaluated the common law rule that the vendor of intoxicating liquor cannot be held liable for injuries resulting from intoxication, and in particular the rule that the seller cannot be held liable for furnishing alcoholic beverages to a customer who injures a third person. A substantial number, if not a majority, have decided that the sale of alcoholic beverages may be the proximate cause of such injuries and that liability may be imposed upon the vendor in favor of the injured third person. * * * The two leading cases abrogating or modifying the common law rule are Waynick v. Chicago's Last Dept. Store, 269 F.2d 322 (7th Cir.1959), and Rappaport v. Nichols, 31 N.J. 188, 156 A.2d 1 (1959). * * * *Rappaport* involved a wrongful death action by a widow against the operators of four taverns for selling liquor to an intoxicated minor who negligently killed her husband in an automobile accident. * * * [T]he court rejected the defendants' contention that their conduct, if negligent, was not the proximate cause of the injuries suffered. It stated: "But a tortfeasor is generally held answerable for the injuries which result in the ordinary course of events from his negligence and it is generally sufficient if his negligent conduct was a substantial factor in bringing about the injuries. The fact that there were also intervening causes which were foreseeable or were normal incidents of the risk created would not relieve the tortfeasor of liability. Ordinarily these questions of proximate and intervening cause are left to the jury for its factual determination." [citations omitted by the court]. * * *

To the extent that the common law rule of nonliability is based on concepts of proximate cause, we are persuaded by the reasoning of the cases that have abandoned that rule. The decisions in those jurisdictions which have abandoned the common law rule invoke principles of proximate cause similar to those established in this state by cases dealing with matters other than the furnishing of alcoholic beverages. * Under these principles an actor may be liable if his negligence is a substantial factor in causing an injury, and he is not relieved of liability because of the intervening act of a third person if such act was reasonably foreseeable at the time of his negligent conduct. * Restatement (Second) of Torts §§ 302, 302A, 431, 447. Moreover, "If the likelihood that a third person may act in a particular manner is the hazard or one of the hazards which makes the actor negligent, such an act whether innocent, negligent, intentionally tortious or criminal does not prevent the actor from being liable for harm caused thereby." Restatement (Second) of Torts § 449. *

Insofar as proximate cause is concerned, we find no basis for a distinction founded solely on the fact that the consumption of an alcoholic beverage is a voluntary act of the consumer and is a link in the chain of causation from the furnishing of the beverage to the injury resulting from intoxication. Under the above principles of proximate cause, it is clear that the furnishing of an alcoholic beverage to an intoxicated person may be a proximate cause of injuries inflicted by that individual upon a third person. If such furnishing is a proximate cause, it is so because the consumption, resulting intoxication, and injury-producing conduct are foreseeable intervening causes, or at least the injury-producing conduct is one of the hazards which makes such furnishing negligent.

The central question in this case, therefore, is not one of proximate cause, but rather one of duty: Did defendant Sager owe a duty of care to plaintiff or to a class of persons of which he is a member? * * *

In the instant case a duty of care is imposed upon defendant Sager by Business and Professions Code section 25602, which provides: "Every person who sells, furnishes, gives, or causes to be sold, furnished, or given away, any alcoholic beverage to any habitual or common drunkard or to any obviously intoxicated person is guilty of a misdemeanor." * * * This provision * * * was adopted for the purpose of protecting members of the general public from injuries to person and damage to property resulting from the excessive use of intoxicating liquor. * * *

The judgment of dismissal is reversed.

NOTES

1. *Subsequent History.* The *Vesely* opinion has apparently been nullified in California, at least in some applications, by a remarkable 1978 statute which stated "the intent of the Legislature to abrogate the holdings in cases such as *Vesely v. Sager* * * * and to reinstate the prior judicial interpretation of this section as it relates to proximate cause for injuries incurred as a result of furnishing alcoholic beverages to an intoxicated person, namely that the furnishing of alcoholic beverages is not the proximate cause of injuries resulting from intoxication, but rather the consumption of alcoholic beverages is the proximate cause of injuries inflicted upon another by an intoxicated person." Cal. Civ. Code § 1714(b) (2014). Courts in a substantial number of states conclude that in at least some circumstances, the seller of intoxicating beverages can be held liable for injuries resulting from the driving of the intoxicated consumer. See

Harper, James and Gray on Torts § 20.5 n.21; *contra*, Felder v. Butler, 292 Md. 174, 438 A.2d 494 (1981) (common law does not provide that the sale of an intoxicating liquor to an inebriated patron is a proximate cause of subsequent injury caused to others by the intoxicated customer).

2. *Proximate Cause and Social Host Liability.* What of the liability of a social host? In Kelly v. Gwinnell, 96 N.J. 538, 476 A.2d 1219 (1984), the New Jersey Supreme Court recognized the differences between holding a social guest liable for serving intoxicating beverages and imposing liability on a bar or restaurant, but it nevertheless recognized a claim, reasoning as follows:

> We therefore hold that a host who serves liquor to an adult social guest, knowing both that the guest is intoxicated and will thereafter be operating a motor vehicle, is liable for injuries inflicted on a third party as a result of the negligent operation of a motor vehicle by the adult guest when such negligence is caused by the intoxication. We impose this duty on the host to the third party because we believe that the policy considerations served by its imposition far outweigh those asserted in opposition. While we recognize the concern that our ruling will interfere with accepted standards of social behavior; will intrude on and somewhat diminish the enjoyment, relaxation, and camaraderie that accompany social gatherings at which alcohol is served; and that such gatherings and social relationships are not simply tangential benefits of a civilized society but are regarded by many as important, we believe that the added assurance of just compensation to the victims of drunken driving as well as the added deterrent effect of the rule on such driving outweigh the importance of those other values.

96 N.J. at 548, 476 A.2d at 1224 (later partially abrogated by N.J. statute limiting liability).

In Ely v. Murphy, 207 Conn. 88, 540 A.2d 54 (1988), a case in which the social guest was a minor, the Connecticut Supreme Court rejected the traditional argument that liability should not be imposed on the social host because "the subsequent injury has been held to have been proximately caused by the intervening act of the immoderate consumer whose voluntary and imprudent consumption of the beverage brings about intoxication and the subsequent injury." The court reasoned that "[i]n view of the legislative determination that minors are incompetent to assimilate responsibly the effects of alcohol and lack the legal capacity to do so, logic dictates that their consumption of alcohol does not * * * constitute the intervening act necessary to break the chain of proximate causation * * * and to insulate one who provides alcohol to minors from liability for ensuing injury."

Most courts continue to reject social host liability, but a growing number are recognizing it, particularly when the guest is a minor.

Modave v. Long Island Jewish Medical Center

United States Court of Appeals for the Second Circuit, 1974.
501 F.2d 1065.

[Plaintiff, injured in an automobile accident, was taken to a private hospital, Long Island Jewish Medical Center ("LIJ"), where, she alleged, she was subjected to malpractice through failure to diagnose a spinal injury, and failure to safeguard her against aggravation of the injury as she was moved about during reception and examination. LIJ had no room to keep her, so she was transferred to a Nassau County hospital, Meadowbrook, where, she claimed, her injury was further aggravated negligently. She sued both LIJ and the county. The jury awarded $50,000 against LIJ and $650,000 against the county. The trial judge set aside the verdict against the county on procedural grounds. The plaintiff then unsuccessfully moved to amend the judgment against LIJ to include the $650,000 awarded against the county.]

■ FRIENDLY, CIRCUIT JUDGE. * * * Plaintiff's motion to amend the judgment against LIJ to include the $650,000 awarded against Nassau County takes off from the unassailable proposition of New York law "that a wrongdoer is liable for the ultimate result, though the mistake or even negligence of the physician who treated the injury may have increased the damage which would otherwise have followed from the original wrong." * In Ferrara v. Galluchio, 5 N.Y.2d 16, 176 N.Y.S.2d 996, 152 N.E.2d 249 (1958), the Court of Appeals applied this principle in a case where malpractice by the defendant x-ray specialists led to plaintiff's consulting a dermatologist who advised her that her radiodermatitis might develop into cancer, with consequent emotional disturbance. The Court stated that the employment of the dermatologist was "a natural consequence of the original wrongdoers' tort because the necessity for such employment was imposed upon the plaintiff by the original wrongdoers' fault." The risk of emotional injury from an alarming remark of the dermatologist, the court concluded, "must be borne by the wrongdoers who started the chain of circumstances without which the cancerophobia would not have developed." * It cannot be questioned that if the driver who caused Miss Modave's injury was negligent, he would be liable for the malpractice of both hospitals. Counsel argues that on a parity of reasoning a first malpractitioner is liable as a matter of law for the malpractice of a second * * *.

Plaintiff reads the malpractice aggravation rule too broadly. It is true that a negligent driver normally is responsible for all the harm occasioned by subsequent malpractice in the course of treatment, whether the malpractice is by one hospital or by two; the driver's negligence is plainly a cause-in-fact of all the subsequent harm, and the intervening malpractice is regarded as being within the scope of the risk created by the negligent conduct. But where a third party has inflicted the original injury, the first hospital to treat the victim, even if negligent, is not necessarily responsible for any subsequent malpractice. At least where apportionment is practicable, the first hospital will be liable for subsequent damage only if its malpractice was a legal cause of the injury suffered at the hands of the second. The distinction that counsel's argument overlooks is the need to show a sufficient causal connection between LIJ's negligence and the harm inflicted by Meadowbrook.[8]

---

[8]   A hypothetical will make this clear. A plaintiff who has suffered a stroke is brought to a hospital where he is given an overdose of medicine, which results in permanent damage to his eyesight. He is then transferred to a second hospital, which has better facilities for stroke victims. The staff of the second hospital negligently fails to recognize the seriousness of his

If proper handling at LIJ would have enabled Miss Modave to have been discharged on the night of the accident without need of further hospitalization and it was her maltreatment at LIJ that necessitated her hospitalization at Meadowbrook, her case against LIJ would indeed fall within the [previous] decisions of the Court of Appeals * * *. But plaintiff sensibly has not pressed any such contention. Her condition was concededly serious enough to require further hospitalization, regardless of the quality of the emergency care she received at LIJ. Going a step further, when malpractice of a first hospital creates a condition not inherent in the original injury and this causes a second hospital to carry out measures which would not otherwise have been needed and which result in further harm, the first hospital might likewise be held liable. There was some evidence in this case to support a theory that the acts of malpractice at Meadowbrook would not have occurred but for the faulty handling at LIJ, * but absent a request to charge in accordance with such a theory, the judge quite properly refrained from submitting it to the jury on his own. * * *

Plaintiff's second attack on the court's charge, presented in tandem with the first, is that the judge should not have permitted the jury to apportion damages in a case in which there was no logical basis for apportioning the harm caused by each defendant. However, there was evidence to support the jury's conclusion that plaintiff's injuries were separable, * and in view of her failure to raise the point below it is not necessary for us to consider whether, upon request, the judge should have instructed the jury more extensively as to the limitations on their prerogative to apportion damages. * * *

We may indeed wonder at the jury's ability to calculate that the damage inflicted by LIJ amounted to $50,000 and the damage at Meadowbrook to $650,000. Had we been the jurors, we might well have availed ourselves of the option, accorded by the trial judge, to find apportionment impracticable and award a judgment against both parties. * But if the jurors found themselves capable of this feat, it is not for us to say them nay. * * *

NOTE

"Danger Invites Rescue." The issue of intervening and superseding cause also frequently appears in cases where the defendant's negligence causes risk or harm to a first victim and then the plaintiff, in an attempt to rescue the first victim, is injured himself. See, e.g., Eckert v. Long Island R. Co., *supra*, at page 343. In the classic case of Wagner v. Int'l Ry. Co., 232 N.Y. 176, 180, 133 N.E. 437, 437 (1921), the plaintiff's cousin was thrown through an open door on a train negligently operated by the defendant. When the train stopped, the plaintiff walked across a railroad bridge in an

---

condition, and, as a result, he suffers brain damage. Plainly the first hospital is liable only for the injury to the plaintiff's eyesight, and the second is liable only for the brain damage. If the malpractice of each had contributed substantially to the same brain injury, both would probably be liable for all the damages attributable to that injury. This, however, would be because it would be impossible for the jury rationally to apportion each tortfeasor's contribution to the single indivisible injury, not because, as counsel insists, the first hospital's malpractice automatically becomes "an original injury" as to the second hospital in any case involving successive acts of malpractice.

attempt to locate the body of his cousin and slipped and fell. In ruling that the jury should be allowed to determine whether the plaintiff's injuries were proximately caused by the defendant's negligence, Judge Cardozo stated:

> Danger invites rescue. The cry of distress is the summons to relief. The law does not ignore these reactions of the mind in tracing conduct to its consequences. It recognizes them as normal. It places their effects within the range of the natural and probable.

Liney v. Chestnut Motors, Inc.

Supreme Court of Pennsylvania, 1966.
421 Pa. 26, 218 A.2d 336.

■ EAGEN, JUSTICE. * * * The defendant operates an automobile sales agency and garage. About ten o'clock a.m. on the day involved, a customer's automobile was delivered to the garage for repairs. The defendant's employees allowed the automobile to remain outside the building, double-parked in the street and with the key in the ignition. About three hours later, it was stolen by an adult stranger who then drove it around the block in such a careless manner that it mounted a sidewalk, struck the plaintiff, a pedestrian thereon, causing her serious injury. Defendant's garage was located in a Philadelphia area experiencing a high and increasing number of automobile thefts in the immediate preceding months.

The lower court's order was correct and we affirm. The complaint failed to state a cause of action against the defendant. Assuming that defendant's employees were negligent in permitting the automobile to remain outside in the street under the circumstances described, it is clear that the defendant could not have anticipated and foreseen that this carelessness of its employees would result in the harm the plaintiff suffered. * In other words, the defendant violated no duty owed to the plaintiff. This being so, the plaintiff was not harmed by the defendant's negligence. * Assuming also that the defendant should have foreseen the likelihood of the theft of the automobile, nothing existed in the present case to put it on notice that the thief would be an incompetent or careless driver. Under the circumstances, the thief's careless operation of the automobile was a superseding cause of the injury suffered, and defendant's negligence, if such existed, only a remote cause thereof upon which no action would lie. *

It is true that the question of proximate cause is generally for the jury. However, if the relevant facts are not in dispute and the remoteness of the causal connection between the defendant's negligence and the plaintiff's injury clearly appears, the question becomes one of law. *

Finally, it is strenuously argued that Anderson v. Bushong Pontiac Co., 404 Pa. 382, 171 A.2d 771 (1961), is controlling. We do not agree. In *Anderson*, several salient facts were present which are absent here. Those facts clearly put the defendant in that case on notice, not only that the automobile was likely to be stolen, but also that it was likely to be stolen and operated by an incompetent driver. * * *

Order affirmed. * * *

NOTES

1. *Compare Ross v. Hartman.* In Ross v. Hartman, 139 F.2d 14 (D.C.Cir.1943), the defendant's agent violated a municipal traffic ordinance by leaving his truck unattended in a public alley with the ignition unlocked and the key in the switch. Within two hours, a thief drove away in the truck and negligently ran over the appellant. The court noted that "the existence of an ordinance changes the situation." It reasoned: "An unlocked motor vehicle creates little more risk of theft than an unlocked bicycle, or for that matter an unlocked house, but it creates much more risk that meddling by children, thieves, or others will result in injuries to the public. The ordinance is intended to prevent such consequences." It deemed "[t]he fact that the intermeddler's conduct was itself a proximate cause of the harm * * * immaterial." The court concluded:

> * * * [T]he conduct of the defendant or his agent was negligent precisely because it created a risk that a third person would act improperly. In such circumstances the fact that a third person does act improperly is not an intelligible reason for excusing the defendant.

Is the existence of the municipal ordinance enough to convincingly distinguish *Ross* from *Liney*?

2. *The Unforeseeability of the Events in Liney.* What makes the harm to the plaintiff in *Liney* unforeseeable? Is it the theft of the automobile at this location? Is it that the thief would drive the automobile in a careless of reckless manner that might cause harm to other drivers and pedestrians? See Cornelius J. Peck, An Exercise Based upon Empirical Data: Liability for Harm Caused by Stolen Automobiles, 1969 Wis. L. Rev. 909, 915 (indicating, *inter alia,* that the accident rate for stolen cars appears to be about 200 times the normal accident rate).

3. *Criminal or Deliberate Wrongdoing.* The court does not rest its decision on the basis that the driver's criminal and deliberate act in stealing the car was a superseding cause. Judge Posner states, "[C]riminal acts are not superseding cause per se. It is true that acts that are either criminal or intentionally tortious (these are overlapping categories) are more likely to be adjudged superseding causes than merely negligent acts." Scottsdale Ins. Co. v. Subscription Plus, Inc., 299 F.3d 618, 620 (7th Cir. 2002). For example, in Watson v. Ky. & Ind. Bridge & Ry. Co., 137 Ky. 619, 633, 126 S.W. 146, 151 (1910), the court found that where the defendant railway company negligently allowed gasoline to flow into the street, the deliberate act of an arsonist in setting fire to the gasoline precluded the defendant railway from being held liable. However, consider also Bell v. Board of Education, *infra* pages 328–29.

Edwards v. Tardif

Supreme Court of Connecticut, 1997.
240 Conn. 610, 692 A.2d 1266.

■ BERDON, JUSTICE. The plaintiff, Craig E. Edwards, as executor of the estate of Agatha M. Edwards, brought this medical malpractice action for damages resulting from the suicide of Agatha M. Edwards (Edwards) against the defendant physicians Daniel Tardif (Tardif) * * * From 1981 to December, 1987, Edwards was treated by Tardif, an internist, for recurring clinical depression. * * * In June 1987, she was admitted to Manchester Memorial Hospital due to severe depression and alcohol abuse. While admitted in the hospital, Edwards expressed thoughts of suicide. * * * During the June, 1987 admission, Tardif served as a consultant with respect to Edwards' illness and, subsequently, continued with her treatment. * * * On October 5, 1988, Edwards telephoned Tardif's office complaining of depression. Ettinger, an internist who practiced with Tardif, was covering for Tardif on that date and returned Edwards' telephone call without first reviewing her medical chart. Ettinger had no prior knowledge of Edwards, had never treated her, and had never discussed her condition with Tardif. During the telephone conversation, Edwards informed Ettinger that she was depressed due to the approaching anniversary of her husband's death and because of difficulties at work. Ettinger did not inquire into the details of the events precipitating Edwards' depression, nor did he ascertain how many previous bouts of depression she had suffered. Rather than scheduling an appointment to evaluate Edwards, Ettinger determined as a result of the telephone conversation that she was depressed and prescribed 100 pills of Tofranil with two refills. Although Ettinger instructed her to contact Tardif in the next few weeks, no other follow-up measures were taken. Eight days later, on October 13, 1988, Edwards committed suicide by overdosing on the Tofranil pills prescribed by Ettinger. Edwards left behind a suicide note expressing her severe depression, torment and anguish.

At trial, the plaintiff presented the expert testimony of Douglas Berv, a psychiatrist and specialist in psychopharmacology. Berv stated that suicide is a known symptom and risk in individuals suffering from depression. He testified that Ettinger's treatment of Edwards fell below the accepted standard of care for internists in several respects. First, he testified that Ettinger prescribed a large amount of Tofranil over the telephone to a patient he had never seen without first having Edwards come in for a psychiatric evaluation and suicide assessment. He further testified that Ettinger had also made an assumption with respect to Edwards' condition and what her treatment should be when the ten month lapse in treatment required a full evaluation of her mental and physical status. Additionally, Berv testified that instead of arranging a psychiatric evaluation for Edwards within a few days after her telephone call, Ettinger suggested that she should call again to schedule an office visit. Berv opined that, had Ettinger conformed to the applicable standard of care, Edwards' death would have been prevented. * * *

Our inquiry in this case focuses on whether Edwards' suicide was an act that broke the chain of causation. "As a general rule, negligence actions seeking damages for the suicide of another will not lie because the act of suicide is considered a deliberate, intentional and intervening act which precludes a finding that a given defendant, in fact, is responsible for the harm." * In other words, suicide generally is an unforeseeable result that serves to preclude civil liability. * This common law rule has been stated as follows: "[I]f one is sane, or if the suicide is during a lucid interval, when one is in full command of all faculties, but life has become unendurable by reason of the injury, it is agreed in negligence cases that the voluntary choice of suicide is an abnormal thing, which supersedes the defendant's liability." *

Conversely, suicide will not break the chain of causation if it was a foreseeable result of the defendant's tortious act. * * * Several other courts have concluded that liability will be imposed on a physician when suicide was one of the foreseeable risks that made the physician's antecedent conduct negligent. * * * Indeed, we have recently "adopted the standard set forth in § 442B of the Restatement [(Second) of Torts] that [w]here the negligent conduct of the actor creates or increases the risk of a particular harm and is a substantial factor in causing that harm, the fact that the harm is brought about through the intervention of another force does not relieve the actor of liability, except where the harm is intentionally caused by a third person and is not within the scope of the risk created by the actor's conduct." Stewart v. Federated Dept. Stores, Inc., 234 Conn. 597, 607–08, 662 A.2d 753 (1995).[6]

Physicians have a duty to exercise the degree of care that physicians in that particular field would exercise in similar circumstances. If the physician's treatment of a patient falls below the relevant standard of care, liability may be imposed if it is reasonably foreseeable that suicide will result if such care is not taken. Accordingly, we hold that a physician may be liable for a patient's suicide when the physician knew or reasonably should have known of the risk of suicide and the physician's failure to render adequate care and treatment proximately causes the patient's suicide.[7] * * *

The judgment is affirmed.

NOTES

1. *"Uncontrollable Impulse" Requirement.* In Hooks SuperX, Inc. v. McLaughlin, 642 N.E.2d 514, 520–21 (Ind.1994), the Indiana Supreme Court stated:

> [S]uicide constitutes an intervening cause * * * if committed by one who is sane enough to realize the effect of his actions * * * [but] only if it is the "voluntary" and "willful" act of the victim. Suicide induced by mental illness so severe that one cannot direct one's conduct does not constitute an intervening cause.

Consider, however, the following response:

> * * * [T]he concern for this distinction is, it is submitted, misplaced. It reflects both a misunderstanding of the implications

---

[6] In *Stewart*, the plaintiff's decedent was murdered by a third party in a parking garage owned and operated by the defendant. Stewart v. Federated Dept. Stores, Inc., 234 Conn. at 599, 662 A.2d 753. The defendant claimed that the trial court improperly refused to direct a verdict in its favor because the third party's actions constituted a superseding intervening cause that broke the chain of causation. * In light of the criminal activities that had previously occurred in the defendant's garage, this court concluded that "the harm that befell [the plaintiff's decedent] had been reasonably foreseeable and within the scope of the risk created by the defendant's negligence." *

[7] * * * Although we conclude that there was sufficient evidence in this case that the defendants breached their duty owed to Edwards, we disagree with the defendants' characterization with respect to whether a physician has a duty to *prevent* suicide. We merely recognize that "a cause of action may exist for *professional malpractice* when a [physician's or other health care provider's] treatment of a suicidal patient falls below the standard of care for the profession, thus giving rise to a traditional malpractice action." * Indeed, were we to adopt the view that a physician has the duty to prevent a patient's suicide, even though the physician's treatment has conformed to or even surpassed the appropriate standard of care, imposition of liability in those circumstances would amount to strict liability. * * *

of mental illness and a distortion of principles of causation. If defendant's negligence caused such injury as to drive the victim to sane despair, the causal connection is more clear, not less, than if the victim's suicidal reaction is senseless. There may be a cause-in-fact question, if it appears that the victim would have killed himself anyway for reasons other than the accident. But if the accident is a cause in fact of the suicide, there is no reason to regard the victim's sanity as impairing proximity.

Harper, James and Gray on Torts § 20.5, n.45.

2. *Suicide as an Intervening Cause following Negligence other than Malpractice.* In Fuller v. Preis, 35 N.Y.2d 425, 322 N.E.2d 263, 363 N.Y.S.2d 568 (1974), plaintiff's decedent developed a seizure disorder after suffering head injuries in an automobile accident caused by defendant's negligence. Seven months later, the decedent, having experienced a variety of losses and stresses in his life, committed suicide after writing a note to his family stating that he believed himself to be sane. How is this case different from the principal case? The New York Court of Appeals allowed recovery.

3. *Alcoholism as an Intervening Cause.* Wheeler v. Glens Falls Ins. Co., 513 S.W.2d 179 (Tenn.1974), was a workers' compensation action where decedent had been injured in a workplace injury but died as a result of the complications of chronic alcoholism. Decedent had a history of alcoholism and had been previously hospitalized for his condition, but there was no evidence of medical treatment for his alcoholism or related diseases for the three years prior to the accident. Following his back and neck injuries, his wife testified that he began drinking heavily to relieve the pain. The court stated that the general rule for recovery in workers' compensation cases is that " 'every natural consequence that flows from the injury likewise arises out of the employment, unless it is the result of an independent intervening cause attributable to claimant's own intentional conduct.' " * The court held that decedent's alcoholism did not constitute such an independent intervening cause:

> In our opinion, the evidence in this case reveals the conduct of the employee Wheeler to be below that which would comprise an intervening, willful intent. The contention of the defendants necessarily assumes that the decedent was a person who was warned not to drink, who understood that warning and its consequences, and who had the ability to make a rational and deliberate choice to violate the prohibition. We cannot, in the face of all the evidence, make the assumption that a chronic alcoholic could meet all these conditions. The evidence paints the picture of a man who drank, not out of a perverse intent to ignore his doctors' advice, but because the pain, despair, and idleness resulting from his injury forced him to do so. * * * We find it difficult to assume from that fact that the decedent willfully and deliberately chose to make that decision. Rather, it seems more to be the choice of a person who, as a chronic alcoholic, was yielding to a natural inability to resist the lure of alcohol. In short, we feel that the evidence indicates that Wheeler had no reasonable control over his decision to continue drinking.

Bell v. Board of Education

Court of Appeals of New York, 1997.
90 N.Y.2d 944, 665 N.Y.S.2d 42, 687 N.E.2d 1325.

■ OPINION OF THE COURT * * * On June 3, 1988, plaintiff's sixth grade class, along with five other fifth and sixth grade classes, attended a drug awareness fair at a park near the school. * Sponsored by defendant Board of Education and the police department, the fair permitted students to walk through the park on their own and participate in program activities that interested them. Seven teachers and four or five aides supervised the group. Before the outing, plaintiff's teacher told his class where to meet so that they might return to school together. Plaintiff testified that at around noon, her teacher gave her permission to leave the park, with friends, for lunch at a nearby pizzeria. At 12:30 p.m., in preparation for return to school, plaintiff's teacher took a head count of his students and discovered that plaintiff was missing. He looked for her in the park, but did not inform any of the other teachers or police officers providing security at the fair that he could not locate her. Plaintiff's teacher and his class left the park at 1:00 p.m., without plaintiff, but stopped first at her house before returning to school. He told plaintiff's mother (who usually met her daughter at school dismissal time to accompany her home) of the disappearance but he did not disclose the incident to school officials.

Meanwhile, at about 12:50 p.m., plaintiff was in the pizzeria when another student told her that her class had left. She hurried to the park but could not find them, and she started to walk home alone. At approximately 1:30 P.M., a block from the park, plaintiff met John Gibson (a student at the nearby junior high school), Chivelle Stallworth and a third boy whose name she did not know. Gibson and Stallworth began accosting her on the street and threatened to hurt her if she left. They then took her to Stallworth's house where they raped and sodomized her for 2½ hours. When they released her, plaintiff ran home and told her mother what had occurred. Plaintiff's mother, who had just informed the school of the disappearance, then called the police. Gibson and Stallworth were arrested later that day. Each pleaded guilty to first degree rape.

After a jury verdict in plaintiff's favor, the Appellate Division, one Justice dissenting, reversed and dismissed the complaint. The court held that as a matter of law, the rape was an unforeseeable superseding event absolving defendant of liability. * We disagree.

Where third-party criminal acts intervene between defendant's negligence and plaintiff's injuries, the causal connection may be severed, precluding liability. * The criminal intervention of third parties may, however, be a "reasonably foreseeable" consequence of circumstances created by the defendant. * While foreseeability is generally an issue for the fact finder, where only one conclusion can be drawn, proximate cause may be decided as a matter of law. *

On this record, we cannot say that the intervening act of rape was unforeseeable as a matter of law. A rational jury hearing the trial testimony could have determined, as the jury in this case did, that the foreseeable result of the danger created by defendant's alleged lack of supervision was injury such as occurred here. A fact finder could have reasonably concluded that the very purpose of the school supervision was to shield vulnerable schoolchildren from such acts of violence. As we have previously recognized, "[w]hen the intervening, intentional act of another is itself the foreseeable harm that shapes the duty imposed, the defendant who fails to guard against such conduct will not be relieved of liability when that act occurs." * * *

C. REASSEMBLING THE COMPONENTS OF CAUSATION

Doe v. Manheimer

Supreme Court of Connecticut, 1989.
212 Conn. 748, 563 A.2d 699.

■ GLASS, JUSTICE. * * * The plaintiff, Jane Doe, worked as a meter reader for the Connecticut Light and Power Company in New London. * * *. At approximately 8 a.m., as she walked along Green Street, she observed a man on the opposite sidewalk who appeared to be looking for directions. She crossed the street to offer assistance. As she came near, the man, a stranger, reached into a satchel, removed a gun, and held it against her. He forced her from the sidewalk through a paved vacant lot that abutted the street. The man then forced her onto adjacent property owned by the named defendant (hereinafter defendant) some fifty to seventy feet from the sidewalk. * * * The area into which the plaintiff was forced was bounded by the defendant's building on one side and a retaining wall in the rear. On the other side, overgrown sumac bushes and tall grass shielded the area from view from the sidewalk and street. Behind the sumac bushes, the abductor viciously assaulted and raped the plaintiff for thirty minutes. * * * The assailant fled after committing the crime and has never been identified or caught. The effect of the sexual assault upon the plaintiff has been severe. She has attempted suicide on several occasions. Her emotional and psychiatric problems have required and continue to require hospital confinement.

The plaintiff brought an action against the defendant for personal injuries sustained in the assault. The complaint alleged causes of action based on common law negligence [and] statutory negligence * * *. In essence, she claimed that the defendant had failed to remove the overgrown vegetation although he knew or should have known that, because the neighborhood was a high crime area, third persons might use the overgrowth to conceal the perpetration of crimes against pedestrians. She asserted that, had the overgrowth not been present, the area in which the assault occurred would have been visible to passing motorists and pedestrians. Consequently, she alleged, the overgrowth caused and contributed to the assault and the duration of the assault.

The action was tried to a jury before the court. * * * Several witnesses described the neighborhood where the sexual assault had been committed as a high crime area. Another rape had occurred in a neighborhood building about three months prior to the sexual assault against the plaintiff. Approximately fourteen months prior to the assault, Clara Manheimer, the defendant's ninety year old mother, had been bound, gagged and robbed in the package store at the front of the building on the defendant's property. Prostitution and drug dealing were more prevalent in that section of New London than in other sections. Further, derelicts and homeless people frequented the site where the assault occurred and the adjacent vacant lot through which the plaintiff had been forced from the sidewalk. * * *

In addition to testimony concerning the assault and the condition of the site, the plaintiff presented George Rand, an environmental psychologist. Rand testified that * * * in his opinion, the physical configuration of the specific site increased the risk of violent crimes between strangers by creating a "protective" zone that reduced or eliminated visibility and, hence, served as an inducement for crime. * * * Melvin Jetmore, a building official for the city of New London and one of the authors of the housing code, testified for the plaintiff that the site of the defendant's property where the rape had occurred violated the housing code due to the presence of an "obnoxious" overgrowth of sumac trees and brush, and various debris including papers, shingles and broken glass. Jetmore testified that prior to the assault, New London had notified the defendant in March, 1983, and again in February, 1984, of the housing code violations, and that Jetmore had specifically told the defendant to remove all the debris and broken glass and "cut all the bushes and trees down." The defendant, however, did not correct the violations.

* * * [T]he jury returned a general verdict in favor of the plaintiff, and awarded her $540,000 in damages. * * * Subsequently, however, the trial court set aside the verdict on the defendant's motion. In setting aside the verdict, the trial court first observed that "[w]ithout the shielding [of the overgrowth], the rape most probably would not have occurred [on the defendant's property]." The court implicitly found that the defendant owed the plaintiff a duty of reasonable care, stating that, "[i]n the neighborhood described in the present case, a trier of fact may . . . find the occurrence of violence reasonably foreseeable in such a sheltered location to be perpetrated by someone lying in ambush or by someone also using the public right of way who harbors an intent to drag into concealment and out of public view some other party also using the public right of way to inflict harm." * * *

Despite finding a legally cognizable duty and a breach of that duty, the trial court nevertheless ruled that "the shielded bushing did not cause the injury. The rape and assault caused the injury and damages." "That shielding [which was described as the building, a retaining wall and sumac trees and/or bushes] could have been provided in that same place and time by some other validly positioned or placed apurtenance [sic]." The court concluded, therefore, that as a matter of law, the jury could not find that the defendant's maintenance of overgrowth on his property was a "substantial factor" in producing the plaintiff's injuries and, hence, the plaintiff had failed to establish proximate cause. * * *

To prevail on a negligence claim, a plaintiff must establish [both] * * * "causation in fact" * * * and proximate cause. * * * This court has often stated that the "test" of proximate cause is whether the defendant's conduct is a "substantial factor" in producing the plaintiff's injury. * See also Ferndale Dairy, Inc. v. Geiger, 167 Conn. 533, 538, 356 A.2d 91 (1975) (defining "substantial factor" as one which "must have continued down to the moment of the damage or, at least, down to the setting in motion of the final active injurious force which immediately produced or preceded the damage"). * That negligent conduct is a "cause in fact," however, obviously does not mean that it is also a "substantial factor" for the purposes of a proximate cause inquiry. The "substantial factor" test, in truth, reflects the inquiry fundamental to all proximate cause questions; that is, "'whether the harm which occurred was of the same general nature as the foreseeable risk created by the defendant's negligence.'" * * *

The "scope of the risk" analysis of "proximate cause" similarly applies where, as here, the risk of harm created by the defendant's negligence allegedly extends to an intervening criminal act by a third party. * "We have consistently adhered to the standard * that a negligent defendant, whose conduct creates or increases the risk of a particular harm and is a substantial factor in causing that harm, is not relieved from liability by the intervention of another person, *except* where the harm is intentionally caused by the third person *and* is not within the scope of the risk created by the defendant's conduct. * * *" "Such tortious or criminal acts may in themselves be foreseeable, [however,] and so within the scope of the created risk * * *." [Restatement (Second) of Torts § 442B cmt. c.] *

Applying these principles, we first note that the defendant has not argued that his conduct was not a "cause in fact" of the plaintiff's injuries. The trial court found that the sexual assault most probably would not have occurred *where it actually occurred* had the overgrown vegetation not been present. The court also found that the jury could have found from the evidence that the rapist "by design and plan premeditated that the sexual assault would occur in that exact location." Further, there was evidence from which the jury could reasonably have found that the assault would not have lasted thirty minutes absent the shielding provided by the overgrowth. * * * Under the circumstances, we have no reason to question the trial court's finding that the injury would not have occurred, where it actually occurred, were it not for the shielding created by the overgrowth. *

We disagree with the plaintiff, however, that there was room for reasonable disagreement over the question whether the condition on the defendant's property proximately caused her injuries. * The plaintiff argues that there was sufficient evidence for the jury to find that the impaired visibility created by the overgrowth, in conjunction with the manner in which the defendant's property was used and the unseemly character of the neighborhood, increased the risk of violent crime between strangers. She claims, therefore, that * * * the assailant's act was within the "scope of the risk" created by the condition of the defendant's property. * * *

[W]e decline to accept the plaintiff's argument suggesting that it was within the "scope of the risk" that the condition of the defendant's land might catalyze a criminal assault. The plaintiff presented expert testimony that conditions of "environmental disorder," such as those present on the defendant's property and within the surrounding neighborhood, stood in a direct and positive relationship with an increased risk of violent crimes between strangers. She also presented evidence tending to indicate that the assailant had planned the crime around the site. Thus, the plaintiff's theory of liability turns in part on the argument that because the overgrowth was instrumental, in a psychological and sociological sense, in fostering the criminal act, the defendant should be held liable. * * * We are not persuaded that a landowner should reasonably foresee that a condition on his property such as overgrown vegetation might provide a substantial incentive or inducement for the commission of a violent criminal assault between strangers. This is true although once such an incident does occur, it necessarily "could" have occurred. Violent crimes are actuated by a host of social and psychological factors. Although, as a matter of fact, it may be true that one of those actuating factors is mere opportunity for concealment, common experience informs us that such a factor is at most incidental. A prudent person who owns land abutting a public way would not, in our opinion, infer from his ordinary experience the possibility that overgrown vegetation will prompt or catalyze a violent criminal act. This theory ascribes far too much speculative imagination to a "reasonable" or "prudent" person. A person of ordinary caution is not required to be accomplished at making such recondite associations. * * *

No different result ensues from the plaintiff's less dramatic argument that the condition on the defendant's property, in connection with the "socio-chemistry" of the area, created a foreseeable "opportunity" for the commission of a violent crime and, hence, the harm inflicted on the plaintiff was within the "scope of the risk." Our cases make it clear that, to be within the "scope of the risk," the harm actually suffered must be of the same "general type" as that which makes the defendant's conduct negligent in the first instance. * It is unexceptional to impose upon a landowner liability resulting from injuries caused directly and without intervening criminal conduct by "dangerous conditions" on the land. Thus, where the plaintiff stumbles on accumulated debris on the defendant's land, and injures himself, the defendant may be liable. * We are not prepared, however, to extend the scope of the foreseeable risk presented by "obnoxious overgrowth" or accumulated debris beyond injury produced by physical contact with such conditions. Thus, the harm suffered by the plaintiff in this case was not of the same general type that allegedly made the defendant negligent. * * *

Finally, we disagree with the plaintiff's assertion that the trial court's conclusion that the occurrence of violence in such a sheltered location was reasonably foreseeable, and that the rape would not have occurred where it did absent the overgrowth, undermined its conclusion that the condition of the defendant's property was not a "substantial factor" of the plaintiff's harm. A review of the trial court's memorandum indicates that the court's prior remarks addressed the issues of duty and factual cause rather than proximate cause. We conclude, therefore, that there was no "room for a reasonable disagreement" that the plaintiff did not establish that the condition on the defendant's land was a proximate cause of the sexual assault. * Accordingly, the trial court did not err in setting aside the jury's verdict in favor of the plaintiff. * * *

NOTES

1.   *Untangling the Reasoning of the Courts.* *Doe* provides an opportunity to review the various prongs of causation analysis and the different tests

for determining duty and proximate causation. It also demonstrates courts' not-always-successful attempts to address the complexities inherent in the intertwining of these concepts.

The Supreme Court tells us that the trial court found that "the plaintiff had failed to establish proximate cause." It noted that the trial judge found that the assault could have occurred at another place and time and have been shielded by something else. Does this sound like proximate cause or cause in fact? An absence of but/for causation or causal linkage? Both? Why does the Supreme Court not consider these issues?

The Supreme Court regards the issue before it as one of proximate causation or scope of liability. Despite past crimes in the same neighborhood and the testimony of the expert witness George Rand, the Supreme Court holds that "[w]e are not persuaded that a landowner should reasonably foresee that * * * overgrown vegetation might provide a substantial incentive or inducement for the commission of a violent criminal assault between strangers." Really? Accepting the court's articulated test of foreseeability, is the issue really one of proximate causation or is it something else?

What policy factors suggest that the defendant landowner should not be held liable for damages arising from her criminal assault? Is crime prevention primarily the responsibility of the landowner? Over the long term, is it likely to help the distressed neighborhood if the defendant is held liable? See *infra* pages 570–571, Note. Under which opinion in this chapter could these important policy factors have been considered explicitly?

2. *Foreseeability of Criminal Attack.* Given the defendant's conduct and the nature of the neighborhood, was the attack on the plaintiff unforeseeable? Re-read Restatement (Second) of Torts §§ 448, 449 (1965) in the court's footnote 5. Do you agree with the court's reasoning under the Restatement that the rape was unforeseeable?

Compare Erickson v. Curtis Investment Co., 447 N.W.2d 165 (Minn.1989), with *Doe v. Manheimer.* In *Erickson,* the plaintiff was raped in a commercial self-serve, multi-level parking garage operated by the defendant. There had been no previous reports of crimes against persons in the garage, but the court found that "[t]he interior [of the garage], with its many levels, its supporting pillars, its stairwells, its relatively low ceilings, and its rows of unoccupied parked cars, provide places in which to hide or to lurk, especially if the interior is dimly lit." The court held that if the jury found that the defendant had been negligent, the court would not be justified in ruling for the defendant as a matter of law on the issue of causation. See also generally O'Brien v. B.L.C. Ins. Co., 768 S.W.2d 64, 68 (Mo.1989) ("The doctrine of intervening cause is not so strong as it seems to have been at one time. The essential question is foreseeability. Even criminal conduct will not always insulate a tortfeasor, if the criminal conduct is reasonably foreseeable.").

3. *Substantial Factor as a Test of Proximate Causation.* In *Doe v. Manheimer,* the Connecticut Supreme Court acknowledges that "[t]his court has often stated that the 'test' of proximate cause is whether the defendant's conduct is a 'substantial factor' in producing the plaintiff's injury." Restatement (Second) of Torts § 435(1) (1965) provides:

If the actor's conduct is a substantial factor in bringing about harm to another, the fact that the actor neither foresaw nor should have foreseen the extent of the harm or the manner in which it occurred does not prevent him from being liable.

Whether the substantial factor test functions solely as part of cause in fact analysis in limiting liability or as a test of proximate cause arguably is unclear. According to *Harper, James and Gray on Torts*, in the view of both the first Restatement of Torts and early twentieth-century scholar Jeremiah Smith, substantial factor "appeared * * * to be, in effect, a test of *proximate* cause." Harper, James and Gray on Torts § 20.6. A comment to the Restatement (Third) of Torts attempts to clarify the role of the substantial factor formulation:

> The "substantial factor" requirement for legal cause in the Second Restatement of Torts has often been understood to address proximate cause, although that was not intended. Because the rules in this Chapter address the grounds for limiting liability with greater precision than the substantial-factor standard, this Restatement does not use that term.

Restatement (Third) of Torts: Liability for Physical and Emotional Harm § 29 cmt. a (2010). A number of states continue to "at least pay lip service" to the idea that substantial factor analysis poses a limitation on liability. Harper, James, and Gray on Torts, *supra*, at § 20.6. See also *supra* pages 248–249, Note.

CHAPTER 5

THE EFFECT OF PLAINTIFF'S CONDUCT AND RELATED ISSUES

In this chapter, we consider how the plaintiff's own conduct affects recovery under a negligence claim through the traditional affirmative defenses of contributory negligence, see *infra* Part A, pages 336–344, and assumption of risk, see *infra* Part D, pages 364–382. In most jurisdictions, principles of comparative fault now replace contributory negligence, at least to some extent, and often replace assumption of risk as well. See *infra* Part B, pages 344–352. In Part C, *infra* pages 352–364, we consider the legal consequences of the plaintiff's failure to take reasonable measures to minimize the extent of injuries to himself when an accident occurs—such as his failure to wear a seatbelt, even if such conduct does not play a role in contributing to the accident itself. Part E, *infra* pages 382–386, addresses the now disfavored concept of imputed contributory negligence. Finally, we turn our attention to how financial responsibility for causing an accident is shared among joint tortfeasors. See *infra* Part F, pages 386–393, and Part G, pages 393–397.

Traditionally, contributory negligence and assumption of risk were affirmative defenses that barred plaintiff's recovery. Today, only four states—Alabama, Maryland, North Carolina, and Virginia—as well as the District of Columbia, continue to regard the plaintiff's contributory negligence as a total bar to recovery in an action against a negligent defendant. However, even in the other forty-six "comparative fault" states, it is critical to understand contributory negligence for two reasons. First, comparative fault does not come into play unless, and until, the jury finds that the plaintiff was negligent in a way that contributed to the accident in question. Second, most comparative fault states apply "modified" comparative fault principles, which provide that once the plaintiff's degree of fault reaches a specified threshold, the plaintiff's contributory negligence continues to bar his recovery entirely. See *infra* pages 350–351, Note.

You already have encountered contributory negligence in a number of the cases that you have read. Recall that in Memorial Hospital of South Bend, Inc. v. Scott, 261 Ind. 27, 36, 300 N.E.2d 50, 56 (1973), *supra* pages 142–145, the Indiana Supreme Court defined contributory negligence as follows:

> The general rule on the issue of the plaintiff's contributory negligence is that the plaintiff must exercise that degree of care that an ordinary reasonable man would exercise in like or similar circumstances. Contributory negligence is conduct on the part of the plaintiff, contributing as a legal cause to the harm he has suffered, *which falls below the standard to which he is required to conform for his own protection*. Restatement [(Second)] of Torts § 463 (1965). (Emphasis in original).

Courts in the nineteenth century generally placed the burden of proof on the plaintiff to prove not only the defendant's negligence but also the plaintiff's own lack of contributory negligence. See Brown v. Kendall, 60 Mass. 292, 297, 6 Cush. 292, 297, *supra* at pages 37–40. During the past century, however, courts generally have required the defendant to plead and prove the facts establishing the plaintiff's contributory negligence:

> The burden of proof rests on each party to a civil action as to each fact essential to his claim or defense. * A party claiming a person failed to exercise due care has the burden of proof on that issue. * The burden of proving all aspects of the affirmative defense of contributory negligence, including causation, rests on the defendant, * unless the elements of the defense may be inferred from the plaintiff's evidence.

Gyerman v. United States Lines Co., 7 Cal.3d 488, 503, 102 Cal.Rptr. 795, 805, 498 P.2d 1043, 1053 (1972).

A. CONTRIBUTORY NEGLIGENCE

Butterfield v. Forrester
Court of King's Bench, 1809.
103 Eng.Rep. 926, 11 East's Reports 60.

* * * This was an action on the case for obstructing a highway, by means of which obstruction the plaintiff, who was riding along the road, was thrown down with his horse, and injured, etc. * * * [T]he defendant, for the purpose of making some repairs to his house, which was close by the road side at one end of the town, had put up a pole across this part of the road, a free passage being left by another branch or street in the same direction. That the plaintiff left a public house not far distant from the place in question at 8 o'clock in the evening in August, when they were just beginning to light candles, but while there was light enough left to discern the obstruction at one hundred yards distance; and the witness, who proved this, said that if the plaintiff had not been riding very hard he might have observed and avoided it; the plaintiff, however, who was riding violently, did not observe it, but rode against it, and fell with his horse and was much hurt in consequence of the accident; and there was no evidence of his being intoxicated at the time. On this evidence Bayley, J. directed the jury, that if a person riding with reasonable and ordinary care could have seen and avoided the obstruction; and if they were satisfied that the plaintiff was riding along the street extremely hard, and without ordinary care, they should find a verdict for the defendant, which they accordingly did. * * *

■ BAYLEY, J. The plaintiff was proved to be riding as fast as his horse could go, and this was through the streets of Derby. If he had used ordinary care he must have seen the obstruction; so that the accident appeared to happen entirely from his own fault.

■ LORD ELLENBOROUGH, C.J. * * * One person being in fault will not dispense with another's using ordinary care for himself. Two things must concur to support this action, an obstruction in the road by the fault of the defendant, and no want of ordinary care to avoid it on the part of the plaintiff. * * *

NOTE

Raisin v. Mitchell. Butterfield generally is regarded as the original contributory negligence case. However, the decision of the Court of Common Pleas thirty years later in Raisin v. Mitchell, 173 Eng.Rep. 979, 9 Car. & P. 613, (Court of Common Pleas, 1839), demonstrates that *Butterfield* was not immediately understood and accepted as dictating a total loss for the plaintiff if both the plaintiff and the defendant were at fault. In *Raisin,* two ships collided in the River Thames. The plaintiff alleged that the defendant's servants "so unskillfully and negligently navigated" the defendant's brig "that it ran against the plaintiff's sloop, and caused it to sink." Counsel for the defendants argued that the plaintiff's crew "did not understand English" and "ought to have given way and allowed the brig to keep her course." Chief Judge Tindal instructed the jury that for the plaintiff to be entitled to damages, "You must be satisfied that the injury . . . was not imputable in any degree to any want of care . . . on the part of the plaintiff." The plaintiff claimed "upwards of £500" in damages to its sloop, but the jury awarded only £250. Plaintiff's counsel protested, no doubt with *Butterfield* in mind, arguing that "[t]here must be some mistake." However, when asked how the jury came up with its verdict, the foreman responded, "[T]here were faults on both sides." Defense counsel argued that this "entitled the defendant to the verdict." However, Chief Judge Tindal responded, "There may be faults [on the plaintiff's part] to a certain extent."

A note to the case by the original reporter indicates that the verdict and the court's opinion "seem to be quite correct and sustainable in point of law . . . ." The reporter quoted Baron Parke in the case of Bridge v. The Grand Junction Ry. Co., 150 Eng.Rep. 1134, 3 Mee. & Wels. 224 (1838):

> There may have been negligence in both parties, and yet the plaintiff may be entitled to recover. The rule of law is laid down with perfect correctness in the case of *Butterfield v. Forrester,* and that rule is, that, although there may have been negligence on the part of the plaintiff, yet, unless he might, by the exercise of ordinary care, have avoided the consequences of the defendants' negligence, he is entitled to recover: if by ordinary care he might have avoided them, he is the author of his own wrong.

Hensel v. Beckward

Court of Appeals of Maryland, 1974.
273 Md. 426, 330 A.2d 196.

■ DIGGES, JUDGE. In Creaser v. Owens, 267 Md. 238, 240–41, 297 A.2d 235 (1972), the most recent case of this Court which discusses Maryland's motor vehicle "boulevard rule," Maryland Code (1957, 1970

Repl. Vol.) Art. 66 ½, § 11–403,[1] we indicated our hope that, with the views expressed there, no longer would this statute give rise to either "lingering doubts about the absoluteness of its application," or, other than through legislative enactment, further "attempts to create new exceptions to it." The present litigation, however, has dashed this hope, as once again we are faced with a case in which the application of the "boulevard rule" is sought to be avoided. Like the Rock of Gibraltar we remain firm and will not allow the legislative mandates contained in this right-of-way statute to be judicially either bypassed or otherwise eroded through new waves of attack.

* * * [T]he accident, which gave rise to this case, occurred on a clear but moonless night in February 1970, when an automobile driven by the respondent, Garfield Beckward, collided with a vehicle driven by the petitioner, Russell William Hensel. * That collision occurred in Allegany County at the unilluminated intersection of Vocke Road, a four-lane divided highway running east and west, and Maryland Route 49, a two-lane highway running north and south with a stop sign which controlled the entry of traffic on Route 49 into its intersection with Vocke Road. The evidence also shows that when Beckward approached that intersection he came to a complete stop on Route 49, whereupon he, together with his wife who was beside him on the front seat, each looked twice, both to the east and to the west, for traffic proceeding on Vocke Road. Seeing no vehicular movement and therefore satisfied as to the apparent safety of moving out into the intersection, Beckward began to drive very slowly across the two eastbound lanes of Vocke Road toward the median, while both he and his wife continued to watch for traffic which might approach from their left. When the Beckwards were about half way across that side of the highway, the petitioner's car suddenly appeared in the illumination of their headlights. This second vehicle was about 20 to 25 feet away when first spotted by the Beckwards, and was proceeding, they say at a fast rate of speed in an easterly direction with unlit headlights. The collision which followed caused Beckward to be catapulted from his automobile onto the road curb, and tragically resulted in his being hospitalized for six months, after which he returned to his home permanently paralyzed from the neck down.

After all the evidence was presented, Judge Getty, relying principally on our decision in *Creaser v. Owens*, directed a verdict, and we think quite correctly, in favor of Hensel on the ground that, under the "boulevard rule," Beckward as the unfavored driver, though he halted at the stop sign, was contributorily negligent as a matter of law

---

[1]   Maryland Code (1957, 1970 Repl. Vol.) Art. 66 ½, § 11–403 in relevant part states:
* * *

(b) *Stopping at entrance to through highway.*—The driver of a vehicle shall come to a full stop as required by this subtitle at the entrance to a through highway and shall yield the right-of-way to other vehicles approaching on the through highway.

(c) *Stopping in obedience to stop signs.*—The driver of a vehicle likewise shall come to a full stop in obedience to a stop sign and yield the right-of-way to a vehicle approaching on the intersecting highway as required herein at an intersection where a stop sign is erected at one or more entrances thereto although not a part of a through highway. * * *

in failing to yield the right-of-way to the Hensel vehicle traveling on the favored highway.

In *Creaser,* a school bus driver, traveling on an unfavored highway, properly stopped at the stop sign and looked for traffic proceeding on the favored highway before venturing into the intersection. Though her visibility beyond 200 feet to her left was obstructed by a hill and a curve in the "boulevard," the bus driver slowly "creeped out" into the intersection, only to be surprised by a speeding car which "jumped" over the hill and collided with the bus. While recognizing the possible harshness of the result, this Court held that because the bus driver failed to yield the right-of-way to the favored driver as required by the "boulevard" statute, the unfavored operator was guilty of contributory negligence as a matter of law. In so ruling we stated:

> In order to make crystal clear our holding here, we emphasize that if an unfavored driver is involved in an accident with a favored vehicle under circumstances where the boulevard law is applicable then in a suit based on that collision the unfavored driver is deemed to be negligent as a matter of law. And, if the unfavored driver is a plaintiff, his suit is defeated unless the doctrine of last clear chance rescues his claim. Whereas, if the unfavored driver is a defendant he is liable except in the rare case when the issue of contributory negligence on the part of the favored driver is properly submitted to a jury, i.e., whether he was guilty of negligence that was a proximate cause of the accident. (all citations omitted) *.

* * * [T]he "boulevard rule," developed over the years, and whose meaning is explained in *Creaser* and similar cases, applies to the facts present here so as to prohibit recovery by the respondent as a matter of law * * *.

NOTES

1. *Traditional Justifications for Contributory Negligence.* How could one justify the rule that contributory negligence totally barred the plaintiff's recovery? Evaluate the following proffered justifications:

   a.   Plaintiff's negligence is an intervening, superseding cause, that insulates the defendant from liability. Would such a conclusion comport with the modern understanding of superseding causation?

   b.   Contributory negligence punishes the plaintiff for his own conduct or prevents a culpable plaintiff from seeking redress from the courts unless he comes with clean hands. How fair and realistic is such an argument?

   c.   Preventing the plaintiff from recovering when he is contributorily negligent discourages accidents. Again, how would you evaluate this argument?

See Harper, James and Gray on Torts § 22.2; William L. Prosser, Comparative Negligence, 41 Cal. L. Rev. 1, 3–4 (1953). For a critical evaluation of the justifications for contributory negligence as a total bar to recovery, see Donald G. Gifford & Christopher J. Robinette, Apportioning

Liability in Maryland Tort Cases: Time to End Contributory Negligence and Joint and Several Liability, 73 Md. L. Rev. 701, 728–40 (2014) [hereinafter, Gifford & Robinette, Apportioning Liability].

Instead of these judicially articulated justifications, William Prosser offers another explanation for the doctrine:

> Probably the true explanation lies merely in the highly individualistic attitude of the common law of the early nineteenth century. The period of development of contributory negligence was that of the industrial revolution, and there is reason to think that the courts found in this defense, along with the concepts of duty and proximate cause, a convenient instrument of control over the jury, by which the liabilities of rapidly growing industry were curbed and kept within bounds.

Prosser, *supra*, at 4.

2. *Contributory Negligence as a Defense to Statutory Claims.* A statutory requirement does not necessarily establish a standard of care the breach of which is remedied in a negligence action. It may instead be deemed remediable by an express or implied cause of action for breach of the statute. See *supra* pages 208–209, Note 3. At common law, if the plaintiff's claim is not formally rooted in negligence, it may be unaffected by the plaintiff's own negligence.

Furthermore, even where the breach of statutory duty is deemed to give rise to a negligence action, courts often recognize an exception to the application of contributory negligence. For example, contributory negligence may not prevent recovery when the legislature passed a statute designed to protect a particularly vulnerable class of people from their inability to protect themselves, or otherwise for the purpose of shifting to one class of actors the entire burden of preventing certain types of accidents. For example, in Koenig v. Patrick Construction Corp., 298 N.Y. 313, 83 N.E.2d 133 (1948), the New York Court of Appeals held that the contributory negligence of the plaintiff, a window cleaner, would not bar his recovery under a state statute requiring his employer to provide safe scaffolding and other equipment. Judge Fuld stated:

> Firmly established is the principle of law that a plaintiff's carelessness is no bar to his recovery under a statute which imposes liability "regardless of negligence." * Obviously, not every statute which commands or prohibits particular conduct is within this principle. Only when the statute is designed to protect a definite class of persons from a hazard of definable orbit, which they themselves are incapable of avoiding, is it deemed to create a statutory cause of action and to impose a liability unrelated to questions of negligence. This rule is based upon the view that, not being dependent upon proof of specific acts of negligence on defendant's part, the cause of action may not be defeated by proof of plaintiff's want of care. Thus, it has been said, "If the defendant's negligence consists in the violation of a statute enacted to protect a class of persons from their inability to exercise self-protective care, a member of such class is not barred by his contributory negligence from recovery for bodily harm caused by the violation of such statute." Restatement of Torts § 483. * * *

Workmen such as the present plaintiff, who ply their livelihoods on ladders and scaffolds, are scarcely in a position to protect themselves from accident. They usually have no choice but to work with the equipment at hand, though danger looms large. The legislature recognized this and to guard against the known hazards of the occupation required the employer to safeguard the workers from injury caused by faulty or inadequate equipment. If the employer could avoid this duty by pointing to the concurrent negligence of the injured worker in using the equipment, the beneficial purpose of the statute might well be frustrated and nullified.

3. *Scope of the Risk and Contributory Negligence.* What role do "scope of the liability" considerations, discussed in the last chapter, play in the case of contributory negligence? In Smithwick v. Hall & Upson Co., 59 Conn. 261, 21 A. 924 (1890), plaintiff, an employee of defendant owner and operator of an icehouse, was seriously injured when a brick wall fell on top of him as a result of defendant's negligence. At the time of the accident, plaintiff was storing ice while standing on the east end of the platform. Plaintiff had been told to stay away from this end of the platform by both his foreman and a co-worker. The foreman did not tell plaintiff why the east end of the platform was not safe, but what he had in mind was the narrowness and unrailed condition of the platform and the possibility that the platform would be slippery because of broken ice. Under these circumstances, the court found that plaintiff's failure to heed the warning did not constitute contributory negligence:

> * * * In the case at bar the conduct of the plaintiff, as we have seen, was, with respect to the danger from the falling wall, not negligent, for the want of knowledge or its equivalent on the part of the plaintiff. * * * Had the injury been occasioned by a misstep or slip from the platform by the carelessness of the plaintiff, or for the want of a railing, the causal connection between the change of position and the injury would, legally speaking, be quite obvious; but, from a legal point of view, no such connection exists between the change of position and the giving way of the wall. * * * Under these circumstances, the failure or neglect to heed the warning does not constitute contributory negligence. *

The defendant in *Smithwick* also claimed, however, that most of plaintiff's injuries resulted not from the falling bricks themselves, but from plaintiff's fall from the platform which—though initiated by the fall of the brick wall—would have been prevented if plaintiff had been on the section of the platform with the railing. The court held that plaintiff's actions did not constitute contributory negligence, but that such conduct might affect the amount of damages to be awarded to him. How does this compare to an injured plaintiff's failure to wear a seat belt in a case arising out of an automobile accident? See Law v. Superior Court, *infra* pages 356–363.

4. *Ameliorating the Harsh Effects of Contributory Negligence: Last Clear Chance.* The draconian nature of the doctrine of contributory negligence as a total bar to plaintiff's recovery—regardless of how slight the plaintiff's negligence—has long been recognized. See generally Harper, James and Gray on Torts § 22.3. In recent decades, most states have replaced this doctrine with the concept of comparative fault, under which a plaintiff's fault reduces, but often does not eliminate, recovery. See *infra* pages 344–

352. Even before the transition to comparative fault, and in those states where contributory negligence remains a complete bar to recovery, courts have identified a variety of doctrines restricting the application of contributory negligence as a complete bar to recovery. Consider the ameliorating concepts described in this and succeeding notes:

In the famous 1842 case of Davies v. Mann, [1842] 152 Eng.Rep. 588 (Ex.), 10 M. & W. 546, plaintiff had fettered the forefeet of an ass which he owned and released it onto a public highway. Defendant's wagon, traveling at "a smartish pace," knocked into the ass and rode over it. Lord Abinger stated that even if the ass were illegally on the road, plaintiff should still be able to recover if "the defendant might, by proper care, have avoided injuring the animal." Thus arose the doctrine of "last clear chance," although it is not clear from the report who had the "last clear chance" to avoid the accident in question.

Under the last clear chance doctrine, the plaintiff's contributory negligence was overridden only "when the defendant had the last clear chance to avoid the injury and negligently failed to take advantage of that chance." Restatement (Third) of Torts: Liability for Physical and Emotional Harm § 9, illus. 2 (2010).

Most jurisdictions that applied the last clear chance doctrine drew a distinction between the rights of plaintiffs who, immediately before the accident, were helpless to avoid the peril which led to their injury, and those who could have saved themselves but were unaware of the danger because of their own negligent inattentiveness. This distinction depended on the state of defendant's knowledge concerning the plaintiff's peril. If the defendant had actual knowledge or "reason to know" of plaintiff's peril and failed to exercise reasonable care to avoid the harm, the defendant would be liable under the last clear chance doctrine to either the helpless plaintiff or the merely inattentive plaintiff.

On the other hand, a defendant who should have known but did not actually know or have "reason to know" of plaintiff's peril was subject to liability under the last clear chance doctrine only to a plaintiff who immediately before the accident was helpless to extricate himself from peril, but not to a merely inattentive plaintiff. In this view, the culpability implied in defendant's actual knowledge of plaintiff's peril (or "reason to know" of it) would override plaintiff's negligence in failing to learn of his peril for purposes of the application of the contributory negligence bar to liability, but defendant's mere negligence would not override plaintiff's mere negligence. (Some jurisdictions recognized an ameliorating doctrine, sometimes called a "humanitarian" doctrine, in which defendant's liability has been recognized in all the permutations discussed above.) See Restatement (Second) of Torts §§ 479 & 480 (1965).

The origins of the doctrine of last clear chance apparently lie in the realm of proximate cause and specifically the "last wrongdoer" rule. See *supra* pages 316–317. Its survival, at least in contributory negligence jurisdictions, may reflect primitive strivings toward a rule of comparative fault as an antidote to the all-or-nothing consequences of the rule of contributory negligence. Yet last clear chance suffers from the same drawback. It, too, is an all-or-nothing rule where it applies, but in the opposite direction. See generally Harper, James and Gray on Torts § 22.14. Most jurisdictions that have adopted comparative fault have abandoned the last clear chance doctrine.

5. *Willful, Wanton or Reckless Misconduct.* Contributory negligence typically has not been regarded as a defense to the defendant's conduct that can be categorized as willful, wanton, or reckless. Harper, James and Gray on Torts § 22.6. Why? On the other hand, the plaintiff's conduct which itself is willful and wanton exposure to risk will bar an action based upon the defendant's willful and wanton conduct. Elliott v. Philadelphia Transp. Co., 356 Pa. 643, 53 A.2d 81 (1947).

6. *Conduct of Rescuers.* Courts rarely find individuals who attempt rescues contributorily negligent. "Rescuers are not prudent; they are heroes." John G. Fleming, The Law of Torts 158 n.18 (9th ed. 1998). For example, in Eckert v. Long Island R.R. Co., 43 N.Y. 502 (1871):

> The evidence showed that the train was approaching in plain view of the deceased, and had he for his own purposes attempted to cross the track, or with a view to save property placed himself voluntarily in a position where he might have received an injury from a collision with the train, his conduct would have been grossly negligent, and no recovery could have been had for such injury. But the evidence further showed that there was a small child upon the track, who, if not rescued, must have been inevitably crushed by the rapidly approaching train. This the deceased saw, and he owed a duty of important obligation to this child to rescue it from its extreme peril, if he could do so without incurring great danger to himself. * * * Under the circumstances in which the deceased was placed, it was not wrongful in him to make every effort in his power to rescue the child, compatible with a reasonable regard for his own safety. * * * He had no time for deliberation. He must act instantly, if at all, as a moment's delay would have been fatal to the child. The law has so high a regard for human life that it will not impute negligence to an effort to preserve it, unless made under such circumstances as to constitute rashness in the judgment of prudent persons. * * * The jury were warranted in finding the deceased free from negligence under the rule as above stated.

The court's opinion states that the decedent "owed a duty of important obligation to this child to rescue it from its extreme peril, if he could do so without incurring great danger to himself. Is the duty referred to a legal duty or only an ethical duty? Compare Stockberger v. United States, 332 F.3d 479, 480 (7th Cir.2003) (Posner, J.) ("The common law traditionally took a hard line, rejecting any legal duty to be a good Samaritan").

7. *Subjective Standards for Measuring the "Reasonable" Conduct of Plaintiffs.* As previously described, see *supra* pages 139–142, negligence law usually measures its standard of conduct by the objective reasonable person standard without taking into account the shortcomings of a particular defendant. Some courts, however, in an effort to alleviate the harsh consequences of contributory negligence, traditionally held that a plaintiff's shortcomings should play a role in deciding whether the plaintiff was contributory negligent. Professor James justified the double standard:

> * * * [I]f the standard of conduct is relaxed for *defendants* who cannot meet a normal standard, then the burden of accident loss resulting from the extra hazards created by society's most dangerous groups (e.g., the young, the novice, the accident prone) will be thrown on the innocent victims of substandard behavior.

Such a conclusion shocks people who believe that the compensation of accident victims is a more important objective of modern tort law than a further refinement of the tort principle, and that compensation should prevail when the two objectives conflict. The application of a relaxed subjective standard to the issue of *plaintiff's* contributory negligence, however, involves no such conflict. * * * For this reason the writer has elsewhere developed the thesis that there should be an explicit double standard of conduct, namely, an external standard for a defendant's negligence, and a (relaxed) subjective standard for contributory negligence. *

Fleming James, Jr., The Qualities of the Reasonable Man in Negligence Cases, 16 Mo. L. Rev. 1, 2 (1951).

B. COMPARATIVE FAULT

Li v. Yellow Cab Co. of California

Supreme Court of California, In Bank, 1975.
13 Cal.3d 804, 119 Cal.Rptr. 858, 532 P.2d 1226.

■ SULLIVAN, JUSTICE. * * * At approximately 9 p.m. on November 21, 1968, plaintiff Nga Li was proceeding northbound on Alvarado in her 1967 Oldsmobile. She was in the inside lane, and about 70 feet before she reached the Third Street intersection she stopped and then began a left turn across the three southbound lanes of Alvarado, intending to enter the driveway of a service station. At this time defendant Robert Phillips, an employee of defendant Yellow Cab Company, was driving a company-owned taxicab southbound in the middle lane on Alvarado. He came over the crest of the hill, passed through the intersection, and collided with the right rear portion of plaintiff's automobile, resulting in personal injuries to plaintiff as well as considerable damage to the automobile.

The court, sitting without a jury, found as facts that defendant Phillips was traveling at approximately 30 miles per hour when he entered the intersection, that such speed was unsafe at that time and place, and that the traffic light controlling southbound traffic at the intersection was yellow when defendant Phillips drove into the intersection. It also found, however, that plaintiff's left turn across the southbound lanes of Alvarado "was made at a time when a vehicle was approaching from the opposite direction so close as to constitute an immediate hazard." The dispositive conclusion of law was as follows: "That the driving of Nga Li was negligent, that such negligence was a proximate cause of the collision, and that she is barred from recovery by reason of such contributory negligence." Judgment for defendants was entered accordingly.

I

"Contributory negligence is conduct on the part of the plaintiff which falls below the standard to which he should conform for his own protection, and which is a legally contributing cause cooperating with the negligence of the defendant in bringing about the plaintiff's harm." Restatement (Second) of Torts § 463. * * * What the effect of such conduct will be is left to a further section, which states the doctrine in its clearest essence: "Except where the defendant has the last clear chance, the plaintiff's contributory negligence *bars recovery* against a defendant whose negligent conduct would otherwise make him liable to the plaintiff for the harm sustained by him." Restatement (Second) of Torts § 467. (Italics added.) * * *

It is unnecessary for us to catalogue the enormous amount of critical comment that has been directed over the years against the "all-or-nothing" approach of the doctrine of contributory negligence. The essence of that criticism has been constant and clear: the doctrine is inequitable in its operation because it fails to distribute responsibility in proportion to fault. * Against this have been raised several arguments in justification but none have proved even remotely adequate to the task. * The basic objection to the doctrine—grounded in the primal concept that in a system in which liability is based on fault, the extent of fault should govern the extent of liability—remains irresistible to reason and all intelligent notions of fairness.

Furthermore, practical experience with the application by juries of the doctrine of contributory negligence has added its weight to analyses of its inherent shortcomings: "Every trial lawyer is well aware that juries often do in fact allow recovery in cases of contributory negligence, and that the compromise in the jury room does result in some diminution of the damages because of the plaintiff's fault. But the process is at best a haphazard and most unsatisfactory one." Prosser, Comparative Negligence, 41 Cal. L. Rev. 1, 4 (1953). * It is manifest that this state of affairs, viewed from the standpoint of the health and vitality of the legal process, can only detract from public confidence in the ability of law and legal institutions to assign liability on a just and consistent basis. * * * 5

It is in view of these theoretical and practical considerations that to this date 25 states, * have abrogated the "all or nothing" rule of contributory negligence and have enacted in its place general apportionment *statutes* calculated in one manner or another to assess liability in proportion to fault. In 1973 these states were joined by Florida, which effected the same result by *judicial* decision. * We are likewise persuaded that logic, practical experience, and fundamental justice counsel against the retention of the doctrine rendering contributory negligence a complete bar to recovery—and that it should be replaced in this state by a system under which liability for damage will be borne by those whose negligence caused it in direct proportion to their respective fault. * * *

II

It is urged that any change in the law of contributory negligence must be made by the Legislature, not by this court. Although the doctrine of contributory negligence is of judicial origin—its genesis being traditionally attributed to the opinion of Lord Ellenborough in

---

5   * * * A contrary conclusion is drawn in an article by Lewis F. Powell, Jr., now [at the time of this opinion] an Associate Justice of the United States Supreme Court. Because a loose form of comparative negligence is already applied in practice by independent American juries, Justice Powell argues, the "all-or-nothing" rule of contributory negligence ought to be retained as a check on the jury's tendency to favor the plaintiff. Powell, Contributory Negligence: A Necessary Check on the American Jury, 43 A.B.A.J. 1005 (1957).

Butterfield v. Forrester (K.B.1809) 103 Eng. Rep. 926—the enactment of section 1714 of the Civil Code[7] in 1872 codified the doctrine as it stood at that date and, the argument continues, rendered it invulnerable to attack in the courts except on constitutional grounds. Subsequent cases of this court, it is pointed out, have unanimously affirmed that—barring the appearance of some constitutional infirmity—the "all-or-nothing" rule is the law of this state and shall remain so until the Legislature directs otherwise. The fundamental constitutional doctrine of separation of powers, the argument concludes, requires judicial abstention. * * *

We have concluded that the foregoing argument, in spite of its superficial appeal, is fundamentally misguided. * * * [I]t was not the intention of the Legislature in enacting section 1714 of the Civil Code, as well as other sections of that code declarative of the common law, to insulate the matters therein expressed from further judicial development; rather it was the intention of the Legislature to announce and formulate existing common law principles and definitions for purposes of orderly and concise presentation and with a distinct view toward continuing judicial evolution. * * *

III

We are thus brought to the second group of arguments which have been advanced by defendants and * * * expose considerations of a practical nature which, it is urged, counsel against the adoption of a rule of comparative negligence in this state * * *.

The most serious of these considerations are those attendant upon the administration of a rule of comparative negligence in cases involving multiple parties. One such problem may arise when all responsible parties are not brought before the court: it may be difficult for the jury to evaluate relative negligence in such circumstances * * *.

A second and related major area of concern involves the administration of the actual process of fact-finding in a comparative negligence system. The assigning of a specific percentage factor to the amount of negligence attributable to a particular party, while in theory a matter of little difficulty, can become a matter of perplexity in the face of hard facts. The temptation for the jury to resort to a quotient verdict in such circumstances can be great. * These inherent difficulties are not, however, insurmountable. Guidelines might be provided the jury which will assist it in keeping focused upon the true inquiry, * and the utilization of special verdicts * or jury interrogatories can be of invaluable assistance in assuring that the jury has approached its sensitive and often complex task with proper standards and appropriate reverence. * * *

Finally there is the problem of the treatment of willful misconduct under a system of comparative negligence. In jurisdictions following the "all-or-nothing" rule, contributory negligence is no defense to an action

---

[7] Section 1714 of the Civil Code has never been amended. It provides as follows: "Everyone is responsible, not only for the result of his willful acts, but also for an injury occasioned to another by his want of ordinary care or skill in the management of his property or person, *except so far as the latter has, willfully or by want of ordinary care, brought the injury upon himself.* The extent of liability in such cases is defined by the Title on Compensatory Relief." (Italics added.)

based upon a claim of willful misconduct * * *. The thought is that the difference between willful and wanton misconduct and ordinary negligence is one of kind rather than degree in that the former involves conduct of an entirely different order, * and under this conception it might well be urged that comparative negligence concepts should have no application when one of the parties has been guilty of willful and wanton misconduct. It has been persuasively argued, however, that the loss of deterrent effect that would occur upon application of comparative fault concepts to willful and wanton misconduct as well as ordinary negligence would be slight, and that a comprehensive system of comparative negligence should allow for the apportionment of damages in all cases involving misconduct which falls short of being intentional. * * *

The existence of the foregoing areas of difficulty and uncertainty * has not diminished our conviction that the time for a revision of the means for dealing with contributory fault in this state is long past due and that it lies within the province of this court to initiate the needed change by our decision in this case. Two of the indicated areas (i.e., multiple parties and willful misconduct) are not involved in the case before us, and we consider it neither necessary nor wise to address ourselves to specific problems of this nature which might be expected to arise. * * *

Our previous comments relating to the remaining two areas of concern (i.e., the status of the doctrines of last clear chance and assumption of risk, and the matter of judicial supervision of the finder of fact) have provided sufficient guidance to enable the trial courts of this state to meet and resolve particular problems in this area as they arise. As we have indicated, last clear chance and assumption of risk (insofar as the latter doctrine is but a variant of contributory negligence) are to be subsumed under the general process of assessing liability in proportion to fault, and the matter of jury supervision we leave for the moment within the broad discretion of the trial courts. * * *

It remains to identify the precise form of comparative negligence which we now adopt for application in this state. Although there are many variants, only the two basic forms need be considered here. The first of these, the so-called "pure" form of comparative negligence, apportions liability in direct proportion to fault in all cases. This was the form adopted by the Supreme Court of Florida in *Hoffman v. Jones*, and it applies by statute in Mississippi, Rhode Island, and Washington. Moreover it is the form favored by most scholars and commentators. * The second basic form of comparative negligence, of which there are several variants, applies apportionment based on fault *up to the point* at which the plaintiff's negligence is equal to or greater than that of the defendant—when that point is reached, plaintiff is barred from recovery. Nineteen states have adopted this form or one of its variants by statute. The principal argument advanced in its favor is moral in nature: that it is not morally right to permit one more at fault in an accident to recover from one less at fault. Other arguments assert the probability of increased insurance, administrative, and judicial costs if a "pure" rather than a "50 percent" system is adopted, but this has been seriously questioned. *

We have concluded that the "pure" form of comparative negligence is that which should be adopted in this state. In our view the "50 percent" system simply shifts the lottery aspect of the contributory negligence rule * to a different ground. As Dean Prosser has noted, under such a system "[i]t is obvious that a slight difference in the proportionate fault may permit a recovery; and there has been much justified criticism of a rule under which a plaintiff who is charged with 49 percent of a total negligence recovers 51 percent of his damages, while one who is charged with 50 percent recovers nothing at all." Prosser, Comparative Negligence, *supra,* 41 Cal. L. Rev. 1, 25 *. In effect "such a rule distorts the very principle it recognizes, i.e., that persons are responsible for their acts to the extent their fault contributes to an injurious result. The partial rule simply lowers, but does not eliminate, the bar of contributory negligence." * * *

For all of the foregoing reasons we conclude that the "all-or-nothing" rule of contributory negligence as it presently exists in this state should be and is herewith superseded by a system of "pure" comparative negligence, the fundamental purpose of which shall be to assign responsibility and liability for damage in direct proportion to the amount of negligence of each of the parties. Therefore, in all actions for negligence resulting in injury to person or property, the contributory negligence of the person injured in person or property shall not bar recovery, but the damages awarded shall be diminished in proportion to the amount of negligence attributable to the person recovering. The doctrine of last clear chance is abolished, and the defense of assumption of risk is also abolished to the extent that it is merely a variant of the former doctrine of contributory negligence; both of these are to be subsumed under the general process of assessing liability in proportion to negligence. Pending future judicial or legislative developments, the trial courts of this state are to use broad discretion in seeking to assure that the principle stated is applied in the interest of justice and in furtherance of the purposes and objectives set forth in this opinion. * * *

■ CLARK, JUSTICE (dissenting). I dissent. For over a century this court has consistently and unanimously held that Civil Code section 1714 codifies the defense of contributory negligence. Suddenly—after 103 years—the court declares section 1714 shall provide for comparative negligence instead. In my view, this action constitutes a gross departure from established judicial rules and role. * * * The majority decision also departs significantly from the recognized limitation upon judicial action—encroaching on the powers constitutionally entrusted to the Legislature. * * * Further, the Legislature is the branch best able to effect transition from contributory to comparative or some other doctrine of negligence. Numerous and differing negligence systems have been urged over the years, yet there remains widespread disagreement among both the commentators and the states as to which one is best. * This court is not an investigatory body, and we lack the means of fairly appraising the merits of these competing systems. Constrained by settled rules of judicial review, we must consider only matters within the record or susceptible to judicial notice. That this court is inadequate to the task of carefully selecting the best replacement system is reflected in the majority's summary manner of eliminating from consideration *all but two* of the many competing proposals—including models adopted by some of our sister states. * * * By abolishing this century old doctrine today, the majority seriously erodes our constitutional function. We are again guilty of judicial chauvinism.

NOTES

1. *Judicial Adoption of Comparative Fault.* The Supreme Court of California rejects the argument "that any change in the law of contributory negligence must be made by the Legislature, not by this court." It does so even though the legislature had codified contributory negligence as a part of its comprehensive Civil Code governing tort liability.

In sharp contrast, the Court of Appeals of Maryland recently "decline[d] to abrogate Maryland's long-established common law principle of contributory negligence," even though the legislature had never codified the principle, relying heavily on the fact that the legislature "has continually considered and failed to pass bills that would abolish or modify the contributory negligence standard" (originally adopted by Maryland courts), thus providing "a clear indication of legislative policy. . . ." Coleman v. Soccer Ass'n of Columbia, 432 Md. 679, 685, 693, 69 A.3d 1149, 1152, 1157 (2013). The court acknowledged "that *stare decisis* should not be construed to inhibit the court "from changing or modifying a common law rule by judicial decision [when] . . . the rule has become unsound in the circumstances of modern life, a vestige of the past, no longer suitable to our people." What "circumstances of modern life" related to whether or not contributory negligence should be a total bar to recovery have changed since the first half of the nineteenth century when the courts in Maryland and elsewhere first adopted this doctrine? What risks are there in interpreting legislative inaction as legislative approval of the status quo? Obviously, the legislature can change the common law if it wants to, as long as the statutory modifications are constitutional, but is it the courts or the legislature that has the primary role in establishing the law governing liability within the tort system? See Gifford & Robinette, Apportioning Liability, 73 Md. L. Rev. at 712–22, 726–28.

2. *Comparison of What?* How is the jury to decide what share of financial responsibility for a plaintiff's damages should be attributed to each party? The answer to this question is by no means self-defining. Is the apportionment to be made by comparing the respective levels of culpability of plaintiff and defendant? Or, by comparing the extent to which each party's fault contributed to the plaintiff's injury? The Restatement of Torts (Third): Apportionment of Liability § 8 (2000) would answer this "either/or" question with an ambiguous "yes":

> Factors for assigning percentages of responsibility to each person whose legal responsibility has been established include
>
> (a) The nature of the person's risk-creating conduct, including any awareness or indifference with respect to the risks created by the conduct * * *
>
> (b) The strength of the causal connection between the person's risk-creating conduct and the harm.

According to the co-reporter for this restatement, the "causal relation referred to in this provision refers to how closely the harm that occurs falls within the risk created by the party's negligence," that is, scope of liability, rather than to any aspect of cause in fact. Telephone Interview with Michael D. Green, Co-reporter, Restatement (Third) of Torts:

Apportionment of Liability (Oct. 10, 2013). Similarly, the Uniform Comparative Fault Act provides that "[i]n determining the percentages of fault, the trier of fact shall consider both the nature of the conduct of each party at fault and the extent of the causal relation between the conduct and the damages claimed." Unif. Apportionment of Tort Responsibility Act § 4, 12 U.L.A. 24 (2003).

Various jurisdictions provide more definitive—albeit conflicting—answers concerning whether percentages of fault are to be determined by degrees of culpability or the extent to which each party contributed to the injury. Compare Wassell v. Adams, 865 F.2d 849 (7th Cir.1989) (Ill. law; per Posner, J.) ("[T]he required comparison is between the respective costs to the plaintiff and to the defendant of avoiding the injury.") and State v. Kaatz, 572 P.2d 775, 782 (Alaska 1977) ("What is to be compared is negligence—conduct, fault, culpability—not causation, either physical or legal.") with Miller v. Am. President Lines, Ltd., 989 F.2d 1450, 1459 (6th Cir.1993) (for purposes of comparative contribution in a maritime personal injury action, "we adopt a comparative causation approach to apportioning damages between tortfeasors") and Moffitt v. Carroll, 640 A.2d 169, 175 (Del.1994) (Delaware statute interpreted to apportion liability "on the basis of the extent of each actor's contribution to the injurious result, i.e. proximate causation"). For more on determining the comparative fault of the plaintiff and the defendant-manufacturer in the context of strict products liability, see *infra* pages 628–629, Note 2.

3. *The Choice between Pure and Modified Comparative Fault. Li* makes clear that a decision to replace contributory negligence with comparative fault leads to a variety of other decisions, most notably, whether the new system should be a "pure" comparative fault approach or a modified one. Most states adopting comparative fault by judicial opinion (approximately a dozen) have opted for pure comparative fault, while the majority of states adopting comparative fault through legislation have chosen a modified approach. See Harper, James and Gray on Torts § 22.15. What might explain judicial preference for the pure approach and legislative preference for the modified approach? The pure form has also been employed for many decades in several federal statutes, including the Federal Employers' Liability Act, 45 U.S.C. § 53 (2012) (since 1908), the Jones Act, 46 U.S.C. § 30104 (2012) (since 1915), and the Death on the High Seas Act, 46 U.S.C. § 30304 (2012) (since 1920), as well as in the common-law jurisdictions of the British Commonwealth.

Modified comparative fault itself has several variations. A majority of modified comparative fault systems apply a version that can be categorized as the "not greater than" approach. In these jurisdictions, the plaintiff's recovery is reduced by the percentage of fault attributable to the plaintiff as long as the plaintiff's fault is "not greater than" that of the defendant. If the plaintiff's fault is greater than the defendant's, the plaintiff recovers nothing. See Harper, James and Gray on Torts §§ 22.15, 22.16. In a minority of modified comparative fault jurisdictions, classified as "not as great as" jurisdictions, the plaintiff's recovery is reduced by the percentage of fault attributable to the plaintiff as long as the plaintiff's percentage of fault is "not as great as" that attributable to the defendant. These two variations of modified comparative fault produce different results only where the jury allocates fifty percent of the fault to the plaintiff and fifty percent to the defendant. How important is this distinction? How frequently would you anticipate that juries allocate fault on a "50–50" basis? South Dakota opts for a third alternative: allowing the plaintiff to recover only when its negligence is "slight" compared with that of the defendant.

See Gifford & Robinette, Apportioning Liability, 73 Md. L. Rev. at 740–45, for a debate between the authors on the respective advantages and disadvantages of pure and modified comparative fault.

4. *Informing the Jury of the Consequences of Its Allocations of Fault.* In some comparative fault jurisdictions, the jury is asked to complete interrogatories or a special verdict form showing the total damages sustained by the plaintiff as well as the percentages of fault attributable to the plaintiff and each defendant. In other jurisdictions, the jury is simply asked to return a general verdict. In either event, should the jury be informed of the consequences of its allocations of fault? For example, assume the jury finds the plaintiff's total compensable damages to be $1,000,000, and that the fault of the plaintiff and the defendant each equals fifty percent. In a "not as great as" modified comparative fault jurisdiction, should the jury be told that such an allocation would result in the plaintiff recovering nothing, but if the jury allocated 50.1 percent of the fault to the defendant, the plaintiff would recover $501,000? Compare Seppi v. Betty, 99 Idaho 186, 193, 579 P.2d 683, 690–91 (1978) (jury should ordinarily be told of consequences) with McGowan v. Story, 70 Wis.2d 189, 234 N.W.2d 325 (1975) (jury should not be told).

5. *Comparing the Plaintiff's Fault with the Fault of Multiple Defendants.* Should the plaintiff's degree of fault be compared with that of each defendant individually or with the combined degrees of negligence of all defendants? Assume the jury assesses the plaintiff's percentage of fault as forty percent and the degree of fault of each of two defendants at thirty percent. In a modified comparative fault jurisdiction with either an "as great as" or "no greater than" rule, the issue of whether the degrees of fault of the defendants are combined will determine whether or not the plaintiff recovers. Compare Elder v. Orluck, 511 Pa. 402, 515 A.2d 517 (1986) (plaintiff barred from recovery only if plaintiff's degree of fault is greater than that of combined defendants) with Stannard v. Harris, 135 Vt. 544, 380 A.2d 101 (1977) (statute construed to provide comparison of plaintiff's degree of fault with that of each individual defendant). Which view seems more consistent with the purposes of comparative fault? Which seems more likely to encourage settlement negotiations among the parties?

6. *Should Judgments of Plaintiff and Defendant Be Set Off Against Each Other?* In a pure comparative fault jurisdiction, it is now possible that in a negligence action, the plaintiff will recover against the defendant and the defendant will recover against the plaintiff on defendant's counterclaim. This could happen, for example, in a routine automobile accident. The same possibility of reciprocal recovery could occur in a "not greater than" modified comparative fault jurisdiction if the jury finds the plaintiff and the defendant to be equally at fault.

Should the amount of the defendant's judgment against the plaintiff on the counterclaim be set off against the plaintiff's recovery on the original claim? Why does it matter? What happens if both parties are insured? If neither party is insured but one defendant is insolvent and judgment-proof? The Third Restatement provides that "[i]f two parties are liable to each other in the same suit, each party is entitled to a setoff of any recovery owed by the other party, except that, in cases in which one or both of the parties has liability insurance, setoff does not reduce the payment of a liability insurer unless an applicable rule of law or statute so provides." Restatement (Third) of Torts: Apportionment of Liability § 9 (2000). See also Jess v. Herrmann, 26 Cal.3d 131, 161 Cal.Rptr. 87, 604 P.2d 208 (1979); Stuyvesant Ins. Co. v. Bournazian, 342 So.2d 471 (Fla.1976).

C. Plaintiff's Opportunity to Minimize Harm

Lange v. Hoyt

Supreme Court of Errors of Connecticut, 1932.
114 Conn. 590, 159 A. 575.

[Consolidated actions brought by Minelda Lange, a minor, through her next friend, for personal injuries and by Minette B. Lange, her mother, for expenses, etc. Plaintiffs had a verdict and defendant appeals.]

■ Avery, J. * * * The plaintiff Minelda sustained a fracture of her left arm, and a fracture and dislocation of the pelvis. Upon the trial, evidence was offered, and the plaintiff claimed, that there was a deformity of the pelvis whereby the right side of the pelvis was displaced upward about one-half inch, so as to diminish the size of the pelvic outlet; and that this deformity was permanent and would interfere with normal childbirth when the plaintiff reached maturity.

It was the claim of the defendant that the condition of the arm and pelvis was aggravated by lack of proper medical treatment after the accident. The plaintiff Minette B. Lange was a believer in Christian Science and had brought her daughter, Minelda, up in the same belief. On the day of the accident, the mother called a medical practitioner who gave first-aid treatment, and advised the removal of the child to the Danbury Hospital. She was removed to the hospital on the same day, where efforts were made by the physicians to reduce the fracture, and a temporary splint was applied, and X-rays taken. The defendant claims that the mother then took the child home against the advice of the physicians; and that, thereafter, medical advice was not had for the child's injuries until the 15th day of May, when a physician visited the plaintiffs on behalf of the defendant and recommended that medical and surgical treatment be secured immediately, but that such medical and surgical treatment was not obtained until May 27th, when Minelda was taken to New York for X-ray examination; and, thereafter, was treated by a surgeon. In substance, the claim of the defendant is that because of lack of surgical treatment from the day of the accident until May 27th, the plaintiff's injuries were aggravated; and that proper treatment by regular physicians and surgeons from the beginning would have effected a substantial cure of her injuries so that no permanent disability would have resulted therefrom.

On the other hand, the plaintiff Minelda Lange claims that she reasonably relied upon her mother to provide such curative agencies as the latter thought necessary; and the mother claimed that on the day of the accident, in addition to first-aid treatment by a regular surgeon, she secured the services of a surgical nurse and had Minelda's arm set by a qualified surgeon at the Danbury Hospital; that from the time of the accident to the time of the trial Minelda was cared for by a competent nurse, had frequent X-rays and treatments by a competent orthopedic surgeon, and between May 2d and May 25th was kept quiet and in bed at home; that no other treatment was suggested by the surgeons nor was she ever informed that further surgical treatments would be useful until the defendant's physician so recommended about May 21st; after which, and as soon as possible, the services of a competent orthopedist and a competent X-ray specialist were engaged on behalf of her daughter.

In view of these claims, the defendant * * * asked the court to inform the jury as to the duty of one injured to exercise ordinary care to cure and restore herself, and assigns error in the charge as delivered upon this subject. The defendant was undoubtedly entitled to have the jury instructed upon this phase of the case. We think, however, the charge as delivered covered the substance of defendant's requests so far as they were proper. * * * It is a rule of general application that one who has been injured by the negligence of another must use reasonable care to promote recovery and prevent any aggravation or increase of the injuries. * * *

The charge of the court is to be tested by the situation disclosed by the claims of proof. Minelda was a child eight years of age, and even if there had been neglect of proper surgical treatment by her mother, the negligence of the parent would not be imputable to the child. * The jury were in substance, told that if they found the negligence of the defendant was a substantial factor in producing Minelda's injuries, she would be entitled to recover, even though negligence on behalf of the parent in failing to obtain proper surgical treatment might have occurred with the negligence of the defendant. As regards the plaintiff Minette B. Lange, the jury were in effect told that she was entitled to recover for expenses incurred by her for nursing, surgery, etc., in connection with her daughter's injuries in so far as the wrongful conduct of the defendant was a substantial factor in producing the injuries. If the injuries were in any way aggravated by the failure of the parent to exercise reasonable care to obtain proper medical and surgical treatment, the parent could not recover for any aggravation of the injuries so caused.

The jury were told that the conduct of both plaintiffs with reference to the presence or absence of reasonable care was to be judged in the light of all the surrounding circumstances including whatever belief as to methods of treatment the jury might have found they conscientiously held. The reference in the last clause of this charge was to the fact that the plaintiff Minette B. Lange was a Christian Scientist and her conduct in the effort to promote the recovery of her daughter was in part at least actuated by the tenets of that belief. While the test of conduct on the part of a plaintiff in promoting a recovery from injuries suffered is one of reasonable care and cannot be made to depend upon the idiosyncrasies of personal belief no matter how honestly held, courts cannot disregard theories as to proper curative methods, held by a large number of reasonable and intelligent people. Reading the charge in the light of the facts claimed to have been proved, it went no farther than saying that, in determining whether the plaintiff Minette B. Lange exercised a reasonable degree of care, the jury were entitled to consider with all the other evidence her conduct in the light of her belief in the doctrines of the Christian Science Church and the extent to which she acted in accordance with them. This was as favorable a charge to the defendant as she was entitled to have upon this feature of the case.

The defendant further complains that the charge was inadequate, in that it did not sufficiently explain to the jury the effect which negligence on the part of the mother in failing to afford proper surgical treatment to her daughter might have as an intervening cause which would relieve the defendant from liability for such part of her injuries as would otherwise have been avoided. * * * Where an injured plaintiff uses reasonable care in the selection of a physician or surgeon, the right of recovery is not affected by the negligence or improper action of the latter. * Primarily the defendant is liable for all the pain, suffering, and injury resulting from his wrongdoing, and to relieve him of any of it there must be some act or neglect intervening sufficient to break the causal connection between the injuries actually suffered, and that wrongdoing; and where the plaintiff has performed his full duty in using reasonable care in employing a physician or surgeon, the latter's neglect or default is not deemed in law sufficient to produce that result. * A child of the age of eight years is necessarily dependent upon her parents as regards the steps to be taken to bring about a recovery from an injury, and, if she is not herself guilty of any negligence or improper conduct, the failure of the parents to take proper steps to that end, by a parity of reasoning, cannot be such a cause of any portion of the injuries as will defeat a recovery for all the results of the defendant's wrongdoing. The charge of the trial court was too favorable to the defendant in suggesting that the mother's negligence in failing to secure surgical attention to her daughter might be such an intervening cause as would defeat a recovery for damages for such part of the latter's injury as might have been avoided thereby.

There is no error. * * *

NOTES

1. *Rule of Avoidable Consequences.* An injured plaintiff may aggravate an injury following the original accident by unreasonably failing to take steps to minimize the damages. For example, she might fail to treat a wound, resulting in infection and the loss of a limb. Under the so-called "rule of avoidable consequences," the plaintiff is not allowed to recover for the "aggravated" portion of injury because of her "duty" to use reasonable care to mitigate damages. See Restatement (Second) of Torts § 918 & illus. 1 (1979) (adopting the doctrine at a time when contributory negligence totally barred recovery). "The plaintiff's 'duty' is measured by the standard of reasonableness in the circumstances." Harper, James, and Gray on Torts § 25.4. The plaintiff is not required to place herself at grave personal risk. In Albert v. Monarch Fed. Sav. & Loan Ass'n, 327 N.J.Super. 462, 465–66, 743 A.2d 890, 892 (App.Div.2000), for example, the court held that the defendant was entitled to a jury instruction on plaintiff's duty to mitigate damages if the evidence supported a finding that surgery would offer "a reasonable prospect of restoration or relief from the disability" when there was no evidence that such surgery would involve undue risk to the plaintiff's health, the possibility of death, or extraordinary suffering.

The Restatement (Third) of Torts: Apportionment of Liability § 3 (2000), comment *b* "abrogates" the rule of avoidable consequences as a total bar to recovery. Instead plaintiff's unreasonable conduct in failing to avoid the consequences of her injury enters into the determination of her degree of comparative fault.

Consider also, in the context of *Langet,* whether a plaintiff suing a physician for negligence in a sterilization procedure and the subsequent wrongful pregnancy must resort to either adoption or abortion in order to mitigate the damages. See, e.g., Smith v. Gore, 728 S.W.2d 738, 751–52 (Tenn.1987) (to impose duties of abortion or adoption in the case of wrongful pregnancy "not only would * * * impermissibly infringe upon Constitutional rights to privacy, * * * but the nature of these alternatives are so extreme as to be unreasonable").

2. *Minimizing Harm and Damage to Property.* Does the obligation to minimize harm in the context of personal injury also apply in cases involving damage to property? In North Bend Lumber Co. v. City of Seattle, 116 Wash. 500, 504–05, 199 P. 988, 989–90 (1921), the Washington Supreme Court held:

> * * * [O]ne is not bound to use his property in anticipation of a situation arising, which, because of the negligence of someone else, known to or suspected by him, may or may not cause him damage. * * * At least, up to the point where one has become morally certain that the negligence of another will injure him he may make any proper and customary use of his property in total disregard of any negligence of that other, whether such negligence be known to him or not. One owns real estate for the use he may make of it. Being the owner, he may make such use of it as he sees fit, so long as he does not injure his neighbor or violate some principle of the doctrine of police regulation. * * *

> The rule which requires one to make a reasonable effort to protect his person from the known negligence of another is a rule of personal conduct, and in the nature of things cannot be extended to the use of property.

A famous discussion of the same issue is contained in LeRoy Fibre Co. v. Chicago, Milwaukee & St. Paul Ry., 232 U.S. 340, 34 S.Ct. 415, 58 L.Ed. 631 (1914). The plaintiff had stored highly flammable flax straw on his own property adjacent to a railroad track. The flax straw was destroyed by a fire caused by the negligent operation of the defendant's locomotive engine. The question before the Supreme Court was whether the jury might consider the plaintiff's storage of the flax as evidence of contributory negligence. Justice McKenna, speaking for a majority of the Court, held that there was no evidence of the plaintiff's contributory negligence to be submitted to the jury:

> That one's uses of his property may be subject to the servitude of the wrongful use by another of his property seems an anomaly. * * * It casts upon him the duty of not only using his own property so as not to injure another, but so to use his own property that it may not be injured by the wrongs of another. * * * The doctrine of contributory negligence is entirely out of place.

Justice Holmes, partially concurring, expressed a substantially different view of the respective property rights of the plaintiff and the defendant:

> If a man stacked his flax so near to a railroad that it obviously was likely to be set fire to by a well-managed train, I should say that he could not throw the loss upon the road by the oscillating result of an inquiry by the jury whether the road had used due care. I should say that although of course he had a right to put his flax where he liked upon his own land, the liability of the railroad for a fire was absolutely conditioned upon the stacks being at a reasonably safe distance from the train. * * *

> If I am right so far, a very important element in determining the right to recover is whether the plaintiff's flax was so near to the track as to be in danger from even a prudently managed engine. Here certainly, except in a clear case, we should call in the jury. I do not suppose that anyone would call it prudent to stack flax within five feet of the engines or imprudent to do it at a distance of half a mile, and it would not be absurd if the law ultimately should formulate an exact measure, as it has tended to in other instances; * but at present I take it that if the question I suggest be material we should let the jury decide whether seventy feet was too near by the criterion that I have proposed. * * *

> I do not think we need trouble ourselves with the thought that my view depends upon differences of degree. * * * Negligence is all degree, * * * and between the variations according to distance that I suppose to exist and the simple universality of the rules in the Twelve Tables or the *Leges Barbarorum*, there lies the culture of two thousand years.

Law v. Superior Court for the County of Maricopa

Supreme Court of Arizona, 1988.
157 Ariz. 147, 755 P.2d 1135.

■ FELDMAN, VICE CHIEF JUSTICE. * * * The basic question presented is whether Arizona should recognize the so-called "seat belt defense." * * *

On the evening of November 8, 1985, Cindy Law was driving her parents' car in Tempe, Arizona. She apparently pulled in front of an automobile operated by James Harder, who swerved violently to avoid a collision. Unfortunately, his evasive maneuver overturned the Harder vehicle. Harder and his wife were not wearing their seat belts and were thrown from their car—James through a closed sunroof. The Harders suffered severe orthopedic injuries as a result of the accident.

The Harders (plaintiffs) brought a negligence action against Cindy Law and her parents (defendants). During the course of discovery, defendants sought information concerning plaintiffs' use and experience with seat belts and shoulder restraints. Plaintiffs objected to these discovery requests on the grounds that the subject was irrelevant [under an intermediate appellate court precedent holding and] * * * that evidence of a passenger's failure to wear a seat belt was inadmissible either to show breach of a duty to minimize damages or to prove contributory negligence.

Defendants moved to compel discovery. In June 1986, the trial judge denied the motion and issued a protective order, concluding that * * * motorists have no duty to wear seat belts. Thus, evidence of a causal connection between the failure to wear seat belts and the extent of plaintiffs' injuries was irrelevant. * * * The court of appeals vacated the trial judge's protective order and held that evidence of seat belt nonuse was admissible so long as defendants could demonstrate a causal relationship between the nonuse and the injuries. * * * In their petition for review, plaintiffs ask us to [decide whether this court should] * * * sanction the introduction of evidence concerning seat belt nonuse as an aid to the apportionment of damages. * * *

I.   An Overview of the Seat Belt Problem.

A.   *The Seat Belt Defense*

* * * As seat belts became a standard automotive fixture, defendants increasingly raised the "seat belt defense." At first, defense attorneys attempted to use the defense as a complete bar to recovery by showing that plaintiff was contributorily negligent. * These efforts were generally unsuccessful. * Courts were unwilling to totally deny recovery based on a finding of contributory negligence when it was almost certain in every case that nonuse of the seat belt was not a cause of the primary accident. *

The focus of defense efforts rapidly shifted to asserting that the victim had failed to properly mitigate damages by not wearing a seat belt. * The mitigation theory sharply split the courts. Some jurisdictions accepted the idea that a plaintiff was responsible to take reasonable pre-accident safety measures. * Most courts refused to bend traditional mitigation concepts to cover the victim's pre-accident conduct. * Arizona followed this majority rule in Nash v. Kamrath, 21 Ariz.App. 530, 521 P.2d 161 (1974). * * *

We must now decide whether the *Nash* position should remain the proper rule for the state of Arizona. In our view, the technological and legal changes that have occurred in the twelve years that passed between *Nash* and the decision in the present case must determine which view of the law represents better policy. One of the most dramatic changes that has occurred in this period is the general acceptance of comparative negligence principles.

B.   *The Growth and Relevance of Comparative Negligence*

* * * Traditional contributory negligence theory, of course, militates for rejection of the seat belt defense. Contributory negligence is conceptualized in terms of conduct by plaintiff which contributed to the occurrence of the accident. * Because seat belt nonuse seldom contributes to the occurrence of the accident, it does not easily fit into the theory of contributory negligence. But see Kington v. Camden, 19 Ariz. App. 361, 507 P.2d 700 (1973) (if driver had fastened her seat belt, she would not have lost control of her vehicle and caused crash). Further, if the seat belt defense is considered a form of contributory negligence, it would totally bar recovery. * * * However, nonuse of a seat belt rarely causes all of plaintiff's injuries. In the typical accident, nonuse simply increases the number or severity of injuries beyond those which would have occurred had the plaintiff used a seat belt. Thus,

under traditional contributory negligence principles, the seat belt defense would have constituted a harsh and untenable policy denying all recovery to nonusers, despite the lack of any causal nexus between seat belt nonuse and some of the injuries.

Comparative negligence theories eliminate most of those problems because an adverse finding on nonuse does not bar recovery but merely reduces the damages in proportion to the contributing factor of seat belt nonuse. Thus, since *Nash*, courts originally unwilling to enforce a total bar to plaintiff's recovery under contributory negligence now are able to make a proportionate reduction of damages under comparative negligence concepts. * This, in fact, furthers the basic goal of comparative negligence theory—to allow an appraisal of all relevant facts in determining the correct damages to be given each claimant in a personal injury case. *

Given this choice, courts able to apply comparative negligence principles to seat belt defense cases broke their analysis into at least two steps. Nonuse of the seat belt generally was not a factor contributing to the accident. However, by failing to use available seat belts, the plaintiff might have enhanced the injuries over those which would have occurred if the belts had been used. * Thus, to ascertain the proper damages, the emphasis switched to this "second collision" between the occupants and their environment. * Even with this new focus, the difficulty of determining the complex calculus of all conceivable causal connections involved in any accident dissuaded some courts from recognizing the defense. * Nevertheless, the rise of comparative negligence undermined much of the theoretical basis for rejection of the defense. * * *

II.   The Seat Belt Defense in Arizona

With the foregoing in mind, we must now decide whether Arizona will adopt some version of the so-called seat belt defense. To do so, we first examine the current validity of the principles underlying the *Nash* decision.

A.   *The Probability of Motor Vehicle Accidents*

Because *Nash* held that motorists could assume that all who use the highways will drive with care, the decision imposed no duty to anticipate injury. Over a lifetime, however, it is almost certain that a motor vehicle accident *will* injure the average motorist. * The clear foreseeability of automobile accidents is the reason most courts now hold automobile manufacturers responsible to make vehicles capable of providing a reasonable level of protection to automobile occupants. * * * Given modern-day conditions, we conclude as a matter of public policy that the law must recognize the responsibility of every person to anticipate and take reasonable measures to guard against the danger of motor vehicle accidents that are not only foreseeable but virtually certain to occur sooner or later. Rejection of the seat belt defense can no longer be based on the antediluvian doctrine that one need not anticipate the negligence of others. There is nothing to anticipate; the negligence of motorists is omnipresent.

B.   *Seat Belts as a Cause of Harm*

In *Nash*, the court noted that seat belts may actually create or enhance injuries instead of preventing them. * There are reports of tragic situations when wearing a seat belt may trap a vehicle occupant in a burning, sinking, or disabled automobile. * Such cases are noteworthy precisely because they are so rare.[29] It is statistically far safer for motorists to remain in their vehicles than to suffer the vagaries of a violent ejection from the automobile. * There are also claims that properly worn seat belts can cause direct and serious harm to users. These assertions focus on abdominal and spinal injuries that may be attributable to seat belt use. However, it is also true that in almost every instance seat belt-induced injuries are far less drastic than those that would have been incurred without the seat belt use. * As a general rule, a motorist is simply better off wearing a seat belt. * We conclude from the technological data that continued non-recognition of the seat belt defense cannot be based on the general concept that seat belts cause harm. The opposite is generally true.

C. The "Duty" to Wear Seat Belts

Nash held there was no duty to wear seat belts. We acknowledge that "duty" to use restraints is generally considered the prime question in cases such as this. * Whatever its relevance to the *Nash* analysis, however, we do not believe that duty in its usual formulation remains a relevant component of the seat belt defense analysis. "Duty" is normally defined in terms of the obligation of care owed to one's neighbors. * * * Because in all but the rarest situation nonuse of a seat belt presents no foreseeable danger to others, it is probably incorrect to conceptualize the seat belt defense in terms of duty. * * *

Everyone has a "duty" to use due care to prevent injury to others. Nonuse of a seat belt is not a question of duty but rather a matter of conduct which only occasionally impinges on others.[33] Thus, we believe that injuries sustained by the plaintiff as a result of his nonuse of an available seat belt are not so much a failure to use care to avoid endangering others but part of the related obligation to conduct oneself reasonably to minimize damages and avoid foreseeable harm to oneself. *

Thus, the seat belt defense would ordinarily raise issues concerning the doctrine of avoidable consequences—a theory that denies recovery for those injuries plaintiff could reasonably have avoided. * Plaintiffs argue that this doctrine is applied only to post-accident conduct and is inapplicable to events preceding the accident—a time when plaintiffs supposedly had a right to assume that others would not act negligently. * Assuming this is ordinarily true, we believe the common law conceptualization of the doctrine of avoidable consequences has been modified by our comparative negligence statute, which applies that doctrine to pre-accident conduct.

---

[29] An agency of the federal government has calculated that the use of seat belt systems by all automobile occupants could reduce fatalities and serious injuries by one-half each year. United States Department of Transportation, National Highway Traffic Safety Administration, Progress and Assessment Report in the National Safety Belt Usage Program (Sept. 1983).

[33] For instance, an adult driver who has a legal duty of due care to passengers in his automobile arguably might be held liable for negligence in failing to fasten the seat belt of a young child riding in the car. The motorist who fails to buckle up while driving and, as a result, loses control so that the car strikes another vehicle, might have negligently breached his duty of due care to other users of the highway. *

D. *The Comparative Negligence Statute*

[In 1984, the Arizona legislature adopted comparative negligence.] * * * The essential question is whether a plaintiff who does not wear an automobile seat belt is at "fault" for injuries enhanced or caused by the failure to use the seat belt. Neither the Arizona comparative negligence statute nor its progenitor uniform law contains any definition of "fault." We do note the instructive definition of this term given in § 1(b) of the Uniform Comparative Fault Act (UCFA), 12 U.L.A. 39–40 (Cum.Supp.1987):

> "Fault" includes acts or omissions that are in any measure negligent or reckless toward the person or property of the actor or others, or that subject a person to strict tort liability. *The term also includes * * * unreasonable failure to avoid an injury or to mitigate damages. * * **

As stated in the official comment to the UCFA, negligent failure to use a seat belt would reduce damages solely for those injuries directly attributable to the lack of seat belt restraint. * Thus, as far as the calculation of damages is concerned, the comparative negligence statutes apply the doctrine of avoidable consequences to pre-accident conduct. * * *

Our examination of the applicable caselaw and our analysis of the concept of "duty" lead us to the conclusion that the seat belt defense is not a question of duty at all. * * * At least under the comparative fault statute, each person is under an obligation to act reasonably to minimize foreseeable injuries and damages. Thus, if a person chooses not to use an available, simple safety device, that person may be at "fault."

E. *Preempting the Role of the Legislature*

Plaintiffs claim that recognition of the seat belt defense is a matter we should leave to the legislature. * * * Some courts hold that creation of a "seat belt defense" is solely a matter for legislative action. * We believe, however, that this court has an obligation to participate in the evolution of tort law so that it may reflect societal and technological changes. * In some cases, this responsibility has compelled us to recognize duties that further public policy and legislative objectives, even though the specifics have not been enacted by the legislature. See, e.g., Ontiveros v. Borak, 136 Ariz. 500, 667 P.2d 200 (1983) [holding that a tavern owner who was negligent in continuing to serve liquor to a patron who was intoxicated could be held liable to those subsequently injured by the patron in an automobile accident].[a]

---

[a]   [Eds. note] In *Ontiveros*, the Arizona Supreme Court found that the common law of Arizona had previously held that tavern owners were not liable under such circumstances. It then justified its willingness to overrule its own precedents:

> However, the common law, which is judge-made and judge-applied, can and will be changed when changed conditions and circumstances establish that it is unjust or has become bad public policy. * * *

> Inherent in the common law is a dynamic principle which allows it to grow and to tailor itself to meet changing needs within the doctrine of stare decisis, which, if correctly understood, was not static and did not forever prevent the courts from reversing themselves or from applying principles of common law to new situations as the need arose. If this were not so, we must succumb to a rule that a judge

Acceptance of the seat belt defense does not require us to violate the proper deference owed the legislature. We neither carry a legislative enactment past the intent which existed at the time of its passage nor recognize an obligation not already reflected in the lives of our citizens. We only acknowledge reality: the use or nonuse of a seat belt is an everyday matter of conduct which plays a significant role in determining the extent of injuries. To hold that we cannot let a jury consider such conduct on the issue of damages is to judicially transmogrify legislative non-action on a common law damage issue into legislative intent to approve nonuse of seat belts. Such a conclusion has never been expressed by the legislature and is very far from the demonstrated legislative objectives in this area. Of course, if we are wrong, and if the legislature intends that in this state one may unreasonably refuse to use a seat belt and nevertheless hold another responsible for the resulting damages, it can easily enact such a policy.

F. *Windfall to the Tortfeasor*

Plaintiffs claim that by recognizing the seat belt defense, we would confer a windfall on tortfeasors. As noted *ante*, the crux of comparative negligence is a proper apportionment of damages based upon the fault of the respective parties. If a victim unreasonably failed to use an available, simple prophylactic device, then he will not be able to recover for damages created or enhanced by the nonuse. * Thus, although some tortfeasors may pay less than they otherwise *would*, they will not pay less than they *should*. We do not believe this rule creates a windfall to the tortfeasor; it is an unavoidable consequence of our comparative negligence system.

G. *Undue Complication of Litigation*

Petitioners maintain that allowing apportionment of damages based on failure to use seat belts will unnecessarily complicate and protract litigation. The defendant must establish several factual predicates before seat belt nonuse may be presented to the jury. * To prove these factors, the defendant may utilize qualified experts in the medical, scientific, and accident reconstruction fields. It is then up to the factfinder to evaluate the evidence and quantify the results under comparative negligence principles.

Of course, this process will take time and create new issues for the jury to decide. These problems are hardly insurmountable. Juries perform this type of operation on a regular basis in many types of civil and criminal cases. The very idea of comparative negligence requires that juries apportion fault. The same is true when juries apportion fault between joint tortfeasors. * In some second impact or so-called "crashworthiness" cases, juries are required to determine the injuries attributable both to the original accident and to a manufacturer's failure to produce an automobile capable of withstanding foreseeable accidents. * Courts almost universally entertain such actions, even

---

should let others "long dead and unaware of the problems of the age in which he lives, do his thinking for him."

Lewis v. Wolf, 122 Ariz. at 568, 596 P.2d at 706 (quoting Mr. Justice Douglas, *Stare Decisis*, 49 Colum. L. Rev. 735, 736 (1949)). * * *

though some recognize the complications produced by injury apportionment. *

There is no doubt that the seat belt defense will complicate and lengthen litigation in some cases. While this certainly does not militate in favor of its acceptance, we believe the problem is no different in principle from that posed by any legal, technological or scientific advance. Neither law nor society can ignore technological change simply because it makes decision more complex.

H.   *Unwanted and Unforeseen Consequences*

As the final argument, plaintiffs assert that introducing evidence of seat belt nonuse would propel our courts into a morass of unforeseen consequences. If seat belt nonuse is relevant, why not introduce evidence of failure to install air bags? Why not hold the plaintiff responsible for failure to buy a large car which is normally much safer in a crash than a small car?

We are faced with a concrete application of comparative negligence principles. We deal in this case only with a plaintiff's use or nonuse of a common, simple safety device *available* in his or her car. In making use of an available seat belt, a motorist need not possess engineering expertise, suffer significant inconvenience, install special equipment or purchase a different vehicle. He or she need use only a few seconds to fasten a convenient safety device. The exact bounds of fault in other fact situations is a matter for the common law to address in its customary evolutionary fashion. *

I.   *Resolution*

We conclude that irrespective of a duty to avoid injuring others, under the theory of comparative "fault," nonuse of a seat belt is a factor that the jury may consider and use to reduce damages under the following conditions:

1. Where the date of the injury is after the effective date of the comparative negligence statute.
2. Where the injured party is of an age and discretion that his or her nonuse could be considered as "fault."
3. When the nonuse was unreasonable under all of the circumstances. * * *
4. Where nonuse either causes injuries which would not have occurred had the restraint been used or enhances those injuries that did occur.
5. Where the evidence shows with reasonable probability the degree of enhancement.

The burden of establishing these matters, as with other matters of comparative negligence, is upon the defendant. * Further, the jury must be clearly instructed that nonuse of a seat belt is an issue bearing upon the extent of damages that may be recovered and not on any other issue. * * *

■ HOLOHAN, JUSTICE, dissenting. * * * Reliance on comparative negligence principles is inconsistent with and serves to confuse that concept as it has been adopted in this state. * * * It is not necessary or correct to use a comparative negligence formula to arrive at the ruling by the court. If the "seat belt defense" is to be adopted, Judge Weis suggests that the doctrine of avoidable consequences is more appropriate:

> Restatement (Second) of Torts § 433 provides for apportionment of damages when plaintiff's conduct was a factor in the harm and comment *f* explains that the doctrine of avoidable consequences is an application of the rule. Because avoidable consequences applies to actions taken after the impact, it has been said to be inapplicable to the seat belt defense. That distinction has not always been observed, however, and should not be controlling in this case. Simply because the correct pigeon-hole for the legal theory is not immediately apparent does not mean that critical evidence should be disregarded. Its relevance is apparent. The test should be not when the challenged activity or non-activity took place; rather, the focus should be whether it played a part in producing the event or was totally unrelated to that event and affected only the injury. The inquiry should not be chronological, but causal. *

Vizzini v. Ford Motor Co., 569 F.2d 754, 770 (3d Cir.1977) (Weis, J., concurring and dissenting). * * *

* * * The important consideration is who should make the decision to impose the duty (or non-duty)? What branch of government under our constitutional system should make such a public policy decision? * * * Public policy exists only as long as there is public support. Courts decide matters, institutionally, without regard to public support. Protecting the constitutional rights of unpopular individuals or groups often involves deciding matters against public opinion, but in doing so, courts perform their well-recognized "judicial function." Courts, however, make poor law makers. They make law on a case-by-case method usually with limited information and without a legislator's concern for public support. * * * [I]n this area of public safety the courts, with the case-by-case method, are powerless to provide a comprehensive program of policy, enforcement and education. The legislative branch is the proper one to deal with this complex problem if there is to be an effective and unified solution. * * *

NOTES

1. *Nonuse of Seat Belt and the Doctrine of Avoidable Consequences.* Some jurisdictions allow the reduction of damages payable to a plaintiff who failed to wear a seat belt under the doctrine of avoidable consequences, rather than under either a contributory negligence or comparative fault approach. E.g., Spier v. Barker, 35 N.Y.2d 444, 363 N.Y.S.2d 916, 323 N.E.2d 164 (1974). What difference does it make whether the plaintiff's damages are reduced under a comparative fault analysis or under the doctrine of avoidable consequences? In a state where contributory negligence remains a complete bar to recovery? In a "modified" comparative fault jurisdiction?

What about head injuries to a motorcyclist who is not wearing a helmet at the time of an accident?

2. *Guidelines and Limits on Recovery for Failure to Use Seat Belt.* The English Court of Appeal reached a different conclusion—and a somewhat unusual one—regarding how the failure to use a seat belt should affect a plaintiff's recovery. In Froom v. Butcher, [1976] Q.B. 286, [1975] 3 W.L.R. 379, [1975] 3 All E.R. 520 (C.A.), Lord Denning reasoned as follows:

> * * * If the plaintiff was to blame in not wearing a seat belt, the damage is in part the result of his own fault. He must bear some share in the responsibility for the damage: and his damages fall to be reduced to such extent as the court thinks just and equitable. * * *

> Th[e] question should not be prolonged by an expensive inquiry into the degree of blameworthiness on either side, which would be hotly disputed. Suffice it to assess a share of responsibility which will be just and equitable in the great majority of cases.

> Sometimes the evidence will show that the failure made no difference. The damage would have been the same, even if a seat belt had been worn. In such case the damages should not be reduced at all. At other times the evidence will show that the failure made all the difference. The damage would have been prevented altogether if a seat belt had been worn. In such cases I would suggest that the damages should be reduced by 25 per cent. But often the evidence will only show that the failure made a considerable difference. Some injuries to the head, for instance, would have been a good deal less severe if a seat belt had been worn, but there would still have been some injury to the head. In such case I would suggest that the damages attributable to the failure to wear a seat belt should be reduced by 15 per cent.

Compare Iowa Code § 321.445(4)(b) (2013) (failure to wear seat belt as required by statute may not be considered evidence of comparative fault; it may be "admitted to mitigate damages," but may reduce plaintiff's recovery by not more than 5 percent of the damages awarded after any reductions for comparative fault); Mich. Comp. Laws Ann. § 257.710e(7) (2014) (failure to wear seat belt "may be considered evidence of negligence" but "shall not reduce the recovery for damages by more than 5 percent").

A few states continue to consider evidence of the plaintiff's failure to use a seat belt inadmissible. E.g., Md. Code Ann., Transp. § 22–412.3(h)(1) (2014).

D. ASSUMPTION OF RISK AND RELATED CONCEPTS

Seigneur v. National Fitness Institute, Inc.

Court of Special Appeals of Maryland, 2000.
132 Md.App. 271, 752 A.2d 631.

■ SALMON, JUDGE. In this case, we are asked to examine the enforceability of an exculpatory clause found in a fitness club's contract.

On September 4, 1998, Gerilynne Seigneur and her husband James filed a complaint in the Circuit Court for Montgomery County against National Fitness Institute, Inc. ("NFI"). The Seigneurs asserted that Ms. Seigneur was injured as a result of NFI's negligence while she was undergoing an initial evaluation at a fitness club owned and operated by NFI. NFI filed a motion to dismiss the complaint based on an exculpatory clause found in its contract with Ms. Seigneur. * * * The motion for summary judgment was granted, and the Seigneurs filed this appeal in which they presented a single issue, *viz*: Does the exculpatory clause in the agreement entered into by the parties validly release NFI from all liability for injuries to Ms. Seigneur caused by NFI's negligence? * We answer that question in the affirmative.

* * * On January 30, 1996, Ms. Seigneur, after deciding to begin a weight loss and fitness program, joined NFI on a one-month trial basis. * * * When she signed her membership contract, Ms. Seigneur had a history of serious lower back problems, including a herniated disc. Moreover, her general physical condition was poor. These facts were disclosed to NFI prior to the accident.

As part of the application process, Ms. Seigneur was required to complete and sign a document entitled "National Fitness, Inc. Health Programs Participation Agreement" ("the Participation Agreement"). Besides informing the customer of NFI's payment and fee collection policies, this agreement contained the following clause:

> Important Information: I, the undersigned applicant, agree and understand that * * * *all exercises shall be undertaken by me at my sole risk and that NFI, Inc. shall not be liable to me for any claims, demands, injuries, damages, actions, or courses of action whatsoever, to my person or property arising out of or connecting with the use of the services and facilities of NFI, Inc., by me,* or to the premises of NFI, Inc. Further, I do expressly hereby forever release and discharge NFI, Inc. from all claims, demands, injuries, damages, actions, or courses of action, and from all acts of active or passive negligence on the part of NFI, Inc., its servants, agents or employees.

Ms. Seigneur signed the Participation Agreement on January 30, 1996. Kim Josties, an NFI employee, then performed an initial evaluation of Ms. Seigneur, in which Ms. Seigneur was first directed to perform various flexibility tests. Ms. Josties next directed her to the weight machines for strength testing. Ms. Seigneur worked on the leg extension machine and then the bench press. She made no complaints after using either of these devices. Ms. Seigneur next used an upper torso weight machine. Ms. Josties placed a ninety-pound weight on this machine and instructed Ms. Seigneur to lift this weight once with her arms. While attempting to lift this load, Ms. Seigneur felt a tearing or ripping sensation in her right shoulder. She instantly reported this to Ms. Josties, but the instructor did not seek immediate medical attention. Instead, Ms. Josties had Ms. Seigneur proceed to the next machine, and shortly thereafter, the initial evaluation was completed.

Ms. Seigneur claims that since this incident, she has had pain and difficulty using her shoulder. In addition, she has undergone shoulder surgery for a condition that her doctor attributed to the use of NFI's upper torso machine.

The Seigneurs' complaint against NFI alleged, *inter alia*, that NFI was vicariously liable because Ms. Josties, as an employee or agent of NFI, was

> negligent in instructing, directing, and/or guiding the [appellant] to lift ninety (90) pounds of weight on the upper

torso machine in the manner previously described, especially in light of the physical condition of the [appellant] and the physical and exercise history and experience of the [appellant], which was, or reasonably should have been known to [Ms. Josties], and in directing the [appellant] to continue with and complete the program evaluation despite her complaint of injury.

The Seigneurs additionally claimed that NFI breached its duty to Ms. Seigneur by negligently hiring Ms. Josties, who "lacked sufficient training, experience, certification and/or other qualifications and knowledge to properly, reasonably and safely instruct, direct and guide [Ms. Seigneur] in lifting weights and in the use of the weight equipment." The Seigneurs also asserted that NFI negligently failed to provide Ms. Josties "with sufficient training and knowledge to properly, reasonably and safely instruct, direct and guide . . . [Ms. Seigneur] in lifting weights and in the use of the weight equipment."

On October 28, 1998, NFI filed a motion to dismiss arguing that the exculpatory clause contained in the Participation Agreement was valid and enforceable and that NFI was entitled to judgment as a matter of law. The Seigneurs responded by arguing that the Participation Agreement was a contract of adhesion and that the exculpatory clause was void as against public policy. * * *

More than one-hundred years ago, it was noted that "the right of parties to contract as they please is restricted only by a few well defined and well settled rules, and it must be a very plain case to justify a court in holding a contract to be against public policy." Estate of Woods, Weeks & Co., 52 Md. 520, 536 (1879). * This legal principle continues to hold true today. * * *

The Court of Appeals, in Wolf v. Ford, 335 Md. 525, 644 A.2d 522 (1994), said:

> It is quite possible for the parties expressly to agree in advance that the defendant is under no obligation of care for the benefit of the plaintiff, and shall not be liable for the consequences of conduct which would otherwise be negligent. There is in the ordinary case no public policy which prevents the parties from contracting as they see fit.

Three exceptions have been identified where the public interest will render an exculpatory clause unenforceable. They are: (1) when the party protected by the clause intentionally causes harm or engages in acts of reckless, wanton, or gross negligence; (2) when the bargaining power of one party to the contract is so grossly unequal so as to put that party at the mercy of the other's negligence; and (3) when the transaction involves the public interest. *

Ms. Seigneur has not alleged that NFI's agents intentionally caused her harm, or engaged in reckless, wanton, or gross acts of negligence. She does assert, however, that the second and third exceptions are applicable.

Appellants argue that NFI "possess[es] a decisive advantage in bargaining strength against members of the public who seek to use its services." She also claims that she was presented with a contract of adhesion and that this is additional evidence of NFI's grossly disproportionate "bargaining power."

It is true that the contract presented to Ms. Seigneur was a contract of adhesion.[4] But that fact alone does not demonstrate that NFI had grossly disparate bargaining power. * As discussed *infra*, there were numerous other competitors providing the same non-essential services as NFI. The exculpatory clause was prominently displayed in the Participation Agreement and Ms. Seigneur makes no claim that she was unaware of this provision prior to her injury.

To possess a decisive bargaining advantage over a customer, the service offered must usually be deemed essential in nature. See Boucher v. Riner, 68 Md.App. 539, 551, 514 A.2d 485 (1986) ("As [teaching the art of parachute jumping] is not of an essential nature, [Parachutes Are Fun, Inc.] had no decisive advantage of bargaining strength against any member of the public seeking to participate."); Winterstein v. Wilcom, 16 Md.App. 130, 138, 293 A.2d 821 (1972) ("Since [facilitating the plaintiff's participation in a drag race] is not of an essential nature, Wilcom had no decisive advantage of bargaining strength against any member of the public seeking to participate."). In Schlobohm v. Spa Petite, Inc., 326 N.W.2d 920 (Minn.1982), the Court said:

> [I]n the determination of whether the enforcement of an exculpatory clause would be against public policy, the courts consider whether the party seeking exoneration offered services of great importance to the public, which were a practical necessity for some members of the public.

As indicated above, courts have found generally that the furnishing of gymnasium or health spa services is not an activity of great public importance nor of a practical necessity. * * * We agree with the views expressed * * *. The services offered by the appellee simply cannot be accurately characterized as "essential." * * *

The Washington metropolitan area, of which Montgomery County is a part, is home to many exercise and fitness clubs. Ms. Seigneur * * * was free to choose among scores of facilities providing essentially the same services. * She also had the option of purchasing her own fitness equipment and exercising at home or of exercising without any equipment by doing aerobic or isometric exercises. Ms. Seigneur's bargaining position was not grossly disproportionate to that of NFI.

* * * [W]hen defining what transactions affect public interests, this Court [has] relied in part on a test enunciated in Tunkl v. Regents of the Univ. of California, 60 Cal.2d 92, 32 Cal.Rptr. 33, 383 P.2d 441 (1963). Quoting *Tunkl*, * * * public interests are affected when the transaction:

> exhibits some or all of the following characteristics. It concerns a business of a type generally thought suitable for public regulation. The party seeking exculpation is engaged in

---

[4] "A contract of adhesion has been defined as one 'that is drafted unilaterally by the dominant party and then presented on a "take-it-or-leave-it" basis to the weaker party who has no real opportunity to bargain about its terms.' " Meyer v. State Farm Fire and Cas. Co., 85 Md.App. 83, 89, 582 A.2d 275 (1990) (quoting Restatement (Second) of Conflict of Laws § 187, cmt. b).

performing a service of great importance to the public, which is often a matter of practical necessity for some members of the public. The party holds himself out as willing to perform this service for any member of the public who seeks it, or at least for any member coming within certain established standards. As a result of the essential nature of the service, in the economic setting of the transaction, the party invoking exculpation possesses a decisive advantage of bargaining strength against any member of the public who seeks his services. In exercising a superior bargaining power the party confronts the public with a standardized adhesion contract of exculpation, and makes no provision whereby a purchaser may pay additional reasonable fees and obtain protection against negligence. Finally, as a result of the transaction, the person or property of the purchaser is placed under the control of the seller, subject to the risk of carelessness by the seller or his agents.

With respect to the just-quoted six-factor test, the Court in *Wolf* held:

> * * * [W]e are concerned that the six-factor test of *Tunkl*, originally intended to be a rough outline in guiding a court's determination as to whether a given transaction affects the public interest, may become too rigid a measuring stick. * * *. We expressly decline, therefore, to adopt the six-factor test set forth in *Tunkl* * * *. This is not to say that the factors listed cannot be considered by a court in determining whether a given transaction involves the public interest, but the six factors are not conclusive. The ultimate determination of what constitutes the public interest must be made considering the totality of the circumstances of any given case against the backdrop of current societal expectations. *

The *Wolf* Court, in refusing to adopt the *Tunkl* test, identified transactions that affect the public interest as those involving

> the performance of a public service obligation, e.g., public utilities, common carriers, innkeepers, and public warehousemen. It also includes those transactions, not readily susceptible to definition or broad categorization, that are so important to the public good that an exculpatory clause would be "patently offensive," such that "the common sense of the entire community would . . . pronounce it" invalid. *

NFI does not provide an essential public service such that an exculpatory clause would be "patently offensive" to the citizens of Maryland. The services offered by a health club are not of great importance or of practical necessity to the public as a whole. * Nor is a health club anywhere near as socially important as institutions or businesses such as innkeepers, public utilities, common carriers, or schools. * * *

We affirm the trial court's ruling that NFI's exculpatory clause is enforceable so as to release NFI from liability for injuries Ms. Seigneur sustained while on its premises.

NOTE

Disclaimer of Liability for Medical Malpractice. In their book *Nudge: Improving Decisions About Health, Welfare, and Happiness* (updated ed., 2009), Richard H. Thaler and Cass R. Sunstein, later head of the federal Office of Information and Regulatory Affairs, propose that health insurers should be able to offer individual consumers/policyholders a choice between a policy that allows the consumer to sue health care providers for negligence and one that provides liability only for intentional or reckless wrongdoing. *Id.* at 209–15. The latter policy, they contend, would be offered at a discount, reflecting the lower cost of medical services when medical malpractice exposure is eliminated. Thaler and Sunstein reason that many consumers would choose the less expensive policy. They also assert that the "deterrent effect of tort liability is overstated." They attribute courts' traditional unwillingness, on public interest grounds, to allow disclaimers of liability in these contexts to "nonlibertarian paternalism, pure and simple." Tom Baker and Timothy D. Lytton have criticized Thaler and Sunstein's proposal, arguing that "patients will often make choices that are not in their best interest." Tom Baker & Timothy D. Lytton, Allowing Patients to Waive the Right to Sue for Medical Malpractice: A Response to Thaler and Sunstein, 104 Nw. U. L. Rev. 233, 234 (2010). They assert that "the preference for immediate gratification will lead patients to overvalue the immediate gains offered by fee reductions, and overconfidence will lead them to underestimate the risk of medical negligence." Further, claim Baker and Lytton, medical negligence disclaimers undervalue the societal benefits of medical malpractice litigation in encouraging safer medical care.

Gross v. Sweet

Court of Appeals of New York, 1979.
49 N.Y.2d 102, 424 N.Y.S.2d 365, 400 N.E.2d 306.

■ FUCHSBERG, JUDGE. * * * Plaintiff Bruce Gross, wishing to learn how to parachute, enrolled in the Stormville Parachute Center Training School, a facility owned and operated by the defendant William Sweet for the purpose of offering instruction in the sport. The ensuing events are essentially undisputed. As a prerequisite for admission into the course, Gross had to pay a fee and sign a form entitled "Responsibility Release." He was then given the standard introductory lesson, which consisted of approximately one hour of on-land training, including oral instruction as well as several jumps off a two and a half foot table. Plaintiff then was equipped with a parachute and flown to an altitude of 2,800 feet for his first practice jump. Upon coming in contact with the ground on his descent, plaintiff suffered serious personal injuries.

The suit is grounded on negligence * * * and gross negligence. In the main, plaintiff claims that defendant failed to provide adequate training and safe equipment, violated certain rules and procedures promulgated by the Federal Aviation Administration governing the conduct of parachute jumping schools and failed to warm him sufficiently of the attendant dangers.

Defendant pleaded the release plaintiff had signed and moved for summary judgment, contending that the terms of the release exculpated the defendant from any liability. Plaintiff, in turn, cross-moved to strike this affirmative defense contending, primarily, that the terms of the release did not specifically bar a suit for personal injuries negligently caused by the defendant. He also urged that, as a matter of policy, the release should not be enforceable as between a student and his teacher, a relationship in which one of the parties holds himself out as qualified and responsible to provide training in a skill and the other party relies on this expertise, particularly in the context of an activity in which the degree of training necessary for safe participation is much greater than might be apparent to a novice. * * *

The appeal is now before us on a certified question: "Was the order of this Court, which reinstated the complaint and granted plaintiff's motion to dismiss the affirmative defense of release, correct as a matter of law?" Our answer is that it was.

We begin with the proposition, too well settled to invoke any dispute, that the law frowns upon contracts intended to exculpate a party from the consequences of his own negligence and though, with certain exceptions, they are enforceable, such agreements are subject to close judicial scrutiny. * To the extent that agreements purport to grant exemption for liability for willful or grossly negligent acts they have been viewed as wholly void *. And so, here, so much of plaintiff's complaint as contains allegations that defendant was grossly negligent, may not be barred by the release in any event. But we need not explore further this possibility for we conclude the complaint in its entirety withstands the exculpatory agreement.

Nor need we consider plaintiff's request that we ignore the release on the grounds that the special relationship of the parties and the public interest involved forbids its enforcement. While we have, for example, had occasion to invalidate such provisions when they were contained in the contract between a passenger and a common carrier, * or in a contract between a customer and a public utility under a duty to furnish telephone service * or when imposed by an employer as a condition of employment, * the circumstances here do not fit within any of these relationships. And, though we note that a recent statute renders void agreements purporting to exempt from liability for negligence those engaged in a variety of businesses that serve the public (e.g., landlords; * caterers; * building service or maintenance contractors; * those who maintain garages or parking garages; * or pools, gymnasiums or places of public amusement or recreation), * defendant's occupation does not fall within any of these classes either. * * *

As the cases make clear, the law's reluctance to enforce exculpatory provisions of this nature has resulted in the development of an exacting standard by which courts measure their validity. So, it has been repeatedly emphasized that unless the intention of the parties is expressed in unmistakable language, an exculpatory clause will not be deemed to insulate a party from liability for his own negligent acts. See Van Dyke Prods. v. Eastman Kodak Co., 12 N.Y.2d 301, 304, 239 N.Y.S.2d 337, 339, 189 N.E.2d 693, 694 (1963) (must be "absolutely clear"); Ciofalo v. Vic Tanney Gyms, 10 N.Y.2d 294, 297, 220 N.Y.S.2d 962, 964, 177 N.E.2d 925, 926 (1961) ("sufficiently clear and unequivocal language"); Boll v. Sharp & Dohme, 281 App.Div. 568, 570–71, 121 N.Y.S.2d 20, 21–22, aff'd 307 N.Y. 646, 120 N.E.2d 836 (1954) ("clear and explicit language"). Put another way, it must appear plainly and precisely that the "limitation of liability extends to negligence or other fault of the party attempting to shed his ordinary responsibility" Howard v. Handler Bros. & Winell, 279 App.Div. 72, 75–76 * (1951). *

Not only does this stringent standard require that the drafter of such an agreement make its terms unambiguous, but it mandates that the terms be understandable as well. Thus, a provision that would exempt its drafter from any liability occasioned by his fault should not compel resort to a magnifying glass and lexicon. * Of course, this does not imply that only simple or monosyllabic language can be used in such clauses. Rather, what the law demands is that such provisions be clear and coherent. *

By and large, if such is the intention of the parties, the fairest course is to provide explicitly that claims based on negligence are included, see Ciofalo v. Vic Tanney Gyms, *supra*, 10 N.Y.2d at 296 (plaintiff "agreed to assume full responsibility for any injuries which might occur to her in or about defendant's premises, 'including but without limitation, any claims for personal injuries resulting from or arising out of the negligence of' the defendant"). That does not mean that the word "negligence" must be employed for courts to give effect to an exculpatory agreement; however, words conveying a similar import must appear. See Theroux v. Kedenburg Racing Ass'n, 50 Misc.2d 97, 99, 269 N.Y.S.2d 789 (1965) (agreement provided for release of liability for any injury "regardless of how such injury . . . may arise, and regardless of who is at fault . . . and even if the loss is caused by the neglect or fault" of the defendant). * * *

The case before us today obviously does not fit within this exception to the strict legal standard generally employed by the courts of this State under which exculpatory provisions drawn in broad and sweeping language have not been given effect. For example, agreements to release from "any and all responsibility or liability of any nature whatsoever for any loss of property or personal injury occurring on this trip," Kaufman v. Am. Youth Hostels, 5 N.Y.2d 1016, 185 N.Y.S.2d 268, 158 N.E.2d 128 (1959), * or to "waive claim for any loss to personal property, or for any personal injury while a member of [a] club" Hertzog v. Harrison Is. Shores, 21 A.D.2d 859, 251 N.Y.S.2d 164 (1964) have not barred claims based on negligence. * * *

With all this as background, the language of the "Responsibility Release" in the case before us, must be viewed as no more explicit than that in *Boll*. In its entirety, it reads:

> I, the undersigned, hereby, and by these covenants, do waive any and all claims that I, my heirs, and/or assignees may have against Nathaniel Sweet, the Stormville Parachute Center, the Jumpmaster and the Pilot who shall operate the aircraft when used for the purpose of parachute jumping for any personal injuries or property damage that I may sustain or which may arise out of my learning, practicing or actually jumping from an aircraft. I also assume full responsibility for any damage that I may do or cause while participating in this sport.

Assuming that this language alerted the plaintiff to the dangers inherent in parachute jumping and that he entered into the sport with apprehension of the risks, it does not follow that he was aware of, much less intended to accept, any *enhanced* exposure to injury occasioned by the carelessness of the very persons on which he depended for his safety. Specifically, the release nowhere expresses any intention to exempt the defendant from liability for injury or property damages which may result from his failure to use due care either in his training methods or in his furnishing safe equipment. Thus, whether on a running reading or a careful analysis, the agreement could most reasonably be taken merely as driving home the fact that the defendant was not to bear any responsibility for injuries that ordinarily and inevitably would occur, without any fault of the defendant, to those who participate in such a physically demanding sport.

In short, instead of specifying to prospective students that they would have to abide any consequences attributable to the instructor's own carelessness, the defendant seems to have preferred the use of opaque terminology rather than suffer the possibility of lower enrollment. But, while, with exceptions not pertinent to this case, the law grudgingly accepts the proposition that men may contract away their liability for negligently caused injuries, they may do so only on the condition that their intention be expressed clearly and in "unequivocal terms." *

Accordingly, the certified question is answered in the affirmative, and the order of the Appellate Division reversing the grant of summary judgment, reinstating the complaint and dismissing the defense based on the release should be affirmed.

■ JONES, J. (dissenting). * * * Despite the unlimited language of the release given by plaintiff, * * * the majority concludes that the agreement does not exonerate defendants from liability for ordinary negligence on their part. * * *

The activity on which plaintiff was about to embark under the tutelage of defendants was a hazardous one at best, but virtually the only claims that he might have had against them should he sustain personal injuries or property damage would be claims resulting from fault or negligence of defendants. The majority reads the agreement "merely as driving home the fact that the defendant was not to bear any responsibility for injuries that ordinarily and inevitably would occur, without any fault of the defendant, to those who participate in such a physically demanding sport." * But of what significance or practical effect is such a release? It is difficult to conceive of any claim other than one predicated on negligence; personal injuries or property damage occasioned without negligence by one or both of the defendants would give rise to no cause of action at all. The release then, if construed as not including claims predicated on negligence, releases nothing and is meaningless and a nullity. A more broadly worded exoneration provision would be difficult to imagine; a requirement that there be included the word "negligence" or a description of the specific acts of misconduct pleaded in the complaint (as plaintiff would contend for) would be a reversion to the "semantic stereotypes," which we have now abjured. * There is therefore no basis for limiting the effect of the release executed by this plaintiff; claims such as the present ones based on ordinary negligence appear to me to be precisely the claims intended by the parties to be included in the language "any and all claims . . . for any personal injuries or property damage that I may sustain or which may arise out of my learning, practicing or actually jumping from an aircraft." * * *

Dalury v. S-K-I, Ltd.

Supreme Court of Vermont, 1995.
164 Vt. 329, 670 A.2d 795.

■ JOHNSON, JUSTICE * * * While skiing at Killington Ski Area, plaintiff Robert Dalury sustained serious injuries when he collided with a metal pole that formed part of the control maze for a ski lift line. Before the season started, Dalury had purchased a midweek season pass and signed a form releasing the ski area from liability. The relevant portion reads:

RELEASE FROM LIABILITY AND CONDITIONS OF USE

1.   I accept and understand that Alpine Skiing is a hazardous sport with many dangers and risks and that injuries are a common and ordinary occurrence of the sport. As a condition of being permitted to use the ski area premises, I freely accept and voluntarily assume the risks of injury or property damage and release Killington Ltd., its employees and agents from any and all liability for personal injury or property damage resulting from negligence, conditions of the premises, operations of the ski area, actions or omissions of employees or agents of the ski area or from my participation in skiing at the area, accepting myself the full responsibility for any and all such damage or injury of any kind which may result.

Plaintiff also signed a photo identification card that contained this same language.

Dalury and his wife filed a complaint against defendants, alleging negligent design, construction, and replacement of the maze pole. Defendants moved for summary judgment, arguing that the release of liability barred the negligence action. The trial court, without specifically addressing plaintiffs' contention that the release was contrary to public policy, found that the language of the release clearly absolved defendants of liability for their own negligence. * * *

On appeal, plaintiffs contend that the release was ambiguous as to whose liability was waived and that it is unenforceable as a matter of law because it violates public policy. We agree with defendants that the release was quite clear in its terms. * * *

Even well-drafted exculpatory agreements, however, may be void because they violate public policy. * * * [W]e conclude that ultimately the "determination of what constitutes the public interest must be made considering the totality of the circumstances of any given case against the backdrop of current societal expectations." * * *

Whether or not defendants provide an essential public service does not resolve the public policy question in the recreational sports context. The defendants' area is a facility open to the public. They advertise and invite skiers and nonskiers of every level of skiing ability to their premises for the price of a ticket. At oral argument, defendants conceded that thousands of people buy lift tickets every day throughout the season. Thousands of people ride lifts, buy services, and ski the trails. Each ticket sale may be, for some purposes, a purely private transaction. But when a substantial number of such sales take place as a result of the seller's general invitation to the public to utilize the facilities and services in question, a legitimate public interest arises.

The major public policy implications are those underlying the law of premises liability. In Vermont, a business owner has a duty "of active care to make sure that its premises are in safe and suitable condition for its customers." * * * We have already held that a ski area owes its customers the same duty as any other business—to keep its premises reasonably safe. *

The policy rationale is to place responsibility for maintenance of the land on those who own or control it, with the ultimate goal of keeping accidents to the minimum level possible. Defendants, not recreational skiers, have the expertise and opportunity to foresee and control hazards, and to guard against the negligence of their agents and employees. They alone can properly maintain and inspect their premises, and train their employees in risk management. They alone can insure against risks and effectively spread the cost of insurance among their thousands of customers. Skiers, on the other hand, are not in a position to discover and correct risks of harm, and they cannot insure against the ski area's negligence.

If defendants were permitted to obtain broad waivers of their liability, an important incentive for ski areas to manage risk would be removed with the public bearing the cost of the resulting injuries. * It is illogical, in these circumstances, to undermine the public policy underlying business invitee law and allow skiers to bear risks they have no ability or right to control.

For these reasons, we * * * do not accept the proposition that because ski resorts do not provide an essential public service, such agreements do not affect the public interest. * A recognition of the principles underlying the duty to business invitees makes clear the inadequacy of relying upon the essential public service factor in the analysis of public recreation cases. While interference with an essential public service surely affects the public interest, those services do not represent the universe of activities that implicate public concerns.

Moreover, reliance on the private nature of defendants' property would be inconsistent with societal expectations about privately owned facilities that are open to the general public. Indeed, when a facility becomes a place of public accommodation, it "render[s] a 'service which has become of public interest' in the manner of the innkeepers and common carriers of old." Lombard v. Louisiana, 373 U.S. 267, 279, 83 S.Ct. 1122, 1128, 10 L.Ed.2d 338 (1963) (Douglas, J., concurring). * Defendants are not completely unfettered, as they argue, in their ability to set the terms and conditions of admission. Defendants' facility may be privately owned, but that characteristic no longer overcomes a myriad of legitimate public interests. Public accommodations laws that prohibit discrimination against potential users of the facility are just one example of limitations imposed by law that affect the terms and conditions of entry. * * *

Defendants argue that the public policy of the state, as expressed in the "Acceptance of inherent risks" statute, 12 Vt. Stat. Ann. 1037, indicates a willingness on the part of the Legislature to limit ski area liability. Therefore, they contend that public policy favors the use of express releases such as the one signed by plaintiff. On the contrary, defendants' allocation of responsibility for skiers' injuries is at odds with the statute. The statute places responsibility for the "inherent risks" of any sport on the participant, insofar as such risks are obvious and necessary. A ski area's own negligence, however, is neither an inherent risk nor an obvious and necessary one in the sport of skiing. Thus, a skier's assumption of the inherent risks of skiing does not abrogate the ski area's duty "to warn of or correct dangers which in the exercise of reasonable prudence in the circumstances could have been foreseen and corrected." *

Brown v. San Francisco Ball Club

District Court of Appeal of California, 1950.
99 Cal.App.2d 484, 222 P.2d 19.

■ WOOD, JUSTICE. This is an appeal by plaintiff from a judgment entered upon a directed verdict for the defendant in an action against San Francisco Ball Club, Inc., for damages for personal injuries sustained while attending a professional baseball game at Seals' Stadium, San Francisco. * * *

Appellant, a woman of 46 years, attended the game as the guest of friends, one of whom furnished and purchased the tickets which were for seats in an unscreened portion of the stadium near the first-base line. The game was in progress when they arrived and about an hour later the accident occurred while the players were changing sides. Appellant was struck by some object and sustained serious injury. Evidence is lacking whether or not it was a baseball, or from what direction it came. However, the motion for directed verdict appears to have been made, and the issues discussed by the parties upon this appeal, upon the assumption that appellant was hit by a baseball, possibly thrown from second to first base, touching the first baseman's glove and passing thence into the stand.

Respondent owned and operated the stadium which had a seating capacity of 18,601, divided into screened and unscreened areas. Approximately 5,000 seats were behind a screen back of the home plate. The remainder were unscreened and in two sections behind the first-base and third-base lines respectively. Tickets for seats were sold at separate windows, one window for each of these three sections, each window marked for a particular section. Patrons decided where they would sit, and went to the appropriate window for their seats. It is generally true of all the games held in this stadium that a great majority of the patrons are situated in the unscreened sections, because they prefer an unobstructed view. The attendance at this particular game was approximately 5,000. There were many vacant seats in each seating area. Most of the spectators were seated in the first-base and third-base unscreened sections, very few in the home-plate screened area. * * *

In baseball, * * * the patron participates in the sport as a spectator and in so doing subjects himself to certain risks necessarily and usually incident to and inherent in the game; risks that are obvious and should be observed in the exercise of reasonable care. This does not mean that he assumes the risk of being injured by the proprietor's negligence but that by voluntarily entering into the sport as a spectator he knowingly accepts the reasonable risks and hazards inherent in and incident to the game. The duty of the proprietor or operator of a baseball stadium toward his patrons is specifically defined, as follows:

> With respect to the law governing cases of this kind, it has been generally held that one of the natural risks assumed by spectators attending professional games is that of being struck by batted or thrown balls; that the management is not required, nor does it undertake to insure patrons against injury from such source. All that is required is the exercise of ordinary care to protect patrons against such injuries * and, in doing so, the management is not obliged to screen all seats, because, as pointed out by the decisions, many patrons prefer to sit where their view is not obscured by a screen. Moreover, the management is not required to provide screened seats for all who may apply for them. The duty imposed by law is performed when screened seats are provided for as many as may be reasonably expected to call for them on any ordinary occasion, * and if * a spectator chooses to occupy an unscreened seat, or * * * is unable to secure a screened seat and consequently occupies one that is not protected, he assumes the risk of being struck by thrown or batted balls; and, if injured thereby, is precluded from recovering damages therefor. As aptly said in Cincinnati Baseball Club Co. v. Eno, 112 Ohio St. 175, 147 N.E. 86 (1925), it is common knowledge that in baseball games hard balls are thrown and batted with such great swiftness they are liable to be thrown or batted outside the lines of the diamond, and spectators occupying positions which may be reached by such balls assume the risk of injury therefrom.

Quinn v. Recreation Park Ass'n, 3 Cal.2d 725, 729–30, 46 P.2d 144, 146 (1935).

It would seem necessarily to follow that respondent fully discharged its duty toward appellant, as concerns the risk to her of being hit by thrown or batted baseballs, when it provided screened seats for all who might reasonably be expected to request them, in fact many more screened seats than were requested. Hence, the injury suffered by her when struck by a thrown ball, while voluntarily occupying an unscreened seat, did not flow from, was not caused by, any failure of performance by respondent of any duty owed her, and did not give rise to a cause of action in her favor against respondent for damages for such injury.

Appellant seeks to take this case out of the application of the rule upon the theory that she was ignorant of the game of baseball and the attendant risks, hence cannot be said to have knowingly assumed the risk. The point is not well taken. Although she had a limited experience with baseball, she was a mature person in possession of her faculties with nothing about her to set her apart from other spectators and require of her a lower standard of self-protection from obvious inherent risks than that required of other spectators. She was, at the time of the accident, 46 years of age; had lived in the San Francisco area since 1926; was about to go to a school for training and to have a job as saleswoman in a real estate office; had seen one baseball game prior to this, in 1928, played in a big field, not a ball park, when she observed the game from an automobile and did not see balls thrown or knocked into the crowd; and had seen kids in the street pitching balls. At the game at which this accident happened she knew there was no screen in front of her seat but failed to notice if any of the seats were behind a screen. She was in attendance for about an hour before the accident, which should have apprised her of the risk of being struck by a ball. Instead of observing, she paid no particular attention to the game and spent her time visiting with a friend. We find nothing here to take appellant outside the usual rule, whether it be said that this "common knowledge" of these obvious and inherent risks are imputed to her or that they are obvious risks which should have been observed by her in the exercise of ordinary care. * * *

Of the cases relied upon by appellant herein, only one, Ratcliff v. San Diego Baseball Club, 27 Cal. App.2d 733, 81 P.2d 625 (1938), relates to the peculiar liability to their patrons of operators of baseball stadiums. That case involved a plaintiff who had elected to occupy a seat within a screened section and was injured while approaching her seat through an unscreened passageway. That case called for the application of a rule of liability materially different from that available to a person injured while occupying a seat in an unscreened section.

We conclude that the evidence herein, viewing it most favorably to the appellant, does not take her outside the application of the rule announced in the *Quinn* case; that she assumed the risk of injury in respect to which she complains; that the injury was not caused by any negligence upon the part of the respondent; and that determination thereof was a proper function of the trial court upon motion for directed verdict.

In the absence of negligence upon the part of the respondent, it is unnecessary to consider the question of contributory negligence upon the part of the appellant.

The judgment is affirmed and the appeal from the order denying a new trial is dismissed.

Blackburn v. Dorta

Supreme Court of Florida, 1977.
348 So.2d 287.

■ SUNDBERG, JUSTICE. [Three consolidated cases are before the Court because of a conflict among the intermediate appellate courts as to whether the doctrine of assumption of risk is still viable as an absolute bar to recovery subsequent to our adoption of the rule of comparative negligence in Hoffman v. Jones, 280 So.2d 431 (Fla.1973).]

* * * Since our decision in *Hoffman v. Jones*, contributory negligence no longer serves as a complete bar to plaintiff's recovery but

is to be considered in apportioning damages according to the principles of comparative negligence. We are now asked to determine the effect of the *Hoffman* decision on the common law doctrine of assumption of risk. If assumption of risk is equivalent to contributory negligence, then *Hoffman* mandates that it can no longer operate as a complete bar to recovery. However, if it has a distinct purpose apart from contributory negligence, its continued existence remains unaffected by *Hoffman*. * * *

At the outset, we note that assumption of risk is not a favored defense. There is a puissant drift toward abrogating the defense. * The argument is that assumption of risk serves no purpose which is not subsumed by either the doctrine of contributory negligence or the common law concept of duty. * It is said that this redundancy results in confusion and, in some cases, denies recovery unjustly. * * * The issue is most salient in states which have enacted comparative negligence legislation. Those statutes provide that the common law defense of contributory negligence no longer necessarily acts as a complete bar to recovery. The effect of these statutes upon the doctrine of assumption of risk has proved to be controversial. Joining the intensifying assault upon the doctrine, a number of comparative negligence jurisdictions have abrogated assumption of risk. * Those jurisdictions hold that assumption of risk is interchangeable with contributory negligence and should be treated equivalently. Today we are invited to join this trend of dissatisfaction with the doctrine. For the reasons herein expressed, we accept the invitation.

At the commencement of any analysis of the doctrine of assumption of risk, we must recognize that we deal with a potpourri of labels, concepts, definitions, thoughts, and doctrines. The confusion of labels does not end with the indiscriminate and interchangeable use of the terms "contributory negligence" and "assumption of risk." In the case law and among text writers, there have developed categories of assumption of risk. Distinctions exist between express and implied; * between primary and secondary; * and between reasonable and unreasonable or, as sometimes expressed, strict and qualified. * It will be our task to analyze these various labels and to trace the historical basis of the doctrine to unravel what has been in the law an "enigma wrapped in a mystery."

It should be pointed out that we are not here concerned with express assumption of risk which is a contractual concept outside the purview of this inquiry and upon which we express no opinion herein. * Included within the definition of express assumption of risk are express contracts not to sue for injury or loss which may thereafter be occasioned by the covenantee's negligence as well as situations in which actual consent exists such as where one voluntarily participates in a contact sport.

The breed of assumption of risk with which we deal here is that which arises by implication or implied assumption of risk. Initially it may be divided into the categories of primary and secondary. The term primary assumption of risk is simply another means of stating that the defendant was not negligent, either because he owed no duty to the plaintiff in the first instance, or because he did not breach the duty owed. Secondary assumption of risk is an affirmative defense to an established breach of a duty owed by the defendant to the plaintiff. *

The concept of primary assumption of risk is the basis for the historical doctrine which arose in the master-servant relationship during the late nineteenth century. * The master was held not to be negligent if he provided a reasonably safe place to work; the servant was said to have assumed the inherent risks that remained. In this context assumption of risk was not an affirmative defense at all. Rather, it was another way of expressing that the master was not negligent, for the servant had the burden of proving that his injury resulted from a risk other than one inherent in a facility or location that was a reasonably safe place to work. * As is often the case in the common law, however, the doctrine mutated into an affirmative defense, with the burden of pleading and proof upon the master. Consequently, even if the servant could show that the master owed and had breached a duty to provide a reasonably safe place to work, the master could escape liability if he could establish that the servant had voluntarily exposed himself to a risk negligently created by the master. Thus, two distinct concepts came to bear the same label with inevitable confusion which has persisted to the present. *

It is apparent that no useful purpose is served by retaining terminology which expresses the thought embodied in primary assumption of risk. This branch (or trunk) of the tree of assumption of risk is subsumed in the principle of negligence itself. Under our Florida jury instructions, the jury is directed first to determine whether the defendant has been negligent, i.e., did he owe a duty to the plaintiff and, if so, did he breach that duty? To sprinkle the term assumption of risk into the equation can only lead to confusion of a jury. * An example of this concept is presented in the operation of a passenger train. It can be said that a passenger assumes the risk of lurches and jerks which are ordinary and usual to the proper operation of the train, but that he does not assume the risk of extraordinary or unusual lurches and jerks resulting from substandard operation of the train. The same issue can be characterized in terms of the standard of care of the railroad. Thus, it can be said that the railroad owes a duty to operate its train with the degree of care of an ordinary prudent person under similar circumstances which includes some lurching and jerking while a train is in motion or commencing to move under ideal circumstances. So long as the lurching or jerking is not extraordinary due to substandard conduct of the railroad, there is no breach of duty and, hence, no negligence on the part of the railroad. The latter characterization of the issue clearly seems preferable and is consistent with the manner in which the jury is instructed under our standard jury instructions.

Having dispensed with express and primary-implied assumption of risk, we recur to secondary-implied assumption of risk which is the affirmative defense variety that has been such a thorn in the judicial side. The affirmative defense brand of assumption of risk can be subdivided into the type of conduct which is reasonable but nonetheless bars recovery (sometimes called pure or strict assumption of risk), and the type of conduct which is unreasonable and bars recovery (sometimes referred to as qualified assumption of risk). * Application of pure or strict assumption of risk is exemplified by the hypothetical situation in which a landlord has negligently permitted his tenant's premises to become highly flammable and a fire ensues. The tenant returns from work to find the premises a blazing inferno with his infant child trapped within. He rushes in to retrieve the child and is injured in so doing. Under the pure doctrine of assumption of risk, the tenant is barred from recovery because it can be said he voluntarily exposed himself to a known risk. Under this view of assumption of risk, the tenant is precluded from recovery notwithstanding the fact that his conduct could be said to be entirely reasonable under the circumstances. * There is little to commend this doctrine of implied-pure or strict assumption of risk, and our research discloses no Florida case in which it has been applied. Certainly, in light of *Hoffman v. Jones,* there is no reason supported by law or justice in this state to give credence to such a principle of law.

There remains, then, for analysis only the principle of implied-qualified assumption of risk, and it can be demonstrated in the hypothetical recited above with the minor alteration that the tenant rushes into the blazing premises to retrieve his favorite fedora. Such conduct on the tenant's part clearly would be unreasonable. Consequently, his conduct can just as readily be characterized as contributory negligence. It is the failure to exercise the care of a reasonably prudent man under similar circumstances. It is this last category of assumption of risk which has caused persistent confusion in the law of torts because of the lack of analytic difference between it and contributory negligence. If the only significant form of assumption of risk (implied-qualified) is so readily characterized, conceptualized, and verbalized as contributory negligence, can there be any sound rationale for retaining it as a separate affirmative defense to negligent conduct which bars recovery altogether? In the absence of any historical imperative, the answer must be no. We are persuaded that there is no historical significance to the doctrine of implied-secondary assumption of risk. As pointed out earlier in this opinion, the affirmative defense developed from a misapplication of principles applicable to the standard of care imposed upon an employer in the master-servant relationship. The opinion of the United States Supreme Court in Tiller v. Atl. Coast Line R.R., 318 U.S. 54, 63 S.Ct. 444, 87 L.Ed. 610 (1943), demonstrates that the doctrine has not only been indiscriminately misapplied historically but also represents a morally unacceptable social policy which was calculated to advance the industrial revolution regardless of the cost in human suffering. Mr. Justice Frankfurter, concurring, put it aptly when he stated:

> The phrase "assumption of risk" is an excellent illustration of the extent to which uncritical use of words bedevils the law. A phrase begins life as a literary expression; its felicity leads to its lazy repetition; and repetition soon establishes it as a legal formula, undiscriminatingly used to express different and sometimes contradictory ideas. Thus, in the setting of one set of circumstances, "assumption of risk" has been used as a shorthand way of saying that although an employer may have violated the duty of care which he owed his employee, he could nevertheless escape liability for damages resulting from his negligence if the employee, by accepting or continuing in the employment with "notice" of such negligence, "assumed the

risk." In such situations "assumption of risk" is a defense which enables a negligent employer to defeat recovery against him. In the setting of a totally different set of circumstances, "assumption of risk" has a totally different meaning. Industrial enterprise entails, for all those engaged in it, certain hazards to life and limb which no amount of care on the part of the employer can avoid. In denying recovery to an employee injured as a result of exposure to such a hazard, where the employer has in no sense been negligent or derelict in the duty owed to his employees, courts have often said that the employee "assumed the risk." Here the phrase "assumption of risk" is used simply to convey the idea that the employer was not at fault and therefore not liable.

Plainly enough only mischief could result from using a single phrase to express two such different ideas. Such ambiguity necessarily does harm to the desirability of clarity and coherence in any civilized system of law. But the greater mischief was that in one of its aspects the phrase "assumption of risk" gave judicial expression to a social policy that entailed much human misery. The notion of "assumption of risk" as a defense—that is, where the employer concededly failed in his duty of care and nevertheless escaped liability because the employee had "agreed" to "assume the risk" of the employer's fault—rested, in the context of our industrial society, upon a pure fiction. And in all English-speaking countries legislation was necessary to correct this injustice. . . . *

We find no discernible basis analytically or historically to maintain a distinction between the affirmative defense of contributory negligence and assumption of risk. The latter appears to be a viable, rational doctrine only in the sense described herein as implied-qualified assumption of risk which connotes unreasonable conduct on the part of the plaintiff. This result comports with the definition of contributory negligence appearing in Restatement (Second) of Torts § 466 (1965). Furthermore, were we not otherwise persuaded to elimination [sic] of assumption of risk as a separate affirmative defense in the context herein described, the decision of this Court in *Hoffman v. Jones,* * would dictate such a result. * * *

Is liability equated with fault under a doctrine which would totally bar recovery by one who voluntarily, but reasonably, assumes a known risk while one whose conduct is unreasonable but denominated "contributory negligence" is permitted to recover a proportionate amount of his damages for injury? Certainly not. Therefore, we hold that the affirmative defense of implied assumption of risk is merged into the defense of contributory negligence and the principles of comparative negligence enunciated in *Hoffman v. Jones,* shall apply in all cases where such defense is asserted. * * *

NOTE

Implied Assumption of Risk and the Third Restatement of Torts. The drafters of Restatement (Third) of Torts: Apportionment of Liability state that the text of § 2 "abandons the traditional doctrine of implied, voluntary assumption of risk that was embodied in Restatement (Second) §§ 496C–

G." Restatement (Third) of Torts: Apportionment of Liability § 2, Reporters' Note, cmt. i (2000). Comment *i* notes that "[w]hen a plaintiff's conduct in the face of a known risk is unreasonable, however, it might constitute plaintiff's negligence."

E. IMPUTED CONTRIBUTORY NEGLIGENCE

Dashiell v. Keauthou-Kona Co.

United States Court of Appeals for the Ninth Circuit, 1973.
487 F.2d 957.

■ TRASK, CIRCUIT JUDGE. This is an appeal from a judgment of the district court, pursuant to a special verdict by a six-member jury, that the contributory negligence of Mrs. Dashiell barred both herself and her husband from recovering for injuries received when the golf cart which Mrs. Dashiell was driving and in which Mr. Dashiell was riding, collided with a truck following a ride down an incline during which Mrs. Dashiell lost control of the cart. * * *

The theories of liability pleaded against the golf course defendants centered around negligent construction of and directions on the cart paths; negligence in supplying a cart that was dangerous to use on steep inclines and in failing to warn of that danger; and negligence in failing to warn of the defects alleged in the braking system and steering mechanism of the cart. * * * The jury found in the form of a special verdict that (1) the golf course defendants were negligent, and their negligence was a proximate cause of the accident; * * * (3) Mr. Dashiell was not contributorily negligent; (4) Mrs. Dashiell was contributorily negligent, and her negligence was a proximate cause of the accident. * * * The trial court found as a matter of law that because the Dashiells were engaged in a joint enterprise, the negligence of Mrs. Dashiell that contributed to the accident so as to bar her recovery must be imputed to her husband so as to bar his recovery. * * *

The appellants argue that the facts of this case do not support a finding of a joint enterprise or venture, and that even if they did, this theory of tort law is so discredited that the Hawaiian courts would not today apply the rule of imputed contributory negligence. * * * Appellees contend that Mrs. Dashiell was acting as agent for her husband while driving the golf cart * * *.

We find that on the facts of this case, at no time did the relationship of joint enterprise or joint venture exist between Mr. and Mrs. Dashiell within the meaning of imputed negligence. This is not a typical case of a business venture of a character similar to a partnership where two or more parties undertake, for some pecuniary purpose, a contractual obligation resulting in the liability of each for the negligence of the other. Because the evidence was insufficient to allow the issue of joint enterprise to go to the jury where a husband and wife were merely enjoying a round of golf, the trial court should have ruled as a matter of law that any contributory negligence of Mrs. Dashiell could not be imputed to her husband. *

The concept of imputed contributory negligence developed on the basis of a fictitious agency applied to defeat the recovery of an injured plaintiff by imputing the negligence of another to him, even though the plaintiff would not have been liable for that negligence had he been sued as a defendant. It had its beginnings in England where it was followed for a relatively short period of time before being overruled. * It has been severely criticized by both courts and commentators in this country. * Prosser notes that

> [e]xcept for vestigial remnants which are at most moribund historical survivals, "imputed contributory negligence" in its own right has now disappeared.

W[illiam L.] Prosser, Law of Torts § 74 (4th ed. 1971). * * *

Several reasons persuade us to reject the imputation of Mrs. Dashiell's negligence to Mr. Dashiell. The Restatement (Second) of Torts § 491 at 548, comment *c*, states the law to be:

> The elements which are essential to a joint enterprise are commonly stated to be four: (1) an agreement, express or implied, among the members of the group; (2) a common purpose to be carried out by the group; (3) a community of pecuniary interest in that purpose, among the members; and (4) an equal right to a voice in the direction of the enterprise, which gives an equal right to control. . . .

In Dias v. Kamalani, 39 Haw. 474, 477–79 (1952), the Supreme Court of Hawaii stated that among other considerations, a joint enterprise is "voluntarily assumed and arising wholly *ex contractu*," and that the factor of joint control "is more readily inferable where the trip is for a business venture than where it is for a pleasure venture." There is no suggestion in the present case that appellants' activities were anything more than social, nor can there be any reasonable inference by reason of the marital relationship alone that appellants undertook any contractual obligation which should cause each to be chargeable for the negligence of the other. ". . . [T]he great weight of modern authority finds no basis for imputing the negligence of one spouse to another merely because of the marital relationship itself." [Fowler] Harper & [Fleming.] James, The Law of Torts § 23.4 (1956). * * *

Additionally, applying the concept of imputed contributory negligence to the facts of this case would needlessly frustrate some basic policies of tort law. Mr. Dashiell was found by the jury to be blameless, and since negligence law is based on personal fault, it would be both illogical and inequitable to deny him recovery unless he were under a duty to control the actions of Mrs. Dashiell as she drove the golf cart. The record reflects no basis on which to find any duty of control. The original purpose of defining the joint enterprise relationship was vicarious liability, in order to increase the number of those liable to provide a financially responsible person to injured third parties. * That purpose is absent when related to the Dashiells; in fact, application of the imputed contributory negligence rule would have the opposite effect of freeing from liability another party who is at fault even though the person denied recovery is blameless. * * *

We reject the bar against Mr. Dashiell's recovery based upon imputation of Mrs. Dashiell's negligence merely by reason of their common recreational interest or any supposed shared right of control of the golf cart. * * *

NOTE

Imputed Contributory Negligence: Driver and Passenger. At one time, the common law of England and some American jurisdictions barred the passenger in an automobile or other vehicle from recovering for the driver's negligence because of imputed contributory negligence. The reasoning was that the passenger had selected the driver and had a measure of control over the driver since the passenger had "employed" that person to drive him. E.g., Thorogood v. Bryan, [1849] 137 Eng.Rep. 458 (C.P.), 8 C.B. 129; see generally Harper, James and Gray on Torts § 23.2. Imputing contributory negligence to the passenger is now repudiated in most jurisdictions. As the court explained in Kalechman v. Drew Auto Rental, Inc., 33 N.Y.2d 397, 353 N.Y.S.2d 414, 308 N.E.2d 886 (1973), the original basis for the rule is no longer realistic:

> One commentator has offered the following explanation of the genesis of the rule: "If the owner of a wagon and team handed the reins over to a passenger and let him drive, control of the horses was within easy reach. If he didn't think the driver reined up fast enough at a railroad crossing, he could reach out and resume control. . . . Actual control was a possibility, not a fiction." [Note, Imputed Negligence in Automobile Accident Cases,] 16 St. John's L. Rev. 222[, 222 (1942)]. But with the advent of the modern automobile there is no longer any basis for assuming that the passenger, no matter what his relationship to the driver may be, has the capacity to assert control over or direct the operation of a moving automobile. The design of the vehicle, the high speeds at which it travels, the split second timing which is often necessary to avoid collision have all combined to erode the assumption that anyone other than the driver can effectively control the operation of the vehicle in traffic.

What other reason do you believe motivate courts to overrule precedents enabling courts to impute the negligence of the driver of an automobile to a passenger?

Handeland v. Brown

Supreme Court of Iowa, 1974.
216 N.W.2d 574.

■ McCORMICK, JUSTICE. In this case of first impression we are required to decide whether a parental claim for medical expense and loss of services, companionship and society under rule 8, Rules of Civil Procedure, is subject to a defense based on the injured child's contributory negligence. Trial court held it is. We disagree and reverse and remand.

Vincent Handeland is the minor son of plaintiff Ronald D. Handeland. On September 10, 1971, Vincent was operating a borrowed motorcycle in Des Moines. He was injured when he collided at an intersection with an automobile driven by defendant Jane Eileen Brown and owned by defendant Dennis Brown.

Litigation ensued. Vincent, through plaintiff as next friend, brought a negligence action against defendants seeking to recover for his injuries. Plaintiff joined the action individually to assert his rule 8 claim based on Vincent's injuries. Rule 8, R.C.P., provides, "A parent, or the parents, may sue for the expense and actual loss of services, companionship and society resulting from injury to or death of a minor child." Defendants pleaded a defense based on Vincent's alleged contributory negligence in bar of plaintiff's claim as well as Vincent's claim. * * * The jury returned its verdict for defendants on both claims. Plaintiff alone appealed. The sole issue, squarely presented, is whether trial court erred in instructing the jury a defense of contributory negligence good against Vincent would also be good against plaintiff.

The position taken by trial court is supported by cases decided in other jurisdictions but not by logic. Our choice is whether we will be persuaded to follow a rule because it is generally followed elsewhere or reject it because we believe it is unsound. The general rule is stated in Restatement (Second) of Torts § 494:

> The plaintiff is barred from recovery for an invasion of his legally protected interest in the health or life of a third person which results from the harm or death of such third person, if the negligence of such third person would have barred his own recovery.

In the Appendix to that section the authors say the rule is supported by the great majority of cases which have considered it. Cases from several jurisdictions are cited for the principle. The authors recognize the rule has been much criticized on the ground the action is independent and not derivative. * * *

Analysis of the cases shows four independent bases relied on by the courts applying the restatement rule: (1) the plaintiff's action is "derivative"; (2) the negligence of the injured party is "imputed" to the plaintiff; (3) the plaintiff receives his cause of action by "assignment" from the injured person; and (4) the rule should be followed because it is well-settled. * * *

The derivative action theory.

Illustrative of cases in the first category is Dudley v. Phillips, 218 Tenn. 648, 405 S.W.2d 468 (1966). There, without saying why, the court held, "[A] cause of action arising in favor of the parent resulting from a tort committed against the child is derivative in nature and such action is subject to the same defenses that are available in the action arising in favor of the child." *Id.* at 471.

We rejected the derivative action rationale as applied to a rule 8 claim in Irlbeck v. Pomeroy, 210 N.W.2d 831, 833 (Iowa 1973) ("Under rule 8 the parent has a cause of action for a legal wrong to himself independent of that of the child."). * In *Irlbeck* we distinguished rule 8 claims from truly derivative actions, such as wrongful death actions, which are brought by one person to redress a wrong done to another rather than himself. A rule 8 claim is brought by a parent to redress a wrong done to himself rather than another. We cannot use the derivative action shibboleth as a basis for adopting the restatement rule.

* * * The eccentricity of the rule in Restatement of Torts (Second) of Torts § 494, is most graphically demonstrated by its effect in this case if Vincent had been operating a motorcycle owned by plaintiff. In that event plaintiff's negligence action against defendants for damages to

the motorcycle would not have been subject to a defense based on Vincent's contributory negligence. * Similarly, if plaintiff had been injured as a passenger on the vehicle his action based on his injuries would not have been subject to that defense. Nor, if Vincent wore clothing owned by his father, would plaintiff's action for its loss have been subject to a defense based on Vincent's contributory negligence. In each of these situations the general principle would be applicable. The merely concurrent negligence of the child would not bar parental redress. By the same logic the father's rule 8 claim should not be subject to a defense predicated on the merely concurrent negligence of the child.

Faced with the choice of following a rule simply because it has generally been followed elsewhere or rejecting it because we believe it is unsound, we choose to reject it. We hold a child's contributory negligence, not the sole proximate cause of his injury, is not a defense to a parental claim under rule 8 for the expense and actual loss of services, companionship and society resulting from injury to or death of the child. * * *

NOTE

Wrongful Death Claims. A number of special contributory negligence problems are presented in connection with claims arising from death. Ordinarily, the right to recover damages for wrongful death is statutory. See *infra* pages 417–418, Notes 1 and 2. Some statutes provide for the inheritance of decedent's claims. Others provide for compensation to certain survivors of decedent for losses resulting from the death. The decedent's contributory negligence generally bars recovery by statutory beneficiaries in a contributory negligence jurisdiction or reduces it in a comparative fault state. See Restatement (Third) of Torts: Apportionment of Liab. § 6(b) (2000).

What is the impact, though, of negligence by a beneficiary under a death statute? The beneficiary's own negligence typically bars or reduces his own recovery as a beneficiary of the wrongful death statute, but does not bar or reduce the estate's recovery under the survival statute, even if the negligent survivor is the representative of the estate who brings suit. For an example of the application of these concepts, see Baca v. Baca, 71 N.M. 468, 379 P.2d 765 (1963). In Teeter v. Missouri Highway & Transp. Comm'n, 891 S.W.2d 817 (Mo.1995), the court held that under comparative negligence, the defendant's liability was not reduced in proportion to the negligence of one of several beneficiaries, but that the defendant might be entitled to contribution from a beneficiary who is a joint tortfeasor. See *infra* Section G for consideration of contribution.

F. JOINT AND SEVERAL LIABILITY AND ALTERNATIVES

Corey v. Havener

Supreme Judicial Court of Massachusetts, 1902.
182 Mass. 250, 65 N.E. 69.

[See *supra* pages 249–250.]

Michie v. Great Lakes Steel Div., National Steel Corp.

United States Court of Appeals for the Sixth Circuit, 1974.
495 F.2d 213.

[See *supra* pages 251–254.]

Walt Disney World Co. v. Wood

Supreme Court of Florida, 1987.
515 So.2d 198.

■ GRIMES, JUSTICE. * * * Aloysia Wood was injured in November 1971 at the grand prix attraction at Walt Disney World (Disney), when her fiancé,[1] Daniel Wood, rammed from the rear the vehicle which she was driving. Aloysia Wood filed suit against Disney, and Disney sought contribution from Daniel Wood. * After trial, the jury returned a verdict finding Aloysia Wood 14% at fault, Daniel Wood 85% at fault, and Disney 1% at fault. The jury assessed Wood's damages at $75,000. The court entered judgment against Disney for 86% of the damages. Disney subsequently moved to alter the judgment to reflect the jury's finding that Disney was only 1% at fault. The court denied the motion. * * *

In Hoffman v. Jones, 280 So.2d 431 (Fla.1973), this Court discarded the rule of contributory negligence, which Florida had followed since at least 1886, and adopted the pure comparative negligence standard. * In adopting comparative negligence, this Court expressly declared two purposes for the change in judicial policy:

   (1)   To allow a jury to apportion fault as it sees fit between negligent parties whose negligence was part of the legal and proximate cause of any loss or injury; and

   (2)   To apportion the total damages resulting from the loss or injury according to the proportionate fault of each party.

     * * *

The * * * issue before us is whether we should now replace the doctrine of joint and several liability with one in which the liability of codefendants to the plaintiff is apportioned according to each defendant's respective fault. According to Disney, this Court in *Hoffman* set for itself the goal of creating a tort system that fairly and equitably allocated damages according to the degrees of fault. Therefore, a defendant should only be held responsible to the extent of his fault in the same way as a plaintiff under comparative negligence.

Joint and several liability is a judicially created doctrine. * This Court may alter a rule of law where great social upheaval dictates its necessity. * The "social upheaval" which is said to have occurred here is the fundamental alteration of Florida tort law encompassed by the adoption of comparative negligence. * Following the adoption of comparative negligence, some states have passed laws eliminating joint and several liability, * and the courts of several others have judicially

---

[1] Wood married her fiancé prior to this action.

abolished the doctrine. * The Kansas Supreme Court in *Brown v. Keill* reasoned:

> There is nothing inherently fair about a defendant who is 10% at fault paying 100% of the loss, and there is no social policy that should compel defendants to pay more than their fair share of the loss. Plaintiffs now take the parties as they find them. If one of the parties at fault happens to be a spouse or a governmental agency and if by reason of some competing social policy the plaintiff cannot receive payment for his injuries from the spouse or agency, there is no compelling social policy which requires the codefendant to pay more than his fair share of the loss. The same is true if one of the defendants is wealthy and the other is not.

Brown, 224 Kan. 195, 203, 580 P.2d 867, 874 (1978).

On the other hand, the majority of courts which have faced the issue in jurisdictions with comparative negligence have ruled that joint and several liability should be retained. * The Illinois Supreme Court in *Coney v. J.L.G. Industries, Inc.*, gave four reasons justifying the retention of joint and several liability:

(1) The feasibility of apportioning fault on a comparative basis does not render an indivisible injury "divisible" for purposes of the joint and several liability rule. A concurrent tortfeasor is liable for the whole of an indivisible injury when his negligence is a proximate cause of that damage. In many instances, the negligence of a concurrent tortfeasor may be sufficient by itself to cause the entire loss. The mere fact that it may be possible to assign some percentage figure to the relative culpability of one negligent defendant as compared to another does not in any way suggest that each defendant's negligence is not a proximate cause of the entire indivisible injury.

(2) In those instances where the plaintiff is not guilty of negligence, he would be forced to bear a portion of the loss should one of the tortfeasors prove financially unable to satisfy his share of the damages.

(3) Even in cases where a plaintiff is partially at fault, his culpability is not equivalent to that of a defendant. The plaintiff's negligence relates only to a lack of due care for his own safety while the defendant's negligence relates to a lack of due care for the safety of others; the latter is tortious, but the former is not.

(4) Elimination of joint and several liability would work a serious and unwarranted deleterious effect on the ability of an injured plaintiff to obtain adequate compensation for his injuries.

Coney v. J.L.G. Indus., Inc., 97 Ill.2d 104, 121–122, 73 Ill. Dec. 337, 345, 454 N.E.2d 197, 205 (1983). * * *

While recognizing the logic in Disney's position, we cannot say with certainty that joint and several liability is an unjust doctrine or that it should necessarily be eliminated upon the adoption of comparative negligence. In view of the public policy considerations bearing on the issue, this Court believes that the viability of the doctrine is a matter which should best be decided by the legislature. Consequently, we approve the decision of the district court of appeal. * * *

■ McDONALD, CHIEF JUSTICE, dissenting. The majority opinion may make social sense, but it defies legal logic. The doctrines of joint and several liability and contributory negligence are consistent with each other. Each tortfeasor, as a part of the whole, is liable for the whole. Comparative negligence, which does not bar, but reduces a recovery to the extent of individual fault, requires a separation of fault between the injured party and the other tortfeasors. It would be a mismatch of legal concepts to have a separation theory for the plaintiffs and a joint liability responsibility for defendants. Comparative negligence recognized the ability of a court to determine and apportion damages in relation to the harm caused. Joint and several, in contrast, presumes the inability of the judiciary to divide fault among parties. We have now said that we can. Accordingly, when the comparative negligence doctrine comes into play, as it did in this case, the law of joint and several liability should be repudiated and each defendant held accountable for only the percentage of damages found by the trier of fact to have been caused by his conduct.

In Hoffman v. Jones, 280 So.2d 431 (Fla.1973), we said "[w]hatever may have been the historical justification for it, today it is almost universally regarded as unjust and inequitable to vest an entire accidental loss on one of the parties whose negligent conduct combined with the negligence of the other party to produce the loss." In furtherance of the principles set forth in *Hoffman*, this Court, recognizing the enactment of section 768.31, Florida Statutes (1975), removed the common law bar against contribution between joint tortfeasors in Lincenberg v. Issen, 318 So.2d 386 (Fla.1975). In doing so, we recognized that the equitable apportionment principle espoused in *Hoffman* should have broader application than permitting a plaintiff recovery for damages if he was partially at fault. As we concluded in *Lincenberg*, "it would be undesirable for this Court to retain a rule that under a system based on fault, casts the entire burden of a loss for which several may be responsible upon only one of those at fault." Instead, "[w]hen the negligence of more than one person contributes to the occurrence of an accident, each person should pay the proportion of the total damages he has caused the other party." I believe these principles, which in *Lincenberg* we discussed in the context of contribution, are equally applicable to the concept of joint and several liability. * * *

I do agree that * * * Florida's courts have consistently applied the doctrine [of joint and several liability] up to the present time. * None of these cases involved a situation where the plaintiff's fault exceeded that of the targeted joint tortfeasor. * * *

All but six states have now made the switch from contributory to comparative negligence. * Of the states that have made this fundamental change, the majority have grappled directly with the viability of joint and several liability under their comparative negligence schemes. I acknowledge from the outset that these states have reached a variety of results. Nevertheless, a survey of the relevant case law from across the nation reveals that those courts that have ruled in favor of retaining joint and several liability following the adoption of comparative negligence have rested their decisions on two fundamental grounds, neither of which I find defensible under Florida's modern tort scheme.

The first ground is the concept that a plaintiff's injury is indivisible. * This idea arises from the ancient common law theory that the plaintiff's loss grew out of one united cause of action in which the act of one defendant was considered the act of all and that the jury could not apportion damages because there was only one wrong. * This unity concept apparently arose from common law realities concerning rules of pleading and joinder. * Under this theory, a concurrent tortfeasor who, like Disney, is one percent at fault is liable for 100 percent of the damages caused by all concurrent tortfeasors based on the idea that each tortfeasor caused the plaintiff's entire loss. This result was palatable under Florida law as it existed prior to *Hoffman* because contributory negligence guaranteed fault-free plaintiffs, the law barred contribution among tortfeasors, and courts did not allocate fault among the various parties. Due to the considerable obstacles confronting a potential plaintiff under such a system, the law compensated a legally "pure" plaintiff for these inherent inequities by allowing him to collect his entire judgment from any defendant guilty of even slight negligence. *

On the other hand, this justification breaks down under Florida's present system. Under pure comparative negligence, even a plaintiff who is ninety-nine percent at fault can bring suit. Thus, the need to compensate necessarily pure plaintiffs for the inherent inequities in the tort system no longer exists. Moreover, * juries routinely allocate fault in every comparative negligence case. The inability to apportion fault, assumed under common law, has been specifically eliminated. It would be an illogical fiction to say that, although fault may be apportioned, causation cannot. * Therefore, the indivisible wrong theory, founded on common law technicalities, is obsolete under pure comparative negligence. Where the reasons for a common law rule no longer exist, the rule should be discarded. *

The second justification cited for retaining joint and several liability is that the doctrine is needed in order to insure that plaintiffs do not bear the risk of being unable to collect their judgments. * I see little validity in this argument either. Between one plaintiff and one defendant, the plaintiff necessarily bears the risk of the defendant being insolvent. I fail to see the justice in shifting the risk simply because there are two defendants, one of whom is solvent or otherwise subject to suit. * As one of our sister courts has cogently noted:

> There is nothing inherently fair about a defendant who is 10% at fault paying 100% of the loss, and there is no social policy that should compel defendants to pay more than their fair share of the loss. Plaintiffs now take the parties as they find them. If one of the parties at fault happens to be a spouse or a governmental agency and if by reason of some competing social policy the plaintiff cannot receive payment for his injuries from the spouse or agency, there is no compelling social policy which requires the codefendant to pay more than his fair share of the

loss. The same is true if one of the defendants is wealthy and the other is not.

Brown v. Keill, 224 Kan. 195, 203, 580 P.2d 867, 874 (1978). I agree. I see no justification for compelling Disney to pay 100 percent of the damage award simply because Mrs. Wood chose to marry the other tortfeasor, an individual whom the jury found to be eighty-five times more at fault than Disney.

Moreover, the familiar axiom that, because it happens to be a solvent business entity, a defendant is necessarily better able to spread the loss than the plaintiff is not true in every case. After all, not every defendant is General Motors or Disney. The doctrine of joint and several liability applies equally to all defendants, whether they be large corporations, small independent businesses, or individuals. * * *

If we are ever to achieve a just and equitable tort system, we must predicate a party's liability upon his or her blameworthiness, not upon his or her solvency or a codefendant's susceptibility to suit. * Those who argue for favoring the plaintiff merely because he or she is the plaintiff have lost sight of the paramount goal of comparative negligence.

By adopting pure comparative negligence in *Hoffman*, this Court set for itself the goal of creating a tort system that fairly and equitably allocates damages. * Basing a defendant's liability upon the ability of others to pay runs counter to *Hoffman*'s pronouncement that the liability of the defendant should not depend upon what damages were suffered, but upon what damages the defendant caused. * Therefore, I would hold that when a plaintiff is partially at fault the doctrine of joint and several liability is abrogated in Florida in favor of a rule that each defendant is liable only for an amount which is equivalent to the total damages multiplied by the percentage of fault by that defendant. * * *

■ OVERTON, JUSTICE, dissenting. * * * To say it is proper for this Court to change the contributory negligence doctrine to comparative negligence by court decision, and then say the judicially established companion doctrine of joint and several liability should be left to the legislature, is both an abdication of our responsibility to address judicially established legal principles and, in this instance, hypocritical.

Our tort system is founded on the principle of fault, with the one whose fault caused injury being liable for the damages he or she caused. In this instance, the tortfeasor that caused only one percent of the injury is required to pay eighty-six percent of the damages. The majority opinion appears to convey the impression that a majority of jurisdictions would allow this type of recovery. That is a false impression. The large majority of jurisdictions recognize the injustice of a rule that would allow a recovery in this circumstance. The majority of jurisdictions which have adopted comparative negligence allow a plaintiff to recover from a defendant on the basis of joint and several liability only if the defendant's negligence is greater than the plaintiff's negligence or if the defendant is at least fifty percent negligent. Joint and several liability, as it is applied to the instant case, is a judicially established rule. As such, it is our responsibility to address it in a manner that will establish sound logical justice for all parties. In my view that can best be achieved by at least eliminating joint and several liability for defendants whose negligence is less than that of the plaintiff.

NOTES

1.   *Several or Proportionate Liability.* Should joint and several liability survive the adoption of comparative negligence? Approximately one dozen states continue to employ the doctrine of joint and several liability when multiple tortfeasors are found liable for the plaintiff's harm. See Gifford & Robinette, Apportioning Liability, 73 Md. L. Rev. at 155 n.325. The polar opposite approach to the result reached by the majority in *Wood* is several or proportionate liability, that is, to hold a defendant liable for only the percentage of damages attributable to its own proportion of fault as determined by the jury. At the time the Restatement (Third) of Torts: Apportionment of Liability was adopted in 2000, the drafters identified sixteen states as several liability jurisdictions. See Restatement (Third) of Torts: Apportionment of Liab. § 17 Reporters' Note, cmt. a, tbl.3 (2000).

2.   *Other Legislative Solutions to Apportioning Joint Liability.* Even more frequently, state legislatures have adopted legislative compromises. These compromise alternatives to joint and several liability take many different forms, but most begin with one of three basic formats. First, a number of state statutes provide "that co-defendants are jointly and severally liable for economic damages, but only severally or proportionately liable for noneconomic damages." Gifford & Robinette, Apportioning Liability, 73 Md. L. Rev. at 757; see, e.g., Neb. Rev. Stat. § 25–21,185.10 (2013) (limiting noneconomic damages to several liability); see also Restatement (Third) of Torts: Apportionment of Liab. § E18 (2000).

A second group of approximately ten statutes "imposes joint and several liability only if the defendant's degree of fault exceeds a statutorily defined threshold, such as twenty percent or fifty percent, but otherwise imposes only proportionate liability." Gifford & Robinette, Apportioning Liability, 73 Md. L. Rev. at 758; see, e.g., Mo. Rev. Stat. § 537.067 (2013) (establishing threshold at fifty-one percent); N.J. Stat. Ann. § 2A:15–5.3 (2014) (establishing threshold at sixty percent). See also Restatement (Third) of Torts: Apportionment of Liab. § D18.

Finally, a third alternative approach is to reallocate the liability of shares of damages that are unpaid because a co-defendant is immune from liability (such as Daniel Wood), judgment-proof, or beyond the jurisdiction of the court:

> The reallocation method re-assesses the uncollectible portion of a judgment against a particular co-defendant to all other parties, including the plaintiff. When *D1* cannot pay the $60,000 share that it should pay because of insolvency or immunity, the logical way to handle it is to reallocate *D1*'s share between *P* and *D2*. With *D1* out of the picture (at least in terms of collection), the share should be allocated to *P* and *D2* according to their respective degrees of fault. *P*'s original allocation of fault was thirty percent and *D2*'s was ten percent. *P* is three times as much at fault as *D2*, and logically *P* should be responsible for three-quarters or seventy-five percent of *D1*'s share and *D2* should be liable for one-quarter or twenty-five percent of *D1*'s share. *D2*, therefore, is liable for twenty-five percent of $60,000—that is,

$15,000—as well as the share originally allocated to it of $10,000. Hence, *D2* is liable for a total of $25,000. If, however, *P* is free from contributory negligence, the co-defendants remain jointly and severally liable.

Both the Uniform Comparative Fault Act[343] and the *Restatement of Torts*[344] endorse one variant of the reallocation method * * *, but fewer than a dozen jurisdictions follow it.[346] In addition, courts have applied proportional reallocation of unpaid shares in decisions under the Comprehensive Environmental Response, Compensation, and Liability Act ("CERCLA").[347]

Gifford & Robinette, Apportioning Liability, 73 Md. L. Rev. at 759–60. See *id.* at 752–64 for a comprehensive description of each of the five alternatives (including both joint and several liability and several liability) and the respective advantages and disadvantages of each approach.

G. CONTRIBUTION AND INDEMNITY

NOTE

Indemnity. The traditional common law rule, beginning with the English case of Merryweather v. Nixan, [1799] Eng.Rep. 1337 (K.B.), 8 Term Rep. 186, 101, was that a defendant who paid damages to a plaintiff in order to satisfy a judgment could not obtain contribution from a jointly liable co-defendant. A reason for this appears to have been the reluctance of the common law to attempt to apportion fault, the same reluctance that delayed the development of comparative negligence as a substitute for the absolute bar of contributory negligence.

Even at common law, however, an innocent defendant who paid a judgment in certain circumstances was traditionally allowed to recover compensation from a negligent co-defendant for the entire amount paid under an aspect of restitution known as "indemnity." The most common example is that of vicarious liability, such as where an employer has paid damages to a third party injured as a result of the negligence of the employer's employee. In this situation, the employer may theoretically recover the damages it has paid from the employee, the actual wrongdoer, although in practice it may be unwise for an employer to attempt to do so. See generally Harper, James and Gray on Torts § 10.2 (including the evolution in a few states of more recent doctrines such as "comparative" or "partial" indemnity). Here, there were no problems concerning apportionment of liability. The indemnity claim and recovery were traditionally for the full amount that the innocent employer had paid, not

---

[343] Unif. Comparative Fault Act § 2(d), 12 U.L.A. 135, 137 (2008) (noting that reallocation avoids unfairness).

[344] Restatement (Third) of Torts: Apportionment of Liab. § C21 cmt. a (2000) (describing the reallocation method as the "fairest means of handling this problem").

[346] See, e.g., Conn. Gen. Stat. Ann. § 52-572 h(g)(1) (West 2013) (applying reapportionment to economic and noneconomic losses). *

[347] 42 U.S.C. §§ 9601-9675 (2006). See, e.g., Town of New Windsor v. Tesa Tuck, Inc., 919 F.Supp. 662, 681 (S.D.N.Y.1996) (stating that courts may use provisions of CERCLA to reallocate "orphan shares" among solvent responsible parties (internal quotation marks omitted)); Charter Twp. of Oshtemo v. Am. Cyanamid Co., 898 F.Supp. 506, 509 (W.D.Mich.1995) (providing that plaintiff and all defendants may be assigned shares in reallocation).

for part of it. "Indemnity claims are similar to contribution claims but see a full recovery instead of a share. . . . The unjust enrichment grounds for recovery are the same as in contribution; only the measure is different." Dan B. Dobbs, 1 Law of Remedies 608 (2d ed. 1993). Frequently, indemnification results from an express contractual agreement between the parties that one party will reimburse the other party for any legal liability. See generally Hendrickson v. Minnesota Power & Light Co., 258 Minn. 368, 372, 104 N.W.2d 843, 848 (1960).

Illinois Compiled Statutes Annotated, Joint Tortfeasor Contribution Act
740 Ill. Comp. Stat. 100/2–5 (West 2014).

§ 2. *Right of Contribution.*

(a) Except as otherwise provided in this Act, where 2 or more persons are subject to liability in tort arising out of the same injury to person or property, or the same wrongful death, there is a right of contribution among them, even though judgment has not been entered against any or all of them.

(b) The right of contribution exists only in favor of a tortfeasor who has paid more than his pro rata share of the common liability, and his total recovery is limited to the amount paid by him in excess of his pro rata share. No tortfeasor is liable to make contribution beyond his own pro rata share of the common liability.

(c) When a release or covenant not to sue or not to enforce judgment is given in good faith to one or more persons liable in tort arising out of the same injury or the same wrongful death, it does not discharge any of the other tortfeasors from liability for the injury or wrongful death unless its terms so provide but it reduces the recovery on any claim against the others to the extent of any amount stated in the release or the covenant, or in the amount of the consideration actually paid for it, whichever is greater.

(d) The tortfeasor who settles with a claimant pursuant to paragraph (c) is discharged from all liability for any contribution to any other tortfeasor.

(e) A tortfeasor who settles with a claimant pursuant to paragraph (c) is not entitled to recover contribution from another tortfeasor whose liability is not extinguished by the settlement.

(f) Anyone who, by payment, has discharged in full or in part the liability of a tortfeasor and has thereby discharged in full his obligation to the tortfeasor, is subrogated to the tortfeasor's right of contribution. This provision does not affect any right of contribution nor any right of subrogation arising from any other relationship.

§ 3. *Amount of Contribution.* The pro rata share of each tortfeasor shall be determined in accordance with his relative culpability. However, no person shall be required to contribute to one seeking contribution an amount greater than his pro rata share unless the obligation of one or more of the joint tortfeasors is uncollectable. In that event, the remaining tortfeasors shall share the unpaid portions of the uncollectable obligation in accordance with their pro rata liability.

If equity requires, the collective liability of some as a group shall constitute a single share.

§ 4. *Rights of Plaintiff Unaffected.* * * * [A] plaintiff's right to recover the full amount of his judgment from any one or more defendants subject to liability in tort for the same injury to person or property, or for wrongful death, is not affected by the provisions of this Act.

§ 5. *Enforcement.* * * * [A] cause of action for contribution among joint tortfeasors may be asserted by a separate action before or after payment, by counterclaim or by third-party complaint in a pending action.

NOTES

1. *Right to Contribution.* Most states now recognize a right of contribution by one tortfeasor who has paid more than her fair share of a judgment against her co-defendants, either as a result of judicial decision or, more commonly, by statute. In some jurisdictions, such as Illinois, the appropriate amount to be paid by each defendant is determined by examining the defendant's relative degrees of fault; in others, the liability to the plaintiff is divided equally ("pro rata") among the defendants. Cf. Southern Md. Oil Co. v. Texas Co., 203 F.Supp. 449, 452 (D.Md.1962).

2. *Right of Contribution against a Defendant Immune from a Direct Action by Plaintiff.* Not infrequently, a defendant seeks contribution from another tortfeasor whose tortious acts were one of multiple causes of the plaintiff's injuries but who is shielded from a direct action brought by the plaintiff by an immunity, such as a family immunity or the immunity created by the exclusivity of the remedy provision of a workers' compensation statute. What if the manufacturer of a machine tool, for example, is successfully sued in a product liability action by a worker who was injured while using the machine? The manufacturer then files a third party action against the worker's employer, seeking contribution, alleging that the employer was responsible for the accident because it failed to instruct the employee properly in the use of the machine, or removed safety guards from the equipment. Should the manufacturer be able to recover from the employer? Why or why not? Compare Dole v. Dow Chem. Co., 30 N.Y.2d 143, 331 N.Y.S.2d 382, 282 N.E.2d 288 (1972) (contribution allowed against employer) and Shor v. Paoli, 353 So.2d 825 (Fla.1977) (contribution action allowed against spouse) with Ramsey v. Georgia-Pacific Corp., 597 F.2d 890, 893 (5th Cir.1979) (Miss. law) (contribution denied against employer) and with Ennis v. Donovan, 222 Md. 536, 161 A.2d 698 (1960) (contribution denied against spouse).

3. *Distinguishing Release from Covenant Not to Sue.* If a single tortfeasor reaches a settlement with the plaintiff and receives a release in exchange for payment of consideration, what is the effect of such a release upon the other defendants? Traditionally, a "release" was seen as the abandonment of a claim—releasing the plaintiff's rights against all tortfeasors. Plaintiffs intending to release only a single tortfeasor and not all possible tortfeasors were encouraged to give the settling tortfeasor a "covenant not to sue" and not a "release."

The modern trend is to examine two factors—(1) the intent of the parties and (2) whether the plaintiff has been wholly compensated—to determine whether the release precludes liability against all joint tortfeasors or only against a single settling tortfeasor. E.g., Gronquist v. Olson, 242 Minn. 119, 64 N.W.2d 159 (1954). If the plaintiff has not been wholly compensated, it is now the usual rule that a release of one tortfeasor does not release the others. See Restatement (Third) of Torts: Apportionment of Liab. § 24 (b) (2000). In jurisdictions following the doctrine of joint and several liability, the release diminishes the claim against the others, ordinarily by the amount of compensation received from the released tortfeasor. See *id.* at § 25.

These rules governing the consequences of settlement are usually accomplished by legislation, such as the enactment by states of one version or another of the Uniform Contribution Among Tortfeasors Act (U.L.A.) § 4 (1939 version or 1955 Revised Version), or its successor, the Uniform Apportionment of Tort Responsibility Act § 7 (2003), e.g., Md. Code Ann., Cts. & Jud. Proc. § 3–1404 (LexisNexis 2013) (1939 version); Mass Gen. L. Ann. ch. 231B, § 4 (2014) (1955 Revised Version). A variation recommended in the Uniform Comparative Fault Act (U.L.A.) § 6 (1977) now provides that the claim of the releasing party against other persons is reduced "by the amount of the released person's equitable share of the obligation." E.g., Iowa Code § 668.7 (2013). Under all these statutes, releases and covenants not to sue are usually treated the same in terms of their effect on plaintiffs' claims against non-settling tortfeasors.

It is important to review the provisions of the applicable contribution statute before entering into settlement agreements. The failure to satisfy prescribed requirements may result in unanticipated losses. A plaintiff who settles with one tortfeasor, for example, may inadvertently forfeit a claim against another defendant, if safeguards specified in the statute are omitted, or a settling defendant may find himself unexpectedly subject to contribution liability to other defendants if the settlement is not properly structured.

4. *"Mary Carter" and Other Contingent Settlement Agreements.* In tort litigation involving multiple defendants, the plaintiff and one or more of the defendants sometimes reach a type of settlement agreement often referred to as a "Mary Carter" agreement (because the validity of this type of agreement was upheld by the court in Booth v. Mary Carter Paint Co., 202 So.2d 8 (Fla.Dist.Ct.App.1967)). See Restatement (Third) of Torts: Apportionment of Liab. § 24 cmt. i (2000). The settling tortfeasor guarantees the plaintiff a minimum recovery, but the plaintiff is required to offset this guaranteed payment in whole or in part with any recovery obtained at trial from the non-settling defendant(s). Such an agreement provides incentive for the settling defendant to cooperate with the plaintiff at trial. Most courts approve the use of Mary Carter agreements because they facilitate settlement, but a few courts, including the Texas Supreme Court, have struck down Mary Carter agreements on public policy grounds. See Elbaor v. Smith, 845 S.W.2d 240 (Tex.1992). According to that court,

> The agreements pressure the "settling" defendant to alter the character of the suit by contributing discovery material,

peremptory challenges, trial tactics, supportive witness examination, and jury influence to the plaintiff's cause. * These procedural advantages distort the case presented before a jury that came to court expecting to see a contest between the plaintiff and the defendants [and] instead see[s] one of the defendants cooperating with the plaintiff.

Courts that allow such agreements often disclose the terms of the agreement to the jury and alter trial processes, for example, reallocating the time allowed each party to question witnesses or the number of its peremptory challenges in an attempt to mirror the actual strategic alignment of the litigants rather than their formal designations as "plaintiff" or "defendants."

The "Mary Carter" agreement is but one form of the wide variety of settlement agreements attempted by plaintiffs and defendants where a defendant's ultimate liability depends upon results at trial. For a discussion of "loan receipt" agreements and "Gallagher" agreements, see Schick v. Rodenburg, 397 N.W.2d 464 (S.D.1986). See also Restatement (Third) of Torts: Apportionment of Liab. § 24 cmt. i (2000).

CHAPTER 6

DAMAGES

Many categories of tortious liability, such as negligence, require the plaintiff to prove "actual damages"—usually either personal injury or property damages—in order to prevail on a claim. Once the plaintiff proves all elements of the tort, including the required element of damages, the plaintiff then can recover other damages, often called "parasitic damages." Other torts, such as intentional torts, do not require proof of actual harm to person or property. Even in the absence of actual damages, the court may find liability and award "nominal" damages. In addition, the plaintiff may recover punitive or exemplary damages if the defendant's conduct is particularly egregious.

This chapter covers the types of damages that may be recovered once liability for negligence or most other torts is established and how they are measured. Part A (*infra* pages 399–411) describes the categories of compensatory damages that the plaintiff may recover in personal injury litigation and how courts place outer limits on the jury's determination of such damages. In Part B (*infra* pages 411–423), we turn to several related "general considerations" affecting the jury's determination of such damages, including the single recovery rule, reducing an award for future expenses to its present discounted value, and the collateral source doctrine. Part C (*infra* pages 423–427) then addresses damages for harm to property. Finally, in Part D (*infra* pages 428–440), we turn to punitive damages, recoverable only if the defendant's conduct is particularly egregious.

In Chapter 8 we consider limitations on liability based on the type of harm sustained by the plaintiff, e.g., when is a plaintiff able to recover for emotional distress in the absence of personal injury or for purely economic harm without proof of personal injury or property damage.

A. COMPENSATORY DAMAGES FOR PERSONAL INJURIES

1. CATEGORIES OF DAMAGES AND JUDICIAL REVIEW

Seffert v. Los Angeles Transit Lines

Supreme Court of California, 1961.
56 Cal.2d 498, 15 Cal.Rptr. 161, 364 P.2d 337.

■ PETERS, JUSTICE. Defendants appeal from a judgment for plaintiff for $187,903.75 entered on a jury verdict. Their motion for a new trial for errors of law and excessiveness of damages was denied.

At the trial plaintiff contended that she was properly entering defendants' bus when the doors closed suddenly catching her right hand and left foot. The bus started, dragged her some distance, and then threw her to the pavement. Defendants contended that the injury resulted from plaintiff's own negligence, that she was late for work and either ran into the side of the bus after the doors had closed or ran after the bus and attempted to enter after the doors had nearly closed.

The evidence supports plaintiff's version of the facts. Several eyewitnesses testified that plaintiff started to board the bus while it was standing with the doors wide open. Defendants do not challenge the sufficiency of the evidence. They do contend, however, that prejudicial errors were committed during the trial and that the verdict is excessive.

* * * [The court finds that there were no prejudicial errors committed by the trial court on the issue of liability.]

The Damages Were Not Excessive

One of the major contentions of defendants is that the damages are excessive, as a matter of law. There is no merit to this contention. * * *

* * * [T]he injury occurred when plaintiff was caught in the doors of defendants' bus when it started up before she had gained full entry. As a result she was dragged for some distance. The record is uncontradicted that her injuries were serious, painful, disabling and permanent. The major injuries were to plaintiff's left foot. The main arteries and nerves leading to that foot, and the posterior tibial vessels and nerve of that foot, were completely severed at the ankle. The main blood vessel which supplies blood to that foot had to be tied off, with the result that there is a permanent stoppage of the main blood source. The heel and shin bones were fractured. There were deep lacerations and an avulsion[3] which involved the skin and soft tissue of the entire foot. These injuries were extremely painful. They have resulted in a permanently raised left heel, which is two inches above the floor level, caused by the contraction of the ankle joint capsule. Plaintiff is crippled and will suffer pain for life.[4] * * * The foot is not only permanently deformed but has a persistent open ulcer on the heel, there being a continuous drainage from the entire area. Medical care of this foot and ankle is to be reasonably expected for the remainder of plaintiff's life.

Since the accident, and because of it, plaintiff has undergone nine operations and has spent eight months in various hospitals and rehabilitation centers. These operations involved painful skin grafting and other painful procedures. One involved the surgical removal of gangrenous skin leaving painful raw and open flesh exposed from the heel to the toe. Another involved a left lumbar sympathectomy in which plaintiff's abdomen was entered to sever the nerves affecting the remaining blood vessels of the left leg in order to force those blood vessels to remain open at all times to the maximum extent. Still another operation involved a cross leg flap graft of skin and tissue from plaintiff's thigh which required that her left foot be brought up to her right thigh and held at this painful angle, motionless, and in a cast for a month until the flap of skin and fat, partially removed from her thigh, but still nourished there by a skin connection, could be grafted to the bottom of her foot, and until the host site could develop enough blood vessels to support it. Several future operations of this nature may be necessary. One result of this operation was to leave a defective area of the thigh where the normal fat is missing and the muscles exposed, and

---

[3]   Defined in Webster's New International Dictionary (2d ed.) as a "tearing asunder; forcible separation."

[4]   Her life expectancy was 34.9 years from the time of trial.

the local nerves are missing. This condition is permanent and disfiguring. Another operation called a debridement, was required. This involved removal of many small muscles of the foot, much of the fat beneath the skin, cleaning the end of the severed nerve, and tying off the severed vein and artery. The ulcer on the heel is probably permanent, and there is the constant and real danger that osteomyelitis may develop if the infection extends into the bone. If this happens the heel bone would have to be removed surgically and perhaps the entire foot amputated.

Although plaintiff has gone back to work, she testified that she has difficulty standing, walking or even sitting, and must lie down frequently; that the leg is still very painful; that she can, even on her best days, walk not over three blocks and that very slowly; that her back hurts from walking; that she is tired and weak; that her sleep is disturbed; that she has frequent spasms in which the leg shakes uncontrollably; that she feels depressed and unhappy, and suffers humiliation and embarrassment.

Plaintiff claims that there is evidence that her total pecuniary loss, past and future, amounts to $53,903.75. This was the figure used by plaintiff's counsel in his argument to the jury, in which he also claimed $134,000 for pain and suffering, past and future. Since the verdict was exactly the total of these two estimates, it is reasonable to assume that the jury accepted the amount proposed by counsel for each item. *

The summary of plaintiff as to pecuniary loss, past and future, is as follows:

Doctor and Hospital Bills		$10,330.5
Drugs and other medical expenses stipulated to in the amount of		2,273.25
Loss of earnings from time of accident to time of trial		5,500.00
		$18,103.75
Future Medical Expenses		
$2,000 per year for next 10 years	20,000.00	
$200 per year for the 24 years	4,800.00	
Drugs for 34 years	1,000.00	
		$25,800.00
		$43,903.75
Possible future loss of earnings		10,000.00
Total pecuniary loss		$53,903.75

There is substantial evidence to support these estimates. The amounts for past doctor and hospital bills, for the cost of drugs, and for a past loss of earnings, were either stipulated to, evidence was offered on, or is a simple matter of calculation. These items totaled $18,103.75. While the amount of $25,800 estimated as the cost of future medical expense, for loss of future earnings and for the future cost of drugs, may seem high, there was substantial evidence that future medical expense is certain to be high. There is also substantial evidence that plaintiff's future earning capacity may be substantially impaired by reason of the injury. The amounts estimated for those various items are not out of line, and find support in the evidence.

This leaves the amount of $134,000 presumably allowed for the nonpecuniary items of damage, including pain and suffering, past and future. It is this allowance that defendants seriously attack as being excessive as a matter of law.

It must be remembered that the jury fixed these damages, and that the trial judge denied a motion for new trial, one ground of which was excessiveness of the award. These determinations are entitled to great weight. The amount of damages is a fact question, first committed to the discretion of the jury and next to the discretion of the trial judge on a motion for new trial. They see and hear the witnesses and frequently, as in this case, see the injury and the impairment that has resulted therefrom. As a result, all presumptions are in favor of the decision of the trial court. * The power of the appellate court differs materially from that of the trial court in passing on this question. An appellate court can interfere on the ground that the judgment is excessive only on the ground that the verdict is so large that, at first blush, it shocks the conscience and suggests passion, prejudice or corruption on the part of the jury. * * *

While the appellate court should consider the amounts awarded in prior cases for similar injuries, obviously, each case must be decided on its own facts and circumstances. Such examination demonstrates that such awards vary greatly. * Injuries are seldom identical and the amount of pain and suffering involved in similar physical injuries varies widely. * * * Basically, the question that should be decided by the appellate courts is whether or not the verdict is so out of line with reason that it shocks the conscience and necessarily implies that the verdict must have been the result of passion and prejudice.

In the instant case, the nonpecuniary items of damage include allowances for pain and suffering, past and future, humiliation as a result of being disfigured and being permanently crippled, and constant anxiety and fear that the leg will have to be amputated. While the amount of the award is high, and may be more than we would have awarded were we the trier of the facts, considering the nature of the injury, the great pain and suffering, past and future, and the other items of damage, we cannot say, as a matter of law, that it is so high that it shocks the conscience and gives rise to the presumption that it was the result of passion or prejudice on the part of the jurors. * * *

The judgment appealed from is affirmed. * * *

■ TRAYNOR, JUSTICE. I dissent. Although I agree that there was no prejudicial error on the issue of liability, it is my opinion that the award of $134,000 for pain and suffering is so excessive as to indicate that it was prompted by passion, prejudice, whim, or caprice.[6] * * *

---

[6]   The award of $53,903.75 for pecuniary loss, past and future, is also suspect. The amount awarded for future medical expenses is $12,196.25 greater than the medical expenses incurred from the time of the accident to the time of trial, a period of nearly two years. The amount awarded for future loss of earnings is $4,500 greater than plaintiff's past loss of

There has been forceful criticism of the rationale for awarding damages for pain and suffering in negligence cases. * Such damages originated under primitive law as a means of punishing wrongdoers and assuaging the feelings of those who had been wronged. * They become increasingly anomalous as emphasis shifts in a mechanized society from ad hoc punishment to orderly distribution of losses through insurance and the price of goods or of transportation. Ultimately such losses are borne by a public free of fault as part of the price for the benefits of mechanization. Cf. * Escola v. Coca Cola Bottling Co., 24 Cal.2d 453, 462, 150 P.2d 436 (1944) (concurring opinion).

Nonetheless, this state has long recognized pain and suffering as elements of damages in negligence cases; * any change in this regard must await reexamination of the problem by the Legislature. Meanwhile, awards for pain and suffering serve to ease plaintiffs' discomfort and to pay for attorney fees for which plaintiffs are not otherwise compensated.

It would hardly be possible ever to compensate a person fully for pain and suffering. " 'No rational being would change places with the injured man for an amount of gold that would fill the room of the court, yet no lawyer would contend that such is the legal measure of damages.' " Zibbell v. Southern Pacific Co., 160 Cal. 237, 255, 116 P.3d 513 (1911). * "Translating pain and anguish into dollars can, at best, be only an arbitrary allowance, and not a process of measurement, and consequently the judge can, in his instructions give the jury no standard to go by; he can only tell them to allow such amount as in their discretion they may consider reasonable. . . . The chief reliance for reaching reasonable results in attempting to value suffering in terms of money must be the restraint and common sense of the jury. . . . " Charles T. McCormick, Damages § 88 (2d ed. 1952). Such restraint and common sense were lacking here.

A review of reported cases involving serious injuries and large pecuniary losses reveals that ordinarily the part of the verdict attributable to pain and suffering does not exceed the part attributable to pecuniary losses. * The award in this case of $134,000 for pain and suffering exceeds not only the pecuniary losses but any such award heretofore sustained in this state even in cases involving injuries more serious by far than those suffered by plaintiff. * * * Although excessive damages is "an issue which is primarily factual and is not therefore a matter which can be decided upon the basis of awards made in other cases" Leming v. Oilfields Trucking Co., 44 Cal.2d 343, 356, 282 P.2d 23, 31 (1955), * awards for similar injuries may be considered as one factor to be weighed in determining whether the damages awarded are excessive. *

The excessive award in this case was undoubtedly the result of the improper argument of plaintiff's counsel to the jury. Though no evidence was introduced, though none could possibly be introduced on the monetary value of plaintiff's suffering, counsel urged the jury to award $100 a day for pain and suffering from the time of the accident to

---

earnings. Yet the evidence indicates that plaintiff's medical care has been largely completed and that the future loss of earnings will not exceed the earnings lost by the prolonged stays in the hospital and the rehabilitation center.

the time of trial and $2,000 a year for pain and suffering for the remainder of plaintiff's life.

The propriety of counsel's proposing a specific sum for each day or month of suffering has recently been considered by courts of several jurisdictions. * * * The reason usually advanced for not allowing such argument is that since there is no way of translating pain and suffering into monetary terms, counsel's proposal of a particular sum for each day of suffering represents an opinion and a conclusion on matters not disclosed by the evidence, and tends to mislead the jury and result in excessive awards. The reason usually advanced for allowing "per diem argument for pain and suffering" is that it affords the jury as good an arbitrary measure as any for that which cannot be measured.

Counsel may argue all legitimate inferences from the evidence, but he may not employ arguments that tend primarily to mislead the jury. * A specified sum for pain and suffering for any particular period is bound to be conjectural. Positing such a sum for a small period of time and then multiplying that sum by the number of days, minutes or seconds in plaintiff's life expectancy multiplies the hazards of conjecture. Counsel could arrive at any amount he wished by adjusting either the period of time to be taken as a measure or the amount surmised for the pain for that period.

> The absurdity of a mathematical formula is demonstrated by applying it to its logical conclusion. If a day may be used as a unit of time in measuring pain and suffering, there is no logical reason why an hour or a minute or a second could not be used, or perhaps even a heart-beat since we live from heart-beat to heart-beat. If one cent were used for each second of pain this would amount to $3.60 per hour, to $86.40 per twenty-four hour day, and to $31,536 per year. The absurdity of such a result must be apparent, yet a penny a second for pain and suffering might not sound unreasonable. . . . The use of the formula was prejudicial error.

Affett v. Milwaukee & Suburban Transport Corp., 11 Wis.2d 604, 613–14, 106 N.W.2d 274, 280 (1960). * * *

I would reverse the judgment and remand the cause for a new trial on the issue of damages. * * *

NOTES

1. *The General Measure of Compensatory Damages.* In Geressy v. Digital Equipment Corp., 980 F.Supp. 640 (E.D.N.Y.1997), Judge Jack B. Weinstein described the appropriate measure of compensatory damages in tort law:

> *Reasonable compensation* is compensation that would make a plaintiff *whole*, as if he or she had never suffered the injury. See, e.g., McDougald v. Garber, 73 N.Y.2d 246, 253–54, 538 N.Y.S.2d 937, 939, 536 N.E.2d 372, 374 (1989) (The purpose of "an award of damages to a person injured by the negligence of another is to compensate the victim. . . . The goal is to restore the injured party, to the extent possible, to the position that would have been occupied had the wrong not occurred."). * * *

Attempts to make the plaintiff whole through money damages are acts of legal fiction which cannot mask the ultimate powerlessness of money to replace what an individual has lost in suffering the unalterable consequences of an injury. The New York Court of Appeals acknowledges that:

> An economic loss can be compensated in kind by an economic gain; but recovery for noneconomic losses such as pain and suffering and loss of enjoyment of life rests on the legal fiction that money damages can compensate for a victim's injury. . . . We accept this fiction, knowing that although money will neither ease the pain nor restore the victim's abilities, this device is as close as the law can come in its effort to right the wrong. We have no hope of evaluating what has been lost, but a monetary award may provide a measure of solace for the condition created. . . .

McDougald, 73 N.Y.2d at 254, 538 N.Y.S.2d at 939–40, 536 N.E.2d at 374–75.

2. *Loss of Earning Capacity.* "A person is entitled to compensation for the lost *capacity* to earn, whether he would have chosen to exercise it or not." Harper, James and Gray on Torts § 25.8. In Earl v. Bouchard Transportation Co., 735 F.Supp. 1167, 1169 (E.D.N.Y.1990), Judge Weinstein described the factors considered by the jury in determining the amount of compensation for the loss of earning capacity:

> * * * In computing the full value of a tort victim's depleted work-capital the jury may consider a variety of factors that differ from plaintiff to plaintiff, such as past earnings, the marketplace value of an individual's skills, the availability of suitable employment, and average work-life expectancy as projected by government statistical tables. This value may be affected as a result of particularized evidence bearing on a plaintiff's pre-accident intentions and proclivities. For example, if the jury credited evidence that before being injured a plaintiff had intended to retire early, a reduction of the full value of an award would be justified under the doctrine of mitigation of damages, which requires tort victims to find alternative employment whenever possible. The award may be increased to the full or close to full value if, on the other hand, the jurors believed that a plaintiff was likely to work beyond that age at which the statistical tables or their common sense experience would normally predict retirement.

The distinction between the loss of earning capacity and the loss of actual income is illustrated both by cases where the plaintiff is employable, but not employed at the time of the accident, e.g., a lawyer who chooses to remain at home and raise young children instead, and by cases where the injured party recovers for loss of earning capacity even if, after suffering a partially disabling injury, he earns as much as or more than he did before the injury. See also *infra* pages 419–420, Note 6.

When an injured plaintiff is self-employed in a business or a profession, he generally is able to show his loss of earning capacity by proving his income before and after the accident. Harper, James and Gray on Torts § 25.8. In many cases, however, the profits of the business are substantially attributable to capital investment or the efforts of other employees. In these cases, courts generally measure the loss by the cost of hiring a substitute to perform the functions previously handled by the injured plaintiff. In some cases, courts have allowed similar proof in instances where a business is new and has not yet established profitability. E.g., Anderson v. Litzenberg, 115 Md.App. 549, 694 A.2d 150 (1997).

3. *Medical and Other Expenses.* A prevailing plaintiff is entitled to recover the reasonable costs of medical and similar expenses resulting from her injury, including both those already incurred at the time of trial and those that will be incurred in the future. See Restatement (Second) of Torts § 924(c) & cmt. f (1979); see also generally Harper, James and Gray on Torts § 25.9. Expert opinion testimony is often necessary to prove both the need for and the reasonableness of such expenditures, particularly in the case of future (as well as past) expenses.

4. *Recovery for "Pain and Suffering."* The frequently used term "pain and suffering" is imprecise, but generally includes several different types of non-economic damages, including physiological pain suffered by the victim at the time of the injury, anguish and terror felt in the face of impending injury or death, the loss of enjoyment of life by an accident victim who is denied the pleasures of normal personal or social activities (unless this loss is compensated as a separate element of damages), and, to varying degrees, the emotional distress and long-term loss of love and companionship resulting from the injury or death of a close family member. Paul C. Weiler et al., American Law Institute, Reporters' Study, Enterprise Responsibility for Personal Injury, Vol. II: Approaches to Legal and Institutional Change 199–200 (1991). Psychic injury and suffering are sometimes referred to as emotional distress or mental anguish.

In Kwasny v. United States, 823 F.2d 194 (7th Cir.1987), Judge Posner offered the following justification for allowing plaintiffs to recover pain and suffering damages:

> We disagree with those students of tort law who believe that pain and suffering are not real costs and should not be allowable items of damages in a tort suit. No one likes pain and suffering and most people would pay a good deal of money to be free from them. If they were not recoverable in damages, the cost of negligence would be less to the tortfeasors and there would be more negligence, more accidents, more pain and suffering, and hence higher social costs. But there is a justified public concern with extravagant tort awards, and it is a duty of an appellate court to keep these awards within reason.

823 F.2d at 197–98 (Ill. law; medical malpractice claim; decedent "was unconscious throughout most of his last illness, and before then his suffering from [defendant's negligence] had been limited to minor problems with swallowing and hoarseness, plus the episode of respiratory arrest and the ensuing tracheotomy and convalescence therefrom. The cumulative pain and discomfort were not trivial but the award of $350,000 to compensate for them was in our view 'manifestly erroneous.' * * * We think $175,000 is the highest reasonable estimate of Mr. Kwasny's pain and suffering due to the government's negligence.").

In his dissent in *Seffert*, Justice Traynor argues that damages can never adequately compensate for the suffering of a plaintiff. Consider in this context the following question asked by a plaintiff's counsel during closing argument: "Who would sell their esophagus for $4 million? * * * " Walters v. Hitchcock, 237 Kan. 31, 33, 697 P.2d 847, 849 (1985) (counsel's question did not constitute a prohibited "golden rule" argument asking jurors to place themselves in the role of the plaintiff).

Some economists have argued that the liability system should not provide pain and suffering damages. E.g., Patricia M. Danzon, Medical Malpractice: Theory, Evidence and Public Policy 153, 160, 171 (1985). They assert that when people buy first-party insurance—such as health, life, and disability insurance—to protect themselves against a variety of calamities, they do not choose to pay the extra dollars that would be necessary to buy protection against non-economic damages resulting from house fires or earthquakes, or from automobile accidents where no other driver is at fault. The extent to which insurance purchasers have a choice in this matter is, however, questionable. Compare, furthermore, the wide acceptance of uninsured and underinsured motorist's coverage that does provide such coverage. See also generally Steven P. Croley & Jon D. Hanson, The Nonpecuniary Costs of Accidents: Pain-and-Suffering Damages in Tort Law, 108 Harv. L. Rev. 1785 (1995).

5. *Variability of Awards of Noneconomic Damages.* Jury awards for non-economic damages are inherently highly variable, as Judge Weinstein has noted:

> As the Second Circuit has observed, "measuring pain and suffering in dollars is inescapably subjective." Gibbs v. United States, 599 F.2d 36, 39 (2d Cir.1979). There is an inherent difficulty in considering such disparate factors as a plaintiff's "ability to dance, bowl, swim, or engage in similar recreational activities, inability to perform customary chores[,] and . . . to engage in the usual family activities." Downie v. United States Lines Co., 359 F.2d 344, 347 n.3 (3d Cir.1966).
>
> Plaintiffs differ. Some are more susceptible to pain than others. Some may be younger, perhaps more deserving in the jury's view, or more vulnerable, or may have led a more difficult life or an easier one. There is an infinite variety of people and reactions to tragedy, further compounding the difficulty of quantifying verdicts.
>
> Even with seemingly objective criteria, such as measurements of the amount of time that a tort victim suffers, different juries produce a seemingly erratic set of verdict data. One scholar in this field, Dean David W. Leebron, attempted to find a correlation between time suffered and the amount of the award. In his research, he was unable to discover any rationale for jury awards for pain and suffering. Dean Leebron found that "the temporal element of the pain and suffering has no statistically significant effect for durations from half a minute up to one week." David W. Leebron, Final Moments: Damages for Pain and Suffering Prior to Death, 64 N.Y.U. L. Rev. 256, 294 (1989). He concluded, "[t]ort awards . . . vary significantly and . . . neither the specific facts of the case nor differing views of the functions of the awards can explain such variation." * See also Oscar G. Chase, Helping Jurors to Determine Pain and Suffering Awards, 23 Hofstra L. Rev. 763, 768 (1995) ("Both anecdotal and empirical evidence indicates that

the disparity between awards for pain and suffering among apparently similar cases defies rational explanation.").

Within the same state verdicts vary widely by geographic area. As Justice Edward T. O'Brien recently observed:

> It is curious that awards for pain and suffering on one side of the East River are uniformly two and three times higher than on the other. Is it that the composition of the two respective communities are so different? I think not. . . .

> * State verdicts vary widely even in the Eastern District of New York depending on the county in which the case is tried.

Geressy v. Digital Equip. Corp., 980 F.Supp. 640, 656–57 (E.D.N.Y.1997).

6. *The Legitimacy of Particular Forms of Argument Regarding Pain and Suffering Damages.* Closing arguments to the jury in personal injury cases are not only analytical, they often include theatric and emotional components . Certain forms of advocacy by plaintiffs' attorneys, such as the arguments described in the opinions in *Seffert,* where plaintiffs' attorneys break down pain and suffering into individual days or even smaller time units, are controversial. Some courts disallow such arguments, e.g., Caley v. Manicke, 24 Ill.2d 390, 182 N.E.2d 206 (1962); while others allow them, e.g., Friedman v. C & S Car Serv., 108 N.J. 72, 527 A.2d 871 (1987) (under court rule); Debus v. Grand Union Stores of Vt., 159 Vt. 537, 547, 621 A.2d 1288, 1290–91 (1993).

Another currently popular technique is the use of "Day-in-the-Life" films or videotapes showing how a plaintiff's life has been affected by her injuries. Compare Bannister v. Town of Noble, Okla., 812 F.2d 1265, 1270 (10th Cir.1987) (Okla. law) (use of film upheld in specific application), with Bolstridge v. Central Maine Power Co., 621 F.Supp. 1202, 1204 (D.Me.1985) (prejudicial effect of film outweighs probative value).

7. *Judicial Control of Damage Verdicts and Remittitur.* The latitude given by the majority in *Seffert* to the jury in its determination of damages is typical. "[T]he majority of jurisdictions in the United States applied a 'shock the conscience' standard to determine the possible excessiveness or insufficiency of jury awards." Geressy v. Digital Equip. Corp., 980 F.Supp. 640, 653 (E.D.N.Y.1997).

Trial courts supervise the size of jury verdicts through use of remittiturs and additurs. See, e.g., Kmart Corp. v. Kyles, 723 So.2d 572, 579 (Ala.1998) ("If the plaintiff does not accept a remittitur of the compensatory damages award from $100,000 to * * * $15,000, the defendants must be granted a new trial."); Donaldson v. Anderson, 109 Nev. 1039, 862 P.2d 1204 (1993) (finding that trial court judgment following verdict awarding parents no damages for loss of consortium in wrongful death of seventeen year old son was "shocking" and "clearly inadequate" and remanding to trial court with instructions to issue $400,000 additur (to be reduced by decedent's comparative fault)). One study found that post-trial judicial actions, whether in the trial court or the appellate court, lowered plaintiffs' awards in only 15 percent of cases in which the plaintiff received a verdict. Michael G. Shanley & Mark A. Peterson, Posttrial Adjustments to Jury Awards 26 (RAND Institute for Civil Justice, 1987).

8. *Statutory Limits on Noneconomic Damages.* More than a dozen states have enacted limits, or "caps," on the amount of pain and suffering or non-economic damages in some or all personal injury actions. E.g., Cal. Civ. Code § 3333.2 (Deering 2014) (noneconomic damages limited to $250,000 in actions against health care providers); Md. Code Ann., Cts. & Jud. Proc. § 11–108 (LexisNexis 2013) (noneconomic damages in personal injury cases limited to $500,000 in 1994 with a $15,000 annual incremental increase thereafter). These limits on noneconomic damages have been challenged on a variety of federal and—sometimes more successfully—state constitutional grounds, with inconsistent results. E.g., Best v. Taylor Mach. Works, 179 Ill.2d 367, 409, 228 Ill.Dec. 636, 657, 689 N.E.2d 1057, 1078 (1997) (Illinois cap held invalid under state constitution); Samsel v. Wheeler Transp. Serv., Inc., 244 Kan. 726, 727, 771 P.2d 71, 72 (1989) (cap upheld against constitutional challenges).

Caps on noneconomic damages have been criticized because they impose the costs of reducing tort compensation and insurance premiums "solely upon a class consisting of these most severely injured by tortious conduct." State ex rel. Ohio Acad. of Trial Lawyers v. Sheward, 86 Ohio St.3d 451, 490, 715 N.E.2d 1062, 1095 (1999). Indeed, the ratio of noneconomic damages to economic damages is likely to be significantly greater in personal injury cases involving modest injuries with small economic losses than it is in cases where the plaintiff has sustained very serious injuries with large medical bills and losses of income.

Caps on noneconomic damages often were enacted as key ingredients in "tort reform" packages in the late 1980s in response to concerns about the availability and affordability of liability insurance. For an account of the interplay between legislative action and judicial reaction in one state, see State ex rel. Ohio Academy of Trial Lawyers v. Sheward, *supra.*

9. *The "American Rule" for Payment of Legal Fees.* Under English law, the courts are authorized to award counsel fees to successful parties in the litigation. In contrast, in all American jurisdictions except for Alaska, attorneys' fees are not ordinarily recoverable in the absence of a statute or enforceable contract providing for the recovery of litigation costs. The argument in favor of the so-called American Rule is that because the outcome of litigation is uncertain, a party should not be penalized for merely defending or prosecuting a lawsuit. In addition, any judicial determination of what constitutes reasonable attorneys' fees would impose substantial new burdens on the courts.

Statutes and court rules frequently allow the prevailing party to recover attorneys' fees if the opposing party's claim or defense is viewed by the court as "frivolous." E.g., Colo. Rev. Stat. § 13–17–102 (2013); Conn. Gen. Stat. Ann. § 52–240a (2013). In addition, many federal and state statutes now allow a successful party to recover attorneys' fees. E.g., 42 U.S.C. § 1988(b) (2012) (civil rights proceedings); 15 U.S.C. § 2310(d)(2) (2012) (consumer protection); see also Hastings Bldg. Prods. Inc. v. Nat'l Aluminum Corp., 815 F.Supp. 228 (W.D.Mich.1993) (allowing costs under Comprehensive Environmental Response, Compensation and Liability Act despite absence of explicit provision).

10. *The Nature of Contingent Fee Agreements.* Because of the "American Rule" for payment of legal fees, personal injury plaintiffs rely on damages awarded for pain and suffering as a source of funds to pay attorneys' fees, ordinarily due under a contingent fee agreement, without sacrificing damages awarded to compensate them for economic losses.

Under a contingent fee agreement, the plaintiff's lawyer agrees to accept a percentage of the eventual recovery as full compensation for her fees. If there is no recovery, the lawyer receives no compensation. Contingent fee agreements assist injured plaintiffs, particularly those with modest resources, in litigating their tort claims. Virtually all lawyers representing plaintiffs in personal injury cases in the United States are paid in this manner. In addition, counsel also often lends plaintiff the out-of-pocket expenses incurred during litigation. According to interviews of Wisconsin attorneys conducted in 1995 by Professor Herbert Kritzer, the most common arrangement is that the attorney's fee is between 15% and 33% if the matter can be settled without filing a lawsuit, between 20% and 43% if a lawsuit is filed but the action does not go to trial, and between 25% and 50% if the lawsuit is tried. Herbert M. Kritzer, The Wages of Risk: The Returns of Contingency Fee Legal Practice, 47 DePaul L. Rev. 267, 286 (1998).

11. *Respective Interests of Attorney and Client.* In addition to providing plaintiffs otherwise unable to afford counsel with the opportunity to have their cases litigated, contingent fee agreements often are believed to align the respective interests of lawyers and their clients. Consider the following excerpts from Circuit Judge Easterbrook's opinion in Kirchoff v. Flynn, 786 F.2d 320, 324, 325 (7th Cir.1986) in which he compares the interests of attorneys and clients under three different types of fee agreements:

> The market for legal services uses three principal plans of compensation: the hourly fee, the fixed fee, and the contingent fee. The contingent fee serves in part as a financing device, allowing people to hire lawyers without paying them in advance (or at all, if they lose). It also serves as a monitoring device. In any agency relation, the agent may pursue his own goals at the expense of the principal's. A fixed fee creates the incentive to shirk; a lawyer paid a lump sum, win or lose, may no longer work hard enough to present his client's case. Fixed fees therefore are used only in cases where the client can monitor the results and the lawyer's work (did the lawyer secure the divorce or not?) or where the client (or the client's general counsel) is sufficiently sophisticated to assess what the lawyer has accomplished.

> An hourly fee creates an incentive to run up hours, to do too much work in relation to the stakes of the case. An hourly fee may be appropriate where it is hard to define output (in litigation, for example, the outcome turns on the merits and not simply the lawyer's skill and dedication), so the hourly method measures and prices the inputs, the attorney's hours. Again, however, it is necessary to monitor the lawyer's work. The general counsel of a corporation or a sophisticated client may measure inputs well * * *.

> The contingent fee uses private incentives rather than careful monitoring to align the interests of lawyer and client. The lawyer gains only to the extent his client gains. This interest-alignment device is not perfect. When the lawyer gains 40 cents to the client's dollar, the lawyer tends to expend too little effort; unless concern for his reputation dominates, he would not put in an extra

$600 worth of time to obtain an extra $1,000 for his client, because he would receive only $400 for his effort. * But imperfect alignment of interests is better than a conflict of interests, which hourly fees may create. The unscrupulous lawyer paid by the hour may be willing to settle for a lower recovery coupled with a payment for more hours. Contingent fees eliminate this incentive and also ensure a reasonable proportion between the recovery and the fees assessed to defendants.

B. GENERAL CONSIDERATIONS

1. SINGLE RECOVERY RULE

Fetter v. Beal
King's Bench, 1698.
1 Raymond's Rep. 339, 91 E.R. 1122.

* * * Special action * * * for a battery committed by the defendant upon the plaintiff, and breaking his skull. The plaintiff declares that he * * * brought an action * * * against the defendant [for battery] and recovered 11£. and no more; and that after that recovery part of his skull by reason of the said battery came out of his head * * *. The defendant pleaded the said recovery in bar. Upon which the plaintiff demurred. And Shower for the plaintiff argued, that this action differed from the nature of the former, and therefore would well lie, notwithstanding the recovery in the other; because the recovery in the former action was only for the bruise and battery, but here there is a maihem by the loss of the skull. As if a man brings an action against another for taking and detaining of goods for two months, and afterwards he brings another action for taking and detaining for two years, the recovery in the former action is not pleadable in bar of the second. * * * And *per totam Curiam,* the jury in the former action considered the nature of the wound, and gave damages for all the damages that it had done to the plaintiff; and therefore a recovery in the said action is good here. And it is the plaintiff's fault, for if he had not been so hasty, he might have been satisfied for this loss of the skull also. Judgment for the defendant * * *.

SAME CASE, SUB NOM
Ferrer v. Beale
King's Bench, 1701.
1 Raymond's Rep. 692, 91 E.R. 1361.

Sir Bartholomew Shower moved in this case for judgment for the plaintiff, because this special subsequent damage is a sufficient foundation for an action, and that for great reason, because the jury could not have consideration of it in giving damages. And he compared it to the case of a nuisance, that a man might have an action for every new dropping of the water from the eaves of the house. 2. There is a maim laid here, and therefore the prior recovery in the action of assault cannot be a bar. Mr. Montague, of the same side said, that if A. breaks a sea wall, and the owner of the land recovers damages for it in an action, and erects a new wall, and before it is dry and settled the sea throws it down again, and overflows the land, & c. for this special subsequent damage the owner may have a new action.

■ HOLT, CHIEF JUSTICE. * * * Every one shall recover damages in proportion to his prejudice which he hath sustained; and if this matter had been given in evidence, as that which in probability might have been the consequence of the battery, the plaintiff would have recovered damages for it. The injury, which is the foundation of the action, is the battery, and the greatness or consequence of that is only in aggravation of damages. * * * [T]his damage, which might probably ensue, might and ought to have been given in evidence, and must be intended to have been given in evidence in the former action, and that the jury gave damages for all the hurt that he suffered; for if the nature of the battery was such, as probably to produce this effect, the jury might give damages for it before it happened. As to the case of the sea wall, the plaintiff would recover damages enough in the first action, to rebuild it; and if he rebuilds it ill, the fault is his own. And as to the nuisance every new dropping is a new nuisance. As to the maihem, that is nothing; for a recovery in battery, & c. is a bar in appeal of maihem, * because in battery the plaintiff may give a maihem in evidence, and recover damages for it. And Holt Chief Justice said, that the original cause was tried before him eight years ago, and the plaintiff and defendant appeared to be both in drink, and the jury did not well know which of them was in fault, and therefore they gave the less damages. The plaintiff could not obtain judgment, the court inclining strongly against him.

NOTES

1. *"Splitting the Cause of Action" in the Modern Context.* The single recovery doctrine is associated with a rule against the "splitting of a cause of action." This issue arises frequently in the contemporary context of illnesses caused by exposure to toxic substances that do not manifest themselves until long after the plaintiff's contact with the substance. Assume the plaintiff develops asbestosis, a fibrous disease of the lungs caused by the inhalation of asbestos dust, and immediately stops working in the occupation that brings her into contact with asbestos. She brings a products liability action against the asbestos manufacturers and recovers damages on the resulting judgment. Some years later, she is diagnosed with mesothelioma—a particularly vicious type of cancer which attacks the pleural membranes that line the lungs, the abdominal cavity, and the heart. If plaintiff files a second action to recover damages for the mesothelioma, does her recovery in the first action for damages caused by asbestos exposure bar recovery? Compare Jackson v. Johns-Manville Sales Corp., 781 F.2d 394, 413 (5th Cir.1986) (under Mississippi law, recovery for mesothelioma allowed in first action brought for asbestosis injuries where plaintiff had better than a 50 percent chance of getting cancer even though disease had not yet manifested itself), with Wilson v. Johns-Manville Sales Corp., 684 F.2d 111, 120–21 (D.C.Cir.1982) (statute of limitations for mesothelioma began to run only after diagnosis of cancer, not when plaintiff was diagnosed years earlier with asbestosis; subsequent action for mesothelioma not barred by rule against claim-splitting). See also *infra*

pages 489–490, Note 2, "Emotional Distress Resulting from Fear of Contracting Latent Diseases," and Note 3, "Medical Monitoring Expenses."

2. *Critiques of the Single Recovery Rule.* The single recovery rule has been criticized on a variety of grounds. See Harper, James and Gray on Torts § 25.2. In 1975, for example, the Michigan Law Revision Commission found that plaintiffs receiving large damage awards "often find themselves a few years later without adequate means for their support after having expended or dissipated the sums which they recovered. Such persons frequently become public charges requiring the expenditure of public funds for their future needs for medical expenses, support and maintenance." Michigan Law Revision Commission, Tenth Annual Report 129 (1975). The National Conference of Commissioners on Uniform State Laws has proposed a model act for the periodic payment of damages. Unif. Periodic Payment of Judgments Act (1990), 14 U.L.A. 228 (2005).

3. *Scheduled Benefits in Settlements.* The constraints of the common law rule against splitting a cause of action obviously do not apply to a settlement agreed upon by both parties. During recent decades, parties in claims involving serious bodily injuries requiring long-term medical treatment and care often have agreed to "structured settlements." Designed with the help of actuaries and medical experts familiar with the plaintiff's anticipated needs, such settlements typically include both an initial lump-sum payment to cover out-of-pocket expenses, past losses, and attorneys' fees, and an annuity intended to cover a claimant's future losses.

Consider a settlement made in 1974 by a university medical center in California, whose admitted negligence during surgery left a 50-year-old woman in an apparently permanent coma. The hospital agreed to provide for the patient's needs for the rest of her life, estimated at 23 1/2 years. The cost of care was said to range from $334 to $380 per day at present prices, and was estimated to reach a total of between $3.5 million and $4.5 million, considering inflation. The settlement also established a contingency fund to pay the patient $100,000 if she should recover, and the payment of $100,000 for existing medical bills and attorneys' fees of $445,000. See Medical Center Agrees to Pay for Injured Patient's Lifetime Care, 31 The Citation 49 (Chicago, IL: Office of the General Counsel of the American Medical Association, June 15, 1975).

4. *Alternative Treatment in Workers' Compensation.* An alternative way of handling prospective loss is widely employed in the administration of workers' compensation laws and various other no-fault plans. Here the notion of single recovery, with all its limitations, is rejected in favor of an award calling for periodic payments (cf. technique sometimes used in handling claims for alimony). This award may be modified from time to time on a showing that disability has increased, decreased, or ceased, or that some other change in the material circumstances has taken place. See, e.g., Conn. Gen. Stat. § 31–315 (2013); N.Y. Workers' Comp. Law §§ 22, 25 & 123 (2014); 77 Pa. Stat. § 772 (2014).

2. FUTURE LOSSES, PRESENT VALUE, AND INFLATION

Feldman v. Allegheny Airlines, Inc.
United States Court of Appeals for the Second Circuit, 1975.
524 F.2d 384.

■ LASKER, DISTRICT JUDGE. On June 7, 1971, an Allegheny Airlines flight crashed in fog while approaching New Haven Airport. Nancy Feldman, a passenger, died, in the crash. Allegheny conceded liability, and the parties submitted the issue of damages to Judge Blumenfeld of the United States District Court for the District of Connecticut. * The airline appeals * from Judge Blumenfeld's judgment awarding $444,056 to Reid Laurence Feldman, as administrator of the estate of his late wife.

Determination of damages in this diversity wrongful death action is governed by Connecticut law * * * which measures recovery by the loss to the decedent of the value of her life rather than by the value of the estate she would have left had she lived a full life. * In accordance with Connecticut law, the judgment represented the sum of (1) the value of Mrs. Feldman's lost earning capacity and (2) the destruction of her capacity to enjoy life's non-remunerative activities, less (3) deductions for her necessary personal living expenses. * * * Damages in a wrongful death action must of necessity represent a crude monetary forecast of how the decedent's life would have evolved. * * * It is clear from Judge Blumenfeld's remarkably detailed and precise analysis that he nevertheless made a prodigious effort to reduce the intangible elements of an award to measurable quantities. It is with reluctance, therefore, that we conclude that his determination of loss of earnings and personal living expenses must be remanded.

I.   Damages for Destruction of Earning Capacity.

Nancy Feldman was 25 years old at the time of her death. From 1968 until shortly before the plane crash, she lived and worked in New Haven while her husband studied at Yale Law School. On Mr. Feldman's graduation from law school in the spring of 1971 the Feldmans moved to Washington, D.C., where they intended to settle. At the time of her death, Mrs. Feldman had neither accepted nor formally applied for employment in Washington, although she had been accepted by George Washington Law School for admission in the Fall of 1971 and had made inquiries about the availability of employment.

A key objection of appellant Allegheny runs to Judge Blumenfeld's calculation of the discount rate at 1.5% in determining the present value of Mrs. Feldman's lost earning capacity on the grounds that the court has no right to take inflation into account in any way in its assessment of damages. The district court decided that the appropriate rate of discount would be the "price of capital," such to be "obtained by adjusting interest rates on 'risk-free' investments so as to exclude the additional interest demanded by the investment market as compensation for investors' assumption of the risk of inflation." *

In calculating the discount rate, the appellee's expert, relied on by the district court, used an average earnings of 4.14% (from mutual savings bank investments) as representative of a prudent, non-sophisticated investment and subtracted 2.87% as the average yearly inflation rate revealed in the Department of Labor's Consumer Price Index over an 18–year period, yielding a 1.27% difference which was rounded up to 1.5%. Judge Blumenfeld corroborated this "inflation-adjusted discount rate" of 1.5% by calculating the real yields of investments since 1940 in federal government securities (with inflation factored out) * * *.

* * * In computing the value of Mrs. Feldman's lost earning capacity, the trial judge found that Mrs. Feldman's professional earnings in her first year of employment would have been $15,040, and that with the exception of eight years during which she intended to raise a family and to work only part time, she would have continued in full employment for forty years until she retired at age 65. The judge further found that during the period in which she would be principally occupied in raising her family, Mrs. Feldman would have remained sufficiently in contact with her profession to maintain, but not increase, her earning ability. Pointing out that under Connecticut law damages are to be based on "the loss of earning *capacity*, not future earnings *per se ...* " * the judge concluded that when a person such as Mrs. Feldman, who possesses significant earning capacity, chooses to forego remunerative employment in order to raise a family, she manifestly values child rearing as highly as work in her chosen profession and her loss of the opportunity to engage in child rearing "may thus fairly be measured by reference to the earning capacity possessed by the decedent." * Applying this rationale, the trial judge made an award for the eight year period of $17,044 per year, the salary which he computed Mrs. Feldman would have reached in the year preceding the first child-bearing year, but did not increase the amount during the period.

We believe the trial judge erred in automatically valuing Mrs. Feldman's loss for the child-bearing period at the level of her salary. As Judge Blumenfeld's opinion points out, the Connecticut cases distinguish clearly between loss of earning capacity and loss of capacity to carry on life's non-remunerative activities. As we read Connecticut law, where a decedent suffers both kinds of loss for the same period each must be valued independently in relation to the elements particular to it.

The court in Floyd v. Fruit Industries, Inc., [144 Conn. 659, 136 A.2d 918 (1957)], equated "earning capacity" with "the capacity to carry on the particular activity of earning money." * Here the evidence established, and the trial court found, that Mrs. Feldman would have worked only part-time while raising a family. In the circumstances, we believe that under the Connecticut rule the plaintiff is entitled to recover "loss of earnings" for the child raising years only to the extent that the court finds that Mrs. Feldman would actually have worked during those years. For example, if the court finds that she would have worked 25% of the time during that period, the plaintiff would properly be credited only with 25% of her salary for each of the eight years.

* * * [W]e conclude that any award in relation to the portion of the child-raising period during which Mrs. Feldman would not have been working must be predicated on her "loss of the enjoyment of life's activities" rather than on loss of earnings, and on remand the district judge should re-evaluate the elements accordingly. * * *

II.   Deductions for Decedent's Necessary Personal Living Expenses.

Where the decedent had been subject to the expense of self-maintenance, Connecticut case law provides for the deduction of "personal living expenses" from damages otherwise recoverable for the loss of earning capacity. * * * The *Floyd* court defined the term "personal living expenses" as:

> . . . those personal expenses which, under the standard of living followed by a given decedent, it would have been reasonably necessary for him to incur in order to keep himself in such a condition of health and well-being that he could maintain his capacity to enjoy life's activities, including the capacity to earn money.

* The trial judge concluded that, under Connecticut law, deductions for Mrs. Feldman's personal living expenses should include the cost, at a level commensurate with her standard of living, of food, shelter, clothing and health care. The judge fixed such costs in Washington, D.C. for the year following her death at $2,750, increasing that figure by 3% per year to the age of retirement. After retirement, living expenses were deducted at the rate of $5,000 annually. These figures were discounted annually by 1.5% to reduce the deduction to present value. Although the process by which the trial judge determined the level of Mrs. Feldman's living expenses was proper, we believe that he substantially underestimated the actual costs of food, shelter, clothing and health care. * * * We recognize the perils involved in an appellate court dealing *de novo* with factual matters. We would not venture to do so in this case if we did not feel we have the right to take judicial notice of the facts of life, including the cost of living for those in the position of the Feldmans in such metropolitan areas as Washington, D.C. We reluctantly conclude that the trial judge was in error in computing living expenses at $2,750 for the year after Mrs. Feldman's death, and building on that base for later years. * * *

The judgment is affirmed in part, reversed in part and remanded.

■ FRIENDLY, CIRCUIT JUDGE (concurring *dubitante*). * * * Both plaintiff's expert and the court allowed for inflation not by building cost-of-living increases into future earnings but by applying a rate of only 1.5% in discounting to present value estimated lost future earnings and other recoverable values calculated in 1971 dollars. The district court derived this 1.5% figure by comparing rates of return on a number of "risk-free" securities issued by the federal government (plaintiff's expert examined other types of "risk-free" fixed income investments and reached similar conclusions) since 1940 with rates of inflation during the same period as reflected by annual changes in the Consumer Price Index. The court subtracted the latter from the former on the theory that the latter amounted to that portion of the return representing what investors have historically demanded as protection against inflation. The difference varied from year to year, but the court determined that 1.5% was a representative figure for the period. This was deemed to be "that part of the annual yield which constitutes payment for the use of capital" or "real yield"—presumably the rate of return which investors would be willing to accept in an inflation-free economy * * *. The distinction drawn between this method and the one more commonly used—adjusting the amount to be discounted so as to include a sum reflecting assumptions about future inflation—apparently given some weight by the majority—is more apparent than real. Plaintiff's expert acknowledged that "another approach" or "alternative calculation" for this problem would be to increase estimated lost future compensation and living expenses to take account of the effects of future inflation and not reduce the rate of return used for discounting by any amount reflecting inflation. The outcome of the calculation under either approach would be very nearly identical. * * *

My guess is also that, even if inflation should be taken into account, neither a Connecticut nor a federal jury would have made an award as large as was made here. * * * However, I am loathe to require a busy federal judge to spend still more time on this diversity case * * *. Although intuition tells me that the Supreme Court of Connecticut would not sustain the award made here, I cannot prove it. I therefore go along with the majority, although with the gravest doubts. * * *

NOTES

1. *Wrongful Death and Survival Actions.* At common law there was no right of recovery following the death of a tort victim. Baker v. Bolton, (1808) 170 Eng.Rep. 1033, 1 Camp. 493. Survivors could recover neither for losses sustained by the decedent during her lifetime nor for losses they would sustain following the decedent's death—including both economic loss and the loss of intangibles such as companionship.

Today, all fifty American states have adopted some form of a wrongful death or survival statute, or both. E.g., Conn. Gen. Stat. §§ 52–555, 52–555a & 52–599 (2013); Fla. Stat. Ann. §§ 768.16–768.26 (West 2014); and Md. Code Ann., Cts. & Jud. Proc., §§ 3–901 to 3–904 (LexisNexis 2013) and Md. Code Ann., Est. & Trusts § 7–401(y) (LexisNexis 2011). The Connecticut statute is somewhat unusual in that it appears to combine some features of both types of death statute. The provisions of the statutes vary considerably, including differences on basic issues such as the types of damages that can be recovered and the appropriate parties to file the action. See generally Harper, James, and Gray on Torts § 24.2. The concepts behind the "wrongful death" action and the "survival" action sometimes are merged, though most statutes continue to distinguish the two. Wrongful death acts typically cover the claims of the decedent's dependents for loss of the support and other benefits they would have received from the decedent but for his death. Survival statutes typically represent the claim the decedent herself would have had for her own losses but for her death.

2. *Recovery for Emotional Loss and Similar Damages by Beneficiaries under Wrongful Death Statute.* Wrongful death statutes determine both the parties that can recover following a wrongful death and the damages that are to be awarded. A particularly important issue is whether the surviving spouse and children can recover for their own non-economic damages resulting from the decedent's death. Some statutes are quite explicit and generous in outlining the types of recoverable damages. The Maryland Wrongful Death Act, for example, specifies that damages "are not limited or restricted by the 'pecuniary loss' or 'pecuniary benefit' rule but may include damages for mental anguish, emotional pain and suffering, loss of society, companionship, comfort, protection, marital care, parental care, filial care, attention, advice, counsel, training, guidance, or education where

applicable * * *." Md. Code Ann., Cts. & Jud. Proc. § 3–904(d) (LexisNexis 2013). In contrast, statutes in some jurisdictions state that damages are limited to pecuniary loss suffered by the designated beneficiaries. See, e.g., N.Y. Est. Powers & Trusts Law § 5–4.3(a) (McKinney 2014); Campbell v. Diguglielmo, 148 F.Supp.2d 269 (S.D.N.Y.2001) (upholding award of $1,500,000 for loss of parental guidance under New York law). In some jurisdictions, statutory language purporting to limit recovery to pecuniary losses has been construed to include at least some damages that could be considered non-economic. E.g., Elliott v. Willis, 92 Ill.2d 530, 534, 65 Ill.Dec. 852, 854, 442 N.E.2d 163, 165 (1982) ("fair and just compensation with reference to the pecuniary injuries" construed to include damages for surviving spouse's loss of companionship and conjugal relations).

3. *Family Members Eligible for Recovery.* Each of us is diminished by the death of someone with whom she is close. But who can recover for emotional loss following a wrongful death? The issue is a matter of statutory interpretation of wrongful death statutes and often such statutes are very specific. The Maryland Wrongful Death Statute, for example, allows recovery for emotional losses sustained as a result of the death of a spouse, minor child, unmarried child under the age of 21 or financially dependent upon the decedent, and the parent of a minor child. Md. Code Ann., Cts. & Jud. Proc. § 3–904(d) (LexisNexis 2013).

When wrongful death statutes are less explicit on the issue of who can recover, the matter is left to judicial interpretation. Should parents be able to recover for their emotional losses resulting from the death of an emancipated adult child? E.g., Schultz v. Grogean, 406 Mass. 364, 548 N.E.2d 180 (1990) (recovery allowed). Should an unborn child of unmarried parents who has not yet reached the stage of viability at the time of the death of the father be able to recover for emotional losses resulting from the death of the father? E.g., Angelini v. OMD Corp., 410 Mass. 653, 575 N.E.2d 41 (1991) (recovery allowed).

4. *Present Discounted Value and Inflation.* As the principal case illustrates, discounting future damages such as lost income or medical expenses to their present value is necessary for an award of damages that makes plaintiff "whole" but does not create a windfall. See also Doca v. Marina Mercante Nicaraguense, S.A., 634 F.2d 30, 40 (2d Cir.1980) (suggesting 2% as appropriate adjusted discount rate to account for inflation, in absence of economic testimony supporting a different rate); O'Shea v. Riverway Towing Co., 677 F.2d 1194, 1198–1201 (7th Cir.1982) (Posner, J.). A certain sum of money is worth more today than the prospect of receiving the same sum of money at some time in the future because of the ability to earn interest on the funds in the meantime. Therefore the question becomes what sum of money today is equal in value to the funds needed by plaintiff to compensate for future losses. Obviously, the answer depends upon two factors: the length of time before the funds will be spent and the *real* rate of interest that will increase the value of currently available funds over time. As discussed in the *Feldman* case, interest rates awarded for current investments include both a *real* rate of interest and an inflationary factor that roughly mirrors the anticipated inflationary increase in wages and medical expenses.

A classic economics text explains how to determine present discounted value of an amount, e.g., medical expenses or loss income, to be paid in the future:

* * * To figure out the value today of $P payable t years from now, ask yourself how much must be invested today at compound interest to grow into $P at the end of t years. Say the interest rate is 6 percent per annum. Applying this each year to the growing amount, a principal amount of $P grows in t years proportionally to P x $(1 + 0.06)^t$. Hence, we need only invert this expression to find present value: the present value of $P payable t years from now is only $P/(1 + 0.06)^t$. Using this formula, we determine that the present value of $100 million paid in 100 years is $294,723.

Paul A. Samuelson & William D. Nordhaus, Economics 286–87 (19th ed. 2009). Obviously, in most personal injury cases, determination of the present discounted value of future income losses and medical expenses will require the summing of a number of individual figures for income losses and medical expenses in future years. To the extent that future quantities are repetitive, formulae, accounting tables, and computer programs are available to ease the burden of calculation. Cf. David Thorndike, Thorndike Encyclopedia of Banking and Financial Tables § 8–1.4 *et seq.* (4th ed. 2001).

The determination of the time value of money cleansed of inflation became easier in 1997 when the United States Department of the Treasury began releasing "inflation-indexed" bonds designed to return to the investor both a designated yield and a return of principal adjusted for inflation. The interest on such bonds is viewed by some courts as "highly significant evidence of the inflation-free time value of money, at least for the life of the bonds." Ramirez v. New York City Off-Track Betting Corp., 112 F.3d 38, 41 n.3 (2d Cir.1997) (Calabresi, J.).

5. *Federal Income Tax.* The Internal Revenue Code excludes from gross income "damages (other than punitive damages) received * * * on account of personal injuries or physical sickness." 26 U.S.C. § 104(a)(2) (2012). This exclusion applies to both compensation for loss of past earnings and estimated future earnings that would have been taxable if the plaintiff had not been injured and had been paid salary or wages. Should the jury be told of these exclusions from federal income tax?

6. *Future Economic Losses and the Gender of the Decedent.* The *Feldman* opinion, issued more than three decades ago, obviously raised the issue of how to determine future income losses at a time when it was assumed that the married female decedent typically would have taken a substantial amount of time away from work in order to raise children. See also *supra* pages 405–06, Note 2, "Loss of Earning Capacity." In discussing this issue, Professor Martha Chamallas writes:

> The basic strategy in calculating loss of future earning capacity is to compare the amount the plaintiff was capable of earning before the injury to the amount plaintiff is capable of earning after the injury. The authorities are generally in agreement that this element of damages is aimed at compensating for loss of potential. * * * By focusing on what plaintiff *could* have earned rather than what plaintiff *would* have earned, the courts have provided a theoretical basis for authorizing awards for persons who do unpaid labor in the home or whose work is not otherwise compensated through the market.

Martha Chamallas, Questioning the Use of Race-Specific and Gender-Specific Economic Data in Tort Litigation: A Constitutional Argument, 63

Fordham L. Rev. 73, 79 (1994) (emphasis added). But according to Chamallas, in reality,

> A common practice in tort litigation for calculating lost future earning capacity is to use separate gender-based tables, one for men and one for women. * Although, in other areas of the law, the use of explicit gender classifications is treated as suspect—both as a matter of policy and of constitutional law *—the use of gender-based tables to determine work-life expectancy has often been uncritically accepted, perhaps because the practice is typically buried within an expert witness's statistical report.

Martha Chamallas, The September 11th Victim Compensation Fund: Rethinking the Damages Element in Injury Law, 71 Tenn. L. Rev. 51, 70 (2003).

7. *Recovery for Pre-Death Terror of Decedent.* Will the decedent's estate be able to recover damages for the decedent's fear and fright experienced in the moments immediately before the decedent's instantaneous death resulting from a collision? See Smallwood v. Bradford, 352 Md. 8, 720 A.2d 586 (1998), allowing jury consideration of such an award, where plaintiff's eyewitness had testified:

> * * * [I]n his attempt to "try to avoid the oncoming car," the decedent started to accelerate and try to speed up onto the right side of the road.

> This evidence of the decedent's defensive maneuvering * * * provides the objective manifestation of the decedent's alleged emotional injury and it is a yardstick by which that injury may be measured. In short, it "provides reasonable assurance that the claim is not spurious." Belcher v. T. Rowe Price Found., Inc., 329 Md. 709, 735, 621 A.2d 872, 885 (1993).

Id. at 19; 720 A.2d at 592.

3. EFFECT ON RECOVERY OF COMPENSATION FROM COLLATERAL SOURCES

Coyne v. Campbell

Court of Appeals of New York, 1962.
11 N.Y.2d 372, 230 N.Y.S.2d 1, 183 N.E.2d 891.

■ FROESSEL, JUDGE. On July 5, 1957 plaintiff sustained a whiplash injury when his automobile was struck in the rear by a motor vehicle driven by defendant. Inasmuch as plaintiff is a practicing physician and surgeon, he received medical treatment, physiotherapy and care from his professional colleagues and his nurse, and incurred no out-of-pocket expenses therefor. Nevertheless, * * * he stated that his special damages for medical and nursing care and treatment amounted to $2,235. The trial court ruled that the value of these services was not a proper item of special damages, and that no recovery could be had therefor since they had been rendered gratuitously. * * * The sole question here presented is the correctness of this ruling. * * *

We find no merit in plaintiff's contention that the medical and nursing services for which damages are sought were supported by consideration. * * * Plaintiff's colleagues rendered the necessary medical services gratuitously as a professional courtesy. It may well be that as a result of having accepted their generosity plaintiff is under a moral obligation to act for them in a similar manner should his services ever be required; such need may never arise, however, and in any event such a moral obligation is not an injury for which tort damages, which "must be compensatory only" * may be awarded. A moral obligation, without more, will not support a claim for legal damages. * * * We are also told that the physiotherapy treatments which plaintiff received from his nurse consumed approximately two hours per week, and that they were given during the usual office hours for which she received her regular salary. Plaintiff does not claim that he was required to or in fact did pay any additional compensation to his nurse for her performance of these duties, and, therefore, this has not resulted in compensable damage to plaintiff.

* * * [I]n Healy v. Rennert, 9 N.Y.2d 202, 206, 213 N.Y.S.2d 44, 46, 173 N.E.2d 777, 778 (1961) * * * the plaintiff had given value for the benefits he received; he paid a premium for the health insurance, and had worked for 18 years, in order to be eligible for the disability retirement benefits. We were not confronted with—and did not attempt to pass upon—a situation where the injured plaintiff received wholly gratuitous services for which he had given no consideration in return and which he was under no legal obligation to repay. In short, insurance, pension, vacation and other benefits which were contracted and paid for are not relevant here. Gratuitous services rendered by relatives, neighbors and friends are not compensable. * * *

The judgment appealed from should be affirmed. * * *

■ FULD, JUDGE (dissenting). It is elementary that damages in personal injury actions are awarded in order to compensate the plaintiff, but, under an established exception, the collateral source doctrine—which we recognized in Healy v. Rennert, 9 N.Y.2d 202, 213 N.Y.S.2d 44, 173 N.E.2d 777 (1961)—a wrongdoer will not be allowed to deduct benefits which the plaintiff may have received from another source. * * * In the *Healy* case *, this court held that, if one is negligently injured by another, the damages recoverable from the latter are diminished neither (1) by the fact that the injured party has been indemnified for his loss by insurance effected by him nor (2) by the fact that his medical expenses were paid by [a] * * * health insurance plan. * * *

I fail to see any real difference between the situation in *Healy* and the case now before us. In neither case was the injured person burdened with any charges for the medical services rendered and, accordingly, when the defendant is required to pay as "damages" for those services or their value, such damages are no less "compensatory" in the one case than in the other. Nor do I understand why a distinction should be made depending upon whether the medical services were rendered gratuitously or for a consideration.[1] What difference should it make

---

[1] I shall assume that in this case the doctors' services were given gratuitously, though a strong argument could be made to the contrary, that is, that they were supported by consideration in that the plaintiff came under a duty to reciprocate and render medical services to his colleagues. Be that as it may, though, I see no basis for labeling the physiotherapy treatments given by the plaintiff's salaried nurse gratuitous. They were given during the nurse's normal working day for which she received wages from the plaintiff. Had

either to the plaintiff or to the defendant whether an injured plaintiff has his medical bills taken care of by an insurer or by a wealthy uncle or by a fellow doctor? Certainly, neither the uncle, who acted out of affection, nor the doctor, impelled by so-called professional courtesy, intended to benefit the tortfeasor.

The crucial question in cases such as this is whether the tortfeasor should, in fairness and justice, be given credit for the amounts, or their equivalent in services, which the plaintiff has received from some collateral source. * * * The rationale underlying the rule is that a wrongdoer, responsible for injuring the plaintiff, should not receive a windfall. Were it not for the fortuitous circumstance that the plaintiff was a doctor, he would have been billed for the medical services and the defendant would have had to pay for them. The medical services were supplied to help the plaintiff, not to relieve the defendant from any part of his liability or to benefit him. * It should not matter, in reason, logic or justice, whether the benefit received was in return for a consideration or given gratuitously, or whether it represented money paid out or its equivalent in services. * * *

NOTES

1. *Types of Collateral Sources.* Should the nature of the collateral source which provides a benefit to plaintiff make a difference? *Coyne* suggests different approaches for collateral benefits that are truly gratuitous and for collateral benefits for which plaintiff paid earlier, such as medical insurance or disability insurance plans. Compare Montgomery Ward & Co. v. Anderson, 334 Ark. 561, 976 S.W.2d 382 (1998); Spizer v. Dixie Brewing Co., 210 So.2d 528, 533 (La.Ct.App.1968). What about collateral benefits provided by government programs, such as Social Security disability benefits or veterans' benefits? E.g., Steckler v. United States, 549 F.2d 1372, 1379 (10th Cir.1977).

2. *Subrogation.* The "double recovery" which the collateral source rules seem to suggest is rarer in reality than might be imagined. Medical and disability insurance contracts typically provide that if plaintiff recovers damages in an action against a third party, the first party insurer, e.g., medical or disability insurer, will be reimbursed for any payments it has made to plaintiff.

In the absence of such a provision the additional recovery by the plaintiff may be viewed as economically efficient by analogy with the return on a lottery ticket, under which winners and losers alike are deemed to have paid for their chance to win a jackpot (plus administrative charges), and to have received what they paid for.

3. *State Legislative Responses to the Collateral Source Rule.* Businesses and liability insurers, particularly during the 1980s, frequently have advocated forcefully for the abrogation of the collateral source rule. Since that time, more than half of all states either have abrogated the rule or modified it. New statutes generally reflect complicated political compromises and exhibit little consistency from one jurisdiction to the next. E.g., Cal. Civ. Code § 3333.1 (2014) (permitting introduction of evidence of

---

she not been required to give such treatments, she would undoubtedly have been free to perform other work for the plaintiff.

payments from certain collateral sources in actions "for personal injury against a health care provider based upon professional negligence," in which case any collateral source so identified loses claims against plaintiff and subrogation rights against defendant); Fla. Stat. Ann. § 768.76 (LexisNexis 2013) (court must deduct from judgment collateral source benefits paid or available to claimant except those for which right of subrogation exists, offset by amounts paid to secure such benefits; also excepted from deduction are Medicaid benefits and benefits under certain state-administered medical service programs, but other Social Security and most other government disability and medical benefits are treated as collateral sources to be included in the reduction of the award).

C. COMPENSATORY DAMAGES FOR HARM TO PROPERTY

Bangert v. Osceola County
Supreme Court of Iowa, 1990.
456 N.W.2d 183.

■ SCHULTZ, JUSTICE. * * * Plaintiffs seek damages against Osceola County for the wrongful removal of trees standing along a half-mile stretch of county roadway. In 1873 pioneers William and Mary Foster traveled by covered wagon to their homestead and built a sod hut on a flat and treeless plain. As a condition for the receipt of a patent to 160 acres of land from the United States, they were required to plant ten acres of trees. At the same time, the Fosters planted the cottonwood trees at issue in this appeal. Over the years these trees grew to 80 feet in height, containing among them the alleged largest cottonwood tree in Iowa. Little did they realize that their grandson Clarence W. Bangert and great-granddaughter and husband Barbara E. and Carl E. Berkenpas, all present owners of the land and plaintiffs here, would be embroiled in this controversy with the county over the removal of the last twenty-eight living trees.

This controversy flared when the county proposed to improve the road. County engineer Rolley Glasgow, described in plaintiffs' brief as "no Johnny Appleseed," and the Osceola Board of Supervisors were determined to remove the row of thirty-one cottonwoods, one plum and four other trees which the county officials claimed were on the county's road easement. Despite a traffic count of only twenty vehicles per day, the county thought it necessary to upgrade the road and avoid possible liability from falling limbs. The plaintiffs protested on numerous occasions and offered several alternatives to removal. Historic, sentimental, and environmental concerns were all rejected and the trees, which could be seen for eight miles, were doomed. On August 7, 1986, when the engineer knew plaintiffs were out of state on vacation, the trees were cut down. Two and half years later the road remains unimproved.

Plaintiffs commenced this action against Osceola County seeking treble damages pursuant to Iowa Code section 658.4 (1985) for the destruction of the twenty-eight healthy cottonwood trees and the plum tree. * * * The county denied liability for the trees, claiming it had a right to remove trees standing on a county road right-of-way easement and that plaintiffs suffered no damages because the trees had no value.

This claim was tried to the court as a law action. * * * [T]he [trial] court held that the county had no right to destroy them. The court awarded plaintiffs treble damages calculated on the trees' commercial market value as lumber plus amounts for crop and fence damages.

Plaintiffs have appealed claiming that the trial court should have taken into account additional factors in calculating damages. * * * They described birds and wildlife, picnics, shade and the trees' landmark status. * * *

We recently stated that it "is impossible to state a simple, all-purpose measure of recovery for loss of trees." Laube v. Estate of Thomas, 376 N.W. 2d 108, 109 (Iowa 1985). "Because of the wide variety in their uses the law has devised a number of alternative measures, to be applied according to the location and use of the . . . trees." We indicated that the loss may be measured by the difference in the value of the realty before and after the destruction of the trees, the commercial market value of the trees or the replacement cost. We did not consider trees with special aesthetic value.

The trial court faced a difficult task in selecting one of the alternate measures. These trees definitely had a special use other than as commercial lumber. The general measure of damages, which is the difference in the value of the realty before and after the destruction of the trees, simply does not fit the situation here. The evidence indicated little damage, if any, to the market value of the real estate. In fact, the county's evidence indicated the removal of the trees would increase, not decrease, the value of plaintiffs' crop land. The trial court properly rejected this method of assessing damages.

The court found that plaintiffs had not established a compensable aesthetic loss. Aesthetic is defined as "[r]elating to that which is beautiful or in good taste." Black's Law Dictionary 52 (5th ed. 1979). We do not dispute the trial court's determination that these trees were not things of beauty. Many of the original trees had died and the one-half mile row of trees was no longer evenly spaced. The court commented that the trees were old and reaching the end of their useful life. The court established damages based on the trees' commercial market value at the time of their destruction at $100 per tree for a total of $2,800, allowed $50 for the plum tree and applied the treble damages provision. No damage was allowed for intrinsic losses arising from plaintiffs' special use of the trees.

Commercial market value as damages is appropriate when the trees have no special use and their only worth to the owner is their value as wood products. * This is not the case here. Plaintiffs had allowed these trees to stand for special purposes other than for commercial use. The record is undisputed that the trees were maintained for sentimental and historic reasons, for shade and windbreaks, as well as for environmental, wildlife and special landmark purposes. Consequently, plaintiffs' damages may be greater and not less than their commercial loss. As the trial court did not consider intrinsic damages other than that due to an aesthetic loss, we remand for consideration of these damages on the present record.

In fixing the appropriate measure of recovery, it is incumbent upon the court to keep in mind "that the principle underlying allowance of damages is that of compensation, the ultimate purpose being to place the injured party in as favorable a position as though no wrong had been committed." Dealers Hobby, Inc. v. Marie Ann Linn Realty Co., 255 N.W.2d 131, 134 (Iowa 1977). While it may be hard to ascertain such a loss with preciseness and certainty, the wronged parties should not be penalized because of that difficulty. Difficulty in ascertaining the amount of damages does not alone constitute a reason for denying recovery or for substituting an inappropriate method. * * *

Plaintiffs in this case approached the issue of damages in two ways. They offered evidence of the value of each tree as well as the cost of replacing them with another variety of tree. * * * Some jurisdictions have allowed additional damages caused by the deprivation of the trees' special value. See Elowsky v. Gulf Power Co., 172 So.2d 643, 645 (Fla.Dist.Ct.App.1965) (owner who worked the night shift allowed compensation for loss of comfort and convenience of a tree that shaded his house); Woodburn v. Chapman, 117 N.H. 906, 908–09, 379 A.2d 1038, 1040 (1977) (additional compensatory damages for a tree's special value as a boundary marker allowed). * Other courts have held that the replacement cost of trees is the proper method of recovery when the trees have a special value to the owner. * On remand we believe it is appropriate for the trial court to reconsider the evidence of damages. If satisfied that an intrinsic loss has occurred that exceeds the trees' lumber value, the court may use either method or a combination of both to arrive at an amount that will compensate plaintiffs for their loss.

* * * We reverse the trial court's determination of actual damages and remand for further consideration and determination of damages. * * *

NOTES

1. *Determining Fair Market Value.* When plaintiff's property is injured or destroyed by defendant's tortious conduct, the general rule is that plaintiff may recover as damages the difference between the fair market value of the property immediately before the injury and immediately after the injury. See generally Harper, James and Gray on Torts § 25.6. Fair market value is the price at which the property would change hands between a willing buyer and a willing seller when both parties have reasonable knowledge of the relevant facts and neither is under any compulsion to buy or sell. The standard is an objective one, using a purely hypothetical buyer and seller. In many cases, in reality, there is no appropriate market for the property in question and market value is "not an existing fact but a legal construct or even a convention." Dan B. Dobbs, Law of Remedies § 3.5 (2d ed. 1993). In the absence of an actual market for the property that has been damaged, courts rely upon expert testimony. In determining fair market value, experts rely upon one or more of several commonly recognized methods for valuing assets including (1) comparable sales, (2) replacement cost less depreciation, and (3) income capitalization. Cf., for use of a combination of tests where none is satisfactory standing alone, Chicago, Milwaukee, St. Paul & Pac. R.R. v. Tindal, 249 F.Supp. 988 (S.D.Iowa 1966).

2. *Inadequacy of Diminution in Market Value as Measure of Damages.* *Bangert* suggests the inadequacy of diminution of market value as the starting point for the determination of damages in some cases. Consider also City of Tyler v. Likes, 962 S.W.2d 489 (Tex.1997) where plaintiff

sought damages for the destruction to her property from floodwaters that allegedly resulted from the City's negligence. Among the items destroyed were family photographs, keepsakes, and correspondence. The Texas Supreme Court stated:

> It is a matter of common knowledge that items such as these generally have no market value which would adequately compensate their owner for their loss or destruction. Such property is not susceptible of supply and reproduction in kind, and their greater value is in sentiment and not in the market place. In such cases the most fundamental rule of damages that every wrongful injury or loss to persons or property should be adequately and reasonably compensated requires the allowance of damages in compensation for the reasonable special value of such articles to their owner taking into consideration the feelings of the owner for such property. *

> * * * The proper measure of * * * damages * * * for those items of small or no market value that "have their primary value in sentiment," * [is] the loss in value to [the plaintiff].

Birmingham Railway Light & Power Co. v. Hinton

Supreme Court of Alabama, 1908.
157 Ala. 630, 47 So. 576.

Action by Walter L. Hinton against the Birmingham Ry. L. & P. Co., to recover as damages the value of certain household goods alleged to have been destroyed by fire set out by one of defendant's locomotives. [Request to] Charge 1, was as follows: If the jury find for the plaintiff they can assess no more than nominal damages in this case. Judgment for plaintiff and defendant appeals. * * *

■ ANDERSON, J.—The witness was the owner of the goods and was familiar with them, and this was the only predicate essential to an opinion from him as to their value. * The plaintiff testified as to the worth of the goods, and this evidence was to be considered by the jury in determining the value of same. It may be that the cost of same could not have been shown as evidence of their value, or, if the witness had no knowledge of their value and based his estimate solely on what they cost, that an opinion advanced by him could be excluded. But it was not shown that Hinton based his valuation solely on the cost of the articles, or that he could not give an opinion of their value regardless of the cost. On the other hand, he stated upon cross-examination that the basis of his estimate was the amount they cost "and what they are really worth." There was no effort to exclude from his consideration the cost of the goods or to show that his opinion was based entirely upon the cost, and, as there was proof of value not based entirely upon the cost of the goods, the jury was authorized to fix the value beyond a nominal sum.

While we treat this case upon the idea that the market value of the goods at the time of destruction was the criterion of their value, and affirm it upon the idea that the jury had some evidence of said market value, yet we do not mean to hold that the marketable value should be the test as to articles of the character in question, or that the owner could not have shown the cost of same as a factor in arriving at their value. Household goods, such as furniture, bedding, and wearing apparel, kept for use and not for sale, and which have in fact been used, may have a real intrinsic value to the owner, and yet little or no market value. In some instances it would be difficult, as well as expensive, to replace them, and yet, if put upon the market there would be little or no demand for them, and in such cases the value should be fixed or ascertained in some rational way, other than by showing what they would bring in a particular market or if hawked off by a secondhand dealer. *

The trial court did not err in refusing charge 1, requested by the defendant. The judgment of the city court is affirmed. * * *

NOTES

1. *Damages for Injury to Personal Property.* What happens if an item of personal property, such as an automobile, may be repaired and restored to the condition it was in before the accident? Some courts still hold that the proper measure of damages is the diminution of market value, but that the cost of reasonable repairs is evidence of the amount of loss of market value. E.g., Am. Tel. and Tel. Co. v. Connecticut Light & Power Co., 470 F.Supp. 105 (D.Conn.1979) (Conn. law). Other courts generally treat the cost of repairs as the measure of damages, but adjust the damage award if the fair market value of the automobile or other item of personal property, even following the repairs, is greater or less than the fair market value before the accident. For example, in Rosenfield v. Choberka, 140 Misc.2d 9, 529 N.Y.S.2d 455 (1988), the court held that the owner of an automobile damaged by defendant's negligence was entitled to recover as damages not only the cost of repairs, but also the difference in its market value before the accident and after the automobile had been repaired. Obviously, in a jurisdiction treating the cost of repairs as the general measure of damages, plaintiff cannot recover an amount greater than the fair market value of the property before the accident. Finally, some courts, e.g., O'Connor v. Schwartz, 304 Minn. 155, 158, 229 N.W.2d 511, 513 (1975); Berg v. Reaction Motors Div., Thiokol Chem. Corp., 37 N.J. 396, 411–12, 181 A.2d 487, 495 (1962), and the Restatement (Second) of Torts § 928 (1979), allow plaintiff to choose between damages measured by diminution of value or, in an appropriate case, the reasonable and necessary cost of repair.

2. *Loss of Household Items.* Loss of market value may be neither practicable nor fair as a measure of plaintiff's loss. Should the jury be allowed to consider the costs of replacing clothing, appliances, and other personal property destroyed by a defendant's tortious conduct? In Farr v. Johnson, 308 So.2d 884, 887 (La.Ct.App.1975), plaintiff was allowed to recover the replacement cost of a television set destroyed by the defendant even though replacement cost was substantially in excess of fair market value. Cf. Maryland Cas. Co. v. Therm-O-Disc, Inc., 137 F.3d 780, 786 (4th Cir.1998) ("Under Maryland law, a homeowner can testify as to the fair market value of common consumer goods, which will usually be close or equal to their replacement cost."). Compare White Consol. Indus. v. Swiney, 237 Va. 23, 30, 376 S.E.2d 283, 287 (1989) (evidence insufficient to sustain damage award for loss of personal property based upon replacement cost in absence of evidence of either rate of depreciation or other proof of fair market value of property immediately before fire).

D. PUNITIVE DAMAGES

Kemezy v. Peters

United States Court of Appeals for the Seventh Circuit, 1996.
79 F.3d 33.

■ POSNER, CHIEF JUDGE. Jeffrey Kemezy sued a Muncie, Indiana policeman named James Peters * * * claiming that Peters had wantonly beaten him with the officer's nightstick in an altercation in a bowling alley where Peters was moonlighting as a security guard. The jury awarded Kemezy $10,000 in compensatory damages and $20,000 in punitive damages. Peters' appeal challenges only the award of punitive damages, and that on the narrowest of grounds: that it was the plaintiff's burden to introduce evidence concerning the defendant's net worth for purposes of equipping the jury with information essential to a just measurement of punitive damages. * * *

The standard judicial formulation of the purpose of punitive damages is that it is to punish the defendant for reprehensible conduct and to deter him and others from engaging in similar conduct. * * * An extensive academic literature, however, elaborates on the cryptic judicial formula, offering a number of reasons for awards of punitive damages. * * *

1. Compensatory damages do not always compensate fully. Because courts insist that an award of compensatory damages have an objective basis in evidence, such awards are likely to fall short in some cases, especially when the injury is of an elusive or intangible character. If you spit upon another person in anger, you inflict a real injury but one exceedingly difficult to quantify. If the court is confident that the injurious conduct had no redeeming social value, so that "overdeterring" such conduct by an "excessive" award of damages is not a concern, a generous award of punitive damages will assure full compensation without impeding socially valuable conduct.

2. By the same token, punitive damages are necessary in such cases in order to make sure that tortious conduct is not underdeterred, as it might be if compensatory damages fell short of the actual injury inflicted by the tort.

These two points bring out the close relation between the compensatory and deterrent objectives of tort law, or, more precisely perhaps, its rectificatory and regulatory purposes. Knowing that he will have to pay compensation for harm inflicted, the potential injurer will be deterred from inflicting that harm unless the benefits to him are greater. If we do not want him to balance costs and benefits in this fashion, we can add a dollop of punitive damages to make the costs greater.

3. Punitive damages are necessary in some cases to make sure that people channel transactions through the market when the costs of voluntary transactions are low. We do not want a person to be able to take his neighbor's car and when the neighbor complains tell him to go sue for its value. * We want to make such expropriations valueless to the expropriator and we can do this by adding a punitive exaction to the judgment for the market value of what is taken. * * *

4. When a tortious act is concealable, a judgment equal to the harm done by the act will underdeter. Suppose a person who goes around assaulting other people is caught only half the time. Then in comparing the costs, in the form of anticipated damages, of the assaults with the benefits to him, he will discount the costs (but not the benefits, because they are realized in every assault) by 50 percent, and so in deciding whether to commit the next assault he will not be confronted by the full social cost of his activity.

5. An award of punitive damages expresses the community's abhorrence at the defendant's act. We understand that otherwise upright, decent, law-abiding people are sometimes careless and that their carelessness can result in unintentional injury for which compensation should be required. We react far more strongly to the deliberate or reckless wrongdoer, and an award of punitive damages commutes our indignation into a kind of civil fine, civil punishment.

Some of these functions are also performed by the criminal justice system. Many legal systems do not permit awards of punitive damages at all, believing that such awards anomalously intrude the principles of criminal justice into civil cases. Even our cousins the English allow punitive damages only in an excruciatingly narrow category of cases. * But whether because the American legal and political cultures are unique, or because the criminal justice system in this country is overloaded and some of its functions have devolved upon the tort system, punitive damages are a regular feature of American tort cases, though reserved generally for intentional torts, including the deliberate use of excess force as here. This suggests additional functions of punitive damages:

6. Punitive damages relieve the pressures on the criminal justice system. They do this not so much by creating an additional sanction, which could be done by increasing the fines imposed in criminal cases, as by giving private individuals—the tort victims themselves—a monetary incentive to shoulder the costs of enforcement.

7. If we assume realistically that the criminal justice system could not or would not take up the slack if punitive damages were abolished, then they have the additional function of heading off breaches of the peace by giving individuals injured by relatively minor outrages a judicial remedy in lieu of the violent self-help to which they might resort if their complaints to the criminal justice authorities were certain to be ignored and they had no other legal remedy.

What is striking about the purposes that are served by the awarding of punitive damages is that none of them depends critically on proof that the defendant's income or wealth *exceeds* some specified level. The more wealth the defendant has, the smaller is the relative bite that an award of punitive damages not actually geared to that wealth will take out of his pocketbook, while if he has very little wealth the award of punitive damages may exceed his ability to pay and perhaps drive him into bankruptcy. To a very rich person, the pain of having to pay a heavy award of damages may be a mere pinprick and so not deter him (or people like him) from continuing to engage in the same type of wrongdoing. * What in economics is called the principle of diminishing marginal utility teaches, what is anyway obvious, that losing $1 is likely to cause less unhappiness (disutility) to a rich person than to a poor one. (This point * * * does not apply to institutions as distinct from natural persons.) But rich people are not famous for being indifferent to money, and if they are forced to pay not merely the cost of the harm to the victims of their torts but also some multiple of that cost they are likely to think twice before engaging in such expensive behavior again. Juries, rightly or wrongly, think differently, so plaintiffs who are seeking punitive damages often present evidence of the defendant's wealth. The question is whether they *must* present such evidence— whether it is somehow unjust to allow a jury to award punitive damages without knowing that the defendant really is a wealthy person. The answer, obviously, is no. A plaintiff is not required to seek punitive damages in the first place, so he should not be denied an award of punitive damages merely because he does not present evidence that if believed would persuade the jury to award him even more than he is asking.

Take the question from the other side: if the defendant is not as wealthy as the jury might in the absence of any evidence suppose, should the plaintiff be required to show this? That seems an odd suggestion too. The reprehensibility of a person's conduct is not mitigated by his not being a rich person, and plaintiffs are never required to apologize for seeking damages that if awarded will precipitate the defendant into bankruptcy. A plea of poverty is a classic appeal to the mercy of the judge or jury, and why the plaintiff should be required to make the plea on behalf of his opponent eludes us. * * *

It ill becomes *defendants* to argue that plaintiffs *must* introduce evidence of the defendant's wealth. Since most tort defendants against whom punitive damages are sought are enterprises rather than individuals, the effect of such a rule would be to encourage plaintiffs to seek punitive damages whether or not justified, in order to be able to put before the jury evidence that the defendant has a deep pocket and therefore should be made to pay a large judgment regardless of any nice calculation of actual culpability. * * * Individual defendants, as in the present case, are reluctant to disclose their net worth in any circumstances, so that compelling plaintiffs to seek discovery of that information would invite a particularly intrusive and resented form of pretrial discovery and disable the defendant from objecting. Since, moreover, information about net worth is in the possession of the person whose net wealth is in issue, the normal principles of pleading would put the burden of production on the defendant—which, as we have been at pains to stress, is just where defendants as a whole would want it. * * *

NOTES

1. *Evidence of Defendant's Wealth.* Compare Adams v. Murakami, 54 Cal.3d 105, 284 Cal.Rptr. 318, 813 P.2d 1348 (1991) (requiring plaintiff to introduce evidence of defendant's financial condition) and Hardaway Mgmt. Co. v. Southerland, 977 S.W.2d 910, 916 (Ky.1998) (parties may not present evidence of the financial condition of either side in an action for punitive damages).

2. *Frequency of Punitive Damage Awards.* Punitive damage awards have attracted considerable publicity and sparked significant controversy in recent decades. The available empirical evidence suggests, however, that

such awards are rare in tort cases. According to Professor Anthony J. Sebok's summary of six major studies conducted since 1985, punitive damages were awarded in between 2% and 9% of all cases in which plaintiffs prevailed on the liability issue. Anthony J. Sebok, Punitive Damages: From Myth to Theory, 92 Iowa L. Rev. 957, 964 (2007). Most punitive damage awards appear to result from "bad faith" contract claims and other business and employment claims, not traditional tort actions. Punitive damages awards in products liability and medical malpractice cases are infrequent.

A 1995 Department of Justice study analyzed 761,919 tort, contract, and real property cases disposed of in the year ending June 30, 1992, in state courts of general jurisdiction in the seventy-five largest counties in the United States. Bureau of Justice Statistics, Special Report: Civil Jury Cases and Verdicts in Large Counties (NCJ 154346) (July 1995). Of these cases, 12,026 were decided by juries, with punitive damages being awarded in 364 of those cases, most of which involved business and employment claims. Punitive damage claims were awarded in thirteen toxic substance cases and three "other" products liability cases. In the latter group, the median punitive damage award was $9,000 and the mean award was $12,000. See also Steven Daniels & Joanne Martin, Myth and Reality in Punitive Damages, 75 Minn. L. Rev. 1 (1990).

3. *Liability of Corporations for Punitive Damages.* Considering the purposes of both vicarious liability and punitive damages, should a corporation be vicariously liable for punitive damages awarded against its employee or officer? Compare Restatement (Second) of Torts § 909 (1979) (principal subject to liability only if it authorized the act, was reckless in employing or retaining an unfit employee, or ratified the act), with Ramos v. Frito-Lay, Inc., 784 S.W.2d 667, 669 (Tex.1990) (employer subject to exemplary damages for actions of "management-level employee in performing a non-managerial task") and Staruski v. Cont'l Tel. Co. of Vt., 154 Vt. 568, 580, 581 A.2d 266, 272 (1990) (vicarious liability for conduct of "governing officer" of corporation).

4. *Insurance Coverage for Punitive Damages.* Given the purposes behind punitive damages analyzed in Judge Posner's opinion in *Kemezy*, should defendants be allowed to insure against punitive damages? Most courts uphold such coverage, e.g., Whalen v. On-Deck, Inc., 514 A.2d 1072 (Del.1986), but others strike down such coverage, at least under some circumstances, as a violation of public policy. E.g., Home Ins. Co. v. Am. Home Prods Corp., 75 N.Y.2d 196, 200, 551 N.Y.S.2d 481, 550 N.E.2d 930 (1990).

5. *Statutory Limitations.* Many states enacted legislation limiting the amount of punitive damages or making recovery more difficult during the late 1980s and 1990s. E.g., 735 Ill. Comp. Stat. Ann. 5/2–1115, 1115.05 (LexisNexis 2014) (no punitive damages for medical malpractice; otherwise, in the absence of criminal conduct subjecting defendant to possible incarceration, punitive damages are limited to three times economic damages); Tex. Civ. Prac. & Rem. Code Ann. §§ 41.001–41.013 (West 2014) (punitive damages ordinarily limited to the greater of $200,000 or twice the amount of economic damages plus the amount of non-economic damages up to $750,000, unless the defendant has committed designated felonies).

Ciraolo v. City of New York

United States Court of Appeals for the Second Circuit, 2000.
216 F.3d 236.

■ CALABRESI, CIRCUIT JUDGE. * * * [Plaintiff sued the City of New York under 42 U.S.C. § 1983 for an unlawful strip search of her person. The jury awarded her $19,645 in compensatory damages and $5,000,000 in punitive damages. The City appealed the award of punitive damages and the court, speaking through Judge Calabresi, reversed on the grounds that the Supreme Court had held in City of Newport v. Fact Concerts, Inc., 453 U.S. 247, 101 S.Ct. 2748, 69 L.Ed.2d 616 (1981) that ordinarily municipalities are immune from punitive damages awards under § 1983.]

■ CALABRESI, CIRCUIT JUDGE, concurring. Although the result the court reaches today is compelled by Supreme Court precedent, I respectfully suggest that the policies behind punitive damages and the purpose of § 1983 would be better furthered by a different outcome. I write separately to explain why I believe this to be so. * * *

The purpose of § 1983 is "not only to provide compensation to the victims of past abuses, but to serve as a deterrent against future constitutional deprivations, as well." Owen v. City of Independence, 445 U.S. 622, 651, 100 S.Ct. 1398, 63 L.Ed.2d 673 (1980). Indeed, the Court in *Newport* recognized that punitive damages serve the dual purpose of deterrence and retribution. See *Newport*, 453 U.S. 247 at 266–67, 101 S.Ct. 2748, 69 L.Ed.2d 616. Nevertheless, and as discussed above, the Court concluded that "the deterrence rationale of § 1983 does not justify making punitive damages available against municipalities," because (1) it was unclear that municipal officials would be deterred by the prospect of damages borne by the taxpayers; (2) voters would still be likely to vote wrongdoing officials out of office absent punitive damages, both because they had done wrong and because of the possibility of compensatory damages; (3) punitive damages assessed directly against the offending officials would be a more effective means of deterrence; and (4) punitive damages could "create a serious risk to the financial integrity" of cities.

The Court's analysis, however, neglected at least one aspect of the deterrence function of punitive damages—an aspect underscored by this case. Punitive damages can ensure that a wrongdoer bears all the costs of its actions, and is thus appropriately deterred from causing harm, in those categories of cases in which compensatory damages alone result in systematic underassessment of costs, and hence in systematic underdeterrence.

It is easy to show why this is so. A rational actor * will undertake an activity when the benefits of doing so exceed the costs. In doing so, it will make some sort of formal or informal, spoken or unspoken, cost-benefit analysis, based on the information it possesses, to determine if a particular activity is worth its price. Such an analysis cannot be even roughly accurate unless approximately all the costs of the activity are borne by the actor. When the perceived benefits of an activity accrue to the actor, but some significant part of the costs is borne by others, the cost-benefit analysis will necessarily be distorted. In such a case, the actor will have an incentive to undertake activities whose social costs exceed their social benefits. In other words, the actor will not be adequately deterred from undesirable activities. And society will suffer.[7]

One goal of the tort system, therefore, is to ensure that actors bear the costs of their activities. * * * In some circumstances, compensatory damages alone will be enough to promote an adequate cost-benefit analysis. In other cases, however, compensatory damages will not come close to equaling all the costs properly attributable to the activity. Costs may not be sufficiently reflected in compensatory damages for several reasons, most of which go to the fact that not all injured parties are in fact compensated by the responsible injurer. For example, a victim may not realize that she has been harmed by a particular actor's conduct, or may not be able to identify the person or entity who has injured her. * Where the injurer makes active efforts to conceal the harm, this problem is of course exacerbated. Moreover, even if a victim is aware of her injury and is able to identify its cause, she may not bring suit. A person will be unlikely to sue if the costs of doing so—including the time, effort, and stress associated with bringing a lawsuit—outweigh the compensation she can expect to receive. A victim is especially unlikely to sue, therefore, in cases where the probable compensatory damages are relatively low. As a result, a harm that affects many people, but each only to a limited degree, will generally be given inadequate weight if only compensatory damages are assessed.

In addition, some victims will not sue even if the damages they could expect to receive would exceed the costs of suing. Victims will differ greatly in their knowledge of and access to the legal process, and those who are relatively poor and unsophisticated, as a practical matter, are frequently unable to bring suit to redress their injuries even if those injuries are grave. A harm that disproportionately affects such victims, therefore, is also particularly likely not to be accurately reflected in compensatory damages.

For these and other like reasons, compensatory damages are, in wide categories of cases, an inaccurate measure of the true harm caused by an activity, and, as a result, making an injurer bear only such damages does not provide adequate deterrence against socially harmful acts. In such circumstances, additional damages, assessed in the cases that *are* brought, may be an appropriate way of making the injurer bear all the costs associated with its activities.

This idea is far from new. Many years ago, in an influential article that was in part responsible for his receipt of the Nobel Memorial Prize in economics, Professor Becker pointed out that charging a thief the cost of what he had stolen would not adequately deter theft unless the thief was caught every time. Since thieves will not always be caught, they must be penalized by more than the cost of the items stolen on the occasions on which they *are* caught. This "multiplier" is essential to render theft unprofitable and properly to deter it. * More recently, scholars have recognized that punitive damages can serve the same

---

[7]   These basic principles of the economic theory of deterrence are widely accepted, and have been applied to both tort and criminal law. See generally, e.g., Gary S. Becker, Crime and Punishment: An Economic Approach, 76 J. Pol. Econ. 169 (1968); see also Guido Calabresi, The Costs of Accidents (1970); A. Mitchell Polinsky & Steven Shavell, Punitive Damages: An Economic Analysis, 111 Harv. L. Rev. 870 (1998).

function in tort law. * Professors Polinsky and Shavell, for example, have argued that punitive damages should be assessed whenever a tortfeasor has a significant likelihood of escaping liability, and have even suggested a formula (simpler to state than to apply) for calculating such damages: total damages should equal the amount of loss in a particular case, multiplied by the inverse of the probability that the injurer will be found liable. * Thus, if the injurer causes harm of $10,000, but will be found liable only one-fifth of the time, total damages—according to Polinsky and Shavell—should equal $50,000 ($10,000 in compensatory damages and $40,000 in punitive damages). Use of such a multiplier, they argue, will cause damages to equal the total harm caused, forcing the injurer to take into account all the costs of its activity and thus decreasing the likelihood that socially harmful activities will persist.[4] * * *

Although widely accepted by economists and acknowledged by some courts, the multiplier function of punitive damages has nonetheless been applied haphazardly at best. One reason this is so is that the twin goals of deterrence and retribution are often conflated, rather than recognized as analytically distinct objectives. The term "punitive damages" itself contributes greatly to the confusion. For *punitive* damages, the term traditionally used for damages beyond what is needed to compensate the individual plaintiff, improperly emphasizes the retributive function of such extracompensatory damages at the expense of their multiplier-deterrent function. It also fails totally to explain the not unusual use of such damages in situations in which the injurer, though liable, was not intentionally or wantonly wrongful. * A more appropriate name for extracompensatory damages assessed in order to avoid underdeterrence might be "socially compensatory damages." For, while traditional compensatory damages are assessed to make the individual victim whole, socially compensatory damages are, in a sense, designed to make society whole by seeking to ensure that all of the costs of harmful acts are placed on the liable actor. *

Indeed, it would not be inappropriate to disaggregate the retributive and deterrent functions of extracompensatory damages altogether and allow separate awards to further the two separate goals. In such a system, socially compensatory damages might be permitted in cases in which all the costs of a defendant's actions were not before the court, whether or not the defendant's conduct was particularly blameworthy. * But a separate award of *punitive* damages would be allowed only in cases where the defendant's conduct was sufficiently reprehensible to deserve punishment apart from whatever assessment was required to compensate the individual victim or society as a whole. *

---

[4] It is possible that, in some circumstances, use of a multiplier formula might overdeter socially useful conduct. Litigation costs borne by the defendant themselves have a deterrent effect that may not be taken into account by a simple multiplier formula. And, although in a legal system that works efficiently, litigation costs would generally be a part of the social cost attributable to the harm caused by the defendant, unnecessary costs of administering such a system may properly be viewed as beyond the actual harm caused. Where a defendant is forced to bear such excess administrative costs, the multiplier formula might overdeter. Despite such failings, however, it seems likely that, in many instances, use of a multiplier will produce more accurate cost allocation than currently occurs.

The majority in *Newport* raised the objection that "punitive damages . . . are in effect a windfall to a fully compensated plaintiff." Newport, 453 U.S. at 267. It is likely that a feeling that such "windfalls" are not warranted—and are distributed arbitrarily among plaintiffs—lies, and properly so, behind much of the current distaste for punitive damages. Of course, socially compensatory damages will have an equivalent deterrent effect on the injurer no matter whom they are paid to. * * * Nevertheless, the existence of such potential windfalls may well induce undesirable behavior on the part of victims and of their lawyers. And there is no good reason why socially compensatory damages should be paid to the individual plaintiff, at least beyond a relatively small part sufficient to induce the victim to undertake the expense of pleading and proving them.

In fact, in order to achieve the goal of social compensation, as well as the goal of optimal deterrence, it would be preferable if such damages were paid into a fund that could then be applied to remedy some of the unredressed social harm stemming from the defendant's conduct. And some states have explicitly recognized this socially compensatory function by mandating that at least a portion of punitive damages awards should go not to the plaintiff, but to the state treasury or to a specified fund. See BMW of North America v. Gore, 517 U.S. 559, 616–18, 116 S.Ct. 1589, 134 L.Ed.2d 809 (1996) (Ginsburg, J., dissenting) (collecting state laws providing for allocation of punitive damages to state agencies). * * *

NOTE

For more on justifying punitive damages as "extracompensatory damages" or "social compensatory damages," see Catherine M. Sharkey, Punitive Damages as Societal Damages, 113 Yale L.J. 347 (2003). Then consider the next opinion.

Philip Morris USA v. Williams

Supreme Court of the United States, 2007.
549 U.S. 346, 127 S.Ct. 1057, 166 L.Ed.2d 940.

■ BREYER, JUSTICE. * * * This lawsuit arises out of the death of Jesse Williams, a heavy cigarette smoker. Respondent, Williams' widow, represents his estate in this state lawsuit for negligence and deceit against Philip Morris, the manufacturer of Marlboro, the brand that Williams favored. A jury found that Williams' death was caused by smoking; that Williams smoked in significant part because he thought it was safe to do so; and that Philip Morris knowingly and falsely led him to believe that this was so. The jury ultimately found that Philip Morris was negligent (as was Williams) and that Philip Morris had engaged in deceit. In respect to deceit, the claim at issue here, it awarded compensatory damages of about $821,000 (about $21,000 economic and $800,000 noneconomic) along with $79.5 million in punitive damages. The trial judge subsequently found the $79.5 million punitive damages award "excessive," * and reduced it to $32 million. Both sides appealed. The Oregon Court of Appeals rejected Philip Morris' arguments and restored the $79.5 million jury award. * * *

Philip Morris * * * said that the trial court should have accepted, but did not accept, a proposed "punitive damages" instruction that specified the jury could not seek to punish Philip Morris for injury to other persons not before the court. In particular, Philip Morris pointed out that the plaintiff's attorney had told the jury to "think about how many other Jesse Williams in the last 40 years in the State of Oregon there have been.... In Oregon, how many people do we see outside, driving home ... smoking cigarettes? ... [C]igarettes ... are going to kill ten [of every hundred]. [And] the market share of Marlboros [i.e., Philip Morris] is one-third [i.e., one of every three killed]." * In light of this argument, Philip Morris asked the trial court to tell the jury that "you may consider the extent of harm suffered by others in determining what [the] reasonable relationship is" between any punitive award and "the harm caused to Jesse Williams" by Philip Morris' misconduct, "[but] you are not to punish the defendant for the impact of its alleged misconduct on other persons, who may bring lawsuits of their own in which other juries can resolve their claims...." * The judge rejected this proposal and instead told the jury that "[p]unitive damages are awarded against a defendant to punish misconduct and to deter misconduct," and "are not intended to compensate the plaintiff or anyone else for damages caused by the defendant's conduct." * In Philip Morris' view, the result was a significant likelihood that a portion of the $79.5 million award represented punishment for its having harmed others, a punishment that the Due Process Clause would here forbid. * * * The Oregon Supreme Court * * * rejected Philip Morris' claim that the Constitution prohibits a state jury "from using punitive damages to punish a defendant for harm to nonparties." * * * Philip Morris then sought certiorari. * * *

In our view, the Constitution's Due Process Clause forbids a State to use a punitive damages award to punish a defendant for injury that it inflicts upon nonparties or those whom they directly represent, i.e., injury that it inflicts upon those who are, essentially, strangers to the litigation. * * * [A] defendant threatened with punishment for injuring a nonparty victim has no opportunity to defend against the charge, by showing, for example in a case such as this, that the other victim was not entitled to damages because he or she knew that smoking was dangerous or did not rely upon the defendant's statements to the contrary. * * * [T]o permit punishment for injuring a nonparty victim would add a near standardless dimension to the punitive damages equation. How many such victims are there? How seriously were they injured? Under what circumstances did injury occur? The trial will not likely answer such questions as to nonparty victims. The jury will be left to speculate. And the fundamental due process concerns to which our punitive damages cases refer—risks of arbitrariness, uncertainty, and lack of notice—will be magnified. * Finally, we can find no authority supporting the use of punitive damages awards for the purpose of punishing a defendant for harming others. We have said that it may be appropriate to consider the reasonableness of a punitive damages award in light of the *potential* harm the defendant's conduct could have caused. But we have made clear that the potential harm at issue was harm potentially caused *the plaintiff.* * * *

Respondent argues that she is free to show harm to other victims because it is relevant to a different part of the punitive damages constitutional equation, namely, reprehensibility. That is to say, harm to others shows more reprehensible conduct. Philip Morris, in turn, does not deny that a plaintiff may show harm to others in order to demonstrate reprehensibility. Nor do we. Evidence of actual harm to nonparties can help to show that the conduct that harmed the plaintiff also posed a substantial risk of harm to the general public, and so was particularly reprehensible—although counsel may argue in a particular case that conduct resulting in no harm to others nonetheless posed a grave risk to the public, or the converse. Yet for the reasons given above, a jury may not go further than this and use a punitive damages verdict to punish a defendant directly on account of harms it is alleged to have visited on nonparties. Given the risks * * * of arbitrariness, the concern for adequate notice, and the risk that punitive damages awards can, in practice, impose one State's (or one jury's) policies (*e.g.*, banning cigarettes) upon other States—all of which accompany awards that, today, may be many times the size of such awards in the 18th and 19th centuries, *—it is particularly important that States avoid procedure that unnecessarily deprives juries of proper legal guidance. We therefore conclude that the Due Process Clause requires States to provide assurance that juries are not asking the wrong question, i.e., seeking, not simply to determine reprehensibility, but also to punish for harm caused strangers.

* * * We have explained why we believe the Due Process Clause prohibits a State's inflicting punishment for harm caused strangers to the litigation. At the same time we recognize that conduct that risks harm to many is likely more reprehensible than conduct that risks harm to only a few. And a jury consequently may take this fact into account in determining reprehensibility.

* * * How can we know whether a jury, in taking account of harm caused others under the rubric of reprehensibility, also seeks to *punish* the defendant for having caused injury to others? Our answer is that state courts cannot authorize procedures that create an unreasonable and unnecessary risk of any such confusion occurring. In particular, we believe that where the risk of that misunderstanding is a significant one—because, for instance, of the sort of evidence that was introduced at trial or the kinds of argument the plaintiff made to the jury—a court, upon request, must protect against that risk. Although the States have some flexibility to determine what *kind* of procedures they will implement, federal constitutional law obligates them to provide *some* form of protection in appropriate cases.

* * * We remand this case so that the Oregon Supreme Court can apply the standard we have set forth. * * *

■ STEVENS, JUSTICE, dissenting. * * * Unlike the Court, I see no reason why an interest in punishing a wrongdoer "for harming persons who are not before the court," should not be taken into consideration when assessing the appropriate sanction for reprehensible conduct. Whereas compensatory damages are measured by the harm the defendant has caused the plaintiff, punitive damages are a sanction for the public harm the defendant's conduct has caused or threatened. There is little difference between the justification for a criminal sanction, such as a fine or a term of imprisonment, and an award of punitive damages. * * * And while in neither context would the sanction typically include a

18 minutes of being moved to a third room he discovered insects in that room as well and had to be moved still again. * * *

It was in November that the plaintiffs checked into the motel. They were given Room 504, even though the motel had classified the room as "DO NOT RENT UNTIL TREATED," and it had not been treated.

The jury awarded each plaintiff $5,000 in compensatory damages and $186,000 in punitive damages, or $1,000 in total damages for each room in the defendant's hotel.

After reviewing these awards against the standard articulated by the Supreme Court in *State Farm Auto Ins. Co. v. Campbell*, and in light of the purposes of punitive damages Judge Posner had described in *Kemezy,* see *supra* pages 428–30, he upheld the award, finding that "[t]he defendant's behavior was outrageous but the compensable harm done was slight and at the same time difficult to quantify because a large element of it was emotional." Judge Posner interpreted the Supreme Court's decision in *Campbell* as not "lay[ing] down a 4-to-1 or single-digit-ratio rule" but merely "a presumption against an award that has a 145-to-1 ratio."

CHAPTER 7

PROTECTION OF OTHERS

The previous chapters focused on liability for unreasonable acts or omissions in the course of affirmative conduct. In this chapter our attention turns in part to the extent, if any, that an omission to act on behalf of others constitutes actionable negligence. This question obviously requires the student to consider whether it is possible in all cases to distinguish meaningfully between acting and omitting to act, and whether an unreasonable omission to act that foreseeably results in harm to others should be treated differently from other unreasonable conduct. Traditional Anglo-American law was reluctant to prescribe what it viewed as affirmative obligations, even when the results appeared heartless. Courts, however, carved out several exceptions to the general rule of non-liability in order to mitigate its harsh consequences. In recent decades, these exceptions expanded significantly.

A related theme deals with the issues of whether, when, and to what extent one may become subject to liability to others for negligence, either in acting or in failing to act, to protect them from harm caused by themselves or by third parties.

A. RESCUES

1. TRADITIONAL PRINCIPLES

Stockberger v. United States

United States Court of Appeals for the Seventh Circuit, 2003.
332 F.3d 479.

■ POSNER, CIRCUIT JUDGE. * * * Maurice Stockberger, an employee of the federal prison at Terre Haute, Indiana, was an insulin-dependent diabetic and known to be such by his coworkers—many of whom, indeed, were medical workers. He had hypoglycemic episodes (episodes in which his blood sugar would fall to dangerously low levels), observed by and known to be such by them, in which he would exhibit personality changes, becoming hostile, suspicious, unresponsive, agitated—and sometimes denying that he had a medical problem. When his coworkers noticed that he was in one of his hypoglycemic states, they would urge him to eat, or to drink Ensure, a nutritious liquid food substitute. On the day of his death, one of his coworkers noticed that Stockberger, who was complaining about feeling ill and said that he wanted to go home, was having one of his hypoglycemic episodes, and offered him Ensure, which he drank. This made him feel better but he said he still wanted to go home. His coworkers wanted him to remain at the prison "until he recovered," but he was adamant about leaving. The coworker who had given him Ensure thought that Stockberger was in no condition to be driving, but he did not offer to drive Stockberger or try to take away his car keys; nor did he try to contact Stockberger's supervisor or wife. The prison had often in the past provided transportation for sick employees, including diabetic employees—including in fact Stockberger. But it had no written policies concerning the treatment of sick employees.

Stockberger got into his pick-up truck and began driving home. He drove very erratically, no doubt because of his hypoglycemia, veering off the road and then back onto it, knocking down traffic signs, and eventually colliding with a tree. His truck burst into flames when it hit the tree, and he died. * * *

The plaintiff's * * * claim is that the prison's action (or rather inaction) in allowing Stockberger to drive in his hypoglycemic condition was a breach of the duty of care imposed by Indiana tort law, the law that, in accordance with the Federal Tort Claims Act, furnishes the rule of decision for the plaintiff's claim. The claim invites consideration of the broader question of the tort duty if any to rescue a person in distress. The common law traditionally took a hard line, rejecting any legal duty to be a good Samaritan. If *A* saw that *B* was about to be struck on the head by a flowerpot thrown from a tenth-story window, and *A* knew that *B* was unaware of the impending catastrophe and also knew that he could save *B* with a shout, yet he did nothing and as a result *B* was killed, still, *A*'s inaction, though gratuitous (there was no risk or other nontrivial cost to *A*) and even reprehensible, would not be actionable. * Yania v. Bigan, 397 Pa. 316, 155 A.2d 343 (1959). * The common law rule has been changed in some states, see, e.g., Vt. Stat. Ann. tit. 12, § 519(a), * but not in Indiana. Statutory modifications of the common law rule are common, such as requiring a driver who has caused an accident to remain at the scene even if he was not culpable, * or forbidding a hospital emergency room to turn away a patient brought to it before his condition has been stabilized. * But none is applicable to this case.

Various rationales have been offered for the seemingly hardhearted common law rule: people should not count on nonprofessionals for rescue; the circle of potentially liable nonrescuers would be difficult to draw (suppose a person is drowning and no one on the crowded beach makes an effort to save him—should all be liable?); altruism makes the problem a small one and liability might actually reduce the number of altruistic rescues by depriving people of credit for altruism (how would they prove they hadn't acted under threat of legal liability?); people would be deterred by threat of liability from putting themselves in a position where they might be called upon to attempt a rescue, especially since a failed rescue might under settled common law principles give rise to liability, on the theory that a clumsy rescue attempt may have interfered with a competent rescue by someone else. * * *

The fact that the prison had sometimes accommodated the needs of a sick employee by providing him with transportation home or to a hospital did not create a contractual duty or reasonable expectation that a hypoglycemic employee would be restrained against his wishes from driving home. Stockberger was adamant that he wanted to go home and intended to do so the same way he had gotten to work, namely by driving his truck. His coworkers may have been negligent in failing to restrain him, just as *A* in our flowerpot hypothetical was negligent in failing to shout, where negligence is determined in Hand formula terms by comparing the burden of precautions (close to zero in both cases) with the harm from failure to take them discounted (multiplied) by the probability of injury. * Probably the burden to Stockberger's coworkers of delaying his departure was less than the risk of a serious accident. The fact that he wanted to go home need not have weighed seriously in the calculus of negligence. His thinking may have been impaired and his coworkers may have known this on the basis of their experience with his previous hypoglycemic episodes, in which he had exhibited irrational thinking.

For the plaintiff to prevail, however, the exceptions to the rule that there is no "good Samaritan" liability would have to be enlarged, to encompass the case in which an employee becomes ill at the workplace for reasons unrelated to his work and the employer fails to use due care to treat the illness. The exception could not be cabined so; its logic would embrace the common situation in which a customer becomes ill in a store, or a guest in a private home. Indeed, either would be the stronger case for imposing a duty of rescue. Employees learn about conditions (including employer provisions for their safety) on the job to an extent that a shopper is unlikely to learn about the dangers of the stores in which he shops or a guest the dangers of his host's home. Employees, moreover, can negotiate for more safety or demand compensation for risks; and to add to wages that reflect risks compensation in tort if the risks materialize would be double counting.

The rule toward which Stockberger's claim gestures is that the owner of premises has a duty of care toward *any* invitee in peril, even if the invitee's illness or injury was in no wise caused or aggravated by the owner or his employees. Such a rule could be defended by reference to hypothetical-contract analysis—by asking whether employees, customers, and guests have a reasonable expectation that if they suddenly collapse on the premises of their employer, business invitor, or host, they will not be left to die; that the employer, business invitor, and host have at least a duty to dial 911. The custodial situation in the case just put, as in a prisoner case, thins the ranks of potential rescuers. And the reasons that support the common law rule are attenuated in these settings, although it could be argued that the employer, business invitor, or social host who is burdened with a duty to care for a sick employee, etc., will be reluctant to invite chronically ill people, such as diabetics; we have also suggested reasons for treating employees differently from other invitees.

Hypothetical-contract analysis is a powerful tool for understanding tort law and determining its scope. It is easy to imagine that if drivers and pedestrians, say, could contract with regard to safety, they would agree that drivers would take cost-justified measures to avoid hitting pedestrians and pedestrians would take cost-justified measures to avoid being hit; for that is the form of contract that would minimize all relevant costs—the costs of accidents and the costs of avoiding accidents. And it is possible that such an analysis would lead to the conclusion that when an invitee suddenly becomes helpless and in peril on the premises of his invitor, the invitor has a duty to take at least minimal steps to save him, since that is the solution that minimizes all the relevant costs. This conclusion might make as much sense as the other exceptions to the common law's rejection of good Samaritan liability, all of which by the way can be rationalized on similar hypothetical-contract grounds—for example, one can easily imagine a contract between potential victims and potential injurers whereby the latter would agree to assist the victim even if the injury itself was not culpable; for the injurer will usually be in the best, and often in the only, position to minimize the costs of the injury to the victim.

Indiana, however, has not yet taken the step of imposing good Samaritan liability on invitors. * * * But the plaintiff in her briefs and at argument has not tried to persuade us that Indiana would adopt the emergent rule. Instead she has tried without success to fit her case into existing Indiana case law. Even if we were *so* confident of the soundness or inevitability of the rule as to be willing to predict its adoption by Indiana, its application to situations in which due care requires restraining a person's freedom of movement would have to be very cautious, probably too cautious to give the plaintiff in this case any relief. The cases that we have cited that imposed liability on invitors for failures to rescue involved extreme situations, such as, in Hutchinson v. Dickie, [162 F.2d 103 (6th Cir.1921)], the failure of a yachtsman to try to rescue a guest who fell overboard.[a] It would not be sensible either to place employers or other invitors on a razor's edge where they face a suit for false imprisonment if they don't let the ill person leave or a suit for negligence if they do, or to turn employers and other invitors into nannies required, for example, to take the car keys away from an employee or customer or social guest because the roads are icy and the individual is known to be an unskillful driver. Stockberger was emphatic in wanting to drive himself home, said that he was feeling better and appeared to be, and could be presumed (for his diabetes was of long standing) to have known his fitness to drive as well as his skeptical coworker did. Of course in such a case there might be a legal duty to persons injured by the employee's foreseeable accident, * but such a case would not present an issue of good Samaritan liability.

Affirmed.

NOTES

1. *Yania v. Bigan.* Suppose an Olympic champion swimmer is sunning himself on a beach at a location where no lifeguard is on duty. He sees a small child drowning and ignores him despite the fact that he could save the child with little or no inconvenience to himself. Is he liable to the child's parents for a negligent failure to rescue?

In the classic case of Yania v. Bigan, 397 Pa. 316, 155 A.2d 343 (1959), cited in *Stockberger*, the plaintiff's decedent, a neighbor of the defendant, was aiding the defendant in pumping water from a trench created when the defendant removed coal from his land. The trench was sixteen to eighteen feet deep, containing water eight to ten feet deep, and the plaintiff's decedent drowned. The defendant had not warned plaintiff's decedent of the depth of the water. The plaintiff alleged that the defendant was negligent in two regards. First, the defendant had urged or enticed the plaintiff's decedent to jump into the water that the defendant knew, or should have known, was eight to ten feet deep. The court responded that because the decedent was not a child, nor was he mentally deficient, his

---

a   [Eds.' note] Compare Harper v. Herman, *infra* pages 464–66.

decision to jump into the water-filled trench was one of volition and freedom of choice and not caused by compulsion.

Of greater interest is the court's conclusion that the defendant was not negligent in failing to rescue Yania. The court acknowledges that a moral obligation may exist, but finds no legal duty to rescue. Why? Richard Epstein offers the following answer:

> Once one decides that * * * an individual is required under some circumstances to act at his own cost for the exclusive benefit of another, then it is very hard to set out in a principled manner the limits of social interference with individual liberty. Suppose one claims [that a duty to rescue] applies only in the "obvious" cases where everyone (or almost everyone) would admit that the duty was appropriate: to the case of the man upon the bridge who refuses to throw a rope to a stranger drowning the waters below. Even if the rule starts out with such modest ambitions, it is difficult to confine it to those limits. Take a simple case first. *X* as a representative of a private charity asks you for $10 in order to save the life of some starving child in a country ravaged by war. There are other donors available but the number of needy children exceeds that number. The money means "nothing" to you. Are you under a legal obligation to give the $10? * * * It is true that the relationship between the gift to charity and the survival of an unidentified child is not so apparent as is the relationship between the man upon the bridge and the swimmer caught in the swirling seas. But lest the physical imagery govern, it is clear that someone will die as a consequence of your inaction in both cases. * * *
>
> * * * Where tests of "reasonableness"—stated with such confidence, and applied with such difficulty—dominate the law of tort, it becomes impossible to tell where liberty ends and obligation begins * * *. In each case, it will be possible for some judge or jury to decide that there was something else which the defendant should have done, and he will decide that on the strength of some cost-benefit formula that is difficult indeed to apply.

Richard A. Epstein, A Theory of Strict Liability, 2 J. Legal Stud. 151, 198–99 (1973).

2. *Statutory Responses to the Common Law Doctrine.* Several states now provide criminal penalties for failure to aid others in distress. A Minnesota statute, for example, provides:

> A person at the scene of an emergency who knows that another person is exposed to or has suffered grave physical harm shall, to the extent that the person can do so without danger or peril to self or others, give reasonable assistance to the exposed person. Reasonable assistance may include obtaining or attempting to obtain aid from law enforcement or medical personnel. A person who violates this subdivision is guilty of a petty misdemeanor.

Minn. Stat. § 604A.01(1) (2013). See also R.I. Gen. Laws § 11–56–1 (2013); Vt. Stat. Ann. tit. 12, § 519 (2014).

3. *Frequency of Non-Rescue.* How important is the no-duty-to-rescue doctrine in the real world? Professor David Hyman argues "that the number of articles written each year on the no-duty rule substantially exceeds the number of non-rescues during the same time period." David A. Hyman, Rescue Without Law: An Empirical Perspective on the Duty to Rescue, 84 Tex. L. Rev. 653, 694 (2006). After an exhaustive empirical study of incidents of rescue and non-rescue, Hyman finds:

> During the past decade, there have been an average of 1.6 documented cases of non-rescue each year in the entire United States. Every year, Americans perform at least 946 non-risky rescues and 243 risky rescues. Every year, at least sixty-five times as many Americans die while attempting to rescue someone else as die from a documented case of non-risky non-rescue.

Id. at 712

2. LIABILITY ARISING FROM DEFENDANT'S CREATION OF RISK

Montgomery v. National Convoy & Trucking Co.
Supreme Court of South Carolina, 1938.
186 S.C. 167, 195 S.E. 247.

■ BAKER, JUSTICE. [* * * "As the truck of appellant National Convoy & Trucking Company undertook to negotiate the hill, traveling in the direction of Charlotte, due to the icy condition of the highway, it stalled and commenced to slide backward down the hill, and it was necessary to jackknife the tractor of the truck in order to avoid sliding down the hill, which entirely blocked the right-hand side of the road traveling in a northerly direction; and there is some testimony that a portion of the tractor extended across the middle of the highway thereby partially blocking travel to the south. The operators of this truck put out a fuse or flare to the rear of the truck and left the scene for help." * * * The court found that there was "no actionable negligence" on the part of the defendant's agents in the truck blocking the highway, the positioning of the truck was instead the result of "the condition of the weather and of the road over which the parties to the action were traveling was an unprecedented and unusual condition, resulting in making the highways extremely and exceedingly slick to the point where the conditions constituted an act of God."]

* * * [A]s respondent's automobile came around a curve at the crest of a long hill, and when the car was sufficiently around the curve on the crest of the hill for the lights of the car to focus on the highway leading down the hill, respondent's chauffeur observed the trucks of appellants, which had completely blocked the highway, said trucks being about fifty-one feet from the point where he could see them. The chauffeur at the time was operating the car at not more than 20 miles per hour, due to the condition of the highway. He applied his brakes and put the car in reverse gear, but by reason of the ice on the highway and decline the car slid on into the trucks, * * * [which were] stalled, completely blocking the traffic line of the highway in a southerly direction. In this collision, respondent received her injuries. There is evidence that the lights of one of the trucks were burning, and fuses or flares burning at the location where the trucks were stalled, but that at the crest of the

hill and curve in the highway there were no lights or other warning attempted to be given the public using the highway traveling in a southerly direction. The agents of appellants operating the trucks knew, or had every reason to know, that once a car had passed the crest of the hill and started down the decline, traveling towards Spartanburg, it would be impossible to stop such automobile or motor vehicle due to the icy condition of the highway, regardless of the rate of speed at which such automobile may be traveling. The trucks of appellant had entirely blocked the highway for fifteen minutes prior to the automobile of respondent reaching the point of the collision, and as aforesaid, there was evidence that appellants failed to warn travelers approaching from the north by the putting out of lights or flares or the flagging of such traffic at the crest of the hill and the curve of the road, the only place, under the conditions of the road on that day, a warning would be of any avail. Several people had congregated at the place where the trucks were stalled, but none was requested to flag oncoming vehicles from the north. * * *

One may be negligent by acts of omission as well as of commission, and liability therefor will attach if the act of omission of a duty owed another, under the circumstances, is the direct, proximate and efficient cause of the injury. * * * One of the acts of negligence alleged in the complaint is the failure of the appellants to warn approaching vehicles of the conditions existing, and this necessarily means that the warning should be given at a point where it would be effective. That appellants recognized that they owed a duty to others using the highway cannot be questioned, since they at some time put out flares and left the lights on their trucks. But if appellants owed a duty to others using the highway, and this cannot be disputed, the performance of such duty was not met by merely having lights at the point where the trucks blocked the highway, but it was incumbent on the appellants to take such precautions as would reasonably be calculated to prevent injury. * * *

In the case at bar it certainly became a question of fact for the jury to pass upon, if the icy condition of the highway (the act of God) was the proximate cause of respondent's injury, or if respondent had shown by the preponderance of the evidence that the act of omission on the part of appellants in failing to warn her of the blocked condition of the highway in time to prevent the injury, combining and concurring with the act of God, was the proximate cause of the injuries suffered by respondent. * * * [G]ranting that appellants were not negligent in blocking the highway, and keeping same blocked, if appellants failed to give a warning of the blocked highway at such a point as would be reasonably expected to be effective, appellants would be liable for the injuries sustained by the respondent. * * * Under the evidence in this case, it cannot be said that the verdict of the jury was contrary to and in violation of certain portions of the judge's charge. * * *

And the judgment of the circuit court is affirmed.

NOTE

Establishing an Affirmative Duty of Care through the Creation of Risk. The Restatement (Third) of Torts: Liability for Physical and Emotional Harm § 39 (2010) provides: "When an actor's prior conduct, even though not tortious, creates a continuing risk of physical harm of a type characteristic of the conduct, the actor has a duty to exercise reasonable care to prevent or minimize the harm."

What is the meaning of the requirement that the actor's initial conduct must create "a continuing risk of physical harm *of a type characteristic of the conduct?*" The Restatement provides the following illustration:

> The Hamford Bus Company serves a town that has a ski resort. Ben rides a Hamford bus to the town in order to go skiing. While Ben is skiing, the Hamford bus driver who transported Ben sees that he has strayed into an area with a substantial avalanche risk. Although Hamford's transportation is a factual cause of the risk to Ben posed by an avalanche, Hamford and its driver have no duty, under this Section, to Ben with respect to the avalanche risk, because Hamford's transportation of Ben does not create a characteristic risk of harm from an avalanche.

Id. at cmt. c, illus. 2.

3. VOLUNTARY UNDERTAKING OF ASSISTANCE

H.R. Moch Co. v. Rensselaer Water Co.

Court of Appeals of New York, 1928.
247 N.Y. 160, 159 N.E. 896.

■ CARDOZO, C. J. The defendant, a water works company under the laws of this State, made a contract with the city of Rensselaer for the supply of water during a term of years. Water was to be furnished to the city for sewer flushing and street sprinkling; for service to schools and public buildings; and for service at fire hydrants, the latter service at the rate of $42.50 a year for each hydrant. Water was to be furnished to private takers within the city at their homes and factories and other industries at reasonable rates, not exceeding a stated schedule. While this contract was in force, a building caught fire. The flames, spreading to the plaintiff's warehouse near by, destroyed it and its contents. The defendant according to the complaint was promptly notified of the fire, "but omitted and neglected after such notice, to supply or furnish sufficient or adequate quantity of water, with adequate pressure to stay, suppress or extinguish the fire before it reached the warehouse of the plaintiff, although the pressure and supply which the defendant was equipped to supply and furnish, and had agreed by said contract to supply and furnish, was adequate and sufficient to prevent the spread of the fire to and the destruction of the plaintiff's warehouse and its contents." By reason of the failure of the defendant to "fulfill the provisions of the contract between it and the city of Rensselaer," the plaintiff is said to have suffered damage, for which judgment is demanded. A motion, in the nature of a demurrer, to dismiss the complaint, was denied at Special Term. The Appellate Division reversed by a divided court.

Liability in the plaintiff's argument is placed on one or other of three grounds. The complaint, we are told, is to be viewed as stating: (1) A cause of action for breach of contract within Lawrence v. Fox, 20 N.Y. 268 [1859]; (2) a cause of action for a common-law tort, within MacPherson v. Buick Motor Company, 217 N.Y. 382, 111 N.E. 1050

(1916) *; or (3) a cause of action for the breach of a statutory duty. These several grounds of liability will be considered in succession.

1. *We think the action is not maintainable as one for breach of contract.*

No legal duty rests upon a city to supply its inhabitants with protection against fire. * That being so, a member of the public may not maintain an action under *Lawrence v. Fox* against one contracting with the city to furnish water at the hydrants, unless an intention appears that the promisor is to be answerable to individual members of the public as well as to the city for any loss ensuing from the failure to fulfill the promise. No such intention is discernible here. On the contrary, the contract is significantly divided into two branches: one a promise to the city for the benefit of the city in its corporate capacity, in which branch is included the service at the hydrants; and the other a promise to the city for the benefit of private takers, in which branch is included the service at their homes and factories. In a broad sense it is true that every city contract, not improvident or wasteful, is for the benefit of the public. More than this, however, must be shown to give a right of action to a member of the public not formally a party. The benefit, as it is sometimes said, must be one that is not merely incidental and secondary. * It must be primary and immediate in such a sense and to such a degree as to bespeak the assumption of a duty to make reparation directly to the individual members of the public if the benefit is lost. The field of obligation would be expanded beyond reasonable limits if less than this were to be demanded as a condition of liability. A promisor undertakes to supply fuel for heating a public building. He is not liable for breach of contract to a visitor who finds the building without fuel, and thus contracts a cold. The list of illustrations can be indefinitely extended. The carrier of the mails under contract with the government is not answerable to the merchant who has lost the benefit of a bargain through negligent delay. The householder is without a remedy against manufacturers of hose and engines, though prompt performance of their contracts would have stayed the ravages of fire. "The law does not spread its protection so far." Robins Dry Dock & Repair Co. v. Flint, 275 U.S. 303, 48 S.Ct. 134, 72 L.Ed. 290 [1927].

So with the case at hand. By the vast preponderance of authority, a contract between a city and a water company to furnish water at the city hydrants has in view a benefit to the public that is incidental rather than immediate, an assumption of duty to the city and not to its inhabitants. * * * Only a few States have held otherwise. * An intention to assume an obligation of indefinite extension to every member of the public is seen to be the more improbable when we recall the crushing burden that the obligation would impose. * The consequences invited would bear no reasonable proportion to those attached by law to defaults not greatly different. A wrongdoer who by negligence sets fire to a building is liable in damages to the owner where the fire has its origin, but not to other owners who are injured when it spreads. The rule in our State is settled to that effect, whether wisely or unwisely. * * * If the plaintiff is to prevail, one who negligently omits to supply sufficient pressure to extinguish a fire started by another, assumes an obligation to pay the ensuing damage, though the whole city is laid low.

A promisor will not be deemed to have had in mind the assumption of a risk so overwhelming for any trivial reward. * * *

2.   *We think the action is not maintainable as one for a common-law tort.*

"It is ancient learning that one who assumes to act, even though gratuitously, may thereby become subject to the duty of acting carefully, if he acts at all." Glanzer v. Shepard, 233 N.Y. 236, 239, 135 N.E. 275, 276 [1922] * The plaintiff would bring its case within the orbit of that principle. The hand once set to a task may not always be withdrawn with impunity though liability would fail if it had never been applied at all. A time-honored formula often phrases the distinction as one between misfeasance and nonfeasance. Incomplete the formula is, and so at times misleading. Given a relation involving in its existence a duty of care irrespective of a contract, a tort may result as well from acts of omission as of commission in the fulfillment of the duty thus recognized by law. * * * If conduct has gone forward to such a stage that inaction would commonly result, not negatively merely in withholding a benefit, but positively or actively in working an injury, there exists a relation out of which arises a duty to go forward. * So the surgeon who operates without pay, is liable though his negligence is in the omission to sterilize his instruments, cf. Glanzer v. Shepard, *supra*; the engineer, though his fault is in the failure to shut off steam; * the maker of automobiles, at the suit of someone other than the buyer, though his negligence is merely in inadequate inspection. MacPherson v. Buick Motor Co., *supra*. The query always is whether the putative wrongdoer has advanced to such a point as to have launched a force or instrument of harm, or has stopped where inaction is at most a refusal to become an instrument for good. *

The plaintiff would have us hold that the defendant, when once it entered upon the performance of its contract with the city, was brought into such a relation with everyone who might potentially be benefited through the supply of water at the hydrants as to give to negligent performance, without reasonable notice of a refusal to continue, the quality of a tort. * * * We are satisfied that liability would be unduly and indeed indefinitely extended by this enlargement of the zone of duty. The dealer in coal who is to supply fuel for a shop must then answer to the customers if fuel is lacking. The manufacturer of goods, who enters upon the performance of his contract, must answer, in that view, not only to the buyer, but to those who to his knowledge are looking to the buyer for their own sources of supply. Every one making a promise having the quality of a contract will be under a duty to the promisee by virtue of the promise, but under another duty, apart from contract, to an indefinite number of potential beneficiaries when performance has begun. The assumption of one relation will mean the involuntary assumption of a series of new relations, inescapably hooked together. * * * We do not need to determine now what remedy, if any, there might be if the defendant had withheld the water or reduced the pressure with a malicious intent to do injury to the plaintiff or another. We put aside also the problem that would arise if there had been reckless and wanton indifference to consequences measured and foreseen. Difficulties would be present even then, but they need not now perplex us. What we are dealing with at this time is a mere negligent omission, unaccompanied by malice or other aggravating elements. The failure in such circumstances to furnish an adequate supply of water is at most the denial of a benefit. It is not the commission of a wrong. * * *

The judgment should be affirmed with costs. * * *

NOTE

Compare Weinberg v. Dinger, 106 N.J. 469, 524 A.2d 366 (1987). In *Weinberg* the plaintiffs were the owners and residents of an apartment complex that was destroyed by fire. Firefighters were unable to extinguish the flames because of inadequate water pressure in nearby hydrants that were installed and maintained by the defendant, a private water company. The court noted that "explicitly or implicitly, the majority of cases denying water company liability ultimately turn on the fear of exposing water companies to unbounded liability." Further, stated the court, "We are mindful of the concern that the water company's added liability insurance cost, ultimately borne by the consumer, constitutes a less efficient method of insuring against fire loss than is afforded by property insurance." With these considerations in mind, the court "abrogate[d] the water company's immunity for losses caused by the negligent failure to maintain adequate water pressure for firefighting[, but] only to the extent of claims that are uninsured or underinsured. To the extent that such claims are insured and thereby assigned to the insurance carrier * * *, we hold that the carrier's subrogation claims are unenforceable against the water company." The court left open, however, the possibility of reconsidering the property insurers' subrogation claims if it could be established that holding the water company liable would reduce fire insurance rates to an extent commensurate with the anticipated increase in liability insurance costs for water companies (and indirectly in the consumers' water rates).

Bloomberg v. Interinsurance Exchange

Court of Appeal of California, 1984.
162 Cal.App.3d 571, 207 Cal.Rptr. 853.

■ ASHBY, J. * * * Appellants' son Seth was a passenger in a car driven by David Camblin, also 16, on the night of September 20, 1980. While traveling on the Golden State Freeway the car developed engine trouble. Camblin pulled the car onto the shoulder of the road, near a callbox. At approximately 1:30 a.m., he placed a call that was answered by the California Highway Patrol (CHP), who transferred it to the Auto Club. The boys returned to the car to await the Auto Club's emergency assistance. An Auto Club tow truck dispatched at approximately 1:30 a.m. failed to locate the stalled car. At about 2:25 a.m., an intoxicated driver * crashed into the car, causing injuries to appellants' son that resulted in his death. * * *

The threshold question is whether respondent owed a duty of care to appellants' son. Determining duty is primarily a question of law. * The duty question must be decided on a case-by-case basis, but each case must be governed by the general rule that everyone is required to use ordinary care to prevent causing injury to others. * A defendant who enters upon an affirmative course of conduct affecting the interests of another is regarded as assuming a duty to act, and will be liable for negligent acts or omissions * because one who undertakes to do an act must do it with care. * As Prosser states: "Where performance clearly has begun, there is no doubt that there is a duty of care." [William] Prosser, Handbook of the Law of Torts § 56 (4th ed. 1971).

* * * Based on these facts we cannot say that respondent owed no duty of care to appellants' son. The undertaking to send the tow truck clearly did affect his interest. Had they not expected respondent to send assistance, the boys may have made other arrangements. They could have called their parents, a friend or even CHP to be driven home or at least to a safer location. * Appellants allege that the Auto Club failed to locate the stalled vehicle due to its negligence. If appellants can prove respondent's negligence, respondent will be held liable for its breach of duty. It was, therefore, error to sustain respondent's demurrer on the ground that respondent owed appellants' son no duty of care.

* * * During oral argument respondent contended that appellants' son was not included in a contract for emergency services made between the Auto Club and appellants. Whether appellants can go forward on a contractual theory depends upon the wording of the contract, which is not in the record before us. Nevertheless, appellants should be given the opportunity * * * to state a cause of action, either solely or alternatively, which describes a negligent undertaking. *

As stated above, respondent's position is that an intoxicated driver caused the death of appellants' son and that the Auto Club in no way contributed to the creation of the situation in which the accident occurred. To the extent that Seth and David relied on respondent to come to their assistance and in so relying made no other arrangements for their rescue, to that extent respondent contributed to the risk of harm. "Anyone legally responsible for the victims of the accident being in their exposed position could [be] found to have contributed in a substantial way to the causation of the accident." Mann v. State of California, 70 Cal.App.3d 773, 777, 139 Cal.Rptr. 82 [1977].

Respondent urges that even if a duty is found to exist on the part of the Auto Club, the actions of an intoxicated driver were a superseding, intervening cause of Seth's death. Generally if the risk of injury might have been reasonably foreseen, a defendant is liable. If an independent, intervening act occurs which is highly unusual or extraordinary, not reasonably likely to happen and hence not foreseeable, it is considered a superseding cause and defendant is not liable. * Among the possible dangers awaiting stranded motorists is injury or death caused by other drivers. In particular, intoxicated drivers are to be expected late at night. * * *

The judgment is reversed.

NOTES

1. *Undertaking Rescue as Basis for Liability.* In United States v. DeVane, 306 F.2d 182 (5th Cir.1962), the decedent's wife had informed the Coast Guard that her husband's fishing vessel was overdue. After a search was begun, the Coast Guard erroneously concluded that the vessel had been located and was in no distress. Upon receiving this news, a friend of the decedent who operated another fishing vessel decided not to undertake the search for the missing boat which he would have otherwise pursued. The

court concluded that the Coast Guard was not under a statutory duty to make any particular rescue efforts but that if it did undertake any such rescue, the United States would be subject to liability under the Federal Tort Claims Act to the family of the decedent if it did so negligently and if, but only if, its negligence worsened the plight of the decedent.

2. *Voluntary Undertaking to Provide Information and Consequent Duty to Warn.* In Mandel v. United States, 793 F.2d 964 (8th Cir.1986), the United States was held liable under the Federal Tort Claims Act for a purely voluntary undertaking for failure to warn. The plaintiff, a counselor for a youth group attending a private camp on grounds adjacent to lands under the jurisdiction of the National Park Service, asked a park ranger for a good swimming location after the ranger voluntarily approached him. The ranger recommended "Mud Cave," a local swimming hole located on another piece of private property, saying, "That's where everyone goes. That's where we recommend for you to go." When the plaintiff dived into the swimming hole, he hit his head on a submerged rock and was permanently paralyzed. The evidence was undisputed that the ranger and the National Park Service did not know of this specific submerged rock, but that they were aware that the river was "laced" with submerged rocks. The court, indicating that the duty of reasonable care included a duty to warn of submerged rocks, held the United States liable.

4. LIABILITY FOR UNREASONABLE FAILURE TO RESCUE REVISITED

Soldano v. O'Daniels
Court of Appeal of California, 1983.
141 Cal.App.3d 443, 190 Cal.Rptr. 310.

■ ANDREEN, JUSTICE. Does a business establishment incur liability for wrongful death if it denies use of its telephone to a good samaritan who explains an emergency situation occurring without and wishes to call the police? * * *

This action arises out of a shooting death occurring on August 9, 1977. Plaintiff's father * [Darrell Soldano] was shot and killed by one Rudolph Villanueva on that date at defendant's Happy Jack's Saloon. This defendant owns and operates the Circle Inn which is an eating establishment located across the street from Happy Jack's. Plaintiff's second cause of action against this defendant is one for negligence.

Plaintiff alleges that on the date of the shooting, a patron of Happy Jack's Saloon came into the Circle Inn and informed a Circle Inn employee that a man had been threatened at Happy Jack's. He requested the employee either call the police or allow him to use the Circle Inn phone to call the police. That employee allegedly refused to call the police and allegedly refused to allow the patron to use the phone to make his own call. Plaintiff alleges that the actions of the Circle Inn employee were a breach of the legal duty that the Circle Inn owed to the decedent. * * *

There is a distinction, well rooted in the common law, between action and nonaction. * It has found its way into the prestigious

Restatement (Second) of Torts (hereafter cited as Restatement), which provides in section 314:

> The fact that the actor realizes or should realize that action on his part is necessary for another's aid or protection does not of itself impose upon him a duty to take such action.

Comment *c* of section 314 is instructive on the basis and limits of the rule and is set forth in the footnote.[4] The distinction between malfeasance and nonfeasance, between active misconduct working positive injury and failure to act to prevent mischief not brought on by the defendant, is founded on "that attitude of extreme individualism so typical of anglo-saxon legal thought." [Francis H.] Bohlen, The Moral Duty to Aid Others as a Basis of Tort Liability, pt. I, 56 U. Pa. L. Rev. 217, 219–20 (1908).

Defendant argues that the request that its employee call the police is a request that it *do* something. He points to the established rule that one who has not created a peril ordinarily does not have a duty to take affirmative action to assist an imperiled person. * It is urged that the alternative request of the patron from Happy Jack's Saloon that he be allowed to use defendant's telephone so that he personally could make the call is again a request that the defendant do something—assist another to give aid. Defendant points out that the Restatement sections which impose liability for negligent interference with a third person giving aid to another do not impose the additional duty to *aid* the good samaritan.[5]

The refusal of the law to recognize the moral obligation of one to aid another when he is in peril and when such aid may be given without

---

4   [The opinion quotes from the Restatement (Second) of Torts:]

The rule stated in this Section is applicable irrespective of the gravity of the danger to which the other is subjected and the insignificance of the trouble, effort, or expense of giving him aid or protection.

The origin of the rule lay in the early common law distinction between action and inaction, or "misfeasance" and "nonfeasance." In the early law one who injured another by a positive affirmative act was held liable without any great regard even for his fault. But the courts were far too much occupied with the more flagrant forms of misbehavior to be greatly concerned with one who merely did nothing, even though another might suffer serious harm because of his omission to act. Hence liability for non-feasance was slow to receive any recognition in the law. It appeared first in, and is still largely confined to, situations in which there was some special relation between the parties, on the basis of which the defendant was found to have a duty to take action for the aid or protection of the plaintiff.

The result of the rule has been a series of older decisions to the effect that one human being, seeing a fellow man in dire peril, is under no legal obligation to aid him, but may sit on the dock, smoke his cigar, and watch the other drown. Such decisions have been condemned by legal writers as revolting to any moral sense, but thus far they remain the law. It appears inevitable that, sooner or later, such extreme cases of morally outrageous and indefensible conduct will arise that there will be further inroads upon the older rule.

Id. at § 314, cmt. c.

5   One who knows or has reason to know that a third person is giving or is ready to give to another aid necessary to prevent physical harm to him, and negligently prevents or disables the third person from giving such aid, is subject to liability for physical harm caused to the other by the absence of the aid which he has prevented the third person from giving.

Id. at § 327.

danger and at little cost in effort has been roundly criticized. Prosser describes the case law sanctioning such inaction as a "refus[al] to recognize the moral obligation of common decency and common humanity" and characterizes some of these decisions as "shocking in the extreme. . . . Such decisions are revolting to any moral sense. They have been denounced with vigor by legal writers." W[illiam] Prosser, Law of Torts § 56 (4th ed. 1971). A similar rule has been termed "morally questionable" by our Supreme Court. Tarasoff v. Regents of Univ. of Cal., 17 Cal.3d 425, 435, n.5, 131 Cal.Rptr. 14, 551 P.2d 334 (1976).

Francis H. Bohlen, in his article "The Moral Duty to Aid Others as a Basis of Tort Liability," commented:

> Nor does it follow that because the law has not as yet recognized the duty to repair harm innocently wrought, that it will continue indefinitely to refuse it recognition. While it is true that the common law does not attempt to enforce all moral, ethical, or humanitarian duties, it is, it is submitted, equally true that all ethical and moral conceptions, which are not the mere temporary manifestations of a passing wave of sentimentalism or puritanism, but on the contrary, find a real and permanent place in * * * settled convictions * * * and become part of the normal habit of thought thereof, of necessity do in time color the judicial conception of legal obligation. . . .
>
> While courts of law should not yield to every passing current of popular thought, nonetheless, it appears inevitable that unless they adopt as legal those popular standards which they themselves, as men, regard as just and socially practicable, but which, as judges, they refuse to recognize solely because they are not the standards of the past of Brian, of Rolle, of Fineux, and of Coke; they will more and more lose their distinctive common law character as part of the machinery whereby free men do justice among themselves.

Bohlen, *supra*, pt. II, 56 U. Pa. L. Rev. 316, 334, 337.

* * * [C]ourts have increased the instances in which affirmative duties are imposed not by direct rejection of the common law rule, but by expanding the list of special relationships which will justify departure from that rule. * * * [Citing cases establishing liability, e.g., of parents for failing to warn baby-sitter of "the violent proclivities of their child"; of the state for failing to warn foster parents of the dangerous tendencies of their ward; and against a sheriff "who had promised to warn decedent before releasing a dangerous person, but failed to do so."] Section 314A of the Restatement lists other special relationships which create a duty to render aid, such as that of a common carrier to its passengers, an innkeeper to his guest, possessors of land who hold it open to the public, or one who has a custodial relationship to another. A duty may be created by an undertaking to give assistance. See Restatement (Second) of Torts § 321 *et seq.* Here there was no special relationship between the defendant and the deceased. It would be stretching the concept beyond recognition to assert there was a relationship between the defendant and the patron from Happy Jack's Saloon who wished to summon aid. But this does not end the matter.

It is time to reexamine the common law rule of nonliability for nonfeasance in the special circumstances of the instant case. * * * The National Advisory Commission on Criminal Justice Standards and Goals, Report on Community Crime Prevention (1973) stated: "Criminal justice professionals readily and repeatedly admit that, in the absence of citizen assistance, neither more manpower, nor improved technology, nor additional money will enable law enforcement to shoulder the monumental burden of combating crime in America." * * * "[T]hat attitude of extreme individualism so typical of anglo-saxon legal thought" may need limited reexamination in the light of current societal conditions and the facts of this case to determine whether the defendant owed a duty to the deceased to permit the use of the telephone.

We turn now to the concept of duty in a tort case. The Supreme Court has identified certain factors to be considered in determining whether a duty is owed to third persons. These factors include:

> the foreseeability of harm to the plaintiff, the degree of certainty that the plaintiff suffered injury, the closeness of the connection between the defendant's conduct and the injury suffered, the moral blame attached to the defendant's conduct, the policy of preventing future harm, the extent of the burden to the defendant and consequences to the community of imposing a duty to exercise care with resulting liability for breach, and the availability, cost, and prevalence of insurance for the risk involved.

Rowland v. Christian, 69 Cal.2d 108, 113, 70 Cal.Rptr. 97, 443 P.2d 561 (1968). * We examine those factors in reference to this case. (1) The harm to the decedent was abundantly foreseeable; it was imminent. The employee was expressly told that a man had been threatened. The employee was a bartender. As such he knew it is foreseeable that some people who drink alcohol in the milieu of a bar setting are prone to violence. (2) The certainty of decedent's injury is undisputed. (3) There is arguably a close connection between the employee's conduct and the injury: the patron wanted to use the phone to summon the police to intervene. The employee's refusal to allow the use of the phone prevented this anticipated intervention. If permitted to go to trial, the plaintiff may be able to show that the probable response time of the police would have been shorter than the time between the prohibited telephone call and the fatal shot. (4) The employee's conduct displayed a disregard for human life that can be characterized as morally wrong:[9] he was callously indifferent to the possibility that Darrell Soldano would die as the result of his refusal to allow a person to use the telephone. Under the circumstances before us the bartender's burden was minimal and exposed him to no risk: all he had to do was allow the use of the telephone. It would have cost him or his employer nothing. It could have saved a life. (5) Finding a duty in these circumstances would promote a policy of preventing future harm. A citizen would not be required to summon the police but would be required, in circumstances

---

[9] The moral right of plaintiff's decedent to have the defendant's bartender permit the telephone call is so apparent that legal philosophers treat such rights as given and requiring no supporting argument. See R[onald] Dworkin, Taking Rights Seriously 99 (1978). The concept flows from the principle that each member of a community has a right to have each other member treat him with the minimal respect due a fellow human being.

such as those before us, not to impede another who has chosen to summon aid. (6) We have no information on the question of the availability, cost, and prevalence of insurance for the risk, but note that the liability which is sought to be imposed here is that of employee negligence, which is covered by many insurance policies. (7) The extent of the burden on the defendant was minimal, as noted.

The consequences to the community of imposing a duty, the remaining factor mentioned in *Rowland v. Christian*, is termed "the administrative factor" by Professor Green in his analysis of determining whether a duty exists in a given case. L[eon] Green, The Duty Problem in Negligence Cases, 28 Colum. L. Rev. 1014, 1035–45 [1929]. * The administrative factor is simply the pragmatic concern of fashioning a workable rule and the impact of such a rule on the judicial machinery. It is the policy of major concern in this case. As the Supreme Court has noted, the reluctance of the law to impose liability for nonfeasance, as distinguished from misfeasance, is in part due to the difficulties in setting standards and of making rules workable. Tarasoff v. Regents of Univ. of Cal., *supra*, 17 Cal.3d at 435, n.5, 131 Cal.Rptr. 14, 551 P.2d 334.

Many citizens simply "don't want to get involved." No rule should be adopted which would require a citizen to open up his or her house to a stranger so that the latter may use the telephone to call for emergency assistance. * * * It does not follow, however, that use of a telephone in a public portion of a business should be refused for a legitimate emergency call. Imposing liability for such a refusal would not subject innocent citizens to possible attack by the "good samaritan," for it would be limited to an establishment open to the public during times when it is open to business, and to places within the establishment ordinarily accessible to the public. Nor would a stranger's mere assertion that an "emergency" situation is occurring create the duty to utilize an accessible telephone because the duty would arise if and only if it were clearly conveyed that there exists an imminent danger of physical harm. See Restatement (Second) of Torts § 327.

Such a holding would not involve difficulties in proof, overburden the courts or unduly hamper self-determination or enterprise. A business establishment such as the Circle Inn is open for profit. The owner encourages the public to enter, for his earnings depend on it. A telephone is a necessary adjunct to such a place. It is not unusual in such circumstances for patrons to use the telephone to call a taxicab or family member. We acknowledge that defendant contracted for the use of his telephone, and its use is a species of property. But if it exists in a public place as defined above, there is no privacy or ownership interest in it such that the owner should be permitted to interfere with a good faith attempt to use it by a third person to come to the aid of another.

The facts of this case come very nearly within section 327 of the Restatement * which provides that if one knows that a third person is ready to give aid to another and negligently prevents the third person from doing so, he is subject to liability for harm caused by the absence of the aid. Section 327 is contained in topic 8 of the Restatement, "Prevention of Assistance by Third Persons." The scope note for this topic provides that the "actor can prevent a third person from rendering aid to another in many ways including the following: ... second, by interfering with his efforts to give aid; third, by injuring or destroying the usefulness of a thing which the third person is using to give aid *or by otherwise preventing him from using it. ...* " * Restatement (Second) of Torts, scope note, p. 145 (emphasis added by court). We conclude that the bartender owed a duty to the plaintiff's decedent to permit the patron from Happy Jack's to place a call to the police or to place the call himself.

It bears emphasizing that the duty in this case does not require that one must go to the aid of another. That is not the issue here. The employee was not the good samaritan intent on aiding another. The patron was.

It would not be appropriate to await legislative action in this area. The rule was fashioned in the common law tradition, as were the exceptions to the rule. * * * The courts have a special responsibility to reshape, refine and guide legal doctrine they have created. * * * The words of the Supreme Court on the role of the courts in a common law system are well suited to our obligation here:

> The inherent capacity of the common law for growth and change is its most significant feature. Its development has been determined by the social needs of the community which it serves. It is constantly expanding and developing in keeping with advancing civilization and the new conditions and progress of society, and adapting itself to the gradual change of trade, commerce, arts, inventions, and the needs of the country." ...

> In short, as the United States Supreme Court has aptly said, "This flexibility and capacity for growth and adaptation is the peculiar boast and excellence of the common law." Hurtado v. California, 110 U.S. 516, 530 * (1884). But that vitality can flourish only so long as the courts remain alert to their obligation and opportunity to change the common law when reason and equity demand it: "The nature of the common law requires that each time a rule of law is applied, it be carefully scrutinized to make sure that the conditions and needs of the times have not so changed as to make further application of it the instrument of injustice. Whenever an old rule is found unsuited to present conditions or unsound, it should be set aside and a rule declared which is in harmony with those conditions and meets the demands of justice." 15 Am. Jur.2d, Common Law, § 2, p. 797. Although the Legislature may of course speak to the subject, in the common law system the primary instruments of this evolution are the courts, adjudicating on a regular basis the rich variety of individual cases brought before them.

Rodriguez v. Bethlehem Steel Corp., 12 Cal.3d 382, 394, 115 Cal.Rptr. 765, 525 P.2d 669 (1974). * * *

The creative and regenerative power of the law has been strong enough to break chains imposed by outmoded former decisions. What the courts have power to create, they also have power to modify, reject and re-create in response to the needs of a dynamic society. The exercise of this power is an imperative function of the courts and is the strength of the common law. It cannot be surrendered to legislative inaction. * * *

The possible imposition of liability on the defendant in this case is not a global change in the law. It is but a slight departure from the "morally questionable" rule of nonliability for inaction absent a special relationship. * * * It is a logical extension of Restatement section 327 which imposes liability for negligent interference with a third person who the defendant knows is attempting to render necessary aid. However small it may be, it is a step which should be taken.

We conclude there are sufficient justiciable issues to permit the case to go to trial and therefore reverse.

B. DUTY TO PROTECT OR WARN THIRD PARTIES

Tarasoff v. Regents of the University of California

Supreme Court of California, 1976.
17 Cal.3d 425, 131 Cal.Rptr. 14, 551 P.2d 334.

■ TOBRINER, JUSTICE. On October 27, 1969, Prosenjit Poddar killed Tatiana Tarasoff. * Plaintiffs, Tatiana's parents, allege that two months earlier Poddar confided his intention to kill Tatiana to Dr. Lawrence Moore, a psychologist employed by the Cowell Memorial Hospital at the University of California at Berkeley. They allege that on Moore's request, the campus police briefly detained Poddar, but released him when he appeared rational. They further claim that Dr. Harvey Powelson, Moore's superior, then directed that no further action be taken to detain Poddar. No one warned plaintiffs of Tatiana's peril. Concluding that these facts set forth causes of action against neither therapists and policemen involved, nor against the Regents of the University of California as their employer, the superior court sustained defendants' demurrers to plaintiffs' second amended complaints without leave to amend. * This appeal ensued. * * *

2. *Plaintiffs can state a cause of action against defendant therapists for negligent failure to protect Tatiana.*

* * * Defendants * * * contend that in the circumstances of the present case they owed no duty of care to Tatiana or her parents and that, in the absence of such duty, they were free to act in careless disregard of Tatiana's life and safety.

In analyzing this issue, we bear in mind that legal duties are not discoverable facts of nature, but merely conclusory expressions, in cases of a particular type, liability should be imposed for damage done. As stated in Dillon v. Legg, 68 Cal.2d 728, 734, * (1968) [*infra* pages 483–488]:

> The assertion that liability must ... be denied because defendant bears no "duty" to plaintiff "begs the essential question—whether the plaintiff's interests are entitled to legal protection against the defendant's conduct.... [Duty] is not sacrosanct in itself, but only an expression of the sum total of

those considerations of policy which lead the law to say that the particular plaintiff is entitled to protection."

Quoting W[illiam L.] Prosser, Law of Torts, 332–33 (3d ed. 1964).

In the landmark case of Rowland v. Christian, 69 Cal.2d 108, 70 Cal.Rptr. 97, 443 P.2d 561 (1968), Justice Peters recognized that liability should be imposed "for injury occasioned to another by his want of ordinary care or skill" * * *. Thus, Justice Peters, quoting from Heaven v. Pender, 11 Q.B.D. 503, 509 (1883) stated: " 'whenever one person is by circumstances placed in such a position with regard to another . . . that if he did not use ordinary care and skill in his own conduct . . . he would cause danger of injury to the person or property of the other, a duty arises to use ordinary care and skill to avoid such danger.' "

We depart from "this fundamental principle" only upon the "balancing of a number of considerations"; major ones "are the foreseeability of harm to the plaintiff, the degree of certainty that the plaintiff suffered injury, the closeness of the connection between the defendant's conduct and the injury suffered, the moral blame attached to the defendant's conduct, the policy of preventing future harm, the extent of the burden to the defendant and consequences to the community of imposing a duty to exercise care with resulting liability for breach, and the availability, cost and prevalence of insurance for the risk involved." *

The most important of these considerations in establishing duty is foreseeability. As a general principle, a "defendant owes a duty of care to all persons who are foreseeably endangered by his conduct, with respect to all risks which make the conduct unreasonably dangerous." Rodriguez v. Bethlehem Steel Corp., 12 Cal.3d 382, 399, 115 Cal.Rptr. 765, 776, 525 P.2d 669, 680 (1974). * As we shall explain, however, when the avoidance of foreseeable harm requires a defendant to control the conduct of another person, or to warn of such conduct, the common law has traditionally imposed liability only if the defendant bears some special relationship to the dangerous person or to the potential victim. Since the relationship between a therapist and his patient satisfies this requirement, we need not here decide whether foreseeability alone is sufficient to create a duty to exercise reasonable care to protect a potential victim of another's conduct.

Although, as we have stated above, under the common law, as a general rule, one person owed no duty to control the conduct of another,[5] * nor to warn those endangered by such conduct, * the courts have carved out an exception to this rule in cases in which the defendant stands in some special relationship to either the person whose conduct needs to be controlled or in a relationship to the foreseeable victim of that conduct. * Applying this exception to the

---

[5] This rule derives from the common law's distinction between misfeasance and nonfeasance, and its reluctance to impose liability for the latter. * Morally questionable, the rule owes its survival to "the difficulties of setting any standards of unselfish service to fellow men, and of making any workable rule to cover possible situations where fifty people might fail to rescue. . . . " W[illiam L.] Prosser, Torts § 56 (4th ed. 1971). Because of these practical difficulties, the courts have increased the number of instances in which affirmative duties are imposed not by direct rejection of the common law rule, but by expanding the list of special relationships which will justify departure from that rule. *

present case, we note that a relationship of defendant therapists to either Tatiana or Poddar will suffice to establish a duty of care; as explained in section 315 of the Restatement Second of Torts, a duty of care may arise from either "(a) a special relation . . . between the actor and the third person which imposes a duty upon the actor to control the third person's conduct, or (b) a special relation . . . between the actor and the other which gives to the other a right of protection."

Although plaintiffs' pleadings assert no special relation between Tatiana and defendant therapists, they establish as between Poddar and defendant therapists the special relation that arises between a patient and his doctor or psychotherapist. * Such a relationship may support affirmative duties for the benefit of third persons. * Thus, for example, a hospital must exercise reasonable care to control the behavior of a patient which may endanger other persons. * A doctor must also warn a patient if the patient's condition or medication renders certain conduct, such as driving a car, dangerous to others. *

Although the California decisions that recognize this duty have involved cases in which the defendant stood in a special relationship *both* to the victim and to the person whose conduct created the danger, * we do not think that the duty should logically be constricted to such situations. Decisions of other jurisdictions hold that the single relationship of a doctor to his patient is sufficient to support the duty to exercise reasonable care to protect others against dangers emanating from the patient's illness. The courts hold that a doctor is liable to persons infected by his patient if he negligently fails to diagnose a contagious disease * or, having diagnosed the illness, fails to warn members of the patient's family. *

Since it involved a dangerous mental patient, the decision in Merchants Nat. Bank & Trust Co. of Fargo v. United States, 272 F.Supp. 409 (D.N.D. 1967) comes closer to the issue. The Veterans Administration arranged for the patient to work on a local farm, but did not inform the farmer of the man's background. The farmer consequently permitted the patient to come and go freely during nonworking hours; the patient borrowed a car, drove to his wife's residence and killed her. Notwithstanding the lack of any "special relationship" between the Veterans Administration and the wife, the court found the Veterans Administration liable for the wrongful death of the wife. * * *

Defendants contend, however, that imposition of a duty to exercise reasonable care to protect third persons is unworkable because therapists cannot accurately predict whether or not a patient will resort to violence. In support of this argument *amicus* representing the American Psychiatric Association and other professional societies cites numerous articles which indicate that therapists, in the present state of the art, are unable reliably to predict violent acts; their forecasts, *amicus* claims, tend consistently to overpredict violence, and indeed are more often wrong than right. * Since predictions of violence are often erroneous, *amicus* concludes, the courts should not render rulings that predicate the liability of therapists upon the validity of such predictions. * * *

We recognize the difficulty that a therapist encounters in attempting to forecast whether a patient presents a serious danger of violence. Obviously we do not require that the therapist, in making that determination, render a perfect performance; the therapist need only exercise "that reasonable degree of skill, knowledge, and care ordinarily possessed and exercised by members of [that professional specialty] under similar circumstances." Bardessono v. Michels, 3 Cal.3d 780, 788, 91 Cal.Rptr. 760, 764, 478 P.2d 480, 484 (1970). * Within the broad range of reasonable practice and treatment in which professional opinion and judgment may differ, the therapist is free to exercise his or her own best judgment without liability; proof, aided by hindsight, that he or she judged wrongly is insufficient to establish negligence.

In the instant case, however, the pleadings do not raise any question as to failure of defendant therapists to predict that Poddar presented a serious danger of violence. On the contrary, the present complaints allege that defendant therapists did in fact predict that Poddar would kill, but were negligent in failing to warn.

Amicus contends, however, that even when a therapist does in fact predict that a patient poses a serious danger of violence to others, the therapist should be absolved of any responsibility for failing to act to protect the potential victim. In our view, however, once a therapist does in fact determine, or under applicable professional standards reasonably should have determined, that a patient poses a serious danger of violence to others, he bears a duty to exercise reasonable care to protect the foreseeable victim of that danger. While the discharge of this duty of due care will necessarily vary with the facts of each case, * in each instance the adequacy of the therapist's conduct must be measured against the traditional negligence standard of the rendition of reasonable care under the circumstances. * * *

The issue in the present context, however, is not whether the patient should be incarcerated, but whether the therapist should take any steps at all to protect the threatened victim; some of the alternatives open to the therapist, such as warning the victim, will not result in the drastic consequences of depriving the patient of his liberty. Weighing the uncertain and conjectural character of the alleged damage done the patient by such a warning against the peril to the victim's life, we conclude that professional inaccuracy in predicting violence cannot negate the therapist's duty to protect the threatened victim.

The risk that unnecessary warnings may be given is a reasonable price to pay for the lives of possible victims that may be saved. We would hesitate to hold that the therapist who is aware that his patient expects to attempt to assassinate the President of the United States would not be obligated to warn the authorities because the therapist cannot predict with accuracy that his patient will commit the crime.

Defendants further argue that free and open communication is essential to psychotherapy; * that "Unless a patient . . . is assured that . . . information [revealed by him] can and will be held in utmost confidence, he will be reluctant to make the full disclosure upon which diagnosis and treatment . . . depends." Sen. Com. on Judiciary, comment on Evid. Code § 1014. The giving of a warning, defendants contend, constitutes a breach of trust which entails the revelation of confidential communications. *

We recognize the public interest in supporting effective treatment of mental illness and in protecting the rights of patients to privacy, * and the consequent public importance of safeguarding the confidential character of psychotherapeutic communication. Against this interest, however, we must weigh the public interest in safety from violent assault. The Legislature has undertaken the difficult task of balancing the countervailing concerns. In Evidence Code § 1014, it established a broad rule of privilege to protect confidential communications between patient and psychotherapist. In Evidence Code section 1024, the Legislature created a specific and limited exception to the psychotherapist-patient privilege: "There is no privilege ... if the psychotherapist has reasonable cause to believe that the patient is in such mental or emotional condition as to be dangerous to himself or to the person or property of another and that disclosure of the communication is necessary to prevent the threatened danger." *

We realize that the open and confidential character of psychotherapeutic dialogue encourages patients to express threats of violence, few of which are ever executed. Certainly a therapist should not be encouraged routinely to reveal such threats; such disclosures could seriously disrupt the patient's relationship with his therapist and with the persons threatened. To the contrary, the therapist's obligations to his patient require that he not disclose a confidence unless such disclosure is necessary to avert danger to others, and even then that he do so discreetly, and in a fashion that would preserve the privacy of his patient to the fullest extent compatible with the prevention of the threatened danger. * * *

For the foregoing reasons, we find that plaintiffs' complaints can be amended to state a cause of action against defendants Moore, Powelson, Gold, and Yandell and against the Regents as their employer, for breach of a duty to exercise reasonable care to protect Tatiana. * * *

NOTES

1. *Legislative Response.* The California legislature responded to *Tarasoff* by enacting Cal. Civ. Code § 43.92 (2014) that prohibits monetary liability unless "the patient has communicated to the psychotherapist a serious threat of physical violence against a reasonably identifiable victim or victims." The statute also explicitly provides that the therapist can only discharge the legal duty by "making reasonable efforts to communicate the threat to the victim * * * *and* to a law enforcement agency."

2. *Rejection of* Tarasoff *in Selected Jurisdictions.* The general principle of *Tarasoff* has been widely accepted in other jurisdictions, even if liability often is rejected under the facts of a specific case. A common limitation is a requirement of specificity as to the threat, or the victim, or both. Cf. Brady v. Hopper, 751 F.2d 329 (10th Cir.1984) (Colo. law). See generally Harper, James and Gray on Torts § 16.12 n.16. In an unusual decision, the Supreme Court of Virginia rejected the underlying reasoning of *Tarasoff.* In Nasser v. Parker, 249 Va. 172, 455 S.E.2d 502 (1995), the decedent, Angela Nasser Lemon, was murdered by George Edwards after she rejected him and attempted to terminate their relationship. Edwards had a previous history of violence toward women, including pointing a gun at Lemon's head. After that incident, she obtained a warrant for Edwards' arrest and left her home. Edwards sought counseling with a psychiatrist who had treated him for seventeen years and agreed to voluntary commitment to a psychiatric hospital. Learning of this, Lemon returned to her home, but shortly thereafter Edwards left the hospital and murdered her. Lemon was not told of Edwards' release. The Supreme Court of Virginia held that no duty to warn Lemon existed. In doing so, it explicitly rejected *Tarasoff*:

> Accordingly, we disagree with the holding of *Tarasoff* that a doctor-patient relationship or a hospital-patient relationship alone is sufficient, as a matter of law, to establish a "special relation" under Restatement § 315(a). Within the context of the Restatement, there is nothing special about the ordinary doctor-patient relationship or hospital-patient relationship. We think there must be added to those ordinary relationships the factor, required by § 319, of taking charge of the patient, meaning that the doctor or hospital must be vested with a higher degree of control over the patient than exists in an ordinary doctor-patient or hospital-patient relationship before a duty arises concerning the patient's conduct.

For a good discussion of the importance of maintaining the confidentiality of patient-therapist disclosures in a different context, cf. Jaffee v. Redmond, 518 U.S. 1, 116 S.Ct. 1923, 135 L.Ed.2d 337 (1996).

Harper v. Herman

Supreme Court of Minnesota, 1993.

499 N.W.2d 472.

■ PAGE, JUSTICE. * * * On Sunday, August 9, 1986, Jeffrey Harper ("Harper") was one of four guests on Theodor Herman's ("Herman") 26-foot boat, sailing on Lake Minnetonka. Harper was invited on the boat outing by Cindy Alberg Palmer, another guest on Herman's boat. Herman and Harper did not know each other prior to this boat outing. At the time Herman was 64 years old, and Harper was 20 years old. Herman was an experienced boat owner having spent hundreds of hours operating boats on Lake Minnetonka similar to the one involved in this action. As owner of the boat, Herman considered himself to be in charge of the boat and his passengers. Harper had some experience swimming in lakes and rivers, but had no formal training in diving.

After a few hours of boating, the group decided to go swimming and, at Herman's suggestion, went to Big Island, a popular recreation spot. Herman was familiar with Big Island, and he was aware that the water remains shallow for a good distance away from its shore. Harper had been to Big Island on one previous occasion. Herman positioned the boat somewhere between 100 to 200 yards from the island with the bow facing away from the island in an area shallow enough for his guests to use the boat ladder to enter the water, but still deep enough so they could swim. * The bottom of the lake was not visible from the boat. After positioning the boat Herman proceeded to set the anchor and lower the boat's ladder which was at its stern.

While Herman was lowering the ladder, Harper asked him if he was "going in." When Herman responded yes, Harper, without warning, stepped onto the side of the middle of the boat and dove into approximately two or three feet of water. As a result of the dive, Harper struck the bottom of the lake, severed his spinal cord, and was rendered a C6 quadriplegic.

Harper then brought suit, alleging that Herman owed him a duty of care to warn him that the water was too shallow for diving. On October 23, 1991, the trial court granted Herman's motion for summary judgment, ruling that the law does not impose such a duty. In reversing the trial court, the court of appeals concluded that Herman voluntarily assumed a duty to exercise reasonable care when he allowed Harper onto his boat, and that the duty of care included warning Harper not to dive because he knew that the water was "dangerously shallow." * The sole issue on appeal is whether a boat owner who is a social host owes a duty of care to warn a guest on the boat that the water is too shallow for diving.

Harper alleges that Herman owed him a duty to warn of the shallowness of the water because he was an inexperienced swimmer and diver, whereas Herman was a veteran boater. Under those circumstances, Harper argues, Herman should have realized that Harper needed his protection.

We have previously stated that an affirmative duty to act only arises when a special relationship exists between the parties. "The fact that an actor realizes or should realize that action on his part is necessary for another's aid or protection does not of itself impose upon him a duty to take such action . . . unless a special relationship exists . . . between the actor and the other which gives the other the right to protection." Delgado v. Lohmar, 289 N.W.2d 479, 483 (Minn.1979). * Accepting, *arguendo*, that Herman should have realized that Harper needed protection, Harper must still prove that a special relationship existed between them that placed an affirmative duty to act on the part of Herman.

Harper argues that a special relationship requiring Herman to act for his protection was created when Herman, as a social host, allowed an inexperienced diver on his boat. Generally, a special relationship giving rise to a duty to warn is only found on the part of common carriers, innkeepers, possessors of land who hold it open to the public, and persons who have custody of another person under circumstances in which that other person is deprived of normal opportunities of self-protection. Restatement (Second) of Torts § 314A (1965). Under this rule, a special relationship could be found to exist between the parties only if Herman had custody of Harper under circumstances in which Harper was deprived of normal opportunities to protect himself.[2] These elements are not present here.

---

[2] Prosser describes a circumstance in which one party would be liable in negligence because another party was deprived of normal opportunities for self-protection as occurring when

> the plaintiff is typically in some respect particularly vulnerable and dependent upon the defendant who, correspondingly, holds considerable power over the plaintiff's welfare. In addition, such relations have often involved some existing or potential economic advantage to the defendant. Fairness in such cases thus may require the defendant to use his power to help the plaintiff, based upon the plaintiff's expectation of protection, which itself may be based upon the defendant's expectation of financial gain.

W. Page Keeton *et al.*, Prosser and Keeton on the Laws of Torts § 56 (5th ed. 1984).

The record before this court does not establish that Harper was either particularly vulnerable or that he lacked the ability to protect himself. Further, the record does not establish that Herman held considerable power over Harper's welfare, or that Herman was receiving a financial gain by hosting Harper on his boat. Finally, there is nothing in the record which would suggest that Harper expected any protection from Herman; indeed, no such allegation has been made.

The court of appeals found that Herman owed Harper a duty to warn him of the shallowness of the water because Herman knew that it was "dangerously shallow." We have previously stated that "[a]ctual knowledge of a dangerous condition tends to impose a special duty to do something about that condition." Andrade v. Ellefson, 391 N.W.2d 836, 841 (Minn.1986) (holding that county was not immune to charge of improper supervision of day care center where children were abused when county knew about overcrowding at the center). However, superior knowledge of a dangerous condition by itself, in the absence of a duty to provide protection, is insufficient to establish liability in negligence. Thus, Herman's knowledge that the water was "dangerously shallow" without more does not create liability. Andrade involved a group of plaintiffs who had little opportunity to protect themselves, children in day care, and a defendant to whom the plaintiffs looked for protection. In this case, Harper was not deprived of opportunities to protect himself, and Herman was not expected to provide protection.

"There are many dangers, such as those of fire and water, . . . which under ordinary conditions may reasonably be expected to be fully understood and appreciated by any child. . . ." Restatement (Second) of Torts § 339 cmt. j (1965). If a child is expected to understand the inherent dangers of water, so should a 20-year-old adult. Harper had no reasonable expectation to look to Herman for protection, and we hold that Herman had no duty to warn Harper that the water was shallow.

Reversed and judgment in favor of defendant reinstated.

NOTES

1. *Potential Liability for Failure to Rescue Social Guest.* Compare Hutchinson v. Dickie, 162 F.2d 103 (6th Cir.1947) (admiralty case). Appellant, owner of a pleasure cabin cruiser, was sued by the wife of the decedent after the decedent fell overboard. She alleged that the appellant was negligent in failing to make a reasonable effort to rescue decedent. The court rejected appellant's argument that he owed no duty to the decedent:

> We take no stock in appellant's contention that he was under no legal obligation to rescue decedent. Dickie was an invited guest upon appellant's cruiser. When appellant heard the cry "Man Overboard" (an undisputed and relevant fact not referred to either in the findings or in the court's opinion) we think it was his duty to use reasonable care to rescue him. This was certainly a moral duty, universally recognized and acted upon. Dickie was drowning and appellant's cruiser was the only instrumentality by which he might be rescued. * * *

In Carey v. Davis, 190 Iowa 720, 180 N.W. 889, 891 (1921), an Iowa case, the court in quoting from Adams v. Chicago G. W. R. Co., 156 Iowa 31, 135 N.W. 21 (1912), said: " * * * whenever one person is by circumstances placed in such a position with regard to another that everyone of ordinary sense * * * would at once recognize that if he did not use ordinary care and skill in his conduct with regard to those circumstances, he would cause danger of injury to the person or property of the other, a duty arises * * * to avoid such danger." * * *

To ask of appellant anything less than ordinary care under the circumstances is so shocking to humanitarian considerations and the commonly accepted code of social conduct that the courts in similar situations have had no difficulty in pronouncing it to be a legal obligation.

2. *Duty to Provide Medical Assistance to Social Guest.* In what circumstances, if any, is one obliged to provide medical assistance to a social guest? In Tiedeman v. Morgan, 435 N.W.2d 86 (Minn.App.1989), the seventeen-year-old plaintiff with a history of heart problems was visiting a fifteen-year-old girl he was dating when he became ill. The girl called "911" but her father subsequently cancelled the call when the plaintiff indicated he was alright. Shortly thereafter, the plaintiff stopped breathing and despite subsequent medical treatment, he was left with severe and permanent brain damage. The plaintiff sued the members of the family for negligence, and the Minnesota Court of Appeals reversed a trial court summary judgment in favor of defendants. The court acknowledged that there was "common law duty of care for those who know or should know of the needs of one in circumstances under their control." Compare Stockberger v. United States, *supra* pages 441–444.

3. *Duty to Protect a Minor.* In Lenoci v. Leonard, 189 Vt. 641, 21 A.3d 694 (2011), the eighteen-year-old defendant, Kayla, accompanied her fifteen-year-old friend, Alex, to a party. Each of the girls lied to her parents about where they were going. At the party, Kayla observed Alex drinking, and was concerned that some young man at the party might "take advantage" of Alex. In fact, during the night, Alex had sex with the nineteen-year-old man who hosted the party. Kayla was aware that they "were intimate but did not know they had intercourse." Alex felt extremely guilty and confessed in a voicemail message to her boyfriend. Two days later, she committed suicide. Alex's parents sued Kayla, alleging that she owed a duty to Alex to prevent the intercourse because "she should have realized she had exposed Alex to an unreasonably risky situation by bringing her to the apartment." The Vermont Supreme Court found that the defendant owed no duty to her now-deceased friend:

> Plaintiff essentially advocates that we find a duty simply because one girl was eighteen and the other was fifteen. The law does not impose such a duty in this situation—a duty for an eighteen-year-old to protect a high school friend who has not reached the age of majority from the consequences of the younger person's independent behavior or to control such behavior. See Restatement (Second) of Torts § 314 ("The fact that the actor realizes or should realize that action on his part is necessary for another's aid or protection does not of itself impose upon him a duty to take such action."). The consequences to the community should such a duty be found would be considerable, transforming every high school friendship at the moment one friend turns eighteen into an in loco parentis relationship. Plaintiff has made

no convincing argument that Kayla was somehow in a position to control Alex's behavior that night by virtue of the less-than-three-year difference in their ages.

Id. at 643.

With *Lenoci,* compare Bjerke v. Johnson, 742 N.W.2d 660, 667 (Minn.2007). The plaintiff, while she was between the ages of 14 and 18, repeatedly visited and sometimes stayed for a couple of weeks at a time at a horse farm owned by the defendant, taking riding lessons and performing farm chores. Later, she lived on the farm for a period of over a year. The defendant's live-in boyfriend sexually abused the plaintiff by developing a long-term sexual relationship with her. The Minnesota Supreme Court held that the defendant owed a duty of care to the plaintiff:

> [A]t least during the times that Bjerke resided full-time at the farm during and after the summer of 1998, Bjerke lacked "normal opportunities for self-protection" because she was a minor child, living apart from her parents and under the daily care and supervision of Johnson. * * * Because Johnson had custody over Bjerke and Bjerke, who, both by virtue of her age and her specific circumstances, lacked normal opportunities for self-protection, we conclude as a matter of law that a special relationship existed from and after the summer of 1998. * * *

> Although we agree with Bjerke that a duty has been shown, we hasten to add that this does not mean that Johnson committed any wrongdoing by taking Bjerke into her custody. Johnson's assumption of the care and custody of Bjerke was generous and admirable. We only conclude that the assumption, however well-meaning, brought with it legal obligations that Johnson would not have otherwise had, obligations sufficient to prevent summary judgment on the issue of a special relationship. * * *

What facts, if any, distinguish *Lenoci* from *Bjerke*?

4. *Duty of Parents to Third Parties.* If a parent knows that his or her child has a propensity for a particular type of dangerous activity likely to harm others, must the parent take reasonable steps to guard against the propensity? See Caldwell v. Zaher, 344 Mass. 590, 183 N.E.2d 706 (1962); Linder v. Bidner, 50 Misc.2d 320, 270 N.Y.S.2d 427 (Sup.Ct. Special Term 1966).

5. *Liability of Business Owner for Failure to Warn Patrons of Risk of Harm by Third Party.* Must a business owner who is aware or should be aware of the risk caused by a third party be liable for failing either to warn a patron of the risk or to prevent the resulting harm? In Gould v. Taco Bell, 239 Kan. 564, 722 P.2d 511 (1986), the defendant was held liable for failing to warn a patron of the risk of assault by another patron when the assault was reasonably to be anticipated. Compare, however, Howe v. Stubbs, 570 A.2d 1203 (Me.1990), where the defendant was held not liable in "the circumstances of the present case" for failure to warn when a motorist's brakes failed on a highway hill adjacent to defendant's property, sending the automobile crashing into the front of the business and injuring plaintiff, despite three similar incidents during the preceding twenty-five years.

C. REQUISITE RELATIONSHIPS

Lamb v. Hopkins

Court of Appeals of Maryland, 1985.
303 Md. 236, 492 A.2d 1297.

■ COLE, JUDGE. * * * On August 8, 1975, Russell J. Newcomer, Jr., was convicted in the Circuit Court for Frederick County of armed robbery and received a five year sentence, four and one-half years of which the court suspended. After Newcomer served six months of this sentence, the court placed him on supervised probation for the remainder of his term (until August 7, 1980). The probation order required Newcomer to obey all laws, not to possess any firearms, and to participate in an alcohol treatment program. * * * [Subsequently, Newcomer was convicted of driving-while-intoxicated-type offenses on two separate occasions.] In response, the State's Division of Parole and Probation (Division) opened Newcomer's file on a "non-active" supervision basis. Furthermore, the field agents (i.e., probation officers) assigned to supervise Newcomer * failed to report these two District Court convictions to the Circuit Court for Frederick County. Thereafter, in September 1979, Newcomer was convicted by the District Court sitting in Frederick County of discharging a firearm and of driving while his license was suspended. These probation violations were similarly not reported to the Circuit Court for Frederick County, nor were they reported to the sentencing judge of the District Court who placed Newcomer on a suspended sentence with supervised probation for one year.

On November 10, 1979, Newcomer, again driving while under the influence of alcohol, collided with a vehicle operated by Cynthia Lou Lamb. This collision rendered the Lambs' then five-month-old daughter, Laura, a quadriplegic.

* * * Alan C. Lamb and Cynthia Lou Lamb, as parents and natural guardians of Laura, filed suit against * * * the director and various employees of the Division, alleging that at the time of the collision Newcomer was on supervised probation under a suspended sentence, and that these defendants proximately caused the minor plaintiff's injuries by failing to petition the sentencing court to incarcerate Newcomer for numerous probation violations. The Division defendants filed a demurrer, alleging that as public officials they were immune from liability, and further that under the amended declaration they neither owed a duty to plaintiffs nor proximately caused the collision. * * * 3 [T]he trial court sustained the demurrer without leave to amend by order dated May 10, 1983, on the ground that the defendants owed no duty to the plaintiffs. * * *

Three basic elements are necessary to state a cause of action in negligence. First, the defendant must be under a duty to protect the plaintiff from injury. * * * Appellants basically contend that an individual who controls a person known by him to be dangerous owes a

---

3 Two months earlier, on January 11, 1983, the plaintiffs settled and satisfied the case as to Newcomer, and filed a joint tortfeasor release. As a result, only the Lambs and the Division defendants remained party to the suit after that date.

duty to exercise due care to those who may be foreseeably harmed by the failure to exercise this level of care, regardless of whether the foreseeably harmed person is readily identifiable. More specifically, the Lambs argue that the probation officers owed them a duty to exercise due care in controlling Newcomer, known by the probation officers to be dangerous. As a result, the Lambs maintain that the trial court erred in sustaining the demurrer to their amended declaration. The appellees, however, counter that they owed no duty of care to the Lambs because the appellees had neither the right nor the ability to control Newcomer's conduct. Absent a special relationship not present here, appellees contend that no basis exists for imposing liability on them for Newcomer's tortious acts. * * *

Section 319 [of the Restatement (Second) of Torts (1965)], entitled "Duty of Those in Charge of Person Having Dangerous Propensities," provides in its entirety: "One who takes charge of a third person whom he knows or should know to be likely to cause bodily harm to others if not controlled is under a duty to exercise reasonable care to control the third person to prevent him from doing such harm." The operative words of this section, such as "takes charge" and "control," are obviously vague, and the Restatement makes no formal attempt to define them. The comment to § 319, however, indicates that the rule stated in that section applies to two situations. First, § 319 applies to those situations where the actor has charge of one or more of a class of persons to whom the tendency to act injuriously is normal. Second, § 319 applies to those situations where the actor has charge of a third person who does not belong to such a class but who has a peculiar tendency so to act of which the actor from personal experience or otherwise knows or should know. Illustrations appended to § 319, which concern the negligent release of an infectious patient from a private hospital for contagious diseases and the escape of a homicidal maniac patient through the negligence of guards employed by a private sanitarium for the insane, provide further guidance regarding the scope of § 319. * * * These illustrations suggest * * * that § 319 has peculiar application to custodial situations. * * *

The Lambs seek to hold the probation officers liable for not reporting the probationer's misconduct to the appropriate courts. They argue that had these officers reported this misconduct to the courts the probationer would not have been in a position to commit the tortious acts because he would have been incarcerated. Initially, we note that the probation officers did not meet the threshold requirement of taking charge of the probationer within the meaning of § 319. The comments and illustrations accompanying § 319 suggest that an actor typically takes charge of a third person by placing him in some form of custody. The more traditional and obvious examples include a correctional institution incarcerating a dangerous criminal, * or a mental institution confining a dangerous patient. * The probationer in this case, of course, was not incarcerated in a correctional institution or confined in a mental hospital, nor had he been negligently released from these facilities, at the time of the 1979 automobile accident. * * * The probationer was essentially free to conduct his day-to-day affairs, and was responsible for reporting certain activities to his probation officers as they arose or as they were scheduled. In addition, unlike in the more typical custodial situations, the officers were evidently not responsible for supervising the probationer on a daily basis. Therefore, because there was no custodial relationship involved in this case, we conclude that the officers did not take charge of the probationer. * * *

The Lambs, asserting that they do not place exclusive reliance upon § 319, contend that [the court orders] impose a duty upon the probation officers * * *

By their nature, they simply impose a duty upon the probation officers to notify the court of any probation violations. * * * [T]he duty the probation officer owes to the court is not extended to the general public, i.e., the Lambs. * * *

Taggart v. State

Supreme Court of Washington, 1992.
118 Wash.2d 195, 822 P.2d 243.

■ CALLOW, J. Shane Sandau and Victoria Taggart were injured by parolees in separate assaults. * * *

Taggart v. State

Parolee Louie Brock assaulted Taggart on April 16, 1985. Brock had an extensive juvenile and adult criminal history. At the age of 15 he was referred to the juvenile court on charges of first degree burglary, having been initially charged with attempted rape. While still a juvenile, Brock was also charged with assault and another attempted rape. Brock's first conviction as an adult was in 1970, at the age of 18, for assault with intent to commit rape. The victim was a 70-year-old woman. At that time, Brock was diagnosed as exhibiting sexual deviation, episodic excessive drinking, antisocial personality, and passive aggressive personality. Brock was released from prison on parole in 1974, only to be arrested 2 months later for the assault and attempted rape of a 75-year-old woman. Both the 1970 and the 1974 attempted rapes involved alcohol abuse. In 1981, Brock was again paroled, and again was arrested within a year, this time for stealing a car, driving while intoxicated, and resisting arrest. At that time Brock was evaluated as being highly susceptible to alcohol abuse, and was reported to have missed counseling appointments and to have no interest or motivation for counseling.

* * * [T]he Board decided to release Brock on parole, effective September 24 [1984]. Upon his release, Brock entered a halfway house for recently released prisoners. He left the halfway house after 4 months. Richardson, who became Brock's parole supervisor, did not require that he obtain further counseling after that. At no time did Richardson require that Brock submit to urinalysis. Her monitoring of Brock consisted of seeing him weekly in her office. Richardson never contacted Brock's employers or girl friend about Brock. If she had, she probably would have learned that Brock was drinking regularly. Brock's assault on Taggart occurred in April 1985, after he had been on parole approximately 7 months. * * *

Sandau v. State

Parolee Keith Geyman repeatedly raped Shane Sandau on September 21, 1984. Sandau was 9 years old at the time. Like Brock, Geyman had an extensive juvenile and adult criminal history. * * *

[Prior to the rape, Geyman's parole officer had recommended that his parole be suspended after repeated violations of parole conditions, but the arrest warrant for the parole violation was never entered into the state's computer. After another series of parole violations came to the attention of the state, a warrant was issued but not acted upon. Shortly thereafter, defendant raped the child.] * * *

The State argues that it owed no duty to Taggart or Sandau as opposed to the general public, and that therefore the public duty doctrine bars their claims based upon negligent parole supervision. We hold that the State has a duty to take reasonable precautions to protect against reasonably foreseeable dangers posed by the dangerous propensities of parolees, and that if injury to Taggart and Sandau was a reasonably foreseeable consequence of paroling Brock and Geyman, then this duty extended to Taggart and Sandau. We therefore reverse and remand the trial courts' dismissals of Taggart's and Sandau's negligent supervision claims. * * *

The public duty doctrine provides that "no liability may be imposed for a public official's negligent conduct unless it is shown that 'the duty breached was owed to the injured person as an individual and was not merely the breach of an obligation owed to the public in general (*i.e.*, a duty to all is a duty to no one).'" Taylor v. Stevens Cy., 111 Wash.2d 159, 163, 759 P.2d 447 (1988). * Numerous exceptions to the doctrine are recognized. * * * a

[Restatement (Second) of Torts §] 319 [provides]: "One who takes charge of a third person whom he knows or should know to be likely to cause bodily harm to others if not controlled is under a duty to exercise reasonable care to control the third person to prevent him from doing such harm." Restatement (Second) of Torts § 319 (1965) (hereinafter § 319). Various features of the relationship between parole officer and parolee are relevant to the question whether parole officers have "taken charge" of the parolees they supervise. Parole officers have the statutory authority under Wash. Rev. Code § 72.04A.080 to supervise parolees. The State can regulate a parolee's movements within the state, require the parolee to report to a parole officer, impose special conditions such as refraining from using alcohol or undergoing drug rehabilitation or psychiatric treatment, and order the parolee not to possess firearms. The parole officer is the person through whom the State ensures that the parolee obeys the terms of his or her parole. Additionally, parole officers are, or should be, aware of their parolees'

---

a   [Eds.' note] The opinion cites Bailey v. Town of Forks, 108 Wash.2d 262, 268, 737 P.2d 1257, 1260 (1987), which identifies the following exceptions to the public duty doctrine:

(1) when the terms of a legislative enactment evidence an intent to identify and protect a particular and circumscribed class of persons (legislative intent), *

(2) where governmental agents responsible for enforcing statutory requirements possess actual knowledge of a statutory violation, fail to take corrective action despite a statutory duty to do so, and the plaintiff is within the class the statute intended to protect (failure to enforce), *

(3) when governmental agents fail to exercise reasonable care after assuming a duty to warn or come to the aid of a particular plaintiff (rescue doctrine), * [and]

(4) where a relationship exists between the governmental agent and any reasonably foreseeable plaintiff, setting the injured plaintiff off from the general public and the plaintiff relies on explicit assurances given by the agent or assurances inherent in a duty vested in a governmental entity (special relationship).

criminal histories, and monitor, or should monitor, their parolees' progress during parole. Because of these factors, we hold that parole officers have "taken charge" of the parolees they supervise for purposes of § 319. When a parolee's criminal history and progress during parole show that the parolee is likely to cause bodily harm to others if not controlled, the parole officer is under a duty to exercise reasonable care to control the parolee and to prevent him or her from doing such harm. * * *

The State argues that nothing less than a full custodial relationship justifies holding parole officers to a duty to protect against parolees. Some courts have adopted such a view, holding that parole officers do not have sufficient control over parolees as to justify imposing on the officers a duty to control the parolees. * Lamb v. Hopkins, 303 Md. 236, 492 A.2d 1297 (1985). * * * We reject this approach and hold that a parole officer takes charge of the parolees he or she supervises despite the lack of a custodial or continuous relationship. * * *

We hold that a parole officer may "take charge" of a parolee, thereby assuming the duty to protect against reasonably foreseeable dangers, despite the absence of a custodial relationship and without exercising the "continuing hourly or daily dominance and dominion" over that parolee. * * * We conclude that parole officers have a duty to protect others from reasonably foreseeable dangers engendered by parolees' dangerous propensities. We emphasize, however, that we are not unmindful of the extremely difficult supervisory tasks that parole officers must perform. Nor in holding that parole officers "take charge" of parolees do we exaggerate the degree of control they exercise over parolees. * * *

In the present case, the parole officers had a duty to take reasonable precautions to protect anyone foreseeably endangered by Brock's and Geyman's dangerous propensities. To establish that this duty extends to them, Taggart and Sandau must show that they were foreseeably endangered. * * * Here, the questions of foreseeability were not so one-sided that they should have been decided by the trial courts. Reasonable juries could have found that Taggart's and Sandau's injuries were foreseeable. Brock had a history of alcoholism and violent attacks against women, and a poor prognosis for recovery from his mental illness. In light of these facts, a jury might conclude that it was reasonably foreseeable that if Brock were not supervised closely he would commit another similar crime. The fact that Taggart herself was not the foreseeable victim of Brock's criminal tendencies does not establish as a matter of law that her injury was not foreseeable. Similarly, Geyman had an extensive criminal history that included violent assaults. He violated the conditions of his parole by quitting his job, changing his address without notifying his parole officer, failing to report to his parole officer, and absconding from parole. Geyman's parole officer knew of these violations, and knew as well that Geyman was reportedly drinking alcohol, which increased the risk of violent behavior, and beating Hazel [Geyman's girlfriend, Sandau's mother] and her children. A jury might conclude that it was reasonably foreseeable that unless Geyman were arrested for violating parole, he would commit further violence against Hazel or her children, including

Sandau. The fact that the violence took the form of raping Sandau, when Geyman's criminal history did not include rape, does not show that injury to Sandau was not foreseeable. Violence against Sandau may have been foreseeable, even though the form of that violence may not have been.

To the extent that the trial courts in these cases dismissed the actions because of the absence of any duty, the courts decided the questions whether Taggart's and Sandau's injuries were foreseeable. In this the trial courts erred. Juries could have reasonably concluded that the duty of Brock's and Geyman's parole officers to protect others foreseeably endangered by Brock and Geyman extended to Taggart and Sandau. * * *

NOTES

1. *Public Duty Doctrine.* The "public duty doctrine" emerged in the decades following the full or partial abrogation of governmental tort immunity, see *infra* pages 521–23, as a means of limiting the liability of states and municipalities. A number of jurisdictions, including Wisconsin, have rejected the "public duty" limitation on liability and hold the government liable on general negligence principles whenever an injury to the plaintiff was foreseeable, even in the absence of a "special" relationship.

In Coffey v. Milwaukee, 74 Wis.2d 526, 247 N.W.2d 132 (1976), a building occupant whose property had been destroyed by fire sued the City of Milwaukee and alleged that the City was "negligent in that certain standpipes provided to furnish the necessary water to fight the fire on the floor where Coffey's offices were located were defective and had not been properly inspected." The City contended that any duties "imposed on the building inspector * * * with respect to fire safety inspections are clearly duties owed to the public in general and not to the specific plaintiff in this case" and that "there can be no liability on the part of a municipality for the breach of such a 'public duty.' " The Supreme Court of Wisconsin held that the argument that the city and its officials could avoid liability under the public duty doctrine was inconsistent with its precedents abolishing municipal immunity. As the court stated, "Any duty owed to the public generally is a duty owed to individual members of the public." The court acknowledged that considerations of public policy sometimes may preclude liability under the specific facts of a particular case. For other opinions rejecting the public duty doctrine, see, e.g., City of Kotzebue v. McLean, 702 P.2d 1309, 1313–14 (Alaska 1985); Ryan v. State, 134 Ariz. 308, 656 P.2d 597 (1982).

2. *Liability of Police Arising from a Special Relationship.* In some circumstances courts will find that a "special relationship" exists between an injured citizen and the police, which justifies the imposition of civil liability. For example, in Sorichetti v. City of New York, 65 N.Y.2d 461, 492 N.Y.S.2d 591, 482 N.E.2d 70 (1985), the defendant, the New York City Police Department, knew of the long history of violence between the plaintiff and her husband. The husband drank excessively and was violent and abusive. The plaintiff had obtained a series of court protection orders and had recently filed for divorce. When the husband came to pick up plaintiff's daughter for visitation, he pointed at the plaintiff and said, "You, I'm going to kill you." The plaintiff went to the police immediately after this threat and again when her daughter was not returned to her on time. The police assured her that they would do something, and repeatedly told her to "wait a little longer." Eventually the child was found in a coma, having been attacked with a knife, a fork, and a screwdriver. On the basis of the protection orders, the police's knowledge of past violent behavior, the specific threats against the victim, and her forbearance and reliance on the police, the court found that a "special relationship" existed between the plaintiff and the defendant that justified liability.

CHAPTER 8

LIMITATIONS ON LIABILITY BASED ON TYPE OF HARM

This chapter considers those instances in which the type of damages sought by the plaintiff brings with it more restrictive rules governing liability. Plaintiffs asserting negligence claims most often cannot recover for psychic or purely commercial harms in the absence of proof of damages for personal injuries or property damages, but there are exceptions. Such denials of recovery for emotional distress or economic loss alone are sometimes categorized as "no duty" or "limited duty" cases. These limitations on liability based on the type of harm sustained by the plaintiff can be regarded as cousins of other limited liability rules, such as those discussed in Chapter 7 that cover liability for failure to rescue or prevent harm to others. In addition, as considered in Chapter 10, the rules that traditionally governed the liability of possessors of land provided for more limited liability than that resulting from application of a general negligence standard.

Part A (*infra* pages 477–490), considers rules and policies governing recovery for psychic harm alone. Part B (*infra* pages 490–495), covers whether there should be recovery for loss of companionship as a result of a non-fatal injury to a family member. In Part C (*infra* pages 495–500), we turn to another type of harm often handled under the rubric of "no duty"—recovery for a child's "wrongful life" or a parent's "wrongful birth" resulting from medical negligence. Finally, Part D (*infra* pages 500–505), covers the law governing whether there can be recovery for purely economic or commercial loss in the absence of personal injury or property damage.

A. RECOVERY FOR PSYCHIC HARM IN THE ABSENCE OF PHYSICAL INJURY (NEGLIGENT INFLICTION OF EMOTIONAL DISTRESS)

Spade v. Lynn & Boston Railroad Co.

Supreme Judicial Court of Massachusetts, 1897.
168 Mass. 285, 47 N.E. 88.

* * * The plaintiff testified in substance that two men somewhat intoxicated were allowed, during a part of the trip from Boston to Chelsea, to stand near her in the car, one of them in a position where he was leaning or lurching toward her in such a way that she was obliged to move to avoid him; that a controversy occurred between one of the intoxicated persons and the conductor about the payment of a fare, and that the conductor said to the intoxicated person, after some other conversation, that if he did not keep quiet he would throw him off the car, even if he broke his head; that as she neared the place where she

was to leave the car, "the first thing I saw was the conductor . . . grab this man by the collar; the next thing I saw was . . . another man from the other end of the car, whom I did not know, come down; but the other man, as he pulled him lurched over on me; then it seemed as though I turned to solid ice. My breath was cut right off. I could not have spoken; I tried to speak, but I chilled so I kept growing stiffer and stiffer, until I did not know, I do not know when they got me off the car." She further stated that nothing had occurred of any sort or description that gave any suggestion of a warning that the conductor was going to rush at the drunken man at this time; that he did it "just as quick as a man could jump"; and that the intoxicated person standing directly in front of her "lurched over so it kind of pushed me back against the car."

The plaintiff further testified:

Q. Your body was not injured in any way by contact with this man?

A. Oh, no, I was not injured. There were not any marks on me, anything like that.

Q. You suffered no pain from this man touching you?

A. No, not any injury from that.

Q. What was the cause of this man's touching you, the one that lurched forward?

A. When the conductor jumped and grabbed this man that I told about, on the opposite side of the car, that made a commotion, and as he twitched him it pushed this other man over on to me.

The jury returned a verdict for the plaintiff; and the defendant alleged exceptions. * * *

■ ALLEN, J. This case presents a question * * * [of] [w]hether, in an action to recover damages for an injury sustained through the negligence of another, there can be a recovery for a bodily injury caused by mere fright and mental disturbance. The jury were instructed that a person cannot recover for mere fright, fear, or mental distress occasioned by the negligence of another, which does not result in bodily injury, but that, when the fright or fear or nervous shock produces a bodily injury, there may be a recovery for that bodily injury, and for all the pain, mental or otherwise, which may arise out of that bodily injury. * * *

The case calls for a consideration of the real ground upon which the liability or nonliability of a defendant guilty of negligence in a case like the present depends. The exemption from liability for mere fright, terror, alarm, or anxiety does not rest on the assumption that these do not constitute an actual injury. They do in fact deprive one of enjoyment and of comfort, cause real suffering, and to a greater or less extent disqualify one for the time being from doing the duties of life. If these results flow from a wrongful or negligent act, a recovery therefor cannot be denied on the ground that the injury is fanciful and not real. Nor can it be maintained that these results may not be the direct and immediate consequence of the negligence. Danger excites alarm. Few people are wholly insensible to the emotions caused by imminent danger, though some are less affected than others.

It must also be admitted that a timid or sensitive person may suffer not only in mind, but also in body, from such a cause. Great emotion may, and sometimes does, produce physical effects. The action of the heart, the circulation of the blood, the temperature of the body, as well as the nerves and the appetite, may well be affected. A physical injury may be directly traceable to fright, and so may be caused by it. We cannot say, therefore, that such consequences may not flow proximately from unintentional negligence; and if compensation in damages may be recovered for a physical injury so caused, it is hard on principle to say why there should not also be a recovery for the mere mental suffering when not accompanied by any perceptible physical effects.

It would seem therefore that the real reason for refusing damages sustained from mere fright must be something different, and it probably rests on the ground that in practice it is impossible satisfactorily to administer any other rule. The law must be administered in the courts according to general rules. * * * A new rule cannot be made for each case, and there must therefore be a certain generality in rules of law, which in particular cases may fail to meet what would be desirable if the single case were alone to be considered.

Rules of law respecting the recovery of damages are framed with reference to the just rights of both parties,—not merely what it might be right for an injured person to receive, to afford just compensation for his injury, but also what it is just to compel the other party to pay. One cannot always look to others to make compensation for injuries received. Many accidents occur, the consequences of which the sufferer must bear alone. And, in determining the rules of law by which the right to recover compensation for unintended injury from others is to be governed, regard must chiefly be paid to such conditions as are usually found to exist. * * * [T]he general conduct of business and of the ordinary affairs of life must be done on the assumption that persons who are liable to be affected thereby are not peculiarly sensitive, and are of ordinary physical and mental strength. * * * [A]s a general rule a carrier of passengers is not bound to anticipate or to guard against an injurious result which would only happen to a person of peculiar sensitiveness. * * * One may be held bound to anticipate and guard against the probable consequences to ordinary people, but to carry the rule of damages further imposes an undue measure of responsibility upon those who are guilty only of unintentional negligence. The general rule limiting damages in such a case to the natural and probable consequences of the acts done is of wide application, and has often been expressed and applied. * * *

We remain satisfied with the rule that there can be no recovery for fright, terror, alarm, anxiety, or distress of mind, if these are unaccompanied by some physical injury; and, if this rule is to stand, we think it should also be held that there can be no recovery for such physical injuries as may be caused solely by such mental disturbance, where there is no injury to the person from without. The logical vindication of this rule is that it is unreasonable to hold persons who are merely negligent bound to anticipate and guard against fright and the consequences of fright; and this would open a wide door for unjust claims, which could not successfully be met. * * *

It is hardly necessary to add that this decision does not reach those classes of actions where an intention to cause mental distress or to hurt the feelings is shown, or is reasonably to be inferred, as, for example in cases of seduction, slander, malicious prosecution, or arrest, and some others. Nor do we include cases of acts done with gross carelessness or recklessness, showing utter indifference to such consequences, when they must have been in the actor's mind. * In the present case no such considerations entered into the rulings or were presented by the facts. The entry therefore must be: Exceptions sustained.

NOTES

1. *Requirement of Physical Impact, Injury, or Manifestation. Spade* came to be understood as a requirement that there be something in the way of physical "impact" before liability would be recognized for psychic harm ("emotional" or "mental" disturbance or "distress") in the absence of an initial physical injury. There has, however, never been a requirement of physical contact between the defendant (or her vehicle) and the plaintiff (or her vehicle), although many laypersons—and even a few claims adjusters—have harbored the notion that there is some such requirement for liability. Impact from "an external force" is sometimes still required, e.g., Gilliam v. Stewart, 291 So.2d 593, 594–95 (Fla.1974). But see strong dissent at 291 So.2d at 596.

Recall that if there has been an initial physical injury, recovery for consequent mental distress has traditionally been allowed as an element of damages for "pain and suffering." In addition, notice of a foreseeable victim's special susceptibility to harm from shock or the like has apparently influenced the imposition of liability for negligently inflicted shock in the absence of impact. See, e.g., Price v. Yellow Pine Paper Mill Co., 240 S.W. 588, 594 (Tex.Civ.App.1922) (victim suffered miscarriage; court characterized defendant's conduct as "willful," because of his prior notice of her pregnancy).

In some jurisdictions, compensation for psychic injury is denied unless it is "manifested" or accompanied by physical injury, e.g., Piorkowski v. Liberty Mut. Ins. Co., 68 Wis.2d 455, 464, 228 N.W.2d 695, 700–01 (1975). Some courts that recite a similar requirement construe it generously. E.g., Quill v. Trans World Airlines, Inc., 361 N.W.2d 438, 443–44 (Minn.App.1985) (in light of the nature of the experience where commercial airliner suddenly plunged downward in tailspin for 34,000 feet, court deemed "sweaty hands, elevated blood pressure and other signs of distress" sufficient evidence to warrant compensation under requirement of "physical injury or symptom").

See also Restatement (Second) of Torts § 436A cmt. c (1965): "[L]ong continued mental disturbance, as for example in the case of repeated hysterical attacks, or mental aberration, may be classified by the courts as illness, notwithstanding their mental character" (and thereby equivalent to "bodily harm"); Vance v. Vance, 286 Md. 490, 500–01, 502–03, 408 A.2d 728, 733–35 (1979) ("In the context of [a requirement for 'physical injury'] * * *, the term 'physical' is not used in its ordinary dictionary sense. * Instead it is used to represent that the injury for which recovery is sought is capable of objective determination"). The Restatement (Third) of Torts: Liability for Physical and Emotional Harm § 4 comment *d* (2010) explicitly rejects the "Second Restatement['s] * * * [approach] that some serious,

long-term conditions—such as nausea, headaches, and hysterical attacks—
that exist at the margin between bodily harm and emotional harm
constituted physical illness, thereby permitting recovery for both the bodily
harm and the emotional harm. That approach has the unfortunate effect of
diluting the definition of bodily harm. By explicitly providing for claims for
negligently inflicted emotional harm * * *, this Restatement does not adopt
that approach and indeed rejects it."

2. *Negligence in Matters Relating to the Handling of Death.* The common
law carved out an exception to the general rule—that the plaintiff could not
recover damages for mental distress resulting from negligence in the
absence of physical impact—for cases involving certain aspects of the
handling of death. Recovery has been allowed, e.g., in the case of a
negligent delivery of a notice that someone had died, Johnson v. State, 37
N.Y.2d 378, 383, 372 N.Y.S.2d 638, 643, 334 N.E.2d 590, 592 (1975); and
when a corpse was negligently mishandled, City of Gladewater v. Pike, 727
S.W.2d 514, 518 (Tex.1987) (negligent misplacement of body). Why these
exceptions?

Steinhauser v. Hertz Corporation

United States Court of Appeals, Second Circuit, 1970.
421 F.2d 1169.

■ FRIENDLY, CIRCUIT JUDGE. On September 4, 1964, plaintiff Cynthia
Steinhauser, a New Jersey citizen then 14 years old, her mother and
father were driving south through Essex County, N. Y. A northbound
car, owned by defendant Hertz Corporation, * * * crossed over a double
yellow line in the highway into the southbound lane and struck the
Steinhauser car heavily on the left side. The occupants did not suffer
any bodily injuries.

The plaintiffs' evidence was that within a few minutes after the
accident Cynthia began to behave in an unusual way. Her parents
observed her to be "glassy-eyed," "upset," "highly agitated," "nervous"
and "disturbed." When Ponzini came toward the Steinhauser car, she
jumped up and down and made menacing gestures until restrained by
her father. On the way home she complained of a headache and became
uncommunicative. In the following days things went steadily worse.
Cynthia thought that she was being attacked and that knives, guns and
bullets were coming through the windows. She was hostile toward her
parents and assaulted them; becoming depressed, she attempted
suicide.

* * * After observation and treatment in three hospitals, with a
final diagnosis of "schizophrenic reaction—acute—undifferentiated,"
she was released in December 1964 under the care of a psychiatrist, Dr.
Royce * * *. His diagnosis, both at the beginning and at the end, was of
a chronic schizophrenic reaction; he explained that by "chronic" he
meant that Cynthia was not brought to him because of a sudden onset
of symptoms. [Since that time, Cynthia has required psychiatric care.]
The evidence was that the need for this will continue, that
reinstitutionalization is likely, and that her prognosis is bad.

As the recital makes evident, the important issue was the existence
of a causal relationship between the rather slight accident and

Cynthia's undoubtedly serious ailment.[1] The testimony was uncontradicted that prior to the accident she had never displayed such exaggerated symptoms as thereafter. However, she had fallen from a horse about two years earlier and suffered what was diagnosed as a minor concussion; she was not hospitalized but missed a month of school. * * *

Dr. Royce testified that a person may have a predisposition to schizophrenia which, however, requires a "precipitating factor" to produce an outbreak. As a result of long observation he believed * * * that the accident was "the precipitating cause" of her serious mental illness. Under cross-examination he stated that prior to the accident Cynthia had a "prepsychotic" personality but might have been able to lead a normal life. * * * In contrast defendants' expert, Dr. Brock, while agreeing that "with a background of fertile soil" schizophrenia can be induced by emotional strain, was of the opinion * * * that Cynthia was already schizophrenic at the time of the accident.

* * * [T]he judge insisted that [plaintiff's counsel] choose between saying "that this plaintiff was perfectly normal and that she got this schizophrenia as a result of the accident" or admitting "that she had schizophrenia before this accident, and that this accident only aggravated a pre-existing condition. There is no in between position." Counsel remarked that there were "a host of other positions" between Cynthia's being "the most perfect child" or being schizophrenic before the accident, but the judge was not persuaded. * * *

* * * The testimony was that before the accident Cynthia was neither a "perfectly normal child" nor a schizophrenic, but a child with some degree of pathology which was activated into schizophrenia by an emotional trauma although it otherwise might not have blossomed. Whatever the medical soundness of this theory may or may not be, * * * plaintiffs were entitled to have it fairly weighed by the jury. * * *

We add a further word that may be of importance on a new trial. Although the fact that Cynthia had latent psychotic tendencies would not defeat recovery if the accident was a precipitating cause of schizophrenia, this may have a significant bearing on the amount of damages. The defendants are entitled to explore the probability that the child might have developed schizophrenia in any event. * * * It is no answer that exact prediction of Cynthia's future apart from the accident is difficult or even impossible. However taxing such a problem may be for men who have devoted their lives to psychiatry, it is one for which a jury is ideally suited.

Reversed for a new trial.

---

[1] The fact that no physical harm was suffered as a result of the accident does not affect plaintiff's right to recover. * * * New York allows such recovery if the "mental injury [is] marked by definite physical symptoms which are capable of clear medical proof," Ferrara v. Galluchio, 5 N.Y.2d 16, 176 N.Y.S.2d 996, 152 N.E.2d 249 (1958). *

Dillon v. Legg

Supreme Court of California, 1968.
68 Cal.2d 728, 69 Cal.Rptr. 72, 441 P.2d 912.

■ TOBRINER, JUSTICE. That the courts should allow recovery to a mother who suffers emotional trauma and physical injury from witnessing the infliction of death or injury to her child for which the tortfeasor is liable in negligence would appear to be a compelling proposition. * * * Nevertheless, past American decisions have barred the mother's recovery. Refusing the mother the right to take her case to the jury, these courts ground their position on an alleged absence of a required "duty" of due care of the tortfeasor to the mother. Duty, in turn, they state, must express public policy; the imposition of duty here would work disaster because it would invite fraudulent claims and it would involve the courts in the hopeless task of defining the extent of the tortfeasor's liability. In substance, they say, definition of liability being impossible, denial of liability is the only realistic alternative. * * *

In the instant case plaintiff's * first cause of action alleged that * * * defendant's negligent operation of his vehicle caused it to "collide with the deceased Erin Lee Dillon resulting in injuries to decedent which proximately resulted in her death." * Plaintiff, as the mother of the decedent, brought an action for compensation for the loss. Plaintiff's second cause of action alleged that she, Margery M. Dillon, "was in close proximity to the . . . collision and personally witnessed said collision." She further alleged that "because of the negligence of defendants . . . and as a proximate cause thereof plaintiff . . . sustained great emotional disturbance and shock and injury to her nervous system" which caused her great physical and mental pain and suffering. Plaintiff's third cause of action alleged that Cheryl Dillon, another infant daughter, was "in close proximity to the . . . collision and personally witnessed said collision." Because of the negligence, Cheryl Dillon "sustained great emotional disturbance and shock and injury to her nervous system," which caused her great physical and mental pain and suffering.

On December 22, 1965, defendant, after he had filed his answer, moved for judgment on the pleadings, contending that "No cause of action is stated in that allegation that plaintiff sustained emotional distress, fright or shock induced by apprehension of negligently caused danger or injury or the witnessing of negligently caused injury to a third person. * Even where a child, sister or spouse is the object of the plaintiff's apprehension no cause of action is stated * *unless the complaint alleges that the plaintiff suffered emotional distress, fright or shock as a result of fear for his own safety.*" * * * The trial court apparently sustained the motion for judgment on the pleadings on the second cause as to the mother because she was not within the zone of danger and denied that motion as to the third cause involving Cheryl because of the possibility that she was within such zone of danger or feared for her own safety. Thus we have before us a case that dramatically illustrates the difference in result flowing from the alleged requirement that a plaintiff cannot recover for emotional trauma in witnessing the death of a child or sister unless she also feared for her own safety because she was actually within the zone of physical impact.

The posture of this case differs from that of Amaya v. Home Ice, Fuel & Supply Co., 59 Cal.2d 295, 298, 29 Cal.Rptr. 33, 35, 379 P.2d 513, 515 (1963) which involved "fright or nervous shock (with consequent bodily illness) induced solely by . . . apprehension of negligently caused danger or injury to a third person" because the complaint here presents the claim of the emotionally traumatized mother, who admittedly was *not* within the zone of danger, as contrasted with that of the sister, who *may have been* within it. The case thus illustrates the fallacy of the rule that would deny recovery in the one situation and grant it in the other. In the first place, we can hardly justify relief to the sister for trauma which she suffered upon apprehension of the child's death and yet deny it to the mother merely because of a happenstance that the sister was some few yards closer to the accident. The instant case exposes the hopeless artificiality of the zone-of-danger rule. In the second place, to rest upon the zone-of-danger rule when we have rejected the impact rule becomes even less defensible. We have, indeed, held that impact is not necessary for recovery. Cook v. Maier, 33 Cal.App.2d 581, 584, 92 P.2d 434, 435–36 (1939). The zone-of-danger concept must, then, inevitably collapse because the only reason for the requirement of presence in that zone lies in the fact that one within it will fear the danger of *impact*. At the threshold, then, we point to the incongruity of the rules upon which any rejection of plaintiff's recovery must rest. * * *

We turn then to an analysis of the concept of duty, which, as we have stated, has furnished the ground for the rejection of such claims as the instant one. * * * The assertion that liability must * * * be denied because defendant bears no "duty" to plaintiff "begs the essential question—whether the plaintiff's interests are entitled to legal protection against the defendant's conduct. . . . It [duty] is a shorthand statement of a conclusion, rather than an aid to analysis in itself. . . . But it should be recognized that 'duty' is not sacrosanct in itself, but only an expression of the sum total of those considerations of policy which lead the law to say that the particular plaintiff is entitled to protection." W. Page Keeton, Prosser and Keeton on the Law of Torts 332–33 (3d ed. 1964). * * *

[T]he idea of court-imposed restrictions on recovery by means of the concept of "duty" contrasted dramatically with the preceding legal system of feudal society. * In the enclosed feudal society, the actor bore responsibility for any damage he inflicted without regard to whether he was at fault or owed a "duty" to the injured person. Thus, at that time, the defendant owed a duty to all the world to conduct himself without causing injury to his fellows. It may well be that the physical contraction of the feudal society imposed an imperative for maximum procurable safety and a corresponding absolute responsibility upon its members. The Industrial Revolution, which cracked the solidity of the feudal society and opened up wide and new areas of expansion, changed the legal concepts. Just as the new competitiveness in the economic sphere figuratively broke out of the walls of the feudal community, so it broke through the rule of strict liability. In the place of strict liability it introduced the theory that an action for negligence would lie only if the defendant breached a duty which he owed to plaintiff. * * * We have pointed out that this late 19th century concept of duty, as applied to the instant situation, has led the courts to deny liability. We have noted that this negation of duty emanates from the twin fears that courts will be flooded with an onslaught of (1) fraudulent and (2) indefinable claims. We shall point out why we think neither fear justified.

1. *This court in the past has rejected the argument that we must deny recovery upon a legitimate claim because other fraudulent ones may be urged.*

The denial of "duty" in the instant situation rests upon the prime hypothesis that allowance of such an action would lead to successful assertion of fraudulent claims. * The rationale apparently assumes that juries, confronted by irreconcilable expert medical testimony, will be unable to distinguish the deceitful from the bona fide. The argument concludes that only a *per se* rule denying the entire class of claims that potentially raises this administrative problem * can avoid this danger.

In the first instance, the argument proceeds from a doubtful factual assumption. Whatever the possibilities of fraudulent claims of physical injury by disinterested spectators of an accident, a question not in issue in this case, we certainly cannot doubt that a mother who sees her child killed will suffer physical injury from shock. "It seems sufficiently obvious that the shock of a mother at danger or harm to her child may be both a real and a serious injury." Prosser and Keeton on the Law of Torts 353 (3d ed. 1964). * * *

In the second instance, and more fundamentally, the possibility that fraudulent assertions may prompt recovery in isolated cases does not justify a wholesale rejection of the entire class of claims in which that potentiality arises. * * * Indubitably juries and trial courts, constantly called upon to distinguish the frivolous from the substantial and the fraudulent from the meritorious, reach some erroneous results. But such fallibility, inherent in the judicial process, offers no reason for substituting for the case-by-case resolution of causes an artificial and indefensible barrier. Courts not only compromise their basic responsibility to decide the merits of each case individually but destroy the public's confidence in them by using the broad broom of "administrative convenience" to sweep away a class of claims a number of which are admittedly meritorious. The mere assertion that fraud is possible, "a possibility [that] exists to some degree in all cases" Klein v. Klein, 58 Cal.2d 692, 695, 26 Cal.Rptr. 102, 104, 376 P.2d 70, 72 (1962), does not prove a present necessity to abandon the neutral principles of foreseeability, proximate cause and consequential injury that generally govern tort law.

Indeed, we doubt that the problem of the fraudulent claim is substantially more pronounced in the case of a mother claiming physical injury resulting from seeing her child killed than in other areas of tort law in which the right to recover damages is well established in California. For example, a plaintiff claiming that fear for his own safety resulted in physical injury makes out a well recognized case for recovery.[4] * Moreover, damages are allowed for "mental

---

[4] California's rule that plaintiff's fear for his own safety is compensable also presents a strong argument for the same rule as to fear for others; otherwise, some plaintiffs will falsely claim to have feared for themselves, and the honest parties unwilling to do so will be penalized. Cf. Fowler V. Harper & Fleming James, Jr., The Law of Torts § 16.15 (1956). Moreover, it is incongruous and somewhat revolting to sanction recovery for the mother if she

suffering," a type of injury, on the whole, less amenable to objective proof than the physical injury involved here; the mental injury can be in aggravation of, or "parasitic to," an established tort. * In fact, fear for another, even in the absence of resulting physical injury, can be part of these parasitic damages. * And emotional distress, if inflicted intentionally, constitutes an independent tort. * The danger of plaintiffs' fraudulent collection of damages for nonexistent injury is at least as great in these examples as in the instant case. In sum, the application of tort law can never be a matter of mathematical precision. In terms of characterizing conduct as tortious and matching a money award to the injury suffered as well as in fixing the extent of injury, the process cannot be perfect. * * * Yet we cannot let the difficulties of adjudication frustrate the principle that there be a remedy for every substantial wrong.

2. *The alleged inability to fix definitions for recovery on the different facts of future cases does not justify the denial of recovery on the specific facts of the instant case; in any event, proper guidelines can indicate the extent of liability for such future cases.*

In order to limit the otherwise potentially infinite liability which would follow every negligent act, the law of torts holds defendant amenable only for injuries to others which to defendant at the time were reasonably foreseeable. * * * This foreseeable risk may be of two types. The first class involves actual physical impact. A second type of risk applies to the instant situation. "In other cases, however, plaintiff is outside the zone of physical risk (or there is no risk of physical impact at all), but bodily injury or sickness is brought on by emotional disturbance which in turn is caused by defendant's conduct. Under general principles recovery should be had in such a case if defendant should foresee fright or shock severe enough to cause substantial injury in a person normally constituted. Plaintiff would then be within the zone of risk in very much the same way as are plaintiffs to whom danger is extended by acts of third persons, or forces of nature, or their own responses (where these things are foreseeable)." Fowler V. Harper & Fleming James, Jr., The Law of Torts, 1035–36.[5]

Since the chief element in determining whether defendant owes a duty or an obligation to plaintiff is the foreseeability of the risk, that factor will be of prime concern in every case. Because it is inherently intertwined with foreseeability such duty or obligation must necessarily be adjudicated only upon a case-by-case basis. We cannot now predetermine defendant's obligation in every situation by a fixed category; no immutable rule can establish the extent of that obligation

---

suffers shock from fear for her own safety and to deny it for shock from the witnessed death of her own daughter. * * *

[5] The concept of the zone of danger cannot properly be restricted to the area of those exposed to *physical* injury; it must encompass the area of those exposed to *emotional* injury. The courts, today, hold that no distinction can be drawn between physical injury and emotional injury flowing from the physical injury; indeed, in the light of modern medical knowledge, any such distinction would be indefensible. As a result, in awarding recovery for emotional shock upon witnessing another's injury or death, we cannot draw a line between the plaintiff who is in the zone of danger of physical impact and the plaintiff who is in the zone of danger of emotional impact. The recovery of the one, within the guidelines set forth *infra*, is as much compelled as that of the other.

for every circumstance of the future. We can, however, define guidelines which will aid in the resolution of such an issue as the instant one.

We note, first, that we deal here with a case in which plaintiff suffered a shock which resulted in physical injury and we confine our ruling to that case. In determining, in such a case, whether defendant should reasonably foresee the injury to plaintiff, or, in other terminology, whether defendant owes plaintiff a duty of due care, the courts will take into account such factors as the following: (1) Whether plaintiff was located near the scene of the accident as contrasted with one who was a distance away from it. (2) Whether the shock resulted from a direct emotional impact upon plaintiff from the sensory and contemporaneous observance of the accident, as contrasted with learning of the accident from others after its occurrence. (3) Whether plaintiff and the victim were closely related, as contrasted with an absence of any relationship or the presence of only a distant relationship.

The evaluation of these factors will indicate the *degree* of the defendant's foreseeability: obviously defendant is more likely to foresee that a mother who observes an accident affecting her child will suffer harm than to foretell that a stranger witness will do so. Similarly, the degree of foreseeability of the third person's injury is far greater in the case of his contemporaneous observance of the accident than that in which he subsequently learns of it. The defendant is more likely to foresee that shock to the nearby, witnessing mother will cause physical harm than to anticipate that someone distant from the accident will suffer more than a temporary emotional reaction. All these elements, of course, shade into each other; the fixing of obligation, intimately tied into the facts, depends upon each case.

In light of these factors the court will determine whether the accident and harm was *reasonably* foreseeable. Such reasonable foreseeability does not turn on whether the particular defendant as an individual would have in actuality foreseen the exact accident and loss; it contemplates that courts, on a case-to-case basis, analyzing all the circumstances, will decide what the ordinary man under such circumstances should reasonably have foreseen. * * * In the instant case, the presence of all the above factors indicates that plaintiff has alleged a sufficient prima facie case. Surely the negligent driver who causes the death of a young child may reasonably expect that the mother will not be far distant and will upon witnessing the accident suffer emotional trauma. * * * We are not now called upon to decide whether, in the absence or reduced weight of some of the above factors, we would conclude that the accident and injury were not reasonably foreseeable and that therefore defendant owed no duty of due care to plaintiff. In future cases the courts will draw lines of demarcation upon facts more subtle than the compelling ones alleged in the complaint before us. * * *

In short, the history of the cases does not show the development of a logical rule but rather a series of changes and abandonments. Upon the argument in each situation that the courts draw a Maginot Line to withstand an onslaught of false claims, the cases have assumed a variety of postures. At first they insisted that there be no recovery for emotional trauma at all. * Retreating from this position, they gave relief for such trauma only if physical impact occurred. They then abandoned the requirement for physical impact but insisted that the victim fear for her own safety, Amaya v. Home Ice, Fuel & Supply Co., 59 Cal.2d 295, 29 Cal.Rptr. 33, 379 P.2d 513, holding that a mother could recover for fear for her children's safety if she simultaneously entertained a personal fear for herself. * They stated that the mother need only be in the "zone of danger." * The final anomaly would be the instant case in which the sister, who observed the accident, would be granted recovery because she was in the "zone of danger," but the *mother*, not far distant, would be barred from recovery. The successive abandonment of these positions exposes the weakness of artificial abstractions which bar recovery contrary to the general rules. As the commentators have suggested, the problem should be solved by the application of the principles of tort, not by the creation of exceptions to them. Legal history shows that artificial islands of exceptions, created from the fear that the legal process will not work, usually do not withstand the waves of reality and, in time, descend into oblivion. * * * To deny recovery would be to chain this state to an outmoded rule of the 19th century which can claim no current credence. No good reason compels our captivity to an indefensible orthodoxy.

The judgment is reversed. * * *

■ BURKE, JUSTICE, dissenting. * * * What if the plaintiff was honestly *mistaken* in believing the third person to be in danger or to be seriously injured? What if the third person had assumed the risk involved? How "close" must the relationship be between the plaintiff and the third person? I.e., what if the third person was the plaintiff's beloved niece or nephew, grandparent, fiancé, or lifelong friend, more dear to the plaintiff than her immediate family? Next, how "near" must the plaintiff have been to the scene of the accident, and how "soon" must shock have been felt? Indeed, what is the magic in the plaintiff's being actually present? Is the shock any less real if the mother does not know of the accident until her injured child is brought into her home? On the other hand, is it any less real if the mother is physically present at the scene but is nevertheless unaware of the danger or injury to her child until after the accident has occurred? No answers to these questions are to be found in today's majority opinion. Our trial courts, however, will not so easily escape the burden of distinguishing between litigants on the basis of such artificial and unpredictable distinctions. * * * As [the] court declared in * * * Waube v. Warrington, 216 Wis. 603, 258 N.W. 497 (1935), * * * to permit recovery by every person who might adversely feel some lingering effect of the defendant's conduct would throw us into "the fantastic realm of infinite liability." * * *

NOTES

1. *Comparison with Cases Involving Intentionally Caused Emotional Distress.* The principal issue posed by the preceding two cases concerns criteria that should be used to establish sufficient evidence of the genuineness of injury to justify recovery in the context of negligence. This same need to distinguish relatively transient or slight symptoms from more seriously disabling injuries also arises when the mental suffering is intentionally caused, but is resolved in a fundamentally different manner.

See *infra* pages 737–745; see also generally Harper, James and Gray on Torts § 9.1.

2. *Emotional Distress Resulting from Fear of Contracting Latent Disease.* Should someone facing a substantially increased risk of a serious disease as a result of exposure to a harmful substance be able to recover for emotional distress even if that individual is not experiencing any physical injury at the current time? Many workers exposed to asbestos sought recovery for emotional distress, in part because of the reality that asbestos manufacturers likely would become bankrupt as a result of hundreds of thousands of claims before the time that the workers would become symptomatic, but virtually all courts denied recovery in the absence of contemporaneous physical injury. E.g., Metro-North Commuter R.R. Co. v. Buckley, 521 U.S. 424, 434, 117 S.Ct. 2113, 2119, 138 L.Ed.2d 560, 571–72 (denying recovery under Federal Employers' Liability Act for emotional distress resulting from fear of contracting asbestos-related diseases despite plaintiff's "physical contact" with asbestos fibers). In a few cases, however, courts have allowed recovery of damages for emotional distress resulting from exposure to harmful substances. E.g., Exxon Mobil Corp. v. Albright, 433 Md. 303, 352, 71 A.3d 30, 60 (2013) ("[T]o recover emotional distress damages for fear of contracting a disease, a plaintiff must show that (1) he or she was exposed actually to a toxic substance due to the defendant's tortious conduct; (2) which led him or her to fear objectively and reasonably that he or she would contract a disease; and (3) as a result of the objective and reasonable fear, he or she manifested a physical injury capable of objective determination"); Ayers v. Jackson Twp., 106 N.J. 557, 577, 525 A.2d 287, 297 (1987) (allowing recovery for claims of emotional distress in the absence of physical injury against defendant township under tort claims act for contamination of water supply resulting from negligent handling of toxic pollutants at township landfill); cf., Potter v. Firestone Tire & Rubber Co., 6 Cal.4th 965, 997, 25 Cal.Rptr.2d 550, 572, 863 P.2d 795, 816 (1993) (allowing recovery for "negligent infliction of emotional distress claims arising out of exposure to carcinogens and/or other toxic substances * * * in the absence of a present physical injury or illness * * * only if the plaintiff pleads and proves that (1) as a result of the defendant's negligen[ce,] * * * the plaintiff is exposed to a toxic substance which threatens cancer; *and* (2) the plaintiff's fears stems from a knowledge, corroborated by reliable medical or scientific opinion, that it is more likely than not that the plaintiff will develop the cancer in the future due to the toxic exposure").

3. *Medical Monitoring Expenses.* Should those exposed to toxic chemicals or other substances creating an increased risk of contracting an illness be able to recover "medical monitoring expenses" to assure timely diagnosis and treatment even if they are asymptomatic? A significant minority of jurisdictions allow such recovery. E.g., Potter v. Firestone Tire & Rubber Co., *supra*, 6 Cal.4th at 1006, 25 Cal.Rptr.2d at 577, 863 P.2d at 822 (recognizing claim for medical monitoring expenses that "is not contingent upon a showing of a present physical injury"); Exxon Mobil Corp. v. Albright, *supra*, 433 Md. at 388, 71 A.3d at 81–82 (concluding that the need for medical testing resulting from exposure to a toxic substance constitutes an invasion of a legally protected interest when "(1) * * * the plaintiff was significantly exposed to a proven hazardous substance through the defendant's tortious conduct; (2) * * * as a proximate result of significant exposure, the plaintiff suffers a significantly increased risk of contracting a latent disease; (3) that increased risk makes periodic diagnostic medical examinations reasonably necessary; and (4) * * * monitoring and testing procedures exist which make the early detection and treatment of the disease possible and beneficial"). The majority of courts, however, do not recognize such claims. E.g., Metro-North Commuter R.R. Co. v. Buckley, *supra,* 521 U.S. at 444, 117 S.Ct. at 2124, 138 L.Ed.2d at 577 (denying recovery under Federal Employers' Liability Act of lump-sum judgment for medical monitoring expenses resulting from asbestos exposure); Caronia v. Philip Morris USA, Inc., 22 N.Y. 3d 439, 452, 982 N.Y.S.2d 40, 5 N.E.3d 11 (2013) (refusing to recognize "a judicially-created independent cause of action for medical monitoring" for those who have not sustained a physical injury). What problems might result from recognition of an independent claim for medical monitoring expenses? Who should recover among the millions of individuals exposed to toxic substances? What is the preclusive effect of a judgment in a later action when the plaintiff becomes ill?

B. RECOVERY FOR LOSS ARISING FROM INJURY TO FAMILY MEMBERS

Ueland v. Pengo Hydra-Pull Corp.

Supreme Court of Washington, 1984.
103 Wash.2d 131, 691 P.2d 190.

■ PEARSON, JUSTICE. This case requires us to decide whether children have a separate cause of action for loss of parental consortium[1] when a parent is injured through the negligence of another. * * *

Eric Ueland, * * * husband of Shelley Ueland and father of the two minor children, Kimberly and William Ueland, suffered severe and permanent mental and physical disabilities when struck by a metal cable during the course of employment as a lineman for Seattle City Light. The Uelands were separated and seeking a divorce at the time of the accident. The minor children, through their mother as guardian, bring this action for loss of consortium with their father as a result of his injuries. * * *

Through legislative act and court decision this state recognizes a wide range of consortium recovery rights. Parents may recover for loss of consortium for injury to a child. Wash. Rev. Code § 4.24.010. * A spouse may bring an action for loss of consortium when the other spouse is injured. Hawkins v. Front St. Cable Ry., 3 Wash. 592, 28 P. 1021 (1892) (allowing a husband to recover for loss of an injured wife's "services" in the household); Lundgren v. Whitney's Inc., 94 Wash. 2d 91, 614 P.2d 1272 (1980) (allowing a wife to recover for loss of consortium when her husband is injured). A child, parent or spouse can bring an action for wrongful death of the other where loss of consortium is an element of the recovery. Wash. Rev. Code § 4.20.020. *

---

[1] Loss of consortium is typically thought of as a "loss of society, affection, assistance and conjugal fellowship, and . . . loss or impairment of sexual relations" in the marital relationship. Black's Law Dictionary 280 (5th ed. 1979). In the parent-child relationship the term consortium refers to the "loss of a parent's love, care, companionship and guidance . . ." Note, The Child's Right To Sue for Loss of a Parent's Love, Care and Companionship Caused by Tortious Injury to the Parent, 56 B.U. L. Rev. 722, 723 (1976). It is consistent with this second definition that we use the term "parental consortium."

The state of the law in this area is anomalous in that a child may recover for loss of consortium if the parent dies as a result of another's negligence, but not if the severely injured parent remains alive but in a vegetative state. Surely the child's loss of the parent's love, care, companionship and guidance is nearly the same in both situations. Also, permitting a husband or wife but not children to recover for loss of consortium erroneously suggests that an adult is more likely to suffer emotional injury than a child. * * *

Prosser * * * criticized this void in the law which has left the child uncompensated for the loss of a parent's love and guidance due to the negligent injury of the parent.

> * * * It is not easy to understand and appreciate this reluctance to compensate the child who has been deprived of the care, companionship and education of his mother, or for that matter his father, through the defendant's negligence. This is surely a genuine injury, and a serious one, which has received a great deal more sympathy from the legal writers than from the judges.

* W[illiam L.] Prosser, Torts § 125 at 896 (4th ed. 1971). * * *

Petitioners draw our attention to numerous arguments against recognizing the cause of action which we now address. First is that creation of such a cause of action lies within the Legislature's, not the court's, domain.   * * * When justice requires, this court does not hesitate to expand the common law and recognize a cause of action. * * * [T]o defer to the Legislature in this instance would be to abdicate our responsibility to reform the common law to meet the evolving standards of justice.

We next address petitioners' second argument, that allowing the action would result in multiple lawsuits. Petitioners are correct to point out that if this cause of action is adopted there could be as many claims as the injured parent has children. * * * We * * * are concerned with the possibility of multiple actions, but * * * hold that the children's claims for loss of parental consortium must be joined with the injured parent's claim whenever feasible. A child may not bring a separate consortium claim unless he or she can show why joinder with the parent's underlying claim was not feasible.

Petitioners' third argument is that damages for such a cause of action would be too speculative to measure and would not compensate the child for the loss suffered. Regarding the speculative nature of the damages, this argument has little merit since evaluating a child's consortium loss is no more speculative than evaluating the loss in the other consortium actions already recognized in this state.

Petitioners direct our attention to cases which say, in effect, that monetary compensation will not enable the child to regain what was lost when the parent was injured. * The Wisconsin Supreme Court, in a recent opinion adopting the child's cause of action, addressed this argument as follows: "Although a monetary award may be a poor substitute for the loss of a parent's society and companionship, * * * we believe that allowing such an award is clearly preferable to completely denying recovery." Theama v. Kenosha, 117 Wis.2d 508, 523, 344 N.W.2d 513 (1984).

Allowing a child to recover for loss of consortium may aid in ensuring the child's continued normal and complete mental development into adulthood. As one writer noted,

> [t]he premise that money can mitigate the impact of a loss may be especially appropriate in the case of a child deprived of a parent's love and guidance. Compensation awarded the child might enable the family to obtain live-in help that could provide not only domestic services, but, incidentally, a measure of guidance and companionship. The child who has suffered an emotional maladjustment as a result of his deprivation would have funds available to pay for needed psychiatric treatment. It is not unrealistic to assume that in many cases monetary compensation could make the difference between a child who suffers a permanent handicap due to the loss of a parent's love and guidance and a child who is able to make a reasonable adjustment to his loss.

* 56 B.U. L. Rev. at 734. Although a monetary award will not enable a child to regain the loss of a parent's love, companionship, and guidance, we believe such an award may enable the child to lessen the impact of the loss. * * *

Some courts limit recovery for loss of parental consortium to minor children dependent on the parent. * Although minors are the group most likely to suffer real harm due to a disruption of the parent-child relationship, we leave this for the jury to consider in fixing damages. This is consistent with our view in wrongful death actions of allowing a child to recover for loss of parental consortium beyond the period of minority. * * *

We conclude that the reasons for recognizing a child's cause of action for loss of parental consortium outweigh any problems such an action may present. Accordingly, we hold that a child has an independent cause of action for loss of the love, care, companionship and guidance of a parent tortiously injured by a third party. * * *

■ DORE, J. (dissenting). * * * Today's decision * * * does not recognize the fact that liability for one's negligence must end someplace. As stated by Judge Breitel in Tobin v. Grossman, 24 N.Y.2d 609, 619, 249 N.E.2d 419, 301 N.Y.S.2d 554 (1969): "Every injury has ramifying consequences, like the ripplings of the waters, without end. The problem for the law is to limit the legal consequences of wrongs to a controllable degree." See also Suter v. Leonard, 45 Cal.App.3d 744, 746, 120 Cal.Rptr. 110 (1975) ("[N]ot every loss can be made compensable in money damages, and legal causation must terminate somewhere"). Using the majority's reasoning, a child should be allowed to recover where the child had no father, and an uncle, who was the child's father figure, was severely, negligently injured. Or a person whose close friend was negligently injured should be allowed to recover where the two had grown up together and had given each other "love, guidance, and companionship." * * * There are many more examples that analytically make sense, yet it is clear that if all injuries were compensated, the courts, and perhaps society, would have great difficulty even functioning.

The majority may argue that for purposes of the present issue, recovery will only be allowed to members of the immediate family. * * * Should a child be allowed to recover for the negligent injury to a sibling? Should a child be allowed to recover where the injury is only temporary? If so, how long does the disability have to be in order for the child to be allowed to recover: one year? one month? one week? * * *

NOTES

1. *Loss of Consortium.* Injuries short of death often result in non-economic damages—both mental distress and loss of companionship—to a spouse.

The common law long recognized the husband's interest in his wife's companionship and allowed him to recover for loss of "consortium"— including intangible elements defined as the " 'constellation of companionship, dependence, reliance, affection, sharing and aid which are legally recognizable, protected rights arising out of the civil contract of marriage.' " Hopson v. St. Mary's Hosp., 176 Conn. 485, 487, 408 A.2d 260, 261 (1979) (quoting Brown v. Kistleman, 177 Ind. 692, 98 N.E. 631 (1912)); see generally Harper, James and Gray on Torts § 8.9. Not until the mid-twentieth century, however, were these same rights extended to the wife. E.g., Hitaffer v. Argonne Co., 183 F.2d 811 (D.C.Cir.1950).

Should a woman who has lived with a man for more than 20 years as "a *de facto* married couple"—and who in fact married him two years after an accident resulting in physical injuries—be allowed to recover for loss of consortium and loss of companionship? In Feliciano v. Rosemar Silver Co., 401 Mass. 141, 514 N.E.2d 1095 (1987), the Massachusetts Supreme Judicial Court denied recovery under such facts.

2. *Recovery for Parents' Loss of Companionship in Personal Injury Actions Involving Children.* Dillon v. Legg, *supra* pages 483–88, explored the issue of recovery by parents for mental disturbance from witnessing an injury to a child.

In Shockley v. Prier, 66 Wis.2d 394, 401, 225 N.W.2d 495, 499 (1975), the parents of an infant who suffered permanent blindness and disfigurement as a result of injuries sustained in the neo-natal unit shortly after the child's birth were awarded damages for loss of "aid, comfort, society and companionship." More often, recovery in similar circumstances is not allowed. E.g., Roberts v. Williamson, 111 S.W.3d 113 (Tex.2003). In *Roberts*, the court distinguished the issue of whether "parents have a claim for loss of consortium in non-fatal injury cases" from whether a child has a claim for loss of consortium when a parent is injured, a right the court had previously recognized:

> Although parents customarily *enjoy* the consortium of their children, in the ordinary course of events a parent does not *depend* on a child's companionship, love, support, guidance, and nurture in the same way and to the same degree that a husband depends on his wife, a wife depends on her husband, or a minor or disabled adult child depends on his or her parent. Of course, it is true that such dependency may exist in a particular situation, but it is not intrinsic to the parent-child relationship as is a minor child's dependency on his or her parents and as is each spouse's

dependency on the other spouse." Norman v. Mass. Bay Transp. Auth., 403 Mass 303, 529 N.E.2d 139, 140–41 (1988). * * *

We concede that serious injury to a child will have emotional consequences for the parents. Tort law, however, cannot remedy every wrong. Sound public policy requires an end at some point to the consequential damages that flow from a single negligent act.

111 S.W.3d at 117–18. See also Harper, James and Gray on Torts § 8.8 n.5. But see Ingraham v. United States, 808 F.2d 1075 (5th Cir.1987); United States v. Dempsey, 635 So.2d 961 (Fla.1994).

3. *Recovery for Child's Loss of Companionship in Personal Injury Actions Involving a Parent. Ueland* poses the issue of whether courts should recognize a right of minor children to recover damages for the loss of companionship of their parents for nonfatal injuries. Many (probably most) courts disagree with the outcome in *Ueland.* For example, in Sizemore v. Smock, 430 Mich. 283, 422 N.W.2d 666 (1988), the court explained why it held that no liability existed in these cases:

We agree that any attempt to draw a meaningful distinction on the basis of the sentimental aspects of the consortium claim between the parties in the parent-child relationship would be specious and unavoidably futile. Nevertheless, * * * we believe that there are compelling conceptual and public policy considerations that militate against this Court further extending a negligent tortfeasor's liability by recognizing a parent's action for loss of society and companionship of a negligently injured child. This determination is not in any way intended to denigrate the unique value inherent in protecting the parent-child relationship.

The consortium action is somewhat of an anomaly in the law of tort in that it is generally the rule that a negligent tortfeasor's liability only extends to an obligation to compensate the person directly injured. * Although it is eminently foreseeable that a negligent injury to one party will result in adverse consequences that affect others to one degree or another, the law cannot redress every injury, and the determination of where to draw the line of liability is essentially a question of policy. * * *

Initially, we question the wisdom of awarding monetary damages to compensate one for a loss of the intangible and sentimental elements of the consortium claim. The efficacy of such an award to either deter negligent conduct or adequately redress the loss suffered is highly questionable. To the extent that the system of tort liability is designed to make one more socially responsible vis-a-vis their relationship with others, it is unlikely that any secondary liability imposed beyond the liability exposure to the primary victim of an injury will do anything to further that objective. Moreover, monetary compensation will not enable the parents to replace the loss they have suffered. Although tort law permits recovery for other intangible injuries, e.g., pain and suffering of the primary injured party, the wisdom of compensating one for such injuries is less compelling when the injury is remote, the loss is intangible, and the liability is secondary. * * *

Compare also Mendillo v. Bd. of Educ. of Town of East Haddam, 246 Conn. 456, 495–96, 717 A.2d 1177, 1196 (1998) (recovery denied), with Salinas v. Fort Worth Cab & Baggage Co., 725 S.W.2d 701 (Tex.1987) (recovery allowed).

C. RECOVERY FOR "WRONGFUL BIRTH" AND "WRONGFUL LIFE"

Greco v. United States

Supreme Court of Nevada, 1995.
111 Nev. 405, 893 P.2d 345.

■ SPRINGER, JUSTICE. * * * The Grecos, mother and child, in this case seek to recover damages from the United States arising out of the negligence of physicians [at Nellis Air Force Base in Nevada] who, they claim, negligently failed to make a timely diagnosis of physical defects and anomalies afflicting the child when it was still in the mother's womb. Sundi Greco asserts that the physicians' negligence denied her the opportunity to terminate her pregnancy and thereby caused damages attendant to the avoidable birth of an unwanted and severely deformed child. On Joshua's behalf, Sundi Greco avers that the physicians' negligence and the resultant denial of Joshua's mother's right to terminate her pregnancy caused Joshua to be born into a grossly abnormal life of pain and deprivation. These kinds of tort claims have been termed "wrongful birth" when brought by a parent and "wrongful life" when brought on behalf of the child for the harm suffered by being born deformed.

The Child's Cause of Action: "Wrongful Life"

We decline to recognize any action by a child for defects claimed to have been caused to the child by negligent diagnosis or treatment of the child's mother. The Grecos' argument is conditional and narrowly put, so: if this court does not allow Sundi Greco [the mother] to recover damages for Joshua's [the child's] care past the age of majority, it should allow Joshua to recover those damages by recognizing claims for "wrongful life." Implicit in this argument is the assumption that the child would be better off had he never been born. These kinds of judgments are very difficult, if not impossible, to make. Indeed, most courts considering the question have denied this cause of action for precisely this reason. * Recognizing this kind of claim on behalf of the child would require us to weigh the harms suffered by virtue of the child's having been born with severe handicaps against "the utter void of nonexistence"; this is a calculation the courts are incapable of performing. * The New York Court of Appeals framed the problem this way:

> Whether it is better never to have been born at all than to have been born with even gross deficiencies is a mystery more properly to be left to the philosophers and the theologians. Surely the law can assert no competence to resolve the issue, particularly in view of the very nearly uniform high value which the law and mankind has placed on human life, rather than its absence.

Becker v. Schwartz, 46 N.Y.2d 401, 413 N.Y.S.2d 895, 900, 386 N.E.2d 807, 812 (1978). We conclude that Nevada does not recognize a claim by a child for harms the child claims to have suffered by virtue of having been born.

The Mother's Cause of Action

With regard to Sundi Greco's claim against her physician for negligent diagnosis or treatment during pregnancy, we see no reason for compounding or complicating our medical malpractice jurisprudence by according this particular form of professional negligence action some special status apart from presently recognized medical malpractice or by giving it the new name of "wrongful birth."[5] Sundi Greco either does or does not state a claim for medical malpractice; and we conclude that she does.

* * * In the case before us, we must accept as fact that Sundi Greco's physicians negligently failed to perform prenatal medical tests or performed or interpreted those tests in a negligent fashion and that they thereby negligently failed to discover and reveal that Sundi Greco was carrying a severely deformed fetus. As a result of such negligence Sundi Greco claims that she was denied the opportunity to terminate her pregnancy and that this denial resulted in her giving birth to a severely deformed child.

It is difficult to formulate any sound reason for denying recovery to Sundi Greco in the case at hand. Sundi Greco is saying, in effect, to her doctors:

> If you had done what you were supposed to do, I would have known early in my pregnancy that I was carrying a severely deformed baby. I would have then terminated the pregnancy and would not have had to go through the mental and physical agony of delivering this child, nor would I have had to bear the emotional suffering attendant to the birth and nurture of the child, nor the extraordinary expense necessary to care for a child suffering from such extreme deformity and disability.

The United States advances two reasons for denying Sundi Greco's claim: first, it argues that she has suffered no injury and that, therefore, the damage element of negligent tort liability is not fulfilled; second, the United States argues that even if Sundi Greco has sustained injury and damages, the damages were not caused by her physicians. To support its first argument, the United States points out that in Szekeres v. Robinson, 102 Nev. 93, 715 P.2d 1076 (1986), this court held that the mother of a normal, healthy child could not recover in tort from a physician who negligently performed her sterilization operation because the birth of a normal, healthy child is not a legally cognizable injury.[6] The United States argues that no distinction can be

---

[5]   One commentator observes that the term "wrongful life," "was a play on the statutory tort of 'wrongful death.'" Alexander M. Capron, Tort Liability in Genetic Counseling, 79 Colum. L. Rev. 618, 634 n.62 (1979). The related concepts of wrongful birth and wrongful pregnancy or conception were similarly inspired. The commentator concludes that the net effect of these terms has been to "spawn confusion" and distort or impair judicial vision.

[6]   We did observe that the mother might have a contractual remedy against the physician for failure to do what he promised to do—sterilize his patient. Szekeres, *supra*, 102 Nev. at 98, 715 P.2d at 1079.

made between a mother who gives birth to a healthy child and a mother who gives birth to a child with severe deformities and that, therefore, *Szekeres* bars recovery.

Szekeres can be distinguished from the instant case. Unlike the birth of a normal child, the birth of a severely deformed baby of the kind described here is necessarily an unpleasant and aversive event and the cause of inordinate financial burden that would not attend the birth of a normal child. The child in this case will unavoidably and necessarily require the expenditure of extraordinary medical, therapeutic and custodial care expenses by the family, not to mention the additional reserves of physical, mental and emotional strength that will be required of all concerned. Those who do not wish to undertake the many burdens associated with the birth and continued care of such a child have the legal right, under *Roe v. Wade* and codified by the voters of this state, to terminate their pregnancies. Roe v. Wade, 410 U.S. 113, 93 S.Ct. 705, 35 L.Ed.2d 147 (1973); Nev. Rev. Stat. § 442.250 (codifying by referendum the conditions under which abortion is permitted in this state). Sundi Greco has certainly suffered money damages as a result of her physician's malpractice.

We also reject the United States' second argument that Sundi Greco's physicians did not cause any of the injuries that Sundi Greco might have suffered. We note that the mother is not claiming that her child's defects were caused by her physicians' negligence; rather, she claims that her physicians' negligence kept her ignorant of those defects and that it was this negligence which caused her to lose her right to choose whether to carry the child to term. The damage Sundi Greco has sustained is indeed causally related to her physicians' malpractice.

Sundi Greco's claim here can be compared to one in which a physician negligently fails to diagnose cancer in a patient. Even though the physician did not *cause* the cancer, the physician can be held liable for damages resulting from the patient's decreased opportunity to fight the cancer, and for the more extensive pain, suffering and medical treatment the patient must undergo by reason of the negligent diagnosis. * The "chance" lost here, was Sundi Greco's legally protected right to choose whether to abort a severely deformed fetus. * If we were to deny Sundi Greco's claim, we would, in effect, be groundlessly excepting one type of medical malpractice from negligence liability. We see no reason to treat this case any differently from any other medical malpractice case. Sundi Greco has stated a prima facie claim of medical malpractice under Nevada law.

Damage Issues

The certified question requires us to decide specifically what types of damages the mother may recover if she succeeds in proving her claim. Courts in these cases have struggled with what items of damages are recoverable because, unlike the typical malpractice claim, claims such as Sundi Greco's do not involve a physical injury to the patient's person. * * *

Extraordinary Medical and Custodial Expenses

This claim for damages relates to the medical, therapeutic and custodial costs associated with caring for a severely handicapped child. * * * Extraordinary care expenses are a foreseeable result of the negligence alleged in this case, and Sundi Greco should be allowed to recover those expenses if she can prove them. This leads us to the question of how to compensate for these kinds of injuries.

* * * We agree with these [cited] authorities and conclude that Sundi Greco may recover extraordinary medical and custodial expenses associated with caring for Joshua for whatever period of time it is established that Joshua will be dependent upon her to provide such care.

The United States contends that if this court allows the mother to recover such extraordinary medical and custodial expenses, then it should require the district court to offset any such award by the amount it would cost to raise a non-handicapped child. To do otherwise, argues the United States, would be to grant the mother a windfall. *

The offset rule has its origins in two doctrines: the "avoidable consequences rule," which requires plaintiffs to mitigate their damages in tort cases, and the expectancy rule of damages employed in contract cases, which seeks to place the plaintiff in the position he or she would have been in had the contract been performed. * We conclude that neither of these doctrines is applicable to the case at bar. To enforce the "avoidable consequences" rule in the instant case would impose unreasonable burdens upon the mother such as, perhaps, putting Joshua up for adoption or otherwise seeking to terminate her parental obligations. *

With regard to the expectancy rule, it would unnecessarily complicate and limit recovery for patients in other malpractice cases if we were to begin intruding contract damage principles upon our malpractice jurisprudence. The rule for compensatory damages in negligence cases is clear and workable, and we decline to depart from it. * * *

Damages for Emotional Distress

Sundi Greco asserts that she is suffering and will continue to suffer tremendous mental and emotional pain as a result of the birth of Joshua. Several jurisdictions allow plaintiffs such as Sundi Greco to recover such damages. * In line with these cases, we agree that it is reasonably foreseeable that a mother who is denied her right to abort a severely deformed fetus will suffer emotional distress, not just when the child is delivered, but for the rest of the child's life. * Consequently, we conclude that the mother in this case should have the opportunity to prove that she suffered and will continue to suffer emotional distress as a result of the birth of her child.

We reject the United States' argument that this court should follow an "offset" rule with regard to damages for emotional distress. Cf. Blake v. Cruz, 108 Idaho 253, 258, 698 P.2d 315, 320 (1984) (requiring damages for emotional distress to be offset by "the countervailing emotional benefits attributable to the birth of the child"). Any emotional benefits are simply too speculative to be considered by a jury in awarding emotional distress damages. As Dean Prosser observes:

> In the case of the wrongful birth of a severely impaired child, it would appear that the usual joys of parenthood would often be substantially overshadowed by the emotional trauma of caring

for the child in such a condition, so that application of the benefit rule would appear inappropriate in this context.

W. Page Keeton *et al.*, Prosser and Keeton on the Law of Torts, § 55 at 371 n.48 (5th ed. 1984) (citations omitted). It is beyond cavil, for example, that "[t]here is no joy in watching a child suffer and die from cystic fibrosis." Schroeder v. Perkel, 87 N.J. 53, 432 A.2d 834, 842 (1981). Moreover, it would unduly complicate the jury's task to require it to weigh one intangible harm against another intangible benefit.

Conclusion

We conclude that a mother may maintain a medical malpractice action under Nevada law based on her physicians' failure properly to perform or interpret prenatal examinations when that failure results in the mother losing the opportunity to abort a severely deformed fetus. Sundi Greco should be given the right to prove that she has suffered and will continue to suffer damages in the form of emotional or mental distress and that she has incurred and will continue to incur extraordinary medical and custodial care expenses associated with raising Joshua. We decline to recognize the tort sometimes called "wrongful life." * * *

■ SHEARING, J., with whom ROSE, J. joins, concurring in part and dissenting in part:

I agree with the majority that a mother should have a malpractice claim against professionals who negligently fail to make a timely diagnosis of fetal defects. However, I would also allow the impaired child a cause of action, with the measure of damages being the extraordinary expenses attributable to the child's impairment. In this case, Joshua was born with congenital defects which result in his suffering paraplegia with no sensation from the hips down and permanent fine and gross motor retardation and mental retardation. It is clear that he will require extraordinary care throughout his life. * * *

Courts have had a great deal of difficulty in dealing with the moral implications of compensating parents or a child for that child's birth, when the plaintiffs' claim is essentially that they would all be better off had the child never been born. One reason the issue of compensation is so knotty is that it runs counter to our conception of the preciousness of human life. * * * The majority, along with other courts, rejects the impaired child's cause of action after wrestling with the question of whether damages exist when that determination requires the comparison of the value of an impaired life to the value of no life at all. * * *

However, not all courts have taken the view that these difficulties are so great as to overcome the public policy objectives of tort law—to compensate injured parties and to deter future wrongful conduct. In Turpin v. Sortini, 31 Cal.3d 220, 240, 182 Cal.Rptr. 337, 344–45, 643 P.2d 954, 958 (1982), the California Supreme Court quoted with approval a lower court opinion which stated:

> The reality of the "wrongful life" concept is that such a plaintiff *exists* and *suffers*, due to the negligence of others. It is neither necessary nor just to retreat into meditation on the mysteries of life. * * *

* * * The California Supreme Court went on to hold that both the child and the parents had a cause of action. However, the court rejected the parents' claim for general damages and allowed [both the parents and the child] only the claim for medical expenses and extraordinary expenses for specialized teaching, training and equipment required because of the impairment. * * *

Th[is] approach * * * is sound. [The [California] court refused] to become mired in philosophical discussions of the meaning and value of life, and focus[ed] on compensating injured parties and deterring future wrongful conduct. Our knowledge in the fields of genetics and obstetrics has grown dramatically, with far-reaching consequences for human life. It is clear that responsive treatments and the counseling necessitated by those treatments will develop in accordance with our ever-increasing capability to test and diagnose. It would, therefore, be anomalous for medical practitioners in these fields to be immune from liability for wrongful conduct or for departing from accepted professional standards. Unquestionably the public policy behind tort law supports compensating impaired children and their parents for the special damages resulting from impairment when the negligence of the medical professional results in the birth of the impaired child. * * *

NOTE

Contrasting Views on Expenses of Rearing Healthy Child. Compare Lovelace Med. Ctr. v. Mendez, 111 N.M. 336, 805 P.2d 603 (1991) (allowing reasonable child-rearing costs for healthy baby born as result of negligent sterilization procedure, without offset for benefits received by parents from presence of child in their lives); and Marciniak v. Lundborg, 153 Wis.2d 59, 450 N.W.2d 243 (1990) (similar); with M.A. v. United States, 951 P.2d 851 (Alaska 1998) (allowing only for injuries incurred through time of childbirth, but not for expenses of raising healthy child); and Burke v. Rivo, 406 Mass. 764, 551 N.E.2d 1 (1990) (child-rearing costs allowed, but offset required for benefits, if any, parents will receive from having the child).

D. RECOVERY FOR ECONOMIC LOSS IN THE ABSENCE OF PERSONAL INJURY OR PROPERTY DAMAGE

Wiltz v. Bayer Cropscience, Ltd. Partnership

United State Court of Appeals for the Fifth Circuit, 2011.
645 F.3d 690.[a]

■ BENAVIDES, J. The Louisiana crawfish industry suffered a precipitous decline when rice seed coated with a pesticide allegedly decimated the 1999–2000 farm-raised crawfish crop. The plaintiffs in this putative class action are buyers and processors of farm-raised crawfish who seek to recover their economic loss from the pesticide manufacturer * * *.

Louisiana crawfish are farmed in rice ponds. The Louisiana farm-raised crawfish crop allegedly suffered a precipitous decline beginning

---

[a] [Eds.' note] Cert. denied, Wiltz v. Cropscience, ___ U.S. ___, 132 S.Ct. 1145, 181 L.Ed.2d 1019 (2012).

in the 1999–2000 crawfish season. According to plaintiff-appellant Tess Wiltz * * *, the decline was caused by the application of rice seed coated with ICON, a pesticide manufactured and sold by defendant-appellee Bayer CropScience, L.P. (Bayer). ICON rice allegedly was introduced in Louisiana rice ponds during the 1999 planting season and taken off the market a few years later.

The plaintiffs buy crawfish from crawfish farmers and then either resell the crawfish live or process them for tail meat. * * * The plaintiffs allege they suffered economic loss when ICON rice drastically reduced the number of crawfish they could buy and process. Although the plaintiffs have submitted evidence suggesting they work closely with crawfish farmers, the plaintiffs have not submitted any evidence suggesting ICON actually harmed *their* crawfish. * * *

In most jurisdictions, the "economic-loss rule" bars recovery in tort when a party suffers economic loss unaccompanied by harm to his own person or property. See, e.g., * Guste v. M/V TESTBANK, 752 F.2d 1019, 1027 (5th Cir.1985) (en banc) ("Courts applying the tort law of Texas, Georgia, Florida, Alabama, Mississippi and Louisiana have consistently denied recovery for economic losses negligently inflicted where there was no physical damage to a proprietary interest."); * Restatement (Third) of Torts: Prods. Liab. § 21 cmt. d (1998) ("A second category of economic loss excluded from the coverage of this Restatement includes losses suffered by a plaintiff but not as a direct result of harm to the plaintiff's person or property"). The economic-loss rule has been characterized as a pragmatic limitation on both proximate causation and the scope of a defendant's duty of care. Compare TESTBANK, 752 F.2d at 1023 (noting the economic loss rule is "a pragmatic limitation imposed by the Court upon the tort doctrine of foreseeability"), with Rardin v. T & D Mach. Handling, Inc., 890 F.2d 24, 26 (7th Cir.1989) ("The issue is not causation; it is duty."), with Roberts v. Benoit, 605 So.2d 1032 (La.1991), on reh'g, 605 So.2d at 1052 ("Regardless if stated in terms of proximate cause, legal cause, or duty, the scope of the duty inquiry is ultimately a question of policy . . . .").

The economic-loss rule has a distinguished lineage traceable at least to Justice Holmes's opinion in Robins Dry Dock & Repair Co. v. Flint, 275 U.S. 303, 308, 48 S.Ct. 134, 72 L.Ed. 290 (1927). In *Robins*, the employees of a dry dock negligently damaged a vessel subject to a charter agreement. * The charterer lost use of the vessel for a period of time and sued the dry dock in tort for economic damages. * The Supreme Court rejected the charterer's claim. The Supreme Court reasoned that the damage to the vessel "was no wrong to the [charterer] but only to those to whom [the vessel] belonged." * The Supreme Court concluded that the harm to the charterer "arose only through their contract with the owners," and that, as a general rule, "a tort to the person or property of one man does not make the tortfeasor liable to another merely because the injured person was under a contract with that other unknown to the doer of the wrong." * * * Although *Robins* * * * interpreted federal maritime law, its reasoning has influenced state tort law as well. *

Courts and commentators have identified several justifications for the economic-loss rule. These justifications tend to echo four themes. First, without some pragmatic limitation on the tort doctrine of foreseeability, a defendant could be held liable for "wave upon wave of successive economic consequences." TESTBANK, 752 F.2d at 1028. * As the Louisiana Supreme Court has recognized, "[b]ecause the list of possible victims and the extent of economic damages might be expanded indefinitely, the court necessarily makes a policy decision on the limitation of recovery of damages." PPG [Indus., Inc. v. Bean Dredging, Inc.], 447 So.2d [1058], 1061–62 (La.1984). It is generally agreed that a line must be drawn somewhere, and the economic-loss rule has the virtue of being predictable and generally applicable. * Second, although the economic-loss rule may produce seemingly unfair outcomes in certain cases, a case-by-case approach is "no less arbitrary." TESTBANK, 752 F.2d at 1028. * This is because a case-by-case approach does not resolve the line-drawing problem but merely postpones it: ultimately, some plaintiffs will be allowed to recover and others will be found too remote. * A case-by-case approach has the additional drawback of producing unpredictable results that are "less judicial and more the product of a managerial, legislative or negotiated function." * Third, the economic-loss rule helps preserve the distinct functions of tort and contract law by allowing parties to allocate economic risks by contract. E. River [S.S. Corp. v. Transamerica Delaval, Inc.], 476 U.S. [858,] 870–71[, 106 S.Ct. 2295, 90 L.Ed.2d 865 (1986)]. * For example, when a defective product malfunctions and causes a purchaser to lose profits but nothing more, that loss "is essentially the failure of the purchaser to receive the benefit of its bargain," and the allocation of that loss is the "core concern" of private contracts and contract law. * Finally, the economic-loss rule promotes first-party loss insurance over third-party liability insurance. * A regime of first-party loss insurance efficiently encourages the party with the best information (that is, the party with knowledge of its own risk of loss) to decide whether to assume, allocate, avoid, or insure against its risk of loss. * First-party loss insurance also is the more feasible way to mitigate disasters "inflicting large and reverberating injuries through the economy." TESTBANK, 752 F.2d at 1029.

* * * [I]n this case, Bayer damaged crawfish owned by crawfish farmers. As a result, the farmers were unable to supply crawfish to the plaintiffs, and the plaintiffs suffered purely economic loss. * * * That the plaintiffs chose to run their business without enforceable supply contracts is not a satisfactory basis for [imposing liability]. * * * The plaintiffs are sophisticated participants in a multimillion-dollar commercial industry. * * * [T]he plaintiffs here could have allocated the risk of a supply disruption by negotiating enforceable supply contracts in the first place. Indeed, by not negotiating such contracts, the plaintiffs would appear to have made a choice to bear the risk of a supply disruption, presumably because they did not think that risk was worth the cost of reallocation or insurance. The plaintiffs' own business calculation is not a sound reason to impose indefinite liability on Bayer. * * *

Accordingly, we affirm the district court's grant of summary judgment.

People Express Airlines, Inc. v. Consolidated
Rail Corp.

Supreme Court of New Jersey, 1985.
100 N.J. 246, 495 A.2d 107.

■HANDLER, J. * * * On July 22, 1981, a fire began in the Port Newark freight yard of defendant Consolidated Rail Corporation (Conrail) when ethylene oxide manufactured by defendant BASF Wyandotte Company (BASF) escaped from a tank car, punctured during a "coupling" operation with another rail car, and ignited. The tank car was owned by defendant Union Tank Car Company (Union Car) and was leased to defendant BASF.

* * * The municipal authorities then evacuated the area within a one-mile radius surrounding the fire to lessen the risk to persons within the area should the burning tank car explode. The evacuation area included the adjacent North Terminal building of Newark International Airport, where plaintiff People Express Airlines' (People Express) business operations are based. Although the feared explosion never occurred, People Express employees were prohibited from using the North Terminal for twelve hours.

The plaintiff contends that it suffered business-interruption losses as a result of the evacuation. These losses consist of cancelled scheduled flights and lost reservations because employees were unable to answer the telephones to accept bookings; also, certain fixed operating expenses allocable to the evacuation time period were incurred and paid despite the fact that plaintiff's offices were closed. No physical damage to airline property and no personal injury occurred as a result of the fire. * * * According to People Express' original complaint, each defendant acted negligently and these acts of negligence proximately caused the plaintiff's harm.

* * * The answer to the allegation of unchecked liability is not the judicial obstruction of a fairly grounded claim for redress. Rather, it must be a more sedulous application of traditional concepts of duty and proximate causation to the facts of each case. * * * The physical harm requirement capriciously showers compensation along the path of physical destruction, regardless of the status or circumstances of individual claimants. Purely economic losses are borne by innocent victims, who may not be able to absorb their losses. * In the end, the challenge is to fashion a rule that limits liability but permits adjudication of meritorious claims. The asserted inability to fix crystalline formulae for recovery on the differing facts of future cases simply does not justify the wholesale rejection of recovery in all cases. * * *

Judicial discomfiture with the rule of nonrecovery for purely economic loss throughout the last several decades has led to numerous exceptions in the general rule. * * * One group of exceptions is based on the "special relationship" between the tortfeasor and the individual or business deprived of economic expectations. Many of these cases are recognized as involving the tort of negligent misrepresentation, resulting in liability for specially foreseeable economic losses[a]

---

[a]   [Eds.' note] See *infra* pages 826–835.

Importantly, the cases do not involve a breach of contract claim between parties in privity; rather, they involve tort claims by innocent third parties who suffered purely economic losses at the hands of negligent defendants with whom no direct relationship existed. Courts have justified their finding of liability in these negligence cases based on notions of a special relationship between the negligent tortfeasors and the foreseeable plaintiffs who relied on the quality of defendants' work or services, to their detriment. The special relationship, in reality, is an expression of the courts' satisfaction that a duty of care existed because the plaintiffs were particularly foreseeable and the injury was proximately caused by the defendant's negligence. * * *

A related exception in which courts have allowed recovery for purely economic losses has been extended to plaintiffs belonging to a particularly foreseeable group, such as sailors and seamen, for whom the law has traditionally shown great solicitude. * * *

These exceptions expose the hopeless artificiality of the *per se* rule against recovery for purely economic reasons. * * * We hold therefore that a defendant owes a duty of care to take reasonable measures to avoid the risk of causing economic damages, aside from physical injury, to particular plaintiffs or plaintiffs comprising an identifiable class with respect to whom defendant knows or has reason to know are likely to suffer such damages from its conduct. A defendant failing to adhere to this duty of care may be found liable for such economic damages proximately caused by its breach of duty.

We stress that an identifiable class of plaintiffs is not simply a foreseeable class of plaintiffs. For example, members of the general public, or invitees such as sales and service persons at a particular plaintiff's business premises, or persons travelling on a highway near the scene of a negligently-caused accident, such as the one at bar, who are delayed in the conduct of their affairs and suffer varied economic losses, are certainly a foreseeable class of plaintiffs. Yet their presence within the area would be fortuitous, and the particular type of economic injury that could be suffered by such persons would be hopelessly unpredictable and not realistically foreseeable. Thus, the class itself would not be sufficiently ascertainable. An identifiable class of plaintiffs must be particularly foreseeable in terms of the type of persons or entities comprising the class, the certainty or predictability of their presence, the approximate numbers of those in the class, as well as the type of economic expectations disrupted. * * *

* * * Plaintiff has set forth a cause of action under our decision, and it is entitled to have the matter proceed to a plenary trial. * * *

NOTES

1. *Exceptions to the Traditional Rule Denying Recovery for "Pure" Economic Loss.* As suggested by *Wiltz, supra* pages 500–502, the overwhelming majority of jurisdictions continue to follow the rule denying recovery in negligence for pure economic loss in the absence of personal injury or property damage. *People Express Airlines* is the rare exception. However, most courts recognize the exceptions noted in *People Express Airlines* and allow liability when there is either a " 'special relationship' between the tortfeasor and the individual or business deprived of economic

expectations" or where "plaintiffs belong[ ] to a particularly foreseeable group, such as sailors and seamen, for whom the law has traditionally shown great solicitude." For example, in Union Oil Co. v. Oppen, 501 F.2d 558 (9th Cir.1974), the plaintiffs were commercial fishermen who sued Union Oil Company and other defendants for their loss of profits resulting from a major oil spill allegedly caused by defendants. The court allowed recovery, identifying the "crucial determinant" as "whether the defendants could reasonably have foreseen that negligently conducted drilling operations might diminish aquatic life and thus injure the business of commercial fishermen." The court cited the traditional exceptions that a party sustaining only an economic loss sometimes can recover from a telegraph company or an attorney who negligently prepares a will. The court also noted the traditional solicitude of courts for those involved in fishing who sustain economic losses as a result of pollution.

2. *The Prospect of Expansive Liability.* In 532 Madison Ave. Gourmet Foods, Inc. v. Finlandia Center, Inc., 96 N.Y.2d 280, 727 N.Y.S.2d 49, 750 N.E.2d 1097 (2001), the New York Court of Appeals followed the traditional rule and rejected claims by businesses for pure economic loss. In one of the three consolidated cases, a section of a 39-story office tower collapsed, allegedly as a result of defendant's negligence, sending bricks, mortar, and other materials onto Madison Avenue in a prime commercial area. City officials closed fifteen heavily traveled blocks of Madison Avenue for two weeks, and some areas—including the location of plaintiff's delicatessen— were inaccessible for five weeks. The Court of Appeals rejected the claims of the plaintiff and others, reasoning that there was "no satisfactory way geographically to distinguish among those who have suffered purely economic losses. * * * [L]imiting the scope of defendants' duty to those who have * * * suffered personal injury or property damage * * * affords a principled basis for reasonably apportioning liability."

Suppose the court had reached a contrary decision and further suppose that after the September 11 terrorist attacks, Congress had not passed legislation limiting the liability of the airlines and others whose negligence arguably contributed to the tragedy. In the weeks that followed September 11, businesses in Manhattan, airlines, and indeed the tourist industry throughout the United States, not to mention investors, suffered huge losses as a result of the terrorist attacks. See Gail Makinen, Cong. Research Serv., RL31617, The Economic Effects of 9/11: A Retrospective Assessment 5 (2002), *available at* http://www.fas.org/irp/crs/RL31617.pdf. What, if anything, does this suggest about the wisdom of the economic loss doctrine?

3. *Economic Damages in Specific Contexts.* For an example of a products liability claim allowing a plaintiff to recover economic losses in the absence of a personal injury or property damage, see 80 South Eighth St. Ltd. P'ship v. Carey-Canada, Inc., 486 N.W.2d 393 (Minn.1992), *infra* pages 619–621. Also, Judge Cardozo's classic opinion in Ultramares Corp. v. Touche, 255 N.Y. 170, 174 N.E. 441 (1931), *infra* pages 828–833, addresses the issue of recovery of purely economic losses under a negligent misrepresentation claim.

CHAPTER 9

LIMITATION OF LIABILITY RESULTING FROM DEFENDANT'S IDENTITY OR RELATIONSHIPS ("IMMUNITIES")

This chapter addresses the issue of when the determination of liability should be altered, not by the nature of the defendant's conduct, but instead by the identity of the defendant or the nature of his relationship with the plaintiff. In an earlier era, immunities often barred liability, but the trend toward total or partial abrogation of such immunities during the latter decades of the twentieth century ranks among the more striking changes in twentieth century tort law.

Particularly difficult issues surround the liability of state, local, and federal governments, and their officers and employees. The topic is a complex one, with various jurisdictions answering these questions inconsistently. Hence, in this general study of tort law, it is possible only to provide an introduction.

A. INTRAFAMILY TORT LIABILITY

Counts v. Counts
Supreme Court of Virginia, 1980.
221 Va. 151, 266 S.E.2d 895.

■ COMPTON, JUSTICE. In this appeal of a tort action, we review the trial court's action in sustaining a plea of interspousal immunity. Here, the husband sued his former wife for compensatory and punitive damages, alleging severe injuries intentionally inflicted upon him by his wife's co-conspirator in an abortive murder-for-hire scheme. We are urged to carve another exception to the foregoing doctrine beyond those fashioned in Surratt v. Thompson, 212 Va. 191, 183 S.E.2d 200 (1971), and Korman v. Carpenter, 216 Va. 86, 216 S.E.2d 195 (1975).[8]

In March of 1977, appellant Robert C. Counts, the plaintiff below, sued Miles Randolph Turner and appellee Lillie Drew Counts, alleging that Turner maliciously injured the plaintiff in January of 1975 pursuant to an agreement between Turner and Mrs. Counts for the

---

[8] In *Surratt* this court refused to apply interspousal immunity to bar a wrongful death action brought by the wife's estate against the husband arising from an automobile accident. In *Korman*, we designed another exception to the doctrine and permitted the estate of a wife, who had been murdered by her husband, to sue the committee of the imprisoned spouse for wrongful death.

murder of Mr. Counts. * * * Mrs. Counts filed a demurrer asserting the action was barred by the doctrine of interspousal immunity. The trial court sustained * * * Mrs. Counts' demurrer and dismissed the action. Plaintiff sought an appeal from the March 1978 order of dismissal as to Mrs. Counts only, and we granted such request. * * *

During the latter part of 1974, while the Countses were married and cohabiting as husband and wife, she solicited Turner to kill Counts, promising to pay Turner $5,000 for the deed. On January 30, 1975, Turner went to the Countses' home in Pulaski County to carry out the conspiracy and attacked plaintiff, intending to kill him. The effort failed, but plaintiff sustained severe mental and physical injuries during the assault. Because Mrs. Counts concealed her part in the conspiracy from her husband, the couple continued to live together until sometime after plaintiff, in March of 1975, discovered his wife's role in the plot. Subsequently, Turner was convicted of maliciously wounding Counts. * * * Charged with conspiring to maliciously wound her husband, the wife was also convicted. She was sentenced to jail and fined. In February of 1977, the Countses' marriage was dissolved by divorce * and this action ensued two weeks later.

In sustaining the ex-wife's plea of immunity, the trial judge examined *Korman* and wrote that "the doctrine of interspousal immunity still is the law of Virginia" except in "automobile cases and under the actual facts of *Korman*." He also was of opinion that "[i]f another exception is to be made to the rule, that must be done either by the Supreme Court of Virginia or by the General Assembly." On appeal, the question is whether the wife is immune from liability in tort for personal injuries intentionally inflicted upon the husband at her direction during the marriage, when the parties are divorced from the bond of matrimony at the time the action is instituted.

Plaintiff urges us to succumb to the current trend and abolish the doctrine of interspousal immunity in its entirety or, in the alternative, to substantially modify the doctrine again to embrace the facts of this case. He points out we have already recognized that a former basis for the doctrine, i.e., the fiction that husband and wife are of "one flesh," is "outmoded," citing Korman v. Carpenter, 216 Va. at 90, 216 S.E.2d at 197. He also notes we said in *Korman* that another justification for the doctrine, that is, preservation of the marriage, becomes irrelevant when one spouse murders the other thus leaving no "marriage to be saved" and no "union to be preserved." * Accordingly, the argument continues, when, as here, the action is brought after the parties are finally divorced, there likewise is no marriage to be preserved, and the common-law doctrine of interspousal immunity * * * should not be applied to bar this suit for a purely personal and malicious tort committed by one spouse against the other during coverture. We reject the plaintiff's invitation to abolish the doctrine *in toto* and we refuse to chisel another exception into the rule to cover the facts of this case.

In *Korman*, we reviewed the history and development of interspousal immunity in Virginia, as articulated in Keister v. Keister, 123 Va. 157, 96 S.E. 315 (1918), through its abrogation in motor vehicle accident litigation in *Surratt*. * We were concerned in *Korman*, as here, with a policy and rule of law designed to protect and encourage the preservation of marriages. * * *

Nevertheless, in *Korman* we forged an exception to the doctrine and permitted the suit to proceed. There we pointed out that in the automobile context of *Surratt*, the court considered "the high incidence of liability insurance covering Virginia-based motor vehicles, together with the mandatory uninsured motorist endorsements to insurance policies" and concluded that the doctrine "could no longer be supported as promotive of the peace and tranquility of the home." We then reasoned that

> in light of *Surratt* it would be an anomaly for us to apply interspousal immunity in this case. We would be invoking the doctrine ostensibly to preserve a family relationship which had been voluntarily terminated by the parties; to promote domestic harmony that had disappeared from the marriage; and to save a marriage which had been terminated by the murder of the wife by the husband. The rule of stare decisis does not require such specious reasoning.

We observed that if the *Surratt* majority "acted properly in abrogating interspousal immunity" in motor vehicle litigation, its abrogation under the facts of *Korman* was "required." We went on to hold "that an action for wrongful death may be maintained, predicated upon injuries to one spouse during marriage arising out of a wrongful act by the other spouse, when such an act results in the termination of the marriage by death, and when the deceased spouse is survived by no living child or grandchild." We concluded by emphasizing we were deciding only "the narrow question" presented by *Korman's* facts and we restricted the precedential scope of the holding, stating we were "not persuaded that permitting a living spouse to sue for torts committed by one on the other, except in automobile accident litigation, would do otherwise than contribute to the destruction of their marriage." We are still not persuaded.

A superficial analysis of *Korman* and the case at bar would reveal no logical justification for abrogating the immunity in the former and applying it in the latter. It would appear on the surface that the policy concern of preserving the marriage would be as irrelevant when the marriage has been ended by divorce as when the marriage has been terminated by death.

But a close examination of the effect on the marriage relationship of permitting a living spouse to sue after divorce for even intentional torts committed during coverture by one on the other dictates a reaffirmance of the immunity doctrine, a concept which is ingrained in the body of law of this State and which is an integral part of the public policy of the Commonwealth to preserve the family unit. Were we to authorize such damage suits, we are confident the availability of such a remedy and the accompanying prospect of a monetary award would contribute to the disruption of many marriages. One example based on an elementary set of assumed facts will serve to illustrate:

The formerly stable marriage of Husband and Wife begins to deteriorate. Finally, in a particularly heated exchange, Husband intentionally strikes Wife causing an injury. Wife then leaves the marital abode and retains an attorney. During the initial consultation, the attorney concludes that Wife is entitled to a divorce on the ground of cruelty and constructive desertion, but nevertheless properly explores the possibility of a reconciliation. Having learned of the injury, the attorney also advises Wife that now in Virginia she may sue Husband and recover damages for her personal injuries, provided she waits to sue until after the divorce is final. Wife, who would otherwise be inclined to seek a reconciliation leading to ultimate preservation of the marriage, is influenced by the prospect of a damage award and decides to quickly sue for divorce so it can become final before the statute of limitations runs on the personal injury claim. Manifestly, it cannot be successfully argued that in such a situation the likelihood of a damage award "would do otherwise than contribute to the destruction of [the parties'] marriage," as we cautioned in *Korman*.[4]

And even if the foregoing scenario did not develop in every situation, the mere availability of such an interspousal action injects into the marriage relationship just one more abrasive and unnecessary ingredient to be added to existing criminal and divorce remedies; the threat would be: "I will not only report your abuse to the criminal prosecutor and seek spousal support in the course of divorcing you, but I will also sue you for damages." We refuse to add by judicial fiat this further impediment to the unity of marriage.

For these reasons, the judgment of the trial court will be affirmed.

■ POFF, JUSTICE, dissenting. I would not abolish the doctrine of interspousal immunity. Nor do I believe one spouse should have a right of action against the other for damages for every intentional tort. But, recognizing that the doctrine is judge-made and may be refined by this Court when necessary to promote the ends of justice, I would allow the suit in this case.

This is not a case of an "uninvited kiss." The plaintiff has suffered grievous injuries as the result of a deliberate tort planned and committed with cold-blooded, criminal intent by the defendant acting through a hired agent. Although the marriage was not terminated by death caused by the tort as in Korman v. Carpenter, 216 Va. 86, 216 S.E.2d 195 (1975), there can be no reasonable doubt that the tort, once discovered by the plaintiff, led to the dissolution of the marriage by divorce. Since we have rejected the "one flesh" fiction as "outmoded," the sole policy underpinning the doctrine is the societal need "to protect and encourage the preservation of marriages." What is left to be preserved here?

The issue here is whether marriage may be asserted as a ground of immunity by a spouse whose willful criminal conduct has destroyed the marriage. * * * The fallacy of the majority's reasoning is that it assumes that all intentional torts are alike and the consequences they produce are the same. How many marriages would survive an interspousal tort committed with intent to kill, maim, disfigure, or disable? Such malicious conduct amounts to a repudiation of the marital contract. The typical victim of such conduct would terminate the marriage regardless of the availability of a right of action for damages. Only a spouse with a

---

[4] We observed in Furey v. Furey, 193 Va. 727, 71 S.E.2d 191 (1952) (interspousal immunity applied to bar suit for antenuptial tort), that an " 'uninvited kiss, no matter how cold and chaste . . . is an assault and battery, and substantial damages may be awarded for such [and that to abrogate the immunity would create] the possibility of recovering . . . monetary damages by an overkissed [wife or] husband.' " 193 Va. at 733 n.5, 71 S.E.2d at 194 n.5, quoting foreign authority.

saintly penchant for absolution or one enervated by fear would decide to continue the marriage. And the decision of such a person would never be substantially influenced by the availability of a right of action for damages. The saintly spouse would not be so venal as to terminate the marriage in order to gain standing to sue; the fearful spouse would forgo the right to monetary damages rather than face the trauma of divorce and the risk of retaliation.

I would hold that when, as here, a spouse has been injured by a tort committed by the other spouse with intent to kill, maim, disfigure, or disable and divorce follows the tort without intervening condonation, the victim may maintain an action for damages against the wrongdoer. If such a rule is an exception to the doctrine of interspousal immunity (and I regard it simply as the kind of refinement the evolving common law necessitates), it does no violence to the policy underlying the doctrine. Instead, it honors the ancient principle that one who suffers a wrong should not be left without a remedy.

Price v. Price

Supreme Court of Texas, 1987.
732 S.W.2d 316.

■ KILGARLIN, JUSTICE. This case presents us with the opportunity to reexamine the validity of the doctrine of interspousal immunity. The case originated as a civil action of negligence for personal injuries brought by Kimberly Parmenter Price against her husband, Duane Price. Duane Price's motion for summary judgment was granted. The court of appeals affirmed that judgment. * We reverse the judgment of the court of appeals and remand this cause to the trial court.

In July of 1983, Kimberly Parmenter, at the time a *feme sole*, was injured when a motorcycle on which she was riding collided with a truck. The motorcycle was driven by Duane Price. Six months after the accident, Duane and Kimberly were married. After marriage, Kimberly brought this action seeking recovery from her husband, Duane, and from the driver of the truck, claiming that the negligence of these drivers had caused her injuries. The driver of the truck and his employer settled. The trial court, in granting summary judgment for Duane, relied on the doctrine that one spouse could not sue another for negligent conduct.

The doctrine of interspousal immunity is a part of the common law, having been judicially created. Its origins are shrouded in antiquity, but the basis of the doctrine is *"that a husband and wife are one person."* Firebrass v. Pennant, 2 Wils. 255, 256 (C.P. 1764). A woman's disability during coverture was an essential ingredient in fostering the doctrine. As was stated in Thompson v. Thompson, 218 U.S. 611, 614–15, 31 S.Ct. 111, 54 L.Ed. 1180 (1910):

> At common law the husband and wife were regarded as one,— the legal existence of the wife during coverture being merged in that of the husband; and, generally speaking, the wife was incapable of making contracts, of acquiring property or disposing of the same without her husband's consent. They could not enter into contracts with each other, *nor were they*

liable for torts committed by one against the other. (emphasis
added).

An earlier thesis on American law expanded the concept of
superiority of the husband over the wife even to the extent of
restraining her liberty or disciplining her. 2 Kent's Com. 174 (8th ed.
1854). While in this, the last quarter of the twentieth century, such
views seem preposterous, recognition that those views were prevalent
in the law makes easily understandable why suits by wives against
husbands were not permitted.

However, the husband/wife unity argument as grounds for the
doctrine was severely impeded by the adoption of what were known as
Married Women Acts. These legislative acts occurred principally in the
latter half of the nineteenth century and early twentieth century. *
These acts, while varying from state to state, generally gave wives the
rights to own, acquire and dispose of property; to contract; and, to sue
in respect to their property and contracts. Most importantly, many of
the statutes specifically abolished the doctrine of the oneness of
husband and wife.

With the demise of the legal fiction of the merger of husband and
wife into a single entity, the doctrine of interspousal immunity found
support in considerations of marital harmony, as well as the potential
for collusive lawsuits. Restatement (Second) of Torts § 895F cmt. d
(1979).

American jurisdictions, in upholding the doctrine, early on
espoused the premise that a civil suit by one spouse against another
would destroy the harmony of the home. One court, in a fire and
brimstone opinion upholding the prohibition against suits between
spouses, foresaw all manner of evil should the immunity doctrine be
terminated. In Ritter v. Ritter, 31 Pa. 396, 398 (1858), that court, while
observing that a favorite maxim at common law was that marriage
makes a man and woman one person at law, also said:

> Nothing could so complete that severance [of the marriage
> relationship] and degradation, as to throw open litigation to
> the parties. The maddest advocate for woman's [sic] rights, and
> for the abolition on earth of all divine institutions, could wish
> for no more decisive blow from the courts than this. The flames
> which litigation would kindle on the domestic hearth would
> consume in an instant the conjugal bond, and bring on a new
> era indeed—an era of universal discord, of unchastity, of
> bastardy, of dissoluteness, of violence, cruelty, and murders.

The second argument for barring interspousal suits, the possibility
of collusive lawsuits, is entirely inconsistent with the subjugation of
wife to husband and preservation of happy homes theses. Nevertheless,
such inconsistency did not seem to trouble the courts. * * *

Without ascribing any reasons for doing so, Texas adopted the
doctrine of interspousal immunity one hundred years ago * * *. The
doctrine remained firmly established as Texas law until Bounds v.
Caudle, 560 S.W.2d 925 (Tex.1977). *Bounds* abrogated the rule as to
intentional torts. In *Bounds*, this court concluded that suits for willful
or intentional torts would not disrupt domestic tranquility since "the
peace and harmony of a home" which had "been strained to the point

where an intentional physical attack could take place" could not be further impaired by allowing a suit to recover damages. * * * Dean William Prosser, a preeminent commentator on tort law, certainly agreed that the doctrine is indefensible. He has stated:

> Stress has been laid upon the danger of fictitious and fraudulent claims, on the very dubious assumption that a wife's love for her husband is such that she is more likely to bring a false suit against him than a genuine one; and likewise the possibility of trivial actions for minor annoyances, which might well be taken care of by finding consent to all ordinary fictions of wedlock—or at least assumption of risk! The chief reason relied upon by all these courts, however, is that personal tort actions between husband and wife would disrupt and destroy the peace and harmony of the home, which is against the policy of the law. This is on the bald theory that after a husband has beaten his wife, there is a state of peace and harmony left to be disturbed; and that if she is sufficiently injured or angry to sue him for it, she will be soothed and deterred from reprisals by denying her the legal remedy—and this even though she has left him or divorced him for that very ground, and although the same courts refuse to find any disruption of domestic tranquility if she sues him for a tort to her property, or brings a criminal prosecution against him. If this reasoning appeals to the reader, let him by all means adopt it. *

* * * It is difficult to fathom how denying a forum for the redress of any wrong could be said to encourage domestic tranquility. It is equally difficult to see how suits based in tort would destroy domestic tranquility, while property and contract actions do not. As to the potential for fraud and collusion, we are unable to distinguish interspousal suits from other actions for personal injury. In Whitworth v. Bynum, 699 S.W.2d 194, 197 (Tex.1985), this court "refuse[d] to indulge in the assumption that close relatives will prevaricate so as to promote a spurious lawsuit." Our system of justice is capable of ascertaining the existence of fraud and collusion. * * *

Other jurisdictions have preceded us in either completely or partially abolishing the doctrine of interspousal immunity. [The court lists precedents from 38 states abrogating the immunity in all or some types of cases.] The doctrine of interspousal immunity has previously been abrogated as to some causes of action in this jurisdiction. We now abolish that doctrine completely as to any cause of action. We do not limit our holding to suits involving vehicular accidents only, as has been done by some jurisdictions and as has been urged upon us in this case. To do so would be to negate meritorious claims such as was presented in Stafford v. Stafford, 726 S.W.2d 14 (Tex.1987). In that case a husband had transmitted a venereal disease to his wife, resulting in an infection that ultimately caused Mrs. Stafford the loss of her ovaries and fallopian tubes, ending for all time her ability to bear children. While we ruled for her, the issue of interspousal immunity had not been preserved for our review. To leave in place a bar to suits like that of Mrs. Stafford or other suits involving non-vehicular torts would amount to a repudiation of the constitutional guarantee of equal protection of the laws. * This we will not do.

Our result today is compelled by the fundamental proposition of public policy that the courts should afford redress for a wrong, and the failure of the rationale supporting the doctrine to withstand scrutiny. We therefore reverse the judgment of the court of appeals upholding the trial court's summary judgment, and remand this cause to the trial court for further proceedings.

NOTES

1. *Interspousal Immunity.* Most states have either abrogated or provided exceptions to the traditional doctrine of interspousal immunity. See Boone v. Boone, 345 S.C. 8, 11–13, 546 S.E.2d 191, 192–93 (2001) (listing decisions from most jurisdictions). A few jurisdictions continue to recognize the immunity in the cases of both intentional and negligent torts. See, e.g., Ga. Code Ann. § 19–3–8 (2013). In other jurisdictions, the immunity continues to apply to some, but not all, intentional torts. See, e.g., Lusby v. Lusby, 283 Md. 334, 390 A.2d 77 (1978) (no interspousal immunity for intentional conduct characterized as "outrageous"; husband and companions ran wife off road by pointing gun at her and crowding her vehicle; he then raped her and helped his companions attempt to rape her).

2. *Insurance Coverage for Intrafamily Torts.* As noted in *Price*, one of the traditionally articulated justifications for intrafamily immunities was to avoid insurance fraud. May an insurer now incorporate into its policies exclusions for torts committed within the family? See, e.g., Farmers Ins. Group v. Reed, 109 Idaho 849, 712 P.2d 550 (1985) (household exclusion clause violates mandatory insurance statute and is consequently "void as against public policy"); see also Nationwide Gen. Ins. Co. v. Seeman, 702 A.2d 915 (Del.1997) (policy provision limiting maximum liability coverage for members of insured's household to $15,000, the minimum required under compulsory insurance laws, held invalid as a violation of public policy); Lewis v. West Am. Ins. Co., 927 S.W.2d 829 (Ky.1996) (similar). Compare Shelter Gen. Ins. Co. v. Lincoln, 590 N.W.2d 726 (Iowa 1999) (upholding the validity of a policy exclusion for injuries to family members in automobile liability policies); Schanowitz v. State Farm Mut. Auto. Ins. Co., 299 Ill.App.3d 843, 234 Ill.Dec. 289, 702 N.E.2d 629 (1998) (similar; umbrella policy; exclusion upheld on ground that claim was covered by uninsured motorist provision of applicable primary automobile liability policy).

Broadbent v. Broadbent

Supreme Court of Arizona, 1995.
184 Ariz. 74, 907 P.2d 43.

■ CORCORAN, JUSTICE. * * * Christopher and his mother, Laura J. Broadbent, went swimming at the family residence on April 13, 1984, their first day of swimming that year. Christopher was wearing "floaties," which are inflatable rings worn on the arms to assist a child in staying afloat. Laura understood that a child could still drown while wearing floaties and should be supervised. At the time of the accident, Christopher was two-and-a-half years old and did not know how to swim. Laura and Christopher were by the side of the pool when the telephone rang. Laura left Christopher alone by the pool to answer the phone. Laura saw Christopher remove his floaties before she answered the phone. Laura talked on the phone 5 to 10 minutes and could not see Christopher from where she was talking. She also did not have on her contact lenses. Laura said that if she stretched the phone cord and her body, she could see the pool area, but when she did this, she could not see Christopher. She dropped the phone, ran toward the pool, and found Christopher floating in the deep end of the pool. Laura administered cardio-pulmonary resuscitation and telephoned for the paramedics. Neither Laura nor the paramedics were able to revive Christopher. The paramedics took Christopher to the hospital where he was finally revived. As a result of this near drowning, Christopher suffered severe brain damage because of lack of oxygen. He has lost his motor skills and has no voluntary movement. * * *

A complaint was filed on behalf of Christopher, as plaintiff, against his mother, alleging that she was negligent and caused his injuries. This action was brought to involve the Broadbents' umbrella insurance carrier in the issue of coverage. In her answer, Laura admitted that she was negligent in her supervision of Christopher, and she moved for summary judgment, arguing that the doctrine of parental immunity applied. * * * The trial court granted Laura's motion for summary judgment and ruled that the parental immunity doctrine applied to the facts of this case. Phillip Broadbent, as Conservator for Christopher, appealed to the court of appeals. The parties stipulated that: (1) the real party in interest was Northbrook Indemnity Company, who provided personal umbrella liability insurance coverage for Laura Broadbent on the date of the accident; (2) Laura may be entitled to indemnity from Northbrook if Laura is liable for the injuries to Christopher; (3) Laura did not want to defend the action but agreed that Northbrook should be permitted to defend; and (4) the only issue in the case was whether the doctrine of parental immunity applied.

The court of appeals ordered that Northbrook be permitted to appear and defend the case. The court of appeals affirmed the trial court, finding that under the parental immunity doctrine the mother was not liable for her child's injuries. * * * The court of appeals noted that it based its decision on an application of the current status of the parental immunity doctrine in Arizona and that any departure or modification of the established case law was "for the supreme court to determine" and not the court of appeals. * We agree and do so in this opinion today.

I.   History and Purpose of the Parental Immunity Doctrine

A.   *The Origins of Parental Immunity*

We begin by stating a few basic facts about the treatment of children under the law and family immunities. Under common law, a child has traditionally been considered a separate legal entity from his or her parent. * Children have generally been allowed to sue their parents in property and contract actions. * * *

The doctrine of parental immunity is an American phenomenon unknown in the English common law. * * * In early American history, children were viewed as "evil and in need of strict discipline," and the courts recognized wide parental discretion. * There was a strong presumption that parental discipline was proper. See, e.g., S.C. Code Ann. § 16–3–40 (Law.Co-op.1976) (statute originating from 1712 that provided a defense to "[k]illing by stabbing or thrusting" if done while chastising or correcting your child). Only recently has the state intervened to protect children. * Viewed against this backdrop, it is not surprising that no American child had sought recovery against a parent for tortious conduct until the late nineteenth century.

In Hewlett v. George, 68 Miss. 703, 711, 9 So. 885, 887 (1891), the Supreme Court of Mississippi held, without citation to legal authority, that a child could not sue her parent for being falsely imprisoned in an insane asylum because of parental immunity, a doctrine which that court created from whole cloth. As its rationale, the court stated:

> [S]o long as the parent is under obligation to care for, guide and control, and the child is under reciprocal obligation to aid and comfort and obey, no such action as this can be maintained. The peace of society, and of the families composing society, and a sound public policy, designed to subserve the repose of families and the best interests of society, forbid to the minor child a right to appear in court in the assertion of a claim to civil redress for personal injuries suffered at the hands of the parent.

* * * [T]he doctrine of parental immunity * * * was soon embraced by almost every state. * However, the courts soon began fashioning several exceptions to the doctrine, and in several states the doctrine has been abolished. * In several situations, parental immunity does not apply: if the parent is acting outside his parental role and within the scope of his employment; if the parent acts willfully, wantonly, or recklessly; if the child is emancipated; if the child or parent dies; if a third party is liable for the tort, then the immunity of the parent does not protect that third party; and if the tortfeasor is standing *in loco parentis*, such as a grandparent, foster parent, or teacher, then the immunity does not apply. * See Restatement (Second) of Torts § 895G at 428–30 (1979) (listing longstanding exceptions to parental immunity doctrine). * * *

C.   *Analysis of the Policy Reasons Advanced in Support of Parental Immunity*

Courts and commentators have postulated many policy reasons for the parental immunity doctrine. The primary justifications for this immunity are:

(1)   Suing one's parents would disturb domestic tranquility;

(2)   Suing one's parents would create a danger of fraud and collusion;

(3)   Awarding damages to the child would deplete family resources;

(4)   Awarding damages to the child could benefit the parent if the child predeceases the parent and the parent inherits the child's damages; and

(5)   Suing one's parents would interfere with parental care, discipline, and control.

Streenz v. Streenz, 106 Ariz. 86, 87 n.1, 471 P.2d 282, 283 n.1 (1970) *
We believe that all of these justifications provide weak support for the
parental immunity doctrine.

The injury to the child, more than the lawsuit, disrupts the family
tranquility. In fact, if the child is not compensated for the tortious
injury, then peace in the family is even less likely. In the seminal
Arizona case on parental immunity, the court recognized that family
tranquility would not be disturbed if the parents had liability
insurance. * This fear of upsetting the family tranquility also seems
unrealistic when we consider how such a lawsuit is initiated. The
parent most often makes the decision to sue himself, and the parent is
in effect prepared to say that he was negligent. *

The danger of fraud and collusion is present in all lawsuits. We
should not deny recovery to an entire class of litigants because some
litigants might try to deceive the judicial system. The system can ferret
out fraudulent and collusive behavior in suits brought by children
against their parents just as the system detects such behavior in other
contexts.

We note, too, that both of these arguments—disturbing domestic
tranquility and danger of fraud and collusion—were also justifications
for spousal immunity, which has been abrogated in Arizona. These
same concerns could justify an immunity from suits brought by one
sibling against another; however, this is an immunity that the courts
have not felt the need to create. Furthermore, one of the justifications
for spousal immunity was that husband and wife were considered a
single legal entity, yet this legal fiction was not applied to the parent-
child relationship. As noted earlier, children have always been able to
maintain actions against their parents in contexts other than
negligence actions, such as contract actions or for willful conduct by the
parent. Therefore, the reliance on spousal immunity as a justification
for parental immunity is not sound. *

A damage award for the child will not deplete, or unfairly
redistribute, the family's financial resources. These cases will generally
not be brought if no insurance coverage is available, and therefore the
worry that the family's resources will be depleted for the benefit of one
child is illusory. The opposite is true. If a child has been seriously
injured and needs expensive medical care, then a successful lawsuit
against the parent and subsequent recovery from the insurance
company could ease the financial burden on the family. It would not be
a viable rule to say that liability only exists where insurance exists, but
we recognize that lawsuits generally will be brought when there is
potential insurance coverage.

The possibility that the parent might inherit money recovered by
the child is remote. This becomes a concern only if the parent inherits
as a beneficiary under intestate succession laws. This is a concern for
the probate courts and the laws of intestate succession, not tort law.
The remedy would be to prohibit inheritance by the parent—not to deny
recovery to the injured child. *

The Arizona courts have embraced the rationale that allowing a
child to sue a parent would interfere with parental care, discipline, and

control. * We have cited with approval the Wisconsin Supreme Court's statement that:

> [a] new and heavy burden would be added to the responsibility and privilege of parenthood, if within the wide scope of daily experiences common to the upbringing of children a parent could be subjected to a suit for damages for each failure to exercise care and judgment commensurate with the risk.

Sandoval v. Sandoval, 128 Ariz. 11, 13, 623 P.2d 800, 802 (1981). * The justification that allowing children to sue their parents would undercut parental authority and discretion has more appeal than the other rationales. However, if a child were seriously injured as a result of the exercise of parental authority, such as by a beating, then it would constitute an injury willfully inflicted, and parents are generally not immune for willful, wanton, or malicious conduct. * Furthermore, such a willful beating would probably constitute child abuse and could be criminally prosecuted. See Ariz. Rev. Stat. § 8–546 (Supp.1994). *

We want to protect the right of parents to raise their children by their own methods and in accordance with their own attitudes and beliefs. The New York Court of Appeals aptly stated this concern:

> Considering the different economic, educational, cultural, ethnic and religious backgrounds which must prevail, there are so many combinations and permutations of parent-child relationships that may result that the search for a standard would necessarily be in vain. . . . For this reason parents have always had the right to determine how much independence, supervision and control a child should have, and to best judge the character and extent of development of their child.

Holodook v. Spencer, 36 N.Y.2d 35, 50, 324 N.E.2d 338, 346, 364 N.Y.S.2d 859, 867 (1974). * Though we recognize the importance of allowing parental discretion, we disagree that our searching for a standard would be "in vain." Parents do not possess unfettered discretion in raising their children.

II.   The Abolishment of Parental Immunity and Adoption of the "Reasonable Parent" Standard for Parent-Child Suits

Although the above concerns make it difficult to draft a proper standard for the type of action a child may maintain against a parent, we will attempt to do so. We need to "fashion an objective standard that does not result in second-guessing parents in the management of their family affairs." * * * If we were to hold that parents are immune for negligent supervision of children, then the issue of liability would revolve around whether an activity could be described as "supervision" and whether lack of supervision was the cause of the injury. This would not involve a consideration of whether the activity infringed on the parents' discretionary decisions regarding care, custody, and control. Almost everything a parent does in relation to his child involves "care, custody, and control." We add that parents always owe a parental duty to their minor child. The issue of liability should revolve around whether the parents have breached this duty and, if so, whether the breach of duty caused the injury.

In accord with the California Supreme Court, "we reject the implication * * * that within certain aspects of the parent-child relationship, the parent has carte blanche to act negligently toward his child. * * * [A]lthough a parent has the prerogative and the duty to exercise authority over his minor child, this prerogative must be exercised within reasonable limits." * We hereby * * * approve of the "reasonable parent test," in which a parent's conduct is judged by whether that parent's conduct comported with that of a reasonable and prudent parent in a similar situation. A parent is not immune from liability for tortious conduct directed toward his child solely by reason of that relationship. See Restatement (Second) of Torts § 895G at 426. And, a parent is not liable for an act or omission that injured his child if the parent acted as a reasonable and prudent parent in the situation would.

III. Application to the Present Case

In this case, the trier of fact may find that the mother, Laura Broadbent, did not act as a reasonable and prudent parent would have in this situation. The finder of fact must determine whether leaving a two-and-a-half year old child unattended next to a swimming pool is reasonable or prudent. We fail to see why parents should not be held liable for negligence in failing to supervise their own children near the pool, when their liability would be clear had the children not been their own. We think that in most cases, if not all, the standard of care owed to a parent's own child is the same as that owed to any other child.

The paradox of parental immunity can be seen if we assume that a neighbor child from across the street was a guest and was injured at the same time and under the same circumstances as Christopher. Should the neighbor child be permitted to sue and recover damages from Laura but Christopher be denied the same opportunity?

A parent may avoid liability because there is no negligence, but not merely because of the status as parent. Children are certainly accident prone, and oftentimes those accidents are not due to the negligence of any party. The same rules of summary judgment apply to these cases as to others, and trial courts should feel free to dismiss frivolous cases on the ground that the parent has acted as a reasonable and prudent parent in a similar situation would. * * * Laura Broadbent is not immune from liability in this case because of the doctrine of parental immunity, which we hereby abolish. * * *

■ FELDMAN, CHIEF JUSTICE, specially concurring. I join in the abrogation of parental immunity and the court's adoption of the reasonable and prudent parent test but write separately to sound a note of caution. Although we abolish a rule of tort immunity, we must bear in mind that "difficult problems" remain in "determining when a physical harm should be regarded as actionable." Restatement (Second) of Torts § 895G cmt. k. If the alleged tortious conduct does not grow out of the family relationship, the question of negligence "may be determined as if the parties were not related." However, there are areas of broad discretion in which only parents have authority to make decisions. In these areas, I agree with the Restatement's view that "the standard of a reasonable prudent parent ... recognize[s] the existence of that discretion and thus ... require[s] that the [parent's] conduct be palpably unreasonable in order to impose liability." If, however, the charged breach of duty falls outside the area of a parent's discretionary authority and is, instead, within the obligation of due care owed by anyone who has supervisory or other responsibility for another's safety, then the test should be much more flexible.

Thus, the parent who decides to enroll a two-year-old child in swimming lessons at a neighborhood pool operates within the realm of parent-child decision-making. Although the child might be hurt during the course of such lessons, the decision to put the child in that position is peculiarly a matter of parental authority rather than a question of supervisory care or performance. Under the proper application of the reasonable and prudent parent test, as a matter of law there should be no liability unless one could say the decision was palpably unreasonable under given circumstances.

The facts of this case illustrate the other side of the coin. The act of leaving an unsupervised two-year-old child, who was unable to swim, at the side of a swimming pool was not an exercise of parental decision-making but an inadvertent act in the performance of duties owed by a caretaker. As the Restatement indicates, the reasonable and prudent parent test extends a great deal of flexibility to the first example but much less, if any, to the second.

NOTE

Parental Immunity. In recent decades, there has been a clear trend toward abolishing or greatly restricting parental immunity, but abrogation of this immunity has proceeded more slowly than in the case of interspousal immunity. See Harper, James and Gray on Torts § 8.11.

Courts generally have allowed parents to be held liable in tort to their children for claims other than ones asserting negligence or other tortious conduct in core parenting activities. For example, many jurisdictions now allow parents to be held liable for injuries arising from automobile accidents, at least where liability insurance coverage is available. See, e.g., Md. Code Ann., Cts. & Jud. Proc. § 5–806 (LexisNexis 2014) (up to mandatory minimum liability insurance coverage limits); Farmers Ins. Group v. Reed, 109 Idaho 849, 712 P.2d 550 (1985); Unah v. Martin, 1984 OK 2, 676 P.2d 1366 (1984); Jilani v. Jilani, 767 S.W.2d 671 (Tex.1988). Courts frequently allow recovery from the parent when the child's injury results from the activities of the parent in a different capacity than that of merely being a parent. See, e.g., Terror Mining Co. v. Roter, 866 P.2d 929, 936–37 (Colo.1994) (liability in a case of an injury arising from "business or employment activities"); Dzenutis v. Dzenutis, 200 Conn. 290, 512 A.2d 130 (1986) (same). Finally, courts are inclined to allow recovery in extreme cases such as those involving sexual abuse, see Hurst v. Capitell, 539 So.2d 264 (Ala.1989), and the intentional killing of the other parent, see Eagan v. Calhoun, 347 Md. 72, 698 A.2d 1097 (1997); cf. similarly, Mahnke v. Moore, 197 Md. 61, 77 A.2d 923 (1951) (right of action against a parent "for injuries resulting from cruel and inhuman treatment or for malicious and wanton wrongs"; decedent father had blown mother's head off with a shotgun in presence of 4½-year-old child, then committed suicide with a shotgun in child's presence a week later).

Most jurisdictions that have limited parental immunity continue to assert it for something like "conduct inherent to parent-child relationship," comprising "an exercise of parental authority and supervision over the child or an exercise of discretion in the provision of care to the child," Cates

v. Cates, 156 Ill.2d 76, 104–05, 189 Ill.Dec. 14, 28, 619 N.E.2d 715, 729 (1993), or "conduct that constitutes the exercise of parental authority, the performance of parental supervision, and the provision of parental care and custody." Broadwell v. Holmes, 871 S.W.2d 471, 476–77 (Tenn.1994). Will the resolution of cases in jurisdictions such as these differ from the outcomes in jurisdictions that have abrogated the immunity?

B. LIABILITY OF CHARITABLE INSTITUTIONS

Another immunity that has substantially faded is charitable immunity. During the latter part of the nineteenth century and the early part of the twentieth century, courts in most American jurisdictions held that these charitable institutions could not be held liable for the negligent acts of their employees. See Harper, James and Gray on Torts §§ 29.16, 29.17. The original justification for this immunity was that allowing a charity to be held liable in tort would divert funds from the purpose intended by donors, to the cost of liability. See Heriot's Hosp. Feoffees v. Ross, (1846) 8 Eng.Rep. 1508, 1510, 12 Clark & F. 507, 513. Charitable immunity, reasoned the courts, encouraged donations and protected churches, hospitals, museums, and similar institutions from being crippled by tort claims and impairing their ability to fulfill their public interest missions.

Beginning with the landmark decision of President & Dirs. of Georgetown Coll. v. Hughes, 130 F.2d 810 (D.C.Cir.1942), most jurisdictions have repudiated or limited the doctrine of charitable immunity. Liability insurance is available to protect charities against financial disaster, and insurance premiums for such coverage are regarded as a routine business expense for charitable institutions, as well as other enterprises. Other jurisdictions limit or constrict the liability of charitable institutions. Among the decisions that have rejected the doctrine altogether are Davis v. Church of Jesus Christ of Latter Day Saints, 258 Mont. 286, 852 P.2d 640 (1993) and Howle v. Camp Amon Carter, 470 S.W.2d 629 (Tex.1971). For examples of limitations on the liability of charities, see Md. Code Ann., Ins. § 19–103 (LexisNexis 2014) (requiring policy provisions that liability insurers of charitable institutions may not assert charitable immunity defense for claims covered by policy); Id., Cts. & Jud. Proc. § 5–632 (LexisNexis 2013) (hospitals "or related institutions" do not have charitable tort immunity unless they carry liability insurance of at least $100,000, in which case their liability is capped at the limits of that insurance); Mass. Gen. Laws ch. 231, § 85k (2012) (liability of charitable institutions limited to $100,000 in case of injuries arising from charitable activities; no limit on recovery for injuries arising from "activities primarily commercial in character").

C. LIABILITY OF THE GOVERNMENT AND ITS OFFICERS

1. LIABILITY OF STATE GOVERNMENTS

NOTES

1. *Sovereign Immunity.* American notions of government immunity trace back to roots in medieval English law that were characterized by the

ancient maxim that "the King can do no wrong." "Just how an immunity that had its roots in feudalism and in a political philosophy associated with the divine right of kings was transplanted to the new republic in America remains something of a mystery." Harper, James and Gray on Torts § 29.2. Later, Justice Holmes explained sovereign immunity in these terms: "A sovereign is exempt from suit, not because of any formal conception or obsolete theory, but on the logical and practical ground that there can be no legal right as against the authority that makes the law on which the right depends." Kawananakoa v. Polyblank, 205 U.S. 349, 353, 27 S.Ct. 526, 527, 51 L.Ed. 834, 836 (1907) (dictum). "But the absence of 'legal right' against the sovereign does not accurately reflect even English history, for the petition of right against the king has been an institutionalized practice since the reign of Edward I. And Holmes's dictum offers no help in solving the problem of whether a modern democratic society *should,* as a matter of either morals or expediency, assume liability and, if so, to what extent." Harper, James and Gray on Torts, § 29.3.

More recently, sovereign immunity most often has been justified on policy grounds. In Opinion of the Justices, 126 N.H. 554, 560, 493 A.2d 1182, 1186–88 (1985), the New Hampshire Supreme Court reviewed the frequently cited policy justifications for sovereign immunity:

> Four considerations support continuation of the immunity doctrine. First, exposure to liability would force the State to obtain funds to satisfy, process, and insure against claims against the State by either increasing revenues or diverting funds from other uses. * If the State incurred significant liability, the payment of these costs could impair the financial ability of the State to render governmental services. Second, exposure to liability for the State's tortious performance of functions that it alone can perform, such as law enforcement, in a sense, would penalize the State for undertaking these obligations. * Unlike an individual or private entity, which can select its activities to minimize its liability exposure, the State may not eschew certain functions, even if the attendant liability exposure is onerous. Third, exposure to liability could inhibit the ability of the legislature and the executive to exercise effectively their discretion. * To allow persons to challenge a governmental policy on the ground that it was negligently developed would force courts to re-evaluate the policy's wisdom and thus to invade the prerogatives of the legislature and the executive. * Finally, exposure to liability for the judiciary's negligent disposition of suits would greatly impair the ability of the courts to render final judgments and could undermine the confidence in the court system that is essential to its effective operation. *

2. *State Torts Claims Acts.* Most states have waived sovereign immunity, at least partially, through legislation. Simultaneously, however, they have imposed limits on the amount of recovery and the circumstances under which the state can be held liable. They have also created procedural barriers to recovery that do not exist in claims against private defendants. For example, the Maryland Torts Claims Act waives the state's sovereign immunity "as to a tort action," but provides that the state's liability cannot "exceed $200,000 to a single claimant for injuries arising from a single transaction or occurrence." Md. Code Ann., State Gov't § 12–104

(LexisNexis 2014). A higher amount may be paid if the recovery is authorized by the state's Board of Public Works upon recommendation of the state attorney general. Immunity is not waived for "[a]ny tortious act or omission * * * that (i) [i]s not within the scope of the public duties of the State personnel; or (ii) [i]s made with malice or gross negligence[.]" Md. Code Ann., Cts. & Jud. Proc. § 5–522 (LexisNexis 2014). Many other states exclude liability when the state official or employee was engaged in a discretionary function. E.g., Nev. Rev. Stat. Ann. § 41.032 (LexisNexis 2013); 42 Pa. Cons. Stat. § 8546 (2014). Often, state torts claims acts require the claimant to file a claim within a shorter statute of limitations than is required for torts claims against other defendants and/or to notify the allegedly liable state agency before filing suit. State torts claims acts typically exclude recovery for punitive damages. Other state torts claims acts simply list torts arising in specific categories of acts or omissions by government officials and employees for which the state can be held liable, such as "the operation of a motor vehicle" or "a dangerous condition of any public building." Colo. Rev. Stat. 24–10–106 (2013). Unless otherwise provided by the legislation, the same terms and conditions apply to the liability of state agencies—including prisons, hospitals, and educational institutions—as to the state itself.

In a few cases, state sovereign immunity has been abrogated by the courts. See, e.g., Stone v. Ariz. Highway Comm'n, 93 Ariz. 384, 381 P.2d 107 (1963); Hicks v. State, 88 N.M. 588, 544 P.2d 1153 (1975). Often in such cases, the legislature subsequently limits the state's liability except under specified circumstances, thus resulting in a liability scheme similar to that which would have resulted if the legislature itself had abrogated sovereign immunity subject to specific terms and conditions. See, e.g., Ariz. Rev. Stat. Ann. §§ 12–820 et seq. (2014); N.M. Stat. Ann. §§ 41–4–1 et seq. (LexisNexis 2014). For an excellent discussion of the history of sovereign immunity, see Muskopf v. Corning Hosp. Dist., 55 Cal.2d 211, 214–15, 11 Cal.Rptr. 89, 91, 359 P.2d 457, 458–59 (1961) (Traynor, J.).

2. LIABILITY OF MUNICIPALITIES

NOTES

1. *Liability of Municipalities.* Traditionally the issue of whether a municipality could be held liable for the tortious conduct of its employees often turned on the question of whether the municipality was engaged in a "governmental" function or a "proprietary" function. On one hand, if the tortious acts or omissions of the municipality's employees resulted from the performance of a function regarded as "governmental," such as the maintenance of streets, the municipality typically was held to be immune. On the other hand, if the municipal function was one that sometimes was performed by a private corporation or other actor, such as the operation of a power plant, sewage system, or toboggan run, the activity was deemed to be a "proprietary" function for which there could be liability. These rules regarding the liabilities of municipalities have been characterized accurately as a "quagmire," Indian Towing Co. v. United States, 350 U.S. 61, 65, 76 S.Ct. 122, 124, 100 L.Ed. 48, 53 (1955), and as "a curious patchwork of immunity and responsibility." Harper, James and Gray on Torts § 29.6. In recent years, the strong trend has been toward the

abrogation of immunities for municipalities. Often state tort claims acts cover the liability of municipalities as well as that of the state itself.

2. *Actions Against State or Local Officials or Municipal (but not State) Governments for Violations of Federal Law.* Section 1983 of Title 42 of the United States Code provides the substantive law basis for most federal suits, including those seeking damages, against local governments and state and local government officials and employees to remedy violations of federal law. 42 U.S.C. § 1983 (2012). The statute, passed in 1871 in response to violence against African Americans, creates a cause of action against any person who, acting under color of state law, violates a person's rights under the federal Constitution or other federal laws. It may be enforced in either state or federal courts. Martinez v. California, 444 U.S. 277, 283–84 n.7, 100 S.Ct. 553, 558 n.7, 62 L.Ed.2d 481, 488 n.7 (1980). In 1978, the United States Supreme Court extended the statute to cover liability of a municipality in certain circumstances (but it has not extended such liability to states). Monell v. Dep't of Soc. Servs., 436 U.S. 658, 685–86, 98 S.Ct. 2018, 2033, 56 L.Ed.2d 611, 632–33 (1978); compare Will v. Mich. Dep't of State Police, 491 U.S. 58, 109 S.Ct. 2304, 105 L.Ed.2d 45 (1989). In *Monell*, the court limited the liability of municipalities under § 1983 to cases in which the plaintiff's injuries resulted from the "execution of a government's policy or custom," excluding vicarious liability for acts of individual municipal officers. This exclusion is particularly significant because of qualified immunities available to municipal officers. See *infra* pages 530–532, Note 1. Thus, the plaintiff often is left without a remedy against either the municipality or the officer or employee who caused the harm.

3. THE FEDERAL TORT CLAIMS ACT

Soldano v. United States

United States Court of Appeals for the Ninth Circuit, 2006.
453 F.3d 1140.

■ FISHER, JUDGE. * * * On June 23, 1998, John Soldano was driving his new Harley-Davidson motorcycle west on the two-lane Big Oak Flat Road in Yosemite National Park, a road familiar to Soldano, who had driven it many times. Sitting behind him as his passenger was his wife, Denise. They were cruising between 30 and 35 m.p.h., consistent with the road's 35 m.p.h. speed limit. As the Soldanos came around a bend in the road approaching the Cascade Creek Bridge, they were startled to find a van stopped in their lane. The van was waiting to turn left across the road's double, solid yellow lines to enter the Cascade Creek Bridge vista point adjacent to the road. John Soldano claims he attempted to brake, but had to veer into the eastbound lane and oncoming traffic when he realized he had insufficient room to stop before colliding with the van. As a result, the Soldanos crashed head-on into another van, and John Soldano suffered severe injuries rendering him a paraplegic. Soldano was also cited for improper crossing of double, solid yellow lines. In a deposition, Soldano * * * described the road as curving around a large, solid granite mountain on his right just before the location of the collision, and said that it was the granite mountain that obstructed his vision of the stopped van. * * *

In April 2001, the Soldanos sued the United States under the FTCA [Federal Tort Claims Act]. Their complaint alleged that the government, through the U.S. Department of the Interior, National Park Service and Superintendent of Yosemite National Park, caused or contributed to the collision by improper design of, and failure to maintain, the road and adjacent area. The Soldanos specifically alleged that the location of the collision "constituted a dangerous condition and concealed trap or hidden hazard causing [the Soldanos] to be surprised by stopped traffic." They faulted the government for the negligent placement of traffic signs, among other things, and alleged that the dangerous condition of the roadway was the proximate cause of their injuries. * * * After a hearing, the district court granted the government's motion for summary judgment, finding that * * * the discretionary function exception to the FTCA barred all of the Soldanos' claims. * * *

The Big Oak Flat Road ("Road") * * * is a part of the national park system of roads. In 1968, the National Park Service created the *Park Road Standards* ("Standards") to establish policies for the design and construction of the nation's park roads. * * * [T]he 1984 Standards set forth the purpose of national park roads:

[P]ark roads are designed with extreme care and sensitivity with respect to the terrain and environment through which they pass—they are laid lightly onto the land.

Each segment of every park road should relate to the resource it traverses in a meaningful way and should constitute an enjoyable and informative experience in itself while providing the visitor the utmost in visual experience. . . . A park road should be fundamentally designed to maintain an overall continuing sense of intimacy with the countryside or area through which it passes. * * *

The placement and use of signs in Yosemite is similarly governed by Park Service policies, in particular those set forth in the *National Park Service Sign Manual* ("Sign Manual"). The Sign Manual delineates a number of factors that park managers are to consider in determining where to place signs. Managers should weigh such potentially competing ends as minimal intrusion, avoidance of unnecessary proliferation of signs and the safety of visitors in deciding whether to use a particular sign at a particular location.

The Yosemite National Park Superintendent, Michael J. Tollefson, has averred that the Park Service's overall road policy decisions made pursuant to the Standards involve balancing preservation of natural resources, visitor enjoyment and safety and the Park Service's limited financial and human resources. The Superintendent has further stated that balancing such considerations requires the exercise of discretion, and that decisions on the Road's design and construction, including the placement of scenic vistas and signs on it, are not governed by mandatory statutes, regulations or policies, but rather by noncompulsory policies as set forth in the 1984 Standards and the Sign Manual. * * *

The Soldanos also allege that the Road was negligently designed at the site of the accident. First, they claim that the Park Service negligently designed the Road by omitting signs warning of the danger of vehicles stopped on a blind curve. Second, they contend that the Road's speed limit was negligently set too high relative to its design, because the Standards permit a 35 m.p.h. speed limit only where a sight distance meets or exceeds 225 feet. Here, the nearly vertical "sideslope" of the Road reduces the sight distance of a vehicle in the position of the Soldanos' to 180 feet. * * * Given the circumstances of the accident and their expert's analysis, the Soldanos have presented evidence sufficient to create triable issues with respect to their claims that the Park Service's design of the Road required warning signs and a lower speed limit at the accident site. We therefore turn to consider whether the district court erred in finding that the discretionary function exception to the FTCA bars these claims.

1. *Discretionary function exception*

"A party may bring an action against the United States only to the extent that the government waives its sovereign immunity." Valdez v. United States, 56 F.3d 1177, 1179 (9th Cir.1995). The FTCA waives the government's sovereign immunity for tort claims arising out of the negligent conduct of government employees acting within the scope of their employment. * Thus, the government can be sued "under circumstances where the United States, if a private person, would be liable to the claimant in accordance with the law of the place where the act or omission occurred." 28 U.S.C. § 1346(b).

The FTCA's waiver of immunity is limited, however, by the discretionary function exception, which bars claims "based upon the exercise or performance or the failure to exercise or perform a discretionary function or duty on the part of a federal agency or an employee of the Government, whether or not the discretion involved be abused." 28 U.S.C. § 2680(a). This exception "restores the government's immunity in situations where its employees are carrying out governmental or 'regulatory' duties," and it "marks the boundary between Congress' willingness to impose tort liability on the United States and the desire to protect certain decision-making from judicial second-guessing." * (citing Berkovitz v. United States, 486 U.S. 531, 536–37, 108 S.Ct. 1954, 100 L.Ed.2d 531 (1988)).

To determine whether the challenged conduct falls within the discretionary function exception, we employ a two-step analysis. First, we determine "whether the challenged actions involve 'an element of judgment or choice.'" Valdez, 56 F.3d at 1179 (quoting United States v. Gaubert, 499 U.S. 315, 322, 111 S.Ct. 1267, 113 L.Ed.2d 335 (1991)). Our inquiry looks to "the nature of the conduct, rather than the status of the actor," and the discretionary element is not met where "a federal statute, regulation, or policy specifically prescribes a course of action for an employee to follow." Berkovitz, 486 U.S. at 536. In such event, our inquiry is at an end, and the discretionary function exception does not apply because "the employee has no rightful option but to adhere to the directive."

However, if an element of choice or judgment is involved, we move to the second step of the analysis and determine "'whether that judgment is of the kind that the discretionary function exception was designed to shield.'" Gaubert, 499 U.S. at 322–23, 111 S.Ct. 1267 (quoting Berkovitz, 486 U.S. at 536, 108 S.Ct. 1954). The exception

" ' protects only governmental actions and decisions based on considerations of public policy.' " * In other words, only those decisions "grounded in social, economic, and political policy" will be protected by the discretionary function exception. Childers v. United States, 40 F.3d 973, 974 (9th Cir.1994). * * * We acknowledge that the distinction between protected and unprotected decisions can be difficult to apprehend, but this is the result of the nature of governmental actions—they fall "along a spectrum, ranging from those 'totally divorced from the sphere of policy analysis,' such as driving a car, to those 'fully grounded in regulatory policy,' such as the regulation and oversight of a bank." Whisnant v. United States, 400 F.3d 1177, 1181 (9th Cir.2005). *

Notwithstanding the occasionally fine line between protected and unprotected activities, general principles exist. In particular, we have declined to find the discretionary function exception applicable "where the challenged governmental activity involves safety considerations under an established policy rather than the balancing of competing public policy considerations." ARA Leisure Servs. v. United States, 831 F.2d 193, 195 (9th Cir.1987). In *ARA Leisure Services*, the Park Service's decision to design the Denali Park Road in Alaska without guardrails was grounded in social, economic and political policy, but the Park Service's failure to maintain a pass on that road in safe condition was not. There was "no clear link between Park Service road policies and the condition" of the pass, so the government's failure to maintain the road fell "in the category of 'ordinary "garden-variety" negligence' " that the FTCA did not immunize from suit. * * *

On the other hand, we have held decisions about the implementation of safety considerations on park roads and trails to be protected, where circumstances clearly showed they were the result of a judgment grounded in social, economic and political policy. In *Valdez v. United States*, Valdez was rendered quadriplegic when he fell down a waterfall in Kings Canyon National Park. Valdez argued that the regulations in Park Service policy manuals were mandatory, such that the Park Service lacked any choice over the challenged conduct. We rejected his argument:

> While the said policy guidelines certainly outline general policy goals regarding visitor safety, the means by which NPS employees meet these goals necessarily involves an exercise of discretion. These guidelines can be considered mandatory only in the larger sense that they set forth broad policy goals attainable only by the exercise of discretionary decisions.

Because the challenged conduct "clearly implicate[d] a choice between the competing policy considerations of maximizing access to and preservation of natural resources versus the need to minimize potential safety hazards," it fell within the discretionary function exception. * * *

Here, we conclude that the discretionary function exception bars the Soldanos' claim that the Park Service negligently designed the Road without warning signs at the site of the accident. The exception does not, however, bar their claim that the Park Service negligently set the speed limit for the Road, relative to the Road's design. Rather, that decision was circumscribed by objective safety criteria and was not the result of a policy decision of the kind protected by the discretionary function exception. * We address these claims in turn.

a. *Design and sign placement*

The Sign Manual sets forth guidelines on the use of signs along park roads:

> The decision to utilize a particular sign at a particular location requires the professional judgment of the park manager—drawing upon available guides, resources, and traffic safety engineering expertise—and considering a variety of other factors, such as the appearance of the road as a whole and its relationship to the natural and/or historical environment through which it passes. * * *

Far from imposing mandatory requirements, the Sign Manual states that decisions about the use and placement of signs are made at the discretion of the park manager, who must weigh competing ends—minimal intrusion, avoidance of unnecessary proliferation of signs and the safety of visitors. * * * The Service must balance a panoply of social, economic and political considerations applicable to the distinctive nature of park roads when determining whether to design a road with a given sign at a particular location. Deciding whether to warn of the potential danger of stopped traffic at the site of the accident is therefore a judgment "of the kind that the discretionary function exception was designed to shield." Gaubert, 499 U.S. at 322–23, 111 S.Ct. 1267 (quoting Berkovitz, 486 U.S. at 536, 108 S.Ct. 1954). The district court did not err in granting summary judgment to the government on the Soldanos' claim that the government negligently designed the Road with insufficient warning signs. *

b. *Design and speed limit*

Setting a safe speed limit for the Road as designed, however, is different, because doing so is essentially a matter of scientific and professional judgment, and "matters of scientific and professional judgment—particularly judgments concerning safety—are rarely considered to be susceptible to social, economic, or political policy." Whisnant, 400 F.3d at 1183. The 1984 Standards specify appropriate speed limits in light of such empirical factors as the elevation and stopping-sight distance of a road. Significantly, they allow a speed limit of 35 mph only where the minimum, actual stopping-sight distance meets or exceeds 225 feet. Here, the Soldanos' expert opined, without contradiction, that the actual stopping-sight distance of the Road is no greater than 180 feet at the location of the accident due to the upward "sideslope" of the Road as it curves around the granite mountain. Plainly, the Road's 35 mph speed limit at the accident location is at odds with the specifications in Table 6 of the Standards, which require a speed limit of no more than 25 mph for roads with the characteristics of the accident site.

"[W]e have generally held that the *design* of a course of governmental action is shielded by the discretionary function exception, whereas the *implementation* of that course of action is not." Whisnant, 400 F.3d at 1181 (original emphasis). The element of choice involved in the Park Service's decision not to implement a speed limit on the Road consistent with the Standards' safety guidelines "resembles more a departure from the safety considerations established in Service policies * * * than a mistaken judgment in a matter clearly involving choices among political, economic, and social factors. . . ." * Nor does the element of choice entail a protected, discretionary selection of the means used to meet a general policy goal. * * *

Thus, although we agree with the district court that the discretionary function exception shields the government from liability arising from challenges to its overall design of the Road and the means by which the Service effected that design—including such placement and configuration choices as the creation of the Cascade Creek Bridge vista point at the site of the accident—we hold that the government is not insulated from the claim that it negligently set an unsafe speed limit for this part of the Road, relative to its design. * * * Accordingly, the government's purported failure to set a safe speed limit on the Road remains a triable issue that is not precluded by the discretionary function exception. Because the district court erred in finding that the discretionary function exception bars the Soldanos' claim that the government negligently set the speed limit for the Road, we reverse the court's summary judgment to that extent and remand for further proceedings. * * *

NOTES

1. *Procedure under Federal Tort Claims Act.* The Federal Tort Claims Act grants federal district courts exclusive jurisdiction to hear claims against the United States under the Act. 28 U.S.C. § 1346(b) (2012). Before filing suit, a claimant must file an administrative claim with the agency concerned within two years after the claim accrues. § 2401(b). Trial is without a jury. §§ 1346(b), 2402. Punitive damages are prohibited, § 2674, and attorneys' fees are limited. § 2678.

2. *FTCA and Strict Liability Claims.* In Laird v. Nelms, 406 U.S. 797, 92 S.Ct. 1899, 32 L.Ed.2d 499 (1972), the Supreme Court held that the claimant could not recover on a strict liability basis under the FTCA for property damage allegedly caused by sonic booms from United States military planes. The court refused to consider a strict liability claim for an "ultrahazardous" [abnormally dangerous] activity, even if the common law of the state where the claim arose might allow such a claim. The court interpreted the statutory language requiring "negligent or wrongful act or omission" not to be satisfied by a strict liability tort. Harper, James and Gray on Torts § 29.13 n.14.

3. *Statutory Exceptions to Liability Generally.* The "discretionary function" provision of subsection 2680(a) of the FTCA is only one of thirteen exceptions to liability listed in the statute. Most of the other exceptions are fairly specific, such as claims arising in a foreign country, from the transmission of mail or the fiscal operations of the Treasury, or from the "combatant activities of the military or naval forces * * * in time of war." Compare certain administrative remedies under the Military Claims Act, 10 U.S.C. §§ 2731 *et seq.* (2012).

4. *Exception for Specified Deliberate Torts.* Subsection 2680(h) of the FTCA excludes liability for "[a]ny claim arising out of assault, battery, false imprisonment, false arrest, malicious prosecution, abuse of process, libel, slander, misrepresentation, deceit, or interference with contract rights" except that liability exists for the first six of these torts if committed by investigative or law enforcement officers. Why? The origins of these exclusions appear to lie in the historical reluctance of courts to hold employers liable for the willful acts of their employees. Now that courts are more willing to hold employers liable under such circumstances, does the blanket statutory exclusion still make sense? What happens if a patient in a federal hospital files a medical malpractice claim under the FTCA, and under local law the claim would sound in battery as well as in negligence? See Moos v. United States, 225 F.2d 705 (8th Cir.1955) (no liability under the Act because the injury resulted from acts that would be battery under Minnesota law). Compare Lane v. United States, 225 F.Supp. 850 (E.D.Va.1964).

Courts have construed the statutory exclusion of liability for "misrepresentation" to include negligent misrepresentation as well as deceit. United States v. Neustadt, 366 U.S. 696, 81 S.Ct. 1294, 6 L.Ed.2d 614 (1961). Thus, liability has been denied where the Federal Aviation Administration negligently evaluated and certified the airworthiness of an aircraft. Knudsen v. United States, 500 F.Supp. 90 (S.D.N.Y.1980). The negligent misrepresentation exception had the potential to preclude liability for many errors of government employees sounding in negligence. Fortunately, however, in Block v. Neal, 460 U.S. 289, 103 S.Ct. 1089, 75 L.Ed.2d 67 (1983), the Supreme Court permitted an action by a recipient of a Farmers Home Administration loan where a government employee inspected the construction work and negligently approved it. The court distinguished the harm resulting from the claimant's reliance on the negligent misrepresentation from the harm resulting by the negligence of the inspector in allowing the construction to proceed. The court held that "the partial overlap between these two tort actions [the negligent misrepresentation claim and the independently sufficient negligence claim] does not support the conclusion that if one is excepted under the Tort Claims Act, the other must be as well."

5. *Injuries Arising from Military Service.* The Supreme Court has judicially created an exception to liability under the FTCA for death or injury of a member of the armed services of the United States incurred in the course of active duty. Feres v. United States, 340 U.S. 135, 71 S.Ct. 153, 95 L.Ed. 152 (1950). The courts have identified three separate justifications for such an exception: (1) those injured or killed during military service receive other government compensation for death or injury, (2) the military requires a uniform federal standard of liability not dependent upon local state tort law, and (3) claims against the government impair the need for military discipline. For an excellent analysis of the justification for the *Feres* doctrine, see Taber v. Maine, 67 F.3d 1029, 1037–53 (2d Cir.1995) (Calabresi, J.). See *supra* pages 114–17.

4. LIABILITY OF PUBLIC OFFICIALS AND EMPLOYEES

NOTES

1. *Immunities of Public Officials at Common Law.* The issues surrounding immunities for public officials are extremely complex and the answers vary greatly from one state to the next. For an analysis of some of the issues, see Ashton v. Brown, 339 Md. 70, 660 A.2d 447 (1995).

In Harlow v. Fitzgerald, 457 U.S. 800, 813–14, 102 S.Ct. 2727, 2736, 73 L.Ed.2d 396, 407–08 (1982), the United States Supreme Court analyzed the issues at play in deciding whether a public official was entitled to immunity under federal law and whether that immunity should be absolute or qualified:

> The resolution of immunity questions inherently requires a balance between the evils inevitable in any available alternative. In situations of abuse of office, an action for damages may offer the only realistic avenue for vindication of constitutional guarantees. * It is this recognition that has required the denial of absolute immunity to most public officers. At the same time, however, it cannot be disputed seriously that claims frequently run against the innocent as well as the guilty—at a cost not only to the defendant officials, but to society as a whole. * These social costs include the expenses of litigation, the diversion of official energy from pressing public issues, and the deterrence of able citizens from acceptance of public office. Finally, there is the danger that fear of being sued will "dampen the ardor of all but the most resolute, or the most irresponsible [public officials], in the unflinching discharge of their duties." Gregoire v. Biddle, 177 F.2d 579, 581 (2d Cir.1949), cert. denied, 339 U.S. 949, 70 S.Ct. 803, 94 L.Ed. 1363 (1950).

The Court then categorized the immunities of public officials under federal law:

> * * * [O]ur decisions consistently have held that government officials are entitled to some form of immunity from suits for damages. As recognized at common law, public officers require this protection to shield them from undue interference with their duties and from potentially disabling threats of liability.

> Our decisions have recognized immunity defenses of two kinds. For officials whose special functions or constitutional status requires complete protection from suit, we have recognized the defense of "absolute immunity." The absolute immunity of legislators, in their legislative functions, see, e.g., Eastland v. United States Servicemen's Fund, 421 U.S. 491, 95 S.Ct. 1813, 44 L.Ed.2d 324 (1975), and of judges, in their judicial functions, see, e.g., Stump v. Sparkman, 435 U.S. 349, 98 S.Ct. 1099, 55 L.Ed.2d 331 (1978), now is well settled. Our decisions also have extended absolute immunity to certain officials of the Executive Branch. These include prosecutors and similar officials, see Butz v. Economou, 438 U.S. 478, 508–12, 98 S.Ct. 2894, 2911–16, 57 L.Ed.2d 895, 917–20 (1978), executive officers engaged in adjudicative functions, id., at 513–17, 98 S.Ct. at 2914–16, 57 L.Ed.2d at 920–23, and the President of the United States, see Nixon v. Fitzgerald, 457 U.S. 731, 102 S.Ct. 2690, 73 L.Ed.2d 349 (1982).

> For executive officials in general, however, our cases make plain that qualified immunity represents the norm. In Scheuer v. Rhodes, 416 U.S. 232, 94 S.Ct. 1683, 40 L.Ed.2d 90 (1974), we acknowledged that high officials require greater protection than those with less complex discretionary responsibilities. Nonetheless, we held that a governor and his aides could receive

the requisite protection from qualified or good-faith immunity. In *Butz v. Economou,* we extended the approach of *Scheuer* to high federal officials of the Executive Branch. Discussing in detail the considerations that also had underlain our decision in *Scheuer,* we explained that the recognition of a qualified immunity defense for high executives reflected an attempt to balance competing values: not only the importance of a damages remedy to protect the rights of citizens, but also "the need to protect officials who are required to exercise their discretion and the related public interest in encouraging the vigorous exercise of official authority." 438 U.S. at 506, 98 S.Ct. at 2911, 57 L.Ed.2d at 916. * * *

The Court went on to hold that high-ranking presidential aides, like Cabinet members, were entitled only to a qualified privilege, specifically stating that "government officials performing discretionary functions generally are shielded from liability for civil damages insofar as their conduct does not violate clearly established statutory or constitutional rights of which a reasonable person would have known."

State law typically provides for somewhat similar immunities. For example, generally, an immunity of some kind is available to executive officials for liability created by the exercise of their *discretionary functions,* as opposed to *ministerial functions.* Ashton, 339 Md. at 116–17, 660 A.2d at 470. In Maryland, and in many other states, this immunity from liability under state tort law is a qualified one that may be overcome by common law malice. Often there are further exceptions to the immunity. Maryland, for example, provides no immunity for actions based on intentional torts or violations of state constitutional provisions. Statutes in Maryland and elsewhere shift the financial responsibility for tort claims against public officials to the local government entity, except when the public official acts with actual malice. Md. Code Ann., Cts. & Jud. Proc. §§ 5–301 to 5–304 (LexisNexis 2014).

State and local officials also are subject to liability under 42 U.S.C. § 1983 (2012) for damages resulting from the violation of federal constitutional rights, and here the immunity available is that described in *Harlow.*

2. *Non-liability of Federal Employees.* Under the so-called "Westfall Act," 28 U.S.C. § 2679(b)(1) (2012), today the remedy against the United States under the FTCA for torts committed by federal employees under state law is made "exclusive of any other civil action * * * for money damages by reason of the same subject matter against the employee * * *." The remedy against the United States is exclusive even if there is no remedy against the United States. See United States v. Smith, 499 U.S. 160, 111 S.Ct. 1180, 113 L.Ed.2d 134 (1991) (remedy against employee precluded even though governmental immunity is not waived under the FTCA because of exceptions to waiver for torts "arising in a foreign country").

Federal employees may nevertheless be subject to liability for the violation of at least certain rights under the federal constitution, under a doctrine announced in Bivens v. Six Unknown Named Agents of Fed. Bureau of Narcotics, 403 U.S. 388, 91 S.Ct. 1999, 29 L.Ed.2d 619 (1971); see Harper, James & Gray on Torts § 29.15A at notes 55 *et seq.* The immunity accorded under the Westfall Act is inapplicable to *Bivens* claims. Cf. Chappell v. Wallace, 462 U.S. 296, 103 S.Ct. 2362, 76 L.Ed.2d 586 (1983). For a similar cause of action under state law against state officials for violation of state constitutional rights, see Widgeon v. Eastern Shore Hosp. Center, 300 Md. 520, 479 A.2d 921 (1984).

3. *Presidential Immunity.* In Nixon v. Fitzgerald, 457 U.S. 731, 102 S.Ct. 2690, 73 L.Ed.2d 349 (1982), the Supreme Court held that the President of the United States has an absolute immunity for civil damages arising out of official conduct during his or her term as president.

What happens, however, if the President is sued for conduct that is not a part of his official duties and that occurred before his Presidency? Those were the circumstances in Clinton v. Jones, 520 U.S. 681, 117 S.Ct. 1636, 137 L.Ed.2d 945 (1997), in which the Supreme Court held that there is no official immunity for unofficial acts when only the personal, private conduct of the President is at issue. The plaintiff had sued President Clinton for conduct occurring before his term in office that she alleged created civil liability for violations of two federal civil rights statutes, as well as for intentional infliction of emotional distress and defamation. The court overrode concerns that the President "might be distracted by the need to participate in litigation during the pendency of his office," and that "burdens will be placed on the President that will hamper the performance of his official duties." The court also refused to stay the proceedings until the completion of Clinton's presidency. President Clinton's answers to questions in the deposition in the case led to his impeachment by the House of Representatives, though he was neither convicted by the Senate nor removed from office. In view of subsequent events, were the conclusions of the Supreme Court sound?

CHAPTER 10

LIABILITY OF POSSESSORS OF LAND

This chapter focuses on cases in which the harm to the plaintiff is caused on premises occupied or owned by the defendant. In these cases, as in the preceding ones, the plaintiff suffered physical harm to interests that are ordinarily legally protected against intentional or negligent invasions. These cases present no new issues concerning the nature of the plaintiff's interest. Traditionally, though, the fact that the defendant was the possessor of the premises on which the plaintiff suffered harm dramatically altered the liability decision. Under traditional common law, the defendant's duty depended on the answers to the following questions: What is the plaintiff's relation to the land? How did she happen to be there when she was hurt? In short, was the plaintiff a "trespasser," a "licensee," or an "invitee"?

In Nelson v. Freeland, 349 N.C. 615, 623–24, 507 S.E.2d 882, 887–88, *infra* pages 554–558 (1998), the Supreme Court of North Carolina recounted the original justifications for handling the liability decision differently depending upon into which one of three categories (trespasser, licensee, or invitee) the land visitor fit:

> The common-law trichotomy * * * emanated from an English culture deeply rooted to the land; tied with feudal heritage; and wrought with lords whose land ownership represented power, wealth, and dominance. * * * [N]ineteenth-century courts * * * restricted the jury's power because juries were comprised mainly of potential land *entrants* who most likely would act to protect the community at large and thereby reign in the landowner's sovereign power over his land. * Thus, the trichotomy was created to disgorge the jury of some of its power by either allowing the judge to take the case from the jury based on legal rulings or by forcing the jury to apply the mechanical rules of the trichotomy instead of considering the pertinent issue of whether the landowner acted reasonably in maintaining his land.

> Additionally, the trichotomy was created at a time when principles of negligence were not in existence. * * * [T]he emergence of negligence law conflicted with the immunity conferred upon landowners under the trichotomy. * Common-law courts, however, decided not to replace the trichotomy with modern principles of negligence law, as they did in almost all other tort areas, but rather "superimposed the new [negligence] principles upon the existing framework of entrant categories." Michael Sears, Abrogation of the Traditional Common Law of Premises Liability, 44 U. Kan. L. Rev. 175, 176 (1995). This combination resulted in our current scheme of premises-liability law which allows judges to maintain control

over jury discretion while, at the same time, utilizing "duty of care" principles set forth in negligence theory. * * *

The seemingly rigid classification system of the common law produced unsatisfying results: of two people hurt on the same premises by the same danger, one might have been able to properly claim that the defendant owed her a duty of reasonable care, while the other victim could not.

When the technical detail of the following cases is mastered, a number of general questions remain: To what extent are the traditional common law classifications effective in altering the course of decisions that would have been made without them on the basis of general negligence principles? Or conversely, to what extent, in some situations at least, are the added concepts useless symbols receiving lip service, but deprived of vitality by suffocation in logomachy designed only for this lethal purpose? What do we seek to accomplish by these added ideas, and by the determination of liability or immunity in the cases in which they are employed? To what social purpose are the added doctrines relevant? Prevention of harm by encouragement of precaution? Distribution of loss? Retribution? Better utilization of economic resources?

In determining liability, the reason for the plaintiff's presence on the land where she was injured is but one factor. Other factors also might play a role in the analysis. Consider the appropriateness of differentiation between various kinds of land occupancy. Should an injury on a vacant lot in a densely populated inner city neighborhood be treated the same as one on a huge tract of timberland in the western United States or on a midwestern family farm? Should the same rules apply to someone injured by manufacturing or mining operations and another injured while strolling along the beach? Is achieving fairness and justice in a particular case best accomplished by a system which strictly classifies visitors to land or by a generalized negligence injury? Can courts and juries be trusted to perform open-ended liability determinations, or do the needs for predictability and avoidance of judgments influenced by hindsight sympathy justify a more rigid structure? And ultimately, do these or other considerations mean that land owners and occupiers should be treated differently from other tortfeasors?

These issues have dominated the judicial debate regarding the handling of tort claims brought by visitors upon land against land possessors for at least the past half century and they remain in dispute in many jurisdictions today. At the current time, slightly fewer than half of all jurisdictions continue to follow the traditional rules applying different rules depending upon the reason that the victim was present on the tortfeasor's property. A slightly larger number of jurisdictions, and the Restatement (Third) of Torts: Liability for Physical and Emotional Harm § 51 (2012) have moved in the direction of handling the liability claims of most land visitors (except for trespassers in a majority of these jurisdictions) under a general negligence standard.

We begin with the duty of care a land possessor owes to visitors under the traditional trichotomy and, in particular, the duty of care owed to trespassers.

A. LIABILITY TO TRESPASSERS UNDER TRADITIONAL LAW CLASSIFYING VISITORS ON LAND

Cain v. Johnson

Supreme Court of Rhode Island, 2000.
755 A.2d 156.

■ WEISBERGER, CHIEF JUSTICE. * * * At approximately 2 a.m. on August 6, 1991, Michael T. Cain (the decedent) and two friends went for a walk along a section of Newport's Cliff Walk. * * * [T]he decedent stepped from the paved walk onto a grassy area on the ocean side of the walk. He fell from the cliff to his death after the ground beneath his feet gave way.

* * * [P]laintiffs, William G. Cain and Mary H. Cain * * *, filed a wrongful death action * * * against defendants, the City of Newport (city), the State of Rhode Island (state), and the university. The plaintiffs alleged that defendants' negligence caused the decedent's death because defendants failed to properly inspect, maintain, and repair the Cliff Walk. * * * [The defendants] moved for summary judgment, arguing that the decedent was a trespasser because the Cliff Walk had closed at 9 p.m. * * * [T]he motion justice granted summary judgment in favor of all defendants * * *. The plaintiffs then appealed the grant of summary judgment. * * *

* * * Pursuant to Newport City Ordinance § 12.32.010(C), the Cliff Walk is "closed for public use between nine p.m. and six a.m. of the following day, daily, and no person shall go upon such public areas during the hours of closing . . . except that the Cliff Walk shall remain open for the purpose of access to the water for fishing." * * * [T]wo signs posted on either end of the walk notify people of the hours that the walk is open to the public. The plaintiffs argue that such notice is insufficient, as there are numerous other unrestricted entrance points along the walk, which stretches approximately 18,000 feet along the Atlantic Ocean. * * *

* * * [T]he decedent was a trespasser even though the Cliff Walk was not so intensively posted as to notify all possible visitors of the hours of operation. * * * [T]he existence of a city ordinance closing a park establishes as a fact that any person in the park after hours is a trespasser, even if the person is completely unaware of the ordinance. * * * Because the decedent was on the Cliff Walk at about 2 a.m., he was a trespasser as a matter of law. * * *

Under Rhode Island law, it is well settled that a landowner owes a trespasser no duty except to refrain from willful or wanton conduct. * It is also well settled that such a duty arises only after a trespasser is discovered in a position of danger. * * * The plaintiffs argue, however, that the holding of the cases above should not be extended to the case at bar. Rather, plaintiffs urge the Court to accept the rule set forth in the Restatement (Second) Torts, § 334 (1965), which provides as follows:

> A possessor of land who knows, or from facts within his knowledge should know, that trespassers constantly intrude upon a limited area thereof, is subject to liability for bodily harm there caused to them by his failure to carry on an

activity involving a risk of death or serious bodily harm with reasonable care for their safety.

Under plaintiffs' definition, the decedent's status as a discovered trespasser, versus an undiscovered trespasser, would be irrelevant. * * * [However, in Previte v. Wanskuck Co., 80 R.I. 1, 90 A.2d 769 (1952),] for example, a wrongful-death action brought by the parents of a young boy who drowned in a pond in Providence, this Court held that "no duty is owed a trespasser by a landowner except to refrain from injuring him wantonly or wilfully after discovering his peril. . . . [W]e see no legal duty imposed on defendant to anticipate the presence of plaintiffs' son as a trespasser on its property."[1] * * * [I]t is clear that a landowner does not owe a trespasser any duty until after the trespasser is discovered in a position of peril. Once the trespasser is discovered, the landowner owes the trespasser a duty to refrain from willfully or wantonly injuring the trespasser.

Because the decedent in the instant case never was discovered in a position of peril, we need not consider whether defendants' conduct rose to the level of willful and wanton conduct. The defendants did not owe the decedent any duty. * * *

The third question posed by the Court asks whether liability arises in light of the nature of the defective condition of the land. The plaintiffs argue that the overall condition that led to the decedent's death was the paved nature of the Cliff Walk. Therefore, plaintiffs argue that even though the precise area of the ground from which the decedent fell was a "natural condition" of the land, the paved nature of the walk rendered it an artificial condition, thereby imposing liability pursuant to the Restatement (Second) Torts § 337, which provides:

A possessor of land who maintains on the land an artificial condition which involves a risk of death or serious bodily harm to persons coming in contact with it, is subject to liability for bodily harm caused to trespassers by his failure to exercise reasonable care to warn them of the condition if

(a) the possessor knows or has reason to know of their presence in dangerous proximity to the condition, and

(b) the condition is of such a nature that he has reason to believe that the trespasser will not discover it or realize the risk involved.

The plaintiffs' argument with respect to this provision, however, must fail for two reasons—(1) because the precise area from which the decedent fell was a natural condition for which defendants could not be held liable, even if this Court were to adopt the foregoing rule, which we have hitherto declined to do, and (2) even if it were considered an artificial condition, it was a condition of such a nature that a trespasser would discover or realize the risk involved. * * *

The area from which the decedent fell is clearly a natural condition of the land. With respect to the duty of care owed by a landowner for

---

[1]   The holding in Previte v. Wanskuck Co., 80 R.I. 1, 90 A.2d 769 (1952), as it related to an infant trespasser was overruled by this Court's decision in Haddad v. First National Stores, Inc., 109 R.I. 59, 64–65, 280 A.2d 93, 96–97 (1971), in which we adopted the attractive nuisance doctrine. Nevertheless, the Court in *Previte* faithfully expounded the common law rule concerning all trespassers.

natural conditions on the land, we have held that "the possessor of land owed a trespasser 'no duty to discover, remedy, or warn of dangerous natural conditions. Perhaps if the possessor sees a trespasser about to encounter extreme danger from such a source, which is known to the possessor and perceptibly not known to the trespasser, there may be a duty to warn (as by shouting). That is about as far as the bystander's duty to a highway traveler would traditionally go, if indeed it would go that far.'" Tantimonico [v. Allendale Mut. Ins. Co.], 637 A.2d [1056,] 1057 [(1994)] (quoting 4 Harper, James & Gray, The Law of Torts § 27.3 at 139 (2d ed. 1986)).

Upon leaving the paved portion of the path, the decedent in the instant case had to walk an additional five feet or so to reach the edge of the cliff. It is from this edge of the cliff where the decedent fell. That area was clearly a natural condition of the land, and liability for it could not be imposed upon defendants, even pursuant to § 337 of the Restatement (Second) Torts.

Even if the area was considered an artificial condition of the land, plaintiffs' argument must fail because the conditions of § 337 cannot be met. Specifically, a visitor to the Cliff Walk certainly should be aware of and appreciate the risks that exist along the edge of a cliff that rises approximately sixty to seventy feet from the ocean. * * * The plaintiffs argue in the instant case that the decedent, as well as other visitors, would not be aware of the risk because the Cliff Walk is open during parts of the year when it would be dark, and, specifically, because it was dark when the decedent visited the cliff. This fact, however, should increase one's awareness of the risks associated with the cliff. Indeed, any visitor along the walk in the dark should be that much more cautious, given the height of the cliff and the inability to see adequately where one is stepping. Accordingly, no liability arises because of the defective condition of the land.

* * * In the instant case, it is clear that a landowner owes a trespasser no duty except to refrain from willful and wanton conduct *after the trespasser has been discovered in a position of peril.* Absolutely no evidence has been presented to suggest that the defendants or any of them were aware of the decedent's position of peril. Accordingly, summary judgment was properly entered. * * *

■ GOLDBERG, J, concurring in part and dissenting in part. * * * The events that led to this tragic death are particularly sad and egregious. Unfortunately, young Cain, a nineteen-year-old college student, was not the first young man to plunge to his death from the Cliff Walk. In 1987, Brian Putney, a student at Salve [University], also died as a result of a fall from the Cliff Walk during the nighttime. A member of Putney's family submitted an affidavit to the hearing justice in this case attesting to promises and representations made to the Putney family that a fence would be erected in the area where Putney fell in order to avoid future casualties of this nature. Nothing was done.

Further, the record before this Court is replete with evidence that every defendant in this case, for more than a decade before Cain's tragic death, had actual knowledge of the extremely dangerous conditions on the Cliff Walk, yet did nothing to remedy this dire situation. Indeed, the record disclosed that Sister Lucille McKillop (Sister McKillop), then the President of Salve, implored the Newport city manager both before and after Putney's fatal plunge to take corrective action respecting the extremely dangerous area of the Cliff Walk adjacent to the college. Beginning as early as 1979, Sister McKillop began a letter-writing campaign to the city through which she expressed her fear that the entire under-support of the Cliff Walk in the area adjacent to Salve was so weakened by erosion that the potential for loss of life was great and that safety measures should take priority over the city's desire to make this attraction available to tourists. In May 1983, the city manager informed Salve that he had directed the director of public works to explore the cost of erecting a chain link fence from Webster Street to Shepard Avenue, the very area of Cain's unfortunate demise. Nothing was done. On October 7, 1987, Sister McKillop again wrote to the city manager of Newport and again urged the city "in the strongest way possible" to act to rectify this problem * * *. [T]he proper definition of the edge of the Cliff Walk with chain link fencing can no longer be put off." Tragically, put off it was. Despite having received written notice of these dangerous conditions and despite the death of Brian Putney, no measures were undertaken to prevent more tragedies.

Further, in July 1989, * * * the National Park Service produced a report that was the culmination of an extensive study of the Cliff Walk commissioned at the request of Congress, designed to evaluate the suitability for including the Cliff Walk in the National Park System. * * * Significantly, the study noted that "[a] fatality on the cliffs in 1987 and a near fatality in 1988 underline the urgency of stabilizing the treadway. The most recent accident involved a twelve year old girl who survived a forty-foot fall from the Cliff Walk. The fall occurred in an area where vegetation masks severe undermining of the cliff." * * *

In addition to this written material, the record before the hearing justice also disclosed that after Cain's body was recovered, a captain of the Newport Fire Department publicly confirmed that the area from which Cain fell was a bad spot, and that to his knowledge, Cain was the third victim. Accordingly, I am satisfied that these defendants had actual notice of the potential for loss of life posed by this particular area of the Cliff Walk and did nothing to forestall this calamity.

Moreover, color photographs in the record depict the area where Cain left the macadam path and fell to his death as a well-worn spot, similar to a man-made overlook, that appears to be a perfectly natural area for a stroller to stop, leave the path, and look out over the Atlantic Ocean. Significantly, this area is defined by an artificial wall at the cliff edge, described in the police report as a "wall next to the walkway where the victim was standing [that] was approximately eight (8) inches tall." Cain fell through a hole that opened up on the landward side of this man-made concrete barrier, in fulfillment of Sister McKillop's chilling prediction that the entire under-support near this man-made structure was in danger of collapse. The existence of this man-made structure defining the cliff edge, in my opinion, belies the argument of the defendants that the decedent fell as a result of a natural condition on the land. * * *

Perhaps the saddest part of this tragedy that resulted in the death of this young man is that following Cain's death, then-Governor Bruce Sundlun ordered immediate action and initiated the installation of a fence for the area. We have been informed that the cost of this repair was $11,960. * * *

Finally, I believe that concerning Newport and the state, Cain was not a trespasser but rather a licensee whose presence on the Cliff Walk was anticipated by the city and the state, and that these defendants should not be relieved from liability by the judicially created technicality known as the trespasser's rule. * * * The plight of the trespasser is one area of the law in which no duty exists, and as a result, a landowner is immunized from liability. * * *

* * * I do not believe that one can hold out an implicit invitation to visit a tourist attraction for the economic benefit of the city/state landowner on the one hand, then seek to escape liability to those who have accepted the invitation and are injured or killed—due to the landowner's negligence—by arguing that the mishap occurred at a time when the park was closed pursuant to an ordinance that is neither enforced nor brought to the public's attention. The fact that Cain was completely ignorant that the Cliff Walk purportedly was closed, in my opinion, is fatal to the city's defense. Accordingly, I am of the opinion that from the standpoint of the City of Newport and the State of Rhode Island, Cain was not a trespasser, but was an implied licensee, and that the grant of summary judgment in favor of the governmental defendants was error. * * *

Under our law, the duty of care owed to a licensee and an invitee is identical and requires the owner to exercise reasonable care to secure the premises against injury that is foreseeable and preventable by undertaking reasonable precautions. Under this rule, "the basic tort test of reasonableness" defines the duty owed by a landowner toward an entrant onto his or her lands, and "the question to be resolved will be whether the owner has used reasonable care for the safety of all persons reasonably expected to be upon his premises." Mariorenzi [v. DiPonte, Inc.,] 114 R.I. 294, 307, 333 A.2d 127, 133 [(1975)]. Thus, under this analysis, I am satisfied that the evidence in this case demonstrates that Cain was reasonably expected to be upon the Cliff Walk that summer evening, that he was not given notice that the Cliff Walk was closed, and that genuine questions of fact remain relative to whether the governmental defendants were in breach of the aforementioned duty of care. * * *

I am of the opinion that Cain, as a tourist visitor to Newport's famed Cliff Walk on that fateful August night, was not a trespasser, but was an implied licensee whose presence on the Cliff Walk was not only anticipated, it was welcomed. Further, I believe that Newport has benefited significantly from the continued vitality of the Cliff Walk as the brightest gem in its tourism crown, and accordingly has always held out an implicit invitation to its summer tourists to come to Newport and visit this attraction.

The record discloses that Cain and his friends entered the Cliff Walk from Forty Steps, a public entrance to the walk at the end of Narragansett Avenue, an area where the city deliberately decided to forgo the placement of signs notifying the public that the park was closed. * * * The fact that there was not a single sign indicating the hours the Cliff Walk was closed to the public at this crucial location defeats any suggestion that Cain was anything but a licensee when he and his friends parked a vehicle on the public street, walked down the very public Forty Steps, and entered the Cliff Walk on a moonlit August night.

Accordingly, in my opinion, the City of Newport may be liable in damages for Cain's tragic death, and the judicially created immunity for trespassers ought not be available under the facts of this case. * * *

NOTES

1. *Justifications for Treating Trespassers Differently.* Assuming, arguendo, that the decedent was properly classified as a trespasser, why should the legal rights of his surviving family members not be determined under the usual standard of reasonable care under all the circumstances, including, here, the time of his presence on the pathway and the fact that the walkway was closed to the public at this hour? For more on the justifications for treating trespassers differently, see *infra* pages 559–60, Note 2.

2. *Children as Trespassers: Attractive Nuisance and Related* Restatement (Second) *Provision.* As early as the mid-nineteenth century, cases in both England and many states recognized that the behavior of children as trespassers would not necessarily preclude their recovery. In Lynch v. Nurdin, (1841) 113 Eng. Rep. 1041 (Q.B.), 1 Q.B. 29, a child between the ages of six and seven and his playmates climbed in and out of a horse-drawn cart and played with the horse, both of which had been negligently left on the street by the defendant's servants. The court acknowledged that the "plaintiff himself has done wrong: he had no right to enter the cart," but still the plaintiff was allowed to recover. The court reasoned that the plaintiff "merely indulged the natural instinct of a child in amusing himself with the empty cart and deserted horse" and that in doing so, he showed as much prudence and thought as a child could be expected to possess. The court concluded: "The most blamable carelessness of his servant having tempted the child, he ought not to reproach the child with yielding to that temptation. He has been the real and only cause of the mischief * * *. His misconduct bears no proportion to that of the defendant which produced it."

A generation later, in the famous case of Sioux City & Pac. R.R. Co. v. Stout, 84 U.S. (17 Wall.) 657, 21 L.Ed. 745 (1873), the United States Supreme Court considered the case of a six year old injured while playing on a railroad turntable. The Supreme Court stated that "while a railway company is not bound to the same degree of care in regard to mere strangers who are unlawfully upon its premises that it owes to passengers conveyed by it, it is not exempt from responsibility to such strangers for injuries arising from its negligence or from its tortious acts." The Court then found a number of factors suggesting that the railroad had been negligent, including the foreseeability that children would be attracted to it, the severity of any resulting injury, and the lack of "any considerable expense or inconvenience" in fixing a broken latch so as to have prevented the injury.

In the infamous case of United Zinc & Chem. Co. v. Britt, 258 U.S. 268, 42 S.Ct. 299, 66 L.Ed. 615 (1922), Justice Holmes cautioned that the principle that allowed child trespassers to recover under some circumstances "must be very cautiously applied." He rejected the application of a standard of reasonable care in a case involving the death of two children who went into water in the basement of the defendant who previously had operated a plant producing sulphuric acid. The water appeared clear, but in fact was dangerously poisoned, and the children died. Justice Holmes ruled that the attractive nuisance doctrine did not establish a duty of reasonable care to the children because the contaminated pool "could not be seen from any place where the children lawfully were and there is no evidence that it was what led them to enter the land." The case was highly criticized, even in its own time. "The *Britt* case with its requirement of 'allurement' has been condemned by every American writer whose views I have read. It has been repeatedly rejected by courts all over the United States, though a few cases are to the contrary. It has been rejected in the Restatement. It has no place in modern law." Laurence H. Eldredge, Modern Tort Problems, 203–04 (1941).

The Restatement (Second) of Torts § 339 provides a rule that is a similar, if less restrictive, standard than the attractive nuisance doctrine outlining when a land possessor owes a duty of reasonable care to trespassing children:

> A possessor of land is subject to liability for physical harm to children trespassing thereon caused by an artificial condition upon the land if
>
> (a) the place where the condition exists is one upon which the possessor knows or has reason to know that children are likely to trespass, and
>
> (b) the condition is one of which the possessor knows or has reason to know and which he realizes or should realize will involve an unreasonable risk of death or serious bodily harm to such children, and
>
> (c) the children because of their youth do not discover the condition or realize the risk involved in intermeddling with it or in coming within the area made dangerous by it, and
>
> (d) the utility to the possessor of maintaining the condition and the burden of eliminating the danger are slight as compared with the risk to children involved, and
>
> (e) the possessor fails to exercise reasonable care to eliminate the danger or otherwise to protect the children.

See also, e.g., Jones v. Billings, 289 A.2d 39 (Me.1972) (adopting standard of Restatement (Second) § 339).

By 2010, Maryland and Vermont were the only states that had adopted neither the attractive nuisance doctrine nor an alternative ameliorative provision suggested by the Restatement (Second) of Torts § 339 (1965) or otherwise adopted by the courts. See Murphy v. Baltimore Gas and Elec. Co., 290 Md. 186, 428 A.2d 459 (1981); Zukatis v. Perry, 165 Vt. 298, 682 A.2d 964 (1996). In Blackburn Ltd. P'ship v. Paul, 438 Md. 100, 90 A.3d 464, 472 (2014), the Court of Appeals of Maryland held the defendant liable to the parents of a child trespasser where the defendant's failure to fence a pool violated a state regulation requiring such fencing. The court found that the state regulation was not just " 'passed for the benefit of the public,' * * * [but] aims to protect a more targeted class of persons." The court "place[d] no significance on the legal status of plaintiffs on the premises. What matters is that they are members of the class to be protected by the statute." However, the court unconvincingly distinguished rather than overruled Osterman v. Peters, 260 Md. 313, 315, 272 A.2d 21, 22 (1971), where the court declined to adopt the attractive nuisance doctrine and held that the "owner of land owes no duty to a trespasser * * *, even one of tender years, except to abstain from willful or wanton misconduct or entrapment * * *."

Herrick v. Wixom

Supreme Court of Michigan, 1899.
121 Mich. 384, 80 N.W. 117.

■ MONTGOMERY, J. This is an action of trespass on the case, * * *. Defendant was possessed of and managed a tent show or circus. * * * Plaintiff went to the circus grounds on the afternoon of this day in company with his cousin. There is testimony to show that while there he and his cousin were invited by a son of the defendant, who had been selling tickets in the ticket wagon, to enter the tent with him, the entertainment being in progress. This plaintiff did, taking a seat on the lower tier of seats. The testimony on the part of defense tended to show that plaintiff was not invited into the show, and that the son of defendant had no authority to invite him in. * * * A part or feature of the entertainment consisted in the ignition and explosion of a giant firecracker attached to a pipe set in an upright position in one of the show rings. This was done by one of the clowns. There is testimony to show that plaintiff sat 30 or 40 feet from the place where the cracker was exploded, but when the same was exploded a part of the firecracker flew and struck plaintiff in the eye, putting it out, whereby he lost the sight and use of the eye. * * * Upon the trial of the cause a verdict of no cause for action was rendered, and judgment for the defendant entered accordingly. Plaintiff brings error. * * *

The circuit judge charged the jury as follows: "The negligence charged in this case is, gentlemen, that Mr. Wixom exploded a firecracker, of the dimensions that the plaintiff claims this firecracker was, in the inside of this tent, and in the presence of his audience. They claim that was negligence. And that is the question for you to determine, under the evidence, and under the rules of law that I have given you and that I shall give you hereafter. Now, you must further find, in order that the plaintiff recover, that the plaintiff was in the tent, where he was injured, by the invitation of some person having authority to allow him to go in there. If he was a mere trespasser, who forced his way in, then the defendant owed him no duty that would enable him to recover under the declaration and proofs in this case. * * *"

We think this instruction faulty, in so far as it was intended to preclude recovery in any event if the plaintiff was found to be a trespasser. It is true that a trespasser who suffers an injury because of a dangerous condition of premises is without remedy. But, where a trespasser is discovered upon the premises by the owner or occupant, he is not beyond the pale of the law, and any negligence resulting in injury will render the person guilty of negligence liable to respond in damages. * In this case the negligent act of the defendant's servant was committed after the audience was made up. The presence of plaintiff was known, and the danger to him from a negligent act was also known. The question of whether a dangerous experiment should be attempted in his presence, or whether an experiment should be conducted with due care and regard to his safety, cannot be made to depend upon whether he had forced himself into the tent. Every instinct of humanity revolts at such a suggestion. For this error the judgment will be reversed, and a new trial ordered. * * *

NOTES

1. *The Distinction between Active Conduct and a Condition of the Property.* Courts are more willing to hold the land possessor liable when the plaintiff's injury results from the active conduct of the defendant than they are when the injury results from a condition on the property. See Harper, James and Gray on Torts § 27.6. It is more likely that a land possessor would be found liable for negligently colliding with the plaintiff with her automobile or shooting him than if she failed to fence an abandoned mineshaft or at least post a warning.

2. *Liability to a Known Trespasser.* Intertwined with the distinction between liability for active intervention and liability for a condition of the property is a second factor, whether the presence of the trespasser is known to the landowner. A leading torts treatise summarizes the often inconsistent results reached by courts as follows:

> Given active intervention, the question then arises what the occupier's duties are with respect to this intervention. * * * Probably all states * * * [now recognize] at least a duty to refrain from wanton or willful misconduct toward a trespasser whose presence is known. Some states have stopped at this point, but many of those that purport to do so have added a gloss that to be actively negligent in the presence of a perceived trespasser amounts to wantonness. This is only a more or less indirect way of requiring the occupier to conduct himself with ordinary care toward a trespasser once the latter's presence has become known. Under one form or another, this is in substance the rule in the vast majority of American jurisdictions. * * *

> Where the trespasser's presence is not perceived, the cases take one of three attitudes. Some courts absolve the occupier of any duty toward the trespasser, even with respect to affirmative activities. This attitude was once quite common, but has steadily been losing ground. At the other extreme, a very few courts have imposed on the occupier whose activities are highly dangerous * * * the duty of care toward trespassers at any place that is exposed to the activity. Taking a middle position, the Restatement (Second) of Torts § 334 and Comments (1965) and a majority of courts impose such a duty where, and only where, the likelihood of trespass at some particular point, or limited locality, on the defendant's premises is considerable. * * * [I]t seems better to proceed on a case-to-case basis, applying the guiding principle of unreasonable danger in all the circumstances, rather than attempting to erect a rigid rule from one or another of the circumstances.

Harper, James and Gray on Torts § 27.6.

3. *Liability of Those Other Than Land Possessors.* In Humphrey v. Twin State Gas & Elec. Co., 100 Vt. 414, 139 A. 440 (1927), the plaintiff was injured when he touched a wire fence that had become electrically charged after wires strung over the land by the defendant, with the permission of Thomas, the owner of the land, fell onto the fence. The evidence was deemed sufficient to establish the defendant's negligence. The defendant resisted the suit on the ground that the plaintiff was a trespasser on the land. The court responded:

> We do not stop to consider this question. He was not an invitee, and for the purposes of this discussion we will assume that he was a trespasser. Being such, he could recover nothing from Thomas for injuries resulting from the condition of the premises, though these existed through the latter's carelessness. This result follows from the fact that Thomas owed him no duty to keep the premises safe for his unlawful use. The defendant takes the position that, so far as the plaintiff's rights go, it stands in Thomas' position and can make the same defense that he could; that it owed the plaintiff no duty, and consequently any negligence proved against it is not actionable so far as the plaintiff can assert. * * * The object of the law being to safeguard and protect the various rights in land, it is obviously going quite far enough to limit the immunity to the one whose rights have been invaded. Nor does logic or justice require more. A trespass is an injury to the possession; and as it is only he whose possession is disturbed who can sue therefore, so it should be that he, alone, could assert the unlawful invasion when suit is brought by an injured trespasser. One should not be allowed "to defend an indefensible act" by showing that the party injured was engaged in doing something which, as to a third person, was unlawful. Authorities sustaining this view of the law are not wanting.

B. LIABILITY TO LICENSEES AND INVITEES UNDER TRADITIONAL LAW CLASSIFYING VISITORS ON LAND

Gautret v. Egerton
Court of Common Pleas, 1867.
L.R. 2 C.P. 371 (Eng).

The declaration in the first of these actions stated that the defendants were possessed of a close of land, and of a certain canal and cutting intersecting the same, and of certain bridges across the said canal and cuttings, communicating with and leading to certain docks of the defendants, which said land and bridges had been and were from time to time used with the consent and permission of the defendants by persons proceeding towards and coming from the said docks; that the defendants, well knowing the premises, wrongfully, negligently, and improperly kept and maintained the said land, canal, cuttings, and bridges, and suffered them to continue and be in so improper a state and condition as to render them dangerous and unsafe for persons lawfully passing along and over the said land and bridges towards the said docks, and using the same as aforesaid; and that Leon Gautret, whilst he was lawfully in and passing and walking along the said close and over the said bridge, and using the same in the manner and for the purpose aforesaid, by and through the said wrongful, negligent, and improper conduct of the defendants as aforesaid, fell into one of the said cuttings of the defendants, intersecting the said close as aforesaid, and thereby lost his life. * * *

[On demurrer to the declarations:]

■ WILLES, J. I am of opinion that our judgment must be for the defendants in each of these cases. * * * The consequences of these accidents are sought to be visited upon these defendants, because they have allowed persons to go over their land, not alleging it to have been upon the business or for the benefit of the defendants, or as the servants or agents of the defendants; nor alleging that the defendants have been guilty of any wrongful act, such as digging a trench on the land, or misrepresenting its condition, or anything equivalent to laying a trap for the unwary passengers; but simply because they permitted these persons to use a way with the condition of which, for anything that appears, those who suffered the injury were perfectly well acquainted. * * * Assuming that these were private docks, the private property of the defendants, and that they permitted persons going to or coming from the docks, whether for their own benefit or that of the defendants, to use the way, the dedication of a permission to use the way must be taken to be in the character of a gift. The principle of law as to gifts is, that the giver is not responsible for damage resulting from the insecurity of the thing, unless he knew its evil character at the time, and omitted to caution the donee. * * * To create a cause of action, something like fraud must be shewn. No action will lie against a spiteful man who, seeing another running into a position of danger, merely omits to warn him. To bring the case within the category of actionable negligence, some wrongful act must be shewn, or a breach of some positive duty: otherwise, a man who allows strangers to roam over his property would be held to be answerable for not protecting them against any danger which they might encounter whilst using the licence. * * *

Judgment accordingly.

Indermaur v. Dames

English Common Pleas, 1866.
L.R. 1 C.P. 274.

■ WILLES, J. This was an action to recover damages for hurt sustained by the plaintiff's falling down a shaft at the defendant's place of business, through the actionable negligence, as it was alleged, of the defendant and his servants. At the trial * * * the plaintiff had a verdict for 400£ damages, subject to leave reserved. * * *

It appears that the defendant was a sugar-refiner, at whose place of business there was a shaft four feet three inches square, and twenty-nine feet three inches deep, used for moving sugar. The shaft was necessary, usual, and proper in the way of the defendant's business. Whilst it was in use, it was necessary and proper that it should be open and unfenced. When it was not in use, it was sometimes necessary, with reference to ventilation, that it should be open. It was not necessary that it should, when not in use, be unfenced; and it might then without injury to the business have been fenced by a rail. Whether it was usual to fence similar shafts when not in use did not distinctly appear; nor is it very material, because such protection was unquestionably proper, in the sense of reasonable, with reference to the safety of persons having a right to move about upon the floor where the shaft in fact was, because in its nature it formed a pit-fall there. At the time of the accident it was not in use, and it was open and unfenced.

The plaintiff was a journeyman gas-fitter in the employ of a patentee who had supplied the defendant with his patent gas-regulator, to be paid for upon the terms that it effected a certain saving: and, for the purpose of ascertaining whether such saving had been effected, the plaintiff's employer required to test the action of the regulator. He accordingly sent the plaintiff to the defendant's place of business for that purpose; and, whilst the plaintiff was engaged upon the floor where the shaft was, he (under circumstances as to which the evidence was conflicting, but) accidentally, and, as the jury found without any fault or negligence on his part, fell down the shaft and was seriously hurt. * * *

It was also argued that the plaintiff was at best in the condition of a bare licensee or guest who, it was urged, is only entitled to use the place as he finds it, and whose complaint may be said to wear the colour of ingratitude, so long as there is no design to injure him. * We think this argument fails, because the capacity in which the plaintiff was there was that of a person on lawful business in the course of fulfilling a contract in which both the plaintiff and the defendant had an interest, and not upon bare permission. * * *

The authorities respecting guests and other bare licensees, and those respecting servants and others who consent to incur a risk, being therefore inapplicable, we are to consider what is the law as to the duty of the occupier of a building with reference to persons resorting thereto in the course of business, upon his invitation, express or implied. The common case is that of a customer in a shop: but it is obvious that this is only one of a class; for, whether the customer is actually chaffering at the time, or actually buys or not, he is, according to an undoubted course of authority and practice, entitled to the exercise of reasonable care by the occupier to prevent damage from unusual danger, of which the occupier knows or ought to know such as a trap-door left open, unfenced, and unlighted.

* * * This protection does not depend upon the fact of a contract being entered into in the way of the shopkeeper's business during the stay of the customer, but upon the fact that the customer has come into the shop in pursuance of a tacit invitation given by the shopkeeper, with a view to business which concerns himself. And, if a customer were, after buying goods, to go back to the shop in order to complain of the quality, or that the change was not right, he would be just as much there upon business which concerned the shopkeeper, and as much entitled to protection during this accessory visit, though it might not be for the shopkeeper's benefit, as during the principal visit, which was. And if, instead of going himself, the customer were to send his servant, the servant would be entitled to the same consideration as the master.

The class to which the customer belongs includes persons who go not as mere volunteers, or licensees, or guests, or servants, or persons whose employment is such that danger may be considered as bargained for, but who go upon business which concerns the occupier, and upon his invitation, express or implied.

Brosnan v. Koufman

Supreme Judicial Court of Massachusetts, 1936[a]
294 Mass. 495, 2 N.E.2d 441.

■ PIERCE, JUSTICE. This is an action of tort for personal injuries sustained by the plaintiff while upon a certain stairway in the Carney building in Boston, which collapsed while the plaintiff was passing over it. * * *

At the trial there was ample evidence to warrant a finding that the plaintiff was in the exercise of due care, as well as a finding that the defendant was negligent in the maintenance of the stairway upon which the plaintiff was injured, if the defendant owed a duty to the plaintiff to exercise reasonable care to maintain the stairway in a reasonably safe condition for travel over it. * * *

Upon the evidence most favorable to the plaintiff it appeared that the Carney building was located upon a parcel of land which had a frontage on Tremont Street and a rear frontage on Pemberton Square, both public highways. The entrance to the building from Tremont Street led into a marble corridor which was about eight feet wide. This corridor extended to a flight of stairs which led to Pemberton Square. The building had been under the control of the defendant since 1921, and this corridor had been used for a long time by a large number of people in walking between Tremont Street and Pemberton Square. The defendant had seen many persons making such use of the corridor. * * *

The evidence showed that as one goes along the corridor from the Tremont Street entrance he passes a bulletin board containing the names of the tenants of the building; that further on, at about fifteen feet from the entrance to the building, he passes three elevators; that beyond the elevators is a stand at which cigars, cigarettes and fruit are sold; that there is also a telephone booth and nearly opposite the elevators is a United States mail box; that beyond the cigar stand there is a right angle turn to the right in the corridor, then more steps, and then another sharp turn, to the left, leading to the iron stairway of seven steps which leads to Pemberton Square. The evidence warranted a finding that the plaintiff had frequently passed over the corridor in question, and at the time of his injury he had entered the building by the Tremont Street entrance for the purpose of mailing letters; that he had done so by using the mail box in the corridor, and that when injured he was about to leave the premises by the Pemberton Square exit. * * *

The only fundamental question is as to whether the plaintiff, in going upon the defendant's premises, was an invitee or business visitor to whom was owed a duty of care with reference to the maintenance of

---

a   [Eds.' note] The Brosnan opinion typifies traditional doctrine. Massachusetts law, however, has since moved forward. Mounsey v. Ellard, 363 Mass. 693, 297 N.E.2d 43 (1973) (abrogating distinction between licensees and invitees, cf. *infra* pages 554–561).

the stairway which collapsed to his physical injury, or whether he was a licensee to whom no such duty was owed. * * *

Persons using a way over private land for their own convenience, with the acquiescence of the owner thereof, are held in many cases to be licensees only, unless the way is so constructed or maintained as to induce people to believe it to be a public street or way. * It is the contention of the plaintiff in the case at bar that invitation was implied from the whole condition of things, including the relation of the corridor to Tremont Street and Pemberton Square, the fact that there was no sign at the entrance to the corridor at Pemberton Square, the presence of the sales stand in the corridor, and particularly the presence of a United States mail receptacle in the corridor, assuming the jury might properly find that the mail box was put there with the purpose and design that it should be used by the public at large, of whom the plaintiff was one.

When a building is adapted for business uses, it is generally held that one who comes upon the premises for a purpose connected with the business carried on or in the interest of the occupant, does so under an implied invitation as one to whom is owed a duty of due care. * If, however, one comes upon such premises for his own convenience, to gratify curiosity, or with the expectation of gratuitous favors, he is at the best a licensee. * The facts in the case at bar * * * establish, on the plaintiff's own testimony, that he was within the corridor for the purpose of mailing his own letters. Leaving out any consideration of the federal statute governing the establishing of mail boxes, the plaintiff has not made out his case. He has not shown that the mailbox was intended for the use of the public generally, rather than for the use of the tenants of the building. It may be noted in this connection that there is no testimony in the record that there was any sign on the outside of the building indicating to the public that there was a mail box within the building, from which an invitation to make use of the box could be implied. * It is not shown that the use of the mail box was for the common or mutual advantage of the defendant and the plaintiff, or that the defendant derived any revenue from its presence or had any direct pecuniary interest in its maintenance, from which it might be implied that he authorized the public having letters to mail to come on the premises to do so. Even though it appears that those using the corridor were not forbidden to use the mail box, such silence would import no more than a tolerance or license to make use of the mail box for personal convenience. * * *

It is immaterial that a cigar stand and public telephone were maintained in the corridor, or that on some other occasion he had come on the premises for purposes connected with the sale of tobacco or with the use of the telephone. Had he done so on the day of the accident he might have been there under an implied invitation of the defendant. * * *

NOTES

1. *Distinguishing Invitees from Licensees.* In off-hand generalization, judicial opinions and text-writers differentiate between "invitees"—to whom the occupier is said to owe an affirmative duty of care to discover unreasonably dangerous conditions and to protect the visitor from them—

and "licensees." As a result of developments since Gautret v. Egerton, *supra*, there is conventionally a duty to warn "licensees" of concealed dangers actually known to the occupier or of which "he has reason to know," and which are likely not to be discovered by the licensee. Restatement (Second) of Torts, §§ 342, 343. (For the difference between "should know" and "reason to know" see Restatement (Second) § 12). There can also be liability to both "invitees" and "licensees" for unreasonably dangerous active conduct, but under somewhat different conditions. *Id.* at §§ 341, 341A. These terms imply that the differentiating criterion is the fact of invitation from the occupier. See, for example, Annotation, Attractive Nuisances, 36 A.L.R. 34 (1925): "In considering the duty of the owner or occupier of premises to persons who come thereon, the law divides them into three categories—trespassers, licensees, and invitees. Invitees * are persons who are invited to come upon the premises. * * * Licensees are persons whose presence is not invited, but tolerated." And some cases expend much effort on determining whether the occupier requested the visitor to come or rather granted the visitor's request for permission. Frequently too, the difference is said to be between a visit for the visitor's benefit only and one for the mutual benefit of visitor and occupier.

In the Restatement (Second) of Torts (1965), Professor Prosser defined "invitee" as either a "public invitee" ("a person who is invited to enter or remain on land as a member of the public for a purpose for which the land is held open to the public") or a "business visitor" ("a person who is invited to enter or remain on land for a purpose directly or indirectly connected with business dealings with the possessor of the lands"). *Id.* at § 332. "Licensee" was redefined as "a person who is privileged to enter or remain on land only by virtue of the possessor's consent." *Id.* at § 330. Comment *b* to § 332 defines "invitation" as "conduct which justifies others in believing that the possessor desires them to enter the land," and "permission" as "conduct justifying others in believing that the possessor is willing that they shall enter if they desire to do so."

Courts continue to experience frustration and reach inconsistent results in trying to distinguish invitees from licensees, particularly in those jurisdictions that still require a prospective economic benefit to the landowner before a visitor is categorized as an invitee, as illustrated by the following discussion from Nelson v. Freeland, 349 N.C. 615, 627, 507 S.E.2d 882, 889–90, *infra* pages 554–558 (1998):

> Consider, for example, the following scenario: A real-estate agent trespasses onto another's land to determine the value of property adjoining that which he is trying to sell; the real-estate agent is discovered by the landowner, and the two men engage in a business conversation with respect to the landowner's willingness to sell his property; after completing the business conversation, the two men realize that they went to the same college and have a nostalgic conversation about school while the landowner walks with the man for one acre until they get to the edge of the property; lastly, the two men stand on the property's edge and speak for another ten minutes about school. If the real-estate agent was injured while they were walking off the property, what is his classification? Surely, he is no longer a trespasser, but did his status change from invitee to licensee once the business conversation ended? What if he was hurt while the two men were

talking at the property's edge? Does it matter how long they were talking?

2. *An Invitation to Perjury?* Recall Justice Pierce's comments about the importance of whether the plaintiff was using the corridor to mail a letter or to use the telephone or to buy tobacco. Is this in effect an invitation to perjury? For example:

> *Client*: I broke my leg on a bad stair in the Carney Bldg. Do you think I can get damages?

> *Lawyer*: Well that depends. Tell me the whole story. What were you doing in the Carney Bldg. and so forth. You know there was a similar accident there in 1936. Terrible. The whole stairway collapsed while a fellow named Brosnan was on it. Hurt him pretty bad. The jury gave him $9,900. But our Supreme Court threw him out. They said he couldn't get anything at all because he went into the building just to mail a letter. If a fellow goes into a building just for his own convenience, he can't expect much from the owner. But the Court said that if the fellow went in there on business with some tenant or to buy tobacco at the stand in the lobby he could have kept the $9,900 verdict. Pretty well settled law here.

> *Client*: Really? That's funny as hell. Why, there are dozens of people in and out of that building all the time. It's just a fluke that it was my leg and not that of one of the dozens of people who go to the dentists, lawyers, finance companies and other tenants in the building. Well, in my case * * * I was walking along Tremont Street to go to the Court House at Pemberton Square and thought I would cut through the building. I mean I found I needed cigarettes and thought I'd get them in the lobby and then go out the Pemberton Square side.

> *Lawyer*: You're sure you went in to buy cigarettes? Because if you were just using the building for a short cut, you'd be out of luck.

> *Client*: Why, I'm positive. You know I was laid up for a couple of months and still haven't paid my medical bills.

> *Lawyer*: Well, I just wanted to make sure. So far you're in the clear. Go on.

Compare "the lecture" given by the criminal defense attorney in Robert Traver's novel, *The Anatomy of a Murder* 30–33 (1958) (attorney tells client, accused of a murder, that a slight variation in how he explains the facts may make the difference between a murder conviction and an acquittal on the grounds of temporary insanity). "Robert Traver" was in fact the pen name of Justice John D. Voelker of the Michigan Supreme Court.

Of course, perjury is conceivable in any case. But in situations like that in *Brosnan v. Koufman*, is the temptation too great? Is it checked by objective facts or the availability of testimony other than that of the plaintiff? May a plaintiff's testimony be influenced by the existence of a statute such as the one quoted in the case that seems to give him not merely permission but a right to enter the building to mail a letter? Does the rule of the *Brosnan* case as applied do more than trap the honest or ignorant? What more?

3. *Limits to Area of Invitation.* Even if the injured party qualifies as an invitee, this status may apply only when he is in an area open to the public. For example, in Morris v. Granato, 133 Conn. 295, 50 A.2d 416 (1946), the plaintiff was a customer at the defendant's restaurant. She mistakenly entered the unmarked men's restroom, believing it to be the women's restroom. Someone brought this to the attention of her companion, and he went to the door, called to her that she had entered the wrong restroom, and returned to the restaurant. The flustered plaintiff turned the wrong direction as she left the men's room and opened an unmarked door, erroneously believing it was the women's restroom, and stepped in. In fact that door led to an unlit cellar. Plaintiff fell down the stairs and was injured. The defendants claimed that the plaintiff was "not an invitee with relation to that part of the restaurant where the cellar door was." The court rejected the argument, concluding, "Whether an invitee exceeded the limits of the invitation depends upon whether his use of the premises went beyond that which the owner might reasonably have contemplated. * * * The jury reasonably could have concluded that the cellar door, four feet away, might be mistaken for a toilet, and could have found that the plaintiff was an invitee as to that part of the restaurant."

4. *Social Guests.* A prime anomaly under the traditional approach to classifying those injured while on the land of others is the situation of the social guest. Social guests are fairly uniformly said to be licensees to whom a lesser duty is owed than that owed to invitees, e.g., Southcote v. Stanley, (1856) 156 Eng.Rep. 1195 (Exch.), 1 Hurl. & N. 247, McMullan v. Butler, 346 So.2d 950 (Ala.1977), even when the host and the guest are really fond of each other and derive mutual pleasure from the visit. The criterion distinguishing an invitee from a licensee is neither invitation nor mutuality of benefit broadly construed, but either business purpose or public invitation. But query: Suppose a lawyer (plaintiff) visits a client's office and after concluding their business says to the client (defendant), "let me take you to dinner and the theatre tonight"; the plaintiff returns to the client's office at six and is hurt by a condition of the floor which would subject the defendant to liability to an invitee. Or suppose that the parties could not agree by dinner time and the client says: "Come over to my place for a drink. I think we can wrap up the loose ends there." The plaintiff accepts the invitation and is hurt by a condition of the floor in the defendant's home.

5. *Police and Fire Personnel and Similar Visitors.* In those jurisdictions still employing the traditional categories of licensee and invitee, classification of public officials, utility meter-readers, and repairpersons has proven particularly troublesome. Postal employees, refuse collectors, inspectors, and meter readers traditionally have been classified as invitees, while police and fire personnel often are categorized as licensees. The distinction is sometimes rationalized on the basis that the first group is visiting the premises for a purpose associated with the business activities of the land occupier. Another explanation is that police and fire personnel arrive at unexpected times and therefore it does not seem feasible to require the occupier of the premises to conduct an inspection and warn of hidden dangers. But inspectors also arrive unexpectedly, and at least business premises should be kept reasonably safe for some visitors, even if others are not expected. In Cook v. Demetrakas, 108 R.I. 397, 275 A.2d 919 (1971), the court suggests a distinction depending upon whether the police officer enters the premises on a routine security check, in which case he might be an invitee, or to chase a thief, in which case he is only a licensee. See also Restatement of Torts, Second § 345(2) (1965) (a public officer or employee who enters land in performance of duty and suffers harm because of condition of land held open to the public is to be treated the same as an invitee).

A separate rule, generally known as the "firefighter's rule," typically bars claims by firefighters and police officers against those whose negligence created the fire or other hazard that injured the officer, particularly if the officer was injured by the condition that occasioned her presence on the premises. Although the rule has sometimes been understood as an application of premises liability theory, courts now justify the "firefighter's rule" on the basis of factors similar to those underlying assumption of risk, as well as on issues of public policy akin to the exclusivity provisions of workers' compensation. See, e.g., Walters v. Sloan, 20 Cal.3d 199, 142 Cal.Rptr. 152, 571 P.2d 609 (1977). Fires and the hazards of fighting crime are viewed as occupational hazards that constitute the occasion for the engagement of fire and police personnel in the first place, and special no-fault compensation systems exist in most jurisdictions for fire and police personnel injured in the course of duty. See also Restatement (Third) of Torts: Liability for Physical and Emotional Harm § 51 cmt. m (2012) (concluding that the firefighter's rule no longer has any basis under premises liability theory if a general negligence standard of liability for land entrants is adopted, but leaving open the question of whether such a rule can be justified by other aspects of the rescuer's occupational role).

C. LIABILITY OF LAND POSSESSORS UNDER A GENERAL NEGLIGENCE STANDARD

Nelson v. Freeland

Supreme Court of North Carolina, 1998.
349 N.C. 615, 507 S.E.2d 882.

■ WYNN, JUSTICE. The sole issue * * * is whether defendant Dean Freeland's ("Freeland") act of leaving a stick on his porch constituted negligence. Indeed, this case presents us with the simplest of factual scenarios—Freeland requested that plaintiff John Harvey Nelson ("Nelson") pick him up at his house for a business meeting the two were attending, and Nelson, while doing so, tripped over a stick that Freeland had inadvertently left lying on his porch. Nelson brought this action against Freeland and his wife seeking damages for the injuries he sustained in the fall. The trial court granted summary judgment for the defendants, and the Court of Appeals affirmed. *

Although the most basic principles of tort law should provide an easy answer to this case, our current premises liability trichotomy—that is, the invitee, licensee, and trespasser classifications—provides no clear solution and has created dissension and confusion amongst the attorneys and judges involved. * * * [D]espite over one hundred years of utilizing the common-law trichotomy, we still are unable to determine unquestionably whether a man who trips over a stick at a friend/business partner's house is entitled to a jury trial—a question ostensibly answerable by the most basic tenet and duty under tort law: the reasonable-person standard of care.

Given that our current premises-liability scheme has confounded our judiciary, we can only assume that it has inadequately apprised landowners of their respective duties of care. Thus, it befalls us to examine the continuing utility of the common-law trichotomy as a means of determining landowner liability in North Carolina. In analyzing this question, we will consider the effectiveness of our current scheme of premises-liability law, the nationwide trend of abandoning the common-law trichotomy in favor of a reasonable-care standard, and the policy reasons for and against abandoning the trichotomy in this state. * * *

In a traditional common-law premises-liability action, the threshold issue of determining the plaintiff's status at the time of the injury is of substantial import. The gravity of this determination stems from the fact that there is a descending degree of duty owed by a landowner based upon the plaintiff's status. * * *

Although the common-law trichotomy has been entrenched in this country's tort-liability jurisprudence since our nation's inception, over the past fifty years, many states have questioned, modified, and even abolished it after analyzing its utility in modern times. * * *

The first significant move toward abolishing the common-law trichotomy occurred in 1957 when England—the jurisdiction giving rise to the trichotomy—passed the Occupier's Liability Act which abolished the distinction between invitees, licensees and so-called contractual visitors. * Shortly thereafter, the United States Supreme Court decided not to apply the trichotomy to admiralty law after concluding that it would be inappropriate to hold that a visitor is entitled to a different or lower standard of care simply because he is classified as a "licensee." See Kermarec v. Compagnie Generale Transatlantique, 358 U.S. 625, 630; 79 S.Ct. 406, 409–10, 3 L.Ed.2d 550, 554 (1959). In so ruling, the Court noted * * *:

> In an effort to do justice in an industrialized urban society, with its complex economic and individual relationships, modern common-law courts have found it necessary to formulate increasingly subtle verbal refinements, to create subclassifications among traditional common-law categories, and to delineate fine gradations in the standards of care which the landowners owe to each. Yet even within a single jurisdiction, the classifications and subclassifications bred by the common law have produced confusion and conflict.

Ultimately, the Court concluded that the numerous exceptions and subclassifications engrafted into the trichotomy have obscured the law, thereby causing it to move unevenly and with hesitation toward " 'imposing on owners and occupiers a single duty of reasonable care in all the circumstances.' " *

Nine years later, the Supreme Court of California decided the seminal case of Rowland v. Christian, 69 Cal.2d 108, 443 P.2d 561, 70 Cal.Rptr. 97 (1968), which abolished the common-law trichotomy in California in favor of modern negligence principles. Specifically, the court in *Rowland* held that the proper question to be asked in premises-liability actions is whether "in the management of his property [the landowner] has acted as a reasonable man in view of the probability of injury to others." * * * The court continued by stating that the trichotomy was "contrary to our modern social mores and humanitarian values, [and it] obscure[s] rather than illuminates the proper considerations which should govern determination of the question of duty."

The *Rowland* decision ultimately served as a catalyst for similar judicial decisions across the country. Indeed, since *Rowland*, twenty-five jurisdictions have either modified or abolished their common-law trichotomy scheme—seven within the last five years. Specifically, eleven jurisdictions have completely eliminated the common-law distinctions between licensee, invitee, and trespasser. * Further, fourteen jurisdictions have repudiated the licensee-invitee distinction while maintaining the limited-duty rule for trespassers. * In summation, nearly half of all jurisdictions in this country have judicially abandoned or modified the common-law trichotomy in favor of the modern "reasonable-person" approach that is the norm in all areas of tort law. * * *

Although the modern trend of premises-liability law in this country has been toward abolishing the trichotomy in favor of a reasonable-person standard, there are some jurisdictions that have refused to modify or abolish it. * One of the primary reasons that some jurisdictions have retained the trichotomy is fear of jury abuse—a fear similar to the reason it was created in the first place. Specifically, jurisdictions retaining the trichotomy fear that plaintiff-oriented juries—like feudal juries composed mostly of land entrants—will impose unreasonable burdens upon defendant-landowners. * This argument, however, fails to take into account that juries have properly applied negligence principles in all other areas of tort law, and there has been no indication that defendants in other areas have had unreasonable burdens placed upon them. Moreover, given that modern jurors are more likely than feudal jurors to be landowners themselves, it is unlikely that they would be willing to place a burden upon a defendant that they would be unwilling to accept upon themselves. *

Another fear held by jurisdictions retaining the trichotomy is that by substituting the negligence standard of care for the common-law categories, landowners will be forced to bear the burden of taking precautions such as the expensive cost associated with maintaining adequate insurance policies. * This argument, however, ignores the fact that every court which has abolished the trichotomy has explicitly stated that its holding was not intended to make the landowner an absolute insurer against all injuries suffered on his property. * Rather, they require landowners only to exercise reasonable care in the maintenance of their premises. *

Lastly, opponents of abolishing the trichotomy argue that retention of the scheme is necessary to ensure predictability in the law. * * *

The jurisdictions eliminating the trichotomy address the aforementioned concerns and provide well-articulated reasons for their decision to abandon the trichotomy. First, these jurisdictions note that the trichotomy was created during feudal times when land formed the principal basis of wealth and when it was desirable to provide a landowner free reign to use and exploit his land, without need for vigilant protection of those who entered his property. * * * After noting the trichotomy's origins, abolishing courts expressed apprehension about applying it in modern times. For example, the Supreme Court of Massachusetts stated:

> Perhaps, in a rural society with sparse land settlements and large estates, it would have been unduly burdensome to obligate the owner to inspect and maintain distant holdings for a class of entrants who were using the property "for their own convenience" but the special immunity which the licensee rule affords landowners cannot be justified in an urban industrial society.

Mounsey v. Ellard, 363 Mass. 693, 706, 297 N.E.2d 43, 51 (1973) (citation omitted). * * * Thus, these courts determined that the social and policy considerations underlying the creation of the common-law trichotomy were no longer viable, and therefore they concluded that it was proper to lay it to rest.

On a more practical level, the trichotomy has been criticized for creating a complex, confusing, and unpredictable state of law. * * * The Supreme Court of Wisconsin made a similar argument in *Antoniewicz* when it asked whether there is any reason why one who invites a guest to a party should have less concern for that individual's well-being than he has for the safety of an insurance salesman delivering a policy to his home. See Antoniewicz v. Reszcynski, 70 Wis.2d 836, 854, 236 N.W.2d 1, 10 (1975). The court then inquired whether the life or welfare of the guest should be regarded in a more sacred manner. Moreover, it queried whether we realistically can say that reasonable people vary their conduct based upon the status of the entrant. * * *

* * * [T]here are numerous advantages associated with abolishing the trichotomy. First, it is based upon principles which no longer apply to today's modern industrial society. Further, the preceding cases demonstrate that the trichotomy has failed to elucidate the duty a landowner owes to entrants upon his property. Rather, it has caused confusion amongst our citizens and the judiciary—a confusion exaggerated by the numerous exceptions and subclassifications engrafted into it. Lastly, the trichotomy is unjust and unfair because it usurps the jury's function either by allowing the judge to dismiss or decide the case or by forcing the jury to apply mechanical rules instead of focusing upon the pertinent issue of whether the landowner acted reasonably under the circumstances. Thus, we conclude that North Carolina should join the twenty-four other jurisdictions which have modified or abolished the trichotomy in favor of modern negligence principles. * * *

Given the numerous advantages associated with abolishing the trichotomy, this Court concludes that we should eliminate the distinction between licensees and invitees by requiring a standard of reasonable care toward all lawful visitors. Adoption of a true negligence standard eliminates the complex, confusing, and unpredictable state of premises-liability law and replaces it with a rule which focuses the jury's attention upon the pertinent issue of whether the landowner acted as a reasonable person would under the circumstances.

In so holding, we note that we do not hold that owners and occupiers of land are now insurers of their premises. Moreover, we do not intend for owners and occupiers of land to undergo unwarranted burdens in maintaining their premises. Rather, we impose upon them only the duty to exercise reasonable care in the maintenance of their premises for the protection of lawful visitors.

Further, we emphasize that we will retain a separate classification for trespassers. We believe that the status of trespasser still maintains viability in modern society, and more importantly, we believe that abandoning the status of trespasser may place an unfair burden on a landowner who has no reason to expect a trespasser's presence. Indeed, whereas both invitees and licensees enter another's land under color of right, a trespasser has no basis for claiming protection beyond refraining from willful injury. * * *

NOTES

1. *Rowland v. Christian.* The movement to replace the system of classifying those injured while on the land of others into trespassers, licensees, and invitees with a general negligence standard began with the California Supreme Court's leading opinion in Rowland v. Christian, 69 Cal.2d 108, 70 Cal.Rptr. 97, 443 P.2d 561 (1968). The court's reasoning proceeded from its statement of the basic principle of liability for negligence:

> * * * [A] person is liable for injuries caused by his failure to exercise reasonable care in the circumstances, * * * [and] in the absence of statutory provision declaring an exception to the fundamental principle * * * no such exception should be made unless clearly supported by public policy. *

> A departure from this fundamental principle involves the balancing of a number of considerations; the major ones are the foreseeability of harm to the plaintiff, the degree of certainty that the plaintiff suffered injury, the closeness of the connection between the defendant's conduct and the injury suffered, the moral blame attached to the defendant's conduct, the policy of preventing future harm, the extent of the burden to the defendant and consequences to the community of imposing a duty to exercise care with resulting liability for breach, and the availability, cost, and prevalence of insurance for the risk involved. * * *

The court noted the incompatibility between these central principles of negligence and the traditional classification system used for plaintiffs in cases against the owners and occupiers of land:

> The departure from the fundamental rule of liability for negligence has been accomplished by classifying the plaintiff either as a trespasser, licensee, or invitee and then adopting special rules as to the duty owed by the possessor to each of the classifications. * * *

> Although in general there may be a relationship between * * *[these] factors and the classifications of trespasser, licensee, and invitee, there are many cases in which no such relationship may exist. Thus, although the foreseeability of harm to an invitee would ordinarily seem greater than the foreseeability of harm to a

trespasser, in a particular case the opposite may be true. The same may be said of the issue of certainty of injury. The burden to the defendant and consequences to the community of imposing a duty to exercise care with resulting liability for breach may often be greater with respect to trespassers than with respect to invitees, but it by no means follows that this is true in every case. In many situations, the burden will be the same, i.e., the conduct necessary upon the defendant's part to meet the burden of exercising due care as to invitees will also meet his burden with respect to licensees and trespassers. The last of the major factors, the cost of insurance, will, of course, vary depending upon the rules of liability adopted, but there is no persuasive evidence that applying ordinary principles of negligence law to the land occupier's liability will materially reduce the prevalence of insurance due to increased cost or even substantially increase the cost.

The Restatement (Third) of Torts: Liability for Physical and Emotional Harm § 51 (2012) now generally provides that "a land possessor owes a duty of reasonable care to entrants on the land * * *." As of 2012, the Restatement identifies approximately half of the states following the traditional system of classification of land entrants with approximately the same number following the general negligence standard.

2. *Liability to Trespassers. Nelson v. Freeland* abolished only the distinction between licensees and invitees, but other jurisdictions, see, e.g., Rowland v. Christian, *supra,* have abolished limitations on the potential liability to all three separate categories of visitors, including trespassers. See Restatement (Third) of Torts: Liability for Physical and Emotional Harm § 51, Table (2012) (identifying slightly more than one-third of the states that apply a general negligence standard as including trespassers within the grand standard).

In Alexander v. Med. Assoc. Clinic, 646 N.W.2d 74 (Iowa 2002), the Iowa Supreme Court considered the issue of whether to apply a general negligence standard in a case brought by a trespasser. The plaintiff had entered an undeveloped, open field adjacent to a residential neighborhood to retrieve his sister's dog and injured his knee when he fell into a ditch. The court rejected the plaintiff's argument that it should discard the traditional trichotomy of standards and instead apply a general negligence standard:

> * * * [T]he common law rule retains validity in modern day life. * * * We agree with one treatise writer that in a society such as ours, "it is considered a socially desirable policy to allow a person to use his own land in his own way, without the burden of watching for and protecting those who come there without permission or right." W. Page Keeton et al., Prosser and Keeton on the Law of Torts § 58 (5th ed. 1984). As one court has stated, "It is unreasonable to subject an owner to a 'reasonable care' test against someone who isn't supposed to be there and about whom he does not know." Wood v. Camp, 284 So.2d 691, 693 (Fla.1973).
>
> The common law rule is also better suited to achieve a reasonable balance between individual property rights and the interests of a trespasser. Under the common law rule, a landowner knows in advance what his duty is; he must refrain from maliciously or

deliberately injuring a trespasser. A duty of reasonable care, in contrast, despite its common usage, is based on a much more amorphous standard, providing little guidance to the landowner. * Carter v. Kinney, 896 S.W.2d 926, 930 (Mo.1995) (refusing to abolish common law classifications, stating "[t]o abandon the careful work of generations for an amorphous 'reasonable care under the circumstances' standard seems—to put it kindly—improvident"). * * *

In summary, we remain unconvinced that the rights of property owners have so little value in today's society that those rights should be diminished in favor of persons trespassing on another's land. The common law standard is just as viable today as it was a century ago: a landowner has a duty not to injure a trespasser maliciously or deliberately, and to use reasonable care after the trespasser's presence becomes known to avoid injuring the trespasser. * This duty strikes an appropriate balance between the interests of the landowner and the trespasser and therefore we decline the plaintiff's invitation to abandon it. * * *

The Restatement (Third) § 52 provides that although a duty of reasonable care is owed to trespassers, only "the duty not to act in an intentional, willful, or wanton manner to cause physical harm" is owed to "flagrant trespassers" so long as the flagrant trespassers are not among those trespassers who "reasonably appear[ ] to be imperiled and (1) helpless; or (2) unable to protect him- or herself." The distinction is justified as follows:

> The idea behind distinguishing particularly egregious trespassers for different treatment is that their presence on another's land is so antithetical to the rights of the land possessor to exclusive use and possession of the land that the land possessor should not be subject to liability for failing to exercise the ordinary duty of reasonable care otherwise owed to them as entrants on the land. * * * A specific rule might reflect that distinction by providing that a flagrant trespasser is one who commits a crime of a certain severity while entering or upon the land. A somewhat broader rule might extend the definition of flagrant trespasser * * * to one who enters the land with a malicious motive or who commits an intentional wrong to the land possessor, or the possessor's family, property, or guests while on the land. Employing a different approach, a jurisdiction might adopt a general standard, for example, that a flagrant trespasser is one whose entrance on the land is sufficiently egregious as to be antithetical to the rights of the land possessor to exclusive possession and use of the land.

Id. at cmt. a. The comment suggests, for example, that while a burglar who is injured on the defendant's premises, see Calvillo-Silva v. Home Grocery, 19 Cal.4th 714, 80 Cal.Rptr.2d 506, 968 P.2d 65 (1998), would be a flagrant trespasser, someone injured while walking in a public park with a posted notice that the park was closed after dusk would not be. See Cain v. Johnson, *supra* pages 537–542.

3. *Recovery of Trespassing Children under a General Negligence Standard.* Sometimes children who would be regarded as trespassers if they were adults are allowed to recover under a general negligence analysis without the benefit of the attractive nuisance doctrine. For example, in

Gould v. DeBeve, 330 F.2d 826 (D.C.Cir.1964), the Court of Appeals allowed a 2½ year old boy to recover after falling through a negligently maintained screen in a third-floor window. The plaintiff and his family were technically trespassers—staying with another family in violation of provisions of the tenant's lease with the landlord. Because the plaintiff was "within the range of foreseeability in terms of those persons to whom injury might result from an unsafe screen," the court stated, "We do not think calling him a trespasser dictates a different result."

Obviously the general negligence standard under Restatement (Third) § 51 would generally supersede the attractive nuisance doctrine and Restatement (Second) of Torts § 339. A comment to Restatement (Third) § 51 notes, however, "That some of the persons likely to be exposed are children who are particularly vulnerable because of their immaturity is relevant to the extent of the precaution required of the land possessor." *Id.* at cmt l.

D. LIABILITY OF LANDLORDS

Sargent v. Ross

Supreme Court of New Hampshire, 1973.
113 N.H. 388, 308 A.2d 528.

■ KENISON, CHIEF JUSTICE. The question in this case is whether the defendant landlord is liable to the plaintiff in tort for the death of plaintiff's four-year-old daughter who fell to her death from an outdoor stairway at a residential building owned by the defendant in Nashua. The defendant resided in a ground-floor apartment in the building, and her son and daughter-in-law occupied a second story apartment serviced by the stairway from which the child fell. At the time of the accident the child was under the care of the defendant's daughter-in-law who was plaintiff's regular baby-sitter.

Plaintiff brought suit against * * * the defendant for negligent construction and maintenance of the stairway which was added to the building by the defendant about eight years before the accident. There was no apparent cause for the fall except for evidence that the stairs were dangerously steep, and that the railing was insufficient to prevent the child from falling over the side. The jury returned a verdict * * * in favor of the plaintiff * * *.

* * * [The] defendant urges that there was * * * no duty owing to the deceased child for the defendant to breach. This contention rests upon the general rule which has long obtained in this and most other jurisdictions that a landlord is not liable, except in certain limited situations, for injuries caused by defective or dangerous conditions in the leased premises. * The plaintiff does not directly attack this rule of nonliability but instead attempts to show, rather futilely under the facts, defendant's control of the stairway. She also relies upon an exception to the general rule of nonliability, to wit, that a landlord is liable for injuries resulting from his negligent repair of the premises. * The issue, as framed by the parties, is whether the rule of nonliability should prevail or whether the facts of this case can be squeezed into the

negligent repair or some other exception to the general rule of landlord immunity.

General principles of tort law ordinarily impose liability upon persons for injuries caused by their failure to exercise reasonable care under all the circumstances. * A person is generally negligent for exposing another to an unreasonable risk of harm which foreseeably results in an injury. * But, except in certain instances, landlords are immune from these simple rules of reasonable conduct which govern other persons in their daily activities. This "quasi-sovereignty of the landowner," F. Harper & F. James, The Law of Torts 1495 (1956), finds its source in an agrarian England of the dark ages. * * * But courts and legislatures alike are beginning to reevaluate the rigid rules of landlord-tenant law in light of current needs and principles of law from related areas. * "Justifiable dissatisfaction with the rule" of landlord tort immunity, F. Harper & F. James, at 1510, compels its reevaluation in a case such as this where we are asked either to apply the rule, and hold the landlord harmless for a foreseeable death resulting from an act of negligence, or to broaden one of the existing exceptions and hence perpetuate an artificial and illogical rule. *

One court recognized at an early date that ordinary principles of tort liability ought to apply to landlords as other persons. "The ground of liability upon the part of a landlord when he demises dangerous property has nothing special to do with the relation of landlord and tenant. It is the ordinary case of liability for personal misfeasance, which runs through all the relations of individuals to each other." Wilcox v. Hines, 100 Tenn. 538, 548–49, 46 S.W. 297, 299 (1898). Most courts, however, while recognizing from an early date that "the law is unusually strict in exempting the landlord from liability," Bowe v. Hunking, 135 Mass. 380, 386 (1883), sought refuge from the rigors of the rule by straining other legal principles such as deceit * and by carving out exceptions to the general rule of nonliability. * Thus, a landlord is now generally conceded to be liable in tort for injuries resulting from defective and dangerous conditions in the premises if the injury is attributable to (1) a hidden danger in the premises of which the landlord but not the tenant is aware, (2) premises leased for public use, (3) premises retained under the landlord's control, such as common stairways, or (4) premises negligently repaired by the landlord. *

As is to be expected where exceptions to a rule of law form the only basis of liability, the parties in this action concentrated at trial and on appeal on whether any of the exceptions applied, particularly whether the landlord or the tenant had control of the stairway. * The determination of the question of which party had control of the defective part of the premises causing the injury has generally been considered dispositive * * *. This was a logical modification to the rule of nonliability since ordinarily a landlord can reasonably be expected to maintain the property and guard against injuries only in common areas and other areas under his control. A landlord, for example, cannot fairly be held responsible in most instances for an injury arising out of the tenant's negligent maintenance of the leased premises. * But the control test is insufficient since it substitutes a facile and conclusive test for a reasoned consideration of whether due care was exercised under all the circumstances. *

There was evidence from which the jury could find that the landlord negligently designed or constructed a stairway which was dangerously steep or that she negligently failed to remedy or adequately warn the deceased of the danger. A proper rule of law would not preclude recovery in such a case by a person foreseeably injured by a dangerous hazard solely because the stairs serviced one apartment instead of two. But that would be the result if the control test were applied to this case, since this was not a "common stairway" or otherwise under the landlord's control. * While we could strain this test to the limits and find control in the landlord, * as plaintiff suggests, we are not inclined to so expand the fiction since we agree that "it is no part of the general law of negligence to exonerate a defendant simply because the condition attributable to his negligence has passed beyond his control before it causes injury * * *." F. Harper & F. James, The Law of Torts § 27.16 (1956). *

The anomaly of the general rule of landlord tort immunity and the inflexibility of the standard exceptions, such as the control exception, is pointedly demonstrated by this case. A child is killed by a dangerous condition of the premises. Both husband and wife tenants testify that they could do nothing to remedy the defect because they did not own the house nor have authority to alter the defect. But the landlord claims that she should not be liable because the stairs were not under her control. Both of these contentions are premised on the theory that the other party should be responsible. So the orthodox analysis would leave us with neither landlord nor tenant responsible for dangerous conditions on the premises. This would be both illogical and intolerable, particularly since neither party then would have any legal reason to remedy or take precautionary measures with respect to dangerous conditions. In fact, the traditional "control" rule actually discourages a landlord from remedying a dangerous condition since his repairs may be evidence of his control. * Nor can there be serious doubt that ordinarily the landlord is best able to remedy dangerous conditions, particularly where a substantial alteration is required. *

* * * [T]he issue of control is relevant to the determination of liability only insofar as it bears on the question of what the landlord and tenant reasonably should have believed in regard to the division of responsibility for maintaining the premises in a safe condition. The basic claim in this case involves only the design or construction of the steps; the maintenance of the stairs was not seriously in issue, except perhaps concerning the lack of precautions, since the evidence was clear that the stairway was dry and free of debris. The inquiry should have centered upon the unreasonableness of the pitch of the steps and the unreasonableness of failing to take precautionary measures to reduce the danger of falls.

Similarly, the truly pertinent questions involved in determining who should bear responsibility for the loss in this case were clouded by the question of whether the accident was caused by a hidden defect or secret danger. * The mere fact that a condition is open and obvious, as was the steepness of the steps in this case, does not preclude it from being unreasonably dangerous, and defendants are not infrequently "held liable for creating or maintaining a perfectly obvious danger of which plaintiffs are fully aware." F. Harper & F. James, *supra* at 1493.

* Additionally, while the dangerous quality of the steps might have been obvious to an adult, the danger and risk would very likely be imperceptible to a young child such as the deceased. * * *

Finally, plaintiff's reliance on the negligent repairs exception to the rule of nonliability * would require us to broaden the exception to include the negligent construction of improvements to the premises. We recognize that this would be no great leap in logic, * but we think it more realistic instead to consider reversing the general rule of nonliability * since "[t]he exceptions have * * * produced a twisting of legal concepts which seems undesirable." Note, 62 Harv. L. Rev. 669, 676 (1949). And "it appears to us that to search for gaps and exceptions in a legal doctrine . . . which exists only because of the somnolence of the common law and the courts is to perpetuate further judicial fictions when preferable alternatives exist. . . . The law of landlord-tenant relations cannot be so frail as to shatter when confronted with modern urban realities and a frank appraisal of the underlying issues." Lemle v. Breeden, 51 Haw. 426, 435, 462 P.2d 470, 475 (1969) (establishing an implied warranty of habitability in dwelling leases). The emphasis on control and other exceptions to the rule of nonliability, both at trial and on appeal, unduly complicated the jury's task and diverted effort and attention from the central issue of the unreasonableness of the risk.

In recent years, immunities from tort liability affording "special protection in some types of relationships have been steadily giving way" in this and other jurisdictions. F. Harper & F. James, *supra* at 1508; see Hurley v. Town of Hudson, 112 N.H. 365, 296 A.2d 905 (1972) (sovereign tort immunity disapproved); Dean v. Smith, 106 N.H. 314, 211 A.2d 410 (1965) and Briere v. Briere, 107 N.H. 432, 224 A.2d 588 (1966) (parental tort immunity abolished); * Welch v. Frisbie Memorial Hosp., 90 N.H. 337, 9 A.2d 761 (1939) (charitable tort immunity not adopted); Gilman v. Gilman, 78 N.H. 4, 95 A. 657 (1915) (husband's tort immunity from wife declared abolished by married woman's act). "Considerations of human safety within an urban community dictate that the landowner's relative immunity, which is primarily supported by values of the agrarian past, be modified in favor of negligence principles of landowner liability." Recent Development, Abrogation of Common-Law Entrant Classes of Trespasser, Licensee, and Invitee, 25 Vand. L. Rev. 623, 640 (1972). "In modern times the immunities have rightly, though gradually, been giving way to the overriding social view that where there is foreseeability of substantial harm landowners, as well as other members of society, should generally be subjected to a reasonable duty of care to avoid it." Taylor v. New Jersey Highway Auth., 22 N.J. 454, 463, 126 A.2d 313, 317 (1956). We think that now is the time for the landlord's limited tort immunity to be relegated to the history books where it more properly belongs.

This conclusion springs naturally and inexorably from our recent decision in Kline v. Burns, 111 N.H. 87, 276 A.2d 248 (1971). *Kline* was an apartment rental claim suit in which the tenant claimed that the premises were uninhabitable. Following a small vanguard of other jurisdictions, we modernized the landlord-tenant contractual relationship by holding that there is an implied warranty of habitability in an apartment lease transaction. As a necessary predicate to our decision, we discarded from landlord-tenant law "that obnoxious legal cliché, caveat emptor." Pines v. Perssion, 14 Wis.2d 590, 596, 111 N.W.2d 409, 413 (1961). In so doing, we discarded the very legal foundation and justification for the landlord's immunity in tort for injuries to the tenant or third persons. * * *

To the extent that *Kline v. Burns* did not do so, we today discard the rule of "caveat lessee" and the doctrine of landlord nonliability in tort to which it gave birth. We thus bring up to date the other half of landlord-tenant law. Henceforth, landlords as other persons must exercise reasonable care not to subject others to an unreasonable risk of harm. * A landlord must act as a reasonable person under all of the circumstances including the likelihood of injury to others, the probable seriousness of such injuries, and the burden of reducing or avoiding the risk. * * * The questions of control, hidden defects and common or public use, which formerly had to be established as a prerequisite to even considering the negligence of a landlord, will now be relevant only inasmuch as they bear on the basic tort issues such as the foreseeability and unreasonableness of the particular risk of harm. * * *

Our decision will shift the primary focus of inquiry for judge and jury from the traditional question of "Who had control?" to a determination of whether the landlord, and the injured party, exercised due care under all the circumstances. Perhaps even more significantly, the ordinary negligence standard should help insure that a landlord will take whatever precautions are reasonably necessary under the circumstances to reduce the likelihood of injuries from defects in his property. "It is appropriate that the landlord who will retain ownership of the premises and any permanent improvements should bear the cost of repairs necessary to make the premises safe...." Kline v. Burns, 111 N.H. 87, 92, 276 A.2d 248, 251 (1971).

* * * We have carefully reviewed the record and conclude that there is sufficient evidence, on the basis of the principles set forth above, to support the verdict of the jury which had the benefit of a view. * Both plaintiff and the wife tenant testified that the stairs were too steep, and the husband tenant testified that his wife complained to him of this fact. While the defendant landlord did not testify, the jury could find that she knew that this steep stairway was frequently used by the young children for whom her daughter-in-law was the regular, daily baby-sitter. In any event, the use of these steps by young children should have been anticipated by the defendant. * * *

Tenney v. Atlantic Associates

Supreme Court of Iowa, 1999.
594 N.W.2d 11.

■ LARSON, JUSTICE. Patricia * * * Tenney arrived home early in the morning of December 5, 1993. She was raped by an unknown intruder who had gained access to her apartment, apparently by the use of keys, on December 4 or early December 5. The door to Tenney's apartment had two locks, including a dead bolt, and both locks were operated by keys. There were no signs of a forced entry. When Tenney originally moved into the apartment, the key provided for her did not open her door, so she returned it. A Park Towne employee gave her two different keys and told Tenney they were the master keys and they would have to have them back in order make copies because they did not have any other keys to Tenney's apartment. Her locks had not been changed after the former tenant moved out, so the same master keys continued to operate her locks.

Tenney's suit alleged Park Towne was negligent in failing to maintain records of access to keys to the apartment, failing to change the lock when she moved in, and failing to maintain adequate security with regard to the keys kept in the manager's office. Park Towne filed a motion for summary judgment, and the district court granted it, holding as a matter of law that (1) Park Towne had not breached a duty to Tenney, and (2) the action of the intruder was a superseding cause of the plaintiff's injuries. * * * Tenney challenges the court's conclusions that the plaintiff failed to establish a duty of care and the acts of the intruder were superseding causes of the plaintiff's injuries. * * *

The district court ruled that, even assuming Park Towne and its tenant had a "special relationship," Restatement (Second) of Torts § 314A (1965), Park Towne still owed no duty of care to the plaintiff to prevent her injuries at the hands of a third party. The reason given by the court was that

> [a] landlord must know or should know of an unreasonable risk of injury [to owe a duty of care]. A landlord is not required to take precautions against a sudden attack from a third person which it has no reason to anticipate [and] [t]here is nothing in the record in this case which would place Park Towne on notice of potential criminal activity, let alone the type of assault which Tenney suffered. * * *

A landlord is not an insurer against every conceivable act by a third party but is required to provide reasonable security against the injury under the circumstances shown by the record. * But the fact that the actor realizes or should realize that action on his part is necessary for another's aid or protection does not of itself impose upon him a duty to take such action. Restatement (Second) of Torts § 314. The rationale of this rule is explained:

> The origin of the rule [generally denying recovery] lay in the early common law distinction between action and inaction, or "misfeasance" and "non-feasance." In the early law one who injured another by a positive affirmative act was held liable without any great regard even for his fault. But the courts were far too much occupied with the more flagrant forms of misbehavior to be greatly concerned with one who merely did nothing, even though another might suffer serious harm because of his omission to act. Hence liability for nonfeasance was slow to receive any recognition in the law. It appeared first in, and is still largely confined to, situations in which there was some *special relation between the parties*, on the basis of which the defendant was found to have a duty to take action for the aid or protection of the plaintiff.

Restatement (Second) of Torts § 314 cmt. c; see also W[illiam L.] Prosser & [W. Page] Keeton, Prosser and Keeton on the Law of Torts §§ 33 & 63 (5th ed. 1984).

The Restatement provides a short list of special relationships that, despite the general rule, create a duty to aid or protect others. This includes the relationship between an innkeeper and his guest. Restatement (Second) of Torts § 314A. The innkeeper-guest relationship, because of its similarity to the landlord-tenant relationship, has prompted an evolution in the law of landlord-tenant relationships.

> Prior to 1970, there was no general tort duty on landlords to protect their tenants against criminal theft or attack. The situation began to change in that year, however, with the landmark decision of *Kline v. 1500 Massachusetts Avenue Apartment Corp.*, [439 F.2d 477 (D.C.Cir.1970)], which imposed a duty of reasonable care upon the owner of an urban multiple unit apartment dwelling to protect its tenants from foreseeable criminal assaults. A growing number of courts have imposed similar duties of reasonable protection upon landlords to protect their tenants, and to protect others perhaps as well, from criminal attack, provided that such assaults are *reasonably foreseeable and preventable*.

Prosser & Keeton § 63.

Kline, the case referred to by Prosser & Keeton, involved facts similar to those in this case, although in *Kline* a tenant was assaulted and robbed in a common hallway, not in her own apartment, as in this case. When Ms. Kline first moved into her apartment, doormen provided security at the entrances and the lobby desk was staffed at all times. Within a few years the doormen were gone, and the desk was left unattended much of the time, "in the face of an increasing number of assaults, larcenies, and robberies being perpetrated against the tenants in and from the common hallways." * The court noted that responsibility for providing security at the main entrance and in the common hallways and elevators was in the landlord, and the lessees of individual apartments were not in a position to provide it.

Kline discussed the rationale driving the rule denying recovery by tenants: generally a private person has no duty to protect another from a criminal attack; the criminal act is a superseding cause of the harm; it is difficult to assess foreseeability of criminal acts; any standard that the landlord must meet would be vague; adverse economic consequences would be incurred by the landlord; and public policy favors allocating protection of citizens to the government. The court continued:

> But the rationale of this very broad general rule falters when it is applied to the conditions of modern day urban apartment living, particularly in the circumstances of this case. The rationale of the general rule exonerating a third party from any duty to protect another from a criminal attack has no applicability to the landlord-tenant relationship in multiple dwelling houses. The landlord is no insurer of his tenants' safety, but he certainly is no bystander. And where, as here, the landlord has notice of repeated criminal assaults and robberies, has notice that these crimes occurred in the portion of the premises exclusively within his control, has every reason to expect like crimes to happen again, and has the exclusive power to take preventive action, it does not seem unfair to

place upon the landlord a duty to take those steps which are within his power to minimize the predictable risk to his tenants.

The court in *Kline* explained the rationale for the changed attitude of courts toward the landlord-tenant relationship:

> This court has recently had occasion to review landlord-tenant law as applied to multiple family urban dwellings. In Javins v. First National Realty Corporation, 428 F.2d 1071, 138 U.S.App.D.C. 369 (D.C.Cir.1970), the traditional analysis of a lease as being a conveyance of an interest in land—with all the medieval connotations this often brings—was reappraised, and found lacking in several respects. This court noted that the value of the lease to the modern apartment dweller is that it gives him "a well known package of goods and services—a package which includes not merely walls and ceilings, but also adequate heat, light and ventilation, serviceable plumbing facilities, *secure windows and doors*, proper sanitation, and proper maintenance." It does not give him the land itself, and to the tenant as a practical matter this is supremely unimportant.

The parallels between innkeepers (who have a special duty of care to guests under Restatement § 314A(2)) and landlords was discussed by the court in *Javins*:

> Even the old common law courts responded with a different rule for a landlord-tenant relationship which did not conform to the model of the usual agrarian lease. Much more substantial obligations were placed upon the keepers of inns (the only multiple dwelling houses known to the common law). Their guests were interested solely in shelter and could not be expected to make their own repairs. "The modern apartment dweller more closely resembles the guest in an inn than he resembles an agrarian tenant, but the law has not generally recognized the similarity." *

In further developing the innkeeper-guest analogy, the *Kline* court said:

> Specifically, innkeepers have been held liable for assaults which have been committed upon their guests by third parties, if they have breached a duty which is imposed by reason of the innkeeper-guest relationship. By this duty, the innkeeper is generally bound to exercise reasonable care to protect the guest from abuse or molestation from third parties, be they innkeeper's employees, fellow guests, or intruders, if the attack could, or in the exercise of reasonable care, should have been anticipated. * * *

We conclude that a landlord, just as any other actor, owes a duty of due care to protect its tenants from reasonably foreseeable harm and must act as a reasonable person under all of the circumstances including the likelihood of injury to others, the probable seriousness of such injuries, and the burden of reducing or avoiding the risk. The questions of control, hidden defects and common or public use, which formerly had to be established as a prerequisite to even considering the negligence of a landlord, will now be relevant only inasmuch as they bear on the basic tort issues such as the foreseeability and unreasonableness of the particular risk of harm. Sargent v. Ross, 113 N.H. 388, 308 A.2d 528, 534 (1973). We agree that this "'reasonable care in all the circumstances standard will provide the most effective way to achieve an allocation of the costs of human injury which conforms to present community values.'" This standard should help ensure that a landlord will take whatever precautions are reasonably necessary under the circumstances to reduce the likelihood of injuries from defects in his property. "It is appropriate that the landlord who will retain ownership of the premises and any permanent improvements should bear the cost of repairs necessary to make the premises safe. . . ." [*Id.*] at 535. *

A duty of care arising out of a landlord-tenant relationship, like that of an innkeeper and guest under Restatement section 314A, does not make the landlord an insurer. Nor will the rule of law be equally applicable in every case.

> The duty in each case is only one to exercise reasonable care under the circumstances. The defendant is not liable where he neither knows nor should know of the unreasonable risk, or of the illness or injury. He is not required to take precautions against a sudden attack from a third person which he has no reason to anticipate, or to give aid to one whom he has no reason to know to be ill. He is not required to take any action where the risk does not appear to be an unreasonable one . . . .

Restatement (Second) of Torts § 314A cmt. e.

* * * For the reasons discussed, the plaintiff must eventually establish that the risk of harm by a third party was reasonably foreseeable to the defendant in order to establish a duty. * * * Galloway v. Bankers Trust Co., 420 N.W.2d 437 (Iowa 1988), involved a sexual assault on a patron in a mall restroom. That case also involved liability under Restatement § 344, and the issue again was foreseeability. In *Galloway* there was evidence of property crimes at the mall, but there were no reports of sexual assaults there. We noted that "[a] history of crimes against persons would, of course, make a stronger case of foreseeability, but we do not believe it is a prerequisite to proof of foreseeability." We concluded in *Galloway* that general crimes in the mall were similar acts, for purposes of establishing foreseeability, and reversed a summary judgment for the mall owners.

In the present case, * * * the issue is whether the plaintiff's resistance to summary judgment presented evidence generating a genuine issue of fact on foreseeability. * * * The answer to interrogatories regarding the plaintiff's two experts not only outlined their opinions as to the acts of negligence on the part of the defendant; they also made it clear that at least one prior act of attempted assault had happened on the premises. * * * One witness, Phillip Schneider, is a professional appraiser experienced in facilities of this type. According to him, the defendant failed to respond adequately after a groundskeeper at Park Towne had entered an apartment with a key and attempted to sexually assault a tenant. (Park Towne continued to employ him for two years afterward.) In addition, Schneider noted the following factors that could reasonably be expected to lead to third-party crimes: failure to do appropriate background check of employees, failure to control access to master keys, failure to change locks prior to new occupancy, failure to maintain adequate security of regular keys, failure to establish and communicate policies to employees regarding keys, failure to maintain written policies with regard to keys, and failure to maintain written policies or communicate policies to employees regarding security. * * *

We conclude the court erred in ruling that defendant owed no duty of care under these circumstances. Whether the defendant breached its duty of care is, of course, a factual matter. * * *

The defendant's motion for summary judgment did not allege the lack of material fact on proximate cause, but the court found as a matter of law that proximate cause could not be established because the intruder's action was a superseding cause. * * *

The general rule is that "if the likelihood that a third person may act in a particular manner is the hazard or one of the hazards which makes the actor negligent, such an act whether innocent, negligent, intentionally tortious, or criminal does not prevent the actor from being liable for harm caused thereby." Restatement (Second) of Torts § 449. Further,

> the happening of the very event the likelihood of which makes the actor's conduct negligent and so subjects the actor to liability cannot relieve him from liability. The duty to refrain from the act committed or to do the act omitted is imposed to protect the other from this very danger. To deny recovery because the other's exposure to the very risk from which it was the purpose of the duty to protect him resulted in harm to him, would be to deprive the other of all protection and to make the duty a nullity.

Restatement (Second) of Torts § 449 cmt. b.

In the present case, the plaintiff's claim is that the violent acts of the intruder were reasonably foreseeable. * * *

NOTE

Arguments against Imposing Liability on Landlords for Criminal Attacks. Compare with *Tenney* the dissenting opinion of Justice Brennan of the Supreme Court of Michigan in Johnston v. Harris, 387 Mich. 569, 576–77, 198 N.W.2d 409, 411–12 (1972):

> Public safety is the business of government.

> Today's decision concedes the failure of government to make the streets and homes of certain areas reasonably safe and in effect transfers the governmental function of public protection to the unfortunate owners of real property in such places.

> Already overburdened by taxes largely laid to pay for public safety, these owners will now be required to maintain additional lighting, guards, enclosures, alarms, locks and take every other precaution to avoid reasonably foreseeable conditions which attract criminals to carry out their nefarious deeds.

At a time when concerned citizens and public officials are seeking ways to involve the broader community in resolving the plight of so-called "high crime areas," our Court would place an additional burden upon the land and the resources of such areas. * * *

No member of this Court lives in such an area. None are voting to increase his own insurance premium, or that of his neighbors. What we do in the name of liberality is regressive. It is a mistake.

CHAPTER 11

LIABILITY OF SUPPLIERS OF PRODUCTS

This chapter concerns the liability of manufacturers, wholesalers, and retailers who distribute defective products that result in physical injuries. The changes that have occurred in this field of tort law are among the most important tort developments of the past century. Many of the rules governing products liability law, and even the language of this branch of the law, were unknown until recent decades.

The chapter emphasizes the development of strict liability in tort for injuries caused by products, but this single theory of recovery does not stand alone. In many jurisdictions negligence often remains an independent ground for recovery, and principles learned while studying negligence—particularly those relating to causation—remain core issues even when the action is one grounded on strict liability. Similarly, products liability law occurs at the intersection of tort law and commercial law. To have a fair picture of how the law handles physical injuries caused by defective products, our study requires us to consider aspects of contract law, or a mixture of contract and tort law, such as those legal principles governing implied and express warranties. Finally, it should be noted that claims based upon misrepresentation—an area of tort law not yet considered—play an increasingly important role in products liability. See *infra* Chapter 15.

A. DEVELOPMENT OF ALTERNATIVE THEORIES OF RECOVERY

Winterbottom v. Wright

Court of Exchequer, 1842.
10 M. & W. 109, 11 L.J. Ex. 415, 152 Eng. Rep. 402.

* * * [T]he defendant was a contractor for the supply of mail-coaches, and had in that character contracted for hire and reward with the Postmaster-General * * *. [I]t had become and was the sole and exclusive duty of the defendant, to wit, under and by virtue of his said contract, to keep and maintain the said mail-coach in a fit, proper, safe, and secure state and condition for the purpose aforesaid: That Nathaniel Atkinson and other persons, having notice of the said contract, were under contract with the Postmaster-General to convey the said mail-coach from Hartford to Holyhead, and to supply horses and coachmen for that purpose * * *[.] That the plaintiff, being a mail-coachman, and thereby obtaining his livelihood, and whilst the said several contracts were in force, having notice thereof, and trusting to and confiding in the contract made between the defendant and the Postmaster-General, and believing that the said coach was in a fit, safe, secure, and proper state and condition for the purpose aforesaid, and not knowing and having no means of knowing to the contrary thereof,

hired himself to the said Nathaniel Atkinson and his co-contractors as mail-coachman, to drive and take the conduct of the said mail-coach, which but for the said contract of the defendant he would not have done. The declaration then averred, that the defendant so improperly and negligently conducted himself, and so utterly disregarded his aforesaid contract, and so wholly neglected and failed to perform his duty in this behalf, that heretofore, to wit, on the 8th of August, 1840, whilst the plaintiff, as such mail-coachman so hired, was driving the said mail-coach from Hartford to Holyhead, the same coach, being a mail-coach found and provided by the defendant[,] * * * being then in a frail, weak, infirm, and dangerous state and condition, to wit, by and through certain latent defects in the state and condition thereof, and unsafe and unfit for the use and purpose aforesaid, and from no other cause, * * * [the mail-coach] gave way and broke down, whereby the plaintiff was thrown from his seat, and in consequence of injuries then received, had become lamed for life. * * *

■ LORD ABINGER, C.B. I am clearly of opinion that the defendant is entitled to our judgment. * * * Here the action is brought simply because the defendant was a contractor with a third person; and it is contended that thereupon he became liable to everybody who might use the carriage. If there had been any ground for such an action, there certainly would have been some precedent of it; but with the exception of actions against innkeepers, and some few other persons, no case of a similar nature has occurred in practice. * * * It is however contended, that this contract being made on the behalf of the public by the Postmaster-General, no action could be maintained against him, and therefore the plaintiff must have a remedy against the defendant. But that is by no means a necessary consequence—he may be remediless altogether.

There is no privity of contract between these parties; and if the plaintiff can sue, every passenger, or even any person passing along the road who was injured by the upsetting of the coach, might bring a similar action. Unless we confine the operation of such contracts as this to the parties who entered into them, the most absurd and outrageous consequences, to which I can see no limit, would ensue. Where a party becomes responsible to the public, by undertaking a public duty, he is liable, though the injury may have arisen from the negligence of his servant or tenant. So, in cases of public nuisances, whether the act was done by the party as a servant, or in any other capacity, you are liable to an action at the suit of any person who suffers. Those, however, are cases where the real ground of the liability is the public duty, or the commission of the public nuisance. There is also a class of cases in which the law permits a contract to be turned into a tort; but unless there has been some public duty undertaken, or public nuisance committed, they are all cases in which an action might have been maintained upon the contract. Thus, a carrier may be sued either in assumpsit or case; but there is no instance in which a party, who was not privy to the contract entered into with him, can maintain any such action. The plaintiff in this case could not have brought an action on the contract; if he could have done so, what would have been his situation, supposing the Postmaster-General had released the defendant? that would, at all events, have defeated his claim altogether. By permitting this action, we should be working this injustice, that after the defendant had done everything to the satisfaction of his employer, and after all matters between them had been adjusted, and all accounts settled on the footing of their contract, we should subject them to be ripped open by this action of tort being brought against him.

■ ALDERSON, B. I am of the same opinion. * * * If we were to hold that the plaintiff could sue in such a case, there is no point at which such actions would stop. The only safe rule is to confine the right to recover to those who enter into the contract: if we go one step beyond that, there is no reason why we should not go fifty. * * *

Then it is urged that it falls within the principle of the case of Levy v. Langridge [(1837) 2 M. & W. 519]. But the principle of that case was simply this, that the father having bought the gun for the very purpose of being used by the plaintiff, the defendant made representations by which he was induced to use it. There a distinct fraud was committed on the plaintiff; the falsehood of the representation was also alleged to have been within the knowledge of the defendant who made it, and he was properly held liable for the consequences. How are the facts of that case applicable to those of the present? Where is the allegation of misrepresentation or fraud in this declaration? It shews nothing of the kind. Our judgment must therefore be for the defendant.

■ GURNEY, B., concurred.

■ ROLFE, B. * * * The duty [with breach of which defendant is charged], therefore, is shewn to have arisen solely from the contract; and the fallacy consists in the use of that word "duty." If a duty to the Postmaster-General be meant, that is true; but if a duty to the plaintiff be intended (and in that sense the word is evidently used), there was none. This is one of those unfortunate cases in which there certainly has been *damnum*, but it is *damnum absque injuriâ*; it is, no doubt, a hardship upon the plaintiff to be without a remedy, but by that consideration we ought not to be influenced. Hard cases, it has been frequently observed, are apt to introduce bad law.

Judgment for the defendant.

NOTES

1. *Common Law Development. Winterbottom* has been consistently treated as the leading case for the proposition that a manufacturer or seller was not liable to a remote purchaser with whom he was not in "privity of contract," even if the seller or manufacturer caused him harm by lack of care in putting out the product. The rationale was that the manufacturer or seller was not under a duty to the remote purchaser—not in privity of contract—to exercise care. But to better understand the development of law, consider to what extent the case actually supports this proposition for which the case is remembered. What features of the case indicate a much narrower principle? Of course, the opinions may express a common-sense judgment of much wider applicability. "The wide acceptance of this rule is remarkable in as much as it was based on dictum by Lord Abinger in a case which involved a contractor rather than a manufacturer, and the matter was before the court on a demurrer." Anderson v. Linton, 178 F.2d 304, 307 (7th Cir.1949).

The judges treat the case as one of first impression with no precedent for the plaintiff's claim, but also no precedent denying his claim. How then is the law determined for such a new case? The court does not mean that *no* new liability can be created—or does it? If not, then what considerations are to guide choice? How well suited was the decision to the life of 1842? How well suited to the present? What kind of life does the decision subsume?

Note that even in 1842 there was troublesome precedent. Is the court's treatment of *Levy v. Langridge* satisfying? What would be plaintiff's argument to show similarity rather than difference?

2.   *Judicial Resources.* In the context of *Winterbottom v. Wright*, consider Professor Atiyah's comment that "It must be remembered that until the establishment of the County Courts in 1846 there were only fifteen common law judges for the entire country" [*i.e.*, England]. P. Atiyah, Accidents, Compensation and the Law 636 (3d ed. 1980).

MacPherson v. Buick Motor Co.

Court of Appeals of New York, 1916.
217 N.Y. 382, 111 N.E. 1050.

■ CARDOZO, J. The defendant is a manufacturer of automobiles. It sold an automobile to a retail dealer. The retail dealer resold to the plaintiff. While the plaintiff was in the car it suddenly collapsed. He was thrown out and injured. One of the wheels was made of defective wood, and its spokes crumbled into fragments. The wheel was not made by the defendant; it was bought from another manufacturer. There is evidence, however, that its defects could have been discovered by reasonable inspection, and that inspection was omitted. There is no claim that the defendant knew of the defect and willfully concealed it. The case, in other words, is not brought within the rule of Kuelling v. Lean Mfg. Co., 183 N.Y. 78, 75 N.E. 1098 (1905). The charge is one, not of fraud, but of negligence. The question to be determined is whether the defendant owed a duty of care and vigilance to anyone but the immediate purchaser.

The foundations of this branch of the law, at least in this state, were laid in Thomas v. Winchester, 6 N.Y. 397 (1852). A poison was falsely labeled. The sale was made to a druggist, who in turn sold to a customer. The customer recovered damages from the seller who affixed the label. "The defendant's negligence," it was said, "put human life in imminent danger." A poison falsely labeled is likely to injure anyone who gets it. Because the danger is to be foreseen, there is a duty to avoid the injury. Cases were cited by way of illustration in which manufacturers were not subject to any duty irrespective of contract. The distinction was said to be that their conduct, though negligent, was not likely to result in injury to anyone except the purchaser. * * *

These early cases suggest a narrow construction of the rule. Later cases, however, evince a more liberal spirit. First in importance is Devlin v. Smith, 89 N.Y. 470 (1882). The defendant, a contractor, built a scaffold for a painter. The painter's servants were injured. The contractor was held liable. He knew that the scaffold, if improperly constructed, was a most dangerous trap. He knew that it was to be used by the workmen. He was building it for that very purpose. Building it for their use, he owed them a duty, irrespective of his contract with their master, to build it with care.

From *Devlin v. Smith* we pass over intermediate cases and turn to the latest case in this court in which *Thomas v. Winchester* was followed. That case is Statler v. Ray Mfg. Co., 195 N.Y. 478, 480 (1909). The defendant manufactured a large coffee urn. It was installed in a restaurant. When heated, the urn exploded and injured the plaintiff. We held that the manufacturer was liable. We said that the urn "was of such a character inherently that, when applied to the purposes for which it was designed, it was liable to become a source of great danger to many people if not carefully and properly constructed."

It may be that *Devlin v. Smith* and *Statler v. Ray Mfg. Co.* have extended the rule of *Thomas v. Winchester*. If so, this court is committed to the extension. The defendant argues that things imminently dangerous to life are poisons, explosives, deadly weapons—things whose normal function it is to injure or destroy. But whatever the rule in *Thomas v. Winchester* may once have been, it has no longer that restricted meaning. A scaffold (*Devlin v. Smith*) is not inherently a destructive instrument. It becomes destructive only if imperfectly constructed. A large coffee urn (*Statler v. Ray Mfg. Co.*) may have within itself, if negligently made, the potency of danger, yet no one thinks of it as an implement whose normal function is destruction. What is true of the coffee urn is equally true of bottles of aerated water.
* * *

Devlin v. Smith was decided in 1882. A year later a very similar case came before the Court of Appeal in England. Heaven v. Pender, [1883] 11 Q.B.D. 503. We find in the opinion of Brett, M. R., afterwards Lord Esher (p. 510), the same conception of a duty, irrespective of contract, imposed upon the manufacturer by the law itself:

> Whenever one person supplies goods, or machinery, or the like, for the purpose of their being used by another person under such circumstances that every one of ordinary sense would, if he thought, recognize at once that unless he used ordinary care and skill with regard to the condition of the thing supplied or the mode of supplying it, there will be danger of injury to the person or property of him for whose use the thing is supplied, and who is to use it, a duty arises to use ordinary care and skill as to the condition or manner of supplying such thing.

He then points out that for a neglect of such ordinary care or skill whereby injury happens, the appropriate remedy is an action for negligence. The right to enforce this liability is not to be confined to the immediate buyer. The right, he says, extends to the persons or class of persons for whose use the thing is supplied. It is enough that the goods "would in all probability be used at once . . . before a reasonable opportunity for discovering any defect which might exist," and that the thing supplied is of such a nature "that a neglect of ordinary care or skill as to its condition or the manner of supplying it would probably cause danger to the person or property of the person for whose use it was supplied, and who was about to use it." * * * Like most attempts at comprehensive definition, it may involve errors of inclusion and of exclusion. But its tests and standards, at least in their underlying principles, with whatever qualification may be called for as they are applied to varying conditions, are the tests and standards of our law.

We hold, then, that the principle of *Thomas v. Winchester* is not limited to poisons, explosives, and things of like nature, to things which in their normal operation are implements of destruction. If the nature of a thing is such that it is reasonably certain to place life and limb in peril when negligently made, it is then a thing of danger. Its nature gives warning of the consequences to be expected. If to the element of danger there is added knowledge that the thing will be used by persons other than the purchaser, and used without new tests, then, irrespective of contract, the manufacturer of this thing of danger is under a duty to make it carefully. That is as far as we are required to go for the decision of this case. There must be knowledge of a danger, not merely possible, but probable. It is *possible* to use almost anything in a way that will make it dangerous if defective. That is not enough to charge the manufacturer with a duty independent of his contract. Whether a given thing is dangerous may be sometimes a question for the court and sometimes a question for the jury. There must also be knowledge that in the usual course of events the danger will be shared by others than the buyer. Such knowledge may often be inferred from the nature of the transaction. But it is possible that even knowledge of the danger and of the use will not always be enough. The proximity or remoteness of the relation is a factor to be considered. We are dealing now with the liability of the manufacturer of the finished product, who puts it on the market to be used without inspection by his customers. If he is negligent, where danger is to be foreseen, a liability will follow.

We are not required at this time to say that it is legitimate to go back of the manufacturer of the finished product and hold the manufacturers of the component parts. To make their negligence a cause of imminent danger, an independent cause must often intervene; the manufacturer of the finished product must also fail in *his* duty of inspection. It may be that in those circumstances the negligence of the earlier members of the series is too remote to constitute, as to the ultimate user, an actionable wrong. * We leave that question open. We shall have to deal with it when it arises. The difficulty which it suggests is not present in this case. There is here no break in the chain of cause and effect. In such circumstances, the presence of a known danger, attendant upon a known use, makes vigilance a duty. We have put aside the notion that the duty to safeguard life and limb, when the consequences of negligence may be foreseen, grows out of contract and nothing else. We have put the source of the obligation where it ought to be. We have put its source in the law.

From this survey of the decisions, there thus emerges a definition of the duty of a manufacturer which enables us to measure this defendant's liability. Beyond all question, the nature of an automobile gives warning of probable danger if its construction is defective. This automobile was designed to go fifty miles an hour. Unless its wheels were sound and strong, injury was almost certain. It was as much a thing of danger as a defective engine for a railroad. The defendant knew the danger. It knew also that the car would be used by persons other than the buyer. This was apparent from its size; there were seats for three persons. It was apparent also from the fact that the buyer was a dealer in cars, who bought to resell. The maker of this car supplied it for the use of purchasers from the dealer just as plainly as the contractor in *Devlin v. Smith* supplied the scaffold for use by the servants of the owner. The dealer was indeed the one person of whom it might be said with some approach to certainty that by him the car would not be used. Yet the defendant would have us say that he was the one person whom it was under a legal duty to protect. The law does not lead us to so inconsequent a conclusion. Precedents drawn from the days of travel by stage coach do not fit the conditions of travel today. The principle that the danger must be imminent does not change, but the things subject to the principle do change. They are whatever the needs of life in a developing civilization require them to be. * * *

We think the defendant was not absolved from a duty of inspection because it bought the wheels from a reputable manufacturer. It was not merely a dealer in automobiles. It was a manufacturer of automobiles. It was responsible for the finished product. It was not at liberty to put the finished product on the market without subjecting the component parts to ordinary and simple tests. * Under the charge of the trial judge nothing more was required of it. The obligation to inspect must vary with the nature of the thing to be inspected. The more probable the danger the greater the need of caution. * * *

■ WILLARD BARTLETT, C.J. (dissenting). * * * I do not see how we can uphold the judgment in the present case without overruling what has been so often said by this court and other courts of like authority in reference to the absence of any liability for negligence on the part of the original vendor of an ordinary carriage to anyone except his immediate vendee. The absence of such liability was the very point actually decided in the English case of *Winterbottom v. Wright,* and the illustration quoted from the opinion of Chief Judge Ruggles in *Thomas v. Winchester* assumes that the law on the subject was so plain that the statement would be accepted almost as a matter of course. In the case at bar the defective wheel on an automobile moving only eight miles an hour was not any more dangerous to the occupants of the car than a similarly defective wheel would be to the occupants of a carriage drawn by a horse at the same speed; and yet unless the courts have been all wrong on this question up to the present time there would be no liability to strangers to the original sale in the case of the horse-drawn carriage. * * *

NOTE

Contemporaneous Cases under Implied Warranty Theories. During the decades following *MacPherson,* the victim injured by a product still faced the often impossible task of proving negligence—unless she had a direct contractual relationship with the defendant. The injured party in privity with the manufacturer could pursue claims based upon warranties, either express or implied. An action for breach of warranty originally was a tort-like claim, brought in an action of trespass on the case for breach of an assumed duty, and closely related to the tort of deceit. J[ames] B. Ames, The History of Assumpsit, 2 Harv. L. Rev. 1, 8 (1888). Beginning with Stuart v. Wilkins, (1778) 99 Eng.Rep. 15 (K.B.); 1 Doug. 18, however, warranties generally came to be regarded as express or implied terms of the contract of sale. The usual remedy for a breach of warranty claim was a contract action, generally with a requirement of privity. In the early twentieth century, warranty provisions were codified as states adopted the Uniform Sales Act (predecessor of the Uniform Commercial Code (U.C.C.)).

Under U.C.C. warranty provisions, recovery was allowed for personal injuries, as well as for economic losses arising from warranty violations.

In addition to *express warranties* arising out of explicit statements or guarantees about product characteristics or qualities, see *infra* page 586, Note 3, goods also became subject to implied warranties. See *infra* pages 585–86, Note 2.Under today's law, the two common types of *implied warranties* are the *implied warranty of merchantability* and the *implied warranty of fitness for a particular purpose*. The general notion of the implied warranty of merchantability is that the goods "are fit for the ordinary purposes for which such goods are used." U.C.C. § 2–314(2)(c). The implied warranty of fitness for a particular purpose arises when the buyer relies on the seller's skill or judgment in selecting suitable goods. U.C.C. § 2–315.

While *MacPherson* abolished any privity requirement for an action based upon negligence, it did not directly alter the privity requirement for products liability actions based upon warranty theories. In Chysky v. Drake Bros. Co., 235 N.Y. 468, 139 N.E. 576 (1923), for example, the plaintiff was a waitress whose mouth was injured when she bit into a piece of cake containing a concealed nail. She sued the defendant manufacturer of the cake, who had sold it to the plaintiff's employer, under an implied warranty theory. The New York Court of Appeals denied recovery because of the lack of privity between the plaintiff and the defendant. In the years following *Chysky*, a number of courts held that, notwithstanding lack of privity, an implied warranty of quality ran to a consumer from a producer of foods. See, e.g., Klein v. Duchess Sandwich Co., 14 Cal.2d 272, 93 P.2d 799 (1939), or from a brand-name distributor. E.g., Armour & Co. v. Leasure, 177 Md. 393, 9 A.2d 572 (1939).

Escola v. Coca Cola Bottling Co.

Supreme Court of California, 1944.
24 Cal.2d 453, 150 P.2d 436.

■ GIBSON, CHIEF JUSTICE. Plaintiff, a waitress in a restaurant, was injured when a bottle of Coca Cola [delivered by an employee of the defendant only 36 hours earlier, exploded] in her hand. She alleged that defendant company, which had bottled and delivered the alleged defective bottle to her employer, was negligent in selling "bottles containing said beverage which on account of excessive pressure of gas or by reason of some defect in the bottle was dangerous . . . and likely to explode." This appeal is from a judgment upon a jury verdict in favor of plaintiff. * * *

Plaintiff * * * rested her case, having announced to the court that being unable to show any specific acts of negligence she relied completely on the doctrine of *res ipsa loquitur*. * * * Under the general rules pertaining to the doctrine * * * it must appear that bottles of carbonated liquid are not ordinarily defective without negligence by the bottling company. * * * The bottle was admittedly charged with gas under pressure, and the charging of the bottle was within the exclusive control of defendant. As it is a matter of common knowledge that an overcharge would not ordinarily result without negligence, it follows under the doctrine of *res ipsa loquitur* that if the bottle was in fact

excessively charged an inference of defendant's negligence would arise.
* * *

The judgment is affirmed. * * *

■ TRAYNOR, JUSTICE. I concur in the judgment, but I believe the manufacturer's negligence should no longer be singled out as the basis of a plaintiff's right to recover in cases like the present one. In my opinion it should now be recognized that a manufacturer incurs an absolute liability when an article that he has placed on the market, knowing that it is to be used without inspection, proves to have a defect that causes injury to human beings. MacPherson v. Buick Motor Co., 217 N.Y. 382, 111 N.E. 1050 (1916), established the principle, recognized by this court, that irrespective of privity of contract, the manufacturer is responsible for an injury caused by such an article to any person who comes in lawful contact with it. * In these cases the source of the manufacturer's liability was his negligence in the manufacturing process or in the inspection of component parts supplied by others.

Even if there is no negligence, however, public policy demands that responsibility be fixed wherever it will most effectively reduce the hazards to life and health inherent in defective products that reach the market. It is evident that the manufacturer can anticipate some hazards and guard against the recurrence of others, as the public cannot. Those who suffer injury from defective products are unprepared to meet its consequences. The cost of an injury and the loss of time or health may be an overwhelming misfortune to the person injured, and a needless one, for the risk of injury can be insured by the manufacturer and distributed among the public as a cost of doing business. It is to the public interest to discourage the marketing of products having defects that are a menace to the public. If such products nevertheless find their way into the market it is to the public interest to place the responsibility for whatever injury they may cause upon the manufacturer, who, even if he is not negligent in the manufacture of the product, is responsible for its reaching the market. However intermittently such injuries may occur and however haphazardly they may strike, the risk of their occurrence is a constant risk and a general one. Against such a risk there should be general and constant protection and the manufacturer is best situated to afford such protection.

The injury from a defective product does not become a matter of indifference because the defect arises from causes other than the negligence of the manufacturer, such as negligence of a submanufacturer of a component part whose defects could not be revealed by inspection, * or unknown causes that even by the device of *res ipsa loquitur* cannot be classified as negligence of the manufacturer. The inference of negligence may be dispelled by an affirmative showing of proper care. * * * An injured person, however, is not ordinarily in a position to refute such evidence or identify the cause of the defect, for he can hardly be familiar with the manufacturing process as the manufacturer himself is. In leaving it to the jury to decide whether the inference has been dispelled, regardless of the evidence against it, the negligence rule approaches the rule of strict liability. It is needlessly circuitous to make negligence the basis of recovery and impose what is in reality liability without negligence. If public policy demands that a manufacturer of goods be responsible for their quality regardless of negligence there is no reason not to fix that responsibility openly. * * * The retailer, even though not equipped to test a product, is under an absolute liability to his customer, for the implied warranties of fitness for proposed use and merchantable quality include a warranty of safety of the product. * This warranty is not necessarily a contractual one, * for public policy requires that the buyer be insured at the seller's expense against injury. * The courts recognize, however, that the retailer cannot bear the burden of this warranty, and allow him to recoup any losses by means of the warranty of safety attending the wholesaler's or manufacturer's sale to him. * Such a procedure, however, is needlessly circuitous and engenders wasteful litigation. Much would be gained if the injured person could base his action directly on the manufacturer's warranty.

The liability of the manufacturer to an immediate buyer injured by a defective product follows without proof of negligence from the implied warranty of safety attending the sale. Ordinarily, however, the immediate buyer is a dealer who does not intend to use the product himself, and if the warranty of safety is to serve the purpose of protecting health and safety it must give rights to others than the dealer. * * * While the defendant's negligence in the *MacPherson* case made it unnecessary for the court to base liability on warranty, Judge Cardozo's reasoning recognized the injured person as the real party in interest and effectively disposed of the theory that the liability of the manufacturer incurred by his warranty should apply only to the immediate purchaser. It thus paves the way for a standard of liability that would make the manufacturer guarantee the safety of his product even when there is no negligence.

This court and many others have extended protection according to such a standard to consumers of food products, taking the view that the right of a consumer injured by unwholesome food does not depend "upon the intricacies of the law of sales" and that the warranty of the manufacturer to the consumer in absence of privity of contract rests on public policy. * Dangers to life and health inhere in other consumers' goods that are defective and there is no reason to differentiate them from the dangers of defective food products. *

In the food products cases the courts have resorted to various fictions to rationalize the extension of the manufacturer's warranty to the consumer: that a warranty runs with the chattel; that the cause of action of the dealer is assigned to the consumer; that the consumer is a third party beneficiary of the manufacturer's contract with the dealer. They have also held the manufacturer liable on a mere fiction of negligence * * *. Such fictions are not necessary to fix the manufacturer's liability under a warranty if the warranty is severed from the contract of sale between the dealer and the consumer and based on the law of torts * as a strict liability. * Warranties are not necessarily rights arising under a contract. An action on a warranty "was, in its origin, a pure action of tort," and only late in the historical development of warranties was an action in assumpsit allowed. [James] Ames, The History of Assumpsit, 2 Harv. L. Rev. 1, 8 (1888); Williston on Contracts § 970 (1936). * * *

As handicrafts have been replaced by mass production with its great markets and transportation facilities, the close relationship between the producer and consumer of a product has been altered. Manufacturing processes, frequently valuable secrets, are ordinarily either inaccessible to or beyond the ken of the general public. The consumer no longer has means or skill enough to investigate for himself the soundness of a product, even when it is not contained in a sealed package, and his erstwhile vigilance has been lulled by the steady efforts of manufacturers to build up confidence by advertising and marketing devices such as trade-marks. * * * The manufacturer's obligation to the consumer must keep pace with the changing relationship between them; it cannot be escaped because the marketing of a product has become so complicated as to require one or more intermediaries. Certainly there is greater reason to impose liability on the manufacturer than on the retailer who is but a conduit of a product that he is not himself able to test. * * *

NOTES

1. *Henningsen v. Bloomfield Motors, Inc.* After Justice Traynor's concurring opinion in *Escola*, the next seminal decision in the development of the law of strict products liability grew from its roots in contract law, not tort law. In Henningsen v. Bloomfield Motors, Inc., 32 N.J. 358, 161 A.2d 69 (1960), the plaintiff Helen Henningsen was injured when the steering wheel of the car she was driving, manufactured by the defendant Chrysler Corporation and purchased from a co-defendant, Bloomfield Motors, an independent automobile dealer, "spun in her hands" causing the car to veer sharply and crash into a highway sign and a brick wall. The plaintiff's husband, Claus, had purchased the car for her as a Mother's Day present. Chrysler argued that "an implied warranty of merchantability is an incident of a contract of sale" and its only contractual privity was with Bloomfield Motors. Helen Henningsen was twice removed from this contractual relationship. Nevertheless, the Supreme Court of New Jersey, echoing Justice Traynor's concurring opinion in *Escola*, concluded:

> With the advent of mass marketing, the manufacturer became remote from the purchaser, sales were accomplished through intermediaries, and the demand for the product was created by advertising media. In such an economy it became obvious that the consumer was the person being cultivated. Manifestly, the connotation of "consumer" was broader than that of "buyer." He signified such a person who, in the reasonable contemplation of the parties to the sale, might be expected to use the product. Thus, where the commodities sold are such that if defectively manufactured they will be dangerous to life or limb, then society's interests can only be protected by eliminating the requirement of privity between the maker and his dealers and the reasonably expected ultimate consumer.

An implied warranty of merchantability, without a requirement that the plaintiff be in privity with the defendant-manufacturer is, for all intents and purposes, strict products liability. Dean Prosser described *Henningsen* as the "fall of the citadel of privity." William L. Prosser, The Fall of the Citadel (Strict Liability to the Consumer), 50 Minn. L. Rev. 791,

791 (1966). In most jurisdictions, strict products liability, as illustrated by the next principal case, soon returned to its tort law roots.

Henningsen is also important because the court struck down the attempts by the manufacturer and the dealer to limit their obligations under implied warranties. Under the guise of providing a warranty to the purchaser, the "8½ inches of fine print" on the reverse side of the contract for the purchase of the automobile attempted to largely eliminate the defendant's obligations under implied warranties. The defendants promised to make

> "good at its factory any part or parts thereof which shall, within ninety (90) days after delivery of such vehicle *to the original purchaser* or before such vehicle has been driven 4,000 miles, whichever event shall first occur, be returned to [the manufacturer] with transportation charges prepaid and which its examination shall disclose to its satisfaction to have been thus defective; *this warranty being expressly in lieu of all other warranties expressed or implied, and all other obligations or liabilities on its part,* and it neither assumes nor authorizes any other person to assume for it any other liability in connection with the sale of its vehicles. . . . " [emphasis supplied by the court]

In other words, Chrysler's obligation under the original warranty went only to Claus Henninsen, "the original purchaser," did not include liability for personal injuries, and was valid for only a short period of time and only when the purchaser complied with highly onerous conditions.

The Supreme Court of New Jersey struck down these disclaimers of liability:

> The terms of the warranty are a sad commentary upon the automobile manufacturers' marketing practices. Warranties developed in the law in the interest of and to protect the ordinary consumer who cannot be expected to have the knowledge or capacity or even the opportunity to make adequate inspection of mechanical instrumentalities, like automobiles, and to decide for himself whether they are reasonably fit for the designed purpose. * But the ingenuity of the Automobile Manufacturers Association, by means of its standardized form, has metamorphosed the warranty into a device to limit the maker's liability. * * *

> The task of the judiciary is to administer the spirit as well as the letter of the law. On issues such as the present one, part of that burden is to protect the ordinary man against the loss of important rights through what, in effect, is the unilateral act of the manufacturer. * * * From the standpoint of the purchaser, there can be no arms length negotiating on the subject. Because his capacity for bargaining is so grossly unequal, the inexorable conclusion which follows is that he is not permitted to bargain at all. He must take or leave the automobile on the warranty terms dictated by the maker. He cannot turn to a competitor for better security.

> * * * In the area of sale of goods, the legislative will has imposed an implied warranty of merchantability as a general incident of sale of an automobile by description. * * * The disclaimer of the implied warranty and exclusion of all obligations except those

specifically assumed by the express warranty signify a studied effort to frustrate that protection. True, the Sales Act authorizes agreements between buyer and seller qualifying the warranty obligations. But quite obviously the Legislature contemplated lawful stipulations (which are determined by the circumstances of a particular case) arrived at freely by parties of relatively equal bargaining strength. The lawmakers did not authorize the automobile manufacturer to use its grossly disproportionate bargaining power to relieve itself from liability and to impose on the ordinary buyer, who in effect has no real freedom of choice, the grave danger of injury to himself and others that attends the sale of such a dangerous instrumentality as a defectively made automobile. In the framework of this case, illuminated as it is by the facts and the many decisions noted, we are of the opinion that Chrysler's attempted disclaimer of an implied warranty of merchantability and of the obligations arising therefrom is so inimical to the public good as to compel an adjudication of its invalidity. * * *

2. *U.C.C. Implied Warranties.* Some courts, like the *Henningsen* court, functionally reached a strict liability result through a warranty analysis. E.g., Spence v. Three Rivers Builders & Masonry Supply, Inc., 353 Mich. 120, 90 N.W.2d 873 (1958); Cf. Back v. Wickes Corp., 375 Mass. 633, 378 N.E.2d 964 (1978) (based on statutory changes in commercial code). Soon, however, as exemplified by the next opinion, Greenman v. Yuba Power Products, Inc., *infra* pages 587–589, most jurisdictions adopted a tort version of strict liability independent of warranty theory. In some jurisdictions, however, implied warranty claims offer an alternative to a strict product liability claim. But see *infra* page 586, Note 4, and pages 590–591, Note 2. Further, if the losses caused by the product are deemed "commercial" or "purely economic" losses, often the implied warranty claim is the only viable claim. But see 80 S. Eighth St. Ltd. P'ship v. Carey-Canada, Inc., *infra* pages 619–621.

Today the statutory Uniform Commercial Code provides for the treatment of express and implied warranty theories as they relate to products and other goods.[a] The most common types of implied warranties are the implied warranty of merchantability and the implied warranty of fitness for a particular purpose. Under U.C.C. § 2–314,

   (2)   Goods to be merchantable must be at least such as

      (a)   pass without objection in the trade under the contract description; and

      (b)   in the case of fungible goods, are of fair average quality within the description; and

      (c)   are fit for the ordinary purposes for which goods of that description are used; * * *.

Section 2–315 provides that "[w]here the seller * * * has reason to know any particular purpose for which the goods are required and that the buyer is relying on the seller's skill or judgment to select or furnish suitable goods, there is * * * an implied warranty that the goods shall be fit for such

---

   a   [Eds.' note] The versions of the U.C.C. warranty provisions included in this note are from the Uniform Commercial Code (The American Law Institute and the National Conference of Commissioners on Uniform State Laws, 2012).

purpose." For example, such a warranty would exist when a customer relied on the pharmacist to recommend an over-the-counter remedy to treat a rash or the salesperson in the hardware section suggested a particular power tool to a customer for a specific home-remodeling project.

3. *Express Warranties.* The requirement of privity between the manufacturer and the injured consumer for *express* warranties began to crumble in the decades following *MacPherson,* far in advance of the *Henningsen* decision. In Baxter v. Ford Motor Co., 168 Wash. 456, 12 P.2d 409 (1932), the plaintiff was injured when a stone struck the windshield of his Ford Model A, causing small pieces of glass to fly into his eye. The plaintiff had purchased his car from an independent dealer, who had acquired it by purchase from the defendant Ford Motor Company. Ford had furnished the dealer with catalogues and printed material which described the windshield as "Shatter-Proof." Despite the lack of privity between the plaintiff and the defendant, the court held that the plaintiff had a right to rely upon the warranties, noting, "It would be unjust to recognize a rule that would permit manufacturers of goods to create a demand for their products by representing that they possess qualities which they, in fact, do not possess, and then, because there is no privity of contract existing between the consumer and the manufacturer, deny the consumer the right to recover if damages result from the absence of those qualities * * *."

Today, U.C.C. § 2–313 provides:

(1)   Express warranties by the seller are created as follows:

(a)   Any affirmation of fact or promise made by the seller to the buyer which relates to the goods and becomes part of the basis of the bargain creates an express warranty that the goods shall conform to the affirmation or promise. * * *

4.   *Parties to whom the Warranties Extend.* In some sense, the *Henningsen* opinion marked the zenith for the ease of recovery under implied warranty theories, soon replaced by the strict liability in tort theory under Restatement § 402A. In many jurisdictions, recovery under implied warranty theories, at least in cases involving the sale of goods, is now governed by provisions of the U.C.C. that are often somewhat more restrictive than the language in *Henningsen.* U.C.C. § 2–318 offers three alternative provisions from which any particular jurisdiction can choose, each specifying to whom warranties under the code extend. The most restrictive of these alternatives, Alternative A, allows an injured party to recover under a U.C.C. warranty only if she is a family member of the purchaser of the product, lives in the same household, or is a guest in the purchaser's home and can reasonably be expected to "use, consume, or be affected by the goods." In contrast, Alternative B more closely mirrors *Henningsen* and provides that an injured party can recover if she "may reasonably be expected to use, consume or be affected by the goods * * *."

5.   *Modification of Warranties.* Because U.C.C. warranties are contractual in nature, an important consideration is the extent to which they may be modified by agreement between the parties. Section 2–316 provides the conditions in which implied warranties can be excluded or modified, including that such modifications must be "conspicuous." Limitations on the implied warranty of merchantability must explicitly mention "merchantability," except that "all implied warranties are excluded by expressions like 'as is', 'with all faults' or other language which in common understanding calls the buyer's attention to the exclusion of warranties and makes plain that there is no implied warranty * * *."

Perhaps most important for purposes of personal injury litigation, under § 2–719, "Limitation of consequential damages for injury to the person in the case of consumer goods is prima facie unconscionable" and therefore invalid.

Finally, two of the three alternative provisions of § 2–315 prevent the seller from limiting the group of beneficiaries, designated in the statutory section, who can recover for a violation of the implied warranties. In other words, the seller's contractual fine print cannot prevent people like Mrs. Henninsen from qualifying as a beneficiary of the implied warranty.

Greenman v. Yuba Power Products, Inc.

Supreme Court of California, In Bank, 1963.
59 Cal.2d 57, 27 Cal.Rptr. 697, 377 P.2d 897.

■ TRAYNOR, JUSTICE. Plaintiff brought this action for damages against the retailer and the manufacturer of a Shopsmith, a combination power tool that could be used as a saw, drill, and wood lathe. He saw a Shopsmith demonstrated by the retailer and studied a brochure prepared by the manufacturer. He decided he wanted a Shopsmith for his home workshop, and his wife bought and gave him one for Christmas in 1955. In 1957 he bought the necessary attachments to use the Shopsmith as a lathe for turning a large piece of wood he wished to make into a chalice. After he had worked on the piece of wood several times without difficulty, it suddenly flew out of the machine and struck him on the forehead, inflicting serious injuries. About 10½ months later, he gave the retailer and the manufacturer written notice of claimed breaches of warranties and filed a complaint against them alleging such breaches and negligence.

After a trial before a jury, the court ruled that there was no evidence that the retailer was negligent or had breached any express warranty and that the manufacturer was not liable for the breach of any implied warranty. Accordingly, it submitted to the jury only the cause of action alleging breach of implied warranties against the retailer and the causes of action alleging negligence and breach of express warranties against the manufacturer. The jury returned a verdict for the retailer against plaintiff and for plaintiff against the manufacturer in the amount of $65,000. The trial court denied the manufacturer's motion for a new trial and entered judgment on the verdict. The manufacturer and plaintiff appeal. Plaintiff seeks a reversal of the part of the judgment in favor of the retailer, however, only in the event that the part of the judgment against the manufacturer is reversed.

Plaintiff introduced substantial evidence that his injuries were caused by defective design and construction of the Shopsmith. His expert witnesses testified that inadequate set screws were used to hold parts of the machine together so that normal vibration caused the tailstock of the lathe to move away from the piece of wood being turned permitting it to fly out of the lathe. They also testified that there were other more positive ways of fastening the parts of the machine together, the use of which would have prevented the accident. The jury could therefore reasonably have concluded that the manufacturer negligently constructed the Shopsmith. The jury could also reasonably have concluded that statements in the manufacturer's brochure were untrue, that they constituted express warranties,[1] and that plaintiff's injuries were caused by their breach.

The manufacturer contends, however, that plaintiff did not give it notice of breach of warranty within a reasonable time and that therefore his cause of action for breach of warranty is barred by section 1769 of the Civil Code. Since it cannot be determined whether the verdict against it was based on the negligence or warranty cause of action or both, the manufacturer concludes that the error in presenting the warranty cause of action to the jury was prejudicial.

Section 1769 of the Civil Code provides: " * * * [I]f, after acceptance of the goods, the buyer fails to give notice to the seller of the breach of any promise or warranty within a reasonable time after the buyer knows, or ought to know of such breach, the seller shall not be liable therefor."

Like other provisions of the Uniform Sales Act, Cal. Civ. Code, §§ 1721–1800, section 1769 deals with the rights of the parties to a contract of sale or a sale. It does not provide that notice must be given of the breach of a warranty that arises independently of a contract of sale between the parties. Such warranties are not imposed by the Sales Act, but are the product of common-law decisions that have recognized them in a variety of situations. * It is true that in many of these situations the court has invoked the Sales Act definitions of warranties, Cal. Civ. Code, §§ 1732, 1735, in defining the defendant's liability, but it has done so, not because the statutes so required, but because they provided appropriate standards for the court to adopt under the circumstances presented. *

The notice requirement of section 1769, however, is not an appropriate one for the court to adopt in actions by injured consumers against manufacturers with whom they have not dealt. * "As between the immediate parties to the sale [the notice requirement] is a sound commercial rule, designed to protect the seller against unduly delayed claims for damages. As applied to personal injuries, and notice to a remote seller, it becomes a booby-trap for the unwary." * * * We conclude, therefore, that even if plaintiff did not give timely notice of breach of warranty to the manufacturer, his cause of action based on the representations contained in the brochure was not barred.

Moreover, to impose strict liability on the manufacturer under the circumstances of this case, it was not necessary for plaintiff to establish an express warranty. * * * A manufacturer is strictly liable in tort when an article he places on the market, knowing that it is to be used without inspection for defects, proves to have a defect that causes injury to a human being. Recognized first in the case of unwholesome food

---

[1] In this respect the trial court limited the jury to a consideration of two statements in the manufacturer's brochure. (1) "WHEN SHOPSMITH IS IN HORIZONTAL POSITION— Rugged construction of frame provides rigid support from end to end. Heavy centerless-ground steel tubing insures perfect alignment of components." (2) "SHOPSMITH maintains its accuracy because every component has positive locks that hold adjustments through rough or precision work."

products, such liability has now been extended to a variety of other products that create as great or greater hazards if defective. *

Although in these cases strict liability has usually been based on the theory of an express or implied warranty running from the manufacturer to the plaintiff, the abandonment of the requirement of a contract between them, the recognition that the liability is not assumed by agreement but imposed by law, * and the refusal to permit the manufacturer to define the scope of its own responsibility for defective products * make clear that the liability is not one governed by the law of contract warranties but by the law of strict liability in tort. Accordingly, rules defining and governing warranties that were developed to meet the needs of commercial transactions cannot properly be invoked to govern the manufacturer's liability to those injured by their defective products unless those rules also serve the purposes for which such liability is imposed.

We need not recanvass the reasons for imposing strict liability on the manufacturer. * * * See F[owler] Harper & F[leming] James, Torts §§ 28.15–28.16; W[illiam L.] Prosser, The Assault Upon the Citadel (Strict Liability to the Consumer), 69 Yale L.J. 1099 (1960); Escola v. Coca Cola Bottling Co., 24 Cal.2d 453, 461, 150 P.2d 436, 440 (1944) (concurring opinion). The purpose of such liability is to insure that the costs of injuries resulting from defective products are borne by the manufacturers that put such products on the market rather than by the injured persons who are powerless to protect themselves. Sales warranties serve this purpose fitfully at best. * In the present case, for example, plaintiff was able to plead and prove an express warranty only because he read and relied on the representations of the Shopsmith's ruggedness contained in the manufacturer's brochure. Implicit in the machine's presence on the market, however, was a representation that it would safely do the jobs for which it was built. Under these circumstances, it should not be controlling whether plaintiff selected the machine because of the statements in the brochure, or because of the machine's own appearance of excellence that belied the defect lurking beneath the surface, or because he merely assumed that it would safely do the jobs it was built to do. It should not be controlling whether the details of the sales from manufacturer to retailer and from retailer to plaintiff's wife were such that one or more of the implied warranties of the sales act arose. * "The remedies of injured consumers ought not to be made to depend upon the intricacies of the law of sales." Ketterer v. Armour & Co., 200 F. 322, 323 (S.D.N.Y.1912). * To establish the manufacturer's liability it was sufficient that plaintiff proved that he was injured while using the Shopsmith in a way it was intended to be used as a result of a defect in design and manufacture of which plaintiff was not aware[a] that made the Shopsmith unsafe for its intended use. * * *

---

[a] [Eds.' note] It was later made clear that plaintiff need not prove lack of awareness, Luque v. McLean, 8 Cal.3d 136, 104 Cal.Rptr. 443, 501 P.2d 1163 (1972).

Restatement (Second) of Torts § 402A (1965).
Special Liability of Seller of Product for Physical Harm to
User or Consumer

(1) One who sells any product in a defective condition unreasonably dangerous to the user or consumer or to his property is subject to liability for physical harm thereby caused to the ultimate user or consumer, or to his property, if

 (a) the seller is engaged in the business of selling such a product, and

 (b) it is expected to and does reach the user or consumer without substantial change in the condition in which it is sold.

(2) The rule stated in Subsection (1) applies although

 (a) the seller has exercised all possible care in the preparation and sale of his product, and

 (b) the user or consumer has not bought the product from or entered into any contractual relation with the seller.

Notes

1. *Adoption of Strict Products Liability.* It is not an exaggeration to say that strict products liability literally swept the country. By the mid-1980s, virtually every state had adopted some form of strict products liability.[b] This development was called "the most radical and spectacular" in American tort law during the twentieth century. Robert W. Miller, Significant New Concepts of Tort Liability—Strict Liability, 17 Syracuse L. Rev. 25, 29 (1965) (quoting American Law Institute Meeting, 32 U.S.L. Week 2623, 2627 (1964)). While most jurisdictions adopted the principle of strict liability in tort, other states accomplished largely the same results but retained the language of implied warranties. See, e.g., Back v. Wickes Corp., 375 Mass. 633, 640, 378 N.E.2d 964, 969 (1978) (Massachusetts warranty law is "congruent in nearly all respects" with principles of Restatement (Second) of Torts § 402A). During the generation following the adoption of § 402A, courts often applied its provisions in a manner similar to statutory interpretation. In 1998, the American Law Institute, drawing upon substantial judicial experience with § 402A, adopted the Restatement (Third) of Torts: Products Liability (1998).

2. *Continuing Importance of Negligence and Warranty Theories of Recovery.* Some states continue to recognize separate causes of action for

---

 [b] [Eds.' note]. See Ogle v. Caterpillar Tractor Co., 716 P.2d 334, 341 n.8 (Wyo.1986) (identifying Delaware, Utah, Virginia, North Carolina, and the District of Columbia as the only American jurisdictions that had not adopted strict tort liability). In fact, three of these jurisdictions had previously adopted strict liability for product claims. See Martin v. Ryder Truck Rental, Inc., 353 A.2d 581, 587–88 (Del.1976); Ernest W. Hahn, Inc. v. Armco Steel Co., 601 P.2d 152, 158 (Utah 1979); and Berman v. Watergate West, Inc., 391 A.2d 1351, 1357 (D.C. 1978). A Virginia statute accomplished similar results by providing that lack of privity is no defense to a claim against a product manufacturer based on implied warranty. Va. Code Ann. § 8.2–318 (2014). Only North Carolina has continued to reject a claim in product liability cases based on strict liability or its equivalent. See Smith v. Fiber Controls Corp., 300 N.C. 669, 678, 268 S.E.2d 504, 510 (1980).

negligence or implied warranties in spite of the adoption of strict liability in tort for products defects. E.g., Denny v. Ford Motor Co., 87 N.Y.2d 248, 263, 639 N.Y.S.2d 250, 259, 662 N.E.2d 730, 739 (1995) (" '[T]he causes of action for strict products liability and breach of implied warranty of merchantability are not identical"); Lance v. Wyeth, 85 A.3d 434 (Pa. 2014) (recognizing claim in negligence for design or marketing of dangerous drug that is separate and distinct from strict liability under Restatement (Second) of Torts §402A)).

Often a single action arising from a product injury includes claims based upon a variety of legal theories. For example, in an action against tobacco companies, plaintiff might assert claims based upon strict products liability, negligence, willful and wanton misconduct, fraud and misrepresentation, express warranty, implied warranty, and concert of action or conspiracy. What respective advantages and disadvantages do claims based upon strict liability, negligence, and implied warranty theories pose for the plaintiff?

The Restatement (Third) of Torts: Products Liability § 2 cmt. n (1998) suggests that plaintiffs should not be allowed to pursue claims based upon different doctrinal labels where the underlying factual predicates of the claims are identical:

> The rules in this Section and in other provisions of this chapter define the bases of tort liability for harm caused by product defects existing at time of sale or other distribution. The rules are stated functionally rather than in terms of traditional doctrinal categories. * * *

> This Restatement contemplates that a well-coordinated body of law governing liability for harm to persons or property arising out of the sale of defective products requires a consistent definition of defect, and that the definition properly should come from tort law, whether the claim carries a tort label or one of implied warranty of merchantability. * * *

See also Freeman v. Hoffman-La Roche, Inc., 260 Neb. 552, 618 N.W.2d 827 (2000) (adopting Restatement (Third) view on this issue); contra, Fleck v. Titan Tire Corp., 177 F.Supp.2d 605 (E.D.Mich.2001) (explicitly rejecting Restatement (Third) view of exclusivity of remedy and permitting plaintiff to proceed on implied warranty under Michigan law after dismissal of design defect, failure to warn, and negligence claims).

3. *What Is a Product?* Restatement (Third) of Torts: Products Liability § 19(a) (1998) defines a product as "tangible personal property distributed commercially for use or consumption. Other items, such as real property and electricity, are products when the context of their distribution and use is sufficiently analogous to the distribution and use of tangible personal property * * *."

It is generally agreed that the seller of a component part, later assembled into something larger, is liable when the component proves defective and causes an injury. See e.g., Roy v. Star Chopper Co., 584 F.2d 1124, 1134 (1st Cir.1978) (applying Rhode Island law) ("The law is clear that a manufacturer of a component part can be held liable under strict liability."). Raw materials can also be subject to product liability actions. See, e.g., Menna v. Johns-Manville Corp., 585 F.Supp. 1178, 1183

(D.N.J.1984) (applying New Jersey law) (asbestos considered a product for strict liability purposes).

Human blood and tissue are specifically excluded from the category of products under Restatement (Third) of Torts: Products Liability § 19(c) (1998). During the past thirty years, state legislatures and courts have generally found that the strong public policy in favor of assuring the availability of blood and tissue outweighs the policy of providing compensation for injuries resulting from their use. See *id.* at cmt. c.

4. *"One Who Sells a Product."* Strict liability under the Restatement (Third) of Torts: Products Liability § 20 (1998) extends to one who "sells or otherwise distributes" a product in a commercial context, including manufacturers, wholesalers, and retailers. It also includes liability for injuries resulting from defects in free samples or products given away for promotional purposes.

The same principles of liability apply to the lease of a new or almost new product as they do to a sale, see, e.g., Stewart v. Budget Rent-A-Car Corp., 52 Haw. 71, 470 P.2d 240 (1970), and even when the product is provided to the consumer on a short-term demonstration basis. See, e.g., First Nat'l Bank of Mobile v. Cessna Aircraft Co., 365 So.2d 966 (Ala.1978). The results are more difficult to reconcile when the defendant is in the position of a bailor, providing the consumer with the product that ultimately causes injury as an incidental part of another transaction. Compare, e.g., Gabbard v. Stephenson's Orchard, Inc., 565 S.W.2d 753, 757 (Mo.Ct.App.1978) (orchard held strictly liable for defective ladder furnished to "you pick" customer) and Shaffer v. Victoria Station, Inc., 91 Wash.2d 295, 299, 588 P.2d 233, 235 (1978) (strict liability applied when customer injured by broken wine glass) with e.g., Keen v. Dominick's Finer Foods, Inc., 49 Ill.App.3d 480, 483, 7 Ill.Dec. 341, 364 N.E.2d 502, 504 (1977) (store not strictly liable when customer injured by shopping cart).

5. *Bystander Recovery.* The language of Restatement (Second) § 402A itself provides liability only "for physical harm thereby caused to the ultimate user or consumer, or to his property * * *." What about harm to a bystander caused by a defective product? Today courts, apparently without exception, allow recovery by foreseeable bystanders. As the California Supreme Court explained in Elmore v. American Motors Corp., 70 Cal.2d 578, 586, 75 Cal.Rptr. 652, 451 P.2d 84, 89 (1969):

> It has been pointed out that an injury to a bystander "is often a perfectly foreseeable risk of the maker's enterprise * * *." 2 Harper and James, The Law of Torts (1956) p. 1572 n.6.

> If anything, bystanders should be entitled to greater protection than the consumer or user where injury to bystanders from the defect is reasonably foreseeable. Consumers and users, at least, have the opportunity to inspect for defects and to limit their purchases to articles manufactured by reputable manufacturers and sold by reputable retailers, whereas the bystander ordinarily has no such opportunities. In short, the bystander is in greater need of protection from defective products which are dangerous, and if any distinction should be made between bystanders and users, it should be made, contrary to the position of defendants, to extend greater liability in favor of the bystanders.

6. *Sales or Service?* Generally strict liability principles do not apply to the sales of services. Often, however, services and products are provided together in one transaction, and separating them is not easy. See Restatement (Third) of Torts: Products Liability § 20 cmt. d (1998). As a general rule, courts usually apply strict liability to sales-service combinations in which the product is used up or consumed. See e.g., Villari v. Terminix Int'l, Inc., 692 F.Supp. 568 (E.D.Pa.1988) (applying Pennsylvania law) (defendant held strictly liable for injuries caused by pesticide). Remember that others in the sales distribution chain, such as the manufacturer and wholesaler of the pesticide, may be strictly liable. However, there is an exception to this general rule for sales-service transactions in the medical context. Courts rarely impose strict liability on doctors and hospitals even if the product is "consumed" during the surgery or other surgical procedure. Cf., Vergott v. Deseret Pharm. Co., 463 F.2d 12 (5th Cir.1972) (applying Texas law) (hospital not strictly liable for broken catheter which resulted in injuries requiring open-heart surgery).

7. *Liability of Successor Corporation.* The liability of successor corporations for injuries caused by products manufactured by their predecessors has become increasingly important for two reasons. First, many contemporary claims arise from exposure to harmful products, such as asbestos, where there is a prolonged time lag between exposure to the product and the manifestation of the disease. During the intervening decades, the original manufacturer often has been acquired by a different corporate entity. Second, manufacturing enterprises today consolidate with increasing frequency.

When the successor corporation gains control of a corporation that otherwise would have incurred liability resulting from its products distributed prior to the acquisition, the new owner will be liable if it gained control of the acquired corporation through the purchase of stock or, if as a result of a merger, the acquired corporation ceased to exist.

If the successor corporation gains control through the acquisition of assets of another corporation, however, the issue of whether the successor corporation is liable is sometimes more difficult to address. On the one hand, it seems fundamentally fair to allow those injured by defective products to recover against a successor corporation that is continuing a predecessor's business, particularly if there is a suggestion that the change in business structure is intended to avoid tort liability. On the other hand, imposing tort liability on a successor corporation that has acquired an ongoing business entity creates incentives to engage in inefficient economic behavior—to dismantle corporations in order to sell their productive assets, thus avoiding successor liability—rather than selling the business as a going concern. As a general rule, most states deny liability of successor corporations for the products of their predecessors, with certain limited exceptions, such as those set out in Restatement (Third) of Torts: Products Liability § 12 (1998); see also Ramirez v. Amsted Indus., Inc., 86 N.J. 332, 431 A.2d 811 (1981) (allowing liability based on the successor corporation's continuation of the predecessor's line of products).

B. MANUFACTURING DEFECTS

Myrlak v. Port Authority of New York and New Jersey

Supreme Court of New Jersey, 1999.
157 N.J. 84, 723 A.2d 45.

■ COLEMAN, J. * * * On July 6, 1991, plaintiff, John Myrlak, was injured when his chair collapsed while he was at work. At that time, plaintiff was forty-three years old, six feet six inches tall, and weighed approximately 325 pounds. * * * Plaintiff usually performed his duties while seated in a movable desk chair that was positioned at a semi-circular console, approximately eight feet long and three feet high. At the time of the accident, plaintiff had been seated in the chair performing his duties for approximately one hour and forty-five minutes. He suddenly heard a loud noise, and the back of his chair cracked and gave way. Plaintiff and the chair fell backwards, causing both to land parallel to the floor. Plaintiff grabbed the arms of the chair and pulled himself forward as he was falling. He injured his lower back and was hospitalized. Although no one other than the plaintiff actually saw the accident, several PATH [Port Authority Trans-Hudson Corporation] employees testified that they heard either a clicking or ratcheting sound, or a loud noise like a grinding of gears. After the accident, those employees observed that the back of the chair had collapsed and was parallel to the floor. A co-worker stated that he touched the back of the chair after the accident and it appeared to be flopping back and forth. Another co-worker testified that he sat in the chair the day following the accident and found it lacked back support.

The chair involved in the accident was manufactured by defendant Girsberger Industries, Inc. * * * [T]he chair that caused plaintiff's accident had been in use for five weeks. * * * Plaintiff was familiar with the chair and its operation. There was no evidence that the chair had been misused by plaintiff or any other PATH employee. The chair, however, was not used exclusively by plaintiff. On the contrary, it was customarily used by several different PATH employees twenty-four hours each day. * * * Plaintiff's expert was unable to duplicate the accident with the chair that was presented as evidence. * * * The expert was unable to identify a specific defect in the chair; nor could he state that a defect caused the accident. * * *

The jury * * * found that plaintiff failed to establish a manufacturing defect in the chair. * * * [The plaintiff appealed, claiming an error in the instructions to the jury.] * * * [T]he Appellate Division * * * reversed the verdict in favor of the manufacturer * * *. We granted defendant Girsberger's petition for certification[.] * * *

In the typical manufacturing defect case, a plaintiff is not required to establish negligence. * In other words, a plaintiff must impugn the product but not the conduct of the manufacturer of the product. * * *

Section 2 of the *Restatement (Third) of Torts: Products Liability* adopts manufacturing defects as one of three categories or theories of product defects. The Restatement defines a manufacturing defect as one in which "the product departs from its intended design though all possible care was exercised in the preparation and marketing of the product." Restatement (Third) of Torts: Products Liability § 2(a). The * * * Restatement's definition[ ] of a manufacturing defect * * * emphasize[s] the safety of the product rather than the reasonableness of the manufacturer's conduct. *

Simply because a plaintiff is not required to prove fault in a strict liability case does not mean that absolute liability will be imposed upon a manufacturer. Although a plaintiff is relieved of proving fault, that plaintiff must nonetheless prove that the product was defective under our common law jurisprudence that was incorporated into the Act. * Based on our well-established case law in this area, a plaintiff must prove that the product was defective, that the defect existed when the product left the manufacturer's control, and that the defect proximately caused injuries to the plaintiff, a reasonably foreseeable or intended user. *

A product is deemed to be defective if it is not reasonably fit, suitable, or safe for the ordinary or foreseeable purpose for which it is sold. * As noted previously, a manufacturing defect under the Act occurs when the product comes off the production line in a substandard condition based on the manufacturer's own standards or identical units that were made in accordance with the manufacturing specifications. *

To prove both the existence of a defect and that the defect existed while the product was in the control of the manufacturer, a plaintiff may resort to direct evidence, such as the testimony of an expert who has examined the product, or, in the absence of such evidence, to circumstantial proof. * The law is "settled in this State that in a products liability case the injured plaintiff is not required to prove a specific manufacturer's defect." Moraca v. Ford Motor Co., 66 N.J. 454, 458, 332 A.2d 599 (1975). Proof that a product is not fit for its intended purposes "requires only proof . . . that 'something was wrong' with the product." Scanlon v. General Motors Corp., 65 N.J. 582, 591, 326 A.2d 673, 678 (1974). The mere occurrence of an accident and the mere fact that someone was injured are not sufficient to demonstrate the existence of a defect. *

Under the Scanlon circumstantial evidence method of proving a product defect, the fact that a product is relatively new does not suffice by itself to establish a defective condition. * The age and prior usage of the product in relation to its expected life span are factors to consider in conjunction with other evidence presented. Generally, the older a product is, the more difficult it is to prove that a defect existed while in the manufacturer's control. * However, age of the product alone may not preclude a finding that the product was defective when the product is "of a type permitting the jury, after weighing all the evidence . . . , to infer that in the normal course of human experience an injury would not have occurred at this point in the product's lifespan had there not been a defect attributable to the manufacturer." Scanlon, 65 N.J. at 593, 326 A.2d at 679. Scanlon held that this critical inference could not be drawn when the product in question, a complicated automobile, was nine months old and had only 4,000 miles of use.

In addition to the direct and circumstantial evidence methods of proving a product defect, a plaintiff has a third option. A plaintiff may establish a defect by "negat[ing] other causes of the failure of the product for which the defendant would not be responsible, in order to make it reasonable to infer that a dangerous condition existed at the time the defendant had control [of the product]." Scanlon, 65 N.J. at 593–94, 326 A.2d at 679. Under that approach, a plaintiff does not have to negate all possible causes of failure, only those likely causes of failure. * * *

The chair had been in use for about five weeks. It was used twenty-four hours a day by at least three different persons of various weights and sizes. Although there was no evidence of misuse, multiple intended users had many opportunities to adjust the tension on the back of the chair to meet their personal needs. It cannot be said that simply because the back of the chair collapsed when plaintiff placed his weight against it, the chair was defective. The accident could not be replicated and no defect was found by any expert. The proofs—direct, circumstantial, and that negating of other causes—simply failed to show that collapse of the chair while the 325-pound plaintiff sat in it meant the chair was defective based on a balancing of the probabilities. * * *

The *Scanlon* rule regarding circumstantial proof of a defect in a strict products liability case was adopted recently in the *Restatement (Third) of Torts: Products Liability*. It provides:

> It may be inferred that the harm sustained by the plaintiff was caused by a product defect existing at the time of sale or distribution, without proof of a specific defect, when the incident that harmed the plaintiff:
>
> (a) was of a kind that ordinarily occurs as a result of a product defect; and
>
> (b) was not, in the particular case, solely the result of causes other than product defect existing at the time of sale or distribution.

Restatement (Third) of Torts § 3 (199[8]). * * *

Although Section 3 of the Restatement is based on a *res ipsa* model, it permits the jury to draw two inferences: that the harmful incident was caused by a product defect, and that the defect was present when the product left the manufacturer's control. The *res ipsa loquitur* doctrine, on the other hand, creates the single inference of negligence. Nevertheless, Section 3 of the Restatement parallels the elements of our *res ipsa loquitur* doctrine. * * * We * * * adopt the indeterminate product defect test announced in Section 3 of the Restatement.

[The Supreme Court upholds those portions of the Appellate Division decision holding that the trial court had improperly excluded other specific] evidence vital to plaintiff's ability to establish a manufacturing defect. Consequently, a new trial is required on plaintiff's strict products liability claims. * * *

[U]pon retrial, plaintiff need not prove a specific defect in the chair if he can establish that the incident that harmed him is of the kind that ordinarily occurs as a result of a product defect, and that the incident was not solely the result of causes other than [a] product defect existing at the time the chair left Girsberger's control. Restatement (Third) of Torts § 3(a) and (b). If plaintiff cannot satisfy those requirements, he is not entitled to have the jury charged regarding an inference of a product defect. * * *

C. DESIGN DEFECTS

Potter v. Chicago Pneumatic Tool Co.

Supreme Court of Connecticut, 1997.
241 Conn. 199, 694 A.2d 1319.

■ KATZ, JUSTICE. * * * The plaintiffs were employed at Electric Boat as "grinders," positions which required use of pneumatic hand tools to smooth welds and metal surfaces.[2] In the course of their employment, the plaintiffs used various pneumatic hand tools, including chipping and grinding tools, which were manufactured and sold by the defendants. The plaintiffs' use of the defendants' tools at Electric Boat spanned approximately twenty-five years, from the mid-1960s until 1987. The plaintiffs suffer from permanent vascular and neurological impairment of their hands, which has caused blanching of their fingers, pain, numbness, tingling, reduction of grip strength, intolerance of cold and clumsiness from restricted blood flow. As a result, the plaintiffs have been unable to continue their employment as grinders and their performance of other activities has been restricted. The plaintiffs' symptoms are consistent with a diagnosis of hand arm vibration syndrome. Expert testimony confirmed that exposure to vibration is a significant contributing factor to the development of hand arm vibration syndrome, and that a clear relationship exists between the level of vibration exposure and the risk of developing the syndrome.

* * * Richard Alexander, a mechanical engineering professor at Texas A & M University, testified that because machinery vibration has harmful effects on machines and on people, engineers routinely research ways to reduce or to eliminate the amount of vibration that a machine produces when operated. Alexander discussed various methods available to control vibration, including isolation (the use of springs or mass to isolate vibration), dampening (adding weights to dampen vibrational effects), and balancing (adding weights to counterbalance machine imbalances that cause vibration). Alexander testified that each of these methods has been available to manufacturers for at least thirty-five years. * * *

After a six week trial, the trial court rendered judgment on jury verdicts in favor of the plaintiffs. Finding that the defendants' tools had been defectively designed so as to render them unreasonably dangerous, the jury awarded the plaintiffs compensatory damages.[3] * * *

I

* * * Products liability law has * * * evolved to hold manufacturers * strictly liable for unreasonably dangerous products that cause injury

---

[2] One expert witness explained the design and purpose of these pneumatic tools: "[T]he machines are connected to an air hose that has air pressure, and you squeeze some kind of a valve and the air pressure is released into what's called an air motor, which is a turbine of sorts. The air propels the motor and rotates the grinding device and you apply the grinding wheel or attachment to the metal that you want to grind."

[3] [The court reduced each verdict to account for the comparative fault of the plaintiff.]

to ultimate users. Nevertheless, strict tort liability does not transform manufacturers into insurers, nor does it impose absolute liability. * * * Strict tort liability merely relieves the plaintiff from proving that the manufacturer was negligent and allows the plaintiff to establish instead the defective condition of the product as the principal basis of liability. *

Although courts have widely accepted the concept of strict tort liability, some of the specifics of strict tort liability remain in question. In particular, courts have sharply disagreed over the appropriate definition of defectiveness in design cases. * As the Alaska Supreme Court has stated: "Design defects present the most perplexing problems in the field of strict products liability because there is no readily ascertainable external measure of defectiveness. While manufacturing flaws can be evaluated against the intended design of the product, no such objective standard exists in the design defect context." Caterpillar Tractor Co. v. Beck, 593 P.2d 871, 880 (Alaska 1979).

Section 402A imposes liability only for those defective products that are "unreasonably dangerous" to "the ordinary consumer who purchases it, with the ordinary knowledge common to the community as to its characteristics." Restatement (Second) of Torts § 402A, cmt. i. * * * In Barker v. Lull Engineering Co., 20 Cal.3d 413, 435, 143 Cal.Rptr. 225, 573 P.2d 443, 457–58 (1978), the California Supreme Court established two alternative tests for determining design defect liability: (1) the consumer expectation analysis; and (2) a balancing test that inquires whether a product's risks outweigh its benefits. Under the latter, otherwise known as the "risk-utility," test, the manufacturer bears the burden of proving that the product's utility is not outweighed by its risks in light of various factors.[8] * * *

In Garthwait v. Burgio, 153 Conn. 284, 289–90, 216 A.2d 189, 192 (1965), this court recognized a products liability cause of action sounding in tort and became one of the first jurisdictions to adopt the rule provided in § 402A. * * * This court has further held that in order to recover under the doctrine of strict liability in tort the plaintiff must prove that:

(1) the defendant was engaged in the business of selling the product;

(2) the product was in a defective condition unreasonably dangerous to the consumer or user;

(3) the defect caused the injury for which compensation was sought;

(4) the defect existed at the time of the sale; and

(5) the product was expected to and did reach the consumer without substantial change in condition.

[Restatement (Second) of Torts § 402A]. *

This court has long held that in order to prevail in a design defect claim, "[t]he plaintiff must prove that the product is unreasonably dangerous." We have derived our definition of "unreasonably

---

[8]   In evaluating the adequacy of a product's design, the *Barker* court stated that "a jury may consider, among other relevant factors, the gravity of the danger posed by the challenged design, the likelihood that such danger would occur, the mechanical feasibility of a safer alternative design, the financial cost of an improved design, and the adverse consequences to the product and to the consumer that would result from an alternative design." *

dangerous" from comment *i* to § 402A, which provides that "the article sold must be dangerous to an extent beyond that which would be contemplated by the ordinary consumer who purchases it, with the ordinary knowledge common to the community as to its characteristics." Restatement (Second) of Torts § 402A, cmt. i. This "consumer expectation" standard is now well established in Connecticut strict products liability decisions. *

The defendants propose that it is time for this court to abandon the consumer expectation standard and adopt the requirement that the plaintiff must prove the existence of a reasonable alternative design in order to prevail on a design defect claim. We decline to accept the defendants' invitation.

In support of their position, the defendants point to the second tentative draft of the Restatement (Third) of Torts: Products Liability (1995) (Draft Restatement [Third]), which provides that, as part of a plaintiff's prima facie case, the plaintiff must establish the availability of a reasonable alternative design. Specifically, § 2(b) of the Draft Restatement (Third) provides:

> [A] product is defective in design when the foreseeable risks of harm posed by the product could have been reduced or avoided by the adoption of a reasonable alternative design by the seller or other distributor, or a predecessor in the commercial chain of distribution, and the omission of the alternative design renders the product not reasonably safe.

The reporters to the Draft Restatement (Third) state that "[v]ery substantial authority supports the proposition that [the] plaintiff must establish a reasonable alternative design in order for a product to be adjudged defective in design." Draft Restatement (Third) § 2, Reporters' Note to cmt. c.

We point out that this provision of the Draft Restatement (Third) has been a source of substantial controversy among commentators. See, e.g., Vargo, The Emperor's New Clothes: The American Law Institute Adorns a "New Cloth" for Section 402A Products Liability Design Defects—A Survey of the States Reveals a Different Weave, 26 U. Mem. L. Rev. 493, 501 (1996) (challenging reporters' claim that Draft Restatement (Third)'s reasonable alternative design requirement constitutes "consensus" among jurisdictions). * Contrary to the rule promulgated in the Draft Restatement (Third), our independent review of the prevailing common law reveals that the majority of jurisdictions *do not* impose upon plaintiffs an absolute requirement to prove a feasible alternative design. *

In our view, the feasible alternative design requirement imposes an undue burden on plaintiffs that might preclude otherwise valid claims from jury consideration. * Such a rule would require plaintiffs to retain an expert witness even in cases in which lay jurors can infer a design defect from circumstantial evidence. Connecticut courts, however, have consistently stated that a jury may, under appropriate circumstances, infer a defect from the evidence without the necessity of expert testimony. * Moreover, in some instances, a product may be in a defective condition unreasonably dangerous to the user even though no feasible alternative design is available. In such instances, the manufacturer may be strictly liable for a design defect notwithstanding the fact that there are no safer alternative designs in existence. See, e.g., O'Brien v. Muskin Corp., 94 N.J. 169, 184, 463 A.2d 298, 306 (1983) ("other products, including some for which no alternative exists, are so dangerous and of such little use that. . . a manufacturer would bear the cost of liability of harm to others"). * * *

Although today we continue to adhere to our long-standing rule that a product's defectiveness is to be determined by the expectations of an ordinary consumer, we nevertheless recognize that there may be instances involving complex product designs in which an ordinary consumer may not be able to form expectations of safety. * In such cases, a consumer's expectations may be viewed in light of various factors that balance the utility of the product's design with the magnitude of its risks. We find persuasive the reasoning of those jurisdictions that have modified their formulation of the consumer expectation test by incorporating risk-utility factors into the ordinary consumer expectation analysis. * Thus, the modified consumer expectation test provides the jury with the product's risks and utility and then inquires whether a reasonable consumer would consider the product unreasonably dangerous. * * * Accordingly, under this modified formulation, the consumer expectation test would establish the product's risks and utility, and the inquiry would then be whether a reasonable consumer would consider the product design unreasonably dangerous. *

In our view, the relevant factors that a jury *may* consider include, but are not limited to, the usefulness of the product, the likelihood and severity of the danger posed by the design, the feasibility of an alternative design, the financial cost of an improved design, the ability to reduce the product's danger without impairing its usefulness or making it too expensive, and the feasibility of spreading the loss by increasing the product's price. * The availability of a feasible alternative design is a factor that the plaintiff may, rather than must, prove in order to establish that a product's risks outweigh its utility. * Furthermore, we emphasize that our adoption of a risk-utility balancing component to our consumer expectation test does not signal a retreat from strict tort liability. In weighing a product's risks against its utility, the focus of the jury should be on the product itself, and not on the conduct of the manufacturer. *

Although today we adopt a modified formulation of the consumer expectation test, we emphasize that we do not require a plaintiff to present evidence relating to the product's risks and utility in every case. As the California Court of Appeals has stated: "There are certain kinds of accidents—even where fairly complex machinery is involved—[that] are so bizarre that the average juror, upon hearing the particulars, might reasonably think: 'Whatever the user may have expected from that contraption, it certainly wasn't that.' " Akers v. Kelley Co., 173 Cal.App.3d 633, 651, 219 Cal.Rptr. 513, 524 (1985). Accordingly, the ordinary consumer expectation test is appropriate when the everyday experience of the particular product's users permits the inference that the product did not meet minimum safety expectations. *

Conversely, the jury should engage in the risk-utility balancing required by our modified consumer expectation test when the particular facts do not reasonably permit the inference that the product did not meet the safety expectations of the ordinary consumer. Furthermore, instructions based on the ordinary consumer expectation test would not be appropriate when, as a matter of law, there is insufficient evidence to support a jury verdict under that test. In such circumstances, the jury should be instructed solely on the modified consumer expectation test we have articulated today.

In this respect, it is the function of the trial court to determine whether an instruction based on the ordinary consumer expectation test or the modified consumer expectation test, or both, is appropriate in light of the evidence presented. * * *

With these principles in mind, we now consider whether, in the present case, the trial court properly instructed the jury with respect to the definition of design defect for the purposes of strict tort liability. The trial court instructed the jury that * * * in determining whether the tools were unreasonably dangerous, it may draw its conclusions based on the reasonable expectations of an ordinary user of the defendants' tools. Because there was sufficient evidence as a matter of law to support the determination that the tools were unreasonably dangerous based on the ordinary consumer expectation test, we conclude that this instruction was appropriately given to the jury. * * *

III

* * * [T]he defendants assert that the trial court improperly prevented the jury from considering the state-of-the-art defense in the context of the plaintiffs' claim of defective design. * * * The trial court instructed the jury that "state of the art is defined as the level of scientific and technological knowledge existing at the time the product in question was designed for manufacture." * The court also instructed the jury that a manufacturer cannot be held to standards that exceed the limit of scientific advances and technology existing at the time of manufacture and, therefore, the defendants could not be found liable if they had proven compliance with the state of the art. The trial court, however, limited the applicability of the state-of-the-art defense solely to the plaintiffs' failure to warn claims. * * *

The question of whether state-of-the-art evidence similarly applies to design defect claims, however, is a matter of first impression for this court. *

We begin our analysis of this issue by recognizing that the term "state of the art" has been the source of substantial confusion. * Several courts have defined state-of-the-art evidence in terms of industry custom; * or in terms of compliance with then existing statutes or governmental regulations. * The majority of courts, however, have defined state-of-the-art evidence as the level of relevant scientific, technological and safety knowledge existing and reasonably feasible at the time of design. *

We also recognize that courts are divided on the issue of whether state-of-the-art evidence is admissible in design defect claims. Several courts have concluded that such evidence is inadmissible in design defect claims because it improperly focuses on the reasonableness of the manufacturer's conduct, which is irrelevant in a strict products liability action. * Conversely, other courts, in construing relevant state tort reform statutes, have stated that a manufacturer's proof of state-of-the-art evidence constitutes a complete defense to a design defect claim. *

Nevertheless, the overwhelming majority of courts have held that, in design defect cases, state-of-the-art evidence is relevant to determining the adequacy of the product's design. * The plaintiffs assert that state-of-the-art evidence has no place in a strict products liability action because it improperly focuses the jury's attention on the manufacturer's conduct. We disagree. We adopt the majority view and hold that such evidence is relevant and assists the jury in determining whether a product is defective and unreasonably dangerous. * * * Accordingly, we conclude that state of the art is a relevant factor in considering the adequacy of the design of a product and whether it is in a defective condition unreasonably dangerous to the ordinary consumer. * * * [We] * * * characterize state of the art as the level of relevant scientific, technological and safety knowledge existing and reasonably feasible at the time of design.

Furthermore, we point out that state of the art refers to what is technologically feasible, rather than merely industry custom. * "Although customs of an industry may be relevant . . . because those customs may lag behind technological development, they are not identical with the state-of-the-art." O'Brien v. Muskin Corp., 94 N.J. 169, 182, 463 A.2d 298, 305 (1983). * See also T.J. Hooper, 60 F.2d 737, 740 (2d Cir.) * (1932) ("[i]ndeed in most cases reasonable prudence is in fact common prudence; but strictly it is never its measure; a whole calling may have unduly lagged in the adoption of new and available devices"). Accordingly, "[a] manufacturer may have a duty to make products pursuant to a safer design even if the custom of the industry is not to use that alternative." O'Brien v. Muskin Corp., 94 N.J. at 182–83, 463 A.2d at 305.

We now apply these principles to the standards for determining design defectiveness that we have addressed in part I of this opinion. Under the ordinary consumer expectation standard, state-of-the-art evidence "helps to determine the expectation of the ordinary consumer." Bruce v. Martin-Marietta Corp., 544 F.2d 442, 447 (10th Cir.1976). * * * In other words, state-of-the-art evidence supplies the jury with a relevant basis on which to determine what the ordinary consumer would expect with respect to safety features available at the time of manufacture.

Furthermore, under the modified consumer expectations standard we have set forth today, such evidence would be admissible as a factor properly to be considered as part of the risk-utility calculus. * * * [S]uch evidence is a relevant factor on both sides of the risk-utility equation: the risks that the product presents to consumers in light of the availability of other safety measures, and the utility of the product in comparison to feasible design alternatives. * Accordingly, state-of-the-art evidence constitutes one of several relevant factors to assist the jury in determining whether a reasonable consumer would consider the product design unreasonably dangerous. * * *

We emphasize that although state-of-the-art evidence may be dispositive on the facts of a particular case, such evidence does not constitute an affirmative defense that, if proven, would absolve the defendant from liability. * In other words, compliance with state of the art would not, as a matter of law, warrant a judgment for a defendant. * * * We therefore conclude that state-of-the-art evidence is merely one factor for the jury to consider under either the ordinary or modified consumer expectation test. Accordingly, if on remand the trial court concludes that sufficient evidence has been produced to warrant an instruction, the jury may properly consider the state of the art in determining whether the defendants' tools were defectively designed and unreasonably dangerous. * * *

D. DEFECTS: FAILURE TO WARN

Liriano v. Hobart Corp.

United States Court of Appeals for the Second Circuit, 1999.
170 F.3d 264.

■ CALABRESI, CIRCUIT JUDGE. * * * Luis Liriano was severely injured on the job in 1993 when his hand was caught in a meat grinder manufactured by Hobart Corporation ("Hobart") and owned by his employer, Super Associated ("Super"). The meat grinder had been sold to Super with a safety guard, but the safety guard was removed while the machine was in Super's possession and was not affixed to the meat grinder at the time of the accident. The machine bore no warning indicating that the grinder should be operated only with a safety guard attached.

Liriano sued Hobart under several theories, including failure to warn. Hobart brought a third-party claim against Super. The [court] * * * dismissed all of Liriano's claims except the one based on failure to warn, and the jury returned a verdict for Liriano on that claim. It attributed five percent of the liability to Hobart and ninety-five percent to Super. The district court then held a partial retrial limited to the issue of whether and to what extent Liriano was responsible for his own injury. On that retrial, the jury assigned Liriano one-third of the fault. * * *

Hobart and Super appealed, arguing (1) that as a matter of law, there was no duty to warn, and (2) that even if there had been a duty to warn, the evidence presented was not sufficient to allow the failure-to-warn claim to reach the jury. * * * Hobart makes two arguments challenging the sufficiency of the evidence. The first concerns the obviousness of the danger that Liriano faced, and the second impugns the causal relationship between Hobart's negligence and Liriano's injury. Each of these arguments implicates issues long debated in the law of torts. With respect to the asserted clarity of the danger, the question is when a danger is so obvious that a court can determine, as a matter of law, that no additional warning is required. With respect to causation, the issue is whether a jury may infer that a defendant's particular negligence was the cause-in-fact of a plaintiff's actual injury from the general fact that negligence like the defendant's tends to cause injuries like the plaintiff's. The obviousness question was the subject of an important but now generally rejected opinion by Justice Holmes, then on the Massachusetts Supreme Judicial Court;[1] the causation

---

[1]   See Lorenzo v. Wirth, 170 Mass. 596, 49 N.E. 1010 (1898), [*supra* pages 155–158].

question is answered in a celebrated opinion of Judge Cardozo, then on the New York Court of Appeals.[2] We examine each in turn.

(1) *Obviousness*

More than a hundred years ago, a Boston woman named Maria Wirth profited from an argument about obviousness as a matter of law that is very similar to the one Hobart urges today. See Lorenzo v. Wirth, 170 Mass. 596, 49 N.E. 1010 (1898). * * * Writing for a majority of the Supreme Judicial Court of Massachusetts, Oliver Wendell Holmes, Jr., held for the defendant. He noted that, at the time of the accident, there had been a heap of coal on the street next to the coal hole, and he argued that such a pile provided sufficient warning to passers-by that they were in the presence of an open hole. "A heap of coal on a sidewalk in Boston is an indication, according to common experience, that there very possibly may be a coal hole to receive it." And that was that.

It was true, Holmes acknowledged, that "blind men, and foreigners unused to our ways, have a right to walk in the streets," and that such people might not benefit from the warning that piles of coal provided to sighted Bostonians. But Holmes wrote that coal-hole cases were simple, common, and likely to be oft repeated, and he believed it would be better to establish a clear rule than to invite fact-specific inquiries in every such case. "In simple cases of this sort," he explained, "courts have felt able to determine what, in every case, however complex, defendants are bound at their peril to know." With the facts so limited, this was an uncomplicated case in which the defendant could, as a matter of law, rely on the plaintiff's responsibility to know what danger she faced.

Justice Knowlton disagreed. His opinion delved farther into the particular circumstances than did Holmes's opinion for the majority. In so doing, he showed that Lorenzo's failure to appreciate her peril might have been foreseen by Wirth and hence that Wirth's failure to warn might constitute negligence. * * * "What kind of conduct is required under *complex* conditions, to reach the usual standard of due care, namely, the ordinary care of persons of common prudence, is a question of fact ... [and thus] a question for a jury." (emphasis added). Even cases involving "obvious" dangers like coal holes, Knowlton believed, might not be resolvable as matters of law when viewed in the fullness of circumstances that rendered the issue less clear than it would be when posed in the abstract.

Holmes commanded the majority of the Supreme Judicial Court in 1898, but Knowlton's position has prevailed in the court of legal history. "'[T]he so-called Holmes view—that standards of conduct ought increasingly to be fixed by the court for the sake of certainty—has been largely rejected ... The tendency has been away from fixed standards and towards enlarging the sphere of the jury.'" Fowler Harper, Fleming James & Oscar Gray, The Law of Torts § 15.3 n.16 (2d ed.1986). * The courts of New York have several times endorsed Knowlton's approach and ruled that judges should be very wary of taking the issue of liability away from juries, even in situations where the relevant dangers might

---

[2] See Martin v. Herzog, 228 N.Y. 164, 126 N.E. 814 (1920), [*supra* pages 196–199].

seem obvious, and especially when the cases in question turn on particularized facts. * * *

If the question before us were * * * simply whether meat grinders are sufficiently known to be dangerous so that manufacturers would be justified in believing that further warnings were not needed, we might be in doubt. On one hand, just as a coal hole was deemed a danger appreciated by most Bostonians in 1898, so most New Yorkers would probably appreciate the danger of meat grinders a century later. Any additional warning might seem superfluous. On the other hand, Liriano was only seventeen years old at the time of his injury and had only recently immigrated to the United States. He had been on the job at Super for only one week. He had never been given instructions about how to use the meat grinder, and he had used the meat grinder only two or three times. And, * * * the mechanism that injured Liriano would not have been visible to someone who was operating the grinder. It could be argued that such a combination of facts was not so unlikely that a court should say, as a matter of law, that the defendant could not have foreseen them or, if aware of them, need not have guarded against them by issuing a warning. That argument would draw strength from the Court of Appeals' direction that the question of whether a warning was needed must be asked in terms of the information available to the injured party rather than the injured party's employer * and its added comment that "in cases where reasonable minds might disagree as to the extent of the plaintiff's knowledge of the hazard, the question is one for the jury."

Nevertheless, it remains the fact that meat grinders are widely known to be dangerous. Given that the position of the New York courts on the specific question before us is anything but obvious, we might well be of two minds as to whether a failure to warn that meat grinders are dangerous would be enough to raise a jury issue. *

But to state the issue that way would be to misunderstand the complex functions of warnings. As two distinguished torts scholars have pointed out, a warning can do more than exhort its audience to be careful. It can also affect what activities the people warned choose to engage in. See James A. Henderson, Jr. & Aaron D. Twerski, Doctrinal Collapse in Products Liability: The Empty Shell of Failure to Warn, 65 N.Y.U. L. Rev. 265, 285 (1990). And where the function of a warning is to assist the reader in making choices, the value of the warning can lie as much in making known the existence of alternatives as in communicating the fact that a particular choice is dangerous. It follows that the duty to warn is not necessarily obviated merely because a danger is clear.

To be more concrete, a warning can convey at least two types of messages. One states that a particular place, object, or activity is dangerous. Another explains that people need not risk the danger posed by such a place, object, or activity in order to achieve the purpose for which they might have taken that risk. Thus, a highway sign that says "Danger—Steep Grade" says less than a sign that says "Steep Grade Ahead—Follow Suggested Detour to Avoid Dangerous Areas."

If the hills or mountains responsible for the steep grade are plainly visible, the first sign merely states what a reasonable person would know without having to be warned. The second sign tells drivers what they might not have otherwise known: that there is another road that is flatter and less hazardous. A driver who believes the road through the mountainous area to be the only way to reach her destination might well choose to drive on that road despite the steep grades, but a driver who knows herself to have an alternative might not, even though her understanding of the risks posed by the steep grade is exactly the same as those of the first driver. Accordingly, a certain level of obviousness as to the grade of a road might, in principle, eliminate the reason for posting a sign of the first variety. But no matter how patently steep the road, the second kind of sign might still have a beneficial effect. As a result, the duty to post a sign of the second variety may persist even when the danger of the road is obvious and a sign of the first type would not be warranted.

One who grinds meat, like one who drives on a steep road, can benefit not only from being told that his activity is dangerous but from being told of a safer way. As we have said, one can argue about whether the risk involved in grinding meat is sufficiently obvious that a responsible person would fail to warn of that risk, believing reasonably that it would convey no helpful information. But if it is also the case— as it is—that the risk posed by meat grinders can feasibly be reduced by attaching a safety guard, we have a different question. Given that attaching guards is feasible, does reasonable care require that meat workers be informed that they need not accept the risks of using unguarded grinders? Even if most ordinary users may—as a matter of law—know of the risk of using a guardless meat grinder, it does not follow that a sufficient number of them will—as a matter of law—also know that protective guards are available, that using them is a realistic possibility, and that they may ask that such guards be used. It is precisely these last pieces of information that a reasonable manufacturer may have a duty to convey even if the danger of using a grinder were itself deemed obvious.

Consequently, the instant case does not require us to decide the difficult question of whether New York would consider the risk posed by meat grinders to be obvious as a matter of law. A jury could reasonably find that there exist people who are employed as meat grinders and who do not know (a) that it is feasible to reduce the risk with safety guards, (b) that such guards are made available with the grinders, and (c) that the grinders should be used only with the guards. Moreover, a jury can also reasonably find that there are enough such people, and that warning them is sufficiently inexpensive, that a reasonable manufacturer would inform them that safety guards exist and that the grinder is meant to be used only with such guards. Thus, even if New York would consider the danger of meat grinders to be obvious as a matter of law, that obviousness does not substitute for the warning that a jury could, and indeed did, find that Hobart had a duty to provide. It follows that we cannot say, as a matter of law, that Hobart had no duty to warn Liriano in the present case. We therefore decline to adopt appellants' argument that the issue of negligence was for the court only and that the jury was not entitled, on the evidence, to return a verdict for Liriano.

(2) *Causation*

On rebriefing following the Court of Appeals decision, Hobart has made another argument as to why the jury should not have been allowed to find for the plaintiff. In this argument, Hobart raises the issue of causation. It maintains that Liriano "failed to present any evidence that Hobart's failure to place a warning [on the machine] was causally related to his injury." Whether or not there had been a warning, Hobart says, Liriano might well have operated the machine as he did and suffered the injuries that he suffered. Liriano introduced no evidence, Hobart notes, suggesting either that he would have refused to grind meat had the machine borne a warning or that a warning would have persuaded Super not to direct its employees to use the grinder without the safety attachment.

Hobart's argument about causation * * * rests on a false premise. It assumes that the burden was on Liriano to introduce additional evidence showing that the failure to warn was a but-for cause of his injury, even after he had shown that Hobart's wrong greatly increased the likelihood of the harm that occurred. But Liriano does not bear that burden. When a defendant's negligent act is deemed wrongful precisely because it has a strong propensity to cause the type of injury that ensued, that very causal tendency is evidence enough to establish a *prima facie* case of cause-in-fact. The burden then shifts to the *defendant* to come forward with evidence that its negligence was *not* such a but-for cause.

We know, as a general matter, that the kind of negligence that the jury attributed to the defendant tends to cause exactly the kind of injury that the plaintiff suffered. Indeed, that is what the jury must have found when it ruled that Hobart's failure to warn constituted negligence. In such situations, * * * the law presumes normality and requires the defendant to adduce evidence that the case is an exception. Accordingly, in a case like this, it is up to the defendant to bring in evidence tending to rebut the strong inference, arising from the accident, that the defendant's negligence was in fact a but-for cause of the plaintiff's injury. See Zuchowicz v. United States, 140 F.3d 381, 388 nn.6–7, 390–91 (2d Cir.1998).

This shifting of the *onus procedendi* has long been established in New York. Its classic statement was made more than seventy years ago, when the Court of Appeals decided a case in which a car collided with a buggy driving after sundown without lights. See Martin v. Herzog, 228 N.Y. 164, 170, 126 N.E. 814, 816 (1920). The driver of the buggy argued that his negligence in driving without lights had not been shown to be the cause-in-fact of the accident. Writing for the Court, Judge Cardozo reasoned that the legislature deemed driving without lights after sundown to be negligent precisely because not using lights tended to cause accidents of the sort that had occurred in the case. The simple fact of an accident under those conditions, he said, was enough to support the inference of but-for causal connection between the negligence and the particular accident. The inference, he noted, could be rebutted. But it was up to the negligent party to produce the evidence supporting such a rebuttal.

The words that Judge Cardozo applied to the buggy's failure to use lights are equally applicable to Hobart's failure to warn: "If nothing else is shown to break the connection, we have a case, prima facie sufficient, of negligence contributing to the result." Under that approach, the fact that Liriano did not introduce detailed evidence of but-for causal connection between Hobart's failure to warn and his injury cannot bar his claim. His *prima facie* case arose from the strong causal linkage between Hobart's negligence and the harm that occurred. See Guido Calabresi, Concerning Cause and the Law of Torts: An Essay for Harry Kalven, Jr., 43 U. Chi. L. Rev. 69 (1975), [*supra* pages 280–281] (describing the concept of "causal link"). And, since the *prima facie* case was not rebutted, it suffices. * * *

The district court did not err. We affirm its decision in all respects.

■ NEWMAN, CIRCUIT JUDGE, concurring. * * * The second circumstance implicated by the previous existence of a safety guard is the one discussed in the Court's opinion—the availability of the option of insisting upon a machine that has a guard, rather than facing only the choice between using a machine with a guard and not using the machine that lacks a guard.

* * * I am not sure that reasonable minds could differ as to the extent of a store employee's knowledge of the hazard of placing his hand in the open spout of a meat-grinder, but I think it likely that the Court of Appeals would rule that reasonable minds might differ on the closely related question concerning the extent of the employee's knowledge of a safer alternative, *i.e.*, avoiding use of a machine from which a safety guard had been removed and requesting a machine with the guard in place. For that reason, * * * I agree that Liriano's case was properly submitted to a jury for its decision.

One final comment is warranted. Those who believe that every decision in human affairs is a rational one, influenced logically by the incentives and disincentives that inhere in a given set of circumstances, will think it perverse that a manufacturer can be liable for failure to warn about the hazard of a meat-grinder originally equipped with a safety guard that has subsequently been removed even though liability might not exist had no such guard been initially installed. Surely, the devout rationalists will say, a rule of law countenancing such seemingly contradictory results will create an incentive for meat-grinder manufacturers not to install safety guards in the first place, thereby obtaining at least the chance to escape liability that, under today's decision, is deemed appropriate for jury consideration. I acknowledge that the disincentive to install a safety guard might exist, but, as with many predictions made on the assumption that a disincentive to take action will result in the action not being taken (or that an incentive to take action will result in the action being taken), I think it is extremely doubtful that meat-grinder manufacturers will elect to forgo safety guards in the hope of avoiding failure-to-warn liability for meat-grinders from which such guards have been removed. * * * Despite the disincentive arguably created by the imposition of liability in this case, manufacturers might well elect to install safety guards simply because they have some concern (humanitarian, not economic) that hands should not be severed by their machines. Moreover, if our decision correctly predicts New York law, manufacturers of meat-grinders equipped with safety guards can readily avoid liability for injuries resulting from use after the guard has been removed by the inexpensive furnishing of some reasonable form of notice of the hazard of using the machine without the guard. Hobart has already acted in this direction by placing on its machine a warning against use if the safety guard has been removed. Thus, the circumstances giving rise to Hobart's liability in this case are unlikely to arise again. * * *

NOTES

1. *Product Modification or Alteration.* The principal case discusses the manufacturer's liability for failure to warn of the risks of removal of safety devices. A distinct question concerns the liability of a manufacturer for harm caused by a product that has been modified after it leaves the manufacturer's hands. See Restatement (Third) of Torts: Products Liability § 2 cmt. p (1998). Subsequent product alteration affects the issues of defectiveness and causation in much the same way as does product misuse. See *infra* pages 621–624, *Ellsworth v. Sherne Lingerie, Inc.* and Notes 1 & 2 following it. If the product has been altered, was it defective at the time it left the manufacturer? Was the cause of injury the product or the subsequent modification? Earlier cases sometimes held that product alterations preclude liability, e.g., Young v. Aeroil Prods. Co., 248 F.2d 185 (9th Cir.1957), but more recent decisions generally uphold liability if the product alteration or modification is foreseeable. E.g., Brown v. U. S. Stove Co., 98 N.J. 155, 174, 484 A.2d 1234, 1244 (1984). See also Restatement (Third) of Torts: Products Liability § 15 cmt. b, § 17 cmt. c (1998).

2. *Are Product Warnings Effective?* Courts generally presume that users of products heed product warnings or instructions. See, e.g., Koonce v. Quaker Safety Prods. & Mfg. Co., 798 F.2d 700, 716 (5th Cir.1986) ("Texas law provides a rebuttable presumption that a user of a product would heed warnings or instructions if they were given"); Levi v. Southwestern La. Elec. Membership Coop., 542 So.2d 1081, 1089 (La.1989) (concluding that worker who knew of hazard of uninsulated electric line would have been more attentive to the danger if there had been a warning).

Professor Howard Latin convincingly argues that consumers and other users of products are unlikely "to read, understand, remember, and follow innumerable product warnings to protect themselves from all product-related risks they may confront" because of a wide variety of factors influencing behavior including information overload, competing demands on time and attention, overconfidence in their ability to avoid harm, and functional illiteracy. Howard Latin, "Good" Warnings, Bad Products, and Cognitive Limitations, 41 UCLA L. Rev. 1193, 1206–20 (1994). Perhaps most strikingly, Latin describes how product users ignore product warnings because they are confident they understand how to use a product safely. In one study, subjects asked to complete a simple construction project were given hammers with three alternative warnings attached:

> (a) *"Caution! A hammer can be made to chip if struck against another hammer face or other hardened surface resulting not only in damage to the hammer but possibly in bodily injury"; (b) "Caution! Do not proceed further. Ask for instructions before you continue this operation. It is important that you do not use this hammer to strike"; or (c) "Caution! Do not proceed further."*[59]

---

[59] Alan L. Dorris & Jerry L. Purswell, Warnings and Human Behavior: Implications for the Design of Product Warnings, 1 J. Prod. Liab. 255, 257 (1977).

The first warning had actually been provided by the manufacturer. The experimenters reported: At the completion of the task, each participant was asked whether a warning label had been on any of the tools. Of the one hundred participants, no one noticed any label of any type. * * *

Uniroyal Goodrich Tire Co. v. Martinez

Supreme Court of Texas, 1998.
977 S.W.2d 328.

■ PHILLIPS, CHIEF JUSTICE. * * * Roberto Martinez, together with his wife and children, sued Uniroyal Goodrich Tire Company ("Goodrich") * * * for personal injuries Martinez suffered when he was struck by an exploding 16″ Goodrich tire that he was mounting on a 16.5″ [16.5 inch] rim. Attached to the tire was a prominent warning label containing yellow and red highlights and a pictograph of a worker being thrown into the air by an exploding tire. The label stated conspicuously: "NEVER MOUNT A 16″ SIZE DIAMETER TIRE ON A 16.5″ RIM," [and further provided a variety of other specific warnings.]

Unfortunately, Martinez ignored every one of these warnings. While leaning over the assembly, he attempted to mount a 16″ tire on a 16.5″ rim without a tire mounting machine, a safety cage, or an extension hose. Martinez explained, however, that because he had removed a 16″ tire from the 16.5″ rim, he believed that he was mounting the new 16″ tire on a 16″ rim. Moreover, the evidence revealed that Martinez's employer failed to make an operable tire-mounting machine available to him at the time he was injured, and there was no evidence that the other safety devices mentioned in the warning were available. * * *

At trial, the Martinezes claimed that the tire manufactured by Goodrich was defective because it failed to incorporate a safer alternative bead design that would have kept the tire from exploding. This defect, they asserted, was the producing cause of Martinez's injuries. * * * The bead is the portion of the tire that holds the tire to the rim when inflated. A bead consists of rubber-encased steel wiring that encircles the tire a number of times. When the tire is placed inside the wheel rim and inflated, the bead is forced onto the bead-seating ledge of the rim and pressed against the lip of the rim, or the wheel flange. When the last portion of the bead is forced onto this ledge, the tire has "seated," and the air is properly sealed inside the tire. The bead holds the tire to the rim because the steel wire, unlike rubber, does not expand when the tire is inflating. * * * The Martinezes' expert, Alan Milner, a metallurgical engineer, testified that a tape bead is prone to break when the spliced portion of the bead is the last portion of the bead to seat. This is commonly called a hang-up. Milner testified that an alternative bead design, a 0.050″ gauge single strand programmed bead, would have prevented Martinez's injuries because its strength and uniformity make it more resistant to breaking during a hang-up. * * *

In 1966, 16.5″ wheel rims were first introduced into the American market. * Milner testified that Uniroyal, Inc. and B.F. Goodrich Company, who in 1986 merged to form [the Uniroyal-Goodrich Tire

Company, referred to by the court as "Goodrich"], soon became aware that mismatching their 16″ tires with the new wheel rims often caused hang-ups that resulted in broken beads. * * * Finally, Milner testified that B.F. Goodrich's own testing department was aware by at least 1976 that a 16″ tire mounted on a 16.5″ rim would explode during a hang-up. * * * Based upon this evidence and his expert opinion, Milner testified that the tire manufactured by Goodrich with a tape bead was defective and unreasonably dangerous. Because Goodrich had also been sued in thirty-four other lawsuits alleging accidents caused by mismatching Goodrich tires, Milner asserted that Goodrich was grossly negligent in failing to adopt the 0.050″ single strand programmed bead in its bias-ply 16″ light truck tires. * * *

The jury found that Goodrich's conduct was the sole proximate cause of Martinez's injuries and that Goodrich was grossly negligent. * * * The court of appeals affirmed * * * [and] rejected Goodrich's argument that Martinez's failure to heed the product's warnings was a complete defense to the product defect claim. * * *

* * * To prove a design defect, a claimant must establish, among other things, that the defendant could have provided a safer alternative design. * Implicit in this holding is that the safer alternative design must be reasonable, *i.e.*, that it can be implemented without destroying the utility of the product. * The newly released Restatement (Third) of Torts: Products Liability carries forward this focus on reasonable alternative design. See Restatement (Third) of Torts: Products Liability § 2(b). Section 2(b) provides:

> A product . . . is defective in design when the foreseeable risks of harm posed by the product could have been reduced or avoided by the adoption of a reasonable alternative design by the seller or other distributor, or a predecessor in the commercial chain of distribution, and the omission of the alternative design renders the product not reasonably safe.

To determine whether a reasonable alternative design exists, and if so whether its omission renders the product unreasonably dangerous (or in the words of the new Restatement, not reasonably safe), the finder of fact may weigh various factors bearing on the risk and utility of the product. * One of these factors is whether the product contains suitable warnings and instructions. * * * Restatement (Third) of Torts: Products Liability § 2 cmt. f.

Goodrich urges this Court to depart from this standard by following certain language from Comment *j* of the Restatement (Second) of Torts. Comment *j* provides in part:

> Where warning is given, the seller may reasonably assume that it will be read and heeded; and a product bearing such a warning, which is safe for use if it is followed, is not in defective condition, nor is it unreasonably dangerous.

Restatement (Second) of Torts § 402A cmt. j (1965). The new Restatement, however, expressly rejects the Comment *j* approach:

> * * * In general, when a safer design can reasonably be implemented and risks can reasonably be designed out of a product, adoption of the safer design is required over a warning that leaves a significant residuum of such risks. * * *

> [W]hen an alternative design to avoid risks cannot reasonably be implemented, adequate instructions and warnings will normally be sufficient to render the product reasonably safe. * *Warnings are not, however, a substitute for the provision of a reasonably safe design.*

Restatement (Third) of Torts: Products Liability § 2 cmt. l. The Reporters' Notes in the new Restatement refer to Comment *j* as "unfortunate language" that "has elicited heavy criticism from a host of commentators." Restatement (Third) of Torts: Products Liability § 2, Reporters' Note, cmt. l. * * *

The drafters of the new Restatement provide the following illustration for why courts have overwhelmingly rejected Comment *j*:

> Jeremy's foot was severed when caught between the blade and compaction chamber of a garbage truck on which he was working. The injury occurred when he lost his balance while jumping on the back step of the garbage truck as it was moving from one stop to the next. The garbage truck, manufactured by XYZ Motor Co., has a warning in large red letters on both the left and right rear panels that reads "DANGER—DO NOT INSERT ANY OBJECT WHILE COMPACTION CHAMBER IS WORKING—KEEP HANDS AND FEET AWAY." The fact that adequate warning was given does not preclude Jeremy from seeking to establish a design defect under Subsection (b). The possibility that an employee might lose his balance and thus encounter the shear point was a risk that a warning could not eliminate and that might require a safety guard. Whether a design defect can be established is governed by Subsection (b).

Restatement (Third) of Torts: Products Liability § 2 cmt. l, illus. 14. * * * For these reasons we refuse to adopt the approach of Comment *j* of the superseded Restatement (Second) of Torts section 402A.

We do not hold, as the dissenting justices claim, that "a product is defective whenever it could be more safely designed without substantially impairing its utility," * or that "warnings are irrelevant in determining whether a product is reasonably safe." * Rather, as we have explained, we agree with the new Restatement that warnings and safer alternative designs are factors, among others, for the jury to consider in determining whether the product as designed is reasonably safe. * * *

* * * The jury heard firsthand how an accident can occur despite the warning label, and how a redesigned tire would have prevented that accident. The jury also heard evidence that Goodrich's competitors had incorporated the single strand programmed bead by the early 1980s, and that Goodrich itself adopted this design in 1991, a year after manufacturing the tire that injured Martinez. Under these circumstances, there is at least some evidence supporting the jury's finding of product defect. * * *

Perez v. Wyeth Laboratories Inc.

Supreme Court of New Jersey, 1999.
161 N.J. 1, 734 A.2d 1245.

■ O'HERN, J. * * * Our medical-legal jurisprudence is based on images of health care that no longer exist. At an earlier time, medical advice was received in the doctor's office from a physician who most likely made house calls if needed. * * * Pharmaceutical manufacturers never advertised their products to patients, but rather directed all sales efforts at physicians. In this comforting setting, the law created an exception to the traditional duty of manufacturers to warn consumers directly of risks associated with the product as long as they warned health-care providers of those risks. For good or ill, that has all changed. * * * Drug manufacturers now directly advertise products to consumers on the radio, television, the Internet, billboards on public transportation, and in magazines. * * *

This appeal concerns Norplant, a Food and Drug Administration (FDA)-approved, reversible contraceptive that prevents pregnancy for up to five years. The Norplant contraceptive employs six thin, flexible, closed capsules that contain a synthetic hormone, levonorgestrel. * The capsules are implanted under the skin of a woman's upper arm during an in-office surgical procedure characterized by the manufacturer as minor. A low, continuous dosage of the hormone diffuses through the capsule walls and into the bloodstream. Although the capsules are not usually visible under the skin, the outline of the fan-like pattern can be felt under the skin. Removal occurs during an in-office procedure, similar to the insertion process. * * *

According to plaintiffs, Wyeth began a massive advertising campaign for Norplant in 1991, which it directed at women rather than at their doctors. Wyeth advertised on television and in women's magazines such as *Glamour, Mademoiselle* and *Cosmopolitan.* According to plaintiffs, none of the advertisements warned of any inherent danger posed by Norplant; rather, all praised its simplicity and convenience. None warned of side effects including pain and permanent scarring attendant to removal of the implants. Wyeth also sent a letter to physicians advising them that it was about to launch a national advertising program in magazines that the physicians' patients may read.

Plaintiffs cite several studies published in medical journals that have found Norplant removal to be difficult and painful. * * * [The trial court had found that "the defendants adequately warned * * * physicians and other health-care professionals of the risks associated with Norplant."]

In 1995, plaintiffs began to file lawsuits in several New Jersey counties claiming injuries that resulted from their use of Norplant. Plaintiffs' principal claim alleged that Wyeth, distributors of Norplant in the United States, failed to warn adequately about side effects associated with the contraceptive. Side effects complained of by plaintiffs included weight gain, headaches, dizziness, nausea, diarrhea, acne, vomiting, fatigue, facial hair growth, numbness in the arms and legs, irregular menstruation, hair loss, leg cramps, anxiety and nervousness, vision problems, anemia, mood swings and depression, high blood pressure, and removal complications that resulted in scarring. * * * After a case management conference, plaintiffs' counsel sought a determination of whether the learned intermediary doctrine applied. * * * The Appellate Division affirmed the trial court's grant of summary judgment in favor of defendants and its determination that the learned intermediary doctrine applied. * * *

In Feldman v. Lederle Laboratories, 97 N.J. 429, 479 A.2d 374 (1984) (*Feldman I*), we considered the relationship between principles of products liability law and pharmaceutical products. In *Feldman I*, we declined to "hold as a matter of law and policy that all prescription drugs that are unsafe are unavoidably so." We explained:

> Drugs, like any other products, may contain defects that could have been avoided by better manufacturing or design. Whether a drug is unavoidably unsafe should be decided on a case-by-case basis; we perceive no justification for giving all prescription drug manufacturers a blanket immunity from strict liability manufacturing and design defect claims under Restatement (Second) of Torts § 402A cmt. k (1965).[a]

> Moreover, even if a prescription drug were unavoidably unsafe, the comment *k* immunity would not eliminate strict liability for failure to provide a proper warning. As Justice Pollock stated in O'Brien v. Muskin Corp., 94 N.J. 169, 183, 463 A.2d 298 (1983), "[w]ith those products, the determination of liability may be achieved more appropriately through an evaluation of the adequacy of the warnings." * * * Thus, a manufacturer who knows or should know of the danger or side effects of a product is not relieved of its duty to warn. Rather, as the comment expressly states, it is only the unavoidably unsafe product *"accompanied by proper . . . warning"* that is not defective. (Emphasis added.)

Feldman, 97 N.J. at 447, 479 A.2d at 383–84.

As explained in Niemiera by Niemiera v. Schneider, 114 N.J. 550, 559, 555 A.2d 1112, 1117 (1989):

> In New Jersey, as elsewhere, we accept the proposition that a pharmaceutical manufacturer generally discharges its duty to warn the ultimate user of prescription drugs by supplying physicians with information about the drug's dangerous

---

[a]   [Eds.' note] Comment *k* to Restatement (Second) of Torts § 402(A) (1965) describes the function of warnings in the case of "unavoidably unsafe" products, such as Norplant:

   k   Unavoidably unsafe products. There are some products which, in the present state of human knowledge, are quite incapable of being made safe for their intended and ordinary use. These are especially common in the field of drugs. An outstanding example is the vaccine for the Pasteur treatment of rabies, which not uncommonly leads to very serious and damaging consequences when it is injected. Since the disease itself invariably leads to a dreadful death, both the marketing and the use of the vaccine are fully justified, notwithstanding the unavoidable high degree of risk which they involve. Such a product, properly prepared, and accompanied by proper directions and warning, is not defective, nor is it *unreasonably* dangerous. * * * The seller of such products, again with the qualification that they are properly prepared and marketed, and proper warning is given * * * is not to be held to strict liability for unfortunate consequences attending their use, merely because he has undertaken to supply the public with an apparently useful and desirable product, attended with a known but apparently reasonable risk. * * *

propensities. * This concept is known as the "learned intermediary" rule because the physician acts as the intermediary between the manufacturer and the consumer. * * *

We observed that there were circumstances, such as in Davis v. Wyeth Laboratories, Inc., 399 F.2d 121 (9th Cir.1968), in which the manufacturer should not be relieved of a duty to warn. * In *Davis*, the manufacturer of a polio vaccine was held to have an independent duty to warn the consumer because in mass immunization clinics such as where the plaintiff received a polio vaccine, there was "no physician present to weigh the risks and benefits of the drug therapy for each patient." * * *

* * * Pressure on consumers is an integral part of drug manufacturers' marketing strategy. From 1995 to 1996, drug companies increased advertising directed to consumers by ninety percent. * In 1997, advertising costs of pharmaceutical products surpassed the half-billion dollar mark for the first time, "easily outpacing promotional efforts directed to physicians." Lars Noah, Advertising Prescription Drugs to Consumers: Assessing the Regulatory and Liability Issues, 32 Ga. L. Rev. 141, 141 (1997). * * *

The difficulties that accompany this [type of advertising] practice are manifest. "The marketing gimmick used by the drug manufacturer often provides the consumer with a diluted variation of the risks associated with the drug product." Even without such manipulation, "[t]elevision spots lasting 30 or 60 seconds are not conducive to 'fair balance' [in presentation of risks]." Given such constraints, pharmaceutical ads often contain warnings of a general nature. However, "[r]esearch indicates that general warnings (for example, see your doctor) in [direct-to-consumer] advertisements do not give the consumer a sufficient understanding of the risks inherent in product use." * * * Jon D. Hanson & Douglas A. Kysar, Taking Behavioralism Seriously: Some Evidence of Market Manipulation, 112 Harv. L. Rev. 1420, 1456 (1999).

Parallel to the developments in drug marketing, the American Law Institute was in the process of adopting the Restatement (Third) of Torts: Products Liability (1997). The comment to Section 6 explains that subsection (d)(1) sets forth the traditional rule of the learned intermediary that drug and medical device manufacturers are liable for failing to warn of a drug's risks only when the manufacturer fails to warn the health-care provider of risks attendant to a specific drug. Restatement (Third) of Torts § 6(d) cmt. a. That same comment also notes that subsection (d)(2) reflects decisional law and provides limited exceptions to the traditional rule by requiring manufacturers to warn patients in certain circumstances. * Because situations may exist when the health-care provider assumes a "much-diminished role as an evaluator or decisionmaker," it is appropriate to impose a duty on the manufacturer to warn the patient directly. *Id.* at § 6(d) cmt. b. Despite the early effort to provide an exception to the doctrine in the case of direct marketing of pharmaceuticals to consumers, the drafters left the resolution of that issue to "developing case law." * * * Thus, under the new Restatement, "warnings may have to be provided to a health-care provider or even to the patient," depending on the circumstances. * * *

* * * [A] recent review summarized the theoretical bases for the [learned intermediary] doctrine as based on four considerations.

> First, courts do not wish to intrude upon the doctor-patient relationship. From this perspective, warnings that contradict information supplied by the physician will undermine the patient's trust in the physician's judgment. Second, physicians may be in a superior position to convey meaningful information to their patients, as they must do to satisfy their duty to secure informed consent. Third, drug manufacturers lack effective means to communicate directly with patients, making it necessary to rely on physicians to convey the relevant information. Unlike [over the counter products], pharmacists usually dispense prescription drugs from bulk containers rather than as unit-of-use packages in which the manufacturer may have enclosed labeling. Finally, because of the complexity of risk information about prescription drugs, comprehension problems would complicate any effort by manufacturers to translate physician labeling for lay patients. For this reason, even critics of the rule do not suggest that pharmaceutical companies should provide warnings only to patients and have no tort duty to warn physicians.

[Lars] Noah, 32 Ga. L. Rev. at 157–59. (footnotes omitted). * * *

First, with rare and wonderful exceptions, the " 'Norman Rockwell' image of the family doctor no longer exists." *Id.* at 180 n.78. * Informed consent requires a patient-based decision rather than the paternalistic approach of the 1970s. * * * Second, because managed care has reduced the time allotted per patient, physicians have considerably less time to inform patients of the risks and benefits of a drug. * * * Third, having spent $1.3 billion on advertising in 1998, * drug manufacturers can hardly be said to "lack effective means to communicate directly with patients," Noah, 32 Ga. L. Rev. at 158, when their advertising campaigns can pay off in close to billions in dividends.

Consumer-directed advertising of pharmaceuticals thus belies each of the premises on which the learned intermediary doctrine rests.

> First, the fact that manufacturers are advertising their drugs and devices to consumers suggests that consumers are active participants in their health care decisions, invalidating the concept that it is the doctor, not the patient, who decides whether a drug or device should be used. Second, it is illogical that requiring manufacturers to provide direct warnings to a consumer will undermine the patient-physician relationship, when, by its very nature, consumer-directed advertising encroaches on that relationship by encouraging consumers to ask for advertised products by name. Finally, consumer-directed advertising rebuts the notion that prescription drugs and devices and their potential adverse effects are too complex to be effectively communicated to lay consumers. Because the FDA requires that prescription drug and device advertising carry warnings, the consumer may reasonably presume that the advertiser guarantees the adequacy of its warnings. Thus, the common law duty to war[n] the ultimate consumer should apply. * * *

Concerns regarding patients' communication with and access to physicians are magnified in the context of medicines and medical devices furnished to women for reproductive decisions. In MacDonald v. Ortho Pharmaceutical Corp., 394 Mass. 131, 475 N.E.2d 65, *cert. denied*, 474 U.S. 920, 106 S.Ct. 250, 88 L.Ed.2d 258 (1985), the plaintiff's use of oral contraceptives allegedly resulted in a stroke. The Massachusetts Supreme Court explained several reasons why contraceptives differ from other prescription drugs and thus "warrant the imposition of a common law duty on the manufacturer to warn users directly of associated risks." For example, after the patient receives the prescription, she consults with the physician to receive a prescription annually, leaving her an infrequent opportunity to "explore her questions and concerns about the medication with the prescribing physician." Consequently, the limited participation of the physician leads to a real possibility that their communication during the annual checkup is insufficient. The court also explained that because oral contraceptives are drugs personally selected by the patient, a prescription is often not the result of a physician's skilled balancing of individual benefits and risks but originates, instead, as a product of patient choice. Thus, "the physician is relegated to a . . . passive role."

* * * When a patient is the target of direct marketing, one would think, at a minimum, that the law would require that the patient not be misinformed about the product. It is one thing not to inform a patient about the potential side effects of a product; it is another thing to misinform the patient by deliberately withholding potential side effects while marketing the product as an efficacious solution to a serious health problem. Further, when one considers that many of these "lifestyle" drugs or elective treatments cause significant side effects without any curative effect, increased consumer protection becomes imperative, because these drugs are, by definition, not medically necessary. * * *

In reaching the conclusion that the learned intermediary doctrine does not apply to the direct marketing of drugs to consumers, we must necessarily consider that when prescription drugs are marketed and labeled in accordance with FDA specifications, the pharmaceutical manufacturers should not have to confront "state tort liability premised on theories of design defect or warning inadequacy." Note, A Question of Competence: The Judicial Role in the Regulation of Pharmaceuticals, 103 Harv. L. Rev. 773, 773 (1990). * * * The FDA is authorized to regulate advertisements for prescription drugs pursuant to 21 U.S.C.A. § 352(n) of the Food, Drug and Cosmetic Act, 21 U.S.C.A. §§ 301–97. * * * Presently, any duty to warn physicians about prescription drug dangers is presumptively met by compliance with federal labeling. * That presumption is not absolute. * Nevertheless, FDA regulations serve as compelling evidence that a manufacturer satisfied its duty to warn the physician about potentially harmful side effects of its product. We believe that in the area of direct-to-consumer advertising of pharmaceuticals, the same rebuttable presumption should apply when a manufacturer complies with FDA advertising, labeling and warning requirements. * * * For all practical purposes, absent deliberate concealment or nondisclosure of after-acquired knowledge of harmful effects, compliance with FDA standards should be virtually dispositive of such claims. * * *

The final issues in this case concern proximate cause, that is, whether misinformation actually affected these patients and, if so, whether the intervention of the physician (without whom the product may not reach the patient) breaks the chain of causation. * * * Although the physician writes the prescription, the physician's role in deciding which prescription drug is selected has been altered. * * * A proximate cause need not be the sole cause of harm. It suffices if it is a substantial contributing factor to the harm suffered. * * * A plaintiff suing under a failure-to-warn theory must presumably establish that she would have heeded an adequate warning if one were given. * * *

To sum up, * * * [t]he direct marketing of drugs to consumers generates a corresponding duty requiring manufacturers to warn of defects in the product. * * * *Norplant* probably does not afford the best context in which to address the general question whether direct-to-consumer marketers of pharmaceutical products are unqualifiedly relieved of a duty to warn consumers of the dangerous propensities of a product. After all, in the case of *Norplant*, the role of the physician can never be insubstantial because only a physician may implant the device. * * *

NOTES

1. *A Contrasting Perspective on the Advertising Exception to the Learned Intermediary Rule.* The court in *Perez v. Wyeth Laboratories* repeatedly quotes Lars Noah, Advertising Prescription Drugs to Consumers: Assessing the Regulatory and Liability Issues, 32 Ga. L. Rev. 141 (1997). Ironically, Professor Noah reaches a conclusion directly opposite that of the Supreme Court of New Jersey:

> Proponents of an advertising exception cannot rebut the two central rationales underlying the learned intermediary doctrine: patients cannot lawfully purchase a prescription drug without receiving authorization from a physician, and physicians are far better situated than manufacturers to communicate with patients. To be sure, consumer-directed drug advertising campaigns may encourage patients to take a more active role in seeking professional treatment and in identifying possible therapies that can be considered by their physicians. In addition, physicians may not in fact successfully communicate risk information about prescription drugs to their patients. * Nonetheless, advocates of an advertising exception fail to appreciate the fact that a medical professional will continue to intervene in the decision to prescribe a drug and make the final judgment about its relative risks and benefits for a particular patient. * It would constitute professional malpractice to do otherwise. * * *
>
> * * * [C]arving out only an advertising exception may do nothing to improve communication with consumers. Even if manufacturers choose to continue advertising and satisfy their duty to provide warnings directly to consumers, such a solution may work to undermine effective dissemination of risk information to patients because the one party best situated to convey such technical information in understandable terms will face reduced incentives to do so if the manufacturers also must provide warnings. * It makes more sense, at least so long as

prescription drugs continue to require the intervention of a medical professional, for courts to focus on the tort duty placed on physicians to secure informed consent, * while letting market mechanisms and regulatory requirements work to supplement rather than supplant the drug information provided to patients. *

Id. at 173, 179.

2. *Warnings and Unavoidably Unsafe Products.* How does the basic purpose of the product warning in *Perez* differ from that in *Uniroyal Goodrich Tire Co. v. Martinez?*

3. *Failure to Warn and "State of the Art."* Of what risks must the manufacturer warn? In Anderson v. Owens-Corning Fiberglas Corp., 53 Cal.3d 987, 281 Cal.Rptr. 528, 810 P.2d 549 (1991), the plaintiff alleged he contracted asbestosis and other lung ailments through exposure to asbestos products while working as an electrician at a navy shipyard from 1941 through 1976. He sued the asbestos product manufacturers for failure to warn of the health consequences of exposure to the product. The court upheld a version of the "state of the art" defense, and ruled that the defendants needed to warn only of risks that were "known or knowable in light of the generally recognized and prevailing best scientific and medical knowledge available at the time of manufacture and distribution." A small minority of cases has allowed recovery for failure to warn even when the risks were neither "known nor knowable." E.g., Beshada v. Johns-Manville Prods. Corp., 90 N.J. 191, 447 A.2d 539 (1982); compare Feldman v. Lederle Labs., 97 N.J. 429, 479 A.2d 374 (1984).

E. RECOVERY FOR ECONOMIC LOSS: THE INTERSECTION OF TORT AND CONTRACT

80 South Eighth Street Limited Partnership v. Carey-Canada, Inc.

Supreme Court of Minnesota, 1992.
486 N.W.2d 393.

■ KEITH, CHIEF JUSTICE. * * * The IDS Center, constructed in 1970–72, is 52 stories high and is comprised of four commercial buildings[.] * * * Two types of asbestos-containing fireproofing, Firebar and Monokote, were used in the construction of the IDS Center. * * * In 1986 and 1987 * * * 80 South Eighth * * * conducted tests which showed that Monokote, even when undisturbed, will release substantial numbers of asbestos fibers into all parts of the IDS Center, thereby posing a health hazard to the occupants of the building. In addition, 80 South Eighth has had to institute costly maintenance procedures to keep the ceiling tiles and light fixtures in the IDS Center free from asbestos fibers.

In 1988, 80 South Eighth brought suit against Grace for compensatory damages to cover the costs of maintenance, removal and replacement of the asbestos in the Center, for punitive damages, and for costs of that suit. 80 South Eighth claims that the original owners, architects, and general contractors had intended to avoid asbestos-containing fireproofing by selecting "cementitious" fireproofing and, were not aware that the Monokote installed in the IDS Center contained asbestos. 80 South Eighth does not seek damages for personal injuries and there are no allegations of personal injuries caused by the asbestos-containing fireproofing used in the building. * * *

Tort actions and contract actions protect different interests. Through a tort action, the duty of certain conduct is imposed by law and not necessarily by the will or intention of the parties. The duty may be owed to all those within the range of harm, or to a particular class of people. On the other hand, contract actions protect the interests in having promises performed. Contract obligations are imposed because of conduct of the parties manifesting consent, and are owed only to the specific parties named in the contract. *

The economic loss doctrine provides a balance between two conflicting societal goals: that of encouraging marketplace efficiency through the voluntary contractual allocation of economic risks with that of discouraging conduct that leads to physical harm. * * *

We agree with Grace that if 80 South Eighth's alleged injuries constitute economic losses, then [the economic loss rule] bars 80 South Eighth's tort claims. Here, 80 South Eighth seeks recovery for costs of maintenance, removal and replacement of the asbestos-containing fireproofing. Such a claim appears to be economic loss * * *. We find that the [economic loss rule] supports a definition of economic loss premised on a product's failure to perform as promised. The underlying assumption * * * in all our cases of economic loss is that commercial parties bring their experiences in the marketplace to the negotiations; that their reasonable contemplation is embodied in the transaction; that at the time of the contract formation they have defined the product, identified the risks, and negotiated a price of the goods that reflects the relative benefits and risks to each party. * * *

Here, however, there is a distinguishing factor. The claim here is not that the fireproofing failed to perform satisfactorily as fireproofing. Such a claim arising from the failure of the product to meet expectations of suitability, quality and performance resulting in damages which a party to a sales contract could reasonably expect would flow from a defect in the product is a benefit of the bargain claim better addressed under contract and the Uniform Commercial Code. Rather, the claim here is that the Monokote introduced into the building asbestos which is highly dangerous to humans. *

* * * We simply do not believe that 80 South Eighth's claim of asbestos contamination is one for economic loss. 80 South Eighth is not seeking enforcement of the benefit of their bargain regarding the fireproofing performance of the Monokote. In seeking the costs of maintenance, removal and replacement, 80 South Eighth seeks the costs of eliminating the risks of injury and of making the building safe for all those who use and occupy this property. * * * Instead, we find persuasive the state and federal decisions which have held that where the claim is for the contamination of the entire building with allegedly dangerous asbestos fibers, the claim is not one for economic loss. *

We believe that allowing 80 South Eighth to proceed in tort for damages relating to the maintenance, removal and replacement of asbestos-containing fireproofing advances both the rationale and public policy objectives of tort law and the Uniform Commercial Code. In the seminal economic loss case, Justice Traynor stated:

The distinction that the law has drawn between tort recovery for physical injuries and warranty recovery for economic loss * * * rests * * * on an understanding of the nature of the responsibility a manufacturer must undertake in distributing his products.

He can appropriately be held liable for physical injuries caused by defects by requiring his goods to match a standard of safety defined in terms of conditions that create unreasonable risks of harm. He cannot be held for the level of performance of his products in the consumer's business unless he agrees that the product was designed to meet the consumer's demands.

Seeley v. White Motor Co., 63 Cal.2d 9, 18, 45 Cal.Rptr. 17, 23, 403 P.2d 145, 151 (1965). Grace's fireproofing continues to provide fireproofing, but it does so by allegedly creating unreasonable risks of harm. Asbestos fibers, if inhaled, can disrupt the normal functioning of the lungs and cause serious health problems. * * * Rather than waiting for an occupant or user of the building to develop an asbestos related injury, we believe building owners should be encouraged to abate the hazard to protect the public. We believe our decision today will do so. * * * We therefore hold that the economic loss doctrine does not bar the owner of a building with asbestos-containing fireproofing from suing the manufacturer of the fireproofing under the tort theories of negligence and strict liability for the costs of maintenance, removal and replacement of the fireproofing. * * *

F. PLAINTIFF'S CONDUCT

Ellsworth v. Sherne Lingerie, Inc.

Court of Appeals of Maryland, 1985.
303 Md. 581, 495 A.2d 348.

■ McAULIFFE, JUDGE. * * * On the morning of February 25, 1980 plaintiff wore a lady's nightgown into the kitchen to make coffee. She admitted that she was wearing the nightgown inside out and as a result the two pockets at the sides were flapping or protruding. * * * [T]he plaintiff placed a tea kettle on the left front small burner of the electric range and turned the burner on "high." * * * The plaintiff reached above the stove to obtain a coffee filter from one of the cupboards, and as she was reaching her gown came very close to or in contact with the exposed portion of the burner. The evidence permitted but did not compel a finding that the ignition source was the left pocket. As a result of the burns, the plaintiff suffered severe and permanent injuries. * * *

Both defendants conceded it was foreseeable that the nightgown would be worn in a kitchen, and a defense expert conceded the likelihood it would be worn in close proximity to an electric range. Defense experts contended, however, that the fabric was safe for use in adult sleepwear * * *. Plaintiff's expert testified that the flammability characteristics of the nightgown caused it to be defective and unreasonably dangerous * * *. [T]he jury rendered a general verdict in favor of the defendants * * *. On appeal the Court of Special Appeals affirmed the lower court. * We granted plaintiff's petition for certiorari to consider the following question[ ]: Whether the trial judge's instructions on misuse of the product * * * constitute[s] reversible error * * *. Comment *h* to § 402 A provides a basis for the "misuse" defense. It states:

> A product is not in a defective condition when it is safe for normal handling and consumption. If the injury results from abnormal handling, as where a bottled beverage is knocked against a radiator to remove the cap; or from abnormal preparation for use, as where too much salt is added to food; or from abnormal consumption, as where a child eats too much candy and is made ill, the seller is not liable.

Most jurisdictions have adopted the Restatement view that misuse or abnormal use is a factor in a strict liability action. * The courts, however, are split on the question of whether the issue of misuse properly arises as a part of a plaintiff's case, or is an affirmative defense. Some courts have referred to misuse as an affirmative defense or part of the defendant's burden of proof. * The recent trend in a number of courts has been to consider the question of misuse as a part of the plaintiff's case, and as being directly related to the issues of defectiveness, or of proximate cause, or both. * * * The problem of understanding the issue of misuse in strict liability cases is further compounded by the absence of agreement as to the meaning of the word. * * * It has been suggested that misuse means any use not intended by the manufacturer, but this is too narrow and fails to take into account a variety of uses reasonably foreseeable although not subjectively intended. It has also been suggested that virtually anything is possible, and thus arguably foreseeable, so that foreseeability as a test is too broad.

We conclude, as have most courts which have considered the issue, that "reasonable foreseeability" is the appropriate test, and thus a seller is required to provide a product that is not unreasonably dangerous when used for a purpose and in a manner that is reasonably foreseeable. * If a product is unreasonably dangerous for such use it is "defective" within the meaning of § 402A of the Restatement, and if that defect is a cause of damage the seller will be responsible. On the other hand, if the product is not unreasonably dangerous when used for a purpose and in a manner that is reasonably foreseeable, it simply is not defective, and the seller will not be liable. *

Misuse of a product may also bar recovery where the misuse is the sole proximate cause of damage, or where it is the intervening or superseding cause. * For example, a high speed electric drill may be defective because a manufacturing defect causes it to short circuit and produce a shock during normal usage. A plaintiff who attaches a brush to that drill and in attempting to clean his teeth suffers injury to his mouth from the high speed of the brush will lose because his misuse is the sole cause of his misfortune, and the defect in the drill is not in any way related to the harm. *

Misuse may also embrace the concept of mishandling. As Comment *g* of § 402A states "the seller is not liable when he delivers the product in a safe condition, and subsequent mishandling . . . make[s] it harmful by the time it is consumed." The burden of proof is upon the plaintiff to show that the product was in a defective condition when it left the hands of the seller.

From what we have said it is apparent that questions of misuse of the product are involved in the determination of whether the product was defective, and whether a defect was the proximate cause of the injury. Because defectiveness and causation are elements which must be proved by the plaintiff, we conclude that misuse is not an affirmative defense. Misuse, therefore, is a "defense" only in the sense that proof of misuse negates one or more essential elements of a plaintiff's case, and may thereby defeat recovery. * * *

Applying these principles to the facts of this case, we conclude the evidence was insufficient to generate an issue of misuse, and that the trial judge erred in allowing the jury to consider misuse of the product as a possible bar to recovery. Clearly, and concededly, Appellant was using the nightgown for a reasonably foreseeable purpose. We conclude that her manner of use of the nightgown, though possibly careless, was reasonably foreseeable as a matter of law. It certainly may be foreseen that wearing apparel, such as nightgowns and robes, will occasionally be worn inside out. It is also foreseeable that a loosely fitting gown will come into contact with sources of ignition in the environment where it may be expected to be worn, and particularly when worn in the kitchen and near a stove. * * *

NOTES

1. *Misuse as a Defense to Products Liability Actions.* Comment *a* to Section 17 of the Restatement (Third) of Torts: Products Liability (1998) is understated in saying that "[c]ertain forms of consumer behavior—product misuse and product alteration or modification—have been the subject of much confusion and misunderstanding." The Third Restatement sorts out the confusion in this manner:

> Early decisions treated product misuse, alteration, and modification, whether by the plaintiff or a third party, as a total bar to recovery against a product seller. Today misuse, alteration, and modification relate to one of three issues in a products liability action. In some cases, misuse, alteration, and modification are important in determining whether the product is defective. In others, they are relevant to the issue of legal cause. Finally, when the plaintiff misuses, alters, or modifies the product, such conduct may constitute contributory fault and reduce the plaintiff's recovery under the rules of comparative responsibility. * * * Jurisdictions differ on the question of who bears the burden of proof regarding conduct that constitutes misuse, modification, and alteration. * * *
>
> * * * The majority position is that all forms of plaintiff's failure to conform to applicable standards of care are to be considered for the purpose of apportioning responsibility between the plaintiff and the product seller or distributor.

Restatement (Third) of Torts: Products Liability § 17 cmts. a, c, d (1998).

2. *Crashworthiness.* What if it is reasonably foreseeable that the defective design of an automobile or other product will increase the probability or severity of injuries in an accident, even if the product defect

was not a cause of the accident? This issue was intensely contested in a series of cases in the 1960s and 1970s, often referred to as "second collision" or "crashworthiness" cases. Compare, e.g., Evans v. Gen. Motors Corp., 359 F.2d 822, 825 (7th Cir.1966) (defendant's duty was "only to ensure that [automobile] was reasonably fit for its intended purpose"; "intended purpose * * * does not include its participation in * * * collisions"); with Nanda v. Ford Motor Co., 509 F.2d 213, 218 (7th Cir.1974) ("when an automobile is so constructed that its occupants are subjected to an unreasonable risk of being severely injured if it becomes involved in an accident that is not of a highly extraordinary kind, the manufacturer is liable for resulting injuries"). Courts now generally hold that while the "intended" use of an automobile does not include participating in a collision, such an event is reasonably foreseeable. Thus, an automobile not otherwise defective that contains a design feature that unreasonably enhances the injuries of occupants or others in the event of a collision may be considered defective, and the design feature may be considered a cause of the enhanced injuries. See generally Restatement (Third) of Torts § 16 cmt. a (1998).

Daly v. General Motors Corp.

Supreme Court of California, 1978.

20 Cal.3d 725, 144 Cal.Rptr. 380, 575 P.2d 1162.

■ RICHARDSON, J. The most important of several problems which we consider is whether the principles of comparative negligence expressed by us in Li v. Yellow Cab Co., 13 Cal.3d 804, 119 Cal.Rptr. 858, 532 P.2d 1226 (1975), apply to actions founded on strict products liability. We will conclude that they do. * * *

In the early hours of October 31, 1970, decedent Kirk Daly, a 36-year-old attorney, was driving his Opel southbound on the Harbor Freeway in Los Angeles. The vehicle, while travelling at a speed of 50–70 miles per hour, collided with and damaged 50 feet of metal divider fence. After the initial impact between the left side of the vehicle and the fence the Opel spun counterclockwise, the driver's door was thrown open, and Daly was forcibly ejected from the car and sustained fatal head injuries. It was equally undisputed that had the deceased remained in the Opel his injuries, in all probability, would have been relatively minor. * * * The sole theory of plaintiff's complaint was strict liability for damages allegedly caused by a defective product, namely, an improperly designed door latch claimed to have been activated by the impact. * * *

Over plaintiffs' objections, defendants were permitted to introduce evidence indicating that: (1) the Opel was equipped with a seat belt-shoulder harness system, and a door lock, either of which if used, it was contended, would have prevented Daly's ejection from the vehicle; (2) Daly used neither the harness system nor the lock; (3) the 1970 Opel owner's manual contained warnings that seat belts should be worn and doors locked when the car was in motion for "accident security"; and (4) Daly was intoxicated at the time of collision, which evidence the jury was advised was admitted for the limited purpose of determining whether decedent had used the vehicle's safety equipment. After relatively brief deliberations the jury returned a verdict favoring all defendants, and plaintiffs appeal from the ensuing adverse judgment.

In response to plaintiffs' assertion that the "intoxication-nonuse" evidence was improperly admitted, defendants contend that the deceased's own conduct contributed to his death. Because plaintiffs' case rests upon strict products liability based on improper design of the door latch and because defendants assert a failure in decedent's conduct, namely, his alleged intoxication and nonuse of safety equipment, without which the accident and ensuing death would not have occurred, there is thereby posed the overriding issue in the case, should comparative principles apply in strict products liability actions? * * *

* * * In Greenman v. Yuba Power Products, Inc., 59 Cal.2d 57, 27 Cal.Rptr. 697, 377 P.2d 897 (1963), * * * [o]ur avowed purpose was "to insure that the costs of injuries resulting from defective products are borne by the manufacturer that put such products on the market rather than by the injured persons who are powerless to protect themselves." * * * From its inception, however, strict liability has never been, and is not now, *absolute* liability. As has been repeatedly expressed, under strict liability the manufacturer does not thereby become the insurer of the safety of the product's user. * On the contrary, the plaintiff's injury must have been caused by a "defect" in the product. * * * Furthermore, we have recognized that though most forms of contributory negligence do not constitute a defense to a strict products liability action, plaintiff's negligence is a complete defense when it comprises assumption of risk. * * *

Those counseling against the recognition of comparative fault principles in strict products liability cases vigorously stress, perhaps equally, not only the conceptual, but also the semantic difficulties incident to such a course. The task of merging the two concepts is said to be impossible, that "apples and oranges" cannot be compared, that "oil and water" do not mix, and that strict liability, which is not founded on negligence or fault, is inhospitable to comparative principles. The syllogism runs, contributory negligence was only a defense to negligence, comparative negligence only affects contributory negligence, therefore comparative negligence cannot be a defense to strict liability. * While fully recognizing the theoretical and semantic distinctions between the twin principles of strict products liability and traditional negligence, we think they can be blended or accommodated. * * *

We pause at this point to observe that where, as here, a consumer or user sues the manufacturer or designer alone, technically, neither fault nor conduct is really compared functionally. The conduct of one party in combination with the product of another, or perhaps the placing of a defective article in the stream of projected and anticipated use, may produce the ultimate injury. In such a case, as in the situation before us, we think the term "equitable apportionment or allocation of loss" may be more descriptive than "comparative fault." * * *

As we have noted, we sought to place the burden of loss on manufacturers rather than ". . . injured persons *who are powerless to protect themselves . . . .*" Greenman, *supra*, at 63. * * * The foregoing goals, we think, will not be frustrated by the adoption of comparative principles. Plaintiffs will continue to be relieved of proving that the manufacturer or distributor was negligent in the production, design, or dissemination of the article in question. Defendant's liability for injuries caused by a defective product remains strict. The principle of protecting the defenseless is likewise preserved, for plaintiff's recovery will be reduced *only* to the extent that his own lack of reasonable care contributed to his injury. The cost of compensating the victim of a defective product, albeit proportionately reduced, remains on defendant manufacturer, and will, through him, be "spread among society." However, we do not permit plaintiff's own conduct relative to the product to escape unexamined, and as to that share of plaintiff's damages which flows from his own fault we discern no reason of policy why it should * * * be borne by others. Such a result would directly contravene the principle announced in Li [v. Yellow Cab Co., 13 Cal.3d 804, 119 Cal.Rptr. 858, 532 P.2d 1226 (1975)], that loss should be assessed equitably in proportion to fault.

We conclude, accordingly, that the expressed purposes which persuaded us in the first instance to adopt strict liability in California would not be thwarted were we to apply comparative principles. What would be forfeit is a degree of semantic symmetry. * * *

A second objection to the application of comparative principles in strict products liability cases is that a manufacturer's incentive to produce safe products will thereby be reduced or removed. While we fully recognize this concern we think, for several reasons, that the problem is more shadow than substance. First, of course, the manufacturer cannot avoid its continuing liability for a defective product even when the plaintiff's own conduct has contributed to his injury. The manufacturer's liability, and therefore its incentive to avoid and correct product defects, remains; its exposure will be lessened only to the extent that the trier finds that the victim's conduct contributed to his injury. Second, as a practical matter a manufacturer, in a particular case, cannot assume that the user of a defective product upon whom an injury is visited will be blameworthy. Doubtless, many users are free of fault, and a defect is at least as likely as not to be exposed by an entirely innocent plaintiff who will obtain full recovery. In such cases the manufacturer's incentive toward safety both in design and production is wholly unaffected. Finally, we must observe that under the present law, which recognizes assumption of risk as a complete defense to products liability, the curious and cynical message is that it profits the manufacturer to make his product so defective that in the event of injury he can argue that the user had to be aware of its patent defects. To that extent the incentives are inverted. We conclude, accordingly, that no substantial or significant impairment of the safety incentives of defendants will occur by the adoption of comparative principles. * * *

A third objection to the merger of strict liability and comparative fault focuses on the claim that, as a practical matter, triers of fact, particularly jurors, cannot assess, measure, or compare plaintiff's negligence with defendant's strict liability. We are unpersuaded by the argument and are convinced that jurors are able to undertake a fair apportionment of liability.

We are strengthened in the foregoing conclusion by the federal experience under the maritime doctrine of "unseaworthiness." For decades, seamen have been permitted to recover from shipowners for injuries caused by defects rendering a vessel "unseaworthy." * * * Nonetheless, comparative principles have been made applicable to suits brought under the "unseaworthiness" doctrine, a form of strict liability, and the degree to which plaintiff's own negligence contributes to his injuries has been considered in determining the amount of his recovery.

* * * [W]e conclude that a system of comparative fault should be and it is hereby extended to actions founded on strict products liability. In such cases the separate defense of "assumption of risk," to the extent that it is a form of contributory negligence, is abolished. While, as we have suggested, on the particular facts before us, the term "equitable apportionment of loss" is more accurately descriptive of the process, nonetheless, the term "comparative fault" has gained such wide acceptance by courts and in the literature that we adopt its use herein.

* * * The judgment is reversed.

■ JEFFERSON, J., concurring in part and dissenting in part. * * * The majority's decision herein will require the jury, on the one hand, to * * * focus on the manufacturer's *product*—disregarding all questions of whether the manufacturer acted unreasonably or negligently—in order to determine defendant manufacturer's liability. On the other hand, the jury must next focus on plaintiff's *conduct*, in order to find that plaintiff was negligent. The jury must then *compare* its focus on plaintiff's negligent *conduct* with its focus on defendant's defective *product*—eliminating, as irrelevant, any consideration of whether defendant's conduct was unreasonable or negligent—to determine the amount of the reduction in plaintiff's total damages. The end result of this configurational analysis by a jury, I submit, based as it must be—on a comparison of noncomparables—will necessarily constitute a patently unfair result.

■ MOSK, J. I dissent. * * * The pure concept of products liability so pridefully fashioned and nurtured by this court for the past decade and a half is reduced to a shambles. * * *

NOTES

1. *Comparative Fault and Unreasonable Failure to Discover Risk.* A sizable number of jurisdictions continue to hold that the plaintiff's unreasonable failure to discover a risk does not constitute contributory negligence or comparative fault in a strict products liability action. For example, in West v. Caterpillar Tractor Co., Inc., 336 So.2d 80 (Fla. 1976), the Supreme Court of Florida stated:

> We recognize that contributory negligence of the user or consumer or bystander in the sense of a failure to discover a defect, or to guard against the possibility of its existence, is not a defense. Contributory negligence of the consumer or user by unreasonable use of a product after discovery of the defect and the danger is a valid defense. * * * The defendant manufacturer may assert that the plaintiff was negligent in some specified manner other than failing to discover or guard against a defect, such as assuming the risk, or misusing the product, and that such negligence was a substantial proximate cause of the plaintiff's injuries or damages. * * *

Id. at 90. Unlike the California Supreme Court, the Florida court reasoned that "the failure of the user to discover the defect in the product or the failure of the user to guard against the possibility of its existence" should not be a defense because "[t]he consumer or user is entitled to believe that the product will do the job for which it was built." *Id.* at 92.

According to Restatement (Third) of Torts: Products Liability, § 17 (1998) cmt. d, a majority of courts now reject the rule "that when the plaintiff's negligence is the failure to discover a product defect, reduction of damages on the basis of apportionment of responsibility is improper" and instead, consistent with *Daly*, hold "that all forms of plaintiff's failure to conform to applicable standards of care are to be considered for the purpose of apportioning responsibility between the plaintiff and the product seller or distributor." Comment *d* notes:

> Before the court will allow any apportionment of responsibility, the defendant must introduce sufficient evidence to support a finding of fault on the part of the plaintiff. Thus, for example, when the defendant claims that the plaintiff failed to discover a defect, there must be evidence that the plaintiff's conduct in failing to discover a defect did, in fact, fail to meet a standard of reasonable care. In general, a plaintiff has no reason to expect that a new product contains a defect and would have little reason to be on guard to discover it.

In Webb v. Navistar Int'l Transp. Corp., 166 Vt. 119, 692 A.2d 343 (1996), the Vermont Supreme Court held that all forms of plaintiff's comparative fault reduce defendant's liability in strict products liability cases. The court reasoned that "there is no reason to impose the cost of a plaintiff's negligence upon the manufacturer to spread among other consumers of the product." *Id.* at 129.

2.   *"Strict" Products Liability and Comparative "Fault."* As argued by Justice Jefferson in his dissent in *Daly*, the application of comparative "fault" in cases where the defendant's liability rests on "strict liability" principles arguably presents a conceptual dilemma. One answer to this dilemma is to assume that the manufacturer-defendant in fact does act with fault in cases where liability is premised on strict products liability:

> In the case of products liability, the fault inheres primarily in the nature of the product. The product is "bad" because it is not duly safe; it is determined to be defective and (in most jurisdictions) unreasonably dangerous. * * * [S]imply maintaining the bad condition or placing the bad product on the market is enough for liability. * * * One does not have to stigmatize conduct as negligent in order to characterize it as fault.

John W. Wade, Products Liability and Plaintiff's Fault—The Uniform Comparative Fault Act, 29 Mercer L. Rev. 373, 377 (1978).

In Murray v. Fairbanks Morse, 610 F.2d 149, 159 (3d Cir.1979), the United States Court of Appeals for the Third Circuit found this reconciliation to be unconvincing and instead proposed what has become a more popular means of comparing the fault of the manufacturer and the plaintiff in strict products liability cases:

> The substitution of the term fault for defect, however, would not appear to aid the trier of fact in apportioning damages between the defect and the conduct of the plaintiff. * * * The jury is not

asked to determine if the defendant deviated from a standard of care in producing his product. There is no proven faulty conduct of the defendant to compare with the faulty conduct of the plaintiff in order to apportion the responsibility for an accident. Although we may term a defective product "faulty," it is qualitatively different from the plaintiff's conduct that contributes to his injury. A comparison of the two is therefore inappropriate. * * *

We believe that if the loss for a particular injury is to be apportioned between the product defect and the plaintiff's misconduct, the only conceptual basis for comparison is the causative contribution of each to the particular loss or injury. In apportioning damages we are really asking how much of the injury was caused by the defect in the product versus how much was caused by the plaintiff's own actions. * * *

G. FEDERAL PREEMPTION

Cipollone v. Liggett Group, Inc.

Supreme Court of the United States, 1992.
505 U.S. 504, 112 S.Ct. 2608, 120 L.Ed.2d 407.

■ STEVENS, JUSTICE. "WARNING: THE SURGEON GENERAL HAS DETERMINED THAT CIGARETTE SMOKING IS DANGEROUS TO YOUR HEALTH." A federal statute enacted in 1969 requires that warning (or a variation thereof) to appear in a conspicuous place on every package of cigarettes sold in the United States.[1] The questions presented to us by this case are whether that statute, or its 1965 predecessor which required a less alarming label, preempted petitioner's common-law claims against respondent cigarette manufacturers.

Petitioner is the son of Rose Cipollone, who began smoking in 1942 and who died of lung cancer in 1984. He claims that respondents are responsible for Rose Cipollone's death because they breached express warranties contained in their advertising, because they failed to warn consumers about the hazards of smoking, because they fraudulently misrepresented those hazards to consumers, and because they conspired to deprive the public of medical and scientific information about smoking. The Court of Appeals held that petitioner's state-law claims were preempted by federal statutes * * *. We now reverse in part and affirm in part. * * *

In July 1965, Congress enacted the Federal Cigarette Labeling and Advertising Act (1965 Act or Act). * * * Section 4 of the Act made it unlawful to sell or distribute any cigarettes in the United States unless the package bore a conspicuous label stating: "CAUTION: CIGARETTE SMOKING MAY BE HAZARDOUS TO YOUR HEALTH." In furtherance of the second purpose, § 5, captioned "Preemption," provided in part:

---

[1] Public Health Cigarette Smoking Act of 1969, Pub. L. 91–222, 84 Stat. 87, as amended, 15 U. S. C. §§ 1331–1340. * * *

(a) No statement relating to smoking and health, other than the statement required by section 4 of this Act, shall be required on any cigarette package.

(b) No statement relating to smoking and health shall be required in the advertising of any cigarettes the packages of which are labeled in conformity with the provisions of this Act.

* * * [Later], Congress enacted the Public Health Cigarette Smoking Act of 1969 (1969 Act or Act), * which amended the 1965 Act in several ways. First, the 1969 Act strengthened the warning label, in part by requiring a statement that cigarette smoking "is dangerous" rather than that it "may be hazardous." * * * Third, and related, the 1969 Act modified the preemption provision by replacing the original § 5(b) with a provision that reads:

(b) No requirement or prohibition based on smoking and health shall be imposed under State law with respect to the advertising or promotion of any cigarettes the packages of which are labeled in conformity with the provisions of this Act. * * *

Article VI of the Constitution provides that the laws of the United States "shall be the supreme Law of the Land; . . . any Thing in the Constitution or Laws of any state to the Contrary notwithstanding." Art. VI, cl. 2. Thus, since our decision in McCulloch v. Maryland, 17 U.S. (4 Wheat.) 316, 427, 4 L.Ed. 579 (1819), it has been settled that state law that conflicts with federal law is "without effect." * Consideration of issues arising under the Supremacy Clause "start[s] with the assumption that the historic police powers of the States [are] not to be superseded by . . . [a] Federal Act unless that [is] the clear and manifest purpose of Congress." * * *

Congress' intent may be "explicitly stated in the statute's language or implicitly contained in its structure and purpose." * In the absence of an express congressional command, state law is preempted if that law actually conflicts with federal law, * or if federal law so thoroughly occupies a legislative field " 'as to make reasonable the inference that Congress left no room for the States to supplement it.' " * * * In our opinion, the preemptive scope of the 1965 Act and the 1969 Act is governed entirely by the express language in § 5 of each Act. * * *

In the 1965 preemption provision regarding advertising (§ 5(b)), Congress spoke precisely and narrowly: "No *statement* relating to smoking and health shall be required *in the advertising* of [properly labeled] cigarettes." Section 5(a) used the same phrase ("No *statement* relating to smoking and health") with regard to cigarette labeling. As § 5(a) made clear, that phrase referred to the sort of warning provided for in § 4, which set forth verbatim the warning Congress determined to be appropriate. Thus, on their face, these provisions merely prohibited state and federal rulemaking bodies from mandating particular cautionary statements on cigarette labels (§ 5(a)) or in cigarette advertisements (§ 5(b)).

Beyond the precise words of these provisions, this reading is appropriate for several reasons. First, as discussed above, we must construe these provisions in light of the presumption against the preemption of state police power regulations. * * * Second, the warning required in § 4 does not by its own effect foreclose additional obligations imposed under state law. That Congress requires a particular warning label does not automatically preempt a regulatory field. * Third, there is no general, inherent conflict between federal preemption of state warning requirements and the continued vitality of state common-law damages actions. * * * All of these considerations indicate that § 5 is best read as having superseded only positive enactments by legislatures or administrative agencies that mandate particular warning labels. * * *

Compared to its predecessor in the 1965 Act, the plain language of the preemption provision in the 1969 Act is much broader. First, the later Act bars not simply "statement[s]" but rather "requirement[s] or prohibition[s] . . . imposed under State law." Second, the later Act reaches beyond statements "in the advertising" to obligations "with respect to the advertising or promotion" of cigarettes.

Notwithstanding these substantial differences in language, both petitioner and respondents contend that the 1969 Act did not materially alter the preemptive scope of federal law. * * * We reject the parties' reading as incompatible with the language and origins of the amendments. * * * The 1969 Act worked substantial changes in the law: rewriting the label warning, banning broadcast advertising, and allowing the FTC to regulate print advertising. In the context of such revisions and in light of the substantial changes in wording, we cannot accept the parties' claim that the 1969 Act did not alter the reach of § 5(b). *

Petitioner next contends that * * * common-law damages actions do not impose "requirement[s] or prohibition[s]" and that Congress intended only to trump "state statute[s], injunction[s], or executive pronouncement[s]." * We disagree; such an analysis is at odds both with the plain words of the 1969 Act and with the general understanding of common-law damages actions. The phrase "[n]o requirement or prohibition" sweeps broadly and suggests no distinction between positive enactments and common law; to the contrary, those words easily encompass obligations that take the form of common-law rules. As we noted in another context, "[state] regulation can be as effectively exerted through an award of damages as through some form of preventive relief. The obligation to pay compensation can be, indeed is designed to be, a potent method of governing conduct and controlling policy." * * *

Moreover, common-law damages actions of the sort raised by petitioner are premised on the existence of a legal duty, and it is difficult to say that such actions do not impose "requirements or prohibitions." * Black's Law Dictionary 1489 (6th ed. 1990) (defining "tort" as "always [involving] a violation of some duty owing to plaintiff"). It is in this way that the 1969 version of § 5(b) differs from its predecessor: Whereas the common law would not normally require a vendor to use any specific *statement* on its packages or in its advertisements, it is the essence of the common law to enforce duties that are either affirmative *requirements* or negative *prohibitions*. We therefore reject petitioner's argument that the phrase "requirement or prohibition" limits the 1969 Act's preemptive scope to positive enactments by legislatures and agencies. * * *

[W]e must fairly but—in light of the strong presumption against preemption—narrowly construe the precise language of § 5(b) and we must look to each of petitioner's common-law claims to determine whether it is in fact preempted. The central inquiry in each case is straightforward: we ask whether the legal duty that is the predicate of the common-law damages action constitutes a "requirement or prohibition based on smoking and health . . . imposed under State law with respect to . . . advertising or promotion," giving that clause a fair but narrow reading. * * * [Justice Stevens then individually analyzes whether subsection 5(b) of the 1969 act preempts each of the plaintiff's common law claims. Only a sampling of this analysis is included here.]

Failure to Warn

To establish liability for a failure to warn, petitioner must show that "a warning is necessary to make a product . . . reasonably safe, suitable and fit for its intended use," that respondents failed to provide such a warning, and that that failure was a proximate cause of petitioner's injury. * * * Petitioner's claims are preempted to the extent that they rely on a state-law "requirement or prohibition . . . with respect to . . . advertising or promotion." Thus, insofar as claims under either failure-to-warn theory require a showing that respondents' post-1969 advertising or promotions should have included additional, or more clearly stated, warnings, those claims are preempted. * * *

Fraudulent Misrepresentation

* * * [P]etitioner's fraudulent-misrepresentation claims that do arise with respect to advertising and promotions (most notably claims based on allegedly false statements of material fact made in advertisements) are not preempted by § 5(b). Such claims are predicated not on a duty "based on smoking and health" but rather on a more general obligation—the duty not to deceive. * * * [B]oth the 1965 and the 1969 Acts explicitly reserved the FTC's authority to identify and punish deceptive advertising practices—an authority that the FTC had long exercised and continues to exercise. * This indicates that Congress intended the phrase "relating to smoking and health" (which was essentially unchanged by the 1969 Act) to be construed narrowly, so as not to proscribe the regulation of deceptive advertising. * * *

To summarize our holding: The 1965 Act did not preempt state-law damages actions; the 1969 Act preempts petitioner's claims based on a failure to warn and the neutralization of federally mandated warnings to the extent that those claims rely on omissions or inclusions in respondents' advertising or promotions; the 1969 Act does not preempt petitioner's claims based on express warranty, intentional fraud and misrepresentation, or conspiracy. * * *

NOTES

1. *Distinguishing Preempted Claims.* How convincing is the attempt of the plurality opinion to distinguish certain claims that establish "requirement[s] or prohibition[s] based on smoking and health * * *

imposed under State law with respect to * * * advertising or promotion" from other claims that do not?

With *Cipollone*, compare Altria Group, Inc. v. Good, 555 U.S. 70, 129 S.Ct. 538, 172 L.Ed.2d 398 (2008). In *Altria* the Supreme Court held that the Federal Cigarette Labeling and Advertising Act (1965) did not eliminate the potential liability of tobacco manufacturers under Maine's Unfair Trade Practices Act for misrepresentations that their products were "light" and had "lowered tar and nicotine." Because the defendant's alleged violation under the state act was the duty not to deceive, it was not "based on smoking and health," a requirement for preemption under the Court's interpretation of the federal act.

2. *Other Ways in which Warning Requirements Benefited Manufacturers.* In addition to preempting at least some common law claims, in what other way might the two federal acts mandating cigarette warning labels serve the interest of tobacco companies in common law litigation against them?

Mutual Pharmaceutical Co. v. Bartlett

Supreme Court of the United States, 2013.
570 U.S. ____, 133 S.Ct. 2466, 186 L.Ed.2d 607.

■ ALITO, J. * * * Under the Federal Food, Drug, and Cosmetic Act (FDCA), * drug manufacturers must gain approval from the United States Food and Drug Administration (FDA) before marketing any drug in interstate commerce. * * * In order for the FDA to consider a drug safe, the drug's "probable therapeutic benefits must outweigh its risk of harm." * The process of submitting an NDA [new-drug application] is both onerous and lengthy. * * * Once a drug—whether generic or brand-name—is approved, the manufacturer is prohibited from making any major changes to the "qualitative or quantitative formulation of the drug product, including active ingredients, or in the specifications provided in the approved application." * Generic manufacturers are also prohibited from making any unilateral changes to a drug's label. *

In 1978, the FDA approved a nonsteroidal anti-inflammatory pain reliever called "sulindac" under the brand name Clinoril. When Clinoril's patent expired, the FDA approved several generic sulindacs, including one manufactured by Mutual Pharmaceutical. * In a very small number of patients, NSAIDs [nonsteroidal anti-inflammatory drugs]—including both sulindac and popular NSAIDs such as ibuprofen, naproxen, and Cox2-inhibitors—have the serious side effect of causing two hypersensitivity skin reactions characterized by necrosis of the skin and of the mucous membranes[.] * * *

In December 2004, respondent Karen L. Bartlett was prescribed Clinoril for shoulder pain. Her pharmacist dispensed a generic form of sulindac, which was manufactured by petitioner Mutual Pharmaceutical. Respondent soon developed an acute case of toxic epidermal necrolysis. The results were horrific. Sixty to sixty-five percent of the surface of respondent's body deteriorated, was burned off, or turned into an open wound. She spent months in a medically induced coma, underwent 12 eye surgeries, and was tube-fed for a year. She is now severely disfigured, has a number of physical disabilities, and is nearly blind.

At the time respondent was prescribed sulindac, the drug's label did not specifically refer to * * * toxic epidermal necrolysis, but did warn that the drug could cause "severe skin reactions" and "[f]atalities." * However, * * * toxic epidermal necrolysis [was] listed as [a] potential adverse reaction[ ] on the drug's package insert. * In 2005—once respondent was already suffering from toxic epidermal necrolysis—the FDA * * * recommended changes to the labeling of all NSAIDs, including sulindac, to more explicitly warn against toxic epidermal necrolysis. *

Respondent sued Mutual in New Hampshire state court, and Mutual removed the case to federal court. Respondent initially asserted both failure-to-warn and design-defect claims, but the District Court dismissed her failure-to-warn claim based on her doctor's "admi[ssion] that he had not read the box label or insert." * After a 2-week trial on respondent's design-defect claim, a jury found Mutual liable and awarded respondent over $21 million in damages. The Court of Appeals affirmed. * As relevant, it found that neither the FDCA nor the FDA's regulations preempted respondent's design-defect claims. * * * We granted certiorari. * * *

* * * [I]t has long been settled that state laws that conflict with federal law are "without effect." * Even in the absence of an express preemption provision, the Court has found state law to be impliedly preempted where it is "impossible for a private party to comply with both state and federal requirements." * In the instant case, it was impossible for Mutual to comply with both its state-law duty to strengthen the warnings on sulindac's label and its federal-law duty not to alter sulindac's label. Accordingly, the state law is preempted.

We begin by identifying petitioner's duties under state law. As an initial matter, respondent is wrong in asserting that the purpose of New Hampshire's design-defect cause of action "is compensatory, not regulatory." * Rather, New Hampshire's design-defect cause of action imposes affirmative duties on manufacturers. * * * [R]espondent's argument conflates what we will call a "strict-liability" regime (in which liability does not depend on negligence, but still signals the breach of a duty) with what we will call an "absolute-liability" regime (in which liability does not reflect the breach of any duties at all, but merely serves to spread risk). New Hampshire has adopted the former, not the latter. * * * New Hampshire requires manufacturers to ensure that the products they design, manufacture, and sell are not "unreasonably dangerous." The New Hampshire Supreme Court has recognized that this duty can be satisfied either by changing a drug's design or by changing its labeling. Since Mutual did not have the option of changing sulindac's design, New Hampshire law ultimately required it to change sulindac's labeling.

Respondent argues that, even if New Hampshire law does impose a duty on drug manufacturers, that duty does not encompass either the "duty to change sulindac's design" or the duty "to change sulindac's labeling." * That argument cannot be correct. New Hampshire imposes design-defect liability only where "the design of the product created a defective condition unreasonably dangerous to the user." * To determine whether a product is "unreasonably dangerous," the New Hampshire Supreme Court employs a "risk-utility approach" under which "a product is defective as designed if the magnitude of the danger outweighs the utility of the product." * That risk-utility approach requires a "multifaceted balancing process involving evaluation of many conflicting factors." * While the set of factors to be considered is ultimately an open one, the New Hampshire Supreme Court has repeatedly identified three factors as germane to the risk-utility inquiry: "the usefulness and desirability of the product to the public as a whole, whether the risk of danger could have been reduced without significantly affecting either the product's effectiveness or manufacturing cost, and the presence and efficacy of a warning to avoid an unreasonable risk of harm from hidden dangers or from foreseeable uses." *

In the drug context, either increasing the "usefulness" of a product or reducing its "risk of danger" would require redesigning the drug: A drug's usefulness and its risk of danger are both direct results of its chemical design and, most saliently, its active ingredients. * * * In the present case, however, redesign was not possible for two reasons. First, the FDCA requires a generic drug to have the same active ingredients, route of administration, dosage form, strength, and labeling as the brand-name drug on which it is based. * * * Second, because of sulindac's simple composition, the drug is chemically incapable of being redesigned. * Given the impossibility of redesigning sulindac, the only way for Mutual to ameliorate the drug's "risk-utility" profile—and thus to escape liability—was to strengthen "the presence and efficacy of [sulindac's] warning." * * * Thus, New Hampshire's design-defect cause of action imposed a duty on Mutual to strengthen sulindac's warnings.

For these reasons, it is unsurprising that allegations that sulindac's label was inadequate featured prominently at trial. Respondent introduced into evidence both the label for Mutual's sulindac at the time of her injuries and the label as revised in 2005 (after respondent had suffered her injuries). * * * And, the District Court repeatedly instructed the jury that it should evaluate sulindac's labeling in determining whether Mutual's sulindac was unreasonably dangerous. * Finally, the District Court clarified in its order and opinion denying Mutual's motion for judgment as a matter of law that the adequacy of sulindac's labeling had been part of what the jury was instructed to consider. * ("if the jury found that sulindac's risks outweighed its benefits, then it could consider whether the warning—regardless of its adequacy—reduced those risks ... to such an extent that it eliminated the unreasonable danger").[2]

Thus, in accordance with New Hampshire law, the jury was presented with evidence relevant to, and was instructed to consider, whether Mutual had fulfilled its duty to label sulindac adequately so as to render the drug not "unreasonably dangerous." In holding Mutual liable, the jury determined that Mutual had breached that duty.

---

[2] That Mutual's liability turned on the adequacy of sulindac's warnings is not unusual. Rather, New Hampshire—like a large majority of States—has adopted comment *k* to § 402A of the Restatement (Second) of Torts, which recognizes that it is "especially common in the field of drugs" for products to be "incapable of being made safe for their intended and ordinary use." * Under comment *k*, "[s]uch a product, properly prepared, and accompanied by proper directions and warning, is not defective, nor is it *unreasonably* dangerous." * * *

The duty imposed by federal law is far more readily apparent. As *PLIVA[, Inc. v. Mensing,]* made clear, federal law prevents generic drug manufacturers from changing their labels. See 564 U.S. ___, ___, 131 S.Ct. 2567, 2577, 180 L.Ed.2d 580, 591 (2011) * See also 21 CFR §§314.94(a)(8)(iii), 314.150(b)(10) (approval for a generic drug may be withdrawn if the generic drug's label "is no longer consistent with that for [the brand-name] drug"). Thus, federal law prohibited Mutual from taking the remedial action required to avoid liability under New Hampshire law.

When federal law forbids an action that state law requires, the state law is "without effect." * Because it is impossible for Mutual and other similarly situated manufacturers to comply with both state and federal law, * New Hampshire's warning-based design-defect cause of action is preempted with respect to FDA-approved drugs sold in interstate commerce. *

The Court of Appeals reasoned that Mutual could escape the impossibility of complying with both its federal- and state-law duties by "choos[ing] not to make [sulindac] at all." * We reject this "stop-selling" rationale as incompatible with our preemption jurisprudence. Our preemption cases presume that an actor seeking to satisfy both his federal- and state-law obligations is not required to cease acting altogether in order to avoid liability. Indeed, if the option of ceasing to act defeated a claim of impossibility, impossibility preemption would be "all but meaningless." *

The incoherence of the stop-selling theory becomes plain when viewed through the lens of our previous cases. In every instance in which the Court has found impossibility preemption, the "direct conflict" between federal- and state-law duties could easily have been avoided if the regulated actor had simply ceased acting.

PLIVA is an obvious example: As discussed above, the *PLIVA* Court held that state failure-to-warn claims were preempted by the FDCA because it was impossible for drug manufacturers like PLIVA to comply with both the state-law duty to label their products in a way that rendered them reasonably safe and the federal-law duty not to change their drugs' labels. * It would, of course, have been possible for drug manufacturers like PLIVA to pull their products from the market altogether. In so doing, they would have avoided liability under both state and federal law: such manufacturers would neither have labeled their products in a way that rendered them unsafe nor impermissibly changed any federally approved label. * * * Adopting the First Circuit's stop-selling rationale would mean that not only *PLIVA*, but also the vast majority—if not all—of the cases in which the Court has found impossibility preemption, were wrongly decided. Just as the prospect that a regulated actor could avoid liability under both state and federal law by simply leaving the market did not undermine the impossibility analysis in *PLIVA*, so it is irrelevant to our analysis here. * * *

The dissent responds that New Hampshire law "merely create[s] an incentive" to alter sulindac's label or composition, * but does not impose any actual "legal obligation." * The contours of that argument are difficult to discern. Perhaps the dissent is drawing a distinction between common-law "exposure to liability," * and a statutory "legal mandate." * But the distinction between common law and statutory law is irrelevant to the argument at hand: In violating a common-law duty, as surely as by violating a statutory duty, a party contravenes the law. While it is true that, in a certain sense, common-law duties give a manufacturer the choice "between exiting the market or continuing to sell while knowing it may have to pay compensation to consumers injured by its product," statutory "mandate[s]" do precisely the same thing: They require a manufacturer to choose between leaving the market and accepting the consequences of its actions (in the form of a fine or other sanction). * * *

* * * Here, as we have tried to make clear, the duty to ensure that one's products are not "unreasonably dangerous" imposed by New Hampshire's design-defect cause of action, * involves a duty to make one of several changes. In cases where it is impossible—in fact or by law—to alter a product's design (and thus to increase the product's "usefulness" or decrease its "risk of danger"), the duty to render a product "reasonably safe" boils down to a duty to ensure "the presence and efficacy of a warning to avoid an unreasonable risk of harm from hidden dangers or from foreseeable uses." * The duty to redesign sulindac's label was thus a part of the common-law duty at issue—not merely an action Mutual might have been prompted to take by the adverse jury verdict here. * * *

■ BREYER, J. & KAGAN, J., dissenting. * * *

■ SOTOMAYOR, J., joined by GINSBURG, J., dissenting. In PLIVA, Inc. v. Mensing, 564 U.S. ___, 131 S.Ct. 2567, 180 L.Ed.2d 580 (2011), this Court expanded the scope of impossibility preemption to immunize generic drug manufacturers from state-law failure-to-warn claims. Today, the Court unnecessarily and unwisely extends its holding in Mensing to preempt New Hampshire's law governing design-defects with respect to generic drugs.

The Court takes this step by concluding that petitioner Mutual Pharmaceutical was held liable for a failure-to-warn claim in disguise, even though the District Court clearly rejected such a claim and instead allowed liability on a distinct theory. Of greater consequence, the Court appears to justify its revision of respondent Karen Bartlett's state-law claim through an implicit and undefended assumption that federal law gives pharmaceutical companies a right to sell a federally approved drug free from common-law liability. Remarkably, the Court derives this proposition from a federal law that, in order to protect consumers, prohibits manufacturers from distributing new drugs in commerce without federal regulatory approval, and specifically disavows any intent to displace state law absent a direct and positive conflict. * * *

I begin with "two cornerstones of our preemption jurisprudence," Wyeth v. Levine, 555 U.S. 555, 565, 129 S.Ct. 1187, 173 L.Ed.2d 51 (2009), that should control this case but are conspicuously absent from the majority opinion. First, " 'the purpose of Congress is the ultimate touchstone' in every preemption case." Second, we start from the "assumption that the historic police powers of the States [are] not to be superseded by [a] Federal Act unless that was the clear and manifest purpose of Congress." * "That assumption," we have explained, "applies with particular force when," as is the case here, "Congress has legislated in a field traditionally occupied by the States." Altria Group, Inc. v. Good, 555 U.S. 70, 77, 129 S.Ct. 538, 172 L.Ed.2d 398 (2008).[1]

The Court applied both of these principles to the Federal Food, Drug, and Cosmetic Act (FDCA) * in *Levine,* where we held that a state failure-to-warn claim against a brand-name drug manufacturer was not preempted by federal law. * Tracing the history of federal drug regulation * * *, the Court explained that federal drug law and state common-law liability have long been understood to operate in tandem to promote consumer safety. * That basic principle, which the majority opinion elides, is essential to understanding this case.

* * * [T]he FDA's permission to market a drug has never been regarded as a final stamp of approval of the drug's safety. Under the FDCA, manufacturers, who have greater "access to information about their drugs" than the FDA, * retain the ultimate responsibility for the safety of the products they sell. In addition to their ongoing obligations to monitor a drug's risks and to report adverse drug responses to the FDA, * * * state common law plays an important "complementary" role to federal drug regulation. * Federal law in this area was initially intended to "supplemen[t] the protection for consumers already provided by state regulation and common-law liability." * * * Congress has not enacted a preemption provision for prescription drugs (whether brand-name or generic) even as it enacted such provisions with respect to other products regulated by the FDA. *

Congress' preservation of a role for state law generally, and common-law remedies specifically, reflects a realistic understanding of the limitations of *ex ante* federal regulatory review in this context. On its own, even rigorous preapproval clinical testing of drugs is "generally . . . incapable of detecting adverse effects that occur infrequently, have long latency periods, or affect subpopulations not included or adequately represented in the studies." [David A.] Kessler[a] & [David C.] Vladeck, A Critical Examination of the FDA's Efforts to Preempt Failure-to-Warn Claims, 96 Geo. L. J. 461, 471 (2008). * * *

Perhaps most significant, state common law provides injured consumers like Karen Bartlett with an opportunity to seek redress that is not available under federal law. "[U]nlike most administrative and legislative regulations," common-law claims "necessarily perform an important remedial role in compensating accident victims." Sprietsma v. Mercury Marine, 537 U.S. 51, 64, 123 S.Ct. 518, 154 L.Ed.2d 466 (2002). While the Court has not always been consistent on this issue, it has repeatedly cautioned against reading federal statutes to "remove all means of judicial recourse for those injured" when Congress did not provide a federal remedy. * And in fact, the legislative history of the FDCA suggests that Congress chose not to create a federal cause of

---

[1] The majority's failure to adhere to the presumption against preemption is well illustrated by the fact that the majority calls on Congress to provide greater clarity with regard to the "difficult preemption questions that arise in the prescription drug context." Certainly, clear direction from Congress on preemption questions is useful. But the whole point of the presumption against preemption is that congressional ambiguity should cut in favor of preserving state autonomy.

[a] [Eds.' note] Dr. Kessler served as Commissioner of the Food and Drug Administration, appointed originally by President George H.W. Bush, a Republican, and later reappointed by President William J. Clinton, a Democrat.

action for damages precisely because it believed that state tort law would allow injured consumers to obtain compensation. *

In light of this background, Mutual should face an uphill climb to show that federal law preempts a New Hampshire strict-liability claim against a generic drug manufacturer for defective design. The majority nevertheless accepts Mutual's argument that "compliance with both federal and state [law was] a physical impossibility." * But if state and federal law are properly understood, it is clear that New Hampshire's design-defect claim did not impose a legal obligation that Mutual had to violate federal law to satisfy.

Impossibility preemption "is a demanding defense," * that requires the defendant to show an "irreconcilable conflict" between federal and state legal obligations. * The logic underlying true impossibility preemption is that when state and federal law impose irreconcilable affirmative requirements, no detailed "inquiry into congressional design" is necessary because the inference that Congress would have intended federal law to displace the conflicting state requirement "is inescapable." * * * [I]mpossibility does not exist where one sovereign's * laws merely create an incentive to take an action that the other sovereign has not authorized because it is possible to comply with both laws. * * * In keeping with the strict standard for impossibility, cases that actually find preemption on that basis are rare. * * *

To assess whether it is physically impossible for Mutual to comply with both federal and state law, it is necessary to identify with precision the relevant legal obligations imposed under New Hampshire's design-defect cause of action. The majority insists that Mutual was required by New Hampshire's design-defect law to strengthen its warning label. In taking this position, the majority effectively re-characterizes Bartlett's design-defect claim as a *de facto* failure-to-warn claim. The majority then relies on that recharacterization to hold that the jury found Mutual liable for failing to fulfill its duty to label sulindac adequately, which *Mensing* forbids because a generic drug manufacturer cannot independently alter its safety label. * But the majority's assertion that Mutual was held liable in this case for violating a legal obligation to change its label is inconsistent with both New Hampshire state law and the record.

For its part, Mutual, in addition to making the argument now embraced by the majority, contends that New Hampshire's design-defect law effectively required it to change the chemical composition of sulindac. Mutual claims that it was physically impossible to comply with that duty consistent with federal law because drug manufacturers may not change the chemical composition of their products so as to create new drugs without submitting a new drug application for FDA approval. * But just as New Hampshire's design-defect law did not impose a legal obligation for Mutual to change its label, it also did not mandate that Mutual change the drug's design.

* * * New Hampshire recognizes strict liability for three different types of product defects: manufacturing defects, design defects, and warning defects. * Because the District Court granted Mutual summary judgment on Bartlett's failure-to-warn claim, only New Hampshire's design-defect cause of action remains at issue in this case. * * *

The design-defect claim that was applied to Mutual subjects the manufacturer of an unreasonably dangerous product to liability, but it does not require that manufacturer to take any specific action that is forbidden by federal law. Specifically, and contrary to the majority, New Hampshire's design-defect law did not require Mutual to change its warning label. A drug's warning label is just one factor in a nonexclusive list for evaluating whether a drug is unreasonably dangerous, * and an adequate label is therefore neither a necessary nor a sufficient condition for avoiding design-defect liability. Likewise, New Hampshire law imposed no duty on Mutual to change sulindac's chemical composition. The New Hampshire Supreme Court has held that proof of an alternative feasible design is not an element of a design-defect claim, * and as the majority recognizes, sulindac was not realistically capable of being redesigned anyway because it is a single-molecule drug. *

To be sure, New Hampshire's design-defect claim creates an incentive for drug manufacturers to make changes to its product, including to the drug's label, to try to avoid liability. And respondent overstates her case somewhat when she suggests that New Hampshire's strict-liability law is purely compensatory. * As is typically true of strict-liability regimes, New Hampshire's law, which mandates compensation only for "defective" products, serves both compensatory and regulatory purposes. * But exposure to liability, and the "incidental regulatory effects" that flow from that exposure, * is not equivalent to a legal mandate for a regulated party to take (or refrain from taking) a specific action. This difference is a significant one: A mandate leaves no choice for a party that wishes to comply with the law, whereas an incentive may only influence a choice. * * *

* * * The fact that imposing strict liability for injuries caused by a defective drug design might make a drug manufacturer want to change its label or design (or both) does not mean the manufacturer was actually required by state law to take either action. And absent such a legal obligation, the majority's impossibility argument does not get off the ground, because there was no state requirement that it was physically impossible for Mutual to comply with while also following federal law. * * * New Hampshire's design-defect law did not require Mutual to do anything other than to compensate consumers who were injured by an unreasonably dangerous drug. * * *

The majority notes that the District Court admitted evidence regarding sulindac's label. But the court did so because the label remained relevant for the more limited purpose of assessing, in combination with other factors, whether sulindac's design was defective because the product was unreasonably dangerous. * * *

* * * Though the majority insists otherwise, it appears to rely principally on an implicit assumption about rights conferred by federal premarket approval under the FDCA. After correctly observing that changing sulindac's chemical composition would create a new drug that would have to go through its own approval process, the majority reasons that Mutual must have been under a state-law duty to change its label because it had no other option to avoid liability while continuing to sell its product. But that conclusion is based on a false premise. A manufacturer of a drug that is unreasonably dangerous

under New Hampshire law has multiple options: It can change the drug's design or label in an effort to alter its risk-benefit profile, remove the drug from the market, or pay compensation as a cost of doing business. If federal law or the drug's chemical properties take the redesign option off the table, then that does not mean the manufacturer suddenly has a legal obligation under state law to improve the drug's label. * * * When a manufacturer cannot change the label or when doing so would not make the drug safe, the manufacturer may still choose between exiting the market or continuing to sell while knowing it may have to pay compensation to consumers injured by its product.[8]

From a manufacturer's perspective, that may be an unwelcome choice. But it is a choice that a sovereign State may impose to protect its citizens from dangerous drugs or at least ensure that seriously injured consumers receive compensation. * * *

It is simply incorrect to say that federal law presupposes that drug manufacturers have a right to continue to sell a drug free from liability once it has been approved. Nothing in the language of the FDCA, which is framed as a prohibition on distribution without FDA approval, * suggests such a right. * * * According to the FDA, while it has formal authority to withdraw approval for a drug based on new adverse information, it is far more common for a manufacturer to stop selling its product voluntarily after the FDA advises the manufacturer that the drug is unsafe and that its risk benefit profile cannot be adequately addressed through labeling changes or other measures. * * *

The most troubling aspect of the majority's decision to once again expand the scope of this Court's traditionally narrow impossibility preemption doctrine is what it implies about the relationship between federal premarket review and state common-law remedies more generally. Central to the majority's holding is an assumption that manufacturers must have a way to avoid state-law liability while keeping particular products in commerce. This assumption, it seems, will always create an automatic conflict between a federal premarket review requirement and state-law design-defect liability because premarket review, by definition, prevents manufacturers from unilaterally changing their products' designs. That is true, for example, of the designs (*i.e.*, the chemical composition) of brand-name drugs under the FDCA no less than it is for generic drugs.

If the creation of such an automatic conflict is the ultimate end-point of the majority's continued expansion of impossibility preemption, then the result is frankly astonishing. Congress adopted the FDCA's premarketing approval requirement in 1938 and then strengthened it in 1962 in response to serious public-health episodes involving unsafe

---

[8] The majority's suggestion that a manufacturer's option of continuing to sell while paying compensation is akin to violating a statutory mandate and then suffering the consequence (such as paying a fine) is flawed. In that scenario, the manufacturer would have violated the law, and the fact that the law is enforced through monetary sanctions (rather than through an injunction or imprisonment) would not change that. Here, no matter how many times the majority insists otherwise, a manufacturer who sells a drug whose design is found unreasonably dangerous based on a balance of factors has not violated a state law requiring it to change its label. In both cases, the manufacturer may owe money. But only in the former will it have failed to follow the law. Cf. Nat'l Fed'n of Indep. Bus. v. Sebelius, 567 U.S. __, __, 132 S.Ct. 2566, 2593–94, 183 L. Ed. 2d 450, 482 (2012) (recognizing that a condition that triggers a tax is not necessarily a "legal command" to take a certain action).

drugs. * Yet by the majority's lights, the very act of creating that requirement in order to "safeguard the consumer," * also created by operation of law a shield for drug manufacturers to avoid paying common-law damages under state laws that are also designed to protect consumers. That is so notwithstanding Congress' effort to disclaim any intent to preempt all state law. The majority's reasoning thus "has the 'perverse effect' of granting broad immunity 'to an entire industry that, in the judgment of Congress, needed more stringent regulation.' " *

This expanded notion of impossibility preemption threatens to disturb a considerable amount of state law. The FDCA's premarket approval process for prescription drugs has provided a model for the regulation of many other products.[15] In some statutes, Congress has paired premarket regulatory review with express preemption provisions that limit the application of state common-law remedies * * *. In other instances, such as with prescription drugs, it has not. Under the majority's approach, it appears that design-defect claims are categorically displaced either way, and Congress' efforts to set the boundaries of preemption more precisely were largely academic. This could have serious consequences for product safety. State design-defect laws play an important role not only in discovering risks, but also in providing incentives for manufacturers to remove dangerous products from the market promptly. * See [George W.] Conk, Is There a Design Defect in the Restatement (Third) of Torts: Products Liability? 109 Yale L. J. 1087, 1130 (2000) ("The tort system can encourage FDA regulatory vigor and competence"). If manufacturers of products that require preapproval are given *de facto* immunity from design-defect liability, then the public will have to rely exclusively on imperfect federal agencies with limited resources and sometimes limited legal authority to recall approved products. And consumers injured by those products will have no recourse. * * *

NOTES

1. *Contrasting Judicial Views of the Objectives of Tort Law.* How do the opinions of Justice Alito (majority opinion) and Justice Sotomayor reflect differing conceptions of the objectives of tort law?

2. *Wyeth v. Levine.* In its prior decision in Wyeth v. Levine, 555 U.S. 555, 129 S.Ct. 1187, 173 L.E.2d 51 (2009), which also raised a preemption defense under the FDCA and the FDA's regulations, the Supreme Court reached a decision that, to say the least, is in tension with the outcome in *Mutual Pharmaceutical.* The majority rejected defenses resting on both the impossibility and obstacle prongs of preemption. Addressing an obstacle defense, in his majority opinion, Justice Stevens wrote:

> Wyeth also argues that requiring it to comply with a state-law duty to provide a stronger warning * * * would obstruct the purposes and objectives of federal drug labeling regulation. Levine's tort claims, it maintains, are preempted because they interfere with "Congress's purpose to entrust an expert agency to make drug labeling decisions that strike a balance between competing objectives." * We find no merit in this argument, which

---

[15] See, *e.g.,* 7 U. S. C. §136a (pesticides); 21 U. S. C. §348 (food additives); §360b (animal drugs); §§360c(a)(1)(C), 360e (certain medical devices); §379e (color additives).

relies on an untenable interpretation of congressional intent and an overbroad view of an agency's power to preempt state law. Wyeth contends that the FDCA establishes both a floor and a ceiling for drug regulation: Once the FDA has approved a drug's label, a state-law verdict may not deem the label inadequate, regardless of whether there is any evidence that the FDA has considered the stronger warning at issue. The most glaring problem with this argument is that all evidence of Congress' purposes is to the contrary. Building on its 1906 Act, Congress enacted the FDCA to bolster consumer protection against harmful products. * Congress did not provide a federal remedy for consumers harmed by unsafe or ineffective drugs in the 1938 statute or in any subsequent amendment. Evidently, it determined that widely available state rights of action provided appropriate relief for injured consumers. * It may also have recognized that state-law remedies further consumer protection by motivating manufacturers to produce safe and effective drugs and to give adequate warnings.

If Congress thought state-law suits posed an obstacle to its objectives, it surely would have enacted an express preemption provision at some point during the FDCA's 70–year history. But despite its 1976 enactment of an express preemption provision for medical devices, * Congress has not enacted such a provision for prescription drugs. * Its silence on the issue, coupled with its certain awareness of the prevalence of state tort litigation, is powerful evidence that Congress did not intend FDA oversight to be the exclusive means of ensuring drug safety and effectiveness. * * *

Id. at 573–75.

In his dissenting opinion in *Wyeth*, Justice Alito revealed analysis that later bore fruit in his majority opinion in *Mutual Pharmaceutical*:

By their very nature, juries are ill equipped to perform the FDA's cost-benefit-balancing function. * * * [J]uries tend to focus on the risk of a particular product's design or warning label that arguably contributed to a particular plaintiff's injury, not on the overall benefits of that design or label; "the patients who reaped those benefits are not represented in court." Indeed, patients like respondent are the only ones whom tort juries ever see, and for a patient like respondent—who has already suffered a tragic accident—Phenergan's risks are no longer a matter of probabilities and potentialities.

In contrast, the FDA has the benefit of the long view. Its drug-approval determinations consider the interests of all potential users of a drug, including "those who would suffer without new medical [products]" if juries in all 50 States were free to contradict the FDA's expert determinations. * And the FDA conveys its warnings with one voice, rather than whipsawing the medical community with 50 (or more) potentially conflicting ones. After today's ruling, however, parochialism may prevail. The problem is well illustrated by the labels borne by "vesicant" drugs, many of which are used for chemotherapy. As a class, vesicants are much more dangerous than drugs like Phenergan, * but the vast majority of vesicant labels—like Phenergan's—either allow or do not disallow IV push. Because vesicant extravasation can have devastating consequences, and because the potentially lifesaving benefits of these drugs offer hollow solace to the victim of such a tragedy, a jury's cost-benefit analysis in a particular case may well differ from the FDA's. * * *

To be sure, state tort suits can peacefully coexist with the FDA's labeling regime, and they have done so for decades. But this case is far from peaceful coexistence. The FDA told Wyeth that Phenergan's label renders its use "safe." But the State of Vermont, through its tort law, said: "Not so." The state-law rule at issue here is squarely preempted. * * *

Id. at 626–28 (Alito, J., dissenting).

3. *State Legislative Changes.* A perception of crisis in the nation's liability insurance system erupted in the mid and late 1980s. "Some businesses saw their insurance premiums double in a period of two years, and others found the coverages they required totally unavailable." David J. Nye & Donald G. Gifford, The Myth of the Liability Insurance Claims Explosion: An Empirical Rebuttal, 41 Vand. L. Rev. 909, 909 n.2 (1988). Although these insurance availability and affordability problems appear in retrospect to have been caused by a variety of factors within the liability insurance and tort systems, see generally David J. Nye, Donald G. Gifford, Bernard L. Webb & Marvin A. Dewar, The Causes of the Medical Malpractice Crisis: An Analysis of Claims Data and Insurance Company Finances, 76 Geo. L.J. 1495, 1511–36 (1988), state legislatures most often responded with legislative changes designed to reduce payments to plaintiffs. See Joseph Sanders & Craig Joyce, "Off to the Races": The 1980s Tort Crisis and the Law Reform Process, 27 Hous. L. Rev. 207 (1990) (with table at 220–22, summarizing legislative changes in 48 states between 1985 and 1988). State legislative efforts to limit tort liability continued into the 1990s.

For example, a bill passed by the Ohio General Assembly and signed into law by the governor in 1996 attempted to change more than 100 sections of the Ohio Revised Code.[a] Many of the provisions addressed issues covering a broad range of tort cases, e.g., caps on damages, Ohio Rev. Code § 2305.01 and collateral benefits, § 2317.45, but others focused specifically on the restrictions of products liability, e.g., statute of repose, Ohio Rev. Code § 2305.10 [C] (in most cases, manufacturer cannot be held liable more than 15 years after initial sale of product, regardless of when plaintiff's injury or disease first manifested itself). For a fascinating narrative of this struggle between the Ohio legislature and its courts for control of the tort system, see State ex rel. Ohio Acad. of Trial Lawyers v. Sheward, 86 Ohio St.3d 451, 715 N.E.2d 1062 (1999) (invalidating much of the "reform" effort).

---

a   [Eds.' note] Am. Sub. H.B. 350, 121st Gen. Assemb., Reg. Sess. (Ohio 1996).

CHAPTER 12

INSURANCE AND THE TORT SYSTEM

By now it should be evident to you that the tort system functions in the context of the insurance system. This means "that when courts talk and reason about a rule of law as though the judgment were to come out of the defendant's pocket, they are often thinking in terms of complete unreality." Harper, James and Gray on Torts § 13.4. The modern day prevalence of liability insurance has played a critical role in the development of tort law, as exemplified by the willingness of courts to adopt a strict liability standard in the products liability arena and to abrogate traditional tort immunities such as those protecting charities, governmental units, and family members. This influence of liability insurance has surfaced throughout your study.

It is obviously impossible to provide a comprehensive examination of insurance law in an introductory torts casebook. The objectives of this chapter are more modest. Several specific issues have been selected to demonstrate the interplay between the tort and insurance systems. How are contracts providing insurance coverage for manufacturers interpreted when confronted with mass toxic torts, where the interval of time between the manufacture of the product and the onset of the disease may be decades? What potential liabilities exist for the insurer itself when the insurer's settlement decisions reflect its own best interests instead of those of the policyholder? In addition, the chapter provides a brief look at issues surrounding the automobile insurance contract, still—in these days of mass toxic torts and sophisticated medical malpractice suits—the most ubiquitous document in the tort system.

A. DEVELOPMENT OF LIABILITY INSURANCE AND ITS IMPACT ON THE TORT SYSTEM

Excerpt, David A. Fischer & Robert H. Jerry, II, Teaching Torts Without Insurance: A Second-Best Solution
45 St. Louis U. L.J. 857, 859–70 (2001).

Not much could be said about tort law before 1850; this would change with the arrival of the Industrial Revolution. * * * Almost as quickly as the new liabilities developed, insurers brought "employers' liability insurance" * to the market. In 1886, an English insurer issued what is thought to be the first policy of liability insurance in the United States; * the insurer promised that it "will pay to the Employer or his legal representatives all such sums for which such Employer shall become liable to his workmen by virtue of the Common Law or any

Statute with the following limitations and conditions. . . ."[12] Additional insurers quickly entered this market, and the total annual premiums written by liability insurers in the United States grew [many]-fold between 1887 and 1906 (from approximately $200,000 to more than $110 million). * As the range of activities on which liabilities were imposed expanded, * the coverage of the liability policy expanded as well; by 1912 one commentator described the typical policy in the United States as providing broad protection "against the legal liability of the Assured arising from bodily injuries resulting from negligence."[15]

Growth in premium volume continued throughout the twentieth century. * By 1998, more than $107 billion was spent annually in the United States on liability insurance, * which amounted to $380 for every person in the nation * and approximately 1.1% of gross domestic product (GDP). * These are large numbers, but the benefits provided by liability insurance are also enormous. Liability insurance gives individuals and firms some measure of security against the risk of financial ruin that can result if one's tortious conduct causes substantial injury to a third party. Indeed, it is difficult to imagine how the modern national and global economies could have matured and developed without the protection afforded to commercial enterprises from the consequences of their acts and neglect upon others.

A policy of insurance is a contract between insurer and policyholder, and like any contract, the insurance policy creates rights and duties between these two parties. In contrast to "first-party" coverage, which insures the policyholder's own interest in a piece of property or a life, liability insurance protects the policyholder against her risk of being liable in tort for damages owed to a third party. Both the first-party and third-party contract protect the policyholder's interests, but when the insurer pays proceeds under the liability insurance contract, the proceeds go not to the policyholder, but to the person to whom the policyholder is indebted by virtue of a judgment or settlement. That is the reason liability insurance is often labeled "third-party" insurance, even though the rights and duties in the contract, like first-party insurance, run between policyholder and insurer. *

Although contract law would afford third-party rights to an intended beneficiary (i.e., a tort victim) of the liability insurance contract, standard liability insurance policies contain a "no-action clause," which expressly states that the contract creates no rights in third parties unless and until a judgment is entered against the policyholder. This means that a victim of a tort cannot sue the insurer directly in tort for the consequences of the policyholder's allegedly wrongful conduct; the tort victim is not in privity with the insurer, and the contract does not bestow third-party rights on the victim. (In a very few states, statutory law provides a direct action to the tort victim against the insurer, and it is not uncommon for state statutes to provide limited direct action rights for discrete kinds of coverages, such as liability insurance for common carriers. *) This means the third-party's tort claim must be brought against the policyholder; if the claim is

---

[12] "Employers' Liability Policy" issued to the Gender and Paeschle Manufacturing Co., Oct. 28, 1886 (copy on file with the Saint Louis University Law Journal). * * *

[15] R.S. Keelob, Liability Policy Forms, in The Business of Insurance: A Text Book and Reference Work Covering All Lines of Insurance 213 (H. Dunham ed., 1912).

The next question must be "certainty with respect to what contingencies?" For an insured is only entitled to indemnity for losses that are covered by its policy. We are aided in our analysis of these policies' coverage by the well-accepted rule that ambiguity in an insurance contract must be construed in favor of the insured. * We believe, however, that although particular terms of the policies are ambiguous as applied to asbestos-related diseases, the principles embodied in the insurance policies provide a sufficient basis upon which to decide this case. In discerning those principles, our guide is—as it must be—the reasonable expectations of Keene when it purchased the policies. * 12 * * *

A.   *Trigger of Coverage*

The first step in the analysis of this problem is to determine what events, from the point of exposure to the point of manifestation, trigger coverage under these policies. In the language of the policies, the question is when did "injury" occur? Both Keene and Hartford advance slightly different versions of the "exposure theory" of coverage. Keene argues that successive coverage is triggered by both exposure to asbestos dust ("inhalation exposure") * and the subsequent development of disease ("exposure in residence"). Keene bases its argument on medical evidence that the body incurs microscopic injury as asbestos fibers become lodged in the lungs and as the surrounding tissue reacts to the fibers thereafter. * * *

INA, Liberty, and Aetna advance the "manifestation" theory of coverage. They argue that coverage is triggered only by the manifestation of either asbestosis, mesothelioma or lung cancer. They assert that their interpretation of the contracts is supported by the ordinary meaning of the terms "bodily injury, sickness or disease." They claim that "bodily injury" does not occur until cellular damage advances to the point of becoming a recognizable disease. INA and Liberty rely on cases in other areas of the law—workmen's compensation, health insurance coverage, and statutes of limitation—that support their interpretation of the term "injury." *

The policy language does not direct us unambiguously to either the "exposure" or "manifestation" interpretation. In the context of asbestos-related disease, the terms "bodily injury," "sickness" and "disease," standing alone, simply lack the precision necessary to identify a point in the development of a disease at which coverage is triggered. The fact that a doctor would characterize cellular damage as a discrete injury does not necessarily imply that the damage is an "injury" for the purpose of construing the policies. At the same time, the fact that an

---

12 Professor ([later] Judge) Keeton has suggested that the legal doctrines governing the construction of insurance contracts fit together under a more general, frequently unstated, principle that can be summarized as follows:

The objectively reasonable expectations of applicants and intended beneficiaries regarding the terms of insurance contracts will be honored even though painstaking study of the policy provisions would have negated those expectations.

[Robert E.] Keeton, Insurance Law Rights at Variance with Policy Provisions, 83 Harv. L. Rev. 961, 967 (1970). Professor Keeton argues that the principle is appropriate in view of the fact that an insurance policy is a contract of adhesion. * As applied to this case, we agree with Judge Keeton and explicitly base our interpretation of these policies on the expectations that Keene could have reasonably formed, as an objective matter, on the basis of the policies' language.

ordinary person would characterize a fully developed disease as an "injury" does not necessarily imply that the manifestation of the disease is the point of "injury" for purposes of construing the policies. In interpreting a contract, a term's ordinary definition should be given weight, but the definition is only useful when viewed in the context of the contract as a whole. * * *

If exposure to asbestos were deemed to constitute a discrete injury and thereby trigger coverage, as Hartford and Keene suggest, the subsequent development of a disease would be characterized best as a consequence of the injury. Future stages of development would not constitute new injuries * and therefore would not trigger additional coverage. * * * The policies state that the insured is covered for "injury" during the policy period. In purchasing such coverage, Keene could have reasonably expected that it was covered for all future liability, except liability for injuries of which Keene could have been aware prior to its purchase of insurance. A latent injury, unknown and unknowable to Keene at the time it purchased insurance, must, at least, be covered by an insurer on the risk at the time it manifests itself. Any other result would violate very reasonable expectations of Keene. Therefore we hold that manifestation of disease is one trigger of coverage under the policies. * * *

This is the same result that courts have reached in determining when an injury or disease begins for purposes of health and accident insurance policies. In those cases, courts have held that a manifestation rule is necessary to protect the reasonable expectations of the insured. * In health and accident insurance policies, as in liability insurance policies, the purpose of the contracts would be defeated if the insured had to bear the risk of disease that is latent at the time a policy is purchased. * None of this implies, however, that insurance policies may not also be triggered prior to manifestation. In fact, we conclude that coverage is also triggered by both inhalation exposure and exposure in residence.

To demonstrate why the policies require that both exposure and manifestation trigger coverage, we begin by positing a rule in which manifestation is the *sole* trigger of coverage. If that interpretation were adopted, * * * Keene would not be covered for diseases manifesting themselves after 1976. * By that time, it was widely known that prolonged inhalation of asbestos has a high probability of causing disease. * From about then on, insurance companies ceased issuing policies that adequately cover asbestos-related disease. Yet we can still expect thousands of cases of those diseases to manifest themselves throughout the rest of the century. If we were to hold that only the manifestation of disease can trigger coverage, the insurance companies would have to bear only a fraction of Keene's total liability for asbestos-related diseases.

The possibility of that result would undermine the function of the insurance policies. When Keene purchased the policies, it could have reasonably expected that it was free of the risk of becoming liable for injuries of which it could not have been aware prior to its purchase of insurance. * There is no doubt that these losses would be covered if the diseases at issue developed spontaneously upon inhalation. Inhalation of asbestos is an "occurrence" that causes injury for which Keene may be held liable. * * * To accept the argument that *only* manifestation triggers coverage—and allow insurers to terminate coverage prior to the manifestation of many cases of disease—would deprive Keene of the protection it purchased when it entered into the insurance contracts. * * * Thus, in order for Keene's rights under the policies to be secure, both inhalation exposure and exposure in residence must also trigger coverage. Regardless of whether exposure to asbestos causes an immediate and discrete injury, the fact that it is part of an injurious process is enough for it to constitute "injury" under the policies. * * *

In sum, the allocation of rights and obligations established by the insurance policies, would be undermined if either the exposure to asbestos or the manifestation of asbestos-related disease were the *sole* trigger of coverage. We conclude, therefore, that inhalation exposure, exposure in residence, and manifestation all trigger coverage under the policies. We interpret "bodily injury" to mean any part of the single injurious process that asbestos-related diseases entail. We now proceed to consider the extent to which an insurer is liable to its policyholder once coverage under its policy is triggered.

B.   *The Extent of Coverage*

* * * As stated above, each policy has a built-in trigger of coverage. Once triggered, each policy covers Keene's liability. There is *nothing* in the policies that provides for a reduction of the insurer's liability if an injury occurs only in part during a policy period. As we interpret the policies, they cover Keene's entire liability once they are triggered. * * * Hartford argues that this allocation of liability allows Keene to "enjoy the benefits of insurance coverage which it has never paid for." * * * [H]owever, * * * [w]ith each policy, Keene paid for insurance against all liability for bodily injury. The policies do not * * * provide that "injury" must occur *entirely* during the policy period for full indemnity to be provided. * * *

C.   *Allocation of Liability*

In any suit against Keene for an asbestos-related disease, it is likely that the coverage of more than one insurer will be triggered. * * * The contribution provision * * * [of each insurer's policy] contains formulae for "contribution by equal shares" and for "contribution by limits," depending upon the provisions of other applicable policies. * These provisions of the policies must govern the allocation of liability among the insurers in any particular case of asbestos-related disease. However, the primary duty of the insurers whose coverage is triggered by exposure or manifestation is to ensure that Keene is indemnified in full. *

D.   *Costs of Defending Suits Against Keene*

The policies provide that the insurer shall defend any suit against Keene for damages due to bodily injury, even if the suit is groundless, false or fraudulent. The insurers' duty to defend Keene and to pay Keene for its defense costs are more broad than their duty to indemnify Keene. As long as a complaint indicates that Keene may be liable for an injury, an insurer must defend Keene if the facts alleged in the complaint indicate that its policy covers the alleged injury. Because we hold that each insurer is fully liable to Keene for indemnification, it follows that each is fully liable for defense costs.[37] * * *

■ WALD, CIRCUIT JUDGE, concurring in part. * * *

* * * [T]he majority opinion exempts asbestos manufacturers from all financial responsibility arising from a suit if the manufacturer had purchased insurance which covered any part of the injury period. * * * I just do not understand why an asbestos manufacturer, which has consciously decided not to insure itself during particular years of the exposure-manifestation period, should have a reasonable expectation that it would be exempt from any liability for injuries that were occurring during the uninsured period. It seems to me logical and fair * * * to distribute the ultimate financial responsibility on a pro rata basis among the various insurance companies on line during the risk period, and to include Keene as a self-insurer for the years when it failed to take out any insurance. * * * If asbestos-related diseases are understood as progressive or cumulative, then all those who voluntarily assumed risk during the period when the diseases progressed must share the responsibility for the judgment and this includes self-insurers. If the risk is to be shared only by the insurance companies, a manufacturing company that purchased insurance intermittently during the risk period would be as secure as those prudent companies that continually purchased insurance. * * *

NOTES

1.   *"Occurrence" as Coverage "Trigger."* Since the early 1940s, liability insurance for businesses has been provided under a standard policy known as the commercial general liability policy or "CGL." See Robert H. Jerry II & Douglas R. Richmond, Understanding Insurance Law §§ 60B[b] & 65[c] (5th ed. 2012). The CGL replaced the earlier practice of writing separate coverage for bodily injury and property damage caused by separate activities, such as landlord's liability or contractor's liability. The CGL provides general coverage for the policyholder regardless of the nature of its business.

Until 1966, the CGL provided coverage for injury caused by an "accident," which was defined as "a sudden and unforeseeable event." Because of uncertainties as to when coverage applied to injuries caused by less abrupt events, such as diseases resulting from leaking chemicals, the language was changed in 1966 to key the coverage to the triggering event of injury from an "occurrence." Obviously, as shown by the principal case, ambiguity still remained in defining the event-triggering coverage.

Courts remain in conflict regarding which event triggers coverage for asbestos-related illnesses under the current version of the CGL. Many courts follow the "triple trigger" or continuous trigger approach adopted by *Keene.* See, e.g, Owens-Illinois, Inc. v. United Ins. Co., 138 N.J. 437, 650 A.2d 974 (1994). Others have followed the "exposure" theory. See, e.g., Insurance Co. of N. Am. v. Forty-Eight Insulations, Inc., 633 F.2d 1212 (6th Cir.1980), *aff'd on rehearing,* 657 F.2d 814 (6th Cir.1981). A few courts hold that it is the manifestation of asbestos-related disease that triggers

---

[37] Nothing we now hold should be read to prevent an insurer from sharing the costs of defense with other insurers under the "other insurance" clauses or under the doctrine of contribution.

coverage, e.g., Eagle-Picher Indus., Inc. v. Liberty Mut. Ins. Co., 682 F.2d 12 (1st Cir.1982).

2. *Claims-Made Policies.* As *Keene* illustrates, the insurer who provides coverage for claims arising in the contexts of certain categories of products torts, environmental claims, and medical malpractice and other kinds of professional liability "often present the * * * difficulty of determining precisely when the actuating event 'occurred' for the purpose of defining coverage." Sparks v. St. Paul Ins. Co., 100 N.J. 325, 330, 495 A.2d 406, 409 (1985). Further, the insurer risks under-pricing its coverage because of its exposure to an indeterminate "tail" of claims—that is, claims filed long after exposure to its product or conduct has ended.

> Insurers' unexpected and dramatically large exposure resulting from asbestos liability led them in 1984 to begin to offer policies on a "claims-made" basis. * Claims-made policies provide coverage for those claims discovered and brought to the attention of the insurer during the policy term, regardless of when the product was manufactured, when the victims was exposed to the product, or when the victim's illness first manifested itself. * * * [M]anufacturers that do not appear to have "long-tail" liability generally still can obtain occurrence policies, but those in fields such as pharmaceuticals, which pose risks of latent diseases, may be forced to purchase claims-made policies. * Even a manufacturer whose products pose a long-term risk sometimes can negotiate to obtain an occurrence policy if its negotiating leverage is sufficiently great, e.g., a large corporation with the need for extensive and diverse insurance coverages.

Donald G. Gifford, The Peculiar Challenges Posed by Latent Diseases Resulting from Mass Products, 64 Md. L. Rev. 613, 648–49 (2003). Insurers also frequently offer claims-made medical malpractice policies.

3. *Pollution Exclusion Coverage.* Another major source of coverage controversy under the CGL has been the "pollution exclusion" provision. In 1973, the CGL was amended to state that coverage would not apply to bodily injury or property damage

> (1) arising out of pollution or contamination caused by oil or (2) arising out of the discharge, dispersal, release or escape of smoke, vapors, soot, fumes, acids, alkalis, toxic chemicals, liquids or gases, waste materials or other irritants, contaminants or pollutants into or upon the land, the atmosphere or any water course of body of water; but this exclusion does not apply if such discharge, dispersal, release or escape is sudden and accidental.

Quoted in Jerry & Richmond, *supra* § 65[c][5][vi].

This "pollution exclusion" has generated and continues to generate considerable litigation and inconsistent judicial interpretations. Jerry and Richmond analyze the basic issue as follows:

> * * * Where does all of this leave us? At one extreme, the 1973 CGL was obviously intended to provide coverage for loss arising out of a train accident where a tank car derails, ruptures, and spills a toxic cargo into a river. Such an incident is "sudden and accidental," outside the scope of the exclusion, and within the policy's coverage. At the other extreme, a company that deliberately deposits toxic wastes into a river commits an

intentional act for which no coverage is provided. The act is intentional, not accidental. Also, the resulting damage from the act is probably known in advance and is certainly foreseeable; thus, it follows that the result is intended as well. *

It is the gray area between these two extremes that is problematic. Consider the example of an underground fuel storage tank. Such tanks have a finite life, and this is known at the time the tank is buried in the ground. Eventually and inevitably, the tank will deteriorate and begin leaking. Thus, it can be said that the leaching of fuel into surrounding soil and the resulting damage is both expectable and foreseeable. Since the burying of the tank is not an accident and the eventual consequences are known, the resulting damage is arguably outside the scope of the coverage; results of acts that have expectable, foreseeable—indeed, certain—consequences are not accidental, and one could argue that such damage is not an "occurrence." Yet from the insured's perspective, no intent exists to cause the leak or the resulting damage. There is a known risk, but the transformation of risk into actual harm is truly accidental. Also, when the tank first suffers a leak, the "rupture" is sudden, not expected or foreseen at the precise moment it occurs. Thus, it is arguable that the resulting liability is within the coverage.

In 1986, the drafters of the CGL again modified the "pollution exclusion" provision, this time adopting the "absolute pollution exclusion," which (1) deleted from the pollution exclusion clause any language creating an exception for "sudden" and accidental releases and (2) eliminated any requirement that the pollution be discharged into or upon land, air, or water. See generally American States Ins. Co. v. Koloms, 177 Ill.2d 473, 227 Ill.Dec. 149, 687 N.E.2d 72 (1997). In short, the 1986 revisions were motivated by the insurance industry's attempt to avoid liability for "traditional environmental contamination," *Id.* at 493, 227 Ill.Dec. at 158, 687 N.E.2d at 81, and specifically to exclude liability for governmental cleanup costs. See Comprehensive Environmental Response, Compensation, and Liability Act (CERCLA), 42 U.S.C. § 9607 (2012).

Early decisions interpreting the 1986 pollution exclusion provision generally denied coverage for environmental damage cases. See, e.g., Park-Ohio Indus. Inc. v. Home Indem. Co., 975 F.2d 1215 (6th Cir.1992) (pollution exclusion clause found to be unambiguous; insured entitled to neither coverage nor defense by insurer); Pipefitters Welfare Educ. Fund v. Westchester Fire Ins. Co., 976 F.2d 1037 (7th Cir.1992) (same). More recently, however, courts often have found the provision ambiguous in cases other than those involving prototypical forms of pollution, and have ruled in favor of the insured. In Lititz Mut. Ins. Co. v. Steely, 567 Pa. 98, 785 A.2d 975 (2001), for example, the court held that the pollution exclusion clause in a policy did not preclude coverage for childhood lead poisoning claims against the landlord/policyholder because the exclusion requires a "discharge, dispersal, release or escape of pollutants." The process by which lead-based paint becomes available for ingestion by children instead occurs through "continual, imperceptible, and inevitable deterioration of paint that has been applied to the interior surface of a residence;" see also Western Alliance Ins. Co. v. Gill, 426 Mass. 115, 686 N.E.2d 997 (1997) (pollution exclusion clause did not bar coverage for carbon monoxide exposure of restaurant patron caused by oven). In Nationwide Mut. Ins. Co. v. Richardson, 270 F.3d 948, 956 (D.C.Cir.2001), the court observed that "many courts [have come] to diametrically opposed conclusions about the clause's clarity and meaning."

C. EXAMPLES OF INSURANCE POLICIES PROVIDING LIABILITY COVERAGE FOR INDIVIDUALS

1. AUTOMOBILE INSURANCE POLICIES

Excerpt, James M. Anderson, Paul Heaton & Stephen J. Carroll, The U.S. Experience with No-Fault Automobile Insurance: A Retrospective

1–2, 8 (RAND Institute for Civil Justice, 2010).

Tort-law scholar Guido Calabresi[a] once asked his readers to imagine an evil deity who demanded 55,000 lives every year in exchange for providing amazing powers of individual transportation without precedent in human history. The personal automobile is the evil deity to which he referred, and we have accepted the bargain but still struggle to allocate the overwhelming costs. In 2006 alone, a staggering 2,575,000 people were injured in automobile accidents in the United States, and 42,642 people were killed. * This enormous toll has long represented the largest single source of accidental injury in the United States. The financial costs compound this human tragedy: Automobile crashes cost $241 billion in 2003, according to the National Safety Council.

The world's largest insurance market has developed as a result of this source of accidental injury and death. U.S. consumers spend more than $110 billion every year on liability insurance for auto accidents—a larger amount than for any other category of insurance expenditure. * Another result has been an enormous amount of litigation. Automobile-accident litigation makes up two-thirds of all injury claims, three-quarters of all lawyers' fees, and three-quarters of all payouts in the personal-injury liability system. * The result of the mixture of insurance and tort law has been a costly system that provides compensation that is very unevenly related to the injuries incurred by the victim. * * *

In practice, widespread insurance use has influenced the actual operation of the traditional system of liability in several important ways.[1] First, insurance adjusters have adopted rules (e.g., drivers who rear-end other vehicles are at fault) to allocate fault. These have minimized more-general analyses of reasonableness and causation in most automobile-accident cases, which are resolved without formal litigation. Rather than undertake a generalized analysis of whether a driver is negligent and therefore liable for an accident—a potentially difficult and open-ended

---

[a] [Eds.' note] Guido Calabresi, Ideals, Beliefs, Attitudes and the Law: Private Law Perspective on a Public Law Problem 1 (1985).

[1] [Chapter 2] Today, every state except Florida, New Hampshire, and Wisconsin requires automobile liability insurance. * In Florida, New Hampshire, and Wisconsin, purchasing insurance is the easiest way to meet the state's financial-responsibility law. Each of these states has financial-responsibility laws that can be satisfied by auto insurance, a surety bond, personal funds, or a certificate of self-insurance. *

inquiry—an insurance adjuster is likely to refer to a simpler set of rules to determine who owes what to whom. * * * Finally, the amount of insurance that the defendant possesses usually serves as a de facto cap on damages. Under the law, an automobile operator is personally liable for whatever losses that he or she causes, whether or not he or she has adequate insurance. However, research has shown that recoveries over insurance policy limits— called "blood money"—are rarely sought by plaintiffs or their attorneys. * * *

NOTE

Automobile Insurance Policies. Insurance coverage for injuries resulting from automobile accidents varies depending upon whether a state is a "no-fault" jurisdiction or a traditional tort liability jurisdiction. In the dozen or so "true" no-fault jurisdictions, the victim of an automobile accident recovers damages for his personal injury or property damage from his own insurer, regardless of whether he or the other driver was at fault, at least until the severity of injuries or amount of damages exceeds a specified threshold. In contrast, in traditional tort liability states, the injured party seeks recovery from the driver or owner of the automobile whose negligence caused the accident, and the liability insurer for the party at fault compensates the victims to the extent of policy limits. For a comparison of how claims for compensation for injuries resulting from an automobile accident would be handled in a "fault" jurisdiction (assuming defendant is insured) with the treatment of claims under a no-fault system, see *infra* pages 682–86.

Automobile insurance policies typically bundle coverages for a variety of claims. In a traditional tort liability state, a policy includes third-party *liability* coverage indemnifying the policyholder for any amounts she may be legally required to pay someone injured as a result of the policyholder's liability, including damages for either *bodily injury* or *property damage.* In addition, the typical automobile policy includes *first-party* coverage, indemnifying the policyholder for losses she may herself suffer, including damage to her own vehicle, resulting from theft, vandalism, or adverse weather, as well as other causes, perhaps subject to a deductible.

Compulsory Insurance

Most jurisdictions require that a person seeking to register a motor vehicle present proof that she has liability insurance covering at least a specified minimum amount of damages. Jerry and Richmond, *supra,* § 132 [a][1]. For example, as of 2014, Maryland required coverage of not less than $30,000 for injury to any one person injured in an accident, a minimum of $60,000 coverage when two or more individuals are injured in an accident, and of at least $15,000 coverage for property damage resulting from an accident. An auto owner purchasing minimum coverage would be said to have policy limits of "30/60/15." Md. Code Ann., Transp. § 17–103(b) (2014). Additional coverages are also required, providing coverage for first party medical, hospital, and disability benefits covering the insured and certain others, and of claims against uninsured and underinsured motorists. *Id.,* Ins. §§ 19–505 to 517 (2014).

What happens if the driving experience of an individual is so bad that no liability insurance carrier would voluntarily insure the driver at any cost? Usually these individuals are able to purchase coverage from an "assigned risk pool" in which all licensed auto insurers in a state are required to participate. Rates offered to such drivers are substantially higher than rates for drivers with better records.

Despite these legal requirements, the evidence indicates that between five and twenty percent of all vehicles operated on U.S. highways are not covered by liability policies. See Alan I. Widiss, Uninsured and Underinsured Motorist Insurance § 1.12 (3d ed. 2005).

Typical Provisions of Automobile Insurance Contracts

Omnibus Clause. Who is covered as an insured under an auto policy? A typical "omnibus clause" of an insurance contract provides:

A. We will pay damages for "bodily injury" or "property damage" for which any "insured" becomes legally responsible because of an auto accident.

B. "Insured" as used in this Part means:

   1. You or any "family member" for the ownership, maintenance or use of any auto. . . .

   2. Any person using "your covered auto."

A provision of the typical policy excludes from liability coverage any person "using a vehicle without a reasonable belief that that person is entitled to do so." Rutgers Cas. Ins. Co. v. Collins, 158 N.J. 542, 730 A.2d 833 (1999). Many coverage disputes involve the question of whether the person using the vehicle had the owner's permission, particularly if the original driver had the permission of the owner but he allowed another person to drive who had no direct contact with the auto owner. See, e.g., Arkwright v. Taulbee, 248 Ga.App. 219, 546 S.E.2d 335 (2001).

"Drive the Other Car" Coverage. The typical auto policy provides coverage for the policyholder or any family member when using "any auto." See Roger C. Henderson and Robert H. Jerry, II, Insurance Law: Cases and Materials, Appendix E, APP–56 (3d ed. 2001). Thus, with the omnibus clause, insurance coverage is provided for the vehicle; in contrast, with the "drive the other car" clause, insurance coverage follows the driver. Most often coverage for other vehicles is limited to those vehicles used only occasionally or infrequently. Otherwise, an additional premium would be justified for coverage of the second vehicle. See Hochgurtel v. San Felippo, 78 Wis.2d 70, 253 N.W.2d 526 (1977) (father's policy covered son's occasional use of non-owned vehicle while making deliveries for employer).

If a driver covered under her own policy is driving a non-owned vehicle insured by another policyholder and the combined policy limits exceed the total damages of plaintiff(s), which policy covers the loss first? Today the standard automobile policy treats the omnibus clause as the primary policy, and "drive the other car" coverage as secondary. Henderson & Jerry, *supra,* APP–58.

Types of Coverage in Standard Automobile Insurance Policies

The following paragraphs provide a very brief summary of some types of coverages typically provided by a standard auto insurance policy. The list is by no means exhaustive; a policy might provide other coverage, e.g., reimbursement for towing expenses.

Third Party or Liability Coverages.

Bodily Injury Liability (BI). This coverage indemnifies the policyholder for any damages, legal costs, and expenses the policyholder must pay as a result of claims and lawsuits for injuries to or death of another.

Property Damage Liability (PD). This coverage pays for the damage to someone else's property, e.g., his automobile or mailbox, which the policyholder becomes legally obligated to pay, as well as legal expenses.

First Party Coverages.

Medical Payments ("MedPay"). Medical payments coverage pays the medical expenses of the policyholder, his family members, or passengers in his car or another car being driven by a covered person following an accident. The coverage pays regardless of who is at fault, but if someone else is liable, the insurer may seek to recoup its expenses from that party.

Personal Injury Protection ("PIP"). Personal Injury Protection typically is the basic insurance coverage in a no-fault state, providing for reimbursement of medical expenses, at least some loss of income, and other costs resulting from auto accident injuries. See *infra*, [ ].

Collision. This coverage pays for damage to the policyholder's automobile from an accident regardless of fault.

Comprehensive. Comprehensive coverage reimburses the policyholder for damage to his automobile resulting from incidents such as vandalism, fire, flood, animals, flying rocks, or debris.

Uninsured/underinsured Motorist Coverage ("UM"). What happens if someone is injured in an automobile accident by a tortfeasor without insurance or without adequate insurance or other assets to pay for the damages? Almost every state either requires proof of uninsured motorist coverage or at least requires the insurer to offer such coverage. See Jerry & Richmond, *supra*, § 135[a]. Under this coverage, the injured person can recover from her own insurer an amount equal to what would have been recovered if the other driver had been insured. In other words, this coverage is a unique first party coverage which allows the policyholder to recover full tort damages, including pain and suffering, up to the amount of the coverage.

Underinsured motorist coverage works much the same way, except it applies when the tortfeasor has insurance but the limits of the insurance are not adequate to cover the damages sustained by the victim.

2. HOMEOWNER'S POLICY

The homeowner's policy ("HO") is similar to the automobile insurance policy in that it combines in a single package both first-party coverages—such as those insuring the homeowner against fire or theft—and personal liability coverage. See Jerry & Richmond, *supra*, § 60B[b]. The liability coverage under the homeowner's policy is broadly construed and, except where coverage is expressly excluded, essentially functions as a comprehensive personal liability policy. See e.g., Berne v. Cont'l Ins. Co., 753 F.2d 27 (3d Cir.1985) (coverage under homeowner's policy for accidental discharge of firearm at bar); Catholic Diocese of Dodge City v. Raymer, 251 Kan. 689, 840 P.2d 456 (1992) (coverage under homeowner's policy for negligent failure to supervise a child after policyholder's child vandalized school owned and operated by plaintiff).

D. LIABILITY FOR "BAD FAITH" FAILURE TO SETTLE

Merritt v. Reserve Insurance Co.

Court of Appeal of California, 1973.
34 Cal.App.3d 858, 110 Cal.Rptr. 511.

■ FLEMING, J. * * *

History of First Suit.

On 3 August 1960 Reserve Insurance issued an automobile liability insurance policy to Stafford Co., which provided personal injury coverage of $100,000 for each person and $300,000 for each accident, and property damage coverage of $25,000. The policy bound Reserve to pay to the limits of its coverage any sums the insured should become legally obligated to pay as damages and to defend any suit seeking damages against the insured. The policy authorized Reserve to investigate, negotiate, and settle any claim or suit against the insured as it deemed expedient.

On the evening of 20 February 1961 a southbound truck owned by Sterling Transit and driven by Merritt collided on Highway 99 near Merced with the rear of Stafford Co.'s southbound truck driven by Bernal, and as a result of the collision Merritt suffered severe and permanent personal injuries. Shortly after the accident, both Reserve, the insurance carrier for Stafford Co., and Transport Indemnity, the insurance carrier for Sterling Transit, undertook separate investigations of the accident. * * *

In June 1961, four months after the accident, Merritt filed suit against Stafford Co. and Bernal for $400,000 damages for personal injuries, and Sterling Transit sued for $24,000 property damages to its vehicle. Stafford Co. forwarded the complaint to Reserve, and the latter then advised Stafford Co. by registered mail that "[t]he amount of damages requested in this suit is $400,000 which is in excess of the limits of coverage provided under your policy with Reserve Insurance Company. This is to advise you, therefore, that you may at your option retain legal counsel to represent your interests in the excess amount." The letter also informed Stafford Co. that Reserve had employed the law firm of Hecker, Dunford & Kenealy to represent Stafford Co. in the defense of the suit. Reserve forwarded its file on the accident to the defending law firm, and that firm concluded from its study of the file that although serious personal injuries were involved, the case was one of non-liability. Thereafter, throughout the course of its employment the firm of Hecker, Dunford & Kenealy consistently and repeatedly advised the carrier that the case was one of non-liability. * * *

Dunford, the firm's attorney who ultimately tried the case, knew that Reserve's personal injury liability under its policy was limited to $100,000 for each person and $300,000 for each accident. * * * Prior to the trial Dunford told Stafford there was nothing to worry about; there was no need to settle; it was not necessary for Stafford to be personally present at the trial. The firm of Hecker, Dunford & Kenealy also consistently advised Reserve and its agents that no possibility for settlement existed * * *. No settlement offer was ever made by Merritt, or Sterling Transit, * * * and the sole demand on behalf of Merritt up to the time of trial was the $400,000 set out in the complaint. On the day the trial started, Merritt sought and received permission to increase his prayer for damages from $400,000 to $650,000. Dunford did not inform Stafford Co. of the increase.

The result of the trial turned out quite differently from what had been anticipated by defense counsel. Merritt testified he was going 45 to 50 miles an hour when he saw a sudden flash of lights in front of him and crashed into Stafford Co.'s slowly moving vehicle before he could stop. The electrical engineer who had inspected Stafford Co.'s vehicle two days after the accident on behalf of Transport Indemnity, the insurance carrier for Sterling Transit, testified that the lighting system on Stafford Co.'s vehicle contained defects that could have caused its rear lights to fail. Plaintiffs discredited the testimony of Bernal, Stafford Co.'s driver, by pointing out improbabilities in his estimate of travel times and by bringing out the fact that Bernal had two felony convictions for smuggling. Plaintiffs discredited Cox's [(a key defense witness's)] testimony through the use of traffic-accident experts, who concluded that Cox's version of the times and distances involved in the accident was physically impossible. Plaintiffs also pointed out that despite Cox's claim to close involvement in the accident, the California Highway Patrol accident report did not list his name as a witness.

The jury returned a verdict of $434,000 for Merritt and $21,000 for Sterling Transit against Stafford Co. and Bernal. The court denied defense motions for a new trial and for judgment notwithstanding the verdict; and this judgment was subsequently affirmed on appeal.

History of Second Suit.

As Stafford Co.'s assignee, Merritt filed the present suit in 1966 against Reserve Insurance, grounded upon Stafford Co.'s right of action against Reserve for bad faith * * * that had resulted in an unsatisfied judgment of $334,000 against Stafford Co. * * * At the trial the circumstances and events connected with the accident and with the conduct of the first suit were reviewed in detail. * * * The judge who presided at the trial of the first suit appeared as an expert witness on behalf of plaintiff in the second suit and gave testimony that the credibility of the witness Cox had been low. Other testimony suggested that the defense's investigation of the accident and defense counsel's preparation for trial and presentation of its defense in court had been inadequate in view of the potential liability to which Stafford Co. had been exposed. The jury returned a verdict of $499,000 in favor of Merritt as assignee of Stafford Co. The court denied a motion for judgment notwithstanding the verdict; and this appeal followed. * * *

Obligations of the Carrier to Its Assured.

* * * Under the policy the carrier [Reserve] assumed two different obligations: (1) to pay to the limits of its coverage sums which the insured should become legally obligated to pay as damages for bodily and property injury; (2) to defend any suit against the insured seeking such damages. In connection with these obligations the carrier reserved the right to investigate, negotiate, and settle any claim or suit as it

deemed expedient. * * * [T]he carrier assumed a third continuing obligation under its liability insurance contract, a duty to deal fairly and in good faith with its assured, the other party to the contract. * * *

Liability insurance policies are universally written with coverages that obligate the carrier to satisfy the assured's legal liability only within specified amounts. It is a consequence of such contracts that the carrier underwrites the risk of the assured's liability for damages to a specified amount, and the assured carries his own risk of liability above that amount. The varying relationship between assured and carrier under a policy of limited liability insurance may be illustrated by reference to the minimum policy coverage required under California law. Vehicle Code section 16059 specifies the minimum allowable coverage for an automobile insurance policy as $15,000 for one personal injury, $30,000 for one accident, and $5,000 for property damage. An assured who contracts for this minimum policy is covered for liability in damages to those amounts, but has assumed his own risk of liability above those amounts. Suppose a claimant files suit seeking $50,000 damages for personal injuries against an assured who holds a minimum policy. At that point both assured and carrier have a common interest in resisting the suit, for if claimant obtains judgment in the amount he seeks the carrier will become liable for $15,000 and the assured liable for $35,000. The defense against the suit presents no problem of good faith, for the interests of carrier and assured are parallel.

But suppose the claimant offers to settle his suit for $10,000. On the tender of this offer a divergence of interest promptly arises between assured and carrier. From the assured's point of view any settlement up to the full amount of his coverage ($15,000) is in his interest, for the settlement eliminates the possibility of any liability attaching to him with respect to the share of the risk he has assumed. No matter how remote the possibility may be of a judgment in excess of $15,000, settlement will always be to the interest of the assured—for the settlement will cost him nothing. On the other hand, from the carrier's point of view settlement of the suit for $10,000 may or may not be to its interest. Mathematically, only if the odds are two to one in favor of claimant's securing a judgment of $15,000 or more, will it be in the carrier's interest to settle. * Thus, when a settlement within policy limits is offered by claimant, the previously parallel interests of assured and carrier diverge, and a conflict of interest arises, for while it is invariably to the assured's financial interest to settle within policy limits, settlement is only to the carrier's financial interest when the relationship between settlement offer and policy limits is mathematically favorable in the light of the probabilities of winning or losing the suit.

Resolution of the conflict of interest between assured and carrier created by a claimant's offer to settle within policy limits is complicated by the fact that under the insurance contract the carrier retains control over the defense of the lawsuit. Customarily, the carrier has selected and employed counsel who defend the suit on behalf of the assured and has reserved to itself the right to investigate, negotiate, and settle the suit against the assured. The assured is not in a position to exercise effective control over the lawsuit or to further his own interests by independent action, even when those interests appear in serious jeopardy. * * *

When an offer is made to settle a claim in excess of policy limits for an amount within policy limits, a genuine and immediate conflict of interest arises between carrier and assured. The normal legal remedy for conflicts in interest is separate representation for the conflicting interests. This remedy, however, possesses only a limited usefulness in the present situation, for while the assured can be advised, as he usually is, that he may employ separate counsel to look after his interests, separate representation usually amounts to nothing more than independent legal advice to the assured, since control of the litigation remains in the hands [of] the carrier. Control of the defense of the lawsuit cannot be split, and independent legal advice to the assured cannot force the carrier to accept a settlement offer it does not wish to accept. In this instance the normal legal remedy of separate representation is an inadequate solution to the conflict in interest. * * *

Since the remedy of separate representation is inadequate * * * the courts have been forced to improvise in order to find a workable solution to the problem of conflict of interest. * The current status of these efforts confirms the carrier in its control over the litigation, but requires the carrier to consider in good faith the interests of the assured equally with its own and evaluate settlement offers within policy limits as though it alone carried the entire risk of loss. The California rule governing the carrier's conduct when conflicts of interest arise from a claimant's offer to settle a claim within policy limits has been formulated in terms of good and bad faith. In Comunale v. Traders & Gen. Ins. Co., 50 Cal.2d 654, 328 P.2d 198 (1958), the Supreme Court said:

> It is generally held that since the insurer has reserved control over the litigation and settlement it is liable for the entire amount of a judgment against the insured, including any portion in excess of the policy limits, if in the exercise of such control it is guilty of bad faith in refusing a settlement. *

The court distinguished good faith from bad faith in the following terms:

> The insurer, in deciding whether a claim should be compromised, must take into account the interest of the insured and give it at let [sic] as much consideration as it does to its own interest. * When there is great risk of a recovery beyond the policy limits so that the most reasonable manner of disposing of the claim is a settlement which can be made within those limits, a consideration in good faith of the insured's interest requires the insurer to settle the claim. Its unwarranted refusal to do so constitutes a breach of the implied covenant of good faith and fair dealing. *

Under this rule a carrier in control of litigation which has rejected a settlement in bad faith may become liable to its assured for the resulting loss. In Crisci v. Security Ins. Co., 66 Cal.2d 425, 58 Cal.Rptr. 13, 426 P.2d 173 (1967), the Supreme Court upheld the imposition of liability on a carrier for bad faith rejection of an offer to settle within policy limits. The test for determining whether the carrier has given good faith consideration to the interests of the assured, said the court, is whether a prudent carrier on a policy of unlimited liability would have accepted the settlement offer. A carrier which unwarrantedly rejects a reasonable settlement offer may become liable to its assured for resulting losses. * * *

When a claimant offers to settle an excess claim within policy limits a conflict of interest immediately arises between carrier and assured. In such circumstances the carrier is required to evaluate the settlement offer in good faith, and good faith requires it to consider the interests of the assured equally with its own or, as some of the cases have said, to evaluate the settlement offer as though the carrier itself were liable for the full amount of the claim. If the carrier rejects the offer to settle within policy limits without having made an honest, intelligent, and knowledgeable evaluation of the offer on its merits, then the carrier has acted in bad faith and may become liable to its assured for consequential damages caused by its bad faith rejection. * * *

If a settlement offer is made in excess of policy limits, what obligations or duties then fall upon the parties to the policy? * * * In resolving such dilemmas the courts have done little more than list a number of factors that may be considered in evaluating the propriety of the carrier's decision. Most of these have been itemized in the court's opinion in Brown v. Guarantee Ins. Co., 155 Cal.App.2d 679, 689, 319 P.2d 69, 75 (1957):

> In deciding whether the insurer's refusal to settle constitutes a breach of its duty to exercise good faith, the following factors should be considered: the strength of the injured claimant's case on the issues of liability and damages; attempts by the insurer to induce the insured to contribute to a settlement; failure of the insurer to properly investigate the circumstances so as to ascertain the evidence against the insured; the insurer's rejection of advice of its own attorney or agent; failure of the insurer to inform the insured of a compromise offer; the amount of financial risk to which each party is exposed in the event of a refusal to settle; the fault of the insured in inducing the insurer's rejection of the compromise offer by misleading it as to the facts; and any other factors tending to establish or negate bad faith on the part of the insurer. * * *

Cause of Action for Bad Faith.

With this background in conflict of interest we turn to the facts of the case at bench. * * * No settlement offer was ever made, either within policy limits, or within policy limits supplemented by the assured's net worth. No demand for settlement was ever presented by the assured to the carrier. * No suggestion that settlement was feasible was ever made prior to judgment by anyone connected with the suit. The case, therefore, does not involve a conflict of interest and does not present a situation in which the carrier can be found to have acted in bad faith toward its assured. * * * Consequently, no cause of action arose on behalf of Stafford Co. against Reserve for bad faith refusal to settle, and the trial court should have entered judgment for defendant

Reserve notwithstanding the verdict on the cause of action for bad faith. * * *

The judgment in favor of plaintiff is reversed, the order denying judgment notwithstanding the verdict is reversed, and the trial court is directed to enter judgment in favor of defendant on the bad faith cause of action. * * *

NOTES

1. *Standard of Liability in Failure to Settle Cases.* Today the liability of the third-party insurer for failure to settle a claim is widely recognized. See generally Kent D. Syverud, The Duty to Settle, 76 Va. L. Rev. 1113 (1990). While most states require that the insurer act in "bad faith" or at least with an absence of "good faith" in order to recover on such a claim, see, e.g., State Farm v. White, 248 Md. 324, 236 A.2d 269 (1967), others employ essentially a negligence standard as to whether the insurer has breached a duty to settle reasonably. See, e.g., Crisci v. Sec. Ins. Co. of New Haven, Conn., 66 Cal.2d 425, 58 Cal.Rptr. 13, 426 P.2d 173 (1967) ("In determining whether an insurer has given consideration to the interests of the insured, the test is whether a prudent insurer without policy limits would have accepted the settlement offer."); Hartford Cas. Ins. Co. v. New Hampshire Ins. Co., 417 Mass. 115, 628 N.E.2d 14 (1994) (adopting test of "whether no reasonable insurer would have failed to settle the case within the policy limits."). Some commentators and even an occasional judge have suggested that insurers ought to be held strictly liable for failure to settle within policy limits. See, e.g., Crisci v. Sec. Ins. Co., 66 Cal.2d at 430–31, 426 P.2d at 177 (in dicta); Syverud, at 1168–72.

How does the potential for a possible failure-to-settle claim affect negotiation in the original tort action?

2. *Assignment of Failure to Settle Claims to Original Plaintiff.* As was the situation in the principal case, in typical "bad faith" claims against an insurance carrier, the insured defendant has assigned its claim against the insurer to the plaintiff in the original action. See, e.g., Crisci, 66 Cal.2d at 428–29, 58 Cal.Rptr. at 16, 426 P.2d at 176 (assignment by defendant to plaintiff, along with payment of $12,000 and transfer of an interest in real property, in order to obtain defendant's release from liability for the excess judgment). In a handful of cases, courts refuse to enforce such assignments of claims. See, e.g., Losser v. Atlanta Int'l. Ins. Co., 615 F.Supp. 58, 61 (D.Utah 1985). Also, courts in several states have interpreted "unfair claims settlement statutes" to create private causes of action for improper failure to settle claims. E.g., Klaudt v. Flink, 202 Mont. 247, 658 P.2d 1065 (1983).

CHAPTER 13

ALTERNATIVE COMPENSATION SYSTEMS AND THEIR COORDINATION WITH THE TORT SYSTEM

This casebook began with an examination of *Ives v. South Buffalo Railway Co.* and the issues it raised about the legitimacy of one alternative compensation system—workers' compensation—in light of the traditional treatment of costs of industrial accidents under American tort law. Today workers' compensation and, in many states, automobile no-fault systems, comfortably co-exist with the tort law system as fora for dealing with accidental injuries:

> In all, the tort liability system compensates accident victims for less than 5% of their economic losses. First-party insurance and workers' compensation make up some of the remaining losses; the victims themselves and their families absorb nearly 40% of medical costs and two thirds of lost wages.

Neal Feigenson, Legal Blame: How Jurors Think and Talk About Accidents 9 (2000).

In this chapter, we survey existing alternatives to common law liability in the United States and consider proposals for expanding no-fault liability to other areas of tort liability. Keep in mind several issues as you read these materials. How do existing no-fault compensation programs coordinate with traditional tort liability? If a no-fault system is adopted, does the need to address issues concerning the cause of the accidental injury and whether it falls within the boundaries of the no-fault plan merely replace the expense of litigating over liability? When should American jurisdictions expand no-fault liability into new areas of accidental injuries and disease? Can such systems be better achieved through the use of strict liability doctrines within the common law tort system or under alternative no-fault compensation systems?

A. THE ARGUMENT FOR NO-FAULT COMPENSATION SYSTEMS

1. GENERAL CRITICISMS OF THE TORT SYSTEM

Excerpts, Stephen D. Sugarman, Doing Away with Tort Law

73 Cal. L. Rev. 558, 559–75, 579–80, 591–96, 603, 604, 616 (1985).

A. *Avoiding Undesirable Accidents: The Ineffectiveness of Tort as a Deterrent*

 1. The Basic Model: Rational Responses to the Threatened Imposition of Tort Damages

Many commentators have tried to justify tort law on the ground that it promotes socially desirable behavior. Specifically, they claim that it prevents injuries * * *. There is, unfortunately, little reason to believe that tort law today actually serves an *important* accident avoidance function. * * * [T]he general model posited is one in which people, like mice put in a psychologist's maze of electrical shocks, are directed away from conduct that brings the sting of tort liability and toward those channels of activity where the sting is avoided. * *However, this simple deterrence model overemphasizes both the amount of overly dangerous activity that would occur without tort liability, and the amount of injury-reduction achieved.* *

 2. Behavior Controls Apart from Tort Law

Self-preservation instincts, market forces, personal morality and governmental regulation combine to control unreasonably dangerous actions independently of tort law. The existence of these forces explains why, if tort liability were simply abolished, there would not be the dramatic increase in injuries that the simple tort-as-deterrent model envisions.

First is the *self-preservation instinct* of would-be injurers. Where conduct is likely to be dangerous to oneself as well as others, the drive to protect one's own body will go a long way towards safeguarding others. * The attention of airline pilots and drivers to safety well illustrates this point; further examples are efforts by store owners and home owners to ensure that their premises are free from hazards. I recognize that this pressure is not universally applicable: manufacturers and physicians mainly endanger others.

Ordinary market forces serve as a second safety control. If buyers have good information and act rationally, the market by itself should provide the goods and services that respond to public willingness to pay for safety. * Unfortunately, there is good reason to think that many consumers are neither well informed about damages nor fully rational actors. * Hence, market pressures alone, although an important influence, will not suffice to achieve the desired level of safety.

Beyond a desire to cater to current buyer preferences, enterprises and professionals have an interest in attracting new customers. This gives them a financial reason to avoid a reputation for providing dangerous products, premises or services. * Bad reviews by consumer organizations or the media, to say nothing of word of mouth complaints, can ruin the marketing of a particular product or service. In addition, a publicized unsafe product line can besmirch a firm's general standing— a matter of considerable importance in a nation of large diversified enterprises. *

Third, *moral inhibitions* serve to block self-satisfying conduct that would be unreasonably dangerous to others. Even if there were no penalties, or no chance of being caught, many peoples' own moral sense—their pride in doing right and the accompanying embarrassment of doing wrong—would protect others from harm. * * *

Regulation, in the form of legally binding *formal behavioral control mechanisms,* is a fourth important force in the realm of accident deterrence. Traditional criminal penalties are but a small part of the overall picture. There has been a proliferation in collective intervention * through safety agencies like CPSC, EPA, FAA, FDA, NHTSA, OSHA, and so on, through the alphabet. Perhaps even more pervasive are state, local and professional control regimes as diverse as building codes, highway engineering departments, and medical quality review boards. * * *

3.   Why the Deterrent Potential of Tort Liability is Undermined

In the deterrence model, education and information should warn the potential tortfeasor when the sting will be applied. Where avoidance hurts less than the sting, he can rationally elect another course of conduct. This is the "law and economics" view. Its model is decidedly one of *general deterrence.* People are led to behave properly before they have any personal encounter with the law. * * * Why does general deterrence fail? * * *

The model of general deterrence requires knowledge. * * * For example, when a state supreme court announces that hosts risk tort liability if they fail to use reasonable care in serving alcoholic beverages, * how many people in the state whose behavior needs modifying even learn of this ruling, let alone remember it? Even in enterprises, key actors may remain quite ignorant of their obligations under tort law. In an important * * * study, George Eads and Peter Reuter report they were "struck in the companies we visited by how few changes in law were transmitted to those involved in design decisions."[32] They noted two manufacturers of potentially highly dangerous products "[b]oth * * * treated the information generated by specific product liability suits as random noise." * * * Even those with broad awareness of tort liability have many reasons to see it as highly unpredictable. These reasons include doctrinal complexity, * rapid legal change, state-to-state variance, the perceived lottery-like nature of secret jury decision-making, * the vagaries of trials, and pervasive rough-and-ready settlement practices. * * *

A further diminution of tort law's effectiveness as a deterrent occurs because people discount the threat of tort liability. * From an economic perspective, some discounting can be quite rational. * Some victims with bona fide claims will not sue. The injured party may be

---

[32] G[eorge] Eads & P[eter] Reuter, Designing Safer Products: Corporate Responses to Product Liability Law and Regulation ix (1983) (RAND Corporation study).

unaware of his legal rights, have an aversion to the idea of litigation, have adequate sources of compensation other than tort damages, or have a small individual loss. Or the victim may not even know who his injurer is. * Sometimes the judicial system will fail to impose liability for conduct which actually was unreasonably dangerous. This can occur where the victim may have lost evidence, a witness is reluctant, or the fact-finding process works imperfectly. Additionally, the tortfeasor likely is aware that many cases can be settled for far less than the cost of damages incurred. * * *

4.   Liability Insurance and Deterrence

Complete liability insurance protection shifts the *direct* economic deterrent pressure of tort law from would-be tortfeasors to insurance companies. This shift complicates tort law's potential for behavioral control. * For most American enterprises, as well as professionals and drivers, protection by liability insurance is the rule. Insurers, however, rarely choose to use significant deductibles or co-insurance provisions to put economic pressure on insureds. * * *

In theory, one might expect the pressure of competition to encourage insurers to individualize pricing wherever possible. They could break the market into finely tuned categories, and set different premiums to reflect the injury potential of each category. The insured, in turn, would have an economic incentive to get into a lower-priced category. Pricing practices could thus make enterprises sensitive to the dangers they create. In practice, however, only a very small proportion of insureds pay premiums sensitive to *changes* in the dangerousness of *their* conduct. * * * Even if a premium hike mattered little, the threat of cancellation might be more effective in promoting care. * * *

Insurance companies themselves can take safety measures such as inspecting premises. More importantly, they can *demand safety measures of insureds*. For example, they can require employee training courses and fire-control systems. Here, too, I am skeptical whether tort law significantly increases accident avoidance. Apart from driver education, insurance companies rarely make safety-related demands before providing individual liability insurance. Doctors, for example, aren't regulated by their insurers. * Likewise, insurers require enterprises to adopt few significant safety measures. * * *

B.   *Making Victims Whole: Tort as a Bizarre Compensation System*

* * * Tort law cannot provide compensation to enormous numbers of accident victims. * Our jurisprudence requires a causal link between the plaintiff and the defendant even where fault is no longer relevant. This problem is not limited to the "DES daughters" sort of litigation, where plaintiffs cannot identify which of many manufacturers provided the drug to their mothers.[a] At least a causal connection exists between the plaintiff group and a limited number of DES manufacturers. But in many accidents there is no plausible defendant. For example, if a driver's mind wanders after a hard day at work, who can be held responsible if he loses control of the car for a minute and crashes into a tree? The object of his thoughts? The tree owner? The car manufacturer? The owner of the road? His boss? Many accidental

---

[a]   [Eds.' note] See *supra* Sindell v. Abbott Labs., 26 Cal.3d 588, 163 Cal.Rptr. 132, 607 P.2d 924 (1980), pages 257–266.

injuries are essentially self-inflicted—not only one-car accidents, but also in home accidents and recreational mishaps. * * *

To further widen the compensation gap, many tort defendants are judgment-proof. Enterprises living on a financial shoestring often go without liability insurance. Many individuals have no funds to satisfy tort judgments. This group includes a distressingly large number of motorists who drive without liability insurance * or who carry a bare statutory minimum. * * *

[L]awyers' talents, plaintiffs' demeanor, defendants' grit, and idiosyncrasies of jury composition combine to hand similar victims altogether dissimilar results. * Geographical bias also pervades the system. * * * It is no wonder, then, that many people view tort law as a lottery. * * *

Compared with other systems of compensation, tort law is too generous to many victims in both small- and large-injury cases. To be sure, many small-injury cases result in no claims at all. However, many others yield substantially more compensation than they warrant because injurers find buying off nuisance claims cheaper than litigation. * * * Similarly, some badly injured tort victims fare fabulously better than do others in our society who have similar needs, but claim against other compensation systems. * * *

Finally, the tort system is fabulously expensive to operate in comparison to modern compensation systems. * First, there are large insurance commissions and other marketing costs that come with privately marketed, often individualized insurance policies. Next, highly individualized and unpredictable rules promote exorbitant claims administration, including investigation costs and lawyer fees. As a result, usually well under half of liability insurance premiums go to paying benefits. * Finally, the tort system imposes a great deal of public expense in the form of judge, jury and administrative time. * * *

C.   *Corrective Justice: The Mirage of Compensation of the Deserving*

* * * The corrective-justice vision compounds the unreality by imagining that people with legal claims naturally want legal redress, * and that they actually find real justice when they sue. To the contrary, in large numbers of cases, the current system functions whimsically and doesn't accord with anyone's sense of justice. The much-vaunted individualized attention to victims * in practice sanctions flagrant horizontal inequity because of settlement practices, trial theatrics, and other reasons already discussed. * * *

There is widespread social consensus in favor of deterring wrongdoing and compensating accident victims. But in the face of current realities it is difficult to argue that tort law well serves these or other more controversial goals. By trying to do many different things, I have argued, tort law ends up doing none of them well. * * *

NOTE

Costs of the Tort System. Tort litigation often is not a simple process, and, as such, it can be costly. Establishing the facts necessary to prove liability in a sophisticated tort action such as a medical malpractice or products liability claim, generally requires months or even years of factual investigation, including the hiring of experts, as well as an extensive discovery process. Similarly, proving damages often requires the use of medical witnesses, economists, and rehabilitation experts.

Most studies conclude that plaintiffs receive roughly half of the total payments made by defendants in the tort system. Professors A. Mitchell Polinsky and Steven Shavell summarize several of these studies:

> Tillinghast-Towers Perrin reports in a nationwide survey of the tort system that victims receive only $0.46 of every dollar paid by defendants.[127] Other authors come to similar conclusions. James Kakalik and Nicholas Pace estimate that in tort litigation generally, victims obtain $0.46 to $0.47 per dollar of tort system expenditures.[128] Also, Kakalik and his coauthors ascertain that in asbestos cases victims obtain $0.37 of every dollar paid by defendants,[129] and Stephen Carroll and his coauthors find that in such cases victims obtain $0.42.[130] Professor Patricia Danzon concludes that for medical malpractice claims victims receive $0.40 for every dollar of defendants' liability insurance payments,[131] and Peter Huber also reports that victims receive $0.40 for such claims.[132] Huber states as well that in product liability litigation, victims obtain $0.40 for every dollar paid by defendants for liability insurance. Professors Joni Hersch and Kip Viscusi observe that in tort litigation in Texas, plaintiffs receive $0.57 for every dollar paid by defendants.[134] Some of these studies do not take into account the administrative costs of insurers, the value of the time spent by litigants, or the operating costs of the judicial system, and therefore overestimate the amount obtained by victims per dollar of total litigation-related expenditures.

A. Mitchell Polinsky & Steven Shavell, The Uneasy Case for Product Liability, 123 Harv. L. Rev. 1437, 1469–70 (2010).

---

[127] See Tillinghast-Towers Perrin, U.S. Tort Costs: 2003 Update 17 (2003) (victims receive $0.22 for economic losses and $0.24 for noneconomic losses). * * *

[128] See James S. Kakalik & Nicholas M. Pace, Rand Inst. for Civil Justice, Costs and Compensation Paid in Tort Litigation ix tbl.S.3 (1986). The numbers reported in the text are based on the net compensation received by plaintiffs compared to the total expenditures on tort litigation * * *.

[129] James S. Kakalik et al., Rand Inst. for Civil Justice, Costs of Asbestos Litigation vii tbl.S.2 (1983).

[130] Stephen J. Carroll et al., Rand Inst. for Civil Justice, Asbestos Litigation 104 (2005).

[131] Patricia M. Danzon, Liability for Medical Malpractice, in 1 Handbook of Health Economics 1339, 1369 (A.J. Culyer & J.P. Newhouse eds., 2000).

[132] * * * [Peter W.] Huber, [Liability: The Legal Revolution and Its Consequences] 151 [(1988)].

[134] Joni Hersch & W. Kip Viscusi, Tort Liability Litigation Costs for Commercial Claims, 9 Am. L. & Econ. Rev. 330, 359 tbl.5 (2007).

2. THE LIMITS OF THE ROLE OF FAULT IN AUTOMOBILE COLLISIONS

Excerpt, David Klein & Julian A. Waller, Causation, Culpability and Deterrence in Highway Crashes

62–64, 71–74,209–10 (Department of Transportation Automobile Insurance and Compensation Study 1970).

* * * The basic concept that has guided safety programs during the past half century—and that remains a major influence today—is that crashes are caused by avoidable inappropriate actions on the part of the driver or the pedestrian. One kind of inappropriate action popularly believed to cause crashes is the deliberate violation of traffic laws. * * * In order clearly to implicate traffic violations as a cause of accidents, one would have to demonstrate that violations occur with greater frequency among drivers who have crashes than among drivers who do not. Although such a relationship has been demonstrated for some kinds of violation and for some types of drivers, * the over-all relationship is not sufficiently strong to implicate violations in general. Indeed, a study * made of overt driving behavior[4] immediately preceding a crash concluded that drivers traveling at substantially greater *or lower* speeds than the general flow of traffic were more likely to crash than those traveling at the same speed as the general flow. Since in many cases—notably on limited-access highways—the general flow exceeds the posted limits by a few miles per hour, the driver who complies with the law by driving at or below the limit conceivably runs a greater risk of a crash than the driver who breaks the speed limit by a slight margin.

When the driver's or the pedestrian's inappropriate response does not involve deliberate violation of the law, it is frequently interpreted as involving "error," carelessness, risk-taking, or some other form of avoidable "improper behavior." * * * As in the case of violations, "improper" driving can be implicated as a causal factor only if it can be demonstrated that it occurs more frequently among drivers involved in crashes than among those not involved. Good evidence on this relationship is lacking, and at least two studies appear to document a lack of any relationship. In one of these, * drivers were covertly observed during one to two miles of city driving and were scored on the basis of safe or unsafe driving behavior. Of the sample, 48% "were judged entirely safe," 41% committed more safe driving acts than unsafe ones, 9% committed an equal number of safe and unsafe acts, and 1% drove unsafely more often than safely. However, when the behavior of these drivers was checked against their official driving records, "comparison of average scores with accident involvement revealed no significant tendency among persons demonstrating different degrees of safeness or unsafeness to have accidents." A similar conclusion appears warranted from the results of the second study as well * * *.

---

[4] Overt driving behavior includes all behavior that can be noted by visual observation as distinct from covert factors, such as blood-alcohol concentration, medical impairment, etc.

[S]everal studies have attempted to determine whether drivers who pass the skill test with high scores differ in subsequent crash experience from those who pass with low scores. These studies have shown that drivers with higher scores do have somewhat fewer crashes than those with lower scores. The differences, however, though statistically significant, are not substantial. * To the extent that basic skill can be evaluated by currently available techniques, therefore, such skill would appear to be a distinguishing factor in crash experience but not an overriding one. * * *

Although it may be possible to characterize an individual as a generally "safe" or generally "unsafe" driver, it is important to note that no individual performs even a thoroughly familiar task at precisely the same level of skill at all times. Everyone * * * has "off days" or "bad moments" during which a normally high level of skill deteriorates sharply, for any of a multiplicity of reasons. Hence a substantial but largely unmeasureable number of violations and crashes occur which involve generally competent drivers who are suffering temporary lapses from their normally adequate levels. *

Common sense would lead to the conclusion that such lapses, if they are indeed temporary and infrequent, might lead to a record of only one or two violations or crashes over a considerable period of time—certainly not a "bad" record. This is undoubtedly true for many drivers, and it probably accounts for a very high proportion of violations and of less severe crashes. Increasingly sophisticated statistical techniques demonstrate, however, that infrequent events, such as violations and crashes, do not distribute themselves in random fashion but may, instead, cluster in a quite "improbable" way. Thus it is possible for a generally "safe" driver to accumulate a "bad" record over a short period of time despite the fact that his lapses from "good" driving behavior are few. * * *

The foregoing analysis has several implications. It indicates that although intentional risk-taking and gross negligence undoubtedly play a part in some crashes—especially the more severe ones—many, if not most, cases of driver error are not intentional or negligent but are beyond conscious control. Some are the result of inherent biological limitations, transitory or permanent, of which the individual is unaware. * Others may be triggered by an environment (of highway, vehicle, etc.) that, at best, fails to inhibit, prevent, or forgive error and, at worst, actually promotes the likelihood or the inevitability of error. * In such cases error may be * * * the cause most easily noted in superficial investigation—but the remote causes, which lie elsewhere, may in fact be not only more significant but also more amenable to change. Still others may result from a combination of these factors. * * *

The very sharp reduction in industrial injuries * * * was accomplished not by educational efforts to make the worker "more careful" but by changes in his environment through the adoption of machinery guards, air brakes and other fail-safe devices, factory fire laws, limitations on the concentration of coal dusts and other hazards in the air, etc. The few industries which still suffer a relatively high rate of industrial injuries are those in which technological devices for environmental safety have not yet been sufficiently developed (e.g., construction) or which for economic or ideological reasons generate

extensive lobbying against their mandatory adoption (e.g., coal mining).
*

As we review the further data on causation, therefore, we must bear in mind that the human behavior involved in causation is itself the outcome of more remote causes, that attempting to change the proximate human behavior may be futile unless these more remote causes are modified, that there may be alternatives to the changing of human behavior, and that in connection with the highway problem these alternatives may be more effective than the traditional efforts to "improve" the driver. * * *

By far the most important inference to be drawn from this report is that efforts need to be shifted from the pre-crash phase of the crash sequence to the crash and post-crash phases—from the prevention or reduction of the number of crashes to the prevention or reduction of the human and economic losses that result from crashes. * * * Given the present level of technology and the present economic and political system, it would appear that primary emphasis should be devoted to vehicle design improvements to increase crash worthiness—essentially an acceleration of some of the efforts that have been going on for the past several years and have already shown positive results. Second priority should be given to improving emergency health services because, relatively speaking, the costs are low and the return in terms of lives saved is high. Third priority should be given to improving the highway system—since highway changes require more time for legislative approval and both more time and more money for implementation. * * *

B. NO-FAULT PLANS: AN OVERVIEW

The following three excerpts describe the basic structure of no-fault compensation systems. The first describes the operation of workers' compensation, the largest category and most long-lived of major alternative compensation systems in the United States. The second excerpt describes a more recent innovation, the National Vaccine Injury Compensation Plan. The third describes automobile no-fault and its complex interactions with the tort system.

1. WORKERS' COMPENSATION

Excerpt, Fowler V. Harper, Fleming James, Jr. & Oscar
S. Gray, Harper, James and Gray on Torts § 11.2
(3d ed. 2007).

[See *supra* pages 15–16.]

2. NATIONAL VACCINE INJURY COMPENSATION PLAN

Excerpt, Donald G. Gifford, William L. Reynolds & Andrew M. Murad, A Case Study in the Superiority of the Purposive Approach to Statutory Interpretation
64 S.C. L. Rev. 221, 246–55 (2012).

There is little doubt about what prompted Congress to pass the National Childhood Vaccine Injury Act of 1986.[a] One manufacturer had withdrawn from the vaccine market in 1984, and several others were suggesting they might do the same. Insurance premiums for manufacturers had skyrocketed, and there were concerns that insurance would no longer be available. Although Congress acknowledged that vaccines had led to "great progress ... in eliminating" childhood diseases, it also recognized that in a few instances vaccinations result in "serious—and sometimes deadly"—side effects.[210] For victims and their families, the common law tort system offered only "opportunities for redress and restitution" that were "limited, time-consuming, expensive, and often unanswered." Despite the fact that "futures have been destroyed and mounting expenses must be met," often no recovery was available within the tort system. In the NCVIA, Congress turned instead to a no-fault compensation system.

The goal of no-fault compensation systems is to benefit both potential tortfeasors and injured parties through an administrative regime that replaces costly, unpredictable tort litigation with a predictable, less-expensive method for awarding compensation. No-fault compensation systems are based upon a hypothetical quid pro quo, also known as the compensation bargain, between potential tortfeasors and the injured parties. Unlike traditional tort litigation, victims are entitled to compensation without having to prove fault or tortious conduct on the part of injurers, and without the fear that affirmative defenses will operate as a bar to recovery. Instead, victims receive compensation through a simple showing that they suffered injuries that fall within the boundaries of the no-fault regime. In exchange for guaranteed compensation, a claimant's recovery is usually limited to a certain percentage of her or his actual *economic* loss. Moreover, compensation for noneconomic loss, such as pain and suffering, is typically unavailable. Thus, the claimant is assured compensation, and the tortfeasor has the benefit of knowing the boundaries of his potential liability, a pair of societal benefits that the less predictable tort system lacks.

The compensation bargain can be examined more closely. No-fault systems, such as the NCVIA, share three objectives. The first is to compensate as many victims of harm-producing behavior as possible. These programs sometimes cover repetitive injuries caused by manufacturers or other businesses.[b] In other instances, no-fault programs, such as automobile no-fault, require participants to purchase

---

[a]   [Eds.' note] 42 U.S.C. §§ 300AA–1 to 34 (2006)] [hereinafter NCVIA].

[210] H.R. Rep. No. 99-908, at 5[–6], *reprinted in* 1986 U.S.C.C.A.N. at 6346–47.

[b]   [Eds.' note] See *infra* pages 705–706, Notes 3 & 5.

insurance to cover the comparatively modest injuries—numerous in the aggregate—that fall within statutorily defined boundaries. As such, compensation as a goal of no-fault compensation systems is inextricably linked to the related concept of loss distribution: the idea that "accident losses will be least burdensome if they are spread broadly among people and over time."[225] The common law tort system, standing alone, does a particularly poor job of fulfilling this instrumental objective. Instead, many victims are forced to absorb most of their losses. * * * For example, before the NVICP [National Vaccine Injury Compensation Plan], many vaccine-injured claimants were simply unable to prove that the manufacturer engaged in tortious conduct, or that the manufacturer caused the victim's loss. In fact, this was one of the primary justifications for passing the NCVIA: "[The no-fault system is] intended to compensate persons with recognized vaccine injuries without requiring the difficult individual determinations of *causation* of injury and without a demonstration that a manufacturer was *negligent* or that a vaccine was *defective*."[229]

This system has ensured that many vaccine-related injuries are compensated; since the no-fault system started receiving claims in 1989, 3,023 injured children have received compensation.[230]

The second objective of no-fault compensation systems in general, and the NVICP in particular, is to limit the liability of businesses or insurers, and to make their liability exposures more predictable. As previously discussed, the original impetus for the NCVIA was primarily to assure vaccine manufacturers that they would not be faced with liability insurance that was either unavailable or unaffordable. This is not surprising. Decades earlier, the National Association of Manufacturers and other business groups came around to supporting the adoption of the workers' compensation statutes because of growing fears about the liability exposure of their members under the common law system. More recently, physicians have advocated for no-fault compensation systems to replace common law handling of medical malpractice claims.[c] Similarly, although many victims of vaccine-related injuries were unable to recover in tort, there had been a number of plaintiffs who prevailed in the tort system and thus recovered large verdicts against the vaccine manufacturers. The unpredictability of such awards, as well as their magnitude, caused liability insurers to increase their premiums.

The third and final objective of no-fault systems is to significantly reduce administrative costs when compared with the tort system. Together with the reduction in the amount of compensation paid to each victim, these cost savings enable a much greater percentage of victims to be compensated without a sharp increase in the amounts manufacturers and their insurers pay. One study showed that before

---

[225] Guido Calabresi, The Costs of Accidents: A Legal and Economic Analysis 39 (Student ed. 1970). * * *

[229] H.R. Rep. No. 99-908, pt. 1, at 12 (1986), *reprinted in* 1986 U.S.C.C.A.N. 6344, 6353 (emphasis added).

[230] Health Res. & Servs. Admin., National Vaccine Injury Compensation Program: Data & Statistics, U.S. Dept. Health & Hum. Services, http://www.hrsa.gov/vaccinecompensation/data.html (last visited Oct. 5, 2012).

[c] [Eds.' note] See *infra* pages 705–706, Notes 4 & 5.

the adoption of the NCVIA, pharmaceutical firms expected to spend between five and seven dollars to transfer a single dollar of compensation to victims of vaccine-related harms.[240] * * *

In contrast to the exorbitant transaction costs inherent in vaccine litigation, the costs of administering the NVICP, according to the Congressional Budget Office, represent approximately 15% of the total cost.[244] Other estimates place the percentage of administrative costs for the NVICP between 10% and 30%.[245]

Further, because no-fault compensation schemes remove the time-consuming, case-by-case determinations of fault necessary in common law tort cases, they can provide quick compensation to victims. For example, a 1996 study showed that uncontested claims in the workers' compensation system—the no-fault system that handles most claims of workers injured in the course of their employment—were typically paid within about three weeks of the date of filing.[249] Contested claims took a bit longer and averaged about four months. In contrast, tort claims handled by the common law judicial system usually take approximately fifteen to twenty months to resolve. In other words, on average, it takes at least four times as long for an injured claimant to receive compensation in the tort system. The ability of no-fault systems to administer claims promptly is a huge benefit for injured parties, especially when the injury renders the victim incapable of performing her job.

B.   *Structural Overview of the National Vaccine Injury Compensation Program*

Two major recurring issues must be addressed when devising an alternative compensation system for product-related injuries. First, the no-fault alternative must designate a "compensable event" to determine which claims are entitled to compensation in the administrative system. Once the claimant has established that he is entitled to compensation, the second major issue that must be addressed is which parties are required to finance the no-fault system. * * *

In any compensation system, the claimant must establish that her injury constitutes a compensable event entitling her to compensation. Recovery in the tort system is premised upon the plaintiff's ability to prove that the defendant's tortious conduct proximately caused the plaintiff's injury. In contrast, no-fault compensation systems provide recovery as long as the injury falls within the statutory or administrative definitions of a compensable event, thus avoiding the

---

[240] See Richard L. Manning, Changing Rules in Tort Law and the Market for Childhood Vaccines, 37 J.L. & Econ. 247, 271 (1994). These figures, according to Manning, were "conservative." *Id.*

[244] Congressional Budget Office, The Economics of U.S. Tort Liability: A Primer 21 (2003), *available at* http://cbo.gov/sites/default/files/cbofiles/ftpdocs/46xx/doc4641/10-22-tortreform-study.pdf.

[245] See James R. Copland, Administrative Compensation for Pharmaceutical-and-Vaccine-Related Injuries, 8 Ind. Health L. Rev. 277, 285 (2011) (11% with 3% going towards attorneys' fees); Robert L. Rabin, The Vaccine No-Fault Act: An Overview, 8 Ind. Health L. Rev. 269, 271 (2011) (between 10% and 30%).

[249] Don Dewees et al., Exploring the Domain of Accident Law: Taking the Facts Seriously 394 (1996) (citing 1 Am. Law Inst., Reporter's Study: Enterprise Responsibility for Personal Injury 119 (1991)).

time-consuming, case-by-case inquiries into fault and causation required by the tort system.

NCVIA established a no-fault compensation system for vaccine-related injuries or deaths. The statute makes clear that a petitioner *must first* seek compensation through the no-fault system before attempting to initiate a civil action for damages against a vaccine manufacturer. As is true of most no-fault regimes, the petitioner is not required to prove tortious conduct on the part of the vaccine manufacturer. Instead, the petitioner must demonstrate that she has suffered an injury, or compensable event, that is within the jurisdiction of the administrative regime. A compensable event is defined by the "Vaccine Injury Table," which lists: (1) the vaccines that are covered under the program; (2) those injuries/disabilities "resulting from the administration of such vaccines" that are entitled to compensation; and (3) the period of time following the vaccination during which the first manifestation of the injury/disability must occur.[262] To establish a prima facie case for compensation, the petitioner must demonstrate that she received a covered vaccine and suffered a "table injury" within the proper time period. The petitioner does not need to prove causation. Instead, after establishing a prima facie case, the petitioner will receive compensation for her injury *unless* the Secretary of HHS can demonstrate that the injury was "unrelated to the administration of the vaccine."[265] Petitioners who cannot establish their compensation entitlements based on the vaccine injury table—for example, those who suffered injuries that are unlisted or occurred outside the coverage period—are not necessarily without recourse. Such claimants may still receive compensation for "non-table" injuries,—injuries not specified in the statute—if they can demonstrate that the vaccine caused their injury.

If the special master determines that that the claimant is entitled to compensation, the claimant may recover damages for both economic and noneconomic harms. Unlike most no-fault compensation systems, in which a fixed schedule caps the claimant's economic recovery, the NVICP provides economic compensation for an *unlimited* amount of certain actual and projected "unreimbursable" expenses, including medical and rehabilitative costs. Injured claimants may also receive compensation for actual and projected lost earnings. Finally, all claimants, regardless of whether they receive an award through the NVICP, are generally entitled to recover reasonable attorneys' fees and costs.

When it comes to recovery for noneconomic injuries, the NVICP also represents a departure from traditional no-fault systems that limit a claimant's recovery to economic loss. The NVICP permits the special master to award up to $250,000 for "pain and suffering" and "emotional distress" on account of a vaccine-related injury. In spite of this "scaled-down discretionary decision" for noneconomic damages, however,

---

[262] See 42 U.S.C. § 300aa–14(a) (2006). See also 42 C.F.R. § 100.3(a) (2011) for the most recent Vaccine Injury Table.

[265] See § 300aa–13(a)(l)(B).

scholars have praised the NVICP for "[assessing] damages in a simple and administratively efficient manner."[276]

After the special master issues a final judgment, the petitioner has two options. The petitioner can accept the master's judgment, precluding her from bringing a civil suit for damages against the vaccine manufacturer. In the alternative, the petitioner may reject the special master's judgment and file a claim for damages. The NCVIA, however, severely limits a vaccine manufacturer's liability in tort actions and thus discourages petitioners from pursuing these claims. Specifically, the NCVIA completely eliminates the manufacturer's liability for: (1) the failure to "provide direct warnings to the injured party"; (2) punitive damages, assuming that the manufacturer did not engage in fraudulent, or otherwise illegal, conduct; and (3) damages resulting from any "injury or death result[ing] from side effects that were unavoidable even though the vaccine was properly prepared and was accompanied by proper directions and warnings." * * *

2. Financing the NVICP

Having discussed the compensation entitlement provisions of the vaccine no-fault system, we now turn to the opposite side of the equation: Who is responsible for financing this compensatory regime? As Professor Rabin explains, "Typically, a no-fault scheme is financed through charges imposed on those parties engaged in the injury-producing activity."[285] The NVICP stays true to this principle and funds the compensation system through an excise tax imposed on all vaccine manufacturers that are covered under the no-fault system. * * * The proceeds from the excise tax are funneled into the Vaccine Injury Compensation Trust Fund, which holds the funds until they are eventually distributed to victims.

3. AUTOMOBILE NO FAULT

Excerpt, James M. Anderson, Paul Heaton & Stephen J. Carroll, The U.S. Experience with No-Fault Automobile Insurance: A Retrospective

2, 14–15, 35 (RAND Institute for Civil Justice, 2010).

* * * Commentators have been seeking a better way to allocate the costs of accidents and compensate victims since almost from the time that Henry Ford's Model T popularized the automobile. * * * Influenced by the example of workers' compensation laws that provided payment to injured workers without a showing of fault, commentators advocated a system of compensation that did not rely on the requirement that an

---

[276] See [Robert L.] Rabin, [Some Thoughts on the Efficacy of a Mass Toxics Administrative Compensation Scheme, 52 Md. L. Rev. 951,] 959 (1993).

[285] [Id.] at 976. Rabin notes that "there is considerable divergence among [compensation] systems" as to whether the assessment funding the compensation system places an equal tax on all units of an injurious product or whether such funding will be variable, based on the "risk-generating character of contributing enterprises." Id. at 976–77. As explained in the text, in enacting the NVICP, Congress opted for the former method of funding, placing a $0.75 excise tax on all vaccine manufacturers who produce a vaccine that is covered under the Act. See 26 U.S.C. § 4131(b) (2006).

injured party show the fault of another driver in order to gain compensation for his or her injuries. * Beginning in 1919, they generally argued for an approach to compensation that did not rely on the tort system and reduced or eliminated compensation for noneconomic losses, such as pain and suffering, to accident victims with less serious injuries. In return, the system would provide assured compensation for accident victims' economic losses without regard for fault. Proponents of this approach argued that it would reduce the overall costs of the system and increase the fraction of the auto-insurance dollar that would go to injured people. The elimination of these disputes would also speed the provision of compensation. Compensation would, thus, be adequate to cover economic loss regardless of fault and would be more equitably distributed among injured parties. Around 1970, this system became known generally as a *no-fault system.* *

Between 1971 and 1976, 16 states adopted some form of mandatory no-fault compensation system. Nine other states either required the purchase of, or required that insurers offer, enhanced first-party insurance covering an insured's economic losses, without any constraint on access to the tort system. Early empirical evaluations of no-fault were generally positive, and it seemed likely that no-fault would be widely adopted. * * *

Variations on No-Fault and Tort Approaches

While automobile-insurance regimes are often divided into tort and no-fault, there are a number of possible variations. A conventional no-fault system has three components: (1) a limitation on the ability to sue under the tort system, (2) a limitation on recovery for noneconomic damages, and (3) a first-party insurance system designed to replace the right to sue. While often spoken of together as being part of a no-fault system, these three components are independent of one another.

Add-On Coverage

Other states are known as *add-on states* because the first-party no-fault coverage is added on to the conventional tort liability system and its required insurance coverages.

- *Mandatory add-on* requires drivers to purchase this first-party coverage in addition to conventional third-party liability coverage.
- *Optional add-on* requires insurance companies to offer first-party policies to drivers, who can choose or decline to purchase the coverage.

In these states, there is no restriction on access to the tort system or noneconomic damages through the tort system.

In conventional tort states, first-party PIP coverage is often available as an optional product, depending on the insurer.[13] The insurer is not required to offer it, but insurers often do. This narrows the distinction between optional-add-on states and tort states.

---

[13] PIP is similar to MedPay in that they are both first-party coverages that do not require any proof of fault. They differ in that PIP typically has much higher policy limits and provides more-comprehensive benefits (including, for example, rehabilitative services and lost income) than MedPay.

Choice

A few states—Kentucky,[14] New Jersey, and Pennsylvania—have a choice system that allows drivers to choose between less-expensive *limited tort insurance* (which restricts the right to recover for noneconomic losses) and more-expensive *full tort insurance* (which allows the insured to retain the full right to recover in tort against third parties).[15] When a driver who has elected full tort is injured by a driver who has elected limited tort, the full tort driver can recover against the limited-tort driver's BI insurance. The limited-tort driver can recover against the other driver only for economic damages that exceed the limited-tort driver's PIP insurance coverage. * * *

Excerpt, Stephen J. Carroll and James S. Kakalik, No-Fault Automobile Insurance: A Policy Perspective

4–7, 9 (RAND Institute for Civil Justice, 1991).

* * * This section compares the traditional and no-fault systems in action and uses results from our larger report to illustrate how each system handles both a typical injury case and a more serious one. *

The Traditional System

In the traditional fault-based system, injured people can seek compensation for all their losses from the driver who caused the accident. These losses include economic and noneconomic loss. However, a driver's responsibility is limited to the extent he or she was at fault.

In the traditional system, consumers can purchase three kinds of injury insurance coverage. Drivers can buy **Bodily Injury (BI)** insurance to pay compensation they owe someone they injured. Drivers can also buy **Uninsured Motorist (UM)** insurance to cover themselves for any compensation due them that they cannot obtain from an uninsured motorist. Finally, drivers may buy a form of no-fault insurance called **Medical Payments (MedPay)**, which covers their own medical costs, typically to low policy limits.

A Typical Injury Case

How does this system work in practice? Suppose you are injured in a car crash in a state that uses the traditional system (a "tort" state). The bill for your medical expenses comes to $701. You also lose $265 in wages because you missed work. (These losses were typical for people injured in auto accidents in the mid-1980s; half of them had smaller economic loss, half greater.)

You typically submit a liability claim to the other driver's BI insurer or, if he did not have BI insurance and you had purchased UM

---

[14] Although Kentucky is technically a choice state, because motorists must specially file a form with the Office of Insurance in order to opt-out of the no-fault system, more than 90 percent of motorists are covered under no-fault. Thus, in practical terms, Kentucky functions like a no-fault state.

[15] Washington, D.C., also has elements of a choice system, but it is unique in that accident victims are permitted to choose, on an accident-by-accident basis, between PIP benefits and tort recovery.

coverage, to your own insurer. You seek compensation for both your economic losses ($966) and your noneconomic loss.

After you negotiate with the other driver's insurer, you usually settle. The settlement amount depends on a variety of factors, such as your share of responsibility for the accident, your injuries, how they affected your everyday activities, and whether you hired an attorney. Our data show that the liability compensation provided someone with about $1,000 in economic losses ranged from nothing to over $25,000. However, let us say you end up with $3,000–$966 for your economic loss and $2,034 for your noneconomic loss. (Our data indicate that people with $1,000 in economic loss who received liability compensation had average compensation that was just over three times their economic loss.) If you hire a lawyer to help you pursue your claim, you will probably receive more than the average, but you will pay some of whatever you receive (typically about one-third) in lawyer fees.

You also submit your medical bills to your own insurer for reimbursement under your MedPay coverage. There is little to negotiate about: MedPay covers your medical costs regardless of who is at fault, and the amount of your bill is clear. So long as costs are below the policy limit, typically in the $1,000 to $5,000 range, you receive the full amount, $701. In sum, you collect $3,701 ($3,000 from liability insurance, either the other driver's BI or your own UM, and $701 from MedPay.)

Incidentally, your employer-provided health-care insurance may have covered most of your medical bills, and your sick pay may have covered the time you had to take off work. But those payments generally do not enter into the determination of what either the other driver's insurance company, or your own, owe to you.

Of course, there is no guarantee that your claim will come out this way. If you had not purchased MedPay auto insurance, you would only get your liability compensation, $3,000. If the other driver was uninsured and if you did not have UM coverage, or if you were totally at fault for the accident, you would get no liability compensation. Your compensation would be limited to your $701 MedPay payment for your medical bills, if you had MedPay coverage. Finally, if you cannot collect liability compensation and do not have MedPay, you get nothing at all from auto insurance.

A More Serious Injury Case

What if the accident is more serious and you are severely injured? The procedure is pretty much the same as above: You submit the same kinds of claims—a liability claim against the other driver's BI insurance or your own UM policy and, if you have MedPay coverage, a claim against it as well. Your compensation depends on your injuries, your economic and noneconomic losses, and your share of fault for the accident. However, an additional factor comes into play: policy limits. The compensation you get from the other driver's BI insurance, or your own UM insurance, and from your MedPay coverage may be capped by policy limits.

Suppose, for example, your medical costs total $50,000, you lose another $50,000 in wages due to time off work, and you incur substantial pain and suffering. Even if the other driver has BI insurance, your compensation will be limited by the amount of coverage provided by his or her BI policy. Odds are that the other driver's policy carries a per-person limit of $50,000 or less. (Over half of all drivers who had BI coverage had a per-person limit of $50,000 or less in 1986.)

If the other driver is uninsured and you have UM, you can collect up to the limit of your own UM policy. Odds are that your UM compensation will be $25,000 or less. (Over half the drivers who had UM coverage had a per-person limit of $25,000 or less in 1986.) You can also collect your MedPay benefits up to its policy limit, say $5,000. (Eighty-six percent of the drivers who had MedPay coverage had a per-person limit of $5,000 or less.)

In sum, you sustain $100,000 in economic loss and substantial noneconomic loss, but your compensation will probably be no greater than $55,000, if the other driver is insured.[2] If the other driver is not insured and you have UM, you receive $30,000; if you are entirely at fault, you receive $5,000. Here, too, if you hire a lawyer to help you pursue your claim, you will pay some of whatever you receive (typically about one-third) in lawyer fees.

No-fault Systems

No-fault systems differ from the traditional system in two ways:

1. No-fault processes serious injury cases differently from less serious injury cases. Seriously injured people can pursue liability claims for all their economic and noneconomic losses; less seriously injured people can seek compensation only for economic losses. The dividing line between serious and less serious injuries is drawn in terms of a threshold. There are two types of threshold:

    A verbal threshold distinguishes claims in terms of a description of the injury (for example, "dismemberment" or "significant and permanent loss of an important bodily function").

    A dollar threshold specifies a dollar amount that medical costs must exceed before an injured person can pursue a liability claim.

2. No-fault also provides enhanced insurance against one's own economic losses. Known as **Personal Injury Protection (PIP)**, this insurance covers economic losses up to the policy limit, without regard to fault. PIP pays only economic losses (such as medical expenses and lost wages), not noneconomic losses.

The Typical Injury Case in a No-Fault System

How does a no-fault system work in practice? Let us look back at the case discussed above and assume that the state no-fault plan has a verbal threshold and provides for a $15,000 PIP benefit level. You had $966 in economic loss ($701 in medical costs and $265 in lost wages). Suppose your injuries are not serious enough to get you over the threshold. Your PIP insurance will compensate you for your medical

---

[2] In principle, you could seek compensation from the other driver's personal assets. However, as a practical matter, this rarely happens.

costs. PIP will also compensate you for 72 percent of your lost wages. *
If you have PIP insurance, you recover $892 from your own insurer,
enough to fully compensate you for your economic loss, taking tax
effects into account. Of course, if you do not have PIP, you get nothing.
(Although all current no-fault states mandate the purchase of PIP
coverage, some people go uninsured.)

If your injuries are sufficiently serious to get you over the
threshold, you can pursue a liability claim against the other driver.
(About 18 percent of the people with approximately $1,000 in economic
losses have injuries that will get them over a verbal threshold.) Once
past the threshold, the liability system's rules and procedures apply;
you will obtain the same liability compensation for noneconomic loss as
under the traditional system, and you will obtain compensation for any
economic loss that exceeds what PIP will compensate. If your liability
compensation for noneconomic loss is $2,034, you will collect that from
the other driver's BI insurer (or your own UM policy). You will also
collect $74 in liability compensation for your economic loss that exceeds
the PIP compensation due you. If you have PIP coverage, you will
recover the $892 from your PIP policy.

The More Serious Injury Case Under No-Fault

What happens to you in the other case—$50,000 in medical costs
and $50,000 in lost wages? Much the same as what happened to you
under the traditional system. However, you first collect from your own
PIP policy up to the limit—$15,000 in this case. You then claim against
the other driver's insurer for your uncompensated economic loss and
your noneconomic losses and collect up to the maximum of the other
driver's liability coverage, say $50,000. Your compensation is $65,000.
You still do not fully recover your economic losses, let alone any
compensation for your noneconomic losses, but you get somewhat more
than you would have under the traditional system, because you collect
PIP rather than MedPay. PIP pays lost wages as well as medical bills
and generally has higher policy limits. * * *

No-fault can yield substantial savings over the traditional system.
No-fault can also increase costs over the traditional system. It all
depends on the particular plan's provisions.

No-fault plans reduce transaction costs, regardless of their specific
provisions. Those plans that ban claims for noneconomic loss reduce
transaction costs by about 80 percent; those that allow seriously injured
people to pursue liability claims for noneconomic loss reduce
transaction costs by about 20 to 40 percent. Since transaction costs
constitute about one-third of total costs, the net reductions from the
latter plans equal approximately 10 percent of the total costs of injury
compensation.

No-fault plans match compensation more closely with economic loss
by increasing the fraction of economic loss that is compensated and by
reducing the amount of compensation paid people in excess of their
economic loss. As a result, injured people with smaller losses tend to
recover amounts approximating their medical costs and lost wages,
while more seriously injured people whose compensation is capped by
policy limits recover a larger share of their economic loss, because they
can collect both enhanced PIP benefits and liability compensation.

No-fault plans generally speed up compensation. Injured people begin receiving payments on average about two months sooner under no-fault than under the traditional system.

C. THE BOUNDARY BETWEEN LIABILITY IN THE NO-FAULT COMPENSATION SYSTEM AND IN TORTS

Inherent in the design of any compensation system is the need to establish both *compensation entitlement boundaries* specifying which victims are entitled to recover benefits, and *liability boundaries* delineating which parties are assessed to provide the necessary funds. Under the common law of torts, the tortious nature of the defendant's conduct and causation, operating together, provide both boundaries. In no-fault compensation systems, however, who recovers and who pays are two separate issues. The legislature and the administrative agency it creates to administer the no-fault compensation system establish the criteria for determining these issues. In this section, we address the issue of compensation entitlement boundaries—who can recover, for what harms, and under what circumstances. Most often, if the harm is not covered under a no fault compensation plan, the injured claimant is able to sue in the common law tort system and recover more generous benefits than those available under the no-fault plan. Accordingly, the defendant typically is the party arguing that the injury falls within those to be compensated under the no-fault plan.

1. WORKERS' COMPENSATION

Blankenship v. Cincinnati Milacron Chemicals, Inc.

Supreme Court of Ohio, 1982.
69 Ohio St.2d 608, 433 N.E.2d 572.

* * * On February 22, 1979, appellants, eight current or former employees of Cincinnati Milacron Chemicals, Inc. (hereinafter Milacron) * * * alleged that while they were stationed at Milacron's chemical manufacturing facility in Reading, Ohio, they were exposed to the fumes and otherwise noxious characteristics of certain chemicals * within the scope of their employment which "rendered [them] sick, poisoned, and chemically intoxicated, [and] causing them pain, discomfort, and emotional distress which will continue for the indefinite future and causing suffering and permanent disability."

In pertinent part, * appellants further alleged in their complaint, that notwithstanding the knowledge of appellees that such conditions existed, the appellees "... failed to correct said conditions, failed to warn ... [appellants]-employees of the dangers and conditions that existed and failed to report said conditions to the various state and federal agencies to which they were required to report by law." Appellants claimed that "[s]uch failure on the part of ... [appellees] was intentional, malicious and in willful and wanton disregard of the health of ... [appellants]" and that "[a]s a direct and proximate result of this ... failure, ... [appellants] have been injured ..." * * * It is undisputed that Milacron is a fully-covered, self-insured employer, in full compliance with all the requirements of the Ohio Workers'

Compensation Act, Ohio Rev. Code §§ 4123.01 *et seq.* Subsequent to the filing of the original complaint and the amended complaint, appellees moved to dismiss the complaint * * *.

The trial court issued an order * * * which granted appellees' motion and dismissed the action with prejudice as to appellees on the ground that the action was barred by relevant sections of the Ohio Constitution and the Ohio Workers' Compensation Act which afforded an employer and his employees total immunity from civil suit. * * * This holding was appealed and subsequently affirmed by the Court of Appeals * * *. In holding that appellees are immune from liability for intentional tortious conduct, the court reasoned that the purpose of Section 35, Article II of the Ohio Constitution, was to abolish civil actions by employees against complying employers for work-related injuries. The court further found that this provision, as implemented by Ohio Rev. Code § 4123.74, means that a court lacks jurisdiction to entertain a civil action for damages against an employer where an employee seeks to circumvent the exclusive nature of the workers' compensation scheme by alleging intentional conduct. * * *

■ WILLIAM B. BROWN, J. * * * The primary focus of the dispute between the parties centers upon the question of whether the Workers' Compensation Act (Ohio Rev. Code §§ 4123.35 *et seq.*) is intended to cover an intentional tort committed by employers against their employees. Section 35, Article II of the Ohio Constitution, serves as a basis for legislative enactments in the area of workers' compensation by providing, in pertinent part:

> For the purpose of providing compensation to workmen and their dependents, for death, injuries or occupational disease, occasioned in the course of such workmen's employment, laws may be passed establishing a state fund to be created by compulsory contribution thereto by employers, and administered by the state, determining the terms and conditions upon which payment shall be made therefrom. Such compensation shall be in lieu of all other rights to compensation, or damages, for such death, injuries, or occupational disease, and any employer who pays the premium or compensation provided by law, passed in accordance herewith, shall not be liable to respond in damages at common law or by statute for such death, injuries or occupational disease. . . .

The constitutional mandate has been implemented by Ohio Rev. Code § 4123.74 which provides:

> Employers who comply with section 4123.35 of the Revised Code shall not be liable to respond in damages at common law or by statute for any injury, or occupational disease, or bodily condition, *received or contracted by any employee in the course of or arising out of his employment* . . . whether or not such injury, occupational disease [or] bodily condition . . . is compensable under sections 4123.01 to 4123.94, inclusive, of the Revised Code. * * *

Clearly, neither the relevant constitutional language nor the pertinent statutory language expressly extend [sic] the grant of immunity to actions alleging intentional tortious conduct by employers against their employees. The General Assembly, however, in enacting Ohio Rev. Code § 4123.95, established a rule of construction which is clearly of assistance in determining the scope of employer immunity. This section provides that: "Sections 4123.01 to 4123.94, inclusive, of the Revised Code, shall be liberally construed in favor of employees and the dependents of deceased employees."

* * * By designating as compensable only those injuries ". . . received or contracted . . . in the course of or arising out of . . . employment . . . ," the General Assembly has expressly limited the scope of compensability. In so doing, the General Assembly surely did not intend to remove all remedies from the employee whose injury is not compensable under the Act. * And, by its use of this phrase, the General Assembly has seemingly allowed the judiciary the freedom to determine what risks are incidental to employment in light of the humanitarian purposes which underlie the Act.

* * * No reasonable individual would equate intentional and unintentional conduct in terms of the degree of risk which faces an employee nor would such individual contemplate the risk of an intentional tort as a natural risk of employment. * Since an employer's intentional conduct does not arise out of employment, Ohio Rev. Code § 4123.74 does not bestow upon employers immunity from civil liability for their intentional torts and an employee may resort to a civil suit for damages. *

This holding not only comports with constitutional and statutory requirements, but it is also consistent with the legislative goals which underlie the Workers' Compensation Act. The workers' compensation system is based on the premise that an employer is protected from a suit for negligence in exchange for compliance with the Workers' Compensation Act. The Act operates as a balance of mutual compromise between the interests of the employer and the employee whereby employees relinquish their common law remedy and accept lower benefit levels coupled with the greater assurance of recovery and employers give up their common law defenses and are protected from unlimited liability. * But the protection afforded by the Act has always been for negligent acts and not for intentional tortious conduct. * Indeed, workers' compensation Acts were designed to improve the plight of the injured worker, and to hold that intentional torts are covered under the Act would be tantamount to encouraging such conduct, and this clearly cannot be reconciled with the motivating spirit and purpose of the Act.

It must also be remembered that the compensation scheme was specifically designed to provide less than full compensation for injured employees. * Damages such as pain and suffering and loss of services on the part of a spouse are unavailable remedies to the injured employee. Punitive damages cannot be obtained. Yet, these damages are available to individuals who have been injured by intentional tortious conduct of third parties, and there is no legitimate reason why an employer should be able to escape from such damages simply because he committed an intentional tort against his employee. In addition, one of the avowed purposes of the Act is to promote a safe and injury-free work environment. * Affording an employer immunity for his intentional behavior certainly would not promote such an environment, for an employer could commit intentional acts with impunity with the knowledge that, at the very most, his workers' compensation premiums may rise slightly. * * *

In conclusion, it is for the trier of fact to initially determine whether the alleged conduct constitutes an intentional injury. In the instant case, the facts will demonstrate whether an intentional tort occurred or whether the injuries received by appellants were incurred in the course of and arising from appellants' employment such that the worker's compensation remedy would be exclusive. These questions of fact, however, are not properly determinable by a * * * motion to dismiss, for the lower court had before it insufficient facts to determine as a matter of law that appellants' complaint was barred. Appellants should be given an opportunity to prove their allegations that their employer committed an intentional tort causing them injury.

For the foregoing reasons, the judgment of the Court of Appeals is reversed, and this cause is remanded for further proceedings according to law. * * *

NOTES

1. *Subsequent History.* The *Blankenship* decision was one of the first volleys in a power struggle between the Ohio Supreme Court and the Ohio General Assembly that lasted more than two decades. The General Assembly attempted to reverse the result in *Blankenship* with legislation on two occasions, and each time the Supreme Court declared the legislation unconstitutional. In 1995, the General Assembly enacted a statute providing that the employer shall not be liable for an intentional tort that occurs during the course of employment except where "the plaintiff proves that the employer committed the tortious act with the intent to injure another or with the belief that the injury was substantially certain to occur." Ohio Rev. Code Ann. § 2745.01 (1995). The Ohio Supreme Court declared the statute unconstitutional on the grounds that the limitation of the employer's liability for intentional torts was not within the powers granted to the legislature under the state constitutional provision giving the legislature the power to enact workers' compensation legislation. Johnson v. BP Chems., Inc., 85 Ohio St.3d 298, 308, 707 N.E.2d 1107, 1114 (1999). However, in 2004, the General Assembly enacted yet another, similar statute limiting employer's liability for intentional torts. Ohio Rev. Code Ann. § 2745.01 (2014). The Ohio Supreme Court subsequently held that this statute was constitutional. Stetter v. R.J. Corman Derailment Servs., L.L.C., 125 Ohio St. 3d 280, 297, 927 N.E.2d 1092, 1110 (2010) ("[T]he General Assembly has not exceeded its authority to change the common law in the area of employer intentional torts."). Compare this conflict between the legislative and judicial branches with that surrounding the decision in *Ives v. South Buffalo Railway Co.*, *supra* pages 3–15, and pages 20–21, Note 2.

While some courts have followed the reasoning of *Blankenship*, others reject it. See, e.g., Mingachos v. CBS, Inc., 196 Conn. 91, 491 A.2d 368 (1985) (although a tort action is not barred against an employer "that deliberately intended to injure its employee," it is not sufficient that the employer's tort was "intentional," unless "the consequences of the act rather than the act itself" are intended).

2. *Recovery from Employer Acting in "Dual Capacity."* What if the employee is injured by actions of the defendant that ordinarily would not be categorized as arising out of the employer/employee relationship? Can a secondary "dual capacity" of the employer in its relationship with the employee establish obligations that are independent of the obligations that arise because of its status as an employer? Consider the case of a hospital operating room technician who is injured when kicked in the shoulder by a patient regaining consciousness after anesthesia. The employee subsequently is treated by a physical therapist employed by the hospital who negligently tears the employee's shoulder muscle, severely injuring him. Can the employee bring a common law tort action asserting medical malpractice for the negligence of its agent? In Wymer v. JH Properties, Inc., 50 S.W.3d 195 (Ky.2001), the Supreme Court of Kentucky held that the employee could bring such an action. Contra Suburban Hosp., Inc. v. Kirson, 362 Md. 140, 763 A.2d 185 (2000). What risks does this so-called dual capacity doctrine create? In recent decades few cases have allowed plaintiffs to recover under the dual capacity doctrine, and those cases where recovery has been allowed generally involve subsequent medical malpractice. Where the employee is injured while working with a machine, tool, or other device manufactured by the employer, attempts to find the employer liable as a product manufacturer have usually been unsuccessful, even when similar machines are sold to the public. See, e.g., Longever v. Revere Copper and Brass, Inc., 381 Mass. 221, 408 N.E.2d 857 (1980).

3. *Additional Reading.* For a study of problems in the administration of one state's workers' compensation system, see Gary T. Schwartz, Waste, Fraud, and Abuse in Workers' Compensation: The Recent California Experience, 52 Md. L. Rev. 983 (1993).

2. AUTOMOBILE NO-FAULT

Licari v. Elliott

Court of Appeals of New York, 1982.
57 N.Y.2d 230, 455 N.Y.S.2d 570, 441 N.E.2d 1088.

■ JASEN, J. The issue raised on this appeal is whether the plaintiff in this negligence action brought to recover damages for personal injuries has established a prima facie case that he sustained a "serious injury" within the meaning of subdivision 4 of section 671 of the Insurance Law, commonly referred to as the "No-Fault" Law.

On February 13, 1979, plaintiff was injured in a motor vehicle accident. After being examined at the hospital, plaintiff was diagnosed as having a concussion, acute cervical sprain, acute dorsal lumbar sprain and a contusion of the chest. He was released two hours later and went home. Later that day, plaintiff consulted his family physician and, after relating the events of the day, was told to rest in bed. On February 15, 1979, plaintiff again consulted his physician and complained that he was coughing up reddish phlegm. Concerned about possible rib damage, his physician had plaintiff admitted to the hospital for tests. The test results showed no rib damage and that plaintiff's lungs were clear. The hospital physician examined plaintiff upon his admission and testified at trial that plaintiff's lungs were clear, reflexes normal, and that he suffered only a "very mild limitation" of movement in the back and neck areas. No further medical testimony was elicited with respect to the extent of plaintiff's limitation of movement. On February 17, 1979, plaintiff stated that he felt better and requested his release from the hospital. He was discharged and returned home. On March 9, 1979, 24 days after the accident, plaintiff returned to his job as a taxi driver. Immediately upon returning to work, plaintiff resumed driving a taxicab 12 hours per day, 6 days a week, as he had prior to the accident. The only proof of limitation with respect to his work performance was plaintiff's own testimony that he was unable to help some of his fares with their luggage "if they happened to have luggage." Plaintiff also testified that he could not help his wife with various household chores as much as he had before the accident. Finally, plaintiff stated he had occasional transitory headaches and dizzy spells which were relieved by aspirin.

After the close of evidence, defendant moved to dismiss the complaint on the ground that plaintiff failed to establish that his injury met any of the threshold requirements of a serious injury as defined in subdivision 4 of section 671 of the Insurance Law. The court reserved decision on the motion and submitted the case to the jury on the theories that, in order to recover, plaintiff had to establish, by a preponderance of the evidence, that he had suffered either a medically determined injury of a nonpermanent nature which prevented him from performing substantially all his daily activities for not less than 90 days during the 180 days immediately following the accident or that as a result of the accident he sustained a significant limitation of use of a body function or system. The jury returned a verdict in favor of plaintiff, finding that plaintiff had proven a serious injury under both definitions. Defendant moved to set aside the verdict on the same ground as his prior motion to dismiss the complaint. The court denied the motion.

On appeal, the Appellate Division reversed and dismissed the complaint, holding that the plaintiff had failed, as a matter of law, to prove a serious injury under either definition. We agree and affirm.

In construing the statutory definition of serious injury, it is necessary to examine the policies and purposes underlying this State's no-fault legislation. The so-called No-Fault Law was adopted by the Legislature to correct certain infirmities recognized to exist under the common-law tort system of compensating automobile accident claimants. * The Legislature provided that "there shall be no right of recovery for non-economic loss [i.e., pain and suffering] except in the case of a serious injury, or for basic economic loss." Insurance Law § 673, sub. 1. The No-Fault Law, as originally enacted, contained a two-part definition of the term "serious injury" keyed to the nature of the injuries and the amount of the medical expenses. The monetary part provided that if reasonable medical costs exceeded $500, a serious injury would be established. This section was repealed in 1977 when experience demonstrated to the Legislature that the $500 threshold provided a target for plaintiffs which was too easily met and that the standard was unsuitable to fulfill the purpose of the No-Fault Law. * It was replaced with the present definition of serious injury as "a personal injury which results in death; dismemberment; significant disfigurement; a fracture; permanent loss of use of a body organ, member, function or system; permanent consequential limitation of use of a body organ or member; significant limitation of use of a body function or system; or a medically determined injury or impairment of a non-permanent nature which prevents the injured person from performing substantially all of the material acts which constitute such person's usual and customary daily activities for not less than ninety days during the one hundred eighty days immediately following the occurrence of the injury or impairment." Insurance Law § 671, sub. 4.

Tacit in this legislative enactment is that any injury not falling within the new definition of serious injury is minor and a trial by jury is not permitted under the no-fault system. We are required then to pass on the threshold question of whether the plaintiff in this case has established a prima facie case that he sustained a serious injury within the meaning of the statute.

Although the statute sets forth eight specific categories which constitute serious injury, we are only concerned on this appeal with construing two of them, to wit: whether the plaintiff suffered a serious injury which resulted in either (1) a "significant limitation of use of a body function or system"; or (2) "a medically determined injury or impairment of a non-permanent nature" which endured for 90 days or more and substantially limited the performance of his daily activities.

We begin our analysis of these two categories of serious injury by recognizing that one of the obvious goals of the Legislature's scheme of no-fault automobile reparations is to keep minor personal injury cases out of court. In support of this policy determination made by the Legislature, it seems only proper that the words contained in these two categories should be construed consistent with the legislative intent. Hence, the word "significant" as used in the statute pertaining to "limitation of use of a body function or system" should be construed to mean something more than a minor limitation of use. We believe that a minor, mild or slight limitation of use should be classified as insignificant within the meaning of the statute.

Likewise in the last category of the statute—"a medically determined injury or impairment of a non-permanent nature which prevents the injured person from performing substantially all of the material acts which constitute such person's usual and customary daily activities for not less than ninety days during the one hundred eighty days immediately following the occurrence of the injury or impairment"—the words "substantially all" should be construed to mean that the person has been curtailed from performing his usual activities to a great extent rather than some slight curtailment. As to the statutory 90/180–day period of disability requirement, it should be considered a necessary condition to the application of the statute. Where the statute is specific, as it is here, that the period of disability must be "for not less than ninety days during the one hundred eighty days immediately following the occurrence of the injury or impairment," the Legislature has made it abundantly clear that disability falling within this threshold period must be proved along with the other statutory requirements in order to establish a prima facie case of serious injury.

There can be little doubt that the purpose of enacting an objective verbal definition of serious injury was to "significantly reduce the number of automobile personal injury accident cases litigated in the courts, and thereby help contain the no-fault premium." Memorandum of State Executive Dept., 1977 McKinney's Session Laws of N.Y., p. 2448. "The verbal definition provided in the [legislation placed] a reasonable restriction and further limitation on the right to sue, in order to preserve the valuable benefits of no-fault, at an affordable cost." 1977 McKinney's Session Laws of N.Y., p. 2450. The Governor voiced his support of these policies when he signed the legislation into law. * While it is clear that the Legislature intended to allow plaintiffs to recover for non-economic injuries in appropriate cases, it had also intended that the court first determine whether or not a prima facie case of serious injury has been established which would permit a plaintiff to maintain a common-law cause of action in tort. *

In light of this mandate, plaintiff's argument that the question of whether he suffered a serious injury is always a fact question for the jury is without merit. It is incumbent upon the court to decide in the first instance whether plaintiff has a cause of action to assert within the meaning of the statute. By enacting the No-Fault Law, the Legislature modified the common-law rights of persons injured in automobile accidents * to the extent that plaintiffs in automobile accident cases no longer have an unfettered right to sue for injuries sustained. Thus, to the extent that the Legislature has abrogated a cause of action, the issue is one for the court, in the first instance where it is properly raised, to determine whether the plaintiff has established a prima facie case of sustaining serious injury. Since the purpose of the No-Fault Law is to assure prompt and full compensation for economic loss by curtailing costly and time-consuming court trials, * requiring that every case, regardless of the extent of the injuries, be decided by a jury would subvert the intent of the Legislature and destroy the effectiveness of the statute. The result of requiring a jury trial where the injury is clearly a minor one would perpetuate a system of unnecessary litigation. "[I]f the procedural system cannot find a way to keep cases that belong in no-fault out of the courthouse, the system is not going to work." [David Herbert] Schwartz, No-Fault Insurance: Litigation of Threshold Questions under the New York Statute—The Neglected Procedural Dimension, 41 Brooklyn L. Rev. 37, 53 (1974). Thus, we believe the Legislature intended that the court should decide the threshold question of whether the evidence would warrant a jury finding that the injury falls within the class of injuries that, under no-fault, should be excluded from judicial remedy. If it can be said, as a matter of law, that plaintiff suffered no serious injury within the meaning of subdivision 4 of section 671 of the Insurance Law, then plaintiff has no claim to assert and there is nothing for the jury to decide. *

Turning to the case before us, plaintiff contends that his injuries were serious within the meaning of the statute in that he was prevented, for at least 90 days, from performing substantially all of the material acts which constituted his usual daily activities. * It is undisputed, however, that plaintiff returned to work 24 days after the accident and that upon his return he immediately resumed his usual schedule of driving a taxi 12 hours per day, 6 days a week. Since plaintiff was able to maintain his daily routine for most of each day after returning to work, it should be abundantly clear that plaintiff was not prevented from performing substantially all of his daily activities

boundaries. They would face financial exposure both within the common law tort system and in terms of assessments to fund the alternative system. Also, their inability to quantify confidently the risk of future tort losses probably would lead liability insurers—generally a cautious, self-protective group—to charge even higher premiums than the absolute degree of financial exposure warranted.

Whenever a no-fault compensation plan has been implemented, claimants who believe they have a strong chance of receiving a larger recovery under the common law have challenged the exclusivity of the compensation plan. For example, in *Licari v. Elliott*, * * *.

In essence, permitting a jury to hear a case that belongs in the no-fault system would destroy no-fault's cost-effectiveness by "perpetuat[ing] a system of unnecessary litigation."[309] No-fault systems reduce transaction costs, permitting a greater number of victims to recover compensation, many of whom would be unable to recover anything through tort litigation. The increased transaction costs associated with defending claims in court that belong in the no-fault system, coupled with the higher compensation awards for cases heard within the tort system, would destroy no-fault's cost effectiveness. That, in turn, would render the goal of providing compensation to *all* injured claimants impossible. * * *

The legal process issue in *Licari*—who should determine in the first instance whether an injured claimant must seek compensation in the no-fault regime or in the courts—is quite similar to the substantive issue posed in *Bruesewitz*: Is it the alternative compensation system or common law courts that should adjudicate most design defect claims? As we know, the Supreme Court held that Congress preempted *all* state law design-defect claims against vaccine manufacturers, thus directing those claims to the no-fault system. * * *

* * * [B]ecause [Justice Breyer] recognized that the plain meaning debate between Scalia and Sotomayor was a "close one," he turned his attention to the congressional goals in passing the NCVIA.

After reviewing the relevant House Committee Report, Justice Breyer determined that Congress had two objectives in mind when it passed the NCVIA. First, Congress "sought to provide generous compensation to those whom vaccines injured"[320] without requiring the claimant to go through the "expensive," "time-consuming" process of common law tort litigation. Second, Congress sought to stabilize a vaccine market where an increase in tort litigation "prompted manufacturers to question their continued participation in the vaccine market."[322] Congress recognized that the withdrawal of more vaccine

---

[309] [Licari v. Elliott, 441 N.E.2d 1088,] 1092 (N.Y.1982) (emphasis added) (quoting David Herbert Schwartz, No-Fault Insurance: Litigation of Threshold Questions Under the New York Statute—The Neglected Procedural Dimension, 41 Brook. L. Rev. 37, 53 (1974)).

[320] See Bruesewitz, 131 S.Ct. at 1084 (citing H.R. Rep. No. 99-908, at 6, 24, *reprinted in* 1986 U.S.C.C.A.N. at 6347, 6365).

[322] [*Id.*] (Breyer, J., concurring) (quoting H.R. Rep. No. 99-908 at 7, *reprinted in* 1986 U.S.C.C.A.N. at 6348) (internal quotation marks omitted) (citing Staff of H.R. Comm. On Energy & Commerce, 99th Cong., Childhood Immunizations 85–86 (Comm. Print. 1986)); see also H.R. Rep. No. 99-908 at 6–7, *reprinted in* 1986 U.S.C.C.A.N at 6347–48 (indicating that as of 1986, there was one manufacturer of polio vaccine, one manufacturer of MMR vaccine, and two manufacturers of DPT vaccine).

manufacturers from the market "would present the very real possibility of vaccine shortages," potentially causing a "genuine public health hazard."[323] Thus, Congress created a no-fault compensation system in which vaccine manufacturers could predictably assess their liability, thereby providing an incentive for manufacturers to remain in the market.

These legislative goals led Justice Breyer to argue that it would be "anomalous" to interpret the statute "as preserving design-defect suits,"[325] because such an interpretation would destroy the viability of the no-fault compensation plan, its effectiveness in capping pharmaceutical manufacturers' liability, and their ability to predict the extent of their liabilities. * * * Justice Breyer * * * made clear that he was basing his holding on the *purpose* underlying the statute. He explained that Congress intended to fulfill its objectives through an administrative no-fault compensation regime, rather than the tort system. Justice Breyer explained:

> To allow a jury in effect to second-guess [an administrator's determination that an injured claimant is entitled to compensation] is to substitute less expert for more expert judgment, thereby threatening manufacturers with liability (indeed, strict liability) in instances where any conflict between experts and nonexperts is likely to be particularly severe—instances where *Congress intended* the contrary.[330]

Justice Breyer recognized that if the NCVIA is to have any utility at all, injured claimants must seek compensation in the no-fault system, and not in the tort system. If injured claimants can pursue tort claims, the NCVIA will not accomplish its dual purpose of stabilizing the vaccine market and compensating a much higher percentage of vaccine victims. Justice Breyer recognized that Congress passed the NCVIA to prevent vaccine manufacturers from leaving the market due to fear of tort liability. Interpreting the NCVIA in a way that did not preempt design-defect claims would thwart this goal by increasing the cost of liability insurance, forcing manufacturers to question their continued participation in the market.

---

[323] Bruesewitz, 131 S. Ct. at 1084 (Breyer, J., concurring) (quoting H.R. Rep. No. 99-908 at 7, *reprinted in* 1986 U.S.C.C.A.N. at 6348) (internal quotation marks omitted).

[325] *Id.* at 1085.

[330] [*Id.*] at 1084 (Breyer, J., concurring) (emphasis added). Congress recognized the inherent risk that when a jury is faced with either imposing a loss on an innocent, young child, or distributing the loss through an innocent manufacturer, it may be more inclined to select the latter option. See H.R. Rep. No. 99-908, at 26 (1986), *reprinted in* 1986 U.S.C.C.A.N. at 6367. The "authoritative" House Report notes:

> [T]he plaintiff is almost invariably a young child, often badly injured or killed, and free from wrongdoing. And, even if the defendant manufacturer may have made as safe a vaccine as anyone reasonably could expect, a court or jury undoubtedly will find it difficult to rule in favor of the "innocent" manufacturer if the equally "innocent" child has to bear the risk of loss with no other possibility of recompense.

Id.; see also [James R.] Copland, [Administrative Compensation for Pharmaceutical-and-Vaccine-Related Injuries, 8 Ind. Health L. Rev. 277,] 282 [(2011)] ("[I]n practice, the tort system's ex post feature likely exacerbates hindsight bias—the tendency to infer causation and negligence inappropriately given injury—particularly when a decision-making body of unsophisticated lay jurors is involved . . . .").

Moreover, Justice Breyer understood that Congress's second purpose in passing the NCVIA was to provide "generous compensation" for vaccine-related injuries.[334] The withdrawal of even a single manufacturer from the system, due to the liability concerns discussed above, would disrupt this goal. Claimants harmed by vaccines produced by non-participating manufacturers would be unable to recover from the NVICP on a no-fault basis. Only those few injured plaintiffs who could prove the common law requirements of fault and causation would be compensated.

Justice Breyer's purposive approach reflects a keen understanding of the structure and objectives of no-fault compensation systems. He recognized that in order to accomplish the congressional goal of compensating a large number of vaccine injuries without regard to fault, vaccine-injured children must seek recompense in the no-fault system. The no-fault system must be the *exclusive* forum for design-defect claims, not simply an alternative to the tort system. This is the lesson of *Licari v. Elliott*: "[I]f the procedural system cannot find a way to keep cases that belong in no-fault out of the courthouse, the system is not going to work."[337]

Subjecting manufacturers to both potential tort liability for claims viewed as strong common law claims and to assessments to fund the NVICP, from which other victims would recover, would impair the congressional objective of establishing a cost-effective no-fault compensation system. If claims of victims such as Hannah Bruesewitz enter the tort system, either manufacturers will leave the market, or pressure from the manufacturers will force lower assessments and hence render less money available to compensate all of those entitled to recompense in the NVICP. As Justice Breyer properly recognized, it is necessary to divert *all* vaccine-injury claims to the no-fault system. Preemption of design-defect claims will promote the goal of providing "generous compensation"[339] to a broad class of children, not just those who can prove a common law tort. Admittedly, a few victims who allege they suffered harms as a result of vaccine exposure, such as Hannah Bruesewitz herself, will be denied compensation, but such a denial reflects the best judgment of Congress and the experts the NVICP retains.

Finally, Justice Breyer reasoned, allowing a jury to "second-guess"[340] the no-fault administrator would destroy the cost-effectiveness of the no-fault regime and "perpetuate a system of unnecessary litigation."[341] Had the Court supported Justice Sotomayor's view and found that the NCVIA did not preempt design-defect claims, then manufacturers would be taxed twice—once for the NCVIA assessment, and a second time for the liability premiums to cover common law liability and the substantial transaction costs inherent in the litigation

---

[334] See Bruesewitz, 131 S.Ct. at 1084 (Breyer, J., concurring) (citing H.R. Rep. No. 99-908, at 6, 24, *reprinted in* 1986 U.S.C.C.A.N. at 6347, 6365).

[337] Licari v. Elliott, 441 N.E.2d 1088, 1092 (N.Y.1982) (alteration in original) (quoting Schwartz, supra note 309, at 53) (internal quotation marks omitted).

[339] [Bruesewitz, 131 S. Ct. at 1084 (Breyer, J., concurring)] (citing H.R. Rep. No. 99-908, at 6, 24, reprinted in 1986 U.S.C.C.A.N. at 6347, 6365).

[340] *Id.* at 1085.

[341] See Licari, 441 N.E.2d at 1092.

process. Meanwhile, victims and their counsel would be able to game the system and choose the approach that offered them the better probability of prevailing and the larger amount of compensation. Congress sought to establish a comprehensive compensation program that would make it financially feasible for the continued production of vaccines, not to give victims the proverbial "two bites at the apple." * * *

D. EVALUATING AUTOMOBILE NO-FAULT

Excerpt, James M. Anderson, Paul Heaton & Stephen J. Carroll, The U.S. Experience with No-Fault Automobile Insurance: A Retrospective

63, 68, 69, 74, 79, 82, 83, 86, 92, 97, 105, 110–11, 115, 117–19, 120–21, 124–25, 127–28, 133 (RAND Institute for Civil Justice, 2010).

Many no-fault proponents claimed that no-fault would reduce claim costs. These proponents argued that no-fault would reduce litigation, limit third-party claims (particularly for noneconomic damages), and simplify the process of determining who was at fault, reducing administrative costs enough to offset the cost of the more-generous first-party benefits available under no-fault. However, a number of researchers have argued that no-fault has actually *increased* insurance costs.[a] * * *

Is a no-fault regime a more or less expensive means of compensating victims for automobile-accident costs? * * * We conclude that auto-insurance premiums and expenditures for compensation are higher under no-fault, at least as it is currently used in the United States. * * * [Automobile insurance] [p]remiums have been consistently higher in states offering PIP coverage, with the highest premiums occurring in no-fault states over the sample period. * * * [T]he premium gap between no-fault and tort stood at $75 in 1987 * * *. More recently, the gap has widened, making premiums under no-fault 50 percent higher than those under tort by 2004. * * *

[W]e now turn to one component affecting the average liability premium: BI claim-payment costs per insured vehicle. These costs primarily reflect compensation for third-party claims for bodily injury resulting from accidents. A key goal of no-fault was to reduce these costs by shifting compensation from the third-party BI liability system to the first-party PIP system by creating a threshold for access to BI compensation. Thus, we would expect BI costs to be substantially lower in no-fault states. The data belie our expectations. * * * Comparing no-fault to tort states, we see that, prior to the early 1990s, BI costs were indeed equal or lower in no-fault states but that, around 1993, this pattern reversed and that, since that time, BI costs have actually been *higher* in no-fault states. * * * It is surprising to observe higher BI costs in no-fault states, given that victims are barred from filing BI claims unless their injuries exceed the relevant threshold. * * *

---

[a] [Eds.' note] E.g., Joseph E. Johnson, George B. Flanigan & Daniel T. Winkler, Cost Implications of No-Fault Automobile Insurance, 59 J. of Risk & Ins.116 (1992); Harvey Rosenfield, Auto Insurance: Crisis and Reform, 29 U. Memphis L. Rev. 69 (1998).

If no-fault does indeed affect insurance costs, then, in addition to observing cross-sectional cost differences between states under different systems, costs within states should also change as vehicles and drivers are moved out of no-fault coverages. That is exactly what we find. Over the period of available data, three states repealed no-fault statutes and reverted to a tort system: Georgia in 1991, Connecticut in 1994, and Colorado in 2003. * * * [The data] reveals a striking pattern of substantial cost decreases in all three states following the repeal of no-fault. * * * Taken together, these facts indicate that no-fault has been a more expensive auto-insurance system. * * *

Does No-Fault Lead to More Accidents?

If a no-fault regime leads to decreased driver safety and more auto accidents, then this factor would explain its rising costs. * * * [Of] eight previous studies of the effect of no-fault on fatal accidents * * *, half the studies claim that no-fault coverage increases fatal accidents, while the other half find no evidence of such an effect. * * * [E]ven among the more methodologically sophisticated recent papers, there is disagreement as to whether no-fault is associated with increases in fatal accidents. * * *

In a companion to this monograph, Heaton and Helland[b] provide new evidence regarding the effects of no-fault on driver safety. In contrast to previous studies that focus on fatal accidents, Heaton and Helland adopt an empirical approach that allows them to estimate the effect of no-fault coverage on both fatal and nonfatal accidents. * * * Heaton and Helland * * * obtain precise estimates suggesting that drivers under no-fault cause similar numbers of accidents and are involved in accidents of similar severity to those under tort. * * *

Does No-Fault Lead to Higher Claiming Rates When Accidents Occur?

If it does not appear that there are more accidents in no-fault states, could it be that there are more claims filed per accident under no-fault? This seems an especially plausible hypothesis because one of the rationales of no-fault was that it would provide a source of compensation for all accidents and not just accidents in which someone else was at fault. * * * No-fault insurance was supposed to make it easier to file claims. * * * While plausible, the data does not support this explanation of the additional costs of no-fault. * * *

Are Costs per Claim Higher for No-Fault?

* * * Our analysis shows that no-fault does, in fact, offer slightly higher reimbursement rates than other regimes. * * *

Did No-Fault Reduce Litigation?

A key premise of no-fault was that it would reduce costs by reducing auto litigation. By diverting all but the most-serious cases from the third-party tort liability system to resolution between the victim and his or her insurer, proponents of no-fault believed that expensive and time-consuming auto-related litigation would be dramatically reduced. * How well has no-fault accomplished the central

---

b [Eds.' note] Paul Heaton & Eric Helland, No-Fault Insurance and Automobile Accidents (2009), *available at* http://www.rand.org/pubs/working_papers/WR551/.

task of reducing litigation? * * * [A]uto accident-related trial litigation is less common in no-fault states.

* * * To summarize up to this point, we have found evidence that no-fault systems provide reimbursement for a larger proportion of economic losses, greater satisfaction with the speed of payment, and faster resolution of third-party claims. Thus, part of the high cost of no-fault may reflect the higher quality of the insurance coverage provided under this regime. We have also shown that * * * total auto litigation volume has become more comparable between tort and no-fault states. * * *

Does No-Fault Create Greater Incentives for Fraud?

* * * [T]he existence of thresholds in no-fault states provides a different impetus for overclaiming that is not present in tort states. In dollar-threshold states, there are particularly strong incentives to exaggerate claims near the threshold value, since such exaggeration allows the claimant to obtain noneconomic damages for not only the marginal dollars expended but also all the previous losses incurred. * * * [W]e are able to observe evidence of threshold overclaiming in some, but not all, dollar-threshold states. * * *

* * * A number of studies have focused on soft-tissue claims as an indicator of overclaiming. * Soft-tissue injuries include sprains and strains of the neck, back, or other parts of the body. These injuries are typically more difficult to verify than other injury types because there are few available objective methods for their diagnosis. * * * Our assumption is that hard injuries, such as fractures, serious lacerations, and burns, cannot be easily falsified and that claims involving these types of injuries are therefore legitimate. Clearly, some proportion of soft-tissue claims are also legitimate, but, other things being equal, we expect overclaiming to be higher in states in which a large proportion of claims involve hard-to-verify injuries. * * * One common pattern we see across both categories of fraud indicators is an increase in prevalence of suspicious claims in no-fault states over time. * * *

Does No-Fault Provide Different Levels of Reimbursement for Noneconomic Damages?

Critics of no-fault argue that a major limitation of the system is the denial of compensation for noneconomic losses to those whose injuries fall below the recovery threshold. Other things being equal, we expect that a lower level of payments for noneconomic losses will reduce costs and premiums, potentially counteracting some of the other factors we have already identified that make no-fault more expensive. * * * However, over time, there has been a gradual convergence between no-fault and tort states, such that insurers under both systems were devoting the same share of payments to compensate noneconomic damages by 2007: 42 percent. * * *

Does No-Fault Encourage Greater Claiming of Medical Services?

* * * When a person is injured in an automobile accident, there are often multiple sources from which the injured or his or her medical provider might be able to recover. For example, the victim might be able to recover from his or her own health insurance, workers' compensation (if the job was job-related), his or her own no-fault PIP auto insurance,

one or more tortfeasors, or their third-party BI insurers. The priority-of-recovery rules in each state will determine who is responsible. This is established by a combination of statute, insurance-policy language, and case law. In general, workers' compensation policies pay first, followed by no-fault automobile policies, and then other sources, including health insurance. Because no-fault plans usually have a higher priority than health insurance, they are more likely to bear the medical costs of an auto accident. * * * Because no-fault PIP insurance usually has a higher priority than health insurance or tort BI insurance, it is more likely to end up bearing medical costs that are auto-accident related. * * *

There is a second reason that medical costs may be higher in no-fault states. Automobile insurers have suggested that no-fault insurance has become an especially attractive payer to health-care providers because it pays a much higher percentage of billed medical costs than medical insurance, which usually includes steep discounts. As medical costs have increased during the past two decades, no-fault automobile insurance was virtually the only insurer that paid the provider's full bill. Thus, medical providers were much more likely to initially bill no-fault insurance prior to seeking recovery against the victim's medical insurance. * * * Claimed medical care is higher in no-fault states than in tort states.

How Likely Is a Claimant to Use a Particular Category of Medical Provider?

* * * [N]o-fault regimes are associated with greater likelihoods of an accident victim visiting almost every category of health-care provider in almost every year for which we have data. Trends in claimed ER use differ substantially across systems. In all years, claimed ER use is more common in no-fault states than in tort states. * * * There is also a higher claimed usage of many types of specialized physicians in no-fault states, in comparison to both tort states and add-on states. * * * [T]he growth in physical-therapist use has been particularly striking in no-fault states * * *. Overall, [our data] suggests that higher medical utilization was an important contributor to the higher costs of no-fault. Claimants in no-fault states were more likely to use almost all types of care, including that of specialized physicians. * * *

Is Medical Cost Inflation Different in No-Fault States?

* * * But why, exactly, have medical claim costs grown so much faster in no-fault states? Anecdotally, stakeholders have suggested several reasons. First, as the practice of medicine has gotten more complex, the business of managing medical care to minimize costs has also grown enormously in complexity. Since PIP is a form of mandatory first-party medical insurance that covers one of the largest medical risks that a person faces, auto insurers are serving as medical insurers. But first-party health insurers have much more specialized expertise in doing this than auto insurers. * * *

E. NO-FAULT COMPENSATION IN OTHER AREAS

NOTES

1. *September 11th Victim Compensation Fund of 2001.* Shortly after the terrorist attacks on the World Trade Center and the Pentagon, and the crash of a hijacked airliner in Shanksville, Pennsylvania, Congress passed the Air Transportation Safety and System Stabilization Act, Public Law 107–42, 115 Stat. 230 (2001). This act entitled the estates of those killed in the terrorist attacks, as well as those who suffered physical harm, to recover compensatory awards on a no-fault basis. Anyone filing a claim against the fund waived the right to file a civil action for damages sustained in the terrorist-related aircraft crashes, but—at least in theory— the decision to pursue a claim against the fund instead of suing other parties potentially liable for the damages was voluntary. The goals of the legislation were both to be "compassionate * * * to meet the needs of victims of September 11" and to respond to the belief that "the airlines were facing imminent bankruptcy and could be effectively judgment proof * * *." Statement by Special Master Kenneth Feinberg, 67 Fed. Reg. 11,233, 11,236 (Mar. 13, 2002).

Awards from the September 11th Victim Compensation Fund were to "take into consideration the harm to the claimant, the facts of the claim, and the individual circumstances of the claimant." 28 C.F.R § 104.41 (2014). Also to be taken into account were the deceased victim's earnings for recent years and the number of dependents that survived the decedent. One of the most controversial provisions of the act provided that the Special Master was required to reduce the award for economic damages by the amount of most types of collateral source payments received by the claimant, such as life insurance proceeds or other financial benefits received as a result of the death. Public Law 107–42, *supra*, § 405(b)(6). In addition, each claimant receiving benefits for a death caused by the attacks was entitled to receive compensation for "noneconomic losses" and the "presumed" award for noneconomic damages was $250,000 plus an additional $100,000 for the spouse and each additional dependent. 28 C.F.R. § 104.44.

The Victim Compensation Fund concluded its activities within a 33– month period. More than 97 percent of the families of victims opted to claim compensation under the fund rather than pursue claims against the airlines that probably would not have succeeded. The Final Report of Special Master Kenneth Feinberg reports:

> In total, the Fund distributed over $7.049 billion to survivors of 2,880 persons killed in the September 11th attacks and to 2,680 individuals who were injured in the attacks or in the rescue efforts conducted thereafter. The average award for families of victims killed in the attacks exceeded $2 million. The average award for injured victims was nearly $400,000.

Final Report of the Special Master for the September 11th Victim Compensation Fund of 2001, Vol. 1, 1 (Nov. 17, 2004), *available at* http:// www.usdoj.gov/final_report.pdf.

The Victim Compensation Fund differed in a number of regards from more traditional no-fault compensation systems. First, the compensation awards and operating expenses were paid for by the federal government not, as more typically is the case, solely from an assessment on parties that causally contributed to the harms. Second, although the determination of the amount of the award began with a "presumptive" award, the administrator, within limits, had the ability to customize the award to the circumstances of each individual case, taking into account factors such as the income of the decedent and the availability of compensation from specified types of collateral sources. Third, the awards included significant compensation for noneconomic damages.

2. *BP Gulf Coast Claims Facility.* In 2010, the explosion of BP's Deepwater Horizon oil rig in the Gulf of Mexico and the resulting massive oil spill led to the creation of another alternative compensation fund. The Gulf Coast Claims facility was created by a "handshake between the chief executive officer of BP and President Barack Obama" in which BP agreed to fund the facility with $20 billion. See Kenneth R. Feinberg, The BP Gulf Oil Spill and the Quest for Complete Justice: Unconventional Responses to Unique Catastrophes, 45 Akron L. Rev. 575, 577 (2012). BP was financially responsible for cleaning up the oil spill and paying damages resulting from it, because the U.S. Coast Guard had designated BP as a "responsible party" under the Oil Pollution Act, 33 U.S.C. §§ 2701 *et seq* (2012).[a]

When the Gulf Coast Claims plan was created, the federal government did not enact statutory provisions or regulations specifying who was entitled to recover, for which harms, and what procedures were to be followed. Kenneth Feinberg, administrator of the September 11 Victims Compensation Fund, was again appointed to administer the fund. The informal nature of both the creation of the Claims Facility and its structure (or lack thereof) led to widespread criticism. For one particularly critical analysis by a leading mass torts scholar, see Linda S. Mullenix, Prometheus Unbound: The Gulf Coast Claims Facility as a Means of Resolving Mass Torts Claims—A Fund Too Far, 71 La. L. Rev. 819 (2011). The open-ended document governing the claims process specified an extremely large class of people eligible for compensation including those sustaining physical injury or death, property damage, lost profits, or lost earning capacity, and those "who use[ ] natural resources that have been injured, destroyed, or lost * * * to obtain food, shelter, clothing, medicine, or other subsistence use." Gulf Coast Claims Facility Protocol for Interim and Final Claims (Nov. 22, 2010), *available at* http://www.propertyinsurancecoveragelaw.com/2010/12/articles/insurance/feinberg-issues-final-protocol-for-claims-to-bp-oil-spill-fund/. Feinberg acknowledged the problems with the Claims Facility:

> Alternative compensation programs make it easy for people to file claims, and tend to attract more claimants than might be seen in court. But they raise more questions of eligibility related to cases of "indirect" injury. For example, should a restaurant in Boston that advertises "the best shrimp scampi in town" receive compensation because it can no longer get shrimp from the Gulf and lost twelve percent of its clientele? * * *

> The 1,200,000 private claims that arose out of the BP oil spill were unlike anything ever before seen. * * * [C]laims were filed

---

[a]   [Eds.' note] Section 2702 (a) of the act provides that "each responsible party for a * * * facility from which oil is discharged * * * is liable for the removal costs and damages * * * that result from such incident. Subsection (b) defines the removal costs and the damages recoverable.

from dentists, chiropractors, veterinarians—every conceivable claim.

Feinberg, *supra*, 45 Akron L. Rev. at 578–79, 582.

3. *Federal Black Lung Program.* In addition to the National Childhood Vaccine Injury Act of 1986, 42 U.S.C. §§ 300AA–1 to 34 (2012), see *supra* pages 676–680, 694–699, Congress has enacted federal statutes establishing no-fault compensation systems as remedies for mass torts, or the possible threat of a mass tort, in several other contexts. These statutes assure the availability of compensation, albeit limited, to those injured. They also limit the liability of potential defendants who Congress believes are carrying on activities beneficial to the nation but might otherwise be shut down because of the threat of legal liability. Like workers' compensation and automobile no-fault, each of the compensation systems provides specified compensation which is less than full tort recovery, designates an administrative agency to implement the program, and precludes recourse to the tort system. For example, the Federal Black Lung Benefits Act, passed in 1969, compensates coal miners and their dependents for the consequences of a disabling disease similar to tuberculosis known as black lung. 30 U.S.C. §§ 901–945 (2012); see also Robert L. Ramsey & Robert S. Habermann, The Federal Black Lung Program—The View From the Top, 87 W.Va. L. Rev. 575 (1985).

4. *Comprehensive Medical Maloccurrence No-Fault Proposals.* Concerns about the manner in which the tort system handles claims arising from injuries resulting from treatment by health care professionals—including (1) damage awards that are sometimes too large and often erratic, (2) many patients with significant injuries who receive no compensation because they cannot prove their injuries resulted from negligence, and (3) the liability system is expensive and inefficient—have spawned a variety of proposals to compensate victims of adverse reactions to medical treatment ("maloccurrences") without regard to fault. See, e.g., Paul C. Weiler, Medical Malpractice on Trial (1991); Clark C. Havighurst & Laurence R. Tancredi, "Medical Adversity Insurance,"—A No-Fault Approach to Medical Malpractice and Quality Assurance, 613 Ins. L.J. 69 (1974); Jeffrey O'Connell, No-Fault Insurance for Injuries Arising from Medical Treatments: A Proposal for Elective Coverage, 24 Emory L.J. 21 (1975).

In a study of New York hospital records—cited in Weiler, *supra,*— Professor Paul Weiler and his colleagues from the medical profession surveyed claiming behavior among those injured in medical maloccurrences while hospitalized. They found that compared with every 1,000 patients injured as a result of a medical maloccurrence, only 125 filed claims. Of those filing claims, sixty ultimately received compensation. Weiler's medical colleagues identified eighty-five instances in which a patient's injury resulted from medical negligence for every 125 claims filed. Nevertheless, it was far more likely that an injury resulting from negligence would be compensated than one not resulting from negligence.

The results of the study led Weiler to propose a no-fault compensation system in which any hospital patient injured by medical treatment who is disabled for more than six months would be entitled to compensation regardless of fault. Weiler, *supra*, at 130. See also Paul C. Weiler, The Case for No-Fault Medical Liability, 52 Md. L. Rev. 908 (1993). Such a patient would recover his economic losses—lost income and medical expenses—not otherwise provided by first-party insurance. In addition, on a no-fault basis, the severely and permanently injured patient would receive modest compensation on the basis of scheduled damages. The amount of such compensation would depend upon the nature of the injured patient's impairment and the patient's age at the time of his injury. Weiler, Medical Malpractice on Trial, *supra*, at 135.

5. *Birth-Related Neurological Injury Plans.* There are few examples in the United States of statutory no-fault compensation systems for injuries resulting from medical maloccurrences. In the late 1980s, in response to obstetricians' claims that liability insurance either was unavailable to them or unaffordable, Virginia and Florida each adopted a no-fault compensation plan for a narrow subset of claims resulting from birth-related neurological injuries. Fla. Stat. §§ 766.301–.316 (2013); Va. Code Ann. §§ 38.2–5000–5021 (2014). See Randall R. Bovbjerg & Frank A. Sloan, No-Fault for Medical Injury: Theory and Evidence, 67 U. Cin. L. Rev. 53 (1998). Each system provides that the no-fault system is the exclusive remedy for babies born with permanent and substantial mental or physical injuries. The proponents of these statutes believed that it was difficult in many cases for the legal process to accurately or fairly determine whether the newborn's injuries resulted from negligence on the part of the physicians and jury damage awards often were quite large. Under the Florida statute, parents or others seeking compensation for such injuries file claims with administrative agencies that investigate the case and issue a recommendation regarding an award, including compensation for medical expenses, custodial care, and rehabilitation. Parents or guardians also may recover a maximum of $100,000 for other losses, including noneconomic losses. The Florida system is financed by a modest assessment on all physicians and hospitals and more substantial payments from physicians who wish to be covered by the provisions of the statute.

Based upon early and limited results from the operation of the statute, Professors Bovbjerg and Sloan note a number of positive results. The statutes, they report, result in much faster administration of claims and much lower administrative costs than the tort system. More cases are compensated under the no-fault system than under the tort system, though still far fewer than the statutes' proponents had predicted. Surprisingly, based upon the small sample available, the amount of compensation for each case appears similar to that under the tort system. Bovbjerg and Sloan report that insurance premiums for Florida obstetricians have declined, even in comparison with their national peers. It should be noted, however, that the pricing of liability insurance involves a wide variety of factors. Attributing a decline in premiums to any single factor, including changes in substantive law, is an iffy proposition.

6. *Elective No-Fault and "Neo No-Fault."* The late Professor Jeffrey O'Connell advocated the adoption of two variations of basic no-fault compensation systems.

Under an elective no-fault plan, a seller could elect, at the time of the sale of a product or service, to obligate itself to offer no-fault benefits for economic losses to any purchaser injured by the product. See Jeffrey O'Connell, Elective No-Fault Liability by Contract: With or Without Enabling Statute, 1975 U. Ill. L. Rev. 59. At the same time, the purchaser would have the option to bind himself to accept no-fault benefits in lieu of a tort claim. Can accident victims be held to the acceptance of no-fault benefits for economic losses in lieu of the possibility of common law tort damages prior to the time of their injuries? See Richard A. Epstein, The Historical Origins and Economic Structure of Workers' Compensation Law, 16 Ga. L. Rev. 775, 789–97 (1982).

In response, in part, to these concerns, Professor O'Connell then proposed a variation that he designated "neo no-fault":

> Under this proposal, any seller of products or services can put in effect an insurance policy or product warranty binding the seller to tender, within ninety days of a claim for an injury resulting from the defendant's product or service, the victim's net economic loss regardless of the existence of tort liability in any particular case. In other words, the seller would bind itself to make the tender regardless of whether the injured party could prove that the defendant's conduct or product was faulty and that he was free from contributory or comparative fault. Net economic loss would include any resulting medical expenses, including rehabilitation and wage loss (possibly with a cap of some fixed amount), beyond the victim's own collateral sources such as accident and health insurance or sick leave. * Benefits would be payable month by month as loss accrued. The victim and anyone with a claim based on the victim's injury, such as members of his family, would be given ninety days from the date of tender to accept such tender *or* to claim in tort. * In other words, upon acceptance of the no-fault tender of net economic loss, the victim would be required to waive his tort claim against the tendering party. * * *
>
> My proposal in no way disadvantages accident victims. They retain exactly the rights they have under tort law, supplemented by an alternative of certain and quicker, but lesser, payment. Any person wishing to assert his tort rights is free to do so. In this regard, the poor are most likely to be without their own collateral sources covering catastrophe; they are also least likely today to pursue a tort remedy and derive some benefit from the tort system. * Thus, my proposal benefits those who most need compensation.

Jeffrey O'Connell, A "Neo No-Fault" Contract In Lieu of Tort: Preaccident Guarantees of Postaccident Settlement Offers, 73 Cal. L. Rev. 898, 907, 913 (1985).

7. *Comprehensive Accident Compensation Systems.* In 1985, Professor Stephen Sugarman suggested going beyond no-fault compensation systems covering injuries occurring in specific contexts. See Stephen D. Sugarman, Doing Away with Tort Law, 73 Cal. L. Rev. 555 (1985), see *supra* 668–671. Instead, he suggested "doing away with tort law" by enhancing compensation programs offered by employers and the government to cover medical expenses and loss of income, and by strengthening governmental regulatory processes to deter harmful conduct.

Since 1972, New Zealand has experimented with a comprehensive no-fault accident compensation system, replacing tort law as a means of compensating for accidental physical injuries. See generally Stephen Todd, Privatization of Accident Compensation: Policy and Politics in New Zealand, 39 Washburn L.J. 404 (2000). Professor Stephen Todd of the University of Canterbury observes:

It was introduced to general approbation and initially, indeed, it worked well enough. Unsurprisingly, however, the scheme has become increasingly controversial as problems concerning the level of coverage, incentives to rehabilitation, methods of funding, and, most critically, overall expense have come to the fore.

The New Zealand system has been repeatedly and significantly modified during the past generation. In basic terms, it now operates as follows:

All New Zealand residents, including residents temporarily overseas, are covered by a cradle-to-grave, no fault, mandatory, state-provided accident rehabilitation and compensation insurance arrangement. * * * The scheme removes the right to sue for personal injury caused by accident, although one can sue for losses from damage to property, or for compensation for mental distress not arising from a personal injury to oneself, and claimants may hope to benefit from awards of exemplary damages against wrongdoers.

The Accident Rehabilitation and Compensation Insurance Corporation (ARCIC), a Crown entity, administers the ACS [accident compensation scheme]. It is responsible for injury prevention, treatment, income maintenance and rehabilitation. It largely funds services supplied by others. It primarily funds:

- the costs of removing the injured from the scene of the accident;

- some, but not all, of the costs associated with medical treatment;

- compensation for loss of earnings at 80 percent of the victim's pre-injury income, up to a set maximum * * *.

- vocational support involving retraining for injured persons; and

- personal support, such as an independence allowance, modifications to homes and cars in the event of permanent incapacity, and a range of care services.

No payments are made under ACS for losses due to sickness as distinct from accident. The state separately provides sickness and invalids benefits, but payments under the ACS for loss of earnings from accident tend to be more generous. * * *

Bryce Wilkinson, New Zealand's Failed Experiment with State Monopoly Accident Insurance, 2 Green Bag 45, 46–47 (1998).

The accident compensation scheme has become controversial in recent years and has been heavily criticized by its opponents. See *id.*; see also Todd, *supra*, at 487–95. Professor Todd concludes, however:

In 1974 the accident compensation scheme in New Zealand represented a great experiment. Now, after twenty-five years of experience, a return to tort seems unthinkable. * * * Certainly, accident compensation has had its problems, but by comparison with the tort system it has to be judged a clear success. * * * The * * * challenge, posing a deeper conceptual problem, is how best to go about rationalizing the boundaries to the scheme.

See also Stephen Todd, Treatment Injury in New Zealand, 86 Chi.-Kent L. Rev. 1169 (2011).

CHAPTER 14

ASSAULT, BATTERY, AND CERTAIN OTHER INTENTIONAL TORTS

When someone intentionally beats up another, there is little question about legal liability in the absence of privilege, although, of course, there may be and usually is very serious dispute as to the facts. The recognition of such liability was an early feature in the development of the common law. Today the traditional doctrines find fresh applications in contemporary contexts as disparate as sports injuries, sexual harassment, and disputes concerning exposure to toxic substances, medical experimentation, and police misconduct.

The party asserting an intentional tort gains advantages that a negligence claim does not offer. Intentional torts frequently possess more "jury appeal" and offer the possibility of punitive damages. Recovery in many jurisdictions is not reduced or eliminated by comparative fault, and judgments for intentional torts are unlikely to be discharged by bankruptcy. 11 U.S.C. § 523(6) (2012) (no discharge for judgments resulting from "willful and malicious injury").

Also included here is a consideration of the allied torts of malicious prosecution and abuse of process. Often not considered in a first year torts course, these torts should encourage you to reflect upon what harm results when the litigation system is misused.

A. BATTERY

Garratt v. Dailey

Supreme Court of Washington, 1955.
46 Wash.2d 197, 279 P.2d 1091.

■ HILL, JUSTICE. The liability of an infant for an alleged battery is presented to this court for the first time. Brian Dailey (age five years, nine months) was visiting with Naomi Garratt, an adult and a sister of the plaintiff, Ruth Garratt, likewise an adult, in the backyard of the plaintiff's home, on July 16, 1951. It is plaintiff's contention that she came out into the backyard to talk with Naomi and that, as she started to sit down in a wood and canvas lawn chair, Brian deliberately pulled it out from under her. The only one of the three persons present so testifying was Naomi Garratt. (Ruth Garratt, the plaintiff, did not testify as to how or why she fell.) The trial court, unwilling to accept this testimony, adopted instead Brian Dailey's version of what happened, and made the following findings:

> III. . . . that while Naomi Garratt and Brian Dailey were in the back yard the plaintiff, Ruth Garratt, came out of her house into the back yard. Some time subsequent thereto defendant,

Brian Dailey, picked up a lightly built wood and canvas lawn chair which was then and there located in the back yard of the above described premises, moved it sideways a few feet and seated himself therein, at which time he discovered the plaintiff, Ruth Garratt, about to sit down at the place where the lawn chair had formerly been, at which time he hurriedly got up from the chair and attempted to move it toward Ruth Garratt to aid her in sitting down in the chair; that due to the defendant's small size and lack of dexterity he was unable to get the lawn chair under the plaintiff in time to prevent her from falling to the ground. That plaintiff fell to the ground and sustained a fracture of her hip, and other injuries and damages as hereinafter set forth.

IV. That the preponderance of the evidence in this case establishes that when the defendant, Brian Dailey, moved the chair in question *he did not have any willful or unlawful purpose* in doing so; that *he did not have any intent to injure the plaintiff, or any intent to bring about any unauthorized or offensive contact with her person* or any objects appurtenant thereto; that the circumstances which immediately preceded the fall of the plaintiff established that the defendant, *Brian Dailey, did not have purpose, intent or design to perform a prank or to effect an assault and battery upon the person of the plaintiff.* *

It is conceded that Ruth Garratt's fall resulted in a fractured hip and other painful and serious injuries. To obviate the necessity of a retrial in the event this court determines that she was entitled to a judgment against Brian Dailey, the amount of her damage was found to be $11,000. Plaintiff appeals from a judgment dismissing the action and asks for the entry of a judgment in that amount or a new trial.

The authorities generally, but with certain notable exceptions, * state that when a minor has committed a tort with force he is liable to be proceeded against as any other person would be. *

In our analysis of the applicable law, we start with the basic premise that Brian, whether five or fifty-five, must have committed some wrongful act before he could be liable for appellant's injuries. * * *

It is urged that Brian's action in moving the chair constituted a battery. A definition (not all-inclusive but sufficient for our purpose) of a battery is the intentional infliction of a harmful bodily contact upon another. The rule that determines liability for battery is given in Restatement of Torts § 13, as:

An act which, directly or indirectly, is the legal cause of a harmful contact with another's person makes the actor liable to the other, if

(a) the act is done with the intention of bringing about a harmful or offensive contact or an apprehension thereof to the other or a third person, and

(b) the contact is not consented to by the other or the other's consent thereto is procured by fraud or duress, and

(c) the contact is not otherwise privileged.

We have in this case no question of consent or privilege. We therefore proceed to an immediate consideration of intent and its place in the law of battery. In the comment on clause (a), the Restatement says:

> *Character of actor's intention.* In order that an act may be done with the intention of bringing about a harmful or offensive contact or an apprehension thereof to a particular person, either the other or a third person, the act must be done for the purpose of causing the contact or apprehension or with knowledge on the part of the actor that such contact or apprehension is substantially certain to be produced. *

We have here the conceded volitional act of Brian, *i.e.*, the moving of a chair. Had the plaintiff proved to the satisfaction of the trial court that Brian moved the chair while she was in the act of sitting down, Brian's action would patently have been for the purpose or with the intent of causing the plaintiff's bodily contact with the ground, and she would be entitled to a judgment against him for the resulting damages. Vosburg v. Putney, 80 Wis. 523, 50 N.W. 403 (1891). *

The plaintiff based her case on that theory, and the trial court held that she failed in her proof and accepted Brian's version of the facts rather than that given by the eyewitness who testified for the plaintiff. After the trial court determined that the plaintiff had not established her theory of a battery (*i.e.*, that Brian had pulled the chair out from under the plaintiff while she was in the act of sitting down), it then became concerned with whether a battery was established under the facts as it found them to be.

In this connection, we quote another portion of the comment on the "Character of actor's intention," relating to clause (a) of the rule from the Restatement heretofore set forth:

> It is not enough that the act itself is intentionally done and this, even though the actor realizes or should realize that it contains a very grave risk of bringing about the contact or apprehension. Such realization may make the actor's conduct negligent or even reckless but unless he realizes that to a substantial certainty, the contact or apprehension will result, the actor has not that intention which is necessary to make him liable under the rule stated in this section.

A battery would be established if, in addition to plaintiff's fall, it was proved that, when Brian moved the chair, he knew with substantial certainty that the plaintiff would attempt to sit down where the chair had been. If Brian had any of the intents which the trial court found, in the italicized portions of the findings of fact quoted above, that he did not have, he would of course have had the knowledge to which we have referred. The mere absence of any intent to injure the plaintiff or to play a prank on her or to embarrass her, or to commit an assault and battery on her would not absolve him from liability if in fact he had such knowledge. * Without such knowledge, there would be nothing wrongful about Brian's act in moving the chair and, there being no wrongful act, there would be no liability.

While a finding that Brian had no such knowledge can be inferred from the findings made, we believe that before the plaintiff's action in such a case should be dismissed there should be no question but that the trial court had passed upon that issue; hence, the case should be remanded for clarification of the findings to specifically cover the question of Brian's knowledge, because intent could be inferred therefrom. If the court finds that he had such knowledge the necessary intent will be established and the plaintiff will be entitled to recover, even though there was no purpose to injure or embarrass the plaintiff. * If Brian did not have such knowledge, there was no wrongful act by him and the basic premise of liability on the theory of a battery was not established.

It will be noted that the law of battery as we have discussed it is the law applicable to adults, and no significance has been attached to the fact that Brian was a child less than six years of age when the alleged battery occurred. The only circumstance where Brian's age is of any consequence is in determining what he knew, and there his experience, capacity, and understanding are of course material. * * *

The remand for clarification gives the plaintiff an opportunity to secure a judgment even though the trial court did not accept her version of the facts, if from all the evidence the trial court can find that Brian knew with substantial certainty that the plaintiff intended to sit down where the chair had been before he moved it, and still without reference to motivation. * * * The cause is remanded for clarification, with instructions to make definite findings on the issue of whether Brian Dailey knew with substantial certainty that the plaintiff would attempt to sit down where the chair which he moved had been, and to change the judgment if the findings warrant it. * * *

NOTES

1. *Battery and the Third Restatement.* The draft Restatement (Third) of Torts provides as follows:

> (1) An actor is subject to liability to another for battery if:
>
> (a) the actor intends to cause a contact with the person of the other;
>
> (b) the actor's conduct causes such a contact;
>
> (c) the contact (i) is offensive or (ii) causes bodily harm to the other; and
>
> (d) the other does not actually consent to the contact * * *.

Restatement (Third) of Torts: Intentional Torts to Persons § 101 (Discussion Draft, April 4, 2014).

2. *Intent.* The Restatement (Third) of Torts: Liability for Physical and Emotional Harm § 1 (2010) provides that "[a] person acts with the intent to produce a consequence if: (a) the person acts with the purpose of producing that consequence; or (b) the person acts knowing that the consequence is substantially certain to result." Which prong of the intent definition does the court apply in *Garratt*?

3. *"Offensive" Battery.* The draft Third Restatement defines contact as offensive if: (a) the contact offends a reasonable sense of personal dignity; or (b) the actor knows that the contact serious offends the other's sense of personal dignity, and it is not unduly burdensome for the actor to refrain from causing the contact." Restatement (Third) of Torts: Intentional Torts to Persons § 101(2) (Discussion Draft, April 4, 2014). For instance, the plaintiff in Alcorn v. Mitchell, 63 Ill. 553 (1872), recovered when the defendant spat in his face while the two were in a courtroom for an earlier trial. In Mink v. Univ. of Chicago, 460 F.Supp. 713, 716–18 (N.D.Ill.1978), the defendant caused the pregnant plaintiffs to ingest diethylstilbestrol (DES) pills without informing them that they were taking DES or were participating in a clinical trial to determine the value of a drug to prevent miscarriages. Years later, when the plaintiffs learned that, as a result of their exposure to DES, their daughters had an increased cancer risk, they were allowed to recover for battery even though they experienced no physical injury. A kiss or grope without consent is the classic case of offensive battery. E.g., Stockett v. Tolin, 791 F.Supp. 1536, 1555–56 (S.D.Fla.1992).

4.   *Single Intent v. Dual Intent.* What must the defendant intend in order to be liable for battery? Must he intend only to cause the contact, which in fact either harms the victim or which she finds offensive? Or must the defendant intend not only to cause the contact but also that his contact will be offensive or harmful to the plaintiff? The "single-intent rule" requires only that the defendant intend to cause the offensive contact. The "double-intent rule," on the other hand, requires that the defendant both intend to cause the contact and that the contact be harmful or offensive to the plaintiff. See Restatement (Third) of Torts: Intentional Torts to Persons § 101, cmt. f (Discussion Draft, April 4, 2014). Which version does the court in *Garratt* implicitly apply?

Consider White v. Univ. of Idaho, 797 P.2d 108, 109 (Idaho 1990), where Professor Neher, an employee of the defendant, "walked up behind [the plaintiff] and touched her back with both of his hands in a movement later described as one a pianist would make in striking and lifting the fingers from a keyboard." Both Neher and the plaintiff "had long been acquainted because of their mutual interest in music, specifically, the piano." The incident occurred while Neher was a social guest in the plaintiff's home. "[H]is intent was to demonstrate the sensation of this particular movement by a pianist, not to cause any harm." Unexpectedly, the plaintiff suffered severe injuries. Is Professor Neher liable under the single-intent rule? The double-intent rule?

According to the drafters of the Restatement (Third) of Torts: Intentional Torts to Persons, which itself adopts the single-intent rule, "Jurisdictions are divided on the choice between the single-intent and the dual-intent rules with most apparently favoring single intent. *Id.* at cmt. f. Compare White v. Univ. of Idaho, 797 P.2d 108 (applying single-intent rule) and Wagner v. State, 122 P.3d 599 (Utah 2005) (applying single-intent rule) with White v. Muniz, 999 P.2d 814 (Colo.2000) (applying double-intent rule). Which rule better protects the plaintiff's interest in personal autonomy? The defendant's interest in having notice of what conduct will lead to liability?

Manning v. Grimsley

United States Court of Appeals for the First Circuit, 1981.
643 F.2d 20.

■ WYZANSKI, SENIOR DISTRICT JUDGE. * * * On September 16, 1975 there was a professional baseball game at Fenway Park in Boston between the defendant, the Baltimore Baseball Club, Inc. playing under the name the Baltimore Orioles, and the Boston Red Sox. The defendant Ross Grimsley was a pitcher employed by the defendant Baltimore Club. Some spectators, including the plaintiff, were seated, behind a wire mesh fence, in bleachers located in right field. In order to be ready to pitch in the game, Grimsley, during the first three innings of play, had been warming up by throwing a ball from a pitcher's mound to a plate in the bullpen located near those right field bleachers. The spectators in the bleachers continuously heckled him. On several occasions immediately following heckling Grimsley looked directly at the hecklers, not just into the stands. At the end of the third inning of the game, Grimsley, after his catcher had left his catching position and was walking over to the bench, faced the bleachers and wound up or stretched as though to pitch in the direction of the plate toward which he had been throwing but the ball traveled from Grimsley's hand at more than 80 miles an hour at an angle of 90 degrees to the path from the pitcher's mound to the plate and directly toward the hecklers in the bleachers. The ball passed through the wire mesh fence and hit the plaintiff.

We, unlike the district judge, are of the view that from the evidence that Grimsley was an expert pitcher, that on several occasions immediately following heckling he looked directly at the hecklers, not just into the stands, and that the ball traveled at a right angle to the direction in which he had been pitching and in the direction of the hecklers, the jury could reasonably have inferred that Grimsley intended (1) to throw the ball in the direction of the hecklers, (2) to cause them imminent apprehension of being hit, and (3) to respond to conduct presently affecting his ability to warm up and, if the opportunity came, to play in the game itself.

The foregoing evidence and inferences would have permitted a jury to conclude that the defendant Grimsley committed a battery against the plaintiff. This case falls within the scope of Restatement (Second) of Torts § 13[9] which provides, *inter alia*, that an actor is subject to liability to another for battery if intending to cause a third person to have an imminent apprehension of a harmful bodily contact, the actor causes the other to suffer a harmful contact. Although we have not found any Massachusetts case which directly supports that aspect of § 13 which we have just set forth, we have no doubt that it would be followed by the Massachusetts Supreme Judicial Court. Section 13 has common law roots that precede the American Revolution, Scott v. Shepherd, 2

---

[9]   The full text of § 13 provides:

An actor is subject to liability to another for battery if

(a) he acts intending to cause a harmful or offensive contact with the person of the other or a third person, or an imminent apprehension of such a contact, and

(b) a harmful contact with the person of the other directly or indirectly results.

Wm.Bl. 892, 96 Eng.Rep. 525 (1773). It is supported by a substantial body of American cases. * * * The whole rule and especially that aspect of the rule which permits recovery by a person who was not the target of the defendant embody a strong social policy including obedience to the criminal law by imposing an absolute civil liability to anyone who is physically injured as a result of an intentional harmful contact or a threat thereof directed either at him or a third person. * It, therefore, was error for the district court to have directed a verdict for defendant Grimsley on the battery count. * * *

NOTE

Intent and Mental Incapacity. What effect should the mental incapacity of a defendant have on her liability for battery and other intentional torts? In the classic case of McGuire v. Almy, 297 Mass. 323, 8 N.E.2d 760 (1937), the Supreme Judicial Court of Massachusetts held that:

> [W]here an insane person by his act does intentional damage to the person or property of another he is liable for that damage in the same circumstances in which a normal person would be liable. This means that in so far as a particular intent would be necessary in order to render a normal person liable, the insane person, in order to be liable, must have been capable of entertaining that same intent and must have entertained it in fact. But the law will not inquire further into his peculiar mental condition with a view to excusing him if it should appear that delusion or other consequence of his affliction has caused him to entertain that intent or that a normal person would not have entertained it.

Id. at 328, 8 N.E.2d at 763; see also Rajspic v. Nationwide Mut. Ins. Co., 104 Idaho 662, 662 P.2d 534 (1983) (defendant may be held liable by reason of insanity despite acquittal on criminal charges). Why?

B. PRIVILEGES

1. CONSENT

O'Brien v. Cunard Steamship Co.

Supreme Judicial Court of Massachusetts, 1891.
154 Mass. 272, 28 N.E. 266.

■ KNOWLTON, J. * * * To sustain the first count, which was for an alleged assault, the plaintiff relied on the fact that the surgeon who was employed by the defendant vaccinated her on ship-board, while she was on her passage from Queenstown to Boston. * * * If the plaintiff's behavior was such as to indicate consent on her part, he was justified in his act, whatever her unexpressed feelings may have been. In determining whether she consented, he could be guided only by her overt acts and the manifestations of her feelings. * It is undisputed that at Boston there are strict quarantine regulations in regard to the examination of emigrants, to see that they are protected from small-pox by vaccination, and that only those persons who hold a certificate from the medical officer of the steamship, stating that they are so protected, are permitted to land without detention in quarantine or vaccination by the port physician. It appears that the defendant is accustomed to have its surgeons vaccinate all emigrants who desire it, and who are not protected by previous vaccination, and give them a certificate which is accepted at quarantine as evidence of their protection. Notices of the regulations at quarantine, and of the willingness of the ship's medical officer to vaccinate such as needed vaccination, were posted about the ship, in various languages, and on the day when the operation was performed the surgeon had a right to presume that she and the other women who were vaccinated understood the importance and purpose of vaccination for those who bore no marks to show that they were protected.

By the plaintiff's testimony, which, in this particular, is undisputed, it appears that about 200 women passengers were assembled below, and she understood from conversation with them that they were to be vaccinated; that she stood about 15 feet from the surgeon, and saw them form in a line, and pass in turn before him; that he "examined their arms, and, passing some of them by, proceeded to vaccinate those that had no mark"; that she did not hear him say anything to any of them; that upon being passed by they each received a card, and went on deck; that when her turn came she showed him her arm; he looked at it, and said there was no mark, and that she should be vaccinated; that she told him she had been vaccinated before, and it left no mark; "that he then said nothing; that he should vaccinate her again"; that she held up her arm to be vaccinated; that no one touched her; that she did not tell him that she did not want to be vaccinated; and that she took the ticket which he gave her, certifying that he had vaccinated her, and used it at quarantine. She was one of a large number of women who were vaccinated on that occasion, without, so far as appears, a word of objection from any of them. They all indicated by their conduct that they desired to avail themselves of the provisions made for their benefit. There was nothing in the conduct of the plaintiff to indicate to the surgeon that she did not wish to obtain a card which would save her from detention at quarantine, and to be vaccinated, if necessary, for that purpose. Viewing his conduct in the light of the surrounding circumstances, it was lawful; and there was no evidence tending to show that it was not. The ruling of the court on this part of the case was correct. * * *

Exceptions overruled.

NOTE

Lack of Consent as an Element of the Tort. Most jurisdictions regard the lack of consent as an essential element of the prima facie tort that the plaintiff must plead and prove. See, e.g., Rains v. Superior Ct., 150 Cal.App.3d 933, 938 198 Cal.Rptr. 249, 253 (1984) ("lack of consent to the particular contact is an essential element of battery"); Wright v. Starr, 42 Nev. 441, 179 P. 877 (1919) (same); Stavroula S. v. Guerriera, 193 A.D.2d 796, 797, 598 N.Y.S.2d 300, 301 (1993) ("lack of consent * * * is the gravamen of the tort of battery"). A minority of jurisdictions, however, regard consent as a privilege or affirmative defense to the intentional torts of battery and assault. See, e.g., Hernandez v. K-Mart Corp., 497 So.2d

1259 (Fla.Dist.Ct.App.1986); Ysaguirre v. Hummert, 667 S.W.2d 741 (Mo.App.1984).

Hernandez v. Schittek

Appellate Court of Illinois, 1999.
305 Ill.App.3d 925, 238 Ill.Dec. 957, 713 N.E.2d 203.

■ KUEHN, JUSTICE. * * * This case began when Hernandez's primary care physician, Dr. Evelyn Yu, found a lump in her left breast. Dr. Yu ordered a mammogram, which confirmed the presence of the lump * * *. The radiology report indicated that the lump was highly suspicious, requiring "excisional biopsy." Dr. Yu then referred Hernandez to a general surgeon, Dr. Schittek.

* * * Dr. Schittek recommended that Hernandez undergo a frozen section biopsy of the lump. In a frozen section biopsy, a portion of the lump is removed. While the patient remains anesthetized, a pathologist microscopically examines the frozen tissue sample. In Hernandez's case, if the pathologist found the presence of cancer within the frozen tissue sample, Dr. Schittek recommended the removal of the upper, outer quarter of the left breast—a procedure known as a quadrantectomy, as well as the removal of certain lymph nodes. If the pathologist did not detect cancer in the frozen tissue sample, then Dr. Schittek only planned to excise the lump. At trial, Dr. Schittek confirmed that there had not been any discussion about what would occur in the event that the frozen section report was inconclusive.

Surgery was scheduled for February 8, 1993. On that date, Hernandez signed a standard consent form for Dr. Schittek's proposed surgical procedures. The form was filled out and witnessed by a registered nurse based upon Dr. Schittek's admission orders. The language of the consent form follows:

> I, the undersigned, authorize Dr. Schittek ... to perform the following operation[-]Left Breast Biopsy, Possible Quadrantectomy and axillary node dissection[-]on Sylvia Hernandez and such additional operations as are considered therapeutically necessary on the basis of findings during the course of said operation.

Hernandez believed that the quadrantectomy would only be performed in the event of cancer.

During surgery, Dr. Schittek made the initial incision and located the lump. * * * Dr. Schittek removed three lump fragments, which were immediately sent to the pathologist, Dr. Victor Aydt, for frozen section microscopic examination. Dr. Schittek closed the wound with sutures. Dr. Aydt was unable to form any conclusive opinions with the samples provided. He indicated that additional lump tissue could be beneficial in reaching a diagnosis. Dr. Aydt did suspect that the lump was malignant. Dr. Aydt then deferred his diagnosis until a permanent section of biopsied tissue could be performed, as the diagnostic quality improves with a permanent section. * * * After informing Hernandez's sister that the pathologist could not reach a definitive conclusion with the sample obtained, Dr. Schittek returned to surgery and performed the quadrantectomy. He * * * remov[ed] approximately one-third of Hernandez's breast. * * *

After surgery, Dr. Schittek spoke with Hernandez's family. Hernandez's sister reports that Dr. Schittek advised that the tissue samples were inconclusive and that he *knew* that the lump was cancerous and that the testing would bear his feelings out. He also apologized to the family, stating that they might be mad at him as he opted to perform the quadrantectomy.

Following Hernandez's discharge from the hospital, the laboratory performed the permanent section analysis * * * [that] verified that the mass was benign * * *. Dr. Schittek called Hernandez at home to advise her that the report indicated that the lump was not cancerous. Thereafter, Hernandez followed up with Dr. Schittek in his office to have a surgical drain removed. Hernandez claims that Dr. Schittek apologized for disfiguring her, while Dr. Schittek denies having made this statement. There really is no dispute that the surgery has left Hernandez with some disfigurement and disability. * * *

Hernandez filed suit against Dr. Schittek. Her first amended complaint was in two counts. Count I made standard medical negligence allegations, while count II alleged surgical battery in that Dr. Schittek exceeded Hernandez's consent in performing the quadrantectomy before determining that the lump was cancerous. * * * At the trial's conclusion, the jury found in Dr. Schittek's favor on both counts of Hernandez's complaint. Hernandez appeals. On appeal, Hernandez initially contends that the trial court erred in failing to direct a verdict in her favor on the civil battery portion of her complaint. The trial court also denied her motion for judgment notwithstanding the jury's verdict on the battery count. * * *

A battery is an unauthorized touching of another's person. * Recovery in a medical battery case is allowed when the patient establishes a complete lack of consent to medical procedures performed, when the treatment is against the patient's will, and/or when the treatment is " 'substantially at variance with the consent given.' " Gaskin v. Goldwasser, 166 Ill.App.3d 996, 1012, 520 N.E.2d 1085, 1094 (1988). * The scope of the patient's consent is critical to a determination of liability, in that the physician's privilege extends to acts substantially similar to those to which the patients [sic] consented. *

The scope of the conversation between patient and physician is not in dispute. Despite the general "possible quadrantectomy" language of the surgical consent form, the parties are in complete agreement that the quadrantectomy was to be performed in the event of a malignancy and that there was no discussion as to what would happen if the frozen section was inconclusive. The parties are therefore in complete agreement with respect to the consent given. In the face of litigation, Dr. Schittek now argues that given the wording of the release, he had *carte blanche* authority to perform the quadrantectomy in any situation but a benign diagnosis. * * * Dr. Schittek clearly believed that he was dealing with a cancerous condition, as his discussions with Hernandez's family and his medical reports reflect. There simply was no need to remove approximately one-third of Hernandez's breast in order to provide another biopsy sample to the pathologist. Dr. Schittek's techniques are actions reflective of his belief in the cancerous nature of this tissue. Without the diagnosis of a malignancy, his actions exceeded the bounds of the consent Hernandez provided.

We conclude that Dr. Schittek's actions in performing the quadrantectomy in the absence of a malignancy diagnosis were " 'substantially at variance with the consent given,' " * and that the evidence, when viewed completely in Dr. Schittek's favor, so overwhelmingly favors Hernandez such that no contrary verdict based on that evidence could possibly stand. * Accordingly, we find that the trial court erred in denying Hernandez's motion for directed verdict as to the battery count and her motion for judgment notwithstanding the verdict. * * *

Hernandez next contends that the trial court erred in refusing to construe the surgical consent form as a matter of law and by failing to instruct the jury as to the meaning and effect of the consent form. * * * Generally speaking, the construction of a written document presents a legal question. * Furthermore, the question of whether or not an ambiguity exists in a written document is generally considered to be a legal question. * Once the trial court determines that the document contains an ambiguity, the construction of the contract becomes a question of fact and extrinsic evidence is admissible with respect to the parties' intent. * If this extrinsic evidence is in dispute, then the issue is one that must be submitted to the jury. * In keeping with this line of reasoning, if the extrinsic facts are uncontroverted, the trial court must determine the contract's meaning as a matter of law without jury submission. * In this case, the trial court determined that the surgical consent form contained ambiguous terms, and the court allowed extrinsic evidence with respect to the parties' intent. Prior to the submission of the case to the jury, the trial court concluded that the phrase "possible quadrantectomy" was ambiguous and that the phrase must be construed by the jury.

Given the parties' previous discussion relative to the presence or absence of a malignancy, the generic usage of the terms "possible quadrantectomy" in the surgical consent form was ambiguous. About this, we agree with the trial court. Therefore, extrinsic evidence on the issue was properly allowed at trial. The extrinsic evidence on this issue was not in dispute. Dr. Schittek and Hernandez both testified to the understanding that the quadrantectomy would be performed in the event of a malignancy. They also testified that there had been no discussion about what Dr. Schittek would do in the event that the pathologist was unable to reach a diagnosis. Dr. Schittek's discharge summary is consistent with this testimony. Since the extrinsic evidence was not in dispute, the trial court should have ruled on the issue of the consent form's meaning as a matter of law.

Furthermore, any arguments with respect to the balance of the surgical consent form, which authorized the performance of "any additional operations as may be therapeutically necessary based on findings during surgery," were improper in light of the evidence. The only procedures performed were the excisional biopsy and the quadrantectomy. The phrase "therapeutically necessary based on findings during surgery" qualifies the additional operations—not the quadrantectomy. Because the consent form was presented to the jury for the determination of its meaning, Dr. Schittek's attorneys were free

that the jury found that Clark had not acted recklessly. We do not agree.

The problem of imposing a duty of care on participants in a sports competition is a difficult one. Players, when they engage in sport, agree to undergo some physical contacts which could amount to assault and battery absent the players' consent. * The courts are wary of imposing wide tort liability on sports participants, lest the law chill the vigor of athletic competition. See, e.g., Ross v. Clouser, 637 S.W.2d 11, 14 (Mo.1982). Nevertheless, "some of the restraints of civilization must accompany every athlete on to the playing field." Nabozny v. Barnhill, 31 Ill.App.3d 212, 215, 334 N.E.2d 258 (1975). "[R]easonable controls should exist to protect the players and the game." Ross v. Clouser, *supra.*

The majority of jurisdictions which have considered this issue have concluded that personal injury cases arising out of an athletic event must be predicated on reckless disregard of safety. See, e.g., Hackbart v. Cincinnati Bengals, Inc., 601 F.2d 516, 524 (10th Cir.1979); Nabozny v. Barnhill, *supra*; * Restatement (Second) of Torts § 500 cmts. e, g (1965).

We adopt this standard. Allowing the imposition of liability in cases of reckless disregard of safety diminishes the need for players to seek retaliation during the game or future games. * Precluding the imposition of liability in cases of negligence without reckless misconduct furthers the policy that "[v]igorous and active participation in sporting events should not be chilled by the threat of litigation." Kabella v. Bouschelle, 100 N.M. 461, 465, 672 P.2d 290 (1983).[5]

Gauvin reads the leading case of *Nabozny v. Barnhill,* to mean that Clark should be held liable, because the jury found that Clark had violated a safety rule, even though the jury found that Clark had not acted willfully, wantonly, or recklessly. Some of *Nabozny's* language might seem to imply that all that is needed to establish an actionable tort is breach of a safety rule. However, "we see *Nabozny* as establishing the standard of conduct to be willfullness or a reckless disregard of safety. . . . This appears clear. . . ." Oswald v. Twp. High School Dist. No. 214, 84 Ill.App.3d 723, 726–27, 40 Ill.Dec. 456, 406 N.E.2d 157 (1980). * The judge below applied the proper rule of law in entering judgment in favor of Clark when the jury found that Clark had not acted recklessly.

Gauvin argues that the judge erred in denying his request for an instruction which tracked the wording of *Nabozny,* in connection with the duty each player owes to all other players to refrain from conduct in violation of a safety rule. * The judge instructed the jurors in terms of recklessness. Because we conclude that the judge was correct in his analysis of *Nabozny* and in his decision to follow the Restatement

---

[5]   Some jurisdictions explain the limitation on liability in sports competitions to cases of reckless conduct in terms of the doctrine of assumption of the risk. * The Legislature has abolished the defense of assumption of the risk in Massachusetts, however. * Because the doctrine has been abolished, "the focus of the analysis in [sport cases] has shifted entirely to the defendant's duty under the circumstances and should no longer be discussed in terms of the plaintiff's assumption of the risk." Blair v. Mt. Hood Meadows Dev. Corp., 291 Or. 293, 301, 630 P.2d 827 (1981). * Thus, in setting out the standard of care, we discuss the policy in terms of the duty.

(Second) of Torts § 500, * there was no error in the denial of the plaintiff's request. * * *

Judgment affirmed.

NOTES

1.   *Basis for Recovery in Injuries Arising from Athletic Contests.* A number of opinions concur generally with *Gauvin.* E.g., Crawn v. Campo, 136 N.J. 494, 497, 643 A.2d 600, 601 (1994) (requiring "reckless or intentional conduct"). Some would apply a negligence standard. E.g., Allen v. Dover Co-Recreational Softball League, 148 N.H. 407, 417 807 A.2d 1274, 1284 (2002); Auckenthaler v. Grundmeyer, 110 Nev. 682, 689, 877 P.2d 1039, 1043–44 (1994); Lestina v. West Bend Mut. Ins. Co., 176 Wis.2d 901, 912–13, 501 N.W.2d 28, 33 (1993). Also, in Hackbart v. Cincinnati Bengals, Inc., 601 F.2d 516, 518–19 (10th Cir.1979), the court of appeals rejected the trial court's reasoning "that professional football is a species of warfare * * * [in which] even intentional batteries are beyond the scope of the judicial process"; cf. Hanson v. Kynast, 38 Ohio App.3d 58, 526 N.E.2d 327 (1987) (recognizing principle); see also Restatement (Second) of Torts § 50 cmt. b & illus. 6 (1965).

In R. v. McSorley, 2000 BCPC 116 (Provincial Court of British Columbia, Criminal Division), the defendant, a professional hockey player, used his stick to slash at an opposing player's head with three seconds left to go in the game, knocking him to the ice. The victim suffered a seizure before regaining consciousness. The two players involved, and their teammates, had been fighting throughout the game. The court found the defendant potentially guilty of criminal assault because he intended to strike the victim in the head. The court further found that stick blows to the head are not permitted in either the written rules, or the unwritten code of the game that often tolerates a greater level of physical violence than do the official rules.

2.   *Mutual Consent to Combat.* What if the plaintiff is injured in a fight, either a prize fight or a simple street-fight? Does the plaintiff's consent to the fight bar him from recovering for any injuries sustained? One position, echoed in Restatement (Second) of Torts § 60 (1965), is that:

> [O]ne who engages in prize fighting, even though prohibited by positive law, and sustains an injury, should not have a right to recover any damages that he may sustain as the result of the combat, which he expressly consented to and engaged in as a matter of business or sport. To enforce the criminal statute against prize fighting, it is not necessary to reward the one that got the worst of the encounter at the expense of his more fortunate opponent.

Hart v. Geysel, 159 Wash. 632, 636, 294 P. 570, 572 (1930). The opposing view is reflected in *Strawn v. Ingram:*

> The rule of law is therefore clear and unquestionable, that consent to an assault is no justification. Where a combat involves a breach of the peace, the mutual consent of the parties thereto is generally regarded as unlawful, and as not depriving the injured party, or for that matter, each injured party, from recovering damages for injuries received from the unlawful acts of the other.

118 W.Va. 603, 605, 191 S.E. 401, 402 (1937) (quoting Cooley on Torts § 97 (4th ed.)).

2. SELF-DEFENSE

Courvoisier v. Raymond

Supreme Court of Colorado, 1896.
23 Colo. 113, 47 P. 284.

■ HAYT, CHIEF JUSTICE. It is admitted, or proven beyond controversy, that appellee received a gunshot wound at the hands of the appellant at the time and place designated in the complaint, and that, as the result of such wound, the appellee was seriously injured. It is further shown that the shooting occurred under the following circumstances:

That Mr. Courvoisier, on the night in question, was asleep in his bed, in the second story of a brick building, situate [sic] at the corner of South Broadway and Dakota streets, in South Denver; that he occupied a portion of the lower floor of this building as a jewelry store. He was aroused from his bed, shortly after midnight, by parties shaking or trying to open the door of the jewelry store. These parties, when asked by him as to what they wanted, insisted upon being admitted, and, upon his refusal to comply with this request, they used profane and abusive epithets toward him. Being unable to gain admission, they broke some signs upon the front of the building, and then entered the building by another entrance, and, passing upstairs, commenced knocking upon the door of a room where defendant's sister was sleeping. Courvoisier partly dressed himself, and, taking his revolver, went upstairs, and expelled the intruders from the building. In doing this he passed downstairs, and out on the sidewalk, as far as the entrance to his store, which was at the corner of the building. The parties expelled from the building, upon reaching the rear of the store, were joined by two or three others. In order to frighten these parties away, the defendant fired a shot in the air; but, instead of retreating, they passed around to the street in front, throwing stones and brickbats at the defendant, whereupon he fired a second, and perhaps a third, shot. The first shot fired attracted the attention of plaintiff, Raymond, and two deputy sheriffs, who were at the Tramway depot, across the street. These officers started toward Mr. Courvoisier, who still continued to shoot; but two of them stopped, when they reached the men in the street, for the purpose of arresting them, Mr. Raymond alone proceeding towards the defendant, calling out to him that he was an officer and to stop shooting. Although the night was dark, the street was well lighted by electricity, and, when the officer approached him, defendant shaded his eyes, and, taking deliberate aim, fired, causing the injury complained of.

The plaintiff's theory of the case is that he was a duly authorized police officer, and in the discharge of his duties at the time; that the defendant was committing a breach of the peace; and that the defendant, knowing him to be a police officer, recklessly fired the shot in question.

The defendant claims that the plaintiff was approaching him at the time in a threatening attitude, and that the surrounding circumstances were such as to cause a reasonable man to believe that his life was in danger, and that it was necessary to shoot in self-defense, and that defendant did so believe at the time of firing the shot. * * *

[The trial court found for the plaintiff.]

The next error assigned relates to the instructions given by the court to the jury, and to those requested by the defendant and refused by the court. The second instruction given by the court was clearly erroneous. The instruction is as follows: "The court instructs you that if you believe, from the evidence, that, at the time the defendant shot the plaintiff, the plaintiff was not assaulting the defendant, then your verdict should be for the plaintiff." The vice of this instruction is that it excluded from the jury a full consideration of the justification claimed by the defendant. The evidence for the plaintiff tends to show that the shooting, if not malicious, was wanton and reckless; but the evidence for the defendant tends to show that the circumstances surrounding him at the time of the shooting were such as to lead a reasonable man to believe that his life was in danger, or that he was in danger of receiving great bodily harm at the hands of the plaintiff, and the defendant testified that he did so believe.

He swears that his house was invaded, shortly after midnight, by two men, whom he supposed to be burglars; that, when ejected, they were joined on the outside by three or four others; that the crowd so formed assaulted him with stones and other missiles, when, to frighten them away, he shot into the air; that, instead of going away, someone approached him from the direction of the crowd; that he supposed this person to be one of the rioters, and did not ascertain that it was the plaintiff until after the shooting. He says that he had had no previous acquaintance with plaintiff; that he did not know that he was a police officer, or that there were any police officers in the town of South Denver; that he heard nothing said at the time, by the plaintiff or anyone else, that caused him to think the plaintiff was an officer; that his eyesight was greatly impaired, so that he was obliged to use glasses; and that he was without glasses at the time of the shooting, and for this reason could not see distinctly. He then adds: "I saw a man come away from the bunch of men and come up towards me, and as I looked around I saw this man put his hand to his hip pocket. I didn't think I had time to jump aside, and therefore turned around and fired at him. I had no doubts but it was somebody that had come to rob me, because, some weeks before, Mr. Wilson's store was robbed. It is next door to mine."

By this evidence two phases of the transaction are presented for consideration: First. Was the plaintiff assaulting the defendant at the time plaintiff was shot? Second. If not, was there sufficient evidence of justification for the consideration of the jury? The first question was properly submitted, but the second was excluded by the instruction under review. The defendant's justification did not rest entirely upon the proof of assault by the plaintiff. A riot was in progress, and the defendant swears that he was attacked with missiles, hit with stones, brickbats, etc.; that he shot plaintiff, supposing him to be one of the rioters. We must assume these facts as established in reviewing the instruction, as we cannot say what the jury might have found had this evidence been submitted to them under a proper charge.

By the second instruction, the conduct of those who started the fracas was eliminated from the consideration of the jury. If the jury believed, from the evidence, that the defendant would have been justified in shooting one of the rioters, had such person advanced towards him, as did the plaintiff, then it became important to determine whether the defendant mistook plaintiff for one of the rioters; and, if such a mistake was in fact made, was it excusable, in the light of all the circumstances leading up to and surrounding the commission of the act? If these issues had been resolved by the jury in favor of the defendant, he would have been entitled to a judgment. Morris v. Platt, 32 Conn. 75 (1864). *

The opinion in the first [case] above cited contains an exhaustive review of the authorities, and is very instructive. The action was for damages resulting from a pistol shot wound. The defendant justified under the plea of self-defense. The proof for the plaintiff tended to show that he was a mere bystander at a riot, when he received a shot aimed at another; and the court held that, if the defendant was justified in firing the shot at his antagonist, he was not liable to the plaintiff, for the reason that the act of shooting was lawful under the circumstances.

Where a defendant, in a civil action like the one before us, attempts to justify on a plea of necessary self-defense, he must satisfy the jury, not only that he acted honestly in using force, but that his fears were reasonable under the circumstances, and also as to the reasonableness of the means made use of. In this case, perhaps, the verdict would not have been different, had the jury been properly instructed; but it might have been, and therefore the judgment must be reversed. * * *

NOTES

1.   *Reasonable Force.* The principal case, of course, involves the use of deadly force when the defendant himself is facing the loss of life or grievous bodily injury. Ordinarily, the person threatened is entitled to use such force as reasonably appears necessary to defend against the attack. See Restatement (Second) of Torts § 63 cmt. j (1965).

2.   *Innocent Bystander.* In Morris v. Platt, 32 Conn. 75 (1864), the defendant fired a pistol shot while being beaten with fists and clubs. His shot struck and killed the plaintiff, an innocent bystander. The court held there was no liability if the defendant reasonably feared he was in danger of death or grievous bodily harm. How does the case differ from *Courvoisier v. Raymond*? With these two cases, compare Roman law which provided: "[I]f in order to defend myself I throw a stone at my attacker and I hit not him but a passerby, I shall be liable * * *, for it is permitted only to use force against an attacker, and even then only so far as is necessary for self-defense and not for revenge." Digest of Justinian 9.2.45.4 (Book Nine: The Lex Aquilia (Alan Watson ed., Univ. of Pa. Press, electronic ed. 2009)).

3.   *Defense of Third Party.* One is justified in using reasonable force in defense of others. It is no longer required that the force be used to defend a member of the defendant's own family or someone otherwise under the defendant's legal protection. What happens, however, if the defendant misperceives the situation—but reasonably so—and the party he seeks to protect would not be entitled to the privilege of self-defense? Compare Restatement (Second) of Torts § 76 cmt. c, illus. 2 (1965) (privilege allowed)

with Webb v. Snow, 102 Utah 435, 447, 132 P.2d 114, 120 (1942) (no privilege).

3. DEFENSE OF PROPERTY

Katko v. Briney

Supreme Court of Iowa, 1971.
183 N.W.2d 657.

■ MOORE, CHIEF JUSTICE. The primary issue presented here is whether an owner may protect personal property in an unoccupied boarded-up farm house against trespassers and thieves by a spring gun capable of inflicting death or serious injury. We are not here concerned with a man's right to protect his home and members of his family. Defendants' home was several miles from the scene of the incident to which we refer *infra*.

Plaintiff's action is for damages resulting from serious injury caused by a shot from a 20-gauge spring shotgun set by defendants in a bedroom of an old farm house which had been uninhabited for several years. Plaintiff and his companion, Marvin McDonough, had broken and entered the house to find and steal old bottles and dated fruit jars which they considered antiques.

At defendants' request plaintiff's action was tried to a jury consisting of residents of the community where defendants' property was located. The jury returned a verdict for plaintiff and against defendants * * *.

For about 10 years, 1957 to 1967, there occurred a series of trespassing and housebreaking events with loss of some household items, the breaking of windows and "messing up of the property in general." The latest occurred June 8, 1967, prior to the event on July 16, 1967 herein involved. Defendants through the years boarded up the windows and doors in an attempt to stop the intrusions. They had posted "no trespass" signs on the land several years before 1967. The nearest one was 35 feet from the house. On June 11, 1967 defendants set "a shotgun trap" in the north bedroom. After Mr. Briney cleaned and oiled his 20–gauge shotgun, the power of which he was well aware, defendants took it to the old house where they secured it to an iron bed with the barrel pointed at the bedroom door. It was rigged with wire from the doorknob to the gun's trigger so it would fire when the door was opened. Briney first pointed the gun so an intruder would be hit in the stomach but at Mrs. Briney's suggestion it was lowered to hit the legs. He admitted he did so "because I was mad and tired of being tormented" but "he did not intend to injure anyone." He gave no explanation of why he used a loaded shell and set it to hit a person already in the house. Tin was nailed over the bedroom window. The spring gun could not be seen from the outside. No warning of its presence was posted.

Plaintiff lived with his wife and worked regularly as a gasoline station attendant in Eddyville, seven miles from the old house. He had observed it for several years while hunting in the area and considered it as being abandoned. He knew it had long been uninhabited. In 1967 the area around the house was covered with high weeds. Prior to July 16, 1967 plaintiff and McDonough had been to the premises and found several old bottles and fruit jars which they took and added to their collection of antiques. On the latter date about 9:30 p.m. they made a second trip to the Briney property. They entered the old house by removing a board from a porch window which was without glass. While McDonough was looking around the kitchen area plaintiff went to another part of the house. As he started to open the north bedroom door the shotgun went off striking him in the right leg above the ankle bone. Much of his leg, including part of the tibia, was blown away. Only by McDonough's assistance was plaintiff able to get out of the house and after crawling some distance was put in his vehicle and rushed to a doctor and then to a hospital. He remained in the hospital 40 days. * * *

Plaintiff testified he knew he had no right to break and enter the house with intent to steal bottles and fruit jars therefrom. He further testified he had entered a plea of guilty to larceny in the nighttime of property of less than $20 value from a private building. He stated he had been fined $50 and costs and paroled during good behavior from a 60–day jail sentence. Other than minor traffic charges this was plaintiff's first brush with the law. On this civil case appeal it is not our prerogative to review the disposition made of the criminal charge against him.

The main thrust of defendants' defense in the trial court and on this appeal is that "the law permits use of a spring gun in a dwelling or warehouse for the purpose of preventing the unlawful entry of a burglar or thief." They repeated this contention in their exceptions to the trial court's instructions 2, 5 and 6. * * *

In the statement of issues the trial court stated plaintiff and his companion committed a felony when they broke and entered defendants' house. In instruction 2 the court referred to the early case history of the use of spring guns and stated under the law their use was prohibited except to prevent the commission of felonies of violence and where human life is in danger. The instruction included a statement breaking and entering is not a felony of violence.

Instruction 5 stated: "You are hereby instructed that one may use reasonable force in the protection of his property, but such right is subject to the qualification that one may not use such means of force as will take human life or inflict great bodily injury. Such is the rule even though the injured party is a trespasser and is in violation of the law himself."

Instruction 6 stated: "An owner of premises is prohibited from willfully or intentionally injuring a trespasser by means of force that either takes life or inflicts great bodily injury; and therefore a person owning a premise is prohibited from setting out 'spring guns' and like dangerous devices which will likely take life or inflict great bodily injury, for the purpose of harming trespassers. The fact that the trespasser may be acting in violation of the law does not change the rule. The only time when such conduct of setting a 'spring gun' or a like dangerous device is justified would be when the trespasser was committing a felony of violence or a felony punishable by death, or where the trespasser was endangering human life by his act." * * *

Prosser on Torts, Third Edition, pages 116–118, states:

... the law has always placed a higher value upon human safety than upon mere rights in property, it is the accepted rule that there is no privilege to use any force calculated to cause death or serious bodily injury to repel the threat to land or chattels, unless there is also such a threat to the defendant's personal safety as to justify a self-defense. . . . spring guns and other man-killing devices are not justifiable against a mere trespasser, or even a petty thief. They are privileged only against those upon whom the landowner, if he were present in person would be free to inflict injury of the same kind.

Restatement of Torts, section 85, page 180, states:

* * * A possessor of land cannot do indirectly and by a mechanical device that which, were he present, he could not do immediately and in person. Therefore, he cannot gain a privilege to install, for the purpose of protecting his land from intrusions harmless to the lives and limbs of the occupiers or users of it, a mechanical device whose only purpose is to inflict death or serious harm upon such as may intrude, by giving notice of his intention to inflict, by mechanical means and indirectly, harm which he could not, even after request, inflict directly were he present.

In Volume 2, Harper and James, The Law of Torts, section 27.3, pages 1440–41, this is found:

The possessor of land may not arrange his premises intentionally so as to cause death or serious bodily harm to a trespasser. The possessor may of course take some steps to repel a trespass. If he is present he may use force to do so, but only that amount which is reasonably necessary to effect the repulse. Moreover if the trespass threatens harm to property only—even a theft of property—the possessor would not be privileged to use deadly force [even if there were no other way to prevent the trespass. Where the owner in person would not be privileged to use deadly force],[a] he may not arrange his premises so that such force will be inflicted by mechanical means. If he does, he will be liable even to a thief who is injured by such device. * * *

The legal principles stated by the trial court in instructions 2, 5 and 6 are well established and supported by the authorities cited and quoted supra. There is no merit in defendants' objections and exceptions thereto. * * *

Affirmed.

NOTES

1. Compare Richard A. Posner, Killing or Wounding to Protect a Property Interest, 14 J.L. & Econ. 201 (1971) (advocating test of reasonableness to be applied to use of deadly mechanical devices where use is necessary to prevent theft or destruction of valuable property, other means of deterrence

---

    [a] [Eds.' note] The court's opinion deletes the bracketed insertion from the original source.

are not practicable, and suitable precautions are taken to minimize the risk of harm to intruders and others).

2. *Use of Force to Eject Once Initial License to Use Property is Revoked.* Reasonable force also may be used to eject those who initially came upon the property with permission or license, but whose license has been lawfully revoked by the landowner or occupier. For example, in Cummins v. St. Louis Amusement Co., 147 S.W.2d 190 (Mo.App.1941), the court ruled that the owner of a motion picture theater could use reasonable force to eject a patron if he became disruptive, in which case the license conferred by the ticket could be properly revoked. The court disagreed, however, with the trial court's instruction that the ticket could be revoked "with or without any good reason therefor."

3. *Use of Force to Recapture Chattels.* When is the use of force privileged to recapture chattels or personal property? May a store owner use force to regain possession of an item stolen from her store? See, e.g., Moore v. Pay 'N Save Corp., 20 Wash.App. 482, 581 P.2d 159 (1978). In order to justify the use of force the following conditions must ordinarily exist:

   (1) The person using the force must have been in previous possession;

   (2) the property must have been tortiously taken either forcibly or by fraud or without claim of right;

   (3) the actor, as against the other, must be entitled to immediate possession;

   (4) the recapture must be effected promptly;

   (5) a request for the return of property must usually be first made; and

   (6) the force used must not be excessive.

Harper, James and Gray on Torts § 3.16.

The second condition precludes the use of force to recapture property under a conditional sales contract, such as when the purchaser has failed to make payments. Under § 9–503 of the Uniform Commercial Code, the secured party may retake possession of the collateral without judicial process, but only if this can be done without breach of peace.

C. ASSAULT

White v. Sander

Supreme Judicial Court of Massachusetts, 1897.
168 Mass. 296, 47 N.E. 90.

These were two actions of tort, one by Benjamin White, and the other by Emma White, his wife, against F. H. Sander, to recover damages for personal injuries caused by a fright caused by defendant throwing a stone into a room where the wife was. The jury returned a verdict for the husband for $179.30, and for the wife for $847.47, and the defendant excepted. Exceptions sustained.

■ ALLEN, J. There was no evidence that the defendant had any intention to injure the female plaintiff, or that he was aware of her condition of health. The house did not belong to her, but to her father, with whom the defendant had an altercation. The defendant's declared purpose was to injure the house, and he threw a large stone against it, in her presence. She then ran into the front room, with her little child, whereupon a large stone was willfully thrown by the defendant, which passed through one of the blinds, all of the blinds upon the front windows being closed. This greatly frightened her, though she was not struck or touched. We do not understand by the bill of exceptions that the defendant knew that she was in that room, or that he had any purpose either to hit or to frighten her, or that it was designed to present to us a case of an intentional injury to her or to her property. These elements being absent, the defendant was not responsible in damages for her fright or the consequent injury to her health. * Under the order taking off the default, the defendant was responsible for nominal damages. Exceptions sustained.

Brower v. Ackerley

Washington Court of Appeals, 1997.
88 Wash.App. 87, 943 P.2d 1141.

■ BECKER, JUDGE. * * * The plaintiff, Jordan Brower, is a Seattle resident active in civic affairs. Christopher and Theodore Ackerley, in their early twenties at the time of the alleged telephone calls, are two sons of the founder of Ackerley Communications, Inc., a company engaged in various activities in Seattle including billboard advertising. Brower perceived billboard advertising as a visual blight. Based on his own investigation, he concluded that Ackerley Communications had erected numerous billboards without obtaining permits from the City of Seattle; had not given the City an accurate accounting of its billboards; and was maintaining a number of billboards that were not on the tax rolls. In January, 1991, Brower presented his findings to the City. When the City did not respond, Brower filed suit in October of 1991 against the City and Ackerley Communications seeking enforcement of the City's billboard regulations.

Within two days an anonymous male caller began what Brower describes as "a campaign of harassing telephone calls" to Brower's home that continued over a period of 20 months. The first time, the caller shouted at Brower in an aggressive, mean-spirited voice to "get a life" and other words to that effect. Brower received at least one more harassing telephone call by January of 1992.

When the City agreed to pursue Brower's complaints about the billboard violations, Brower dropped his suit. In April of 1992, the City made a public announcement to the effect that Ackerley Communications had erected dozens of illegal billboards. Within a day of that announcement, Brower received an angry telephone call from a caller he identified as the same caller as the first call. In a loud, menacing voice, the caller told Brower that he should find a better way to spend his time. Two days later there was another call telling Brower to "give it up."

In July of 1992, shortly after the City Council passed a moratorium on billboard activity, Brower received another angry anonymous call. The male voice swore at him and said, "You think you're pretty smart, don't you?" Brower says he seriously wondered whether he was in any danger of physical harm from the caller. Over the following months Brower continued to receive calls from an unidentified male who he says "belittled me, told me what a rotten person I was, and who used offensive profanity."

On July 19, 1993, the City Council passed a new billboard ordinance. At about 6:30 that evening an angry-voiced man telephoned Brower and said "dick" in a loud voice and hung up. At about 7:30 p.m. the same caller called and said, "I'm going to find out where you live and I'm going to kick your ass." At 9:43 p.m. Brower received another call from a voice disguised to sound, in Brower's words, "eerie and sinister". The caller said "Ooooo, Jordan, oooo, you're finished; cut you in your sleep, you sack of shit." Brower recorded the last two calls on his telephone answering machine.

Brower made a complaint to the police, reporting that he was very frightened by these calls. Because Brower had activated a call trapping feature of his telephone service after the third telephone call, the police were able to learn that the call had originated in the residence of Christopher Ackerley. When contacted by the police, Christopher Ackerley denied making the calls. He said Brower's telephone number was in his apartment, and that his brother Ted Ackerley had been in the apartment at the time and perhaps had made the calls.

The City filed no criminal charges based on the police report. Brower then brought this civil suit against Christopher and Theodore Ackerley seeking compensation for the emotional distress he suffered as the result of the telephone calls. According to Brower, he interpreted the calls of July 19 as a death threat, and felt "hunted down". He experienced feelings of panic, terror, and insecurity as well as a rising pulse, light-headedness, sweaty palms, sleeplessness, and an inability to concentrate that lasted for some time afterward: "Every day I come home, I worry that someone has burned our house down, or if my wife is late from work, whether she has been harmed."

The Ackerleys moved for summary judgment. Brower responded primarily with his own declaration describing the telephone calls and his reaction to them. The trial court dismissed all claims. Brower appeals, arguing that his declaration raises a genuine issue of material fact as to his claims of assault, negligence, and the tort of outrage. The Ackerleys respond that the telephone calls described by Brower do not amount to civil assault, and that the distress Brower claims he suffered as a result was insufficiently severe to support his other causes of action.

Damages for mental and emotional distress are generally available merely upon proof of an intentional tort such as assault. * In such cases, there is no requirement that emotional distress be severe or manifested by physical symptoms in order to be compensable as an element of damages. * Therefore, we initially examine Brower's proof to determine whether he has presented proof of an intentional tort.

Assault

The elements of civil assault have not been frequently addressed in Washington cases. The gist of the cause of action is "the victim's apprehension of imminent physical violence caused by the perpetrator's action or threat."[5] In the 1910 case of Howell v. Winters,[6] the Supreme Court relied on a definition provided in Cooley, Torts (3d ed.):

> An assault is an attempt, with unlawful force, to inflict bodily injuries upon another, accompanied with the apparent present ability to give effect to the attempt if not prevented. Such would be the raising of the hand in anger, with an apparent purpose to strike, and sufficiently near to enable the purpose to be carried into effect; the pointing of a loaded pistol at one who is in its range; the pointing of a pistol not loaded at one who is not aware of that fact and making an apparent attempt to shoot; shaking a whip or the fist in a man's face in anger; riding or running after him in threatening and hostile manner with a club or other weapon; and the like. The right that is invaded here indicates the nature of the wrong. Every person has a right to complete and perfect immunity from hostile assaults that threaten danger to his person; "A right to live in society without being put in fear of personal harm."[7]

The discussion in *Howell* accords with the Restatement (Second) of Torts, which defines assault, in relevant part, as follows:

> (1) An actor is subject to liability to another for assault if
>
>> (a) he acts intending to cause a harmful or offensive contact with the person of the other or a third person, or an imminent apprehension of such a contact, and
>>
>> (b) the other is thereby put in such imminent apprehension.[8]

According to section 31 of the Restatement, words alone are not enough to make an actor liable for assault "unless together with other acts or circumstances they put the other in reasonable apprehension of an imminent harmful or offensive contact with his person."[9] The comments to section 31 indicate infliction of emotional distress is a better-suited cause of action when mere words cause injury, "even though the mental discomfort caused by a threat of serious future harm on the part of one who has the apparent intention and ability to carry out his threat may be far more emotionally disturbing than many of the attempts to inflict minor bodily contacts which are actionable as assaults."[10]

The Ackerleys argue that dismissal of Brower's assault claim was appropriate because the threatening words were unaccompanied by any physical acts or movements. Brower acknowledges that words alone cannot constitute an assault, but he contends the spoken threats became assaultive in view of the surrounding circumstances including the fact that the calls were made to his home, at night, creating the impression that the caller was stalking him.

---

[5] St. Michelle v. Robinson, 52 Wash.App. 309, 313, 759 P.2d 467 (1988).

[6] Howell v. Winters, 58 Wash. 436, 437–38, 108 P. 1077 (1910).

[7] *Id.* at 438 (quoting T. Cooley, Torts 278 (3d ed.)).

[8] Restatement (Second) of Torts § 21.

[9] *Id.* § 31.

[10] *Id.* § 31 cmt. a.

Whether the repeated use of a telephone to make anonymous threats constitutes acts or circumstances sufficient to render the threats assaultive is an issue we need not resolve because we find another issue dispositive: the physical harm threatened in the telephone calls to Brower was not imminent.

To constitute civil assault, the threat must be of imminent harm. As one commentator observes, it is "the immediate physical threat which is important, rather than the manner in which it is conveyed."[11] The Restatement's comment is to similar effect: "The apprehension created must be one of imminent contact, as distinguished from any contact in the future."[12] The Restatement gives the following illustration: "A threatens to shoot B and leaves the room with the express purpose of getting his revolver. A is not liable to B."[13]

The telephone calls received by Brower on July 19 contained two explicit threats: "I'm going to find out where you live and I'm going to kick your ass"; and later, "you're finished; cut you in your sleep." The words threatened action in the near future, but not the imminent future.

The immediacy of the threats was not greater than in the Restatement's illustration where A must leave the room to get his revolver. Because the threats, however frightening, were not accompanied by circumstances indicating that the caller was in a position to reach Brower and inflict physical violence "almost at once,"[14] we affirm the dismissal of the assault claim. * * *

NOTE

Apprehension without Fear. What if a nine-year old child attempts to punch a defensive lineman from a professional football team? The football player "is confident that he can avoid any blow" from the child and he experiences no fear. Has the child committed an assault? See Restatement (Third) of Torts: Intentional Torts to Persons § 103 cmt. c, illus. 1, 5 (Discussion Draft, April 4, 2014). According to the drafters of the Restatement:

> Apprehension does not require belief that the actor will succeed in inflicting the harmful or offensive contact. At times, a person might be aware that a harmful or offensive contact is imminent and yet know or believe that something will prevent the contact— for instance, the person's own action to avoid the contact, or the intervention of a third person. Nonetheless, the requirement of apprehension is satisfied if the person believes the harmful or offensive contact is imminent unless something further occurs, such as the person's ducking or fleeing to avoid contact, the person's employing self-defense, or outside intervention.

Id. at cmt. c.

---

[11] W. P. Keeton, Prosser and Keeton on the Law of Torts 45 (5th ed. 1984).

[12] Restatement (Second) of Torts § 29 cmt. b.

[13] *Id.* § 29 cmt. c, illus. 4.

[14] *Id.* § 29 cmt. b.

a pattern of grossly abusive, threatening, and degrading conduct. Shields began regularly using the harshest vulgarity shortly after his arrival at the Nash facility. In response, Bruce and Davis informed Shields that they were uncomfortable with obscene jokes, vulgar cursing, and sexual innuendo in the office. Despite these objections, Shields continued to use exceedingly vulgar language on a daily basis. Several witnesses testified that Shields used the word "f——" as part of his normal pattern of conversation, and that he regularly heaped abusive profanity on the employees. Linda Davis testified that Shields used this language to get a reaction. Gene Martin, another GTE employee, testified that Shields used the words "f——" and "motherf——er" frequently when speaking with the employees. On one occasion when Bruce asked Shields to curb his language because it was offensive, Shields positioned himself in front of her face, and screamed, "I will do and say any damn thing I want. And I don't give a s—— who likes it." Another typical example is when Gene Martin asked Shields to stop his yelling and vulgarity because it upset the female employees, and Shields replied "I'm tired of walking on f——ing eggshells, trying to make people happy around here." There was further evidence that Shields's harsh and vulgar language was not merely accidental, but seemed intended to abuse the employees.

More importantly, the employees testified that Shields repeatedly physically and verbally threatened and terrorized them. There was evidence that Shields was continuously in a rage, and that Shields would frequently assault each of the employees by physically charging at them. When doing so, Shields would bend his head down, put his arms straight down by his sides, ball his hands into fists, and walk quickly toward or "lunge" at the employees, stopping uncomfortably close to their faces while screaming and yelling. * * * A number of witnesses testified that Shields frequently yelled and screamed at the top of his voice, and pounded his fists when requesting the employees to do things. Bruce testified that Shields would "come up fast" and "get up over her"—causing her to lean back—and yell and scream in her face for her to get things for him. Shields included vulgar language in his yelling and screaming. * * *

Bruce also testified that Shields called her into his office every day and would have her stand in front of him, sometimes for as long as thirty minutes, while Shields simply stared at her. Bruce was not allowed to leave Shields's office until she was dismissed, even though Shields would periodically talk on the phone or read papers. This often occurred several times a day. Bruce testified that it made her nauseated and intimidated her. * * * Shields required Bruce and Davis, both general clerks at GTE, to purchase vacuum cleaners with company funds and to vacuum their offices daily, despite the fact that the company had a cleaning service that performed janitorial services such as vacuuming. The purpose of this seemed not to clean, but to humiliate. * * *

In considering whether the evidence establishes more than an ordinary employment dispute, we will also address GTE's argument that because none of Shields's acts standing alone rises to the level of outrageous conduct, the court of appeals erred in holding that, considered cumulatively, the conduct was extreme and outrageous. *

As already noted, the employees demonstrated at trial that Shields engaged in a course of harassing conduct directed at each of them, the totality of which caused severe emotional distress. It is well recognized outside of the employment context that a course of harassing conduct may support liability for intentional infliction of emotional distress. * In such cases, courts consider the totality of the conduct in determining whether it is extreme and outrageous. See [Duty v. General Fin. Co., 154 Tex. 16, 18–19, 273 S.W.2d 64, 65–66 (Tex.1954)] (analyzing creditor's entire course of conduct, including repetitive threatening phone calls and letters). Similarly, in the employment context, courts and commentators have almost unanimously recognized that liability may arise when one in a position of authority engages in repeated or ongoing harassment of an employee, if the cumulative quality and quantity of the harassment is extreme and outrageous. * When such repeated or ongoing harassment is alleged, the offensive conduct is evaluated as a whole. * * * We agree with the overwhelming weight of authority in this state and around the country that when repeated or ongoing severe harassment is shown, the conduct should be evaluated as a whole in determining whether it is extreme and outrageous. Accordingly, we hold that the court of appeals did not err in doing so.

We now consider whether Shields's conduct, taken as a whole, amounts to extreme and outrageous conduct. * * * We recognize that, even when an employer or supervisor abuses a position of power over an employee, the employer will not be liable for mere insults, indignities, or annoyances that are not extreme and outrageous. Restatement (Second) of Torts § 46 cmt. e (1965). But Shields's ongoing acts of harassment, intimidation, and humiliation and his daily obscene and vulgar behavior, which GTE defends as his "management style," went beyond the bounds of tolerable workplace conduct. * * * Occasional malicious and abusive incidents should not be condoned, but must often be tolerated in our society. But once conduct such as that shown here becomes a regular pattern of behavior and continues despite the victim's objection and attempts to remedy the situation, it can no longer be tolerated. It is the severity and regularity of Shields's abusive and threatening conduct that brings his behavior into the realm of extreme and outrageous conduct. Conduct such as being regularly assaulted, intimidated, and threatened is not typically encountered nor expected in the course of one's employment, nor should it be accepted in a civilized society. An employer certainly has much leeway in its chosen methods of supervising and disciplining employees, but terrorizing them is simply not acceptable. If GTE or Shields was dissatisfied with the employees' performance, GTE could have terminated them, disciplined them, or taken some other more appropriate approach to the problem instead of fostering the abuse, humiliation, and intimidation that was heaped on the employees. Accordingly, the trial court properly submitted the issue to the jury, and there was some evidence to support the jury's conclusion that Shields's conduct was extreme and outrageous.

B. *Intent*

GTE argues that the employees failed to establish that GTE, as opposed to Shields, possessed the requisite intent to support GTE's liability. The jury found that Shields intentionally inflicted emotional distress on the employees. The jury further found that Shields was acting in the scope of his employment. GTE contends that these findings are insufficient to support GTE's liability because the jury never found that GTE acted with the requisite intent. * * * GTE further contends that the jury's finding that Shields was acting in the scope of his employment is insufficient for liability because, GTE argues, an employer is never liable for an employee's intentional or malicious acts that are unforeseeable considering the employee's duties, and there was no finding that Shields's intentional acts were foreseeable by GTE.

Generally, a master is vicariously liable for the torts of its servants committed in the course and scope of their employment. * This is true even though the employee's tort is intentional when the act, although not specifically authorized by the employer, is closely connected with the servant's authorized duties. * If the intentional tort is committed in the accomplishment of a duty entrusted to the employee, rather than because of personal animosity, the employer may be liable. * Shields's acts, although inappropriate, involved conduct within the scope of his position as the employees' supervisor. * * * GTE has cited no evidence that Shields's actions were motivated by personal animosity rather than a misguided attempt to carry out his job duties. The jury concluded that Shields's acts were committed in the scope of his employment, and there is some evidence to support this finding. Thus, GTE is liable for Shields's conduct. * * *

C.   *Severe Emotional Distress*

GTE next contends that any distress the employees suffered was not severe. GTE argues that the employees' complaints of embarrassment, fear, stomach aches, loss of sleep, and headaches "are problems that are normally dealt with by each of us in everyday life."

Emotional distress includes all highly unpleasant mental reactions such as embarrassment, fright, horror, grief, shame, humiliation, and worry. * Severe emotional distress is distress that is so severe that no reasonable person could be expected to endure it. * The employees testified that, as a result of being exposed to Shields's outrageous conduct, they experienced a variety of emotional problems, including crying spells, emotional outbursts, nausea, stomach disorders, headaches, difficulty in sleeping and eating, stress, anxiety, and depression. The employees testified that they experienced anxiety and fear because of Shields's continuing harassment, especially his charges and rages. Each employee sought medical treatment for these problems, and all three plaintiffs were prescribed medication to alleviate the problems. An expert witness testified that each of them suffered from post-traumatic stress disorder. This evidence is legally sufficient to support the jury's finding that the employees suffered severe emotional distress. * * *

[W]e affirm the court of appeals' judgment. * * *

NOTES

1.   *Intentional Infliction of Emotional Distress.* Life is filled with at least transitory emotional distress and, regrettably, much of it is intentionally inflicted. Most vicissitudes of daily life do not belong in the courts. Yet the terms used to define the tort of intentional infliction of emotional distress, such as "outrageous" and "severe," seem very open-ended. How then does the law of torts distinguish the tort from the mere insult? Recovery has been allowed for more than a century where the suffering is of a kind likely to cause physical injury and such injury results. In Wilkinson v. Downton, [1897] 2 Q.B. 57, for example, the defendant, as a practical joke, falsely informed the plaintiff that her husband had been seriously injured in an accident, and she suffered "violent shock to her nervous system, producing vomiting and other more serious and permanent physical consequences at one time threatening her reason * * *." In the first half of the twentieth century, courts were reluctant to allow recovery in the absence of what they regarded as "physical" injury.

Today cases allowing recovery for intentional infliction of emotional distress frequently fall into a number of discrete factual patterns. The text of the *Bruce* case provides examples of at least two such categories: overzealous debt collection practices and sexual harassment. Other areas where the courts often allow recovery include strong-arm tactics, e.g., State Rubbish Collectors Ass'n v. Siliznoff, 38 Cal.2d 330, 338, 240 P.2d 282, 286 (1952) (trade group threatened to beat-up plaintiff unless dues were paid) and outrageous professional conduct, e.g., Rockhill v. Pollard, 259 Or. 54, 485 P.2d 28 (1971) (following an automobile accident, defendant doctor examined an unconscious 10 month old and the mother only in a cursory fashion, attributed child's vomiting to overeating, and made them wait outside in freezing rain).

The use of racial epithets may or may not be found to constitute intentional infliction of emotional distress, depending upon the surrounding circumstances (and the court). Recovery was allowed in Murray v. Wal-Mart, Inc., 874 F.2d 555 (8th Cir.1989) where the defendant's store manager pushed plaintiff back into the store, accused her of shoplifting, denied her access to heart medication, and used profanity and racial slurs. See also Wiggs v. Courshon, 355 F.Supp. 206 (S.D.Fla.1973) (recovery allowed for racial slurs); but see Bradshaw v. Swagerty, 1 Kan.App.2d 213, 563 P.2d 511 (1977) (recovery denied when plaintiff's lawyer used racial slurs; court stated that the words were " 'mere insults' of the kind which must be tolerated in our roughened society").

Courts rarely allow recovery for the intentional infliction of emotional distress caused by family members or intimate friends, even when the facts are such that the conduct is offensive and intentional and the resulting emotional distress is severe. See Ira M. Ellman & Stephen D. Sugarman, Spousal Emotional Abuse as a Tort?, 55 Md. L. Rev. 1268, 1343 (1996) ("it is probably a mistake for the courts to make tort law available for claims between divorcing spouses, apart from cases in which the abusive conduct is criminal").

2.   *Outrageous Misconduct.* As the *Brower* and *GTE Southwest* cases suggest, liability for intentional infliction of emotional distress

> has been found only where the conduct has been so outrageous in character, and so extreme in degree, as to go beyond all possible bounds of decency, and to be regarded as atrocious, and utterly intolerable in a civilized community. Generally, the case is one in which the recitation of the facts to an average member of the community would arouse his resentment against the actor, and lead him to exclaim, "Outrageous!"

The liability clearly does not extend to mere insults, indignities, threats, annoyances, petty oppressions, or other trivialities. * * * There is no occasion for the law to intervene in every case where some one's feelings are hurt.

Restatement (Second) of Torts § 46 cmt. d (1965).

Snyder v. Phelps

United States Supreme Court, 2011.
562 U.S. ___, 131 S.Ct. 1207, 179 L.Ed.2d 172.

■ ROBERTS, CHIEF JUSTICE * * * Fred Phelps founded the Westboro Baptist Church in Topeka, Kansas, in 1955. The church's congregation believes that God hates and punishes the United States for its tolerance of homosexuality, particularly in America's military. The church frequently communicates its views by picketing, often at military funerals. In the more than 20 years that the members of Westboro Baptist have publicized their message, they have picketed nearly 600 funerals. * Marine Lance Corporal Matthew Snyder was killed in Iraq in the line of duty. Lance Corporal Snyder's father selected the Catholic church in the Snyders' hometown of Westminster, Maryland, as the site for his son's funeral. Local newspapers provided notice of the time and location of the service.

Phelps became aware of Matthew Snyder's funeral and decided to travel to Maryland with six other Westboro Baptist parishioners (two of his daughters and four of his grandchildren) to picket. On the day of the memorial service, the Westboro congregation members picketed on public land adjacent to public streets near the Maryland State House, the United States Naval Academy, and Matthew Snyder's funeral. The Westboro picketers carried signs that were largely the same at all three locations. They stated, for instance: "God Hates the USA/Thank God for 9/11," "America is Doomed," "Don't Pray for the USA," "Thank God for IEDs," "Thank God for Dead Soldiers," "Pope in Hell," "Priests Rape Boys," "God Hates Fags," "You're Going to Hell," and "God Hates You."

The church had notified the authorities in advance of its intent to picket at the time of the funeral, and the picketers complied with police instructions in staging their demonstration. The picketing took place within a 10- by 25-foot plot of public land adjacent to a public street, behind a temporary fence. * That plot was approximately 1,000 feet from the church where the funeral was held. Several buildings separated the picket site from the church. * The Westboro picketers displayed their signs for about 30 minutes before the funeral began and sang hymns and recited Bible verses. None of the picketers entered church property or went to the cemetery. They did not yell or use profanity, and there was no violence associated with the picketing. * The funeral procession passed within 200 to 300 feet of the picket site. Although Snyder testified that he could see the tops of the picket signs as he drove to the funeral, he did not see what was written on the signs until later that night, while watching a news broadcast covering the event.

Snyder filed suit against Phelps * * *. Snyder alleged five state tort law claims [including] * * * intentional infliction of emotional distress * * *. At trial, Snyder described the severity of his emotional injuries.

He testified that he is unable to separate the thought of his dead son from his thoughts of Westboro's picketing, and that he often becomes tearful, angry, and physically ill when he thinks about it. * Expert witnesses testified that Snyder's emotional * anguish had resulted in severe depression and had exacerbated pre-existing health conditions.

A jury found for Snyder on the intentional infliction of emotional distress * * * claim[ ], and held Westboro liable for $2.9 million in compensatory damages and $8 million in punitive damages. Westboro filed several post-trial motions, including a motion contending that the jury verdict was grossly excessive and a motion seeking judgment as a matter of law on all claims on First Amendment grounds. The District Court remitted the punitive damages award to $2.1 million, but left the jury verdict otherwise intact. *

In the Court of Appeals, Westboro's primary argument was that the church was entitled to judgment as a matter of law because the First Amendment fully protected Westboro's speech. The Court of Appeals agreed. * The court reviewed the picket signs and concluded that Westboro's statements were entitled to First Amendment protection * * *. To succeed on a claim for intentional infliction of emotional distress in Maryland, a plaintiff must demonstrate that the defendant intentionally or recklessly engaged in extreme and outrageous conduct that caused the plaintiff to suffer severe emotional distress. * The Free Speech Clause of the First Amendment—"Congress shall make no law . . . abridging the freedom of speech"—can serve as a defense in state tort suits, including suits for intentional infliction of emotional distress. See, *e.g.*, Hustler Magazine, Inc. v. Falwell, 485 U.S. 46, 50–51, 108 S.Ct. 876, 99 L.Ed.2d 41 (1988). *

Whether the First Amendment prohibits holding Westboro liable for its speech in this case turns largely on whether that speech is of public or private concern, as determined by all the circumstances of the case. "[S]peech on 'matters of public concern' . . . is 'at the heart of the First Amendment's protection.'" Dun & Bradstreet, Inc. v. Greenmoss Builders, Inc., 472 U.S. 749, 758–59 (1985) (opinion of Powell, J.). * * * " '[N]ot all speech is of equal First Amendment importance,'" however, and where matters of purely private significance are at issue, First Amendment protections are often less rigorous. * That is because restricting speech on purely private matters does not implicate the same constitutional concerns as limiting speech on matters of public interest * * *.

Speech deals with matters of public concern when it can "be fairly considered as relating to any matter of political, social, or other concern to the community," * or when it "is a subject of legitimate news interest; that is, a subject of general interest and of value and concern to the public." * * *

The "content" of Westboro's signs plainly relates to broad issues of interest to society at large, rather than matters of "purely private concern." * The placards * * * may fall short of refined social or political commentary, the issues they highlight—the political and moral conduct of the United States and its citizens, the fate of our Nation, homosexuality in the military, and scandals involving the Catholic clergy—are matters of public import. The signs certainly convey Westboro's position on those issues, in a manner designed * * * to reach as broad a public audience as possible. And even if a few of the signs—such as "You're Going to Hell" and "God Hates You"—were viewed as containing messages related to Matthew Snyder or the Snyders specifically, that would not change the fact that the overall thrust and dominant theme of Westboro's demonstration spoke to broader public issues.

Apart from the content of Westboro's signs, Snyder contends that the "context" of the speech—its connection with his son's funeral—makes the speech a matter of private rather than public concern. The fact that Westboro spoke in connection with a funeral, however, cannot by itself transform the nature of Westboro's speech. Westboro's signs, displayed on public land next to a public street, reflect the fact that the church finds much to condemn in modern society. Its speech is "fairly characterized as constituting speech on a matter of public concern," * and the funeral setting does not alter that conclusion. * * *

Westboro's choice to convey its views in conjunction with Matthew Snyder's funeral made the expression of those views particularly hurtful to many, especially to Matthew's father. The record makes clear that the applicable legal term—"emotional distress"—fails to capture fully the anguish Westboro's choice added to Mr. Snyder's already incalculable grief. But Westboro conducted its picketing peacefully on matters of public concern at a public place adjacent to a public street. * * *

That said, "[e]ven protected speech is not equally permissible in all places and at all times." * Westboro's choice of where and when to conduct its picketing is not beyond the Government's regulatory reach—it is "subject to reasonable time, place, or manner restrictions" that are consistent with the standards announced in this Court's precedents. * * *

Simply put, the church members had the right to be where they were. Westboro alerted local authorities to its funeral protest and fully complied with police guidance on where the picketing could be staged. The picketing was conducted under police supervision some 1,000 feet from the church, out of the sight of those at the church. The protest was not unruly; there was no shouting, profanity, or violence.

The record confirms that any distress occasioned by Westboro's picketing turned on the content and viewpoint of the message conveyed, rather than any interference with the funeral itself. A group of parishioners standing at the very spot where Westboro stood, holding signs that said "God Bless America" and "God Loves You," would not have been subjected to liability. It was what Westboro said that exposed it to tort damages.

Given that Westboro's speech was at a public place on a matter of public concern, that speech is entitled to "special protection" under the First Amendment. Such speech cannot be restricted simply because it is upsetting or arouses contempt. "If there is a bedrock principle underlying the First Amendment, it is that the government may not prohibit the expression of an idea simply because society finds the idea itself offensive or disagreeable." * * *

The jury here was instructed that it could hold Westboro liable for intentional infliction of emotional distress based on a finding that

Westboro's picketing was "outrageous." "Outrageousness," however, is a highly malleable standard with "an inherent subjectiveness about it which would allow a jury to impose liability on the basis of the jurors' tastes or views, or perhaps on the basis of their dislike of a particular expression." *Hustler*, 485 U.S. at 55. * * * What Westboro said, in the whole context of how and where it chose to say it, is entitled to "special protection" under the First Amendment, and that protection cannot be overcome by a jury finding that the picketing was outrageous. For all these reasons, the jury verdict imposing tort liability on Westboro for intentional infliction of emotional distress must be set aside. * * *

■ ALITO, JUSTICE (dissenting). * * * Respondents and other members of their church have strong opinions on certain moral, religious, and political issues, and the First Amendment ensures that they have almost limitless opportunities to express their views. They may write and distribute books, articles, and other texts; they may create and disseminate video and audio recordings; they may circulate petitions; they may speak to individuals and groups in public forums and in any private venue that wishes to accommodate them; they may picket peacefully in countless locations; they may appear on television and speak on the radio; they may post messages on the Internet and send out e-mails. And they may express their views in terms that are "uninhibited," "vehement," and "caustic." It does not follow, however, that they may intentionally inflict severe emotional injury on private persons at a time of intense emotional sensitivity by launching vicious verbal attacks that make no contribution to public debate. To protect against such injury, "most if not all jurisdictions" permit recovery in tort for the intentional infliction of emotional distress (or IIED). * * * It is well established that a claim for the intentional infliction of emotional distress can be satisfied by speech. * * *

On the morning of Matthew Snyder's funeral, respondents could have chosen to stage their protest at countless locations. They could have picketed the United States Capitol, the White House, the Supreme Court, the Pentagon, or any of the more than 5,600 military recruiting stations in this country. They could have returned to the Maryland State House or the United States Naval Academy, where they had been the day before. * * * But of course, a small group picketing at any of these locations would have probably gone unnoticed. The Westboro Baptist Church, however, has devised a strategy that remedies this problem. As the Court notes, church members have protested at nearly 600 military funerals. * * * This strategy works because it is expected that respondents' verbal assaults will wound the family and friends of the deceased and because the media is irresistibly drawn to the sight of persons who are visibly in grief. The more outrageous the funeral protest, the more publicity the Westboro Baptist Church is able to obtain. * * * Neither classic "fighting words"[b] nor defamatory statements are immunized when they occur in a public place, and there is no good reason to treat a verbal assault based on the conduct or character of a private figure like Matthew Snyder any differently. * * *

---

b   [Eds.' note] The Supreme Court has held that " 'fighting' words—those which by their very utterance * * * tend to incite to incite an immediate breach of the peace" are within the "well-defined and narrowly limited classes of speech, the prevention and punishment of which have never been thought to raise any Constitutional problem." Chaplinsky v. New Hampshire, 315 U.S. 568, 571–72, 62 S.Ct. 766, 769, 86 L.Ed. 1031, 1035 (1942).

Allowing family members to have a few hours of peace without harassment does not undermine public debate. I would therefore hold that, in this setting, the First Amendment permits a private figure to recover for the intentional infliction of emotional distress caused by speech on a matter of private concern. * * *

NOTES

1. *The Goals of Tort Law and Constitutional Restrictions on Liability.* Is the issue of whether the father should be able to recover for his understandably severe emotional distress the same as whether the state could constitutionally criminally prosecute the defendants for their conduct? Does the Supreme Court focus exclusively on the loss minimization or deterrence goal of tort law and ignore other goals such as compensation and corrective justice or civil recourse? Compare Justice Sotomayor's dissenting opinion in Mutual Pharm. Co. v. Bartlett, *supra* pages 637–642 and Note 1 following her opinion.

2. *Liability for Political Cartoons Caricaturing Public Persons.* In *Snyder*, the U.S. Supreme Court relied on its earlier decision in Hustler Magazine, Inc. v. Falwell, 485 U.S. 46, 108 S.Ct. 876, 99 L.Ed.2d 41 (1988). In that case, the distributor of Campari Liqueur ran a series of advertisements featuring interviews with various celebrities about their "first times." By the end of each advertisement, it was clear that the celebrity was discussing her or his first time drinking Campari, but the advertisements clearly and deliberately played on the sexual double entendre. The defendant Hustler Magazine ran a parody of these ads featuring the plaintiff, a nationally known evangelical pastor, in which he allegedly described his "first time" as a "drunken incestuous rendezvous with his mother in an outhouse." In small print at the bottom of the page, the defendant's publication stated that its depiction was "ad parody—not to be taken seriously." The plaintiff sued for intentional infliction of emotional distress, and the jury awarded him both $100,000 compensatory damages and $50,000 punitive damages.

The Supreme Court held that the First Amendment prevented the defendant from being held liable for intentional infliction of emotional distress. For nearly a quarter-century before *Hustler*, the Court had held that the First Amendment constrained plaintiffs from recovering for the torts of defamation and invasion of privacy in some circumstances. See *infra* pages 902–930 (constitutional limits on defamation) and 934–935, 950–951, 959–963, 965–966, 967–973 (constitutional limits on invasion of privacy). The Court held that the judgment in favor of Reverend Falwell was not consistent with the First Amendment:

> * * * [I]n the world of debate about public affairs, many things done with motives that are less than admirable are protected by the First Amendment. * * * The art of the cartoonist is often not reasoned or evenhanded, but slashing and one-sided. * * * Despite their sometimes caustic nature, from the early cartoon portraying George Washington as an ass down to the present day, graphic depictions and satirical cartoons have played a prominent role in public and political debate. * * * Lincoln's tall, gangling posture, Teddy Roosevelt's glasses and teeth, and Franklin D. Roosevelt's jutting jaw and cigarette holder have been memorialized by political cartoons with an effect that could not have been obtained

by the photographer or the portrait artist. From the viewpoint of history it is clear that our political discourse would have been considerably poorer without them.

Respondent contends, however, that the caricature in question here was so "outrageous" as to distinguish it from more traditional political cartoons. There is no doubt that the caricature of respondent and his mother published in *Hustler* is at best a distant cousin of the political cartoons described above, and a rather poor relation at that. If it were possible by laying down a principled standard to separate the one from the other, public discourse would probably suffer little or no harm. But we doubt that there is any such standard, and we are quite sure that the pejorative description "outrageous" does not supply one. "Outrageousness" in the area of political and social discourse has an inherent subjectiveness about it which would allow a jury to impose liability on the basis of the jurors' tastes or views, or perhaps on the basis of their dislike of a particular expression. An "outrageousness" standard thus runs afoul of our longstanding refusal to allow damages to be awarded because the speech in question may have an adverse emotional impact on the audience. * * *

E. False Imprisonment

McCann v. Wal-Mart Stores, Inc.

United States Court of Appeals for the First Circuit, 2000.
210 F.3d 51.

■ Boudin, Circuit Judge. * * * On December 11, 1996, Debra McCann and two of her children—Jillian, then 16, and Jonathan, then 12—were shopping at the Wal-Mart store in Bangor, Maine. After they returned a Christmas tree and exchanged a CD player, Jonathan went to the toy section and Jillian and Debra McCann went to shop in other areas of the store. After approximately an hour and a half, the McCanns went to a register and paid for their purchases. One of their receipts was time stamped at 10:10 p.m.

As the McCanns were leaving the store, two Wal-Mart employees, Jean Taylor and Karla Hughes, stepped out in front of the McCanns' shopping cart, blocking their path to the exit. Taylor may have actually put her hand on the cart. The employees told Debra McCann that the children were not allowed in the store because they had been caught stealing on a prior occasion. In fact, the employees were mistaken; the son of a *different* family had been caught shoplifting in the store about two weeks before, and Taylor and Hughes confused the two families.

Despite Debra McCann's protestations, Taylor said that they had the records, that the police were being called, and that the McCanns "had to go with her." Debra McCann testified that she did not resist Taylor's direction because she believed that she had to go with Taylor and that the police were coming. Taylor and Hughes then brought the McCanns past the registers in the store to an area near the store exit. Taylor stood near the McCanns while Hughes purportedly went to call the police. During this time, Debra McCann tried to show Taylor her identification, but Taylor refused to look at it.

After a few minutes, Hughes returned and switched places with Taylor. Debra McCann told Hughes that she had proof of her identity and that there must be some proof about the identity of the children who had been caught stealing. Hughes then went up to Jonathan, pointed her finger at him, and said that he had been caught stealing two weeks earlier. Jonathan began to cry and denied the accusation. At some point around this time Jonathan said that he needed to use the bathroom and Hughes told him he could not go. At no time during this initial hour or so did the Wal-Mart employees tell the McCanns that they could leave.

* * * Eventually, [a] security officer, Rhonda Bickmore, arrived at the store and informed Hughes that the McCanns were not the family whose son had been caught shoplifting. Hughes then acknowledged her mistake to the McCanns, and the McCanns left the store at approximately 11:15 p.m. In due course, the McCanns brought suit against Wal-Mart for false imprisonment (a defamation claim was also made but was rejected by the jury).

The jury awarded the McCanns $20,000 in compensatory damages on their claim that they were falsely imprisoned in the Wal-Mart store by Wal-Mart employees. Wal-Mart has now appealed the district court's denial of its post-judgment motions for judgment as a matter of law and for a new trial, * * * arguing that the McCanns did not prove false imprisonment under Maine law and that the court's jury instructions on false imprisonment were in error. * * *

Both of Wal-Mart's claims of error depend on the proper elements of the tort of false imprisonment. Although nuances vary from state to state, the gist of the common law tort is conduct by the actor which is intended to, and does in fact, "confine" another "within boundaries fixed by the actor" where, in addition, the victim is either "conscious of the confinement or is harmed by it." Restatement (Second) of Torts § 35 (1965). * * *

While "confinement" can be imposed by physical barriers or physical force, much less will do—although how much less becomes cloudy at the margins. It is generally settled that mere threats of physical force can suffice, Restatement § 40; and it is also settled * * * that the threats may be implicit as well as explicit, see id. cmt. a; *, and that confinement can also be based on a false assertion of legal authority to confine. Restatement § 41. Indeed, the Restatement provides that confinement may occur by other unspecified means of "duress." Id. § 40A.

* * * [W]e think that a reasonable jury could conclude that Wal-Mart's employees intended to "confine" the McCanns "within boundaries fixed by" Wal-Mart, that the employees' acts did result in such a confinement, and that the McCanns were conscious of the confinement.

The evidence, taken favorably to the McCanns, showed that Wal-Mart employees stopped the McCanns as they were seeking to exit the store, said that the children were not allowed in the store, told the McCanns that they had to come with the Wal-Mart employees and that

Wal-Mart was calling the police, and then stood guard over the McCanns while waiting for a security guard to arrive. The direction to the McCanns, the reference to the police, and the continued presence of the Wal-Mart employees (who at one point told Jonathan McCann that he could not leave to go to the bathroom) were enough to induce reasonable people to believe either that they would be restrained physically if they sought to leave, or that the store was claiming lawful authority to confine them until the police arrived, or both.

Wal-Mart asserts that under Maine law, the jury had to find "actual, physical restraint," a phrase it takes from Knowlton v. Ross, 114 Me. 18, 22, 95 A. 281, 283 (1915) * * *.

Taking too literally the phrase "actual, physical restraint" would put Maine law broadly at odds with not only the *Restatement* but with a practically uniform body of common law in other states that accepts the mere threat of physical force, or a claim of lawful authority to restrain, as enough to satisfy the confinement requirement for false imprisonment (assuming always that the victim submits). * * *

Affirmed.

NOTES

1. *Confinement within Boundaries.* In the classic case of Bird v. Jones, (1845) 115 Eng.Rep. 668, 669 (K.B.), the court held that preventing the plaintiff from proceeding forward on a public highway did not constitute false imprisonment. Justice Coleridge stated:

> A prison may have its boundary large or narrow, visible and tangible * * *; it may itself be moveable or fixed: but a boundary it must have * * *. [I]t is one part of the definition of freedom to be able to go whithersoever one pleases; but imprisonment is something more than the mere loss of this power; it includes the notion of restraint within some limits defined by a will or power exterior to our own.

What about depriving the victim of the ability to leave a locality or even a state? See Helstrom v. N. Slope Borough, 797 P.2d 1192, 1199 (Alaska 1990) ("[T]he deprivation of a plane ticket at the instigation of the Borough, effectively preventing Helstrom from leaving Barrow, sufficiently confined him.").

2. *Shopkeepers' Privilege.* Most states provide that store proprietors who have reasonable grounds to suspect someone of shoplifting or other theft may detain the suspect for a reasonable period of time in order to investigate the matter in a reasonable manner. Most often statutes provide this privilege, but some jurisdictions reach the same result under the common law. Did such a privilege apply in *McCann v. Wal-Mart Stores*? Why or why not?

Scofield v. Critical Air Medicine, Inc.

Court of Appeal of California, 1996.
45 Cal.App.4th 990, 52 Cal.Rptr.2d 915.

■ KLEIN, P. J. * * * On December 29, 1990, Nancy Scofield, the mother of Erin, Laura, and David, was killed in a truck accident in Baja

§ 11. Therefore, ". . . it is not necessary that any damage result from it other than the confinement itself, since the tort is complete with even a brief restraint of the plaintiff's freedom." * Also, false imprisonment has been characterized as a "dignitary tort," designed to allow recovery by one who either "knows of the dignitary invasion" or is actually harmed by it. * * * In view of the nature of the interest protected, it is appropriate a cause of action may be brought even where the damage is purely nominal. As Witkin observes, "[t]he advantages of . . . an award [of nominal damages], other than psychological, are two: (1) The plaintiff is entitled to costs [citation]; (2) he may be entitled to punitive damages [citation]." Bernard E. Witkin, Summary of Cal. Law, Torts § 1316 (9th ed. 1988). * * *

Frequently, emotional distress is the primary injury resulting from an intentional tort such as false imprisonment, and that injury clearly is compensable. * * * In addition to recovery for emotional suffering and humiliation, one subjected to false imprisonment is entitled to compensation for other resultant harm, such as loss of time, physical discomfort or inconvenience, any resulting physical illness or injury to health, business interruption, and damage to reputation, as well as punitive damages in appropriate cases. Prosser & Keeton, Torts § 11. * * *

The judgment is affirmed. * * *

F. ALIEN TORT STATUTE

Kiobel v. Royal Dutch Petroleum Co.

Supreme Court of the United States, 2013.
569 U.S. ___, 133 S.Ct. 1659, 185 L.Ed.2d 671.

■ ROBERTS, CHIEF JUSTICE. * * * Petitioners were residents of Ogoniland, an area of 250 square miles located in the Niger delta area of Nigeria and populated by roughly half a million people. When the complaint was filed, respondents Royal Dutch Petroleum Company and Shell Transport and Trading Company, p.l.c., were holding companies incorporated in the Netherlands and England, respectively. Their joint subsidiary, respondent Shell Petroleum Development Company of Nigeria, Ltd. (SPDC), was incorporated in Nigeria, and engaged in oil exploration and production in Ogoniland. According to the complaint, after concerned residents of Ogoniland began protesting the environmental effects of SPDC's practices, respondents enlisted the Nigerian Government to violently suppress the burgeoning demonstrations. Throughout the early 1990's, the complaint alleges, Nigerian military and police forces attacked Ogoni villages, beating, raping, killing, and arresting residents and destroying or looting property. Petitioners further allege that respondents aided and abetted these atrocities by, among other things, providing the Nigerian forces with food, transportation, and compensation, as well as by allowing the Nigerian military to use respondents' property as a staging ground for attacks.

Following the alleged atrocities, petitioners moved to the United States where they have been granted political asylum and now reside as legal residents. * They filed suit in the United States District Court for the Southern District of New York, alleging jurisdiction under the Alien Tort Statute [ATS] and requesting relief under customary international law. The ATS provides, in full, that "[t]he district courts shall have original jurisdiction of any civil action by an alien for a tort only, committed in violation of the law of nations or a treaty of the United States." 28 U.S.C. §1350. According to petitioners, respondents violated the law of nations by aiding and abetting the Nigerian Government in committing (1) extrajudicial killings; (2) crimes against humanity; (3) torture and cruel treatment; (4) arbitrary arrest and detention; (5) violations of the rights to life, liberty, security, and association; (6) forced exile; and (7) property destruction. The District Court dismissed the first, fifth, sixth, and seventh claims, reasoning that the facts alleged to support those claims did not give rise to a violation of the law of nations. The court denied respondents' motion to dismiss with respect to the remaining claims * * *.

The Second Circuit dismissed the entire complaint, reasoning that the law of nations does not recognize corporate liability. * We granted certiorari to consider that question. * After oral argument, we directed the parties to file supplemental briefs addressing an additional question: "Whether and under what circumstances the [ATS] allows courts to recognize a cause of action for violations of the law of nations occurring within the territory of a sovereign other than the United States." * * *

Passed as part of the Judiciary Act of 1789, the ATS was invoked twice in the late 18th century, but then only once more over the next 167 years. * The statute provides district courts with jurisdiction to hear certain claims, but does not expressly provide any causes of action. We held in Sosa v. Alvarez-Machain, 542 U.S. 692, 714, 124 S. Ct. 2739, 159 L. Ed. 2d 718 (2004), however, that the First Congress did not intend the provision to be "stillborn." The grant of jurisdiction is instead "best read as having been enacted on the understanding that the common law would provide a cause of action for [a] modest number of international law violations." We thus held that federal courts may "recognize private claims [for such violations] under federal common law." * * *

The question here is not whether petitioners have stated a proper claim under the ATS, but whether a claim may reach conduct occurring in the territory of a foreign sovereign. Respondents contend that claims under the ATS do not, relying primarily on a canon of statutory interpretation known as the presumption against extraterritorial application. That canon provides that "[w]hen a statute gives no clear indication of an extraterritorial application, it has none," * and reflects the "presumption that United States law governs domestically but does not rule the world." * This presumption "serves to protect against unintended clashes between our laws and those of other nations which could result in international discord." * * *

We typically apply the presumption to discern whether an Act of Congress regulating conduct applies abroad. * * * [T]he danger of unwarranted judicial interference in the conduct of foreign policy is magnified in the context of the ATS, because the question is not what Congress has done but instead what courts may do. * * * These concerns, which are implicated in any case arising under the ATS, are all the more pressing when the question is whether a cause of action under the ATS reaches conduct within the territory of another sovereign. These concerns are not diminished by the fact that *Sosa* limited federal courts to recognizing causes of action only for alleged violations of international law norms that are " 'specific, universal, and obligatory.' " * * *

The question under *Sosa* is not whether a federal court has jurisdiction to entertain a cause of action provided by foreign or even international law. The question is instead whether the court has authority to recognize a cause of action under U.S. law to enforce a norm of international law. The reference to "tort" does not demonstrate that the First Congress "necessarily meant" for those causes of action to reach conduct in the territory of a foreign sovereign. In the end, nothing in the text of the ATS evinces the requisite clear indication of extraterritoriality.

Nor does the historical background against which the ATS was enacted overcome the presumption against application to conduct in the territory of another sovereign. * We explained in *Sosa* that when Congress passed the ATS, "three principal offenses against the law of nations" had been identified by Blackstone: violation of safe conducts, infringement of the rights of ambassadors, and piracy. * See 4 W. Blackstone, Commentaries on the Laws of England 68 (1769). The first two offenses have no necessary extraterritorial application. Indeed, Blackstone—in describing them—did so in terms of conduct occurring within the forum nation. See *ibid.* (describing the right of safe conducts for those "who are here"); * * * *id.*, at 245–248 (recognizing the king's power to "receiv[e] ambassadors at home" and detailing their rights in the state "wherein they are appointed to reside"). * Two notorious episodes involving violations of the law of nations occurred in the United States shortly before passage of the ATS. Each concerned the rights of ambassadors, and each involved conduct within the Union. * * * The two cases in which the ATS was invoked shortly after its passage also concerned conduct within the territory of the United States. * These prominent contemporary examples—immediately before and after passage of the ATS—provide no support for the proposition that Congress expected causes of action to be brought under the statute for violations of the law of nations occurring abroad.

The third example of a violation of the law of nations familiar to the Congress that enacted the ATS was piracy. Piracy typically occurs on the high seas, beyond the territorial jurisdiction of the United States or any other country. * * * Petitioners contend that because Congress surely intended the ATS to provide jurisdiction for actions against pirates, it necessarily anticipated the statute would apply to conduct occurring abroad. Applying U.S. law to pirates, however, does not typically impose the sovereign will of the United States onto conduct occurring within the territorial jurisdiction of another sovereign, and therefore carries less direct foreign policy consequences. * * * We do not think that the existence of a cause of action against them is a sufficient basis for concluding that other causes of action under the ATS reach conduct that does occur within the territory of another sovereign; pirates may well be a category unto themselves. * * *

Finally, there is no indication that the ATS was passed to make the United States a uniquely hospitable forum for the enforcement of international norms. As Justice Story put it, "No nation has ever yet pretended to be the *custos morum* of the whole world . . . ." United States v. The La Jeune Eugenie, 26 F. Cas. 832, 847 (No. 15,551) (CC. Mass.1822). * * *

The United States was, however, embarrassed by its potential inability to provide judicial relief to foreign officials injured in the United States. * * * The ATS ensured that the United States could provide a forum for adjudicating such incidents. * Nothing about this historical context suggests that Congress also intended federal common law under the ATS to provide a cause of action for conduct occurring in the territory of another sovereign.

Indeed, far from avoiding diplomatic strife, providing such a cause of action could have generated it. * * * Moreover, accepting petitioners' view would imply that other nations, also applying the law of nations, could hale our citizens into their courts for alleged violations of the law of nations occurring in the United States, or anywhere else in the world. The presumption against extraterritoriality guards against our courts triggering such serious foreign policy consequences, and instead defers such decisions, quite appropriately, to the political branches.

We therefore conclude that the presumption against extraterritoriality applies to claims under the ATS, and that nothing in the statute rebuts that presumption. * * * [P]etitioners' case seeking relief for violations of the law of nations occurring outside the United States is barred. On these facts, all the relevant conduct took place outside the United States. And even where the claims touch and concern the territory of the United States, they must do so with sufficient force to displace the presumption against extraterritorial application. * Corporations are often present in many countries, and it would reach too far to say that mere corporate presence suffices. If Congress were to determine otherwise, a statute more specific than the ATS would be required.

The judgment of the Court of Appeals is affirmed.

■ BREYER, JUSTICE, with whom JUSTICES GINSBURG, SOTOMAYOR, AND KAGAN join, concurring in the judgment. * * * Unlike the Court, I would not invoke the presumption against extraterritoriality. Rather, guided in part by principles and practices of foreign relations law, I would find jurisdiction under this statute where (1) the alleged tort occurs on American soil, (2) the defendant is an American national, or (3) the defendant's conduct substantially and adversely affects an important American national interest, and that includes a distinct interest in preventing the United States from becoming a safe harbor (free of civil as well as criminal liability) for a torturer or other common enemy of mankind. * * * In this case, however, the parties and relevant conduct lack sufficient ties to the United States for the ATS to provide jurisdiction.

Our decision in *Sosa* frames the question. In *Sosa* the Court specified that the Alien Tort Statute (ATS), when enacted in 1789, "was intended as jurisdictional." * We added that the statute gives today's courts the power to apply certain "judge-made" damages law to victims of certain foreign affairs-related misconduct, including "three specific offenses" to which "Blackstone referred," namely "violation of safe conducts, infringement of the rights of ambassadors, and piracy." * We held that the statute provides today's federal judges with the power to fashion "a cause of action" for a "modest number" of claims, "based on the present-day law of nations," and which "rest on a norm of international character accepted by the civilized world and defined with a specificity comparable to the features" of those three "18th-century paradigms." * * *

Recognizing that Congress enacted the ATS to permit recovery of damages from pirates and others who violated basic international law norms as understood in 1789, *Sosa* essentially leads today's judges to ask: Who are today's pirates? * We provided a framework for answering that question by setting down principles drawn from international norms and designed to limit ATS claims to those that are similar in character and specificity to piracy. * * * And just as a nation that harbored pirates provoked the concern of other nations in past centuries, * so harboring "common enemies of all mankind" provokes similar concerns today. * * *

As I have indicated, we should treat this Nation's interest in not becoming a safe harbor for violators of the most fundamental international norms as an important jurisdiction-related interest justifying application of the ATS in light of the statute's basic purposes—in particular that of compensating those who have suffered harm at the hands of, *e.g.*, torturers or other modern pirates. Nothing in the statute or its history suggests that our courts should turn a blind eye to the plight of victims in that "handful of heinous actions." * International norms have long included a duty not to permit a nation to become a safe harbor for pirates (or their equivalent). * * *

Applying these jurisdictional principles to this case, however, I agree with the Court that jurisdiction does not lie. The defendants are two foreign corporations. * * * Their only presence in the United States consists of an office in New York City (actually owned by a separate but affiliated company) that helps to explain their business to potential investors. * The plaintiffs are not United States nationals but nationals of other nations. The conduct at issue took place abroad. And the plaintiffs allege, not that the defendants directly engaged in acts of torture, genocide, or the equivalent, but that they helped others (who are not American nationals) to do so.

Under these circumstances, even if the New York office were a sufficient basis for asserting general jurisdiction, * it would be farfetched to believe, based solely upon the defendants' minimal and indirect American presence, that this legal action helps to vindicate a distinct American interest, such as in not providing a safe harbor for an "enemy of all mankind." Thus I agree with the Court that here it would "reach too far to say" that such "mere corporate presence suffices." * I consequently join the Court's judgment but not its opinion.

NOTES

1. *Bases of the Opinions.* The opinions of Chief Justice Roberts and Justice Breyer obviously focus on two different issues. What does Chief

Justice Roberts believe the most important issue is in *Kiobel*? Justice Breyer?

2. *The Continuing Vitality of the Alien Tort Statute and Human Rights Violations.* During the last thirty years, human rights activists saw the Alien Tort Statute as a powerful tool for fighting human rights violations throughout the world, and many courts agreed. E.g., Abebe-Jira v. Negewo, 72 F.3d 844 (11th Cir.1996) (affirming judgment in favor of Ethiopian prisoners who were tortured); Kadic v. Karadžić, 70 F.3d 232 (2d Cir.1995) (reversing dismissal of claims alleging that Serbian military leader orchestrated torture, rape, and other abuses).

To what extent does the decision in *Kiobel* impose limitations on the use of the Alien Torts Statute for these purposes? What if a former leader of a foreign government that actively participated in human rights violations now lives in the United States? What if a corporation headquartered in the United States aided and abetted a foreign government in committing human rights violations in another country? How do these examples differ from those present in *Kiobel* that have been called "foreign cubed" —when a foreign plaintiff sues a foreign defendant for harm perpetrated on foreign soil? Would Chief Justice Roberts and Justice Breyer reach different results in any of these cases? Professor Oona Hathaway suggests that liability may remain "for 'foreign squared' cases— cases in which the plaintiff or defendant is a U.S. national or where the harm occurred on U.S. soil." Hathaway continues:

> Thus cases like that filed against U.S. corporation ExxonMobil by fifteen Indonesian villagers that alleged the company colluded in brutal oppression in violation of the law of nations arguably survive this decision entirely intact. In fact, the Chief Justice's acknowledgement that "mere corporate presence" does not suffice to subject that corporation to liability in U.S. courts seems to imply that corporations with more than mere presence *can* be subject to that same liability.

Oona Hathaway, *Kiobel Commentary: The door remains open to "foreign squared" cases,* SCOTUSblog (Apr. 18, 2013, 4:27 PM), http://www. scotusblog.com/2013/04/kiobel-commentary-the-door-remains-open-to-foreign-squared-cases/ (last visited Oct. 4, 2014).

G. TRESPASS TO CHATTELS AND CONVERSION

Pearson v. Dodd

United States Court of Appeals for the District of Columbia, 1969.
410 F.2d 701.

■ J. SKELLY WRIGHT, CIRCUIT JUDGE. This case arises out of the exposure of the alleged misdeeds of Senator Thomas Dodd of Connecticut by newspaper columnists Drew Pearson and Jack Anderson. * * * The undisputed facts in the case were stated by the District Court as follows:

> ... On several occasions in June and July, 1965, two former employees of the plaintiff, at times with the assistance of two members of the plaintiff's staff, entered the plaintiff's office without authority and unbeknownst to him, removed

numerous documents from his files, made copies of them, replaced the originals, and turned over the copies to the defendant Anderson, who was aware of the manner in which the copies had been obtained. The defendants Pearson and Anderson thereafter published articles containing information gleaned from these documents. * * *

The District Court ruled that appellants' receipt and subsequent use of photocopies of documents which appellants knew had been removed from appellee's files without authorization established appellants' liability for conversion. * * *

Conversion is the substantive tort theory which underlay the ancient common law form of action for trover. A plaintiff in trover alleged that he had lost a chattel which he rightfully possessed, * and that the defendant had found it and converted it to his own use. With time, the allegations of losing and finding became fictional, leaving the question of whether the defendant had "converted" the property the only operative one. *

The most distinctive feature of conversion is its measure of damages, which is the value of the goods converted. * The theory is that the "converting" defendant has in some way treated the goods as if they were his own, so that the plaintiff can properly ask the court to decree a forced sale of the property from the rightful possessor to the converter. *

Because of this stringent measure of damages, it has long been recognized that not every wrongful interference with the personal property of another is a conversion. * Where the intermeddling falls short of the complete or very substantial deprivation of possessory rights in the property, the tort committed is not conversion, but the lesser wrong of trespass to chattels. *

The Second Restatement of Torts has marked the distinction by defining conversion as:

> ... An intentional exercise of dominion or control over a chattel which so seriously interferes with the right of another to control it that the actor may justly be required to pay the other the full value of the chattel. *

Less serious interferences fall under the Restatement's definition of trespass.[30]

The difference is more than a semantic one. The measure of damages in trespass is not the whole value of the property interfered with, but rather the actual diminution in its value caused by the

---

[30] Restatement (Second) of Torts § 217 (1965): "A trespass to a chattel may be committed by intentionally (a) dispossessing another of the chattel, or (b) using or intermeddling with a chattel in the possession of another."

[32] To support an action of trespass to a chattel where the invasion of interests does not result in its destruction or in a dispossession thereof, it was early held there must be some physical harm to the chattel or to its possessor. Unlike the action of trespass quare clausum fregit in the case of land, no action could be maintained for a mere harmless intermeddling with goods. The possessor's proprietary interest in the inviolability of his personal property did not receive that protection which the similar interest in the possession of land or the dignitary interest in the inviolability of the person receives. . . .

1 F. Harper & F. James, The Law of Torts, § 2.3.

interference. * More important for this case, a judgment for conversion can be obtained with only nominal damages, whereas liability for trespass to chattels exists only on a showing of actual damage to the property interfered with.³² Here the District Court granted partial summary judgment on the issue of liability alone, while conceding that possibly no more than nominal damages might be awarded on subsequent trial. Partial summary judgment for liability could not have been granted on a theory of trespass to chattels without an undisputed showing of actual damages to the property in question.

It is clear that on the agreed facts appellants committed no conversion of the physical documents taken from appellee's files. Those documents were removed from the files at night, photocopied, and returned to the files undamaged before office operations resumed in the morning. Insofar as the documents' value to appellee resided in their usefulness as records of the business of his office, appellee was clearly not substantially deprived of his use of them.

This of course is not an end of the matter. It has long been recognized that documents often have value above and beyond that springing from their physical possession. * They may embody information or ideas whose economic value depends in part or in whole upon being kept secret. The question then arises whether the information taken by means of copying appellee's office files is of the type which the law of conversion protects. The general rule has been that ideas or information are not subject to legal protection,³⁴ but the law has developed exceptions to this rule. Where information is gathered and arranged at some cost and sold as a commodity on the market, it is properly protected as property. * Where ideas are formulated with labor and inventive genius, as in the case of literary works * or scientific researches, * they are protected. Where they constitute instruments of fair and effective commercial competition, those who develop them may gather their fruits under the protection of the law. *

The question here is not whether appellee had a right to keep his files from prying eyes, but whether the information taken from those files falls under the protection of the law of property, enforceable by a suit for conversion. In our view, it does not. The information included the contents of letters to appellee from supplicants, and office records of other kinds, the nature of which is not fully revealed by the record. Insofar as we can tell, none of it amounts to literary property, to scientific invention, or to secret plans formulated by appellee for the conduct of commerce. Nor does it appear to be information held in any way for sale by appellee, analogous to the fresh news copy produced by a wire service. *

Appellee complains, not of the misappropriation of property bought or created by him, but of the exposure of information either (1) injurious to his reputation or (2) revelatory of matters which he believes he has a right to keep to himself. Injuries of this type are redressed at law by

---

³⁴ * The traditional rule has been that conversion will lie only for the taking of tangible property, or rights embodied in a tangible token necessary for the enforcement of those rights. * This overly restrictive rule has recently been relaxed in favor of the reasonable proposition that any intangible generally protected as personal property may be the subject matter of a suit for conversion. *

suit for libel and invasion of privacy respectively, where defendants' liability for those torts can be established under the limitations created by common law and by the Constitution.[40]

Because no conversion of the physical contents of appellee's files took place, and because the information copied from the documents in those files has not been shown to be property subject to protection by suit for conversion, the District Court's ruling that appellants are guilty of conversion must be reversed. * * *

Moore v. Regents of the University of California

Supreme Court of California, 1990.
51 Cal.3d 120, 793 P.2d 479, 271 Cal.Rptr. 146.

■ PANELLI, JUSTICE. * * * The plaintiff is John Moore (Moore), who underwent treatment for hairy-cell leukemia at the Medical Center of the University of California at Los Angeles (UCLA Medical Center). The five defendants are: (1) Dr. David W. Golde (Golde), a physician who attended Moore at UCLA Medical Center; (2) the Regents of the University of California (Regents), who own and operate the university; (3) Shirley G. Quan, a researcher employed by the Regents; (4) Genetics Institute, Inc. (Genetics Institute); and (5) Sandoz Pharmaceuticals Corporation and related entities (collectively Sandoz).

Moore first visited UCLA Medical Center on October 5, 1976, shortly after he learned that he had hairy-cell leukemia. After hospitalizing Moore and "withdr[awing] extensive amounts of blood, bone marrow aspirate, and other bodily substances," Golde * confirmed that diagnosis. At this time all defendants, including Golde, were aware that "certain blood products and blood components were of great value in a number of commercial and scientific efforts" and that access to a patient whose blood contained these substances would provide "competitive, commercial, and scientific advantages."

On October 8, 1976, Golde recommended that Moore's spleen be removed. Golde informed Moore "that he had reason to fear for his life, and that the proposed splenectomy operation . . . was necessary to slow down the progress of his disease." Based upon Golde's representations, Moore signed a written consent form authorizing the splenectomy.

Before the operation, Golde and Quan "formed the intent and made arrangements to obtain portions of [Moore's] spleen following its removal" and to take them to a separate research unit. * * * These research activities "were not intended to have . . . any relation to [Moore's] medical . . . care." However, neither Golde nor Quan informed Moore of their plans to conduct this research or requested his permission. Surgeons * * * removed Moore's spleen on October 20, 1976. Moore returned to the UCLA Medical Center several times * * * at Golde's direction and based upon representations "that such visits were necessary and required for his health and well-being, and based upon the trust inherent in and by virtue of the physician-patient relationship. . . ." On each of these visits Golde withdrew additional samples of "blood, blood serum, skin, bone marrow aspirate, and

---

[40] We have held that appellee is not entitled to summary judgment for invasion of privacy. * * *

sperm." * * * "In fact, [however,] throughout the period of time that [Moore] was under [Golde's] care and treatment, ... the defendants were actively involved in a number of activities which they concealed from [Moore]. ... " Specifically, defendants were conducting research on Moore's cells and planned to "benefit financially and competitively ... [by exploiting the cells] and [their] exclusive access to [the cells] by virtue of [Golde's] ongoing physician-patient relationship. ... "

Sometime before August 1979, Golde established a cell line from Moore's T-lymphocytes.[10] On January 30, 1981, the Regents applied for a patent on the cell line, listing Golde and Quan as inventors. * * * Moore admits in his complaint that "the true clinical potential of each of the lymphokines ... [is] difficult to predict, [but] ... competing commercial firms in these relevant fields have published reports in biotechnology industry periodicals predicting a potential market of approximately $3.01 Billion Dollars by the year 1990 for a whole range of [such lymphokines]. ... " With the Regents' assistance, Golde negotiated agreements for commercial development of the cell line and products to be derived from it. [Under an agreement with Genetics Institute, the Institute acquired exclusive rights to the biological materials and the research related to them in exchange for a minimum payment of $330,000 over three years to Golde and the Regents, as well as the rights to 75,000 shares of common stock. Later other researchers were added to the agreement, and the compensation was increased.] * * *

Based upon these allegations, Moore attempted to state 13 causes of action. * Each defendant demurred to each purported cause of action. The superior court, however, expressly considered the validity of only the first cause of action, conversion. * * * [T]he superior court sustained Genetics Institute's and Sandoz's demurrers * * * on the grounds that Moore had not stated a cause of action for conversion * * *. [T]he Court of Appeal reversed, holding that the complaint did state a cause of action for conversion. * * *

Moore repeatedly alleges that Golde failed to disclose the extent of his research and economic interests in Moore's cells before obtaining consent to the medical procedures by which the cells were extracted. These allegations, in our view, state a cause of action against Golde for invading a legally protected interest of his patient. This cause of action can properly be characterized either as the breach of a fiduciary duty to disclose facts material to the patient's consent or, alternatively, as the

---

[10] A T-lymphocyte is a type of white blood cell. T-lymphocytes produce lymphokines, or proteins that regulate the immune system. Some lymphokines have potential therapeutic value. If the genetic material responsible for producing a particular lymphokine can be identified, it can sometimes be used to manufacture large quantities of the lymphokine through the techniques of recombinant DNA. *

While the genetic code for lymphokines does not vary from individual to individual, it can nevertheless be quite difficult to locate the gene responsible for a particular lymphokine. Because T-lymphocytes produce many different lymphokines, the relevant gene is often like a needle in a haystack. * Moore's T-lymphocytes were interesting to the defendants because they overproduced certain lymphokines, thus making the corresponding genetic material easier to identify. * * *

Cells taken directly from the body (primary cells) are not very useful for these purposes. Primary cells typically reproduce a few times and then die. One can, however, sometimes continue to use cells for an extended period of time by developing them into a "cell line," a culture capable of reproducing indefinitely. * * *

performance of medical procedures without first having obtained the patient's informed consent. * * * [W]e hold that a physician who is seeking a patient's consent for a medical procedure must, in order to satisfy his fiduciary duty * and to obtain the patient's informed consent, disclose personal interests unrelated to the patient's health, whether research or economic, that may affect his medical judgment. * * *

Moore also attempts to characterize the invasion of his rights as a conversion—a tort that protects against interference with possessory and ownership interests in personal property. He theorizes that he continued to own his cells following their removal from his body, at least for the purpose of directing their use, and that he never consented to their use in potentially lucrative medical research. Thus, to complete Moore's argument, defendants' unauthorized use of his cells constitutes a conversion. As a result of the alleged conversion, Moore claims a proprietary interest in each of the products that any of the defendants might ever create from his cells or the patented cell line.

* * * In effect, what Moore is asking us to do is to impose a tort duty on scientists to investigate the consensual pedigree of each human cell sample used in research. * To impose such a duty, which would affect medical research of importance to all of society, implicates policy concerns far removed from the traditional, two-party ownership disputes in which the law of conversion arose. * Invoking a tort theory originally used to determine whether the loser or the finder of a horse had the better title, Moore claims ownership of the results of socially important medical research, including the genetic code for chemicals that regulate the functions of every human being's immune system. *

We have recognized that, when the proposed application of a very general theory of liability in a new context raises important policy concerns, it is especially important to face those concerns and address them openly. * Moreover, we should be hesitant to "impose [new tort duties] when to do so would involve complex policy decisions," * especially when such decisions are more appropriately the subject of legislative deliberation and resolution. * This certainly is not to say that the applicability of common law torts is limited to the historical or factual contexts of existing cases. But on occasions when we have opened or sanctioned new areas of tort liability, we "have noted that the 'wrongs and injuries involved were both comprehensible and assessable within the existing judicial framework.'" *

Accordingly, we first consider whether the tort of conversion clearly gives Moore a cause of action under existing law. We do not believe it does. Because of the novelty of Moore's claim to own the biological materials at issue, to apply the theory of conversion in this context would frankly have to be recognized as an extension of the theory. Therefore, we consider next whether it is advisable to extend the tort to this context.

"To establish a conversion, plaintiff must establish an actual interference with his *ownership* or *right of possession*. . . . Where plaintiff neither has title to the property alleged to have been converted, nor possession thereof, he cannot maintain an action for conversion." * Since Moore clearly did not expect to retain possession of his cells following their removal, * to sue for their conversion he must have retained an ownership interest in them. But there are several reasons to doubt that he did retain any such interest. First, no reported judicial decision supports Moore's claim, either directly or by close analogy. Second, California statutory law drastically limits any continuing interest of a patient in excised cells. Third, the subject matters of the Regents' patent—the patented cell line and the products derived from it—cannot be Moore's property.

* * * [T]he laws governing such things as human tissues, * transplantable organs, * blood, * fetuses, * pituitary glands, * corneal tissue, * and dead bodies * deal with human biological materials as objects sui generis, regulating their disposition to achieve policy goals rather than abandoning them to the general law of personal property. It is these specialized statutes, not the law of conversion, to which courts ordinarily should and do look for guidance on the disposition of human biological materials. * * *

Lacking direct authority for importing the law of conversion into this context, Moore relies, as did the Court of Appeal, primarily on decisions addressing privacy rights. * These opinions hold that every person has a proprietary interest in his own likeness and that unauthorized, business use of a likeness is redressible as a tort. * * * Moore, adopting the analogy originally advanced by the Court of Appeal, argues that "[i]f the courts have found a sufficient proprietary interest in one's persona, how could one not have a right in one's own genetic material, something far more profoundly the essence of one's human uniqueness than a name or a face?" However, as the defendants' patent makes clear—and the complaint, too, if read with an understanding of the scientific terms which it has borrowed from the patent—the goal and result of defendants' efforts has been to manufacture lymphokines. * Lymphokines, unlike a name or a face, have the same molecular structure in every human being and the same, important functions in every human being's immune system. Moreover, the particular genetic material which is responsible for the natural production of lymphokines, and which defendants use to manufacture lymphokines in the laboratory, is also the same in every person; it is no more unique to Moore than the number of vertebrae in the spine or the chemical formula of hemoglobin. * * *

Finally, the subject matter of the Regents' patent—the patented cell line and the products derived from it—cannot be Moore's property. This is because the patented cell line is both factually and legally distinct from the cells taken from Moore's body. * Federal law permits the patenting of organisms that represent the product of "human ingenuity," but not naturally occurring organisms. * Human cell lines are patentable because "[l]ong-term adaptation and growth of human tissues and cells in culture is difficult—often considered an art . . . ," and the probability of success is low. * It is this *inventive effort* that patent law rewards, not the discovery of naturally occurring raw materials. Thus, Moore's allegations that he owns the cell line and the products derived from it are inconsistent with the patent, which constitutes an authoritative determination that the cell line is the product of invention. * * *

Moore's novel claim * * * to apply the theory of conversion within this context must frankly be recognized as a request to extend that theory. * * * [T]he novelty of Moore's claim demands express consideration of the policies to be served by extending liability * rather than blind deference to a complaint alleging as a legal conclusion the existence of a cause of action. * * * Of the relevant policy considerations, two are of overriding importance. The first is protection of a competent patient's right to make autonomous medical decisions. * * * The second important policy consideration is that we not threaten with disabling civil liability innocent parties who are engaged in socially useful activities, such as researchers who have no reason to believe that their use of a particular cell sample is, or may be, against a donor's wishes. * * * The assertion of rights by sources would affect not only the researcher who obtained the original specimen, but perhaps other researchers as well. "Biological materials are routinely distributed to other researchers for experimental purposes, and scientists who obtain cell lines or other specimen-derived products, such as gene clones, from the original researcher could also be sued under certain legal theories [such as conversion]. Furthermore, the uncertainty could affect product developments as well as research. Since inventions containing human tissues and cells may be patented and licensed for commercial use, companies are unlikely to invest heavily in developing, manufacturing, or marketing a product when uncertainty about clear title exists." * * *

* * * [T]he threat of liability for conversion might help to enforce patients' rights indirectly. This is because physicians might be able to avoid liability by obtaining patients' consent, in the broadest possible terms, to any conceivable subsequent research use of excised cells. Unfortunately, to extend the conversion theory would utterly sacrifice the other goal of protecting innocent parties. * Since conversion is a strict liability tort,[38] it would impose liability on all those into whose hands the cells come, whether or not the particular defendant participated in, or knew of, the inadequate disclosures that violated the patient's right to make an informed decision. In contrast to the conversion theory, the fiduciary-duty and informed-consent theories protect the patient directly, without punishing innocent parties or creating disincentives to the conduct of socially beneficial research.

Research on human cells plays a critical role in medical research. * * * These efforts are beginning to bear fruit. Products developed through biotechnology that have already been approved for marketing in this country include treatments and tests for leukemia, cancer, diabetes, dwarfism, hepatitis-B, kidney transplant rejection, emphysema, osteoporosis, ulcers, anemia, infertility, and gynecological tumors, to name but a few. * The extension of conversion law into this area will hinder research by restricting access to the necessary raw materials. Thousands of human cell lines already exist in tissue repositories * * *. At present, human cell lines are routinely copied and distributed to other researchers for experimental purposes, usually free of charge. * This exchange of scientific materials, which still is

---

[38] " 'The foundation for the action for conversion rests neither in the knowledge nor the intent of the defendant. . . . [Instead,] "the tort consists in the breach of what may be called an absolute duty; the act itself . . . is unlawful and redressible as a tort." ' " * Byer v. Canadian Bank of Commerce, 8 Cal.2d 297, 300, 65 P.2d 67 (1937). * See also City of Los Angeles v. Superior Court, 85 Cal.App.3d 143, 149, 149 Cal.Rptr. 320 (1978) ("[c]onversion is a species of strict liability in which questions of good faith, lack of knowledge and motive are ordinarily immaterial").

relatively free and efficient, will surely be compromised if each cell sample becomes the potential subject matter of a lawsuit. * * *

If the scientific users of human cells are to be held liable for failing to investigate the consensual pedigree of their raw materials, we believe the Legislature should make that decision. Complex policy choices affecting all society are involved, and "[l]egislatures, in making such policy decisions, have the ability to gather empirical evidence, solicit the advice of experts, and hold hearings at which all interested parties present evidence and express their views. . . ." * Legislative competence to act in this area is demonstrated by the existing statutes governing the use and disposition of human biological materials. * * *

Finally, there is no pressing need to impose a judicially created rule of strict liability, since enforcement of physicians' disclosure obligations will protect patients against the very type of harm with which Moore was threatened. So long as a physician discloses research and economic interests that may affect his judgment, the patient is protected from conflicts of interest. Aware of any conflicts, the patient can make an informed decision to consent to treatment, or to withhold consent and look elsewhere for medical assistance. As already discussed, enforcement of physicians' disclosure obligations protects patients directly, without hindering the socially useful activities of innocent researchers.

For these reasons, we hold that the allegations of Moore's third amended complaint state a cause of action for breach of fiduciary duty or lack of informed consent, but not conversion. * * *

■ MOSK, J. I dissent. * * * [T]he majority assert in effect that Moore cannot have an ownership interest in the Mo cell line because defendants patented it. * The majority's point wholly fails to meet Moore's claim that he is entitled to compensation for defendants' unauthorized use of his bodily tissues *before* defendants patented the Mo cell line * * *. I do not question that the cell line is primarily the product of defendants' inventive effort. Yet likewise no one can question Moore's crucial contribution to the invention—an invention named, ironically, after him: but for the cells of Moore's body taken by defendants, *there would have been no Mo cell line.* * * *

Our society values fundamental fairness in dealings between its members, and condemns the unjust enrichment of any member at the expense of another. This is particularly true when, as here, the parties are not in equal bargaining positions. * * *

The second reason why the nondisclosure cause of action is inadequate for the task that the majority assign to it is that it fails to solve half the problem before us: it gives the patient only the right to *refuse* consent, i.e., the right to prohibit the commercialization of his tissue; it does not give him the right to *grant* consent to that commercialization on the condition that he share in its proceeds. * * * Reversing the words of the old song, the nondisclosure cause of action thus accentuates the negative and eliminates the positive: the patient can say no, but he cannot say yes and expect to share in the proceeds of his contribution. * * *

NOTE

Conversion of Intangible Property. Liability for conversion may exist even when the plaintiff's alleged property interest is in intangible property. E.g., CRS Recovery, Inc. v. Laxton, 600 F.3d 1138 (9th Cir.2010) (recognizing internet domain names as subject to conversion under California law); Astroworks, Inc. v. Astroexhibit, Inc., 257 F.Supp.2d 609, 618 (S.D.N.Y.2003) (conversion of intellectual property comprising idea reduced to practice, viz., copyrighted and trademarked website); Anderson v. Century Prods. Co., 943 F.Supp. 137, 152–53 (D.N.H.1996) (potential liability for conversion of baby carriage design); Quincy Cablesystems, Inc. v. Sully's Bar, Inc., 650 F.Supp. 838, 848 (D.Mass.1986) (potential liability of taverns for unauthorized interception, with satellite dish antennas, and use of cable television network's program signals); Nat'l Sur. Corp. v. Applied Sys., Inc., 418 So.2d 847 (Ala.1982) (computer program as the subject of conversion); Thyroff v. Nationwide Mut. Ins. Co, 8 N.Y.3d 283, 864 N.E.2d 1272 (2007) (allowing claim for conversion by insurance agent when his former employer denied his access to electronic records consisting of customer lists and other personal information that were indistinguishable from printed records).

CompuServe Inc. v. Cyber Promotions, Inc.

United States District Court for the Southern District of Ohio, 1997.
962 F.Supp. 1015.

■ GRAHAM, JUDGE. This case presents novel issues regarding the commercial use of the Internet, specifically the right of an online computer service to prevent a commercial enterprise from sending unsolicited electronic mail advertising to its subscribers.

Plaintiff CompuServe Incorporated ("CompuServe") is one of the major national commercial online computer services. It operates a computer communication service through a proprietary nationwide computer network. * * * CompuServe * * * provides its subscribers with a link to the much larger resources of the Internet. This allows its subscribers to send and receive electronic messages, known as "e-mail," by the Internet. Defendants Cyber Promotions, Inc. and its president Sanford Wallace are in the business of sending unsolicited e-mail advertisements on behalf of themselves and their clients to hundreds of thousands of Internet users, many of whom are CompuServe subscribers. CompuServe has notified defendants that they are prohibited from using its computer equipment to process and store the unsolicited e-mail and has requested that they terminate the practice. Instead, defendants have sent an increasing volume of e-mail solicitations to CompuServe subscribers. CompuServe has attempted to employ technological means to block the flow of defendants' e-mail transmissions to its computer equipment, but to no avail. * * *

For the reasons which follow, this Court holds that where defendants engaged in a course of conduct of transmitting a substantial volume of electronic data in the form of unsolicited e-mail to plaintiff's proprietary computer equipment, where defendants continued such practice after repeated demands to cease and desist, and where defendants deliberately evaded plaintiff's affirmative efforts to protect its computer equipment from such use, plaintiff has a viable claim for trespass to personal property and is entitled to injunctive relief to protect its property.

The Court will begin its analysis of the issues by acknowledging, for the purpose of providing a background, certain findings of fact recently made by another district court in a case involving the Internet:

1. The Internet is not a physical or tangible entity, but rather a giant network which interconnects innumerable smaller groups of linked computer networks. It is thus a network of networks. * * *

4. Some of the computers and computer networks that make up the network are owned by governmental and public institutions, some are owned by non-profit organizations, and some are privately owned. The resulting whole is a decentralized, global medium of communications—or "cyberspace"—that links people, institutions, corporations, and governments around the world. * * *

11. No single entity—academic, corporate, governmental, or non-profit—administers the Internet. It exists and functions as a result of the fact that hundreds of thousands of separate operators of computers and computer networks independently decided to use common data transfer protocols to exchange communications and information with other computers (which in turn exchange communications and information with still other computers). There is no centralized storage location, control point, or communications channel for the Internet, and it would not be technically feasible for a single entity to control all of the information conveyed on the Internet.

American Civil Liberties Union v. Reno, 929 F.Supp. 824, 830–832 (E.D.Pa.1996). * * *

[S]ome companies, like defendant Cyber Promotions, Inc., have begun using the Internet to distribute advertisements by sending the same unsolicited commercial message to hundreds of thousands of Internet users at once. Defendants refer to this as "bulk e-mail," while plaintiff refers to it as "junk e-mail." In the vernacular of the Internet, unsolicited e-mail advertising is sometimes referred to pejoratively as "spam."[1]

CompuServe subscribers use CompuServe's domain name "CompuServe.com" together with their own unique alpha-numeric identifier to form a distinctive e-mail mailing address. That address may be used by the subscriber to exchange electronic mail with any one of tens of millions of other Internet users who have electronic mail capability. E-mail sent to CompuServe subscribers is processed and stored on CompuServe's proprietary computer equipment. Thereafter, it becomes accessible to CompuServe's subscribers, who can access CompuServe's equipment and electronically retrieve those messages.

Over the past several months, CompuServe has received many complaints from subscribers threatening to discontinue their

---

[1] This term is derived from a skit performed on the British television show Monty Python's Flying Circus, in which the word "spam" is repeated to the point of absurdity in a restaurant menu.

subscription unless CompuServe prohibits electronic mass mailers from using its equipment to send unsolicited advertisements. CompuServe asserts that the volume of messages generated by such mass mailings places a significant burden on its equipment which has finite processing and storage capacity. CompuServe receives no payment from the mass mailers for processing their unsolicited advertising. * * *

In an effort to shield its equipment from defendants' bulk e-mail, CompuServe has implemented software programs designed to screen out the messages and block their receipt. In response, defendants have modified their equipment and the messages they send in such a fashion as to circumvent CompuServe's screening software. Allegedly, defendants have been able to conceal the true origin of their messages by falsifying the point-of-origin information contained in the header of the electronic messages. Defendants have removed the "sender" information in the header of their messages and replaced it with another address. Also, defendants have developed the capability of configuring their computer servers to conceal their true domain name and appear on the Internet as another computer, further concealing the true origin of the messages. By manipulating this data, defendants have been able to continue sending messages to CompuServe's equipment in spite of CompuServe's protests and protective efforts.

Defendants assert that they possess the right to continue to send these communications to CompuServe subscribers. CompuServe contends that, in doing so, the defendants are trespassing upon its personal property. * * *

CompuServe predicates this * * * motion for a preliminary injunction on the common law theory of trespass to personal property or to chattels, asserting that defendants' continued transmission of electronic messages to its computer equipment constitutes an actionable tort. * * *

The Restatement [(Second) of Torts] § 217(b) states that a trespass to chattel may be committed by intentionally using or intermeddling with the chattel in possession of another. Restatement § 217, Comment e defines physical "intermeddling" as follows:

> ... intentionally bringing about a physical contact with the chattel. The actor may commit a trespass by an act which brings him into an intended physical contact with a chattel in the possession of another[.]

Electronic signals generated and sent by computer have been held to be sufficiently physically tangible to support a trespass cause of action. * It is undisputed that plaintiff has a possessory interest in its computer systems. Further, defendants' contact with plaintiff's computers is clearly intentional. Although electronic messages may travel through the Internet over various routes, the messages are affirmatively directed to their destination. * * *

A plaintiff can sustain an action for trespass to chattels, as opposed to an action for conversion, without showing a substantial interference with its right to possession of that chattel. * Harm to the personal property or diminution of its quality, condition, or value as a result of defendants' use can also be the predicate for liability. * * * In the present case, any value CompuServe realizes from its computer equipment is wholly derived from the extent to which that equipment can serve its subscriber base. Michael Mangino, a software developer for CompuServe who monitors its mail processing computer equipment, states by affidavit that handling the enormous volume of mass mailings that CompuServe receives places a tremendous burden on its equipment. * Defendants' more recent practice of evading CompuServe's filters by disguising the origin of their messages commandeers even more computer resources because CompuServe's computers are forced to store undeliverable e-mail messages and labor in vain to return the messages to an address that does not exist. * To the extent that defendants' multitudinous electronic mailings demand the disk space and drain the processing power of plaintiff's computer equipment, those resources are not available to serve CompuServe subscribers. Therefore, the value of that equipment to CompuServe is diminished even though it is not physically damaged by defendants' conduct.

Next, plaintiff asserts that it has suffered injury aside from the physical impact of defendants' messages on its equipment. Restatement [(Second) of Torts] § 218(d) also indicates that recovery may be had for a trespass that causes harm to something in which the possessor has a legally protected interest. * * * [T]he receipt of a bundle of unsolicited messages at once can require the subscriber to sift through * * * all of the messages in order to find the ones he wanted or expected to receive. These inconveniences decrease the utility of CompuServe's e-mail service and are the foremost subject in recent complaints from CompuServe subscribers. * * * Many subscribers have terminated their accounts specifically because of the unwanted receipt of bulk e-mail messages. * Defendants' intrusions into CompuServe's computer systems, insofar as they harm plaintiff's business reputation and goodwill with its customers, are actionable under Restatement § 218(d). * * *

[T]he owner of personal property can create a privilege in the would-be trespasser by granting consent to use the property. A great portion of the utility of CompuServe's e-mail service is that it allows subscribers to receive messages from individuals and entities located anywhere on the Internet. Certainly, then, there is at least a tacit invitation for anyone on the Internet to utilize plaintiff's computer equipment to send e-mail to its subscribers. * * *

Defendants argue that plaintiff made the business decision to connect to the Internet and that therefore it cannot now successfully maintain an action for trespass to chattels. * * * On or around October 1995, CompuServe notified defendants that it no longer consented to the use of its proprietary computer equipment. Defendants' continued use thereafter was a trespass. * * *

Further, CompuServe expressly limits the consent it grants to Internet users to send e-mail to its proprietary computer systems by denying unauthorized parties the use of CompuServe equipment to send unsolicited electronic mail messages. * * * Defendants * * * have used plaintiff's equipment in a fashion that exceeds that consent. The use of personal property exceeding consent is a trespass. * * *

Based on the foregoing, plaintiff's motion for a preliminary injunction is granted. * * *

NOTE

Compare Intel Corp. v. Hamidi, 30 Cal.4th 1342, 71 P.3d 296, 1 Cal.Rptr.3d 32 (2003) where the California Supreme Court held that a series of six email messages sent by a former employee over the employer's email system, which criticized the plaintiff's employment practices, did not constitute trespass to chattels where the emails neither damaged the recipient computer system nor impaired its functioning. The court distinguished its opinion from *CompuServe* because the plaintiff was not an internet service provider (ISP). However, the court did question whether the interests served by the court's decision in *CompuServe* "were properly considered injuries to the ISP's possessory interest in its personal property, the type of property interest the tort is primarily intended to protect" and whether it was appropriate to count injuries to "CompuServe's business interests—reputation, customer goodwill, and employee time * * * as harms to the chattel (the server)."

H. MALICIOUS PROSECUTION AND ABUSE OF PROCESS

South Arkansas Petroleum Co. v. Schiesser

Supreme Court of Arkansas, 2001.
343 Ark. 492, 36 S.W.3d 317.

■ GLAZE, JUSTICE. This appeal is brought by South Arkansas Petroleum Co., Inc. (SAPCO), from a jury verdict which found SAPCO liable for malicious prosecution and abuse of process committed against appellee Dana Schiesser. The jury awarded Schiesser $110,000.00 in compensatory damages and $250,000.00 in punitive damages. Schiesser initiated the lawsuit against SAPCO after she successfully defended herself against felony theft charges. The charges were based upon allegations by SAPCO's executive officers, Clint and Jim Johnson, which they had reported to the Monticello police and the Drew County prosecuting attorney. On appeal, SAPCO argues Schiesser proved neither malicious prosecution nor abuse of process.

We first address SAPCO's arguments as they relate to malicious prosecution. To prevail on her claim of malicious prosecution, Schiesser was required to prove the following elements: (1) a proceeding instituted or continued by the defendant against the plaintiff; (2) termination of the proceeding in favor of the plaintiff; (3) absence of probable cause for the proceeding; (4) malice on the part of the defendant; and (5) damages. McLaughlin v. Cox, 324 Ark. 361, 922 S.W.2d 327 (1996). Here, SAPCO does not question elements (2) and (5), but it does question whether Schiesser proved the other three.

SAPCO first submits that there is no substantial evidence that it instituted or continued the criminal charges against Schiesser; in making this argument, it relies on comment *g* to the Restatement (Second) of Torts, § 653 (1977). Section 653 sets out the elements of the tort of malicious prosecution, and comment *g* provides in relevant part as follows:

> [A] private person who gives to a public official information of another's supposed criminal misconduct ... obviously causes the institution of such subsequent proceedings as the official

may begin on his own initiative, but giving the information or even making an accusation of criminal misconduct does not constitute a procurement of the proceedings initiated by the officer if it is [left] entirely to his discretion to initiate the proceedings or not.

SAPCO contends that the Monticello police obtained a warrant for Schiesser's arrest on their own initiative, and there was no evidence that the prosecuting attorney filed charges against Schiesser upon any basis other than the prosecuting attorney's own discretion. SAPCO cites Matthews v. Blue Cross & Blue Shield of Michigan, 456 Mich. 365, 572 N.W.2d 603 (1998), because of its reliance on comment g to the Restatement. There, the Michigan court stated the settled rule that a prosecutor's exercise of his or her independent discretion in initiating and maintaining the prosecution is a complete defense to an action for malicious prosecution. Comment g to the Restatement, however, further provides that, when a private person makes an accusation of criminal misconduct about another to an official, the person must believe the accusation or information is true. "If, however, the information is known by the giver to be false, an *intelligent exercise of the officer's discretion becomes impossible*, and a prosecution based upon it is procured by the person giving the false information." Restatement (Second) of Torts § 653 cmt. g (emphasis added). Despite SAPCO's attempt to distinguish "the Restatement approach," Arkansas law is consistent with comment *g* and the Michigan case, as well. In *McLaughlin,* this court stated the absence of probable cause is an essential element in a claim for malicious prosecution, and it is only when the defendant makes a full, fair, and truthful disclosure of all facts known to him to competent counsel (or the prosecuting attorney) and then acts bona fide upon such advice, that this will be a good defense to a claim of malicious prosecution. *

SAPCO's argument that the evidence entitles it to the so-called "advice-of-counsel" defense, as related above in comment *g* and our *McLaughlin* decision, is futile. In short, SAPCO's owner, Clint Johnson, gave law enforcement officials information alleging criminal misconduct on Schiesser's part, but was not forthcoming with all the pertinent information which he had in his possession when he first reported the alleged theft to Monticello police.

Before contacting Monticello Police Investigator John Dement, Clint Johnson checked some of the store's daily reports during a period beginning in June 1996, and ending in January 1997, and found that these reports reflected $7,809 in "overrings." Based on that, and without looking at each day's shift reports (which would have shown which employee did the overrings), Clint Johnson concluded Schiesser had stolen that amount of money. On June 26, 1997, Clint and Jim Johnson confronted Schiesser about the overrings; she replied that she did not take any money, but that "she would repay it not to have her name drug [sic] through the mud." Both of the Johnsons accused Schiesser of stealing money, and told her if she did not repay the money, they would prosecute her. Schiesser subsequently decided not to pay any money because she denied having taken it.

In July 1997, Clint Johnson went to Officer Dement's office in order to file a complaint against Schiesser; he provided Dement with paperwork which he claimed supported SAPCO's allegations of theft. Although the daily reports Clint Johnson gave Dement showed Schiesser had entered "overrings" on them between June 1996 and January 1997, Schiesser was indisputably out of the country and out of state on a number of those days. Clint Johnson was apprised of these errors by reading the daily reports, but he never gave that information to Dement. Clint Johnson also conceded Schiesser could not be shown to have been in the store on other days that Clint Johnson had daily reports purportedly bearing Schiesser's signature. Thus, while Clint Johnson knew Schiesser could not have signed a number of the daily reports he gave Dement, Johnson, for whatever reason, failed to give this exculpatory information to Dement. It is also worthy to mention that, on one of the days Schiesser was accused of stealing money, the amount missing was supposedly $728.00. Such amount was clearly fictitious, because the store had never sold merchandise that totaled more than $350.00 in one day. This error, too, was known by Clint Johnson, but not given to Officer Dement before charges were filed against Schiesser. * * * In sum, we conclude that the record soundly and convincingly supports the view that the State filed felony charges based largely on the misleading information the Johnsons gave, as well as the information they failed to give, to the police, magistrate judge, and prosecuting attorney. Based upon such information, it is fair to conclude SAPCO procured and thereby instituted the criminal charges against Schiesser, charges of which she was later acquitted for lack of evidence.

SAPCO next argues that, irrespective of the evidence, Schiesser failed to prove the third element of malicious prosecution, namely, that there was an absence of probable cause to bring the criminal charges against her. * * * SAPCO submits the novel argument that because the State's criminal case against Schiesser survived Schiesser's directed verdict motions, those rulings constituted a binding determination of the existence of probable cause in a later malicious prosecution action. * * * This argument is wholly without merit. * * *

* * * [T]he trial judge in the criminal action against Schiesser viewed only the evidence in favor of the State when ruling on Schiesser's directed-verdict motions, and merely found sufficient evidence to submit the case to a jury. As already discussed above, whether Schiesser stole SAPCO's money was clearly in dispute, thus making it a factual question for the jury. Given these circumstances, SAPCO is simply wrong in its contention that such probable cause issue was fully and finally decided and, as a matter of law, could not later be litigated in a civil malicious prosecution action. *

In SAPCO's third point, it asserts that Schiesser's evidence fell short of showing SAPCO possessed malice—the fourth element of malicious prosecution—when it caused officials to initiate criminal charges against Schiesser. SAPCO largely relies on Officer Dement's testimony that * * * Clint Johnson seemed to be truthful and did not appear to be acting out of hatred, ill will, or vindictiveness. *

Once again, we are left to point out that when Clint Johnson first accused Schiesser of stealing money, he withheld considerable information that tended to show she never took SAPCO's money. Johnson conceded this fact, but offered no sound reason for his failure to disclose this exculpatory information to either Dement or the prosecuting attorney. In addition, SAPCO's other owner, Jim Johnson, admitted he did not know that Schiesser stole the money, but met with her to tell her that, as manager, she was responsible for the money, and if she repaid the money, his son (Clint) would not bring criminal charges against her. * From this testimony, the jury could have inferred ill will on the Johnsons' part * * *. Moreover, while SAPCO claims more than $7,800.00 was stolen, it never clearly showed that amount of money was illicitly taken or that the overrings were anything more than mistakes. * * * Here, malice may be inferred from the lack of probable cause, for the reasons already discussed, but especially because Clint Johnson was shown to have deliberately failed to inform the police that Schiesser was out of the country and state on several occasions when money was "stolen." Also, as just discussed, Jim Johnson made it clear that his purpose was to get the money repaid, even though he had no proof that Schiesser had stolen it. In addition, Linda Kay Reed, another SAPCO employee, testified that she was unaware of any policy that a manager was responsible for the repayment of missing funds. Finally, Schiesser herself testified that while on her cruise in the Bahamas, she made an unflattering comment about Clint Johnson; that comment somehow made its way back to Johnson, and he treated her differently after she returned from the cruise. From these facts, as presented to the jury, there was sufficient evidence regarding the lack of probable cause and Johnson's improper motive for instituting the suit from which the jury could conclude that SAPCO acted maliciously.

SAPCO's last point for reversal is that Schiesser's evidence was insufficient to support the jury's finding of abuse of process. Again, we disagree. In order to prevail on an abuse of process claim, a plaintiff must show the following: (1) a legal procedure set in motion in proper form, even with probable cause and ultimate success; (2) the procedure is perverted to accomplish an ulterior purpose for which it was not designed; and (3) a willful act is perpetrated in the use of process which is not proper in the regular conduct of the proceeding. * This court has stated that the test of abuse of process is whether a judicial process is used to extort or coerce. * The key to the tort is the improper use of process after its issuance in order to accomplish a purpose for which the process was not designed. * Thus, it is the purpose for which the process is used, once issued, that is important in reaching a conclusion. *

In Routh Wrecker Serv., Inc. v. Washington, 335 Ark. 232, 980 S.W.2d 240 (1998), this court held that there was sufficient evidence to support a jury's finding of abuse of process when the defendant, Routh Wrecker, had Washington arrested, apparently for theft, when Washington stopped payment on a check he had written for a car being sold at auction by Routh. Washington had stopped payment because when he went to pick up the car, its battery, spare tires, and some tools were missing. Despite the fact that Washington never took the car from Routh's lot, Routh swore out an affidavit that Washington had not returned the car to the lot. In addition, when Washington's father contacted Ronald Routh about the charges, Routh replied that "all he wanted was his money and that he would drop the charges if he was paid." * * * "We further observe[ ] that the use of criminal prosecution to extort payment of money or recovery of property is a classic example of the tort of abuse of process." * This court held that, because Routh allowed the case to proceed for the coercive purpose of collecting Washington's money, there was sufficient evidence to survive Routh's motion for directed verdict on abuse of process. *

The facts of the instant case present a similar situation. As noted above, Clint Johnson testified that his intention was to get his money back. Although Johnson knew that Schiesser could not have stolen the money on several occasions for which she was accused, and although he had no direct proof that she had taken any of the money, he contacted the police department in order to procure an arrest warrant. In ruling on SAPCO's motion for directed verdict, the trial judge found that Johnson "gave testimony before [the magistrate judge] at the probable cause hearing that Schiesser had taken all this money when, in fact, the documents show that other people completed the reports. He did not reveal that. [Instead] he continued to pursue criminal process at that point in time, for unwarranted and perverted purposes." Viewing this evidence and giving all inferences in the light most favorable to Schiesser, we hold there was substantial evidence from which the jury could conclude that SAPCO used the criminal process, after its issuance, to accomplish an ulterior purpose for which the process was not designed. * * *

For the reasons above, we affirm.

NOTES

1. *Lack of Probable Cause.* The issue of probable cause has much in common with the issue of reasonable care in a negligence case. Both may involve (1) a determination of the facts, in the sense of what actually happened, from conflicting evidence and (2) an evaluation of a party's conduct as to its reasonableness under the circumstances. In both types of cases, the first question is left to the jury where the evidence permits a dispute; but the second question receives divergent treatments. In the negligence field, the evaluation of conduct is also generally left to the jury (within bounds imposed by the court). In malicious prosecution, it is for the court to say whether given facts amount to probable cause. This potentially gives the judge greater control of the latter issue than she has of negligence.

2. *Favorable Termination of Prior Proceeding.* To recover under a malicious prosecution claim, it is also necessary to show that the prior proceeding terminated in the plaintiff's favor. What if the complaining witness fails to appear and testify in the earlier prosecution? See Jones v. State Farm Mut. Auto. Ins. Co., 578 So.2d 783, 785–86 (Fla.Dist.Ct.App.1991). What if the prior claim in a civil action is settled? See Thompson v. Beecham, 72 Wis.2d 356, 241 N.W.2d 163 (1976), but compare Blase v. Appicelli, 195 Mich.App. 174, 181, 489 N.W.2d 129, 133 (1992) ("[A] settlement or compromise brought about by duress or coercion will not bar an action for malicious prosecution.").

3. *Abuse of Process.* What are the differences between the requirements of malicious prosecution and abuse of process? See generally Harper, James and Gray on Torts § 4.9. For the abuse of process tort, is it necessary to show that the previous action was initiated without probable cause? See Jackson v. District of Columbia, 710 F.Supp. 13 (D.D.C.1989); Drill Parts

and Serv. Co. v. Joy Mfg. Co., 619 So.2d 1280, 1286–88 (Ala.1993). That the previous action terminated favorably to the party seeking relief for abuse of process? See DeLaurentis v. City of New Haven, 220 Conn. 225, 597 A.2d 807 (1991); Berman v. Karvounis, 308 Md. 259, 518 A.2d 726 (1987).

Schiesser illustrates the most common application of the tort: the use of criminal process to extort money. There are many other possible applications including its use against an attorney filing a medical malpractice action in circumstances indicating he had no belief in the merits of the claims but was motivated primarily by the prospect of a nuisance settlement, Dunn v. Koehring Co., 546 F.2d 1193 (5th Cir.1977) (Miss. law); against a religious sect that procured the initiation of proceedings by converts against "deprogrammers" primarily for the purpose of destroying them financially and discouraging the continuation of their efforts, Alexander v. Unification Church of Am., 634 F.2d 673 (2d Cir.1980) (N.Y. law); against a husband in a divorce proceeding who sued his wife's attorney solely to cause him to be disqualified from representing the wife because of a conflict of interest, Millennium Equity Holdings, LLC v. Mahlowitz, 456 Mass 627 629, 925 N.E.2d 513, 517 (2010); and against a teachers' association that—as a form of work stoppage—subpoenaed eighty-seven teachers for the first day of an administrative hearing concerning charges that the teachers had engaged in an illegal strike, even though it was clear that it would be impossible for that many witnesses to testify. Bd. of Educ. v. Farmingdale Classroom Teachers Ass'n, 38 N.Y.2d 397, 380 N.Y.S.2d 635, 343 N.E.2d 278 (1975).

4. *Spoliation of Evidence.* The litigation process obviously is impaired if a party negligently or intentionally destroys relevant evidence. A minority of jurisdictions recognize an independent tort, known as spoliation of evidence, against a party who destroys evidence. For example, in Rizzuto v. Davidson Ladders, Inc., 905 A.2d 1165, 1179 (Conn.2006), the Connecticut Supreme Court held that a plaintiff proving the following elements could recover for spoliation of evidence: (1) the defendant's knowledge of a pending or impending civil action involving the plaintiff; (2) the defendant's destruction of evidence; (3) in bad faith, that is, with intent to deprive the plaintiff of his cause of action; (4) the plaintiff's inability to establish a prima facie case without the spoliated evidence; and (5) damages.

The court went on to state that to establish proximate cause, the plaintiff "must prove that the defendant's intentional, bad faith destruction of evidence rendered the plaintiff *unable* to establish a prima facie case in the underlying litigation." Once the plaintiff meets this evidentiary burden, stated the court, the defendant may rebut a presumption that the plaintiff would have prevailed in the underlying action if the lost or destroyed evidence had been available. The court then indicated that the plaintiff could recover the entire amount of compensatory damages that it would have received if it had prevailed in the original litigation.

Most states do not recognize spoliation as a separate tort action against first party opponents—particularly when the adversely affected party knew or should have known about the spoliation either before or during the litigation of the underlying claim. E.g., Cedars-Sinai Med. Ctr. v. Super. Ct., 18 Cal. 4th 1, 74 Cal.Rptr.2d 248, 954 P.2d 511 (Cal.1998); MetLife Auto & Home v. Basil Chevrolet, 1 N.Y.3d 478, 807 N.E.2d 865, 775 N.Y.S.2d 754 (N.Y.2004); Martino v. Wal-Mart Stores, 908 So.2d 342 (Fla.2005). In *Cedars*, the California Supreme Court, in overruling its earlier landmark decision recognizing an independent tort claim, identified the following policy considerations for denying tort recovery:

1) Judicial preference for using non-tort remedies to punish litigation misconduct;

2) Prevention of attacks on final judgment on grounds that evidence was falsified or destroyed;

3) The uncertainties of proving harm in spoliation cases;

4) Costs to plaintiffs of erroneous determinations in subsequent spoliation actions and cost to defendants and courts of meritless actions;

5) Jury confusion when simultaneously trying underlying and spoliation claims; and

6) Duplicative proceedings with the potential for inconsistent results.

954 P.2d at 517–18.

Wilson v. Hayes

Supreme Court of Iowa, 1990.
464 N.W.2d 250.

■ LAVORATO, JUSTICE. Two doctors [Drs. Kathleen Wilson and Michael Wilson] brought suit against an attorney alleging malicious prosecution and abuse of process. The claims arose out of a medical malpractice action that the attorney brought against the doctors on behalf of his client. The client claimed that the doctors' negligence resulted in his wife's death. The underlying malpractice suit was eventually disposed of without trial, and this action followed. * * * [The Wilsons] claim that Hayes' conduct in initiating the original lawsuit and then continuing the case constituted malicious prosecution. In addition they contend that Hayes committed an abuse of process when he sought a personal release instead of dismissing the lawsuit. * * * The [trial] court held that the Wilsons had failed to prove by a preponderance of the evidence the essential elements of each tort. The Wilsons appealed and Hayes cross-appealed. * * *

A. *Malicious Prosecution.*

* * * Malicious prosecution began as a remedy for unjustifiable criminal proceedings. Gradually the remedy was extended to the wrongful institution of civil suits. * In fact, the Restatement refers to the civil side of the remedy as the "wrongful use of civil proceedings." See Restatement (Second) of Torts, Wrongful Use of Civil Proceedings, §§ 674–681B (1977). * * * The remedy's primary purpose is to provide relief in those cases in which a plaintiff brings a meritless suit and has an improper motive for bringing it. * Courts have not favored the remedy and so have construed its requirements strictly against the malicious prosecution plaintiff. According to Prosser, two competing social interests underlie the remedy: the individual interest in freedom from unjustifiable litigation and the social interest in supporting resort to the law. [William L.] Prosser, [Law of Torts] § 119 [(5th ed. 1984) (hereinafter Prosser)]

It is only in recent years that litigants have used the remedy against attorneys. One commentator suggests the remedy focuses on the intent of the original plaintiff rather than on the attorney's conduct in screening lawsuits. * For that reason it is suggested the remedy is ill-equipped to deter lawyers from filing groundless suits. * This in turn may account for the reluctance of the courts to hold lawyers liable for malicious prosecution. *

We recently summarized the elements of a malicious prosecution suit in a civil setting:

> To prevail on a claim for malicious prosecution, the plaintiff must establish each of the following six elements: (1) a previous prosecution, (2) instigation of that prosecution by the defendant, (3) termination of that prosecution by acquittal or discharge of the plaintiff, (4) want of probable cause, (5) malice on the part of defendant for bringing the prosecution, and (6) damage to plaintiff.

Royce v. Hoening, 423 N.W.2d 198, 200 (Iowa 1988); see also Restatement (Second) of Torts §§ 674, 681A (setting forth comparable elements).

The fighting issue here concerns Hayes' conduct in initiating and continuing the malpractice action. Specifically, did he have probable cause? And did he act with malice or an improper purpose?

While we have addressed the question of probable cause to file suit from a litigant's standpoint, we have not developed a standard for reviewing an attorney's decision to file suit. Such a standard requires a careful consideration of the attorney's duty to the client and freedom of access to the courts:

> [In developing a standard for reviewing a lawyer's decision to file suit], we must be ever mindful that an attorney's role is to facilitate access to our judicial system for any person seeking legal relief. As such, probable cause is not to be judged merely upon some personal assessment of a claim's merit. It must encompass consideration of the law's desire to fully meet the client's needs. While an attorney is under an ethical duty to avoid suit where its only purpose is to harass or injure, if a balance must be struck between the desire of an adversary to be free from unwarranted accusations and the need of the client for undivided loyalty, the client's interests must be paramount. . . .

We thus emphasize that any standard of probable cause must insure that the attorney's "duty to his client to present his case vigorously in a manner as favorable to the client as the rules of law and professional ethics will permit" is preserved. . . .

We recognize that through an effort to protect every citizen's free access to the courts some innocent persons may suffer the publicity, expense and other burdens of defending ill-founded lawsuits. While this is regrettable, the chilling effect that a broad rule of attorney liability would have upon the legal system, and ultimately upon its popular acceptance as a means of dispute resolution, appears to outweigh the value of the protection it would afford to those who might be deemed "innocent" defendants.

Wong v. Taber, 422 N.E.2d 1279, 1285–86 (Ind.App.1981). *

In keeping with this philosophy, the *Restatement* has formulated a special rule to govern review of an attorney's conduct in commencing and continuing a lawsuit:

> An attorney who initiates a civil proceeding on behalf of his client or one who takes any steps in the proceeding is not liable if he has probable cause for his action; and even if he has no probable cause and is convinced that his client's claim is unfounded, he is still not liable if he acts primarily for the purpose of aiding his client in obtaining a proper adjudication of his claim. An attorney is not required or expected to prejudge his client's claim, and although he is fully aware that its chances of success are comparatively slight, it is his responsibility to present it to the court for adjudication if his client so insists after he has explained to the client the nature of the chances.
>
> If, however, the attorney acts without probable cause for belief in the possibility that the claim will succeed, and for an improper purpose, as, for example, to put pressure upon the person proceeded against in order to compel payment of another claim of his own or solely to harass the person proceeded against by bringing a claim known to be invalid, he is subject to the same liability as any other person.

Restatement (Second) of Torts § 674 cmt. d (1977). In short, under this rule the lawyer avoids liability if the lawyer either had probable cause or acted primarily to have the client's claim judicially determined. * * *

Comment *c* to section 676 gives examples of improper purposes: the person bringing suit is aware the claim has no merit; the proceedings are begun because of hostility or ill will; the matter is initiated solely for the purpose of depriving the person against whom it is brought of a beneficial use of property; or, suit is brought for the purpose of forcing a settlement which has no relation to the merits of the claim (a "nuisance" suit). * * *

We think the Restatement's approach to attorney liability for malicious prosecution is sound. So we adopt the rule stated in comment *d* to section 674 of the Restatement. We also adopt the rule that a finding of an improper purpose must be supported by evidence independent of the evidence establishing a want of probable cause. In other words, in cases of malicious prosecution against attorneys an improper purpose may not be presumed from a want of probable cause. * * * There are a number of reasons why we think this approach is sound. First, we have already mentioned the attorney's duty to facilitate access to the court for any person seeking legal relief and the lawyer's duty to vigorously present the client's case. Any broad rule of attorney liability would have a chilling effect on both. * * * Second, statute of limitations problems present serious dilemmas to attorneys. There may be only enough time to file suit based on the information the client gives. Should a lawyer refuse to handle a case that seems to have merit merely because there is not enough time to investigate and research? These circumstances create a "catch 22" situation for the lawyer. The attorney could fail to file and possibly create grounds for legal malpractice. Or the attorney could file and possibly create grounds for a malicious prosecution action. * * * Sixth, an attorney's identification with a client is professional, not personal. In this sense an attorney's role does not differ from that in other professional relationships. For example, no reasonable person would impute a patient's conduct to a treating physician. And no reasonable person would levy criticism against a physician for furnishing needed medical services, even when the patient might seek such treatment for injuries resulting from objectionable or even outrageous conduct. Last, we think Iowa Rule of Civil Procedure 80(a) provides an adequate alternative remedy for baseless litigation. * * * A violation of Rule 80(a) subjects the offending lawyer to sanctions including "the amount of the reasonable expenses incurred because of the filing of [the enumerated documents], including a reasonable attorney fee." An attorney who files a suit without first conducting a reasonable investigation may escape liability for malicious prosecution if the suit turns out to be groundless. But such an attorney may incur sanctions under rule 80(a). With these principles in mind we turn to the record in this case. * * *

These facts * * * support the court's conclusion that the Wilsons had failed to prove by a preponderance of the evidence that probable cause to initiate the suit was lacking. Hayes had before him the facts according to the Rashids [plaintiffs in the medical malpractice action] as well as documentary evidence tending to support these facts. Hayes also had the opinion of a qualified expert with whom Hayes had consulted in previous cases. Given this information, we think a reasonably prudent and careful attorney could conclude that filing the suit was justified.

* * * [U]nder the Restatement rule we adopt today, an improper purpose—the counterpart of malice—cannot be inferred from a lack of probable cause. So under this rule, even had the district court found a lack of probable cause, it would need to find from independent evidence that Hayes initiated the suit for an improper purpose. We find no such independent evidence in the record. * * *

B. *Abuse of process.*

Abuse of process is similar to malicious prosecution in that the basis for both is the improvident use of courts. Note, A Lawyer's Duty to Reject Groundless Litigation, 26 Wayne L. Rev. 1561, 1565 (1980). The focus, however, is slightly different:

> Malicious prosecution occurs when an action is instituted without foundation. Conversely, abuse of process may be found when [legal process] is . . . used to attain a collateral objective beyond that anticipated by the process. An ulterior motive does not alone satisfy the requirement for an action in abuse of process; a definite act or threat outside the process is required.

Id. at 1555–56. *

We have defined abuse of process as the use of " 'legal process, whether criminal or civil, against another primarily to accomplish a purpose for which it is not designed. . . .' " Schmidt v. Wilkinson, 340 N.W.2d 282, 284 (Iowa 1983) (quoting Restatement (Second) of Torts

§ 682). The essence of this tort is an improper purpose for using the legal process. The improper purpose must result from " 'some act or threat directed to an immediate objective not legitimate in the use of the process. . . .' " *Id.* (quoting Restatement (Second) of Torts § 682, Reporters' Notes (1977)).

An improper purpose or use " 'is ordinarily an attempt to secure from another some collateral advantage not properly includable in the process itself. . . .' " *Id.* at 284–85. * Simply put, the improper purpose relates to an extortion or coercion attempt by one person to do some other thing. An abuse of process can occur even though there is probable cause to bring the action and the original action terminates in favor of the plaintiff. *

Abuse of process has two elements: (1) legal process and (2) use of the legal process in an improper or unauthorized manner. Tomash v. John Deere Indus. Equip. Co., 399 N.W.2d 387, 390 (Iowa 1987). A third element, while not specifically mentioned in our cases, requires that the plaintiff suffered damages as a result of the abuse. * The first element can generally be shown by the use of a legal process against the plaintiff. * The second element—improper motive in using the legal process—is more difficult to prove. The plaintiff must prove that the defendant used the legal process *primarily* for an impermissible or illegal motive. * * *

In previous cases we have taken a very restrictive view of the primary purpose element. We have done so in the interest of protecting the right of ready access to courts. * So abuse of process will not lie for a civil action which inconveniences a defendant, or for one filed in expectation of settlement (a "nuisance" suit). Additionally, there is no abuse of process when the action is filed to intimidate and embarrass a defendant knowing there is no entitlement to recover the full amount of damages sought. * * *

The Wilsons contend that Hayes had an improper or illegal motive for continuing the suit: to secure a release for himself which would avoid a suit against him. In support of their contention, the Wilsons argue that Hayes violated several ethical rules and these violations would supply the "primarily" improper motive. Specifically, the Wilsons claim that Hayes' attempt to secure the release constituted a conflict of interest between Hayes and Namen [Rashid]. The Wilsons suggest that at a minimum Hayes should have told Namen about the conflict and should have advised Namen to consult with another attorney about it. * * * We seriously doubt whether the release request constitutes evidence of improper purpose for abuse of process purposes. Settlement is included in the "goals of proper process," even though the suit is frivolous. * The district court also found that Hayes continued to pursue the case in the district court and on appeal for legitimate reasons and not "primarily" to secure a release. We think there is substantial evidence to support these findings. * * *

For all these reasons we conclude the judgment of the district court as to both claims must be affirmed. * * *

NOTES

1. *Malicious Prosecution and Civil Cases.* In most jurisdictions, the tort of malicious prosecution has now been expanded to cover not only frivolous criminal proceedings, but also civil actions. Sometimes the tort is identified by a different name such as "wrongful civil proceeding," Restatement (Second) of Torts §§ 674–81 (1977), or "malicious abuse of process." E.g., One Thousand Fleet Ltd. P'ship v. Guerriero, 346 Md. 29, 694 A.2d 952 (1997).

In approximately one-third of American jurisdictions, recovery for malicious prosecution arising out of a civil action requires a showing of "special damage"—an injury resulting from the civil action that fairly directly interferes with plaintiff's person or property or otherwise goes beyond the usual costs and aggravation of civil litigation. Examples of special damage include attachment of property, involuntary bankruptcy proceedings, or commitment proceedings. See Harper, James and Gray on Torts § 4.8. In Engel v. CBS, Inc., 93 N.Y.2d 195, 711 N.E.2d 626, 689 N.Y.S.2d 411 (1999), the attorney-plaintiff argued that the inconvenience and costs imposed by the defendant CBS's additional lawsuit, which was designed to create professional conflicts of interest for the plaintiff if he pursued other advocacy against CBS, constituted the special damage required for a malicious prosecution action. The Court of Appeals rejected this argument but suggested that more specific allegations of undermining plaintiff's attorney-client relationship might so qualify.

A claim for malicious prosecution generally cannot be asserted as a counterclaim in the original civil action because the tort requires a termination of the preceding action favorable to the plaintiff in the malicious prosecution action. E.g., H & H Farms, Inc. v. Hazlett, 6 Kan.App.2d 263, 627 P.2d 1161 (1981).

2. *Non-Tort Sanctions for Frivolous Litigation.* The party who cannot prove the elements of malicious prosecution or abuse of process is not necessarily without remedy. Today state and federal rules of court and statutes provide compensation for costs sustained by the victim of frivolous litigation and sanctions against those who initiate such litigation. Many states have adopted rules similar to Federal Rule of Civil Procedure 11 which allows recovery for attorney's fees and other litigation expenses in the original action if the judge finds the claims (or the defenses) to be frivolous. See James W.M. Moore, Moore's Federal Practice—Civil § 54.171(3)(h)(ii) (Daniel R. Coquillette et al. eds., 3d ed. 2014). See also Jeffrey A. Parness, Choices About Attorney Fee-Shifting Laws: Further Substance/Procedure Problems Under *Erie* and Elsewhere, 49 U. Pitt. L. Rev. 393, 394 nn.2 & 3 (1988) (noting an "explosion" in court rules allowing fee-shifting in cases of frivolous litigation).

CHAPTER 15

MISREPRESENTATION

The earlier chapters of this casebook addressed tortious liability for personal injuries and property damage. In the next two chapters, we switch our focus to torts imposing liability for specified conduct interfering with the functioning of the commercial marketplace.

Misrepresentation law has its origins in the tort of deceit, a precursor of intentional misrepresentation. As one treatise describes it, "The type of interest protected by the law of deceit is the interest in formulating business judgments without being misled by others—in short, in not being cheated." Harper, James and Gray on Torts § 7.1.

The concept of misrepresentation, broadly defined, plays a role in many areas of tort law. For example, both the physician who obtains informed consent to a medical procedure using incomplete or misleading descriptions of the likely consequences—and the defendant sued for battery after obtaining consent to physical contact based upon false statements—use misrepresentation as an integral part of their tortious conduct. Today, concepts first developed in the common law of misrepresentation provide the foundation for federal and state statutes that provide analogous remedies in areas such as securities regulation, consumer protection, and the purchase and sale of land.

A. ORIGINS

Pasley v. Freeman

Court of King's Bench, 1789.
100 Eng.Rep. 450, 3 Term Rep. 51.

* * * [The plaintiff's complaint alleged that the defendant Joseph Freeman "wrongfully and deceitfully encourage[d] and persuade[d] * * * John Pasley and Edward" to extend credit to John Christopher Falch for Falch's purchase of various goods. In encouraging John Pasley and Edward to do so, the defendant "falsely, deceitfully, and fraudulently * * * assert[ed] and affirm[ed]" that Falch was a trustworthy and creditworthy individual. "John Pasley and Edward, confiding in and giving credit to the * * * assertion and affirmation of the said Joseph, and believing the same to be true, * * * did * * * sell and deliver the last mentioned goods, wares, and merchandizes, upon trust and credit, to the said John Christopher. . . . [I]n truth and in fact, at the time of the said Joseph's making his said last-mentioned assertion and affirmation, the said John Christopher was not then and there a person safely to be trusted and given credit to in that respect, and the said Joseph well knew the same * * *." John Christopher failed to pay the sum owed and, in fact, "was, and still is, wholly unable to pay the said sum of money last mentioned, or any part thereof * * *."]

* * *

■ GROSE, J.—Upon the face of this count in the declaration, no privity of contract is stated between the parties. * * * Then this is an action against the defendant for making a false affirmation, or telling a lie, respecting the credit of a third person, with intent to deceive, by which the third person was damnified * * *. It is admitted, that the action is new in point of precedent: but it is insisted that the law recognizes principles on which it may be supported. The principle on which it is contended to lie is, that wherever deceit or falsehood is practised to the detriment of another, the law will give redress.

* * * The tort * * * is said to be an action upon the case analogous to the old writ of deceit. * * * [O]n looking into the old books for cases in which the old action of deceit has been maintained upon the false affirmation of the defendant, * * * I have not met with any case of an action upon a false affirmation, except against a party to a contract, and where there is a promise, either express or implied, that the fact is true * * *. [I]n this very case, if the action lies, the plaintiffs will stand in a peculiarly fortunate predicament, for then they will have the responsibility both of Falch and the defendant. And they will be in a better situation than they would have been if, in the conversation that passed between them and the defendant, instead of asserting that Falch might safely be trusted, the defendant had said, "if he do not pay for the goods, I will": for then undoubtedly an action would not have lain against the defendant.[a]

* * * The misrepresentation stated in the declaration is respecting the credit of Falch; * * * but credit to which a man is entitled is matter of judgment and opinion, on which different men might form different opinions, and upon which the plaintiffs might form their own; to mislead which no fact to prove the good credit of Falch is falsely asserted. * * * [I]t is not an assertion of a fact peculiarly in the knowledge of the defendant. Whether Falch deserved credit depended on the opinion of many; for credit exists on the good opinion of many. Respecting this, the plaintiffs might have inquired of others, who knew as much as the defendant; it was their fault that they did not, and they have suffered damage by their own * * * gross negligence that they gave credence to the assertion of the defendant, without taking pains to satisfy themselves that that assertion was founded in fact * * * I am therefore of opinion, that this action * * * cannot be maintained.

■ BULLER, J.—* * * Fraud without damage, or damage without fraud, gives no cause of action; but where these two concur, an action lies. * * * Every deceit comprehends a lie; but a deceit is more than a lie on account of the view with which it is practised, it's [sic] being coupled with some dealing, and the injury which it is calculated to occasion, and does occasion, to another person. * * * These cases * * * shew that, if there be fraud or deceit, the action will lie; and that knowledge of the falsehood of the thing asserted is fraud and deceit. * * *

* * * [T]he plaintiffs had an interest in knowing what the credit of Falch was. * * * All that is required of a person in the defendant's situation is, that he shall give no answer, or that if he do, he shall answer according to the truth as far as he knows. * * * [T]he law * * * requires that, if it be answered at all, it shall be answered honestly. * * * And if a man will wickedly assert that which he knows to be false, and thereby draws his neighbour into a heavy loss, even though it be

under the specious pretence of serving his friend, I say *ausis talibus istis non jura subserviunt.*

■ ASHHURST, J.— * * * It is admitted that a fraudulent affirmation, when the party making it has an interest, is a ground of action * * *. But it was argued that the action lies not unless where the party making it has an interest, or colludes with one who has. * * * [T]he gi[s]t of the action is the injury done to the plaintiff, and not whether the defendant meant to be a gainer by it: what is it to the plaintiff whether the defendant was or was not to gain by it; the injury to him is the same. * * *

■ LORD KENYON, CH. J. * * * [I]n this case the plaintiffs had no means of knowing the state of Falch's credit but by an application to his neighbours. * * * It is admitted that the defendant's conduct was highly immoral, and detrimental to society. And I am of opinion that the action is maintainable on the grounds of deceit in the defendant, and injury and loss to the plaintiffs.

[The judgment for the plaintiffs was affirmed.]

NOTE

Historical Significance. "This decision * * * marks a new point of departure in the law of fraud. Prior to that time the use of the action of deceit upon a false representation, if not strictly limited to situations where the false representation was made by a seller to his vendee as an inducement to the sale, was at least restricted to situations where the party injured was brought into legal relations with the persons making the false representation." 1 Thomas A. Street, The Foundations of Legal Liability 392 (1906).

B. MISREPRESENTATION OF FACT

Dezero v. Turner

Supreme Court of Vermont, 1941.
112 Vt. 194, 22 A.2d 173.

■ JEFFORDS, JUSTICE. This is an action in tort for deceit. The plaintiff in his complaint alleges that he sold to the defendant and installed in the home of the latter a certain oil burning heating system upon the following express representations of the defendant: "I (defendant) have an interest in an estate being probated in the Fair Haven Probate Court and I have just received $1500.00 from this estate, and I have this money now in my possession and I will keep $825.75 of this money and pay it to you immediately after you have installed the heating system in my home on the Gleason Road." Then follow allegations of falsity of the above representations, scienter by the defendant, reliance by the plaintiff on the representations, installation of the heating system, failure to pay for the same on demand, total loss of the goods and labor of installation resulting from the facts previously alleged, to the damage of the plaintiff.

The defendant in his demurrer to the complaint specified as reasons for its claimed insufficiency that there was no false representation alleged of any existing fact to secure credit but merely an allegation of a promise to pay for services at some future time. The demurrer was sustained and the cause passed to this Court under P.L. 2072.

Certain false representations alleged to have been made by the defendant were that he had an interest in an estate and had received a stated amount of money from the estate which he then possessed. There can be no question but that these alleged false statements, admitted by the demurrer to have been made, were of existing facts which the jury could reasonably find were spoken for the purpose of securing credit for the transaction in question alleged to have been given in reliance upon said representations. Consequently grounds for an action of fraud or deceit are set forth and the pleading is not defective because these false representations were followed by others looking to the future, reliance upon which is also alleged. The false statements of existing facts alleged in the complaint could be found by the jury to have constituted a material inducement to the dealings between the parties and the right of the plaintiff to recover would not be changed because the jury could also find that he was induced to some extent in the matter by the alleged future representations. It is not essential that a misrepresentation of a material fact be the sole cause or inducement of the contract or transaction in question. It is enough that it constitute a material inducement. * * *

Judgment reversed and cause remanded.

NOTE

Advantages of Proving Misrepresentation. Advantages of the tort action for intentional misrepresentation include the possibility of punitive damages and the fact that a judgment for fraud is not dischargeable in bankruptcy. 11 U.S.C. § 523(2) (2012); see, e.g., Abbott v. Regents of Univ. of Cal., 516 F.2d 830 (9th Cir.1975) (fraudulent application for student loan).

Lazar v. Superior Court of Los Angeles County

Supreme Court of California, 1996.
12 Cal.4th 631, 909 P.2d 981, 49 Cal.Rptr.2d 377.

■ WERDEGAR, JUSTICE. * * * Andrew Lazar alleged [that he] * * * lived and worked in Long Island, * * * [where] he was employed * * * [as president of] a family-owned restaurant equipment company. * * *

In September 1989, a vice-president of real party in interest Rykoff-Sexton, Inc. (Rykoff or defendant) contacted Lazar and tried to persuade him to come to work in Los Angeles as Rykoff's West Coast general manager for contract design. Rykoff * * * intensively recruited Lazar * * * [and] brought Lazar and his wife to Los Angeles to visit Rykoff's offices, to visit realtors and to see the city.

During this recruitment process, Lazar told Rykoff he was concerned about relocating to Los Angeles, as the move would entail relinquishing a secure job as president of the family company where he had worked all his adult life, separating his children from their friends at an important time of their lives and leaving his home of 40 years. As a condition of agreeing to relocate, Lazar required Rykoff's assurance that his job would be secure and would involve significant pay increases.

In response to Lazar's concerns, Rykoff made representations to Lazar that led him to believe he would continue to be employed by Rykoff so long as he performed his job and achieved goals. Rykoff represented that Lazar would enjoy continued advancement within the organization, would be welcomed as part of the Rykoff "family" and, as a Rykoff employee, would enjoy security and a strong future. Rykoff represented that Lazar would have a long-term relationship with the company. Additionally, Rykoff implied the current head of the department in which Lazar would work had plans to retire and Lazar would be groomed to assume that position.

Rykoff further represented that the company was very strong financially and anticipated solid growth and a stable, profitable future. In particular, Rykoff represented that the department in which Lazar would work was a growth division within the company and that Rykoff had plans to expand it. Rykoff also stated Rykoff would pay Lazar $130,000 annually to start and, if Lazar performed his job, his yearly income would quickly rise to $150,000. Rykoff told Lazar he would receive annual reviews and raises accordingly.

Lazar asked for a written employment contract, but was refused. Rykoff stated a written contract was unnecessary because "our word is our bond." In or about February 1990, Lazar accepted Rykoff's offer of employment on terms including the foregoing.

Rykoff's representations to Lazar regarding the terms on which he would be retained, Rykoff's financial health and Lazar's potential compensation were false and, when making them, Rykoff's agents knew they were false. Rykoff had in the immediately preceding period experienced its worst economic performance in recent history, and the company's financial outlook was pessimistic. In fact, Rykoff was planning an operational merger that would eliminate Lazar's position. Rykoff had no intention of retaining Lazar so long as he performed adequately. Instead, Rykoff secretly intended to treat Lazar as if he were an "at will" employee, subject to termination without cause. Rykoff knew the promised compensation increases would not be given, as company policy limited annual increases to 2 to 3 percent.

Based on Rykoff's representations, Lazar resigned his New York position and, in May 1990, commenced employment at Rykoff. The following month, Lazar bought a home in California and moved his family there.

Lazar performed his job at Rykoff in an exemplary manner. He obtained sales increases in his assigned region, and soon after he commenced employment his West Coast region achieved its sales budget for the first time. Lazar accomplished continued improvement in sales and lowered overall operating costs within his department.

In April 1992, Rykoff failed to pay Lazar certain bonus compensation to which he had become entitled under a company incentive program. Subsequently, in July, Lazar was terminated. Rykoff told Lazar his job was being eliminated owing to management reorganization. A Rykoff vice-president told Lazar his termination was not performance related and was for cause. * * *

As a consequence of Rykoff's conduct and Lazar's reliance on Rykoff's representations, Lazar lost past and future income and employment benefits. He lost contact with the New York employment market so that reemployment there is difficult or impossible. Lazar is burdened with payments on Southern California real estate he can no longer afford. Lazar and his family have experienced emotional distress, with both psychological and physical manifestations.

* * * Lazar set forth [a] cause[ ] of action [among others] for * * * fraud and deceit * * *. Rykoff demurred * * *. The trial court sustained Rykoff's demurrer in its entirety * * *. The Court of Appeal * * * direct[ed] the superior court to vacate its order, insofar as it sustained Rykoff's demurrers to Lazar's cause[ ] of action for * * * fraud and deceit * * *. We granted Rykoff's petition for review. * * *

"The elements of fraud, which give rise to the tort action for deceit, are (a) misrepresentation (false representation, concealment, or nondisclosure); (b) knowledge of falsity (or 'scienter'); (c) intent to defraud, i.e., to induce reliance; (d) justifiable reliance; and (e) resulting damage." 5 Witkin, Summary of Cal. Law: Torts § 676 (9th ed. 1988). * "Promissory fraud" is a subspecies of the action for fraud and deceit. A promise to do something necessarily implies the intention to perform; hence, where a promise is made without such intention, there is an implied misrepresentation of fact that may be actionable fraud. * * * In such cases, the plaintiff's claim does not depend upon whether the defendant's promise is ultimately enforceable as a contract. "If it is enforceable, the [plaintiff] . . . has a cause of action in tort as an alternative at least, and perhaps in some instances in addition to his cause of action on the contract." Restatement (Second) of Torts, § 530(1), cmt. c. * Recovery, however, may be limited by the rule against double recovery of tort and contract compensatory damages. *

Lazar's allegations, if true, would establish all the elements of promissory fraud. As detailed above, Lazar alleges that, in order to induce him to come to work in California, Rykoff intentionally represented to him he would be employed by the company so long as he performed his job, he would receive significant increases in salary, and the company was strong financially. Lazar further alleges that Rykoff's representations were false, and he justifiably relied on them in leaving secure New York employment, severing his connections with the New York employment market, uprooting his family, purchasing a California home and moving here.

Lazar alleges that Rykoff knew its representations regarding the terms upon which he would be retained in Rykoff's employ, potential salary increases and the financial strength of the company were false at the time they were made. He also alleges that, at the time Rykoff represented to him his job would be permanent and secure, Rykoff was planning an operational merger likely to eliminate Lazar's job, and Rykoff had no intention of retaining him so long as he performed adequately. Instead, Lazar alleges, Rykoff secretly intended to treat him as if he were subject to termination without cause. Lazar further alleges Rykoff knew the purported potential salary increases would not materialize, because company policy was to limit annual increases to 2 or 3 percent. These allegations adequately state a cause of action for promissory fraud as traditionally understood. * * *

Lazar's reliance on Rykoff's misrepresentations was truly detrimental, such that he may plead all the elements of fraud. * * * Rykoff used misrepresentations to induce Lazar to change employment, a result Rykoff presumably could *not* have achieved truthfully (because Lazar had required assurances the Rykoff position would be secure and would involve significant increases in pay). Moreover, Lazar's decision to join Rykoff left Lazar in worse circumstances than those in which he would have found himself had Rykoff not lied to him. (Allegedly, Lazar's secure living and working circumstances were disrupted, and Lazar became the employee of a financially troubled company, which intended to treat him as an at-will employee.) * * *

Consistent with the foregoing, as to his *fraud* claim Lazar may properly seek damages for the costs of uprooting his family, expenses incurred in relocation, and the loss of security and income associated with his former employment in New York. * * *

NOTE

Statement of Intention as Material Fact. What is the misrepresentation of existing fact in Lazar? Could a promise to pay be turned into such a misrepresentation by showing that, when it was made, the defendant (a) had the formed intention not to pay? (b) had no reasonable prospect of resources from which to pay? Consider Edgington v. Fitzmaurice, (1885) 29 Ch. D. 459, 483 (C.A.) (per Bowen, L.J.) ("* * * [T]he state of a man's mind is as much a fact as the state of his digestion.").

Cabot v. Christie
Supreme Court of Vermont, 1869.
42 Vt. 121.

* * * The plaintiff gave evidence tending to show that he bought the farm at the time and for the price stated in the declaration, and that the defendant made representations in respect to the number of acres, *as of his own knowledge*, designedly intending to induce the plaintiff to suppose and believe, and thereby the plaintiff was induced to and did suppose and believe, that the farm contained at least one hundred and thirty acres of land, and relying thereupon, the plaintiff made the purchase; that the defendant knew that there was not one hundred and thirty acres, or he didn't know that there was that quantity; that in fact there was only one hundred and seventeen acres and a few rods in the farm; that the plaintiff had no knowledge of the quantity except from the defendant's representation.

The defendant gave evidence tending to show that he supposed there was one hundred and thirty acres and a little more in the farm, derived from what he had heard said, and from various deeds in his possession of various grantors and of various parcels, *but that he did not know, and did not profess or represent to the plaintiff that he knew, how many acres there were in fact*; that he gave the plaintiff all the information and sources of information he had on the subject, neither making any false representation, nor fraudulent concealment, nor any undertaking as to the number of acres in the farm. There was no evidence or claim that the farm was sold by the acre; but it appeared that it was sold in lump, or as a farm entire.

The plaintiff requested the court to charge the jury: *First,* That under the declaration, the plaintiff is entitled to recover if he proves a warranty of the number of acres in the farm, or if he proves a fraudulent representation of the number of acres. *Second,* That the fraudulent representation may be proved either by evidence of false representations, known to the defendant to be false, and relied upon by the plaintiff, or by proof of an absolute representation of the number of acres, which representation was made with intent that the plaintiff should rely upon it, and was made upon professed knowledge, but without actual knowledge, and which was in fact false, but was relied upon by the plaintiff as true.

The court complied with said requests only so far as is shown by the charge, and charged as follows:

> In order to entitle the plaintiff to recover, he must satisfy the jury that the defendant knew the farm did not contain one hundred and thirty acres, or that he did not believe it contained one hundred and thirty acres; and that in order to induce the plaintiff to buy the farm, he falsely represented it to contain one hundred and thirty acres; and that the plaintiff was by such false representation induced to make the purchase, believing it to contain that quantity.

> If he honestly believed it contained one hundred and thirty acres, the plaintiff can not recover, though the defendant was in error about it. Honest mistake is not fraud. *Incorrect* is not the same as *false.* You must find that he represented the quantity different from what he knew or believed to be true, with the fraudulent intent. Also, that the plaintiff was thus induced to make the purchase. That is, that the plaintiff would not have made the purchase if the defendant had not represented it to be one hundred and thirty acres. Inquire as to these several points. Fraud is not presumed, but must be proved.

The jury returned a verdict for the defendant. The plaintiff excepted to the charge in the respects in which it failed to comply with or was against said requests. In other respects the charge was satisfactory. The declaration counted both upon a false warranty of the defendant in regard to the number of acres contained in the farm, and a warranty in regard to said quantity. * * *

■ STEELE, J.

I.   The plaintiff can not recover upon the ground of a parol warranty of the quantity of the land. If the quantity was warranted it should be provable by the deed. It is true that a deed of conveyance need not contain all the stipulations of the parties. For example, the agreements as to consideration and mode of payment need not be embraced in the deed, for the instrument purports to be the deed of but one of the parties. But it does purport to contain the covenants of the grantor with respect to the property conveyed. To add a new covenant by parol proof would be a palpable violation of the familiar rule that written contracts are not to be varied by oral testimony. Such a parol stipulation, it has been held, could not be proved in respect to an ordinary bill of sale of personal property.

Nor is the plaintiff entitled to recover in this action upon the ground of mistake. A mutual and material mistake, by which the purchaser was misled as to the quantity of land, would be a more appropriate ground for relief in a court of chancery than in a court of law.

If, then, the plaintiff was entitled to recover at all in this case, it was by reason of some fraud on the part of the defendant by which the bargain was induced.

II.   The plaintiff complains of the ruling of the county court upon the subject of fraud. It is conceded that the quantity of land was represented incorrectly. The court properly told the jury that this, in itself, would not amount to fraud. To entitle the plaintiff to a recovery upon that ground, the defendant must have made some representation upon the subject that he did not believe to be true. The plaintiff claims, and his evidence tended to prove, that the defendant did make such a representation by stating the quantity of land as a matter within his own knowledge, when, in fact, as the defendant concedes, it was a matter upon which he had only a belief.

We think it very clear that a party may be guilty of fraud by stating his belief as knowledge. Upon a statement of the defendant's mere belief, judgment, or information, the plaintiff might have regarded it prudent to procure a measurement of the land before completing his purchase. A statement, as of knowledge, if believed, would make a survey or measurement seem unnecessary. A representation of a fact, *as of the party's own knowledge*, if it proved false, is, unless explained, inferred to be *willfully* false and made with an intent to deceive, at least in respect to the knowledge which is professed. A sufficient explanation however sometimes arises from the nature of the subject itself, or from the situation of the parties being such that the statement of knowledge could only be understood as an expression of strong belief or opinion. But the quantity of land in a farm is a matter upon which accurate or approximately accurate knowledge is not at all impossible or unusual. If the defendant had only a belief or opinion as to the quantity of land, it was an imposition upon the plaintiff to pass off such belief as knowledge. So, too, if he made an absolute representation as to the quantity, which was understood and intended to be understood as a statement upon knowledge, it is precisely the same as if he had distinctly and in terms professed to have knowledge as to the fact. It is often said that a representation is not fraudulent if the party who makes it believes it to be true. But a party who is aware that he has only an opinion how a fact is, *and represents that opinion as knowledge*, does not believe his representation to be true. As is well said in a note to the report of the case of Taylor v. Ashton, (1843) 11 Mees. & Wels. 418 (Phila. Ed.), the belief of a party to be an excuse for a false representation must be "a belief in the representation as made. The *scienter* will, therefore, be sufficiently established by showing that the assertion was made as of the defendant's own knowledge, and not as mere matter of opinion with regard to facts of which he was aware that he had no such knowledge." The same principle of law has been repeatedly recognized. *

In the case before us, the plaintiff, under the charge of the court, was denied the benefit of this rule of law, although there was evidence tending to show every necessary element of a fraud of the nature we have been considering. The plaintiff's request was refused, and the jury were instructed that the plaintiff could only recover in case they found "that the defendant represented the quantity of land different from what he knew or believed to be true." Under these instructions it would be immaterial whether he made the representation as a matter of knowledge or as a matter of opinion so long as he kept within his belief as to the quantity of land. In this we think there was error. The court properly instructed the jury that the representation, to warrant a recovery, must have been relied on and have been an inducement to the purchase. The subsequent remark, that the jury, to hold the defendant, must find that the plaintiff would not have made the purchase but for the representation, we regard as probably inadvertent.

What the plaintiff would have done but for the false representation, is often a mere speculative enquiry, and is not the test of the plaintiff's right. If the false representations were material and relied upon, and were intended to operate and did operate as one of the inducements to the trade, it is not necessary to enquire whether the plaintiff would or would not have made the purchase without this inducement.

The judgment of the county court is reversed and the cause is remanded.

NOTES

1. *Representation Susceptible of Knowledge.* The demarcation between whether a statement is one of fact or opinion relates not only to the form of the expression, but also to whether the underlying assertion is one that is "susceptible of knowledge" or can be proved or disproved. For example, in Control Data Corp. v. Garrison, 305 Minn. 347, 352, 233 N.W.2d 740, 744 (1975), the defendant building contractor represented to a prospective purchaser of the building that it was structurally sound. Within a year, the building settled badly, possibly because supporting pilings had sheared underground during the construction process. The court acknowledged "that the determination of whether a piling driven into the ground has remained intact would be difficult." Nevertheless, it ruled that this fact was "susceptible of knowledge," regardless of how burdensome or difficult the determination of the fact might be. What should be the result if the matter is not actually susceptible of knowledge but plaintiff reasonably believed it is, e.g., because of defendant's superior knowledge of the field in question? See Clements Auto Co. v. Service Bureau Corp., 444 F.2d 169 (8th Cir.1971).

2. *Liability for Misrepresentation of Opinion.* According to the drafters of the Restatement (Third) of Torts: Liability for Economic Harm (Tentative Draft No. 2, 2014),

A false statement of opinion may result in liability only if

(a) the parties are in a fiduciary or confidential relationship, or

> (b) the defendant claims to have expertise or other knowledge not accessible to the plaintiff, and offers the opinion to provide a basis for reliance by the plaintiff.

Id. at § 14. For an example of the second exception to the general rule that an opinion does not result in liability, see Seeger v. Odell, *infra* pages 818–20. In addition, comment *a* to the proposed Restatement provision provides that "[a] statement of opinion may imply that its maker has knowledge of facts to support it . . . [and] that factual implication * * * can support liability for fraud * * *. *Id.* at § 14 cmt. a. See also Damon v. Sun Co., *infra* pages 807–09.

3. *Misrepresentations of Law.* "Misrepresentations of law have often been called statements of 'opinion' on which no one has a right to rely. * But * * * the statement may imply the existence of external facts. For one thing it may imply the existence or nonexistence of an applicable statute, regulation, or judicial decision, * and this is one kind of external fact that may seem very important to the person addressed by the statement. * * * Beyond that, the statement of law may imply the existence of facts that have legal significance but are not part of the law itself, * for example, that a corporation has taken the steps required to qualify it to do business within the state * * * or that the actions and agreement necessary for the formation of a contract have been completed. The modern tendency is to treat either kind of statement as one of fact * * * at least where the statement is made by one who is apparently in a position to know the facts that are implied. *" Harper, James and Gray on Torts § 7.8.

In Rosenberg v. Cyrowski, 227 Mich. 508, 512–13, 198 N.W. 905, 906 (1924), the plaintiffs were real estate agents who had agreed with Paul Cyrowksi to sell certain property owned by him. They asked the defendant, Cyrowski's brother, an attorney, to prepare a written contract documenting that Paul Cyrowksi had agreed to a three percent commission. The defendant advised the plaintiffs that they did not need a written agreement. Subsequently, when the property was sold and the commission was not paid, the plaintiffs sued the defendant attorney for misrepresentation. The court held that even though the defendant was under no obligation to give legal advice to the plaintiffs, if "he knew he was not stating the truth" and plaintiffs relied on such statements, they could recover. The court stated that "the general rule that 'fraud cannot be predicated upon misrepresentations as to matters of law' * * * 'may be rendered inapplicable by the existence of peculiar facts and circumstances.'"

4. *Predictions as Representations of Existing Fact.* Predictions are apt to be regarded as opinion. E.g., Connellan v. Himelhoch, 506 F.Supp. 1290 (E.D.Mich.1981) (estimate of future profits). Courts often take a different view, however, when a statement about a product's future performance is made by one in a position to know the facts about the product's characteristics. E.g., Omega Eng'g, Inc. v. Eastman Kodak Co., 908 F.Supp. 1084, 1098 (D.Conn.1995) (estimates by manufacturer of battery's shelf life, delivered with disclaimers, but purporting to be based on product research).

5. *Judgments about People.* Judgments as to the capacity of people may be regarded as speculative and therefore not providing the basis for a misrepresentation action. E.g., Parker v. Arthur Murray, Inc., 10 Ill.App.3d 1000, 1004, 295 N.E.2d 487, 490 (1973) (representations to plaintiff that he had "exceptional potential to be a fine and accomplished dancer" and that

he was a "natural born dancer" and a "terrific dancer," in connection with sale of a course of dancing lessons, considered "mere expression of opinion," pertaining to "future or contingent events, expectations or probabilities," "speculation or opinion," rather than "averment of fact").

6. *Statements of Value.* Statements of *value* are often treated as "puffery," dealers' talk or opinion. For example, in Rodio v. Smith, 123 N.J. 345, 587 A.2d 621 (1991), the New Jersey Supreme Court held that the slogan "You're in good hands with Allstate" is not a representation of fact. But often the circumstances—such as an uninformed buyer's reliance on the seller's apparent knowledge—invest statements of "value" with actionable implications of "fact." See, e.g., Briggs v. Carol Cars, Inc., 407 Mass. 391, 396, 553 N.E.2d 930, 933 (1990) (dealer's representation that used car "was in good condition reasonably implied that it was safe and operable and that the vehicle's oil requirements would be far less than they turned out to be").

C. DAMAGE CLAIMS AND OTHER REMEDIES: THE ROLE OF FAULT

Reno v. Bull

Court of Appeals of New York, 1919.
226 N.Y. 546, 124 N.E. 144.

■ MCLAUGHLIN, J. Action to recover damages for fraud and deceit, by reason of which it is claimed plaintiff was induced to purchase fifty shares, each of the par value of $100, of the capital stock of the American Oriental Company, a Maine corporation. Plaintiff had a verdict for $6,000, and from the judgment entered thereon defendants appealed to the Appellate Division, where the same was unanimously affirmed, and by permission they now appeal to this court. * * *

After a careful consideration of the record, the briefs and argument of respective counsel, I have reached the conclusion that there are at least two errors of this character which are so fundamental that they necessitate the reversal of the judgment. They are instructions given to the jury as to the duty and obligations of the defendants and as to the measure of damages.

As to the duty and obligations of the defendants: At the time the stock was purchased, they were, with others, directors of the corporation. It had a plant, which cost several hundred thousand dollars, for refining crude oil, located on San Francisco bay * * *. The corporation * * * made an arrangement with the Charles D. Barney & Co., prominent bankers in New York and Philadelphia, to offer [preferred stock] * * * for sale. Prior to the offering, Barney & Co. prepared a circular, or prospectus, signed by them, which consisted of a letter from one Ertz, the president of the corporation, addressed to Barney & Co., which contained statements as to the capacity of the plant, probable earnings of the corporation, crude oil supplied in the state of California, advantages in securing trade in the Orient and large dividends that would be received by holders of the preferred stock. The circular also contained the names of the directors, the advisory committee, and other matters unnecessary to state. This circular was adopted and approved by the directors of the corporation. The statements contained in the circular, which the plaintiff claimed were and which the jury have found to be false, were: (a) that the plant was well built, fully completed and had a capacity of refining 2,000 barrels of crude oil per day; (b) that there was an abundance of crude oil in the state of California; and (c) that there was a profitable Oriental market for the sale of the refined products. In connection with these alleged false statements, it was also claimed that the defendants were liable, by reason of a statement made by Ertz, the president of the corporation, to the plaintiff, at or immediately prior to the time he purchased the stock, to the effect that the corporation would begin business with $1,000,000 cash capital.

No evidence was offered at the trial, nor was the claim there made, or upon the argument before us, that the defendants or any of them had actual knowledge of the alleged false statements set forth in the circular or the statement made by the president, or that they had any connection with such statements other than as directors of the corporation, and all except one of them testified at the trial that they, at the time the circular was issued, believed the statements therein made to be true.

The action, as indicated, was to recover for fraud and deceit, and to maintain it the plaintiff had to prove that the defendants, as directors, by adopting and authorizing Barney & Co. to issue the circular, made the representations alleged; that such representations were false; that they knew they were false; that they were made for the purpose of deceiving the public, and that he, believing the same to be true, made the purchase and was thereby damaged; in other words, the plaintiff had to prove, as this court has recently said, "Representation, falsity, *scienter,* deception and injury." Ochs v. Woods, 221 N.Y. 335, 117 N.E. 305 (1917). This rule is so well settled in this state that the citation of authorities seems almost unnecessary. * The jury should have been so instructed. The trial court, however, in utter disregard of this rule, said to the jury that it was the duty of the defendants, when they, as directors of the corporation, approved of the circular, to know the truth of the facts stated therein and if they did not know whether such facts were true, they were bound to know if they had a reasonable opportunity to ascertain the same. He said,

> It is their duty before they allow these representations to be made to the public ... to know the facts ... * * * In other words, if although they did not know these facts and did not know them to be false, if they authorized the issuance of the prospectus, and authorized the statements to be made, then they are liable * * *. If they authorized a false statement to be made, when by common prudence and the exercise of ordinary care, they could have discovered that these representations were false, then they are just as liable as if they had actual personal knowledge that they were false.

When the instructions thus given are subjected to the rule above stated, it at once becomes apparent that the same were erroneous. Erroneous, because there was substituted as the test of defendants' liability, negligence, instead of a purpose to deceive. Negligence and fraud are not synonymous terms; nor in legal effect are they equivalent terms. Fraud presupposes a willful purpose resorted to with intent to deprive another of his legal rights. It is positive in that the purpose concurs with the act, designedly and knowingly committed. Negligence, whatever be its grade, does not include a purpose to do a wrongful act. It may be some evidence of, but is not, fraud. * Fraud always has its origin in a purpose, but negligence is an omission of duty minus the purpose.

* * * In the instant case, the defendants, in approving the circular and authorizing Barney & Co. to offer the stock for sale, acted solely for the corporation. * * * So far as they were concerned, the corporation alone was interested in the sale. Barney & Co. was its agent and not the agent of the defendants. *

The rule as to the measure of damages was not the one to be applied. The court said to the jury that if the plaintiff were entitled to recover, then he should be awarded "the difference between the value of the stock at the time it was sold to him . . . and the value of the stock as it would have been at that time if the representations were true." The purpose of an action for deceit is to indemnify the party injured. All elements of profit are excluded. The true measure of damage is indemnity for the actual pecuniary loss sustained as the direct result of the wrong. * The plaintiff paid $5,000 for the stock purchased by him. If he were entitled to recover at all, it was the difference between that amount and the value of the stock which he received with interest from that time. He was not entitled to anything else. * * *

Judgments reversed. * * *

NOTES

1.   *Derry v. Peek*, (1889) 14 App. Cas. 337 (H.L.), a classic case, was a shareholder's action in deceit against the directors of a corporation, alleging misrepresentation in the prospectus, reliance, and consequent injury and loss. Compare the following excerpts from the opinion by Lord Herschell:

> This action is one which is commonly called an action of deceit, a mere common law action." * * * I think it important that it should be borne in mind that such an action differs essentially from one brought to obtain rescission of a contract on the ground of a misrepresentation of a material fact. * * * Where rescission is claimed it is only necessary to prove that there was misrepresentation; then, however honestly it may have been made, however free from blame the person who made it, the contract, having been obtained by misrepresentation, cannot stand. In an action of deceit, on the contrary, it is not enough to establish misrepresentation alone * * *.

> There is another class of actions which I must refer to also for the purpose of putting it aside. I mean those cases where a person within whose special province it lay to know a particular fact, has given an erroneous answer to an enquiry made with regard to it by a person desirous of ascertaining the fact for the purpose of determining his course accordingly, and has been held bound to make good the assurance he has given. * * * In cases like this it has been said that the circumstance that the answer was honestly

made in the belief that it was true affords no defence to the action. * * *

I may pass now to Foster v. Charles, [1830] 7 Bing. 105. It was there contended that the defendant was not liable, even though the representation he had made was false to his knowledge, because he had no intention of defrauding or injuring the plaintiff. This contention was not upheld by the Court. * * * Willfully to tell a falsehood, intending that another shall be led to act upon it as if it were the truth, may well be termed fraudulent, whatever the motive which induces it, though it be neither gain to the person making the assertion nor injury to the person to whom it is made. * * *

I proceed to state briefly the conclusions to which I have been led. * * * First, in order to sustain an action of deceit, there must be proof of fraud, and nothing short of that will suffice. Secondly, fraud is proved when it is shewn that a false representation has been made (1) knowingly, or (2) without belief in its truth, or (3) recklessly, careless whether it be true or false. Although I have treated the second and third as distinct cases, I think the third is but an instance of the second, for one who makes a statement under such circumstances can have no real belief in the truth of what he states. To prevent a false statement being fraudulent, there must, I think, always be an honest belief in its truth. * * * Thirdly, if fraud be proved, the motive of the person guilty of it is immaterial.

2.   *Federal Securities Acts.* "[T]he federal securities acts[9] impose civil liability on a wide group of persons—including officers, directors, accountants, and underwriters,[10]—for false statements and certain omissions in a registration statement without requiring scienter. The issuer's liability is strict, that of other classes of defendants defeasible if certain named defenses are affirmatively established, among which is that such person 'had, after reasonable investigation, reasonable ground to believe and did believe' in the truth of the false statement."[11] Harper, James and Gray on Torts § 7.5.

3.   *Rescission as a Remedy.* The notion underlying rescission—either at law or in equity—as a remedy for misrepresentation, is that the bargain, being tainted with fraud, is voidable at the election of the victim. The election is exercised by the victim returning what she has received in the transaction, or by making tender of it if return is not accepted. She is then entitled to get back what she has parted with, in an appropriate legal action. See Restatement (Third) of Torts: Liability for Economic Harm § 9 cmt. (b)(1) (Tentative Draft No. 2, 2014). Cancellation or rescission is by no means the only remedy equity has to offer in cases of fraud. Reformation, specific performance of the bargain as represented, the constructive trust device, receivership, and any other appropriate relief may be granted in a proper case.

---

[9]   Securities Act of 1933, 15 U.S.C. §§ 77a–77aa (2006); Securities Exchange Act of 1934, 15 U.S.C. §§ 78a–78jj (2012).

[10]   Section 11 of the Securities Act of 1933 * * * 15 U.S.C. § 77k(a) (2000); * * * Louis Loss and Joel Seligman, Fundamentals of Securities Regulation 1228 (5th ed. 2004).

[11]   15 U.S.C. § 77k(b)(3) (2012). * * *

4. *Misrepresentation as Defense to Contract Claim.* The party misled by a misrepresentation also has the option of waiting until an action is brought against her for misrepresentation and then setting up the misrepresentation as a defense to the contract claim. E.g., Kovach v. McLellan, 564 So.2d 274 (Fla.Dist.Ct.App.1990) (defense against mortgage foreclosure). Misrepresentation may also be used to nullify a defense. For example, misrepresentation may void a release. E.g., Vickers v. Gifford-Hill & Co., Inc., 534 F.2d 1311 (8th Cir.1976).

5. *Innocent Misrepresentations.* As indicated above, rescission may be based upon innocent misrepresentation. See Restatement of Restitution § 28(b) (1937); Seneca Wire & Mfg. Co. v. A.B. Leach & Co., 247 N.Y. 1, 159 N.E. 700 (1928). Under contract law, an innocent material misrepresentation that induces a party's "manifestation of assent" may make a contract voidable. Restatement (Second) of Contracts § 164 (1981). Innocent misrepresentations thus may provide the grounds for a contract defense, rescission, or equitable estoppel.

In the case of products, of course, the breach of an express warranty leads to strict liability for even an "innocent" misrepresentation. See *supra* page 586, Note 3. What distinctions exist between an action for breach of warranty and a damage claim for innocent misrepresentation?

Restatement (Third) of Torts: Products Liability § 9 (1998) provides:

> One engaged in the business of selling or otherwise distributing products who, in connection with the sale of a product, makes a fraudulent, negligent, or innocent misrepresentation of material fact concerning the product is subject to liability for harm to persons or property caused by the misrepresentation.

A few courts have allowed recovery of damages for innocent misrepresentation even when a disclaimer of warranty or the lack of privity or similar relationship required under state statutory provisions precluded an action for express warranty. See, e.g., Clements Auto Co. v. Service Bureau Corp., 444 F.2d 169 (8th Cir.1971); see also generally Restatement (Third) of Torts: Products Liability § 9 Reporters' Note cmt. b (1998). In *Clements Auto Co. v. Service Bureau Corp.*, the court ruled that under Minnesota law, "the element of *scienter*, or intent to deceive, or even recklessness, is not necessary to actionable fraud," and that in the case of statements made of one's own knowledge, it is "immaterial" whether the statement is made "innocently or knowingly." The court went on to hold that disclaimers of warranties and other contract provisions were ineffective to preclude the fraud action. See also Restatement (Second) of Torts § 552C (1977) (providing restitution damages for certain innocent misrepresentations occurring during a sale, rental, or exchange transaction).

D. CONCEALMENT AND NON-DISCLOSURE

Laidlaw v. Organ

Supreme Court of the United States, 1817.
2 Wheat. 178, 15 U.S. 178, 4 L.Ed. 214.

[The plaintiff Organ purchased a large quantity ("111 hogsheads") of tobacco from the defendant, a broker who sold tobacco on commission.

The sale was not completed until February 19, 1815. On the evening of February 18, a British fleet arriving in New Orleans carried the first news of the signing of the Treaty of Ghent between the American and British commissioners, ending what has become known in the United States as the War of 1812. The news was made public by the distribution of handbills on February 19, 1815, and plaintiff knew of this fact when he met with Girault, an agent for the defendant, on February 19. The peace treaty, by opening new markets for tobacco grown in the American south, subsequently resulted in an increase of between 30 and 50 percent in the price of tobacco.

It appears from the facts that Girault was not aware of the peace treaty when he met with plaintiff on February 19. Girault asked plaintiff during the negotiations whether there was any news calculated to enhance the price or value of tobacco. The statement of facts in the trial court indicates that there was "no evidence that the plaintiff had asserted or suggested anything to the said Girault, calculated to impose upon him with respect to said news, and to induce him to think or believe that it did not exist."

The tobacco was delivered to the plaintiff on February 20, but later in the day the defendant seized the tobacco by force even though the plaintiff had paid for it. Plaintiff brought suit to re-acquire possession of the tobacco. The jury found for the plaintiff, and the defendant appealed.]

■ MARSHALL, CHIEF JUSTICE. The question in this case is, whether the intelligence of extrinsic circumstances, which might influence the price of the commodity, and which was exclusively within the knowledge of the vendee, ought to have been communicated by him to the vendor? The court is of opinion that he was not bound to communicate it. It would be difficult to circumscribe the contrary doctrine within proper limits, where the means of intelligence are equally accessible to both parties. But at the same time, each party must take care not to say or do anything tending to impose upon the other. The court thinks that the absolute instruction of the judge was erroneous, and that the question whether any imposition was practised by the vendee upon the vendor ought to have been submitted to the jury. For these reasons the judgment must be reversed, and the cause remanded to the district court of Louisiana, with directions to award a *venire facias de novo* [new trial].

NOTE

Superior Knowledge. The drafters of the Restatement (Third) of Torts: Liability for Economic Harm note:

> One party often knows more than the other about the subject of an exchange between them. That difference, without more, creates no obligation of disclosure. Better information is a legitimate advantage at the bargaining table, and the law encourages its acquisition.

Restatement (Third) of Torts: Liability for Economic Harm § 13 cmt. d (Tentative Draft No. 2, 2014).

Swinton v. Whitinsville Savings Bank

Supreme Judicial Court of Massachusetts, 1942.
311 Mass. 677, 42 N.E.2d 808.

■ QUA, JUSTICE. The declaration alleges that on or about September 12, 1938, the defendant sold the plaintiff a house in Newton to be occupied by the plaintiff and his family as a dwelling; that at the time of the sale the house "was infested with termites, an insect that is most dangerous and destructive to buildings"; that the defendant knew the house was so infested; that the plaintiff could not readily observe this condition upon inspection; that "knowing the internal destruction that these insects were creating in said house," the defendant falsely and fraudulently concealed from the plaintiff its true condition; that the plaintiff at the time of his purchase had no knowledge of the termites, exercised due care thereafter, and learned of them about August 30, 1940; and that, because of the destruction that was being done and the dangerous condition that was being created by the termites, the plaintiff was put to great expense for repairs and for the installation of termite control in order to prevent the loss and destruction of said house.

There is no allegation of any false statement or representation, or of the uttering of a half truth which may be tantamount to a falsehood. There is no intimation that the defendant by any means prevented the plaintiff from acquiring information as to the condition of the house. There is nothing to show any fiduciary relation between the parties, or that the plaintiff stood in a position of confidence toward or dependence upon the defendant. So far as appears the parties made a business deal at arm's length. The charge is concealment and nothing more; and it is concealment in the simple sense of mere failure to reveal, with nothing to show any peculiar duty to speak. * * *

If this defendant is liable on this declaration every seller is liable who fails to disclose any nonapparent defect known to him in the subject of the sale which materially reduces its value and which the buyer fails to discover. Similarly it would seem that every buyer would be liable who fails to disclose any nonapparent virtue known to him in the subject of the purchase which materially enhances its value and of which the seller is ignorant. * The law has not yet, we believe, reached the point of imposing upon the frailties of human nature a standard so idealistic as this. That the particular case here stated by the plaintiff possesses a certain appeal to the moral sense is scarcely to be denied. Probably the reason is to be found in the facts that the infestation of buildings by termites has not been common in Massachusetts and constitutes a concealed risk against which buyers are off their guard. But the law cannot provide special rules for termites and can hardly attempt to determine liability according to the varying probabilities of the existence and discovery of different possible defects in the subjects of trade. * * *

The order sustaining the demurrer is affirmed, and judgment is to be entered for the defendant. *

NOTE

See also Note following *Ollerman v. O'Rourke Co., infra* page 817.

Campbell v. Booth

Court of Civil Appeals of Texas, 1975.
526 S.W.2d 167.

■ CLAUDE WILLIAMS, CHIEF JUSTICE. Waylon E. Campbell and Margaret J. Campbell brought this action against Don L. Booth and Janet B. Booth for damages, both actual and exemplary, alleged to have resulted from affirmative fraudulent concealment in the sale of real estate. * * *

Mr. and Mrs. Booth, the owners of the property in question, placed the property in the hands of a real estate broker to negotiate a sale. Mr. and Mrs. Campbell, on one or more occasions, inspected the house. During these inspection tours, made in company with the real estate agent, the Campbells did not observe anything out of the ordinary nor did they smell any offensive odors. The Campbells made an offer to purchase the house, and a contract for such sale was signed on August 31, 1973. A few days after the signing of the contract, Mr. and Mrs. Campbell and Mr. Campbell's mother again toured the house and did not detect any offensive odors. The sale was consummated about September 25, 1973, and the Booths vacated the premises about October 1, 1973. At the time the Booths left the house, it was locked, and there is no evidence that anyone entered the premises until about one week later on October 7, 1973, when the Campbells returned to take possession. On that date, when the Campbells opened the house, they immediately detected the offensive odor for the first time. This odor was determined to have been caused by canine urine which permeated most of the carpets in the house. * * * Thereafter, the carpets were taken up and removed. Samples of the damaged carpet were made and introduced into evidence. After replacing the damaged carpet with new carpet, the Campbells moved into the house. Mr. Campbell testified that he would not have entered into the contract for the purchase of the house had he been aware of the condition of the rugs which was discovered following the sale.

Mr. Campbell said that neither he nor his wife had any reason to suspect that there was anything wrong with the carpet prior to the closing of the contract of sale. When he and his wife entered the house, about two weeks later, they were confronted with the smell which they described as "horrible." He said: "It just smelled horrible. It wasn't just a little smell like the house had been closed up a week and without substantial ventilation, it just smelled horrible." At the time the Campbells inspected the house, prior to the purchase of same, they knew that the Booths had several dogs, two Dobermans, and a smaller dog as well as several cats. At that time they did not know that the dogs were allowed in the house but did see the cats in a closet. Mr. Campbell said that on one of his inspection trips through the house that he noticed at least one candle which was burning and that his wife and the agent who was showing the house also saw it. Concerning deodorizers, Mr. Campbell testified that he observed "airwick around all over the place," which he described as "little pull-up deals" and which would act as a deodorizer. He said that at least two of these were left in the house, one in the kitchen and one in the bathroom and that they had been pulled up but they did not get rid of the odor altogether. * * *

Appellees contend that the case is governed by the rule that fraud, because of silence as to a material fact, can only exist where the defrauded party did not have an equal opportunity to discover the true facts. That rule, however, does not apply to cases where, as here, the fraud resulted from affirmative acts of concealment. * * * [T]he evidence is sufficient to lead only to the conclusion that appellees utilized the scented candles and other deodorizers for the purpose of masking odors caused by animal urine so that a favorable atmosphere would thereby be created when potential purchasers of the house were present. * * * [W]e conclude that there is more than a mere suspicion or surmise concerning the elements of fraudulent concealment and also of damages resulting therefrom. The trial court should have submitted these issues to the jury.

The judgment of the trial court is reversed and remanded.

■ AKIN, J. (dissenting). * * * Plaintiffs allege that defendants fraudulently concealed the condition of the carpet from plaintiffs. With reference to fraudulent concealment, plaintiffs have suggested two theories: (a) that scented candles were burned during their three inspection tours of the house, thereby masking the odor of the alleged urine and (b) that the plaintiffs had used a powerful deodorant known as "Odors Away" plus Airwicks to conceal the alleged odor. Plaintiffs conclude from these inferences and the actual presence of the malodorous carpet that defendants fraudulently concealed the condition of the carpet from plaintiffs. I cannot agree. * * *

At the time the Campbells inspected the house, prior to the purchase contract being signed, they knew that the Booths had three dogs and two cats. They were aware that the cats and at least one of the dogs were kept in the house. The evidence here presents the classic *caveat emptor* situation. Not only did the Campbells know that the Booths had these dogs and cats but the contract of sale contained the following provisions:

> This contract is made and entered into subject to the purchaser having five (5) working days from the date of acceptance of this contract in which to make inspections * * *

This clause, coupled with the fact that the Campbells were aware that the Booths had both dogs and cats and the fact that Mr. Campbell was in the real estate business, should have placed them on reasonable notice to inspect the carpeting for alleged animal urine damage. Plaintiffs were on notice of this possibility, had ample opportunity to inspect the carpet, and should have done so. I conclude, therefore, that there was no evidence of probative value of any fraudulent concealment upon which a jury verdict could be based. The trial judge was, therefore, correct in withdrawing this case from the jury and instructing a verdict in favor of defendants. * * *

NOTE

Misrepresentation by Concealment. Affirmative acts of concealment of defects, or of other unattractive qualities of the object of a transaction, have long been considered the equivalent of fraudulent misrepresentation. See, e.g., Southern v. Floyd, 89 Ga.App. 602, 80 S.E.2d 490 (1954) (seller concealed break in furnace boiler with temporary filling); Griffith v. Byers

Constr. Co., 212 Kan. 65, 510 P.2d 198 (1973) (defendant-developer graded, developed, and advertised for sale, for use as homesites, part of an abandoned oil field containing salt water disposal areas that were concealed by the grading); see also Nicolet, Inc. v. Nutt, 525 A.2d 146 (Del.1987) (alleged conspiracy among members of trade associations to actively suppress medical information on hazards of exposure to asbestos). A classic example of common law concealment has been the tampering with an automobile's odometer, now also subject to statutory penalties and actions for damages under 49 U.S.C. §§ 32701 *et seq.* (2012).

Damon v. Sun Co.

United States Court of Appeals for the First Circuit, 1996.
87 F.3d 1467.

■ TORRUELLA, CHIEF JUDGE. * * * Defendant Sun Oil Company, Inc. (R & M) ("Sun") * * * built a gasoline station with underground storage tanks on the property and operated a retail gasoline station thereafter until November 1977. On or about December 19, 1974, a leaking underground pipe leading from the underground storage tanks to the pumps released approximately 2,000 gallons of gasoline. Sun's regional manager of operations, Robert Laubinger ("Laubinger"), was on the property after the leak was discovered. On November 21, 1979, the plaintiffs, Roy and Eleanor Damon, purchased the property from Sun for $90,000. The plaintiffs had a right to examine the property by terms of the Agreement of Sale. The Damons owned the property from 1979 to March 25, 1992 and operated a retail service station at the property from June 12, 1980 to January 31, 1991.

On January 31, 1991, the plaintiffs leased the property to K. Rooney, Inc. ("Rooney"). Since then, Rooney has operated a retail service station on the property. In November 1991, Rooney began upgrading the station * * *. As digging commenced, the Abington Fire Department observed petroleum product pooling in the surface excavations, shut down the construction and notified the Massachusetts Department of Environmental Protection ("DEP"). * * * As a result of the discovery of the pollution, Rooney refused to pay rent from November 1991 to March 1992. [Rooney subsequently purchased the property for $345,000, substantially discounted from the option price in the rental agreement between Rooney and plaintiffs of $600,000.] * * *

The district court's additional findings of fact included the following. A rupture of an elbow joint in the pipe which connects the tanks and the pumps caused the 1974 spill, which closed the station for approximately six weeks. In June or July 1979, Damon attempted to reach Richard Bunzell ("Bunzell"), whose name was given on the "For Sale" sign at the station. After some unsuccessful attempts to reach Bunzell, a Sun telephone operator referred Damon to Laubinger, Sun's regional manager for service station maintenance. The questions Damon asked Laubinger * * * included * * * whether Sun had experienced any problems with the station, particularly with the underground tanks. Laubinger knew of the 1974 spill, but did not reveal it. Rather, he answered that it was a "good station" which just needed to be run by a good operator to be successful. After his phone conversation with Laubinger, Damon contacted Bunzell and, after some negotiation, accepted his offer of $90,000. In late August 1979, Damon and Bunzell met at the property to view the property. Damon asked about a depression he noticed in the blacktop near the pumps and Bunzell explained it was caused by the installation of the first stage of a vapor recovery system. In response to Damon's question of whether Sun had had any problems with the underground storage tanks, Bunzell stated, "No, we've had no problems with it. It's all good." * * *

The Damons brought suit against Sun, alleging common law misrepresentation * * *. The district court, after a four day bench trial, found for the Damons on * * * the misrepresentation * * * count[ ], awarding them $245,000 plus reasonable attorney's fees and costs. * * *

* * * Here, the alleged false representations are the statements made by Sun's representatives that it was a "good" station, upon which Damon relied in his purchasing decision. The alleged harm suffered was that the Damons bought a gas station in 1979 that would have been worth more in 1992 if what the defendant's representatives stated had in fact been true. The damages were measured by the difference between the value of the property if it had been uncontaminated, as the defendant represented, and the actual value of the property as contaminated. * * *

Our review of the record leads us to affirm the district court's finding that the statements were factual in nature. * * * The court found that Damon asked Bunzell if Sun had had any problems with the underground storage tanks, to which Bunzell responded that Sun had had "no problems with it. It's all good." * * * The district court also found that although Laubinger knew about the 1974 spill—indeed, he visited the property at the time—he did not reveal the information to Damon. Instead, he responded to Damon's questions about whether Sun had any problems with the station, particularly with the underground tanks, by stating "that it was a 'good station' which just needed to be run by a good operator to be successful." * * *

Next, in discussing whether the Bunzell and Laubinger statements were opinions or fact, the district court noted that Damon's questions were not just about the current conditions on the property. If they had been, their statements that it was a good station would presumably have been opinion. Rather, the district court specified that the questions also went to whether there had been problems in the station in the past of which Damon should be aware, with the underground tanks specifically. In that context, reading the record in the light most favorable to the Damons, we do not find that the district court erred in finding that the Sun representatives' statements that it was a "good station" were factual. Indeed, we are hard put to see how, where there has been a spill of 2,000 gallons in 1974, which Sun knew of, statements five years later that it was a "good station" and that Sun had had "no problems with it" in reply to a question regarding the underground tanks are not misrepresentations of fact. * * *

Sun tries to fend off this conclusion by pointing out that "[s]ellers . . . are not liable in fraud for failing to disclose every latent defect known to them which reduces materially the value of the property and of which the buyer is ignorant." Nei v. Burley, 388 Mass. 307, 310, 446 N.E.2d 674, 676 (1983). However, it is well established that "in Massachusetts . . . a party who discloses partial information that may be misleading has a duty to reveal all the material facts he [or she] knows to avoid deceiving the other party." V.S.H. Realty, Inc. v. Texaco, Inc., 757 F.2d 411, 415 (1st Cir.1985); cf. Nei, 446 N.E.2d at 676 * * *. Accordingly, we find Maxwell v. Ratcliffe, 356 Mass. 560, 562, 254 N.E.2d 250, 252 (1969), analogous to the Damons' position. In that case, potential buyers of a house asked whether the cellar was dry, and the brokers represented that it was, when they had, or should have had, knowledge that there was periodic water seepage. The Court found that "because the question of the dryness of the cellar had been raised expressly, there was special obligation on the brokers to avoid half truths and to make disclosure at least of any facts known to them or with respect to which they had been put on notice." *

Sun also seeks support from the fact that Damon signed an agreement representing that he had inspected the property and would indemnify Sun from and against liability for violation of environmental laws. However, "Massachusetts case law unequivocally rejects assertion of an 'as is' clause as an automatic defense against allegations of fraud." V.S.H. Realty, Inc., 757 F.2d at 418 (noting also that Uniform Commercial Code § 2–316, which allows disclaimers in the sale of goods between merchants, does not preclude claims based on fraud) * * *.

* * * [W]e affirm the decision of the district court on all points.

B.N. v. K.K.

Court of Appeals of Maryland, 1988.
312 Md. 135, 538 A.2d 1175.

■ ADKINS, JUDGE. This is a case certified to us by the United States District Court for the District of Maryland pursuant to the Maryland Uniform Certification of Questions of Law Act. * The certified question is:

Does Maryland Recognize A Cause of Action for Either Fraud, Intentional Infliction Of Emotional Distress, Or Negligence Resulting From the Sexual Transmission Of A Dangerous, Contagious, and Incurable Disease, Such As Genital Herpes? * * *

In this case, appellant, B.N. (Ms. N.), has sued appellee, K.K. (Dr. K.), in the United States District Court, under that court's diversity jurisdiction. 28 U.S.C. § 1332. * * * Between July and December 1983, Ms. N. was employed as a nurse at Johns Hopkins Hospital in Baltimore. For part of the period, Dr. K. also worked there. From July through October of that year, Ms. N. and Dr. K. "were involved in an intimate boyfriend-girlfriend relationship" and "engaged in acts of sexual intercourse." While this was going on, Dr. K. knew he had genital herpes, but never disclosed that fact to Ms. N., who neither knew nor had any reason to believe that Dr. K. "was a carrier of genital herpes." On or about 1 October 1983, Ms. N. and Dr. K. engaged in sexual intercourse. On that date Dr. K. knew that his disease was active and would be transmitted to Ms. N. through sexual intercourse. That result in fact occurred and was caused by Dr. K.'s conduct, Ms. N. never having engaged in sexual contact with anyone but Dr. K. during the relevant period. On the basis of these general allegations, as well as some others contained in particular counts, to some of which we shall later refer, Ms. N. charged Dr. K. with fraud * * *.

It is true that this tort is usually applied in a business setting, or to one in which some pecuniary loss is claimed. Restatement (Second) of Torts § 525 cmt. h (1977). Obviously, this is not that kind of case. But a business setting and pecuniary loss are not necessarily required. See Fleming James & Oscar S. Gray, Misrepresentation—Part I, 37 Md. L. Rev. 286, 286 (1977) (misrepresentation "usually, but not necessarily, involves a business transaction between" the parties). * * *

In Maharam v. Maharam, 123 A.D.2d 165, 510 N.Y.S.2d 104 (1986), a husband concealed from his wife the fact that he had genital herpes. She sued him for wrongful transmission of the disease. The court concluded that she had established a cause of action in fraud, in part because the marital relationship imposed upon him a duty to speak. * Dr. K. distinguishes this case from * * * Maharam because here, according to him, there was no duty to speak since there was no marital or other confidential relationship between the parties. Of course, concealment cannot be the basis of an action in deceit if there is no duty to speak. But if there is such a duty, the concealment can result in liability to the same extent that an actual denial of the existence of the fact would. * See also Restatement (Second) of Torts § 557A (1977). * The question, then, is whether Dr. K. had such a duty.

The parties debate that issue in terms of whether there was a confidential relationship between them. * * * Its resolution is essentially one of fact, for absent some relationship, such as a fiduciary one, which is presumptively confidential, the nature of the relationship—whether one party justifiably placed confidence in the other and whether the other accepted that placement—is for a fact-finder to decide. * Other courts have found relationships of trust and confidence in purely personal relationships.

> The term [fiduciary] connotes the idea of trust or confidence, contemplates good faith, rather than legal obligation as the basis of the transaction; refers to the integrity, the fidelity of the party trusted, rather than his credit or ability. It has been held to include those informal relations which exist whenever one party trusts and relies on another, as well as technical fiduciary relations.

Brown v. Foulks, 232 Kan. 424, 430, 657 P.2d 501, 505–06 (1983). See also Lowrance v. Patton, 710 P.2d 108, 111–12 (Okla.1985) ("The relationship need not be legal but it may be either moral, social, domestic or merely personal. Therefore, a fiduciary relationship which is recognized and enforced equitably does not rest on any particular legal relationship"); and Thigpen v. Locke, 363 S.W.2d 247, 253 (Tex.1963) ("a relationship of trust and confidence may be shown to arise informally from purely personal relationships"). And see Jewish Ctr. of Sussex Cnty. v. Whale, 165 N.J. Super. 84, 397 A.2d 712 (Ch.Div.1978), aff'd, 172 N.J. Super. 165, 411 A.2d 475 (App.Div.1980), aff'd, 86 N.J. 619, 432 A.2d 521 (1981) (nature of relationship between clergyman and congregation is such that the former, when seeking a spiritual leadership position, has the duty to disclose prior acts of moral turpitude).

We are not about to decide that only a marital relationship would impose a duty to disclose a contagious disease transmitted by sexual relations. We have recognized that if the likelihood of physical harm is present, certain tort duties may arise under circumstances in which they otherwise would not. * Also, the Restatement (Second) of Torts § 557A and cmt. a (1977) states that "[o]ne who by . . . nondisclosure of a fact that it is his duty to disclose causes physical harm to the person . . . is subject to liability . . . " in a tort action of deceit. It may be that an ongoing "intimate boyfriend-girlfriend relationship" may give rise to a duty to speak under circumstances like those alleged in this case. As the Kathleen K. v. Robert B., 150 Cal.App.3d 992, 997, 198 Cal.Rptr. 273, 276–77 (Cal.App.1984) court said, "a certain amount of trust and confidence exists in any intimate relationship. . . ."

But the existence of a confidential relationship is not essential to Ms. N.'s cause of action for fraud because * * * Dr. K. had a general tort duty, at the least, to disclose his condition before engaging in intercourse with her. See Restatement (Second) of Torts § 557A cmt. a (1977). That duty he breached, according to the allegations of the complaint. That is, whether the relationship between Ms. N. and Dr. K. was "confidential" in the eyes of the law or whether it was not, it was a relationship which had to make Dr. K. aware that to engage in sexual intercourse with Ms. N. without disclosing his condition would be highly likely to produce severe harm to a readily and clearly identifiable person. *

Whether Ms. N. reasonably relied upon the implicit representation of good health that resulted from Dr. K.'s nondisclosure is a question of fact depending to some degree on the nature of their relationship; she has alleged reasonable reliance. The implicit misrepresentation was obviously a material one; Ms. N. asserts that she never would have engaged in sex with Dr. K. had she known the truth; she also avers that she suffered damage directly from the misrepresentation. Consequently, she has also stated a cause of action for fraud that is recognized in Maryland.

NOTES

1. *A Fiduciary or Confidential Relationship.* A proposed section to the Restatement (Third) of Torts: Liability for Economic Harm provides that one party to a transaction has a duty "to disclose material information" if "the actor is in a fiduciary or confidential relationship with another that obliges the actor to make disclosures." Restatement (Third) of Torts: Liability for Economic Harm § 13(c) (Tentative Draft No. 2, 2014). A comment to the provisions explains:

> "Confidential relationships" are defined less formally than fiduciary relationships but have similar consequences * * *. They arise when one party is bound to act in good faith for the benefit of the other because they have a relationship of trust; typically one of the parties has gained a position of substantial influence over the other. Such relationships often develop within families.

Restatement (Third) of Torts: Liability for Economic Harm § 13, cmt. b (Tentative Draft No. 2, 2014). Courts have applied this duty to disclose to the relationships between a physician and a patient, e.g., Nixdorf v.

Hicken, 612 P.2d 348, 354 (Utah 1980). and between long-time social friends, e.g., Bickhardt v. Ratner, 871 F.Supp. 613, 618–19 (S.D.N.Y.1994).

2. *Duty to Disclose Presence of a Sexually Transmitted Disease.* The failure to disclose the presence of a sexually transmitted disease to a spouse or paramour may give rise to liability in negligence (as distinguished from negligent misrepresentation or fraud) to those foreseeably endangered by the risk of infection. This negligence liability (as distinguished from fraud) is based on the general proposition that a person with any contagious disease should take reasonable care to prevent its spread. See Mussivand v. David, 45 Ohio St.3d 314, 544 N.E.2d 265 (1989) (potential liability in negligence to paramour's spouse; no liability to the spouse in fraud because reliance by the spouse on the defendant would not have been justifiable in the circumstances, their relationship not being one based on "friendship or trust").

Ollerman v. O'Rourke Co.

Supreme Court of Wisconsin, 1980.
94 Wis.2d 17, 288 N.W.2d 95.

■ ABRAHAMSON, JUSTICE. * * * [T]he buyer alleges that on or about May 15, 1974 he entered into a written offer to purchase a vacant lot * * * for an agreed price of $12,600; that on or about June 4, 1974, the seller conveyed the lot to the buyer by a warranty deed; that the buyer purchased the lot to build a house; and that in the process of excavating for the house, a well on the property was uncapped and water was released.

The complaint further alleges that the seller is a corporation engaged in the business of developing and selling real estate; that it is experienced in matters of real estate; that it had owned and subdivided the area of real estate in which the subject lot is located; that it was offering the subject lot and other lots in the same area for public sale; that it is familiar with the particular area of real estate in which the lot is located; that the area is zoned residential and that the seller knew it was zoned residential.

The complaint further states that the buyer "was a stranger to the area"; that he was inexperienced in matters of real estate transactions; that he purchased the lot to construct a house; that he did not know of the existence of a well under the land surface hidden from view; that if he had known of the well, he either would not have purchased the property or would have purchased it at a lower price; that the well constituted a defective condition of the lot; that the well made the property worth less for residential purposes than he had been led to believe; that the well made the property unsuitable for building without added expense; and that the seller's failure to disclose the existence of the well was relied upon by the buyer and he was thereby induced to buy this lot in ignorance of the well.

The buyer further alleges that he incurred additional expenses for water control and construction costs because of the well * * *.

Additional allegations applicable to what is labeled in the complaint as the "first cause of action" are that the seller, through its agents, knew of the existence of the underground well and, in order to induce buyer to buy the land, "falsely and with intent to defraud," failed to disclose this fact which it had a duty to disclose and which would have had a material bearing on the construction of a residence on the property. * * * The circuit court, without disclosing its rationale, overruled the seller's motion to dismiss the amended complaint for failure to state a claim upon which relief can be granted. * * * On appeal, the seller argues that the complaint fails to state a claim upon which relief can be granted [on the grounds that] * * * the complaint does not state a claim for actionable intentional misrepresentation because, as a matter of law, the seller had no duty to disclose the existence of the well. * * *

We discuss first whether the complaint states a claim for intentional misrepresentation. Initially we observe, as did the seller, that the complaint does not allege the first two elements of the tort of intentional misrepresentation, namely that the seller made a representation of fact and that the representation was untrue. The gravamen of the wrong is the nature of the false words used and the reliance which they may reasonably induce. In lieu of these allegations of false words, the complaint recites that the seller failed to disclose a fact, the existence of the well. The general rule is that silence, a failure to disclose a fact, is not an intentional misrepresentation unless the seller has a duty to disclose.[7] If there is a duty to disclose a fact, failure to disclose that fact is treated in the law as equivalent to a representation of the nonexistence of the fact. In Southard v. Occidental Life Ins. Co., 31 Wis.2d 351, 359, 142 N.W.2d 844, 848 (1966), we said:

> A person in a business deal must be under a duty to disclose a material fact before he can be charged with a failure to disclose. Restatement (Second) of Torts § 551(1) states the rule as follows: "One who fails to disclose to another a thing [Sic; "a fact" in Restatement] which he knows may justifiably induce the other to act or refrain from acting in a business transaction is subject to the same liability to the other as though he had represented the nonexistence of the matter which he has failed to disclose, if, but only if, he is under a duty to the other to exercise reasonable care to disclose the matter in question."[8]

The question thus presented in the case at bar is whether the seller had a duty to disclose to the buyer the existence of the well. If there is a duty to disclose, the seller incurs tort liability for intentional misrepresentation (i.e. the representation of the non-existence of the fact), if the elements of the tort of intentional misrepresentation are proved. *

---

[7] Restatement (Second) of Torts § 551, cmt. b (1977) states: ". . . In the absence of a duty of disclosure . . . one who is negotiating a business transaction is not liable in deceit because of his failure to disclose a fact that he knows his adversary would regard as material. . . . "

[8] Comment *d* to sec. 551 of the Restatement explains that "reasonable care to disclose" refers to the means of transmitting the information to the proper party if there is a duty to disclose:

> d. Under the rule stated in this Subsection the person under a duty of disclosure is not subject to liability merely because he has failed to bring the required information home to the person entitled to it. His duty is to exercise reasonable care to do so. If reasonable care is exercised, the fact that the information does not reach the person entitled to it does not subject him to liability. . . .

551(2)(e) is the "catch-all" provision setting forth conditions under which a duty to disclose exists; it states that a party to a transaction is under a duty to exercise reasonable care to disclose to the other "facts basic to the transaction, if he knows that the other is about to enter into it under a mistake as to them, and that the other, because of the relationship between them, the customs of the trade or other objective circumstances, would reasonably expect a disclosure of those facts." Section 551, comment *l* recognizes the difficulty of specifying the factors that give rise to a reasonable expectation of disclosure:

> The continuing development of modern business ethics has, however, limited to some extent this privilege to take advantage of ignorance. There are situations in which the defendant not only knows that his bargaining adversary is acting under a mistake basic to the transaction, but also knows that the adversary, by reason of the relation between them, the customs of the trade or other objective circumstances, is reasonably relying upon a disclosure of the unrevealed fact if it exists. In this type of case good faith and fair dealing may require a disclosure.

> It is extremely difficult to be specific as to the factors that give rise to this known, and reasonable, expectation of disclosure. In general, the cases in which the rule stated in Clause (e) has been applied have been those in which the advantage taken of the plaintiff's ignorance is so shocking to the ethical sense of the community, and is so extreme and unfair, as to amount to a form of swindling, in which the plaintiff is led by appearances into a bargain that is a trap, of whose essence and substance he is unaware. In such a case, even in a tort action for deceit, the plaintiff is entitled to be compensated for the loss that he has sustained.

Section 551(2)(e) of the Restatement (Second) of Torts limits the duty to disclose to disclosure of those "facts basic" to the transaction. Section 551 comment *j* differentiates between basic facts and material facts as follows:

> A basic fact is a fact that is assumed by the parties as a basis for the transaction itself. It is a fact that goes to the basis, or essence, of the transaction, and is an important part of the substance of what is bargained for or dealt with. Other facts may serve as important and persuasive inducements to enter into the transaction, but not go to its essence. These facts may be material, but they are not basic. * * *

This court has moved away from the rule of caveat emptor in real estate transactions, as have courts in other states. * * * An analysis of the cases of this jurisdiction and others indicates that the presence of the following elements is significant to persuade a court of the fairness and equity of imposing a duty on a vendor of real estate to disclose known facts: the condition is "latent" and not readily observable by the purchaser; the purchaser acts upon the reasonable assumption that the condition does (or does not) exist; the vendor has special knowledge or means of knowledge not available to the purchaser; and the existence of the condition is material to the transaction, that is, it influences whether the transaction is concluded at all or at the same price. * * *

The seller's position is that imposing a duty to disclose on a vendor of real estate dealing at arm's length with a purchaser would result in an element of uncertainty pervading real estate transactions; that there would be chaos if a vendor were subject to liability after parting with ownership and control of the property; that a rash of litigation would ensue; and that a purchaser could protect himself or herself by inspection and inquiry and by demanding warranties.

The seller's arguments are not persuasive in light of the facts alleged in the complaint and our narrow holding in this case. * Where the vendor is in the real estate business and is skilled and knowledgeable and the purchaser is not, the purchaser is in a poor position to discover a condition which is not readily discernible, and the purchaser may justifiably rely on the knowledge and skill of the vendor. Thus, in this instant case a strong argument for imposing a duty on the seller to disclose material facts is this "reliance factor." The buyer portrayed in this complaint had a reasonable expectation of honesty in the marketplace, that is, that the vendor would disclose material facts which it knew and which were not readily discernible. Under these circumstances the law should impose a duty of honesty on the seller.

In order to determine whether the complaint in the case at bar states a claim for intentional misrepresentation we hold that a subdivider-vendor of a residential lot has a duty to a "non-commercial" purchaser to disclose facts which are known to the vendor, which are material to the transaction, and which are not readily discernible to the purchaser. A fact is known to the vendor if the vendor has actual knowledge of the fact or if the vendor acted in reckless disregard as to the existence of the fact. * * *

The seller's brief asserts that the well is not a material fact because it does not constitute a defective condition; that the existence of the well was well known in the community; * and that the buyer should have made inquiry about the lot. These are matters to be raised at trial, not on a motion to dismiss. The buyer must prove at trial that the existence of the well was a material fact and that his reliance was justifiable. * * *

For the reasons set forth, we hold that the allegations of the complaint state a claim upon which relief can be granted and that the motion to dismiss the complaint was properly overruled. * * *

NOTE

Failure to Disclose Termite Damage. With Swinton v. Whitinsville Savings Bank, *supra* pages 804, compare Saporta v. Barbagelata, 220 Cal.App.2d 463, 33 Cal.Rptr. 661 (1963); Mulkey v. Waggoner, 177 Ga.App. 165, 338 S.E.2d 755 (1985).

E. PLAINTIFF'S CONDUCT: JUSTIFIABLE RELIANCE

Seeger v. Odell

Supreme Court of California, 1941.
18 Cal.2d 409, 115 P.2d 977.

■ TRAYNOR, JUSTICE. * * * [The plaintiffs were an elderly couple who owned a lot. Mary Gibbs, the holder of a note and mortgage on the plaintiffs' property, secured a final judgment of foreclosure on the property. Shortly thereafter, the defendant and Gibbs asked the plaintiffs to attend a conference regarding the property where the original holders of the note and mortgage, William A. McAdoo and R.T. Colter, also were present.] * * * At the conference, McAdoo, Colter, Gibbs and Odell were represented by their attorney, Ben H. Neblett. Neblett told plaintiffs that as an attorney he had superior knowledge of many facts concerning the land and that they could rely upon all he had to say. McAdoo and Colter had previously secured a money judgment against plaintiffs in another action, and Neblett stated that, acting on behalf of Colter and McAdoo, he had secured an execution on plaintiffs' land to satisfy the judgment, that the sheriff had levied on the land and sold it to McAdoo and Colter for the amount of the judgment debt * * *. Neblett went on to assure the plaintiffs, however, that he and his clients were plaintiffs' friends and would make an unselfish proposal solely to enable the plaintiffs to receive some return from the land out of which they would otherwise get nothing. The proposal was that plaintiffs join with Mary Gibbs in a lease of the land to Odell for the purpose of drilling for oil, with the understanding that they would receive a specific royalty from the oil produced.

The complaint further alleges: The plaintiffs believed Neblett's representation that their land had been sold at an execution sale to Colter and McAdoo. They therefore joined in executing a lease to Odell and made no attempt to pay the mortgage debt or to exercise the equity of redemption after the foreclosure sale, although during this period many persons offered to lease the land from them with advances sufficient to cover the mortgage indebtedness. After Mary Gibbs bought in the property at the foreclosure sale in August, 1933, Odell took possession under his lease and drilled a well, from which he has received profits of more than $100,000.

The complaint alleges further: No execution actually had been levied on the land. The representation that the land had been sold to McAdoo and Colter was known to be false by Neblett and his clients. It was made to induce the plaintiffs to refrain from paying the mortgage indebtedness or from exercising their equity of redemption and to induce them to join in leasing the property to Odell. Plaintiffs did not discover the falsity of the representations until May, 1936. The records covering the facts involved were situated in a city at some distance from the city where plaintiffs reside. They are both elderly; neither drives an automobile; and they had no reason to suspect that the representations were false. Following the discovery of the misrepresentation, plaintiffs notified Odell of their rescission of the lease. They then brought this action against Odell, McAdoo, Colter, and Gibbs, asking that the foreclosure sale to Mary Gibbs be set aside, that the title to the property be quieted in them except as to existent sub-leases in the hands of innocent sublessees, and that a judgment be awarded them for all moneys received as royalties by Mary Gibbs or her assigns from the oil well and for all moneys received by Odell from the oil well. Plaintiffs offer to do all things required of them by the court, including the paying of the mortgage indebtedness on the property. * * *

It is well established in California and other jurisdictions that a person who has been induced by fraudulent misrepresentations to enter into a contract or to make a conveyance may have the contract or conveyance set aside and secure a restitution of those benefits lost to him by the transaction. * * * It must appear, however, not only that the plaintiff acted in reliance on the misrepresentation but that he was justified in his reliance. * He may not justifiably rely upon mere statements of opinion, including legal conclusions drawn from a true state of facts *, unless the person expressing the opinion purports to have expert knowledge concerning the matter or occupies a position of confidence and trust. * If, however, the opinion or legal conclusion misrepresents the facts upon which it is based or implies the existence of facts which are nonexistent, it constitutes an actionable misrepresentation. *

Negligence on the part of the plaintiff in failing to discover the falsity of a statement is no defense when the misrepresentation was intentional rather than negligent. * As a general rule negligence of the plaintiff is no defense to an intentional tort. * The fact that an investigation would have revealed the falsity of the misrepresentation will not alone bar his recovery, * and it is well established that he is not held to constructive notice of a public record which would reveal the true facts. * The purpose of the recording acts is to afford protection not to those who make fraudulent misrepresentations, but to *bona fide* purchasers for value. Nor is a plaintiff held to the standard of precaution or of minimum knowledge of a hypothetical, reasonable man. Exceptionally gullible or ignorant people have been permitted to recover from defendants who took advantage of them in circumstances where persons of normal intelligence would not have been misled. * "No rogue should enjoy his ill-gotten plunder for the simple reason that his victim is by chance a fool." Chamberlin v. Fuller, 59 Vt. 247, 9 A. 832, 836 (1887). If the conduct of the plaintiff in the light of his own intelligence and information was manifestly unreasonable, however, he will be denied a recovery. * "He may not put faith in representations which are preposterous, or which are shown by facts within his observation to be so patently and obviously false that he must have closed his eyes to avoid discovery of the truth. . . . " W[illiam L.] Prosser, Torts, 749.

In the present case the allegations of the plaintiffs' complaint, if true, are sufficient to establish the right to relief on the basis of a fraudulent misrepresentation. * * * The fact that an examination of the record would have revealed to plaintiffs the falsity of the representation or that they may have been negligent in failing to make further investigations does not bar their right to relief. The misrepresentation is not such that its falsity must have been so obvious to the plaintiffs as to preclude any justifiable reliance thereon by them. The defendants cannot urge as a defense that plaintiffs were more credulous than the average person. * * *

Because of the alleged fraudulent misrepresentation plaintiffs ask for a setting aside of the foreclosure sale to Mary Gibbs and a rescission of the lease to Odell, with an accounting of the profits received by these defendants from the property. * * * As a condition of restitution, however, the plaintiffs must restore to the defendants any benefits which they have received as a result of the transaction. * Plaintiffs must therefore pay to Mary Gibbs the amount of the mortgage debt before they can recover the property. A restoration of the royalties received by plaintiffs is not necessary since they need not restore property which is rightfully theirs. * It is well established that a court granting equitable relief has the power to make its decrees contingent upon compliance by the plaintiff with certain conditions. * The interests of the defendants can thus be well protected by a decree making any relief granted to plaintiffs conditional upon their paying the mortgage debt. * * *

Defendants finally contend that plaintiffs are barred from a recovery by the statute of limitations and laches. In California the statute of limitations in an action based upon fraud begins to run from the time when the fraud was discovered or should reasonably have been discovered. * It is necessary for a plaintiff to allege facts showing that suit was brought within a reasonable time after discovery of the fraud without unnecessary delay and that failure to make the discovery sooner was not due to negligence. * The present action was brought more than three years after the date when the misrepresentation was allegedly made but only sixty days after it was discovered. Plaintiffs allege that the discovery did not occur sooner because of their advanced age, the considerable distance of the available records from their home, and the absence of any occasion on their part to examine the records or otherwise inquire into the truth of the representation. The alleged facts, if believed, would justify a trial court in finding that the plaintiffs were sufficiently diligent in discovering the fraud, and that the action was brought within a reasonable time thereafter.

The judgment is reversed.

NOTES

1.   *Justifiable Reliance.* To recover in a misrepresentation action, the plaintiff must prove not only that she relied on the misrepresentations of the defendant, but also that her reliance was justifiable. Why, based upon the opinion, is the term "justifiable" preferable to the word "reasonable" in this context? Cf. Field v. Mans, 516 U.S. 59, 71–75, 116 S.Ct. 437, 444–46, 133 L.Ed.2d 351, 362–65 (1995); Guiggey v. Bombardier, 615 A.2d 1169, 1173 (Me.1992). Some courts purport to require diligence on the part of victims of fraud, as a requisite of justifiable reliance, if the facts in question are not "peculiarly within" the fraudulent party's knowledge. Cf. Mallis v. Bankers Trust Co., 615 F.2d 68, 80–81 (2d Cir.1980), cert. denied, 449 U.S. 1123, 101 S.Ct. 938, 67 L.Ed.2d 109 (1981).

Should the standard of diligence expected from a sophisticated business institution be different from that expected of the ordinary consumer? See Hercules & Co. v. Shama Rest. Corp., 613 A.2d 916, 933 (D.C.1992) (recognizing "support for the proposition" that the "reasonableness" requirement has been eliminated for reliance by consumers on misrepresentations of entrepreneurs, but retaining *caveat emptor*, and the reasonableness requirement, in the "commercial arena" involving "sophisticated business institutions dealing with each other on a level playing field"). Compare Nader v. Allegheny Airlines, Inc., 626 F.2d 1031, 1032–1033, 1036 (D.C.Cir.1980), where lawyer and consumer advocate Ralph Nader had a "confirmed reservation" on a flight operated by Allegheny Airlines. However, when the plaintiff Nader arrived at the boarding area shortly before the scheduled take-off, he was told that the flight was already full. The plaintiff filed suit, alleging common law intentional misrepresentation, among other claims. After an earlier round of appeals, including an appeal to the United States Supreme Court on collateral issues, the trial court found that the defendant Allegheny had a duty to disclose "that its policy of deliberate overbooking qualified the meaning of a 'confirmed reservation'[.] * * * [I]ts failure to disclose amounted to a false representation, and * * * Nader had proved the other elements of the tort of fraudulent misrepresentation." It awarded Nader $10 in compensatory damages and $15,000 in punitive damages. In reversing the judgment, the Court of Appeals stated:

> The plaintiff Nader was an extraordinarily knowledgeable passenger, an able lawyer and a famous and distinguished advocate of consumer rights, including the rights of airline passengers. * * * [T]he evidence demonstrates that Nader "knew the facts" that a confirmed reservation did not exclude the possibility that he might not be boarded. "(O)ne who has special knowledge, experience and competence may not be permitted to rely on statements for which the ordinary man might recover." W[illiam L.] Prosser, Law of Torts § 108 at 717 (4th ed. 1971). It cannot be said that Nader relied on his confirmed reservation with Allegheny as a guarantee of passage.

Id. at 1037–1038.

2. *Intentional Misrepresentation and Comparative Fault.* The drafters of the Restatement (Third) of Torts: Liability for Economic Harm § 11 cmt. d (Tentative Draft No. 2, 2014) state:

> Requiring justifiable reliance creates some tension with the usual rule that contributory negligence is no defense to an intentional-tort claim. * * * The requirement does not impose a duty of active investigation on a plaintiff, and does not entitle a defendant to exploit a plaintiff's foolishness with impunity; if the defendant has deliberately preyed on the plaintiff's inattention, that inattention should not be considered an instance of unjustifiable reliance.

At least one court has applied comparative fault principles to a plaintiff's intentional misrepresentation action. Bank Brussels Lambert v. Chase Manhattan Bank, N.A., 1999 WL 710778 (S.D.N.Y.1999). A few states now apply comparative fault to intentional torts in general. See, e.g., Blazovic v. Andrich, 124 N.J. 90, 107, 590 A.2d 222, 231 (1991); see also generally Restatement (Third) of Torts: Apportionment of Liability § 1(c) (2000) (intentional torts should not necessarily preclude comparison with culpability of plaintiff's conduct, but should be included within a single system of apportioning liability). Most jurisdictions continue to reject the application of contributory negligence or comparative fault to intentional misrepresentation actions. E.g., Gen. Motors Acceptance Corp. v. Central Nat'l Bank of Mattoon, 773 F.2d 771, 782 (7th Cir.1985); Carroll v. Gava,

98 Cal.App.3d 892, 159 Cal.Rptr. 778 (1979); Radford v. J.J.B. Enters., Ltd., 163 Wis.2d 534, 472 N.W.2d 790 (App.1991).

3. *Indirect Reliance and Fraud on the Market.* Restatement (Second) of Torts § 533 (1977) allows the plaintiff to satisfy the reliance element by proving "indirect reliance" in a situation in which the defendant makes a false representation to a third party who the defendant knows or has reason to expect will communicate the information to the plaintiff in such a manner as to influence the plaintiff's conduct in a transaction.

The United States Supreme Court extended this same basic idea one step further when it allowed defrauded investors to recover in class actions brought under federal securities fraud statutes without proving that particular investors individually relied, either directly or indirectly, on the security issuer's misrepresentations or omissions. Basic Inc. v. Levinson, 485 U.S. 224, 108 S.Ct. 978, 99 L.Ed.2d 194 (1988). Instead, the Court enabled plaintiffs to establish the reliance element by proving that they had purchased securities at market prices that were higher because of the defendant's misrepresentations or omissions, even though the defendant's statements were never communicated, either directly or indirectly, to the investors.

Courts in common law misrepresentation actions, however, typically refuse to substitute "fraud on the market" as an alternative to proving plaintiff's reliance and hold that "actual receipt and consideration of any misstatement remains central to the case of any plaintiff seeking to prove that he or she was deceived by the misstatement or omission." Kaufman v. i-Stat Corp., 165 N.J. 94, 118, 754 A.2d 1188, 1200 (2000). In *Kaufman*, the Supreme Court of New Jersey explained:

> The doctrine of indirect reliance has developed with careful consideration given to its impact. Indirect reliance occurs when a single communication, an inducement to engage in a fraudulent transaction, is clearly communicated to the defrauded party. The price of a publicly traded stock, however, synthesizes a great variety of information and conveys as much of that information as possible. But the information is jumbled. No one piece of information survives clearly enough that the share price can be said to have passed it on clearly. Until study or experience can prove that an impersonal mechanism can communicate a single idea clearly, indirect reliance should not be expanded to include this theoretical model of market performance and excuse this plaintiff from her obligation to show individual reliance on the alleged misrepresentation.

F. MEASURE OF DAMAGES

Selman v. Shirley

Supreme Court of Oregon, 1938.
161 Or. 582, 85 P.2d 384.

■ ROSSMAN, JUSTICE. * * * The property with which this suit is concerned is 160 acres of land * * * [that] the plaintiffs agreed to purchase * * * for a consideration of $2,000 * * *. The findings state: "The defendant, H. E. Shirley, knowingly and falsely represented to plaintiff that there was [sic] at least 4000 cords of wood on said premises; that said representations was [sic] false and was [sic] made by defendant H. E. Shirley with the intention of inducing plaintiffs to purchase said premises; that the plaintiffs in purchasing said premises relied upon said representations."

We have read carefully the transcript of evidence and are well satisfied that it fully supports the above findings. The uncontradicted testimony also indicates that Shirley represented that timber of that kind was worth fifty cents a cord as stumpage. These were material representations, and it is clear that the plaintiffs would not have signed the contract of purchase had they not been deceived into the belief that 4,000 cords of firewood were upon the place. * * * As a matter of fact there were only 200 cords of wood upon the property. * * *

The plaintiffs also claim that they were deceived by a representation that a stream which they saw upon their visit to the land in May, 1933, flowed throughout the year and supplied enough water to irrigate ten acres. Besides inquiring about the timber, the plaintiffs had also inquired of Blakely [defendant's real estate agent] about the stream. In a letter to them Blakely stated: "This stream does run the year round and the owner told me the next day after you were here that it is a dandy trout stream and that he has caught lots of trout in it. There is plenty of water in this stream, as I told you, to irrigate ten acres of the farm. You need have no fear that you wouldn't always have good water in this creek." Blakely knew nothing concerning the stream from his own observations and swore that the letter was a true narrative of Shirley's statement. A witness who had overheard the conversation between the two men corroborated Blakely, stating that Shirley had said, "It was a year round stream and that he (Shirley) had irrigated ten acres." * * * However, the witnesses swore that the stream dries up in the summer months and, under the best of circumstances, does not flow sufficient water to irrigate even a small garden patch. The circuit court found that Shirley had made the statement contained in Blakely's letter, but made no finding concerning its truthfulness. We are satisfied that the evidence warrants a conclusion that the representation was false.

The findings state that the property was "of the fair market value of $2,000 at the time said contract was entered into, to-wit: July 1, 1933; that plaintiffs have suffered no damages, having agreed to pay $2,000 for said premises." The sole issue upon which we deem it necessary to express an opinion is whether the plaintiffs are entitled to (1) the benefits of their bargain; or (2) no damages because the market value of the land equals the sum which they agreed to pay.

* * * [T]he plaintiffs retained possession of the property after they discovered the fraud which had been practiced upon them. It has been many times stated by this court that a defrauded party is not required to rescind the contract in order to sue for deceit, and that if he affirms the contract he does not thereby waive his right to recover damages for the fraud which had been practiced upon him.

The plaintiffs argue that they are entitled to the benefit of their bargain which contemplated that they should have, not only 160 acres of land, but also a growth of timber upon the land aggregating 4000 cords and a good irrigating stream; and that the rule which measures their damages should be based upon that premise. The defendants contend that this court has rejected the benefit-of-the-bargain rule in favor of the rule which grants damages equal only to the out-of-pocket loss. The rule championed by the plaintiffs would certainly be available if this action were based upon a warranty and were, therefore, contractual in nature. * * *

The rule which gives to the defrauded party the benefit of his bargain is favored by the textbook writers. The following is quoted from Williston on Contracts (Rev. Ed.) § 1392:

> Not all courts allow the same damages to a buyer who has been induced to buy by fraudulent representations and sues for the deceit as to a buyer who sues for breach of warranty. The contrary view, confining the damages in deceit to the value of what the plaintiff parted with, less the value of what he received, has the support of the Supreme Court of the United States, and of some state courts. * * * At first sight it may seem that the latter rule is clearly and universally correct, confining as it does the plaintiff's recovery to a restitution of what he lost by entering into the transaction. The real explanation of the broader rule, at least in cases of sales of goods, seems to be that the defendant in deceit is not simply a fraudulent person; he is a warrantor of the truth of his statements. The injured person may, because of fraud, elect to rescind the transaction and claim restitution of what he has parted with, or he may demand that the representations be made good. Ordinary warranties where no fraud exists may be enforced by action of tort. The addition of the element of deceit cannot deprive the injured person of the rights which would be his if this element were lacking, and if the representation on which he relied were a warranty and nothing more. * * * A practical reason for the enforcement of the broader rule may be found in the fact that under the other rule a fraudulent person can in no event lose anything by his fraud. He runs the chance of making a profit if he successfully carries out his plan and is not afterward brought to account for it; and if he is brought to account, he at least will lose nothing by his misconduct. . . . Any universal statement, therefore, that the damages for fraudulent misrepresentation are the difference between the law governing sales of goods and that governing other transactions may explain some apparently inconsistent decisions. * * *

The rule is thus stated in 27 C.J., Fraud, § 243, p. 92:

> The measure of the damages sustained by the purchaser where a purchase has been induced by fraud, is according to the weight of authority, the difference between the real value of the property purchased and the value which it would have had had the representations been true. This rule is based upon the theory that a defrauded party is entitled to the benefit of his bargain and should be placed in the same position that he would have occupied had the false representations upon which he acted been true. * * *

However, the Restatement of the Law of Torts § 549, embraces the out-of-pocket-loss rule. We quote from it the following:

> The measure of damages which the recipient of a fraudulent misrepresentation is entitled to recover from its maker as damages under the rule stated in § 525 is the pecuniary loss which results from the falsity of the matter misrepresented, including
>
> (a) the difference between the value of the thing bought, sold or exchanged and its purchase price or the value of the thing exchanged for it * * *.

Williston on Contracts (Rev. Ed.) § 1392, referring to the section of the Restatement just quoted, declares that it "adopts the minority rule." Professor Williston continues that under the maxim adopted by the Restatement, "if fraudulent representations constitute a warranty also, recovery may be had on that basis"; that is, the defrauded party obtains the benefit of his bargain. * * *

We come now to an effort to reconcile our decisions and to deduce a rule therefrom. First of all, it is evident that the party guilty of fraud is liable for such damages as naturally and proximately resulted from the fraud. This is the universal rule. Next, our decisions warrant the conclusions: (1) If the defrauded party is content with the recovery of only the amount that he actually lost, his damages will be measured under that rule; (2) if the fraudulent representation also amounted to a warranty, recovery may be had for loss of the bargain because a fraud accompanied by a broken promise should cost the wrongdoer as much as the latter alone; (3) where the circumstances disclosed by the proof are so vague as to cast virtually no light upon the value of the property had it conformed to the representations, the court will award damages equal only to the loss sustained; and (4) where, * * * the damages under the benefit-of-the-bargain rule are proved with sufficient certainty, that rule will be employed.

In the present instance, the plaintiffs are clearly the victims of a fraud. The representations which deceived them concerned the quality or condition of the property; they were willful, were phrased in positive terms and were made in writing. They were made with knowledge upon the part of Shirley that the plaintiffs were ignorant of the facts and desired information. A determination of the value of the property, had it been as represented, does not carry one into the field of conjecture, but resort may be had to values for which Shirley and other witnesses vouched; that is, 4,000 cords of stumpage were worth $2,000. Had Shirley's representations been true, the plaintiffs would now have, not only the land, but also the timber. They should not be compelled, because Shirley was dishonest, to be content with the land only. Through false representations Shirley should not be permitted to obtain for the logged-off land a sum which would have been refused him had he been honest and truthful. In this case we are satisfied that Shirley must have known that through his deceit the plaintiffs would lose the benefit of the bargain which he was inducing them to enter into. Thus, we get back to the one rule which is of universal application: the party guilty of the fraud is liable for such damages as naturally and proximately result from the fraud. We conclude that the plaintiffs are entitled to damages awarded upon the basis of 50 cents per cord for the difference between the represented 4,000 cords and the actual 200 cords. The balancing of these accounts will indicate that there is now $650 owing to the plaintiffs. * * * It may appear that under these circumstances the plaintiffs will obtain the land for virtually nothing. There is, however, substantial evidence in the record indicating that without the timber and water for irrigation the land possesses virtually no value. While it is true that Shirley, Blakely and two other real estate agents expressed the opinion that this logged-off tract was worth $2,000, the effect of this evidence is greatly discredited by the representation, which induced the plaintiffs to make the purchase, that the land plus the 4,000 cords and served by a good irrigating stream was worth $2,000. But, be this as it may, courts ought not to be overnice in trying to save one who has willfully deceived another from the vicissitudes resulting from his wrong. * * *

■ BELT, JUSTICE (dissenting). * * * The measure of damages set forth in the majority opinion enables plaintiffs to acquire the 160-acre ranch for $100. If the representation had been 8,000 cords of wood, plaintiffs would get the ranch for nothing and the sum of $1,900 in addition. As stated in Curtis v. Buzard, 254 Pa. 61, 98 A. 777 (1916): "One defrauded 'can deduct from the purchase-money the difference between what he agreed and what it was then actually worth, and in our opinion no more, for if he could exceed that measure of damages a vendee of land might get a man's land for nothing, by showing that had the land been as represented it would have been worth enough more than its actual value to wipe out all the purchase-money, and thus give the vendee the land for nothing.' " * * *

Neither am I able to agree that the land without the timber as represented is "virtually of no value." The conclusion as expressed in the majority opinion is contrary to the findings of the trial court and is not supported by the record. * * *

NOTE

Measure of Recovery in Action Based Upon Misrepresentation. The principal case outlines both the "benefit of the bargain" measure of recovery—with its origins in contract and warranty law—and the "out-of-pocket-loss" rule, reflecting more traditional measures of tort recovery. The combination rule of the Oregon court was adopted in § 549 of the Restatement (Second) of Torts (1977) and has been followed by several states including Idaho, Maryland, Massachusetts, New Jersey and Washington. A majority of states appear to provide only for the benefit of the bargain. Other states restrict plaintiff's recovery to out-of-pocket losses. In either case, consequential damages often are recoverable.

G. RELATIONSHIPS THAT REQUIRE CARE: LIABILITY FOR NEGLIGENT MISREPRESENTATION

The 1889 decision of Derry v. Peek, *supra* pages 800–801, Note 1, established the principle that no recovery was available for economic losses caused by negligent misrepresentations. Beginning in the early twentieth century, however, American courts sometimes allowed recovery for negligent misrepresentation under restricted circumstances.

Glanzer v. Shepard

Court of Appeals of New York, 1922.
233 N.Y. 236, 135 N.E. 275.

■ CARDOZO, J. Plaintiffs bought of Bech, Van Siclen & Co., a corporation, 905 bags of beans. The beans were to be paid for in accordance with weight sheets certified by public weighers. Bech, Van Siclen & Co., the seller, requested the defendants, who are engaged in business as public weighers, to make return of the weight and furnish the buyers with a copy. * * * The defendants did as bidden. They certified the weight of the 905 bags to be 228,380 pounds, and were paid for the service by the seller. Their return recites that it has been made "by order of" Bech, Van Siclen & Co., "for G. Bros.[the purchaser and plaintiff]." * * * The plaintiffs, upon attempting a resale, found that the actual weight was less by 11,854 pounds than the weight as certified in the return. Upon learning this, they brought suit against the defendants * * * for $1,261.26, the amount overpaid. The trial judge * * * ordered judgment for the plaintiffs. The Appellate Term reversed upon the ground that the plaintiffs had no contract with the defendants, and must seek their remedy against the seller. The Appellate Division reversed the Appellate Term, and reinstated the verdict. The defendants are the appellants here.

We think the law imposes a duty toward buyer as well as seller in the situation here disclosed. The plaintiffs' use of the certificates was not an indirect or collateral consequence of the action of the weighers. It was a consequence which, to the weighers' knowledge, was the end and aim of the transaction. Bech, Van Siclen & Co. ordered, but Glanzer Brothers were to use. The defendants held themselves out to the public as skilled and careful in their calling. They knew that the beans had been sold, and that on the faith of their certificate payment would be made. They sent a copy to the plaintiffs for the very purpose of inducing action. All this they admit. In such circumstances, assumption of the task of weighing was the assumption of a duty to weigh carefully for the benefit of all whose conduct was to be governed. We do not need to state the duty in terms of contract or of privity. Growing out of a contract, it has none the less an origin not exclusively contractual. Given the contract and the relation, the duty is imposed by law. Cf. MacPherson v. Buick Motor Co., 217 N.Y. 382, 390 (1916). * * *

Here the defendants are held, not merely for careless words *, but for the careless performance of a service—the act of weighing—which happens to have found in the words of a certificate its culmination and its summary. * The line of separation between these diverse liabilities is difficult to draw. It does not lose for that reason its correspondence with realities. Life has relations not capable always of division into inflexible compartments. The moulds expand and shrink.

We state the defendants' obligation, therefore, in terms, not of contract merely, but of duty. Other forms of statement are possible. They involve, at most, a change of emphasis. We may see here, if we please, a phase or an extension of the rule in Lawrence v. Fox, 20 N.Y. 268 (1859), as amplified recently in Seaver v. Ransom, 224 N.Y. 233, 120 N.E. 639 (1918). If we fix our gaze upon that aspect, we shall stress the element of contract, and treat the defendants' promise as embracing the rendition of a service, which, though ordered and paid for by one, was either wholly or in part for the benefit of another. * * * These other methods of approach arrive at the same goal, though the paths may seem at times to be artificial or circuitous. We have preferred to reach the goal more simply. The defendants, acting, not casually nor as mere servants, but in the pursuit of an independent calling weighed and certified at the order of one with the very end and aim of shaping the conduct of another. Diligence was owing, not only to him who ordered, but to him also who relied. * * *

The judgment should be affirmed with costs. * * *

Ultramares Corp. v. Touche

Court of Appeals of New York, 1931.
255 N.Y. 170, 174 N.E. 441.

■ CARDOZO, C.J. The action is in tort for damages suffered through the misrepresentations of accountants, the first cause of action being for misrepresentations that were merely negligent and the second for misrepresentations charged to have been fraudulent.

In January, 1924, the defendants, a firm of public accountants, were employed by Fred Stern & Co., Inc., to prepare and certify a balance sheet exhibiting the condition of its business as of December 31, 1923. * * * Fred Stern & Co., Inc., which was in substance Stern himself, was engaged in the importation and sale of rubber. To finance its operations, it required extensive credit and borrowed large sums of money from banks and other lenders. All this was known to the defendants. The defendants knew also that in the usual course of business the balance sheet when certified would be exhibited by the Stern Company to banks, creditors, stockholders, purchasers, or sellers, according to the needs of the occasion, as the basis of financial dealings. Accordingly, when the balance sheet was made up, the defendants supplied the Stern Company with thirty-two copies certified with serial numbers as counterpart originals. Nothing was said as to the persons to whom these counterparts would be shown or the extent or number of the transactions in which they would be used. In particular there was no mention of the plaintiff, a corporation doing business chiefly as a factor, which till then had never made advances to the Stern Company, though it had sold merchandise in small amounts. The range of the transactions in which a certificate of audit might be expected to play a part was as indefinite and wide as the possibilities of the business that was mirrored in the summary.

By February 26, 1924, the audit was finished and the balance sheet made up. It stated assets in the sum of $2,550,671.88 and liabilities other than capital and surplus in the sum of $1,479,956.62, thus showing a net worth of $1,070,715.26. Attached to the balance sheet was a certificate as follows:

> * * * We have examined the accounts of Fred Stern & Co., Inc., for the year ending December 31, 1923, and hereby certify that the annexed balance sheet is in accordance therewith and with the information and explanations given us. We further certify that, subject to provision for federal taxes on income, the said statement, in our opinion, presents a true and correct view of

the financial condition of Fred Stern & Co., Inc., as at December 31, 1923.

TOUCHE, NIVEN & CO.

Public Accountants.

Capital and surplus were intact if the balance sheet was accurate. In reality both had been wiped out, and the corporation was insolvent. The books had been falsified by those in charge of the business so as to set forth accounts receivable and other assets which turned out to be fictitious. The plaintiff maintains that the certificate of audit was erroneous in both its branches. The first branch, the asserted correspondence between the accounts and the balance sheet, is one purporting to be made as of the knowledge of the auditors. The second branch, which certifies to a belief that the condition reflected in the balance sheet presents a true and correct picture of the resources of the business, is stated as a matter of opinion. In the view of the plaintiff, both branches of the certificate are either fraudulent or negligent. As to one class of assets, the item of accounts receivable, if not also as to others, there was no real correspondence, we are told, between balance sheet and books, or so the triers of the facts might find. If correspondence, however, be assumed, a closer examination of supporting invoices and records, or a fuller inquiry directed to the persons appearing on the books as creditors or debtors, would have exhibited the truth.

The plaintiff, a corporation engaged in business as a factor, was approached by Stern in March, 1924, with a request for loans of money to finance the sales of rubber. Up to that time the dealings between the two houses were on a cash basis and trifling in amount. As a condition of any loans the plaintiff insisted that it receive a balance sheet certified by public accountants, and in response to that demand it was given one of the certificates signed by the defendants and then in Stern's possession. On the faith of that certificate the plaintiff made a loan which was followed by many others. The course of business was for Stern to deliver to the plaintiff documents described as trust receipts which in effect were executory assignments of the moneys payable by purchasers for goods thereafter to be sold. When the purchase price was due, the plaintiff received the payment, reimbursing itself therefrom for its advances and commissions. Some of these transactions were effected without loss. Nearly a year later, in December, 1924, the house of cards collapsed. In that month, the plaintiff made three loans to the Stern Company, one of $100,000, a second of $25,000, and a third of $40,000. For some of these loans no security was received. For some of the earlier loans the security was inadequate. On January 2, 1925, the Stern Company was declared a bankrupt.

This action, brought against the accountants in November, 1926, to recover the loss suffered by the plaintiff in reliance upon the audit, was in its inception one for negligence. On the trial there was added a second cause of action asserting a fraud also. The trial judge dismissed the second cause of action without submitting it to the jury. As to the first cause of action, he reserved his decision on the defendants' motion to dismiss, and took the jury's verdict. They were told that the defendants might be held liable if with knowledge that the results of the audit would be communicated to creditors they did the work negligently, and that negligence was the omission to use reasonable and ordinary care. The verdict was in favor of the plaintiff for $187,576.32. On the coming in of the verdict, the judge granted the reserved motion. The Appellate Division * affirmed the dismissal of the cause of action for fraud, but reversed the dismissal of the cause of action for negligence, and reinstated the verdict. * * *

The two causes of action will be considered in succession, first the one for negligence and second that for fraud.

1.   We think the evidence supports a finding that the audit was negligently made, though in so saying we put aside for the moment the question whether negligence, even if it existed, was a wrong to the plaintiff. To explain fully or adequately how the defendants were at fault would carry this opinion beyond reasonable bounds. A sketch, however, there must be, at least in respect of some features of the audit, for the nature of the fault, when understood, is helpful in defining the ambit of the duty. [The court describes several suspicious entries in the books and accounts of Fred Stern & Co. and unconvincing explanations from its employees.] * * *

* * * The adverse [to the defendant] verdict * * * was not wrong upon the evidence before us, if duty be assumed.

We are brought to the question of duty, its origin and measure. The defendants owed to their employer a duty imposed by law to make their certificate without fraud, and a duty growing out of contract to make it with the care and caution proper to their calling. Fraud includes the pretense of knowledge when knowledge there is none. To creditors and investors to whom the employer exhibited the certificate, the defendants owed a like duty to make it without fraud, since there was no notice in the circumstances of its making that the employer did not intend to keep it to himself. *

A different question develops when we ask whether they owed a duty to these to make it without negligence. If liability for negligence exists, a thoughtless slip or blunder, the failure to detect a theft or forgery beneath the cover of deceptive entries, may expose accountants to a liability in an indeterminate amount for an indeterminate time to an indeterminate class. The hazards of a business conducted on these terms are so extreme as to enkindle doubt whether a flaw may not exist in the implication of a duty that exposes to these consequences. * * *

The assault upon the citadel of privity is proceeding in these days apace. * * * In the field of the law of contract there has been a gradual widening of the doctrine of Lawrence v. Fox, 20 N.Y. 268 (1859), until today the beneficiary of a promise, clearly designated as such, is seldom left without a remedy. * Even in that field, however, the remedy is narrower where the beneficiaries of the promise are indeterminate or general. Something more must then appear than an intention that the promise shall redound to the benefit of the public or to that of a class of indefinite extension. The promise must be such as to "bespeak the assumption of a duty to make reparation directly to the individual members of the public if the benefit is lost." Moch Co. v. Rensselaer Water Co., 247 N.Y. 160, 164, 159 N.E. 896, 897 (1928). * In the field of the law of torts a manufacturer who is negligent in the manufacture of a chattel in circumstances pointing to an unreasonable risk of serious bodily harm to those using it thereafter may be liable for negligence though privity is lacking between manufacturer and user. * A force or instrument of harm having been launched with potentialities of danger manifest to the eye of prudence, the one who launches it is under a duty to keep it within bounds. * * * We are now asked to say that a like liability attaches to the circulation of a thought or a release of the explosive power resident in words. * * *

In Glanzer v. Shepard, 233 N.Y. 236, 135 N.E. 275 (1922), * * * [w]e held that the weighers were liable at the suit of the buyer for the moneys overpaid. Here was something more than the rendition of a service in the expectation that the one who ordered the certificate would use it thereafter in the operations of his business as occasion might require. Here was a case where the transmission of the certificate to another was not merely one possibility among many, but the "end and aim of the transaction." * * * The intimacy of the resulting nexus is attested by the fact that, after stating the case in terms of legal duty, we went on to point out that viewing it as a phase or extension of *Lawrence v. Fox* * we could reach the same result by stating it in terms of contract. * The bond was so close as to approach that of privity, if not completely one with it. Not so in the case at hand. No one would be likely to urge that there was a contractual relation, or even one approaching it, at the root of any duty that was owing from the defendants now before us to the indeterminate class of persons who, presently or in the future, might deal with the Stern Company in reliance on the audit. In a word, the service rendered by the defendant in *Glanzer v. Shepard* was primarily for the information of a third person, in effect, if not in name, a party to the contract, and only incidentally for that of the formal promisee. In the case at hand, the service was primarily for the benefit of the Stern Company, a convenient instrumentality for use in the development of the business, and only incidentally or collaterally for the use of those to whom Stern and his associates might exhibit it thereafter. Foresight of these possibilities may charge with liability for fraud. The conclusion does not follow that it will charge with liability for negligence. * * *

From the foregoing analysis the conclusion is, we think, inevitable that nothing in our previous decisions commits us to a holding of liability for negligence in the circumstances of the case at hand, and that such liability, if recognized, will be an extension of the principle of those decisions to different conditions, even if more or less analogous. The question then is whether such an extension shall be made.

The extension, if made, will so expand the field of liability for negligent speech as to make it nearly, if not quite, coterminous with that of liability for fraud. Again and again, in decisions of this court, the bounds of this latter liability have been set up, with futility the fate of every endeavor to dislodge them. Scienter has been declared to be an indispensable element, except where the representation has been put forward as true of one's own knowledge, * or in circumstances where the expression of opinion was a dishonorable pretense. * Even an opinion, especially an opinion by an expert, may be found to be fraudulent if the grounds supporting it are so flimsy as to lead to the conclusion that there was no genuine belief back of it. Further than that this court has never gone. Directors of corporations have been acquitted of liability for deceit, though they have been lax in investigation and negligent in speech. Reno v. Bull, 226 N.Y. 546, 124 N.E. 144 (1919). * This has not meant, to be sure, that negligence may not be evidence from which a trier of the facts may draw an inference of fraud, Derry v. Peek, [L.R.] 14 A.C. 337, 369, 375, 376 (1889), but merely that if that inference is rejected, or, in the light of all the circumstances, is found to be unreasonable, negligence alone is not a substitute for fraud. Many also are the cases that have distinguished between the willful or reckless representation essential to the maintenance at law of an action for deceit, and the misrepresentation, negligent or innocent, that will lay a sufficient basis for rescission in equity. * * *

* * * A representation even though knowingly false does not constitute ground for an action of deceit unless made with the intent to be communicated to the persons or class of persons who act upon it to their prejudice. * * *

Liability for negligence if adjudged in this case will extend to many callings other than an auditor's. Lawyers who certify their opinion as to the validity of municipal or corporate bonds with knowledge that the opinion will be brought to the notice of the public will become liable to the investors, if they have overlooked a statute or a decision, to the same extent as if the controversy were one between client and adviser. Title companies insuring titles to a tract of land, with knowledge that at an approaching auction the fact that they have insured will be stated to the bidders, will become liable to purchasers who may wish the benefit of a policy without payment of a premium. These illustrations may seem to be extreme, but they go little, if any, farther than we are invited to go now. Negligence, moreover, will have one standard when viewed in relation to the employer, and another and at times a stricter standard when viewed in relation to the public. Explanations that might seem plausible, omissions that might be reasonable, if the duty is confined to the employer, conducting a business that presumably at least is not a fraud upon his creditors, might wear another aspect if an independent duty to be suspicious even of one's principal is owing to investors. * * *

Our holding does not emancipate accountants from the consequences of fraud. It does not relieve them if their audit has been so negligent as to justify a finding that they had no genuine belief in its adequacy, for this again is fraud. It does no more than say that if less than this is proved, if there has been neither reckless misstatement nor insincere profession of an opinion, but only honest blunder, the ensuing liability for negligence is one that is bounded by the contract, and is to be enforced between the parties by whom the contract has been made. We doubt whether the average business man receiving a certificate without paying for it and receiving it merely as one among a multitude of possible investors, would look for anything more.

2.   The second cause of action is yet to be considered.

The defendants certified as a fact, true to their own knowledge, that the balance sheet was in accordance with the books of account. If their statement was false, they are not to be exonerated because they believed it to be true.[a] We think the triers of the facts might hold it to be false.

Correspondence between the balance sheet and the books imports something more, or so the triers of the facts might say, than correspondence between the balance sheet and the general ledger, unsupported or even contradicted by every other record. The correspondence to be of any moment may not unreasonably be held to signify a correspondence between the statement and the books of original entry, the books taken as a whole. If that is what the certificate means, a jury could find that the correspondence did not exist, and that the defendants signed the certificates without knowing it to exist and even without reasonable grounds for belief in its existence. The item of $706,000, representing fictitious accounts receivable, was entered in the ledger after defendant's employee Siess had posted the December sales. He knew of the interpolation, and knew that there was need to verify the entry by reference to books other than the ledger before the books could be found to be in agreement with the balance sheet. The evidence would sustain a finding that this was never done. By concession the interpolated item had no support in the journal, or in any journal voucher, or in the debit memo book, which was a summary of the invoices, or in anything except the invoices themselves. The defendants do not say that they ever looked at the invoices, seventeen in number, representing these accounts. They profess to be unable to recall whether they did so or not. They admit, however, that, if they had looked, they would have found omissions and irregularities so many and unusual as to have called for further investigation. When we couple the refusal to say that they did look with the admission that if they had looked, they would or could have seen, the situation is revealed as one in which a jury might reasonably find that in truth they did not look, but certified the correspondence without testing its existence.

In this connection we are to bear in mind the principle already stated in the course of this opinion that negligence or blindness, even when not equivalent to fraud, is none the less evidence to sustain an inference of fraud. At least this is so if the negligence is gross. * * * We conclude, to sum up the situation, that in certifying to the correspondence between balance sheet and accounts the defendants made a statement as true to their own knowledge, when they had, as a jury might find, no knowledge on the subject. If that is so, they may also be found to have acted without information leading to a sincere or genuine belief when they certified to an opinion that the balance sheet faithfully reflected the condition of the business. * * *

NOTES

1. *Liability for Negligent Misrepresentation.* Since Derry v. Peek, *supra* pages 800–801, requiring *scienter* for deceit, liability for negligent

---

[a] [Eds.' note] But cf. Aaron Brodsky, The Twilight Zone Between Negligence and Fraud in the Accountants' Cases, 3 Intramural L. Rev. N.Y.U. 11, 13 (1947) ("This portion of the opinion does not recognize an important distinction between negligence and fraud. If a person pretends that he knows his statement is true when he merely believes that it is probably true, he has not the sort of belief which would remove his case from the realm of consciousness of false representation. But if he believes it is definitely true, and says it is, but it isn't, then the element of scienter is lacking and he shouldn't be held liable for fraud.").

misrepresentation has been relatively rare. "Some relationships between the parties are generally deemed to require care on the part of one of them in ascertaining and communicating facts to the other." Harper, James and Gray on Torts § 7.6.

Today courts follow one of three approaches in determining the extent of liability of accountants for negligent misrepresentation. The first approach, exemplified by Walpert, Smullian & Blumenthal, P.A. v. Katz, 361 Md. 645, 762 A.2d 582 (2000), is based on *Ultramares*, as clarified by a subsequent New York case, Credit Alliance Corp. v. Arthur Andersen & Co., 65 N.Y.2d 536, 493 N.Y.S.2d 435, 483 N.E.2d 110 (1985). In order to recover from an accounting firm for negligent misrepresentation under this test, the plaintiff must prove that:

(1) the defendants were aware that the financial reports they prepared were to be used for a particular purpose or purposes;

(2) in the furtherance of which a known party or parties was intended to rely; and

(3) there must have been some conduct on the part of the accountants linking to that party or parties, which evinces the accountants' understanding of that party or parties' reliance.

In short, courts interpret *Ultramares* as not requiring strict privity or third-party beneficiary status.

The second approach, followed by a majority of jurisdictions, is outlined in Restatement (Second) of Torts § 552 (1977). Here, accounting firms or other suppliers of commercial information are held liable when the third-party plaintiff is actually known as a member of the limited group for whose benefit the information is being supplied; further, the information must be relied upon in a transaction that the supplier of the information intends to influence or knows that the recipient of the information intends to influence. Under this rule, the accountant who regularly conducts audits and furnishes financial statements and opinions routinely required by lenders, investors, purchasers or others, is not liable unless she is informed that an identified third party or third parties will be using the statement for a particular purpose.

The third approach, adopted by only a few states, uses a "foreseeability" standard and holds accountants and similar professionals liable in the same manner as other tortfeasors. E.g., H. Rosenblum, Inc. v. Adler, 93 N.J. 324, 461 A.2d 138 (1983) (later overturned by statute). This approach serves the traditional tort goals of (1) compensation or loss distribution—the injured victim of the accountant's negligence is compensated by the wrongdoer—and (2) loss minimization—the rule provides substantial incentives for accountants to exercise due care. Further, this standard recognizes that the role of the auditor has expanded from that of a "watchdog for management to an independent evaluator of the adequacy and fairness of financial statements issued by management to stockholders, creditors and others." The disadvantages of this approach, of course, are the concerns expressed by Judge Cardozo in *Ultramares*.

The typical application of the negligent misrepresentation claim is to persons hired to provide professional services involving the furnishing of specialized information. Liability for negligent misrepresentation is accordingly imposed, ordinarily, between parties in a non-adversarial relationship with each other. There are, however, rare exceptions; for an example of liability for negligent misrepresentation of parties negotiating "at arm's-length," see Martens Chevrolet, Inc. v. Seney, 292 Md. 328, 439 A.2d 534 (1982).

Courts occasionally extend the negligent misrepresentation liability of professionals such as title abstractors and surveyors to persons neither in privity with them nor for whose specific benefit the professionals were retained by others, to include persons whose reliance on the representation was merely foreseeable. In doing so, the courts appear to be influenced both by the limited class of individuals likely to be harmed by such negligence and the importance to the public of reliance upon these professions. In Williams v. Polgar, 391 Mich. 6, 22, 215 N.W.2d 149, 157 (1974), the Michigan Supreme Court held that a title abstractor, hired by the seller of the land, was liable to "those persons an abstractor could reasonably foresee as relying on the accuracy of the abstract," including the purchaser of the land or another person in the subsequent chain of title injured by the abstractor's negligence. Similarly, in Rozny v. Marnul, 43 Ill.2d 54, 66, 250 N.E.2d 656, 662 (1969), the Supreme Court of Illinois allowed a private purchaser of land to recover from a negligent surveyor on the rationale that "[t]he situation is not one fraught with such an overwhelming potential liability as to dictate a contrary result, for the class of persons who might foreseeably use this plat is rather narrowly limited, if not exclusively so, to those who deal with the surveyed property as purchasers or lenders. Injury will ordinarily occur only once and to the one person then owning the lot."

2. *"Negligent Misrepresentations" Resulting in Physical Harm.* The ordinary rules of negligence apply when physical harm is a foreseeable result of a "negligent misrepresentation." E.g., Freeman v. United States, 509 F.2d 626 (6th Cir.1975) (air traffic controller negligently gave wrong information about location and direction to pilot of plane carrying parachutists who consequently jumped, to their death, over Lake Erie instead of target airfield). The distinction is not one between "negligence in word and negligence in deed," but rather "whether the plaintiff's financial loss is caused through physical injury or whether it is caused directly." Hedley Byrne & Co. v. Heller & Partners Ltd., [1964] A.C. 465, 516, 517 (Devlin, L.).

CHAPTER 16

BUSINESS TORTS

When does tort law provide compensation for injury to business relationships? This question is not new to our study. The misrepresentation and product liability torts obviously protect the integrity of the business relationship. In addition, the materials on compensation for merely economic damages addressed damages to business relationships. This chapter considers a sampling of additional torts that focus specifically on the protection of business relationships: interference with contract and with reasonable economic expectancies, injurious falsehood, the prima facie tort, and unfair competition. In many cases common law remedies co-exist alongside extensive federal and state statutory regulation.

Two concerns restrain the development of common law liability in these areas. First, will recognition of liability expose a potential defendant to what Chief Judge Cardozo described in Ultramares Corp. v. Touche, *supra* pages 828–833, as "liability in an indeterminate amount for an indeterminate time to an indeterminate class"? Second, will the looming prospect of liability inhibit legitimate competition or otherwise stifle legitimate enterprise?

A. INTERFERENCE WITH CONTRACT AND REASONABLE ECONOMIC EXPECTANCIES

Tata Consultancy Services v. Systems Int'l, Inc.
United States Court of Appeals for Sixth Circuit, 1994.
31 F.3d 416.

■NELSON, DAVID A., J. * * * The plaintiff, the Tata Consulting Services Division of Tata Sons Ltd. of Bombay, India, provides computer consulting services to clients around the world. Defendant Systems International, Inc., doing business as Syntel, Inc., is a Michigan corporation that engages in the same type of business. * * *

Tata claims * * * that Syntel and its agents enticed Tata employees to violate their employment contracts by jumping ship in favor of Syntel * * *. Evidence presented by way of deposition shows that Tata invests considerable time and effort in recruiting personnel from leading technical institutes in India. * * * Candidates are informed that newly-hired Tata employees have an initial service commitment of three years, a portion of which is devoted to training in India. * * * Employees with a sufficient level of expertise are often asked to accept "deputations" to work for Tata clients overseas under temporary visas. Each such employee normally agrees to return to India following the deputation and to remain in Tata's employ for twice the period of the deputation or a maximum of two years, whichever is less. * * *

In the course of this litigation Tata has taken the depositions of 16 former employees who, like others who were not deposed, left Tata to work for Syntel. More than half of those deposed were persuaded to quit before completing their initial three-year employment obligations, and all of them left Tata's employ before completing the additional periods of employment to which they had committed themselves by accepting deputations overseas.

In November of 1987 Tata complained to Syntel about the latter's interference with Tata's contractual relationships with its employees. Tata's senior personnel manager in Bombay, Joseph Abraham, telephoned Mr. Desai [President and co-owner of Syntel] at that time and threatened litigation if the raiding did not stop. Mr. Abraham has said in an affidavit that Mr. Desai was told he was interfering with Tata's contractual rights. The Abraham affidavit also indicates that Mr. Desai was specifically told of the existence of contracts obligating Tata employees to return to India following completion of their assignments in the United States. * * *

The deposition of Anuradha Krishnamurthy, a computer consultant * * *, provides something of a case study in how, as Tata sees it, the defendants wrongfully interfered with Tata's contractual relationships. Ms. Krishnamurthy * * * was hired by Tata as a trainee in February of 1986. She went through an initial training program of six to eight weeks' duration, and, perhaps because of her advanced education, was able to skip the second phase of Tata's formal training regimen. * * * [I]n July of 1988, Tata deputed her to work with one of its clients in the United States. * * * Ms. Krishnamurthy entered into a written deputation agreement in which she promised that upon completion of her assignment to the United States she would continue in Tata's employ for a term not less than twice the period of her employment in the United States, but not more than 24 months. Ms. Krishnamurthy testified that she knew it was important to Tata that she return to India after her deputation so that the valuable experience gained in the United States could be shared with others. * * *

Ms. Krishnamurthy * * * decided not to continue the Tata deputation. This decision followed a series of telephone conversations initiated by Syntel President Bharat Desai * * * [in which he] told her a little about Syntel and * * * [eventually] offered her a job. Notwithstanding her unexpired contractual obligation to Tata, Ms. Krishnamurthy subsequently agreed to go to work for Mr. Desai at a higher rate of pay than she had been receiving from Tata. * * *

Turning to another matter[,] * * * there is evidence that some Tata employees were "enticed" to work for Syntel, as the district court put it, by promises of help in obtaining H-1 visas, good for a substantially longer term in the United States than the temporary B-1 visas procured by Tata. * There is also evidence that Syntel offered to help Tata employees obtain the green cards necessary for permanent residence in this country. * * *

In April of 1990 Tata brought suit against Syntel[.] * * * The complaint set forth claims for relief [including] * * * tortious interference with Tata's contractual relationships with its employees * * *. Judgment was * * * entered dismissing with prejudice all of the claims in the complaint. * * * This appeal followed. * * *

The parties are in agreement that Tata's tortious interference claims are governed by the law of Michigan. They are also in agreement that the following summary of Michigan's law on tortious interference is, as far as it goes, accurate:

> The elements of tortious interference with a contractual relationship are (1) a contract, (2) a breach, and (3) instigation of the breach without justification by the defendant.

> One who alleges tortious interference with a contractual or business relationship must allege the intentional doing of a per se wrongful act or the doing of a lawful act with malice and unjustified in law for the purpose of invading the contractual rights or business relationship of another.

Wood v. Herndon & Herndon Investigations, Inc., 186 Mich.App. 495, 499–500, 465 N.W.2d 5, 8 (1990). *

* * * [T]he defendants argue that they did not intentionally commit any act that was wrongful per se; that they acted lawfully and without malice; that they merely outbid Tata for the services of the people they hired, doing so to further their own economic interests; and that nothing they did was unethical, fraudulent, or otherwise unjustified or improper. The district court accepted these arguments. * * *

The Supreme Court of Michigan * * * first imposed liability for tortiously interfering with another's contract in Morgan v. Andrews, 107 Mich. 33, 64 N.W. 869 (1895), * * * [in which the court quoted] the following passage * * * which was taken * * * from Lumley v. Gye, 2 El. & Bl. (Q.B. 1853) 216, 118 Eng.Rep. 749, 22 L.J.Q.B. (N.S.) 463:

> Merely to persuade a person to break his contract may not be wrongful in law or fact; still, if the persuasion be used for the indirect purpose of injuring the plaintiff, *or benefiting the defendant at the expense of the plaintiff*, it is a malicious act, which, in law and in fact, is a wrongful act, and therefore an actionable act, if injury issues from it.

* * * [In] Wilkinson v. Powe, 300 Mich. 275, 1 N.W.2d 539 (1942), the * * * Michigan Supreme Court * * * reinstated a jury verdict against dairy operators who had persuaded neighboring farmers to cancel milk-hauling contracts with the plaintiff so that the defendants could pick up the milk instead. Noting that the *Morgan* court had long since approved the rule of *Lumley v. Gye*, and quoting again the passage about the defendant's persuading a person to break a contract for the indirect purpose of "benefiting the defendant at the expense of the plaintiff," the court went on to declare that

> A prima facie case is established when plaintiff proves the intentional procurement of a breach of contract, and, upon such proof, it becomes incumbent upon defendant to show justification. *

"No categorical answer can be made to the question of what will constitute justification," the court said, "and it is usually held that this question is one for the jury." * Acknowledging that the defendants in the case before it would clearly have been within their legal rights if they had merely refused to accept further deliveries of milk by the plaintiff, the court pointed out that the defendants had done more: they had sent the farmers letters that "showed active solicitation of a breach of the contract[,] and their refusal to accept delivery of milk was merely another step in bringing about the breach." It was the showing of "active solicitation" that completed the plaintiff's prima facie case[7] and made it incumbent on the defendants to persuade the jury that the solicitation had been justified. * * *

Mr. Justice Traynor's opinion in Imperial Ice Co. v. Rossier, 18 Cal.2d 33, 112 P.2d 631 (1941) * * * held that an ice distributor's complaint against an ice manufacturer stated a cause of action for procuring the breach of a covenant not to compete because "[t]he plaintiff's complaint alleged that the defendant *intentionally and actively* induced the seller to violate his contract in order to sell ice to it." * * * [T]he * * * court commented as follows on the matter of active inducement:

> Had defendants merely sold ice to Coker without actively inducing him to violate his contract, his distribution of the ice in the forbidden territory in violation of his contract would not then have rendered defendants liable. They may carry on their business of selling ice as usual without incurring liability for breaches of contract by their customers. It is necessary to prove that they intentionally and actively induced the breach." *Imperial Ice*, 112 P.2d at 634.

* * * [T]he California court issued the following caution:

> It is well established, however, that a person is not justified in inducing a breach of contract simply because he is in competition with one of the parties to the contract and seeks to further his own economic advantage at the expense of the other.

Further support for the view that a desire to further one's own economic interests does not constitute justification for actively inducing another to violate his contractual undertakings may be found in the commentary on §768 of Restatement (Second) of Torts *:

> (2) The fact that one is a competitor of another for the business of a third person does not prevent his causing a breach of an existing contract with the other from being an improper interference if the contract is not terminable at will.

---

[7]   The plaintiff had to show malice, of course, but legal malice can be inferred from the intentional doing of a wrongful act without justification:

> The great weight of authority in this country and in England is to the effect that, if A has a legal contract with B, either for the rendition of service or any other purpose, and C, having knowledge of the existence thereof, intentionally and knowingly, and without reasonable justification or excuse, induces B to break the contract, by reason of which A sustains damage, an action will lie by A against C to recover the same. . . . The action of C is malicious, in that, with the knowledge of A's rights, he intentionally and knowingly and for unworthy or selfish purposes, destroys them by inducing B to break his contract. It is a wrongful act, done intentionally, without just cause, or excuse, and from this a malicious motive is to be inferred. This does not necessarily mean actual malice or ill will, but the intentional doing of a wrongful act without legal or social justification.

Wilkinson, 300 Mich. 275 at 282–83, 1 N.W.2d 539. *

As applied to the case at bar, the significance of the body of law we have described is obvious. If an employee of Tata approached Syntel about a job, without having been solicited to do so by Syntel or anyone acting on its behalf, Syntel might well be justified in hiring the applicant whether or not his employment contract with Tata had expired. But if the approach came from Syntel—if Syntel sought out the Tata employee, in other words, and actively solicited him to come to work for Syntel knowing that the employee could not do so without breaking an existing contract with Tata—the hiring of the employee away from Tata might well be unjustified. Malice could be inferred from the wrongful act of inducing breach of the contract, and it would be no defense that Syntel acted not out of hatred or ill-will toward Tata, but solely in the interest of feathering its own economic nest at the expense of a competitor. Indeed, "the indirect purpose of . . . benefiting the defendant at the expense of the plaintiff" would be critical to a finding of malice. * * *

* * * Jim-Bob, Inc. v. Mehling, [178 Mich.App. 71, 96, 443 N.W.2d 451, 462 (1989),] disavowed any suggestion * * * that one who interferes with another's contractual rights is necessarily "shielded from liability" if his acts "are in furtherance of legitimate personal or business interests."[11] In the words of the *Jim-Bob* court,

> [T]he fact that certain actions are taken with the intent that they inure to the personal or pecuniary benefit of the defendant cannot, per se, in our view, weave a broad and impenetrable blanket of immunity from liability for those actions. Certainly, in nearly all cases of interference, the defendant hopes to benefit by way of a resulting advancement of its personal or business interests. But these ends do not necessarily justify the means undertaken. A defendant may not, with impunity, sabotage the contractual agreements of others, and that defendant's cry that its actions were motivated by purely business interests cannot, standing alone, operate as a miracle cure making all that was wrong, right. On the contrary, the defendant's motive is but one of several factors which must be weighed in assessing the propriety of the defendant's actions. Such factors include (1) the nature of the defendant's conduct, (2) the nature of the plaintiff's contractual interest, (3) the social utility of the plaintiff's and the defendant's respective interests, and (4) the proximity of the defendant's conduct to the interference." *Id.* at 462–63 (citing Restatement (Second) of Torts § 767 and comments thereto).

The approach taken by the Court of Appeals in *Jim-Bob* seems entirely consistent with that taken by the Supreme Court in Wilkinson v. Powe, 300 Mich. 275, 1 N.W.2d 539 (1942), *supra*. There, it will be recalled, the Supreme Court said that there can be no categorical

---

[11] In the context of employment contracts, th[is] principle * * * is inconsistent with the following passage from Restatement (Second) of Agency, § 312, comment *a*:

> In the absence of a privilege, one who intentionally causes a servant or other agent to break a contract of employment is liable to the employer. Privileges to do this are rare; *business competition does not give rise to one.* (Emphasis supplied.)

answer to the question of what will constitute justification, "and it is usually held that this question is one for the jury." * * *

Up to this point, our analysis has been predicated on the assumption that Tata's contracts with its employees were binding for the time periods agreed to. The district court, however, concluded that the contracts "lack mutuality as to the term of employment and would not be enforceable for a term certain under Michigan law." The court therefore treated the contracts as establishing nothing more than a business expectancy or at-will relationship, deserving of less protection against tortious interference than enforceable bilateral contracts would receive. See Kand Med., Inc. v. Freund Med. Prods., Inc., 963 F.2d 125 (6th Cir.1992), holding that less protection is accorded under Ohio law to an "exitable" contract—i.e., a contract terminable at will—than to one that the contracting party is not entitled to terminate at will. * * *

On the record before us, we are not persuaded that Tata's employees were legally free to terminate their contracts whenever they pleased. The contracts were not lacking in mutuality, Tata not having reserved the right to discharge an employee during the term of his contract except for cause. * * *

The duration of the contracts, moreover, does not appear unreasonable. A three-year commitment is certainly not unusual, as anyone who has enlisted in the armed forces of the United States can attest, and a post-deputation commitment not exceeding two years in length does not, on its face, seem oppressive. * * * It is true that Tata could end a deputation without having to show good cause for doing so, but termination of a deputation did not mean termination of employment. Upon his return to India the employee would still be entitled to receive his salary, and he would still be obligated to work for Tata until the expiration of the agreed term. * * *

* * * All in all, it seems to us, there is enough doubt about the propriety of Syntel's conduct * * * to make summary judgment in favor of these defendants inappropriate as far as the claim of tortious interference with the employment contracts is concerned. * * *

NOTES

1. *Origins of Interference with Contract.* The roots of the interference with contract cause of action lie in earlier times—before the dominance of the market economy, when status was more important than contractual relations. See generally Harper, James and Gray on Torts § 6.5. Under Roman law, the head of the family could sue for harm done, generally physical violence, to members of the family—including his wife and children—and to slaves. Labor shortages caused by the Great Plague in the fourteenth century resulted in the Ordinance of Labourers, 1349, 23 Edw. III 3, cc. 1–8, and the Statute of Labourers, 1350, 25 Edw. III 2, cc. 1–7, which made it unlawful to entice another's servants to leave their employment, whether by force or persuasion. Until the case of Lumley v. Gye, (1853) 118 Eng.Rep. (Q.B.) 749, 2 El. & Bl. 216, the principle extended no further than allowing recovery of damages for the seduction, beating, or enticing from employment of a person in the menial or domestic service of another.

In *Lumley*, Miss Johanna Wagner, a famous opera singer, contracted with the plaintiff to appear exclusively at his theater for a period of time. The defendant, though aware of the contract, persuaded the plaintiff to refuse to perform, but without using force, fraud or other means illegal in themselves. A divided court ruled that the defendant committed a tort for which damages were recoverable, finding the defendant's actions wrongful and malicious, merely because the defendant was aware of the plaintiff's contract.

2. *Interference with Performance Other than Inducing Breach.* A third-party defendant may be held liable whenever he prevents a party from fulfilling its contractual obligations or adds to the burden of a party's performance, even if the nature of the defendant's activity is something other than inducing the party to breach its contractual obligation. See, e.g., Samedan Oil Corp. v. Intrastate Gas Gathering, Inc., 78 S.W.3d 425 (Tex.App.2001) (defendant natural gas well operator disconnected pipeline to processing plant, interfering with performance of plant's gas purchase contracts with third parties); Examination Mgmt. Servs., Inc. v. Kirschbaum, 927 P.2d 686 (Wyo.1996) (defendant withheld payments due plaintiff, which plaintiff needed to pay his contractors).

3. *The Pennzoil-Texaco Case.* What was at the time the largest civil judgment in the history of American tort law resulted from a suit for interference with contract. In Texaco, Inc. v. Pennzoil, Co., 729 S.W.2d 768 (Tex.App.1987), the defendant Texaco attempted a take-over bid for the Getty Oil Co. despite knowledge of an agreement between Pennzoil and Getty for Pennzoil to acquire a substantial interest in Getty. Pennzoil brought an action against Texaco for interference with contract, and the state trial jury awarded $7.53 billion in compensatory damages and $3 billion in punitive damages. Texaco filed an action in federal court to prevent Pennzoil from filing a judgment lien against its property because such a lien would have driven it into bankruptcy, but the United States Supreme Court ultimately prevented federal court interference in the collection of the state court judgment. See Texaco, Inc. v. Pennzoil Co., 626 F.Supp. 250 (S.D.N.Y.1986), modified and remanded, 784 F.2d 1133 (2d Cir.1986), rev'd and remanded, 481 U.S. 1, 107 S.Ct. 1519, 95 L.Ed.2d 1 (1987). Eventually the parties settled for a mere $3 billion. Timothy S. Feltham, Note, Tortious Interference with Contractual Relations: The *Texaco Inc. v. Pennzoil Co.* Litigation, 33 N.Y.L. Sch. L. Rev. 111, 120–22 (1988).

Top Service Body Shop, Inc. v. Allstate Insurance Co.

Supreme Court of Oregon, En Banc, 1978.
283 Or. 201, 582 P.2d 1365.

■ LINDE, JUSTICE. Plaintiff, the operator of an automobile body repair shop in Coos Bay, Oregon, sued defendant insurance company for general and punitive damages for injuries alleged to result from defendant's wrongful practices in directing insurance claimants to have repairs made at body shops other than plaintiff's. The complaint pleaded [a] cause[ ] of action grounded in * * * tortious interference with plaintiff's business * * *. Defendant answered by general denials and an affirmative defense to the tort claim asserting a privilege of acting in its own legitimate financial interests. Plaintiff replied that defendant's methods and intent took its actions beyond any such privilege. The trial resulted in jury verdicts for plaintiff in amounts of $20,000 compensatory and $250,000 punitive damages on the tort claim * * *. On defendant's motion, the trial court entered judgments notwithstanding the verdicts on both causes of action, primarily for failure of proof. The court also allowed defendant's alternative motion for a new trial * * *. On appeal, plaintiff assigns as error the rulings on these motions * * *. We affirm.

I.   The claim of tortious interference.

* * * Tort claims for wrongful interference with the economic relationships of another have an ancient lineage. Their history has been traced from interference with members of another's household in Roman law or with his tenants in English law, with his workmen after the 1349 Ordinance of Labourers, with prospective workmen or customers, with existing contracts for personal services, Lumley v. Gye, 118 Eng.Rep. 749 (QB 1853), and with contracts generally, * to contemporary forms not dependent on the existence of a contract. * * *

* * * Either the pursuit of an improper objective of harming plaintiff or the use of wrongful means that in fact cause injury to plaintiff's contractual or business relationships may give rise to a tort claim for those injuries. However, efforts to consolidate both recognized and unsettled lines of development into a general theory of "tortious interference" have brought to the surface the difficulties of defining the elements of so general a tort without sweeping within its terms a wide variety of socially very different conduct.[3] * * *

* * * Dean John W. Wade [,] * * * [who succeeded William Prosser as Reporter for the Restatement (Second) of Torts, revised] the Restatement chapter dealing with the tort of interference with existing or prospective contracts or, as the Reporter described it, "interference with advantageous economic relations," [and] proposed significant changes in the analysis. * As the Restatement now stands, such interference would give rise to liability if it is both intentional and affirmatively improper (replacing reliance on lack of "privilege" in the definition of the tort), and a purpose to harm the injured party would be one factor making the interference improper.[8]

---

[3]   During one period of history, the tort of interference with contracts was a main legal weapon against labor organization. * In the contemporary context, a broad generalization similarly could make prima facie torts of otherwise lawful activities designed to persuade others to stop smoking cigarettes or eating certain foods, or using certain pesticides, or doing business in South Africa [during the apartheid regime], or buying grapes [to support the labor-organizing efforts of the United Farm Workers against grape growers during the "boycott" extending from 1965 through 1970] or other products, leaving the defense in each case to a showing of privilege. * * *

[8]   § 766. Intentional Interference with Performance of Contract by Third Person.

One who intentionally and improperly interferes with the performance of a contract (except a contract to marry) between another and a third person by inducing or otherwise causing the third person not to perform the contract, is subject to liability to the other for the pecuniary loss resulting to the other from the third person's failure to perform the contract.

§ 766B. Intentional Interference with Prospective Contractual Relation.

One who intentionally and improperly interferes with another's prospective contractual relation (except a contract to marry) is subject to liability to the other

* * * In Wampler v. Palmerton, 250 Or. 65, 439 P.2d 601 (1968), intentional interference with an existing contract was assumed to be prima facie tortious, unless it was justified or privileged as promoting some legitimate interest. In that case, corporate officers were held to have such a privilege in advising the corporation. * A similar approach was followed in North Pac. Lumber Co. v. Moore, 275 Or. 359, 551 P.2d 431 (1976), but the court held that it was plaintiff's burden to prove both that defendant intentionally interfered with plaintiff's prospective sales and that defendant had no privilege to do so. In that case, defendant was plaintiff's competitor, and the court assumed that its privilege as a competitor might be overcome by proof that it had made use of customer and market information obtained by hiring one of plaintiff's employees. The effect is that the propriety of defendant's objective or motive is really a part of plaintiff's case rather than an affirmative defense of "privilege." However, even when defendant's objectives are not improper, for instance the pursuit of competition or other legitimate interests, defendant may still be liable for using improper means to achieve these objectives.

Meanwhile, the decision in Nees v. Hocks, 272 Or. 210, 536 P.2d 512 (1975), rejected the concept that every intentional infliction of harm is prima facie a tort unless justified. Finding that this concept was no longer needed to escape the rigidity of the common-law forms of pleading, the court concluded that it created as many difficulties as it solved. However, the court found that the plaintiff had effectively pleaded and proved that her discharge by defendant was tortious by reason of an improper motive.

We conclude that the approach of *Nees v. Hocks* is equally appropriate to claims of tort liability for intentional interference with contractual or other economic relations. In summary, such a claim is made out when interference resulting in injury to another is wrongful by some measure beyond the fact of the interference itself. Defendant's liability may arise from improper motives or from the use of improper means. They may be wrongful by reason of a statute or other regulation, or a recognized rule of common law,[11] or perhaps an established standard of a trade or profession. No question of privilege arises unless the interference would be wrongful but for the privilege; it becomes an issue only if the acts charged would be tortious on the part

---

for the pecuniary harm resulting from the loss of the benefits of the relation when the interference consists of

(a) inducing or otherwise causing a third person not to enter into or continue the prospective relation or

(b) preventing the other from acquiring or continuing the prospective relation.

[Restatement (Second) of Torts (Tent. Draft No. 23, 1977).]

[11] Commonly included among improper means are violence, threats or other intimidation, deceit or misrepresentation, bribery, unfounded litigation, defamation, or disparaging falsehood. See * * * Restatement (Second) of Torts § 766 cmts. j, k, § 767 cmt. c (Tent. Draft No. 23, 1977). As the latter comment points out, in a claim of improper interference with plaintiff's contractual relations, it is not necessary to prove all the elements of liability for another tort if those elements that pertain to the defendant's conduct are present. For instance, fraudulent misrepresentations made to a third party are improper means of interference with plaintiff's contractual relations whether or not the third party can show reliance injurious to himself. *

of an unprivileged defendant. Even a recognized privilege may be overcome when the means used by defendant are not justified by the reason for recognizing the privilege. * To this extent we agree with the analysis of the second Restatement. *

In the present case, Top Service pleaded both improper motives and improper means of interference. It alleged that Allstate sought to and did induce Top Service's patrons not to have Top Service repair their automobiles, making false statements about the quality of plaintiff's workmanship and threats about withdrawing insurance coverage or subjecting the settlement of claims to possible arbitration. It also alleged that this was done "with the sole design of injuring Plaintiff and destroying his business," and in an endeavor to "compel Plaintiff to abandon the same." If proved, along with damages and causation, these allegations satisfy the elements of the tort we have reviewed above. * * *

Taken most favorably to plaintiff, as is proper after a verdict for plaintiff, the evidence showed that Allstate has a practice of designating certain repair shops in the locality as "competitive shops" to which it prefers to send insurance claimants for whose repairs Allstate is obligated; that Top Service at one time was a "drive-in" shop for Allstate, where claimants would be directed for an estimate by an Allstate insurance adjuster; that after a dispute Top Service's owner decided that it would not continue as a drive-in shop for Allstate; and that thereafter Allstate adjusters would actively discourage claimants under its insurance policies from taking work to be paid for by Allstate to Top Service, sending them instead to other shops on its preferred list. As specific bases for an inference of destructive purpose, Top Service lists two occasions when Allstate adjusters disparaged the quality of Top Service's work (apart from its relative cost), although Allstate personnel had generally considered Top Service a high quality shop; Allstate's willingness to disappoint its own insured who preferred Top Service; one occasion when Allstate took its option to "total" a car, i.e., to pay off its value, when the insured wanted it repaired at Top Service; and finally Allstate's resort to "improper and unlawful means" to direct business away from Top Service to other shops. Without setting forth here the excerpts of the record cited by plaintiff, we agree with the trial court that these acts were wholly consistent with Allstate's pursuit of its own business purposes as it saw them and did not suffice to support an inference of the alleged improper purpose to injure Top Service. The court's ruling on this point was not error.

Wal-Mart Stores, Inc. v. Sturges

Supreme Court of Texas, 2001.
52 S.W.3d 711.

■ HECHT, JUSTICE. Texas, like most states, has long recognized a tort cause of action for interference with a prospective contractual or business relation even though the core concept of liability—what conduct is prohibited—has never been clearly defined. Texas courts have variously stated that a defendant may be liable for conduct that is "wrongful," "malicious," "improper," of "no useful purpose," "below the behavior of fair men similarly situated," or done "with the purpose of harming the plaintiff," but not for conduct that is "competitive," "privileged," or "justified," even if intended to harm the plaintiff. Repetition of these abstractions in the case law has not imbued them with content or made them more useful, and tensions among them, which exist not only in Texas law but American law generally, have for decades been the subject of considerable critical commentary. * * *

[The plaintiffs entered into a contract to purchase a tract of land known as "Tract 2" from Bank One. The contract gave the plaintiffs the right to terminate the purchase if they were not able to lease the property. The plaintiffs were aware that a chain of food stores, Fleming Foods of Texas, was interested in building a food store in the area. The defendant Wal-Mart Corporation, which operated a store on an adjoining piece of property, had the right to approve or disapprove intended uses of Tract 2 under restrictions contained in two recorded easements.

Meanwhile, Wal-Mart itself had hired a realtor to help it acquire Tract 2 for purposes of expansion. When the realtor informed Wal-Mart of the plaintiffs' contract with Bank One to purchase Tract 2, he suggested to Wal-Mart that it deny the request to modify the easement, and Wal-Mart did so. Wal-Mart further instructed its realtor to contact Fleming and tell its manager of store development, who had been working on the possible lease of Tract 2, that if Wal-Mart could not acquire Tract 2, it would close its existing store on the adjoining parcel. Without the continued operation of the nearby Wal-Mart store, Fleming would not be interested in acquiring Tract 2 for construction of its grocery store. Fleming cancelled its letter of intent to lease the property from the plaintiffs, and the plaintiffs opted out of their contract with Bank One.]

The plaintiffs sued Wal-Mart for tortiously interfering with their prospective lease with Fleming * * *. The jury found Wal-Mart liable * * *. [T]he trial court rendered judgment on the interference claim, awarding actual and punitive damages * * *. All parties appealed. The court of appeals affirmed the award of actual damages * * *. We granted Wal-Mart's petition for review.

II

* * * We will focus on Wal-Mart's argument that there is no evidence of wrongful interference: that is, in the language of the jury charge, no evidence that Wal-Mart acted "with the purpose of harming Plaintiffs." To resolve this issue, we must understand what kind of conduct is legally harmful and constitutes tortious interference. Whenever two competitors vie for the same business advantage, as Wal-Mart and Sturges did over the acquisition of Tract 2, one's success over the other can almost always be said to harm the other. Wal-Mart's evidentiary challenge here raises the question of what harm must be proved to constitute tortious interference. To answer this question, we look to the historical development of the interference torts in other jurisdictions and in Texas and survey every Texas case involving a claim of intentional interference with prospective relations. We then analyze the evidence in this case.

A

The origins of civil liability for interference have been traced to Roman law that permitted a man to sue for violence done to members of his household. The common law also recognized such liability as early as the fourteenth century and extended it to include driving away a business's customers or a church's donors. But a common-law cause of action was strictly limited to cases in which actual violence or other such improper means were used. For centuries the common law continued to allow civil actions for interference with one's customers or other prospective business relationships, but as the Restatement (Second) of Torts § 766B cmt. b (1979) summarizes, "in all of them the actor's conduct was characterized by violence, fraud or defamation, and was tortious in character."

The common law departed from this requirement in 1853 in the English case of Lumley v. Gye, 2 El. & Bl. 216, 118 Eng.Rep. 749 (Q.B. 1853). * * * Forty years later in Temperton v. Russell, 1 Q.B. 715 (1893), the English court reaffirmed its decision in *Lumley*, holding that trade union officials could be liable to a building materials supplier for threatening his customers with labor disturbances if they continued to purchase supplies from him. * The court announced that the rule in *Lumley* would apply not only to interference with all contracts, regardless of the subject matter, but to interference with prospective or potential relations as well.

Temperton's treatment of interference with prospective relations as simply another aspect of interference with contract was a mistake. It is one thing for *A* and *B* to compete for *C's* business, and quite another for *A* to persuade or force *C* to break his contract with *B*. Tortious interference with contract contemplates that competition may be lawful and yet limited by promises already made. Absent any such promises, competitors should be free to use any lawful means to obtain advantage. * * * *Lumley's* holding that unlawful conduct was not a prerequisite for liability for tortious interference with contract was understandable; *Temperton's* extension of the same rule to situations involving only prospective relations was not.

The use of "malice" to denote the touchstone of liability for tortious interference with contract was not well explained in *Lumley* and the cases that followed. "Malice" appeared at first to signify malevolence, although it soon became apparent that that definition would not work. * * * [L]awful conduct is not made tortious by the actor's ill will towards another, nor does an actor's lack of ill will make his tortious conduct any less so. "Malice" obviously meant that character of conduct that would not justify inducing a breach of contract, but that was an obviously circular definition (a person is not justified in inducing a breach of contract if he acts with malice, that is, if he acts in such a way that does not justify inducing a breach of contract). Exactly what conduct was culpable, and therefore "malicious," went undefined.

As clumsy as the idea of "malice" was in describing liability for tortious interference with contract, it made no sense at all in trying to describe liability for tortious interference with prospective advantage. Competitors could quite naturally be expected, well within the bounds of law, to try to achieve the best for themselves and, consequently, harm to each other. In a society built around business competition, interference with prospective business relations has never been thought to be wrongful in and of itself. That some liability factor was essential has never been in doubt. If that factor was not unlawful conduct, discarded by *Lumley* for tortious interference with contract, then it was not clear what it should be. * * *

[T]he Restatement (Second) of Torts did little to solve them. Concluding that "it has seemed desirable to make use of a single word that will indicate for this tort the balancing process expressed by the two terms, 'culpable and not justified,' " [Restatement (Second) of Torts intro to ch. 37, at 6] the *Restatement* chose "improper" as a word "neutral enough to acquire a specialized meaning of its own" for purposes of defining the interference torts. The *Restatement* separated interference with contract and interference with prospective business relations, previously combined as one, but it used the same new standard—"improper"—to define liability for each. Hence, section 766B states with respect to intentional interference with prospective contractual relations:

> One who intentionally and improperly interferes with another's prospective contractual relation (except a contract to marry) is subject to liability to the other for the pecuniary harm resulting from loss of the benefits of the relation, whether the interference consists of (a) inducing or otherwise causing a third person not to enter into or continue the prospective relation or (b) preventing the other from acquiring or continuing the prospective relation.

The *Restatement* then states that whether conduct was "improper" for both interference torts should be determined from consideration of the same broad factors:

> In determining whether an actor's conduct in intentionally interfering with a contract or a prospective contractual relation of another is improper or not, consideration is given to the following factors: (a) the nature of the actor's conduct, (b) the actor's motive, (c) the interests of the other with which the actor's conduct interferes, (d) the interests sought to be advanced by the actor, (e) the social interests in protecting the freedom of action of the actor and the contractual interests of the other, (f) the proximity or remoteness of the actor's conduct to the interference, and (g) the relations between the parties. *Id.* § 767.

The second *Restatement*, like the first, provided that lawful competition was not tortious interference with a prospective business relation although it might be tortious interference with any contract not terminable at will.

Thus, the second *Restatement* abandoned the confusing and overlapping notions of "malice," "privilege," and "justification," but it made little more than a formal distinction between the two interference torts, setting the liability standard for both at "improper" conduct, and it continued the idea that the considerations for determining what was improper were, except for lawful competition, similar for both torts. Commentators since have criticized the *Restatement* as overstating case law. Professor Perlman's analysis of the cases suggests that the interference tort [with prospective relations] should be limited to cases in which the defendant's acts are independently unlawful and that if improper motivation is to give rise to liability, it should be based only on objective indicia of activity producing social loss. In most cases, tort law will provide the standard for judging the unlawfulness of the means. At the same time, those courts that have emphasized unlawful means have recognized that sources other than traditional tort law also might define the lawfulness of the defendant's behavior. Incorporation of such sources seems right. [Harvey S.] Perlman, Interference with Contract and Other Economic Expectancies: A Clash of Tort and Contract Doctrine, 49 U. Chi. L. Rev. 61, 97–98 (1982).

Likewise, Professor Keeton summarized:

* * * [V]iolence or intimidation, defamation, injurious falsehood or other fraud, violation of the criminal law, and the institution or threat of groundless civil suits or criminal prosecutions in bad faith, all have been held to result in liability, and there is some authority which limits liability to such cases.

W. Page Keeton *et al.*, Prosser & Keeton on the Law of Torts § 130. * * *

                                        B

* * * It appears that in most Texas cases in which plaintiffs have actually recovered damages for tortious interference with prospective business relations, the defendants' conduct was either independently tortious * * * or in violation of state law. * * * [W]e see no need for a definition of tortious interference with prospective business relations that would encompass other conduct. The historical limitation of the tort to unlawful conduct—"the actor's conduct was characterized by violence, fraud or defamation, and was tortious in character," see Restatement (Second) of Torts § 766B cmt. b (1979)—provides a viable definition and preserves the tort's utility of filling a gap in affording compensation in situations where a wrong has been done. The concepts of malice, justification, and privilege have not only proved to be overlapping and confusing, they provide no meaningful description of culpable conduct, as the Restatement (Second) of Torts concluded more than twenty years ago.

We therefore hold that to recover for tortious interference with a prospective business relation a plaintiff must prove that the defendant's conduct was independently tortious or wrongful. By independently tortious we do not mean that the plaintiff must be able to prove an independent tort. Rather, we mean only that the plaintiff must prove that the defendant's conduct would be actionable under a recognized tort. Thus, for example, a plaintiff may recover for tortious interference from a defendant who makes fraudulent statements about the plaintiff to a third person without proving that the third person was actually defrauded. * * * Likewise, a plaintiff may recover for tortious interference from a defendant who threatens a person with physical harm if he does business with the plaintiff. The plaintiff need prove only that the defendant's conduct toward the prospective customer would constitute assault. Also, a plaintiff could recover for tortious interference by showing an illegal boycott, although a plaintiff could not recover against a defendant whose persuasion of others not to deal with the plaintiff was lawful. Conduct that is merely "sharp" or unfair is not actionable and cannot be the basis for an action for tortious interference with prospective relations, and we disapprove of cases that suggest the contrary. * These examples are not exhaustive, but they illustrate what conduct can constitute tortious interference with prospective relations. * * *

In reaching this conclusion we treat tortious interference with prospective business relations differently than tortious interference with contract. It makes sense to require a defendant who induces a breach of contract to show some justification or privilege for depriving another of benefits to which the agreement entitled him. But when two parties are competing for interests to which neither is entitled, then neither can be said to be more justified or privileged in his pursuit. If the conduct of each is lawful, neither should be heard to complain that mere unfairness is actionable. Justification and privilege are not useful concepts in assessing interference with prospective relations, as they are in assessing interference with an existing contract.

III

With this understanding of what conduct is prohibited by the tort of interference with prospective contractual or business relations and what conduct is not prohibited, we return to the evidence of this case. * * * We must look to see whether there is evidence of harm from some independently tortious or unlawful activity by Wal-Mart.

The plaintiffs tell us that their interference claim is based on the telephone conversation between Hudson, Wal-Mart's realtor, and Callaway, Fleming's manager of store development. Specifically, the plaintiffs complain of Hudson's "ultimatum" to Callaway that if Wal-Mart were not able to acquire Tract 2 for expansion, it would relocate its store. The plaintiffs contend that Hudson's statement was false and therefore fraudulent. To be fraudulent a statement must be material and false, the speaker must have known it was false or acted recklessly without regard to its falsity, the speaker must have intended that the statement be acted on, and hearer [sic] must have relied on it. The plaintiffs do not dispute that Wal-Mart had undertaken to identify stores which could not be expanded and to relocate them, that it attempted to acquire Tract 2 as an alternative to relocating the * * * store, and that as Hudson told Callaway, if Wal-Mart could not acquire Tract 2 it would relocate. The only evidence the plaintiffs cite in support of their contention is that at the time Hudson called Callaway Wal-Mart had not begun efforts to relocate; that as a general matter Wal-Mart preferred to expand rather than relocate; and that there was room on Tract 1 for some expansion of the store. The fact that Wal-Mart had not begun to relocate its store when Hudson talked with Callaway is no evidence that his statement was false. The plaintiffs point to no evidence that Wal-Mart's general preference for expansion over relocation, or the possibilities for some expansion on Tract 1, would have made it decide not to relocate. Indeed, if Tract 1 had been adequate for Wal-Mart's intended expansion, it would not have needed to acquire Tract 2. Thus, no evidence supports the plaintiffs' contention that Hudson's statement to Callaway was fraudulent or that Hudson intended to deceive Callaway, and the plaintiffs do not contend that Wal-Mart's conduct was otherwise illegal or tortious. The record contains no evidence to indicate that Wal-Mart intended the plaintiffs any harm other than what they would necessarily suffer by Wal-Mart's successful acquisition of Tract 2, which they were both pursuing, by entirely lawful means. We therefore conclude that there is no evidence to support a judgment for the plaintiffs on their interference claim. * * *

NOTES

1.   *Determining Whether Interference Is Improper.* Compare the court's holding in *Wal-Mart Stores, Inc.* regarding the type of conduct necessary for a finding of improper interference with prospective contractual relations with the more inclusive, open-ended test suggested by the Restatement (Second) of Torts § 767 (1979) quoted in the opinion. Comment *c* to section 767 notes that some of the factors included in the section, "like fraud and physical violence, are tortious to the person immediately affected by them; others, like persuasion and offers of benefits, are not tortious to him. Under the same circumstances interference by some means is not improper while interference by other means is improper; and, likewise, the same means may be permissible under some circumstances while wrongful in others." See also Crandall Corp. v. Navistar Int'l Transp. Corp., 302 S.C. 265, 395 S.E.2d 179 (1990) (recognizing action for intentional interference with prospective contractual relations "for an improper purpose or by improper methods * * *. If a defendant acts for more than one purpose, his improper purpose must predominate * * *.").

Comment *c* to section 767 further states:

> * * * Violation of recognized ethical codes for a particular area of business activity or of established customs or practices regarding disapproved actions or methods may also be significant in evaluating the nature of the actor's conduct as a factor in determining whether his interference with the plaintiff's contractual relations was improper or not.

Restatement (Second) of Torts § 767 cmt. c (1979); see also Harris v. Perl, 41 N.J. 455, 197 A.2d 359 (1964); Adler, Barish, Daniels, Levin & Creskoff v. Epstein, 482 Pa. 416, 393 A.2d 1175 (1978) (A.B.A. Code of Professional Responsibility); contra, Della Penna v. Toyota Motor Sales, U.S.A., Inc., 11 Cal.4th 376, 45 Cal.Rptr.2d 436, 902 P.2d 740 (1995).

2.   *Protests and Boycotts.* Businesses injured by protests and boycotts sometimes try to use either the interference with contract or the interference with advantageous economic relations tort to end the boycott or recover damages. Generally, First Amendment interests trump the tort law interest. For example, in Missouri v. Nat'l Org. for Women, 620 F.2d 1301, 1317 (8th Cir.1980), *cert. denied*, 449 U.S. 842, 101 S.Ct. 122, 66 L.Ed.2d 49 (1980), the state of Missouri sought to end the boycott by the National Organization for Women (NOW) of the state, motivated by Missouri's failure to ratify the proposed United States constitutional amendment granting equal rights to women. Evidence showed that Missouri hotels and restaurants had suffered revenue losses. The substantive basis for the relief sought was primarily based on federal statutory law, but the plaintiffs also pursued state tort law actions. The Supreme Court held that "the right to petition is of such importance that it is not an improper interference when exercised by way of a boycott." In Women's Health Care Servs., P.A. v. Operation Rescue-National, 773

F.Supp. 258, 262–63 (D.Kan.1991), the federal district court granted a preliminary injunction to prevent Operation Rescue from physically blockading abortion clinics with the intention to "shut them down" on both federal grounds and state grounds, including interference with contract (the court of appeals upheld the injunctive relief on the state law claims, 24 F.3d 107 (10th Cir.1994)). See Hill v. Colorado, 530 U.S. 703, 120 S.Ct. 2480, 147 L.Ed.2d 597 (2000) and Schenck v. Pro-Choice Network, 519 U.S. 357, 117 S.Ct. 855, 137 L.Ed.2d 1 (1997) for recent Supreme Court opinions on the permissibility of restrictions on those seeking to prevent or discourage patient access to abortion clinics.

B. INJURIOUS FALSEHOOD

Auvil v. CBS "60 Minutes"
United States Court of Appeals for the Ninth Circuit, 1995.
67 F.3d 816.

■ PER CURIAM. * * * On February 26, 1989, CBS's weekly news show "60 Minutes" aired a segment on daminozide, a chemical growth regulator sprayed on apples. The broadcast, entitled " 'A' is for Apple," also addressed the slow pace of government efforts to recall the chemical. The broadcast was based largely on a Natural Resources Defense Council ("NRDC") report, entitled *Intolerable Risk: Pesticides in Our Children's Food* ("*Intolerable Risk*"), which outlined health risks associated with the use of a number of pesticides on fruit, especially the risks to children. " 'A' is for Apple" focused on the NRDC report's findings concerning daminozide, as well as the EPA's knowledge of daminozide's carcinogenity. Scientific research had indicated that daminozide, more commonly known by its trade name, Alar, breaks down into unsymmetrical dimethylhydrazine (UDMH), a carcinogen.[2]

The segment opened with the following capsule summary from Ed Bradley, a "60 Minutes" commentator:

The most potent cancer-causing agent in our food supply is a substance sprayed on apples to keep them on the trees longer and make them look better. That's the conclusion of a number of scientific experts. And who is most at risk? Children, who may someday develop cancer from this one chemical called daminozide. Daminozide, which has been sprayed on apples for more than 20 years, breaks down into another chemical called UDMH. * * *

Following the "60 Minutes" broadcast, consumer demand for apples and apple products decreased dramatically. The apple growers and others dependent upon apple production lost millions of dollars. Many of the growers lost their homes and livelihoods. * * *

The district court * * * granted summary judgment to CBS because the growers did not produce evidence sufficient to create a triable issue of fact as to the falsity of the broadcast. The growers appeal the district court's summary judgment ruling that they failed to offer evidence

---

[2] Alar cannot be removed either by washing the fruit or peeling it. In addition, the substance remains in the flesh of the apple and, as a result, can be found in processed apple products, including apple juice and applesauce.

sufficient to present a genuine issue of fact for trial on the falsity of the CBS broadcast. * * *

To establish a claim of product disparagement, also known as trade libel, a plaintiff must allege that the defendant published a knowingly false statement harmful to the interests of another and intended such publication to harm the plaintiff's pecuniary interests. Restatement (Second) of Torts § 623A (1977). Accordingly, for a product disparagement claim to be actionable, the plaintiff must prove, *inter alia,* the falsity of the disparaging statements. See Restatement (Second) of Torts §§ 623A, 651(1)(c) (1977).

Existing case law on product disparagement provides little guidance on the falsity prong. Nonetheless, as a tort whose actionability depends on the existence of disparaging speech, the tort is substantively similar to defamation. Therefore, we reference defamation cases to arrive at a decision in the instant matter.

" 'A' is for Apple" was based on *Intolerable Risk,* a scientific report disseminated by the NRDC. The report discussed the findings of cancer research studies on various chemicals used on fruit and questioned the EPA's hesitance in removing Alar from the market.[6] The broadcast contained a number of factual assertions, several of which are pointed out by the growers to support their claim that the broadcast falsely disparaged their product. On the subject of daminozide's cancer-causing potential, the growers point to the following statements:

> The most potent cancer-causing agent in our food supply is a substance sprayed on apples to keep them on the trees longer and make them look better.

> We know that [daminozide and other chemicals] do cause cancer.

> Just from these eight pesticides, what we're finding is that the risk of developing cancer is approximately 250 times what EPA says is an acceptable level of cancer in our population. * * *

The growers offered evidence showing that no studies have been conducted to test the relationship between ingestion of daminozide and incidence of cancer in *humans.* Such evidence, however, is insufficient to show a genuine issue for trial regarding the broadcast's assertions that daminozide is a potent carcinogen. Animal laboratory tests are a legitimate means for assessing cancer risks to humans. * * * The growers' only challenge to the scientific studies is their claim that animal studies cannot be relied on to indicate cancer risk for humans. Because animal studies can be relied upon, their evidence that no studies have been conducted on the effects of daminozide on humans does not create a genuine issue for trial on the falsity of the broadcast's assertions regarding daminozide's carcinogenicity.

On the subject of cancer risks to children from the use of daminozide on apples, the growers point to the following factual assertions to support their falsity claim:

---

[6] Neither party disputes that the broadcast disparaged apples. The broadcast communicated that daminozide is a potent human carcinogen that poses a significant risk to children. Because the broadcast focused on the use of daminozide on apples, the disparaging statements made during the broadcast about daminozide reflect negatively on apples.

What we're talking about is a cancer-causing agent used on food that EPA knows is going to cause cancer for thousands of children over their lifetime. * * *

[O]ver a lifetime, one child out of every 4,000 or so of our preschoolers will develop cancer just from these eight pesticides.

[The NRDC study] says children are being exposed to a pesticide risk several hundred times greater than what the agency says is acceptable.

The growers offered evidence showing that no scientific study has been conducted on cancer risks to children from the use of pesticides. However, CBS based its statements regarding cancer and children on the NRDC's findings that the daminozide found on apples is more harmful to children because they ingest more apple products per unit of body weight than do adults. The growers have provided no affirmative evidence that daminozide does not pose a risk to children. The fact that there have been no studies conducted specifically on the cancer risks to children from daminozide does nothing to disprove the conclusion that, if children consume more of a carcinogenic substance than do adults, they are at higher risk for contracting cancer. The growers' evidence, therefore, does not create a genuine issue as to the falsity of the broadcast's assertion that daminozide is more harmful to children.

Despite their inability to prove that *statements* made during the broadcast were false, the growers assert that summary judgment for CBS was improper because a jury could find that the broadcast contained a provably false *message*, viewing the broadcast segment in its entirety. They further argue that, if they can prove the falsity of this implied message, they have satisfied their burden of proving falsity. The growers' contentions are unavailing. Their attempt to derive a specific, implied message from the broadcast as a whole and to prove the falsity of that overall *message* is unprecedented and inconsistent with Washington law. * * * The Washington courts' view finds support in the Restatement, which instructs that a product disparagement plaintiff has the burden of proving the "falsity of the *statement.*" Restatement (Second) of Torts § 651(1)(c) (1977) (emphasis added). This standard refers to individual statements and not to any overall message. Therefore, we must reject the growers' invitation to infer an overall message from the broadcast and determine whether that message is false.

We also note that, if we were to accept the growers' argument, plaintiffs bringing suit based on disparaging speech would escape summary judgment merely by arguing, as the growers have, that a jury should be allowed to determine both the overall message of a broadcast and whether that overall message is false. Because a broadcast could be interpreted in numerous, nuanced ways, a great deal of uncertainty would arise as to the message conveyed by the broadcast. Such uncertainty would make it difficult for broadcasters to predict whether their work would subject them to tort liability. Furthermore, such uncertainty raises the spectre of a chilling effect on speech.[11]

---

[11] There is an additional problem with the growers' arguments: their approach allows disparagement plaintiffs to construct an overall message that lends itself easily to proof of

Because the growers have failed to raise a genuine issue of material fact regarding the falsity of statements made during the broadcast of " 'A' is for Apple," the district court's decision granting CBS's motion for summary judgment is affirmed.

NOTES

1. *Injurious Falsehood.* The Restatement (Second) of Torts § 623A *et seq.* (1977) identifies a tort of "injurious falsehood" which encompasses false and derogatory statements about a variety of interests including not only products, but also interests in other property. Disparagement of the quality of products is also known as "trade libel." *Id.* § 626. In Anheuser-Busch, Inc. v. John Labatt Ltd., 89 F.3d 1339, 1347 (8th Cir.1996), the court affirmed verdict for the plaintiff Anheuser-Busch in an injurious falsehood claim against the defendant Labatt based upon the defendant's advertising slogan, "If It's Not Labatt's, It's Not Ice Beer."

2. *Disparagement of Title.* The Restatement (Second) of Torts also provides for an action for disparagement of property, frequently known by the traditional term, "slander of title." *Id.* § 624; see also Horning v. Hardy, 36 Md.App. 419, 373 A.2d 1273 (1977). In TXO Prod. Corp. v. Alliance Res. Corp., 187 W.Va. 457, 419 S.E.2d 870 (1992), aff'd 509 U.S. 443, 113 S.Ct. 2711, 125 L.Ed.2d 366 (1993), the appellant alleged that the appellee TXO Production Corporation had filed a "frivolous" declaratory judgment action, purported to clear a "cloud" in the title to leased oil and gas rights that the appellant and the appellee had agreed to develop. The appellant counterclaimed asserting a slander of title claim and alleging that in fact the appellant's real purpose was to create a "cloud on the title," thus reducing royalty payments owed under their agreement. The court traced the origins of the action for slander of title:

> * * * [T]he slander of title cause of action was especially important 400 years ago when many transfers of land were oral transfers (i.e., feoffment with livery of seisin), and when, the Domesday Book notwithstanding, land records were much less complete than they are today.

The court upheld the trial court judgment for the appellant and adopted essentially the Restatement (Second) of Torts formulation for what the Restatement refers to as "disparagement of title" (slander of title):

> From the Restatement, we can deduce the elements of slander of title:
>
> 1. publication of
>
> 2. a false statement
>
> 3. derogatory to plaintiff's title

---

falsity. The instant case provides a cogent example. Rather than proving the falsity of statements made during " 'A' is for Apple" by challenging the studies upon which factual assertions made during the broadcast were based, the growers request that we analyze the message that the studies *conclusively* show that apples cause cancer in humans. Accordingly, the growers offered evidence that the studies are *not conclusive*, that there are no studies tracing the specific link between ingestion of daminozide and incidence of cancer in humans. It is considerably easier to prove the falsity of an assertion that studies are conclusive, rather than to prove the falsity of the studies themselves.

4.   with malice

5.   causing special damages

6.   as a result of diminished value in the eyes of third parties.

Id. at 466, 419 S.E.2d at 879. See Restatement (Second) of Torts §§ 623A and 624 (1977).

C. PRIMA FACIE TORT

Advance Music Corp. v. American Tobacco Co.

Court of Appeals of New York, 1946.
296 N.Y. 79, 70 N.E.2d 401.

■ LOUGHRAN, CHIEF JUDGE. The amended complaint in this action is attacked by motion under rule 106 of the Rules of Civil Practice for insufficiency on its face. Three separately stated causes of action are pleaded therein.

By way of inducement, the first cause makes these allegations: The plaintiff is a corporation engaged in the business of publishing musical compositions. Its revenue is chiefly derived from sales of sheet music made to the public and from licenses for use of its compositions in the entertainment field. It expends large sums of money for advertising in an effort to create a general impression that its compositions are or will be among the most popular song successes of the day. Methods employed by the plaintiff to that end include performances of its compositions by bandleaders and entertainers through the media of radio, phonograph recordings and motion pictures. Jobbers, dealers and the general public normally purchase musical compositions which are currently made popular by means of advertising of that kind. Sheet music is handled by jobbers and dealers on consignment. Premature return or other failure to promote sales thereof brings about serious loss to the publisher.

In respect of the wrong asserted by the plaintiff, the first cause of action goes on to say: The defendants—a tobacco company and an advertising concern—are the creators of a commercial coast-to-coast radio program which is broadcast each Saturday night. "A wide listening audience estimated to be in excess of fifteen million people per week is attracted to this program by reason of the constant representations . . . made by the defendants that said program consists of the rendition of the nine or ten most popular songs of the week in the relative order of their popularity based upon an extensive and accurate survey conducted throughout the nation." Weekly lists of the songs thus classified by the defendants upon their radio program are widely circulated by them, "so that the public, dealers, jobbers, motion picture companies, phonograph companies, electrical transcription companies, radio station performers and entertainers, and others, may be induced to rely upon such lists and purchase and use the music stated to be the most popular." In pursuing this course, the defendants act wantonly and without good faith. Their selections and ratings of the nine or ten most popular songs of the week "are in fact the choice or result of caprice or of other considerations foreign to a selection based on an accurate and extensive survey of the nation-wide popularity of such songs and the relative order of their popularity for the current week of such broadcast." Songs published by the plaintiff which are among the first nine or ten most popular musical compositions of the nation are either passed over by the defendants or placed on their radio program and weekly lists in an improper order of popularity.

In respect of the damages complained of by the plaintiff, the first cause of action sets forth the following particulars: Music jobbers and dealers, bandleaders, entertainers, supervisors of radio programs, phonograph recording companies and motion picture producers in choosing songs are largely influenced by the selections and ratings which the defendants disseminate by way of their radio program and weekly lists. On that account, jobbers and dealers prematurely return songs of the plaintiff and thereby prevent distribution thereof to retail outlets for sale to the public. For the same reason, most users of music are induced to accept the songs heralded by the defendants and to neglect songs published by the plaintiff. In consequence of all this, the measures taken by the plaintiff for exploitation of its songs are frustrated; the value of its musical compositions is depreciated; its revenue is diminished; and its property rights and business prestige are impaired.

The foregoing parts of the first cause of action are incorporated by reference into the second cause of action and are there followed by the further allegation that "the aforesaid acts and representations on the part of the defendants are made with intent to injure the plaintiff." Thus in sum and substance the second cause of action constitutes a statement to this effect: The defendants are wantonly causing damage to the plaintiff by a system of conduct on their part which warrants an inference that they intend harm of that type. So read, the second cause of action is, we think, adequate in its office as a plaintiff's pleading.

In Skinner & Co. v. Shew & Co. [1893] 1 Ch. 413, 422, Lord Justice Bowen said: "At Common Law there was a cause of action whenever one person did damage to another wilfully and intentionally, and without just cause or excuse." So, in Aikens v. State of Wisconsin, 195 U.S. 194, 25 S.Ct. 3, 49 L.Ed.at 154 (1904), the court said: "It has been considered that, *prima facie*, the intentional infliction of temporal damages is a cause of action, which, as a matter of substantive law, whatever may be the form of pleading requires a justification if the defendant is to escape." 195 U.S. at 204, 25 S.Ct. at 5, 49 L.Ed. at 159 (Holmes, J.). These broad propositions were approved by Sir Frederick Pollock as authority for his doctrine that all willful harm is actionable unless the defendant justify or excuse his conduct. F. Pollock, The Law of Torts 17, 18 (14th ed. 1939).

On the other hand, the view that all intentional wrongdoing is prima facie tortious has been rejected by other high authorities who contrariwise maintain that every plaintiff must bring his case under some accepted head of tort liability. "The only adequate answer to many claims for damages [said Sir John Salmond] is the mere *ipse dixit* of the law that no such cause of action is recognized." J. Salmond, Torts 15–16, note m (10th ed.1945). So, Mr. P. A. Landon, as editor of the fourteenth edition of Pollock's Law of Torts, says: "The law is to-day, as it has always been, that only that harm which falls within one of the specified categories of wrong-doing entitles the person aggrieved to a legal remedy. The categories of tort (not, of course, the categories of particular torts) are closed." F. Pollock, *supra,* at 14.

This difference over the general principles of liability in tort was composed for us in Opera on Tour, Inc. v. Weber, 285 N.Y. 348, 34 N.E.2d 349 (1941). We there adopted from Aikens v. State of Wisconsin, *supra,* the declaration that *"prima facie,* the intentional infliction of temporal damages is a cause of action, which . . . requires a justification if the defendant is to escape." The above second cause of action alleges such a prima facie tort and, therefore, is sufficient in law on its face. * * * The justification that is required in a case like this must, of course, be one which the law will recognize. *

The judgment of the Appellate Division should be reversed and the order of Special Term affirmed, with costs in this court and in the Appellate Division.

NOTES

1.   *Motive.* In Twin Labs., Inc. v. Weider Health & Fitness, 900 F.2d 566 (2d Cir.1990), the plaintiff, a producer of bodybuilding supplements, filed a lawsuit alleging a prima facie tort claim against a competitor when the competitor's wholly owned subsidiary refused to place the plaintiff's advertisements in its two bodybuilding magazines. The court held that under New York law, the claim failed because the plaintiff failed to establish that the "sole motive" in refusing the advertising was "disinterested malevolence." The court stated that the defendant's conduct must not only be harmful, but also must be "done with sole intent to harm." According to the court, other motives such as " 'profit, self-interest, or business advantage' will not suffice under the doctrine of prima facie tort."

2.   *Recognition of Prima Facie Tort.* The principle behind the prima facie tort is reflected in several sections of the Restatement (Second) of Torts, e.g., § 870 (liability for injury caused intentionally by conduct "generally culpable and not justifiable under the circumstances"). A few states have followed New York's lead in recognizing the prima facie tort. E.g., Lord v. Souder, 748 A.2d 393, 402–03 (Del.2000) (recognizing principle, but refusing to apply it to facts of case); Nazeri v. Mo. Valley Coll., 860 S.W.2d 303, 315 (Mo.1993) (dicta, recognizing action as "a particular and limited theory of recovery with specific elements").

D. UNFAIR COMPETITION: OTHER ASPECTS

Pennsylvania State University v. University Orthopedics, Ltd.

Superior Court of Pennsylvania, 1998.
706 A.2d 863.

■ CAVANAUGH, JUDGE. * * * UO [University Orthopedics] is a professional medical corporation located in State College, Pennsylvania, which provides orthopedic and sports medicine services. PSU [Pennsylvania State University] is a state-supported institution of higher education based in State College, Pennsylvania, which, through its College of Medicine, operates a network of health care facilities throughout the State College and central Pennsylvania area. Through the Penn State Center for Sports Medicine located in State College, PSU offers orthopedic and sports medicine services to the general public. The dispute in this case arose over UO's use of the word "university" in conjunction with its medical practice. PSU's health care services are grouped under the name "University Health Services" and it employs the word "university" in connection with many of the medical services it offers. PSU alleged the use of "university" by UO was designed to cause consumers of medical services to believe that UO was affiliated with PSU. UO has used "university" not only as part of its logo, but in a variety of promotional materials and advertisements. * * *

On December 9, 1994 PSU filed an equity action against UO seeking injunctive relief and damages. PSU's complaint contained four counts * * *. With respect to PSU's claim of unfair competition and trademark infringement, the court found that PSU failed to raise a "passing off" theory of liability.[1] As such, it concluded that PSU was required to prove that it had a legal right to the exclusive use of the word "university." The court then found that "university" was a generic term and that UO was entitled to summary judgment on the issues of unfair competition and trademark infringement. * * * Following the entry of summary judgment, PSU filed this appeal. * * *

Here, the trial court found that "university" was a generic term and PSU does not challenge that determination. After reviewing the record and pertinent legal authority, we agree with the trial court that "university" is a generic term. * * * A generic term is one that is * * * so commonly descriptive of a product or service that it does not identify the specific source of the product or service. * "University" has been defined as an institution of higher learning providing facilities for teaching and research and authorized to grant academic degrees. Webster's New Collegiate Dictionary 1271 (1979). Here, the primary significance of "university" indicates a nature or class—institutions of higher learning—rather than specific origin—PSU. The term fits squarely within the definition of generic: PSU is a species of the broader, general, generic term "university." This conclusion, however, does not end our analysis. * * *

We begin our analysis by examining PSU's complaint, in light of the trial court's conclusion that it failed to plead a claim of "passing off." After reviewing the complaint, we find that PSU did, in fact, specifically raise the "passing off" theory and pled sufficient facts to establish a claim of unfair competition. PSU alleged that its use of the word "university" in conjunction with its medical services, including orthopedic and sports medicine services, has come to indicate to actual and potential consumers that such services originate with PSU or from those affiliated with PSU. It further alleged that UO exploited a nonexistent relationship with PSU by advertising its orthopedic and sports medicine services using the word "university" and by suggesting or implying an affiliation with PSU. It also alleged UO's use of the word "university" was a deception of the public, that it was a false representation of fact likely to cause confusion as to the actual provider

---

[1] Under a "passing off" theory, a plaintiff alleges the public was confused or deceived into mistakenly purchasing a competitor's product or service in the belief it was the product or service of the plaintiff.

of the medical services and that UO was passing itself off as having an affiliation with PSU.

* * * There was also evidence that UO distributed advertisements at PSU sporting events. UO indicated in some advertisements that one of its physicians served as "Team Surgeon for Penn State athletes since 1989." Finally, the evidence submitted by PSU indicates that actual confusion occurred between its center for sports medicine and UO's practice. PSU documented at least 34 instances, over a seven-month period, when consumers of medical services or members of the medical community mistakenly contacted its Center for Sports Medicine, believing they were contacting UO. * * * In Hanover Star Milling Company v. Metcalf, 240 U.S. 403, 413, 36 S.Ct. 357, 360, 60 L.Ed.713 (1916), the Supreme Court said,—"This essential element (i.e., 'passing off' or deception) is the same in trademark cases as in cases of unfair competition unaccompanied with trademark infringement. In fact, the common law of trademarks is but a part of the broader law of unfair competition." The action for unfair competition "exists today separate and apart from any statutory rights which the owner of the trademark possesses." House of Westmore, Inc. v. Denney, 151 F.2d 261, 265 (3d Cir.1945). In Manz v. Philadelphia Brewing Co., 37 F.Supp. 79, 80 (E.D. Pa. 1940), it was recognized that ". . . trade-names can only be protected against use or imitation on the ground of unfair competition." The gist of the action lies in the deception practiced in "passing off" the goods of one for that of another. * * *

The law of unfair competition also requires that a company, entering a field already occupied by a rival of established reputation, "must do nothing which will unnecessarily create or increase confusion between his goods or business and the goods or business of the rival." *Id.* Moreover, the trading on another's business reputation by use of deceptive selling practices or other means is enjoinable on the grounds of unfair competition. If the particular use in question is reasonably likely to produce confusion in the public mind, equity will restrain the unfair practice and compel an accounting of the profits gained thereby. *

As with federal law, descriptive, geographical and generic words, as well as words of common or general usage belong to the public and are not capable of exclusive appropriation. * However, a competitor's use of a name, label, symbol or trademark may be enjoined where the mark has acquired a secondary meaning. In order to establish secondary meaning, it must be shown that people in the trade or the purchasing public perceives the word or name as standing for the business of a particular company. * A generic term, even where it has developed a secondary meaning, is never granted trademark protection. * Nonetheless, an action for unfair competition on the basis of a likelihood of confusion may still lie.

* * * PSU argues that it does not have to prove it possesses a right to the exclusive use of the term "university"; and that even if "university" is a generic term, there are sufficient facts to support a claim of "passing off." We agree with the trial court insofar as it concluded that PSU did not establish it possessed a legal right to the exclusive use of the word "university." A generic term by definition is incapable of exclusive appropriation. Nonetheless, as we have already

concluded that summary judgment was improperly entered with respect to PSU's federal claim, we also now conclude, based upon the averments of fact in PSU's complaint and the documentary evidence submitted by PSU, that summary judgment was erroneously entered on PSU's common law unfair competition claim under a "passing off" theory. There exists [sic] genuine issues of material fact as to whether UO's use of the generic term "university," in conjunction with its medical practice, would be reasonably likely to cause confusion or the likelihood of confusion among the public and whether consumers of medical services viewing UO's name and advertisements would be reasonably likely to assume an affiliation with PSU. As such, the grant of summary judgment on this claim was improper. * * *

We conclude the trial court erred in entering summary judgment in favor of UO on * * * its claim for common law unfair competition * * *. The court erroneously concluded that PSU had failed to plead the theory of "passing off" in relation to its claims for unfair competition and that PSU was required to prove an exclusive right to use of the word "university" in order to obtain relief. * * * Accordingly, we reverse the court's order entering summary judgment in favor of UO and remand the case for further proceedings consistent with this Opinion. * * *

NOTES

1. *Lanham Act.* The Trademark Act of 1946, also known as the Lanham Act, 15 U.S.C. §§ 1051–1127 (2012) provides comprehensive federal regulation of trademarks. A trademark is a word, name, symbol, device or other designation that is distinctive to goods or services and which is used in a manner to identify such goods or services and to distinguish them from others. Restatement (Third) of Unfair Competition § 9 (1995). Trademarks are also regulated by state statutes. Section 43(a) of the Lanham Act creates causes of action for a wide variety of unfair competition claims beyond those based strictly on trademark, such as injurious falsehood and "passing off."

Other federal and state statutes regulate competitive conduct beyond the Lanham Act and provide private causes of actions to injured plaintiffs. Patent and copyright statutes, like many of the provisions of the Lanham Act, protect intellectual property interests. See 17 U.S.C. §§ 101 *et seq.* (2012) (copyright); 35 U.S.C. § 1 (2012) (patent). In addition, conduct that threatens to reduce or eliminate competition may impose liability under federal or state antitrust law. See, e.g., Sherman Antitrust Act, 15 U.S.C. §§ 1–7 (2012) (conspiracy in restraint of trade, attempt to monopolize); Clayton Antitrust Act, 15 U.S.C. §§ 12–17 (2012).

2. *State Law and Unfair Competition.* A comprehensive study of unfair competition obviously is beyond the scope of this section. Today, statutes in every single state govern the area. See Restatement (Third) of Unfair Competition § 1, Statutory Note (1995) (listing state statutes). Yet a variety of common law actions remain. See, e.g., McCoy v. Mitsuboshi Cutlery, Inc., 67 F.3d 917, 925 n.2 (Fed.Cir.1995) (under Texas law, recognizing common law torts for "passing off," trade-secret misappropriation, and misappropriation of business opportunity). In addition, unfair competition also becomes subject to tort liability when it takes the form of another tort. E.g., Evenson v. Spaulding, 150 F. 517 (9th Cir.1907) (physical interference); Hayes v. Irwin, 541 F.Supp. 397 (N.D.Ga.1982), aff'd 729 F.2d 1466 (11th Cir.1984), cert. denied 469 U.S. 857, 105 S.Ct. 185, 83 L.Ed.2d 119 (1984) (defamation and disparagement).

CHAPTER 17

DEFAMATION

The actions of libel and slander afford redress for harm to reputation resulting from defamatory statements.

The rules and principles governing defamation are, to a considerable degree, ancient ones, crystallized in the struggles for jurisdiction among the early English courts. Separate systems of rules developed for slander—oral defamation, within the jurisdiction of the ecclesiastical courts and later the common law courts—and for libel—written defamation, originally a matter of concern to the Court of the Star Chamber because of its potential to encourage sedition. This legacy of the early common law of defamation remains influential in determining many basic issues in contemporary defamation actions.

The tort of defamation, however, has undergone revolutionary changes in the United States since 1964 as a result of developments in constitutional law. Defamation law has always presented a conflict between the protection of plaintiffs' interest in reputation and defendants' ability to communicate freely with others. In a series of cases beginning with *New York Times v. Sullivan, infra* pages 902–911, the Supreme Court recognized that the impact of defamation actions on defendants' freedom to communicate could raise constitutional concerns. These Supreme Court decisions have required states to alter important aspects of the law of defamation.

A. BASIS OF LIABILITY

Idema v. Wager

United States District Court for the Southern District of New York, 2000.
120 F.Supp.2d 361.

■ McMAHON, JUDGE. On January 29, 1999, an article with the headline, "Militant Sues Red Hook" was published by defendant Richard K. Wager ("Wager"), publisher of defendant *The Poughkeepsie Journal* ("*Journal*"). * The *Journal* has a daily circulation of 45,000 * * *. At the time of publication, the plaintiffs, Jonathon Keith Idema ("Idema") and Counterr Group, Inc. ("Counterr"), a police and military training organization headed by Idema, had commenced a civil suit against the Town of Red Hook in the Supreme Court of Dutchess County in New York. * * * On January 30, 1999, after reading the article, Idema faxed a letter to Wager. He demanded a retraction and written apology to the plaintiffs for use of word "militant" to describe them. He claimed that the defendants wanted to associate them with members of the Communist party, or in the alternative, with individuals who advocate the overthrow of the United States government by force. On February 1, 1999, Wager's faxed response to Idema was: "After careful review of the facts, we believe our reporting has been fair." On February 5, 1999, Idema forwarded a certified mail letter to Wager. Again, he requested a retraction and an apology for use of the word "militant" to describe him and his organization. He also threatened to commence action for libel and defamation. As the reader will surmise, whatever response he received from defendants was unsatisfactory, and he made good his threat. * * *

The first cause of action sounds in libel and defamation. Plaintiffs allege that the defendants' use of word "militant" in its headline discredited plaintiffs' profession and professionalism, and exposed them to "hate, ridicule, and contempt." * * *

Defamation is the injury to one's reputation either by written expression, which is libel, or by oral expression, which is slander. * The law of defamation serves to protect an individual's right to one's reputation. * To establish a prima facie case of personal injury based on the publication of libel or slander, all of the following elements are required: 1) a false and defamatory statement of and concerning the plaintiff; 2) publication by defendant of such a statement to a third party; 3) fault on part of the defendant; and 4) injury to plaintiff. * * *

[T]his court needs to determine whether the use of the word "militant" in the headline is susceptible of being defamatory at all. The relevant inquiry focuses on whether the allegedly defamatory word or phrase constitutes a fact or an opinion. In making this determination (which is, again, a question of law for the Court *), courts use a three-part inquiry: (1) whether the specific language used was precise and readily understood; (2) whether statements are susceptible of being proven false; and (3) whether context of statements signals to reader that what is being conveyed is likely to be opinion or fact. [See *infra* pages 926–930].

Plaintiff argues, citing Flamm v. American Association of University Women, 201 F.3d 144 (2d Cir.2000), (1) that Defendant's use of the word "militant" reasonably implies that Plaintiff engages in "revolutionary socialism", and (2) that the accusation "can be proven false." However, the libelous innuendo at issue in *Flamm* is too dissimilar to serve as a basis for this Plaintiff's challenge. In *Flamm*, Defendant American Association of University Women published a directory of attorneys which included a description of the attorney Flamm as " 'an ambulance chaser' with an interest only in 'slam-dunk cases.' " The *Flamm* court found that these phrases "reasonably" implied that Flamm "[e]ngaged in the unethical solicitation of clients" and that the accusation could be proven false. The phrase "ambulance chaser" as applied to an attorney cannot be read without a negative inference, whereas the use of the word "militant" to describe this Plaintiff carries no clear inference at all. Therefore, where "ambulance chaser" conveys an obvious, negative message which * * * "militant" may not.

The word "militant" used in the headline of which plaintiff complains is not defamatory as a matter of law and will not support an action for defamation. The word itself has many meanings and shades of meaning, ranging from the religious ("the Church Militant[,]" a term used to refer to Christians who are currently alive and, presumably, fighting the forces of evil in the name of Jesus), to the political ("Militant Civil Rights Activist[,]" referring to those who fight with soldierly zeal to combat for the cause of equal rights). Susan B. Anthony, Martin Luther King, Jr., and Mother Teresa have each been called "militant" in the service of their respective causes, yet society regards them as noble, not nutty. Thus, contrary to plaintiffs' assertion, the word does not have a "precise and readily understood meaning" such that the reader would immediately perceive it to be derogatory. * Standing alone, the word carries no connotation whatever of Communism, extremism or belonging to what plaintiffs describe as "the fringe elements of society." Nor does it suggest any design to overthrow the Government. Indeed, the word is far less precise than the phrase "fellow traveler of fascism," which has been held not to have a precise and unambiguous meaning and not to be susceptible of being proven false. See Buckley v. Littell, 539 F.2d 882, 894 (2d Cir.1976). Therefore, the average reader would be more likely to conclude that the word was used as an opinion about plaintiff, rather than as a fact.

* * * [T]he Court is required to put the word back in its allegedly libelous context—what is referred to as a totality of circumstances test. * Thus * * * the effect of the headline and the article on the ordinary reader must be examined together under a totality of circumstances. * Circumstances that tend to establish the false and defamatory nature of a word or phrase include the "tone" of the reportage, * and the content of the headline and the article. * The content of the headline and article are examined using the common usage or meaning of the specific language used in the challenged statement. * The challenged language should not be construed with the close precision expected from lawyers and judges, because the ordinary reader would not stop to analyze. * Nonetheless, whether the common usage or meaning of the challenged language ascribed to it is capable of a defamatory meaning is to be determined by the courts. * And in determining what is the common usage or meaning of challenged specific language, courts must not find defamatory interpretation where none exists or strain to interpret it in its mildest and most inoffensive sense. * Only where reasonable minds could disagree over the tone and content of an article and its headline must the claim go to the jury, "to determine in what sense the words were used and understood by the ordinary reader." *

The instant complaint does not even present a close question, let alone one over which reasonable minds could differ. * * * To adopt the plaintiff's interpretation of the word "militant" as referring to "revolutionary Socialism," would not explain any statement in the article, but would add "an entirely new and independent thought" that finds no support in the body of the article. * Nothing in the language of the article, plain or implied meaning, would subject the plaintiff to contempt, aversion or affect him in his calling as a criminologist or police instructor. Nothing in the story supports plaintiffs' reading of the word "militant" as advocating the overthrow of the Government or being on the lunatic fringe of society. * * * Thus, because nothing in the article would subject them to hatred, contempt or aversion, the use of the word "militant" in the headline would not do so. * * * Because plaintiffs have failed to satisfy the first element needed to sustain a claim of libel under New York law, it is not necessary to analyze any of the other elements. The first cause of action is dismissed. * * *

NOTES

1. *Can a Plaintiff Be Defamation-Proof?* If the tort of defamation protects against a loss of reputation, can the pre-existing reputation of the plaintiff be so bad as to preclude recovery of damages for defamation? Consider Cardillo v. Doubleday & Co., 518 F.2d 638 (2d Cir.1975), where the plaintiff, a prison inmate described by the court as a "habitual criminal," brought suit against the author of a book about organized crime that claimed the plaintiff had participated in a series of robberies. In a later opinion, however, the same court suggested that "the doctrine of 'libel-proof' defendants" is a "narrow one" that should be limited to the facts of the *Cardillo* case. Buckley v. Littell, 539 F.2d 882, 889 (2d Cir.1976), cert. denied, 429 U.S. 1062, 97 S.Ct. 785, 50 L.Ed.2d 777 (1977). See also Brandt v. Super. Ct., 67 Cal.2d 437, 443, 62 Cal.Rptr. 429, 433, 432 P.2d 31, 35 (1967) ("A man with a very bad reputation may be libeled").

2. *A Defamatory Photograph.* In Burton v. Crowell Pub. Co., 82 F.2d 154, 154–155 (2d Cir.1936), the defendant published a pictorial advertisement for Camel cigarettes featuring the plaintiff. Judge Learned Hand described the photograph as follows:

> * * * [T]he plaintiff was a widely known gentleman steeple-chaser, and the text quoted him as declaring that "Camel" cigarettes "restored" him after "a crowded business day." * * * [The second picture] represented him coming from a race to be weighed in; he is carrying his saddle in front of him with his right hand under the pommel and his left under the cantle; the line of the seat is about twelve inches below his waist. Over the pommel hangs a stirrup; over the seat at his middle a wide girth falls loosely in such a way that it seems to be attached to the plaintiff and not the saddle. So regarded, the photograph becomes grotesque, monstrous, and obscene * * *.

Judge Hand readily acknowledged that readers viewing the advertisement would recognize that it was an "optical illusion" and "that it was the camera, and the camera alone, that had made this unfortunate mistake." Nevertheless, the judge concluded that the photograph "exposed the plaintiff to overwhelming ridicule" and that "[s]uch a caricature affects a man's reputation, if by that is meant his position in the mind of others; the association so established may be beyond repair; he may become known indefinitely as the absurd victim of this unhappy mischance." If it was clear to the reader that the plaintiff's appearance was an unfortunate mistake, how could the photograph have been false and defamatory? A leading torts treatise offers this explanation:

> The advertisement, it is submitted, is defamatory, not because the ridicule need not flow from a false factual assertion, but because * * * there really was a false factual communication. For an instant it seems to the viewer that a grotesque appendage is attached. This is factual. That the viewer's belief in it is only transitory is irrelevant. * * * In context, the depiction is sufficient to trigger ridicule that is not merely transitory.

Harper, James and Gray on Torts §5.2.

Excerpt, Thomas A. Street, The Foundations of Legal Liability
300 (1906).

Where the language alleged to be defamatory does not appear to be such on its face, the plaintiff is required to state fully in his declaration the circumstances which make the words actionable. This is done by setting forth, in addition of course to the words actually used, what is called the inducement, the colloquium, and the innuendo. The first term is applied to the narrative of the extrinsic circumstances under which the words were used and which are necessary to be known before the defamatory meaning can attach. The office of the colloquium is to connect the spoken or written words with the circumstances disclosed in the inducement, while the innuendo interprets the meaning of the language used in the light of the surrounding circumstances and discloses its sting to the court. The purpose of all this elaborate apparatus is merely to enable the court to ascertain with certainty the meaning which the language was really intended and understood to have. Consequently, it is settled that there can be no enlargement of the meaning of words by innuendo beyond that which they may properly bear under the facts disclosed in the inducement and colloquium.

Ball v. Roane
Court of Queen's Bench, 1592.
78 Eng.Rep. 559, Cro.Eliz. 308.

Action for these words: "There was never a robbery committed within forty miles of Wellingborough, but thou hadst thy part in it." After verdict it was moved in arrest of judgment, that the action did not lie, because it was not averred there was any robbery committed within forty miles, &c. for otherwise it is no slander—*Et sic opinio Cur'*; and judgment for the defendant. Mich. 36. & 37. Eliz. 6. R. Placito 11.

Ball v. Roane
Court of Queen's Bench, 1593.
78 Eng.Rep. 591, Cro. Eliz. 342.

Action for Words. "There was never a purse cut within twenty miles of Wellingborough, but thou hadst thy part in it." And avers, that such a purse was cut, &c. and he had no part in it.—And it was moved, that an action lieth not; for it is not said he had a part of it as a partaker in the felony; for he may have a part in it in the loss, and so it is no slander.—But it was adjudged for the plaintiff; for the words shall be taken to be spoken in the worst sense, in disgrace and reproach of the plaintiff.—*Nota*, Serjeant Yelverton cited a case, Pasch. 32. Eliz. Sir Edward Hastings brought an action for these words: "You have procured a perjured man to seek my blood;" and ruled, that an action did not lie. But Fenner said the case was not adjudged, but ended by his arbitrament.

Anthony Theobald v. Brook

Court of Queen's Bench, 1597.
78 Eng.Rep. 859, Cro.Eliz. 618.

Action for these words, which the defendant spake to one Gurney: "Bring me to the constable's house, for I am robbed this night: and bring me to Bonaventure Theobalds' house to arrest him; for old Theobalds (innuendo the plaintiff) setteth his sons to rob me (*innuendo dictum Bonaventure, et quendam Johannem, filium ipsuis Anthonii*) from time to time." The defendant pleaded not guilty and found against him. After verdict it was moved in arrest of judgment, that the words were not actionable, because it is not alleged that any of Anthony's sons robbed him; and it is but an intent of setting to rob, and no act done: the words also are insensible.—But notwithstanding it was held by The Court, that the words were very slanderous, and that the action was maintainable. And so it had been adjudged in this court, that "one such lay in wait to murder me;" or, that "he sent his servant to murder me." Wherefore it was adjudged for the plaintiff.—Note. Error was hereof brought, because it is not precisely affirmed *of* the plaintiff, but it is said Old Theobalds, and he doth not name the plaintiff, and an innuendo will not serve. Whereupon it was reversed.

NOTE

Mitior Sensus. Would those hearing the statement about the plaintiff likely believe that he had committed a crime? Does the court here strain to find that the words might have a more innocent explanation? In the past, judges sought to give words an innocent meaning under the doctrine of *mitior sensus* (i.e., words should be construed in the "milder sense"). This doctrine, however, has been in decline since the eighteenth century and now largely has disappeared (except to some extent in Illinois). In modern times, the court determines whether the words are capable of being interpreted in a defamatory manner, and the jury decides whether in fact they were so understood.

B. "OF AND CONCERNING THE PLAINTIFF"

Peck v. Tribune Co.

Supreme Court of the United States, 1909.
214 U.S. 185, 29 S.Ct. 554, 53 L.Ed. 960.

■ HOLMES, JUSTICE. This is an action on the case for a libel. The libel alleged is found in an advertisement printed in the defendant's newspaper, The Chicago Sunday Tribune, and so far as is material is as follows: "Nurse and Patients Praise Duffy's. Mrs. A. Schuman, One of Chicago's Most Capable and Experienced Nurses, Pays an Eloquent Tribute to the Great Invigorating, Life-Giving, and Curative Properties of Duffy's Pure Malt Whisky." Then followed a portrait of the plaintiff, with the words, "Mrs. A. Schuman," under it. Then, in quotation marks, "After years of constant use of your Pure Malt Whiskey, both by myself and as given to patients in my capacity as nurse, I have no hesitation in recommending it as the very best tonic and stimulant for all weak and run-down conditions," etc., etc., with the words "Mrs. A. Schuman, 1576

Mozart St., Chicago, Ill.," at the end, not in quotation marks, but conveying the notion of a signature, or at least that the words were hers. The declaration alleged that the plaintiff was not Mrs. Schuman, was not a nurse, and was a total abstainer from whisky and all spirituous liquors. There was also a count for publishing the plaintiff's likeness without leave. The defendant pleaded not guilty. At the trial, subject to exceptions, the judge excluded the plaintiff's testimony in support of her allegations just stated, and directed a verdict for the defendant. His action was sustained by the Circuit Court of Appeals. *

Of course, the insertion of the plaintiff's picture in the place and with the concomitants that we have described imported that she was the nurse and made the statements set forth * * *. Many might recognize the plaintiff's face without knowing her name, and those who did know it might be led to infer that she had sanctioned the publication under an alias. There was some suggestion that the defendant published the portrait by mistake, and without knowledge that it was the plaintiff's portrait, or was not what it purported to be. But the fact, if it was one, was no excuse. If the publication was libelous, the defendant took the risk. As was said of such matters by Lord Mansfield, "Whatever a man publishes, he publishes at his peril." The King v. Woodfall, Lofft, 776, 781. * The reason is plain. A libel is harmful on its face. If a man sees fit to publish manifestly hurtful statements concerning an individual, without other justification than exists for an advertisement or a piece of news, the usual principles of tort will make him liable, if the statements are false or are true only of someone else. *

The question, then, is whether the publication was a libel. It was held by the Circuit Court of Appeals not to be, or at most to entitle the plaintiff only to nominal damages, no special damage being alleged. It was pointed out that there was no general consensus of opinion that to drink whisky is wrong, or that to be a nurse is discreditable. It might have been added that very possibly giving a certificate and the use of one's portrait in aid of an advertisement would be regarded with irony, or a stronger feeling, only by a few. But it appears to us that such inquiries are beside the point. It may be that the action for libel is of little use, but, while it is maintained, it should be governed by the general principles of tort. If the advertisement obviously would hurt the plaintiff in the estimation of an important and respectable part of the community, liability is not a question of a majority vote.

We know of no decision in which this matter is discussed upon principle. But obviously an unprivileged falsehood need not entail universal hatred to constitute a cause of action. No falsehood is thought about or even known by all the world. No conduct is hated by all. That it will be known by a large number, and will lead an appreciable fraction of that number to regard the plaintiff with contempt, is enough to do her practical harm. Thus, if a doctor were represented as advertising, the fact that it would affect his standing with others of his profession might make the representation actionable, although advertising is not reputed dishonest, and even seems to be regarded by many with pride. * It seems to us impossible to say that the obvious tendency of what is imputed to the plaintiff by this advertisement is not seriously to hurt her standing with a considerable and respectable class in the community. Therefore it was the plaintiff's right to prove her case and go to the jury, and the defendant would have got all that it could ask if it had been permitted to persuade them, if it could, to take a contrary view. * * *

Judgment reversed.

NOTES

1. *Damage to Reputation among Whom?* To constitute defamation, among which group must the plaintiff's reputation be damaged? Suppose a naval officer is portrayed in a movie as a warm-hearted, courageous, and impetuous hero in such a way as to endear him to the movie-going public but to make him seem undisciplined and irresponsible to his fellow officers. Is there defamation? See Kelly v. Loew's, Inc., 76 F.Supp. 473 (D.Mass.1948) (holding that the movie was in fact defamatory to the officer)

Do those who would be likely to think less of the plaintiff because of a defamatory charge have to be "right-thinking" people? Consider the case of the inmate incarcerated for narcotics offenses who newspapers reported "planned to cooperate with prosecutors and testify against" an organized crime figure. Michtavi v. N.Y. Daily News, 587 F.3d 551, 551–52 (2d Cir.2009) (N.Y. law) (stating that the "population of right-thinking persons unambiguously excludes those who would think ill of one who legitimately cooperates with law enforcement" and finding the defendant's reporting not defamatory as a matter of law). Compare Grant v. Reader's Digest Assn., 151 F.2d 733, 735 (2d Cir.1945) (L. Hand, J.) ("We do not believe . . . that we need say whether 'right-thinking' people would harbor similar feelings * * *. It is enough if there be some, as there certainly are, who would feel so, even though they would be 'wrong-thinking' people if they did"; reversing dismissal of libel claim brought by a lawyer against a publisher who had accused him of being "a legislative representative for the * * * Communist Party").

Would it be defamatory to call an ardent and life-long Democrat a Republican or vice versa? Suppose the Democrat lived in an extremely liberal locale, or the Republican in an extremely conservative area?

2. *"Of and Concerning the Plaintiff."* The requirement that the words be published "of and concerning" the plaintiff has for the most part, like other aspects of interpreting the challenged statement, been worked out along the lines of the objective test so consistently espoused by Holmes. See Restatement (Second) of Torts § 564 (1977) (test whether recipient "correctly, or mistakenly but reasonably, understands" the statement to mean what is claimed).

3. *Strict Liability at Common Law.* Justice Holmes notes that "[t]here was some suggestion that the defendant published the portrait by mistake, and without knowledge that it was the plaintiff's portrait, or was not what it purported to be. But the fact, if it was one, was no excuse." At common law, defamation was a strict liability tort. In many cases, this aspect of defamation law has been dramatically altered as a result of United States Supreme Court decisions during the past fifty years. See *infra* pages 902–926.

Farrell v. Triangle Publications, Inc.

Supreme Court of Pennsylvania, 1960.
399 Pa. 102, 159 A.2d 734.

■ JONES, CHIEF JUSTICE. On January 29, 1958, *The Inquirer*, Philadelphia's morning newspaper of wide circulation, published the following under the headline "$900,000, Trash Deal 'Split' for Commissioners Probed":

> The Delaware county District Attorney's office yesterday began investigating a report that a $900,000 slice of the canceled $1,600,000 Upper Darby incinerator deal was earmarked for division among a number of township commissioners and others.
>
> This startling development arose on the eve of the opening today of the Delaware county grand jury investigation into the abortive deal that was quickly dropped after an expose by the *Inquirer*. Investigators studying the report of the $900,000 jackpot declined to elaborate, but it was learned they would question the 13 commissioners, former office holders. . . .

John H. Farrell, the plaintiff, was at the time one of the Commissioners of Upper Darby Township, of whom there were thirteen. Farrell brought this action against Triangle Publications, Inc., the publisher of the *Philadelphia Inquirer*, for damages on the ground that the article libeled him. The defendant * * * assert[ed] that it failed to state a cause of action. The court sustained the preliminary objections and entered judgment for the defendant. This appeal followed.

The sole question involved is whether the article referred to Farrell as an object of its charges and insinuations with sufficient particularity to invest him with a cause of action for libel. That the article was defamatory cannot be seriously disputed.

Where a defamatory publication or utterance is directed toward a class or group whose membership is so numerous that no one individual member can reasonably be deemed an intended object of the defamatory matter, no cause of action for libel or slander arises therefrom. * For example, if someone should speak or write defamatorily of all the members of one of the professions, such as the law, medicine or ministry, no particular lawyer, doctor or minister could maintain a personal action for the defamation for the reason that no one would be sufficiently identified as an object thereof to justifiably warrant a conclusion that his individual reputation had been substantially injured. Where, however, a defamatory publication or utterance is directed toward a comparatively small class or group all of whose constituent members may be readily identified and the recipients of the defamatory matter are likely to identify some, if not all, of them as intended objects of the defamation, an individual member of the group may sue for the damages done his reputation thereby. *

If a newspaper should publish defamatory statements about a person by referring to him by name, it would, of course, lay itself open to liability for damages to the injured person in a suit for libel. That being so, it would indeed be irrational, as well as unconscionable, to permit a publication to escape responsibility under the libel law simply by confining the objects of its defamation to "a number of," "some of," or even to "one of" a relatively small group of persons all of whom are readily identifiable by recipients of the defamatory matter. To hold otherwise would be to make liability for libel depend upon the form of the defamation rather than its content.

On the other hand, if it is clear that, because of the large number in the group referred to in the printed matter, or for any other reason, a recipient of a defamatory publication could not reasonably conclude that it referred to the particular person claiming to have been libeled thereby, the complaint should be dismissed for failure to state a cause of action. But, if the defamatory publication can reasonably be interpreted as referring to a particular complainant, whether recipients did so conclude is for a jury to determine. *

The Restatement (Second) of Torts § 564, states the principle as follows:

Applicability of Defamatory Communication to Plaintiff: A defamatory communication is made concerning the person to whom its recipient correctly, or mistakenly but reasonably, understands it as intended to refer.

Illustrations:

2. A newspaper publishes the statement that some member of B's household has committed murder. In the absence of any circumstances indicating that some particular member of B's household was referred to, the newspaper has defamed each member of B's household. * * *

Here, the ordinary reader of the *Philadelphia Inquirer* could naturally and reasonably infer that the defamatory publication referred to the plaintiff, among others. Certain it is that a substantial number of readers, particularly those residents in Upper Darby Township, knew that the plaintiff was one of the thirteen commissioners of the township. Moreover, it is not unreasonable to conclude that many other Upper Darby readers of the *Inquirer* who, prior to the defamatory article, had not known the identity of all of the township's commissioners, were impelled by the scandalous nature of the charges to make inquiry and find out who the commissioners were—a process which would almost inevitably lead to connecting the plaintiff's name with the alleged corruption in office.

The fact that the article did not state that all of the commissioners of the township were parties to the reported corrupt deal could not operate to exclude the plaintiff from being one of the relatively small and officially designated group to which the article indisputably made reference. The publication also declared that the district attorney's office would question all thirteen of the commissioners, one of whom was the plaintiff. That statement at least implied that, in the mind of the district attorney, none of the commissioners was above suspicion of knowledge, guilty or otherwise, of the alleged "split." The effect of the article could be to impugn the integrity and honesty of the plaintiff in the estimation of the public. Even persons favorably disposed toward him might, upon reading the article, reasonably conclude that the plaintiff was one of the commissioners referred to as being corrupt. This would be a sufficient maligning of his reputation to give him a cause of action for libel.

* * * We hold that, under the facts pleaded, the trial court should have concluded as a matter of law that the publication was defamatory and that the plaintiff was sufficiently referred to so that a recipient might reasonably conclude that the plaintiff was an object of the defamation. Whether recipients did so conclude is a question for a jury to determine. The court was therefore in error in dismissing the complaint and in entering judgment for the defendant.

C. LIBEL AND SLANDER

Davies and Wife v. Solomon
Court of Queen's Bench, 1871.
L.R. 7 Q.B. 112 (Eng.).

[Action of slander for the following words:] "I can prove that John Davies' wife * * * had connection with a man named Labrach two years ago, but I would rather have the tongue cut out of my mouth than separate man and wife," whereby the plaintiff Isabella was injured in her character and reputation, and became alienated from and deprived of the cohabitation of her husband, and lost and was deprived of the companionship and ceased to receive the hospitality of divers friends, and especially of her husband, John Davies, "and one M.D. and one G.H.T. and one A.J.M.," who have by reason of the premises withdrawn from the companionship and ceased to be hospitable to or friendly with the plaintiff Isabella. * * *

Demurrer and joinder in demurrer. * * *

■ BLACKBURN, J. The sole difficulty in deciding the case is caused by the opinion of Lord Wensleydale in Lynch v. Knight., 9 H.L.C. 577. He held that no action would lie for slander of a wife when the only special damage alleged was the loss to the plaintiff of the consortium of her husband. In the present case, however, it is unnecessary to decide this question, for the declaration, after alleging the loss of cohabitation by the wife, proceeds to aver that "she lost, and was deprived of the companionship, and ceased to receive the hospitality of divers friends."

Now, first, was that consequence such as might reasonably and naturally be expected to follow from the speaking of slanderous words? Judging from the habits and manners of society, of all the consequences that might be expected to result from a statement that a woman had committed adultery, or had been guilty of unchastity, the most natural would be that those who had invited her and given her hospitality would thenceforth cease to do so. Then Moore v. Meagher, 1 Taunt. 39, decides that the loss of the hospitality of friends is sufficient special damage to sustain an action like the present; and the hospitality, as the word is there used, means simply that persons receive another into their houses, and give him meat and drink gratis. Perhaps such a definition may rather extend the signification of the word, but it is true in effect—for if they do not receive him, or if they make him pay for his entertainment, that is not hospitality. In Roberts v. Roberts, 5 B. & S. 384; 33 L.J. (Q.B.) 249, it is to be observed, that the loss suffered by the plaintiff in being excluded from a religious society, was not temporal, and was therefore held not to be enough. But in the present case is a matter of temporal change—small though it be—laid in the declaration.

It is also argued, that inasmuch as this action is brought by the wife, the husband being merely joined for conformity, the damage necessary to give the right to recover must be damage to her alone, and that the loss of hospitality which she has hitherto enjoyed, is only pecuniary loss to her husband and not to her. * * * I am, however, unwilling to agree with such artificial reasoning, and I think the real damage in this case is to the wife herself. Notwithstanding that it is the husband's duty to support his wife, he is only bound to provide her with necessaries suitable to his station in life; and she might, by visiting friends in a higher position than himself, enjoy luxuries which he either could not or might not choose to afford her * * *. I am therefore of opinion that the declaration is good; and the demurrer must be overruled.[a]

Thorley v. Lord Kerry

Court of Exchequer Chamber, 1812.
4 Taunt. 355, 128 Eng.Rep. 367.

[The defendant sent by messenger an unsealed letter to the plaintiff, which the messenger read, stating that the plaintiff "under the cloak of religious and spiritual reform, hypocritically, and with the grossest impurity, deals out his malice, uncharitableness, and falsehoods." The plaintiff sued for libel and gained a verdict and judgment. On writ of error:]

■ MANSFIELD, C.J. * * * There is no doubt that this was a libel, for which the Plaintiff in error might have been indicted and punished; because, though the words impute no punishable crimes, they contain that sort of imputation which is calculated to vilify a man, and bring him, as the books say, into hatred, contempt, and ridicule; for all words of that description an indictment lies; and I should have thought that the peace and good name of individuals was sufficiently guarded by the terror of this criminal proceeding in such cases. The words, if merely spoken would not be of themselves sufficient to support an action. But the question now is whether an action will lie for these words so written, notwithstanding that such an action would not lie for them if spoken * * *.

[T]he distinction has been made between written and spoken slander as far back as Charles the Second's time, and the difference has been recognized by the Courts for at least a century back. It does not appear to me that the rights of parties to a good character are insufficiently defended by the criminal remedies which the law gives, and the law gives a very ample field for retribution by action for words spoken in the cases of special damage, of words spoken of a man in his trade or profession, of a man in office, of a magistrate or officer; for all these an action lies. But for mere general abuse spoken, no action lies.

---

[a]   [Eds.' note] Adultery and fornication were not crimes in the temporal courts of England or many of our states. See Buys v. Gillespie, 2 Johns. 115, 3 Am.Dec. 404 (N.Y.1807). Many states by statute or judicial decision made it slander per se to charge a woman with unchastity. See also *infra* pages 882–883, Note 2.

In the arguments both of the judges and counsel, in almost all the cases in which the question has been, whether what is contained in a writing is the subject of an action or not, it has been considered, whether the words, if spoken, would maintain an action. It is curious that they have also adverted to the question, whether it tends to produce a breach of the peace: but that is wholly irrelevant, and is no ground for recovering damages. So it has been argued that writing shews more deliberate malignity; but the same answer suffices, that the action is not maintainable upon the ground of the malignity, but for the damage sustained. So, it is argued that written scandal is more generally diffused than words spoken, and is therefore actionable; but an assertion made in a public place, as upon the Royal Exchange, concerning a merchant in London, may be much more extensively diffused than a few printed papers dispersed, or a private letter: it is true that a newspaper may be very generally read, but that is all casual. These are the arguments which prevail on my mind to repudiate the distinction between written and spoken scandal; but that distinction has been established by some of the greatest names known to the law, Lord Hardwicke, Hale, I believe, Holt C.J., and others. Lord Hardwicke C.J. especially has laid it down that an action for a libel may be brought on words written, when the words, if spoken, would not sustain it. Co. Dig. tit. Libel, referring to the case in Fitzg. 122, 253, says, there is a distinction between written and spoken scandal. By his putting it down there as he does, as being the law, without making any query or doubt upon it, we are led to suppose that he was of the same opinion.

I do not now recapitulate the cases, but we cannot, in opposition to them, venture to lay down at this day, that no action can be maintained for any words written, for which an action could not be maintained if they were spoken: upon these grounds we think the judgment of the Court of King's Bench must be affirmed. The purpose of this action is to recover a compensation for some damage supposed to be sustained by the Plaintiff by reason of the libel. The tendency of the libel to provoke a breach of the peace, or the degree of malignity which actuates the writer, has nothing to do with the question. If the matter were for the first time to be decided at this day, I should have no hesitation in saying, that no action could be maintained for written scandal which could not be maintained for the words if they had been spoken.

Judgment affirmed.

NOTE

Television, Radio, and the Internet. Should radio and television be considered slander or libel? Restatement (Second) of Torts § 568A cmt. a (1977) provides, in part, "The wide dissemination that results from broadcasting over radio and television, together with the prestige and potential effect upon the public mind of a standardized means of publication that many people tend automatically to accept as conveying truth, are such as to put the broadcaster upon the same footing as the publisher of a newspaper." In the past, courts sometimes held that broadcast statements were to be treated as libel if they were read from a script, but as slander if they were spontaneous. Today it is generally— though not universally—accepted that defamatory radio and television broadcasts are libel, regardless of whether they are spoken from a script.

What about e-mail or other internet postings? In W.J.A. v. D.A., 416 N.J.Super. 380, 4 A.3d 601 (App.Div.2010), the court quoted from an earlier precedent and held that internet postings are libel:

> [The] [d]efendant's postings are written words published through a "mechanical device" (the computer) akin to the typewriter. As a general proposition, it may take more aforethought to type an internet posting than it does to blurt out spoken words. Also, unlike spoken words that evaporate, internet postings have permanence, as the posts can remain on that particular site for an indefinite period and can easily be copied and forwarded. The name "the world wide web" is an indication that unlike spoken words, Internet postings have the widest distribution possible— globally. While the image of "town crier" standing and speaking on his soapbox has literary appeal, the Internet is more akin to the town crier handing out printed papers.

Id. at 385–86; see also Varian Med. Sys., Inc. v. Delfino, 113 Cal.App.4th 273, 6 Cal.Rptr.3d 325, 343 (Cal.App.2003) (holding that internet communications are libel because they are "publications *by writing*" (emphasis in original); Flood v. Times Newspapers, Ltd., *The Times* (London), Oct. 23, 2009, at 93, col.4 (Q.B.D.) ("What could be found on the internet about a person might become like a tattoo, permanently blighting a person's prospects"); but see Glenn H. Reynolds, Libel in the Blogosphere: Some Preliminary Thoughts, 84 Wash. U. L. Rev. 1157, 1165 (2006) (arguing that online defamatory statements should be treated like slander, not libel).

What about posts on Twitter? On one hand, tweets are evanescent in that they tend to be replaced by newer tweets on an individual user's screen. On the other hand, a permanent record remains and is available by using a search engine. Those who tweet tend to be careless as if they were speaking, but tweets can be widely circulated through "re-tweeting." See Julie Hilden, Should the Law Treat Defamatory Tweets the Same Way It Treats Printed Defamation?, JUSTICIA.COM (Oct. 3, 2011), *available at* http://verdict.justia.com/2011/10/03/should-the-law-treat-defamatory-tweets-the-same-way-it-treats-printed-defamation (last visited, Oct. 7, 2014).

Text-messages? What about a programmed parrot? Cf. Silvertop v. The Stepney Guardians, cited in Chicken v. Ham (H.L.), A.P. Herbert, Uncommon Law 71, 75 (1935).

Biondi v. Nassimos

Superior Court of New Jersey, Appellate Division, 1997.
300 N.J.Super. 148, 692 A.2d 103.

■ SKILLMAN, JUDGE. This appeal involves the "slander per se" doctrine. At the time of the alleged slander, plaintiff Thomas J. Biondi was Chairman of the New Jersey Board of Examiners of Master Plumbers (the Board). Defendant Antoine Nassimos regularly attended the Board's public meetings, apparently acting as a liaison between the New Jersey Society of Professional Energy and Environmental Contractors (NJSPEEC) and the Board. On September 23, 1993, Nassimos attended a public meeting at which the Board announced a decision that Joseph Fichner, Jr., a licensed master plumber and member of the NJSPEEC, had committed various acts of occupational misconduct, fraud and misrepresentation. * Based on these violations, the Board ordered Fichner to pay substantial fines and to make restitution to various customers, and also imposed "an inactive five year suspension" of his license. Later in the meeting when the public was given the opportunity to speak, Nassimos charged the Board with improperly releasing information about its decision in the *Fichner* matter prior to taking official action. Nassimos also charged that it was improper for plaintiff, as a member of the Board, to be affiliated with the New Jersey Association of Plumbing, Heating & Cooling Contractors. According to plaintiff, Nassimos then said "words to the effect of: 'I have information that the Chairman, Mr. Biondi, has mob connections and that if I don't stop complaining against him and the Board, he will order a hit on me.'" In response, plaintiff said to Nassimos: "I think you've overstepped your bounds. I might have to consult an attorney."

On November 3, 1993, plaintiff filed this action against Nassimos and the NJSPEEC. Plaintiff's complaint alleged that Nassimos' statement that plaintiff "has mob connections" and would "order a hit" on him was "intended by Mr. Nassimos and were understood by the listeners to indicate and designate someone as a member of organized crime, as the perpetrator of uncounted serious crimes, as one who makes his living through a life of crime, as one who directs others to commit crimes, . . . and as one who is involved in crimes including, but not limited to murder, extortion, gambling and bribery of public officials."

After the trial court denied defendants' motion for summary judgment, a trial was commenced before a jury. However, the trial court declared a mistrial shortly before the close of plaintiff's case. Prior to the second trial, defendants renewed their motion for summary judgment. At oral argument on the motion, plaintiff conceded that he did not have any "special damages" and was "stuck with a slander per se case." This time the court granted defendants' motion, concluding that a statement that a person has "connections with [the] mafia" does not constitute an allegation of criminal activity and therefore does not constitute slander per se. Plaintiff appeals from the summary judgment dismissing his complaint. * We affirm.

At the outset, we note that the issue presented in this appeal is not whether Nassimos' statements that plaintiff has "mob connections" and may "order a hit" upon him are defamatory but rather whether they constitute "slander per se." We have no doubt that a jury could find these statements to be defamatory, that is, as "tend[ing] so to harm the reputation of another as to lower him in the estimation of the community or to deter third persons from associating or dealing with him." Ward v. Zelikovsky, 136 N.J. 516, 529, 643 A.2d 972, 978 (1994) (quoting Restatement (Second) of Torts § 559 (1977)). * * *

However, plaintiff cannot prevail merely by showing that Nassimos' statements were defamatory because he has not offered any evidence of the type of damages generally required to establish a cause of action for slander. To establish a slander claim under the common law, a plaintiff is required to show "special damages," which is defined as "harm of a material or pecuniary nature." Ward v. Zelikovsky, 136

N.J. at 540, 643 A.2d at 984. Plaintiff admittedly has no evidence that he suffered such "special damages" as a result of Nassimos' statements. Moreover, even if our Supreme Court were prepared to modify the common law rule requiring special damages to establish a cause of action for slander by allowing a plaintiff in a slander action, as in most libel actions, * to prove any form of actual damage to reputation, either pecuniary or non-pecuniary, * plaintiff presented no evidence that he suffered any damage to his reputation as a result of Nassimos' outburst at the Board meeting. Plaintiff testified at his deposition that when he attended a meeting of the New Jersey Association of Plumbing, Heating and Cooling Contractors, other members referred to him as "Don Thomasso" and "Godfather," asked whether they had to "kiss [his] ring," and insisted that he sit at the head of the table. However, plaintiff did not show the kind of damage to reputation ordinarily required to establish a cause of action for defamation, because he did not present evidence that anyone had refused to associate with him or that any of his business or personal relationships had been "seriously disrupted." * Therefore, his claim is maintainable only if Nassimos' statements constituted slander per se.

The slander per se doctrine is limited to defamatory statements which impute to another person (1) a criminal offense; (2) a loathsome disease; (3) conduct, characteristics or a condition that is incompatible with his business, trade or office; or (4) serious sexual misconduct. Restatement (Second) of Torts §§ 570–74 (1977). * If a defamatory statement constitutes slander per se, a plaintiff may establish a cause of action not only without proving "special damages," that is, damages of a pecuniary nature, but without proving any form of actual damage to reputation. * This is sometimes referred to as the "presumed damages" doctrine. *

The slander per se doctrine has been severely criticized by scholarly commentators, who recommend the elimination of both the "presumed damages" rule applicable to slander per se cases and the "special damages" rule applicable to all other slander cases. * The commentators conclude that these archaic common law rules should be replaced by a single uniform rule that a plaintiff must prove actual damage to reputation, either pecuniary or non-pecuniary, to establish any cause of action for defamation. * * *

Therefore, even though the slander per se doctrine continues to be a part of New Jersey's law of defamation,[3] the Court's characterization of the doctrine as "a relic from tort law's previous age" and its conclusion that "the trend should be toward elimination . . . of the per se categories," Ward v. Zelikovsky, 136 N.J. at 541, 643 A.2d at 984, suggests that lower courts should invoke the slander per se doctrine only in cases where it clearly applies.

---

[3] Missouri and Kansas have eliminated slander per se and the corollary "presumed damages" rule. Consequently, these states now require a showing of actual damage to reputation to establish any cause of action for defamation. *

We also note that the First Amendment precludes an award of presumed damages for a defamatory statement involving an "issue of public concern." See Dun & Bradstreet, Inc. v. Greenmoss Builders, Inc., *infra* pages 919–23; Gertz v. Robert Walsh, Inc., *infra* pages 912–919. However, defendants have not argued that Nassimos' statements about plaintiff involved any "issue of public concern."

Plaintiff argues that Nassimos' statements that he has "mob connections" and would "order a hit" upon Nassimos unless Nassimos stopped complaining about plaintiff and the Board constituted slander per se because they implied that he had committed a crime. The Restatement of Torts describes this category of slander per se as follows:

> One who publishes a slander that imputes to another conduct constituting a criminal offense is subject to liability to the other without proof of special harm if the offense imputed is of a type which, if committed in the place of publication, would be
>
> (a) punishable by imprisonment in a state or federal institution, or
>
> (b) regarded by public opinion as involving moral turpitude.

Restatement (Second) of Torts § 571 (1977). However, it does not constitute slander per se "to suggest that another is capable of committing a crime" or "to charge another with a criminal intention or design, if no criminal act is charged." Restatement (Second) of Torts § 571 cmt. c (1977).

We are satisfied that a statement that a person has "mob connections" does not constitute an assertion that he has committed a crime. It is not uncommon for the mass media to report that an entertainer or other celebrity has "mob ties" or "mob connections." The ordinary understanding of such a story is not that the celebrity himself has committed crimes but rather that he associates with criminals. Consequently, even though a statement that a person has "mob connections" may be defamatory, it is not slander per se because it does not allege the commission of a crime. *

Nassimos' further alleged comment that he had information plaintiff would "order a hit on me" if Nassimos did not "stop complaining against him and the Board" is not slander per se because it merely alleges plaintiff's intention to commit a crime sometime in the future rather than a past criminal act. See Restatement (Second) of Torts, § 571 cmt. c. Although plaintiff argues that this comment implied that he was a member of an ongoing criminal enterprise because only such a person could "order a hit," we believe that such a comment could be just as easily construed to mean that plaintiff would ask his "mob connections" to kill Nassimos as a favor or in exchange for the payment of money. * The circumstance that Nassimos' comment was uttered in the midst of a heated personal attack upon plaintiff, as Chairman of the Board, for allegedly leaking information about a decision in a pending disciplinary matter, reduces the possibility that the audience reasonably could have understood Nassimos was asserting that plaintiff had committed a crime. * In view of the disfavor with which the slander per se doctrine is currently held, courts should not permit speculative inferences regarding the possible meaning of an alleged defamatory statement to support a verdict in favor of a plaintiff who is unable to show any actual damage to his reputation.

Affirmed.

NOTES

1.   *Special Damages and Presumed Damages.* Liability for slanderous statements other than those falling within the categories of slander per se requires that the plaintiff plead and prove special damages. Restatement (Second) of Torts § 575 (1977). This requirement probably had its origin in the struggle for jurisdiction over slander cases between the royal and ecclesiastical courts. Once special damages were proved, it was evident that the matter had resulted in "temporal" as contrasted to merely "spiritual" damages, and the exercise of jurisdiction by royal courts was accordingly appropriate. Similarly it was clear from the nature of the "slander per se" categories themselves that slander about these subjects was likely to result in temporal and not merely spiritual harm.

Special damages ordinarily represent the loss of something having economic or pecuniary value. Examples include the loss of business, e.g., Ellsworth v. Martindale-Hubbell Law Directory, 68 N.D. 425, 280 N.W. 879 (1938); denial of employment, e.g., Stuempges v. Parke, Davis & Co., 297 N.W.2d 252, 258–59 (Minn.1980); loss of credit, e.g., Prettymam v. Shockley, 4 Harr. 112, 4 Del. 112 (1844); and loss of material hospitality, e.g., victuals, Davies v. Solomon, *supra* pages 875–876. See also Nelson v. Melvin, 236 Iowa 604, 19 N.W.2d 685 (1945) (loss of marriage). Mental distress—even though resulting in physical illness—traditionally has not been regarded as a basis for special damages for purposes of defamation, but once special damages are proven, and the slander therefore is actionable, the plaintiff can recover for emotional distress as parasitic damages. E.g., Carter v. Willert Home Prods., Inc., 714 S.W.2d 506 (Mo.1986).

Once the case for defamation was established at common law—a claim for libel, slander per se, or slander together with special damages—the plaintiff also was entitled to recover for *general damages,* that is, damages to compensate the plaintiff for injury to reputation, loss of business generally, and wounded feelings and the bodily suffering caused by such feelings. Juries were allowed to award damages not only for harm to reputation that was proven to have occurred, but also, in the absence of specific proof, for harm to reputation that would normally be assumed to flow from the defamatory publication. Since *New York Times Co. v. Sullivan* and its aftermath, *infra* pages 902–25, the United States Supreme Court has limited the ability of state courts to award presumed damages in certain circumstances.

2.   *Categories of Slander Per Se.* In order to provide the basis for slander per se, the crime imputed must in some jurisdictions be one involving "moral turpitude." See, e.g., Great Coastal Express, Inc. v. Ellington, 230 Va. 142, 148–49, 334 S.E.2d 846, 850 (1985) (holding that commercial bribery involves moral turpitude and citing precedents that petty larceny and making false statements to obtain unemployment benefits also involve moral turpitude, while drunkenness, illegal possession of liquor, gambling, and assault and battery do not); compare Earley v. Winn, 129 Wis. 291, 310, 109 N.W. 633, 640 (1906) (slander for having charged plaintiff with having whipped her mother; also, reportedly, for having sold watered milk).

At common law, slander per se for imputing a loathsome disease required both that the disease be contagious and that it warrant social ostracism, such as leprosy or venereal disease. In modern times, actions in this category have been rare.

To provide the basis for a claim of slander per se, comments relating to the plaintiff's business or trade must be ones particularly harmful to the plaintiff's reputation because of the specific demands or qualifications of plaintiff's profession. For example, courts have held that it is slander per se to accuse a minister, a navigator, or a schoolmaster of alcohol abuse, but not a business person. See Harper, James and Gray on Torts § 5.12.

Today there are few successful cases brought under the serious sexual misconduct category of slander per se. Examples of such cases include French v. Jadon, Inc., 911 P.2d 20, 32 (Alaska 1996) (liability for slander asserting that plaintiff traded sex for drugs).

3. *The "Spurious Rule" of Libel per Quod.* The doctrines discussed in the principal case are historically peculiar to slander, but are nevertheless echoed in some jurisdictions in libel actions as well. In a handful of jurisdictions, including New York, statements that are defamatory only if the words they contain are supplemented by facts extrinsic to the statements themselves are sometimes called "libel *per quod*," with consequences that vary among the jurisdictions. In some, also including New York, plaintiffs must not only plead and prove the extrinsic facts, but must ordinarily for such defamation establish "special damages." For instance, in *Idema v. Wager,* excerpted at *supra* pages 865–67, the defendant prevailed not only on the grounds discussed in that excerpt, but also on the ground that plaintiff had failed to establish "special" damages, which the court considered necessary for libel not "actionable per se." The court stated in this connection:

> The challenged language is actionable per se if it tends to expose another to "public hatred, shame, obloquy, contempt, ridicule, aversion, ostracism, degradation, or disgrace" or "to induce an evil opinion of one in the minds of right-thinking persons and to deprive one of one's confidence and friendly intercourse in society" or tends to disparage a person in the way of his office, profession or trade. * It is not clear from the face of the headline that the word "militant" is used in any negative sense that would expose the plaintiff to "public shame, ridicule, or ostracism." And a reading of the article and the headline together does not suggest to a reasonable reader what it apparently suggests to an overly sensitive Idema: that "militant" defines only fringe, lunatic elements in society. In fact, the article refers to the Plaintiff as the "operator of a former anti-terrorist training facility" which was once "featured by CBS as the most professional organization of its kind." Therefore, because the word "militant" is not clearly libelous on its face, the headline is not actionable per se. *

120 F.Supp.2d at 367.

> This doctrine of libel per quod has been heavily criticized:

> The requirement for special damages in the case of "libel per quod" is clearly contrary to the historical rule as developed in England and to the apparent weight of authority in this country; furthermore it tends to ignore the distinction between slander and libel. * * *

Because of its obvious technical confusion, few doctrines have been treated with such open contempt by commentators and judges alike as the "libel per quod" special damages rule. * * * Professor Eldredge called it, properly, a "spurious rule." * Despite the tact normally displayed by federal judges in describing state law that they are called on to apply, some of them have made little effort to conceal their scorn for this rule. It was, for instance, generally assumed on the basis of dicta in Maryland opinions that the rule applied in Maryland. In Sauerhoff v. Hearst Corp., 388 F.Supp. 117, 118 (D.Md.1974), the District Court, attempting to deal with Maryland law, said, "[H]erein the irrational animals known as libel 'per quod' and libel 'per se,' and the Merlinesque touchstones which attach to them, must be identified, whether or not their existence can be rationally justified." The Fourth Circuit majority opinion * * * quoted this comment "upon these juristic fetishes" with apparent approval, and topped it with a reference to a deceased colleague's saying about "rustic relics of ancient asininity." Sauerhoff v. Hearst Corp. (Baltimore News Am. Div.), 538 F.2d 588, 590 (4th Cir.1976).

Harper, James and Gray on Torts § 5.9A. See also Laurence H. Eldredge, The Spurious Role of Libel Per Quod, 79 Harv. L. Rev. 733, 742–43 (1966).

D. PUBLICATION

Bals v. Verduzco

Supreme Court of Indiana, 1992.
600 N.E.2d 1353.

■ DICKSON, JUSTICE. Should employee evaluation information communicated intracompany to management personnel be considered "published" for purposes of a defamation action? * * *

Both plaintiff-appellant Daniel I. Bals and defendant-appellee Albert Verduzco were employees of Inland Steel Company, with Bals under the direct supervision of Verduzco. Bals was terminated following a series of employee evaluation reports submitted by Verduzco. Bals commenced this action against Verduzco alleging defamation * * *. Trial was held on the defamation action, and at the conclusion of the plaintiff's case in chief, the trial court granted the defendant's motion for judgment. It concluded that Verduzco's submission of the employee evaluation reports did not constitute a publication necessary to sustain a defamation action. The Court of Appeals affirmed. * * *

    1.   Publication

In an action for defamation, the plaintiff must show that the defamatory matter was "published," that is, communicated to a third person or persons. * There is substantial conflict among other jurisdictions over whether or not intracompany documents can satisfy the publication element of a defamation claim. * Many jurisdictions * hold that communications between employees or officers of the same corporation are not communications to a third person as required by the law of defamation. Grounded in agency theory, this approach views the corporation as simply communicating with itself.

On the other hand, a significant number of courts hold that intracompany communications may constitute publication for purposes of a defamation action. These jurisdictions consider damage to one's reputation within a corporate community to be just as devastating as that effected by defamation spread to the outside. Although corporate officers might be the embodiment of the corporation, it is argued, they remain individuals with distinct personalities and opinions which might be affected just as surely as those of other employees by the spread of injurious falsehoods. This approach is consistent with Restatement (Second) of Torts § 577 cmt. i (1977):

> i.   *Communication by one agent to another agent of the same*
>   *principal.* The communication within the scope of his
>   employment by one agent to another agent of the same
>   principal is a publication not only by the first agent but
>   also by the principal and this is true whether the principal
>   is an individual, a partnership or a corporation. . . . * * *

Upon employment, an individual does not relinquish the value of a good reputation. To the contrary, a person's suitability for continued employment and advancement at work may be substantially influenced by the reputation one earns. When intracompany communications injure an employee's occupational reputation, the result may be among the most injurious of defamations. We cannot deprive access to the courts for an employee who suffers very real and significant injuries as a result of intracompany defamatory falsehoods which would otherwise be actionable. Refusing to characterize such communication as a publication for a defamation action is an unacceptable legal fiction that interferes with an Indiana employee's * * * right to a remedy for injury to reputation. We hold that employee evaluation information communicated intracompany to management personnel may be considered published for purposes of a defamation action.

[The court sustained the lower court's judgment on the grounds that a qualified privilege or defense was "available to protect personnel evaluation information communicated in good faith." See *infra* pages 893–897.]

NOTES

1. *Publication and Transcription.* Should an executive or lawyer who dictates an "angry letter" to her administrative assistant and throws it away be liable for defamation? Should she be disadvantaged because she finds it more efficient to transcribe her correspondence than to use a word processor herself?

2. *"Compelled Self-Publication."* What if an employer, in firing an employee, makes statements to the employee alone that would be defamatory if shared with a third-party. Subsequently, while seeking new employment, the employee believes he is compelled to explain the basis for his previous termination of employment. Can the employer be held liable for this "compelled self-publication"? Compare McKinney v. Cnty. of Santa Clara, 110 Cal.App.3d 787, 797–98, 168 Cal.Rptr. 89, 94 (1980) (imposing liability) with Layne v. Builders Plumbing Supply Co., 210 Ill.App.3d 966, 976, 155 Ill.Dec. 493, 569 N.E.2d 1104, 1111 (1991) (rejecting liability).

Zeran v. America Online, Inc.

United States Court of Appeals for the Fourth Circuit, 1997.
129 F.3d 327.

■ WILKINSON, CHIEF JUDGE. * * * On April 25, 1995, an unidentified person posted a message on an AOL [America Online] bulletin board advertising "Naughty Oklahoma T-Shirts." The posting described the sale of shirts featuring offensive and tasteless slogans related to the April 19, 1995, bombing of the Alfred P. Murrah Federal Building in Oklahoma City. Those interested in purchasing the shirts were instructed to call "Ken" at Zeran's home phone number in Seattle, Washington. As a result of this anonymously perpetrated prank, Zeran received a high volume of calls, comprised primarily of angry and derogatory messages, but also including death threats. Zeran could not change his phone number because he relied on its availability to the public in running his business out of his home. Later that day, Zeran called AOL and informed a company representative of his predicament. The employee assured Zeran that the posting would be removed from AOL's bulletin board but explained that as a matter of policy AOL would not post a retraction. The parties dispute the date that AOL removed this original posting from its bulletin board.

On April 26, the next day, an unknown person posted another message advertising additional shirts with new tasteless slogans related to the Oklahoma City bombing. Again, interested buyers were told to call Zeran's phone number, to ask for "Ken," and to "please call back if busy" due to high demand. The angry, threatening phone calls intensified. * * * By April 30, Zeran was receiving an abusive phone call approximately every two minutes. Meanwhile, an announcer for Oklahoma City radio station KRXO received a copy of the first AOL posting. On May 1, the announcer related the message's contents on the air, attributed them to "Ken" at Zeran's phone number, and urged the listening audience to call the number. After this radio broadcast, Zeran was inundated with death threats and other violent calls from Oklahoma City residents. Over the next few days, Zeran talked to both KRXO and AOL representatives. He also spoke to his local police, who subsequently surveilled his home to protect his safety. By May 14, after an Oklahoma City newspaper published a story exposing the shirt advertisements as a hoax and after KRXO made an on-air apology, the number of calls to Zeran's residence finally subsided to fifteen per day.

* * * On April 23, 1996, [Zeran] filed this * * * suit against AOL * * *. AOL answered Zeran's complaint and interposed 47 U.S.C. § 230 as an affirmative defense. AOL then moved for judgment on the pleadings * * *. The district court granted AOL's motion, and Zeran filed this appeal.

II

* * * Zeran seeks to hold AOL liable for defamatory speech initiated by a third party. He argued to the district court that once he notified AOL of the unidentified third party's hoax, AOL had a duty to remove the defamatory posting promptly, to notify its subscribers of the message's false nature, and to effectively screen future defamatory material. Section 230 entered this litigation as an affirmative defense pled by AOL. The company claimed that Congress immunized

interactive computer service providers from claims based on information posted by a third party.

The relevant portion of § 230 states: "No provider or user of an interactive computer service shall be treated as the publisher or speaker of any information provided by another information content provider." 47 U.S.C. § 230(c)(1). * By its plain language, § 230 creates a federal immunity to any cause of action that would make service providers liable for information originating with a third-party user of the service. Specifically, § 230 precludes courts from entertaining claims that would place a computer service provider in a publisher's role. Thus, lawsuits seeking to hold a service provider liable for its exercise of a publisher's traditional editorial functions—such as deciding whether to publish, withdraw, postpone or alter content—are barred.

The purpose of this statutory immunity is not difficult to discern. Congress recognized the threat that tort-based lawsuits pose to freedom of speech in the new and burgeoning Internet medium. The imposition of tort liability on service providers for the communications of others represented, for Congress, simply another form of intrusive government regulation of speech. Section 230 was enacted, in part, to maintain the robust nature of Internet communication and, accordingly, to keep government interference in the medium to a minimum. * * * None of this means, of course, that the original culpable party who posts defamatory messages would escape accountability. * * * Congress made a policy choice, however, not to deter harmful online speech through the separate route of imposing tort liability on companies that serve as intermediaries for other parties' potentially injurious messages.

Congress' purpose in providing the § 230 immunity was thus evident. Interactive computer services have millions of users. * The amount of information communicated via interactive computer services is therefore staggering. The specter of tort liability in an area of such prolific speech would have an obvious chilling effect. It would be impossible for service providers to screen each of their millions of postings for possible problems. Faced with potential liability for each message republished by their services, interactive computer service providers might choose to severely restrict the number and type of messages posted. Congress considered the weight of the speech interests implicated and chose to immunize service providers to avoid any such restrictive effect.

* * * § 230 responded to a New York state court decision, Stratton Oakmont, Inc. v. Prodigy Servs. Co., 1995 WL 323710 (N.Y.Sup.Ct.1995). There, the plaintiffs sued Prodigy—an interactive computer service like AOL—for defamatory comments made by an unidentified party on one of Prodigy's bulletin boards. The court held Prodigy to the strict liability standard normally applied to original publishers of defamatory statements, rejecting Prodigy's claims that it should be held only to the lower "knowledge" standard usually reserved for distributors. The court reasoned that Prodigy acted more like an original publisher than a distributor both because it advertised its practice of controlling content on its service and because it actively screened and edited messages posted on its bulletin boards.

Congress enacted § 230 to remove the disincentives to self-regulation created by the *Stratton Oakmont* decision. Under that court's holding, computer service providers who regulated the dissemination of offensive material on their services risked subjecting themselves to liability, because such regulation cast the service provider in the role of a publisher. Fearing that the specter of liability would therefore deter service providers from blocking and screening offensive material, Congress enacted § 230's broad immunity "to remove disincentives for the development and utilization of blocking and filtering technologies that empower parents to restrict their children's access to objectionable or inappropriate online material." 47 U.S.C. § 230(b)(4). In line with this purpose, § 230 forbids the imposition of publisher liability on a service provider for the exercise of its editorial and self-regulatory functions.

Zeran argues, however, that the § 230 immunity eliminates only publisher liability, leaving distributor liability intact. Publishers can be held liable for defamatory statements contained in their works even absent proof that they had specific knowledge of the statement's inclusion. * According to Zeran, interactive computer service providers like AOL are normally considered instead to be distributors, like traditional news vendors or book sellers. Distributors cannot be held liable for defamatory statements contained in the materials they distribute unless it is proven at a minimum that they have actual knowledge of the defamatory statements upon which liability is predicated. *

Zeran contends that he provided AOL with sufficient notice of the defamatory statements appearing on the company's bulletin board. This notice is significant, says Zeran, because AOL could be held liable as a distributor only if it acquired knowledge of the defamatory statements' existence.

Because of the difference between these two forms of liability, Zeran contends that the term "distributor" carries a legally distinct meaning from the term "publisher." Accordingly, he asserts that Congress' use of only the term "publisher" in § 230 indicates a purpose to immunize service providers only from publisher liability. He argues that distributors are left unprotected by § 230 and, therefore, his suit should be permitted to proceed against AOL. We disagree. Assuming *arguendo* that Zeran has satisfied the requirements for imposition of distributor liability, this theory of liability is merely a subset, or a species, of publisher liability, and is therefore also foreclosed by § 230.

The terms "publisher" and "distributor" derive their legal significance from the context of defamation law. Although Zeran attempts to artfully plead his claims as ones of negligence, they are indistinguishable from a garden variety defamation action. Because the publication of a statement is a necessary element in a defamation action, only one who publishes can be subject to this form of tort liability. Restatement (Second) of Torts § 558(b) (1977). * Publication does not only describe the choice by an author to include certain information. In addition, both the negligent communication of a defamatory statement and the failure to remove such a statement when first communicated by another party—each alleged by Zeran here under a negligence label—constitute publication. Restatement (Second) of

Torts § 577. * In fact, every repetition of a defamatory statement is considered a publication. *

In this case, AOL is legally considered to be a publisher. "[E]very one who takes part in the publication . . . is charged with publication." Even distributors are considered to be publishers for purposes of defamation law:

> Those who are in the business of making their facilities available to disseminate the writings composed, the speeches made, and the information gathered by others may also be regarded as participating to such an extent in making the books, newspapers, magazines, and information available to others as to be regarded as publishers. They are intentionally making the contents available to others, sometimes without knowing all of the contents—including the defamatory content—and sometimes without any opportunity to ascertain, in advance, that any defamatory matter was to be included in the matter published.

W. Page Keeton *et al.*, Prosser & Keeton on The Law of Torts § 113 (5th ed. 1984). AOL falls squarely within this traditional definition of a publisher and, therefore, is clearly protected by § 230's immunity.

Zeran contends that decisions like *Stratton Oakmont* and Cubby, Inc. v. CompuServe, Inc., 776 F.Supp. 135 (S.D.N.Y.1991), recognize a legal distinction between publishers and distributors. He misapprehends, however, the significance of that distinction for the legal issue we consider here. It is undoubtedly true that mere conduits, or distributors, are subject to a different standard of liability. As explained above, distributors must at a minimum have knowledge of the existence of a defamatory statement as a prerequisite to liability. But this distinction signifies only that different standards of liability may be applied *within* the larger publisher category, depending on the specific type of publisher concerned. * * *

Zeran simply attaches too much importance to the presence of the distinct notice element in distributor liability. The simple fact of notice surely cannot transform one from an original publisher to a distributor in the eyes of the law. To the contrary, once a computer service provider receives notice of a potentially defamatory posting, it is thrust into the role of a traditional publisher. The computer service provider must decide whether to publish, edit, or withdraw the posting. In this respect, Zeran seeks to impose liability on AOL for assuming the role for which § 230 specifically proscribes liability—the publisher role. * * *

If computer service providers were subject to distributor liability, they would face potential liability each time they receive notice of a potentially defamatory statement—from any party, concerning any message. Each notification would require a careful yet rapid investigation of the circumstances surrounding the posted information, a legal judgment concerning the information's defamatory character, and an on-the-spot editorial decision whether to risk liability by allowing the continued publication of that information. Although this might be feasible for the traditional print publisher, the sheer number of postings on interactive computer services would create an impossible burden in the Internet context. * Because service providers would be subject to liability only for the publication of information, and not for its removal, they would have a natural incentive simply to remove messages upon notification, whether the contents were defamatory or not. * Thus, like strict liability, liability upon notice has a chilling effect on the freedom of Internet speech.

Similarly, notice-based liability would deter service providers from regulating the dissemination of offensive material over their own services. Any efforts by a service provider to investigate and screen material posted on its service would only lead to notice of potentially defamatory material more frequently and thereby create a stronger basis for liability. Instead of subjecting themselves to further possible lawsuits, service providers would likely eschew any attempts at self-regulation.

More generally, notice-based liability for interactive computer service providers would provide third parties with a no-cost means to create the basis for future lawsuits. Whenever one was displeased with the speech of another party conducted over an interactive computer service, the offended party could simply "notify" the relevant service provider, claiming the information to be legally defamatory. In light of the vast amount of speech communicated through interactive computer services, these notices could produce an impossible burden for service providers, who would be faced with ceaseless choices of suppressing controversial speech or sustaining prohibitive liability. Because the probable effects of distributor liability on the vigor of Internet speech and on service provider self-regulation are directly contrary to § 230's statutory purposes, we will not assume that Congress intended to leave liability upon notice intact. * * *

For the foregoing reasons, we affirm the judgment of the district court.

NOTE

Retraction. If a publisher retracts a statement in a timely manner upon request, what should the effect be on liability? Many state statutes limit liability in such a case. E.g., Cal. Civ. Code § 48a (Deering 2014); Fla. Stat. § 770.02 (2013); see also Harper, James and Gray on Torts § 5.19 n.1 for a listing of additional statutes.

E. ISSUES OF TRUTH AND REPUBLICATION AT COMMON LAW

Olinger v. American Savings and Loan Ass'n

United States Court of Appeals for the District of Columbia Circuit, 1969.
133 U.S.App.D.C. 107, 409 F.2d 142.

■ PER CURIAM: This action was brought to recover damages stemming from an alleged libel, invasion of privacy, and malicious interference with peace of mind. The District Court granted appellee's motion for summary judgment. We remand solely on the libel theory.

The facts, viewed in the light most favorable to appellant, are as follows. Appellant, a career Air Force officer, was divorced from his wife in January 1966. By the terms of the decree, he was ordered to make support and alimony payments totaling $550 per month. A deed of trust, held by appellee, on the couple's former house in Maryland obligated both appellant and his former wife. Subsequent to the divorce, however, the couple agreed orally that Mrs. Olinger would continue to live in the house and would keep up the payments on it.

After remarrying, appellant was transferred to Germany. Although he regularly made his support and alimony payments, the deed of trust payments fell into arrears. After several telephone conversations with the former Mrs. Olinger, appellee instructed the trustees to foreclose on the property. They so informed both appellant and his former wife and initiated the necessary legal proceedings. Upon receiving notification of the impending foreclosure, appellant, through his attorney, informed appellee that he would be willing to effectuate a friendly sale of the property. In subsequent conversations with appellant's attorney, appellee's representative (Lowery) accused appellant of leaving the country without providing for his family and of having adulterous relationships. He also stated his intention, based on the advice of a retired Air Force Colonel, to write a letter concerning these matters to appellant's commanding officer, though he conceded that the value of the property exceeded the balance due on the loan. Despite the attorney's objections, Lowery did write such a letter, the substance of which forms the basis of this action. * * * Appellant was called before his superior officers in Germany to account for the charges contained in the letter. The embarrassment and humiliation of this experience and of other comments and discussion regarding the letter allegedly aggravated appellant's pre-existing nervous condition, resulting in his hospitalization.

* * * [W]e conclude that the facts, viewed in this light, would support a verdict in appellant's favor on the libel theory. * * * Appellee, while not here contesting the defamatory nature of the publication, has taken great pains to demonstrate the truth of each and every statement in the letter. Truth, of course, is a complete defense to a charge of libel. * It is clear, however, that at least one of the statements in the letter was "true" only because it was prefaced by "Mrs. Olinger reports that . . . ." Appellant has asserted that he was willing to effectuate a friendly sale of the house and, indeed, that Lowery had been made aware of this intention. He further asserts that he and his former wife had reached an agreement whereby she was to keep up the payments on the house. Nonetheless Lowery's letter included the following recital: "Mrs. Olinger reports that Col. Olinger is unwilling to permit her to sell the property and he will not keep the payments current on the first and second trust."

The law affords no protection to those who couch their libel in the form of reports or repetition. In the first place repetition of a defamatory statement is a publication in itself, regardless whether the repeater names the source. * As a corollary, and more germane to the instant case, the repeater cannot defend on the ground of truth simply by proving that the source named did, in fact, utter the statement. * To quote the Restatement of Torts:

> When one person repeats a defamatory statement which he attributes to some other person, it is not enough for the person

who repeats it to prove that the statement was made by the other person. He must prove the truth of the defamatory charges which he has thus repeated.[5]

The statement in question contains two charges: (1) that appellant was unwilling to permit his former wife to sell the house, and (2) that he was not keeping the payments current on the first and second trusts. It is apparent that both charges are at least capable of defamatory meaning. It is for the jury to determine whether the statement was so understood by the recipients of the letter * and whether the charges it contains are, in fact, true. * Since these are genuine issues of material fact, * we remand for further proceedings not inconsistent with this opinion.

NOTES

1. *Truth as a Defense at Common Law.* The principal case states the common law rule that the truth of the defamatory statement is a defense to liability. Why? It has not always been so, at least in some contexts. For some time the rule in England was that truth was not a defense and that evidence of the truthfulness of the statement was not even admissible in a criminal libel prosecution. See Harper, James and Gray on Torts § 5.20. Indeed, it was often said that "The greater the truth the greater the libel." By the early nineteenth century, however, it was generally established that there was no civil liability for true statements.

At common law, truth was an affirmative defense to be pleaded and proved by the defendant. How easy is it for a defamed individual to prove a negative, particularly if the statements attribute to plaintiff a continuing course of conduct or general lack of character? In *Philadelphia Newspapers, Inc. v. Hepps, infra* pages 923–26, the United States Supreme Court considered constitutional challenges to placing the burden on certain defendants to prove the truth of the statement asserted to be defamatory.

2. *Republication of Defamatory Statements.* It is well established that every republication of a defamatory statement is a separate tort for which the republisher is liable, even if the defamatory remarks are attributed to another person. Restatement (Second) of Torts § 578 cmt. c (1977). This is true even if the republisher labels the statement as a "rumor" or "report." See, e.g., Lawrence v. Bauer Publ'g & Printing Ltd., 176 N.J.Super. 378, 389, 423 A.2d 655, 660–61 (App.Div.1980) ("[n]or may defendants shield themselves from liability by literally relying on other sources * * *. Surrounding the defamatory sting of their words with terms such as 'reportedly,' 'may be,' or 'could possibly be' will not protect a publisher.")

3. *Fair Reporting Privilege.* One category of republication is immune from liability under a common law affirmative defense known as the fair reporting privilege. Fair reports of proceedings in courts, legislative proceedings, and proceedings before executive officers are privileged, even if the publisher knows or suspects that the statements repeated defame someone. See, e.g., Piscatelli v. Van Smith, 424 Md. 294, 309, 35 A.3d 1140, 1149 (2012); Gobin v. Globe Publ'g Co., 216 Kan. 223, 531 P.2d 76 (1975). To receive the benefit of this privilege, the account must be "accurate and complete or a fair abridgment of the occurrence reported." Restatement

---

[5]   * Restatement of Torts § 582 cmt. d (1938).

(Second) of Torts § 611 and cmt. a (1977). Courts generally hold that this privilege can be lost if the publisher is acting with "malice," in one sense or another. See *infra* page 911, Note 2.

In Edwards v. Nat'l Audubon Soc'y, Inc., 556 F.2d 113 (2d Cir.1977), the Second Circuit Court of Appeals, in dicta, went further and suggested that the press has a "right of neutral reportage," notwithstanding doubts about the truth of the accusations reported. Other courts have rejected the application of such a privilege. See, e.g., Khawar v. Globe Int'l, Inc., 19 Cal.4th 254, 79 Cal.Rptr.2d 178, 965 P.2d 696 (1998); Ortega v. Post-Newsweek Stations, Fla., Inc., 510 So.2d 972 (Fla.Dist.Ct.App.1987).

F. PRIVILEGED OCCASIONS UNDER COMMON LAW

Nodar v. Galbreath

Supreme Court of Florida, 1984.
462 So.2d 803.

■ BOYD, CHIEF JUSTICE. * * * The complaint alleged that defendant/petitioner Joseph J. Nodar committed a slander of the plaintiff/respondent Patricia Galbreath by making certain remarks, heard by others, impugning her professional ability. The plaintiff is a public high school teacher. Prior to and at the time of the communication charged as defamatory, the son of the defendant was a student in a class taught by the plaintiff. The class was a special tenth-grade English class for gifted students. The publication alleged as having been defamatory was made at a meeting of the governing board of the Broward County school district, specifically a portion of the school board meeting specially set aside for receiving the comments of members of the public. Attached to the complaint was a transcript of petitioner's statement to the school board, the most pertinent parts of which are set out in the footnote.[1]

The record shows that the defendant was dissatisfied with the instruction his son was receiving in the class and believed that it was not in accord with the established curriculum for the tenth-grade gifted English class. The theory of the complaint was that the publication was a false and defamatory statement tending to impugn plaintiff's abilities in connection with her business or profession and thus was slander per se. A second count alleged that the statements were made with express malice and sought punitive damages. The jury found the remarks

---

[1] Although the entire statement provides a context which is important to an understanding of the statements, in the interest of brevity we provide only the portions said to be defamatory. These excerpts are but a small fraction of the entire statement:

We expressed our concerns about the curriculum of the English class, the gifted English class, explained to them what was going on in the way of an education for these children, including my son, the harassment my son has been receiving from this particular teacher, because of our investigation or inquiry as to his grades and why his grades are going down. He has been harassed since then, he has been abused by her verbally, and his grades have been dropping. . . . My son is being victimized by these two teachers. . . . Now, there is a lot of money funded for this program and, for example, my son, we pay for his books that he has to bring into class to read, we pay for his pencils, we pay for his paper, and the only thing he gets is an unqualified teacher, that's all he's got, and that's all the rest of the children in that class have— an unqualified teacher. . . .

defamatory and maliciously made and returned verdicts for $5,000 compensatory damages and $5,000 punitive damages.

By motion to dismiss and by answer to the complaint the defense raised [several] issues * * *. Through special verdict interrogatories the trial court submitted to the jury the questions of (1) whether the statements were fact or opinion; (2) whether the defendant had a qualified privilege; and (3) whether he abused or lost the privilege due to express malice. The jury found that the statements were matters of fact, that the defendant when he spoke had a qualified privilege, but that he exceeded the bounds of the privilege because of his malice toward the teacher. On appeal the district court affirmed. * * *

[W]e cannot conclude that one who accepts a position as a teacher in a public high school thereby effects the same kind of surrender of the right to vindicate defamation as does one who seeks or accepts an elected or policymaking position with a public body or government institution. * * *

Petitioner argues that his remarks were privileged as a matter of law. We find that there are several legal grounds for holding that the defendant's remarks were made upon a conditionally privileged occasion. "One who publishes defamatory matter concerning another is not liable for the publication if (a) the matter is published upon an occasion that makes it conditionally privileged and (b) the privilege is not abused." Restatement (Second) of Torts § 593 (1976) [sic].[a] The law of Florida embraces a broad range of the privileged occasions that have come to be recognized under the common law. * "A communication made in good faith on any subject matter by one having an interest therein, or in reference to which he has a duty, is privileged if made to a person having a corresponding interest or duty, even though it contains matter which would otherwise be actionable, and though the duty is not a legal one but only a moral or social obligation." * 19 Fla. Jur.2d, Defamation and Privacy § 58 (1980). *

This general rule of privilege finds expression in several established common-law legal grounds for holding that the defendant's statements to the school board were protected by a qualified privilege. The remarks of the defendant, addressed in person to a school board at a school board meeting concerning the curriculum and instruction in an English class at a public high school in which his son was enrolled and his son's difficulties with the class clearly came within the scope of the privilege based on mutuality of interest of speaker and listener. * The concern of a parent for the welfare of his child provides a privilege for the occasion of speaking to one having the power or duty to take action for the benefit of the child. Restatement (Second) of Torts § 597 (1977).

Another ground for holding that the statement was conditionally privileged would be that the statement was made for the protection of the recipient's interest in receiving information on the performance of its employee. See Restatement (Second) of Torts § 595 (1977). In this connection, the value of the defendant's defamatory information to the school board in overseeing the operation of the public schools must be weighed against the extent of the harm likely to be done to the

---

[a] [Eds.' Note] The correct date for the cited provisions of the Restatement (Second) of Torts is 1977. We have corrected the dates of the subsequent citations.

plaintiff's reputation as a result of the communication. * Under the American Law Institute's approach, the interest of the school board in the performance of a teacher, its employee, would give rise to a privilege in another to provide information concerning that performance even without a legal duty or a family relationship and even though the information is not requested but merely volunteered, if the publication is "within the generally accepted standards of decent conduct." Restatement (Second) of Torts § 595 (1977). Under the common law of Florida, a communication to an employer regarding his employee's performance is conditionally privileged, and the mode, manner, or purpose of the communication would go to the question of abuse or forfeiture of the privilege. Analogous situations include communications for bona fide commercial purposes where the interest to be protected is the recipient's. *

Another recognized legal ground for holding that the defendant's statements were privileged is that they were the statements of a citizen to a political authority regarding matters of public concern, i.e., the school curriculum and the performance of a public employee.[5] [b] All of these grounds of qualified privilege have existed in the law of Florida for many generations and have served to provide broad protection for freedom of speech and of the press long before the creation of the remedy fashioned in *New York Times v. Sullivan.*

Where the circumstances surrounding a defamatory communication are undisputed, or are so clear under the evidence as to be unquestionable, then the question of whether the occasion upon which they were spoken was privileged is a question of law to be decided by the court. * Here the circumstances and content of the statement were clear and undisputed. Therefore the defendant's statements to the school board were qualifiedly privileged as a matter of law and the trial judge erred in submitting the question of privilege to the jury. The trial court should have instructed the jury that the statements were made on a privileged occasion.

The legal conclusion that the defendant's remarks were privileged brings us to the question of express malice. If the statements were made without express malice—that is, if they were made for a proper purpose in light of the interests sought to be protected by legal recognition of the privilege—then there can be no recovery. * * *

The evidence was insufficient to show express malice and there should have been a directed verdict on this ground. There was some confusion below about the concept of express malice, the trial court giving the jury the definition from Montgomery v. Knox, 23 Fla. 595, 3 So. 211 (1887): "ill will, hostility, evil intention to defame and injure." Where a person speaks upon a privileged occasion, but the speaker is

---

[5] Yet another arguable ground would be the privilege of every person to express to other persons his fair comment and criticism on any public, governmental, political, social, or cultural matters. * Although we recently said that there is no qualified privilege "to defame a private person merely because the defamatory communication is directed to a matter of public or general concern," Miami Herald Publishing Co. v. Ane, 458 So.2d 239, 241 (Fla.1984), we acknowledged that past cases had recognized the privilege of fair comment where there were "additional factors." We need not decide whether this case presents such additional factors because there are numerous other grounds of privilege.

[b] [Eds.' note] See *infra* Note at page 930 regarding the continuing viability of the common law fair comment privilege.

motivated more by a desire to harm the person defamed than by a purpose to protect the personal or social interest giving rise to the privilege, then it can be said that there was express malice and the privilege is destroyed. Strong, angry, or intemperate words do not alone show express malice; rather, there must be a showing that the speaker used his privileged position "to gratify his malevolence." Myers v. Hodges, 53 Fla. 197, 213, 44 So. 357, 362 (1907). * If the occasion of the communication is privileged because of a proper interest to be protected, and the defamer is motivated by a desire to protect that interest, he does not forfeit the privilege merely because he also in fact feels hostility or ill will toward the plaintiff. * Restatement (Second) of Torts §§ 599, 603 cmt. a (1977). The incidental gratification of personal feelings of indignation is not sufficient to defeat the privilege where the primary motivation is within the scope of the privilege. * * *

The words themselves, we believe, are not so extreme as to demonstrate express malice. Petitioner merely said that the teacher had harassed and verbally abused his son, that she was unqualified to teach the course, and that her performance as a teacher was victimizing his son. While we must accept the unchallenged conclusion of the jury that these words were defamatory, the words do not inherently demonstrate express malice. The accusation that the teacher gave the student a poor mark in retaliation for the father's complaints about her teaching, while clearly capable of stating defamatory meaning, does not show express malice. Examples of cases where the false and defamatory words themselves were so extreme as to intrinsically show express malice are Loeb v. Geronemus, 66 So.2d 241 (Fla. 1953) (defendants said plaintiff was guilty of evil conduct, was of low moral character, was a disgrace, a troublemaker, was not respectable, had been compelled to leave Chicago) and Brown v. Fawcett Publ'ns, Inc., 196 So.2d 465 (Fla.Dist.Ct.App.1967) (defendant said plaintiff was a murderer, rapist, and sodomite).

The fact that the defendant's remarks to the school board were preceded by many months of personal conversations, telephone calls, and letters to the teacher and her superiors does not demonstrate express malice. Indeed, it seems to us that this evidence tends to support rather than negate the claim of privilege, as it shows that defendant tried to seek redress of his grievances through private communications before he publicly revealed his complaints at the school board meeting. The series of personal visits, telephone calls, and letters, far from exhibiting a pattern of malicious harassment, demonstrates a degree of parental concern for the effectiveness of public schools which our state, through its courts of law, should attempt to encourage rather than discourage.

We therefore hold that the plaintiff's evidence was insufficient as a matter of law to carry the burden of proving express malice. * * *

NOTE

Occasions for Exercise of Qualified Privilege. The criteria for deciding when a common law qualified privilege or conditional privilege applies are flexible and capable of being applied to a wide range of situations. Occasions for the exercise of the privilege have been categorized into three groups:

(1) those in which the interest, the protection of which makes the occasion privileged, is one of the person publishing the defamatory matter,

(2) those in which the interest to be protected is an interest of the person to whom the defamatory matter is published, or of a third person, and

(3) those occasions which are privileged for the protection of a public interest.

Harper, James and Gray on Torts § 5.26.

Qualified privileges most frequently apply in recurring fact patterns. Many cases accord a qualified privilege to reports, charges and accusations among members of religious and charitable foundations and within professional societies, e.g., Gabauer v. Woodcock, 520 F.2d 1084 (8th Cir.1975) (labor union); Schreidell v. Shoter, 500 So.2d 228 (Fla.Dist.Ct.App.1986) (rabbi's action against member of board of directors of synagogue), and within corporations and other businesses, e.g., Bainhauer v. Manoukian, 215 N.J.Super. 9, 520 A.2d 1154 (App.Div.1987) (communications among hospital physicians about serious alleged professional deficiencies of colleague). Qualified privileges also generally attach in two other areas in which defamation allegations frequently arise: employment references, e.g., Vickers v. Abbott Labs., 308 Ill.App.3d 393, 241 Ill.Dec. 698, 719 N.E.2d 1101 (1999), and credit reports. See Restatement (Second) of Torts § 595 cmt. h (1977).

Kennedy v. Cannon

Court of Appeals of Maryland, 1962.
229 Md. 92, 182 A.2d 54.

■ SYBERT, JUDGE. This appeal questions whether the trial court erred in directing a verdict for the defendant, an attorney, in a suit for slander on the grounds that the allegedly slanderous statement was privileged as part of the defendant's duty as counsel to his client, and that no malice on the part of the defendant had been shown.

The appellee, Robert Powell Cannon (defendant below), was summoned to the Wicomico County jail in Salisbury at the request of Charles L. Humphreys, a Negro who had been arrested early that morning and charged with the rape of the appellant, Jane Linton Kennedy, a white, married woman. After conferring with the prisoner, appellee made a telephone call to Richard L. Moore, managing editor of the *Salisbury Times*, a daily newspaper published in Salisbury, with a circulation of about 23,000. He inquired concerning any information the newspaper might have received in regard to the charge against Humphreys and was informed by Mr. Moore that "we had talked to the authorities and had gotten a story together, and the story said that Humphreys had signed a statement admitting intercourse with the woman who was involved." Mr. Moore told the appellee that the information had been given by the State's Attorney. Thereupon, the appellee proceeded to tell Mr. Moore everything that Humphreys had related to him, including an assertion by Humphreys that Mrs. Kennedy had consented to the intercourse. When informed that it would be impossible to print matter of that type, and at such great length, appellee agreed, with some reluctance, to the publication as part of the news article of additional material quoting the appellee as to Humphreys' claim. The article which was published that afternoon included in the information furnished by the State's Attorney the identity of the appellant, the fact that she is a white woman, the fact that she had accused Humphreys, a Negro, of raping her, and a statement that Humphreys had signed an admission of the intercourse. The article then quoted appellee as having said, "He [Humphreys] emphatically denies the charge. He says that the woman submitted to his advances willingly."

As a result of the publication of the statement appellant alleged she suffered humiliation and harassment by annoying phone calls from unknown persons and eventually was forced to move with her family out of the community and the State. She instituted a suit against appellee alleging that the words spoken by him to the newspaper charged her with the crime of adultery, were slanderous per se under Art. 88, § 1, Code (1957), and were not privileged.

The appellee admitted on the witness stand that the newspaper article correctly quoted his statement to the editor. He sought to justify its publication on the ground that the physical safety of his client required it. He stated he feared the possibility of a lynching if only the material released by the State's Attorney were published. Recalling a lynching which had occurred in Salisbury under similar circumstances some 25 years previously, he said he felt that the account should include a denial of the charge based upon his client's claim of consent by the woman. At the conclusion of the testimony before a jury, the trial court granted appellee's motion for a directed verdict, expressing the opinion that when the State had undertaken to publish a statement about the case damaging to his client, the appellee was justified and privileged in replying as he did. Appellant appeals from the judgment for costs entered in favor of appellee.

The question raised here is whether appellee's statement comes within the ambit of * * * slander or whether a recovery by appellant is barred because the statement was privileged. * * *

The privilege afforded an attorney in a judicial proceeding and its rationale are discussed in the leading case of Maulsby v. Reifsnider, 69 Md. 143, 151, 14 A. 505 (1888), where this Court stated:

> . . . All agree, that counsel are privileged and protected to a certain extent, at least, for defamatory words spoken *in a judicial proceeding*, and words thus spoken are not actionable, which would in themselves be actionable, if spoken elsewhere. He is obliged in the discharge of a professional duty to prosecute and defend the most important rights and interests, the life it may be, or the liberty or the property of his client, and it is absolutely essential to the administration of justice that he should be allowed the widest latitude in commenting on the character, the conduct and motives of parties and witnesses and other persons directly or remotely connected with the subject-matter in litigation. And to subject him to actions of slander by everyone who may consider himself aggrieved, and to the costs and expenses of a harassing litigation, would be to fetter and restrain him in that open and

fearless discharge of duty which he owes to his client, and which the demands of justice require. Not that the law means to say, that one, because he is counsel in the trial of a cause, has the right, abstractly considered, deliberately and maliciously to slander another, but it is the fear that if the rule were otherwise, actions without number might be brought against counsel who had not spoken falsely and maliciously. It is better therefore to make the rule of law so large that counsel acting *bona fide* in the discharge of duty, shall never be troubled, although by making it so large, others who have acted *mala fide* and maliciously, are included. The question whether words spoken by counsel were spoken maliciously or in good faith, are, and always will be, open questions, upon which opinion may differ, and counsel, however innocent, would be liable if not to judgments, to a vexatious and expensive litigation. The privilege thus recognized by law is not the privilege merely of counsel, but the privilege of clients, and the evil, if any, resulting from it must be endured for the sake of the greater good which is thereby secured. But this privilege is not an absolute and unqualified privilege, and cannot be extended beyond the reason and principles on which it is founded. . . . (Emphasis added.)

The Court went on to hold that the words, to be privileged, must also be relevant to the judicial proceeding in which they were spoken.

The statement just quoted reflects the view of a majority of the jurisdictions in this country, although the semantics in this area of tort law have changed somewhat since the date of the *Maulsby* case. What was characterized in that case as a qualified privilege for communications, conditioned on their being pertinent or relevant to a judicial proceeding, without regard to the motive of the speaker, is referred to by modern text writers and in case law as an absolute privilege. * This absolute immunity extends to the judge as well as to witnesses and parties to the litigation, for defamatory statements uttered in the course of a trial or contained in pleadings, affidavits, depositions, and other documents directly related to the case. F. Harper & F. James, The Law of Torts, § 5.22 (1956), and cases there cited. An absolute privilege is distinguished from a qualified privilege in that the former provides immunity regardless of the purpose or motive of the defendant, or the reasonableness of his conduct, while the latter is conditioned upon the absence of malice and is forfeited if it is abused. *

Appellee in this case contends that under the *Maulsby* case, his statement was absolutely privileged. It is not disputed that the statement was relevant to the criminal proceeding. The essential question to be answered is whether it was published in—that is, as part of—a "judicial proceeding."

The term "judicial proceeding" is broad enough to cover all steps in a criminal action, so that when Humphreys was arrested and charged with rape it would be a valid conclusion that the judicial proceeding had commenced. * However, this does not necessarily mean that every statement made by an attorney after the inception of a judicial proceeding will be privileged.

Appellee cites the oft quoted rule from Restatement of Torts § 586:

> An attorney at law is absolutely privileged to publish false and defamatory matter of another in communications preliminary to a proposed judicial proceeding, or in the institution of, or during the course and as a part of a judicial proceeding in which he participates as counsel, if it has some relation thereto.

However, the extension of this absolute privilege to statements not made in the judicial proceeding itself is limited both by the comments on the rule of the Restatement itself, and by the decisions. The scope of the privilege is restricted to communications such as those made between an attorney and his client, or in the examination of witnesses by counsel, or in statements made by counsel to the court or jury. Restatement of Torts § 586 cmts. a and c. * Appellee cites no authorities which would extend the privilege beyond a communication to one actually involved in the proceeding, either as judge, attorney, party or witness. On the other hand, it has been held that such absolute privilege will not attach to counsel's extra-judicial publications, related to the litigation, which are made outside the purview of the judicial proceeding. * Nor will the attorney be privileged for actionable words spoken before persons in no way connected with the proceeding. * * *

All of the above cited cases make it obvious that aside from any question of ethics, an attorney who wishes to litigate his case in the press will do so at his own risk. We hold that appellee had no absolute privilege in regard to the statement made by him to the newspaper.

However, the argument is made (and the language of the trial court's opinion shows that it was persuasive there) that the forum had been chosen by the State's Attorney, and not by appellee, and that he had a right, perhaps even a duty to his client, to publish the statement in question. This argument raises indirectly the contention that because of the attorney-client relationship, at least a qualified privilege existed in the absence of a showing of malice or abuse of the privilege.

There may well be a qualified privilege based upon an attorney-client relationship which would justify an otherwise slanderous communication to certain other persons, to protect the rights of society or one to whom a legal or moral duty is owed. However, the communication *must be made in a proper manner and to proper parties only*, i.e., to parties having a corresponding interest or duty. * It may be conceded that appellee indeed had a duty to act upon the information he had gained as to the statement given by the State's Attorney to the newspaper, particularly in light of Humphreys' statement to him. However, the means he chose to fulfill that duty were not proper, nor did he release the communication to a party having a corresponding interest or duty in the matter; and it cannot be said that his action was within the scope of his professional acts as an attorney in a pending case. * Other steps more consonant with Canon 20, Canons of Professional Ethics, were open to appellee. He could have requested the transfer of Humphreys to the jail of another jurisdiction for safekeeping until trial. He could have sought to have the objectionable matter, contained in the proposed article, kept out of publication. Even if this attempt were unsuccessful, other tactics were possible to the attorney who eventually defended the case, e.g., a request for change of venue, *voir dire* examination of prospective jurors in regard to the article, and preservation of the question of the prejudicial effect of the article, for appellate review.

The solicitude of appellee for his client is understandable, and the initial act of the State's Attorney in releasing his statement to the press must be disapproved. Nevertheless, as we have stated, appellee's legal duty in no way justified the publication of his defamatory reply statement. To hold otherwise would open the door to the universally condemned "trial by press," a procedure forbidden to counsel and subversive of the fair and orderly conduct of judicial proceedings. * * *

We hold that as a matter of law appellee had neither an absolute nor a qualified privilege in regard to the defamatory statement. Since the words spoken were slanderous *per se* they required no proof of special damage and carried the implication of malice. * * *

NOTES

1. *Legislative Privilege.* At common law, an absolute privilege protects members of state and national legislative bodies for defamatory statements made during the course of debate, committee hearings or deliberations, or discussions of legislative problems. Restatement (Second) of Torts § 590A (1977). To receive protection, the statement must be in reference to a legitimate object of legislative concern. This common law privilege is incorporated in the Constitution of the United States Article I, Section 6, which provides that "for any speech, or debate in either house [Senators and Representatives] shall not be questioned in any other place." The Supreme Court delineated the scope of this constitutional immunity in Hutchinson v. Proxmire, 443 U.S. 111, 99 S.Ct. 2675, 61 L.Ed.2d 411 (1979). Senator Proxmire awarded "Golden Fleece of the Month Awards" to publicize what he regarded as wasteful federal spending. The plaintiff had received federal grants for his research on aggressive behavior among primates. The Court found that Proxmire was "wholly immune" for his statements on the Senate floor, but not immune for statements contained in press releases and constituent newsletters that were not "essential to the deliberations of the Senate" and were not "part of the legislative process."

2. *Executive Privilege.* The common law immunity of absolute privilege extends to presidents, governors, cabinet members, and other representatives of the executive branch as well. Restatement (Second) of Torts § 591 (1977). In Spalding v. Vilas, 161 U.S. 483, 16 S.Ct. 631, 40 L.Ed. 780 (1896), the Supreme Court sustained a claim of absolute privilege by the Postmaster General, stating:

> In exercising the functions of his office, the head of an executive department, keeping within the limits of his authority, should not be under an apprehension that the motives that control his official conduct may at any time become the subject of inquiry in a civil suit for damages. It would seriously cripple the proper and effective administration of public affairs as entrusted to the executive branch of the government, if he were subjected to any such restraint. * * *

Judge Learned Hand explained the justification for an *absolute* privilege in this manner:

> The justification for doing so is that it is impossible to know whether the claim is well founded until the case has been tried, and that to submit all officials, the innocent as well as the guilty, to the burden of a trial and to the inevitable danger of its outcome, would dampen the ardor of all but the most resolute, or the most irresponsible, in the unflinching discharge of their duties.

Gregoire v. Biddle, 177 F.2d 579, 581 (2d Cir.1949) (not a defamation action).

In Barr v. Matteo, 360 U.S. 564, 79 S.Ct. 1335, 3 L.Ed.2d 1434 (1959), the Supreme Court extended the privilege to "any federal official" on "matters committed by law to his control or supervision" made "within the outer perimeter of * * * [the official's] line of duty." In Doe v. McMillan, 412 U.S. 306, 93 S.Ct. 2018, 36 L.Ed.2d 912 (1973), however, the Court indicated that the absolute immunity extends to officials of "suitable rank," not to "policemen and like officials," who "apparently enjoy a more limited privilege."

As previously explained, Westfall Act (Federal Employees Liability Reform and Tort Compensation Act of 1988, Pub. L. 100–694, amending 28 U.S.C. §§ 2671, 2674, 2679(b) and (d) (2012)) now makes the Federal Tort Claims Act the exclusive remedy for state tort claims based on the acts or omissions of all federal employees within the scope of their office or employment. A tort remedy against the employee is precluded even if the FTCA provides no remedy against the United States. See *supra* pages 532–33, Note 2. The Federal Tort Claims Act explicitly excludes liability for libel and slander. 28 U.S.C. § 2680(h) (2012). Accordingly, both high-level and low-level employees of the United States now enjoy absolute statutory immunity for defamatory statements and need not rely on the complexities of common law privilege for defense against such claims.

3. *Administrative Proceedings and Privilege.* An absolute privilege similar to that for judicial proceedings also extends to proceedings before administrative agencies exercising quasi-judicial powers. See, e.g., Field v. Kearns, 43 Conn.App. 265, 682 A.2d 148 (1996) (absolute immunity for statement made during bar grievance proceedings); compare Jacobs v. Frank, 60 Ohio St.3d 111, 573 N.E.2d 609 (1991) (qualified privilege only); Preiser v. Rosenzweig, 538 Pa. 139, 646 A.2d 1166 (1994) (no privilege for proceedings before Fee Dispute Committee of local bar association where bar association is private organization).

G. CONSTITUTIONAL REQUIREMENTS

New York Times Co. v. Sullivan
Supreme Court of the United States, 1964.
376 U.S. 254, 84 S.Ct. 710, 11 L.Ed.2d 686.

■ BRENNAN, JUSTICE. We are required in this case to determine for the first time the extent to which the constitutional protections for speech and press limit a State's power to award damages in a libel action brought by a public official against critics of his official conduct.

Respondent L. B. Sullivan is one of the three elected Commissioners of the City of Montgomery, Alabama. He testified that he was "Commissioner of Public Affairs and the duties are supervision of the Police Department, Fire Department, Department of Cemetery and Department of Scales." He brought this civil libel action against the four individual petitioners, who are Negroes and Alabama clergymen, and against petitioner the New York Times Company, a New York corporation which publishes the *New York Times*, a daily newspaper. A jury in the Circuit Court of Montgomery County awarded him damages of $500,000, the full amount claimed, against all the petitioners, and the Supreme Court of Alabama affirmed. *

Respondent's complaint alleged that he had been libeled by statements in a full-page advertisement that was carried in the *New York Times* on March 29, 1960. * Entitled "Heed Their Rising Voices," the advertisement began by stating that "As the whole world knows by now, thousands of Southern Negro students are engaged in widespread non-violent demonstrations in positive affirmation of the right to live in human dignity as guaranteed by the U. S. Constitution and the Bill of Rights." It went on to charge that "in their efforts to uphold these guarantees, they are being met by an unprecedented wave of terror by those who would deny and negate that document which the whole world looks upon as setting the pattern for modern freedom. . . ." Succeeding paragraphs purported to illustrate the "wave of terror" by describing certain alleged events. The text concluded with an appeal for funds for three purposes: support of the student movement, "the struggle for the right-to-vote," and the legal defense of Dr. Martin Luther King, Jr., leader of the movement, against a perjury indictment then pending in Montgomery.

The text appeared over the names of 64 persons, many widely known for their activities in public affairs, religion, trade unions, and the performing arts. Below these names, and under a line reading "We in the south who are struggling daily for dignity and freedom warmly endorse this appeal," appeared the names of the four individual petitioners and of 16 other persons, all but two of whom were identified as clergymen in various Southern cities. The advertisement was signed at the bottom of the page by the "Committee to Defend Martin Luther King and the Struggle for Freedom in the South," and the officers of the Committee were listed.

Of the 10 paragraphs of text in the advertisement, the third and a portion of the sixth were the basis of respondent's claim of libel. They read as follows:

Third paragraph:

In Montgomery, Alabama, after students sang "My Country, 'Tis of Thee" on the State Capitol steps, their leaders were expelled from school, and truckloads of police armed with shotguns and tear-gas ringed the Alabama State College Campus. When the entire student body protested to state authorities by refusing to re-register, their dining hall was padlocked in an attempt to starve them into submission.

Sixth paragraph:

Again and again the Southern violators have answered Dr. King's peaceful protests with intimidation and violence. They have bombed his home almost killing his wife and child. They have assaulted his person. They have arrested him seven times—for "speeding," "loitering" and similar "offenses." And now they have charged him with "perjury"—a *felony* under which they could imprison him for *ten years.* . . .

Although neither of these statements mentions respondent by name, he contended that the word "police" in the third paragraph referred to him as the Montgomery Commissioner who supervised the Police Department, so that he was being accused of "ringing" the campus with police. He further claimed that the paragraph would be read as imputing to the police, and hence to him, the padlocking of the dining hall in order to starve the students into submission. * As to the sixth paragraph, he contended that since arrests are ordinarily made by the police, the statement "They have arrested (Dr. King) seven times" would be read as referring to him; he further contended that the "They" who did the arresting would be equated with the "They" who committed the other described acts and with the "Southern violators." Thus, he argued, the paragraph would be read as accusing the Montgomery police, and hence him, of answering Dr. King's protests with "intimidation and violence," bombing his home, assaulting his person, and charging him with perjury. Respondent and six other Montgomery residents testified that they read some or all of the statements as referring to him in his capacity as Commissioner.

It is uncontroverted that some of the statements contained in the two paragraphs were not accurate descriptions of events which occurred in Montgomery. Although Negro students staged a demonstration on the State Capitol steps, they sang the National Anthem and not "My Country, 'Tis of Thee." Although nine students were expelled by the State Board of Education, this was not for leading the demonstration at the Capitol, but for demanding service at a lunch counter in the Montgomery County Courthouse on another day. Not the entire student body, but most of it, had protested the expulsion, not by refusing to register, but by boycotting classes on a single day; virtually all the students did register for the ensuing semester. The campus dining hall was not padlocked on any occasion, and the only students who may have been barred from eating there were the few who had neither signed a preregistration application nor requested temporary meal tickets. Although the police were deployed near the campus in large numbers on three occasions, they did not at any time "ring" the campus, and they were not called to the campus in connection with the demonstration on the State Capitol steps, as the third paragraph implied. Dr. King had not been arrested seven times, but only four; and although he claimed to have been assaulted some years earlier in connection with his arrest for loitering outside a courtroom, one of the officers who made the arrest denied that there was such an assault.

On the premise that the charges in the sixth paragraph could be read as referring to him, respondent was allowed to prove that he had not participated in the events described. Although Dr. King's home had in fact been bombed twice when his wife and child were there, both of these occasions antedated respondent's tenure as Commissioner, and the police were not only not implicated in the bombings, but had made every effort to apprehend those who were. Three of Dr. King's four arrests took place before respondent became Commissioner. Although Dr. King had in fact been indicted (he was subsequently acquitted) on two counts of perjury, each of which carried a possible five-year sentence, respondent had nothing to do with procuring the indictment.

Respondent made no effort to prove that he suffered actual pecuniary loss as a result of the alleged libel.[3] One of his witnesses, a former employer, testified that if he had believed the statements, he doubted whether he "would want to be associated with anybody who would be a party to such things that are stated in that ad," and that he would not re-employ respondent if he believed "that he allowed the Police Department to do the things that the paper say he did." But neither this witness nor any of the others testified that he had actually believed the statements in their supposed reference to respondent.

The cost of the advertisement was approximately $4,800, and it was published by the Times upon an order from a New York advertising agency acting for the signatory Committee. The agency submitted the advertisement with a letter from A. Philip Randolph, Chairman of the Committee, certifying that the persons whose names appeared on the advertisement had given their permission. Mr. Randolph was known to the Times' Advertising Acceptability Department as a responsible person, and in accepting the letter as sufficient proof of authorization it followed its established practice. There was testimony that the copy of the advertisement which accompanied the letter listed only the 64 names appearing under the text, and that the statement, "We in the south . . . warmly endorse this appeal," and the list of names thereunder, which included those of the individual petitioners, were subsequently added when the first proof of the advertisement was received. Each of the individual petitioners testified that he had not authorized the use of his name, and that he had been unaware of its use until receipt of respondent's demand for a retraction. The manager of the Advertising Acceptability Department testified that he had approved the advertisement for publication because he knew nothing to cause him to believe that anything in it was false, and because it bore the endorsement of "a number of people who are well known and whose reputation" he "had no reason to question." Neither he nor anyone else at the Times made an effort to confirm the accuracy of the advertisement, either by checking it against recent Times news stories relating to some of the described events or by any other means.

Alabama law denies a public officer recovery of punitive damages in a libel action brought on account of a publication concerning his official conduct unless he first makes a written demand for a public retraction and the defendant fails or refuses to comply. * Respondent served such a demand upon each of the petitioners. None of the individual petitioners responded to the demand, primarily because each took the position that he had not authorized the use of his name on the advertisement and therefore had not published the statements that

---

[3]   Approximately 394 copies of the edition of the *Times* containing the advertisement were circulated in Alabama. Of these, about 35 copies were distributed in Montgomery County. The total circulation of the *Times* for that day was approximately 650,000 copies.

respondent alleged had libeled him. The Times did not publish a retraction in response to the demand, but wrote respondent a letter stating, among other things, that "we . . . are somewhat puzzled as to how you think the statements in any way reflect on you," and "you might, if you desire, let us know in what respect you claim that the statements in the advertisement reflect on you." Respondent filed this suit a few days later without answering the letter. * * *

The trial judge submitted the case to the jury under instructions that the statements in the advertisement were "libelous per se" and were not privileged, so that petitioners might be held liable if the jury found that they had published the advertisement and that the statements were made "of and concerning" respondent. The jury was instructed that, because the statements were libelous per se, "the law . . . implies legal injury from the bare fact of publication itself," "falsity and malice are presumed," "general damages need not be alleged or proved but are presumed," and "punitive damages may be awarded by the jury even though the amount of actual damages is neither found nor shown." * * * In affirming the judgment, the Supreme Court of Alabama sustained the trial judge's rulings and instructions in all respects. * * *

Because of the importance of the constitutional issues involved, we granted the separate petitions for certiorari of the individual petitioners and of the Times. * We reverse the judgment. We hold that the rule of law applied by the Alabama courts is constitutionally deficient for failure to provide the safeguards for freedom of speech and of the press that are required by the First and Fourteenth Amendments in a libel action brought by a public official against critics of his official conduct. * We further hold that under the proper safeguards the evidence presented in this case is constitutionally insufficient to support the judgment for respondent. * * *

II

Under Alabama law as applied in this case, a publication is "libelous per se" if the words "tend to injure a person . . . in his reputation" or to "bring [him] into public contempt"; the trial court stated that the standard was met if the words are such as to "injure him in his public office, or impute misconduct to him in his office, or want of official integrity, or want of fidelity to a public trust. . . . " The jury must find that the words were published "of and concerning" the plaintiff, but where the plaintiff is a public official his place in the governmental hierarchy is sufficient evidence to support a finding that his reputation has been affected by statements that reflect upon the agency of which he is in charge. Once "libel per se" has been established, the defendant has no defense as to stated facts unless he can persuade the jury that they were true in all their particulars. * His privilege of "fair comment" for expressions of opinion depends on the truth of the facts upon which the comment is based. * Unless he can discharge the burden of proving truth, general damages are presumed, and may be awarded without proof of pecuniary injury. A showing of actual malice is apparently a prerequisite to recovery of punitive damages, and the defendant may in any event forestall a punitive award by a retraction meeting the statutory requirements. Good motives and belief in truth do not negate an inference of malice, but are relevant only in mitigation of punitive damages if the jury chooses to accord them weight. *

The question before us is whether this rule of liability, as applied to an action brought by a public official against critics of his official conduct, abridges the freedom of speech and of the press that is guaranteed by the First and Fourteenth Amendments. Respondent relies heavily, as did the Alabama courts, on statements of this Court to the effect that the Constitution does not protect libelous publications. * Those statements do not foreclose our inquiry here. None of the cases sustained the use of libel laws to impose sanctions upon expression critical of the official conduct of public officials. * * * The general proposition that freedom of expression upon public questions is secured by the First Amendment has long been settled by our decisions. * * *

Thus we consider this case against the background of a profound national commitment to the principle that debate on public issues should be uninhibited, robust, and wide-open, and that it may well include vehement, caustic, and sometimes unpleasantly sharp attacks on government and public officials. * The present advertisement, as an expression of grievance and protest on one of the major public issues of our time, would seem clearly to qualify for the constitutional protection. The question is whether it forfeits that protection by the falsity of some of its factual statements and by its alleged defamation of respondent.

Authoritative interpretations of the First Amendment guarantees have consistently refused to recognize an exception for any test of truth—whether administered by judges, juries, or administrative officials—and especially one that puts the burden of proving truth on the speaker. * The constitutional protection does not turn upon "the truth, popularity, or social utility of the ideas and beliefs which are offered." N.A.A.C.P. v. Button, 371 U.S. 415, 445, 83 S.Ct. 328, 344, 9 L.Ed.2d 405, 425 (1963). As Madison said, "Some degree of abuse is inseparable from the proper use of every thing; and in no instance is this more true than in that of the press." 4 Elliot's Debates on the Federal Constitution 571 (1876). * * * That erroneous statement is inevitable in free debate, and that it must be protected if the freedoms of expression are to have the "breathing space" that they "need . . . to survive," N.A.A.C.P. v. Button, 371 U.S. at 433, 83 S.Ct. at 338, 9 L.Ed.2d at 418. * * *

There is no force in respondent's argument that the constitutional limitations * * * apply only to Congress and not to the States. It is true that the First Amendment was originally addressed only to action by the Federal Government, and that Jefferson, for one, while denying the power of Congress "to controul the freedom of the press," recognized such a power in the States. * But this distinction was eliminated with the adoption of the Fourteenth Amendment and the application to the States of the First Amendment's restrictions. *

What a State may not constitutionally bring about by means of a criminal statute is likewise beyond the reach of its civil law of libel. * The fear of damage awards under a rule such as that invoked by the Alabama courts here may be markedly more inhibiting than the fear of prosecution under a criminal statute. * Alabama, for example, has a criminal libel law * * *. Presumably a person charged with violation of this statute enjoys ordinary criminal-law safeguards such as the requirements of an indictment and of proof beyond a reasonable doubt. These safeguards are not available to the defendant in a civil action.

The judgment awarded in this case—without the need for any proof of actual pecuniary loss—was one thousand times greater than the maximum fine provided by the Alabama criminal statute, and one hundred times greater than that provided by the Sedition Act. And since there is no double-jeopardy limitation applicable to civil lawsuits, this is not the only judgment that may be awarded against petitioners for the same publication.[18] Whether or not a newspaper can survive a succession of such judgments, the pall of fear and timidity imposed upon those who would give voice to public criticism is an atmosphere in which the First Amendment freedoms cannot survive. * * *

The state rule of law is not saved by its allowance of the defense of truth. * * * A rule compelling the critic of official conduct to guarantee the truth of all his factual assertions—and to do so on pain of libel judgments virtually unlimited in amount—leads to a comparable "self-censorship." Allowance of the defense of truth, with the burden of proving it on the defendant, does not mean that only false speech will be deterred.[19] * * * Under such a rule, would-be critics of official conduct may be deterred from voicing their criticism, even though it is believed to be true and even though it is in fact true, because of doubt whether it can be proved in court or fear of the expense of having to do so. They tend to make only statements which "steer far wider of the unlawful zone." * The rule thus dampens the vigor and limits the variety of public debate. It is inconsistent with the First and Fourteenth Amendments.

The constitutional guarantees require, we think, a federal rule that prohibits a public official from recovering damages for a defamatory falsehood relating to his official conduct unless he proves that the statement was made with "actual malice"—that is, with knowledge that it was false or with reckless disregard of whether it was false or not. * * * Such a privilege for criticism of official conduct * is appropriately analogous to the protection accorded a public official when he is sued for libel by a private citizen. In Barr v. Matteo, 360 U.S. 564, 575, 79 S.Ct. 1335, 1341, 3 L.Ed.2d 1434, 1443 (1959), this Court held the utterance of a federal official to be absolutely privileged if made "within the outer perimeter" of his duties. The States accord the same immunity to statements of their highest officers, although some differentiate their lesser officials and qualify the privilege they enjoy. * But all hold that all officials are protected unless actual malice can be proved. The reason for the official privilege is said to be that the threat of damage suits would otherwise "inhibit the fearless, vigorous, and effective administration of policies of government" and "dampen the ardor of all but the most resolute, or the most irresponsible, in the unflinching discharge of their duties." *Id.* at 571, 79 S.Ct. at 1339, 3 L.Ed.2d at 1441. Analogous considerations support the privilege for the citizen-critic of government. It is as much his duty to criticize as it is the official's duty to administer. * * * It would give public servants an

---

[18] The Times states that four other libel suits based on the advertisement have been filed against it by others who have served as Montgomery City Commissioners and by the Governor of Alabama; that another $500,000 verdict has been awarded in the only one of these cases that has yet gone to trial; and that the damages sought in the other three total $2,000,000.

[19] Even a false statement may be deemed to make a valuable contribution to public debate, since it brings about "the clearer perception and livelier impression of truth, produced by its collision with error." John Stuart Mill, On Liberty 15 (Oxford: Blackwell, 1947). *

unjustified preference over the public they serve, if critics of official conduct did not have a fair equivalent of the immunity granted to the officials themselves.

We conclude that such a privilege is required by the First and Fourteenth Amendments.

III

We hold today that the Constitution delimits a State's power to award damages for libel in actions brought by public officials against critics of their official conduct. Since this is such an action, * the rule requiring proof of actual malice is applicable. While Alabama law apparently requires proof of actual malice for an award of punitive damages, * where general damages are concerned malice is "presumed." Such a presumption is inconsistent with the federal rule. * * * Since the trial judge did not instruct the jury to differentiate between general and punitive damages, it may be that the verdict was wholly an award of one or the other. But it is impossible to know, in view of the general verdict returned. Because of this uncertainty, the judgment must be reversed and the case remanded. *

Since respondent may seek a new trial, we deem that considerations of effective judicial administration require us to review the evidence in the present record to determine whether it could constitutionally support a judgment for respondent. * * * [W]e consider that the proof presented to show actual malice lacks the convincing clarity which the constitutional standard demands, and hence that it would not constitutionally sustain the judgment for respondent under the proper rule of law. The case of the individual petitioners requires little discussion. Even assuming that they could constitutionally be found to have authorized the use of their names on the advertisement, there was no evidence whatever that they were aware of any erroneous statements or were in any way reckless in that regard. The judgment against them is thus without constitutional support.

As to the Times, we similarly conclude that the facts do not support a finding of actual malice. * * * The Times' failure to retract upon respondent's demand * * * is * * * not adequate evidence of malice for constitutional purposes. Whether or not a failure to retract may ever constitute such evidence, there are two reasons why it does not here. First, the letter written by the Times reflected a reasonable doubt on its part as to whether the advertisement could reasonably be taken to refer to respondent at all. Second, it was not a final refusal, since it asked for an explanation on this point—a request that respondent chose to ignore. * * *

Finally, there is evidence that the Times published the advertisement without checking its accuracy against the news stories in the Times' own files. The mere presence of the stories in the files does not, of course, establish that the Times "knew" the advertisement was false, since the state of mind required for actual malice would have to be brought home to the persons in the Times' organization having responsibility for the publication of the advertisement. With respect to the failure of those persons to make the check, the record shows that they relied upon their knowledge of the good reputation of many of those whose names were listed as sponsors of the advertisement, and upon the letter from A. Philip Randolph, known to them as a responsible individual, certifying that the use of the names was authorized. * * * We think the evidence against the Times supports at most a finding of negligence in failing to discover the misstatements, and is constitutionally insufficient to show the recklessness that is required for a finding of actual malice. *

We also think the evidence was constitutionally defective in another respect: it was incapable of supporting the jury's finding that the allegedly libelous statements were made "of and concerning" respondent. Respondent relies on the words of the advertisement and the testimony of six witnesses to establish a connection between it and himself. * * * There was no reference to respondent in the advertisement, either by name or official position. A number of the allegedly libelous statements—the charges that the dining hall was padlocked and that Dr. King's home was bombed, his person assaulted, and a perjury prosecution instituted against him—did not even concern the police; despite the ingenuity of the arguments which would attach this significance to the word "They," it is plain that these statements could not reasonably be read as accusing respondent of personal involvement in the acts in question. The statements upon which respondent principally relies as referring to him are the two allegations that did concern the police or police functions: that "truckloads of police . . . ringed the Alabama State College Campus" after the demonstration on the State Capitol steps, and that Dr. King had been "arrested . . . seven times." These statements were false only in that the police had been "deployed near" the campus but had not actually "ringed" it and had not gone there in connection with the State Capitol demonstration, and in that Dr. King had been arrested only four times. The ruling that these discrepancies between what was true and what was asserted were sufficient to injure respondent's reputation may itself raise constitutional problems, but we need not consider them here. Although the statements may be taken as referring to the police, they did not on their face make even an oblique reference to respondent as an individual. * * * [N]one of [the witnesses] suggested any basis for the belief that respondent himself was attacked in the advertisement beyond the bare fact that he was in overall charge of the Police Department and thus bore official responsibility for police conduct. * * *

For good reason, "no court of last resort in this country has ever held, or even suggested, that prosecutions for libel on government have any place in the American system of jurisprudence." City of Chi. v. Tribune Co., 307 Ill. 595, 601, 139 N.E. 86, 88 (1923). The present proposition would sidestep this obstacle by transmuting criticism of government, however impersonal it may seem on its face, into personal criticism, and hence potential libel, of the officials of whom the government is composed. There is no legal alchemy by which a State may thus create the cause of action that would otherwise be denied for a publication which, as respondent himself said of the advertisement, "reflects not only on me but on the other Commissioners and the community." Raising as it does the possibility that a good-faith critic of government will be penalized for his criticism, the proposition relied on by the Alabama courts strikes at the very center of the constitutionally protected area of free expression. * We hold that such a proposition may not constitutionally be utilized to establish that an otherwise impersonal attack on governmental operations was a libel of an official responsible for those operations. Since * * * there was no other evidence to connect the statements with respondent, the evidence was constitutionally insufficient to support a finding that the statements referred to respondent. * * *

Reversed and remanded.

■ [BLACK, JUSTICE, concurred on the ground that the press should have "absolute immunity for criticism of the way public officials do their public duty." JUSTICE GOLDBERG concurred similarly. JUSTICE DOUGLAS joined both these opinions.]

NOTES

1. *"Public Officials."* Under *New York Times Co. v. Sullivan,* what individuals qualify as "public officials"? In Rosenblatt v. Baer, 383 U.S. 75, 85–86, 86 S.Ct. 669, 675–676, 15 L.Ed.2d 597, 606, n.13 (1966), the Supreme Court set the standard as follows:

> * * * [T]he "public official" designation applies at the very least to those among the hierarchy of government employees who have, or appear to the public to have, substantial responsibility for or control over the conduct of governmental affairs.

> * * * Where a position in government has such apparent importance that the public has an independent interest in the qualifications and performance of the person who holds it, beyond the general public interest in the qualifications and performance of all government employees * * * the *New York Times* malice standards apply.

The status of "public official" sometimes has been broadly interpreted by the courts to include functionaries such as public school teachers, e.g., Kelley v. Bonney, 221 Conn. 549, 606 A.2d 693 (1992); *contra* Nodar v. Galbreath, *supra* pages 893–96, and police officers, e.g., Cibenko v. Worth Publishers, Inc., 510 F.Supp. 761 (D.N.J.1981). What about a candidate for public office? See, e.g., Monitor Patriot Co. v. Roy, 401 U.S. 265, 91 S.Ct. 621, 28 L.Ed.2d 35 (1971).

2. *Comparing "Actual Malice" and "Express Malice."* Note that the Supreme Court's understanding of "actual malice" in *New York Times Co. v. Sullivan* is different from the concept of "express malice" that was historically necessary to overcome a common law qualified privilege. See *supra* pages 895–96. See generally Harper, James and Gray on Torts § 5.27. Increasingly, however, state courts either adopt the constitutional "actual malice" test for defining when a common law qualified privilege has been overcome, see, e.g., Marchesi v. Franchino, 283 Md. 131, 387 A.2d 1129 (1978), or provide that the type of conduct traditionally associated with either label is sufficient to overcome a common law privilege. See, e.g., Crump v. P & C Food Mkts., Inc., 154 Vt. 284, 293, 576 A.2d 441, 447 (1990); Soentgen v. Quain & Ramstad Clinic, P.C., 467 N.W.2d 73, 79 (N.D.1991). This trend has not escaped criticism. For example, Harper, James & Gray argue that while "assimilation of these concepts may promote simplification in the law, * * * [t]he policy objectives of the constitutional requirement * * * are quite different from the purposes of some of the qualified privileges, e.g., that accorded reports of mercantile credit agencies." Harper, James and Gray on Torts § 5.27.

3. *Critical View of New York Times Co. v. Sullivan.* For a critical view of the Supreme Court's decision, see Richard A. Epstein, Was *New York Times v. Sullivan* Wrong? 53 U. Chi. L. Rev. 782 (1986).

Gertz v. Robert Welch, Inc.

Supreme Court of the United States, 1974.
418 U.S. 323, 94 S.Ct. 2997, 41 L.Ed.2d 789.

■ POWELL, JUSTICE. * * * In 1968 a Chicago policeman named Nuccio shot and killed a youth named Nelson. The state authorities prosecuted Nuccio for the homicide and ultimately obtained a conviction for murder in the second degree. The Nelson family retained petitioner Elmer Gertz, a reputable attorney, to represent them in civil litigation against Nuccio.

Respondent publishes *American Opinion*, a monthly outlet for the views of the John Birch Society. Early in the 1960's the magazine began to warn of a nationwide conspiracy to discredit local law enforcement agencies and create in their stead a national police force capable of supporting a Communist dictatorship. As part of the continuing effort to alert the public to this assumed danger, the managing editor of *American Opinion* commissioned an article on the murder trial of Officer Nuccio. * * * In March 1969 respondent published the resulting article under the title "FRAME-UP: Richard Nuccio And The War On Police." The article purports to demonstrate that the testimony against Nuccio at his criminal trial was false and that his prosecution was part of the Communist campaign against the police.

In his capacity as counsel for the Nelson family in the civil litigation, petitioner attended the coroner's inquest into the boy's death and initiated actions for damages, but he neither discussed Officer Nuccio with the press nor played any part in the criminal proceeding. Notwithstanding petitioner's remote connection with the prosecution of Nuccio, respondent's magazine portrayed him as an architect of the "frame-up." * * * The article stated that petitioner had been an official of the "Marxist League for Industrial Democracy, originally known as the Intercollegiate Socialist Society, which has advocated the violent seizure of our government." It labeled Gertz a "Leninist" and a "Communist-fronter." It also stated that Gertz had been an officer of the National Lawyers Guild, described as a Communist organization that "probably did more than any other outfit to plan the Communist attack on the Chicago police during the 1968 Democratic Convention."

These statements contained serious inaccuracies. The implication that petitioner had a criminal record was false. Petitioner had been a member and officer of the National Lawyers Guild some 15 years earlier, but there was no evidence that he or that organization had taken any part in planning the 1968 demonstrations in Chicago. There was also no basis for the charge that petitioner was a "Leninist" or a "Communist-fronter." And he had never been a member of the "Marxist League for Industrial Democracy" or the "Intercollegiate Socialist Society." The managing editor of *American Opinion* made no effort to verify or substantiate the charges against petitioner. Instead, he appended an editorial introduction stating that the author had "conducted extensive research into the Richard Nuccio Case." And he

included in the article a photograph of petitioner and wrote the caption that appeared under it: "Elmer Gertz of Red Guild harasses Nuccio."
* * *

Petitioner filed a diversity action for libel in the United States District Court for the Northern District of Illinois. * * * After answering the complaint, respondent filed a pretrial motion for summary judgment, claiming a constitutional privilege against liability for defamation. It asserted that petitioner was a public official or a public figure and that the article concerned an issue of public interest and concern. * * * The editor denied any knowledge of the falsity of the statements concerning petitioner and stated that he had relied on the author's reputation and on his prior experience with the accuracy and authenticity of the author's contributions to *American Opinion.* The District Court denied respondent's motion for summary judgment * * *. It thought that respondent's claim to the protection of the constitutional privilege depended on the contention that petitioner was either a public official under the *New York Times* decision or a public figure under Curtis Publishing Co. v. Butts, 388 U.S. 130, 87 S.Ct. 1975, 18 L.Ed.2d 1094 (1967), apparently discounting the argument that a privilege would arise from the presence of a public issue. After all the evidence had been presented but before submission of the case to the jury, the court ruled in effect that petitioner was neither a public official nor a public figure. It added that, if he were, the resulting application of the *New York Times* standard would require a directed verdict for respondent. * * * The jury awarded $50,000 to petitioner. Following the jury verdict and on further reflection, the District Court concluded that the *New York Times* standard should govern this case even though petitioner was not a public official or public figure. It accepted respondent's contention that that privilege protected discussion of any public issue without regard to the status of a person defamed therein. Accordingly, the court entered judgment for respondent notwithstanding the jury's verdict. * * *

Petitioner appealed to contest the applicability of the *New York Times* standard to this case. * * * [T]he Court of Appeals for the Seventh Circuit * * * agreed with the District Court that respondent could assert the constitutional privilege because the article concerned a matter of public interest, citing this Court's intervening decision in Rosenbloom v. Metromedia, Inc., 403 U.S. 29, 91 S.Ct. 1811, 29 L.Ed.2d 296 (1971). The Court of Appeals read *Rosenbloom* to require application of the *New York Times* standard to any publication or broadcast about an issue of significant public interest, without regard to the position, fame, or anonymity of the person defamed, and it concluded that respondent's statements concerned such an issue. * After reviewing the record, the Court of Appeals endorsed the District Court's conclusion that petitioner had failed to show by clear and convincing evidence that respondent had acted with "actual malice" as defined by *New York Times.* There was no evidence that the managing editor of *American Opinion* knew of the falsity of the accusations made in the article. In fact, he knew nothing about petitioner except what he learned from the article. The court correctly noted that mere proof of failure to investigate, without more, cannot establish reckless disregard for the truth. Rather, the publisher must act with a "high degree of awareness of . . . probable falsity." St. Amant v. Thompson, 390 U.S.

727, 731, 88 S.Ct. 1323, 1325, 20 L.Ed.2d 262, 267 (1968). * The evidence in this case did not reveal that respondent had cause for such an awareness. The Court of Appeals therefore affirmed. * For the reasons stated below, we reverse. * * *

III

We begin with the common ground. Under the First Amendment there is no such thing as a false idea. However pernicious an opinion may seem, we depend for its correction not on the conscience of judges and juries but on the competition of other ideas. * But there is no constitutional value in false statements of fact. Neither the intentional lie nor the careless error materially advances society's interest in "uninhibited, robust, and wide-open" debate on public issues. * * *

Although the erroneous statement of fact is not worthy of constitutional protection, it is nevertheless inevitable in free debate. * * * Our decisions recognize that a rule of strict liability that compels a publisher or broadcaster to guarantee the accuracy of his factual assertions may lead to intolerable self-censorship. Allowing the media to avoid liability only by proving the truth of all injurious statements does not accord adequate protection to First Amendment liberties. * * *

The need to avoid self-censorship by the news media is, however, not the only societal value at issue. If it were, this Court would have embraced long ago the view that publishers and broadcasters enjoy an unconditional and indefeasible immunity from liability for defamation. * Such a rule would, indeed, obviate the fear that the prospect of civil liability for injurious falsehood might dissuade a timorous press from the effective exercise of First Amendment freedoms. Yet absolute protection for the communications media requires a total sacrifice of the competing value served by the law of defamation.

The legitimate state interest underlying the law of libel is the compensation of individuals for the harm inflicted on them by defamatory falsehood. * * * Some tension necessarily exists between the need for a vigorous and uninhibited press and the legitimate interest in redressing wrongful injury. * * * The *New York Times* standard defines the level of constitutional protection appropriate to the context of defamation of a public person. Those who, by reason of the notoriety of their achievements or the vigor and success with which they seek the public's attention, are properly classed as public figures and those who hold governmental office may recover for injury to reputation only on clear and convincing proof that the defamatory falsehood was made with knowledge of its falsity or with reckless disregard for the truth. This standard administers an extremely powerful antidote to the inducement to media self-censorship of the common-law rule of strict liability for libel and slander. And it exacts a correspondingly high price from the victims of defamatory falsehood. Plainly many deserving plaintiffs, including some intentionally subjected to injury, will be unable to surmount the barrier of the *New York Times* test. Despite this substantial abridgment of the state law right to compensation for wrongful hurt to one's reputation, the Court has concluded that the protection of the *New York Times* privilege should be available to publishers and broadcasters of defamatory falsehood concerning public officials and public figures. * We think that these decisions are correct, but we do not find their holdings justified solely by reference to the interest of the press and broadcast media in immunity from liability. Rather, we believe that the *New York Times* rule states an accommodation between this concern and the limited state interest present in the context of libel actions brought by public persons. For the reasons stated below, we conclude that the state interest in compensating injury to the reputation of private individuals requires that a different rule should obtain with respect to them.

Theoretically, of course, the balance between the needs of the press and the individual's claim to compensation for wrongful injury might be struck on a case-by-case basis. * * * But this approach would lead to unpredictable results and uncertain expectations, and it could render our duty to supervise the lower courts unmanageable. Because an ad hoc resolution of the competing interests at stake in each particular case is not feasible, we must lay down broad rules of general application. * * * With that caveat we have no difficulty in distinguishing among defamation plaintiffs. The first remedy of any victim of defamation is self-help—using available opportunities to contradict the lie or correct the error and thereby to minimize its adverse impact on reputation. Public officials and public figures usually enjoy significantly greater access to the channels of effective communication and hence have a more realistic opportunity to counteract false statements than private individuals normally enjoy.[9] Private individuals are therefore more vulnerable to injury, and the state interest in protecting them is correspondingly greater.

More important than the likelihood that private individuals will lack effective opportunities for rebuttal, there is a compelling normative consideration underlying the distinction between public and private defamation plaintiffs. An individual who decides to seek governmental office must accept certain necessary consequences of that involvement in public affairs. He runs the risk of closer public scrutiny than might otherwise be the case. And society's interest in the officers of government is not strictly limited to the formal discharge of official duties. * * *

Those classed as public figures stand in a similar position. Hypothetically, it may be possible for someone to become a public figure through no purposeful action of his own, but the instances of truly involuntary public figures must be exceedingly rare. For the most part those who attain this status have assumed roles of special prominence in the affairs of society. Some occupy positions of such persuasive power and influence that they are deemed public figures for all purposes. More commonly, those classed as public figures have thrust themselves to the forefront of particular public controversies in order to influence the resolution of the issues involved. In either event, they invite attention and comment.

Even if the foregoing generalities do not obtain in every instance, the communications media are entitled to act on the assumption that public officials and public figures have voluntarily exposed themselves to increased risk of injury from defamatory falsehood concerning them.

---

[9] Of course, an opportunity for rebuttal seldom suffices to undo harm of defamatory falsehood. Indeed, the law of defamation is rooted in our experience that the truth rarely catches up with a lie. But the fact that the self-help remedy of rebuttal, standing alone, is inadequate to its task does not mean that it is irrelevant to our inquiry.

No such assumption is justified with respect to a private individual. He has not accepted public office or assumed an "influential role in ordering society." Curtis Publishing Co. v. Butts, 388 U.S. at 164, 87 S.Ct. at 1996, 18 L.Ed.2d at 1116 (Warren, C.J., concurring in result). He has relinquished no part of his interest in the protection of his own good name, and consequently he has a more compelling call on the courts for redress of injury inflicted by defamatory falsehood. Thus, private individuals are not only more vulnerable to injury than public officials and public figures; they are also more deserving of recovery.

For these reasons we conclude that the States should retain substantial latitude in their efforts to enforce a legal remedy for defamatory falsehood injurious to the reputation of a private individual. * * * We hold that, so long as they do not impose liability without fault, the States may define for themselves the appropriate standard of liability for a publisher or broadcaster of defamatory falsehood injurious to a private individual. This approach provides a more equitable boundary between the competing concerns involved here. It recognizes the strength of the legitimate state interest in compensating private individuals for wrongful injury to reputation, yet shields the press and broadcast media from the rigors of strict liability for defamation. * * *

IV

Our accommodation of the competing values at stake in defamation suits by private individuals allows the States to impose liability on the publisher or broadcaster of defamatory falsehood on a less demanding showing than that required by *New York Times*. This conclusion is not based on a belief that the considerations which prompted the adoption of the *New York Times* privilege for defamation of public officials and its extension to public figures are wholly inapplicable to the context of private individuals. Rather, we endorse this approach in recognition of the strong and legitimate state interest in compensating private individuals for injury to reputation. But this countervailing state interest extends no further than compensation for actual injury. For the reasons stated below, we hold that the States may not permit recovery of presumed or punitive damages, at least when liability is not based on a showing of knowledge of falsity or reckless disregard for the truth.

The common law of defamation is an oddity of tort law, for it allows recovery of purportedly compensatory damages without evidence of actual loss. Under the traditional rules pertaining to actions for libel, the existence of injury is presumed from the fact of publication. Juries may award substantial sums as compensation for supposed damage to reputation without any proof that such harm actually occurred. The largely uncontrolled discretion of juries to award damages where there is no loss unnecessarily compounds the potential of any system of liability for defamatory falsehood to inhibit the vigorous exercise of First Amendment freedoms. Additionally, the doctrine of presumed damages invites juries to punish unpopular opinion rather than to compensate individuals for injury sustained by the publication of a false fact. More to the point, the States have no substantial interest in securing for plaintiffs such as this petitioner gratuitous awards of money damages far in excess of any actual injury.

We would not, of course, invalidate state law simply because we doubt its wisdom, but here we are attempting to reconcile state law with a competing interest grounded in the constitutional command of the First Amendment. It is therefore appropriate to require that state remedies for defamatory falsehood reach no farther than is necessary to protect the legitimate interest involved. It is necessary to restrict defamation plaintiffs who do not prove knowledge of falsity or reckless disregard for the truth to compensation for actual injury. * * * [A]ctual injury is not limited to out-of-pocket loss. Indeed, the more customary types of actual harm inflicted by defamatory falsehood include impairment of reputation and standing in the community, personal humiliation, and mental anguish and suffering. Of course, juries must be limited by appropriate instructions, and all awards must be supported by competent evidence concerning the injury, although there need be no evidence which assigns an actual dollar value to the injury.

We also find no justification for allowing awards of punitive damages against publishers and broadcasters held liable under state-defined standards of liability for defamation. In most jurisdictions jury discretion over the amounts awarded is limited only by the gentle rule that they not be excessive. Consequently, juries assess punitive damages in wholly unpredictable amounts bearing no necessary relation to the actual harm caused. And they remain free to use their discretion selectively to punish expressions of unpopular views. Like the doctrine of presumed damages, jury discretion to award punitive damages unnecessarily exacerbates the danger of media self-censorship, but, unlike the former rule, punitive damages are wholly irrelevant to the state interest that justifies a negligence standard for private defamation actions. They are not compensation for injury. Instead, they are private fines levied by civil juries to punish reprehensible conduct and to deter its future occurrence. In short, the private defamation plaintiff who establishes liability under a less demanding standard than that stated by *New York Times* may recover only such damages as are sufficient to compensate him for actual injury.

V

Notwithstanding our refusal to extend the *New York Times* privilege to defamation of private individuals, respondent contends that we should affirm the judgment below on the ground that petitioner is either a public official or a public figure. There is little basis for the former assertion. Several years prior to the present incident, petitioner had served briefly on housing committees appointed by the mayor of Chicago, but at the time of publication he had never held any remunerative governmental position. Respondent admits this but argues that petitioner's appearance at the coroner's inquest rendered him a "de facto public official." Our cases recognize no such concept. Respondent's suggestion would sweep all lawyers under the *New York Times* rule as officers of the court and distort the plain meaning of the "public official" category beyond all recognition. We decline to follow it.

Respondent's characterization of petitioner as a public figure raises a different question. That designation may rest on either of two alternative bases. In some instances an individual may achieve such pervasive fame or notoriety that he becomes a public figure for all purposes and in all contexts. More commonly, an individual voluntarily injects himself or is drawn into a particular public controversy and thereby becomes a public figure for a limited range of issues. In either case such persons assume special prominence in the resolution of public questions.

Petitioner has long been active in community and professional affairs. He has served as an officer of local civic groups and of various professional organizations, and he has published several books and articles on legal subjects. Although petitioner was consequently well known in some circles, he had achieved no general fame or notoriety in the community. * * * Absent clear evidence of general fame or notoriety in the community, and pervasive involvement in the affairs of society, an individual should not be deemed a public personality for all aspects of his life. It is preferable to reduce the public-figure question to a more meaningful context by looking to the nature and extent of an individual's participation in the particular controversy giving rise to the defamation.

In this context it is plain that petitioner was not a public figure. He played a minimal role at the coroner's inquest, and his participation related solely to his representation of a private client. He took no part in the criminal prosecution of Officer Nuccio. Moreover, he never discussed either the criminal or civil litigation with the press and was never quoted as having done so. He plainly did not thrust himself into the vortex of this public issue, nor did he engage the public's attention in an attempt to influence its outcome. We are persuaded that the trial court did not err in refusing to characterize petitioner as a public figure for the purpose of this litigation.

We therefore conclude that the *New York Times* standard is inapplicable to this case and that the trial court erred in entering judgment for respondent. Because the jury was allowed to impose liability without fault and was permitted to presume damages without proof of injury, a new trial is necessary. We reverse and remand for further proceedings in accord with this opinion. * * *

■ BURGER, CHIEF JUSTICE, dissenting. The doctrines of the law of defamation have had a gradual evolution primarily in the state courts. * * * Agreement or disagreement with the law as it has evolved to this time does not alter the fact that it has been orderly development with a consistent basic rationale. In today's opinion the Court abandons the traditional thread so far as the ordinary private citizen is concerned and introduces the concept that the media will be liable for negligence in publishing defamatory statements with respect to such persons. * * * I would prefer to allow this area of law to continue to evolve as it has up to now with respect to private citizens rather than embark on a new doctrinal theory which has no jurisprudential ancestry. * * *

■ The dissenting opinions of JUSTICES DOUGLAS and BRENNAN are omitted.

■ WHITE, JUSTICE, dissenting. For some 200 years—from the very founding of the Nation—the law of defamation and right of the ordinary citizen to recover for false publication injurious to his reputation have been almost exclusively the business of state courts and legislatures. * * * But now, using that Amendment as the chosen instrument, the Court—in a few printed pages, has federalized major aspects of libel law by declaring unconstitutional in important respects the prevailing defamation law in all or most of the fifty States. * * * Scant, if any, evidence exists that the First Amendment was intended to abolish the common law of libel, at least to the extent of depriving ordinary citizens of meaningful redress against their defamers. * * *

NOTES

1.   *Subsequent Case History.* On retrial, the jury awarded the plaintiff compensatory damages of $100,000 and punitive damages in the amount of $300,000. The award was upheld by the Seventh Circuit Court of Appeals, 680 F.2d 527 (7th Cir.1982), cert. denied, 459 U.S. 1226, 103 S.Ct. 1233, 75 L.Ed.2d 467 (1983). The court upheld the jury's finding that the editor of *American Opinion* acted with actual malice because he solicited a writer with a "a known and unreasonable propensity to label persons or organizations as Communist, to write the article; and after the article was submitted, made virtually no effort to check the validity of statements that were defamatory * * *."

2.   *State Responses. Gertz v. Welch* obviously does not establish the substantive rules for liability in defamation, but rather only the constitutional limitations on such liability rules. Following *Gertz,* most states decided to permit private victims of defamation to recover on a showing of negligence. E.g., Stone v. Essex Cnty. Newspapers, Inc., 367 Mass. 849, 330 N.E.2d 161 (1975); see also Turf Lawnmower Repair, Inc. v. Bergen Record Corp., 139 N.J. 392, 406 n.1, 655 A.2d 417, 424 n.1 (1995) (with citations to 42 jurisdictions where negligence is said to be the standard for private plaintiffs whether or not the subject of the speech is of public concern); Harper, James and Gray on Torts § 5.0 n.34. Some states went further and applied the "actual malice" standards to private plaintiffs, as well as public officials and public figures. E.g., Diversified Mgmt., Inc. v. Denver Post, Inc., 653 P.2d 1103 (Colo.1982) (if "matter involved is of public or general concern"); cf. Chapadeau v. Utica Observer-Dispatch, Inc., 38 N.Y.2d 196, 341 N.E.2d 569, 379 N.Y.S.2d 61 (1975) (holding that "where the content of the article is arguably within the sphere of legitimate public concern," plaintiff must prove "that the publisher acted in a grossly irresponsible manner without due consideration for the standards of information gathering and dissemination ordinarily followed by responsible parties").

Dun & Bradstreet, Inc. v. Greenmoss Builders, Inc.

Supreme Court of the United States, 1985.
472 U.S. 749, 105 S.Ct. 2939, 86 L.Ed.2d 593.

■ POWELL, JUSTICE. In Gertz v. Robert Welch, Inc., 418 U.S. 323, 94 S.Ct. 2997, 41 L.Ed.2d 789 (1974), we held that the First Amendment restricted the damages that a private individual could obtain from a publisher for a libel that involved a matter of public concern. More specifically, we held that in these circumstances the First Amendment prohibited awards of presumed and punitive damages for false and defamatory statements unless the plaintiff shows "actual malice," that is, knowledge of falsity or reckless disregard for the truth. The question presented in this case is whether this rule of *Gertz* applies when the false and defamatory statements do not involve matters of public concern.

Petitioner Dun & Bradstreet, a credit reporting agency, provides subscribers with financial and related information about businesses. All the information is confidential; under the terms of the subscription agreement the subscribers may not reveal it to anyone else. On July 26, 1976, petitioner sent a report to five subscribers indicating that respondent, a construction contractor, had filed a voluntary petition for bankruptcy. This report was false and grossly misrepresented respondent's assets and liabilities. That same day, while discussing the possibility of future financing with its bank, respondent's president was told that the bank had received the defamatory report. He immediately called petitioner's regional office, explained the error, and asked for a correction. In addition, he requested the names of the firms that had received the false report in order to assure them that the company was solvent. Petitioner promised to look into the matter but refused to divulge the names of those who had received the report.

After determining that its report was indeed false, petitioner issued a corrective notice on or about August 3, 1976, to the five subscribers who had received the initial report. The notice stated that one of respondent's former employees, not respondent itself, had filed for bankruptcy and that respondent "continued in business as usual." Respondent told petitioner that it was dissatisfied with the notice, and it again asked for a list of subscribers who had seen the initial report. Again petitioner refused to divulge their names.

Respondent then brought this defamation action in Vermont state court. It alleged that the false report had injured its reputation and sought both compensatory and punitive damages. The trial established that the error in petitioner's report had been caused when one of its employees, a 17-year-old high school student paid to review Vermont bankruptcy pleadings, had inadvertently attributed to respondent a bankruptcy petition filed by one of respondent's former employees. Although petitioner's representative testified that it was routine practice to check the accuracy of such reports with the businesses themselves, it did not try to verify the information about respondent before reporting it.

After trial, the jury returned a verdict in favor of respondent and awarded $50,000 in compensatory or presumed damages and $300,000 in punitive damages. Petitioner moved for a new trial. It argued that in Gertz v. Robert Welch, Inc., 418 U.S. at 349, 94 S.Ct. at 3011, 41 L.Ed.2d at 810, this Court had ruled broadly that "the States may not permit recovery of presumed or punitive damages, at least when liability is not based on a showing of knowledge of falsity or reckless disregard for the truth," and it argued that the judge's instructions in this case permitted the jury to award such damages on a lesser showing. The trial court indicated some doubt as to whether *Gertz* applied to "non-media cases," but granted a new trial * * *. The Vermont Supreme Court reversed. * * * [T]he court held "that as a matter of federal constitutional law, the media protections outlined in *Gertz* are inapplicable to nonmedia defamation actions." * Recognizing disagreement among the lower courts about when the protections of *Gertz* apply, * we granted certiorari. * We now affirm. * * *

We have never considered whether the *Gertz* balance obtains when the defamatory statements involve no issue of public concern. To make this determination, we must employ the approach approved in *Gertz* and balance the State's interest in compensating private individuals for injury to their reputation against the First Amendment interest in protecting this type of expression. This state interest is identical to the one weighed in *Gertz*. * * *

The First Amendment interest, on the other hand, is less important than the one weighed in *Gertz*. We have long recognized that not all speech is of equal First Amendment importance. * It is speech on "'matters of public concern'" that is "at the heart of the First Amendment's protection." First Nat'l Bank of Bos. v. Bellotti, 435 U.S. 765, 776, 98 S.Ct. 1407, 1415, 55 L.Ed.2d 707, 717 (1978). * * * In contrast, speech on matters of purely private concern is of less First Amendment concern. * As a number of state courts, including the court below, have recognized, the role of the Constitution in regulating state libel law is far more limited when the concerns that activated *New York Times* and *Gertz* are absent. * In such a case,

> [t]here is no threat to the free and robust debate of public issues; there is no potential interference with a meaningful dialogue of ideas concerning self-government; and there is no threat of liability causing a reaction of self-censorship by the press. * * *

Harley-Davidson Motorsports, Inc. v. Markley, 279 Ore. 361, 366, 568 P.2d 1359, 1363 (1977). *

While such speech is not totally unprotected by the First Amendment, * its protections are less stringent. In *Gertz*, we found that the state interest in awarding presumed and punitive damages was not "substantial" in view of their effect on speech at the core of First Amendment concern. * This interest, however, *is* "substantial" relative to the incidental effect these remedies may have on speech of significantly less constitutional interest. The rationale of the common-law rules has been the experience and judgment of history that "proof of actual damage will be impossible in a great many cases where, from the character of the defamatory words and the circumstances of publication, it is all but certain that serious harm has resulted in fact." W[illiam L.] Prosser, Law of Torts § 112 (4th ed.1971). * As a result, courts for centuries have allowed juries to presume that some damage occurred from many defamatory utterances and publications. * This rule furthers the state interest in providing remedies for defamation by ensuring that those remedies are effective. In light of the reduced constitutional value of speech involving no matters of public concern, we hold that the state interest adequately supports awards of presumed and punitive damages—even absent a showing of "actual malice." *

The only remaining issue is whether petitioner's credit report involved a matter of public concern. * * * [P]etitioner's credit report concerns no public issue. * It was speech solely in the individual interest of the speaker and its specific business audience. * This particular interest warrants no special protection when—as in this case—the speech is wholly false and clearly damaging to the victim's business reputation. * Moreover, since the credit report was made available to only five subscribers, who, under the terms of the subscription agreement, could not disseminate it further, it cannot be said that the report involves any "strong interest in the free flow of commercial information." Virginia Pharmacy Bd. v. Virginia Citizens Consumer Council, Inc., 425 U.S. 748, 764, 96 S.Ct. 1817, 1827, 48 L.Ed.2d 346, 360 (1976). There is simply no credible argument that this type of credit reporting requires special protection to ensure that "debate on public issues [will] be uninhibited, robust, and wide-open." New York Times Co. v. Sullivan, 376 U.S. at 270, 84 S.Ct. at 720, 11 L.Ed.2d at 701.

In addition, the speech here, like advertising, is hardy and unlikely to be deterred by incidental state regulation. * It is solely motivated by the desire for profit, which, we have noted, is a force less likely to be deterred than others. * Arguably, the reporting here was also more objectively verifiable than speech deserving of greater protection. * In any case, the market provides a powerful incentive to a credit reporting agency to be accurate, since false credit reporting is of no use to creditors. Thus, any incremental "chilling" effect of libel suits would be of decreased significance. *

We conclude that permitting recovery of presumed and punitive damages in defamation cases absent a showing of "actual malice" does not violate the First Amendment when the defamatory statements do not involve matters of public concern. Accordingly, we affirm the judgment of the Vermont Supreme Court.

■ The separate concurring opinions of CHIEF JUSTICE BURGER and JUSTICE WHITE are omitted.

■ BRENNAN, JUSTICE, with whom JUSTICES MARSHALL, BLACKMUN, and STEVENS join, dissenting. * * * The question presented here is narrow. Neither the parties nor the courts below have suggested that respondent Greenmoss Builders should be required to show actual malice to obtain a judgment and actual compensatory damages. Nor do the parties question the requirement of *Gertz* that respondent must show fault to obtain a judgment and actual damages. The only question presented is whether a jury award of presumed and punitive damages based on less than a showing of actual malice is constitutionally permissible. * * *

Relying on the analysis of the Vermont Supreme Court, respondent urged that this pruning be accomplished by restricting the applicability of *Gertz* to cases in which the defendant is a "media" entity. Such a distinction is irreconcilable with the fundamental First Amendment principle that "[t]he inherent worth of . . . speech in terms of its capacity for informing the public does not depend upon the identity of its source, whether corporation, association, union, or individual." First Nat'l Bank of Bos. v. Bellotti, 435 U.S. 765, 777, 98 S.Ct. 1407, 1416, 55 L.Ed.2d 707, 718 (1978). * * * Perhaps most importantly, the argument that *Gertz* should be limited to the media misapprehends our cases. We protect the press to ensure the vitality of First Amendment guarantees. * This solicitude implies no endorsement of the principle that speakers other than the press deserve lesser First Amendment protection. * * *

The free speech guarantee gives each citizen an equal right to self-expression and to participation in self-government. * * * Accordingly, at least six Members of this Court (the four who join this opinion and Justice White and The Chief justice) agree today that, in the context of defamation law, the rights of the institutional media are no greater and no less than those enjoyed by other individuals or organizations engaged in the same activities. * * *

The five Members of the Court voting to affirm the damages award in this case have provided almost no guidance as to what constitutes a protected "matter of public concern." * * *

NOTE

For more on the distinction between speech that is a matter of public concern and speech that is not, compare Snyder v. Phelps, *supra* pages 745–749.

Philadelphia Newspapers, Inc. v. Hepps

Supreme Court of the United States, 1986.
475 U.S. 767, 106 S.Ct. 1558, 89 L.Ed.2d 783.

■ O'CONNOR, JUSTICE. * * * Maurice S. Hepps is the principal stockholder of General Programming, Inc. (GPI), a corporation that franchises a chain of stores—known at the relevant time as "Thrifty" stores—selling beer, soft drinks, and snacks. Mr. Hepps, GPI, and a number of its franchisees are the appellees here. * Appellant Philadelphia Newspapers, Inc., owns the *Philadelphia Inquirer* (*Inquirer*). The *Inquirer* published a series of articles * * * [asserting] that appellees had links to organized crime and used some of those links to influence the State's governmental processes, both legislative and administrative. * * *

Appellees brought suit for defamation against appellants in a Pennsylvania state court. Consistent with *Gertz*, Pennsylvania requires a private figure who brings a suit for defamation to bear the burden of proving negligence or malice by the defendant in publishing the statements at issue. * As to falsity, Pennsylvania follows the common law's presumption that an individual's reputation is a good one. Statements defaming that person are therefore presumptively false, although a publisher who bears the burden of proving the truth of the statements has an absolute defense. *

The parties first raised the issue of burden of proof as to falsity before trial, but the trial court reserved its ruling on the matter. Appellee Hepps testified at length that the statements at issue were false, and he extensively cross-examined the author of the stories as to the veracity of the statements at issue. After all the evidence had been presented by both sides, the trial court concluded that Pennsylvania's statute giving the defendant the burden of proving the truth of the statements violated the Federal Constitution. The trial court therefore instructed the jury that the plaintiffs bore the burden of proving falsity. * * *

[T]he appellees here brought an appeal directly to the Pennsylvania Supreme Court. That court viewed *Gertz* as simply requiring the plaintiff to show fault in actions for defamation. It concluded that a showing of fault did not require a showing of falsity, held that to place the burden of showing truth on the defendant did not unconstitutionally inhibit free debate, and remanded the case for a new trial. * We noted probable jurisdiction and now reverse. *

II

* * * [The Court reviews *New York Times Co. v. Sullivan* and its progeny.] One can discern in these decisions two forces that may reshape the common-law landscape to conform to the First Amendment. The first is whether the plaintiff is a public official or figure, or is instead a private figure. The second is whether the speech at issue is of public concern. When the speech is of public concern and the plaintiff is a public official or public figure, the Constitution clearly requires the plaintiff to surmount a much higher barrier before recovering damages from a media defendant than is raised by the common law. When the speech is of public concern but the plaintiff is a private figure, as in *Gertz*, the Constitution still supplants the standards of the common law, but the constitutional requirements are, in at least some of their range, less forbidding than when the plaintiff is a public figure and the speech is of public concern. When the speech is of exclusively private concern and the plaintiff is a private figure, as in *Dun & Bradstreet*, the constitutional requirements do not necessarily force any change in at least some of the features of the common-law landscape.

Our opinions to date have chiefly treated the necessary showings of fault rather than of falsity. Nonetheless, as one might expect given the language of the Court in *New York Times*, a public-figure plaintiff must show the falsity of the statements at issue in order to prevail in a suit for defamation. *

Here, as in *Gertz*, the plaintiff is a private figure and the newspaper articles are of public concern. In *Gertz*, as in *New York Times*, the common-law rule was superseded by a constitutional rule. We believe that the common law's rule on falsity—that the defendant must bear the burden of proving truth—must similarly fall here to a constitutional requirement that the plaintiff bear the burden of showing falsity, as well as fault, before recovering damages.

There will always be instances when the factfinding process will be unable to resolve conclusively whether the speech is true or false; it is in those cases that the burden of proof is dispositive. Under a rule forcing the plaintiff to bear the burden of showing falsity, there will be some cases in which plaintiffs cannot meet their burden despite the fact that the speech is in fact false. The plaintiff's suit will fail despite the fact that, in some abstract sense, the suit is meritorious. Similarly, under an alternative rule placing the burden of showing truth on defendants, there would be some cases in which defendants could not bear their burden despite the fact that the speech is in fact true. Those suits would succeed despite the fact that, in some abstract sense, those suits are unmeritorious. Under either rule, then, the outcome of the suit will sometimes be at variance with the outcome that we would desire if all speech were either demonstrably true or demonstrably false.

This dilemma stems from the fact that the allocation of the burden of proof will determine liability for some speech that is true and some that is false, but *all* of such speech is *unknowably* true or false. Because the burden of proof is the deciding factor only when the evidence is ambiguous, we cannot know how much of the speech affected by the allocation of the burden of proof is true and how much is false. In a case presenting a configuration of speech and plaintiff like the one we face here, and where the scales are in such an uncertain balance, we believe that the Constitution requires us to tip them in favor of protecting true speech. To ensure that true speech on matters of public concern is not deterred, we hold that the common-law presumption that defamatory speech is false cannot stand when a plaintiff seeks damages against a media defendant for speech of public concern. * * * Because * * * a "chilling" effect would be antithetical to the First Amendment's protection of true speech on matters of public concern, we believe that a private-figure plaintiff must bear the burden of showing that the speech at issue is false before recovering damages for defamation from a media defendant. * * *

We recognize that requiring the plaintiff to show falsity will insulate from liability some speech that is false, but unprovably so. Nonetheless, the Court's previous decisions on the restrictions that the First Amendment places upon the common law of defamation firmly support our conclusion here with respect to the allocation of the burden of proof. * * *

We note that our decision adds only marginally to the burdens that the plaintiff must already bear as a result of our earlier decisions in the law of defamation. The plaintiff must show fault. A jury is obviously more likely to accept a plaintiff's contention that the defendant was at fault in publishing the statements at issue if convinced that the relevant statements were false. As a practical matter, then, evidence offered by plaintiffs on the publisher's fault in adequately investigating the truth of the published statements will generally encompass evidence of the falsity of the matters asserted. *

We recognize that the plaintiff's burden in this case is weightier because of Pennsylvania's "shield" law, which allows employees of the media to refuse to divulge their sources. * * *

For the reasons stated above, the judgment of the Pennsylvania Supreme Court is reversed, and the case is remanded for further proceedings not inconsistent with this opinion.

■ BRENNAN, JUSTICE, with whom JUSTICE BLACKMUN joins, concurring [opinion omitted].

■ STEVENS, JUSTICE, with whom THE CHIEF JUSTICE and JUSTICES WHITE and REHNQUIST join, dissenting.

The issue the Court resolves today will make a difference in only one category of cases—those in which a private individual can prove that he was libeled by a defendant who was at least negligent. For unless such a plaintiff can overcome the burden imposed by *Gertz v. Robert Welch, Inc.*, he cannot recover regardless of how the burden of proof on the issue of truth or falsity is allocated. By definition, therefore, the only litigants—and the only publishers—who will benefit from today's decision are those who act negligently or maliciously. * * *

In my view, as long as publishers are protected by the requirement that the plaintiff has the burden of proving fault, there can be little, if any, basis for a concern that a significant amount of true speech will be deterred unless the private person victimized by a malicious libel can also carry the burden of proving falsity. The Court's decision trades on the good names of private individuals with little First Amendment coin to show for it.

I respectfully dissent.

NOTES

1. *Truth as a Defense: Private Plaintiff/Private Matter.* Since *Philadelphia Newspapers, Inc. v. Hepps,* at least one state supreme court has stated that "The treatment of truth as an affirmative defense remains where the plaintiff is a private figure." Newberry v. Allied Stores, Inc., 108 N.M. 424, 430, 773 P.2d 1231, 1237 (1989).

2. *Media Defendants.* Note that in *Philadelphia Newspapers,* Justice O'Connor explicitly holds "that the common-law presumption that defamatory speech is false cannot stand when a plaintiff seeks damages against a *media* defendant for speech of public concern." (emphasis added) Compare this with Justice Brennan's claim in his dissenting opinion in *Dun & Bradstreet, supra* pages 922–23, "at least six Members of this Court * * * agree today that, in the context of defamation law, the rights of the institutional media are no greater and no less than those enjoyed by other individuals or organizations engaged in the same activities." The Supreme Court has yet to resolve this apparent inconsistency, and lower courts and commentators reach different conclusions.

H. EXPRESSION OF OPINION AS DEFAMATION

Milkovich v. Lorain Journal Co.

Supreme Court of the United States, 1990.
497 U.S. 1, 110 S.Ct. 2695, 111 L.Ed.2d 1.

■ REHNQUIST, CHIEF JUSTICE. * * * Petitioner Milkovich, now retired, was the wrestling coach at Maple Heights High School in Maple Heights, Ohio. In 1974, his team was involved in an altercation at a home wrestling match with a team from Mentor High School. Several people were injured. In response to the incident, the Ohio High School Athletic Association (OHSAA) held a hearing at which Milkovich and H. Don Scott, the Superintendent of Maple Heights Public Schools, testified. * * * OHSAA placed the Maple Heights team on probation * * * [and] also censured Milkovich for his actions during the altercation. Thereafter, several parents and wrestlers sued OHSAA * * * seeking a restraining order against OHSAA's ruling on the grounds that they had been denied due process in the OHSAA proceeding. Both Milkovich and Scott testified in that proceeding. The court overturned OHSAA's probation and ineligibility orders on due process grounds.

The day after the court rendered its decision, respondent Diadiun's column appeared in the *News-Herald,* a newspaper * * * owned by respondent Lorain Journal Co. The column bore the heading "Maple beat the law with the 'big lie' " * * *. The column contained the following passages:

> . . . [A] lesson was learned (or relearned) yesterday by the student body of Maple Heights High School, and by anyone who attended the Maple-Mentor wrestling meet of last Feb. 8. * * * It is simply this: If you get in a jam, lie your way out. * * * The teachers responsible were mainly head Maple wrestling coach, Mike Milkovich, and former superintendent of schools H. Donald Scott. . . . Anyone who attended the meet, whether

> he be from Maple Heights, Mentor, or impartial observer, knows in his heart that Milkovich and Scott lied at the hearing after each having given his solemn oath to tell the truth. * * *

Petitioner commenced a defamation action against respondents * * * alleging that the headline of Diadiun's article and the * * * passages quoted above "accused plaintiff of committing the crime of perjury, an indictable offense in the State of Ohio, and damaged plaintiff directly in his life-time occupation of coach and teacher, and constituted libel per se." * * * [Eventually,] the Ohio Court of Appeals in the instant proceedings affirmed a trial court's grant of summary judgment in favor of respondents, concluding that "it has been decided, as a matter of law, that the article in question was constitutionally protected opinion." * The Supreme Court of Ohio dismissed petitioner's ensuing appeal for want of a substantial constitutional question. * We granted certiorari, * to consider the important questions raised by the Ohio courts' recognition of a constitutionally required "opinion" exception to the application of its defamation laws. We now reverse. * * *

As the common law developed in this country, apart from the issue of damages, one usually needed only allege an unprivileged publication of false and defamatory matter to state a cause of action for defamation. * The common law generally did not place any additional restrictions on the type of statement that could be actionable. Indeed, defamatory communications were deemed actionable regardless of whether they were deemed to be statements of fact or opinion. See, e.g., Restatement (Second) of Torts, §§ 565–567 (1977). As noted in Restatement § 566, comment a:

> Under the law of defamation, an expression of opinion could be defamatory if the expression was sufficiently derogatory of another as to cause harm to his reputation, so as to lower him in the estimation of the community or to deter third persons from associating or dealing with him. . . . This position was maintained even though the truth or falsity of an opinion—as distinguished from a statement of fact—is not a matter that can be objectively determined and truth is a complete defense to a suit for defamation.

However, due to concerns that unduly burdensome defamation laws could stifle valuable public debate, the privilege of "fair comment" was incorporated into the common law as an affirmative defense to an action for defamation. "The principle of 'fair comment' afforded legal immunity for the honest expression of opinion on matters of legitimate public interest when based upon a true or privileged statement of fact." F. Harper & F. James, Law of Torts § 5.28 (1956). As this statement implies, comment was generally privileged when it concerned a matter of public concern, was upon true or privileged facts, represented the actual opinion of the speaker, and was not made solely for the purpose of causing harm. * "According to the majority rule, the privilege of fair comment applied only to an expression of opinion and not to a false statement of fact, whether it was expressly stated or implied from an expression of opinion." Restatement § 566 cmt. a. Thus under the common law, the privilege of "fair comment" was the device employed to strike the appropriate balance between the need for vigorous public discourse and the need to redress injury to citizens wrought by invidious or irresponsible speech.

[The court reviews *New York Times Co.* v. *Sullivan* and its progeny, *supra* pages 902–925.] * * *

Respondents would have us recognize, in addition to the established safeguards discussed above, still another First-Amendment-based protection for defamatory statements which are categorized as "opinion" as opposed to "fact." For this proposition they rely principally on the following dictum from our opinion in *Gertz v. Robert Welch,* [*supra* pages 912–919]:

> Under the First Amendment there is no such thing as a false idea. However pernicious an opinion may seem, we depend for its correction not on the conscience of judges and juries but on the competition of other ideas. But there is no constitutional value in false statements of fact.

418 U.S. at 339–40, 94 S.Ct. at 3007, 41 L.Ed.2d at 805 (footnote omitted).

Judge Friendly appropriately observed that this passage "has become the opening salvo in all arguments for protection from defamation actions on the ground of opinion, even though the case did not remotely concern the question." Cianci v. New Times Publ'g Co., 639 F.2d 54, 61 (2d Cir.1980). Read in context, though, the fair meaning of the passage is to equate the word "opinion" in the second sentence with the word "idea" in the first sentence. Under this view, the language was merely a reiteration of Justice Holmes' classic "marketplace of ideas" concept. See Abrams v. United States, 250 U.S. 616, 630, 40 S.Ct. 17, 22, 63 L.Ed.1173, 1180 (1919) (dissenting opinion) ("[T]he ultimate good desired is better reached by free trade in ideas— . . . the best test of truth is the power of the thought to get itself accepted in the competition of the market").

Thus, we do not think this passage from *Gertz* was intended to create a wholesale defamation exemption for anything that might be labeled "opinion." See *Cianci,* at 62, n.10 (The "marketplace of ideas" origin of this passage "points strongly to the view that the 'opinions' held to be constitutionally protected were the sort of thing that could be corrected by discussion"). Not only would such an interpretation be contrary to the tenor and context of the passage, but it would also ignore the fact that expressions of "opinion" may often imply an assertion of objective fact.

If a speaker says, "In my opinion John Jones is a liar," he implies a knowledge of facts which lead to the conclusion that Jones told an untruth. Even if the speaker states the facts upon which he bases his opinion, if those facts are either incorrect or incomplete, or if his assessment of them is erroneous, the statement may still imply a false assertion of fact. Simply couching such statements in terms of opinion does not dispel these implications; and the statement, "In my opinion Jones is a liar," can cause as much damage to reputation as the statement, "Jones is a liar." As Judge Friendly aptly stated: "[It] would be destructive of the law of libel if a writer could escape liability for accusations of [defamatory conduct] simply by using, explicitly or implicitly, the words 'I think.' " * It is worthy of note that at common law, even the privilege of fair comment did not extend to "a false statement of fact, whether it was expressly stated or implied from an expression of opinion." Restatement (Second) of Torts § 566 cmt. a (1977).

Apart from their reliance on the *Gertz* dictum, respondents do not really contend that a statement such as, "In my opinion John Jones is a liar," should be protected by a separate privilege for "opinion" under the First Amendment. But they do contend that in every defamation case the First Amendment mandates an inquiry into whether a statement is "opinion" or "fact," and that only the latter statements may be actionable. They propose that a number of factors developed by the lower courts (in what we hold was a mistaken reliance on the *Gertz* dictum) be considered in deciding which is which. But we think the " 'breathing space' " which " 'freedoms of expression require in order to survive,' " Philadelphia Newspapers v. Hepps, *supra* pages 923–926, (quoting *New York Times*), is adequately secured by existing constitutional doctrine without the creation of an artificial dichotomy between "opinion" and fact.

Foremost, we think *Hepps* stands for the proposition that a statement on matters of public concern must be provable as false before there can be liability under state defamation law, at least in situations, like the present, where a media defendant is involved. * Thus, unlike the statement, "In my opinion Mayor Jones is a liar," the statement, "In my opinion Mayor Jones shows his abysmal ignorance by accepting the teachings of Marx and Lenin," would not be actionable. *Hepps* ensures that a statement of opinion relating to matters of public concern which does not contain a provably false factual connotation will receive full constitutional protection. *

Next, * * * protection [is provided] for statements that cannot "reasonably [be] interpreted as stating actual facts" about an individual. * This provides assurance that public debate will not suffer for lack of "imaginative expression" or the "rhetorical hyperbole" which has traditionally added much to the discourse of our Nation. *

The *New York Times-Butts-Gertz* culpability requirements further ensure that debate on public issues remains "uninhibited, robust, and wide-open." *New York Times*, 376 U.S. at 270. Thus, where a statement of "opinion" on a matter of public concern reasonably implies false and defamatory facts regarding public figures or officials, those individuals must show that such statements were made with knowledge of their false implications or with reckless disregard of their truth. Similarly, where such a statement involves a private figure on a matter of public concern, a plaintiff must show that the false connotations were made with some level of fault as required by *Gertz*. * * *

We are not persuaded that, in addition to these protections, an additional separate constitutional privilege for "opinion" is required to ensure the freedom of expression guaranteed by the First Amendment. The dispositive question in the present case then becomes whether a reasonable factfinder could conclude that the statements in the Diadiun column imply an assertion that petitioner Milkovich perjured himself in a judicial proceeding. We think this question must be answered in the affirmative. As the Ohio Supreme Court itself observed: "[T]he clear impact in some nine sentences and a caption is that [Milkovich] 'lied at

the hearing after . . . having given his solemn oath to tell the truth.' " *
This is not the sort of loose, figurative, or hyperbolic language which
would negate the impression that the writer was seriously maintaining
that petitioner committed the crime of perjury. Nor does the general
tenor of the article negate this impression.

We also think the connotation that petitioner committed perjury is
sufficiently factual to be susceptible of being proved true or false. A
determination whether petitioner lied in this instance can be made on a
core of objective evidence by comparing, *inter alia*, petitioner's
testimony before the OHSAA board with his subsequent testimony
before the trial court. * * *

Reversed.

NOTE

Fair Comment. A privilege known as "fair comment" existed at
common law to protect opinions about matters of public interest, including
not only those involved in political debate, but also those involved in other
areas of endeavor including artistic, literary and scientific matters. See
Carr v. Hood, (1808) 170 Eng.Rep. 983 (K.B.). Some cases continue to refer
to a separate privilege of fair comment. E.g., Piscatelli v. Van Smith, 424
Md. 294, 314–16, 35 A.3d 1140, 1151–53 (2012); Gaylord Entm't Co. v.
Thompson, 958 P.2d 128 (Okla.1998). For all intents and purposes,
however, the protection of opinion once afforded by the fair comment
doctrine now appears to overlap the constitutional protection afforded by
Gertz, even though the Court limited the impact of the "opinion" passage
from *Gertz*.

CHAPTER 18

INVASION OF PRIVACY

"Invasion of privacy" is a comparatively new tort. Drawing together seemingly unrelated theories from earlier cases, Samuel D. Warren and Louis D. Brandeis first identified a coherent concept of "invasion of privacy" as an aspect of tort law in an 1890 article in the *Harvard Law Review*. See *infra*. This common law right to privacy is now recognized in most states, and the same value is reflected in numerous statutes providing private rights of action.

Decades after the Warren and Brandeis article, Dean William Prosser spelled out a four-fold classification of "privacy" torts, see William L. Prosser, Privacy, 48 Cal. L. Rev. 383 (1960), that was subsequently incorporated in the Restatement (Second) of Torts after a spirited debate. See *id.* §§ 652A–652E (1977). Dean John W. Wade, Prosser's successor as Reporter, was concerned about how best to limit the concept of privacy to rights against only those invasions that were unreasonable. Others worried about the use of the word "privacy" to describe interests that seem to have nothing to do with privacy. Further, Prosser's classification of privacy torts leaves unanswered the question whether an overarching concept of privacy exists that should be afforded protection in instances that do not fit into Prosser's four categories. Harper, James and Gray on Torts § 9.6A; Danielle Keats Citron, Mainstreaming Privacy Torts, 98 Cal. L. Rev. 1805 (2010); Edward J. Bloustein, Privacy as an Aspect of Human Dignity: An Answer to Dean Prosser, 39 N.Y.U. L. Rev. 962 (1964). Finally, one of the major issues in privacy law during recent decades has paralleled similar tensions in the law of defamation—the extent to which the tort is significantly limited by the constitutional protections afforded the freedoms of speech and press.

A. PUBLIC DISCLOSURE OF PRIVATE FACTS

Excerpt, Samuel D. Warren & Louis D. Brandeis, The Right to Privacy
4 Harv. L. Rev. 193, 196 (1890).

* * * The press is overstepping in every direction the obvious bounds of propriety and of decency. Gossip is no longer the resource of the idle and of the vicious, but has become a trade, which is pursued with industry as well as effrontery. To satisfy a prurient taste the details of sexual relations are spread broadcast in the columns of the daily papers. To occupy the indolent, column upon column is filled with idle gossip, which can only be procured by intrusion upon the domestic circle. The intensity and complexity of life, attendant upon advancing civilization, have rendered necessary some retreat from the world, and man, under the refining influence of culture, has become more sensitive to publicity, so that solitude and privacy have become more essential to the individual; but modern enterprise and invention have, through

invasions upon his privacy, subjected him to mental pain and distress, far greater than could be inflicted by mere bodily injury. Nor is the harm wrought by such invasions confined to the suffering of those who may be made the subjects of journalistic or other enterprise. * * * Each crop of unseemly gossip * * * becomes the seed of more, and, in direct proportion to its circulation, results in a lowering of social standards and of morality.

Even gossip apparently harmless, when widely and persistently circulated, is potent for evil. It both belittles and perverts. It belittles by inverting the relative importance of things, thus dwarfing the thoughts and aspirations of a people. * * * Triviality destroys at once robustness of thought and delicacy of feeling. No enthusiasm can flourish, no generous impulse can survive under its blighting influence.

NOTE

Judicial Recognition of Privacy Tort. Courts did not rush to recognize the new privacy tort. The highest courts of Michigan and New York expressly rejected it. See Atkinson v. John E. Doherty & Co., 121 Mich. 372, 383–84, 80 N.W. 285, 289 (1899); Roberson v. Rochester Folding Box Co., 171 N.Y. 538, 556, 64 N.E. 442, 447 (1902). Judge O'Brien of the New York Court of Appeals felt so strongly about the issue he wrote a law review article defending the *Roberson* decision. A few years later, however, the Georgia Supreme Court recognized the privacy tort. See Pavesich v. New Eng. Life Ins. Co., 122 Ga. 190, 201–02, 50 S.E. 68, 72–73 (1905). With the imprimatur of the first Restatement of Torts in the 1930s, the pace of recognition accelerated. See Restatement of Torts § 867 (1939); Prosser, *supra*, 48 Cal. L. Rev. at 386.

Shulman v. Group W Productions, Inc.

Supreme Court of California, 1998.
18 Cal.4th 200, 74 Cal.Rptr.2d 843, 955 P.2d 469.

■ WERDEGAR, JUSTICE. More than 100 years ago, Louis Brandeis and Samuel Warren complained that the press, armed with the then recent invention of "instantaneous photographs" and under the influence of new "business methods," was "overstepping in every direction the obvious bounds of propriety and of decency." [Samuel] Warren & [Louis] Brandeis, The Right to Privacy, 4 Harv. L. Rev. 193, 195–96 (1890). * * * Today, of course, the newspapers of 1890 have been joined by the electronic media; today, a vast number of books, journals, television and radio stations, cable channels and Internet content sources all compete to satisfy our thirst for knowledge and our need for news of political, economic and cultural events—as well as our love of gossip, our curiosity about the private lives of others, and "that weak side of human nature which is never wholly cast down by the misfortunes and frailties of our neighbors." * Moreover, the "devices" available for recording and transmitting what would otherwise be private have multiplied and improved in ways the 19th century could hardly imagine.

Over the same period, the United States has also seen a series of revolutions in mores and conventions that has moved, blurred and, at times, seemingly threatened to erase the line between public and private life. While even in their day Brandeis and Warren complained that "the details of sexual relations are spread broadcast in the columns of the daily papers," * today's public discourse is particularly notable for its detailed and graphic discussion of intimate personal and family matters—sometimes as topics of legitimate public concern, sometimes as simple titillation. * * *

On June 24, 1990, plaintiffs Ruth and Wayne Shulman, mother and son, were injured when the car in which they and two other family members were riding on interstate 10 in Riverside County flew off the highway and tumbled down an embankment into a drainage ditch on state-owned property, coming to rest upside down. Ruth, the most seriously injured of the two, was pinned under the car. Ruth and Wayne both had to be cut free from the vehicle by the device known as "the jaws of life." A rescue helicopter operated by Mercy Air was dispatched to the scene. The flight nurse, who would perform the medical care at the scene and on the way to the hospital, was Laura Carnahan. Also on board were the pilot, a medic and Joel Cooke, a video camera operator employed by defendants Group W Productions, Inc., and 4MN Productions. Cooke was recording the rescue operation for later broadcast. Cooke roamed the accident scene, videotaping the rescue. Nurse Carnahan wore a wireless microphone that picked up her conversations with both Ruth and the other rescue personnel. Cooke's tape was edited into a piece approximately nine minutes long, which, with the addition of narrative voice-over, was broadcast on September 29, 1990, as a segment of *On Scene: Emergency Response.* * * *

[The opinion then describes how the program portrayed the accident scene.] While Ruth is still trapped under the car, Carnahan asks Ruth's age. Ruth responds, "I'm old." On further questioning, Ruth reveals she is 47, and Carnahan observes that "it's all relative. You're not that old." During her extrication from the car, Ruth asks at least twice if she is dreaming. At one point she asks Carnahan, who has told her she will be taken to the hospital in a helicopter: "Are you teasing?" At another point she says: "This is terrible. Am I dreaming?" She also asks what happened and where the rest of her family is, repeating the questions even after being told she was in an accident and the other family members are being cared for. While being loaded into the helicopter on a stretcher, Ruth says: "I just want to die." Carnahan reassures her that she is "going to do real well." But Ruth repeats: "I just want to die. I don't want to go through this."

Ruth and Wayne are placed in the helicopter, and its door is closed. * * * Carnahan, speaking into what appears to be a radio microphone, transmits some of Ruth's vital signs and states that Ruth cannot move her feet and has no sensation. The video footage during the helicopter ride includes a few seconds of Ruth's face, covered by an oxygen mask. The helicopter lands on the hospital roof. With the door open, Ruth states while being taken out: "My upper back hurts." Carnahan replies: "Your upper back hurts. That's what you were saying up there." Ruth states: "I don't feel that great." Carnahan responds: "You probably don't." Finally, Ruth is shown being moved from the helicopter into the hospital. * * *

The accident left Ruth a paraplegic. When the segment was broadcast, Wayne phoned Ruth in her hospital room and told her to turn on the television because "Channel 4 is showing our accident now." Shortly afterward, several hospital workers came into the room to mention that a videotaped segment of her accident was being shown. Ruth was "shocked, so to speak, that this would be run and I would be exploited, have my privacy invaded, which is what I felt had happened." She did not know her rescue had been recorded in this manner and had never consented to the recording or broadcast. * * * Asked at deposition what part of the broadcast material she considered private, Ruth explained: "I think the whole scene was pretty private. It was pretty gruesome[;] * * * it's not for the public to see this trauma that I was going through."

Ruth and Wayne sued the producers of *On Scene: Emergency Response*, as well as others. The first amended complaint included two causes of action for invasion of privacy, one based on defendants' unlawful intrusion by videotaping the rescue in the first instance and the other based on the public disclosure of private facts, i.e., the broadcast. * * * The trial court granted the media defendants' summary judgment motion, basing its ruling on plaintiffs' admissions that the accident and rescue were matters of public interest and public affairs. * * * The Court of Appeal reversed and remanded for further proceedings, but on limited grounds and as to some causes of action only. * * *

Influenced by Dean Prosser's analysis of the tort actions for invasion of privacy, Prosser, Privacy, 48 Cal. L. Rev. 381 (1960), and the exposition of a similar analysis in the Restatement (Second) of Torts §§ 652A–652E * * *, California courts have recognized both of the privacy causes of action pleaded by plaintiffs here: (1) public disclosure of private facts, and (2) intrusion into private places, conversations or other matters. * * *

I.   Publication of Private Facts

The claim that a publication has given unwanted publicity to allegedly private aspects of a person's life is one of the more commonly litigated and well-defined areas of privacy law. * * * [T]he Restatement * * * provides that "[o]ne who gives publicity to a matter concerning the private life of another is subject to liability to the other for invasion of his privacy, if the matter publicized is of a kind that (a) would be highly offensive to a reasonable person, and (b) is not of legitimate concern to the public." Restatement (Second) of Torts § 652D.

* * * [U]nder California common law the dissemination of truthful, newsworthy material is not actionable as a publication of private facts. * Restatement (Second) of Torts § 652D. If the contents of a broadcast or publication are of legitimate public concern, the plaintiff cannot establish a necessary element of the tort action, the lack of newsworthiness. To so state, however, is merely to begin the necessary legal inquiry, not to end it. It is in the determination of newsworthiness—in deciding whether published or broadcast material is of legitimate public concern—that courts must struggle most directly to accommodate the conflicting interests of individual privacy and press freedom.

Although we speak of the lack of newsworthiness as an element of the private facts tort, newsworthiness is at the same time a constitutional defense to, or privilege against, liability for publication of truthful information. * Indeed, the danger of interference with constitutionally protected press freedom has been and remains an ever-present consideration for courts and commentators struggling to set the tort's parameters, and the requirements of tort law and the Constitution have generally been assumed to be congruent. See Restatement (Second) of Torts § 652D cmt. d (newsworthiness standard developed in common law but now expresses constitutional limit as well); Virgil v. Time, Inc., 527 F.2d 1122, 1128–30 (9th Cir.1975) (accepting Restatement test of newsworthiness as constitutional standard). * Little is to be gained, therefore, in attempting to keep rigorously separate the tort and constitutional issues as regards newsworthiness, and we have not attempted to do so here. Tort liability, obviously, can extend no further than the First Amendment allows; conversely, we see no reason or authority for fashioning the newsworthiness element of the private facts tort to *preclude* liability where the Constitution would allow it.

Delineating the exact contours of the constitutional privilege of the press in publication of private facts is, however, particularly problematic, because this privilege has not received extensive attention from the United States Supreme Court. The high court has considered the issue in only one case involving the common law public disclosure tort, Cox Broadcasting Corp. v. Cohn, 420 U.S. 469, 95 S.Ct. 1029, 43 L.Ed.2d 328 (1975) (*Cox Broadcasting*), and its holding in that case was deliberately and explicitly narrow. In *Cox Broadcasting*, a criminal court clerk, during a recess in court proceedings relating to a rape-murder case, allowed a television reporter to see the indictment, which contained the name of the victim. The television station broadcast an account of the court proceedings, using the victim's name; the victim's father alleged the broadcast to be a tortious publication of private facts. The Georgia Supreme Court, relying on a Georgia statute prohibiting publication or broadcast of a rape victim's identity, held the broadcast of the victim's name was not privileged as newsworthy; the court viewed the statute as showing that the victim's identity was not a matter of legitimate public concern. The state court further held the statute did not itself infringe on the station's First Amendment rights.

The federal high court reversed, but—recognizing the important interests on both sides of the newsworthiness question—proceeded cautiously and on limited grounds. "Rather than address the broader question of whether truthful publications may ever be subjected to civil or criminal liability consistently with the First and Fourteenth Amendments, or to put it another way, whether the State may ever define and protect an area of privacy free from unwanted publicity in the press, it is appropriate to focus on the narrower interface between press and privacy that this case presents, namely, whether the State may impose sanctions on the accurate publication of the name of a rape victim obtained from public records—more specifically, from judicial records which are maintained in connection with a public prosecution and which themselves are open to public inspection. We are convinced that the State may not do so." Cox Broadcasting, 420 U.S. at 491, 95 S.Ct. at 1044, 43 L.Ed.2d at 347. * * *

Newsworthiness—constitutional or common law—is also difficult to define because it may be used as either a descriptive or a normative term. "Is the term 'newsworthy' a descriptive predicate, intended to refer to the fact there is widespread public interest? Or is it a value predicate, intended to indicate that the publication is a meritorious contribution and that the public's interest is praiseworthy?" * A position at either extreme has unpalatable consequences. If "newsworthiness" is completely descriptive—if all coverage that sells papers or boosts ratings is deemed newsworthy—it would seem to swallow the publication of private facts tort, for "it would be difficult to suppose that publishers were in the habit of reporting occurrences of little interest." At the other extreme, if newsworthiness is viewed as a purely normative concept, the courts could become to an unacceptable degree editors of the news and self-appointed guardians of public taste. * * *

Our prior decisions have not explicitly addressed the type of privacy invasion alleged in this case: the broadcast of embarrassing pictures and speech of a person who, while generally not a public figure, has become involuntarily involved in an event or activity of legitimate public concern. We nonetheless draw guidance from those decisions, in that they articulate the competing interests to be balanced. First, the analysis of newsworthiness does involve courts to some degree in a normative assessment of the "social value" of a publication. * All material that might attract readers or viewers is not, simply by virtue of its attractiveness, of *legitimate* public interest. Second, the evaluation of newsworthiness depends on the degree of intrusion and the extent to which the plaintiff played an important role in public events, * and thus on a comparison between the information revealed and the nature of the activity or event that brought the plaintiff to public attention. "Some reasonable proportion is . . . to be maintained between the events or activity that makes the individual a public figure and the private facts to which publicity is given. Revelations that may properly be made concerning a murderer or the President of the United States would not be privileged if they were to be made concerning one who is merely injured in an automobile accident." Restatement (Second) of Torts § 652D cmt. h. Courts balancing these interests in cases similar to this have recognized that, when a person is involuntarily involved in a newsworthy incident, not all aspects of the person's life, and not everything the person says or does, is thereby rendered newsworthy. * * *

* * * To observe that the newsworthiness of private facts about a person involuntarily thrust into the public eye depends, in the ordinary case, on the existence of a logical nexus between the newsworthy event or activity and the facts revealed is not to deny that the balance of free press and privacy interests may require a different conclusion when the intrusiveness of the revelation is greatly disproportionate to its relevance. Intensely personal or intimate revelations might not, in a given case, be considered newsworthy, especially where they bear only slight relevance to a topic of legitimate public concern. * * *

We agree at the outset with defendants that the subject matter of the broadcast as a whole was of legitimate public concern. Automobile accidents are by their nature of interest to that great portion of the public that travels frequently by automobile. The rescue and medical treatment of accident victims is also of legitimate concern to much of the public, involving as it does a critical service that any member of the public may someday need. The story of Ruth's difficult extrication from the crushed car, the medical attention given her at the scene, and her evacuation by helicopter was of particular interest because it highlighted some of the challenges facing emergency workers dealing with serious accidents.

The more difficult question is whether Ruth's appearance and words as she was extricated from the overturned car, placed in the helicopter and transported to the hospital were of legitimate public concern. Pursuant to the analysis outlined earlier, we conclude the disputed material was newsworthy as a matter of law. One of the dramatic and interesting aspects of the story as a whole is its focus on flight nurse Carnahan, who appears to be in charge of communications with other emergency workers, the hospital base and Ruth, and who leads the medical assistance to Ruth at the scene. Her work is portrayed as demanding and important and as involving a measure of personal risk (e.g., in crawling under the car to aid Ruth despite warnings that gasoline may be dripping from the car). The broadcast segment makes apparent that this type of emergency care requires not only medical knowledge, concentration and courage, but an ability to talk and listen to severely traumatized patients. One of the challenges Carnahan faces in assisting Ruth is the confusion, pain and fear that Ruth understandably feels in the aftermath of the accident. For that reason the broadcast video depicting Ruth's injured physical state (which was not luridly shown) and audio showing her disorientation and despair were substantially relevant to the segment's newsworthy subject matter.

* * * That the broadcast *could* have been edited to exclude some of Ruth's words and images and still excite a minimum degree of viewer interest is not determinative. Nor is the possibility that the members of this or another court, or a jury, might find a differently edited broadcast more to their taste or even more interesting. The courts do not, and constitutionally could not, sit as superior editors of the press. * * *

The broadcast details of Ruth's rescue of which she complains were, as a matter of law, of legitimate public concern because they were substantially relevant to the newsworthy subject of the piece and their intrusiveness was not greatly disproportionate to their relevance. That analytical path is dictated by the danger of the contrary approach; to allow liability because this court, or a jury, believes certain details of the story as broadcast were not important or necessary to the purpose of the documentary, or were in poor taste or overly sensational in impact, would be to assert impermissible supervisory power over the press.

* * * Summary judgment for the defense was proper as to plaintiffs' cause of action for publication of private facts (the second cause of action). * * *

Doe v. Methodist Hospital

Supreme Court of Indiana, 1997.
690 N.E.2d 681.

■ SHEPARD, CHIEF JUSTICE. Over the last century, courts and commentators have developed a quadripartite formulation for the tort of invasion of privacy. In this case we consider whether one branch of that tort, public disclosure of private facts, may form the basis of a civil action in Indiana. On the facts of this case, we decline to recognize that it may.

"John Doe" appeals the trial court's entry of summary judgment for appellee Cathy Duncan, whom Doe had sued for invasion of privacy. * * *

Doe is a letter carrier for the U.S. Postal Service. In early 1990, he was rushed from his workplace to Methodist Hospital because of a suspected heart attack. During the ambulance ride, he informed the paramedics that he had tested positive for the human immunodeficiency virus (HIV), and they recorded that information in his medical records. Doe had previously disclosed his HIV status to a small circle of close friends and co-workers, but he had not shared that information with his co-workers generally. For several years rumors had circulated in the workplace, sometimes with a negative connotation, that Doe was gay. On that basis alone, some co-workers had speculated that he was HIV positive.

While Doe was in the hospital, co-worker Logan Cameron allegedly checked on Doe's condition by calling his own wife, Lizzie Cameron, who worked at Methodist Hospital. Doe contends that Lizzie reviewed his confidential medical records, discovered he was HIV positive, and disclosed that information to her husband Logan. Doe further alleges that Logan Cameron related the information to some of Doe's co-workers, including Duncan.

Becky Saunders, who was also a letter carrier, stated that Duncan approached her and said: "I heard that [John Doe] has AIDS. Is it true?" * According to Saunders, Duncan said that she received the information either from someone who worked in a clinic or from someone who knew someone who worked in a clinic. We accept, for the purposes of this appeal, Saunders' statement that she was not previously aware of Doe's HIV status.

Duncan also approached co-worker Ron Okes in what he characterized as an attempt to verify the rumor. Okes was a close friend of Doe, and Doe had previously told him in confidence that he was HIV positive. Okes did not confirm Duncan's gossip. A few days later, Duncan approached Okes again. She told him she had gone to Doe's significant other, * who was also a co-worker, and apologized for spreading the rumor. *

Doe and his significant other apparently complained to postal supervisors, and the Postal Service seems to have taken responsible action. According to Okes' testimony, the supervisors separately confronted Duncan and Logan Cameron about the incidents, perhaps in the presence of Doe and his partner. Duncan left her meeting in tears, and was ultimately transferred to a different work station.

Doe sued Duncan for invasion of privacy. * * * Duncan moved for summary judgment, which the trial court granted. Doe appealed, and the Court of Appeals affirmed. * We granted Doe's petition for transfer, and now affirm the judgment of the trial court. * * *

Although Warren and Brandeis had written in terms of a comprehensive interest in privacy, the far-flung cases they cited never coalesced into a unified tort. The first Restatement managed to articulate a two-dimensional interest in "not having [one's] affairs known to others or [one's] likeness exhibited to the public." Restatement of Torts § 867. By 1960, Professor Prosser had concluded that invasion of privacy was "not one tort, but a complex of four." [William L.] Prosser, Privacy, 48 Cal. L. Rev. 383, 389 (1960).

The Second Restatement adopted this view, describing four distinct injuries: (1) intrusion upon seclusion, (2) appropriation of likeness, (3) public disclosure of private facts, and (4) false-light publicity. Restatement (Second) of Torts § 652A (1977). The Second Restatement also candidly acknowledged that these four separate wrongs were only tenuously related. They were united only in their common focus on some abstract notion of being left alone. *Id.* § 652A cmt. b.

Taken separately, each wrong more closely resembles other distinct torts, rather than separate branches of a single privacy tort. See, e.g., Restatement of Torts § 867 cmt. a. Often the privacy tort seems to function as little more than a "lite" version of trespass, outrage, or defamation—promising the same great take with only half the facts. See, e.g., Lovgren v. Citizens First National Bank, 126 Ill.2d 411, 128 Ill.Dec. 542, 546, 534 N.E.2d 987, 991 (Ill.1989) ("It has been said that all defamation cases can be analyzed as false-light cases, but not all false-light cases are defamation cases."). Moreover, recognizing one branch of the privacy tort does not entail recognizing all four. * * *

The only branch of the privacy tort at issue in this case is disclosure. This cause of action has been recognized in most states, see Diane L. Zimmerman, Requiem for a Heavyweight: A Farewell to Warren and Brandeis's Privacy Tort, 68 Cornell L. Rev. 291, 365–67 (1983) * * *. On the other hand, a few states have refused to recognize disclosure. * Even where the cause of action has been recognized, the success rate of plaintiffs has been extremely low, perhaps because of its stringent elements. *Id.* at 293 n.5 (finding only 18 state cases in which plaintiff's claim succeeded or survived a motion for summary judgment or dismissal).

While we have recited the Second Restatement's four-part definition of the privacy tort, * we have never directly confronted disclosure as an actionable invasion of privacy. * * * Consistent with the national trend, defendants in three of the four reported Indiana decisions involving disclosure * * * were exonerated. * In the fourth case the court merely held that the plaintiff's claim against one of two defendants survived a motion for summary judgment. *

In this case, Doe would have us impose upon Hoosiers a legal duty to refrain from publicly disclosing the private affairs of others. We can identify two main interests that such a duty would protect. First, a person has an interest in reputation, in being able to interact effectively with other people. Second, a person has an interest in mental well-being, in avoiding the emotional distress that could result from disclosures. Each of these interests must be balanced against competing public and private interests.

A.   Reputation

Under one view, the primary harm that can result from a public disclosure of private facts is an injury to a person's reputation. The Restatement explains that "[e]very individual has some phases of his life and his activities and some facts about himself that he does not expose to the public eye." Restatement (Second) of Torts § 652D cmt. b (1977). When someone else exposes those facts, the Restatement recognizes injury to reputation as the main compensable harm that can result. See *id.* § 652H cmt. a. * * *

1.   *The Interest in Reputation.* Some commentators have derided the reputational interest as an interest in cultivating a undeserved reputation. Judge Posner, for example, has declared that "we have no right, by controlling the information that is known about us to manipulate the opinions that other people hold of us." [Richard A.] Posner, The Right of Privacy, 12 Ga. L. Rev. 393, 408 (1978). * * * Still, the reputational interest protected by disclosure actions should not be lightly dismissed. Truthful disclosures can be socially disruptive and personally dangerous. In many real-life situations, the maintenance of a social organization—such as a workplace—sometimes depends upon the ability of individuals to censor themselves and minimize internecine strife. Moreover, while truthful disclosures can shatter undeserved reputations, they can also incite undeserved abuse. Defamation law has traditionally addressed similar injuries to reputation. * * * Defamation rules apply, however, only to statements that are false as well as defamatory. * * * To the extent the disclosure sub-tort protects an interest in reputation, it fills this supposed gap, as truth is not a defense in a disclosure action. Indeed, one commentator largely attributes the emergence of the sub-tort to "the general common law defense of truth in civil defamation actions and the concomitant unavailability of a remedy thereunder for highly embarrassing truthful disclosures." David Elder, The Law of Privacy, § 3.1 (1991). In other words, disclosure sometimes serves as an alternative action for truthful defamation.

2.   *Truthful Defamation.* That alternative feature of the disclosure sub-tort, however, brings it into potential conflict with the libel provision of the Indiana Bill of Rights: "In all prosecutions for libel, the truth of the matters alleged to be libelous may be given in justification." Ind. Const. art. I, § 10. The text of Section 10 is not lacking in ambiguity. Nevertheless, our review of its history suggests a very strong policy against any civil liability based on truthful defamation.

[The court undertakes an extensive review of the role of truth as a defense against both criminal and civil actions against libel in Great Britain, the United States, and specifically in Indiana.] * * * With the rise of the enlightenment in the sixteenth and seventeenth centuries, the English government increasingly used criminal libel law to suppress dissent. * On the theory that truthful statements were at least as dangerous to public peace as false ones, the Star Chamber, and later the common law courts, abrogated the defense of truth in criminal libel. * * * The influence of the British experience is manifest. * * * In

Britain, criminal libel became "almost exclusively" an instrument for the suppression of political dissent. * Perhaps the fear of a similar use of the law by elites in early Indiana led the framers of the 1816 Constitution to guarantee the availability of a truth defense where political speech was concerned. * * * Nevertheless, whether the framers of the 1851 Constitution intended the new Section 10 to guarantee a truth defense in civil as well as criminal actions for libel is open to doubt. * * * At the least, one can say that the truth-in-libel provision of the 1851 Indiana Constitution commands real caution about proposals to recognize a civil cause of action for libel that impose liability for truthful statements.

B.   Emotional Health

There is a second interest that the public disclosure sub-tort protects, an interest in emotional health. Doe alleged that he suffered "embarrassment, humiliation, and mental distress" as a result of the disclosure of his HIV status. Warren and Brandeis, in fact, focused most of their attention in their article on these injuries, expressing a concern for "peace of mind" and the embittering of life. [Samuel] Warren & [Louis] Brandeis, The Right to Privacy, 4 Harv. L. Rev. 193, 200, 204 (1891).

Indiana law, however, already provides protection for emotional injuries with a civil action for intentional infliction of emotional distress, also known as "outrage."[a]

* * * [U]nder the Second Restatement a plaintiff does not have to prove any [emotional distress] in a public disclosure action. He needs only to show that the disclosed matter was private and not of legitimate concern to the public, and that the disclosure would be highly offensive to a reasonable person. Restatement (Second) of Torts § 652D (1977). In this sense, disclosure is a sort of strict liability version of outrage. It is outrage "lite."

At least one court has required plaintiffs in disclosure actions to establish the elements of outrage as well as disclosure. Writing for the Supreme Court of Oregon, Justice Hans Linde reasoned that disclosure should not be treated differently from other causes of action based on emotional injuries. See Anderson v. Fisher Broadcasting Cos., 300 Or. 452, 712 P.2d 803, 807–14 (1986). Under the Oregon rule, a plaintiff has to prove that a defendant's disclosure was "designed to cause severe mental or emotional distress." * * * Justice Linde seems right. * * * [W]e do not discern anything special about disclosure injuries. Perhaps Victorian sensibilities once provided a sound basis of distinction, but our more open and tolerant society has largely outgrown such a justification. In our "been there, done that" age of talk shows, tabloids, and twelve-step programs, public disclosures of private facts are far less likely to cause shock, offense, or emotional distress than at the time Warren and Brandeis wrote their famous article.

With these policies in mind, we turn to Doe's request that we recognize the sub-tort of disclosure, examining the facts and arguments advanced. According to the Second Restatement, a person is subject to liability for public disclosure of private facts if the person (1) gives

---

[a]   [Eds.' note] Outrage is also known as intentional infliction of emotional distress. See *supra* pages 737–750.

"publicity", (2) to a matter that (a) concerns the "private life" of another; (b) would be "highly offensive" to a reasonable person; and (c) is not of legitimate public concern. Restatement (Second) of Torts § 652D (1977). On appeal, Duncan argues that Doe's claim must fail with regard to Okes because of the "private life" element and with regard to Saunders because of the "publicity" element. We agree with both contentions. *

A key issue contested in the briefs is whether "publicity" requires disclosure to the general public or whether more isolated disclosures are also actionable. According to the Second Restatement, "publicity" in disclosure law is not the same as "publication" in defamation law. Restatement (Second) of Torts § 652D cmt. a. "Publication" can consist of communication to just one individual. *Id.* § 577(1). In contrast, "publicity" requires communication of the information "to the public at large, or to so many persons that the matter must be regarded as substantially certain to become one of public knowledge." *Id.* at § 652D cmt. a. A paradigmatic example is a creditor who posts in a shop window a sign declaring that a named individual owes him a certain sum of money, as in Brents v. Morgan, 221 Ky. 765, 299 S.W. 967 (1927).

The Restatement explicitly observes that communication "to a single person or even to a small group of persons" is not actionable. Restatement (Second) of Torts § 652D cmt. a. * Most courts have followed this definition of "publicity," ignoring the Restatement's suggestion that courts could extend coverage "to a simple disclosure," Restatement (Second) of Torts § 652D cmt. a. * Obviously, Duncan's two disclosures do not satisfy a requirement of dissemination to the general public.

On the other hand, a few courts, including Indiana's neighbors, have adopted a looser definition of "publicity." In the seminal *Beaumont* case, the Supreme Court of Michigan held that even if a disclosure were not made to the general public, it could still be actionable if made to a "particular public" with a special relationship to the plaintiff, such as co-workers, family members, or neighbors. Beaumont v. Brown, 401 Mich. 80, 103, 257 N.W.2d 522, 531 (Mich.1977). The court sought to identify a nexus between the information disclosed and the relationship between the plaintiff and the class to whom the disclosure was made. The question was whether a particular disclosure would be embarrassing given the plaintiff's relationship with the "particular public" at issue. In the most liberal application of *Beaumont*, the D.C. Circuit, applying a Kentucky privacy statute, held that disclosure of a person's infidelity to that person's spouse was actionable given the obvious detrimental impact that particular information could have on the intimate marital relationship. McSurely v. McClellan, 243 U.S.App.D.C. 270, 753 F.2d 88 (D.C.Cir.1985), cert. denied, 474 U.S. 1005, 106 S.Ct. 525, 88 L.Ed.2d 457 (1985). * * *

Even under the more flexible *Beaumont* standard, however, we conclude that Doe could not maintain a disclosure action against Duncan. Indeed, Doe could not sue Duncan based on her communications with Okes under any definition of "publicity" because Doe had already disclosed his HIV status to Okes. According to the Second Restatement, "[t]here is no liability when the defendant merely gives further publicity to information about the plaintiff that is already public." Restatement (Second) of Torts § 652D cmt. b. * Doe could hardly have been embarrassed and humiliated by Duncan's attempted disclosure to Okes of information Doe had already disclosed to him. *

In addition, Duncan's disclosure to Saunders, without more, cannot form the basis of a disclosure action even under the *Beaumont* doctrine. To designate a person or a group of persons as a "particular public," that person or persons must have a special relationship with the plaintiff such that the disclosure would be particularly damaging. * * * [N]othing in the record indicates that knowledge of Doe's HIV status would be more relevant or damaging to his relationship with Saunders than with any of the other letter carriers. There is simply no basis for narrowing the definition of "particular public" from the set of all Doe's letter-carrier colleagues to just Saunders.

Conclusion

Indiana recognizes a number of the claims described generically as invasions of privacy. The version of these torts involving disclosure of truthful but private facts encounters a considerable obstacle in the truth-in-defense provisions of the Indiana Constitution. The facts and the complaint in this particular case do not persuade us to endorse the sub-tort of disclosure.

We affirm the trial court. * * *

NOTE

Rejection of Public Disclosure Tort. As the principal case notes, some states reject altogether the public disclosure of private embarrassing facts tort and, in those jurisdictions recognizing the tort, successful claims are rare. In Howell v. New York Post Co., 81 N.Y.2d 115, 124, 596 N.Y.S.2d 350, 355, 612 N.E.2d 699, 704 (1993), the New York Court of Appeals held that "[t]here is * * * no cause of action in this state for publication of truthful but embarrassing facts." The plaintiff was a patient in a psychiatric facility photographed by the defendant's photographer with a telephoto lens for a picture accompanying a story about another patient who was walking with the plaintiff, Hedda Nussbaum, Nussbaum was the "adoptive" mother of a six-year old child whose death resulted from child abuse perpetrated by Nussbaum's lover. The photograph of Nussbaum and the plaintiff was contrasted with an earlier photo of Nussbaum showing Nussbaum physically and emotionally abused. The plaintiff had alleged that it was important to her recovery that her hospitalization remain a secret from her family and friends. The New York privacy statute, originally adopted as a response to the Warren and Brandeis privacy article, *supra* pages 931–932, prohibited only using a person's name or picture for "advertising" or "trade" purposes. The New York courts have refused to recognize common law invasion of privacy torts.

B. INTRUSION UPON SECLUSION

Hamberger v. Eastman

Supreme Court of New Hampshire, 1964.
106 N.H. 107, 206 A.2d 239.

The plaintiffs, husband and wife, brought companion suits for invasion of their privacy against the defendant who owned and rented a dwelling house to the plaintiffs. The plaintiffs allege that the defendant installed and concealed "a listening and recording device" in their bedroom, which was in the dwelling house rented to them by the defendant and that this device was connected to the defendant's adjacent residence by wires "capable of transmitting and recording any sounds and voices originating in said bedroom." * * *

■ KENISON, CHIEF JUSTICE. The question presented is whether the right of privacy is recognized in this state. There is no controlling statute and no previous decision in this jurisdiction which decides the question. Inasmuch as invasion of the right of privacy is not a single tort but consists of four distinct torts, it is probably more concrete and accurate to state the issue in the present case to be whether this state recognizes that intrusion upon one's physical and mental solitude or seclusion is a tort. * * *

The four kinds of invasion comprising the law of privacy include: (1) intrusion upon the plaintiff's physical and mental solitude or seclusion; (2) public disclosure of private facts; (3) publicity which places the plaintiff in a false light in the public eye; (4) appropriation, for the defendant's benefit or advantage, of the plaintiff's name or likeness. In the present case, we are concerned only with the tort of intrusion upon the plaintiffs' solitude or seclusion. *

"It is evident that these four forms of invasion of privacy are distinct, and based on different elements. It is the failure to recognize this which has been responsible for much of the apparent confusion in the decisions. Taking them in order—intrusion, disclosure, false light, and appropriation—the first and second require the invasion of something secret, secluded or private pertaining to the plaintiff; the third and fourth do not. The second and third depend upon publicity, while the first does not, nor does the fourth, although it usually involves it. The third requires falsity or fiction; the other three do not. The fourth involves a use for the defendant's advantage which is not true of the rest." W[illiam L.] Prosser, Torts § 112 (3d ed. 1964).

The tort of intrusion upon the plaintiff's solitude or seclusion is not limited to a physical invasion of his home or his room or his quarters. As Prosser points out, the principle has been carried beyond such physical intrusion "and extended to eavesdropping upon private conversations by means of wire tapping and microphones." * * * The right of privacy has been upheld in situations where microphones have been planted to overhear private conversations. *

We have not searched for cases where the bedroom of husband and wife has been "bugged" but it should not be necessary—by way of understatement—to observe that this is the type of intrusion that would be offensive to any person of ordinary sensibilities. What married "people do in the privacy of their bedroom is their own business so long as they are not hurting anyone else." * The Restatement, Torts § 867 provides that "a person who unreasonably and seriously interferes with another's interest in not having his affairs known to others . . . is liable to the other." As is pointed out in comment *d*[,] "[L]iability exists only if the defendant's conduct was such that he should have realized that it would be offensive to persons of ordinary sensibilities. It is only where the intrusion has gone beyond the limits of decency that liability accrues. These limits are exceeded where intimate details of the life of one who has never manifested a desire to have publicity are exposed to the public. . . ."

The defendant contends that the right of privacy should not be recognized on the facts of the present case as they appear in the pleadings because there are no allegations that anyone listened or overheard any sounds or voices originating from the plaintiffs' bedroom. The tort of intrusion on the plaintiffs' solitude or seclusion does not require publicity and communication to third persons although this would affect the amount of damages, as Prosser makes clear. * The defendant also contends that the right of privacy is not violated unless something has been published, written or printed and that oral publicity is not sufficient. Recent cases make it clear that this is not a requirement. *

If the peeping Tom, the big ear and the electronic eavesdropper (whether ingenious or ingenuous) have a place in the hierarchy of social values, it ought not to be at the expense of a married couple minding their own business in the seclusion of their bedroom who have never asked for or by their conduct deserved a potential projection of their private conversations and actions to their landlord or to others. Whether actual or potential such "publicity with respect to private matters of purely personal concern is an injury to personality. It impairs the mental peace and comfort of the individual and may produce suffering more acute than that produced by a mere bodily injury." R[oscoe] Pound, Jurisprudence 58 (1959). The use of parabolic microphones and sonic wave devices designed to pick up conversations in a room without entering it and at a considerable distance away makes the problem far from fanciful. *

It is unnecessary to determine the extent to which the right of privacy is protected as a constitutional matter without the benefit of statute. * For the purposes of the present case it is sufficient to hold that the invasion of the plaintiffs' solitude or seclusion, as alleged in the pleadings, was a violation of their right of privacy and constituted a tort for which the plaintiffs may recover damages to the extent that they can prove them. "Certainly, no right deserves greater protection, for, as Emerson has well said, 'solitude, the safeguard of mediocrity, is to genius the stern friend.'" [Michael J.] Ezer, Intrusion on Solitude: Herein of Civil Rights and Civil Wrongs, 21 Law in Transition 63, 75 (1961).

The motion to dismiss should be denied. * * *

NOTE

Invasions of Privacy Through Use of Technology. Hamberger v. *Eastman* is only one example of perhaps the simplest application of the intrusion upon seclusion tort, seeking damages for the use of enhanced technology to intrude upon activities traditionally considered private. See also, e.g., Wolfson v. Lewis, 924 F.Supp. 1413, 1428 (E.D.Pa.1996) (use of "shotgun mike" and videotaping through windows of family residence by newsgathering organization); Lewis v. LeGrow, 258 Mich.App. 175, 670 N.W.2d 675 (2003) (hidden videotaping of sexual activity between defendant and several plaintiffs in defendant's bedroom without the consent of plaintiffs); Geraci v. Conte, No. 72440, 1998 WL 323564 (Ohio App. June 18, 1998) (one-way mirror used to observe high school students changing clothes at swimming party). New technologies, such as tiny hidden cameras and cell phones that contain cameras, no doubt will lead to an increasing number of such claims. See, e.g., "Brigid Schulte, Patients Secretly Taped by Johns Hopkins Doctor Win $190 Million Settlement but Want Answers," Washington Post (July 21, 2014), *available at* http://www.washingtonpost.com/news/local/wp/2014/07/21/betrayed-trust-patients-secretly-taped-by-doctor-win-190-million-settlement-but-want-answers/ (gynecologist surreptitiously videotaped "private parts" of patients).

Shulman v. Group W Productions, Inc.

Supreme Court of California, 1998.
18 Cal.4th 200, 74 Cal.Rptr.2d 843, 955 P.2d 469.

* * *   [See *supra* pages 932–934 for facts and procedural history of case.]

Of the four privacy torts identified by Prosser, the tort of intrusion into private places, conversations or matter is perhaps the one that best captures the common understanding of an "invasion of privacy." It encompasses unconsented-to physical intrusion into the home, hospital room or other place the privacy of which is legally recognized, as well as unwarranted sensory intrusions such as eavesdropping, wiretapping, and visual or photographic spying. See Restatement (Second) of Torts § 652B cmt. b. and illustrations. It is in the intrusion cases that invasion of privacy is most clearly seen as an affront to individual dignity. "[A] measure of personal isolation and personal control over the conditions of its abandonment is of the very essence of personal freedom and dignity, is part of what our culture means by these concepts. A man whose home may be entered at the will of another, whose conversations may be overheard at the will of another, whose marital and familial intimacies may be overseen at the will of another, is less of a man, has less human dignity, on that account. He who may intrude upon another at will is the master of the other and, in fact, intrusion is a primary weapon of the tyrant." Edward J. Bloustein, Privacy as an Aspect of Human Dignity: An Answer to Dean Prosser, 39 N.Y.U. L. Rev. 962, 973–74 (1964). *

Despite its conceptual centrality, the intrusion tort has received less judicial attention than the private facts tort, and its parameters are less clearly defined. The leading California decision is Miller v. National Broadcasting Co., 187 Cal.App.3d 1463, 232 Cal.Rptr. 668 (1986).

Miller, which like the present case involved a news organization's videotaping the work of emergency medical personnel, adopted the Restatement's formulation of the cause of action: "One who intentionally intrudes, physically or otherwise, upon the solitude or seclusion of another or his private affairs or concerns, is subject to liability to the other for invasion of his privacy, if the intrusion would be highly offensive to a reasonable person." Restatement (Second) of Torts § 652B; *Miller,* 187 Cal.App.3d at 1482, 232 Cal.Rptr. at 678.

As stated in *Miller* and the Restatement, therefore, the action for intrusion has two elements: (1) intrusion into a private place, conversation or matter, (2) in a manner highly offensive to a reasonable person. We consider the elements in that order.

We ask first whether defendants "intentionally intrude[d], physically or otherwise, upon the solitude or seclusion of another," that is, into a place or conversation private to Wayne or Ruth. * "[T]here is no liability for the examination of a public record concerning the plaintiff . . . [or] for observing him or even taking his photograph while he is walking on the public highway. . . . " Restatement § 652B cmt. c. * To prove actionable intrusion, the plaintiff must show the defendant penetrated some zone of physical or sensory privacy surrounding, or obtained unwanted access to data about, the plaintiff. The tort is proven only if the plaintiff had an objectively reasonable expectation of seclusion or solitude in the place, conversation or data source. *

Cameraman Cooke's mere presence at the accident scene and filming of the events occurring there cannot be deemed either a physical or sensory intrusion on plaintiffs' seclusion. Plaintiffs had no right of ownership or possession of the property where the rescue took place, nor any actual control of the premises. Nor could they have had a reasonable expectation that members of the media would be excluded or prevented from photographing the scene; for journalists to attend and record the scenes of accidents and rescues is in no way unusual or unexpected. *

Two aspects of defendants' conduct, however, raise triable issues of intrusion on seclusion. First, a triable issue exists as to whether both plaintiffs had an objectively reasonable expectation of privacy in the interior of the rescue helicopter, which served as an ambulance. Although the attendance of reporters and photographers at the scene of an accident is to be expected, we are aware of no law or custom permitting the press to ride in ambulances or enter hospital rooms during treatment without the patient's consent. * Other than the two patients and Cooke, only three people were present in the helicopter, all Mercy Air staff. As the Court of Appeal observed, "[i]t is neither the custom nor the habit of our society that any member of the public at large or its media representatives may hitch a ride in an ambulance and ogle as paramedics care for an injured stranger." *

Second, Ruth was entitled to a degree of privacy in her conversations with Carnahan and other medical rescuers at the accident scene, and in Carnahan's conversations conveying medical information regarding Ruth to the hospital base. Cooke, perhaps, did not intrude into that zone of privacy merely by being present at a place where he could hear such conversations with unaided ears. But by placing a microphone on Carnahan's person, amplifying and recording what she said and heard, defendants may have listened in on conversations the parties could reasonably have expected to be private.

The Court of Appeal held plaintiffs had no reasonable expectation of privacy at the accident scene itself because the scene was within the sight and hearing of members of the public. The summary judgment record, however, does not support the Court of Appeal's conclusion; instead, it reflects, at the least, the existence of triable issues as to the privacy of certain conversations at the accident scene, as in the helicopter. The videotapes (broadcast and raw footage) show the rescue did not take place "on a heavily traveled highway," as the Court of Appeal stated, but in a ditch many yards from and below the rural superhighway, which is raised somewhat at that point to bridge a nearby crossroad. From the tapes it appears unlikely the plaintiffs' extrication from their car and medical treatment at the scene could have been observed by any persons who, in the lower court's words, "passed by" on the roadway. Even more unlikely is that any passersby on the road could have heard Ruth's conversation with Nurse Carnahan or the other rescuers. *

Whether Ruth expected her conversations with Nurse Carnahan or the other rescuers to remain private and whether any such expectation was reasonable are, on the state of the record before us, questions for the jury. We note, however, that several existing legal protections for communications could support the conclusion that Ruth possessed a reasonable expectation of privacy in her conversations with Nurse Carnahan and the other rescuers. A patient's conversation with a provider of medical care in the course of treatment, including emergency treatment, carries a traditional and legally well-established expectation of privacy. * Moreover, California's Invasion of Privacy Act, Cal. Pen. Code, § 630–637.6, prohibits the recording of any "confidential communication" without the consent of all parties thereto. * * *

Ruth's claim, of course, does not require her to prove a statutory violation, only to prove that she had an objectively reasonable expectation of privacy in her conversations. Whether the circumstances of Ruth's extrication and helicopter rescue would reasonably have indicated to defendants, or to their agent, Cooke, that Ruth would desire and expect her communications to Carnahan and the other rescuers to be confined to them alone, and therefore not to be electronically transmitted and recorded, is a triable issue of fact in this case. * * * We cannot say, as a matter of law, that Cooke should not have perceived he might be intruding on a confidential communication when he recorded a seriously injured patient's conversations with medical personnel.

We turn to the second element of the intrusion tort, offensiveness of the intrusion. In a widely followed passage, the *Miller* court explained that determining offensiveness requires consideration of all the circumstances of the intrusion, including its degree and setting and the intruder's "motives and objectives." * The *Miller* court concluded that reasonable people could regard the camera crew's conduct in filming a man's emergency medical treatment in his home, without seeking or obtaining his or his wife's consent, as showing "a cavalier disregard for ordinary citizens' rights of privacy" and, hence, as highly offensive. * We agree with the *Miller* court that all the circumstances of an intrusion, including the motives or justification of the intruder, are pertinent to the offensiveness element. * * * Although, as will be discussed more fully later, the First Amendment does not immunize the press from liability for torts or crimes committed in an effort to gather news, * the constitutional protection of the press does reflect the strong societal interest in effective and complete reporting of events, an interest that may—as a matter of tort law—justify an intrusion that would otherwise be considered offensive. * * *

In deciding, therefore, whether a reporter's alleged intrusion into private matters (i.e., physical space, conversation or data) is "offensive" and hence actionable as an invasion of privacy, courts must consider the extent to which the intrusion was, under the circumstances, justified by the legitimate motive of gathering the news. Information-collecting techniques that may be highly offensive when done for socially unprotected reasons—for purposes of harassment, blackmail or prurient curiosity, for example—may not be offensive to a reasonable person when employed by journalists in pursuit of a socially or politically important story. * * *

The mere fact the intruder was in pursuit of a "story" does not, however, generally justify an otherwise offensive intrusion; offensiveness depends as well on the particular method of investigation used. At one extreme, " 'routine . . . reporting techniques,' " such as asking questions of people with information ("including those with confidential or restricted information") could rarely, if ever, be deemed an actionable intrusion. * At the other extreme, violation of well-established legal areas of physical or sensory privacy—trespass into a home or tapping a personal telephone line, for example—could rarely, if ever, be justified by a reporter's need to get the story. Such acts would be deemed highly offensive even if the information sought was of weighty public concern; they would also be outside any protection the Constitution provides to newsgathering. * Between these extremes lie difficult cases, many involving the use of photographic and electronic recording equipment. * * *

On this summary judgment record, we believe a jury could find defendants' recording of Ruth's communications to Carnahan and other rescuers, and filming in the air ambulance, to be " 'highly offensive to a reasonable person.' " * With regard to the depth of the intrusion, * a reasonable jury could find highly offensive the placement of a microphone on a medical rescuer in order to intercept what would otherwise be private conversations with an injured patient. In that setting, as defendants could and should have foreseen, the patient would not know her words were being recorded and would not have occasion to ask about, and object or consent to, recording. * * *

For much the same reason, a jury could reasonably regard entering and riding in an ambulance—whether on the ground or in the air—with two seriously injured patients to be an egregious intrusion on a place of expected seclusion. Again, the patients, at least in this case, were hardly in a position to keep careful watch on who was riding with them, or to inquire as to everyone's business and consent or object to their presence. A jury could reasonably believe that fundamental respect for human dignity requires the patients' anxious journey be taken only with those whose care is solely for them and out of sight of the prying eyes (or cameras) of others.

Nor can we say as a matter of law that defendants' motive—to gather usable material for a potentially newsworthy story—necessarily privileged their intrusive conduct as a matter of common law tort liability. A reasonable jury could conclude the producers' desire to get footage that would convey the "feel" of the event—the real sights and sounds of a difficult rescue—did not justify either placing a microphone on Nurse Carnahan or filming inside the rescue helicopter. Although defendants' purposes could scarcely be regarded as evil or malicious (in the colloquial sense), their behavior could, even in light of their motives, be thought to show a highly offensive lack of sensitivity and respect for plaintiffs' privacy. * A reasonable jury could find that defendants, in placing a microphone on an emergency treatment nurse and recording her conversation with a distressed, disoriented and severely injured patient, without the patient's knowledge or consent, acted with highly offensive disrespect for the patient's personal privacy comparable to, if not quite as extreme as, the disrespect and insensitivity demonstrated in *Miller.*

Turning to the question of constitutional protection for newsgathering, one finds the decisional law reflects a general rule of *nonprotection*: the press in its newsgathering activities enjoys no immunity or exemption from generally applicable laws. Cohen v. Cowles Media Co., 501 U.S. 663, 669–70, 111 S.Ct. 2513, 2518–19, 115 L.Ed.2d 586, 597 (1991); * Dietemann v. Time, Inc., 449 F.2d 245, 249 (9th Cir.1971) (First Amendment is not a license for electronic intrusion; investigative journalism can be successfully practiced without secret recording); Shevin v. Sunbeam Television Corp., 351 So.2d 723, 725–27 (Fla.1977) (* * * Florida statute prohibiting nonconsensual recording of private conversations may constitutionally be applied to news reporters). * * *

Courts have impliedly recognized that a generally applicable law might, under some circumstances, impose an "impermissible burden" on newsgathering. Miller, 187 Cal.App.3d at 1493, 232 Cal.Rptr. 668, 685 * * *. No basis exists, however, for concluding that * * * the intrusion tort places such a burden on the press, either in general or under the circumstances of this case. * * * More specifically, nothing in the record or briefing here suggests that reporting on automobile accidents and medical rescue activities depends on secretly recording accident victims' conversations with rescue personnel or on filming inside an occupied ambulance. * * *

As should be apparent from the above discussion, the constitutional protection accorded newsgathering, if any, is far narrower than the protection surrounding the publication of truthful material; consequently, the fact that a reporter may be seeking "newsworthy" material does not in itself privilege the investigatory activity. The reason for the difference is simple: The intrusion tort, unlike that for publication of private facts, does not subject the press to liability for the contents of its publications. Newsworthiness, as we stated earlier, is a complete bar to liability for publication of private facts and is evaluated with a high degree of deference to editorial judgment. The same deference is not due, however, when the issue is not the media's right to publish or broadcast what they choose, but their right to intrude into secluded areas or conversations in pursuit of publishable material. * * *

As to constitutional policy, we repeat that the threat of infringement on the liberties of the press from intrusion liability is minor compared with the threat from liability for publication of private facts. * * * [N]o constitutional precedent or principle of which we are aware gives a reporter general license to intrude in an objectively offensive manner into private places, conversations or matters merely because the reporter thinks he or she may thereby find something that will warrant publication or broadcast. * * * In contrast to the broad privilege the press enjoys for publishing truthful, newsworthy information in its possession, the press has *no* recognized constitutional privilege to violate generally applicable laws in pursuit of material. Nor, even absent an independent crime or tort, can a highly offensive intrusion into a private place, conversation, or source of information generally be justified by the plea that the intruder hoped thereby to get good material for a news story. * * *

In short, the state may not intrude into the proper sphere of the news media to dictate what they should publish and broadcast, but neither may the media play tyrant to the people by unlawfully spying on them in the name of newsgathering. Summary judgment for the defense was proper as to plaintiffs' cause of action for publication of private facts (the second cause of action), but improper as to the cause of action for invasion of privacy by intrusion (the first cause of action). * * *

NOTES

1. *Galella v. Onassis.* The widow of President John F. Kennedy was the successful plaintiff in an earlier invasion of privacy claim against someone involved in newsgathering. In Galella v. Onassis, 487 F.2d 986, 991–92 (2d Cir.1973), the defendant fancied himself as among the "paparazzi," news photographers who "make themselves as visible to the public and obnoxious to their photographic subjects as possible in order to aid in the advertisement and wide sale of their works." Over a period of years, the defendant pursued the Kennedys, jumping in the path of the plaintiff's young son riding a bicycle in Central Park, approaching the plaintiff in a power boat while she was swimming, invading the children's schools, and "jumping and posturing around while taking pictures" of the plaintiff on numerous occasion. The defendant claimed that the First Amendment provided immunity from any liability while he was gathering news. The court of appeals disagreed, and affirmed the district court's granting of an injunction prohibiting the defendant from entering a zone surrounding the plaintiff and her children, albeit restricting the zone more narrowly than the original injunction from the district court.

2. *Intrusion upon Seclusion and Workplace Privacy.* In Sanders v. American Broadcasting Companies, Inc., 20 Cal.4th 907, 912–13, 85 Cal.Rptr.2d 909, 912–13, 978 P.2d 67, 70–71 (1999), the Supreme Court of California considered a case in which an investigative reporter posed as an employee of a telepsychic operation where psychics gave readings over the telephone for which the customer was charged on a per-minute basis. The plaintiff was a psychic and co-worker who discussed his personal aspirations with the posing psychic, not recognizing she was a reporter.

These conversations were videotaped with a camera hidden in the reporter's hat and recorded with a microphone hidden in her brassiere. One conversation took place in the plaintiff's workspace, one of more than 100 similar cubicles used by the telepsychics, and the other took place in an adjoining aisle near her cubicle. The evidence showed that conversations in one cubicle could be overheard in nearby cubicles. The California Supreme Court reversed judgment for the defendant, reasoning that:

> * * * [P]rivacy, for purposes of the intrusion tort, is not a binary, all-or-nothing characteristic. There are degrees and nuances to societal recognition of our expectations of privacy: the fact that the privacy one expects in a given setting is not complete or absolute does not render the expectation unreasonable as a matter of law. * * *

> [A]n employee may, under some circumstances, have a reasonable expectation of visual or aural privacy against electronic intrusion by a stranger to the workplace, despite the possibility that the conversations and interactions at issue could be witnessed by coworkers or the employer.

3. *Testing for HIV without Patient's Consent.* In Doe v. High-Tech Inst., Inc., 972 P.2d 1060, 1071 (Colo.App.1998), the court found that the unauthorized testing of the plaintiff's blood sample for the human immunodeficiency virus (HIV) constituted an actionable intrusion upon seclusion. The plaintiff was a student in the defendant's medical assistant training program. The plaintiff informed the instructor that he had tested positive for HIV as the result of an anonymous blood test and requested that the instructor treat the information as confidential. Soon thereafter, all students were tested for rubella, and the defendant's instructor, without the plaintiff's knowledge, requested that the laboratory also test the plaintiff's blood for HIV. When the test was positive, the lab, as required by Colorado law, informed the Department of Health and the defendant. The court disregarded the defendant's argument that the plaintiff's interest affected by the intrusion upon seclusion tort ended once the blood was drawn. Instead, the court concluded:

> * * * [A] person has a privacy interest in his or her blood sample and in the medical information that may be obtained from it. * * * Although intrusion upon seclusion clearly encompasses an intrusion upon a physical space held in seclusion by a person, the element of seclusion also encompasses intrusions into a person's private concerns based upon a reasonable expectation of privacy in that area. See Phillips v. Smalley Maintenance Services, Inc., 435 So.2d 705 (Ala.1983) (intrusion by employer into employee's sexual history). * * *

The court therefore recognized a general privacy interest in one's health information. Because of the sensitivity of such information, it concluded that the unauthorized HIV test under the circumstances of the case "would be considered by a reasonable person as highly invasive, and therefore, such is sufficient to constitute an unreasonable or offensive intrusion."

C. FALSE LIGHT

Peoples Bank & Trust Co. of Mountain Home v. Globe International, Inc.

United States District Court for the Western District of Arkansas, 1992.
786 F.Supp. 791.

■ WATERS, CHIEF JUDGE. The plaintiff, Peoples Bank and Trust Company of Mountain Home, conservator of the estate of Nellie Mitchell, an aged person, by amended complaint filed September 24, 1991, brought defamation, invasion of privacy, and intentional infliction of emotional distress claims against the defendant, Globe International, Inc. d/b/a "*Sun.*" Mrs. Mitchell is a 96-year-old resident of Mountain Home, Arkansas. She has operated a newsstand on the town square since 1963. Prior to that she delivered newspapers on a paper route, and according to the evidence, still makes deliveries to certain "downtown" business establishments and select customers. It appears that Nellie, as she is known to almost everyone in this small Ozark Mountain town, is a town "landmark" or "treasure". * * *

The basis of the plaintiff's claims is an article and picture that appeared in the October 2, 1990, edition of the *Sun*. The October 2 edition published a photograph of the plaintiff in conjunction with a story entitled:

SPECIAL DELIVERY

World's oldest newspaper carrier, 101, quits because she's pregnant! *I guess walking all those miles kept me young*

The "story" purports to be about a "papergal Audrey Wiles" in Stirling, Australia, who had been delivering papers for 94 years. Readers are told that Ms. Wiles became pregnant by "Will" a "reclusive millionaire" she met on her newspaper route. "I used to put Will's paper in the door when it rained, and one thing just kind of led to another." In words that could certainly have described Nellie Mitchell, the article, which was in the form and style of a factual newspaper account, said:

[S]he's become like a city landmark because nearly everyone at one time or another has seen her trudging down the road with a large stack of papers under her arm.

A photograph of Nellie, apparently "trudging down the road with a large stack of papers under her arm" is used in conjunction with the story. The picture used in the October 2 edition of the *Sun* had been used by the defendant in a reasonably factual and accurate article about Mrs. Mitchell published in another of the defendant's publications, the *Examiner*, in 1980.

* * * The jury found that the defendant's conduct had invaded Mrs. Mitchell's privacy by placing her in a false light and had amounted to an intentional infliction of emotional distress. The jury awarded the plaintiff $650,000 in compensatory damages and $850,000 in punitive damages. The jury rendered a verdict in favor of the defendant on the defamation claim. Judgment was entered against the defendant on the jury verdict. Pending before the court is defendant's motion for judgment as a matter of law or, alternatively, for remittitur of the jury

award or, alternatively for new trial. * * * The motion will be denied for the reasons set forth below. * * *

Testimony at trial indicated that most of the defendant's articles are created "TOH" or "top of the head," in the words of John Vadar, editor of the *Sun*. That is, the authors, none of whom use their real name, are given a headline and a picture and then "make up" the accompanying stories. In fact, according to the evidence, the editor and perhaps others "make up" a series of headlines for stories to appear in each issue, and they are placed on a table. The "reporters" or perhaps, according to defendant's contentions at the trial, their "authors of fiction" select from this list the stories they wish to write.[1] John Vadar, indicated that, when the picture of Mrs. Mitchell was selected, it was assumed she was dead. The *Sun's* stated policy was to illustrate its articles with pictures of individuals from other countries who would not be damaged by the publication being circulated in the United States. The use of Mrs. Mitchell's picture was merely a "mistake."

Although defendant's contention during the trial was that Nellie Mitchell could not have been defamed because the publication contained only fiction readily recognized as such by reasonable readers, some of its "authors" testified that some of the articles were factual or at least based on fact, and it became obvious that even they could not tell the difference. Some of defendant's own witnesses could not agree which articles were purely fantasy and which were true or at least had some factual basis. * * *

With regard to the extent of emotional distress suffered by Mrs. Mitchell, she testified that she was mad, upset, embarrassed, and humiliated by the article. Further, Mrs. Mitchell indicated she had been teased about being pregnant. Betty Mitchell, Nellie Mitchell's daughter, testified that her mother "almost suffered a stroke." There was also testimony to the effect that Mrs. Mitchell attempted to buy up the papers so others could not see them. * * *

It may be, as defendant in essence argues, that Mrs. Mitchell does not show a great deal of obvious injury, but a reasonable juror might conclude, after hearing the evidence and viewing the *Sun* issue in question, that Nellie Mitchell's experience could be likened to that of a person who had been dragged slowly through a pile of untreated sewage. After that person had showered and a few weeks have passed, there would be little remaining visible evidence of the ordeal which the person had endured and the resulting damages incurred, but few would doubt that substantial damage had been inflicted by the one doing the dragging. * * * The court concludes that reasonable jurors could find that it is "worth" a great deal to suddenly find your likeness buried in the slime of which this publication was made, directly in front of an article describing the relative tastiness of adult human flesh compared to that of children. * * *

---

[1] In this respect, Paul Greenberg, Pulitzer-prize winning journalist[,] testified in a deposition used as evidence in this case, while being questioned by defendant's attorney:

> Q. If the author testifies that he made up a story, isn't that fiction?
>
> A. Sir, it's false. All things that are false are not necessarily fiction.
>
> Q. Tell me the difference between "false" and "fiction."
>
> A. I can give you an illustration. William Faulkner wrote fiction. *Pravda* published falsehoods.

[T]he Arkansas Supreme Court has specifically adopted a cause of action for false light invasion of privacy and has held that both a defamation claim and a false light claim may be brought in the same suit. In Dodrill v. Arkansas Democrat Co., 265 Ark. 628, 590 S.W.2d 840 (1979), cert. denied, 444 U.S. 1076, 100 S.Ct. 1024, 62 L.Ed.2d 759 (1980), * * * the plaintiff had asserted both a defamation claim and a false light invasion of privacy claim. The court noted that "[t]he invasion of privacy claim stands upon a different footing than the defamation claim." * The court further noted:

> The right to recover for an invasion of privacy is conditioned upon the complaining party's demonstrating that (1) the false light in which he was placed by the publicity would be highly offensive to a reasonable person, and (2) that the defendant had knowledge of or acted in reckless disregard as to the falsity of the publicized matter and the false light in which the plaintiff would be placed. . . . A cause of action both for "false light" invasion of privacy and for defamation can be joined in the same action. . . . However, there can be but one recovery for any particular publication. . . . *

The court further held that in light of Time, Inc. v. Hill, 385 U.S. 374, 87 S.Ct. 534, 17 L.Ed.2d 456 (1967) [which prohibited recovery for "false reports of matters of public interest in the absence of proof that the defendant published the report with knowledge of its falsity or in reckless disregard of the truth"], "actual malice must be demonstrated by one seeking to recover for invasion of privacy." * * *

Defendant's second and third arguments both concern the actual malice standard as applied in this case. Defendant concedes that the court properly instructed the jury on the definition of actual malice. However, defendant argues that there was no evidence of intentional conduct on the part of *Globe*. * * *

In this latter argument the defendant appears to ignore the reckless prong of the definition of actual malice. * * * [A]ctual malice [in the circumstances of this case is] defined as intentional conduct or conduct that "recklessly failed to anticipate, that readers could construe the publicized matter as conveying actual facts or events concerning Mrs. Mitchell." Plaintiff argues that the defendant's method of publishing—not distinguishing between truth or fiction, off the top of their head, out of whole cloth—demonstrates at the very least reckless disregard. * * * After hearing the testimony in this case, the court believes the jury could have, and apparently did, find that the defendant intended their readers to construe the article in question as conveying actual facts or events concerning Mrs. Mitchell or at the very least that the defendant recklessly failed to anticipate that the article would be so construed. The court believes the publication methods utilized by the defendant make it reasonable for the jury to draw such a conclusion. After all, as already noted, there was evidence from which the jury could believe that defendant's own employees who actually wrote the articles, when asked, couldn't always tell the difference between fact and fantasy.

The defendant could very easily indicate to its readers in some fashion that the material conveyed in the *Sun* is fiction if it really intended that its readers recognize that the articles are false and made up fantasy. The court believes that it could be inferred from the manner of publication that the defendant intends its readers to believe its articles are conveying actual facts or at the very least leave the reader in doubt as to what portions are factual and what portions are pure fantasy.[4]

Additionally, the defendant argues the jury verdicts are inconsistent since the jury found in its favor on the defamation claim. Defendant argues that it is inconsistent to find no defamation but find false light because both required a finding that the statement could be understood as describing actual facts or events concerning the plaintiff, or actual conduct of the plaintiff. * In the defamation claim this was made one of the essential elements of the claim. * With regard to the false light claim, this requirement was incorporated into the definition of actual malice as follows: "actual malice means that Globe International intended, or recklessly failed to anticipate, that readers would construe the publicized matter as conveying actual facts or events concerning Mrs. Mitchell. A finding of actual malice requires more than mere negligence."

Although it is true that both defamation and false light required a similar finding that the matter could be construed as conveying actual facts or events concerning the plaintiff, the other elements of the offenses were different. False light contains only two elements: (1) that the false light in which she was placed by the publicity would be highly offensive to a reasonable person, and (2) actual malice * * *. The definition of defamatory statement, Instruction Number 8, stated, *inter alia,* "a publication is defamatory if it exposes a person to public hatred, contempt and ridicule, or if it causes him or her to be shunned or avoided. In other words, a statement is defamatory if it tends to harm the reputation of that person so as to lower him or her in the esteem of the community, or to deter others from associating or dealing with him or her."

The jury could easily have found the statements at issue to be highly offensive and yet not defamatory as the term was defined. Additionally, the two torts, although very similar, do protect, or at least are meant to protect, different interests. * * *

The court believes and finds that there was ample evidence to warrant submission of this issue to the jury. Certainly, reasonable minds could differ and the court will not substitute its own judgment for that of the jury.[a] * * *

---

[4] Although the court would certainly not allow a newspaper poll to affect in any way its judgment in this matter, it is interesting to note the responses to a poll contained in the December 10, 1991, issue of the *Arkansas Democrat-Gazette.* Readers were asked: "Do you believe the stories in the supermarket tabloids are real?" The response: Yes—53.1%, No—46.9%. While the article reporting the poll contained the disclaimer that it did not purport to be a "scientific survey and reflects only the opinion of those who choose to participate," it at least indicates that over one-half of those who bothered to respond either believed articles in supermarket tabloids to be true or lied about it. It, of course, might be that only people who read and believe supermarket tabloids respond to call[s] in telephone polls.

[a] [Eds.' note] The Eighth Circuit Court of Appeals affirmed the district court's judgment in all respects except it found that the trial court committed an abuse of discretion in failing to grant a remittitur on the compensatory damages award of $650,000. The court of appeals upheld the punitive damage award of $850,000. 978 F.2d 1065 (8th Cir.1992). On remand, the

Machleder v. Diaz

United States Court of Appeals for the Second Circuit, 1986.
801 F.2d 46.

■ CARDAMONE, CIRCUIT JUDGE. * * * On May 22, 1979 WCBS-TV, a Manhattan television station owned and operated by CBS, Inc. (CBS), aired a report on its 6 o'clock news dealing with the dumping of toxic chemicals at a site in Newark, New Jersey. The broadcast highlighted the investigation of CBS reporter Arnold Diaz, then WCBS-TV's New Jersey investigative correspondent, and focused on his interview with plaintiff, Irving Machleder, the owner of a company that uses hazardous chemicals in its blending operations. As a result of this broadcast, Machleder brought a diversity action in the United States District Court for the Southern District of New York (Duffy, J.) alleging libel [and] false light invasion of privacy * * *. A district court jury awarded the plaintiff $250,000 in compensatory damages and $1,000,000 in punitive damages on his false light privacy claim.

The invasion of Machleder's privacy that he claims cast him in a false light arose from what plaintiff alleges was Diaz' "ambush" or "confrontational" interview. Ambush interview is a derogatory descriptive term for a controversial investigative reporting technique in which a reporter and his news crew intercept an "unsuspecting newsworthy subject on the street and [bombard] him with incriminating accusations ostensibly framed as questions." Note, The Ambush Interview: A False Light Invasion of Privacy?, 34 Case W. Res. L. Rev. 72, 72 (1983). * * *

[Defendant Diaz and his film crew observed hundreds of rusting drums, many marked "hazardous" and "flammable" on a lot overgrown with weeds. Some of the barrels leaked into a nearby waterway, and the area stank. Defendant and his film crew believed that the drums were on property owned by Flexcraft, and he advanced toward the Flexcraft plant.]

* * * Diaz approached Irving Machleder—with audio and video cameras rolling—and asked him if he knew anything about the chemical barrels dumped next to his building. Machleder replied that he did not want to be filmed for television and began to move away. Diaz and his crew followed. Machleder became agitated, shouting "get that damn camera out of here. . . . I don't want, I don't need, I don't need any publicity." When Machleder reached the door of his office he said to Diaz, "We don't . . . we didn't dump 'em;" Diaz asked, "Who did?" and Machleder responded, "You call the Housing Department. They have all the information." According to Diaz, he was then invited into the office by Bruce Machleder [Irving's brother], who told him that the presence of the barrels had previously been reported to the [authorities]. * * * That evening Diaz' report, as noted, was televised on WCBS-TV's 6 o'clock Report. * * *

On May 29, 1979 Machleder's attorney sent a letter to CBS demanding a retraction of the Diaz Report and, when CBS refused to

---

district court—somewhat reluctantly—granted a substantial remittitur in the amount of $500,000, leaving a compensatory damage award of $150,000. 817 F.Supp. 72 (W.D.Ark.1993).

retract any part of it, the present litigation was commenced. * * * Ruling on post-trial motions * * *, the district court held *, that the jury's compensatory award of $250,000 on the false light invasion of privacy claim was neither excessive nor outrageous, that CBS acted with actual malice in broadcasting the report, and that the punitive damage award of $1,000,000 was not excessive. CBS appeals from the compensatory and punitive damages verdict awarded by the jury for the false light invasion of privacy claim. * * * No appeal has been taken from the district court's dismissal of Machleder's libel claim after the jury rendered a verdict in favor of CBS * * *.

* * * To establish a false light cause of action the published matter must be false—and, in addition, it must be highly offensive to a reasonable person. * * * The first requirement is that the published material contain a false portrayal. The very name of this tort, *"false light,"* indicates that something false must be demonstrated, and the commentators agree that falsity must be shown to state a false light cause of action. * Restatement (Second) of Torts § 652E cmt. b (1977). For 150 years the common law of England recognized the tort of false light invasion of a person's privacy and required a showing of falsity before an injunction would issue. In Byron v. Johnston, 35 Eng.Rep. 851 (1816), a publisher advertised for sale certain poems that he represented as being the work of the famous English poet, Lord Byron who, as plaintiff, succeeded in obtaining an injunction restraining their publication because the poems were falsely held out to be his works. Moreover, we recently held that "[I]n a false light case . . . the gravamen of the tort is falsity. . . . " Lerman v. Flynt Distributing Co., Inc., 745 F.2d 123, 135 (2d Cir.1984), cert. denied, 471 U.S. 1054, 105 S.Ct. 2114, 85 L.Ed.2d 479 (1985).

It follows logically that if falsity is required to state a false light claim, truth must be a defense. It is at this pivotal juncture that a false light claim parts from the other three invasions of an individual's right to privacy—intrusion, public exposure of private facts and appropriation—and moves closer to the common law tort of defamation. * * * [T]ruth—as it is in defamation—is a complete defense to a false light invasion of privacy cause of action. See Cox Broadcasting Corp. v. Cohn, 420 U.S. 469, 498–99, 95 S.Ct. 1029, 1047–48, 43 L.Ed.2d 328, 351–52 (1975) (Powell, J., concurring).

New Jersey has adopted the common law approach set forth in the Restatement (Second) of Torts § 652E which requires falsity to sustain a cause of action for false light invasion of privacy. * Section 652E of the Restatement provides:

> One who gives publicity to a matter concerning another that places the other before the public in a false light is subject to liability to the other for invasion of his privacy, if
>
> (a) the false light in which the other was placed would be highly offensive to a reasonable person, and
>
> (b) the actor had knowledge of or acted in reckless disregard *as to the falsity of the publicized matter and the false light in which the other would be placed.* (emphasis added).

For liability to attach under Section 652E the published matter must be false, though not necessarily defamatory. * Comment *a* to

§ 652E states, "[I]t is essential to the rules stated in this Section that the matter published concerning the plaintiff is not true." * * *

In order for a plaintiff to succeed on a false light claim without unduly impinging on the First Amendment guarantees of freedom of the press, falsity and the requisite level of fault must be demonstrated. In Time, Inc. v. Hill, 385 U.S. at 374, 87 S.Ct. at 534, the Supreme Court considered a false light invasion of privacy action involving a New York statute which provided a cause of action to a person whose name or picture was used by another without consent for purposes of trade or advertising. It ruled that "the constitutional protections for speech and press preclude the application of the New York statute to redress *false reports* of matters of public interest in the absence of proof that the defendant published the report with knowledge of its falsity or in reckless disregard of the truth." * Because the New York courts had construed the relevant statute to allow truth as a complete defense when the publication involved a matter of public interest, the Court did not address whether the First Amendment would be violated if truth were not a defense to this kind of privacy claim. Yet, because the fault standard devised by the Court requires knowledge of or reckless disregard of falsity, the logic seems inescapable that the First Amendment also requires a plaintiff to prove falsity. * * *

Regardless of the particular fault standard to be applied, it is clear that when publishing or broadcasting a newsworthy matter of public interest a media defendant may not be held liable for the tort of false light invasion of a person's privacy without proof of falsity and some level of fault. Cf. Philadelphia Newspapers, Inc. v. Hepps, 475 U.S. 767, 106 S.Ct. 1558, 89 L. Ed.2d 783 (1986) (First Amendment requires a plaintiff to prove falsity in defamation cases. Falsity may never be presumed nor may defendant be required to prove truth.). * * *

Irving Machleder asserts that CBS deliberately created a false light portrayal of him in order to sensationalize an "otherwise uneventful story." He argues that, in furtherance of this goal, CBS selectively chose those parts of the interview that tended to portray him as intemperate and evasive or as an illegal dumper, and excised those portions that would explain his behavior. For example, Machleder pointed out that CBS cut from the news report his statement, "I don't want to be on television, I'm sorry, I'm sorry," preferring the subsequent more hostile and incriminating statement, "Get that damn camera out of here." He maintains that had the broadcast included the earlier statement, the viewing audience would have understood the later statement to be the result of intimidation and pressure rather than an implied admission of guilt. Although plaintiff's argument has superficial merit, recovery for a false light tort may not be predicated on a rule that holds a media defendant liable for broadcasting truthful statements and actions because it failed to include additional facts which might have cast the plaintiff in a more favorable or balanced light. * * * A court cannot substitute its judgment for that of the press by requiring the press to present an article or broadcast in what the court believes is a balanced manner. It may only assess liability when the press so oversteps its editorial freedom that it contains falsity and does so with the requisite degree of fault. * * *

Having established that principle, we turn to examine whether any vitality remains in the false light privacy tort when injury to reputation is at stake. Because both the defamation and false light privacy torts share the common elements of publication and falsity, a good deal of overlapping exists between them. But important distinctions remain so that the answer to the question of whether the older tort claim has swallowed whole the newer is "no". Yet, in many cases a successful false light claim might also give rise to liability for defamation. For example, while a false light claim may be defamatory, it need not be. * Further, false light law makes no distinction between oral or written words as defamation does. Nor is there a distinction in privacy invasion false light cases between slander *per se* and slander requiring proof of special damages. * * *

With the above principles in mind we turn to the facts of this case. The first issue to be addressed is whether the news account giving rise to the claim was false. In order to answer this question, we begin by examining the trial court's charge to the jury on defamation and false light, and then scrutinizing the jury verdict sheet. * * * There is one theory for reconciling the jury's verdict as to the false light claim and the libel claim. In support of his false light claim, the plaintiff alleged that the broadcast portrayed him as intemperate and evasive *or* as an illegal dumper. In contrast, his defamation claim was based on the allegation that he was portrayed as an illegal dumper. Thus, the jury could have found that the plaintiff was an illegal dumper, but was not, as portrayed, intemperate and evasive. * * *

Here we find that the evidence was insufficient. Any portrayal of plaintiff as intemperate and evasive could not be false since it was based on his own conduct which was accurately captured by the cameras. Further, the only evidence on plaintiff's temperment [sic] came from a business associate who, though he had done business with the plaintiff, saw Machleder only for 15 minutes every three months. This was clearly insufficient evidence to establish that the film showing plaintiff's actions depicted him in a false light. Since proof of falsity was required, and the film footage (virtually unedited except for omission from the interview of plaintiff's statement, "I don't want to be on television, I'm sorry, I'm sorry," according to CBS's uncontroverted allegation) was accurate, the false light claim must fail.

Having found that the district court erred in not granting defendant's judgment notwithstanding the verdict, we discuss briefly whether the published matter was highly offensive to a reasonable person, merely to indicate that a portrayal of this type—even had it been false—would not give rise to liability on a false light claim.

Comment *c* to the Restatement of Torts § 652E makes clear that "[i]t is only when there is such a major misrepresentation of his character, history, activities or beliefs that serious offense may reasonably be expected to be taken by a reasonable man in his position, that there is a cause of action for invasion of privacy." *

We hold that the district court that ruled on the motions erred in concluding that the "alleged portrayal of Machleder as intemperate and evasive in response to Diaz's questions [could not] be deemed inoffensive as a matter of law," * and in denying summary judgment on the false light claim on that basis. By the same token, the trial court erred in denying CBS' motions for a directed verdict and judgment notwithstanding the verdict since no reasonable juror could have concluded that the alleged portrayal was highly offensive. * * *

In order to avoid a head-on collision with First Amendment rights, courts have narrowly construed the highly offensive standard. A brief review of several cases illustrates that the alleged portrayal of Irving Machleder as intemperate and evasive fails to meet such standard. Those decisions that have found false light portrayals offensive to a reasonable person are considerably more insulting than CBS's portrayal of Irving Machleder. * Time, Inc. v. Hill, 385 U.S. at 378, 87 S.Ct. at 537 (false portrayal of family held hostage, depicting violence and verbal sexual insult); Douglass v. Hustler Magazine, Inc., 769 F.2d 1128 (7th Cir.1985) (unauthorized use of model's nude photograph in *Hustler* Magazine falsely portrayed her as a lesbian and willing to be associated with *Hustler* magazine). Again, courts have declined to recognize portrayals as highly offensive in cases more egregious than Machleder's. * * *

Because the jury found in plaintiff's libel action that the defamatory statements, i.e., of illegal dumping, were not substantially false, the illegal dumping portrayal will not support a false light verdict. As a matter of law, we conclude that the portrayal of Irving Machleder as intemperate and evasive is not false and is not highly offensive to a reasonable person. Thus, on either ground a finding of liability for false light invasion of privacy must be reversed and the action dismissed. * * * The judgment of the district court awarding compensatory and punitive damages for a false light invasion of privacy is reversed and plaintiff's complaint dismissed. * * *

NOTE

Continued Recognition as a Separate Tort. Does the false light category add anything significant to the substantive law of privacy? A false statement may, of course, constitute defamation or an injurious falsehood. If it does neither of these things, it might nevertheless invade a person's privacy if it recites a fact that, *if true,* would constitute an unjustified disclosure of private matters. Is that not the only thing that would render the statement actionable *as an invasion of privacy*? And if so, does the false light concept deserve separate recognition as a branch of the law of privacy?

When we come to constitutional privilege, however, falsity may assume importance. If the fact disclosed is a matter of public interest and therefore protected by the First Amendment, a state may not hold it actionable unless the statement of purported fact was knowingly false or made with reckless disregard of its truth or falsity, or perhaps meets lower *Gertz* standards, *supra* 912–919, all of which would include a requirement that the statement must be false. See Philadelphia Newspapers, Inc. v. Hepps, *supra* pages 923–925.

A distinction between the interests protected by defamation and false light torts is suggested by Gary T. Schwartz, Explaining and Justifying a Limited Tort of False Light Invasion of Privacy, 41 Case W. Res. L. Rev. 885, 898 (1991):

In a defamation action, the plaintiff complains that the defendant's statement has diminished his reputation; the statement's falsity comes in by showing that this diminution is not justified. In a false light action, the defendant's falsehood brings about a mismatch or conflict between the plaintiff's actual identity and his identity in the minds of others, a conflict that itself can be offensive or disorienting.

The filming of the humorous but controversial, commercially released movie *Borat*, spawned both false light and appropriation claims. The lead character, Borat, is a citizen of Kazakhstan who travels to the United States at the request of his government to film a documentary about life in America, with the goal of improving the culture of his own country. During the film, Borat interacts with many Americans in varying contexts, none of whom know that he really is an actor. In one scene, Borat attends an actual Pentecostal religious camp meeting and acts as though he has been converted and begins to speak in tongues. The plaintiff in *Johnston v. One American Productions, Inc.*, who was a real life participant at the meeting (not an actress) and was unaware that Borat was an actor playing a role, is shown as she raises her "arms in praise to God for Borat's conversion." Johnston v. One America Prods., Inc., Civil Action No. 2:07CV042–P–B, 2007 WL 2433927 at *1 (N.D.Miss. August 22, 2007). The movie, at this point, arguably appears to be mocking the religious observance. The parties disagreed as to whether the plaintiff was placed in a false light:

> The defendants argue that the plaintiff was not portrayed in a false light because it is true that she voluntarily raised her hands [in] religious praise in response to the character Borat's apparent conversion to her religion. The plaintiff counters, however, that the issue is not whether she does and did raise her hands in praise upon the conversion of another; rather, the issue is whether she is reasonable to believe that viewers of the movie would question whether she knowingly and voluntarily participated in a mocking of her religion.

The court denied the defendants' motion to dismiss the claim, concluding that there were jury questions of

(1)   whether the Pentecostal scene portraying the plaintiff waving her arms in religious praise in response to Borat's apparent conversion would be highly objectionable to a reasonable person in the plaintiff's position, * such that a person in the plaintiff's position would believe others would believe she willingly participated in a mocking of her religion; and

(2)   whether "the defendant [knew] that the plaintiff, as a reasonable [person], would be justified in the eyes of the community in feeling seriously offended and aggrieved by the publicity." * * *

Are *Diaz* and *Johnston* distinguishable?

In recent decades, cases in which the plaintiff actually recovers on the false light tort, such as Peoples Bank & Trust Co. of Mountain Home v. Globe International, Inc., *supra*, are rare. Many states explicitly have rejected recognition of the false light tort. E.g., Jews for Jesus, Inc. v. Rapp, 997 So.2d 1098, 1100 (Fla.2008) (declining to recognize tort because it is "largely duplicative of defamation" but "without many of the First Amendment protections"); Renwick v. News & Observer Publ'g Co., 310 N.C. 312, 326, 312 S.E.2d 405, 413 (1984) (false light tort is "constitutionally suspect").

D. APPROPRIATION

White v. Samsung Electronics America, Inc.
United States Court of Appeals for the Ninth Circuit, 1992.
971 F.2d 1395.

■ GOODWIN, SENIOR CIRCUIT JUDGE. * * * Plaintiff Vanna White is the hostess of "Wheel of Fortune," one of the most popular game shows in television history. An estimated forty million people watch the program daily. Capitalizing on the fame which her participation in the show has bestowed on her, White markets her identity to various advertisers.

The dispute in this case arose out of a series of advertisements prepared for Samsung by Deutsch. The series ran in at least half a dozen publications with widespread, and in some cases national, circulation. Each of the advertisements in the series followed the same theme. Each depicted a current item from popular culture and a Samsung electronic product. Each was set in the twenty-first century and conveyed the message that the Samsung product would still be in use by that time. By hypothesizing outrageous future outcomes for the cultural items, the ads created humorous effects. For example, one lampooned current popular notions of an unhealthy diet by depicting a raw steak with the caption: "Revealed to be health food. 2010 A.D." * * *

The advertisement which prompted the current dispute was for Samsung video-cassette recorders (VCRs). The ad depicted a robot, dressed in a wig, gown, and jewelry which Deutsch consciously selected to resemble White's hair and dress. The robot was posed next to a game board which is instantly recognizable as the Wheel of Fortune game show set, in a stance for which White is famous. The caption of the ad read: "Longest-running game show. 2012 A.D." Defendants referred to the ad as the "Vanna White" ad. Unlike the other celebrities used in the campaign, White neither consented to the ads nor was she paid.

Following the circulation of the robot ad, White sued Samsung and Deutsch in federal district court under * * * the California common law right of publicity * * *. The district court granted summary judgment against White * * *.

White next argues that the district court erred in granting summary judgment to defendants on White's common law right of publicity claim. In Eastwood v. Superior Court, 149 Cal.App.3d 409, 417, 198 Cal.Rptr. 342, 347 (1983), the California court of appeal stated that the common law right of publicity cause of action "may be pleaded by alleging (1) the defendant's use of the plaintiff's identity; (2) the appropriation of plaintiff's name or likeness to defendant's advantage, commercially or otherwise; (3) lack of consent; and (4) resulting injury." The district court dismissed White's claim for failure to satisfy *Eastwood's* second prong, reasoning that defendants had not appropriated White's "name or likeness" with their robot ad. We agree that the robot ad did not make use of White's name or likeness. However, the common law right of publicity is not so confined. The *Eastwood* court did not hold that the right of publicity cause of action could be pleaded only by alleging an appropriation of name or likeness. *Eastwood* involved an unauthorized use of photographs of Clint Eastwood and of his name. Accordingly, the *Eastwood* court had no occasion to consider the extent beyond the use of name or likeness to which the right of publicity reaches. That court held only that the right of publicity cause of action "may be" pleaded by alleging, *inter alia,* appropriation of name or likeness, not that the action may be pleaded *only* in those terms.

The "name or likeness" formulation referred to in *Eastwood* originated not as an element of the right of publicity cause of action, but as a description of the types of cases in which the cause of action had been recognized. The source of this formulation is Prosser, Privacy, 48 Cal. L. Rev. 383, 401–07 (1960), one of the earliest and most enduring articulations of the common law right of publicity cause of action. In looking at the case law to that point, Prosser recognized that right of publicity cases involved one of two basic factual scenarios: name appropriation, and picture or other likeness appropriation. Even though Prosser focused on appropriations of name or likeness in discussing the right of publicity, he noted that "[i]t is not impossible that there might be appropriation of the plaintiff's identity, as by impersonation, without the use of either his name or his likeness, and that this would be an invasion of his right of privacy." At the time Prosser wrote, he noted however, that "[n]o such case appears to have arisen."

Since Prosser's early formulation, the case law has borne out his insight that the right of publicity is not limited to the appropriation of name or likeness. * * * In Carson v. Here's Johnny Portable Toilets, Inc., 698 F.2d 831 (6th Cir.1983), the defendant had marketed portable toilets under the brand name "Here's Johnny"—Johnny Carson's signature "Tonight Show" introduction—without Carson's permission. The district court had dismissed Carson's Michigan common law right of publicity claim because the defendants had not used Carson's "name or likeness." In reversing the district court, the sixth circuit found "the district court's conception of the right of publicity . . . too narrow" and held that the right was implicated because the defendant had appropriated Carson's identity by using, *inter alia,* the phrase "Here's Johnny."

These cases teach not only that the common law right of publicity reaches means of appropriation other than name or likeness, but that the specific means of appropriation are relevant only for determining whether the defendant has in fact appropriated the plaintiff's identity. The right of publicity does not require that appropriations of identity be accomplished through particular means to be actionable. * * *

Although the defendants in these cases avoided the most obvious means of appropriating the plaintiffs' identities, each of their actions directly implicated the commercial interests which the right of publicity is designed to protect. As the *Carson* court explained:

> [t]he right of publicity has developed to protect the commercial interest of celebrities in their identities. The theory of the right is that a celebrity's identity can be valuable in the promotion of

products, and the celebrity has an interest that may be protected from the unauthorized commercial exploitation of that identity. . . . If the celebrity's identity is commercially exploited, there has been an invasion of his right whether or not his "name or likeness" is used.

It is not important *how* the defendant has appropriated the plaintiff's identity, but *whether* the defendant has done so. * * * A rule which says that the right of publicity can be infringed only through the use of nine different methods of appropriating identity merely challenges the clever advertising strategist to come up with the tenth.

Indeed, if we treated the means of appropriation as dispositive in our analysis of the right of publicity, we would not only weaken the right but effectively eviscerate it. The right would fail to protect those plaintiffs most in need of its protection. Advertisers use celebrities to promote their products. The more popular the celebrity, the greater the number of people who recognize her, and the greater the visibility for the product. The identities of the most popular celebrities are not only the most attractive for advertisers, but also the easiest to evoke without resorting to obvious means such as name, likeness, or voice. * * *

Viewed separately, the individual aspects of the advertisement in the present case say little. Viewed together, they leave little doubt about the celebrity the ad is meant to depict. The female-shaped robot is wearing a long gown, blond wig, and large jewelry. Vanna White dresses exactly like this at times, but so do many other women. The robot is in the process of turning a block letter on a game-board. Vanna White dresses like this while turning letters on a game-board but perhaps similarly attired Scrabble-playing women do this as well. The robot is standing on what looks to be the Wheel of Fortune game show set. Vanna White dresses like this, turns letters, and does this on the Wheel of Fortune game show. She is the only one. Indeed, defendants themselves referred to their ad as the "Vanna White" ad. We are not surprised.

Television and other media create marketable celebrity identity value. Considerable energy and ingenuity are expended by those who have achieved celebrity value to exploit it for profit. The law protects the celebrity's sole right to exploit this value whether the celebrity has achieved her fame out of rare ability, dumb luck, or a combination thereof. We decline Samsung and Deutch's invitation to permit the evisceration of the common law right of publicity through means as facile as those in this case. Because White has alleged facts showing that Samsung and Deutsch had appropriated her identity, the district court erred by rejecting, on summary judgment, White's common law right of publicity claim. * * *

IV. The Parody Defense

In defense, defendants cite a number of cases for the proposition that their robot ad constituted protected speech. The only cases they cite which are even remotely relevant to this case are Hustler Magazine v. Falwell, 485 U.S. 46, 108 S.Ct. 876, 99 L.Ed.2d 41 (1988) and L.L. Bean, Inc. v. Drake Publishers, Inc., 811 F.2d 26 (1st Cir.1987). Those cases involved parodies of advertisements run for the purpose of poking fun at Jerry Falwell and L.L. Bean, respectively. This case involves a true advertisement run for the purpose of selling Samsung VCRs. The ad's spoof of Vanna White and Wheel of Fortune is subservient and only tangentially related to the ad's primary message: "buy Samsung VCRs." Defendants' parody arguments are better addressed to non-commercial parodies. * The difference between a "parody" and a "knock-off" is the difference between fun and profit.

In remanding this case, we hold only that White has pleaded claims which can go to the jury for its decision. * * *

Comedy III Productions, Inc. v. Gary Saderup, Inc.

Supreme Court of California, 2001.
25 Cal. 4th 387, 106 Cal. Rptr. 2d 126, 21 P.3d 797.

■ MOSK, J.   * * * Plaintiff Comedy III Productions, Inc. (hereafter Comedy III), brought this action against defendants Gary Saderup and Gary Saderup, Inc. (hereafter collectively Saderup), seeking damages and injunctive relief for violation of section 990 and related business torts.* * *

[The California Supreme Court previously held that the statutory right to publicity, "derived from the law of privacy, did not survive the death of the person whose identity was exploited and was not descendible to his or her heirs of assignees." The Legislature responded by enacting Section 990 that provides, "Any person who uses a deceased personality's name, voice, signature, photograph, or likeness, in any manner, on or in products, merchandise or goods, or for purposes of advertising or selling, or soliciting purchases of, products, merchandise, goods, or services, without prior consent * * * shall be liable for any damages * * *.]

Comedy III is the registered owner of all rights to the former comedy act known as *The Three Stooges*, who are deceased personalities within the meaning of the statute. Saderup is an artist with over 25 years' experience in making charcoal drawings of celebrities. * * * Without securing Comedy III's consent, Saderup sold lithographs and T-shirts bearing a likeness of *The Three Stooges* reproduced from a charcoal drawing he had made. These lithographs and T-shirts did not constitute an advertisement, endorsement, or sponsorship of any product. * * *

Saderup contends the statute applies only to uses of a deceased personality's name, voice, photograph, etc., for the purpose of advertising, selling, or soliciting the purchase of, products or services. He then stresses * * * that the lithographs and T-shirts at issue in this case did not constitute an advertisement, endorsement, or sponsorship of any product. He concludes the statute therefore does not apply in the case at bar. As will appear, the major premise of his argument—his construction of the statute—is unpersuasive. * * * We * * * give effect to the plain meaning of the statute: it makes liable any person who, without consent, uses a deceased personality's name, voice, photograph, etc., either (1) "on or in" a product, *or* (2) in "advertising or selling" a product. The two uses are not synonymous: * * * there is an obvious difference between "placing a celebrity's name on a 'special edition' of a vehicle, and using that name in a commercial to endorse or tout the same or another vehicle."

Applying this construction of the statute to the facts at hand, we agree with the Court of Appeal that Saderup sold more than just the incorporeal likeness of *The Three Stooges*. Saderup's lithographic prints of *The Three Stooges* are themselves tangible personal property, consisting of paper and ink, made as products to be sold and displayed on walls like similar graphic art. Saderup's T-shirts are likewise tangible personal property, consisting of fabric and ink, made as products to be sold and worn on the body like similar garments. By producing and selling such lithographs and T-shirts, Saderup thus used the likeness of *The Three Stooges* "on . . . products, merchandise, or goods" within the meaning of the statute." * * *

Saderup next contends that enforcement of the judgment against him violates his right of free speech and expression under the First Amendment. * * * The right of publicity is often invoked in the context of commercial speech when the appropriation of a celebrity likeness creates a false and misleading impression that the celebrity is endorsing a product. * Because the First Amendment does not protect false and misleading commercial speech, * and because even non-misleading commercial speech is generally subject to somewhat lesser First Amendment protection, * the right of publicity may often trump the right of advertisers to make use of celebrity figures.

But the present case does not concern commercial speech. As the trial court found, Saderup's portraits of *The Three Stooges* are expressive works and not an advertisement for or endorsement of a product. Although his work was done for financial gain, "[t]he First Amendment is not limited to those who publish without charge. . . . [An expressive activity] does not lose its constitutional protection because it is undertaken for profit." Guglielmi v. Spelling-Goldberg Productions (1979) 25 Cal.3d 860, 868, 160 Cal.Rptr. 352, 603 P.2d 454 (1979) (Bird, C. J.).

The tension between the right of publicity and the First Amendment is highlighted by recalling the two distinct, commonly acknowledged purposes of the latter. First, " 'to preserve an uninhibited marketplace of ideas' and to repel efforts to limit the " 'uninhibited, robust and wide-open" debate on public issues.' " Guglielmi, *supra*, 25 Cal.3d at 866. Second, to foster a "fundamental respect for individual development and self-realization. The right to self-expression is inherent in any political system which respects individual dignity. Each speaker must be free of government restraint regardless of the nature or manner of the views expressed unless there is a compelling reason to the contrary." *Id.*

The right of publicity has a potential for frustrating the fulfillment of both these purposes. Because celebrities take on public meaning, the appropriation of their likenesses may have important uses in uninhibited debate on public issues, particularly debates about culture and values. And because celebrities take on personal meanings to many individuals in the society, the creative appropriation of celebrity images can be an important avenue of individual expression. As one commentator has stated:

> Entertainment and sports celebrities are the leading players in our Public Drama. We tell tales, both tall and cautionary, about them. We monitor their comings and goings, their

missteps and heartbreaks. We copy their mannerisms, their styles, their modes of conversation and of consumption. Whether or not celebrities are "the chief agents of moral change in the United States," they certainly are widely used— far more than are institutionally anchored elites—to symbolize individual aspirations, group identities, and cultural values. Their images are thus important expressive and communicative resources: the peculiar, yet familiar idiom in which we conduct a fair portion of our cultural business and everyday conversation.

Michael Madow, Private Ownership of Public Image: Popular Culture and Publicity Rights 81 Cal. L. Rev. 125, 128 (1993).

As Madow further points out, the very importance of celebrities in society means that the right of publicity has the potential of censoring significant expression by suppressing alternative versions of celebrity images that are iconoclastic, irreverent, or otherwise attempt to redefine the celebrity's meaning. * A majority of this court recognized as much in *Guglielmi*: "The right of publicity derived from public prominence does not confer a shield to ward off caricature, parody and satire. Rather, prominence invites creative comment." * * *

Nor do Saderup's creations lose their constitutional protections because they are for purposes of entertaining rather than informing. As Chief Justice Bird stated in *Guglielmi*, invoking the dual purpose of the First Amendment: "Our courts have often observed that entertainment is entitled to the same constitutional protection as the exposition of ideas. That conclusion rests on two propositions. First, 'the line between informing and entertaining is too elusive for the protection of the basic right. Everyone is familiar with instances of propaganda through fiction. What is one man's amusement, teaches another doctrine.'" Guglielmi, *supra*, 25 Cal.3d at 867. "Second, entertainment, as a mode of self-expression, is entitled to constitutional protection irrespective of its contribution to the marketplace of ideas. 'For expression is an integral part of the development of ideas, of mental exploration and of the affirmation of self. The power to realize his potentiality as a human being begins at this point and must extend at least this far if the whole nature of man is not to be thwarted.'" *Id.* * * *

But having recognized the high degree of First Amendment protection for noncommercial speech about celebrities, we need not conclude that all expression that trenches on the right of publicity receives such protection. The right of publicity, like copyright, protects a form of intellectual property that society deems to have some social utility. "Often considerable money, time and energy are needed to develop one's prominence in a particular field. Years of labor may be required before one's skill, reputation, notoriety or virtues are sufficiently developed to permit an economic return through some medium of commercial promotion. * For some, the investment may eventually create considerable commercial value in one's identity." [Lugosi v. Universal Pictures, 25 Cal.3d 813, 834–35, 160 Cal.Rptr. 323, 336, 603 P.2d 425, 438 (Bird, C. J., dissenting)].

The present case exemplifies this kind of creative labor. Moe and Jerome (Curly) Howard and Larry Fein fashioned personae collectively known as *The Three Stooges*, first in vaudeville and later in movie shorts, over a period extending from the 1920's to the 1940's. * The three comic characters they created and whose names they shared—Larry, Moe, and Curly—possess a kind of mythic status in our culture. * * * Through their talent and labor, they joined the relatively small group of actors who constructed identifiable, recurrent comic personalities that they brought to the many parts they were scripted to play. * * *

In sum, society may recognize, as the Legislature has done here, that a celebrity's heirs and assigns have a legitimate protectible interest in exploiting the value to be obtained from merchandising the celebrity's image, whether that interest be conceived as a kind of natural property right or as an incentive for encouraging creative work. * * *

It is admittedly not a simple matter to develop a test that will unerringly distinguish between forms of artistic expression protected by the First Amendment and those that must give way to the right of publicity. Certainly, any such test must incorporate the principle that the right of publicity cannot, consistent with the First Amendment, be a right to control the celebrity's image by censoring disagreeable portrayals. Once the celebrity thrusts himself or herself forward into the limelight, the First Amendment dictates that the right to comment on, parody, lampoon, and make other expressive uses of the celebrity image must be given broad scope. The necessary implication of this observation is that the right of publicity is essentially an economic right. What the right of publicity holder possesses is not a right of censorship, but a right to prevent others from misappropriating the economic value generated by the celebrity's fame through the merchandising of the "name, voice, signature, photograph, or likeness" of the celebrity.

Beyond this precept, how may courts distinguish between protected and unprotected expression? Some commentators have proposed importing the fair use defense from copyright law, 17 U.S.C. § 107, which has the advantage of employing an established doctrine developed from a related area of the law. * * * [T]he first fair use factor—"the purpose and character of the use" * does seem particularly pertinent to the task of reconciling the rights of free expression and publicity. As the Supreme Court has stated, the central purpose of the inquiry into this fair use factor

> is to see, in Justice Story's words, whether the new work merely "supersede[s] the objects" of the original creation, * or instead adds something new, with a further purpose or different character, altering the first with new expression, meaning, or message; it asks, in other words, whether and to what extent the new work is "transformative." * Although such transformative use is not absolutely necessary for a finding of fair use, * the goal of copyright, to promote science and the arts, is generally furthered by the creation of transformative works.

Campbell v. Acuff-Rose Music, Inc., 510 U.S. 569, 579, 114 S.Ct. 1164, 1171, 127 L.Ed.2d 500 (1994).

This inquiry into whether a work is "transformative" appears to us to be necessarily at the heart of any judicial attempt to square the right of publicity with the First Amendment. * * * When artistic expression takes the form of a literal depiction or imitation of a celebrity for commercial gain, directly trespassing on the right of publicity without adding significant expression beyond that trespass, the state law interest in protecting the fruits of artistic labor outweighs the expressive interests of the imitative artist. *

On the other hand, when a work contains significant transformative elements, it is not only especially worthy of First Amendment protection, but it is also less likely to interfere with the economic interest protected by the right of publicity. As has been observed, works of parody or other distortions of the celebrity figure are not, from the celebrity fan's viewpoint, good substitutes for conventional depictions of the celebrity and therefore do not generally threaten markets for celebrity memorabilia that the right of publicity is designed to protect. * Accordingly, First Amendment protection of such works outweighs whatever interest the state may have in enforcing the right of publicity. The right-of-publicity holder continues to enforce the right to monopolize the production of conventional, more or less fungible, images of the celebrity.

Cardtoons [v. Major League Baseball Players Association], 95 F.3d 959 [(10th Cir.1996)], * * * is consistent with this "transformative" test. There, the court held that the First Amendment protected a company that produced trading cards caricaturing and parodying well-known major league baseball players against a claim brought under the Oklahoma right of publicity statute. The court concluded that "[t]he cards provide social commentary on public figures, major league baseball players, who are involved in a significant commercial enterprise, major league baseball," and that "[t]he cards are no less protected because they provide humorous rather than serious commentary." The Cardtoons court weighed these First Amendment rights against what it concluded was the less-than-compelling interests advanced by the right of publicity outside the advertising context—especially in light of the reality that parody would not likely substantially impact the economic interests of celebrities—and found the cards to be a form of protected expression. * * *

We emphasize that the transformative elements or creative contributions that require First Amendment protection are not confined to parody and can take many forms, from factual reporting * to fictionalized portrayal; * see also Parks v. Laface Records, 76 F. Supp.2d 775, 779–82 (E.D.Mich.1999) (use of civil rights figure Rosa Parks in song title is protected expression), from heavy-handed lampooning, see Hustler Magazine v. Falwell 485 U.S. 46, 108 S.Ct. 876, 99 L.Ed.2d 41 (1988),[a] to subtle social criticism. *

Another way of stating the inquiry is whether the celebrity likeness is one of the "raw materials" from which an original work is synthesized, or whether the depiction or imitation of the celebrity is the very sum and substance of the work in question. We ask, in other words, whether a product containing a celebrity's likeness is so

---

[a]   [Eds.' note] See *supra* pages 749–750, Note 2.

transformed that it has become primarily the defendant's own expression rather than the celebrity's likeness. And when we use the word "expression," we mean expression of something other than the likeness of the celebrity.

We further emphasize that in determining whether the work is transformative, courts are not to be concerned with the quality of the artistic contribution—vulgar forms of expression fully qualify for First Amendment protection. * On the other hand, a literal depiction of a celebrity, even if accomplished with great skill, may still be subject to a right of publicity challenge. The inquiry is in a sense more quantitative than qualitative, asking whether the literal and imitative or the creative elements predominate in the work.

Furthermore, in determining whether a work is sufficiently transformative, courts may find useful a subsidiary inquiry, particularly in close cases: does the marketability and economic value of the challenged work derive primarily from the fame of the celebrity depicted? If this question is answered in the negative, then there would generally be no actionable right of publicity. When the value of the work comes principally from some source other than the fame of the celebrity—from the creativity, skill, and reputation of the artist—it may be presumed that sufficient transformative elements are present to warrant First Amendment protection. If the question is answered in the affirmative, however, it does not necessarily follow that the work is without First Amendment protection—it may still be a transformative work.

In sum, when an artist is faced with a right of publicity challenge to his or her work, he or she may raise as affirmative defense that the work is protected by the First Amendment inasmuch as it contains significant transformative elements or that the value of the work does not derive primarily from the celebrity's fame.

Turning to the present case, we note that the trial court, in ruling against Saderup, stated that "the commercial enterprise conducted by [Saderup] involves the sale of lithographs and T-shirts which are not original single works of art, and which are not protected by the First Amendment; the enterprise conducted by [Saderup] was a commercial enterprise designed to generate profits solely from the use of the likeness of The Three Stooges which is the right of publicity . . . protected by section 990." Although not entirely clear, the trial court seemed to be holding that *reproductions* of celebrity images are categorically outside First Amendment protection. * * * [T]hat a reproduction receives no First Amendment protection—is patently false: a reproduction of a celebrity image that, as explained above, contains significant creative elements is entitled to as much First Amendment protection as an original work of art. The trial court and the Court of Appeal therefore erred in this respect.

Rather, the inquiry is into whether Saderup's work is sufficiently transformative. Correctly anticipating this inquiry, he argues that all portraiture involves creative decisions, that therefore no portrait portrays a mere literal likeness, and that accordingly all portraiture, including reproductions, is protected by the First Amendment. We reject any such categorical position. Without denying that all portraiture involves the making of artistic choices, we find it equally undeniable, under the test formulated above, that when an artist's skill and talent is manifestly subordinated to the overall goal of creating a conventional portrait of a celebrity so as to commercially exploit his or her fame, then the artist's right of free expression is outweighed by the right of publicity. * * *

On the other hand, we do not hold that all reproductions of celebrity portraits are unprotected by the First Amendment. The silkscreens of Andy Warhol, for example, have as their subjects the images of such celebrities as Marilyn Monroe, Elizabeth Taylor, and Elvis Presley. Through distortion and the careful manipulation of context, Warhol was able to convey a message that went beyond the commercial exploitation of celebrity images and became a form of ironic social comment on the dehumanization of celebrity itself. * Such expression may well be entitled to First Amendment protection. Although the distinction between protected and unprotected expression will sometimes be subtle, it is no more so than other distinctions triers of fact are called on to make in First Amendment jurisprudence. *

Turning to Saderup's work, we can discern no significant transformative or creative contribution. His undeniable skill is manifestly subordinated to the overall goal of creating literal, conventional depictions of The Three Stooges so as to exploit their fame. Indeed, were we to decide that Saderup's depictions were protected by the First Amendment, we cannot perceive how the right of publicity would remain a viable right other than in cases of falsified celebrity endorsements.

Moreover, the marketability and economic value of Saderup's work derives primarily from the fame of the celebrities depicted. While that fact alone does not necessarily mean the work receives no First Amendment protection, we can perceive no transformative elements in Saderup's works that would require such protection.

Saderup argues that it would be incongruous and unjust to protect parodies and other distortions of celebrity figures but not wholesome, reverential portraits of such celebrities. The test we articulate today, however, does not express a value judgment or preference for one type of depiction over another. * * * Stated another way, we are concerned not with whether conventional celebrity images should be produced but with who produces them and, more pertinently, who appropriates the value from their production. Thus, under section 990, if Saderup wishes to continue to depict *The Three Stooges* as he has done, he may do so only with the consent of the right of publicity holder.

The judgment of the Court of Appeal is affirmed.

NOTE

The Supreme Court Considers Appropriation and Constitutional Concerns. In Zacchini v. Scripps-Howard Broadcasting Co., 433 U.S. 562, 563, 97 S.Ct. 2849, 2851, 53 L.Ed.2d 965, 968 (1977), plaintiff Hugo Zacchini was an entertainer who "perform[ed] a 'human cannonball' act in which he was shot from a cannon into a net some 200 feet away." Defendant, owner of a local television station, aired a movie clip of the entire 15–second act, even though plaintiff had asked the reporter working for the defendant not to film it. Plaintiff sued for damages claiming unlawful appropriation of his professional property and noted that the "human cannonball" act was "invented by his father and . . . performed only by his family for the last fifty years." The Supreme Court rejected defendant's claim that its broadcast of the film of plaintiff's act was constitutionally protected by the First and Fourteenth Amendments:

> * * * [T]he State's interest is closely analogous to the goals of patent and copyright law, focusing on the right of the individual to reap the reward of his endeavors and having little to do with protecting feelings or reputation. * * * An entertainer such as petitioner usually has no objection to the widespread publication of his act as long as he gets the commercial benefit of such publication. Indeed, in the present case petitioner did not seek to enjoin the broadcast of his act; he simply sought compensation for the broadcast in the form of damages.

Most often the creative efforts of artists, entertainers, writers, musicians, and others will be protected by federal copyright law. In the *Zacchini* case, however, plaintiff had not "fixed" his act in some tangible form, such as videotape or film, as required by the copyright law. See 17 U.S.C. § 102 (2012).

THE LITIGATION PROCESS

Tort law is inextricably intertwined with the procedures of the civil trial process. In your first-year Civil Procedure course, you will study the civil litigation process in great detail. Here we provide only a brief overview to help you understand the litigation process and the procedural terms you will encounter in reading your torts cases. The trial procedures used in federal courts and in each of the state court systems vary, so this brief description provides only a simplified overview of typical processes in tort litigation.

In most cases, the lawyer for the plaintiff wants the case to be heard and decided by the jury. Participants in the tort process traditionally assume that juries—consisting of ordinary citizens—are inclined to favor the interests of accident victims in litigation against defendants—usually either businesses or individuals that jurors typically (and usually accurately) believe are insured. Conversely, the lawyer representing the defendant wants to prevent the jury from deciding the case. Accordingly, much of the tort litigation process can be understood as the struggle between the plaintiff's attorney and defense counsel as to whether the case will be decided by the jury or whether instead it will be decided by the judge "as a matter of law."

Most claims for accident compensation are resolved without the filing of a lawsuit. See David M. Engel, Perception and Decision at the Threshold of Tort Law: Explaining the Infrequency of Claims, 62 DePaul L. Rev. 293, 294, 301 (2013).

The tort litigation process begins when the plaintiff files a *complaint* (historically sometimes called a petition) with the clerk of courts. As you will explore in your Civil Procedure class, the complaint asserts the facts that the plaintiff alleges entitle her to relief from the court, generally consisting of monetary damages to be paid by the defendant. At the same time the complaint is filed with the court, it is delivered to or *served upon* the defendant. Today service is usually accomplished through certified mail.

Assuming that the defendant is not prepared to admit liability and quickly settle the case, the defense attorney typically responds in one of two ways. First, the defense counsel may file a *motion to dismiss* arguing that even if all the facts stated in the plaintiff's complaint are true, these facts do not satisfy the legal requirements entitling the plaintiff to recover. Traditionally, it was often said that the defendant filed a *demurrer* or demurred to the complaint. A demurrer was a challenge to the legal sufficiency of an earlier pleading filed by the other party that essentially argued "so what?" A party could demur to any of a variety of pleadings, not just the complaint.

If the trial court grants the defendant's motion to dismiss or demurrer, the plaintiff may seek the court's permission to amend the complaint in order to correct the fatal deficiency. Otherwise, the dismissal ends (at least for the time) the proceeding in the trial court. However, the plaintiff may appeal the order dismissing the case to an appellate court. Today, the vast majority of states have so-called *"intermediate appellate courts,"* but in a few states, the appeal proceeds directly to the *state's highest court* (usually called the *"supreme court"*). The appellate court reviews whether the trial court judge erred as a matter of law in dismissing the plaintiff's complaint. In those jurisdictions with intermediate appellate courts, some states allow the losing party to appeal to the next level, the state's highest court, as a matter of right, but more often that court has discretion as to whether or not to hear the appeal from the intermediate appellate court.

If the trial judge denies the defendant's motion to dismiss, in most instances the defendant cannot appeal immediately to a higher court. Instead, she must wait until there is a final judgment from the trial court. For example, if the trial court awards a final judgment to the plaintiff following a trial, the defendant can then appeal, arguing that the trial court should have granted her motion to dismiss before trial.

The defendant's second possible response to the filing of the complaint is to respond with an *answer* denying some or all the factual allegations included in the plaintiff's complaint. In addition, in tort cases, the defendant sometimes asserts an *affirmative defense* to the plaintiff's complaint. When raising an affirmative defense, the defendant argues that even if the facts of the plaintiff's complaint are true and satisfy the requirements of liability for a tort claim, there is some other recognized legal basis why the plaintiff is not entitled to recover. Finally, in the same pleading, the defendant may also file a *counterclaim*, asserting that the facts show that the defendant should be able to recover compensation from the plaintiff as a result of harm suffered by the defendant from the same "transaction or occurrence" (e.g., the accident), described in the plaintiff's complaint.

The attorneys for both parties then begin preparing for the possibility of trial, even though most cases are resolved before trial.[1] This preparation includes factual investigation, legal research, and discovery. *Discovery* consists of a series of legally sanctioned processes to force the other party and other witnesses to share information and documents. For example, the defendant can take the *deposition* or oral testimony of the plaintiff or ask the plaintiff to answer *interrogatories* or written questions.

As the parties learn more about the facts during their continuing investigations and the discovery process, the facts in dispute between the parties narrow. One of the parties, usually the defendant, may then file a *motion for a summary judgment*, arguing that there is no longer a genuine dispute between the parties as to the material facts of the case, and that based on these facts, the moving party is entitled to judgment as a matter of law. Again, as was the case with the motion to dismiss, if the motion is granted, the party against whom the motion is granted (usually the plaintiff) may appeal.

If the motion for summary judgment is denied, often the parties settle at this point. Otherwise, the parties continue preparation for trial and often pursue additional discovery.

---

[1] In 2004, only 1.8 percent of federal civil cases were resolved by trial, compared to 11.5 percent in 1962. See Marc Galanter, The Vanishing Trial: An Examination of Trials and Related Matters in Federal and State Courts, 1 J. Empirical Legal Stud. 459, 461 (2004).

Once the trial begins, the judge has the responsibility to decide "matters of law" and the fact-finder, either the judge or the jury, resolves factual disputes and applies the law to the facts. Historically a jury consisted of twelve members, but today most jurisdictions allow for juries with fewer members, often six. The judge—and usually the attorneys—question prospective jurors in a process known as *voir dire* and attempt to uncover anything that might bias a juror in favor of one party or the other. Each party typically is able to "strike" or eliminate some prospective jurors, either by "showing cause" (potential bias) or often, in a specified small number of instances, "peremptorily" (without showing any cause).

After the jury is chosen, each attorney has the opportunity to deliver an *opening statement*—not an argument, but a preview of what the attorney expects the evidence will show. The plaintiff's attorney then calls the witnesses whose testimony she expects will prove the facts necessary to satisfy the requirements of liability and establish the amount of harm suffered by her client. After the plaintiff's attorney questions each of these witnesses on *direct examination*, the defense attorney has the opportunity to *cross-examine* the witness. Plaintiff's counsel may also introduce into evidence photographs, documents, or tangible objects relevant to the case. Often the defense attorney will dispute the admissibility of the testimony of a particular witness or other evidence and, as described below, decisions as to the admissibility of evidence may eventually be appealed.

After the plaintiff's attorney completes the presentation of the plaintiff's witnesses, the defense counsel usually asks the judge to grant a *directed verdict* (called a motion for judgment as a matter of law in federal courts and in some state courts) in the defendant's favor. In order to grant the motion for a directed verdict, the trial court judge must find that no reasonable jury could find that the plaintiff's evidence satisfied the requirements necessary to hold the defendant liable. If the trial court grants the defendant's motion for a directed verdict, the plaintiff may appeal.

Assuming that the trial court denies the defendant's motion for a directed verdict at the close of the plaintiff's case, the defendant then proceeds to call witnesses and otherwise introduce evidence. The defense counsel engages in direct examination of its witnesses, and the plaintiff's attorney has the opportunity to cross-examine the defense witnesses. The plaintiff's attorney also may call rebuttal witnesses to challenge the testimony of the defense witnesses.

At the conclusion of the defendant's case, the defense attorney and often the plaintiff's attorney file competing motions for directed verdicts (see *supra* for standards for granting a motion for a directed verdict). Again, the granting of a motion for a directed verdict concludes the case and the losing party may then appeal.

Assuming that the court denies the parties' respective motions for directed verdicts, the attorney for the plaintiff makes her *closing argument* to the jury, arguing how the testimony and evidence presented during trial should lead the jury to find a verdict in favor of the plaintiff. The defense counsel counters with his closing argument explaining why the plaintiff is not entitled to recover.

Following the closing arguments, the trial court judge orally delivers *instructions of law* to the jury, explaining what the jury must find in order to grant a verdict in favor of the plaintiff. The judge usually meets with counsel for both parties prior to the closing arguments to solicit their *requests for jury instructions*, that is, each counsel's proposal as to what the jury should be told about the law governing the case. The judge's decision to grant or deny a requested jury instruction often later provides an important basis for appealing the trial court's judgment. After the jury receives its instructions, it "retires" to consider the case and to arrive at a verdict.

Once the jury returns to the courtroom with a verdict, the trial is not over! Indeed, for purposes of beginning the process that leads to the appellate opinions you read in law school, the fun is just beginning. Assume that the jury returns with a verdict for the plaintiff. The defendant typically moves for a *judgment notwithstanding verdict—* traditionally called a *judgment n.o.v. (non obstante veredicto)* and, like a motion for a directed verdict, referred to as a "judgment as a matter of law" in the federal courts. The legal standard for the judgment notwithstanding verdict is the same as the standard for the motion for the directed verdict, i.e., that no reasonable jury could have reached the decision that the jury did. Often trial court judges are reluctant to grant a motion for a directed verdict before the case is submitted to the jury, hoping and expecting that the jury will reach the "right result" and the judge will be let off the hook. If the court grants the defendant's motion for a judgment notwithstanding verdict, the result of the verdict is flipped—instead of the plaintiff prevailing as the jury said it should, the defendant now wins. The trial court's decision to either grant or deny the motion for judgment notwithstanding verdict is grounds for appeal by the losing party. Note that when the court denies a directed verdict, the non-prevailing party generally cannot appeal; she can only appeal after she raises the same issues in a motion for a judgment notwithstanding verdict and this subsequent motion is denied. Don't forget to file your motion for a judgment notwithstanding verdict if you plan on appealing!

The other principal post-trial motion is a *motion for a new trial*. The trial court judge may grant such a motion when she concludes that the jury's verdict is either "against the weight of the evidence" or the jury's award of damages is excessive. In other words, the judge grants a motion for a new trial when she thinks the jury got it wrong, but she is not convinced that the jury verdict is so far out-of-line as to warrant a judgment notwithstanding verdict that reverses the result reached by the jury.

Also, the judge may grant a motion for a new trial if she believes that there was a legal error in the trial proceedings that prejudiced the case of the losing party. For example, either an incorrect decision to allow or disallow the admission of certain evidence or an error in the jury instructions that prejudiced the losing party might be grounds for a new trial. The judge's decision to grant or deny a motion for a new trial is appealable. If counsel believes the judge made a legal error during the trial, he must *preserve* the grounds of appeal by both *objecting* at the time of the error and incorporating the error in his motion for a new trial.

If the trial judge denies the motion for judgment notwithstanding verdict and/or the motion for a new trial filed by the party that did not prevail in the jury's verdict, the trial court judge *enters judgment* on the jury's verdict.

The losing party may then file its *notice of appeal*. Each party files written *briefs* with the appellate court arguing why precedents and other legal authorities justify a decision in its favor. Appellate courts sometimes also hear oral argument from counsel. The appellate court often (but unfortunately, not nearly always) issues a published written opinion justifying the court's decisions. Like the editors of your other law school casebooks, in this casebook we select a handful of such decisions and provide excerpts from the opinions in those cases.

INDEX